Notable Native Americans

Wapiti regional library

Notable Native Americans

Sharon Malinowski
Editor

George H. J. Abrams
Consulting Editor & Author of Foreword

Gale Research Inc.

An International Thomson Publishing Company

ITP

NEW YORK • LONDON • BONN • BOSTON • DETROIT • MADRID
MELBOURNE • MEXICO CITY • PARIS • SINGAPORE • TOKYO
TORONTO • WASHINGTON • ALBANY NY • BELMONT CA • CINCINNATI OH

STAFF

Sharon Malinowski, *Editor*

Judy Galens, Joseph M. Palmisano, Shirelle Phelps, and Joseph C. Tardiff, *Editors*
Ned Burels, Mark F. Mikula, Anna J. Sheets, and Melissa Ann Walsh, *Associate Editors*
Dawn R. Barry, *Assistant Editor*
Neil Schlager, *Managing Editor, Multicultural Team*

Victoria B. Cariappa, *Research Manager*
Mary Rose Bonk, *Research Supervisor*
Norma Sawaya, *Editorial Associate*

Marlene H. Lasky, Manager, *Permissions*
Margaret A. Chamberlain, *Picture Permissions Specialist*
Susan Brohman and Barbara A. Wallace, *Permissions Associates*

Cynthia Baldwin, *Product Design Manager*
Pamela A. E. Galbreath, *Art Director*
Marty Somberg, *Graphic Designer*

⊗™ This book is printed on acid-free paper that meets the minimum requirements of American National Standard for Information Sciences-
Permanence Paper for Printed Library Materials, ANSI Z39.48-1984.

Library of Congress Catalog Card Number 94-36202
A CIP record is available from the British Library

ISBN 0-8103-9638-6

Printed in the United States of America.

Library of Congress Cataloging-in-Publication Data

Notable Native Americans / Sharon Malinowski, editor, George H.J.
Abrams, consulting editor and author of foreward. -- 1st ed.
        p. cm.
        Includes index.
        ISBN 0-8103-9638-6 (alk. paper) : $65.00
        1. Indians of North America--Biography. 2. Indians of North
America--History. I. Malinowski, Sharon. II. Abrams, George H.J.,
1939-
E89.N67 1994
920'.00297--dc20   94-36202
    [B]   CIP

I(T)P™ Gale Research Inc., an International Thomson Publishing Company.
        ITP logo is a trademark under license.

10 9 8 7 6 5 4 3 2 1

Contents

Preface

Based upon a need for reference sources in the area of Native American biography in both academic and public libraries, Gale presents this extensive compilation of biographical and bibliographical information on more than two hundred and sixty-five notable Native North American men and women throughout history, from all fields of endeavor—politics, law, journalism, science, medicine, religion, art and literature, athletics, education, and entertainment. Approximately thirty percent of the entries focus on historical figures and seventy percent on contemporary or twentieth-century individuals. Signed narrative essays, ranging from one to three pages in length, include Indian names and their English translations as well as name varients, plus a list of reference sources. Wherever possible, photographs or illustrations accompany the entries.

Preparation

Before preparing this edition of *Notable Native Americans,* an advisory board was assembled to assist in the compilation of a list of featured entrants. More than fourteen hundred names were considered for possible inclusion in this volume; lists were compiled for review by the advisory board, whose recommendations were then incorporated. This list was then reviewed by the consulting editor. Mailings were made to all living entrants with known addresses so that information might be as complete and accurate as possible.

Entry Format

The entries featured in *Notable Native Americans* provide in-depth biographical and bibliographical information on a selection of both historical and contemporary figures who are recognized as notable by the Native American community and are collectively unavailable in any other single reference source. The format of each entry is designed for ease of use—by students, teachers, scholars, librarians, and the general public.

Additional Features

A list of featured entires provides a quick guide to the biographies presented in thes publication. In addition to a subject index, which provides reference to other individuals, battles, treaties, movements, and organizations discussed within the entries, there is a listing of entries according to tribal group or nation plus a listing of entries according to occupations or tribal roles, which will assist the reader in quickly finding information on a variety of topics.

Acknowledgements

The editor gratefully acknowledges George H. J. Abrams and the members of the advisory board for their expertise and collaboration; Neil Schlager and the Multicultural Team members for their indispensable editorial support, especially Melissa Walsh for her generous and skillful assistance in project management; Carol Bimberg, Jeffrey Muhr, and David Schulte for their technical assistance; and Aarti Stephens, Jeff Hill, and Mary L. Onorato for their administrative support.

Suggestions Are Welcome

The editor hopes that you find *Notable Native Americans* a useful reference tool and welcomes comments and suggestions on any aspects of this work. Please send comments to: The Editor, *Notable Native Americans,* Gale Research, Inc., 835 Penobscot Building, 645 Griswold St., Detroit, MI 48226-4094; or call toll-free at 800-347-GALE; or fax to 313-961-6741.

Acknowledgements

Photographs and illustrations appearing in *Notable Native Americans* were received from the following sources:

UPI/Bettmann: **pp. 3, 22, 24, 31, 33, 57, 80, 105, 111, 159, 184, 195, 209, 222, 224, 232, 254, 258, 263, 269, 272, 274, 291, 296, 298, 310, 326, 358,386, 434**; Photograph by Tama Rothchild, courtesy of Paula Gunn Allen: **p. 7**; The Bettmann Archive: **pp. 10, 37, 106, 54, 219, 228, 306, 320, 335, 338, 353, 356, 392, 400, 411, 427**; AP/Wide World Photos: **pp. 118, 129, 182, 256,262, 283, 301, 323, 378, 399, 407, 421, 433, 439, 453, 474**; Courtesy of Fred Begay: **p. 27**; Courtesy of Robert LaFollett Bennett: **p. 33**; Drawing by Loren Zephier: **pp. 34, 205, 472**; Courtesy of the Colorado Historical Society: **p. 37**; Courtesy of Brugier Collection: **p. 42**; The Granger Collection, New York: **pp. 47, 93, 155, 160, 285, 308, 349, 362, 364, 443, 449, 460, 466**; Drawing by George Varian: **p. 49**; Courtesy of Joseph Bruchac III: **p. 58**; Reuters/Bettmann: **p. 64**; Courtesy of the National Archives: **p. 108, 187, 259**; Courtesy of Gladys Cardiff: **p. 68**; Courtesy of the Library of Congress: **p. 74**; Photograph by Carolyn Forbes: **p. 87**; The Granger Collection: **pp. 95, 192, 265, 299, 317, 351, 367, 374, 390, 414, 416, 430**; Photograph by John A. Anderson, 1898: **p. 99**; Photograph by Edward Curtis, courtesy of National Archives: **p. 66**; Photograph by Thorney Lieberman: **p. 140**; Photograph © Thorney Lieberman: **p. 141**; Photograph by Carolyn L. Forbes, courtesy of Jack Forbes: **p. 152**; Photograph by Mike Long, courtesy of Diane Glancy, reprinted by permission of Holy Cow! Press: **p. 167**; Archive Photos/Fotos International: **p. 170**; Photograph by Robyn Stoutenburg: **p. 179**; Courtesy of Norbert S. Hill, Jr.: **p. 197**; Photograph by Rich Powers: **p. 200**; Photograph by Craig Locklear, courtesy of Otellie Loloma: **p. 245**; Photograph by The Photography Studio, courtesy of Linda Lomhaftewa: **p. 247**; Courtesy of Smithsonian Institution: **p. 250**; Painting of Duane Niatum by Nita Walker after a photograph by Mary Randlett, reprinted by permission of Holy Cow! Press: **p. 289**; Photograph by M. Foster, reprinted by permission of Simon J. Ortiz: **p. 303**; Courtesy of Everett R. Rhoades: **p. 360**; Courtesy of The Kansas State Historical Society: **p. 370**; Photograph by Arthur Murata: **p. 372**; Archive Photos: **p. 380**; Courtesy of the Saul Zaentz Company, all rights reserved: **p. 382**; Photograph by Marcie Keegan: **p. 385**; Courtesy of Kate Shanley: **p. 394**; © 1981 Linda Fry Poverman: **p. 396**; Courtesy of Ross O. Swimmer: **p. 418**; Courtesy of Luci Tapahonso: **p. 425**; Courtesy of Floyd Westerman: **p. 457**; Photograph of Roberta Hill Whiteman © by Ernest Whiteman, reprinted by permission of Holy Cow! Press: **p. 459**.

Advisory Board

George H. J. Abrams
Consulting Editor
Seneca anthropologist
Hackensack, New Jersey

Sherman Alexie
Spokane/Coeur d'Alene poet and fiction writer
Spokane, Washington

JoAllyn Archambault
Yankton Dakota Sioux anthropologist
Chair, American Indian Program
National Museum of Natural History
Smithsonian Institution
Washington, D.C.

Beth Brant
Mohawk poet and fiction writer
Melvindale, Michigan

Edward D. Castillo
Cahuilla-Luiseño educator
Director, Native American Studies Program
Sonoma State University
Rohnhert Park, California

Janice White Clemmer
Wasco/Shawnee/Delaware educator
Department of Secondary Education
Brigham Young University
Provo, Utah

Anne Medicine
Oneida/Seneca educator
Assistant Dean of Graduate Studies
Stanford University
Palo Alto, California

Beatrice Medicine
Lakota Sioux anthropologist
Coordinator of Women's Perspectives
Royal Commission on Aboriginal Peoples
Ottawa, Ontario, Canada

Cheryl Metoyer-Duran
Cherokee educator
Rupert Costo Chair in History
University of California, Riverside

Elizabeth Anne Parent
Athabascan and Yupik educator
Director, American Indian Studies Program
San Francisco State University

Kathryn W. Shanley
Assiniboine scholar
English Department
University of Washington, Seattle

Ofelia Zepeda
Tohono O'odham educator and linguist
Director, American Indian Studies Program
University of Arizona, Tuscon

Introduction

Race, Culture, and Law: The Question of American Indian Identity
by George H. J. Abrams

One of the initial questions raised in the study of American Indians is, "Who is an Indian?" While the answer may seem naive and deceptively simple, it becomes increasingly obvious as one begins an inquiry into this issue that there is no easy resolution to the complexity of determining the individual and collective identity within the contemporary American Indian community or, equally important, how individuals of Indian descent are perceived by non-Indians, including the general public, social scientists, and others. This brief discourse on the subject raises several issues that directly and collaterally involve the subject of race, culture, and law as they relate to the increasingly complex issues of American Indian identity.

One of the three criteria, in addition to culture and law, which are generally agreed upon in the determining of American Indian identity, is the arguable factor of race. Those who have studied the issue of race can generally be classified into either the "lumpers" or the "splitters." Lumpers view Indians as part of the general group of Asians or Mongolians; the splitters separate Indians into a distinct population category known by a number of names, including "Amerindians." Some splitters have also categorized Indians as being composed of a number of separate races occupying the western hemisphere. Today, most scientists, based upon prevailing evidence, consider American Indians a branch of the Asian population.

In reaction to the despised term "race," Ashley Montegu and other scientists proposed that an alternative term, "ethnic group," be substituted, believing that the latter has fewer negative connotations. Nevertheless, confusion reigns in the erroneous and often interchangeable usage by the lay public of the terms race and ethnic group, since most contemporary scholars do not equate the two. Perhaps one of the more extreme splitters was Stanley Garn who, thirty years ago, proposed that there were hundreds, if not thousands, of racial categories composed of gene clusters isolated by geographical location and cultural features. In more recent times, Stephen Jay Gould, the Harvard biologist and paleontologist, suggested a total elimination of racial classification as scientifically indefensible, favoring instead the adoption of "population clines" representing geographical divisions based on diversity.

During the 1930s, some activist American Indian individuals and organizations sought the assistance of many outside organizations, including the American Nazis, in their struggle against federal government policies. In an astounding and magnanimous pronouncement, the German-American Bund declared that American Indians were members of the Aryan race (Philip, 1977; 173).

The First Indians

With the exception of radical creationists who believe that Indians were divinely created separately in this hemisphere, most American Indians would reluctantly acknowledge that there was an Asian origin or, even more remotely, an African origin for the ancestral population of the western hemisphere. Increasingly indisputable linguistic and genetic evidence is accumulating to demonstrate the unquestionable Asian origins of the American Indian. Moreover, each tribal group in the western hemisphere has or has had a traditional belief system, mythology, or oral history that adequately explains its genesis, with some tribes having several versions. It is unlikely that the contrary opinions in the arguments between faith and science regarding the racial origins of the American Indians will be soon be resolved.

Another major issue in the discussion of the origins of the American Indian is when the first human populations arrived in the western hemisphere. The ultraconservative and traditional archaeological view, for the most part, generally supports the date of approximately 12,000 BP (Before Present) for the first arrival of humans across the Bering Land Bridge, called Beringia. More liberal archaeological interpretations are beginning to see a much earlier date for the initial appearance of American Indians as additional evidence continues to be discovered in both North and South America, ranging from 20,000 to 50,000+ BP (Jaffe, 1992).

Early History

It has been repeatedly demonstrated throughout history that once two or more distinct populations come together, whether in conflict or peace, one of the first things that happens is the exchange of genes. This is undoubtedly what must have happened when the early Norse settlers of Greenland and Nova Scotia and the occasional Basque fishermen encountered the American Indian tribesmen on the northeast coasts of North America. Some scholars believe that there may also have been some sporadic Asian contact on the northwest coast and Mexico, which may have had arguable genetic and cultural influence on Indians in those areas. The same process is applied to African influence on various areas in Middle and South America.

Eventually, the same process of outside racial and cultural influences occurred with the establishment of the first permanent European colonies. One of the romantic stories involving the origin of the Lumbee Indians of North Carolina is that they are the descendants of the English settlers of Roanoke Island, people who mysteriously disappeared and are said to have voluntarily abandoned their settlement to join the neighboring Indians or were made captives of local tribal groups (Sider, 1993).

Many tribal groups also incorporated into their ranks frontier adventurers, early hunters and trappers, numerous colonials who sought refuge from white settlements (such as escaped slaves and indentured servants), those seeking escape from colonial legal authorities, or war captives. Extensive literature on the subject of captives tells us that most were adopted as tribal members to replace those family members lost in warfare, although some were either killed in blood revenge, assigned to servitude or slavery, or otherwise relegated to a lesser social status or class (Namias, 1993). A growing body of literature is beginning to review the relationship between American Indians and blacks, including blacks who have become Indians, and black Buffalo Soldiers who fought against American Indians (Forbes, 1993; Burton, 1991; Katz, 1986).

One of the definite impressions that emerges from reading the biographies in this publication is that of an increasing number of mixed-blood individuals as one approaches the twentieth century, as a result of an early French fur trapper, a white or Indian captive from another tribe, a runaway or fugitive, or someone who sought escape from the confines of Euro-American society. In other cases, thousands of former black slaves, who had been removed from the South to Indian Territory, were enrolled on so-called Freedmen Rolls within the various Five Civilized Tribes of Oklahoma (Abel, 1915; Perdue, 1979). Having been assigned reservation lands and tribal enrollment following the Civil War, the Freedmen Cherokees, among others, continue their affiliation with their former owners to this day. The degree of intermarriage between slaves or former slaves and their Indian owners remains a controversial and on-going subject of study.

In the early period, when outsiders, either white or black, became associated with a tribal group, they often became a permanently recognized member of the community. At that time, there was no need for considerations of tribal enrollment or a specified "degree of Indian blood." Only later were these legal definitions seen as necessary in order to define tribal membership. In these early instances, adoption into a tribal group meant that the individual was culturally and legally a member of the tribe, an Indian in every way but genetically. Public adoption was accomplished by acceptance into a family, clan, or traditional kinship unit, which the community recognized by the granting of a name to the adoptee, symbolizing their total cultural integration into the group.

Only in more recent times has the honorific adoption of individuals, such as politicians, entertainers, and other white "friends," made the traditional process considerably less important or permanent culturally than it had been. In some instances, there is the need for contemporary tribal groups to publicly recognize the contributions that a non-Indian individual is felt to have made to the tribe. Too often now, however, there is a carnival, or less than serious, atmosphere accompanying such honorific adoptions. Even though honorific, the adoption process has been expanded to such a liberal degree as to become practically meaningless in many instances. Contrary to what some adoptees may believe or advertise, this type of adoption does not enroll an individual as a legal member of the tribal group and does not entitle the individual to share in tribal money, land, or other resources. If such adoptions did enroll such individuals, the process of tribal adoptions would become considerably more selective and rare. In addition, some unscrupulous adoptees, or people who claim to have been adopted, have used the adoption by a tribe for nefarious financial and political purposes, claiming to be legitimate tribal members, or members of the traditional religion, identifiers which the unsuspecting and often gullible non-Indian public would not question. Also, some Indian people have eagerly participated in the adoption of non-Indians for financial benefit.

Very early in the history of the incorporation of outsiders, some of the intermarried white men, or so-called "squawmen," began to assume property ownership through their spouses and, in some cases, control and representation in the political life of the tribe. The passage of the General Allotment, or Dawes, Act of October 18, 1888, excluded intermarried white men from acquiring "any right to any tribal property, privilege, or interest whatever to which any member of such tribe is entitled." Excluded from the provision were the Five Civilized Tribes of Indian Territory (later Oklahoma). Section II of the Act proffered United States citizenship to Indian women married to white men, without jeopardizing any rights to tribal property. It should be noted that this legislation was silent on the situation of Indian men married to white women, of which there were a growing number (Cohen, 1944).

Throughout the legal history of United States involvement in the issues of intermarriage and tribal membership, various tribal groups have retained the inherent right to determine the methods and criteria by which they will regulate and control tribal membership. The following cases illustrate the complexity of the legal, racial, and cultural identity of American Indians.

The Case of Pocahontas

In 1784, Patrick Henry suggested that intermarriage between colonials and Indians be encouraged in Virginia by way of a system of cash stipends and tax incentives. Henry's ideas did not prevail. The miscegenation laws instead kept the various races in the state apart, especially since "the one-drop rule," which viewed any person of the least descent from a black or Indian ancestor as being of that race, had already been long ingrained into the social and legal fabric of the American colonies (Davis, 1991).

In the State of Virginia, being one of the thousands of people descended from Pocahontas (often erroneously identified as a "princess") is considered a genealogical feature of which to be exceptionally proud. Pocahontas' marriage to John Rolfe (not John Smith as is commonly believed) in 1613 was followed by her fatal visit to England in 1616. She died of smallpox just prior to her return to America the following year and was buried at Gravesend, England. Pocahontas was survived by her only child, Thomas Rolfe, who was raised in England by his uncle and eventually returned to Virginia, where he settled on land inherited from his father and his grandfather, Powhatan. In Virginia, Rolfe apparently had only peripheral and sporadic interaction with his Powhatan Indian relatives, finally turning against them in English interests. In Virginia he married a fellow colonial, established a plantation, and died an Englishman. It is through Thomas Rolfe and his only child, Jane Rolfe Bolling, that the numerous and socially prominent descendants of Pocahontas are derived (Barbour, 1969).

Early in the colonial period, the issue of racial classification and triracial miscegenation became a major concern. Eventually, a body of statutes were developed, providing the basis of the State of Virginia Codes which enacted formal legal classifications of American Indians and others. These antimiscegenation laws, of course, were designed to protect the racial purity of whites, the last enacted during a period of extreme nativism following World War I. In 1924, the Virginia General Assembly passed "An Act to Preserve Racial Integrity" which incorporated the earlier antimiscegenation laws of the state but also instituted one of the most severe interpretations of racial identity. It stipulated that "every person not a colored person having one fourth or more of American Indian blood shall be deemed an American Indian; except that members of Indian tribes existing in this Commonwealth having one fourth or more of Indian blood and less than one sixteenth of Negro blood shall be deemed tribal Indians" (*Loving v.Virginia*,1967; 1014, fn 4).

As one interesting consequence of the creation of the Virginia law of 1924, the numerous individuals less than one-sixteenth descendants of Pocahontas were specifically excluded from the Virginia miscegenation laws, providing: "It shall hereafter be unlawful for any white person in this State to marry any save a white person with no other admixture of blood than white and American Indian. For the purpose of this act, the term 'white person' shall apply only to the person who has no trace whatsoever of any blood other than Caucasian; but persons who have one-sixteenth or less of the blood of the American Indian and have no other non-Caucasic blood shall be deemed to be white persons" (Virginia Code Annotated 20-54, 1960).

At a later time, John Rolfe and Pocahontas could have been prosecuted for committing a felony, and their child declared illegitimate and legally unable to marry a white person, simply because Virginia declared that all marriages of white persons with non-white persons were void. In special consideration of the situation of Pocahontas' descendants, the Virginia Bureau of Vital Statistics, in enacting the so-called "Pocahontas Exemption," stated: "When the Racial Integrity law was being enacted, it was the desire of all to recognize as an integral and honored part of the white race the descendants of John Rolfe and Pocahontas, and to protect also other white citizens of Virginia who are descendants in part of members of the civilized tribes of Oklahoma and who are of no other admixture than white and Indian" (Plecker, supra note 91; 25-26).

Had the one-drop social rule that normally applied to blacks continued to be applied in the case of Indians, it could have proved to be inconvenient and embarrassing for a multitude of individuals who are Pocahontas' descendants. Included among Pocahontas' descendants are various collateral relatives of President George Washington, Martha Dandridge Custis Washington, a brother-in-law and son-in-law of President Thomas Jefferson, Virginia Governor Thomas Mann Randolph of "Edge Hill," Senator John Randolph of Roanoke, Mrs. Benjamin Harrison IV, Mrs. Gouverneur Morris, Sr., George Wythe Randolph, the Confederate Secretary of War, Mrs. Robert E. Lee, the second Mrs. Woodrow Wilson, the golfer Dr. Cary Middlecoff, and possibly Patricia, Countess Mountbatten of Burma (Brown et al, 1985; personal communication). It would seem obvious that none of the above individuals are Indians, and none claimed to be such although they are documented as being of minuscule American Indian ancestry.

The antimiscegenation statutes of Virginia, the last in the United States, were finally struck down in the Supreme Court's ruling in *Loving v. Virginia* (1967). In this case, Richard Perry Loving, a white man, had in 1958 married his childhood sweetheart, Mildred Jeter, in the District of Columbia, in order to evade Virginia's laws. Mrs. Loving was a triracially mixed resident of Virginia and self-identified as black. In an earlier miscegenation case dealing directly with an Indian, that of *Stevens v. United States* (1944), miscegenation law was upheld when the Tenth Circuit ruled that the prosecution of a full-blooded Oklahoma Indian who married a black person did not violate the fourteenth amendment of the Constitution or the Civil Rights Act of 1866.

Patterson v. Council of the Seneca Nation of Indians (1927)

Various court cases have tested the methods by which tribes have legally determined tribal membership. Usually these methods were based on some form of traditional kinship system that was in existence before the arrival of the Europeans. In some cases, these variable systems were later formalized as an accommodation to the legal requirements of state or federal governments, with the cooperation of tribal governments who increasingly came to see that it was important to delineate their membership, following a period of fraudulent treaties negotiated by individuals who had questionable authority to do so. It was also necessary in order to regulate annuity distribution, determine who legally represented the tribe in negotiations with other governments, and who had legal claims to Indian land and its resources as legally recognized members of the group.

In the State of New York the traditionally matrilineal Iroquois tribes, comprising the Mohawk, Oneida, Onondaga, Cayuga, Seneca, and Tuscarora, had begun to formalize their tribal membership systems as early as the 1840s, a period in which a great degree of both intertribal and racial mixing had already occurred (Upton, 1980). In effect, what came to be formally recognized in the Iroquois situation was that a New York Iroquois is a legal member of a specific tribal group and clan, if his mother was a member of that tribe. The tribe, race, or nationality of the father was not officially important, or often, in the early data, unrecorded. As is often heard today, "You always know who your mother is, but not necessarily your father." In fact, the first question an Iroquois is likely to be asked by another Iroquois is, "Who is your mother?" This continues to be the time-honored method for determining one's social relationship to other Iroquois.

In addition, determining the degree of Indian blood or "blood quantum," which was later to become so important to other federally recognized tribes, was not a matter of record for the New York Iroquois and has not been to the present. Consequently, at the present time among the Seneca Nation, there is a growing number of tribal members who are of minimal Seneca ancestry, in at least one case one-one hundred twenty-eighth Seneca "blood." Under the current system, legal recognition as a tribal member will continue into infinity, with the actual degree of Seneca ancestry becoming increasingly minute.

By the mid-1800s, distinct tribal enumerations of membership among the Seneca were being conducted. There is evidence that in the early years of the U.S. census, intermarried members of other tribes, descendants of adopted female captives, and resident whites were enrolled, their descendants now extricably meshed into the fabric of the Seneca. Community rumors abound regarding individuals and families that originated from other tribal groups in the relatively distant past, implying that they should not be on the tribal roll. This partially explains the interest in tribal genealogy, especially in determining descent from early culture heros. To paraphrase Dorothy Parker: "Indians and elephants never forget."

The ideal matrilineal rule within the Seneca Nation has been internally challenged a number of times over the past one hundred years or more, usually by politically prominent Seneca men married to white women by whom, because of the matrilineal rule, their children were not legally recognized by the tribe as members. As a consequence, these descendants of male Senecas, while they may be socially accepted as members of the reservation community, could not inherit their father's reservation lands, could not participate or vote in the tribal political system, and could not share in any annuities or other benefits associated with tribal membership.

One of the earliest cases in Indian law to challenge a tribe's descent rule was *Patterson v. Council of the Seneca Nation of Indians* (245 N.Y. 433, 157 N.E. 734 [1927]; Cohen, 133-134). The case was brought by an enrolled Seneca man who wished to have the Seneca children of white mothers legally recognized as Indians and enrolled as members of the tribe. The Supreme Court ultimately upheld the traditional matrilineal rule of the Seneca Nation, concluding: "The conclusion is inescapable that the Seneca Tribe remains a separate nation; that its powers of self-government are retained with the sanction of the state; that the ancient customs and usages of the nation except in a few particulars, remain, unabolished, the law of the Indian land; that in its capacity of a sovereign nation the Seneca Nation is not subservient to the orders and directions of the courts of New York state; that, above all, the Seneca Nation retains for itself the power of determining who are Senecas, and in that respect is above interference and dictation" (738).

Santa Clara Pueblo v. Martinez (1978)

Some fifty years after the Seneca case, an equally famous situation emerged at the Santa Clara Pueblo community in New Mexico. In this landmark case, the Pueblo had established their traditional patrilineal rule in 1939 as the legal method of determining tribal membership. Here, a Santa Clara man whose children had a white mother were legally members of the pueblo; whereas, the children of a full-blood Santa Clara woman married to a Navajo in 1941, though they were raised in the community and spoke the Tewa language, were not eligible for enrollment as Santa Clara.

Suit was brought against the Pueblo of Santa Clara and its governor, Lucario Padilla, by Mrs. Julia Martinez on behalf of her daughter, Audrey Martinez, to challenge the patrilineal rule at Santa Clara. Above the issue of tribal enrollment, it was charged that the daughter was being denied federal services in health and education, and denied equal protection under Title II of the Indian Bill of Rights.

Initially, the federal district court ruled in a broad interpretation that the Indian Bill of Rights precluded all tribal sovereign immunity, and ruled against the Martinez family. In their appeal to the Tenth Circuit, the court affirmed the jurisdiction question but reversed the lower court in supporting the Martinez'. The court, applying an interpretation of equal protection to the Indian Bill of Rights, pointed out the sex discrimination involved in the tribe's patrilineal rule. The Pueblo of Santa Clara appealed to the United States Supreme Court which ruled in their favor. The Supreme Court upheld the tribes' sovereign right to determine the internal rules governing membership, and stated that tribes can only be sued after specific Congressional mandate (Wunder, 1994).

The Present

The determination of many individuals (of real, imagined, or minimal Indian ancestry) to be recognized as American Indians has caused a major reaction in the Indian community. To some extent the romantic Rousseauesque image of the American Indian as the Natural Man living in an unspoiled Eden has drawn many to suddenly recognize some remote Indian ancestry which they now feel needs to be claimed as their racial and cultural identification. Often this claim centers on some remote and mysterious ancestor, usually a Cherokee Indian grandmother or great-grandmother, who was forced to hide her racial identity in order to be accepted in the white community. In some cases, the precise identity of this Indian ancestor is not entirely clear, occasionally deriving from a long extinct tribal group, such as the Yamassee or Timucua.

There are, however, instances where individual quests for their Indian "roots" have legitimate basis in fact. For example, there have been thousands of Indian children and infants who have been taken away from their tribal communities and adopted by whites. As adults, some have successfully sought out their Indian origins, in some cases happily, and in others not. Also, there have been aggressive attempts by several tribes to have Indian adoptees returned to their tribes of origin, the feeling being that a form of continuing cultural genocide and destruction of Indian identity has been practiced in removing such children from an Indian environment. In several recent cases, the courts have supported the return of Indian adoptees to their tribes of origin.

The long history of impostors who have assumed Indian personalities continues to the present day. Earlier such individuals as Grey Owl, Red Fox, and Buffalo Child Long Lance (Smith, 1982) received considerable notoriety, since they were accepted by both whites and Indians, and were represented in the public forum as professional Indians and the voice of the "true Indian." The lucrative business and political importance of being an Indian has contributed to the inclusion of such individuals into the ranks of professional scholars, the arts, political circles, and others.

Since the advent of affirmative action programs, when identification as a minority became critical in academia and funding circles, there has been an increased number of individuals who now claim American Indian identity on the basis of a minuscule minority ancestry, or others who have deliberately fabricated this identity. As a result, an informal network of Indian scholars and political activists called the "Indian identity police" has been organized to investigate claims to Indian ancestry, especially those who are prominent on the national scene. A few of those who have been researched and "outed," including individuals in the national arts and academic areas, have threatened legal suit. Recently, a series of articles in a national Indian newspaper has exposed a number of these individuals who are writers (Reynolds, 1993).

Indians in the New Age

Inventing Indians and cultural fictions is not a new phenomenon. Although there is considerable historical depth to this movement, there now appears to be a strong and growing parallel of new Indian cultural identification with the New Age, resulting in the blurring of Indian tribal distinctiveness, and the creation of the homogenized Indian. Recently, some scholars have begun to reveal what they believe to be the newly created cultural and historical fallacies in contemporary Indian life and belief, to the dismay of many American Indians (Clifton, 1990; Deloria, 1992). The ultimate effect of selective incorporation of fabricated Indian culture, history, and religion into the New Age is to minimize and trivialize the beliefs, artifacts, and identity of American Indians. It is often pointed out that this process is not intended to demean Indian culture and identity; rather, New Agers insist on being advocates of Indian belief. In one case, the exposure of the Chief Seattle speech as fraud has dismayed the environmentalists and New Agers who often quoted this in their literature (Murray, 1993).

The flourishing of the present New Age movement, with its attraction to American Indian traditional beliefs, has resulted in a negative reaction on the part of many Indian religious people. It has been suggested that the various tribal religions are not proselytizing religions, and that their beliefs are held closely among members. At a recent meeting of the American Anthropological Association, a session was held on the subject of New Age and the American Indian. It was attended by many New Age believers who lamented that Indians were not more cooperative and supportive of efforts to popularize New Age beliefs, and that Indians continued to be secretive and exclusive in not allowing eager outsiders to attend and participate in their ceremonies. Additionally, there was regret that Indians were not more open to exploitation of their beliefs, since Indian religions were perhaps one of the last sources of inspiration in a troubled and endangered world.

There is often a liberal usage of the material paraphernalia associated with Indians, including the sweat bath, yarn mandalas and ojo de dios, the recently invented ubiquitous Oneida dream catcher (which actually may have originated in a much earlier date among Canadian Algonquians), feather fans, talking stones, use of the circle as a focal point of ceremony, drums, flutes, and rattles. Some features of stereotyped Indian belief have achieved a prominent place in the New Age, including bastardized concepts of Indian environmentalism, respect for the aged and Mother Earth, and Indians being especially attuned to societal concerns. Many Indians have been appalled, having seen the result of the movement to adopt some form of their beliefs, incorporate them into a hodge podge along with Oriental mysticism, astrology, palm reading, "crystal fondling," talking stones, and other features. As one Seneca man stated when discussing a local Indian woman's New Age business on the reservation, "This must be the mishmash of mumbo jumbo that Indians believe on Mars."

Some of the practitioners of the New Age movement claim divine knowledge has been imparted to them in a variety of ways, such as through earlier Indian ancestors of which they are the current incarnation, or from being admitted into secret ceremonies of tribal religion. Often, such practitioners adopt Indian names, usually "Princess," "Chief," "Dancing

Fawn," or "Soaring Eagle," to give some authentication to their knowledge of the sacred beliefs of the American Indian or a specific group. Unfortunately, there are well known examples of Indians themselves who are actively participating, profiting, and encouraging the misapplied application of strongly held Indian beliefs (Quinn, 1990).

The Future

In an excellent article, Lawrence Wright (1994) outlined the current situation regarding the American Indian. As the House Subcommittee on Census, Statistics, and Postal Personnel prepares for the census for the year 2000, one authority has predicted the possibility that continuing the ill-defined ethnic and racial categories that have been employed in the past could further confuse the ongoing race debate (Wright). In past censuses, the questionable criterion of "self-identification" of individuals claiming American Indian ancestry has undoubtedly skewed and inflated the population figures and accompanying social data. Although this may ultimately have been a positive contribution to federal and state allocations of money for Indian programs, it nevertheless gave a false picture regarding the Indian population in the United States. As one congressman remarked: "The numbers drive the dollars."

At the present time, there are four officially recognized racial groups in the United States: White, Black, Asian and Pacific Islander, and American Indian or Alaskan Native. These categories were established in 1977 by the Office of Management and Budget (OMB) under Statistical Directive 15, an important document which is central to racial classification in the United States. Numerous racial and ethnic groups have lobbied to have special consideration made to reassign or designate separate categories for their people. In addition to attempts at having the Laotians and Cambodians added under the Asian and Pacific Islander category, the Arab American Institute, representing various Middle Eastern nationalities currently enumerated under the white category, is now lobbying to have their classification considered a separate and distinct category.

In the case of American Indians, various Hawaiian politicians have been working to have Native Hawaiians relocated from the Asian and Pacific Islander category to that of the American Indian or Alaska Native category. Senator Daniel K. Akaka, a Native Hawaiian, has pointed out that the erroneous idea is perpetuated that Native Hawaiians are an immigrant class or that they no longer exist as a definable group. He argues that this situation would be corrected by the reassignment of the Native Hawaiian to the classification of aboriginal peoples. Akaka does not discuss the special tax exemptions, gambling casinos, and other privileges that are owing to federally recognized tribal groups in the other forty-nine states, although others have pointed this out. No special provisions have been mentioned in possible reassignments of the American Samoans, the Guamese, or the Puerto Rican populations. The National Congress of the American Indians (NCAI), the largest and most representative of tribal groups in the United States, is actively opposing Akaka's proposals, seeing them as a possible threat to American Indian identity and allocations of money for specially funded programs designated for Indians.

The additional suggestion of a "multiracial" category being added to Directive 15 is also seen by many American Indians, and others, as a threat to the present order of racial classification. Proponents of the new category believe that this addition would more realistically reflect the complex racial composition of the United States. If such a change were implemented, the vast majority of those now self-identified as American Indians would be more appropriately assigned to the multiracial category, drastically reducing the total numbers now enumerated as Indians in the federal census. In addition, an estimated seventy-five to ninety percent of blacks could also be reassigned to the multiracial box, due to the estimated numbers who claim mixed ancestry, essentially an abandonment of the racist one-drop rule. Based on data of previous censuses, it is demonstrated that Indians have a significantly higher percentage of interracial marriages than other minority groups, and that their numbers have grown a demographically impossible two hundred and fifty-nine percent from 1960 to 1990 (Wright). Nevertheless, most tribal groups are recording a growing number of out-marriages among tribal members, and a rapid overall population increase.

The Hispanic category also presents a conundrum with regard to American Indian ancestry. In the case of those whose origins are from Mexico, Guatemala, Peru, and many other Latin American countries, most, but not all, derive from Indian ancestry. Currently, there are significantly more Mayan Indians, refugees from internecine violence in Guatemala, residing in Florida than there are native Seminole and Miccosuki Indians.

The process of federal recognition, by which the government establishes a formal relationship with an Indian group, extending special status, such as federal services and tax-free reservation lands, is a major hurdle much sought after by many Indian based communities, especially triracial groups in the East. The process represents important outside recognition of Indian identity, and inclusion into the larger Indian world. Although some advocates for these groups decry the arduous process involved in federal recognition, other unquestioned Indian groups and individuals think that the federal recognition process is much too lax and liberal, allowing less than "real Indians" into a much cherished Indian identity. Also, with more and more groups being formally recognized by the federal government, the potential share of money allocated for services to all tribal groups is lessened.

The interconnected issues of race and identity will continue to vex legislators, governments, and tribes at least into the next century. For American Indians the basic and overriding issues are self-identity and group identity. The processes of acculturation, assimilation, and amalgamation, along with vacillating government policies to minimize or eliminate the racial, legal, and cultural identity of the American Indian will continue. The subject requires an in depth treatment and scholarly inquiry. As for all of their existence, the American Indians have been able to persevere and retain a dynamic identity. They will continue to do so in the foreseeable future.

Bibliography:

Abel, Annie Heloise, *The American Indian as Slaveholder and Secessionist*, Cleveland, Arthur H. Clarke and Company, 1915.

Barbour, Philip L., *Pocahontas and her World*, Boston, Houghton Mifflin Company, 1969.

Brown, Stuart E., Jr., Lorraine F. Myers, and Eileen M. Chappel, *Pocahontas Descendants, and Supplement (1987)*, Berryville, Virginia, The Pocahontas Foundation, 1985.

Burton, Art, *Black, Red and Deadly: Black and Indian Gunfighters of the Indian Territory, 1870-1907*, Austin, Eakin Press, 1991.

Cohen, Felix S., *Handbook of Federal Indian Law*, Washington, United States Government Printing Office, 1942; reissued, Albuquerque, University of New Mexico Press, 1971.

Davis, F. James, *Who is Black? One Nation's Definition*, University Park, Pennsylvania State University Press, 1991.

Deloria, Vine, Jr., "Comfortable Fictions and the Struggle for Turf: An Essay Review of *The Invented Indian: Cultural Fictions and Goverment Policies*," *American Indian Quarterly*, summer 1992; 397-410.

Forbes, Jack D., *Africans and Native Americans: The Language of Race and the Evolution of Red-Black Peoples*, Urbana and Chicago, University of Illinois Press, 1993.

The Invented Indian: Cultural Fictions and Government Policies, edited by James A. Clifton, New Brunswick, Transaction Publishers, 1990.

Jaffe, A. J., *The First Immigrants from Asia: A Population History of the North American Indians*, New York, Plenum Press, 1992.

Katz, William Loren, *Black Indians: A Hidden Heritage*, New York, Atheneum, 1986.

McAuliffe, Dennis, Jr., *The Deaths of Sybil Bolton: An American History*, New York, Random House, 1994.

Murray, Mary, "The Little Green Lie: How a Hoax Becomes a Best-Selling Book When it Serves a Special Cause," *Reader's Digest*, July 1993; 100-104.

Namias, June, *White Captives: Gender and Ethnicity on the American Frontier*, Chapel Hill, University of North Carolina Press, 1993.

Perdue, Theda, *Slavery and the Evolution of Cherokee Society, 1540-1866*, Knoxville, University of Tennessee Press, 1979.

Philip, Kenneth R., *John Collier's Crusade for Indian Reform, 1920-1954*, Tucson, University of Arizona Press, 1977.

Plecker, W. A., *The New Family and Race Improvement*, New Family Series, Virginia Health Bulletin, 17:5, 1925.

Quinn, William W., Jr., "The Southeast Syndrome: Notes on Indian Descendant Recruitment Organizations and Their Perceptions of Native American Culture," *American Indian Quarterly*, 14: 2, 1990; 147-154.

Reynolds, Jerry, "Indian Writers: Real or Imagined," *Indian Country Today*, September 8, 1993; A-1, A-3; September 15, 1993; A-1, A-3; October 6, 1993; A-1, A-2.

Sider, Gerald M., *Lumbee Indian Histories: Race, Ethnicity, and Indian Identity in the Southern United States*, Cambridge, Cambridge University Press, 1993.

Smith, Donald B., *Long Lance: The True Story of an Impostor*, Lincoln, University of Nebraska Press, 1982.

United States Supreme Court Reports, *Loving v. Virginia* (388 US 1, 18 L ed 2d 1010-1018, 87 S Ct 1817 [1967]).

Upton, Helen M., *The Everett Report in Historical Perspective: The Indians of New York*, Albany, New York State American Revolution Bicentennial Commission, 1980.

Viola, Herman J., *Ben Nighthorse Campbell: An American Warrior*, The Library of the American Indian, New York, Orion Books, 1993.

Wadlington, Walter, "The Loving Case: Virginia's Antimiscegenation Statute in Historical Perspective," *Virginia Law Review*, 52, 1966; 1189-1223.

Wright, Lawrence, "One Drop of Blood," *New Yorker*, July 25, 1994; 46-55.

Wunder, John R., "Retained by the People: A History of American Indians and the Bill of Rights," *Bicentennial Essays on the Bill of Rights*, Oxford, Oxford University Press, 1994.

Featured Entries

George H. J. Abrams
Contemporary Seneca anthropologist

Hank Adams
Contemporary Assiniboine/Dakota Sioux activist

Sherman Alexie
Contemporary Spokane/Coeur d'Alene poet and fiction writer

Elsie Allen
Twentieth-century Pomo basket weaver, scholar, educator, cultural consultant, and writer

Paula Gunn Allen
Contemporary Laguna Pueblo/Sioux novelist, poet, and professor

American Horse
Nineteenth-century Oglala Lakota Sioux tribal leader

Owanah Anderson
Contemporary Choctaw administrator, activist, writer, and editor

William Apess
Nineteenth-century Pequot minister, activist, and writer

Anna Mae Pictou Aquash
Twentieth-century Micmac political activist

JoAllyn Archambault
Contemporary Yankton Dakota Sioux anthropologist, artist, and museum program director

Amos Bad Heart Bull
Nineteenth-century Oglala Lakota Sioux tribal historian and artist

Louis W. Ballard
Contemporary Quapaw-Cherokee music educator and composer

Dennis J. Banks
Contemporary Anishinabe Ojibwa activist, teacher, and author

Barboncito
Nineteenth-century Navajo leader, ceremonial singer, and war chief

Fred Begay
Contemporary Navajo physicist

Harrison Begay
Contemporary Navajo artist

John Kim Bell
Contemporary Mohawk symphony orchestra conductor, composer, and foundation director

Clyde Bellecourt
Contemporary Ojibwa activist

Ramona Bennett
Contemporary Puyallup tribal leader, activist, and educator

Robert LaFollette Bennett
Contemporary Oneida lawyer and administrator

Big Foot
Nineteenth-century Minniconjou Sioux tribal leader

Black Elk
Nineteenth- and twentieth-century Oglala Lakota Sioux spiritual leader

Black Hawk
Eighteenth- and nineteenth-century Northern Sauk and Fox resistance leader

Black Kettle
Nineteenth-century Southern Cheyenne tribal leader

Ethel Blondin-Andrew
Contemporary Dene cabinet minister

Gertrude Simmons Bonnin
Nineteenth- and twentieth-century Yankton Sioux writer, educator, musician, and activist

Lionel R. Bordeaux
Contemporary Lakota Sioux educational leader and university president

Elias Boudinot
Nineteenth-century Cherokee editor, translator, author, orator, and religious and political figure

Billy Bowlegs
Nineteenth-century Seminole chief

Beth Brant
Contemporary Mohawk writer and poet

Joseph Brant
Eighteenth-century Mohawk tribal leader

Molly Brant
Eighteenth-century Mohawk tribal leader

Louis R. Bruce, Jr.
Twentieth-century Oglala Sioux/Mohawk government official

Joseph Bruchac III
Contemporary Abenaki author, poet, and storyteller

Diane M. Burns
Contemporary Anishinabe Ojibwa/Chemehuevi poet and artist

Barney Furman Bush
Contemporary Shawnee/Cayuga poet and teacher

Ben Nighthorse Campbell
Contemporary Northern Cheyenne political figure

Captain Jack
Nineteenth-century Modoc tribal leader

Gladys Cardiff
Contemporary Cherokee poet

Douglas Cardinal
Contemporary Blackfeet architect

Harold Cardinal
Contemporary Cree tribal leader and author

Tantoo Cardinal
Contemporary Métis actress

Edward Castillo
Contemporary Cahuilla-Luiseño educator and activist

Duane Champagne
Contemporary Turtle Mountain Chippewa sociologist and professor

Alfred Chato
Nineteenth- and twentieth-century Chiracahua Apache subchief and U.S. Army scout

Dean Chavers
Contemporary Lumbee educator and fund raiser

Maria Chona
Nineteenth- and twentieth-century Papago oral historian, medicine woman, and basket maker

C. Blue Clark
Contemporary Creek historian and university administrator

Henry Roe Cloud
Twentieth-century Winnebago educator and administrator

Cochise
Nineteenth-century Chiracahua Apache tribal leader

Mangas Coloradas
Nineteenth-century Mimbreno Apache tribal leader

Elizabeth Cook-Lynn
Contemporary Crow Creek Sioux poet and professor

George Copway
Nineteenth-century Ojibway missionary, writer, and lecturer

Helen Quintana Cordero
Contemporary Cochiti Pueblo potter and figurine maker

Cornplanter
Eighteenth- and nineteenth-century Seneca tribal leader

Crazy Horse
Nineteenth-century Oglala Brulé Sioux military and tribal leader

Crow Dog
Nineteenth-century Brulé Lakota Sioux warrior and tribal leader

Mary Crow Dog
Contemporary Lakota Sioux activist

Crowfoot
Nineteenth-century Blackfeet tribal leader

Curly
Nineteenth-century Crow scout

Charles Brent Curtis
Nineteenth- and twentieth-century Kansa/Kaw-Osage attorney, legislator, and vice president

Datsolalee
Nineteenth-century Washo basket weaver

Frank Day
Twentieth-century Maidu painter and tribal historian

Ada E. Deer
Contemporary Menominee social worker, activist, educator, and government official

Deganawida
Sixteenth-century Huron prophet, leader, and statesman

Delaware Prophet
Eighteenth-century Delaware spiritual leader

Ella Cara Deloria
Twentieth-century Yankton Sioux ethnologist, linguist, and novelist

Vine Deloria, Jr.
Contemporary Yankton Sioux writer

Vine Deloria, Sr.
Twentieth-century Standing Rock Yankton Sioux minister

William G. Demmert, Jr.
Contemporary Tlingit/Dakota Sioux professor and administrator

Lena Frank Dick
Twentieth-century Washoe basket weaver

Olive Patricia Dickason
Contemporary Métis historian, teacher, and writer

Angel DeCora Dietz
Nineteenth- and twentieth-century Winnebago artist, illustrator, and writer

Henry Chee Dodge
Nineteenth- and twentieth-century Navajo tribal leader

Michael Anthony Dorris
Contemporary Modoc writer, educator, and anthropologist

Edward P. Dozier
Twentieth-century Santa Clara Pueblo anthropologist, linguist, educator, activist, and writer

Frank C. Dukepoo
Contemporary Hopi-Laguna geneticist

Dull Knife
Nineteenth-century Northern Cheyenne tribal leader

Gabriel Dumont
Nineteenth-century Métis tribal leader

Charles Alexander Eastman
Nineteenth- and twentieth-century Santee Sioux writer and physician

John E. Echohawk
Contemporary Pawnee attorney and rights activist

Walter R. Echo-Hawk
Contemporary Pawnee attorney

Charles Edenshaw
Nineteenth- and twentieth-century Haida artist and tribal leader

Louise Erdrich
Contemporary Chippewa novelist and poet

Gary Dale Farmer
Contemporary Cayuga actor, producer, and activist

Donald L. Fixico
Contemporary Shawnee, Sauk/Fox, Creek, and Seminole professor

Harry Fonseca
Contemporary Maidu artist

Philip Fontaine
Contemporary Sagkeeng Ojibway leader and activist

Jack D. Forbes
Contemporary Renapé Powhatan/Lenapé Delaware ethnohistorian, educator, and writer

Billy Frank, Jr.
Contemporary Nisqually activist

Gall
Nineteenth-century Hunkpapa Lakota Sioux warrior and tribal leader

Hanay Geiogamah
Contemporary Kiowa/Delaware playwright, editor, and choreographer

Dan George
Twentieth-century Burrard Squamish actor and tribal leader

Geronimo
Nineteenth-century Bedonkohe Chiricahua Apache warrior and tribal leader

Tim Giago
Contemporary Oglala Sioux publisher and author

James Gladstone
Twentieth-century Blood Blackfeet political figure

Diane Glancy
Contemporary Cherokee writer and educator

Carl Nelson Gorman
Contemporary Navajo artist and lecturer

R. C. Gorman
Contemporary Navajo artist

Graham Greene
Contemporary Oneida actor

Janet Campbell Hale
Contemporary Coeur d'Alene novelist, poet, and educator

Handsome Lake
Eighteenth-century Seneca spiritual leader

Helen Hardin
Twentieth-century Santa Clara Pueblo artist

Chitto Harjo
Nineteenth-century Creek warrior

Joy Harjo
Contemporary Muscogee Creek writer, educator, musician, and artist

Suzan Shown Harjo
Contemporary Cheyenne administrator

Elijah Harper
Contemporary Cree provincial legislator

LaDonna Harris
Contemporary Comanche political activist and economic developer

Ned Hatathli
Twentieth-century Navajo educator

Ira Hamilton Hayes
Twentieth-century Pima military hero

William L. Hensley
Contemporary Inuit leader

Charlotte Heth
Contemporary Cherokee ethnomusicologist and administrator

J. N. B. Hewitt
Nineteenth- and twentieth-century Tuscarora ethnologist

Hiawatha
Fourteenth-century Mohawk or Onondaga tribal leader

Rosella Hightower
Contemporary Choctaw ballerina, dance teacher, and director

Thomson Highway
Contemporary Cree playwright and artistic director

Norbert S. Hill, Jr.
Contemporary Oneida educator

Geary Hobson
Contemporary Cherokee, Quapaw, and Chickasaw writer and educator

Linda Hogan
Contemporary Chickasaw poet, novelist, and essayist

George Horse Capture, Sr.
Contemporary Gros Ventre museum curator, writer, consultant, and cultural conservator

Allan Houser
Twentieth-century Fort Sill Chiricahua Apache artist

Oscar Howe
Twentieth-century Yankton Sioux artist and professor

Hump
Nineteenth-century Minniconjou Sioux tribal leader

Ishi
Nineteenth- and twentieth-century Yahi (Southern Yana) survivor and research informant

Alice Mae Jemison
Twentieth-century Seneca/Cherokee activist and politician

Emily Pauline Johnson
Nineteenth- and twentieth-century Mohawk author

Basil H. Johnston
Contemporary Ojibway (Chippewa) author and educator

Ted Jojola
Contemporary Isleta Pueblo educator and administrator

Peter Jones
Nineteenth-century Ojibwa Missisauga ruling chief, missionary, and author

William Jones
Nineteenth- and twentieth-century Fox ethnologist and writer

Joseph
Eighteenth- and nineteenth-century Nez Percé tribal leader

Joseph (the Younger)
Nineteenth- and twentieth-century Nez Percé tribal leader

Betty Mae Tiger Jumper
Contemporary Seminole nurse, tribal leader, journalist, and storyteller

Fred Kabotie
Twentieth-century Hopi artist and teacher

William Wayne Keeler
Twentieth-century Cherokee tribal leader and businessman

Kenojuak
Contemporary Inuit artist

Keokuk
Eighteenth- and nineteenth-century Sauk and Fox tribal leader

Kicking Bird
Nineteenth-century Kiowa tribal leader

Kirke Kickingbird
Contemporary Kiowa attorney and educator

Clara Sue Kidwell
Contemporary Choctaw/Chippewa author, educator, and historian

Thomas King
Contemporary Cherokee writer and educator

Francis La Flesche
Nineteenth- and twentieth-century Omaha ethnologist

Susan La Flesche Picotte
Nineteenth- and twentieth-century Omaha physician and community leader

Susette La Flesche Tibbles
Nineteenth- and twentieth-century Omaha advocate of Indian rights

Lame Deer
Twentieth-century Minniconjou herbal healer, tribal leader, and activist

Arlinda Faye Locklear
Contemporary Lumbee attorney

Charles Loloma
Twentieth-century Hopi jewelry designer and potter

Otellie Loloma
Twentieth-century Hopi artist and potter

Linda Lomahaftewa
Contemporary Hopi/Choctaw artist and educator

K. Tsianina Lomawaima
Contemporary Creek educator and anthropologist

Looking Glass
Nineteenth-century Nez Percé tribal leader

Phil Lucas
Contemporary Choctaw film producer, director, writer, and actor

Peter MacDonald
Contemporary Navajo tribal leader

Wilma Pearl Mankiller
Contemporary Cherokee tribal leader

George Manuel
Twentieth-century Shuswap tribal leader, activist, and author

Manuelito
Nineteenth-century Navajo tribal leader

Mungo Martin
Nineteenth- and twentieth-century Kwakiutl tribal leader and artist

Maria Montoya Martinez
Twentieth-century Tewa San Ildefonso Pueblo potter

Massasoit
Seventeenth-century Wampanoag tribal leader

John Joseph Mathews
Twentieth-century Osage tribal leader and writer

D'Arcy McNickle
Twentieth-century Flathead writer, historian, and activist

Russell C. Means
Contemporary Lakota Sioux activist

Beatrice A. Medicine
Contemporary Lakota Sioux anthropologist

Billy Mills
Contemporary Oglala Sioux athlete

N. Scott Momaday
Contemporary Kiowa writer, poet, and educator

Carlos Montezuma
Nineteenth- and twentieth-century Yavapai physician and activist

Norval Morrisseau
Contemporary Ojibwa artist

Mountain Wolf Woman
Twentieth-century Winnebago writer

Mourning Dove
Twentieth-century Colville Salishan writer and activist

Raymond Nakai
Contemporary Navajo tribal leader

Nampeyo
Nineteenth- and twentieth-century Hano potter

Nora Naranjo-Morse
Contemporary Tewa Pueblo poet and potter

Lloyd Kiva New
Contemporary Cherokee artist, fabric designer, artisan, administrator, and arts educator

Duane Niatum
Contemporary Klallam poet, short story writer, and essayist

Richard Oakes
Twentieth-century Mohawk political activist

Alanis Obomsawin
Contemporary Abenaki filmmaker and singer

Samson Occom
Eighteenth-century Mohegan preacher, diarist, epistolarist, and hymn lyricist

Barney Old Coyote
Contemporary Crow educator and administrator

Earl Old Person
Contemporary Blackfeet tribal leader

Opechancanough
Sixteenth- and seventeenth-century Powhatan-Renapé leader

Alfonso Ortiz
Contemporary San Juan Tewa educator, author, and anthropologist

Simon J. Ortiz
Contemporary Acoma Pueblo poet, writer

Osceola
Nineteenth-century Seminole tribal leader

Oshkosh
Nineteenth-century Menominee tribal leader

Ouray
Nineteenth-century Uncompahgre Ute tribal leader

Elizabeth Anne Parent
Contemporary Athabascan and Yupik educator

Arthur C. Parker
Nineteenth- and twentieth-century Seneca anthropologist and activist

Ely Samuel Parker
Nineteenth-century Seneca tribal leader, military leader, government official, and engineer

Quanah Parker
Nineteenth- and twentieth-century Comanche tribal leader

Jeanine Pease-Windy Boy
Contemporary Crow educator, administrator, and college president

Leonard Peltier
Contemporary Ojibwa-Lakota activist and political prisoner

Petalésharo
Nineteenth-century Pawnee tribal leader

Helen White Peterson
Contemporary Oglala Sioux government advisor

Archie Phinney
Twentieth-century Nez Percé anthropologist and activist

Peter Pitseolak
Twentieth-century Inuk photographer

Plenty Coups
Nineteenth- and twentieth-century Crow chief and tribal leader

Pocahontas
Seventeenth-century Powhatan-Renapé diplomat

Pontiac
Eighteenth-century Ottawa-Chippewa tribal leader

Popovi Da
Twentieth-century San Ildefonso Pueblo artist

Alexander Lawrence Posey
Nineteenth- and twentieth-century Creek poet, journalist, and humorist

Poundmaker
Nineteenth-century Cree tribal leader

Powhatan
Sixteenth- and seventeenth-century Powhatan-Renapé leader

Pushmataha
Eighteenth- and nineteenth-century Choctaw tribal leader

Rain-in-the-Face
Nineteenth-century Hunkpapa Sioux tribal leader and warrior

Red Cloud
Nineteenth-century Oglala Sioux tribal leader and warrior

Red Jacket
Eighteenth- and nineteenth-century Seneca tribal leader

Ben Reifel
Twentieth-century Brulé Sioux political figure

Carter Revard
Contemporary Osage poet and professor

Everett Ronald Rhoades
Contemporary Kiowa physician, administrator, and educator

John Rollin Ridge
Nineteenth-century Cherokee poet, editor, and journalist

Louis Riel
Nineteenth-century Métis resistance leader

David Risling
Contemporary Hoopa, Yurok, and Karok educator

Will Rogers
Nineteenth- and twentieth-century Cherokee entertainer and humorist

Roman Nose
Nineteenth-century Cheyenne tribal leader

Wendy Rose
Contemporary Hopi/Miwok poet, artist, and educator

Sacagawea
Eighteenth- and nineteenth-century Lehmi-Shoshone interpreter and guide

Buffy Sainte-Marie
Contemporary Cree singer, composer, actress, and activist

Ramona Sakiestewa
Contemporary Hopi weaver

Samoset
Seventeenth-century Abenaki tribal leader

Will Sampson, Jr.
Twentieth-century Creek actor and artist

Sanapia
Twentieth-century Comanche medicine woman

Joe Sando
Contemporary Jemez Pueblo author, historian, and educator

Satanta
Nineteenth-century Kiowa war chief

Katherine Siva Saubel
Contemporary Cahuilla educator and tribal leader

Fritz Scholder
Contemporary Luiseño artist

Seattle
Nineteenth-century Suquamish/Duwamish tribal chief

Sequoyah
Eighteenth- and nineteenth-century Cherokee linguist

Kathryn W. Shanley
Contemporary Assiniboine (Nakota) scholar

Leslie Marmon Silko
Contemporary Laguna Pueblo novelist and poet

Jay Silverheels
Twentieth-century Mohawk actor

Sitting Bull
Nineteenth-century Hunkpapa Sioux tribal leader and warrior

Juane Quick-to-See Smith
Contemporary Salish/Cree/Shoshone artist

Smohalla
Nineteenth-century Wanapam spiritual leader

Reuben Snake, Jr.
Twentieth-century Winnebago tribal and religious leader

David Sohappy, Sr.
Twentieth-century Yakima fisherman and activist

Spokane Garry
Nineteenth-century Spokane tribal leader, scholar, and Christian convert

Spotted Tail
Nineteenth-century Brulé Sioux warrior and civil leader

Squanto
Seventeenth-century Wampanoag translator and guide

Standing Bear
Nineteenth-century Ponca tribal leader

Ross Swimmer
Contemporary Cherokee tribal leader, government official, attorney, and businessman

Maria Tallchief
Contemporary Osage ballerina

Mary TallMountain
Contemporary Koyukon Athabaskan poet and fiction writer

Luci Tapahonso
Contemporary Navajo poet

Tecumseh
Eighteenth-century Shawnee warrior and tribal leader

Kateri Tekakwitha
Seventeenth-century Mohawk Catholic nun and candidate for sainthood

Grace F. Thorpe
Contemporary Sauk and Fox activist and craftsperson

Jim Thorpe
Nineteenth- and twentieth-century Sauk and Fox athlete and Olympic champion

Clifford Earl Trafzer
Contemporary Wyandot historian, educator, and author

John Trudell
Contemporary Santee Sioux activist, actor, and musician

Pablita Velarde
Contemporary Santa Clara Pueblo artist

Victorio
Nineteenth-century Mimbreno Apache tribal leader

Gerald Vizenor
Contemporary Ojibwa (Chippewa) author and teacher

Nancy Ward
Eighteenth- and nineteenth-century Cherokee warrior and tribal leader

Washakie
Nineteenth-century Shoshoni tribal leader

Stand Watie
Nineteenth-century Cherokee political leader and
Confederate general

Annie Dodge Wauneka
Contemporary Navajo health educator and tribal leader

James Welch
Contemporary Blackfeet/Gros Ventre novelist

Floyd Westerman
Contemporary Sisseton-Wahpeton Dakota Sioux songwriter
and performer

Roberta Hill Whiteman
Contemporary Oneida poet and educator

Sarah Winnemucca
Nineteenth-century Northern Paiute interpreter, lecturer, and
diplomat

Elizabeth Woody
Contemporary Wasco/Navajo poet, writer, artist, and
photographer

Rosita Worl
Contemporary Tlingit tribal leader, anthropologist, and
activist

Wovoka
Nineteenth- and twentieth-century Numu (Northern Paiute)
spiritual leader

Rosebud Yellow Robe
Twentieth-century Dakota-Brulé/Hunkpapa Sioux author
and performer

Young Man Afraid of His Horses
Nineteenth-century Oglala Sioux tribal leader

Peterson Zah
Contemporary Navajo leader

Ofelia Zepeda
Contemporary Tohono O'odham educator and linguist

Entries Listed by Tribal Groups/Nations

Abenaki

Joseph Bruchac III
Alanis Obomsawin
Samoset

Apache

Alfred Chato (Chiracahua)
Cochise (Chiracahua)
Mangas Coloradas (Mimbreno)
Geronimo (Bedonkohe Chiricahua)
Allan Houser (Fort Sill Chiricahua)
Victorio (Mimbreno)

Athabascan

Elizabeth Anne Parent

Blackfeet

Douglas Cardinal
Crowfoot
James Gladstone
Earl Old Person
James Welch

Cahuilla

Edward Castillo
Katherine Siva Saubel

Cayuga

Barney Furman Bush
Gary Dale Farmer

Chemehuevi

Diane M. Burns

Cherokee

Louis W. Ballard
Elias Boudinot
Gladys Cardiff
Diane Glancy
Charlotte Heth
Geary Hobson
Alice Mae Jemison
William Wayne Keeler
Thomas King
Wilma Pearl Mankiller
Lloyd Kiva New

John Rollin Ridge
Will Rogers
Sequoyah
Ross Swimmer
Nancy Ward
Stand Watie

Cheyenne

Black Kettle (Southern)
Ben Nighthorse Campbell (Northern)
Dull Knife (Northern)
Suzan Shown Harjo
Roman Nose

Chickasaw

Geary Hobson
Linda Hogan

Chippewa

Louise Erdrich
Clara Sue Kidwell
Pontiac

Choctaw

Owanah Anderson
Rosella Hightower
Clara Sue Kidwell
Linda Lomahaftewa
Phil Lucas
Pushmataha

Comanche

LaDonna Harris
Quanah Parker
Sanapia

Cree

Harold Cardinal
Elijah Harper
Thomson Highway
Poundmaker
Buffy Sainte-Marie
Juane Quick-to-See Smith

Creek

C. Blue Clark

Donald L. Fixico
Chitto Harjo
Joy Harjo (Muscogee)
K. Tsianina Lomawaima
Alexander Lawrence Posey
Will Sampson, Jr.

Crow

Curly
Barney Old Coyote
Jeanine Pease-Windy Boy
Plenty Coups

Dakota

Hank Adams
JoAllyn Archambault
William G. Demmert, Jr.
Charles Alexander Eastman (Santee)
John Trudell (Santee)
Floyd Westerman (Sisseton-Wahpeton)
Rosebud Yellow Robe

Delaware

Delaware Prophet
Jack D. Forbes (Lenapé)
Hanay Geiogamah

Duwamish

Seattle

Gros Ventre

George Horse Capture, Sr.
James Welch

Haida

Charles Edenshaw

Hano

Nampeyo

Hoopa

David Risling

Hopi

Frank C. Dukepoo
Fred Kabotie
Charles Loloma
Otellie Loloma

Linda Lomahaftewa
Wendy Rose
Ramona Sakiestewa

Huron

Deganawida

Inuit

William L. Hensley
Kenojuak

Inuk

Peter Pitseolak

Kansa

Charles Brent Curtis

Karok

David Risling

Kiowa

Hanay Geiogamah
Kicking Bird
Kirke Kickingbird
N. Scott Momaday
Everett Ronald Rhoades
Satanta

Koyukon Athabaskan

Mary TallMountain

Kwakiutl

Mungo Martin

Lakota

American Horse (Oglala)
Amos Bad Heart Bull (Oglala)
Big Foot (Minniconjou)
Black Elk (Oglala)
Lionel R. Bordeaux
Louis R. Bruce, Jr. (Oglala)
Crazy Horse (Oglala Brulé)
Crow Dog (Brulé)
Mary Crow Dog
Gall (Hunkpapa)
Tim Giago (Oglala)
Hump (Minniconjou)
Lame Deer (Minniconjou)

Russell C. Means
Beatrice A. Medicine
Billy Mills (Oglala)
Leonard Peltier
Helen White Peterson (Oglala)
Rain-in-the-Face (Hunkpapa)
Red Cloud (Oglala)
Sitting Bull (Hunkpapa)
Spotted Tail (Brulé)
Rosebud Yellow Robe (Brulé/Hunkpapa)
Ben Reifel (Brulé)
Young Man Afraid of His Horses (Oglala)

Lehmi

Sacagawea

Luiseño

Edward Castillo
Fritz Scholder

Lumbee

Dean Chavers
Arlinda Faye Locklear

Maidu

Frank Day
Harry Fonseca

Menominee

Ada E. Deer
Oshkosh

Métis

Tantoo Cardinal
Olive Patricia Dickason
Gabriel Dumont
Louis Riel

Micmac

Anna Mae Pictou Aquash

Miwok

Wendy Rose

Modoc

Captain Jack
Michael Anthony Dorris

Mohawk

John Kim Bell
Beth Brant
Joseph Brant
Molly Brant
Louis R. Bruce, Jr.
Hiawatha
Emily Pauline Johnson
Richard Oakes
Jay Silverheels
Kateri Tekakwitha

Mohegan

Samson Occom

Nakota

Hank Adams (Assiniboine)
JoAllyn Archambault (Yankton)
Gertrude Simmons Bonnin (Yankton)
Ella Cara Deloria (Yankton)
Vine Deloria, Jr. (Yankton)
Vine Deloria, Sr. (Standing Rock Yankton)
Oscar Howe (Yankton)
Kathryn W. Shanley (Assiniboine)

Navajo

Barboncito
Fred Begay
Harrison Begay
Ethel Blondin-Andrew (Dene)
Henry Chee Dodge
Carl Nelson Gorman
R. C. Gorman
Ned Hatathli
Peter MacDonald
Manuelito
Raymond Nakai
Luci Tapahonso
Annie Dodge Wauneka
Elizabeth Woody
Peterson Zah

Nez Percé

Joseph
Joseph (the Younger)
Looking Glass
Archie Phinney

Nisqually

Billy Frank, Jr.

Numu (Northern Paiute)

Sarah Winnemucca
Wovoka

Ojibwa/Ojibway

Dennis J. Banks (Anishinabe)
Clyde Bellecourt
Diane M. Burns (Anishinabe)
Duane Champagne (Turtle Mountain Chippewa)
George Copway
Philip Fontaine (Sagkeeng)
Basil H. Johnston (Chippewa)
Peter Jones (Missisauga)
Norval Morrisseau
Leonard Peltier
Gerald Vizenor (Chippewa)

Omaha

Francis La Flesche
Susan La Flesche Picotte
Susette La Flesche Tibbles

Oneida

Robert LaFollette Bennett
Graham Greene
Norbert S. Hill, Jr.
Roberta Hill Whiteman

Onondaga

Hiawatha

Osage

Charles Brent Curtis
John Joseph Mathews
Carter Revard
Maria Tallchief

Ottawa

Pontiac

Papago

Maria Chona

Pawnee

John E. Echohawk
Walter R. Echo-Hawk
Petalésharo

Pequot

William Apess

Pima

Ira Hamilton Hayes

Pomo

Elsie Allen

Ponca

Standing Bear

Powhatan-Renapé

Jack D. Forbes
Opechancanough
Pocahontas
Powhatan

Pueblo

Paula Gunn Allen (Laguna)
Helen Quintana Cordero (Cochiti)
Edward P. Dozier (Santa Clara)
Frank C. Dukepoo (Laguna)
Helen Hardin (Santa Clara)
Ted Jojola (Isleta)
Maria Montoya Martinez (Tewa/San Ildefonso)
Nora Naranjo-Morse (Tewa)
Alfonso Ortiz (San Juan Tewa)
Simon J. Ortiz (Acoma)
Popovi Da (San Ildefonso)
Joe Sando (Jemez)
Leslie Marmon Silko (Laguna)
Pablita Velarde (Santa Clara)

Puyallup

Ramona Bennett

Quapaw

Louis W. Ballard
Geary Hobson

Salishan

Sherman Alexie (Spokane/Coeur d'Alene)
Dan George (Squamish)
Janet Campbell Hale (Coeur d'Alene)
D'Arcy McNickle (Flathead)
Mourning Dove (Colville)
Duane Niatum (Klallam)
Seattle (Suquamish)
Juane Quick-to-See Smith
Spokane Garry (Spokane)

Sauk and Fox

Black Hawk
Donald L. Fixico

William Jones
Keokuk
Grace F. Thorpe
Jim Thorpe

Seminole

Billy Bowlegs
Donald L. Fixico
Betty Mae Tiger Jumper
Osceola

Seneca

George H. J. Abrams
Cornplanter
Handsome Lake
Alice Mae Jemison
Arthur C. Parker
Ely Samuel Parker
Red Jacket

Shawnee

Barney Furman Bush
Donald L. Fixico
Tecumseh

Shoshone

Sacagawea
Juane Quick-to-See Smith
Washakie

Shuswap

George Manuel

Sioux

Paula Gunn Allen
Louis W. Ballard
Elizabeth Cook-Lynn (Crow Creek)

Tlingit

William G. Demmert, Jr.
Rosita Worl

Tohono O'odham

Ofelia Zepeda

Tuscarora

J. N. B. Hewitt

Uncompahgre Ute

Ouray

Wampanoag

Massasoit
Squanto

Wanapam

Smohalla

Wasco

Elizabeth Woody

Washo/Washoe

Datsolalee
Lena Frank Dick

Winnebago

Henry Roe Cloud
Angel DeCora Dietz
Reuben Snake, Jr.
Mountain Wolf Woman

Wyandot

Clifford Earl Trafzer

Yahi

Ishi (Southern Yana)

Yakima

David Sohappy, Sr.

Yavapai

Carlos Montezuma

Yupik

Elizabeth Anne Parent

Yurok

David Risling

Entries Listed by Occupations/Tribal Roles

Activist

Hank Adams
Elsie Allen
Owanah Anderson
William Apess
Anna Mae Pictou Aquash
Dennis J. Banks
Barboncito
Clyde Bellecourt
Ramona Bennett
Gertrude Simmons Bonnin
Mary Crow Dog
Ada E. Deer
Angel DeCora Dietz
Edward P. Dozier
John E. Echohawk
Gary Dale Farmer
Philip Fontaine
Billy Frank, Jr.
William L. Hensley
Alice Mae Jemison
Susan La Flesche Picotte
Susette La Flesche Tibbles
Lame Deer
George Manuel
D'Arcy McNickle
Russell C. Means
Carlos Montezuma
Mourning Dove
Richard Oakes
Arthur C. Parker
Leonard Peltier
Petalésharo
Helen White Peterson
Archie Phinney
Buffy Sainte-Marie
Reuben Snake, Jr.
David Sohappy, Sr.
Standing Bear
Grace F. Thorpe
John Trudell
Sarah Winnemucca
Rosita Worl

Actor

Dennis J. Banks
Tantoo Cardinal
Gary Dale Farmer
Dan George
Graham Greene
Phil Lucas
Russell C. Means
Will Rogers

Buffy Sainte-Marie
Will Sampson, Jr.
Jay Silverheels
John Trudell
Floyd Westerman

Administrator (Business)

Louis R. Bruce, Jr.
William Wayne Keeler
Lloyd Kiva New
Ross Swimmer

Administrator (Education)

John Kim Bell
Lionel R. Bordeaux
Louis R. Bruce, Jr.
C. Blue Clark
Henry Roe Cloud
William G. Demmert, Jr.
Charlotte Heth
Ted Jojola
Lloyd Kiva New
Jeanine Pease-Windy Boy
Alexander Lawrence Posey
Rosita Worl

Administrator (Government)

Owanah Anderson
Robert LaFollette Bennett
Louis R. Bruce, Jr.
Henry Roe Cloud
William G. Demmert, Jr.
Suzan Shown Harjo
LaDonna Harris
Barney Old Coyote
Helen White Peterson
Everett Ronald Rhoades

Anthropologist

George H. J. Abrams
JoAllyn Archambault
Michael Anthony Dorris
Edward P. Dozier
K. Tsianina Lomawaima
Beatrice A. Medicine
Alfonso Ortiz
Arthur C. Parker
Archie Phinney
Rosita Worl

Archaeologist

Arthur C. Parker

Architect

Douglas Cardinal

Artist

JoAllyn Archambault
Amos Bad Heart Bull
Harrison Begay
Frank Day
Lena Frank Dick
Angel DeCora Dietz
Charles Edenshaw
Harry Fonseca
Carl Nelson Gorman
R. C. Gorman
Helen Hardin
Joy Harjo
Allan Houser
Oscar Howe
Fred Kabotie
Kenojuak
Charles Loloma
Otellie Loloma
Linda Lomahaftewa
Mungo Martin
Norval Morrisseau
Lloyd Kiva New
Popovi Da
Wendy Rose
Ramona Sakiestewa
Will Sampson, Jr.
Fritz Scholder
Juane Quick-to-See Smith
Pablita Velarde
Elizabeth Woody

Athlete

Ben Nighthorse Campbell
Billy Mills
Jim Thorpe

Basket maker

Elsie Allen
Maria Chona
Datsolalee
Lena Frank Dick

Choreographer

Hanay Geiogamah
Rosella Hightower

Composer/Conductor

Louis W. Ballard
John Kim Bell
Samson Occom

Dancer

Rosella Hightower
Maria Tallchief

Editor

Owanah Anderson
Elias Boudinot
Hanay Geiogamah
Janet Campbell Hale
N. Scott Momaday
Duane Niatum
Alexander Lawrence Posey
John Rollin Ridge

Educator

George H. J. Abrams
Elsie Allen
Paula Gunn Allen
Louis W. Ballard
Fred Begay
Ramona Bennett
Gertrude Simmons Bonnin
Beth Brant
Joseph Bruchac III
Barney Furman Bush
Edward Castillo
Duane Champagne
Dean Chavers
Henry Roe Cloud
Elizabeth Cook-Lynn
Ada E. Deer
William G. Demmert, Jr.
Olive Patricia Dickason
Angel DeCora Dietz
Michael Anthony Dorris
Edward P. Dozier
Frank C. Dukepoo
Donald L. Fixico
Jack D. Forbes
Diane Glancy
Janet Campbell Hale
Joy Harjo
Ned Hatathli
Charlotte Heth
Norbert S. Hill, Jr.
Geary Hobson
Linda Hogan
Allan Houser
Oscar Howe
Basil H. Johnston
Ted Jojola
Fred Kabotie
Kirke Kickingbird
Clara Sue Kidwell
Thomas King
Charles Loloma
Otellie Loloma
Linda Lomahaftewa
K. Tsianina Lomawaima
N. Scott Momaday
Lloyd Kiva New
Barney Old Coyote
Alfonso Ortiz
Elizabeth Anne Parent
Jeanine Pease-Windy Boy
Carter Revard
Everett Ronald Rhoades
David Risling

Wendy Rose
Sanapia
Joe Sando
Katherine Siva Saubel
Kathryn W. Shanley
Reuben Snake, Jr.
Spokane Garry
Clifford Earl Trafzer
Gerald Vizenor
Roberta Hill Whiteman
Sarah Winnemucca
Rosita Worl
Ofelia Zepeda

Entertainer

Frank C. Dukepoo
Gabriel Dumont
Will Rogers

Ethnologist

J. N. B. Hewitt
William Jones
Francis La Flesche

Fiction writer

Sherman Alexie
Paula Gunn Allen
Joseph Bruchac III
Michael Anthony Dorris
Louise Erdrich
Janet Campbell Hale
Betty Mae Tiger Jumper
Mourning Dove
Duane Niatum
Simon J. Ortiz
Leslie Marmon Silko

Filmmaker

Joy Harjo
Phil Lucas
Alanis Obomsawin

Fisherman

Billy Frank, Jr.
David Sohappy, Sr.

Geneticist

Frank C. Dukepoo

Health Service worker

Maria Chona
Betty Mae Tiger Jumper
Annie Dodge Wauneka

Herbalist

Lame Deer
Sanapia

Historian

Maria Chona
C. Blue Clark
Olive Patricia Dickason
Donald L. Fixico
Jack D. Forbes
Clara Sue Kidwell
D'Arcy McNickle
Joe Sando
Clifford Earl Trafzer

Informant

Ishi
Kicking Bird
Stand Watie

Jewelry designer

Ben Nighthorse Campbell
Charles Loloma

Journalist

Betty Mae Tiger Jumper
Alexander Lawrence Posey
John Rollin Ridge

Lawyer

Robert LaFollette Bennett
Charles Brent Curtis
John E. Echohawk
Walter R. Echo-Hawk
Kirke Kickingbird
Arlinda Faye Locklear

Legislator

Ethel Blondin-Andrew
Ben Nighthorse Campbell
Ada E. Deer
James Gladstone
Elijah Harper
William L. Hensley

Linguist

Edward P. Dozier
Sequoyah
Sarah Winnemucca
Ofelia Zepeda

Military figure

Alfred Chato
Ira Hamilton Hayes
Ely Samuel Parker
Stand Watie

Museum program/exhibit developer

George H. J. Abrams
JoAllyn Archambault
George Horse Capture, Sr.

Musician

Louis W. Ballard
John Kim Bell
Gertrude Simmons Bonnin
Joy Harjo
Alanis Obomsawin
Buffy Sainte-Marie
John Trudell

Performing artist

Emily Pauline Johnson
Will Rogers
Buffy Sainte-Marie
Floyd Westerman
Rosebud Yellow Robe

Photographer

Peter Pitseolak
Elizabeth Woody

Physician

Charles Alexander Eastman
Susan La Flesche Picotte
Carlos Montezuma
Everett Ronald Rhoades

Physicist

Fred Begay

Playwright

Hanay Geiogamah
Thomson Highway

Poet

Sherman Alexie
Paula Gunn Allen
Barney Furman Bush
Gladys Cardiff
Elizabeth Cook-Lynn
Janet Campbell Hale
Joy Harjo
Emily Pauline Johnson
Duane Niatum
Simon J. Ortiz
Carter Revard
Leslie Marmon Silko
Mary TallMountain
Luci Tapahonso
Roberta Hill Whiteman
Elizabeth Woody

Political figure

Hank Adams
Ethel Blondin-Andrew
Elias Boudinot
Joseph Brant
Ben Nighthorse Campbell
Charles Brent Curtis

Ada E. Deer
Philip Fontaine
LaDonna Harris
William L. Hensley
Alice Mae Jemison
Keokuk
Kirke Kickingbird
Ely Samuel Parker
Alexander Lawrence Posey
Ben Reifel
Reuben Snake, Jr.
Ross Swimmer
Stand Watie

Potter

Helen Quintana Cordero
Charles Loloma
Otellie Loloma
Maria Montoya Martinez
Nampeyo
Nora Naranjo-Morse

Producer/Director

Gary Dale Farmer
Rosella Hightower
Phil Lucas
Alanis Obomsawin

Publisher

Joseph Bruchac III
Tim Giago

Religious figure

William Apess
George Copway
Peter Jones
Susan La Flesche Picotte
Samson Occom
Spokane Garry
Kateri Tekakwitha

Resistance leader

Barboncito
Black Hawk
Billy Bowlegs
Captain Jack
Gabriel Dumont
Pontiac
Louis Riel
Roman Nose

Sociologist

Duane Champagne

Songwriter

Buffy Sainte-Marie

Floyd Westerman

Spiritual leader

Black Elk
Delaware Prophet
Vine Deloria, Sr.
Dull Knife
Handsome Lake
Smohalla
Wovoka

Translator/Interpreter

Elias Boudinot
Henry Chee Dodge
Pocahontas
Sacagawea
Samoset
Squanto
Sarah Winnemucca

Tribal leader

American Horse
Barboncito
Ramona Bennett
Big Foot
Black Kettle
Molly Brant
Harold Cardinal
Alfred Chato
Cochise
Mangas Coloradas
Cornplanter
Crazy Horse
Crow Dog
Crowfoot
Deganawida
Henry Chee Dodge
Dull Knife
Gabriel Dumont
Charles Edenshaw
Philip Fontaine
Gall
Geronimo
Elijah Harper
Hiawatha
Hump
Peter Jones
Joseph
Joseph (the Younger)
Betty Mae Tiger Jumper
William Wayne Keeler
Keokuk
Kicking Bird
Lame Deer
Looking Glass
Peter MacDonald
Wilma Pearl Mankiller
George Manuel
Manuelito

Mungo Martin
Massasoit
John Joseph Mathews
Raymond Nakai
Earl Old Person
Opechancanough
Osceola
Oshkosh
Ouray
Ely Samuel Parker
Quanah Parker
Petalésharo
Plenty Coups
Pontiac
Poundmaker
Powhatan
Pushmataha
Rain-in-the-Face
Red Cloud
Red Jacket
Roman Nose
Samoset
Satanta
Katherine Siva Saubel
Seattle
Sitting Bull
Reuben Snake, Jr.
Spokane Garry
Standing Bear
Ross Swimmer
Tecumseh
Victorio
Nancy Ward
Washakie
Stand Watie
Annie Dodge Wauneka
Rosita Worl
Young Man Afraid of His Horses
Peterson Zah

Warrior

Barboncito
Black Hawk
Black Kettle
Billy Bowlegs
Joseph Brant
Captain Jack
Alfred Chato
Cochise
Mangas Coloradas
Crazy Horse
Crow Dog
Dull Knife
Gall
Geronimo
Chitto Harjo
Keokuk
Kicking Bird
Pontiac
Rain-in-the-Face
Red Cloud

Roman Nose
Satanta
Spotted Tail
Tecumseh
Victorio
Nancy Ward
Washakie
Young Man Afraid of His Horses

Writer

George H. J. Abrams
Sherman Alexie
Elsie Allen
Paula Gunn Allen
Owanah Anderson
William Apess
Dennis J. Banks
Gertrude Simmons Bonnin
Elias Boudinot
Beth Brant
Joseph Bruchac III
Diane M. Burns
Harold Cardinal
George Copway
Ella Cara Deloria
Vine Deloria, Jr.
William G. Demmert, Jr.
Olive Patricia Dickason
Angel DeCora Dietz
Michael Anthony Dorris
Edward P. Dozier
Charles Alexander Eastman
Louise Erdrich
Jack D. Forbes
Tim Giago

Diane Glancy
Janet Campbell Hale
Joy Harjo
Geary Hobson
Linda Hogan
George Horse Capture, Sr.
Emily Pauline Johnson
Basil H. Johnston
Peter Jones
William Jones
Clara Sue Kidwell
Thomas King
Francis La Flesche
Phil Lucas
George Manuel
John Joseph Mathews
D'Arcy McNickle
N. Scott Momaday
Mountain Wolf Woman
Mourning Dove
Nora Naranjo-Morse
Samson Occom
Alfonso Ortiz
Simon J. Ortiz
Alexander Lawrence Posey
John Rollin Ridge
Will Rogers
Wendy Rose
Joe Sando
Mary TallMountain
Luci Tapahonso
Clifford Earl Trafzer
Gerald Vizenor
James Welch
Elizabeth Woody
Rosebud Yellow Robe

Contributors

Abrams, George H. J. Please see entry. Seneca anthropologist and educator; researcher/consultant to the President, Christian A. Johnson Endeavor Foundation, New York, New York; visiting scholar, Museum Studies Department, Graduate School of Arts and Science, New York University, New York, New York; founding director of the Seneca-Iroquois National Museum; contributor to several books, including *Iroquois Culture, History and Prehistory: Proceedings of the 1965 Conference on Iroquois Research* (1967), *Ways of Effectively Addressing Cultural Responsibilities: Proceedings of the Native American Museums Program National Workshop* (1983), and *Museums, and the Making of "Ourselves": The Role of Objects in National Identity* (1994); author of several essays in such periodicals as *American Anthropologist, Western Historical Quarterly*, and *Geographic Review*; consulting editor of *Notable Native Americans*, 1995; member/board of directors, American Indian Development, Inc., Denver, Colorado; member of the American Indian Advisory Board, Denver Museum of Natural History, Denver, Colorado; member/board of advisors, Mohawk-Caughnawaga Museum, Fonda, New York. **Essays:** Charles Curtis, Arthur Caswell Parker, and Ely Samuel Parker.

Andreassi, Diane. Newspaper reporter, editor, and free-lance writer for a number of publications. **Essays:** Frank C. Dukepoo, Tim Giago, and Kirke Kickingbird.

Begay, David. Teaches at the Navajo Community College, Tsaile, Arizona. **Essay:** Billy Mills (with Nancy C. Maryboy).

Bernardis, Timothy. Professor of Crow Studies and library director, since the library's inception in 1985, at Little Big Horn College, Montana; author of a Crow tribal catalog for the Smithsonian Institution and a Crow bibliography (with Peter Nabokov) to be published by Scarecrow Press. **Essay:** Plenty Coups.

Cannon, Charles. Free-lance writer based in Chicago, Illinois. **Essays:** Nicholas Black Elk, Ella Cara Deloria, Susan La Flesche Picotte, and Alexander Lawrence Posey.

Carter, Christina E. Librarian specializing in Native American studies at the University of New Mexico General Library. **Essays:** C. Blue Clark, Ada Deer, Leonard Peltier, and Sacagawea.

Carter, Bill. Teaches history at Arizona State University in Tempe. **Essays:** Dan George and Will Sampson, Jr.

Clay, Catherine A. Information specialist and free-lance writer based in Lake Alfred, Florida. **Essays:** American Horse, Owanah Anderson, Chato, Maria Chona, Henry Roe Cloud, Crow Dog, Henry Chee Dodge, Donald Fixico, Philip Fontaine, Tsianina Lomawaima, Phil Lucas, Ouray, and Poundmaker.

Clegg, Blanche Cox. Archivist at Southern Utah University in Cedar City. **Essays:** Nampeyo, Nora Naranjo-Morse, Ramona Sakiestewa, Luci Tapahonso, Sarah Winnemucca, and Elizabeth Woody.

Conliff, Steven Edwin. Free-lance writer and editor of Mahican (Stockbridge) and Oneida descent; edited the anthology *Blacklisted News: Secret Histories from Chicago '68 to 1984* (1983); member of the Delaware Indian Heritage Committee. **Essays:** George H. J. Abrams, Curly, J.N.B. Hewitt, Roman Nose, Samoset, Victorio, and Winnemucca.

Cullum, Linda. Assistant Public Services Librarian at Lake Superior State University Library, Sault Ste. Marie, Michigan; contributor to *Library Journal* and *American Reference Books Annual*. **Essays:** Beth Brant, Diane M. Burns, and Janet Campbell.

Davies, Wade. Doctoral student of twentieth-century Native American history, specializing in the Navajo Nation and health care issues, at Arizona State University in Tempe. **Essay:** Fred Begay.

di Filippo, JoAnn. Graduate student pursuing a M.A. degree in American Indian Studies at the University of Arizona; economic consultant to several American Indian communities; founder of The Sunset Foundation, a non-profit organization designed to assist American Indian youths in cultural enrichment programs; member of the Tohono O'odham Judiciary Staff; court-appointed legal representative for Children-In-Need on the Tohono O'odham Reservation, Sells, Arizona. **Essays:** Geronimo, N. Scott Momaday, Simon J. Ortiz, Elizabeth Anne Parent, and Ofelia Zepeda.

Floyd, Kay A. Free-lance writer and administrative assistant at Lake Superior State University, Sault Ste. Marie, Michigan. **Essays:** Deganawida, Handsome Lake, and Pontiac.

Forbes, Jack D. Please see entry. Powhatan-Renápe and Delaware-Lenápe chair and professor of Native American Studies at the University of California, Davis; author of *Columbus and Other Cannibals* (1992), *Africans and Native Americans* (1993), *Apache, Navaho and Spaniard* (1994), and *Only Approved Indians* (1995). **Essays:** Opechancanough and Powhatan.

Gallman, Jason. Free-lance writer and graduate student in literature at Purdue University, West Lafayette, Indiana. **Essays:** Black Kettle, Joseph Bruchac III, Billy Frank, Jr., Ted Jojola, Kenojuak, Thomas King, George Manuel, Mungo Martin, Barney Old Coyote, Archie Phinney, Peter Pitseolak, David Risling, and Katherine Siva Saubel.

Gelatt, Roberta Kaplin. Free-lance writer, community volunteer, and an aspiring author of young adult fiction from La Crosse, Wisconsin. **Essays:** Maria Montoya Martinez and Roberta Hill Whiteman.

Gibb, Alice. Writer and editor based in Ailsa Craig, Ontario, whose essays have appeared in newspapers, periodicals, and history books. **Essays:** Ethel Blondin-Andrew and Norval Morrisseau.

Hadella, Paul. Professor of English at Southern Oregon State College; runs Talent House Press, an independent poetry publisher. **Essay:** Sherman Alexie.

Hellstern, Russell. Real estate broker; photographer; free-lance writer with special interest in history and American Indian culture. **Essays:** Billy Bowlegs, Helen Quintana Cordero, and Mourning Dove.

Huseboe, Arthur R. Professor of English and executive director of the Center for Western Studies at Augustana College, Sioux Falls, South Dakota; holds the National Endowment for the Humanities Chair in Regional Heritage; former president of the Western Literature Association. **Essay:** Charles Alexander Eastman.

Jaskoski, Helen. Teaches in the English Department at California State University-Fullerton; editor emeritus of *SAIL--Studies in American Indian Literature.* In addition to scholarship on American Indian, African American, Jewish American, and Asian American literature, she has published poetry, fiction, and articles on poetry and healing; her book *Poetry/Mind/Body* is published by University Press of America. **Essays:** Wendy Rose and Kathryn Winona Shanley.

Jersyk, Julie Henderson. Librarian at Northeastern University, Boston, Massachusetts. **Essays:** Delaware Prophet, Squanto, and Tecumseh.

Kasee, Cynthia R. Educator with a Ph.D. in American Indian Studies from Union Institute College, Cincinnati, Ohio; contributor to *Directory of Minority Women: Native American Women* and *Encyclopedic Series of the American Wars: Revolutionary War*, both published by Garland Press; founded the Native American Awareness Society of Thomas More College, Crestview Hills, Kentucky; member of the Association of American Indian/Alaska Native College Professors and the National Congress of Native Americans. **Essays:** Anna Mae Pictou Aquash, LaDonna C. Harris, Ira Hamilton Hayes, George P. Horse Capture, Emily Pauline Johnson, Betty Mae Tiger Jumper, Carlos Montezuma, Richard Oakes, Alfonso Ortiz, Quanah Parker, Janine Pease-Windy Boy, Buffy Sainte-Marie, Reuben Snake, Jr., John Trudell, Nancy Ward, and Annie Dodge Wauneka.

Kunesh, Tom (tpkunesh). Mixed-blood Standing Rock Hunkpapa Lakota; public relations person for the Chattanooga InterTribal Association. **Essays:** JoAllyn

Archambault, Black Hawk, Tantoo Cardinal, Graham Greene, Arlinda Faye Locklear, and Seattle.

Lealand, Brett A. Multidisciplinary artist of Sephardic descent living in New England. **Essays:** Louis W[ayne] Ballard, John Kim Bell, Mary Molly Brant, Cochise, Alanis Obomsawin, Fritz Scholder, Maria Tallchief, Kateri Tekakwitha, Gerald Robert Vizenor, and James Welch.

Little, John E. Free-lance writer based in Lawrenceville, New Jersey. **Essays:** Edward Pasqual Dozier, Keokuk, Kicking Bird, Francis La Flesche, Susette La Flesche Tibbles, John Joseph Mathews, Red Jacket, and Standing Bear.

Maryboy, Nancy C. Teaches at the Navajo Community College, Tsaile, Arizona. **Essay:** Billy Mills (with David Begay).

Marecki-Arriola, Denise. Free-lance writer from Forest Grove, Oregon, specializing in Native American history. **Essays:** Manuelito, Satanta, David Sohappy, Sr., and Garry Spokane.

Maxfield, Doris. Free-lance writer based in Linden, Michigan. **Essays:** Pushmataha and Will Rogers.

McAuliffe, Claudeen E. Teaches supervisory and management courses at Milwaukee Area Technical College and Waukesha County Technical College, Wisconsin; member of the Taino Indian Council in Puerto Rico. **Essays:** Elsie Allen, Mangas Coloradas, Norbert S. Hill, Jr., Petalésharo, and Sanapia.

McDermott, John D. Historical consultant from Sheridan, Wyoming; former policy director of the President's Advisory Council on Historic Preservation; author of *Dangerous Duty* (1993), a story of military posts that protected the Oregon Trail in Wyoming's South Pass area. **Essays:** Big Foot, Dull Knife, and Joseph the Younger.

McIntosh, Kenneth W. Adjunct professor, University of Tulsa; member of American Indian Historians' Association and Oklahoma Historical Society; author of "Geronimo's Friend: Angie Debo and the New History," *Chronicles of Oklahoma*, summer 1988. **Essay:** Chitto Harjo.

Meredith, Howard. Cherokee and Akokisa research associate, Cookson Institute; head of American Studies Department of the University of Science and Arts of Oklahoma; member of board of directors of Red Earth and Hall of Fame of Famous American Indians; author of *Hasinai*, 1988; *Modern American Indian Tribal Government*, 1993; and *Southern Plains Alliances*, in press. **Essays:** Ramona Bennett, Charlotte Anne Wilson Heth, Geary Hobson, Allan Houser, and William Jones.

Noah, Phyllis "Picturestone." Cherokee free-lance writer and editor; editor of *Close Encounters of the Fourth and Fifth Kind* (1991); public relations representative for Native

American art festivals and pow wows; traditional dancer. **Essays:** Helen Bagshaw Hardin, Ned A. Hatathli, William L. Hensley, Linda Hogan, Clara Sue Kidwell, Charles Loloma, Otellie, Loloma, Linda Lomahaftewa, Peter MacDonald, Raymond Nakai, Popovi Da, and Everett Ronald Rhoades.

Noguera, Susan. Free-lance writer in Livonia, Michigan; contributor to *Black Writers* (1994); and *Theater and Stage Actors and Producers.* **Essay:** Diane Glancy.

Parker, Sandra Sac. Free-lance writer in Okmulgee, Oklahoma; news editor of the *Cherokee Observer*; speaker and writer on Native American history. **Essays:** William Wayne Keeler and Lloyd Kiva New.

Pfeffer, Wendy. Free-lance writer in Pennington, New Jersey; author of children's books, including *The Gooney War* (1990), *All About Me* (1990), *The World of Nature* (1990), *From Tadpole to Frog* (1994), and *Goldfish* (forthcoming). **Essays:** William G. Demmert, Jr., Angel DeCora Dietz, Gary Dale Farmer, Jay Silverheels, and Juane Quick-to-See Smith.

Ratner, Megan. Free-lance writer in New York City. **Essay:** Mountain Wolf Woman.

Reddish, Jennifer Gray. Free-lance writer and poet; managing editor of *Tribal College: Journal of American Indian Higher Education*; editor of *Tribal College Student*; contributor to *News From Indian Country*; recently interned with a member of Parliament while attending the London School of Economics, University of London, and with the U.S. State Department at the American Embassy in Bangkok, Thailand. **Essays:** Duane Champagne and Elizabeth Cook-Lynn.

Rosenberg, Ruth. Assistant professor of English specializing in Native American literature at Brooklyn College. **Essays:** Amos Bad Heart Bull, Dennis J. Banks, Harrison Begay, Clyde Bellecourt, Robert LaFollette Bennett, Barney Furman Bush, Gladys Cardiff, Douglas Joseph Cardinal, Harold Cardinal, Mary Crow Dog, Frank Day, Michael A. Dorris, Harry Fonseca, Hanay Geiogamah, Suzan Shown Harjo, Thomson Highway, Fred Kabotie, Lame Deer, Duane Niatum, Carter Revard, and Peterson Zah.

Ruppert James. Associate professor of English and Alaska Native studies, University of Alaska-Fairbanks; served in Germany as a senior Fulbright lecturer and Fulbright lecturer at the University of Erlangen-Nurnberg and at the American Institute, University of Munich, respectively; former president of the Association for the Study of American Indian Literatures; author of "D'Arcy McNickle" in *Western Writers Series* (1988), *Guide to American Poetry Explication: Volume 1, Colonial and Nineteenth-Century* (1989), and *Racconti dal Grande Nord* (1993); contributor to several journals related to Native and multicultural studies. Essays: D'Arcy McNickle and Mary TallMountain.

Sawicki, Lori J. Free-lance writer and editor in Ann Arbor, Michigan; author of children's books. **Essays:** Datsolalee and Peter Jones.

Scarry, John. Professor of English, Hostos Community College, CUNY; member of board of editors, *Journal of Basic Writing*; author and editor of books and articles on singers and the history of musical performance; published reviews and essays on Joy Harjo in *Parabola* and *World Literature Today*; co-author of *The Writer's Workplace*. **Essay:** Joy Harjo.

Shepherd, Kenneth R. Historian, free-lance writer, and editor based in Southgate, Michigan; adjunct instructor in history, Henry Ford Community College, Dearborn, Michigan. **Essay:** Pocahontas.

Stiefer, Sandy J. Free-lance writer in Aurora, Ohio. **Essays:** Osceola and Oshkosh.

Symes, Martha. Archaeologist in Hackensack, New Jersey. **Essays:** Cornplanter, Hiawatha, and Alice Mae Lee Jemison.

Tower, Christopher B. Free-lance writer and journalist in Gull Lake, Michigan; recently received grant to write a book of short fiction related to Native Americans. **Essays:** Barboncito, Louis R. Bruce, Jr., Dean Chavers, Lena Frank Dick, Olive Patricia Dickason, James Gladstone, Carl Nelson Gorman, Rudolph Carl Gorman, Rosella Hightower, Oscar Howe, Joe Simon Sando, Pablita Velarde, and Young Man Afraid of His Horses.

Turek, Michael F. Historian, free-lance writer, and consultant in Toppenish, Washington; employment history includes positions at: the Intertribal Bison Cooperative, the Huna Traditional Tribal Council and Division of Subsistence (Alaska Department of Fish and Game), the Yakama Indian Nation, the Native American Fish and Wildlife Society, and several national parks; presently conducting research for an history book centering on national parks and Native Americans. **Essays:** Rosita Worl, Crowfoot, Hank Adams, Gabriel Dumont, Elijah Harper, Joseph, Looking Glass, Earl Old Person, Smohalla, and Washakie.

Van Dyke, Annette. Assistant professor of interdisciplinary studies and women's studies, Sangamon State University, Springfield, Illinois; author of *The Search for a Woman-Centered Spirituality* (1992) and articles on Native American women. **Essays:** Paula Allen Gunn, Louise Erdich, and Leslie Marmon Silko.

Viles, Philip H., Jr. Chief Justice of the Cherokee Nation (Oklahoma); preparing book on the subjects and sculptors of National Statuary Hall, U.S. Capital Building. **Essays:** Elias Boudinat, John Rollin Ridge, Stand Watie, Ross Swimmer, and Jim Thorpe.

Weil, Tina. Doctoral student, Arizona State University; completed M.A. thesis entitled *The Forgotten Homefront: Arizona Indians During World War II*; fields of study include U.S. history and women's history. **Essay:** Louis David Riel, Jr.

Welburn, Ron. Cherokee and Conoy poet, music critic, and educator; instructor of American literature, University of Massachusetts at Amherst; published book reviews in *Choice*, *MELUS*, and *Studies in American Indian Literatures*. **Essays:** William Apess, Gertrude Simmons Bonnin, and Samson Occom.

White, Fred. Free-lance writer in Pasadena, California. **Essay:** Charles Edenshaw.

Wild, Peter. Professor, Department of English, University of Arizona; writer of poetry and literary criticism; former cowboy and firefighter. **Essays:** Massasoit and Sequoyah.

Wilson, Darryl Babe. Pit River doctoral student of American Indian studies, University of California at Davis; poet and storyteller; attended the 1972 United Nations Conference on Human Environment in Stockholm, Sweden; co-director of the 1991 California American Studies Conference at Fullerton; author of poems contained in *Wellen auf dem Meer der Zeit* (Waves upon the Ocean of Time, 1974); published numerous articles related to Native American culture; co-editor of *Dear Christopher* (1992); co-author of anthology, *Voices from the Earth* (forthcoming). **Essays:** Edward D. Castillo, Jack D. Forbes, Wilma Pearl Mankiller, and Clifford Earl Trafzer.

Winsell, Keith A. Race relations and ethnic history specialist with a Ph.D. and M.L.S.; director of Library Services at Sinte Gleska University on the Rosebud Sioux Reservation in South Dakota; formerly director of American Minority Studies at St. Olaaf College in Northfield, Minnesota, and of the Amistad Research Center at Tulane University in New Orleans. **Essays:** Lionel Bordeaux, Ben Nighthorse Campbell, Crazy Horse, Gall, Ishi, Spotted Tail, and Wovoka.

Wroble, Lisa A. Free-lance writer of fiction and nonfiction for children and adults; contributor to *Twentieth Century Young Adult Writers* and *DLB: British Children's Writers*; reviewer for the *ALAN Review*; Michigan board member for the Society of Children's Book Writers and Illustrators; member of the Children's Literature Association. **Essays:** Joseph Brant, Captain Jack (Kintpuash), George Copway, and Basil H. Johnston.

Zimmerman, Karen P. Archivist in the I.D. Weeks Library, University of South Dakota; historian; author of *South Dakota: An Annotated Bibliography* (1993), and *The Sioux and Other Native American Cultures of the Dakotas* (1993). **Essays:** Vine Deloria, Jr., Vine Deloria, Sr., Walter R. Echo Hawk, John E. Echohawk, Hump, Russell C. Means, Beatrice A. Medicine, Helen White Peterson, Rain-in-the-Face, Red Cloud, Ben Reifel, Sitting Bull, Floyd Red Crow Westerman, and Rosebud Yellow Robe Frantz.

Notable
Native
Americans

George H. J. Abrams

1939-

Seneca anthropologist and educator
Also known as Ha-Doh-Jus ["Grown Up" or "Adult"]

George H. J. Abrams has helped his people to salvage significant national integrity from the modern Seneca catastrophe, the Kinzua Dam construction. In the 1950s, Iroquois traditionalists' resistance to the flooding of ancestral land and cemeteries failed; but, it fueled resurgent Indian nationalism. Defining progress, reconstructing history, sometimes reliving its recurring conflicts and consequences, can be painful; modern American Indians and non-Indian academics often have become belligerents. Abrams made them, briefly, partners.

Abrams was born May 4, 1939, on the Allegany Indian Reservation in Salamanca, New York. He was an anthropology graduate student at the State University of New York at Buffalo in 1964 when the U.S. Army Corps of Engineers, while constructing the Kinzua Dam, reached the Cornplanter Grant cemetery. This small plot, just across the Pennsylvania state line from the Allegany Reservation, was still inhabited by descendants of the Seneca chief,Cornplanter, half-brother of the Seneca prophet Handsome Lake.

A member of the Great Blue Heron Clan and the youngest of five children, all enrolled members of the Seneca Nation, Abrams was raised by his maternal grandmother who taught Abrams his ancestral language and Gai-wiio, the traditional religion of the Iroquois founded by Handsome Lake. Without his participation, an ambitious last-minute analysis of the remains removed for reburial from the Cornplanter Cemetery and later the Allgany Reservation would have been unfeasible. This osteological and archaeological study verified the ageing and sexing techniques archaeologists (and those dependant on their conclusions) routinely used in the study of large cemetary populations. It allowed Abrams' coworker, the late Dr. Audrey Sublett, to conclude her long survey of Seneca physiology and genetic change. Remarkably, the project was accomplished entirely with the written permission of Cornplanter's heirs and the tribal council of the Seneca Nation of Indians. All procedures were accomplished in strict accordance with the conditions they requested.

Perhaps because of his status within the tribe, Indians accepted Abrams' work as valid. On June 12, 1965, when the soon-to-be-flooded Coldspring Longhouse was desanctified and its sacred eternal fire was moved to Steamburg on the Allegany Reservation, he attended and recorded the innovative and private Iroquois ceremony. "[R]eligious cohesiveness was demonstrated in a rather dramatic and unusual manner," Abrams reported, adding: "By allotting a portion of the ceremony to representatives of each of the Iroquois Longhouses, overall Iroquois religious unity was demonstrated and reaffirmed."

After receiving his bachelor's and master's degrees in anthropology, Abrams traveled west to the University of Arizona, where he attended the Ph.D. program as a John Hay Whitney fellow. He also attended the University of New Mexico Law School under the American Indian graduate scholarship program and Western Washington State University in Bellingham, where he was a professor. In Denver, he served as a member of the Natural History Museum's American Indian Advisory Board and as a director of the educational networking group, American Indian Development, Inc.

In 1977 Abrams became a trustee of both the Heye Foundation Museum of the American Indian in New York City, and of the New York State Archaeological Association. That same year, he was asked by his home reservation to become the founding director of the Seneca-Iroquois National Museum, a tribal museum of the Seneca Nation. In 1978 he became chairman of the Seneca Nation Library's Board of Trustees, as well as the North American Indian Museums Association. During the 1980s, he was involved with many of the most prestigious institutions studying Native Americans, including the Smithsonian Institution and Chicago's Newberry Library Center for the History of the American Indian. Abrams also became active in community affairs. In 1979, he served as chairman of the Allegany Reservation's Johnson-O'Malley Local Indian Education Committee; and in 1980, he was a member of the board of advisors of the Mohawk-Caughnawaga Museum in Fonda, New York. From establishing museums and other educational projects, Abrams progressed to involvement in reservation politics. Elected to the Seneca Nation Board of Education in 1987, he served a year as President, later becoming a Seneca Internal Taxation Committee member and a Planning Commissioner. From 1990 to 1992 he was special assistant to the director of the National Museum of the American Indian at the Smithsonian Institution. Subsequently, Abrams became associated with the philanthropic Christian A. Johnson Endeavor Foundation in New York, while his daughter attended college. Also in New York, Abrams was a visiting scholar with the Museum Studies Department at the Graduate College of Arts and Sciences, New York University.

In 1994 Abrams challenged conservative curatorial "political correctness." He advanced the case that the Museum of the American Indian should repatriate to the Six Nations in Brantford, Ontario, wampum belts, identified as crucial to Iroquois National identity. Hoarding grave plunder while neglecting their own records often has passed for professionalism among twentieth-century preservationists. Some experts worry that information might get lost if institutions consider spiritual sensitivities and return human remains and venerated relics to descendant Indian Nations. Abrams, however, rose to a prominent professional position where he contributed otherwise unobtainable insights into Iroquois ritual, innovation, and resilience without trampling sacred convictions. Although museums and schools sometimes lack up-to-date material or culturally sensitive personnel, Abrams recommends that interested students of Native American affairs interact with them, plus read widely but specialize.

SELECTED WRITINGS BY ABRAMS:

"The Cornplanter Cemetery," *Pennsylvania Archaeologist,* 1965; 59-73.
"Moving of the Fire: A Case of Iroquois Ritual Innovation," in *Iroquois Culture, History and Prehistory,* edited by Elizabeth Tooker, Albany, New York State Museum and Science Service, 1967; 23-24.
"Red Jacket," in *World Book Encyclopedia,* 1976.
The Seneca People, Phoenix, Indian Tribal Series, 1976.
"The Case for Wampum Repatriation from the Museum of the American Indian to the Six Nations Confederacy, Brantford, Ontario, Canada," in *Museums and the Making of "Ourselves,"* edited by Flora E. S. Kaplan, London, Leister University Press, 1994; 351-384.

SOURCES:

Books

Native North American Almanac, edited by Duane Champagne, Detroit, Gale Research, 1994.
Reference Encyclopedia of the American Indian, sixth edition, edited by Barry T. Klein, West Nyack, New York, Todd Publications, 1993.
Wallace, Anthony F. C., *The Death and Rebirth of the Seneca,* New York, Vintage/Random House, 1969.
Wilson, Edmund, *Apologies to the Iroquois,* New York, Vintage/Random House, 1959, 1960.

Periodicals

Albrecht, Brian E., "Who Owns the Past?" (Part 1: "Indians Can't Rest in Peace: Looters Can't Resist Lure of Burial Grounds;" Part 2: "Striking Pay Dirt: Despite the Horror of Many, Grave Robbing is Big Business"), *Cleveland Plain Dealer,* May 6-7, 1990.
Sublett, Audrey J., "The Cornplanter Cemetery: Skeletal Analyses," *Pennsylvania Archaeologist,* 1965; 74-92.

Other

Abrams, George H. J., interviews with Steven E. Conliff conducted September 2 and September 9, 1994.

—*Sketch by Steven Edwin Conliff*

Hank Adams
1943-
Assiniboine/Dakota Sioux activist

Hank Adams was one of the leaders in the struggle over Indian fishing rights in the Northwest. He was born in northeast Montana, May 16, 1943, on the Fort Peck Indian Reservation at a place known as Wolf Point, or Poverty Flats. Growing up on the Quinault Indian Reservation on Washington's Olympic Peninsula, Adams attended Moclips High School where he was student body president, editor of the school newspaper and annual, and a member of the football and basketball teams. After graduating in 1961, Adams studied communications skills at the University of Washington from 1961 to 1963. He then moved to California, becoming involved in politics and the Democratic Party. He supported President John F. Kennedy and during the 1968 Democratic primary worked on Robert F. Kennedy's presidential campaign. From 1965 to 1967, Adams worked with Ralph Nader and the staffs of U.S. senators, including Robert F. Kennedy, acquainting Congress with Indian issues. A result of his work was the creation of the Select Senate Subcommittee on Indian Education.

Fights for Treaty and Fishing Rights

Adams began his activist career in the early 1960s, becoming involved in the Red Power movement and joining the National Indian Youth Council, an organization created by Native American college students. Many of the young, college educated Indian leaders to emerge during the 1960s and 1970s were members of the council. After receiving his draft notice in April of 1964, Adams refused induction into the U.S. Army, declaring that he would not serve in the military until Indian treaty rights were recognized. His attempt failed, however, and after serving in the Army Adams joined the fight for Indian fishing rights in the Northwest. As chairman of the National Indian Youth Council's Washington State Project, Adams organized fish-ins and demonstrations protesting the state's policies on Indian fishing rights.

Many of Washington's Indians live on small, widely scattered reservations in the densely populated, urban Puget Sound lowlands. Traditionally fishing folk with villages on the rivers and along the coasts, the Indians gave up most of their land when they signed treaties in the 1850s. But they did retain their right to fish at their usual and accustomed

Hank Adams

tles on these two rivers. In January of 1971, Adams and a colleague, Michael Hunt, were fishing on the Puyallup River, the scene of recent battles between police and Indian fishermen. Sometime after midnight, while watching a set net for a friend, Adams was shot in the stomach. Adams claimed two white men had shot him, but police disputed his account and the assailant was never found. After recovering from the gunshot wound Adams continued to fight for Indian fishing rights.

Along with his fight for Indian fishing rights, Adams worked at establishing tribal fishery programs. He requested technical assistance, management services, and funding from the federal government for these programs. Adams argued that federally funded Indian fishery programs should be included in the economic development plans of Northwest Indian tribes. He also envisioned a corps of Native American fishery biologists and enforcement officers to regulate the fisheries.

The battle for the recognition of Indian treaty fishing rights was strengthened with a decisive victory in 1974 when Federal Judge George Boldt ruled in favor of the Indians in the landmark decision, *U.S. v. Washington.* Judge Boldt ruled that treaty Indians were entitled to 50 percent of the commercially harvested catch in Washington State. Boldt's decision forced the state of Washington into recognizing Indian treaty fishing rights.

Adams' role as a political activist, organizer, and leader helped bring about the recognition of Indian treaty fishing rights in the Northwest. As a visionary, Adams was calling for tribal involvement in off-reservation fishery management at a time when Indian tribes had no role in resource management off their reservations. Tribal, federal, and state co-management of natural resources has now become accepted practice.

Adams has had numerous articles published in newspapers and journals, and his views have also been communicated in film and on television. He has been involved in monitoring and lobbying the Washington state legislature; twice entered primary elections as a congressional candidate; and in 1973 served as a special liaison between the White House and the Indians occupying Wounded Knee, South Dakota, helping to negotiate a settlement.

places. In the early 1960s, Adams and other Indians were claiming that the treaties signed in the 1850s still guaranteed them the right to fish at traditional sites. State officials, sport and commercial fishermen disagreed, leading to the fishing rights battles. In 1964, Adams helped organize a march on the Washington State Capitol in Olympia. The march included actor Marlon Brando and over 1,000 Indians. This demonstration captured the public's attention and was followed by other marches and fish-ins. In 1968, Adams became the director of the Survival of American Indians Association, a local, western Washington organization primarily concerned with Indian fishing rights.

Fishing Rights Struggle Turns Violent

Throughout the late 1960s and into the mid-1970s, Adams continued to campaign against state regulation of Indian fishing at traditional sites. Two of the best known sites in western Washington were on the Nisqually River near a place called Frank's Landing, and on the Puyallup River near the city of Tacoma. Frank's Landing, a six-acre tract on the Nisqually River below the small Nisqually Indian Reservation, had been purchased by Willie Frank to replace lands he lost in the government's Fort Lewis acquisition. Frank's Landing was the scene of fish-ins and sometimes violent confrontations between state officials and Nisquallis. The fishing sites on the Puyallup River were also scenes of violent confrontations between Indians and law enforcement officers. From 1968 to 1971, Adams was regularly arrested and jailed for his role in the fishing rights bat-

SOURCES:

Books

Cohen, Fay G., *Treaties on Trial: The Continuing Controversy over Northwest Indian Fishing Rights,* Seattle, University of Washington Press, 1986; 66, 69, 81.
Dictionary of Indians of North America, Volume 1, St. Clair Shores, Michigan, Scholarly Press, 1978; 16-17.
Native North American Almanac, edited by Duane Champagne, Detroit, Gale Research, 1994; 996-997.
Steiner, Stan, *The New Indians,* New York, Dell, 1968; 59-61.

Uncommon Controversy: Fishing Rights of the Muckleshoot, Puyallup and Nisqually Indians, Seattle, University of Washington Press, 1970; 112.

—Sketch by Michael F. Turek

Sherman Alexie

Sherman Alexie
1966-
Spokane/Coeur d'Alene poet and fiction writer

Sherman Alexie is one of the most exciting young Native American writers to emerge in the 1990s. The son of a Spokane father and a part-Coeur d'Alene mother, Alexie grew up on the Spokane Indian Reservation in Wellpinit, Washington. At 18 he left the reservation to attend college at Gonzaga University in Spokane. After two years he transferred to Washington State University in Pullman, where he majored in American Studies. He credits his creative writing instructor at Washington State, Alex Kuo, for encouraging him to seek publication for his writing. Alexie returned to the reservation during summer breaks from college, and life on the reservation—synonymous with poverty, unemployment, alcoholism, and despair—remains an important focus of his poetry and fiction.

Success Comes Quickly

In 1990, Alexie's poems began to appear in literary magazines little known outside poetry circles. By 1993, the literary establishment was heralding him as the standard-bearer for a new generation of Native American writers: he had published four books; his chapbook, *I Would Steal Horses,* had won Slipstream Press' fifth annual chapbook contest; and leading magazines such as *Esquire* and *Vanity Fair* had featured his work. The Washington State Arts Commission awarded him a poetry fellowship in 1991, and the National Endowment for the Arts awarded him a creative writing fellowship in 1992.

This talented writer's rise from obscurity to national prominence is remarkable. A laudatory notice in the *New York Times Book Review* set the tone for a flood of reviews to come. Writing about *The Business of Fancydancing,* Alexie's 1992 debut collection of fiction and poetry, James R. Kincaid declared, "Mr. Alexie's is one of the major lyric voices of our time." As important as favorable reviews have been in establishing Alexie's reputation, his own tireless promotion of his books has also attributed to his success. In an interview in January of 1994, Alexie estimated that he had given 290 readings throughout the United States in 1992 and 1993, performing to audiences ranging in size from six to 1,000.

Timing has also been a factor in Alexie's rise. His emergence as an important writer coincided with the controversial five-hundredth anniversary of Columbus' discovery of the New World. With the literary establishment courting native reactions to the Quincentennial, the time was right for the appearance of a powerful new writer who would command the spotlight. *Old Shirts & New Skins,* which represents a veritable catalog of native grievances, contains the scathing poem, "Postcards to Columbus." This volume of poetry, with its militant tone, voices some of Alexie's most direct protests against the 500 years of oppression that Native Americans have endured. In *Old Shirts & New Skins,* Alexie targets his anger at incidents such as the nineteenth-century Sand Creek massacre, Hollywood's treatment of Native Americans, as well as life on the reservation.

The Element of Humor

In *The Lone Ranger and Tonto Fistfight in Heaven,* Alexie's 1993 collection of short fiction, he writes: "Survival = Anger x Imagination. Imagination is the only weapon on the reservation." Also necessary for survival is the ability to laugh at most of life's miseries. As intense as Alexie's writing often is, none of his books is devoid of humor. Two works particularly reveal his comic sensibility: *The Lone Ranger and Tonto Fistfight in Heaven* and *The Business of Fancydancing.* In his 1969 *Custer Died for Your Sins,* Native American essayist, Vine Deloria, Jr., challenged the stereotype of the "granite-faced grunting redskin ... perpetuated by American mythology," claiming that "Indian people are exactly opposite of the popular stereotype." Although it may be true, as Deloria pointed out, that laughter is a defining element of everyday American Indian life, no native writer before Alexie has consistently brought this element to the forefront. "Indians have found a humorous side of nearly every problem...," writes Deloria. "The more desperate the problem, the more humor is directed to describe it." Problems as desperate as racist state troopers, commodity food, the Bureau of Indian Affairs (BIA), and cancer are all given the comic treatment in Alexie's work.

SELECTED WRITINGS BY ALEXIE:

The Business of Fancydancing, Brooklyn, Hanging Loose Press, 1992.

First Indian on the Moon, Brooklyn, Hanging Loose Press, 1993.

The Lone Ranger and Tonto Fistfight in Heaven, New York, Atlantic Monthly Press, 1993.

Old Shirts & New Skins, Los Angeles, UCLA American Indian Studies Center, 1993

SOURCES:

Books

Deloria, Vine, Jr., *Custer Died for Your Sins,* London, Macmillan, 1969; 146-147.

Periodicals

"Fancydancer," *New Yorker,* May 10, 1993; 38-41.

Kincaid, James R., "Who Gets to Tell Their Stories?" *New York Times Book Review,* May 3, 1992; 28.

Smith, Patricia Clark, review of *The Business of Fancydancing, American Book Review,* 14, December 1992-January 1993; 8.

Ullman, Leslie, "Betrayals and Boundaries: A Question of Balance," *Kenyon Review,* 15, summer 1993; 182-191.

Other

Alexie, Sherman, interview with Paul Hadella, conducted January 24, 1994.

—*Sketch by Paul Hadella*

Elsie Allen
1899-1990
Pomo basket weaver, scholar, educator, cultural consultant, and writer
Also known as "Pomo Sage"

Elsie Allen was a well-known basket weaver of Pomo heritage who lived for more than 90 years. Her ancestors inhabited the area around California's Russian River— including Sonoma, Mendocino, and Lake counties—just north of what is now the city of San Francisco. This region is especially rich in willows, sedges, and other plants suitable for basketmaking. Over the centuries, the Pomo people gained worldwide recognition for their skill in cultivating, harvesting, preparing, and weaving these plant materials into decorative and functional baskets. Following in the tradition of generations of Pomo basket makers, Allen helped to keep this unique art alive; she also fostered an appreciation for Pomo traditions both within and beyond the United States.

From the 1840s to the turn of the twentieth century, increasing numbers of white settlers profoundly changed the Pomo way of life and reduced the people to a few scattered bands in the California area. Many Pomo gave up their traditional hunter-gatherer existence and took jobs as farm laborers. Allen was born to two laborers, , on September 22, 1899, near Santa Rosa. As a young child, she lived an isolated but happy existence with her grandmother near the village of Cloverdale, speaking only the Pomo language. Allen's father died when she was about eight years old, and after her mother married her second husband, Richard Burke (who was half Pomo and half English), the new family moved north to Hopland. Elsie Allen began work in the fields at the age of ten.

Struggled with Education and Career

About a year later, she began her formal education at the Indian boarding school in Covelo, located in northern Mendocino County, a full 80 miles away from home. Leaving her family and traveling such a long distance to the school proved to be traumatic for Allen. Her inability to speak English—the only language spoken at the school—made life there very difficult. In addition, soon after arriving in Covelo, Allen lost all of her belongings in a fire. Forced to wear boys' clothes, perform seemingly meaningless activities, and abandon her native tongue, she had little incentive for learning. After a year she returned home.

When Allen was 13, she began attending a new government Indian school near her home in Hopland. Under the tutelage of a patient teacher, she studied the English language and, for the next three years, continued her education while working in the fields to supplement the family income. Convinced that there were more challenging opportunities for a young woman than the predictable future of a farm laborer, she sought advice from a Catholic priest in Ukiah. He took her to San Francisco to work as a domestic in the home of two older women. When she protested over the restrictions her new employers placed on her, they promptly fired her. However, she easily obtained employment at St. Joseph's Hospital in San Francisco in 1918, during the labor shortage that followed the close of World War I.

Elsie married a northern Pomo named Arthur Allen in 1919. Between 1920 and 1928, they had four children: Genevieve, Leonard, Dorothy, and George. She returned to work in the fields while raising her family.

Allen had watched both her mother and grandmother make baskets while she was a child and began gathering and preparing materials for weaving when she was older. When her grandmother passed away in 1924, Allen lost an important link to her people's past; because it was traditional for a woman's baskets and materials to be buried with her, Allen was left with few weaving examples to follow after her grandmother's death. However, Allen's mother, Annie, continued the family custom. She actively pursued the craft of basketmaking, displaying her works at fairs and promoting the art in the California region. When her health began to decline, Annie adamantly insisted that her baskets not be buried with her, so that they might be enjoyed and studied by future generations. Elsie Allen met with much resistance from her relatives and other members of the Pomo nation over this issue, but she respected her mother's dying wish— and she promised her mother that she, too, would carry on the tradition.

Allen did not have much time to devote to basketmaking until she reached the age of 62. Her activities expanded to teaching the art at California's Mendocino Art Center—to Indians and non-Indians alike. She was resolute in her belief that this art and its associated traditions not be lost to antiquity.

Maintained Tradition of Female Influence

Throughout history, women of the Pomo nation held high status in civil matters. A female chief exercised authority over women's issues and concerns. Allen maintained this tradition through her membership in the Pomo and Hintil women's clubs, working for her people by promoting education, cultural preservation, and Indian rights in the community.

Allen's community regarded her as a cultural scholar, and she became known as "Pomo Sage," acquiring an honorary Doctor of Divinity degree. One of her most notable achievements was her association from 1979 to 1981 with the Native American Advisory Council, working on Sonoma State University's Warm Springs Cultural Resources Study, a cultural and historical record of the Makahmo and Mahilakawna (Dry Creek/West Creek) Pomo.

The Native American Advisory Council later formed a partnership with the U.S. Army Corps of Engineers in the Warm Springs Dam-Lake Sonoma Project. The proposed dam and lake, intended to provide flood control, fresh water, and recreational facilities in the Russian River area, carried with it the potential to destroy indigenous plants that native peoples valued for medicinal, economic, ceremonial, and artistic uses. As a member of the council, Allen contributed to an ethnobotanical mitigation study—an examination of the plant lore of the Pomo tribe and the impact of environmental changes on the area and its people—and was instrumental in organizing a large scale relocation of endangered plants.

Some observers have suggested that Allen's most notable contribution was rescuing the art of Pomo basketmaking from oblivion. Her baskets are on display in both public and private collections around the world. In 1972 she authored *Pomo Basketmaking: A Supreme Art for the Weaver,* which recounts her own life story and documents in detailed pictures and print the fine art of Pomo basketmaking. She died in 1990.

SOURCES:

Books

Allen, Elsie, *Pomo Basketmaking: A Supreme Art for the Weaver,* Healdsburg, California, Naturegraph Publishers, 1972.
Native American Women, edited by Gretchen M. Bataille, New York, Garland Publishing, 1993; 5-6.

Other

Peri, David W., Scott M. Patterson, and Jennie L. Goodrich, *Ethnobotanical Mitigation: Warm Springs Dam-Lake Sonoma, California,* compiled by Elgar Hill for the U.S. Army Corps of Engineers, San Francisco District, Environmental Analysis and Planning, 1982.

—Sketch by Claudeen E. McAuliffe

Paula Gunn Allen
1939-
Laguna Pueblo/Sioux novelist, poet, and professor

Paula Gunn Allen is one of the foremost scholars of Native American literature as well as a talented poet and novelist. She also collects and interprets Native American mythology. She describes herself as a "multicultural event," citing her Pueblo/Sioux/Lebanese/Scottish-American ancestry. Her father, E. Lee Francis, born of Lebanese parents at Seboyeta, a Spanish-Mexican land grant village north of Laguna Pueblo, spoke only Spanish and Arabic until he was ten. Due to the lack of a Marionite rite in the area, he was raised Roman Catholic. He owned the Cubero Trading Company and was Lieutenant Governor of New Mexico from 1967 through 1970. Her mother, Ethel, is Laguna Pueblo, Sioux, and Scots. She converted to Catholicism from Presbyterianism to marry Francis.

Allen's great-grandfather, a Scots man named Kenneth Gunn, immigrated into the area in the 1800s and married her great-grandmother, Meta Atseye, whose Indian name was Corn Tassel. Meta had been educated at the Carlisle Indian School to be, as Allen says in her introduction to *Spider Woman's Granddaughters,* "a literate, modest, excruciatingly exacting maid for well-to-do white farmers' and ranchers' wives," but "became the farmer-rancher's wife instead." Her grandmother, half Laguna, half Scottish-American, Presbyterian, first married a Sioux (Ethel's father) and then remarried a German Jewish immigrant, Sidney Solomon Gottlieb. Her mother grew up speaking and writing both English and Mexican Spanish.

Allen was born in Albuquerque, New Mexico, and grew up in Cubero, New Mexico, a Spanish-Mexican land grant

Paula Gunn Allen

Contributions to Native American Literary Scholarship

Allen is recognized as a major scholar, literary critic, and teacher of Native American literature. Her teaching positions include San Francisco State University, the University of New Mexico, Fort Lewis College in Durango, California, the University of California at Berkeley, and the University of California at Los Angeles, where she was a professor of English. Allen's 1983 *Studies in American Indian Literature: Critical Essays and Course Designs,* an important text in the field, has an extensive bibliography in addition to information on teaching Native American literatures. *The Sacred Hoop: Recovering the Feminine in American Indian Traditions,* published in 1986, contains her 1975 germinal essay "The Sacred Hoop: A Contemporary Perspective," which was one of the first to detail the ritual function of Native American literatures as opposed to Euro-American literatures. Allen's belief in the power of the oral tradition embodied in contemporary Native American literature to effect healing, survival, and continuance underlies all of her work.

Allen writes from the perspective of a Laguna Pueblo woman from a culture in which the women are held in high respect. The descent is matrilineal—women owned the houses, and the major deities are female. A major theme of Allen's work is delineation and restoration of this woman-centered culture. Her work abounds with the mythic dimensions of women's relationship to the sacred, as well as the plight of contemporary Native American women, many of whom have lost the respect formerly accorded to them.

Elaborating on the roles and power of Native American women, Allen's "Who Is Your Mother: Red Roots of White Feminism" was published in *Sinister Wisdom* in 1984. In this startling article, Allen articulated Native American contributions to democracy and feminism, countering a popular idea that societies in which women's power was equal to men's never existed. She also has been a major champion to restore the place of gay and lesbian Native Americans in the community. These ideas were first published in 1981 in a ground-breaking essay in *Conditions,* "Beloved Women: Lesbians in American Indian Cultures," and then reworked for the *Sacred Hoop.*

Allen says that her focus on women is intended to affect the consciousness of Euro-American women rather than men because, until the last ten years or so, the women in her culture were never considered weak, and she wants others to know that women were not held down in all cultures. Allen feels some ambivalence about the feminist movement because of this misunderstanding and the cultural chauvinism of Euro-American women, which has been personally hurtful to her and other Native women, but she admits that feminists provide the best audience for her work and have given her much support. In her family, the woman-centered tradition was so strong that her grandfather wanted to name her mother Susan B. Anthony.

Allen was awarded a National Endowment for the Arts writing fellowship in 1978, and she received a postdoctoral fellowship grant from the Ford Foundation-National Research Council in 1984. Also at this time, she served as

village abutting the Laguna and Acoma reservations and the Cibola National Forest. She attended mission schools in Cubero and San Fidel, but she did most of her schooling at a Sisters of Charity boarding school in Albuquerque, from which she graduated in 1957. Her 1983 novel *The Woman Who Owned the Shadows* and some of her poetry draws from this experience of being raised Catholic. However, Allen is well aware of the conflicting influences in her background: Catholic, Native American, Protestant, Jewish, and Marionite. In an interview with Joseph Bruchac for *Survival This Way,* Allen says: "Sometimes I get in a dialogue between what the Church taught me, the nuns taught me, and what my mother taught me, what my experience growing up where I grew up taught me. Often you can't reconcile them." Her novel speaks to this confusion as the main character attempts to sort through the varying influences to reclaim a Native American women's spiritual tradition. On her journey, her protagonist uses traditional Laguna Pueblo healing ceremonies as well as psychotherapy, the Iroquois story of Sky Woman, and the aid of a psychic Euro-American woman.

Allen received both her bachelor's degree in English (1966) and her Master of Fine Arts degree in creative writing (1968) from the University of Oregon after beginning her studies at Colorado Women's College. She had three children and is divorced. She received her doctorate in American studies with an emphasis on Native American literature (1975) from the University of New Mexico. Two other writers from Laguna Pueblo are related to Allen—a sister, Carol Lee Sanchez, and a cousin, Leslie Marmon Silko.

associate fellow at the Stanford Humanities Institute, coordinating the "Gynosophic Gathering, A Woman Identified Worship Service," in Berkeley. She is active in the antinuclear and anti-war movements as well as the feminist movement. She won an American Book Award in 1990 for *Spider Woman's Granddaughters: Traditional Tales and Contemporary Writings by Native American Women,* which is an attempt to correct the lack of stories by and/or about Native Women in literature collections. In her 1991 *Grandmother of the Light: A Medicine Woman's Sourcebook,* Allen expands her interest in the ritual experience of women as exhibited in the traditional stories. She traces the stages in a woman's spiritual path using Native American stories as models for walking in the sacred way.

Contributions to Native American Poetry

Besides her extensive work as a scholar, Allen is the author of numerous volumes of poetry. Because of her multicultural background, Allen can draw on varying poetic rhythms and structures, which emanate from such sources as country-western music, Pueblo corn dances, Catholic masses, Mozart, Italian opera, and Arabic chanting. In her work, a finely detailed sense of place resonates with landscapes from the city, the reservation, and the interior. She has been recognized by critics such as A. LaVonne Ruoff for her purity of language and emotional intensity.

Allen became interested in writing in high school when she discovered the work of Gertrude Stein, whom she read extensively and tried to copy. Other influences have been the Romantic poets, Shelley and Keats. Allen took up writing more seriously in college when she read Robert Creeley's *For Love* and discovered that he was teaching at the University of New Mexico, where she was a student. She took his poetry class, although she considered herself a prose writer at the time. Creeley introduced her to the work of the poets Charles Olson, Allen Ginsberg, and Denise Levertov—all of whom have been major influences on Allen. She left New Mexico to finish her bachelor's degree at the University of Oregon and studied with Ralph Salisbury, who was Cherokee, though she did not know it at the time. Feeling isolated and suicidal, Allen says that the presence of a Santee Sioux friend, Dick Wilson, and the discovery of N. Scott Momaday's *House Made of Dawn* made all the difference to her. Recent influences upon her work have been Adrienne Rich, Patricia Clark Smith, and E. A. Mares.

Allen's 1982 *Shadow Country* received an honorable mention from the National Book Award Before Columbus Foundation. Allen uses the theme of shadows—the not dark and not light—to bridge her experience of mixed heritage as she attempts to respond to the world in its variety. Allen's poetry has an infusion of spirits common to Native American literature, but represents not only her Native American heritage, but her multicultural heritage. She also uses her poetry to respond to personal events in her life, such as her mother's suffering with lupus ("Dear World" in *Shadow Country*) and the death of one of her twin sons ("On the Street: Monument" in *Shadow Country*). In the interview

with Bruchac, Allen says, "My poetry has a haunted sense to it ... a sorrow and grievingness in it that comes directly from being split, not in two but in twenty, and never being able to reconcile all the places that I am." Allen's multicultural vision allows her to mediate between her different worlds to make a rich contribution to Native American literature as a scholar, writer, and educator.

SELECTED WRITINGS BY ALLEN:

Novels

The Woman Who Owned the Shadows, San Francisco, Spinsters/Aunt Lute Books, 1983.

Verse

The Blind Lion, Berkeley, California, Thorp Springs Press, 1974.
Coyote's Daylight Trip, Albuquerque, New Mexico, La Confluencia, 1978.
A Cannon Between My Knees, New York, Strawberry Hill Press, 1981.
Star Child, Marvin, South Dakota, Blue Cloud Quarterly, 1981.
Shadow Country, Los Angeles, University of California Indian Studies Center, 1982.
Wyrds, San Francisco, Taurean Horn, 1987.
Skin and Bones, Albuquerque, New Mexico, West End Press, 1988.

Editor

From the Center: A Folio; Native American Art and Poetry, New York, Strawberry Hill Press, 1981.
Studies in American Indian Literature: Critical Essays and Course Design, New York, Modern Language Association, 1983.
Spider Woman's Granddaughters: Traditional Tales and Contemporary Writing by Native American Women, New York, Fawcett, 1990.
The Voice of the Turtle: American Indian Literature 1900-1970, New York, Ballantine Press, 1994.

Other

Sipapu: A Cultural Perspective, Albuquerque, New Mexico, University of New Mexico Press, 1975.
The Sacred Hoop: Recovering the Feminine in American Indian Traditions, Boston, Beacon Press, 1986.
Grandmothers of the Light: A Medicine Woman's Sourcebook, Boston, Beacon Press, 1991.
Indian Perspectives, Southwest Parks and Monuments Association, 1992.

SOURCES:

Books

American Indian Women: Telling Their Lives, edited by Gretchen M. Bataille and Kathleen M. Sands, Lincoln, Nebraska, University of Nebraska Press, 1984.

Bruchac, Joseph, "I Climb the Mesas in My Dreams: An Interview with Paula Gunn Allen," in *Survival This Way: Interviews with American Indian Poets,* Tucson, Arizona, Sun Tracks and University of Arizona Press, 1987; 1-24.

Crawford, C. F., John F. William Balassi, and Annie O. Ersturox, "Paula Gunn Allen," in *This About Vision: Interviews with Southwestern Writers,* Albuquerque, University of New Mexico Press, 1990; 95-107.

Hanson, Elizabeth J., *Paula Gunn Allen,* Western Writers Series, Boise, Idaho, Boise State University, 1990.

Milton, John R., "Paula Gunn Allen (Laguna-Sioux-Lebanese)," in *Four Indian Poets,* Vermillion, South Dakota, 1974.

Ruoff, A. LaVonne Brown, *American Indian Literatures: An Introduction, Bibliographic Review and Selected Bibliography,* New York, Modern Language Association, 1990; 92-94.

Ruoff, A. LaVonne Brown, *Literatures of the American Indian,* New York, Chelsea House Publishers, 1991; 95-96.

"Paula Gunn Allen, 'The Autobiography of a Confluence,'" in *I Tell You Now: Autobiographical Essays by Native American Writers,* edited by Brian Swann and Arnold Krupat, Lincoln, Nebraska, University of Nebraska Press, 1987; 141-154.

Van Dyke, Annette, "The Journey Back to Female Roots: A Laguna Pueblo Model," in *Lesbian Texts and Contexts,* edited by Karla Jay and Joanne Glasgow, New York University Press, 1990; 339-354.

Van Dyke, Annette, "Curing Ceremonies: The Novels of Leslie Marmon Silko and Paula Gunn Allen," in *The Search for a Woman-Centered Spirituality,* New York University Press, 1992.

Van Dyke, Annette, "Paula Gunn Allen," *Contemporary Lesbian Writers of the United States: A Bio-Bibliographical Critical Sourcebook,* edited by Sandra Pollack and Denise Knight, Westport, Connecticut, Greenwood Press, 1993.

Winged Words: American Writers Speak, edited by Laura Coltelli, Lincoln, Nebraska, University of Nebraska Press, 1990; 11-39.

Periodicals

Aal, Katharyn Machan, "Writing as an Indian Woman: An Interview with Paula Gunn Allen," *North Dakota Quarterly,* spring 1989; 149-161.

Allen, Paula Gunn, "Beloved Woman: The Lesbians in American Indian Cultures," *Conditions,* 1981; 65-67.

Allen, Paula Gunn, "Who Is Your Mother? Red Roots of White Feminism," *Sinister Wisdom,* winter 1984; 34-46.

Ballinger, Franchot, and Brian Swann, "A *MELUS* Interview: Paula Gunn Allen," *MELUS,* summer 1983; 3-25.

Caputi, Jane, "Interview with Paula Gunn Allen," *Trivia, a Journal of Ideas,* fall 1990; 50-67.

—Sketch by Annette Van Dyke

American Horse
(?)-1876
Oglala Lakota Sioux leader
Also known as Iron Plume, Iron Shield, and Number Two

American Horse was one of the Lakota leaders during the Indian wars of the 1860s and 1870s. He is perhaps best remembered for his death at Slim Buttes, in revenge for the defeat of George Armstrong Custer and the U.S. Seventh Cavalry at Little Big Horn. He was known among his people as Iron Shield, but also was thought to be called Iron Plume according to newspapermen who reported on the Indian wars. He was often confused with the younger American Horse ["Wasechun-tashunka"], the son of Sitting Bear. The younger American Horse was active in the Ghost Dance Movement of 1889, well after the elder American Horse died, and was a member of the True Oglala, also called the Bear People. Although some writers speculated that the younger American Horse was either a son or nephew to the elder man, George Hyde in *Red Cloud's Folk: A History of the Oglala Sioux Indians,* documented from interviews with He-Dog that the younger man was no relation to the elder American Horse.

It is not known when the elder American Horse was born. Historians have speculated that he was born as early as 1801 or as late as 1840. He was the son of Old Smoke, the leader of the Smoke People, who also were referred to as the Iteschicha ["Bad Faces"]. Chief Old Smoke's sister was Walks-As-She-Thinks, who was the mother of the famous Chief Red Cloud. Although not much is known about American Horse's early life, sources indicate his cousin Red Cloud and fellow Lakota Crazy Horse were life-long friends. During the 1830s and 1840s, the Oglala people split into two factions, the Smoke People and the Bear People, over a dispute about the leadership of the tribe. The latter group followed Chief Bull Bear, while the Smoke People were led by Chief Old Smoke. After the dispute, the Smoke People moved north of Fort Laramie, toward the Black Hills of the Dakotas. They used the Powder River country for buffalo hunting and fought frequently with the Crow Indians over that territory. Some of the Smoke people remained at Fort Laramie. Chief Old Smoke, who was described as fat and jovial, reportedly took up farming there just before he died in 1864.

American Horse Becomes a Leader

American Horse was one of a select group of "shirt-wearers," who assisted the Oglala chiefs with their duties. Billy Garnett, a white trader, watched the ceremony at which American Horse, Crazy Horse, Young-Man-Afraid and Sword were made "shirt-wearers" in 1865. Steven Ambrose in *Crazy Horse and Custer* described the ceremony. After a

American Horse

feast, one of the wise and knowledgeable elders would describe the duties of a "shirt-wearer." Such warriors were duty-bound to lead warriors in peace and in war, keeping the peace and respecting the rights of the weak. "They must be wise and kind and firm in all things, counseling, advising, and then commanding. If their words were not heard, they could use blows to enforce their orders; in extreme cases, they even had the right to kill. But they must never take up arms against their own people without thought and counsel and must always act with caution and justice."

Following the speeches, each of the warriors was presented with a shirt made from the hides of two bighorn sheep and decorated with scalps they had won in battle, feathers and quill work. After receiving the shirts more speeches were made where the warriors were told to care for the poor, widows, orphans and those who had little power. The four men were chosen, Ambrose said, "because they were greathearted, generous, strong, and brave, and ... would do their duty gladly and with good heart." Although they were not considered chiefs by their people, the shirt-wearers were looked upon as leaders.

With the California Gold Rush in 1849, settlers began moving west of the Mississippi in greater numbers. In 1862, Congress passed the Homestead Act, which provided western emigrants 160 acres of public land in the plains territory for $10, if they promised to live there and farm the land for at least five years. During the next three years, some 300,000 settlers crossed the plains. While Indians periodically attacked settlers, stole livestock and raided newly-built

towns, there was no organized warfare because the army was needed for the Civil War.

At about the same time, gold was discovered in Montana. Government treaties with the Indians in the 1850s had set aside the northern Wyoming area for Lakota hunting grounds. Ignoring those treaties, John M. Bozeman blazed a shorter trail to the Montana gold fields through the Lakota territory near the Powder River and Big Horn Mountains in 1862. In 1863 and 1864, he led settlers and miners across the same trail despite attacks from Indians who were protecting their land. In 1865, the Civil War ended and many projects to expand westward settlement began, including a transcontinental railroad, and forts built along the trails travelled by the settlers. Two of those forts were planned for the Bozeman Trail.

The government, well aware that its plans for westward expansion could be thwarted by an Indian war, directed that a peace treaty be signed with the Lakota. In October 1865, Major General S. R. Curtis and Newton Edmunds managed to get some of the southern Lakotas to sign a treaty that listed all the Lakota bands, including those northern bands hostile to the invading whites. When attacks along the Bozeman Trail continued, the military realized that many of the Indians under such leaders as American Horse, Red Cloud and Crazy Horse had not agreed to the peace.

In January 1866, Colonel Henry E. Maynadier, commander at Fort Laramie, was ordered to do everything possible to get hostile groups to sign the treaty. When only a few of the bands came in to sign, E. B. Taylor of the Indian Office joined Maynadier in June 1866. He sent word to the Oglalas that they would receive guns and ammunition if they signed the treaty. It was enough to entice Red Cloud and some of his followers to Fort Laramie. However, Taylor attempted to deceive the group and did not tell them about the planned army forts. At the same time the talks were proceeding at Fort Laramie, Colonel Henry B. Carrington and 700 soldiers were making their way to the Powder River to build the first of the forts. When word reached the chiefs at Fort Laramie, they walked out of the negotiations in a rage.

The Fetterman Fight

In August, 1866, Carrington reached Piney Creek, which was about halfway between the Powder and Bighorn Rivers, where he began building Fort Phil Kearny. Two infantry companies were sent further north on the Bozeman Trail to begin work on Fort C. F. Smith leaving Carrington 350 soldiers. Fort Phil Kearny was one of the strongest forts ever built during the war for the Plains and provided a clear view all around to prevent any sneak attacks. However, not knowing anything about Indian warfare, Carrington built the fort about five miles away from his supply of wood.

Red Cloud set up his camp with some 1,000 followers along the Powder River, close enough to the fort to harass the soldiers daily. As one of Red Cloud's chief lieutenants and a shirt-wearer, American Horse certainly was part of that group, although most historians do not mention him specifically. Charles King, in "Custer's Last Battle," noted that in the 1870s, one of the reservations established in the Black Hills "was the bailiwick of the hero of the Phil Kearny massacre, old Red Cloud, and here were gathered most of his tribe ... and many of his chiefs; some 'good,' like Old-Man-Afraid-of-His-Horses and his worthy son, but most of them crafty, cunning, treacherous, and savage, like Red Dog, Little-Big-Man, American Horse, and a swarm of various kinds of Bulls and Bears and Wolves."

The Lakota coordinated their efforts to harass the soldiers at the fort, particularly when they ventured out to get wood for fuel and construction. Throughout the summer, the Indians attacked vulnerable soldiers, killing one or two during each attack. By September, the number of attacks increased. Martin F. Schmitt and Dee Brown in *Fighting Indians of the West* said that when the Indians were not attacking the soldiers they "raided wagon trains, stampeding or capturing horses and mules. They heaped hay on Carrington's beloved mowing machines and set them afire, stole most of his beef herd, shot up the herders, sent pursuing soldiers limping and crawling back to the fort with arrows driven into their bodies."

By December 1866, the number of Indians in Red Cloud's camp had increased to about 2,000. Following Red Cloud's orders, the shirt-wearers planned to use decoys to lure as many of the soldiers into the open as possible for an ambush. In late December after two failed ambushes, the decoys again attacked a group going for wood. Carrington sent Captain William J. Fetterman and 80 soldiers to the rescue, but ordered him not to pursue the Indians past Lodge Trail Ridge. Convinced that he could destroy the entire Lakota nation with only a few men, Fetterman disobeyed orders. The shirt-wearers led by Crazy Horse took charge of the decoys on December 21 and led Fetterman's troops past Lodge Trail Ridge and into Peno Valley where the rest of Red Cloud's forces waited. After about 20 minutes of fighting, Fetterman's entire detachment was killed. A relief column was able to retrieve about half of the bodies while a messenger was sent to Fort Laramie for reinforcements. The next day, Carrington himself led a detachment to retrieve the rest of the bodies. When the reinforcements arrived, Carrington was recalled and Captain H. W. Wessells took over command.

For the next two years, Red Cloud, American Horse and other Lakotas harassed the soldiers at both Fort Phil Kearny and Fort C. F. Smith. In April, 1868, a new peace treaty was drawn up that required Fort Phil Kearny to be burned to the ground. The Lakota returned to the Powder River after the treaty was signed to hunt. In the summer of 1870, American Horse joined Red Cloud and a group of other Lakota leaders on a trip to Washington, where the 1868 treaty was explained in more detail. On the way, the Lakota leaders saw the number of white people inhabiting the country and, although they spoke in anger to the government officials they met, many of the leaders agreed to move to a reservation on the Missouri River. While Red Cloud moved to a reservation, American Horse, Sitting Bull, Crazy Horse, Black Moon, Gall and Man-Afraid-of-His-Horse, chose to remain free to follow the buffalo. There are some references

to American Horse at the Spotted Tail Agency and the Red Cloud Agency during the early 1870s, but he apparently only was visiting and did not live at either Agency for any length of time.

Custer's Last Stand

In 1874, George Custer made a discovery during a reconnaissance mission in the Black Hills that eventually led to his death. Gold was discovered in the Black Hills and drew a new wave of miners and speculators to Indian lands. Although the government broke its treaty with the Indians by allowing whites into the Black Hills, it was decided to send a new delegation to the Lakota to negotiate the purchase of the sacred land. Some 7,000 Lakota came to the council with the government in September 1875. Because the Black Hills were (and are today) important to the Lakota religion, the Indians were in no mood to sell. Red Cloud said he would not take less than $70 million as well as beef herds to last seven generations. Others just called for war. No agreement was reached and the miners continued to swarm into the Black Hills. By the New Year, "there were eleven thousand whites in Custer City alone," according to Schmitt and Brown.

In December, 1875, the Lakota were told to move to one of the agencies immediately. Because it was winter, when no one moved about on the northern plains, the Indians remained where they were. Unfamiliar with the area and the tribal customs, the Interior Department ordered the military to force the Indians to the reservations. General George Crook, known to the Indians as "Three Stars", was transferred to the region. On March 17, 1865, a detachment of his soldiers surprised a small Lakota camp under the leader He-Dog and destroyed all the tepees and winter stores of food. He-Dog moved his people to Crazy Horse's village. The following month Sitting Bull held a council to talk of war. At the same time General Crook attempted to recruit scouts at the Red Cloud Agency. Several of the older chiefs prevented the young warriors from going with Crook, who finally hired Crow scouts to lead him through the Black Hills. Crook led his troops east in search of more Indians while General Terry made his way to the Big Horn. Terry ordered Custer and the Seventh Calvary to find the Indians' trail and follow it until he found them or Terry himself. As the Indians under Sitting Bull prepared for war and hunted meat, many of the reservation Indians joined them. There were several minor skirmishes between soldiers and Lakotas before summer that year. By June, the Indians made camp at the Little Horn in the Big Horn Mountains.

Depending upon who tells the story, either Custer surprised Sitting Bull's camp or Sitting Bull cleverly ambushed the Seventh Calvary. Whichever version actually occurred, 189 enlisted soldiers, 13 officers and four civilians died on June 25, 1876 at the Little Big Horn, according to official military records. Others have indicated 266 soldiers were killed with another 54 wounded. Historians do not specifically mention American Horse at the battle with Custer, but evidence discovered a few months later indicates he and his band of Lakota probably were participants in the massacre.

After the celebration of their victory, the Lakota broke up into smaller bands and began their usual summer hunting for buffalo. In the fall, many started moving toward the Agencies. American Horse and his band travelled with the Minniconjous leader Roman Nose. In all, there were some 200 warriors in their camp along with many women and children. They had good conduct certificates identifying them as part of the Spotted Tail Agency and planned to go there for the winter.

The Death of American Horse

The military wanted vengeance for those who had died at the Little Big Horn. When military reinforcements arrived, General Crook began moving down the Rosebud while Terry moved toward Yellowstone in hopes of finding some of the escaping Indians. Crook travelled light with as few provisions as possible so that he could move faster. By September, his supplies were depleted and his troops were slaughtering horses for food. On September 7, he sent Captain Anson Mills, known to the Indians as Bear Coat, and a detachment of 150 men to Deadwood to replenish supplies. Late in the afternoon, scout Frank Grouard found fresh signs of Indians at a stream near Slim Buttes and reported it to Mills. The general had accidently come across American Horse's camp of some 35 to 37 lodges. He decided to attack it. On the morning of September 9, Mills surprised the sleeping Indians by stampeding the tribe's horses through the camp. Many of the Indians escaped into the surrounding bluffs and started firing back. Believing that Crazy Horse had heard the first shots and come to the rescue, Mills sent a message back to Crook asking for help.

Mills was able to hold the camp until Crook arrived. While herding the horses through the Indian camp that morning, Private W. J. McClinton spotted Custer's Seventh Cavalry guidon hanging on American Horse's tepee. He turned it over to Mills, who later was given American Horses' tepee as a reward. The soldiers also found articles of soldiers' clothing, gloves labeled with the name of Colonel Keogh of the Seventh Cavalry who was with Custer, a large number of guns and ammunition, about 175 ponies many of which were branded with "U.S." or "7 C," cavalry saddles, a letter addressed to a private in the Seventh Cavalry as well as several tons of meat and other supplies. It was considered more than sufficient proof that American Horse had taken part in the massacre in June. But, according to news reporters at the scene, some of the Indians later said American Horse had not taken part in that battle and that other Indians had brought these things to their camp.

When Crook arrived about 11 o'clock that morning with his 2,000 troops, there was still a small group of Indians in a gulch a few yards away from the lodges. They had managed to kill some of Mills' pack mules and harassed the soldiers taking over their camp. When talking failed to get the Indians to come out, Crook ordered Lieutenant William P. Clark to assault the gulch, but reporters traveling with the army hampered the operation. After some two hours of exchanging shots, Crook heard the squaws' death-chants and ordered the shooting stopped. John G. Bourke in *On the Border with Crook* described the scene around him. "The women and pappooses [sic], covered with dirt and blood, were screaming in an agony of terror; behind and above us were the oaths and yells of the surging soldiers; back of the women lay what seemed, as near as we could make out, to be four dead bodies still weltering in their gore." During the afternoon, Sitting Bull, who was camped nearby, came to rescue the Lakota at Slim Buttes. After exchanging fire with the soldiers he withdrew, realizing he was badly outnumbered.

Further discussions with the hidden Indians resulted in 13 women and children surrendering. Cyrus Townsend Brady in *The Sioux Indian Wars from the Powder River to the Little Big Horn* said that later it was learned that "even the women had used guns, and had displayed all the bravery and courage of the Sioux." Crook asked the women to return to the gulch to tell the remaining holdouts that they would be treated well if they surrendered. A young warrior came out and received the same assurances, so he went back and helped American Horse out of the gulch along with about nine more women and children. The dead left behind in the gulch included two warriors, one woman and a child. American Horse had been shot in his gut and he was trying to hold his intestines in while he moved toward Crook. He also was biting down on a piece of wood to keep from crying out. He handed Crook his gun and sat down by one of the fires. He refused help from Crook's surgeon, but his wife apparently tried to stem the flow of blood with her shawl.

American Horse died that night. Mari Sandoz in *Crazy Horse: The Strange Man of the Oglalas,* reported American Horse said, "It is always the friendly ones who are struck," before he died. Other writers indicate American Horse said nothing before he died. Some sources reported soldiers scalped him after he died. A total of ten Indians, at least half of them women or children, died in the battle at Slim Buttes, while three soldiers were killed and another 20 were wounded. It was the first of many defeats for the Lakota.

SOURCES:

Ambrose, Stephen E., *Crazy Horse and Custer,* New York, Doubleday, 1975; 124-127, 211-227.

Biographical Dictionary of Indians of the Americas, second edition, Newport Beach, California, American Indian Publishers, 1991, 20-21.

Bourke, John G., *On the Border with Crook,* Scribner's, 1891; 16, 242-255, 270-322, 362-380.

Brady, Cyrus Townsend, *The Sioux Indian Wars from the Powder River to the Little Big Horn,* Indian Head Books, 1992; 304-311.

Brown, Dee, *Bury My Heart at Wounded Knee,* New York, Bantam, 1972; 283-289.

Dillon, Richard H., *North American Indian Wars,* Facts On File, 1983; 216-217.

Encyclopedia of Indians of the Americas, Volume 2, Scholarly Press, 1974; 129-130.

Hyde, George E., *Red Cloud's Folk: A History of the Oglala Sioux Indians,* Norman, University of Oklahoma Press, 1967; 40-41, 50-55, 58-59, 64-67, 86-91, 96-98, 114-117, 274-276, 312-318.

"John M. Bozeman," in *Encyclopaedia Britannica,* Volume 2, Encyclopaedia Britannica, 1992; 448-449.

King, Charles, "Custer's Last Battle," in *The Custer Reader,* edited by Paul Andrew Hutton, Lincoln, University of Nebraska Press, 1992; 345-362.

King, Captain Charles, *Campaigning with Crook,* Norman, University of Oklahoma Press, 1964; 116-124.

Knight, Oliver, *Following the Indian Wars: The Story of the Newspaper Correspondents among the Indian Campaigners,* Norman, University of Oklahoma Press, 1960; 233, 257-288.

Native North American Almanac, edited by Duane Champagne, Detroit, Gale Research, 1994; 1000.

Peters, Joseph P., *Indian Battles and Skirmishes on the American Frontier 1790-1898,* Argonaut Press, 1966; 6-24, 5-65, 36-41.

Sandoz, Mari, *Crazy Horse: The Strange Man of the Oglalas,* Lincoln, University of Nebraska Press, 1992; 335-341.

Schmitt, Martin F., and Dee Brown, *Fighting Indians of the West,* Bonanza Books, 1968; 11, 15-26, 113-117, 120, 137-141, 161-169, 178-179.

200 Years: A Bicentennial Illustrated History of the United States, U.S. News and World Report, 1975; 59-67.

Utley, Robert M., *Frontier Regulars: The United States Army and the Indian, 1866-1891,* Macmillan, 1973; 267-271.

Utley, Robert M., "Indian-United States Military Situation, 1848-1891," in *Handbook of North American Indians,* Volume 4, edited by William C. Sturtevant, Washington, D.C., Smithsonian Institution, 1988; 174-176.

Vaughn, J. W., *Indian Fights: New Facts on Seven Encounters,* Norman, University of Oklahoma Press, 1966; 184-196.

Vestal, Stanley, *Sitting Bull, Champion of The Sioux,* Norman, University of Oklahoma Press, 1980; 184-189.

Waldman, Carl, *Who Was Who in Native American History,* New York, Facts On File, 1990; 4-5.

—*Sketch by Catherine A. Clay*

Owanah Anderson
Contemporary
Choctaw administrator, activist, writer, and editor

Owanah Anderson, who considers her most important role to be helping people connect with each other, is perhaps best known for her work in advancing the status of Native American women. She founded the Ohoyo Resource Center in 1979, which assisted Native American women in achieving their educational and employment goals, and

since 1984 she has been involved with Native American ministries of the Episcopal church. Born in Choctaw County, Oklahoma, Anderson attended school in Boswell, Oklahoma, and graduated from high school as the class valedictorian. With the help of a scholarship, she majored in journalism at the University of Oklahoma in Norman.

Anderson has held a variety of jobs in media and business throughout her professional career. In 1977, she was the co-chairperson of the Texas delegation to the Houston Women's Conference. Between 1977 and 1980, she served on the United States Department of Health, Education, and Welfare Committee on Rights and Responsibilities of Women, where she focused or consulted on issues involving the Indian Health Service and Women's Educational Equity. From 1978 to 1981, she was a member of President Jimmy Carter's Advisory Committee on Women. By 1979, she had become more involved specifically with Indian issues. "You have a responsibility to the tribe and its people, and eventually you discharge it," Anderson said during an interview with Catherine A. Clay.

To fulfill some of that responsibility, Anderson founded and acted as director of the Ohoyo Resource Center for the U.S. Department of Education. Ohoyo is the Choctaw word for "woman," and the center provided a women's network offering leadership training, conferences, and other employment-related services. One of her projects at the center was overseeing the 1982 publication of *Ohoyo One Thousand: A Resource Guide of American Indian/Alaska Native Women,* which lists biographies of more than 1,000 Native American women from more than 230 different tribes or bands. The book helps identify women who have achieved some level of success and recognition in their chosen careers by including information about the women's skills and their involvement in various issues. In 1982, Anderson edited *Words of Today's American Indian Women: Ohoyo Makachi,* which features the speeches and discussion at the 1981 women's conference in Tahlequah, Oklahoma. Although the center closed in 1983, the network of Native American women was continued among its members.

In 1980, Anderson served as the only American Indian representative to the Commission on Security and Cooperation in Europe held in Madrid, Spain. In 1981, she received the Ann Roe Howard Award from the Harvard University Graduate School of Education. She was also appointed by the governor to the Texas Indian Commission, on which she served from 1982 to 1988. Anderson became a member of the North Texas Women's Hall of Fame in 1984 and was honored by the National Coalition of Women of Color in 1987. Also during the eighties, she acted as the chairperson of the National Committee on Indian Work for the Episcopal church. In 1989, she was awarded an honorary doctorate degree from Seabury-Western Theological Seminary in Evanston, Illinois.

Leads Ministry for Episcopal Church

Anderson moved to New York City in 1984 to join the staff of the presiding bishop to head up the American Indian

Ministries of the Episcopal church. In the ministry, she has global involvement with indigenous Anglicans from all over the world. Her travels take her from New York to Oklahoma to Alaska and as far away as New Zealand. She also oversees an annual program budget of $1.5 million for the Episcopal mission among American Indians. In addition, she has been involved in the development of the Anglican Indigenous People's Network of the Pacific Rim. Among other things, the network helps the indigenous people from around the Pacific (e.g., Native Hawaiians, Maori of New Zealand, American Indians, and the Aboriginals of Australia) learn how much they have in common with each other.

In 1988, Anderson wrote *Jamestown Commitment,* which recounts the Anglican church's efforts to share the gospel with Native Americans in the early years of the European expansion into the New World. The work describes the many occasions where tribal leaders asked the church to send missionaries to teach the tribes Christianity as well as English. Those early efforts often are criticized for helping to end the practice of traditional Native American religions. However, Anderson explained to Clay that the requests for missionaries formed an important aspect of Native American history that should be told. She also pointed out that traditional Native American religions have many parallels with Christianity.

In addition to her work with the Episcopal church, Anderson has served on the board of directors for the Association of American Indian Affairs since 1987. The association is the oldest of the Indian advocacy organizations in the United States. Since the late 1980s, she also has been involved with HONOR, a national treaty rights organization which insures that the federal government abides by its many treaties with various Native American tribes.

Anderson admitted to Clay that she has a love-hate relationship with New York City. With her grown children and grandchildren living in Texas and Native American friends scattered from Washington to Alaska, New York has seemed like a lonely place, where it is not easy to get to know people. However, she enjoys the theater, opera, and the energy of the city. Anderson is the widow of Henry J. Anderson, a north Texas attorney who died in 1983.

SOURCES:

Books

Native American Women, edited by Gretchen M. Bataille, New York, Garland Publishing, 1993.
Native North American Almanac, edited by Duane Champagne, Detroit, Gale Research, 1994.

Other

Anderson, Owanah, "Biographical Brief," 1994.
Anderson, interview with Catherine A. Clay conducted July 24, 1994.

—Sketch by Catherine A. Clay

William Apess
1798-1839
Pequot minister, activist, and writer

William Apess was the first Native American to write and publish his own autobiography, *A Son in the Forest,* and was the most prolific writer in the English language among Indians in the nineteenth century. He exemplifies Native Americans whose acculturation to the white man's way was characterized by emotional and spiritual trauma as he early in life internalized the values of the conquering Americans, but utilized a religious zeal to construct a renewed sense of Native American identity and selfhood.

As a Pequot Indian, Apess inherited the defeat and nearly total annihilation of his people during the Pequot War of 1637, survivors of which were sold into slavery in the West Indies or were dispersed to live a hidden existence in southeastern Connecticut. By the late eighteenth century, the Pequots lived on two reservations, where they took care of their families often through day labor and domestic work, and where a vanquished sense of tribal pride made them ripe victims for alcohol abuse and depression. Yet, Native Americans were among the general population that responded during the eighteenth and early nineteenth centuries to evangelical Christianity. Apess was but one of several Native Americans who became prominent as ministers, and he remains outstanding for his prolific literary acumen.

Apess was born on January 31, 1798, in Colrain, Massachusetts. His father, William, a half-blooded descendant of King Philip, was a shoemaker by trade; his mother, Candace, was a Pequot who may have had part African ancestry. Nineteenth-century records show that the spelling of the surname was *Apes* with one "s" until son William inexplicably added the letter for his later publications. Apess' parents went to Colrain from Colchester, Connecticut, and Apess biographer Barry O'Connell speculates one reason for this was to elude Candace Apes' slave master, who did not manumit her until 1805. Eventually, the family returned to its former home where upon the parents' separating, young William lived with his maternal grandparents.

Apess' boyhood with his grandparents was marked by abuse resulting in a severely broken arm, indenture to neighboring households and escapes from them, occasional friendships with local ruffians, and little formal schooling. Around 1809, at the height of the Second Great Awakening, an extremely sensitive religious disposition began to emerge as he sought to attend revivalist meetings and was impressionably receptive to the rhetorical conventions espoused by Calvinists about Christian salvation. The youthful Apess found himself more inclined toward what he called the "noisy Methodists." Their fervor stimulated his growing personal convictions about the rightness of spontaneous expression in worship, the loving grace of Christ as the savior of mankind, and about Native Americans as one of the Ten Lost Tribes of Israel.

Apess' religious zeal in part contributed to his confused identity as an Indian when, berry-picking one afternoon with his adoptive white family, he encountered suntanned white women whom he thought were cruel Indians, and fled. Nor did an interest in Christianity prevent his being periodically flogged by various masters, who vacillated in permitting Apess to attend Methodist meetings. In early 1813 Apess finally ran away to New York City with another indentured youth and, prodded by unscrupulous drinking soldiers, enlisted in the Army as a drummer. Initially opposing their blasphemies, as he says in his autobiography, *A Son of the Forest,* "in little time I became almost as bad as any of them, could drink rum, play cards, and act as wickedly as any. I was at times tormented with the thoughts of death, but God had mercy on me and spared my life."

Apess' militia unit marched to Plattsburgh, New York, to prepare a siege of Montreal. Although he was officially a drummer as well as being under the legal age for Army service, Apess saw action in a few battles. After mustering out of his militia, he traveled and worked in southern Canada, socializing with several Native American families there, and eventually worked his way southward through Albany en route to Connecticut.

By age 19 Apess faced anew the ravages of sinful behavior and resumed earnestly attending religious meetings. One outstanding experience confirmed his religious faith more than previous conversion experiences. Leaving the southeastern Connecticut home of maternal relatives to visit his father, who had resettled in Colrain, Apess became lost one night in a swamp. This experience became profoundly significant for his convictions, for he felt himself called to preach the Gospel and increasingly, even before his baptism in 1818, received opportunities to exhort congregations of Native Americans, whites, and blacks to repent and seek salvation. Although at this time he was legally forbidden to preach without a license, he proselytized throughout Connecticut and in the Albany area. In December 1821 Apess married Mary Wood of Salem, Connecticut, a self-effacing woman ten years his senior "of nearly the same color as myself." Religious exhorting and the need to support his wife and growing family forced him into lengthy separations from them. Only on a few occasions, such as one preaching tour in the Albany area, was his family able to be near him. Apess preached to worshippers on Long Island, in New York City, in the Albany-Troy region, in Utica, and in southern and coastal New England. In 1829, after the Methodist Episcopal church refused to ordain him, he was befriended by the Protestant Methodists who performed his ordination.

Writing, Preaching, and Activism

In 1829 the first edition of Apess' autobiography, *A Son of the Forest,* was published. This record of his life up to that time can best be described as a conversion narrative for the way its author draws attention to how his childhood hardships and later behavioral excesses shaped his personality for baptism and his quest for heavenly reward. Conversion narratives, or testimonies, are a kind of spiritual memoir demonstrating to the reader how the author arrives at a state of grace. *A Son of the Forest* had no precedence as a published full-length personal narrative written by an Indian. Its very title creates a literary appeal for audiences who looked upon literacy among peoples of color in the United States as an exotic phenomenon and as proof that Native Americans and African Americans were capable of becoming civilized according to the white man's way.

Apess' literary style is similar to that of his religious and political contemporaries, and its maturity and clarity are remarkable for someone who could only attend school during the winter months for only six years. That he slightly revised the 1831 edition of *A Son of the Forest* and the second editions of his other writings attests to his concern for detail and a desire to represent himself as literarily and humanly respectable. Apess came to preaching and writing in an era when white politicians, educators, and religious leaders intensely debated the fate of the Indian and the slave; he lived amidst schemes for Indian removal from the South and the repatriation of slaves to Africa. And he was acutely aware that his congregations included as many repentant sinners as curious onlookers who simply wanted to witness an Indian preacher.

A Son of the Forest includes a lengthy Appendix in which Apess rearranged and paraphrased much of the text of a book entitled *A Star in the West,* published in 1816 by Elias Boudinot (not the Cherokee writer-editor of the same name). The argument advanced concerns about the similarities between the biblical Hebrews and Native Americans according to customs and character traits, and Apess used this text because he agreed with its Ten Lost Tribes thesis.

In the 1830s Apess wrote prolifically about religious, historical, and political issues. *The Increase of the Kingdom of Christ: A Sermon* was printed in 1831 with an appendix, *The Indians: The Ten Lost Tribes.* John the Baptist, the preacher in the wilderness and forerunner of Christ, is the model for *The Increase* as Apess presents a detailed and cogently organized statement on the theme of the Native American as among God's chosen people.

Another book, *The Experiences of Five Christian Indians of the Pequot Tribe,* was published in 1833, revealing Apess' skills as a writer, life historian, and editor. Its five testimonies confront the legacy of degradation imposed on Pequots as a people and as tribal individuals. Apess' personal statement, opening this collection, condenses what he wrote in *A Son of the Forest* while forcefully challenging whites about their racism. In the second testimony, Mary Apes, his wife, describes her parents and presents her own observations about the advantages of piety. In the third, Apess rendered the statement of a Hannah Caleb. The remaining two testimonies are remarkable in singular ways. "The Experience of Sally George," about a woman who was related to Apess, may have been written prior to *A Son of the Forest,* and Apess wrote it partly in her voice and partly from an objective point of view. In "The Experience of Ann Wampy," he describes the title character's life and includes a passage approximating her speech mannerisms in what is an early example of oral history, a method of historical inquiry that faithfully presents a record of the spoken word. The first edition of *Experiences* also includes Apess' militant essay, "An Indian's Looking-Glass for the White Man." Here Apess attacks the racial hypocrisy of white Christians who live in a world overwhelmingly populated by peoples of color and proceeds to remind Christians of the non-white identity of Jesus. The acuity of his remarks in this daring essay recalls David Walker's *Appeal* (1829) and the statements of Malcolm X in the twentieth century.

Apess responded to disparate rumors about conditions affecting the Mashpee Wampanoag Indians on Cape Cod by visiting their community in 1833. He quickly became embroiled in the "Mashpee Revolt" against the Commonwealth of Massachusetts and its energetic efforts to deny the right of this tribe any form of self-government and representation while it tacitly encouraged corruption and greed by white landowners and squatters. Apess served a 30-day jail sentence for leading a group of Indian men in removing timber from a trespassing white man's wagon. In his annotations to *On Our Own Ground: The Complete Writings of William Apess, A Pequot,* Barry O'Connell describes Apess as playing more a catalytic role to advance Indian rights rather than his being the revolt's architect. After a peaceful solution was achieved, Apess published a documentary history and exposé of the incident, *Indian Nullification of the Unconstitutional Laws of Massachusetts Relative to the Marshpee Tribe; or, The Pretended Riot Explained* in 1835, consisting of his observations in addition to the reprinting of letters, depositions and petitions to governing officials by the Wampanoag selectmen, and letters reprinted from regional newspapers. The *Indian Nullification* is one of the outstanding legal-related documents by a private individual in the nineteenth century.

The final extant writing by Apess, *Eulogy on King Philip, as Pronounced at the Odeon, in Federal Street, Boston,* was initially printed in 1836. By this time, he began to use the additional 's' in documents for his name: the 1837 edition of *Experiences* (which happens to exclude the "Looking-Glass" essay), also carries this unexplained alteration. The *Eulogy* is a long speech attributing to the seventeenth-century Wampanoag leader the qualities befitting a martyred American patriot slain in the process of defending his country from invaders.

For many years, Apess scholars could only speculate about his fate after 1838, for which an inventory of his household goods survives as the result of a debt action in Barnstable, not far from the Mashpee community. However, in recent years a published obituary came to light describing Apess' death in late April 1839 in New York City from "apoplexy." Details of his autopsy suggest a head injury possibly related to alcohol, which he managed to avoid for two decades. Whatever the fatal circumstances, William Apess in his last years gained little consolation that Native Americans would receive justice in their lost country.

SELECTED WRITINGS BY APESS:

On Our Own Ground: The Complete Writings of William Apess, a Pequot, edited by Barry O'Connell, Amherst, University of Massachusetts Press, 1992.

SOURCES:

Books

Bates, Ernest Sunderland, "William Apes," in *Dictionary of American Biography,* Volume 1, edited by Allen Johnson, New York, Charles Scribner's Sons, 1928; 323.

A Biobibliography of Native American Writers, 1772-1924 (Native American Bibliography Series, No. 2), compiled by Daniel F. Littlefield, Jr., and James W. Parins, Metuchen, New Jersey, Scarecrow Press, 1981.

Ruoff, A. LaVonne Brown, "Three Nineteenth-Century American Indian Autobiographies," in *Redefining American Literary History,* edited by A. LaVonne Brown Ruoff and Jerry W. Ward, New York, Modern Language Association, 1990; 251-269.

Wiget, Andrew, *Native American Literature,* Boston, Twayne, 1985; 50-52.

Periodicals

McQuaid, Kim, "William Apes, Pequot: An Indian Reformer in the Jackson Era," in *New England Quarterly,* 50, 1977; 605-625.

Moon, Randall, "William Apess and Writing White," in *Studies In American Indian Literatures,* 5, winter 1993; 45-54.

O'Connell, Barry, "William Apess and the Survival of the Pequot People," in *Algonkians of New England: Past and Present* (Dublin Seminar for New England Folklife Annual Proceedings 1991), edited by Peter Benes, Boston, Boston University, 1992; 89-100.

Other

"Death of Apes," *Gazette & Mercury* (Greenfield, Massachusetts), May 7, 1839.

—Sketch by Ron Welburn

Anna Mae Pictou Aquash
1945-1976(?)
Micmac political activist

From the era of Native American political activism and militancy during the early 1970s, there is no more haunting figure than Anna Mae Pictou Aquash. Mother, wife, social worker, daycare teacher, American Indian Movement (AIM) member, her image is powerful as much for her untimely death as for her life's work. Found murdered on the Pine Ridge Reservation during a time of tremendous social and political upheaval, she has become an icon of the indigenous rights movement.

Childhood on a Micmac Reserve

Anna Mae Pictou was born on March 27, 1945 to Mary Ellen Pictou and Francis Thomas Levi, both Micmac Indians. She came into the world in a small Indian village just outside the town of Shubenacadie, Nova Scotia, Canada. Levi left before Anna Mae was born, and Mary Ellen's third grade education was not enough on which to raise her children in financial security. Still a young woman herself, Mary Ellen Pictou admitted to being a little too unsettled to offer her girls much in the way of discipline. Pictou spent her early years in this atmosphere of poverty and uncertainty.

Pictou's mother married Noel Sapier, a Micmac traditionalist in 1949. A strong believer in the retention of what little was left of Micmac culture and religion, Sapier brought discipline and emotional security to the family. He moved them to Pictou's Landing, another small Micmac reserve, and tried to make a living between seasonal farmhand jobs and traditional craftwork. Although she knew they were still very poor, Pictou learned the richness of her people's culture.

Poverty often breeds disease, and conditions were very poor at Pictou's Landing. In 1953, Anna Mae was plagued with recurrent eye infections. By the time an Indian Department physician recognized the signs of tuberculosis of the eye, Anna Mae had already developed tuberculosis of the lung. She recovered but she was physically weak for sometime afterward.

In 1956, Noel Sapier died of cancer, and a new phase of Pictou's childhood began. Until then, she had encountered racism mostly during trips to nearby towns. Now she went to an off-reserve school and was shocked by her reception. Although reserve schools were notoriously below standards, Pictou's prior A-average schoolwork was still well above failing when she started in her new school. By the end of her first year, however, she was failing all her subjects. In later years, she would often talk about how the constant jeers, racial slurs, and lewd comments had ruined her school years. Pictou was not alone; most of her Micmac tribespeople followed the same pattern of failure when they enrolled in off-reserve schools.

Pictou's difficulties with verbal and sometimes physical threats from classmates continued in high school. She steadily performed at lower and lower grade levels, but she stayed in school, something that many of her Indian classmates had not done. Her school problems were compounded in 1956, when her mother ran away to another reserve to marry Wilford Barlov. Pictou and her siblings came home to find that they had been abandoned. Because it was common for Micmacs to work as migrant farmhands throughout the Maritime Provinces and New England, and Pictou herself had worked summers as a harvester, she dropped out of school and turned to the only profession she knew, working the potato and berry harvest.

New Life in Boston

At the age of 17, Pictou decided to move to Boston to seek her fortune. Reportedly on something of a dare, she went there with Jake Maloney, a young Micmac she knew but had never dated. They found themselves in Boston in 1962, a strange, noisy, bustling world for people used to reserve life. The presence of so many other Micmacs made the transition somewhat easier, though, and the couple soon settled in. Pictou began working in a factory and set up house with Jake. They considered themselves married and started a family. In 1964 and 1965, Pictou gave birth to daughters Denise and Deborah. Just after Deborah's birth, the couple married in New Brunswick and moved to another Micmac reserve. Although they had liked life in Boston, they had mixed feelings about raising their daughters in such a big city, and they moved back and forth between Boston and the Maritimes several times. During their stays in Canada, they immersed themselves in Micmac tradition, learning much from Jake's step-uncle, one of the last Micmacs to remember many of their old ways.

Becomes a Community Organizer

In 1968, Natives were calling for equal rights, cultural recognition, and the upholding of promises made in treaties. Pictou worked as a volunteer in the Boston Indian Council's headquarters while holding down her factory job. Her council work centered on helping young, urban Natives develop self-esteem, a technique that seemed to help them avoid alcohol abuse. It was a topic close to Pictou's own life. She had seen the havoc drinking caused in Indian communities and during the initial period after her breakup with Jake Maloney, she herself frequently drank.

At the Indian Council Pictou heard about a planned protest by AIM. A number of New England AIM members were joining with national leader Russell Means to protest the "official" version of Thanksgiving by converging on the Mayflower II, a reconstruction of the Pilgrims' vessel. Pictou participated in the protest and the event galvanized her resolve to work for Native rights.

Pictou, along with her daughters, moved to Bar Harbor, Maine, to work in the Teaching and Research in Bicultural Education School Project (TRIBES). The girls attended the school and Pictou taught. The curriculum aimed at keeping young Indians in school by teaching traditional subjects as well as Indian history, values, and beliefs to foster pride in the students. Although the project was successful, it was closed in 1972, when funding was cut. The family returned to Boston, where Anna Mae enrolled in the New Careers program at Wheelock College. This program was designed to include classroom instruction and community work. Pictou's assignment was teaching at a daycare center in Roxbury, a predominately African-American section of Boston. She excelled in the program and in her work, and was eventually offered a scholarship to attend Brandeis University. Pictou declined the offer, preferring to continue her work in the Black and Indian communities.

Around this time, she met a Nogeeshik Aquash, a Chippewa artist from Ontario. Together, they raised her daughters and became more involved in the growing Indian rights movement. When AIM and other allied groups marched on Washington, D.C., in 1972, on the Trail of Broken Treaties, Pictou and Nogeeshik were there. Several months later, in April of 1973, AIM occupied the small, historic settlement of Wounded Knee, South Dakota. In 1890, it had been the site of an infamous massacre of Minneconjou Sioux by General George Custer's old regiment of the Seventh Cavalry. It was chosen for this historical significance to garner public attention for AIM's efforts against the reputedly corrupt administration of tribal chairman of the Oglala Sioux, Richard "Dick" Wilson.

When word of the occupation and resulting siege by federal troops reached Boston, Pictou and Nogeeshik left for South Dakota. Arriving several days later, they immediately busied themselves by sneaking food and medical supplies to the occupiers. Initially, they camped at Crow Dog's Paradise, the home of medicine men Henry Crow Dog and Leonard Crow Dog. Later, inside one of the stores at Wounded Knee, Anna Mae would help deliver Pedro, the first son of Mary Brave Bird, who would soon marry Leonard Crow Dog. On April 12, 1973, Pictou married Nogeeshik Aquash in a traditional Lakota (Sioux) ceremony presided over by Nicholas Black Elk and Wallace Black Elk.

The standoff at Wounded Knee ended with the indictment of AIM leaders Dennis Banks and Russell Means. The Aquashes returned to Boston, where they continued their work for the movement. Aquash was on her way to becoming a national AIM leader. In 1974, she moved to St. Paul to work in the AIM office there. Within a year, she was involved in the Menominee Indian takeover of an abandoned Alexian Brothers Catholic Monastery in protest of the termination of their federal Indian status. The conflict in Gresham, Wisconsin, ended peacefully and Aquash emerged as a figure who would be constantly under FBI observation.

Back to Wounded Knee

During the summer of 1975, Aquash and AIM security chief Leonard Peltier attended an AIM conference in Farmington, New Mexico, to lend support to Navajo protests over mining in the Four Corners area. From there, they were called back to Pine Ridge to help organize security for Lakota traditionalists and AIM supporters who were being attacked by Wilson's provisional police force. They camped on the property of the Jumping Bull family. On June 26, 1975, a fight broke out between two FBI agents and AIM members. Two agents and a young Indian were killed. AIM members scattered as an international manhunt began for the FBI agents' killers.

Three months later, in September of 1975, Aquash was arrested with several others during a raid on the Rosebud Reservation. Fearing the worst, she jumped bail and went "underground." In November, she was leaving the Port Madison Reservation in Washington state when federal agents began watching the two vehicles in the AIM caravan. In Oregon, just one mile short of the Idaho border, state troopers stopped the group and Aquash was again arrested. She was extradited to South Dakota in handcuffs to face charges from the raid at Rosebud, as well as federal charges of transporting and possessing firearms and dangerous

weapons, including dynamite. Since she had not been indicted on the earlier charges, the South Dakota judge gave her bond; she fled again on November 24, 1975.

On February 24, 1976, a Lakota rancher found Aquash's dead body while riding the perimeter of his property. Her body's deteriorated condition indicated that she had been dead for some time. The body was initially taken to the Pine Ridge Public Health Service for an autopsy. The cause of her death was deemed exposure, and, as no one was able to identify her, she was buried as a "Jane Doe." Her hands were cut off and sent to FBI headquarters in Washington, D.C., for possible identification. A week later, Anna Mae Aquash was identified. When her family was informed, they called on AIM to help them secure a second autopsy. On March 11, 1976, another post-mortem revealed a .32 caliber bullet hole at the base of Anna Mae's skull. Her death was now officially a homicide. Aquash was reburied with traditional rites, and the investigation of her murder began.

Although two senators brought the matter before Congress and the Department of Justice, and although Canadian authorities demanded full accounting for the murder of one of their citizens on the federal land of a friendly neighboring country, the investigation never went far. The murder of Anna Mae Aquash remains unsolved, but she is remembered as a powerful symbol of an era of Native rights activism.

SOURCES:

Brand, Johanna, *The Life and Death of Anna Mae Aquash,* Toronto, James Lorimer, 1978.
Matthiessen, Peter, *In the Spirit of Crazy Horse,* New York, Viking Books, 1983.
Native American Women, edited by Gretchen M. Bataille, New York, Garland Publishing, 1993.
Native North American Almanac, edited by Duane Champagne, Detroit, Gale Research, 1994.
Weyler, Rex, *Blood of the Land,* New York, Everest House Publishing, 1982.

—*Sketch by Cynthia R. Kasee*

JoAllyn Archambault
1942-
Yankton Dakota Sioux anthropologist, artist, and museum program director

JoAllyn Archambault is a preeminent anthropologist and program director at the Smithsonian Institution. She was born February 13, 1942, in Claremore, Oklahoma, into a mixed-blood Standing Rock Dakota (enrolled), Creek, Irish and French family. Since 1986 she has served as the director of the American Indian Program at the National Museum of Natural History, part of the Smithsonian Institution in Washington, D.C. Her work at the museum involves the preservation and promotion of Native American art and culture, and political anthropology. She acts as an ethnic liaison and supervises Native fellowship interns in addition to a $110,000 annual program budget. She is also responsible for the redesign of the North American Indian Ethnology Halls for the "Changing Cultures in a Changing World" exhibit, covering over 20,000 square feet at a projected cost of $9.2 million.

Academic and Professional Career

She attended University of California at Berkeley, receiving her B.A. in 1970, M.A. in 1974, and Ph.D. in 1984, all in the field of anthropology. From 1970 to 1975, she received a Ford Foundation doctoral fellowship for American Indians. Her dissertation, *"The Gallup Ceremonial": A Study of Patronage within a Contemporary Context of Indian-White Relationships,* was based on the annual tourist event held in Gallup, New Mexico (centrally between the Hopi and Navajo reservations to the west and north with the Ute, the Jicarilla to the northeast, Pueblo to the east, Zuni to the south, and Apache to the southwest), which is sponsored by whites for whites but focusses upon Native Americans. The primary feature of the Gallup Ceremonial that Archambault examines is the patron-client/white-native system of distribution of art goods, including white referrals to dealers, white control of commissions and of the entire economy based on white art dealer control of access to the economic and retail gates outside of the native economy. She asserts that although natives have been dependent in recent times upon Anglo modes of contact, the demise of the patronage structure occurred as natives became more sophisticated and business-savvy, resulting in the takeover and establishment of their own dealer contacts. In her study she demonstrated that the old patron-client system depended upon white control of business access, and was based upon the economic system developed by European traders who first established themselves among the tribes and later within the reservation system. This system of control, she asserts, was shifting and dying.

Her interests since then have included research in several urban and reservation communities, including reservation land use, health evaluation, expressive art, material culture, contemporary native culture, and the Sundance among eight different Plains' groups. Archambault indicates that she has provided a wide array of assistance about conservation, architecture, public programming, and research projects to tribes and to Indian controlled museums, archives and other types of cultural projects.

Prior to her work in Washington, Archambault served as a full-time lecturer in Native American studies at the University of California at Berkeley between 1976 and 1979, at which time she became chair of the ethnic studies department at California College of Arts and Crafts. She served as a part-time research associate at the Center for the Study of Race, Crime and Social Policy at Cornell University in Ithaca, New York, from 1980 to 1982; and in 1983, she moved to the University of Wisconsin in Milwaukee where she became assistant professor of anthropology until 1986. She has also taught at several other colleges and universities, including Oglala Lakota College in Pine Ridge, South Dakota, California State University at Hayward, the University of New Mexico, Navajo Community College in Tsaile, New Mexico, Mills College in Oakland, California, and Johns Hopkins University. Archambault has lectured worldwide, presenting papers at numerous academic institutions from New York to Kunming, China, on a variety of Native American issues.

Art

Working with the National Museum of Natural History, Archambault has curated and implemented four major exhibits: "Plains Indian Arts: Change and Continuity" in 1987, "100 Years of Plains Indian Painting" in 1989, "Indian Basketry and Their Makers" in 1990, and "Seminole!" in 1990. She also contributed to the Southwest Museum's Quincentennial exhibit, "Grandfather, Hear Our Voices" in 1992.

Professional Affiliations

A member of the American Anthropological Association, Archambault has served on its Commission on Native American Reburial as well as the University of California Joint Academic-Senate-Administration Committee on Human Skeletal Remains. In addition to membership in the American Ethnological Society and the Anthropological Society of Washington, Archambault belongs to the Council for Museum Anthropology, Native American Art Studies Association, the Society for Applied Anthropology, Studies in American Indian Literature, and the Plains Anthropological Society.

SELECTED WRITINGS BY ARCHAMBAULT:

Books

"Beadwork" and "Quillwork," in *Native American in the Twentieth Century,* edited by Mary Davis, New York, Garland Publishing, 1994.

"Women and Power in Native North America: A Commentary," in *Women and Power in Native North America,* edited by L. Ackerman, University of Oklahoma Press, 1994.

"The Plains Indian Sundance" and "Plains Indian Art," in *Handbook of the American Indian,* "Plains" Volume, Washington, D.C., Smithsonian Institution, forthcoming.

Periodicals

"Art and Value in American Plains Indian Cultures," *Texas Journal of Ideas, History and Culture,* 11:2, 1989.

SOURCES:

Books

Kasee, Cynthia, "JoAllyn Archambault," in *Native American Women,* edited by Gretchen M. Bataille, New York, Garland Publishing, 1993; 12-13.
Native North American Almanac, edited by Duane Champagne, Detroit, Gale Research, 1994; 1004.

Reference Encyclopedia of the American Indian, sixth edition, edited by Barry T. Klein, New York, Todd Publications, 1993; 460.

Other

Archambault, JoAllyn, interview with tpkunesh conducted on May 19, 1994.

—Sketch by tpkunesh

Amos Bad Heart Bull
1869-1913
Oglala Lakota Sioux tribal historian and artist
Also known as Eagle Lance and Tatanka Cante Sica ["Bad Heart Buffalo"]

Amos Bad Heart Bull was called "the Herodotus of his people" by Helen Blish, who rescued his 400 pictographs by having had them photographed before their interment. Through her intervention *A Pictographic History of the Oglala Sioux* was published to relate the transition of these proud Plains warriors into reservation Indians. The illustrations from this book have been featured in every television documentary about the Ghost Dance, the Battle of the Little Big Horn, and the deaths of Sitting Bull and Crazy Horse. The artist's pictures of Crazy Horse, his cousin, are the only surviving likenesses of him since Crazy Horse never allowed himself to be photographed. Fortunately, Blish was able to interview two of the artist's uncles, He Dog (Sunka Bloka) and Short Bull (Tatanka Ptecela), on the Pine Ridge Reservation in South Dakota, to learn a little about his life. Short Bull and He Dog told her that Amos Bad Heart Bull the Elder had been a band historian, a keeper of the winter count, and had created a hide chronicle on which the outstanding single event of each year was recorded. Since he died young, the task of bringing up his son fell to them, and to their brothers, Little Shield and Only Man. They told him stories of the battles they had fought in, and observed his interest in collecting treaties and documents about Indian-white encounters.

Self-Taught Artistry

Without any formal instruction, Bad Heart Bull began creating annotated drawings. Although he had been given no education, he taught himself to write using a system devised by the missionaries for the transcription of Lakota. He also learned English from the soldiers at Fort Robinson, where he had enlisted as a scout for the United States Army in 1890. From a clothing dealer in Crawford, Nebraska, he bought a used ledger in which he began his 415 drawings using black pen, indelible pencil, and blue, yellow, green, and brown crayons, and red ink. In some instances he painted with a brush so fine that the strokes can be seen only under magnification. In addition, some of the pictures are touched with a gray or brown wash in places. He worked at

this project for about two decades recording the civic, religious, social, economic, and military life of the Oglala.

His technical innovations permitted multiple perspectives of an event. He portrayed masses of people engaged in dramatic actions by assuming a panoramic view. Depicting hundreds of men and horses in battle, or in religious ceremonies, or in processionals to a buffalo hunt from above, he captured tribal activities in long-shots or topographic views. Then, he would render close-ups of some aspect on the same page, framed and set-off to one side, so that one could study the psychological impact of the sweeping event upon an individual participant by means of a near-view insert. He experimented with other than stylized profile renditions, using full-face depictions, rear-views, rendering wounded horses from below, or showing dancers in three-quarter view. Another innovation was his use of foreshortening. These techniques added drama and realism to his pictures.

Each set of drawings tells part of a heroic epic. The first group shows tribal events before 1856. The councilmen (wakicunza) and their marshals (akicita) are shown deliberating in the camp council, a buffalo hunt, a sun dance, and the eight warrior societies in their regalia are shown. The next set of pictures tells the story of the conflicts with the Crow, their hereditary enemies on the Plains in sporadic skirmishes from 1856 to 1875. The third set narrates the defeat of U.S. General George A. Custer on the Little Big Horn River in Montana. The next group of pictures shows the reorganization of Oglala society as it was forced to accept reservation existence. It opens with the ceremonies: the Sacred Bow, the Victory Dance, the Dance of the Black Tailed Deer, the Horse Dance, and the Vision Quest. These are followed by eight depictions of courting scenes, and ten of games. This section closes with the transition to agriculture. The next to last set depicts the Ghost Dance and the Battle of Wounded Knee. And the final set shows the fourth of July being celebrated in 1898 and in 1903 on the Pine Ridge Reservation. By grouping his pictures in these narrative sequences, the artist has conveyed the history of his band over 60 years. Because he preserved the most minute details of daily life, this constitutes an unparalleled historical record.

Rescued for Posterity

In 1926, Helen Blish was a graduate student at the University of Nebraska searching for examples of Plains art. From W. O. Roberts of the Pine Ridge Agency, she learned about Bad Heart Bull's drawings, which had been given, after the artist's death in 1913, to his sister, Dolly Pretty Cloud. Speaking through an interpreter, Blish spent her summer vacations from teaching in a Detroit high school, studying the art of Pretty Cloud's brother, kept in a trunk on the dirt floor of the one-room cabin on the reservation. It was only after much persuasion that she was permitted to rent it for a modest annual fee and to analyze the renderings for her master's thesis under the noted art historian, Hartley Burr Alexander.

Following Lakota custom, the prized ledger book was buried with Pretty Cloud upon her death in 1947. Fortunately, though, Blish's work had been given to the American Museum of Natural History in New York City before her death in 1941. In 1959, the University of Nebraska Press decided to publish Bad Heart Bull's pictorial history and attempted to get permission to disinter the ledger, to no avail. However, it was found that Alexander had photographed the priceless document page-by-page in 1927; therefore, these illustrations were collated with Blish's manuscript and was published in book form. Mari Sandoz, the biographer of Bad Heart Bull's cousin, Crazy Heart, encouraged the project from its inception, and wrote its introduction in the last year of her life. She said, "Without doubt, the Amos Bad Heart Bull picture history is the most comprehensive, the finest statement as art and as report of the North American Indian so far discovered anywhere."

SOURCES:

Blish, Helen H., *A Pictographic History of the Oglala Sioux,* Lincoln, University of Nebraska Press, 1967.

Dockstader, Frederick J., *Great North American Indians,* New York, Van Nostrand Reinhold, 1977.

The Indians' Book, edited by Natalie Cirtis Burlin, New York, Harper, 1923.

Sandoz, Mari, *Crazy Horse: The Strange Man of the Oglalas,* Lincoln, University of Nebraska Press, 1942.

—*Sketch by Ruth Rosenberg*

Louis W. Ballard
1931-
Quapaw-Cherokee music educator and composer

Louis Wayne Ballard is one of the most visible Native American composers. His compositions include many types of music, but they always incorporate Native American themes. As a music curriculum specialist for the U.S. Bureau of Indian Affairs, Ballard also has been a pioneer in developing ethnic-centered educational materials. He has travelled extensively establishing bicultural music programs in schools, and has lectured on Indian art and music at colleges around the United States.

Ballard was born July 8, 1931, in Miami, Oklahoma. His mother was of Quapaw-French ancestry and his father was of Cherokee-Scot heritage. Ballard was surrounded by

Louis W. Ballard

music from a very young age. He learned Native songs and dances as a youth attending tribal ceremonials, for example, and his mother wrote children's songs and was a pianist. As he matured, his grandmother encouraged him to learn to play piano, and he soon began taking piano lessons at a mission chapel near where she lived. An adept student, he began writing out his own musical ideas and composing not long afterward. Ballard studied music at Bacone College and Northeast Oklahoma Agricultural and Mechanical College, and went on to earn his bachelor's degree from the University of Tulsa. During his undergraduate years, he performed various jobs to help finance his education, including that of janitor, dishwasher, ambulance driver, drugstore clerk, and waiter. He also worked as a nightclub pianist and a singer.

While at the University of Tulsa in the early 1950s, Ballard discovered the music of Bela Bartok. Ballard was strongly influenced in his own writing by Bartok's use of Hungarian themes. In fact, Ballard became determined to incorporate ethnicity into his own work by using Indian tribal themes and motifs. His initial goal was to foster greater appreciation for the music of his people. As his career developed, he broadened this objective toward a desire to bring Indian music into the mainstream of musical expression and awareness via American folk music. In 1967, Ballard completed his master's degree in music at the University of Oklahoma, where he had been awarded the F. B. Parriott fellowship for his accomplishments.

Earned Recognition for Compositions

A versatile composer, Ballard has written various types of music for nearly all instruments, from ballet to choral arrangements, including chamber and orchestral works. Though he won a number of prestigious awards for different genres, he enjoyed notable success with ballet. Koshare, a ballet based upon an ancient Hopi creation story, premiered in Barcelona, Spain, in 1960 and was first performed in the United States seven years later. Also in 1967, his ballet *The Four Moons* was featured during the celebration of the state of Oklahoma's sixtieth anniversary. In addition, Ballard's *Mid-Winter Fires,* an instrumental, highlighted the White House Conference on Children and Youth in 1969 and the University of Colorado Conference on American Indian Music in 1971.

In 1969, Ballard won the Marion Nevins MacDowell Award for his woodwind quartet *Ritmo Indio,* and was later nominated for a Pulitzer Prize for his piece *Desert Trilogy.* In 1972, he became the first professional musician to be awarded the Indian Achievement Award created by the Indian Council Fire. Two of his most popular pieces are his cantata based on the life of actor Will Rogers, *Portrait of Will,* and his choral work *Scenes from Indian Life.*

During the mid-1970s, Ballard served as the music department dean for the Institute of American Indian Arts in Santa Fe, New Mexico. He also became the music curriculum specialist for the U.S. Bureau of Indian Affairs, where he presided over the program development for all reservation schools. In this role, he insisted that all students utilize Indian instruments and compositions to learn the cultural content as well as the unique musical style of each tribe. As a result, he became known for his applied emphasis on ethnicity in music education.

In his development of educational materials, and perhaps in pursuit of his own early interests, Ballard has collected a great number of ceremonial and dance songs, Indian lullabies, and love songs. Ballard also created classroom educational materials in the form of a film and a phonodisc recording. *American Indian Music for the Classroom* includes a spoken introduction by the composer, a teacher's guide, Indian land areas map, study photographs, and an 18-page bibliography.

Ballard also acts as music consultant and president of First American Indian Films, Inc. The company released a film entitled *Discovering American Indian Music,* which includes a composition by Ballard and depicts the social and ceremonial functions of music. While authentically dressed Indians portraying various tribes across the United States perform dances with song, modern Native life is also addressed. Ballard lives in Santa Fe, New Mexico, with his wife, who is a concert pianist, and three children.

SOURCES:

Books

Biographical Dictionary of the Indians of the Americas, Newport Beach, California, American Indian Publishers, 1983; 37-38.

Native North American Almanac, edited by Duane Champagne, Detroit, Gale Research, 1994; 1006.
Reference Encyclopedia of the American Indian, sixth edition, West Nyack, New York, Todd Publications, 1993; 464-465.

Other

American Indian Music for the Classroom (phonodisc and phono cassette tape), Canyon C 3001-3004.
Wilets, Bernard, *Discovering American Indian Music* (motion picture), BFA Educational Media, 1971.

—Sketch by Brett A. Lealand

Dennis J. Banks
1937-
Anishinabe Ojibwa activist, teacher, and author
Also known as Nowacumig

A founder and current field director of the American Indian Movement (AIM), Dennis J. Banks was born on the Leech Lake Indian Reservation in northern Minnesota on April 12, 1937. At Bureau of Indian Affairs (BIA) boarding schools, he and his younger brother, Mark, lost their native language. He entered the United States Air Force in 1953, serving in Japan. The ties he forged with the Japanese people and the alliances he formed with Buddhist leaders led later to his sponsoring sacred runs in Japan and publishing his award-winning autobiography, *Sacred Soul,* there in 1988.

Banks Becomes an Activist

Unable to find steady employment in the Minneapolis-St. Paul area following his discharge from the service in the late 1950s, Banks began to drink. Apprehended in a grocery-store robbery, Banks was imprisoned for more than two and one-half years while his white accomplice was freed. Finally released in 1968, by July of that year, Banks and George Mitchell, and Clyde Bellecourt had formed the American Indian Movement in Minneapolis to assist Indians in exercising their civil rights, improving their economic and social conditions, and reclaiming their Indian traditions.

In November of 1969, he participated with AIM members 200 others in the occupation of Alcatraz Island in the San Francisco Bay. They demanded that all surplus federal land be returned to the control of Indians and seeking to have the island turned into a cultural center. On Thanksgiving in 1970, AIM sponsored in a day of mourning at Plymouth, Massachusetts; in the spring of 1971, they set up camp at Mount Rushmore to dramatize Lakota claims to the Black Hills; and in the fall of 1972, Banks, Bellecourt,

Dennis J. Banks

Banks urged AIM members to discipline themselves so as not to discredit the Movement. Despite his efforts, bad publicity, deliberately instigated by Douglass Durham, an infiltrator who had attached himself to Banks as his pilot and bodyguard, subverted his efforts. Durham admitted on March 5, 1975, in Des Moines, Iowa, that he was an FBI informant; on March 12, he identified the agents to whom he had reported. Durham had instigated crimes and then released denunciations to the press. However, on July 26, 1975, a South Dakota court found him guilty for his involvement in the Custer courthouse riot. Rather than serve a 15-year sentence, he fled to California. Governor Edmund G. Brown granted him amnesty until his term expired in 1983.

Banks earned an associate of arts degree at the University of California, Davis, and began teaching at Deganawida-Quetzecoatl (DQ) University. There, Banks served as the first American Indian university chancellor. He also taught at Stanford University in Palo Alto, California, and has lectured worldwide about Native American issues and culture.

In March of 1983, Banks was granted sanctuary on the Onondaga Reservation near Syracuse, New York. There he ran six miles a day, coached young runners, chopped firewood, conducted drives for food and clothing donations. A year later, he surrendered himself and was sentenced to three years in the South Dakota penitentiary on October 8, 1984.

Serves Pine Ridge Reservation

Upon his parole December 9, 1985, Banks worked at the Loneman School as an alcoholism counselor, hosted a weekly show on the radio station KILI sponsoring talks against drug use, and tried to find jobs for the unemployed by luring businesses to the reservation.

In 1987, Banks succeeded in having grave desecration laws upgraded from a misdemeanor to a felony in Kentucky and Indiana. He coordinated reburial ceremonies for 1,200 disturbed sites in Uniontown, Kentucky.

In 1991, he moved to Northern Kentucky where he heads the organization he founded in 1978, Sacred Run. As director and coach, he has led spiritual runs totalling 43,000 miles (as of the fall of 1993). In 1988, Banks led runners 3,600 miles across North America and then ran 2,000 miles through Japan, beginning in Hiroshima on the forty-third anniversary of the dropping of the atomic bomb. In 1990, they ran Europe through 13 countries from England to Moscow in the then U.S.S.R. In 1991, Sacred Run crossed Canada from Vancouver to Kahnawake in Quebec. In 1992, they ran from Alaska to New Mexico. In 1993, runners ran 6,000 miles in Australia and then travelled to New Zealand's North Island to run another 1,000 miles. In 1994, Banks led the Walk for Justice from California to Washington, D.C., to plead for the liberation of political prisoner, Leonard Peltier, as well as to bring attention to a variety of other Native issues.

Banks has also appeared in three movies: *War Party,* in 1988; *Thunderheart,* in 1991; and *The Last of the Mohi-*

Mitchell, and Mad Bear Anderson led the Trail of Broken Treaties march across the United States to Washington, D.C. Although meetings with the administration had been pre-arranged, federal officials refused to meet with AIM leaders. Since they were also denied appropriate housing, which had been promised them in advance, they went to the BIA building to protest. When riot squads tried to evict them, they occupied these offices for five days.

On February 28, 1973, the historic take-over of Wounded Knee, site of the 1890 massacre, began. For 71 days AIM withstood tanks, heavy artillery, helicopter strafing, and roadblocks. The siege did not end until May 9, 1973. In 1973, at the national convention in White Oak, Oklahoma, Banks was elected leader of AIM. Peter Matthiessen describes Banks in *In the Spirit of Crazy Horse* as a "handsome man with an intense, brooding expression" who "was quickly established as the most thoughtful and articulate leader in the new Movement."

An incident occurred in February of 1973 that would result in another imprisonment for Banks. On February 6, Sarah Bad Heart Bull requested the help of AIM at the Custer courthouse in South Dakota. When she protested the release of the murderer of her son, Wesley Bad Heart Bull, police clubbed her. The infuriated Indians set fire to some cars and a building; and it was on charges of arson and assault that Banks was to be, after many trials, imprisoned again in 1985. On February 12, 1974 an eight-month trial began which resulted in Banks' acquittal of the ten felony changes lodged against him because the prosecution had used illegal wiretaps, falsified documents, and perjured witnesses.

cans, in 1992. He has also produced a tape recording featuring Native American music, *Still Strong.*

SOURCES:

Books

Contemporary Newsmakers, Detroit, Gale Research, 1986.
Crow Dog, Mary, *Lakota Woman,* New York, Harper Perennial, 1991.
Current Biography Yearbook 1992, New York, H. W. Wilson, 1992.
Matthiessen, Peter, *In The Spirit of Crazy Horse,* New York, Viking, 1983.

Periodicals

Los Angeles Times, June 15, 1986; 10.
People, May 28, 1984; 85.
Printup, Wade, "Run for Land and Life: Japan," *Turtle Quarterly,* winter-spring 1989; 4-14.
Trahant, LeNora Begay, "Walk for Justice Supporters Move through Utah," *News from Indian Country,* April, 1994; 1-2.

—*Sketch by Ruth Rosenberg*

Barboncito
1820(?)-1871
Navajo leader, ceremonial singer, and war chief
Also known as Little Bearded One, Daagi'i
(Dághaa'í) ["The One with the Mustache"],
Hastíin Bidaghaa'i ["The Man with the Mustache"], Hashké yich'i' Dahilwo' ["He Is Anxious
to Run at Warriors"], Bisahalani ["The Orator"],
and Hoozhooji Naatá ["Blessing Speaker"]

Barboncito was a Navajo war chief who headed the Navajo resistance of the mid-1860s with his brother Delgadito and Manuelito, another Navajo war chief. A staunch but peaceful opponent to white encroachment on Native American homelands, Barboncito was beloved among his people for his eloquence, his leadership skills, and his inspirational role as a religious singer. He is remembered for signing the 1868 treaty with the U.S. government insuring the Navajos—or "The Dine" (the people)—the lands on which they still live today.

Barboncito was born to the Ma'iideeshgiizhnii ["Coyote Pass"] clan. He was born at Cañon de Chelly, in present-

day northeastern Arizona, where the mountains of the area produced a major stronghold for the Navajos, ensuring them a formidable defensive position. He quickly rose to become one of the council chiefs of the Navajo people.

Signed First Treaty

Once the United States occupied Santa Fe, in New Mexico territory, around the time of the Mexican War, the Navajos signed their first treaty with the white settlers. Barboncito was one of the chiefs to sign the Doniphan Treaty of 1846, agreeing to peaceful relations and beneficial trade with the whites. Despite the treaty, fighting continued between Navajos and whites because Doniphan had failed to obtain all the signatures of all the Navajo chiefs. Furthermore, the U.S. Army did not possess sufficient military strength to quell skirmishes between Navajos and nearby Spanish-Mexicans, who sought to enslave the Indians. Leaders on both sides tried to put an end to the traditional warfare to no avail. Attacks and negotiations by U.S. troops sent mixed signals to Navajos, who believed the Anglo-American settlers were unlawfully seizing Indian land.

Barboncito, also known as "The Orator" and "Blessing Speaker," did not participate in these skirmishes. In the late 1850s, he acted as a mediator between the Navajos and the whites and argued for putting an end to the escalating warfare. Navajos and whites fought over the grazing lands of Canyon Bonito near Fort Defiance, located in what is now the eastern part of the state of Arizona. The Navajos had let their horses graze in these pastures for centuries, but the white newcomers also wanted the lands for their horses. In 1860 U.S. soldiers slaughtered a number of Navajo horses, leading the Navajos to raid army herds to replenish their losses. The United States then responded by destroying the homes, crops, and livestock of the Navajo people.

Retaliated Against White Aggression

The Anglo-American attack on the Navajos forced Barboncito to action. He soon earned the war name Hashké yich'i' Dahilwo' ["He Is Anxious to Run at Warriors."] With the help of Manuelito, he led over 1,000 Navajo warriors in a retaliatory attack on Fort Defiance. The great war skills of Barboncito and Manuelito nearly won them the fort, but they were driven off by the U.S. Army and pursued into the Chuska Mountains. In the mountains, the U.S. troops were unable to withstand the Navajo hit-and-run attacks.

Stalemated, Indians and whites sat down at a peace-council once again. Barboncito, Manuelito, Delgadito, Armijo, Herrero Grande, and 17 other chiefs met Colonel Edward R. S. Canby at Fort Fauntleroy, 35 miles south of Fort Defiance. They all agreed to the terms of a treaty in 1861. For a time, the Navajos and the whites tried to forge the bonds of friendship. Despite the treaty, though, an undercurrent of distrust caused conflict between the two groups to continue.

When the U.S. military diverted most of its forces east for the Civil War, the Navajos increased their efforts at what the whites considered to be "cattle-rustling and general marauding." The United States led an extensive campaign to "burn-and-imprison" the Navajos, administered by Colonel Christopher "Kit" Carson and Ute mercenaries, traditional enemies of the Navajos. Barboncito made peaceful overtures to General James H. Carleton, Carson's commanding officer, in 1862, but the assault against the Navajo people dragged on.

When this ruthless practice proved unsuccessful, Carleton ordered Carson to bodily move the entire nation of Navajo clans from their homes in the Arizona area to a region known as Bosque Redondo, in the arid lowlands of southeastern New Mexico—all despite protests from the Indian Bureau and Carson himself. Carleton is widely quoted as having said that he aimed to transform the Navajos from "heathens and raiders" to "settled Christians" under the watchful eye of troops stationed at nearby Fort Sumner.

Carleton met with Barboncito and other chiefs in April of 1863. He informed the Navajos that they could prove their peaceful intentions by going to Bosque Redondo. Barboncito replied, as quoted in *Bury My Heart at Wounded Knee:* "I will not go to the Bosque. I will never leave my country, not even if it means that I am killed." And despite U.S. Army efforts to force him from his home, Barboncito stayed.

Last Holdout in Resistance Movement

Barboncito led the resistance movement at Cañon de Chelly against Carson and the whites with the aid of Delgadito and Manuelito. Again Carson launched a scorched earth campaign against the Navajos and "Dinetah" ["Navajo Land"]. Carson destroyed fields, orchards, and hogans—an earth-covered Navajo dwelling—and he confiscated cattle from the Continental Divide to the Colorado River. Though only 78 of the 12,000 Navajo people were killed, Carson's efforts crushed the Navajo spirit. By 1864 Carson had devastated Cañon de Chelly, hacking down thousands of peach trees and obliterating acres of corn fields. Eventually, a shortage of food and supplies forced the Navajos to surrender their sacred stronghold.

That same year, the "Long Walk" began, in which 8,000 Navajo people—two-thirds of the entire tribe—were escorted by 2,400 soldiers across 300 miles to Bosque Redondo, New Mexico. About 200 of the Indians died en route. The remaining 4,000 Navajos escaped west with Manuelito, who eventually surrendered in 1866 (two months before Barboncito). Barboncito was the last Navajo chief to be captured and led to Bosque Redondo. Once he found conditions there worse than imagined, he escaped and returned to Cañon de Chelly, but he was recaptured.

The "Long Walk" to Bosque Redondo was horrifying and traumatic for the Navajos. Disease, blight, grasshoppers, drought, supply shortages, infertile soil, and quarrels with Apaches plagued the tribe, and an estimated 2,000 people died of hunger or illness at the relocation settlement. As a ceremonial singer with knowledge of his people's ancient beliefs, Barboncito knew that it went against the wisdom of tradition for the Navajo to leave their sacred lands, to cross the rivers, or to abandon their sacred mountains and shrines.

Forced to do so—forced to become dependent on whites for food and other supplies—was spiritually destructive for the Navajo tribespeople and for Barboncito. He stayed as long as he could in the sacred lands, but on November 7, 1866, he, too, led his small band of 21 followers to Bosque Redondo.

During their stay there, Barboncito led ceremonies that the Navajos believed helped them to return home. The most frequently practiced ceremony of that time was called "Ma'ii Bizee naast'a" ["Put a Bead in Coyote's Mouth"]. According to historical records, the Indians formed a large circle with Barboncito and a female coyote, who faced east, in the center. Barboncito caught the coyote and placed in its mouth a white shell, tapered at both ends with a hole in its center. As he set the coyote free, she turned clockwise and walked westward. This was seen as a sign that the Navajo people, the Dine, would be set free.

Negotiated for Final, Lasting Peace

In 1868 Barboncito, Manuelito, and a delegation of chiefs traveled to Washington, D.C., after General Carleton had been transferred from Fort Sumner at Bosque Redondo and could no longer inflict his policies on the Navajo. Barboncito was granted great status by the whites—more authority than would have been accorded him by tribal custom. He played a leading role in negotiations with General William T. Sherman and Colonel Samuel F. Tappan, telling them that the creator of the Navajo people had warned the tribe never to go east of the Rio Grande River. He explained the failures of Bosque Redondo: even though they dug irrigation ditches, the crops failed; rattlesnakes did not warn victims away before striking as they did in Navajo Country; people became ill and died. Barboncito told the white negotiators that the Navajos wished to return home.

But the U.S. government was not inclined to return all of "Navajo Country" to the Navajos. Sherman provided Barboncito and the other chiefs with three choices: to go east to Oklahoma (then known as Indian Territory), to relocate in New Mexico and be governed by the laws of that territory, or to return to a diminished portion of their original lands. The Navajos chose the last option. On June 1, 1868, the Navajo leaders, including Barboncito, signed a treaty with the U.S. government. As reprinted in Wilcombe Washburn's *American Indian and the United States: A Documentary History,* the agreement begins: "From this day forward all war between the parties to this agreement shall forever cease."

Although he was the last to surrender, Barboncito was the first to sign the document with his "X" mark. He died on March 16, 1871, at Cañon de Chelly, having established himself as a distinguished chief and a skillful negotiator. The Navajo still live at Cañon de Chelly.

SOURCES:

Biographical Dictionary of the Indians of the Americas, second edition, Newport Beach, California, American Indian Publishers, 1991; 39-40.

Brown, Dee, *Bury My Heart at Wounded Knee,* New York, Holt, 1970.

Dockstader, Frederick J., *Great North American Indians,* New York, Van Nostrand Reinhold, 1977; 25-26.

The Encyclopedia of North American Indian Tribes, edited by Bill Yenne, New York, Crescent Books, 1986.

Handbook of the North American Indians, edited by William C. Sturtevant, Washington, D.C., Smithsonian Institution, 1983.

Insight Guides: Native America, edited by John Gattuso, Boston, Houghton Mifflin, 1993.

The Native Americans: An Illustrated History, edited by Betty Ballantine and Ian Ballantine, Atlanta, Turner Publishing, 1993.

Native North American Almanac, edited by Duane Champagne, Detroit, Gale Research, 1994; 1008.

Waldman, Carl, *Atlas of the North American Indian,* New York, Facts On File, 1985.

Waldman, Carl, *Who Was Who in Native American History,* New York, Facts on File, 1990; 15.

Washburn, Wilcombe E., *The American Indian and the United States: A Documentary History,* Volume 4, New York, Random House, 1973; 2526-2532.

—Sketch by Christopher B. Tower

Fred Begay

Fred Begay

1932-

Navajo physicist

Fred Begay is a nuclear physicist and educator who has served as a technical staff member at the Los Alamos National Laboratory since 1971. He has directed his scientific research primarily toward the use of laser, electron, and ion beams to demonstrate the application of thermonuclear fusion as a technique to provide future economical and environmentally safe and clean electrical power source. Since the 1960s, he has participated in scientific investigations and published dozens of articles covering experimental and theoretical physics topics such as high energy neutrons, gamma rays, and solar wind in space, thermonuclear fusion, elementary particles, quantum theory, general relativity, and fractal geometry. He has been invited to provide advice on science and technology matters to the U.S. Department of Energy, the National Science Foundation, the U.S. National Academy of Sciences, the Navajo government, and the university community. Also, Begay has presented numerous lectures on physics and science education as a guest lecturer and visiting professor, and has encouraged numerous young Native American students to pursue a career in science and mathematics.

Begay was born in 1932 at Towaoc, Colorado, which is located on the Ute Mountain Indian Reservation. Since he was not born in a hospital, the U.S. government school officials estimated his birthday to be July 2. His father, Chee Begay, was Navajo and Ute, as was his mother, Joy Joe. Both his parents practiced Navajo medicine and provided traditional health care to Navajo communities in the northern regions of the Navajo Reservation. During the 1930s Begay was trained in Navajo medicine by his parents. In 1942 Begay began his modern education and was trained as a farmer at the U.S. Vocational Indian School, which is located on the Southern Ute Indian Reservation in southern Colorado.

In 1951 Begay joined the U.S. Army Air Corps and served as a non-commissioned officer in an air-rescue squadron in Korea. In 1952 he married Helen Etcitty from Lukachukai, Arizona, and raised seven children (two boys and five girls). In 1955 Begay began his college education at the University of New Mexico (UNM) in Albuquerque, which provided an opportunity for World War II and Korean veterans to complete their high school education and begin their college education. Under this program, he completed his B.S. degree in physics and mathematics in 1961, his M.S. degree in physics in 1963, and his Ph.D. in physics in 1971. His studies in graduate school included mathematical physics and nuclear physics. He was the first Navajo to earn a Ph.D. in physics.

Joins Staff of Los Alamos National Laboratory

After spending ten years conducting NASA-funded space physics experiments using NASA's earth satellites, Begay was invited to join the physics staff at the Los Alamos

National Laboratory in 1971 to begin his research into the alternative use of laser, electron, and ion beams to heat thermonuclear plasmas. He has held teaching and research sabbatical appointments at the Stanford Linear Accelerator Center, Stanford University (research in elementary particles, 1975), and at the University of Maryland (research in plasma physics, 1987-1988). He has been invited to speak on the comparative analysis of the Navajo and modern view on nature and the environment at the Society for Applied Anthropology, the American Association of Physics Teachers, and other scientific and university institutions.

Begay has volunteered his time to advise the Navajo government on science and technology matters. For example, from 1974 to 1976, he was chairman of the Navajo Nation's Environmental Protection Commission which had to review and approve comprehensive environmental impact statements on the $6-billion coal-gasification project. From 1974 to 1978, he was science education advisor to the president of the Navajo Community College. Also, since 1974 he has served as president of the Navajo Science and Engineering Research Council (NSERC), which provides an opportunity for Navajo professionals with doctorates in science, engineering, and medicine to provide advice on science and technology matters to the Navajo government.

Begay has devoted his life to encouraging minority students to begin and complete their pre-college and college education. He has discovered that fractal geometry can be used as a teaching and learning tool for teachers and students to understand the fundamental structure of mathematics and its use in applied mathematics. Since 1991, he has served as co-principal investigator for a National Science Foundation-funded $10-million minority undergraduate science and mathematics project at Arizona State University. This NSF project provides an opportunity for undergraduate students to conduct basic and applied research at the university, and at government and industrial research laboratories. For his efforts in science education and human resource development, Begay has been awarded the America Indian Science and Engineering Society's Ely Parker Award in 1992, and the National Science Foundation's Lifetime Achievement Award in 1994.

Begay has made fundamental contributions to nuclear fusion, plasma physics, and science and mathematics education. His life as a physicist and an educator are documented in the following films: *Nation within a Nation* (Hearst Metrotone New, 1972) *In Our Native Land* (Sandia Laboratories, 1972), and *The Long Walk of Fred Begay* (British Broadcasting Corporation, 1978).

SOURCES:

Books

Native American Biographies, Globe Fearon, 1994.
Native North American Almanac, edited by Duane Champagne, Detroit, Gale Research, 1994.
Science, Addison-Wesley, 1989.

Periodicals

Begay, Fred, "Computational Model for Relativistic Electron Beam-Dense Carbon Plasma Heating Experiments," *Physica Scripta,* 1989; 80-82.
National Geographic, 172:5, 1987; 602.

Other

Begay, Fred, interview with Wade M. Davies, conducted August 10, 1994.
Research Highlights, 1992, Washington, D.C., U.S. Department of Energy, Los Alamos National Laboratory, 1992.
The Long Walk of Fred Begay, "Nova," 602, Journal Graphics, 1979.

—Sketch by Wade M. Davies

Harrison Begay
1917-
Navajo artist
Also known as Haskay Yah Ne Yah ["Warrior Who Walked Up to His Enemy"]

Harrison Begay is one of the most famous of all Navajo painters. His watercolors and silkscreen prints have been widely collected. His work, which has won 13 major awards, has a sinuous delicacy of line and is noted for its meticulous detail, restrained palette, and elegance of composition. His style has been so influential that disciples, like Baji Whit thorne, say that by studying his paintings one learns not only technique but also religion. The Navajo conception of the orderly balance of irreconcilable forces is exemplified in Begay's style, which is at once serenely still and vitally active.

Herds Family's Sheep

Harrison Begay was born on November 15, 1917, at White Cone, Arizona, to Black Rock and Zonnie Tachinie Begay. His mother belonged to the Red Forehead Clan, and his father adopted the Zuni Deer Clan. He was said to have been related to Manuelita, the esteemed medicine man. The boy herded his family's flock of sheep near Greasewood, where he still lives. In 1927, he was sent to school at Fort Wingate, from which he ran away to spend the next four years at home, studying alone as he tended the sheep. In 1934, he attended Fort Defiance Indian School in New Mexico, and later Tohatchi Indian School. He graduated from high school in 1939 as salutatorian.

The institution that conferred distinction upon him was Dorothy Dunn's studio at the Santa Fe Indian School.

Among Begay's classmates were other Navajo painters: Gerald Nailor, Quincy Tahoma, and Andy Tsinajinnie. They were taught to depict pastoral landscapes and tribal traditions in smoothly-brushed forms placed flat on the picture plane. In *American Indian Painting,* Dunn summed up Begay's work as "at once decorative and lifelike, his color clear in hue and even in value, his figures placid yet inwardly animated.... [H]e seemed to be inexhaustibly resourceful in a quiet reticent way."

In 1940, Begay married Ramona Espinosa; the couple divorced in 1945. Also in 1940, he attended Black Mountain College in Blueridge, North Carolina, to study architecture for one year. In 1941, he enrolled in Phoenix Junior College in Arizona.

Serves in the United States Army

Begay was one of the 21,767 Native American veterans of the U.S. Army in World War II. From 1942 to 1945, Begay served in the signal corps. He participated in the Normandy campaign and was stationed in Iceland and in Europe. Upon his discharge, he stayed in Colorado until September of 1947. While there, he was briefly tutored by an artist in Denver. The army had trained him to be a radio technician, but his artistic talent enabled him to make a living as a full-time painter since his return to the reservation in 1947.

Works in Arts and Crafts Shops

He was given space to paint at Clay Lockett's Arts and Crafts Shop in Tucson, Arizona. He also painted in Parkhurst's Shop in Santa Fe, New Mexico, and in Woodard's Shop in Gallup, New Mexico. He prefers to work in watercolors, usually casein paints because oil painting takes too long. A prolific artist, he regularly exhibits at the Philbrook Art Center each May, and at the Gallery in New Mexico that sponsors exhibits for five days in August each year at the Intertribal Indian Ceremonials. He won two grand awards at the Intertribal festivities and has been a consistent winner at state and tribal fairs. The French government honored him with its Palmes d'Academiques in 1945.

Begay cofounded TEWA Enterprises, which made silkscreen prints of his work. His fine-lined, flat-colored designs were eminently suitable for serigraph reproduction. This method of duplication also made his work affordable to the general public. Begay has also specialized in sensitive renditions of animals such as fawns, antelope, deer, sheep, and horses. He is also fond of depicting looms as subjects, as in his often reproduced painting, "Two Weavers" of 1946.

In 1959, Begay had an Enemyway chant performed for him. He paid the singer who conducted the rite to protect warriors against the ghosts of slain enemies with a set of three paintings of the Navajo sacred mountains. A similar set of the four sacred mountains, each associated with a different color and a different direction, is now owned by the Museum of Northern Arizona at Flagstaff. In order to compose these paintings, Begay studied the Navajo origin myths recorded by Washington Matthews.

In addition to Begay's considerable achievements in the art world, he is also the state champion long distance runner having broken the record in the mile race.

SOURCES:

Dockstader, Frederick J., *Indian Art in America,* Greenwich, Connecticut, New York Graphic Society, 1966.

Dunn, Dorothy, *American Indian Painting,* Albuquerque, University of New Mexico Press, 1968.

Fawcett, David M., and Lee A. Callander, *Native American Painting: Selections from the Museum of the American Indian,* Emerson, New Jersey, ALE Associates, 1982.

Wade, Edwin L., *The Arts of the North American Indian: Native Traditions in Evolution,* New York, Hudson Hills Press, 1986.

Wyman, Leland C., "Navajo Ceremonial System," in *Handbook of the North American Indians,* Volume 10, edited by Alfonso Ortiz, Washington, D.C., Smithsonian Institution, 1983.

—Sketch by Ruth Rosenberg

John Kim Bell
1952-
Mohawk symphony orchestra conductor, composer, and foundation director

John Kim Bell became the first Native North American professional symphony orchestra conductor. It was unusual for Natives to have access to the kinds of fostered development, training, and opportunities he had acquired in his youth on the reservation. When Bell realized this, he took a sabbatical from conducting to create the Canadian Native Arts Foundation (CNAF), which provides scholarships for young students of the arts.

Bell was born October 8, 1952 on the Kahnawake (Kanawake) Mohawk Reservation near Montreal, Quebec. It was created in the early 1700s as a Jesuit mission for converted Iroquois by the French. Beginning at an early age, Bell studied keyboard, violin, and saxophone. He began his conducting career at age 18 when, after a year of accompanying local auditions for a Broadway musical touring company, he was hired as an assistant conductor-thus becoming the youngest professional conductor in the United States. He attended Ohio State University on scholarship and graduated in 1975 with a bachelor's degree in music. Ohio State granted him the William Oxley Thompson Alumni Award in 1987 for his achievements.

In 1980 Bell became the first Native North American professional symphony conductor when he received an

29

appointment to conduct with the Toronto Symphony. After a year of working with the symphony, in addition to his extensive experience conducting Broadway musicals, he went on to study at the Academia Musicale Chigiana in Sienna, Italy. There he received a Certificate of Performance in 1981.

Bell's position as the only Native symphony conductor placed him in the limelight as the subject of a Canadian Broadcasting Company (CBC) documentary. Aired in 1983, the film reached a great number of Indians, all interested to know how they or their children might be able to access an education or a career in the arts. Bell was flooded with requests for information, and it started to make him actively question the place relegated to Native (aboriginal) peoples in Canadian society. During an interview with *Canadian Business,* for example, he asked such questions as: "Do native people have to be relegated to making moccasins? Can you be a native and a business executive? Can you be a native and conduct?" Realizing the severely limited opportunities fostered by poverty and isolation among Indians, he set his mind to helping those less fortunate than himself.

Formed the Canadian Native Arts Foundation

Working from a card table in his basement, Bell used $35,000 of his own funds to launch the CNAF in 1985. The following year he secured a personal loan of $85,000 and received grants of over $150,000 from the Canadian government. Since he knew that government funding is often unstable, Bell aggressively pursued, and ultimately obtained, corporate financial backing.

Bell's primary objective for the CNAF was to provide Native youth with scholarships in the arts, much as he had received early in his college education. Instead of approaching private sector sponsors for direct, tax-deductible contributions, Bell felt there would be a greater willingness to participate and a broader community benefit if sponsors were to use their promotional budgets to support fundraising performances. This strategic planning evidenced great success, when just five years after he was showcased in the CBC documentary, Bell's foundation raised $1 million for the production of his contemporary Native ballet, *In the Land of Spirits.* Bell produced and co-composed the piece, which premiered at the Native Arts Center of Ottawa in 1988. *In the Land of Spirits* also became the first recorded Native ballet.

In addition to his Broadway musical and symphony conducting, Bell has conducted for ballet and dance. He has been guest conductor for the Native Ballet of Canada, as well as conductor for Eglevsky Ballet Company and Dance Theatre of Harlem in New York City. Bell was also assistant conductor and conductor to the Panovs in 1972, a Soviet ballet team on tour in the United States. Moreover, he gained some experience in opera when in 1974 he was apprentice opera coach for the Chautauqua Opera Association. Bell has expanded his compositional skills further by composing two Canadian television film scores having Native themes. The first was a PBS docudrama titled *The Trial of Standing Bear* and the second was a production of CFTO titled *Divided Loyalties,* initially aired in 1989.

SOURCES:

Books

Canadian Who's Who, edited by Kieren Simpson, Toronto, University of Toronto Press, 1993; 79.
Native North American Almanac, edited by Duane Champagne, Detroit, Gale Research, 1994; 1009.

Periodicals

Canadian Business, 62, September 1989; 92.

—Sketch by Brett A. Lealand

Clyde Bellecourt
Contemporary
Ojibwa activist

Clyde Bellecourt, one of the cofounders of the American Indian Movement (AIM), grew up on the reservation with seven sisters and four brothers, none of whom ever had enough to eat. In the ninth grade, unable to tolerate the racist attitudes in the public school he had been forced to attend, he dropped out in despair. At the age of 15, he looked for jobs in the city when work was unavailable on the reservation. Unable to find employment in the city, he became involved in robberies and burglaries and eventually found himself in prison.

Begins Hunger Strike in Prison

Sentenced to Minnesota's Stillwater State Prison, he began a hunger strike, determined to die. A fellow inmate, Eddie Benton Benai, tried unsuccessfully to get him to eat by dropping a candy bar into Bellecourt's cell every day. Clyde refused to touch them, and they piled up. Then one day Benai brought him a book about his Ojibwa heritage; the story revived his will to live and restored his pride in being an Indian. And in 1962, he began educating his fellow inmates about their distinguished traditions. He told Peter Matthiessen in *In the Spirit of Crazy Horse,* "I guess we had the first real Indian Studies Program in the country."

Released from prison in 1964, Bellecourt tried to organize the "Red Ghetto" of Minneapolis, who were humiliated in the schools, harassed by police, discriminated against by employers, unfairly treated by the courts, to protest for their civil rights. In July of 1968, Eddie Benton Benai, George Mitchell, Dennis Banks, and Vernon Bellecourt and Clyde Bellecourt formed a coalition called Concerned Indian Americans (CIA) by incorporating a nonprofit organization with an all-Indian board and staff, which elected Vernon Bellecourt the national director. When the group realized its

Clyde Bellecourt

acronym would be CIA, a respected elder suggested that since they were always talking about what they aimed to do, they should call it "aim." A veteran suggested that they take as their symbol an upside-down American flag since this is an internationally recognized distress symbol; and the world knew, even if Americans did not recognize, the unjust situation of Native Americans. They also determined to grow their hair and wear it in braids to signify their warrior status. They relinquished their neckties and adopted wooden chokers; and, to symbolize their reborn pride, they wore red jackets with thunderbird emblems on the back.

With a small grant from the Urban League, funds from church groups, and a donation from the Northern State Power Company for which Bellecourt worked, he bought two-way radios to monitor police calls, and cameras and tape recorders to secure evidence of the violent treatment Indians received at the hands of the law enforcers. They recorded vicious beatings, began filing suits against the police department, and would have attorneys and bondsmen waiting at the police station. Bellecourt's street patrol advised Indians who had been arrested that they were entitled to legal defense and to a jury trial and that they need not let themselves be coerced into pleading guilty. His vigilance dramatically reduced the number of arrests; but he, himself, was beaten more than 30 times by infuriated police.

AIM "Survival Schools"

With the support of Minnesota's judicial system, an alternative to reform school was offered to juvenile offend-

ers who were tribal people. Begun in 1970, an intensive course in Indian heritage counteracted the misinformation these youngsters had been given in white history books; they learned the truth about their heroic leaders and were spiritually fortified by learning the traditional stories of their own culture. The old ceremonies, which had been so long outlawed, were revived. The Bellecourt brothers visited Leonard Crow Dog, and through him met other Lakota holy men such as Lame Deer, Frank Fools Crow, and Pete Catches, who still practiced yuwipi, and the sun dance, and the pipe ceremony, who still remembered the traditional songs, and who taught them the power of the drum. A reciprocal empowerment ensued. The elders were able to transmit the old ways to the young; and they, infused with these values, became involved with tribal people whenever they were in trouble.

The Reclamation of Alcatraz Island

From November of 1969, until June of 1971, AIM members occupied the abandoned federal penitentiary on Alcatraz Island in San Francisco Bay. About 200 Indians participated and issued a proclamation stating that they claimed it "by the right of discovery." They elaborated ironically the ten ways in which it was suitable for an Indian reservation: first, it was isolated; second, it had no fresh water; third, it had no sanitation facilities; fourth, it had no means of employment; fifth, it had no health care facilities; sixth, the soil was rocky; seventh, there were no plants or game animals; eighth, there were no educational facilities; ninth, the population exceeded the land base; and, tenth, Indians have always been treated as prisoners.

During this symbolic 19-month takeover, they broadcast on Radio Free Alcatraz. They wanted to use the building for a cultural center. Instead of negotiation, armed force was used to evict them as trespassers. But the action enlisted new members to their cause, such as John Trudell and Russell Means, who subsequently founded an AIM chapter in Cleveland. Other demonstrations followed at Mount Rushmore in South Dakota, at Plymouth Rock in Massachusetts, and at the fishing rights struggle in the Pacific Northwest. Wherever treaty rights had been violated, these young militants staged symbolic protests. Bellecourt said that the drum that had been silenced for so long was now being heard from coast to coast. When Fort Lawton, outside Seattle, was taken over, Richard Oakes, the young Mohawk leader of the Alcatraz occupation came to advise them against making any of the mistakes they had made in San Francisco Bay. The murder of this gentle, soft-spoken man in Santa Clara, California, on September 20, 1972, was denounced in a press conference held by Means, Sid Mills, a wounded Vietnam veteran and Yakima leader in the fishing-rights fight, and Hank Adams, an Assiniboine-Sioux who had been shot in the stomach by the Tacoma police.

The Trail of Broken Treaties March

From across the country came a four-mile-long procession of Native people to arrive in Washington, D.C., on

November 3, 1972, just before the presidential election, to dramatize the unkept promises of more than 300 treaties made with Indians. To Bellecourt, this seemed the fulfillment of an Ojibwa prophecy that one cay all the tribes on this Turtle Continent would unite in brotherhood. They had not intended to take over the BIA building, but had simply gone there to apply for decent housing for their holy men who had come with them. Instead, riot squads broke in to drive them out. Their attempts to deal as representatives of sovereign nations over denied treaty rights was turned into a confrontation totally misrepresented by the media. President Richard Nixon never gave them a hearing even though a polite reception had been promised before they set out. The damage done to the building by armed federal agents was blamed on the Indians who were accused of vandalism. To cover up its mishandling of the incident, the BIA Commissioner and his staff were fired, and the government paid the Indians $66,000 to leave Washington. From then on, the FBI targeted AIM; and on January 11, 1973, a Nixon aide informed them that the government would not make treaties with its own citizens. Counterintelligence agents were sent to infiltrate AIM meetings.

Wounded Knee II

At the site of the mass grave of the 1890 ghost-dancers in Pine Ridge, the poorest tribe in the United States declared itself the Independent Oglala Nation on February 28, 1973, and invited AIM to help them take their stand. The government sent tanks, paramilitary units, heavy artillery, and set up road blocks around the reservation. On March 13, a federal grand jury issued indictments against Clyde Bellecourt and others; a group of attorneys in St. Paul formed a legal defense fund on March 22 to assist and filed a suit on April 16 stating that the military siege was attempting to starve the people into submission. In response, the government tightened the blockade, turned off the water, and arrested anyone attempting to bring medicine or food into Wounded Knee.

Unlike the more militant AIM members, Bellecourt was so opposed to violence that he had not carried a weapon at Wounded Knee. He had always counseled pacifism, and still sought a peaceful solution. He was shot in the stomach by an advocate of violence, Craig Camp, whom Means believed the FBI had paid to do this. Bellecourt's life was saved by John Fire Lame Deer's doctoring. Bellecourt ennobled himself by refusing to testify against his attacker in court. After extended litigation, the charges against Bellecourt for his participation at Wounded Knee were finally dismissed.

SOURCES:

Matthiessen, Peter, *In the Spirit of Crazy Horse,* New York, Penguin, 1983.

Native American Testimony: A Chronicle of Indian-White Relations from Prophecy to the Present, 1492-1992, edited by Peter Nabokov, New York, Penguin, 1992.

—*Sketch by Ruth Rosenberg*

Ramona Bennett
1938-
Puyallup tribal leader, activist, and educator

A leader in the Native American community, Ramona Bennett was the chairperson of the Puyallup tribe from 1971 through 1978. In addition, Bennett served as the Puyallup tribal administrator for 11 years. She is an articulate speaker on fishing rights, tribal sovereignty, American Indian child welfare, and health issues, as well as Native American educational concerns.

Bennett was born in Seattle, Washington on April 28, 1938. After completing her high school education at the local public school, she attended Evergreen State College in Seattle, earning a bachelor's degree in liberal arts. Bennett then went on to the University of Puget Sound, where she received a master's degree in education.

While Bennett served on the Puyallup Tribal Council, she worked in tribal community organization with the Puyallup, Nisqually, and Muckleshoot tribes, whose original territory extended along the Puyallup, the Nisqually, and the Green Rivers, near Commencement Bay in Washington. Currently, these tribes occupy substantially smaller reserve areas within the northwestern portion of Washington state. In the 1960s, these tribal peoples became involved in a controversial battle concerning American Indian fishing rights. The State of Washington had attempted to regulate American Indian fishing on the Puyallup River, thus breaking the 1855 Treaty of Point Elliot, which guarantees Native Americans in the area unrestricted use the land and its natural resources, including fisheries. The tribes refused to honor Washington state fishing laws and consequently, the tension between Anglo-Americans and Puyallup, Nisqually, and Muckleshoot fishermen led to violent confrontations on the rivers. Relations between Anglo-Americans and local Native Americans were further weakened due to the state's reduction of reserve areas without U.S. Congressional approval. These occurrences led to the founding of the Survival of American Indians Association in 1964. Bennett was one of the Association's founders and also became one of the first officers in the newly established organization.

The fishing rights issue was temporarily resolved by the U.S. Supreme Court. Their decision confirmed the treaty-protected right of tribal peoples to fish off the reservation, as well as on the reservation, but declared that the state had the right to regulate Native American fishing as long as the state's actions were not discriminatory. Continued demonstrations by area tribes kept the State of Washington from assuming complete control of the fisheries, and in 1973, the United States Supreme Court struck down their earlier decision, finding it discriminatory. The issue was finally resolved with the landmark case, *United States v. Washington* (1974), which supported Native American fishing rights as well as initiated efforts to clear reservation boundary issues.

In the meantime, Bennett, as Puyallup Tribal Chairperson, remained active throughout the 1970s. By court order, she governed portions of Tacoma—a Washington city containing part of the Puyallup Reservation within its border—with the mayor of that city. As a governing member of the community, Bennett was instrumental in finding effective solutions to differences between Anglo-American systems of governance and the Puyallup Tribe.

Bennett has served on several regional and national boards, including the National Coalition to Support Indian Treaties. In recent years, she has served as the school administrator of Wa-He-Lut Indian School in Olympia, Washington. As an educator and leader, she is dedicated to teaching people methods for overcoming cross-cultural differences.

Bennett believes that Anglo-American knowledge of Puyallup and other Indian peoples' cultural perspectives—including language, tribal logic, and world view, as well as relationships within and upon the earth—is critical to a peaceful coexistence. She feels that ignoring Native American concepts is dangerous for everyone. In particular, Bennett has noted that treaties cannot be disregarded without endangering the fabric of life for all concerned.

SOURCES:

Josephy, Alvin M., Jr., *Now that the Buffalo's Gone: A Study of Today's American Indians,* New York, Knopf, 1982.
Native North American Almanac, edited by Duane Champagne, Detroit, Gale Research, 1994.
Report on Trust Responsibility, and the Federal-Indian Relationship; Including Treaty Review, Final Report of the American Indian Policy Review Commission, Washington, D.C., U.S. Government Printing Office, 1976.
Uncommon Controversy: Fishing Rights of the Muckleshoot, Puyallup, and Nisqually Indians; A Report for the American Friends Service Committee, Seattle, University of Washington Press, 1970.

—Sketch by Howard Meredith

Robert LaFollette Bennett
1912-
Oneida lawyer and administrator

Robert L. Bennett was the second Native American appointed to the position of commissioner of the Bureau of Indian Affairs (BIA). His predecessor, Ely Samuel Parker (Hasanoanda of the Seneca, also known as Donehogawa) had also been a member of the Iroquois Confederacy. Both of them had studied law, and had served in the armed forces—Parker in the Civil War, Bennett in World War II. Born on the Oneida Reservation, November 16, 1912, near

Robert LaFollette Bennett

Green Bay, Wisconsin, where his father had a farm, Bennett learned early to negotiate between a mother who was ambitious for his success in the white world, and a grandmother, who spoke only Oneida and was suspicious of white ways. Over the grandmother's objections, he was enrolled in a private school where he was the only Native American student. By participating in many activities, he made himself popular with his classmates. After his father died, Bennett, at the age of 15, was sent to Haskell Institute, a Kansas boarding school operated by the BIA. He arrived without even a change of clothing, determined to make something of himself. When he graduated in 1931, with an associate's degree in business administration, the country was in the Depression and few jobs were available. Haskell offered him a clerkship at a dollar a day with free room and board. Many years later, he became a member of Haskell's Board of Regents.

Robert LaFollette Bennett Begins Career in Public Service

Bennett was a junior clerk in the Washington, D.C., office of the BIA; for a time, he served on the Navajo Reservation in Arizona and Ute Reservation in Colorado. Upon his return to Washington, he continued administrative work during the day and enrolled in law school before working hours, earning his law degree in 1941 from Southeastern University School of Law in Washington. From 1941 to 1943, he served as administrative assistant on the Navajo Reservation until he was drafted and entered the Marine Corps. He was designated the most outstanding recruit in his training platoon; and after the war, he worked with Native American veterans, helping them to obtain an education and other benefits through the G.I. Bill. Bennett also organized American Legion Posts for the Utes and the Navajos. For a time he served as placement officer for the BIA in South Dakota setting up employment opportunities for Indians. He eventually became assistant area director at Aberdeen, South Dakota. In 1962, he was promoted to area director and sent to Juneau, Alaska. There he energetically protected indigenous land claims. For his vigorous support of their rights, he was awarded the Indian Achievement Award in 1962; and in 1966, he was given the Outstanding American Indian Citizen Award.

Presides Over Bureau of Indian Affairs

In 1966, President Lyndon B. Johnson appointed Bennett to head the enormous Bureau of Indian Affairs. Bennett helped set up a coalition of all the federal groups who could render services to the Indian people, enlisted the Vice President in a National Council of Indian Opportunity, and sent messages to Congress. He worked to transfer self-governance to the tribes and fought Termination. Simultaneously he engaged in campaigns to preserve tribal culture and to convince the public of the competence of Native peoples to manage their own affairs as well as to prove themselves capable citizens. He maintained close contacts with all constituencies, traveling the continent to visit all the tribes and discuss problems with tribal leaders. After three energetic years of service, he resigned from Washington politics to live in Albuquerque. In 1969, he founded the American Indian Athletic Hall of Fame, becoming its first president. From 1970 until 1975, he was the director of the American Indian Law Center at the University of New Mexico Law School in Albuquerque, and recruited many Native Americans into legal careers. In 1988, he was chosen Outstanding Member of the Oneida Tribe of Wisconsin.

SOURCES:

Biographical Dictionary of Indians of the Americas, Newport Beach, California, American Indian Publishers, 1983.

Native North American Almanac, edited by Duane Champagne, Detroit, Gale Research, 1994.

Reference Encyclopedia of the American Indian, edited by Barry T. Klein, West Nyack, New York, Indian Publications, 1993.

—*Sketch by Ruth Rosenberg*

Big Foot
1825(?)-1890
Minniconjou Sioux tribal leader
Also known as Si Tanka and Spotted Elk

The son of Lone Horn, Big Foot became chief of the Minniconjou ("Planters by the River") after the death of his

Big Foot

father in 1874. One of the seven subdivisions of the Teton Sioux, the Minniconjou lived in northwestern South Dakota with the Hunkpapa, another band of the Teton Sioux led by Sitting Bull. Native accounts of Big Foot describe him as a great hunter. He was also a skilled horseman who possessed a string of fine ponies, most often obtained from the Crow or other enemies. He was best known, however, for his political and diplomatic successes. An able negotiator, Big Foot was skilled at settling quarrels between rival parties and was often in great demand among other Teton bands.

Big Foot

After the Sioux War for the Black Hills in 1876-77, the Minniconjou were placed on the Cheyenne River Reservation in South Dakota. Being a person accustomed to finding ways of reconciling disparate views, Big Foot sought means to adapt to white ways. According to Native accounts, Big Foot was among the first American Indians to raise corn in accordance with government standards. Moreover, he traveled to Washington, D.C. and requested that a mission school be established near the forks of the Cheyenne River. While the Indian Bureau tentatively agreed, the matter was set aside and eventually forgotten.

Ghost Dance

In 1889 Kicking Bear introduced the Ghost Dance religion to the Minniconjou. The ritual dance was developed by the Paiute medicine man Wovoka, after speaking to the creator. It was believed that the Ghost Dance would restore the world to its aboriginal state; it promised for the return of Native ancestors and all plant and animal life. Devastated by war, hunger, and disease, the Minniconjou welcomed the new religion. While their dancing never became violent, several other Sioux, who were angered by the 1883 prohibition of the Sun Dance and other "barbarous" customs by the Secretary of the Interior as well as the 1889 reduction of Sioux holdings to six small reservations, turned the Ghost Dance into a movement advocating violence against their white oppressors. Consequently, the U.S. Office of Indian Affairs outlawed the Ghost Dance in 1890.

Later that same year, Big Foot and his followers moved to Cherry Creek where they had planned on joining Chief Hump and his band of Minniconjou in their dancing. The latter, however, defected and surrendered his band to the agency on December 9, 1890. Disillusioned, Big Foot and his tribe moved back to their camp below the forks of the Cheyenne River. While he did not participate in the Ghost Dance thereafter, many of his tribesmen continued to dance, spurred on by the medicine man Yellow Bird.

On December 15, 1890, the Standing Rock Reservation police killed Sitting Bull over a dispute regarding the Ghost Dance ceremony. After hearing of Sitting Bull's death, Big Foot decided to migrate to the Pine Ridge Reservation. On December 28, the Minniconjou were intercepted by an army detachment under the command of Major Samuel Whitside. Big Foot, who was suffering from pneumonia at the time, ordered his band's surrender. His tribe was then escorted to Wounded Knee Creek where they set up camp. Shortly thereafter, Colonel James Forsyth arrived and assumed command of the situation. On the morning of December 29, when the colonel ordered the tribe to surrender their weapons, a fight erupted in which Big Foot and nearly 200 Sioux men, women, and children were killed, along with 25 soldiers.

SOURCES:

Books

Hyde, George, *A Sioux Chronicle,* Norman, University of Oklahoma Press, 1956.

McGregor, James H., *The Wounded Knee Massacre: From the View Point of the Sioux,* Rapid City, South Dakota, Fenske Printing, 1940.

Sneve, Virginia Driving Hawk, *They Led a Nation: The Sioux Chiefs,* Sioux Falls, South Dakota, Brevet Press, 1975.

Utley, Robert M., *The Last Days of the Sioux Nation,* New Haven, Connecticut, Yale University Press, 1963.

Waldman, Carl, *Who Was Who in Native American History,* New York, Facts on File, 1990.

Periodicals

McDermott, John D., "Wounded Knee: Centennial Voices," *South Dakota History,* 20, winter 1990; 245-298.

—Sketch by John D. McDermott

Black Elk
1863(?)-1950
Oglala Lakota Sioux spiritual leader

Nicholas Black Elk, more widely known simply as "Black Elk," was a Lakota Sioux spiritual leader of the Oglala band. He started as a traditional Lakota holy man, or *wicasa wakan,* and went on to spend the greater part of his life as a devout and involved Roman Catholic. He is often remembered in connection with the 1932 book by the poet John Neihardt that bears his name: *Black Elk Speaks.* In this book he remembered pre-reservation Sioux spiritual life and spoke at length about his boyhood and young adulthood. He again explained traditional Sioux religious life in a book by Joseph Epes Brown published in 1953 entitled *The Sacred Pipe.* The latter book does not treat Black Elk's private life, and the former ends his narrative at the age of about 25, when he witnessed the 1890 massacre at Wounded Knee. Yet Black Elk lived well past 80 years of age, and although the image presented to the world in *Black Elk Speaks* has strongly informed non-Indian depictions of Sioux culture, it runs counter to the way Black Elk is remembered in his own community.

Early Life and Faith

Black Elk witnessed many dramatic and cataclysmic events during his childhood and young adult years. Although there is some doubt as to his actual date of birth, he told Neihardt he was born in December of 1863 on the Little Powder river, which runs through eastern Montana and Wyoming. Black Elk's concern for matters of the spirit had precedents in his family. His father, also called Black Elk, was a medicine-person, too. When his son was a toddler, the elder Black Elk was wounded at the Fetterman Fight (1866), in which a U.S. cavalry unit was routed by their Sioux, Arapaho, and Cheyenne opponents under the leadership of the great Oglala chief, Red Cloud. Black Elk also claimed to have been cousin to another great Oglala chief, Crazy Horse.

In May of 1876, the elder Black Elk lost faith in Red Cloud and took his family to join Crazy Horse. This enabled the young Black Elk to witness and participate in Custer's defeat at the battle of Little Big Horn in June. After the murder of Crazy Horse in 1877, Black Elk's band was among those to flee to Canada and join Sitting Bull. In the years thereafter, Black Elk witnessed the extermination of the buffalo and the beginning of the reservation era.

In 1886, Black Elk joined Buffalo Bill's Wild West Show and toured the U.S. and Europe. In the summer of 1889, he returned and found his people suffering greatly but placing their faith in a new religious movement that had spread from the west. Black Elk had earned community status as a spiritual leader and had already led dances and rituals. Now he threw his spiritual power behind the Ghost Dance, the messianic movement that had been spread by the Paiute Indian Wovoka. The Ghost Dancers, who burgeoned in numbers across the Northern Plains in 1889 and 1890, believed that their dancing could bring about a day where the white people would be gone and the buffalo would return. A Northern Plains innovation that Black Elk helped introduce was the wearing of Ghost Shirts, which were supposed to render bullets harmless to the wearer. Unfortunately, the Ghost Dance made the U.S. soldiers in charge of overseeing reservation life exceedingly nervous. The Army's panicky morale led in December 1890 to the last, and among the most horrible, of the massacres in the struggle to confine Native Americans to reservations: Wounded Knee.

The most formative event of the young Black Elk's life, however, was the vision he experienced when he was nine years old. This great vision was his spiritual calling, a calling that led him first to learn the traditional role of a *wicasa wakan,* then to become a Ghost Dance adherent and leader, and finally to become a devoted spiritual advisor in the Catholic community. An important part of his vision was an admonition by the Six Grandfathers, that he should lead his people down the good road of life, peace, and prosperity by nurturing the sacred tree and keeping the nation's hoop intact. The meaning of the vision is not so easy to understand. It is long and complex (the version in the Neihardt book occupies some 20 pages) and Black Elk struggled to understand and carry out the meaning of his vision throughout his long life.

Conversion to Catholicism

The next major formative experience in Black Elk's life came in 1904. Black Elk was called to doctor a sick boy and had begun traditional healing rituals when a Catholic priest arrived at the scene and ejected Black Elk, throwing his drum and rattle out and saying, "Satan, get out!" Black Elk remained outside and waited for the priest. When he came out, the priest invited Black Elk to come with him to Holy Rosary Mission (which had been established in 1888 at the behest of Red Cloud). Two weeks later, Black Elk was still at the mission, wanting to be baptized. He accepted the Catholic faith on December 6, 1904, the feast day of St. Nicholas, and from that day on he was called Nicholas or "Nick" Black Elk.

Shortly after his conversion, Black Elk became a catechist, entrusted with instructing new converts, preaching, and, if the need arose and no priest was present, administering the sacraments. In this capacity he was a member of the Society of St. Joseph, an organization of Catholic men who sponsored prayer meetings and an annual summer conference, the Catholic Sioux Congress. He learned his Bible well, often citing Bible stories and verses. He was enthusiastic and energetic in winning over new souls to the faith. In the years following his conversion he did not dwell on or even discuss his pre-Christian life and occupation. It is likely that he did not see the incompatibility of traditional Sioux and Christian spiritualities that many missionaries of the late nineteenth and early twentieth centuries perceived. According to his daughter, Lucy Looks Twice, Black Elk applied the term *wicasa wakan* to Catholic priests as well as to medicine-people.

By the time John Neihardt arrived at Black Elk's door to write down his 'life story', Black Elk had not been a practicing medicine-man for almost 30 years. After *Black Elk Speaks*

was published in 1932, Black Elk and some of those close to him—most notably his Jesuit priest friends—seemed to have serious contentions with the book. The book ends with Black Elk's words, "And I, to whom so great a vision was given in my youth—you see me now a pitiful old man who has done nothing, for the nation's hoop is broken and scattered. There is no center any longer, and the sacred tree is dead." Yet Black Elk had accomplished a great deal since his youth. He responded in a letter of January 26, 1934: "A white man made a book and told what I had spoken of olden times, but the new times he left out.... In the last thirty years I am different from what the white man wrote about me. I am a Christian. I was baptized thirty years ago.... Thirty years ago I was a real Indian and knew a little about the Great Spirit—the *Wakantanka....* I made medicine for sick people. I was proud, perhaps I was brave, perhaps I was a good Indian; but now I am better.... St. Paul also turned better when he was converted."

Black Elk died on August 17, 1950. He had told Joseph Epes Brown that there would be unusual phenomena in the sky on the day that he died, and those present at the wake reported seeing falling stars and unusually bright northern lights. Some also reported seeing symbols in the sky, including a figure eight and a hoop. In the words of his old friend and fellow Catholic organizer, John Lone Goose, "Maybe the Holy Spirit shined upon him because he was such a holy man."

Black Elk's spiritual power was energetic and broad enough to span two distinct religious traditions. He learned the intricacies and contemplated the mysteries of both traditions with the zeal of someone with true spiritual thirst, the same thirst that prodded him never to forget his great vision and always to seek to decipher it. He will be remembered and revered in a truly ecumenical sense, as a holy man, a *wicasa wakan,* of merging cultures in a changing America.

SOURCES:

Neihardt, John, *Black Elk Speaks,* Washington Square Press, 1959.
Steltenkamp, Michael F., *Black Elk: Holy Man of the Oglala,* Norman, University of Oklahoma Press, 1993.

—Sketch by Charles Cannon

Black Hawk
1767-1838
Northern Sauk and Fox resistance leader
Also known as Black Sparrow Hawk and Ma-ka-tai-me-she-kia-kiak

Black Hawk led the Algonquian tribes in northwestern Illinois and southern Wisconsin in their struggle against their tribal leaders' land concessions and compromises with

Black Hawk

the United States. He was born into the Thunder Clan in 1767 in Sauk Sautenuk/Saukenuk, Virginia Colony (now Rock Island, Illinois). His father was Pyesa, keeper of the Sauk band's medicine bundle. Black Hawk developed into a brave warrior, taking his first scalp at the age of 17 in war parties against the Osage (Wazhazhe) and Cherokee to the south. Two years later, in 1786, his father was killed in a raid on the Cherokee, and Black Hawk became keeper of the band's medicine bundle. He married a woman named Assheweque ["Singing Bird"], and with her he had three children, including his son Whirling Thunder.

Black Hawk

The politics that governed Black Hawk's life began in 1804, when the leaders of the southern Sauk and Fox of the Missouri fell under the influence of alcohol brought to the negotiations by U.S. government representatives. They signed the Treaty of St. Louis, conceding all tribal lands east of the Mississippi—50,000,000 acres—to the United States of America. Black Hawk contended that the tribal leaders of the southern Sac and Fox of the Missouri did not speak for or represent the northern Sac and Fox of the Mississippi, a separate tribal group. He refused to move from his villages in Illinois and Wisconsin to Iowa. Before the U.S. could take action against him, Black Hawk became a supporter of Tecumseh's (Shawnee) idea of a Native tribal confederacy, and like Tecumseh sided with the British in the War of 1812. After the war, in response to his hostile actions, the U.S. government parleyed with Keokuk, a younger rival chief of the Fox clan and a U.S. accommodationist.

These two military and political losses completed Black Hawk's alienation from both the U.S. and Keokuk. Over the next decade the situation deteriorated still further. In 1816 the U.S. Army, anticipating the need to protect new white settlers, built Fort Armstrong at Rock Island, Illinois, within Black Hawk's traditional homeland. Two years later, the Illinois Territory became the twenty-first state. During the 1820s, while the state was still sparsely populated, Black Hawk strengthened his British ties by making frequent trading trips back and forth to Canada. Because of this, he and his followers were sometimes called the "British Band."

Keokuk continued to negotiate with the U.S. government for Sauk and Fox land. In 1829, he advised peace to his people and surrendered to the U.S. as a neutral. In company with two other Sac and Fox chiefs, Keokuk ceded the Rock River land area to the U.S. in exchange for land west of the Mississippi in what is now Iowa and an annuity for the tribe. He also warned the U.S. government of Black Hawk's warlike intentions. Black Hawk's band returned from their winter hunt in the spring of 1829 to Saukenuk, their Rock River village, to find their land and homes occupied by white squatters. Shocked and enraged, Black Hawk and his followers nonetheless stayed and shared their village with the newcomers for the remainder of that summer and for the next two years.

Black Hawk's War

Black Hawk's attempt to preserve the Sauk homeland from white settlers had failed. In the summer of 1831, the U.S. government sought to make the invasion complete. On June 26, U.S. Army troops bombarded Saukenuk to force the removal of Black Hawk's 2,000-people village across the Mississippi in accordance with Keokuk's agreement. Warned in advance of the attempt, however, Black Hawk and his villagers had escaped the previous night into Iowa and remained there through March 1832. Black Hawk received spiritual and political support for his resistance from the Winnebago prophet, White Cloud, and counted more than 2,000 people, including 600 warriors, among his followers. However, he received no aid in the struggle against U.S. encroachment from the British.

On April 5, 1832, Black Hawk's band of 1,000 crossed the Mississippi River back into Illinois and headed north, trying to win support from other tribes in the area. The Winnebagos and Potowatomis, however, declared their neutrality and refused to support Black Hawk. In response, the U.S. Army and state militias were called up. Among the volunteers to fight were such future political notables as Abraham Lincoln, Zachary Taylor, Jefferson Davis, and Daniel Boone's son, Nat. A month later, Black Hawk was ready to admit defeat and surrender. On May 14, 1832, as his truce party approached the U.S. troops under a white flag, nervous soldiers fired on them. His warriors retaliated and handily won the battle, which became known as Stillman's Run, after the panicked flight of Major Isaiah Stillman's men. Happy in their victory, but cautious about reprisals, Black Hawk and White Cloud headed back north to Wisconsin. For the next two months, however, the combined U.S. forces kept Black Hawk's band on the run with minor skirmishes along the way. With no aid from other tribes, lacking food, and losing troops to desertion, Black Hawk continued to press north into Wisconsin.

On July 21, 1832, the U.S. Army and Wisconsin militia, aided by Winnebago informers, attacked Black Hawk in the Battle of Wisconsin Heights, near present-day Sauk City, northwest of Madison. Many natives were killed, but others escaped by raft across the Wisconsin River, pushing westward toward the Bad Axe River that flows into the Mississippi. On August 1, 1832. the U.S. steamship *Warrior,* supported by cannon and soldiers on the riverbank, attacked natives at the mouth of the Bad Axe River who were trying to parley under a truce flag. About 28 natives were killed. The following day Black Hawk argued for a northward march to the land of the Anishinabe and the Chippewa. Most of his band refused to follow him, so Black Hawk left with White Cloud and around 50 followers. On August 3, 1832, the 1,300-man U.S. Army attacked with cannon, artillery and sharpshooters, slaughtering the 300 natives who had stayed behind. Dakota tribesmen killed those Sauk, Fox, and Winnebago who reached the western bank of the Mississippi. This fight became known as the Massacre at Bad Axe River.

Exhausted and demoralized, Black Hawk, White Cloud and the remaining native resistance fighters surrendered at Fort Crawford (present-day Prairie du Chien) Wisconsin, on August 27, 1832. In his surrender speech, quoted in several books of familiar quotations, Black Hawk stated, "I fought hard, but your guns were well aimed. The bullets flew.... My warriors fell around me; it began to look dismal. I saw my evil day at hand. The sun rose dim on us in the morning, and at night it sank in a dark cloud, and looked like a ball of fire. That was the last sun that shone on Black Hawk. His heart is dead, and no longer beats in his bosom. He is now a prisoner to the white men."

Prisoner of War

From Wisconsin, Black Hawk was taken to Jefferson Barracks, Missouri, and then held as a prisoner of war in Fort Monroe, Virginia. In 1833 he was taken to Washington, D.C., to meet President Andrew Jackson. He later toured cities in the eastern U.S. In the end, Black Hawk was allowed to return to Iowa as a hostage under the trusteeship of Keokuk, the U.S.-recognized leader of the Sauk. This, coupled with an injunction against assuming a leadership role, was the ultimate humiliation.

Black Hawk became something of a celebrity after his surrender. His portrait was painted by the famous painter of Native Americans, George Catlin, in 1832. It now hangs in the National Museum of American Art, part of the Smithsonian Institution, in Washington D.C. He dictated his autobiography, *Life of Ma-ka-tai-me-she-kia-kiak: The Autobiography of Black Hawk,* to the trader Antoine LeClaire in 1833. In 1833 and 1837 Charles Bird King painted two more portraits of Black Hawk, which were widely distributed. Black Hawk died, in his own words, "an obscure member of a nation that formerly honored and respected [his] opin-

ions," on October 3, 1838, at Iowaville on the Des Moines River, at the age of 71.

The Sauk and Fox tribes suffered the fate that Black Hawk had foreseen for them. In the peace treaty of 1832-33 that ended Black Hawk's war, the U.S., with Keokuk's cooperation, took the remaining 6,000,000 acres of Sauk and Fox lands in Illinois and eastern Iowa, as well Winnebago lands in southern Wisconsin. By 1837, all their neighboring tribes had flown to lands west of the Mississippi. In 1842, the Sauk and Fox ceded away all land in Iowa, and accepted a smaller reservation in Kansas. Six years after that, Keokuk died there in disgrace. The Sauk ceded away their Kansas lands in 1867 and accepted a smaller reservation in Oklahoma Indian Territory.

Black Hawk himself was not allowed to rest in peace in the land to which his people had fled. His remains were stolen from his burial ground and obtained by the governor of the Iowa Territory who displayed them in his office. They were later recovered and placed on display in the Burlington Historical Society, Illinois, which burnt to the ground in 1855.

SOURCES:

Brown, Dee, *Bury My Heart at Wounded Knee,* New York, Holt, 1970; 5.

Native North American Almanac, edited by Duane Champagne, Detroit, Gale Research, 1994; 1013.

Native Americans: An Annotated Bibliography, compiled by Frederick E. Hoxie and Harvey Markowitz, Salem, 1991; 137.

A Concise Dictionary of Indian Tribes of North America, edited by Barbara A. Leitch, Algonac, Michigan, Reference Publications, 1979; 409-410.

History of the Indian Tribes of North America, three volumes, edited by Thomas L. McKenney and James Hall, [Philadelphia], 1836-1844.

Dictionary of the American Indian, edited by John L. Stoutenburgh, Jr., Theosophical Library, 1960; 34.

Waldman, Carl, *Who Was Who in Native American History,* New York, Facts on File, 1990; 27-28.

Waters, Frank, *Brave Are My People: Indian Heroes Not Forgotten,* foreword by Vine Deloria, Jr., Clear Light, 1993; 69-77.

—Sketch by tpkunesh

Black Kettle
1803(?)-1868
Southern Cheyenne tribal leader
Also known as Moka-ta-va-tah

Black Kettle was a Cheyenne chief noted for his attempts to negotiate peace with the United States during the

Black Kettle

period of intense frontier conflict between 1860 and 1868. Despite his demonstrations of good faith, he was betrayed numerous times by United States troops and was later criticized by military leaders in order to justify their massacres of Cheyennes at locations such as Sand Creek and Washita. Black Kettle was attacked by mainstream newspaper such as the *New York Times* for supposedly waging war against the United States. However, his reputation was restored by twentieth-century historians, who have argued that such charges were unfounded. As a result of their scholarship, Black Kettle is generally considered to be the greatest of all the Cheyenne peace chiefs.

Black Kettle

Cheyenne scholars have uncovered conflicting evidence concerning the birth and parentage of Black Kettle. According to some accounts, he was born around 1812 and was the son of High-Backed Wolf, a principal chief of the Cheyenne nation. Other records suggest, however, that Black Kettle was born around 1807 and was the son of Swift Hawk Lying Down, who was not a Cheyenne chief. Little information is known about Black Kettle's early life. Several historical documents suggest that William S. Harney, a general in the United States army, adopted Black Kettle when he was about 15 years of age and maintained a strong friendship with him that would last until the Cheyenne leader's death. Before Black Kettle became a chief, he fought in several intertribal battles and won a reputation as a fierce warrior. In 1948, for instance, he led a campaign against the Utes, acquiring his first wife in the battle. Five

years later, he carried the sacred Medicine Arrows into battle against the Delawares, showing the high level of respect his fellow Cheyennes had for him.

Principle Chief of the Southern Cheyenne

By 1860 Black Kettle had attained the honorable position of principal chief of the Cheyenne nation. When Commissioner A. B. Greenwood met with the Cheyenne chiefs at Fort Wise to negotiate a peace treaty, it was Black Kettle who, according to one agent, best understood the terms of the agreement and signed the treaty first. The legality of this settlement, however, was called into question three years later when the chiefs of the Dog Soldiers—a Cheyenne military society that often opposed Black Kettle's attempts to make peace with the whites—claimed that the treaty was a swindle and that Black Kettle denied signing it. According to Stan Hoig's profile of Black Kettle in *The Peace Chiefs of the Cheyennes,* however, this questioning of Black Kettle's reputation as a peacemaker was groundless.

During the summer of 1864, Black Kettle continued his efforts to bring peace to the central plains. With the help of George Bent, the son of a white trader who was married to Black Kettle's niece, Black Kettle wrote a letter to Major Edward Wynkoop, the commander at Fort Lyon, calling for a peace conference and an exchange of prisoners. Wynkoop offered to negotiate with Black Kettle, but he brought with him his garrison force and two howitzers, angering the Dog Soldiers. Still, Black Kettle proceeded with his attempts to reach an agreement, placing his trust in Wynkoop. The major himself had a great respect for the Cheyenne leader. According to George Grinnell's *The Fighting Cheyennes,* Wynkoop described Black Kettle as "one who had stamped on every lineament, the fact that he was born to command, he while all the balance of the council were snarling like wolves, sat calm, dignified, immovable with a slight smile on his face." The two fighters arranged a deal: Wynkoop agreed to hold back his forces for three or four days while Black Kettle secured the white prisoners who had been captured. According to Cheyenne custom, Black Kettle had no authority to take the white captives without purchasing their freedom himself. Using his own ponies, Black Kettle bought the freedom of four white children, who ranged from four to 17 years of age.

Having fulfilled his part of the bargain, Black Kettle formed a delegation consisting of two other Cheyennes—White Antelope and Bull Bear—and four Arapaho chiefs, which accompanied Wynkoop to Denver for a council with John Evans, Governor of the Colorado Territory, at Camp Weld on September 28, 1864. Asked by Evans to speak first, Black Kettle articulated the peaceful intentions of the delegation, stressing the need for mutual understanding. Evans refused to acknowledge such pleas and accused the Cheyennes and Arapahos of starting the war in the central plains and forming an alliance with the Sioux, who, for the most part, resisted any effort to make peace with the whites. Making no attempt to reconcile differences, Evans informed the delegation that the plains would soon be filled with United States soldiers and advised Black Kettle to fight on the side of the army.

Faced with no other alternative, Black Kettle agreed to help the soldiers. As a result of an outbreak of scurvy at nearby Camp Lyon, Major Scott J. Anthony, a fellow officer to Wynkoop, told Black Kettle that the Cheyennes should remain at their encampment 40 miles to the north, near Sand Creek. Anthony guaranteed that they would be safe from United States troops at this location. Satisfied with the agreement, Black Kettle led his delegation back to the Sand Creek village.

As the sun rose on the morning of November 28, 1864, Colonel John Chivington, with Anthony's full support, attacked the Cheyenne village. Notified by a squaw that troops were approaching, Black Kettle held up a large American flag—one that was given to him by Greenwood at the earlier meeting—in front of his tepee, along with a white flag of surrender. The United States troops continued their fire on the village. After the vast majority of the women and children had fled, Black Kettle and his wife attempted to follow the others in their retreat. However, they were surrounded by the troops and Black Kettle's wife was shot. Black Kettle ran back to the sand bar where she had fallen, but after concluding that she was dead, he fled to a creek bank where other Cheyennes were hiding. When the troops finally withdrew at dusk, Black Kettle returned to his wife, finding that although she had been shot at least eight more times, she had miraculously survived.

Black Kettle and his wife, along with the remaining Cheyennes, retreated to the Dog Soldier camps, leaving behind over 100 who had been massacred by the soldiers. Among those killed in the battle were several Cheyenne chiefs, including Standing-in-Water, War Bonnet, White Antelope, Yellow Wolf, Knock Knee, and One Eye. Their village destroyed and most of their horses and mules captured, the few survivors followed Black Kettle south of the Arkansas River. Meanwhile, the Dog Soldiers, who were already against making peace with the whites, went on their own rampage of violence, dismantling frontier settlements and transportation lines throughout Kansas—acts that would later be attributed falsely to Black Kettle.

One year after the massacre, the peace emissaries for the Little Arkansas council located Black Kettle on the Cimarron River south of Fort Dodge and invited him to negotiations. The commission—headed by Black Kettle's longtime friend, General Harney—examined Black Kettle's wife's nine wounds and presented Black Kettle with a horse as a reparation gift. With the help of William Bent and Kit Carson, the commission drafted a treaty that provided the Cheyennes and the Arapahos with a new reserve area in the northwestern part of Indian Territory, or what is now Oklahoma.

The Death of Black Kettle

During the next two years, the United States army wavered in its policy toward Black Kettle. While Wynkoop, the new Cheyenne and Arapaho agent, delivered a trainload of annuity goods and made some efforts to make reparations for the horses lost at Salt Creek, other military officials con-

tinued to levy charges of aggression against the Cheyennes. Black Kettle, for instance, was accused of murders and thefts that were, most likely, committed by either Sioux or Dog Soldiers.

Despite the threats of the Dog Soldiers, Black Kettle agreed to attend a new treaty council at Medicine Lodge Creek in October of 1867. Although more than 300 hostile Dog Soldiers surrounded the camp, Black Kettle proceeded with the negotiations, admitting to the Commission that he had no authority over the Dog Soldiers and could not prevent their attack. To make matters worse, the Dog Soldier leaders threatened to kill Black Kettle's horses if he did not attend an important Cheyenne religious ceremony known as the Medicine Arrow rites. Black Kettle, though aware of the potential for violence, attempted to bring the two parties together, convincing the Commission to remain a few more days while he attended the ceremonies. When the talks finally resumed, Black Kettle was able to convince the Dog Soldiers to sign a treaty stipulating that they give up the country between the Arkansas South Platte rivers under the condition that they be allowed to roam and hunt there as long as there were buffalo.

After a peaceful winter, tensions again mounted when the government failed to make a delivery of food and ammunition that was promised in the Medicine Lodge agreement. Wynkoop soon arrived with a shipment of food, but he did not provide the Cheyennes with ammunition until late in the summer. Shortly after the ammunition did arrive, however, a whiskey-drinking war party consisting of Sioux, Arapahos, and Cheyennes on their way to a conflict with the Pawnees came in contact with some white settlers along the Saline and Solomon rivers and committed several atrocities. Despite a full confession by Chief Little Rock, a member of Black Kettle's band, who named the individuals involved, war-minded whites used these acts to stifle further peace talks.

Black Kettle's further efforts to negotiate a lasting peace with the United States were, for the most part, unsuccessful. He died in combat with U.S. Troops. In November of 1868, Black Kettle decided to move his small village of about 50 lodges farther down the Washita River so that he could be closer to other tribes. Not suspecting that troops would pursue the Cheyennes in the harsh winter conditions, Black Kettle's village was easily surrounded on the night of November 26 by the Seventh United States Cavalry under the command of Lieutenant Colonel George Armstrong Custer. At dawn, Custer's troops attacked the unsuspecting village, killing most of the Cheyennes and their elderly leader.

SOURCES:

Berthrong, Donald J., *The Southern Cheyennes,* Norman, University of Oklahoma Press, 1963.

Grinnell, George Bird, *The Fighting Cheyennes,* Norman, University of Oklahoma Press, 1956.

Hoig, Stan, *The Peace Chiefs of the Cheyennes,* Norman, University of Oklahoma Press, 1980.

Stands In Timber, John, and Margot Liberty, *Cheyenne Memories,* New Haven, Yale University Press, 1967.

—*Sketch by Jason Gallman*

Black Sparrow Hawk
See Black Hawk

Ethel Blondin-Andrew
1951-
Dene cabinet minister

Ethel Blondin-Andrew, a Dene Indian from the Arctic, was the first aboriginal woman to sit in Canada's House of Commons. Elected by a landslide victory in 1988 to represent the Western Arctic, Blondin-Andrew was named Secretary of State for youth and training by Prime Minister Jean Chretien in November of 1993. A high-profile cabinet minister, Blondin-Andrew was outspoken in campaigning for aboriginal rights and in her defence of trapping and the fur industry. As fellow caucus member Sheila Copps noted in a *HomeMaker's* profile of Blondin-Andrew: "Anyone who can get themselves elected as an aboriginal woman in this country is someone who knows how to overcome obstacles."

Blondin-Andrew describes herself as a "snotty-nosed kid from the bush" in *HomeMaker's,* and her childhood was typical for many Dene and Inuit of her generation. She was born on March 25, 1951, in Fort Norman, Northwest Territories, to a young, unmarried mother, Cecilia Modeste. At three months, Blondin-Andrew was custom adopted by her aunt and uncle, Joseph Blondin and Marie Therese (Tatti), and raised with their children. The relative Blondin-Andrew most credits with shaping her determination to succeed in life, however, was her grandmother Catherine Blondin. "Because of my grandmother's influence, I always felt that I was equal to anybody," related Blondin-Andrew in *HomeMaker's.*

As a youngster, Blondin-Andrew spent happy years in the family's bush camp before being sent away to residential school in Inuvik at age nine. Three years later, she was diagnosed with tuberculosis of the spine and moved to a sanatorium in Edmonton, Alberta. When she recovered, Blondin-Andrew returned to the family's new home, purchased for $80, in the isolated community of Fort Franklin near Great Bear Lake. These years, in a poorly-heated house without electricity or running water, "were difficult times, but they built up my threshold for misery, and gave me a useful perspective," the politician noted in *HomeMaker's.*

Selected for Leadership Training

It was at the young age of 14 that Blondin-Andrew was selected for leadership training and sent to Grandin College, a co-ed high school in Fort Smith. Her achievements there seemed threatened when she found herself pregnant and unmarried at age 17. Sent to a home for unwed mothers, Blondin-Andrew stubbornly refused to give up her son. By age 21, she had married and was studying at the University of Alberta while raising her three children, Troy, Tanya, and Tim Townsend. Graduating with her Bachelor of Education degree in 1974, Blondin-Andrew taught in remote native communities around the Northwest Territories for several years. She was appointed an aboriginal languages specialist for the Department of Education in Yellowknife. Her first marriage ended in divorce.

Elected to Parliament by Landslide Victory

Blondin-Andrew became a senior civil servant in the mid-1980s when she was appointed manager and then acting director of the Public Service Commission of Canada's indigenous development program in Ottawa, which trained natives for government jobs. When the program ended, Blondin-Andrew returned to Yellowknife to become assistant deputy minister in the territorial government's Department of Culture and Communications. But Blondin-Andrew decided the best way to implement real change for her people was to run for elected office. Despite her lack of political experience and money, Liberal Party candidate Blondin-Andrew defeated her two male opponents by a landslide in the 1988 election.

Blondin-Andrew was named aboriginal affairs critic for the Liberal opposition government, and quickly earned widespread respect and media attention for her sharp questioning of Prime Minister Brian Mulroney during the Mohawk land dispute at Oka, Quebec. Blondin-Andrew also chaired her party's Western/Northern caucus and co-chaired the party's leadership convention. When the Liberals were elected to office in 1993, Blondin-Andrew was given the junior cabinet post of Secretary of State, responsible for youth and training. She took time from her political duties in August of 1993 to marry Leon Andrew, a Fort Norman trapper. Five months later, Blondin-Andrew charged her husband with two counts of spousal assault, stating that while she was sympathetic to her husband's problems, women could not allow themselves to be victimized. The couple reconciled while Andrew served his jail sentence. As a cabinet minister, Blondin-Andrew has continued working to legislate change for Canada's native peoples. As Copps noted, "Aboriginal issues have a greater profile in the party and the country because of Ethel."

SOURCES:

Books

Bejermi, John, *Canadian Parliamentary Handbook,* Ottawa, Borealis Press, 1992.

Canadian Parliamentary Guide, edited by Kathyrn O'Handley, Toronto, Globe and Mail Publishing, 1994.

Canadian Who's Who, edited by Kieran Simpson, Toronto, University of Toronto Press, 1993.

Periodicals

Brockman, Aggie, "Striking a Delicate Balance," *Up Here,* October/November, 1993; 43-47, 59-61.

"Dene MP Has Earned Widespread Respect," *Calgary Herald,* January 13, 1991; A8.

Johnson, Doug, "Blondin-Andrew Pleased at Appointment," *Windspeaker,* November 22-December 5, 1993; 2.

Winsor, Hugh, "MP Faced Hard Choice Over Abuse by Husband," *Globe and Mail,* February 13, 1993; A3.

Yaffe, Barbara, "Welcome to the Middle Ages, Pt. 11," *HomeMaker's,* January/February, 1993; 84-90.

—Sketch by Alice Gibb

Gertrude Simmons Bonnin

Gertrude Simmons Bonnin
1876-1938
Yankton Sioux writer, educator, musician and activist

Also known as Zitkala-Sa ["Red Bird"]

Staunchly independent, an accomplished writer and musician, and an activist for Native American rights, Gertrude Bonnin was perhaps the most dynamic Native American of the first quarter of the twentieth century. Her stature as a feminist encouraged and occasionally disconcerted her contemporaries such as Charles Eastman, Carlos Montezuma, and Arthur C. Parker. As a writer she shared her storytelling traditions, especially for young readers, while also contributing essays and personal reflections that expressed chagrin at the betrayal and denigrations created by the white man's social and educational institutions. Her life came to exemplify the almost irreconcilable difficulties confronting educated Indians who must live in both the red and the white worlds.

Particular details of Gertrude Bonnin's early life seem to have been self-generated. Critic Dexter Fisher, a Bonnin scholar, and Agnes Picotte, a Lakota educator, offer the following clarifications: Bonnin's mother, Tate I Yohin Win ("Reaches for the Wind"), also known as Ellen, was a Yankton Sioux of the Nakota cultural and linguistic group. Ellen was married three times to white men; her husband Felker was Gertrude's father. Before Gertrude's birth on February 22, 1876 (not 1873 as Gertrude would later indicate) on the Yankton Reservation in South Dakota, Felker abandoned his wife, who then returned to the Yankton Agency, where she eventually married John Haysting Simmons. Young Gertrude grew up as a Simmons. As a young woman she gave herself

the name Zitkala-Sa, which means "Red Bird" in the Lakota language. The suffix "Sa" is most often printed with an accent above the S for a "szhea" pronunciation, but some printings of the suffix place an *umlaut* above the vowel.

As a child at the Yankton Agency, Gertrude listened to the traditional stories of Iya, the notorious glutton, Iktomi, the foolish one, Blood Clot Boy, and the various animals that she would write about in her first book, *Old Indian Legends.* She lived according to traditional Yankton ways as much as the reservation permitted. In 1884, she accepted an opportunity to get a white child's education by attending White's Manual Labor Institute in Wabash, Indiana. This development began a lifelong struggle between traditional ways and progressive endeavors. Ellen Simmons distrusted missionaries' efforts to educate Indian children and fiercely opposed her daughter for being attracted to a school "in the land of red apples." Upon her daughter's return from White's Institute, the rift between them widened when Gertrude announced her decision to again leave the reservation to continue her schooling. In 1888-1889 she attended the Santee Normal Training School in Nebraska. She returned to White's later, before moving on to another Quaker institution, Earlham College in Indiana, in 1895. She lived in a social milieu of Christian acculturation, which she bravely maintained in balance with her traditional upbringing and knowledge. At Earlham she applied herself vigorously to studying music, becoming a respectable violinist. In early 1896 her oration, "Side by Side," gained her second place in statewide oratory honors among students, and the March issue of *The Word Corner,* the school paper at the Santee Agency, printed the oration as her first publication. Gertrude's educational precocity took her to study briefly in

Boston at the New England Conservatory of Music. By the end of the century she was teaching at the Carlisle Indian School in Pennsylvania, performing along with the many Sioux musicians in its orchestra.

First Collection of Stories Published

Despite the strained relations with her mother, Gertrude Simmons frequently returned home to stay in touch with her heritage. Around 1900 she felt a surge of obligation to recall and preserve her Nakota culture, and in 1901 Ginn and Company, located in Boston, published 14 of her stories as *Old Indian Legends,* under her chosen name of Zitkala-Sa. Meanwhile, she wrote and published in such sophisticated periodicals as the *Atlantic, Harper's, Everybody's,* and *Red Man and Helper* the essays and reflections that gave her a wide readership and also brought notoriety for her relentless exposures of the hypocrisies whites espoused about Indian education and the bitter experiences schools created for Indian youngsters. She disagreed with Carlisle founder Richard Henry Pratt, who advocated teaching Indians agrarian skills and domestic responsibilities. Her position, which was that Indian youths should be taught academic subjects, was remarkably similar to that of her African-American contemporary, scholar and educator W. E. B. DuBois. On the subject of religion, her essay, "Why I Am A Pagan," used the storytelling technique to defend her way of life to a Sioux preacher who had traded his traditions for the doctrines of Christianity.

Sometime also in 1900 Gertrude Simmons met Carlos Montezuma, who although nicknamed the "fiery Apache," was actually a Yavapai Indian from Arizona and an 1889 graduate of the Chicago Medical College. Montezuma was so impressed by her that in 1901 he asked her to marry him. Both were strong-willed individuals, and although they broke the engagement that summer, they continued corresponding— sometimes with fierce debate—for decades. For instance, she once rebuked his idea of creating an Indian organization that would be all-male. Her letters to Carlos Montezuma are in his collected papers at the State Historical Society of Wisconsin, but none of his letters to her seem to have survived. By means of the Montezuma collection's letters, Montezuma biographer Peter Iverson interprets her indecision about marriage as a disinclination toward the institution, but he also considers that Gertrude Simmons wanted to marry a man who shared her Yankton cultural heritage. On a visit to her mother in late 1901, she met Captain Raymond Bonnin, a Nakota like herself who was on the staff of the Indian Bureau. They married in 1902, and the following year their son, Raymond Ohiya Bonnin, was born. (Similar to Charles Eastman's Sioux name, Ohiya in the Nakota dialect means "Winner.")

The active writing and musical career of Zitkala-Sa, as she had begun signing her prose, declined for several years as she and her husband worked on various reservations, including the Uintah and Ouray Reservation in Utah between 1903 and 1916. She did, however, take time in 1913 to collaborate with classical music composer William Hanson on an opera, "Sun Dance," that premiered in Vernal, Utah, that year. Indians and whites avidly enjoyed this opera, and it was occasionally performed elsewhere in Utah and in neighboring states. After the work lay dormant for nearly two decades, the New York Light Opera Guild premiered it in 1937, selecting it as its American opera for that year. Operas about American folk life gained popularity during the twenties and thirties, yet none about Native Americans except this one were co-authored by a Native American.

Bonnin's Activism and Organizations

Gertrude Bonnin was not a founding member of the Society of American Indians (SAI), a self-help organization that began in 1911 at Ohio State University. But she became one of its earliest supporters and active correspondents, rising eventually to positions on its staff. The organizers of the SAI, the most important of the pan-Indian groups during this time, wanted a forum that would reach beyond issues affecting individual tribes; they saw themselves as advocates for issues affecting the greater number of Indian reservation and community populations. The SAI began issuing its quarterly, the *American Indian* magazine, in 1916, and Bonnin's poem, "The Indian's Awakening," appeared in it. At its conference in Cedar Rapids, Iowa, that September, Gertrude Bonnin was elected secretary. She also began corresponding with Arthur C. Parker, the Seneca ethnologist who was SAI's president.

Bonnin also joined non-Indian national civic organizations such as the League of American Pen Women and the General Federation of Women's Clubs. Her work in Native American issues proved exciting, useful and challenging for her. She was among several progressive Indians and white religious leaders and public officials who debated the merits of peyote with Indian religious traditionals, some educated Indians, and white anthropologists. While in Utah, Bonnin opposed the usage of peyote as a spiritual practice, which the Utes had initiated. In keeping with her opposition to peyote usage, Bonnin supported the Congressional Indian bill of 1918, which was designed for the suppression of the plant. The defenders of peyote ostensibly lost when the bill was passed, but enforcement of the bill proved ineffectual. Eventually, peyote usage precipitated the establishment in 1924 of the Native American Church, which used and defended peyote as a sacred medicine.

Another endeavor that Bonnin began while living in Utah was her support for both the Indian Service and the Community Center movement. The Indian Service consisted of Native Americans, many of whom were educated in mission and trade schools on or off reservations, who worked on the reservations or in similar Indian communities performing the kind of support services work that Bonnin and her husband were doing. These Indians could have pursued alternatives that would have given them personal advantages, and Bonnin sympathized with and lauded their devotion to community and tribal ties and encouraged those who remained as they made their career sacrifices. As for the Community Center movement, Bonnin believed that community centers such as the one at Fort Duchesne in Utah could contribute to fostering the improvement of Indians if Indians themselves, along with whites, educators and missionaries, were willing to work together. She encouraged nonpartisanship at the centers. The movement failed during a time when tribalism increased and pan-Indian agendas were set aside.

With Gertrude's role in the SAI, the Bonnins relocated in 1916 to Washington, D.C., where "Gertie," as she was affectionately called, continued to help Native Americans make adjustments to white society as best as they could. Although she was a respected leader, she continued experiencing the distrust of reservation Indians because she straddled the Native American and white communities. Professional challenges for Bonnin in the SAI came about in 1918. One involved her role in the peyote controversy. A second had to do with growing "personal and religious" differences with Marie Baldwin (Ojibway), the SAI treasurer. At the SAI's annual meeting, where Bonnin was re-elected as secretary in addition to being elected treasurer, Bonnin joined the chorus of Indian voices calling for the abolition of the Indian Bureau, the federal organization despised for its paternalism and autocracy. Factionalism and individual tribal issues that drew members to their home reservations and communities accelerated and as a result the viability of the SAI weakened. Bonnin's commitment to its principles and her desire to make it fulfill its promise as an effective organization increased as the enthusiasm of its other members waned or they became otherwise preoccupied. She successfully pushed the *American Indian* magazine to devote a special issue to the Sioux in 1917, an issue for which she wrote "A Sioux Woman's Love For Her Grandchild" and the editorial in which she attacked the Indian Bureau as "unAmerican." Eventually, Bonnin assumed the editorship of this periodical, writing editorials addressing the importance of land retention and Indian self-determination. She served with the SAI in this capacity until 1920, when, opposed to the declining organization's new political direction under Thomas Sloan (Omaha), a lawyer who defended peyotism, she resigned from her activities and membership.

As if in partial summation of her activities, Bonnin gathered several of her writings for a new book, *American Indian Stories,* published by Hayworth Press in 1921 under the name, Zitkala-Sa. These autobiographical essays and stories had already appeared at the beginning of the century, and "A Warrior's Daughter," a fiction, was among them. Four entries had never been published, although one, "America's Indian Problem," was simultaneously printed in the book and in the December issue of *Edict* magazine. Bonnin probably felt her early writings were still timely for their pro-Indian self-determination stance. In 1924 the Indian Rights Association, an organization that Bonnin supported for many years, published a small volume, *Oklahoma's Poor Rich Indians, an Orgy of Graft and Exploitation of the Five Civilized Tribes, Legalized Robbery,* which Bonnin co-authored with Charles H. Fabens and Matthew K. Sniffen. This study reported on Indians being murdered and swindled out of the recently discovered oil-rich land on which they had been living since forced there from the southern states in the nineteenth century.

Fights with New Vigor for Indian Rights

Otherwise relegated to peripheral influence among her former pan-Indian associates, Bonnin fought with new vigor for Indian rights, encouraged by the Indian Citizenship Act of 1924. She helped found the National Council of American Indians in 1926 and became its first president; her husband was elected secretary-treasurer. The National Council's main objective was to make "a constructive effort to better the Red Race and make its members better citizens of the United States." It became Bonnin's platform for calling upon Indians to support rights issues, to encourage racial consciousness and pride, and promote pan-Indianism. Despite Bonnin's efforts, educated Indians during the period between the two world wars continued to be involved with tribal issues rather than national Indian concerns. As a pan-Indian organization, the NCAI thus languished for many years, and because of Bonnin's charismatic self-reliance and overt leadership, potential Indian allies felt their participation precluded. (After the demise of the National Council, a new reform organization, the National Congress of American Indians—which would have an identical acronym—was established in 1944.) The stasis of her organization and the criticism confronting her from time to time did not lessen her interests. She supported the ideas of John Collier (excepting his tolerance of peyote usage) before and during his celebrated tenure as Indian Commissioner under Franklin Roosevelt's New Deal, because he respected the integrity of Native American cultural traditions.

Gertrude Bonnin continued lecturing on Indian reform and Indian rights until her health began to fail. The NCAI dissolved when she died on January 26, 1938, in Washington, D.C. Later that year the Indian Confederation of America, a New York City-based group, honored her memory at its annual pow wow. Her reputation as an incisive writer and activist at the forefront of the struggle to gain respect for Native Americans has gained wider appreciation since the efforts of Dexter Fisher, author of a 1979 doctoral dissertation about her, the republication of her two books, and scholarly articles on her writing style and narrative strategies. Whether under her "American name" or the Zitkala-Sa sobriquet she used for much of her writing, Gertrude Bonnin remains one of America's outstanding human rights activists.

SELECTED WRITINGS BY BONNIN:

(As Zitkala-Sa), *Old Indian Legends* (originally published 1902), Lincoln, Bison Books, University of Nebraska Press, 1985.

(As Zitkala-Sa), *American Indian Stories* (originally published 1921), Lincoln, Bison Books, University of Nebraska Press, 1985.

SOURCES:

Books

A *Biobibliography of Native American Writers, 1772-1924* (Native American Bibliography Series No. 2), compiled by Daniel F. Littlefield, Jr., and James W. Parins, Metuchen, New Jersey, Scarecrow Press, 1981.

A *Biobibliography of Native American Writers, 1772-1924: A Supplement* (Native American Bibliography Series No. 5), compiled by Daniel F. Littlefield, Jr., and James

W. Parins, Metuchen, New Jersey, Scarecrow Press, 1985.

Fisher, Dexter, "Foreword," in *American Indian Stories* by Zitkala-Sa, Lincoln, Bison Books, University of Nebraska Press, 1985; v-xx.

Fisher, Dexter, "The Transformation of Tradition: A Study of Zitkala Sa and Mourning Dove, Two Transitional American Indian Writers," in *Critical Essays on Native American Literature,* edited by Andrew Wiget, Boston, G. K. Hall, 1985; 202-211.

Hertzberg, Hazel W., *The Search for an American Indian Identity: Modern Pan-Indian Movements,* Syracuse, Syracuse University Press, 1971.

Indians of Today, edited by Marion Gridley, Crawfordsville, Indiana, 1936.

Iverson, Peter, *Carlos Montezuma and the Changing World of American Indians,* Albuquerque, University of New Mexico Press, 1982.

Notable American Women—1607-1950: A Biographical Dictionary, edited by Edward T. James, Cambridge, Massachusetts, Belknap Press of Harvard University Press, 1971.

Picotte, Agnes, "Foreword," in *Old Indian Legends* by Zitkala-Sa, Lincoln, Bison Books, University of Nebraska Press, 1985; ix-xviii.

Ruoff, A. LaVonne Brown, *American Indian Literatures: An Introduction, Bibliographic Review, and Selected Bibliography,* New York, Modern Language Association, 1990.

Stout, Mary, "Zitkala-Sa: The Literature of Politics," in *Coyote Was Here: Essays in Contemporary Native American Literary and Political Mobilization,* edited by Bo Scholer, Denmark, Seklos, 1984; 70-78.

Periodicals

Cutter, Martha J., "Zitkala-Sa's Autobiographical Writings: The Problems of Canonical Search for Language and Identity," *MELUS,* 19:1, spring 1994; 31-44.

Fisher, Dexter, "Zitkala-Sa: The Evolution of a Writer," *American Indian Quarterly,* 5:3, August 1979; 229-238.

Zitkala-Sa, "Why I Am a Pagan," *Atlantic,* December 1902; 801-803.

—Sketch by Ron Welburn

Lionel R. Bordeaux
1940-
Lakota Sioux educational leader and university president

Lionel R. Bordeaux has been an active spokesman for Native American educational rights since the early 1970s. During that period he has also served as president of Sinte Gleska University (named for the nineteenth century Lakota civic leader and negotiator, Spotted Tail) located on the Rosebud Sioux Reservation in South Dakota.

Bordeaux was born on the Rosebud Reservation on February 9, 1940. He and his wife Barbara have four adult children. Bordeaux graduated from the St. Francis Indian Mission School and earned his B.S. degree in history and social science at Black Hills State University in 1964. He later earned a master's degree at the University of South Dakota. While working on a doctoral dissertation in educational administration at the University of Minnesota, he was designated to become the first president of the newly established Sinte Gleska College.

Early employment experience included positions with the Bureau of Indian Affairs (BIA) between 1964 and 1972. He was an education specialist, vocational counselor, management intern, and teacher-counselor at locations in New Mexico, Texas, the Pine Ridge Reservation in South Dakota, and in Washington, D.C. In addition to more than two decades as a college president, he has served in Rosebud Sioux tribal government for eight years as a council member and as a chair of both the tribal education committee and education board.

Among Bordeaux's numerous organizational affiliations have been that of board member of the South Dakota State Education and Planning Commission, the Regents of Haskell Indian Junior College in Lawrence, Kansas, and the New York based Phelps-Stokes Fund. He has also served as president of both the American Indian Higher Education Consortium (tribal college) and the National Indian Education Association.

Years as College President

Sinte Gleska University is an institution that reflects the ideology and goals of its namesake (Spotted Tail). It was first conceptualized about 1968 by Stanley Red Bird, a Lakota elder, and Gerald Mohatt, now an administrator at the University of Alaska. In part, it was a response to the problems of distance and retention of Native American students at other colleges and universities. In 1970, a community board of directors was selected and a tribal charter was granted in 1971. With Mohatt as the first director, 26 courses were offered in 11 locations throughout the reservation. The central offices were in an abandoned BIA building in Rosebud. Early funding was uncertain because the State of South Dakota considered such ventures a responsibility of the federal government. The BIA did not fully support the concept of the institution.

Administrators sought a Lakota director of the scholastic activity; and Bordeaux, a Ph.D. candidate at the University of Minnesota, was invited to apply and was inaugurated as president on February 3, 1973. The challenges the new president faced are summarized by Wayne J. Stein in *Tribally Controlled Colleges:* "Concerns for funding, curriculum development, personnel development, student service needs, tribal politics, national politics." A great deal of

Bordeaux's efforts were devoted to representing the new college in various ways on the national level.

Within a few months, the college faced a significant local threat. Tribal chair, Robert Burnette, considered Stanley Red Bird and Lionel Bordeaux to be supporters of his predecessor as chairman, Webster Two Hawk. As a result, both Red Bird and Bordeaux were dismissed in December of 1973. Bordeaux and others appeared before the tribal council and were able to get a 19-2 reversal of the decision. A few months later, Burnette again dismissed Bordeaux. After college supporters picketed the tribal government and made impassioned appeals, the decision was revoked by the same wide margin. The institution has retained stability and autonomy since that date.

The college graduated its first class in August of 1973. From the beginning, as Stein observes, "President Bordeaux played a major role on the national scene to generate funding for tribal colleges and with the American Indian Higher Education Consortium staff to create legislation for such funding." Sinte Gleska College was awarded North Central Association accreditation in 1977. A later graduate education program elevated it to university status. The institution, and nearly 30 others, has remained alive because of federal legislation in October of 1978 supporting tribal colleges.

The special role of the Rosebud Sioux institution has received acknowledgement in many ways. In July of 1994, a New York Times reporter offered his impressions of the campus: "There are no ivy walls or fraternity houses on the campus of Sinte Gleska University.... But the college is the jewel of the Rosebud reservation." The human potential of the reservation is being developed and Bordeaux recognizes that there is also a need to develop a "strong land ethic," to find productive ways of using over 1,200 square miles of sparsely populated area on the reservation.

More than two decades of solid performance has resulted in many forms of regional and national recognition for Bordeaux as well. He co-chaired the 1992 White House Conference on Indian Education and was selected as an outstanding educator of the year by the South Dakota Indian Education Association. Augustana College in Sioux Falls, South Dakota, honored him with a Doctorate in Humane Letters in 1989 and he has been selected to the South Dakota Hall of Fame.

SOURCES:

Books

Stein, Wayne J., "Sinte Gleska College," in *Tribally Controlled Colleges, Making Good Medicine,* New York, Peter Lang, 1992; 57-74.

Periodicals

Johnson, Dirk, "In Bleak Area in South Dakota, Indians Put Hopes in Classroom," *New York Times,* July 3, 1991; A11.

—Sketch by Keith A. Winsell

Elias Boudinot
1803(?)-1839
Cherokee editor, translator, author, orator, and religious and political figure
Also known as Buck Watie, Stag Watie, Galagina (Galegina, Galgina, Kulakinah, Kilakina, Kullageenah) ["Buck," "Male Deer," or "Young Stag Deer"]

At age 25, Elias Boudinot became the first editor of the bilingual newspaper *Cherokee Phoenix,* which began publication in the Cherokee Nation East (now Georgia) in 1828. Much of the paper was printed in English, but at least a quarter of each issue was in Cherokee. Boudinot resigned as editor in 1832, after a disagreement with tribal authorities about whether the newspaper should be a vehicle for discussion on the issue of removal of the Cherokees to Indian Territory. The *Cherokee Phoenix* ceased publication in 1835 under pressure from Georgia authorities. Boudinot then became a prime mover in the Treaty Party and was a signer of the Treaty of New Echota in 1835. This treaty was not authorized and had the effect of ceding tribal land, a capital offense. The tragic consequence of the treaty was the Trail of Tears, during which over one-fifth of the tribe died en route to Indian Territory. Boudinot moved west in 1837, where he continued in a publishing venture with Dr. Samuel Worcester that resulted in the first book ever published in Oklahoma. When the main body of the Cherokees completed their journey in 1839, Boudinot was assassinated, along with his relatives Major Ridge and John Ridge, in retribution for his role in the treaty.

Elias Boudinot was born in the old Cherokee Nation (the area is now part of the state of Georgia) around 1803 (some say 1805). His father was David Oowatie, and Stand Watie, the noted Confederate general, was his younger brother. His Indian name was Galagina (pronounced Killke-nah). He assumed the name of Elias Boudinot, a prominent Revolutionary statesman and his benefactor, at Boudinot's request. The education of the Cherokee Elias Boudinot began at the school of the Moravian Mission at Spring Place (now part of Murray County, Georgia). The Moravians had been active among the Cherokees starting in 1800, when two Moravian brothers travelled from Salem, North Carolina, to Tellico, the Cherokee capital, to address tribal officials with the proposition of setting up a school among them. Around age 15, Boudinot travelled to the Foreign Mission School in Cornwall, Connecticut, spending one night with his benefactor en route.

After graduation, he announced his intention to marry a white girl from Cornwall. Boudinot's cousin John Ridge had caused a controversy in the community two years earlier by marrying a white girl, which prompted the local newspaper to call for closure of the Cornwall Mission

Elias Boudinot

School. It was with this background that Boudinot asked Harriet Ruggles Gold to be his bride. The marriage was strongly opposed by many Cornwall residents, and the bride's brother burned the two in effigy as Harriet went into temporary hiding for her own safety. During that same demonstration, the church bells tolled a death knell and members of the church choir, to which Harriet belonged, were asked to wear black mourning bands for their lost sister. Harriet's family also struggled with approval of this union, and Harriet became seriously ill. As she grew steadily worse, her parents rethought their position and approved the union, trusting they were following God's will. Eventually, Harriet's health was restored and marriage plans proceeded.

Harriet was very religious and longed to do missionary work. Her love for Boudinot and for a life of religious work combined to help the couple weather the storm. Boudinot had taken classes at Andover Theological Seminary in Massachusetts, it being his goal to take the gospel of Christianity to his people. Love prevailed, and the couple were married in the home of her parents on March 28, 1826. However, this incident resulted in the closing of the Cornwall School in the autumn of 1826. Harriet Gold Boudinot died ten years later at age 31, after bearing six children. In 1836, Boudinot married Delight Sargent, also a white woman; they remained childless.

Returned to Georgia and Edited the *Cherokee Phoenix*

With his course at Cornwall and his study at Andover Theological Seminary, Boudinot was one of the best-edu-

cated citizens of the Cherokee Nation. He went on a fund-raising speaking tour before teaching at a mission school in High Tower, Cherokee Nation, from 1826 to 1827. In 1828 he became editor of the *Cherokee Phoenix,* which made use of the Cherokee alphabet Sequoyah had developed. By 1833, Boudinot published a novel in Cherokee, *Poor Sarah; or, The Indian Woman.*

In 1827, Boudinot was named clerk of the Cherokee National Council (legislature). The major issue facing the council was increasing pressure from the U.S. government to remove the Cherokees from their ancestral land in Georgia to Indian Territory in Oklahoma. The Cherokee council, meeting in October 1829, decided to stand firm, alarmed at the loss of their ancestral land. The resolution that was adopted (drafted by Major Ridge, Boudinot's uncle) called for the death penalty for any tribal member who thereafter undertook "to cede any part of their tribal domain." The Boudinot-Ridge-Watie faction was apparently content with this posture until 1831, when the council named John Ross principal chief (over John Ridge) for an indefinite period. Ross and his majority believed they could retain their land by using the U.S. court system and by eventually treating with Georgia and/or the U.S. government to keep their lands.

In March 1832, Boudinot and his cousin John Ridge travelled to Boston and other northern cities to speak and raise support for the Cherokee cause. In the meantime, Georgia continued its encroachment and its efforts to enforce the Georgia Compact, which would move the Cherokees to the West. Upon his return to the Cherokee Nation in the summer of 1832, Boudinot assessed the situation and the deteriorating fortunes of his tribe and began to change his position on removal. He resigned as editor of the *Phoenix* in September, under pressure from the tribal government. He wanted to use the newspaper as an instrument of discussion, but John Ross forbade the editor to print a word in favor of removal.

Reversed Position on Removal

At this time, Boudinot and his family began considering their own situation. They ultimately decided that a treaty with the U.S. government, ceding land in exchange for new land in the West, was their best hope. They formed the "Treaty Party" and made a trip to Washington, D.C., in 1835 to negotiate unofficially on behalf of the Cherokees. On December 29, the Treaty of New Echota was signed by Boudinot, John Ridge, Major Ridge, Stand Watie, and 15 others, none of whom had authority to do so. The treaty provided for surrender of Cherokee lands and removal of the people to Indian Territory (now Oklahoma). The lawful government of the Cherokee Nation was outraged and sent petitions with signatures of more than 90 percent of the tribal members to the Senate, pleading against ratification. Nonetheless, the treaty passed on May 23, 1836, by one vote.

Boudinot and his family were able to choose their time for passage to the West, since they were part of a favored group who had signed the Treaty of New Echota. They travelled to Indian Territory in September 1837, along with John

Ridge and his family. When they arrived, they joined Dr. Samuel Austin Worcester, a medical missionary, in Park Hill, near the capitol at Tahlequah.

Joined Worcester in Publishing Venture

Worcester, known as the "Cherokee Messenger" among the Cherokees, had worked with Boudinot since 1826 in the old Cherokee Nation. He established the new Worcester Mission in 1836. Worcester worked fervently among the Cherokees, learning the language with Boudinot as his interpreter. Together they wrote textbooks and translated several books of the Bible into Cherokee. Worcester was imprisoned in Georgia for helping the Cherokees and became famous through the U.S. Supreme Court case *Worcester v. Georgia.* This case, decided in 1832, established tribal sovereignty and protected Cherokees from Georgia laws. The decision also freed Worcester, although Georgia ignored it until Worcester was pardoned in early 1833.

One of the conditions of Worcester's pardon was that he leave Georgia. When he did, he took his printing press to the new nation with him, with the intention of teaching and preaching among the Cherokee. In 1835 he set up his press at Union Mission, on the west banks of the Grand River south of the present-day Pryor, Oklahoma, in Mayes County. Textbooks, religious tracts, the *Cherokee Almanac,* and other items were published here. Most notably, the collaboration of Boudinot and Worcester produced the first book published in what is now Oklahoma in August 1835. The title was "I Stutsi in Natsoku," or "The Child's Book." In 1836, the press was moved to the recently established community of Park Hill and Worcester's mission work continued. Boudinot had served as his interpreter and assistant for several years and together they issued more than 13 million printed pages.

Assassinated for Role in Treaty of New Echota

The work continued until Boudinot's assassination on June 22, 1839, on the same day that his relatives John Ridge and Major Ridge were killed; only Stand Watie escaped the plot. Boudinot was lured from the home he was building at Park Hill by three men who wanted him to go with them to the home of Dr. Worcester for medicine. He was killed by the three as they approached the mission. No one was ever brought to justice for his murder (or for the deaths of the Ridges), but it was assumed that the responsibility lay with Ross sympathizers, although not Ross personally. Boudinot is buried in the Worcester Mission Cemetery at Old Park Hill, near Tahlequah, Oklahoma, the capital of the Cherokee Nation since 1839. The site is approximately 300 yards north of the spot where he died, and the cemetery is the only remaining part of the mission. At Boudinot's death, his wife Delight took all six children east to escape the violence in the Cherokee Nation. They were placed with relatives of Harriet Gold Boudinot. The best-known of the children was Elias Cornelius Boudinot. He studied engineering and then law, became active in politics, and was eventually elected to the Confederate Congress.

SOURCES:

Books

Biographical Dictionary of Indians of the Americas, second edition, Newport Beach, California, American Indian Publishers, 1991.

Boudinot, Elias, *Poor Sarah; or, The Indian Woman,* New Echota, Cherokee Nation East, United Brethren's Missionary Society, 1833.

Cherokee Cavaliers: Forty Years of Cherokee History as Told in the Correspondence of the Ridge-Watie-Boudinot Family, edited by Edward Everett Dale and Gaston Litton, Norman, University of Oklahoma Press, 1939.

Dictionary of American Biography, edited by John A. Garraty, New York, Charles Scribner's Sons, 1951.

Dockstader, Frederick J., *Great North American Indians,* New York, Van Nostrand Reinhold, 1977.

Gabriel, Ralph Henry, *Elias Boudinot, Cherokee & His America,* Norman, University of Oklahoma Press, 1941; 91, 95, 98, 106, 109, 133.

Native North American Almanac, edited by Duane Champagne, Detroit, Gale Research, 1994.

Starr, Emmet, *Old Cherokee Families: "Old Families and Their Genealogy,"* Norman, University of Oklahoma Foundation, 1972; 381, 473

Schwarze, Edmund, *History of the Moravian Missions among the Southern Indian Tribes,* Bethlehem, Pennsylvania, Moravian Historical Society, 1923.

Waldman, Carl, *Who Was Who in Native American History,* New York, Facts on File, 1990.

Wardell, Morris L., *A Political History of the Cherokee Nation, 1838-1907,* Norman, University of Oklahoma Press, 1977.

Wilkins, Thurmond, *Cherokee Tragedy: The Story of the Ridge Family and of the Decimation of a People,* New York, Macmillan, 1970; 296.

Woodward, Grace Steele, *The Cherokees,* Norman, University of Oklahoma Press, 1963.

Periodicals

Ballenger, T. L., "Restoration of the Worcester Cemetery, Old Park Hill," *Chronicles of Oklahoma,* 31:2, summer 1953.

Ballenger, T. L., "The Illinois River," *Chronicles of Oklahoma,* 46:4, winter 1968-1969; 456-457.

Beeson, Leola Selman, "Homes of Distinguished Cherokee Indians," *Chronicles of Oklahoma,* 11:3, September 1933; 927-932.

Clark, Robert L., "The Centennial of Oklahoma Printing," *Chronicles of Oklahoma,* 48:2, summer 1970; 209-211.

Colbert, Thomas Burnell, "Visionary or Rogue? The Life & Legacy of Elias Cornelius Boudinot," *Chronicles of Oklahoma,* 45:3, fall 1987; 268-269, 279.

Delly, Lillian, "Episode at Cornwall," *Chronicles of Oklahoma,* 51:4, winter 1973-1974; 444-450.

Foreman, Grant, "The Murder of Elias Boudinot," *Chronicles of Oklahoma,* 12:1, March 1934.

Wilson, T. Paul, "Confederate Delegates of the Five Civilized Tribes," *Chronicles of Oklahoma,* 53:3, fall 1975; 358-360.

—Sketch by Philip H. Viles, Jr.

Billy Bowlegs
1810-1859(?)
Seminole chief
Also known as Halpatter Micco (Halpuda Mikko) ["The Alligator Chief"]

Billy Bowlegs

Billy Bowlegs was one of the most influential Seminole Indian chiefs during the Third Seminole Indian War, also called the "Billy Bowlegs War." His father, Secoffee, and his mother were both full-blooded Mikasuki Seminole. The name Bowlegs has nothing to do with the shape of his legs. His English name was believed to be Billy Bolek, and black slaves that escaped from southern plantations translated his name to the white settlers as Bowlegs. He was one of the last chiefs to be removed from the Florida Territory to Indian Territory (now Oklahoma) reservations so that white settlers could have access to south Florida lands. Bowlegs was an accomplished politician as well as a warrior, capable of negotiating peace when conflicts occurred. His people received adequate recognition at the end of the Third Seminole War because of his compassion for their well-being.

During his years as chief, Bowlegs made contact with Cuban fishermen and Spanish traders along the Gulf of Mexico coast. He could speak both Spanish and English. He was intelligent and wise when dealing with his people and their difficulties. He cared for them and continually tried to limit the loss of Indian life in his wars with the military. Billy Bowlegs was never captured in all the U.S. government's efforts to open Florida for settlement. His contributions to the Seminole Indian heritage is remembered with pride.

Bowlegs Learns about War at a Young Age

The Seminole Wars grew out of border conflicts between the expanding United States and Spanish Florida. As white English-speaking settlers moved into Georgia, North Carolina, and Alabama during the middle of the eighteenth century, they came into contact with the Seminoles and began to push them out of their traditional lands. The Indians escaped by occupying land in northern Florida, then owned by Spain. As the United States continued to grow, however, pressure on the Seminoles increased. In addition, the tribes served as havens for escaped slaves and criminals. These runaways found life to be better in the swamps than on the plantations. They had more freedom and benefitted the Seminoles by teaching them farming and ranching and serving as interpreters between the Indians and the white settlers and military.

In the spring of 1818 Major General Andrew Jackson, an experienced Indian fighter, led 3,000 troops into Spanish Florida to coerce the Seminoles out of areas that whites wanted to settle and to recover the runaway slaves for their owners. This action began the First Seminole Indian War. A treaty was reached in 1818, and some of the Seminoles began to be moved westward to reservations. Many of the bands, however, did not want to be moved. They wanted to stay in Florida, where they had established themselves as excellent hunters and farmers, and fled south into central Florida between Fort Myers and Fort Lauderdale. As long as Florida remained Spanish territory, the Seminoles stood a chance of staying in their chosen land. In 1819, however, Spain decided to cede the Florida territory to the United States.

Bowlegs was only a child at this time, but he learned first-hand the ways that the U.S. military and the Washington government could manipulate the Indians. He saw the treaty lands shrink to allow farmers access to reservation lands. Laws were passed that discriminated against Indians. To avoid prison or death sentences, the Indians were forced to move to reservations west of the Mississippi River. Bowlegs concluded the military and Washington government could not be trusted.

Bowlegs Becomes Chief During Second Seminole War

The bands of Seminoles in Florida from 1818 to 1835 were spread over central and southern Florida. They ranged from Tampa Bay and Fort Myers south along the Gulf of Mexico and then east through the Big Cypress Swamp and Everglades to the Atlantic coast. During this period the government in Washington encouraged expansion and settlement in Florida, displacing some of the Seminoles again. The treaty of Payne's Landing, signed in 1832, called for the removal of all the Seminole to lands in the west. Small bands of warriors, refusing to recognize these terms, tried to keep the newcomers from taking the lands set aside by the treaty that ended the first war. Fearful of these reprisals, the settlers appealed to Washington for men, supplies, and money to raise a civilian militia. The Seminoles in turn prepared for more military campaigns that would attempt to remove their people to western reservations.

From 1835 to 1842 the battles and attacks continued. Bowlegs fought beside many of the tribe's most skilled warriors and leaders, including Osceola, Micanopy, Jumper, Alligator, Wildcat, Arpeika (Sam Jones), Prophet (Otalke Thlocco), and Tigertail. He followed his father into a hereditary leadership position and became a chief around the age of 20. Bowlegs learned to negotiate with military officers. When negotiations broke down, he raided white settlements during the night and hid in the Big Cypress Swamp during the day. He camped in the hammocks, areas of land above the surrounding lowland swamp and waterways, of the Everglades, Big Cypress Swamp, and areas near Lake Okeechobee. Some of these areas were large enough to farm and establish a village, and had the additional advantage that the Seminoles could see any approaching soldiers.

The army quickly became tired and frustrated chasing Bowlegs and his band of warriors through the Florida swamps. The soldiers found travelling and fighting in the southern swamps difficult and lost battles due to weather conditions, sickness, and lack of adequate supplies. So they changed their tactics; they began to a policy of kidnapping chiefs under a flag of truce and sending them to the Indian Territory. Without leadership, the remaining Indians soon surrendered and were moved west. By 1842, most of the chiefs and their bands of warriors, women, and children had been captured or killed. Many of the Seminoles abandoned their traditional ways after relocation, accepting white culture and becoming one of the so-called Five Civilized Tribes.

The Second Seminole War officially ended when the federal government passed the Armed Occupation Act on August 4, 1842, opening land for settlement that was previously occupied by Indians. In James Covington's book, *The Billy Bowlegs War,* he states this law really meant that a huge "grab bag of land" extending from present-day Gainesville and St. Augustine south to the Peace River was open to settlement by any adventurers willing to risk the wrath of the remaining Seminoles.

Third Seminole Indian War

After the Second Seminole War ended in 1842, some additional lands were set aside in Florida for the two small remaining bands of Indians. It had become too costly in both money and human lives to continue their deportation. The

Seminoles were difficult to find in the Big Cypress Swamp and areas east to the Everglades. In addition, they were able to sustain themselves by hunting and by planting crops such as corn, rice, beans, pumpkins, and squash, which could be stored and used when they returned to that area. These hammocks could support bands of 50 to 200 Seminoles for short periods.

In the years between the second and third wars, conferences were held between the military and Bowlegs to find solutions to the problems of relocating the Indians to western reservations. The Seminoles wanted to remain in Florida on the lands set aside by treaty after the first and second wars. However, settlers continued to complain about raids conducted on their farms and ranches. Livestock and crops were being stolen and resistance by the white settlers often ended in death on both sides. On the other hand, settlers and ranchers continually encroached on Indian land.

The Seminoles were aware of the superior strength of the military. Bowlegs used any tactic to stall the confrontation he knew would eventually occur if the Indians refused to negotiate. When the government offered something to the Indians in payment for them to give up their land, Bowlegs took long periods of time before giving counteroffers. He also occasionally made unreasonable claims to draw out the negotiations. In 1849, however, trouble broke out again in central and western Florida. The authorities sent for Bowlegs to explain the Indian raids on the settlers and exerted pressure on him and the remaining Seminoles to relocate. Bowlegs made a counter offer: to find the responsible raiders and bring them in for punishment. The authorities tried this method several times. The responsible Indian raiders were hanged and peace prevailed for a short time.

More settlers were now coming to Florida as lands were opened in the northern and central regions. When the military began surveying the Seminole lands in central and south Florida, hostilities broke out again. These survey crews were seen by the Indians as a direct threat to their existence. Bowlegs in particular recognized the methods that brought about the First Seminole War in north Florida. After the surveying was completed, the military came to talk about the treaty and, as a result, the Indians were forced from lands already set aside for them.

In July, 1852, the commanding general in the region, General Luther Blake, took Bowlegs to Washington to meet with President Millard Fillmore and other government officials. General Blake also tried to impress Bowlegs with the strength of the Washington leadership and to show him how impossible it was to continue to resist the move to the western Indian reservations. Bowlegs and other Seminole leaders, including Chocote, Tustenuggee, Toslatchee, Emathla, and Nokose received gifts and agreed to leave Florida. Under the terms of the agreement, they were to persuade other Seminoles to follow them to the reservation. Money and small tracts of farmland were offered to the bands if the Indians agreed to move to the reservation lands. When Bowlegs returned to Florida, however, he recanted, refusing to relocate. Another trip to Washington in 1855, was also a failure; he returned to Florida saying he would never leave his homelands.

In December 1855, First Lieutenant George L. Hartsuff and his detachment of 12 soldiers left Fort Myers. Their assignment was simply to locate villages and not to provoke any action. When they came across a large planted field, however, Hartsuff and his men took some of the bananas and crops and carelessly trampled the fields with their horses. When Bowlegs discovered the theft several days later, he went looking for the group. Forty Seminoles under Bowlegs killed four soldiers and wounded four others, including Hartsuff. This began the Third Seminole War, in which Bowlegs was the primary Seminole leader.

The Seminoles under Bowlegs waged a guerilla war, attacking the military's weak points to limit the loss of Indian life and property. Their raids were not well-organized but occurred whenever the opportunity presented itself. The Seminoles attacked the government survey crews and soldiers as they moved into Indian areas. The Indians then retreated into the swamp to hide in the remote hammocks. The soldiers had problems locating the Indians and moving their equipment over the water-logged ground. Many troopers fell ill from the heat. In addition, supplies arrived haphazardly, and Washington resisted requests for additional aid because of the money and lives already expended in trying to move the Seminoles.

In August of 1856, the western Seminoles finally reached an agreement on territory, land, and compensation. The U.S. government relocated Creek Indians from Georgia to share the land with the Seminoles. Bowlegs remained in Florida and continued his resistance. For several years he successfully continued his pattern of raiding and ambushing the military. Eventually, however, the determination of the settlers put pressure on Washington to do something to bring a quick end to the conflict. Additional troops and money were sent to Florida. Military forts were established from west central Florida to the Atlantic east coast, and supply lines were reorganized. The Seminole camps and towns, although usually found abandoned, were destroyed, along with crops and stores of grain and meat.

By the end of 1857, Bowlegs and his followers were one of the last bands still fighting. The other groups, led by Sam Jones, Chipco, Tiger, and others, had surrendered and been moved out west. The military tried to open peace negotiations by bringing Seminole Indian Chief Jumper and other leaders back to Florida to talk to Billy Bowlegs, but he was not yet ready to surrender his land. In November of that year, a large detachment was sent to locate Bowlegs. They found a town of about 40 dwellings and a large cache of grain, pumpkins, and other foods. Some of Bowlegs' personal belongings were also found, including a tintype photograph of Bowlegs in Washington. Soldiers killed several Indian warriors and sent the women and children who were captured to Oklahoma. Bowlegs caught up with the detachment and ambushed them several times on their way back to Fort Myers.

Again in February 1858, another group of Seminoles from Oklahoma returned to Florida to try to persuade Bowlegs to surrender. By this time, Bowlegs and his band were reduced to a few warriors with women and children left in several camps. He knew his group could not hold out any longer. The Seminole Indian population in Florida had now been reduced to several hundred people. War, disease, and short supplies of meat and grain had further diminished the tattered natives.

On May 8, 1858, the Third Seminole Indian War officially ended. It was the last Indian war east of the Mississippi River. Billy Bowlegs and his followers were sent to Fort Myers on the Gulf coast and then taken to Egmont Key, an island at the mouth of Tampa Bay. They were held there for a time while the military waited for any additional Indians who might surrender. They then sailed by boat to New Orleans, and from there traveled to the Seminole reservations. A small number of Seminoles avoided capture and remained hidden in the swamps. The military gave up its efforts to find them, and the settlers moved onto the lands that could be cultivated or ranched.

Several accounts exist of Billy Bowlegs' death. One story has him remaining on the reservation and helping the military during the Civil War until his death in 1861. Another story pictures him dying of smallpox in 1859. Bowlegs will be remembered for his heroic efforts in leading the battles with his people while trying to prevent the loss of their homelands. He caused years of frustration for the government in Washington and in Florida.

SOURCES:

Coe, Charles H., *Red Patriots: The Story of the Seminoles,* University Press of Florida, 1974

Covington, James W., *The Billy Bowlegs War,* Mickler House Publishers, 1981.

Covington, James W., *The Seminoles of Florida,* University Press of Florida, 1993.

Gifford, John C., *Billy Bowlegs and the Seminole War,* Triangle Company, 1925.

Mahon, John K., *History of the Second Seminole War* 1835-1842, revised edition, University of Florida Press, 1967.

Swanton, John R., *The Indians of the Southeastern United States,* United States Government Printing Office, 1946.

—Sketch by Russell Hellstern

Beth Brant
1941-
Mohawk writer and poet
Also known as Degonwadonti

Beth Brant explores her Native American heritage, as well as her love of family and interest in female relationships in her short stories, poetry, and critical essays, which have been published extensively in periodicals, anthologies, and other collections. She is the author of two books, *Mohawk Trail* and *Food & Spirits: Stories,* and the editor of a collection of writing and art entitled *A Gathering of Spirit: A Collection by North American Women.* And these writings have earned Brant numerous awards, including grants from the Michigan Council for the Arts, the Ontario Arts Council, and the National Endowment for the Arts. A full-time writer and the mother of three daughters, grandmother of four grandsons, and foster parent, Brant resides in Melvindale, Michigan, with her partner, Denise Dorsz.

Brant was born on May 6, 1941, in Detroit, Michigan. The daughter of a Native father and Irish/Scots mother—and the descendant of tribal leaders Molly Brant and Joseph Brant—she is a Bay of Quinte Mohawk from the Tyendinaga Reserve in Deseronto, Ontario. Her paternal grandparents moved to the Detroit area with the hope that their children, of which there were nine, would find more opportunities away from the reservation. Brant grew up in her grandparents' house in Detroit along with her parents, Joseph and Hazel Brant, brother, and sister. Her father worked first in an automobile factory and, later, as a teacher. Brant writes poignantly about her family and childhood experiences in many of her works.

Brant moved quickly from childhood into adulthood when she dropped out of high school and married at 17; she had three daughters from this marriage: Kim, Jennifer, and Jill. And when the marriage ended in divorce, Brant worked as a waitress, salesclerk, cleaning woman, and at other unskilled jobs in order to support herself and her children.

Inspirational Eagle Instigates Writing Career

It wasn't until 1981, when Brant was 40 years old, that she began her life as a writer. She traces the origins of this decision to a motor trip through the Mohawk Valley when, as described in the Afterword to *Mohawk Trail,* "a Bald Eagle flew in front of her car, sat in a tree, and instructed her to write." She has been writing steadily since this time, displaying a style that ranges from humorously light-hearted—particularly in her recollections of her family—to angry, intense, and spiritual. Her first book-length publication was *Mohawk Trail* (1985), a miscellany of poems and stories, both fictional and autobiographical. In it, Brant establishes several of the dominant themes that appear throughout her work, such as her love of her family and of the Mohawk people; her interest in women's relationships, both sexual and platonic; and her depiction of the suffering and alienation experienced by those outside the mainstream of the dominant culture.

Brant gained national recognition with her next publication, *A Gathering of Spirit: A Collection by North American Women,* published in 1988. Originally appearing as a special issue of the periodical *Sinister Wisdom* in 1993 before being published in book form, it was the first anthology of contemporary Indian women's art and literature. Striving to present a representative compilation, Brant not only solicited entries from established writers, but also advertised for contributions in tribal newspapers and in women's prisons; the work of Native lesbians is featured as well. Ground-breaking in conception and scope, the work has enjoyed four printings and remains an important collection.

In 1991, Brant published *Food & Spirits,* a collection of stories preceded by a long poem that celebrates the healing power of words, another thematic strand in her works. Once again, her protagonists are on the margins of society: all are Native and most are women, although a young child, an elderly man, and a man dying of AIDS are featured as well.

In addition to these book-length works, Brant's creative and critical writings have been published extensively in numerous anthologies and periodicals, particularly those with Native and/or feminist perspectives. In addition, one of her short stories, "Turtle Gal," has been adapted for radio and was aired by the Canadian Broadcasting Corporation (CBC) in 1990. Despite these achievements, being a writer has not come easily to Brant. She observed in *New Voices from the Longhouse* that "economic realities, Indian invisibility, the lack of 'formal, Euroamerican education' have taken their toll." And yet she acknowledges that these same struggles have shaped her artistry: "These things have made me the kind of writer I am. I like to think I am continuing the long journey of being a storyteller that my people first began. And I want to tell the stories that nobody wants to hear—stories of working-class lives, gay lives, Indian lives—stories that refuse to fit an image of romance or sentimentality."

Encourages Other Writers

Teaching and mentoring have also played a significant role in Brant's life. She was a lecturer at the University of British Columbia in 1989 and 1990, has been a guest lecturer in women's studies and native studies at the New College of the University of Toronto, and was a writer-in-residence at the Kanhiote Library on the Tyendinaga Mohawk Reserve in Canada in 1993. She has also lectured and given readings at universities and cultural centers throughout North America.

In addition to teaching, Brant has participated in a number of creative writing workshops, such as the Women of Color Writing Workshop held in Vancouver in 1991, the 1991 Michigan Festival of Writers in East Lansing, the International Feminist Book Fair held in Amsterdam in 1992, and the Flight of the Mind Writing Workshop in Eugene, Oregon in 1992. These experiences have led Brant to form creative writing workshops for groups of Indian women, women in prison, and high school students. Always seeking ways to help others express themselves, Brant has participated in a project called Returning the Gift, which was designed to create new opportunities for Native writers to share their work. The project included a 1992 meeting of 250 writers in Norman, Oklahoma, various outreach programs, and the formation of an organization known as the Native Writer's Circle of the Americas.

Brant is involved with a number of other projects as well. She co-founded Turtle Grandmother, a clearinghouse for manuscripts, both published and unpublished, by Native American women and a source of information about Native women. She is also an AIDS activist, working for People with AIDS (PWA) and giving AIDS education workshops throughout the Indian community.

SELECTED WRITINGS BY BRANT:

Mohawk Trail, Ithaca, Firebrand Books, 1985.

(Editor) *A Gathering of Spirit: A Collection by North American Women,* Ithaca, Firebrand Books, 1988.

Food & Spirits: Stories, Ithaca, Firebrand Books, 1991.

"Giveaway: Native Lesbian Writers," *Signs: Journal of Women in Culture and Society,* 18, summer 1993; 944-947.

"Grandmothers of a New World," *Women of Power,* 16, spring 1990; 40-47.

Writing As Witness, Toronto, Women's Press, 1995.

SOURCES:

Books

All My Relations: An Anthology of Contemporary Canadian Native Fiction, edited by Thomas King, Norman, University of Oklahoma Press, 1992.

Bruchac, Carol, Linda Hogan, and Judith McDaniel, *The Stories We Hold Secret: Tales of Women's Spiritual Development,* New York, Greenfield Review Press, 1986.

Dykewords: An Anthology of Lesbian Writing, edited by the Lesbian Writing and Publishing Collective, Toronto, Women's Press, 1990.

Living the Spirit: A Gay American Indian Anthology, edited by Will Roscoe, New York, St. Martin's Press, 1988.

Native American Women, edited by Gretchen M. Bataille, New York, Garland Publishing, 1993; 34-36.

Native North American Almanac, edited by Duane Champagne, Detroit, Gale Research, 1994; 760, 1019.

New Voices from the Longhouse: An Anthology of Contemporary Iroquois Writing, edited by Joseph Bruchac, New York, Greenfield Review Press, 1989.

Petrone, Penny, *Native Literature in Canada: From the Oral Tradition to the Present,* Toronto, Oxford University Press, 1990.

Songs from This Earth on Turtle's Back: Contemporary American Indian Poetry, edited by Joseph Bruchac, New York, Greenfield Review Press, 1983.

Talking Leaves: Contemporary Native American Short Stories, edited by Craig Lesley, New York, Dell, 1991.

Women's Studies Encyclopedia, Volume 2, edited by Helen Tierney, New York, Greenwood Press, 1990; 221.

Periodicals

Bataille, Gretchen M., review of *Food & Spirits: Stories, Choice,* December 1991; 589.

"Bearing Witness/Sobreviviendo: An Anthology of Native American/Latina Art and Literature," edited by Jo Cochran and others, *Calyx: A Journal of Art and Literature by Women* (special issue), 8, 1984; 101-104.

Blicksilver, E., review of *Mohawk Trail, Choice,* October 1985; 289.

Kuda, Marie, review of *Food & Spirits: Stories, Booklist,* May 15, 1991; 1779.

LaFromboise, Teresa, and Elizabeth Anne Parent, review of *A Gathering of Spirit: Writing and Art by North American Indian Women, Signs: Journal of Women in Culture and Society,* 10, summer 1985; 782-785.

Review of *Food & Spirits: Stories, Publisher's Weekly,* April 26, 1991; 55.

—Sketch by Linda Cullum

Joseph Brant
1742-1807
Mohawk tribal leader
Also known as Thayendanégea ["He Places Two Bets"]

Joseph Brant was a Mohawk chief and officer of the British army who led Indian troops into battle during the Revolutionary war. He was born in 1742 in the forest along the upper Ohio River, while his parents were on a hunting trip. His father, Tehowaghwengaraghkwin, was a Mohawk Wolf clan chief. His mother was either a full- or half-blood Indian. After his father's death, his mother married Nichaus Brant, an established and respected Mohawk Indian whose family had used the English surname for several generations. Brant's family connection with Sir William Johnson, British Superintendent of Indian Affairs in the colony of New York, gave him the ability to move with ease back and forth between the world of a British gentleman and the fields and councils of Indian tribal life while retaining his credibility to both groups. During and after the Revolutionary War he negotiated in both Canada and the United States for land rights for his native people.

Transitions from Indian to White Society

Brant spent his childhood in the clan's long-established residence at Canajoharie near the Ohio River. This provided the young man with access to both white and Indian cultures: the Indians in the town had been in contact with white settlers, yet life to the west along the Ohio River was still wild. It offered Brant freedom to learn hunting, fishing, swimming, trapping, and canoeing, in preparation for his role as an adult hunter-warrior. When his half-sister Molly married Johnson, described by Dale Van Every in *A Company of Heroes* as having "long been regarded by the Iroquois as the greatest living white man," the English trader and ambassador took

Joseph Brant

an interest his young brother-in-law. At the age of 12 Brant was summoned to live with them at Fort Johnson in the Mohawk River valley of upstate New York.

Brant adjusted from the wilderness of the Ohio frontier to the complexities of the white man's world with ease. At the age of 13 Brant served with Johnson at the Battle of Lake George during the French War. At age 17, he was among Johnson's troops during the Niagara campaign of 1759. Two years later Johnson sent Brant to Eleazar Wheelock's Indian Charity School in Lebanon, Connecticut, the forerunner of Dartmouth College. Again, Brant had no trouble adjusting to his new environment. While at Wheelock's school Brant became a Christian convert and spent time translating parts of the Bible into Mohawk. In *Great Indian Chiefs,* Albert Britt mentions that Brant was much praised for this work: "He assisted the Rev. Mr. Stewart in the revision of the *Indian Prayer Book and Psaltery.* He also wrote a *History of the Bible,* an *Indian Catechism,* a *Liturgy,* and a *Primer,* presenting copies of the last two to the library of Harvard University."

Recognized as a Leader among Both Indians and Whites

Brant left school in 1763 at age 21, when Molly sent word to Wheelock's school that he should return to Fort Johnson. Rumors of war were thick in the air; Pontiac, an Ottawa chief, was organizing bands to attack the British presence in the Great Lakes area. Brant led a company of Mohawk and Oneida volunteers, together with troops organized by Johnson and led by Andrew Montour, against Pontiac's followers. After the war, Brant did not return to school;

instead, he became an advocate in the land difficulties faced by his people. Van Every states "[h]is position as an official Indian Service interpreter, his access to Johnson's attention, and his firsthand acquaintance with he way white men spoke and thought added to the effectiveness of his efforts."

Sir William Johnson died in 1774 and his nephew was appointed as replacement. Brant served the new Superintendent of Indian Affairs as secretary. Shortly thereafter he was commissioned a British colonel and led forces in raids meant to devastate the materials and food supplies to the American troops. Composed of members of the fragmented Iroquois League, British soldiers and Tory compatriots, Brant's company fought at Cherry Valley, Minisink and the Battle of Oriskany, among others. At the end of the war he was rewarded with a land grant at Anaquaqua, along the Grand River in Ontario. He retired a British officer on half pay. Many Mohawk and other Indians from the Iroquois League followed him to Anaquaqua. The area eventually became the Six Nations Reserve.

Brant had three wives and nine children during his lifetime. He married his first wife, Christine, at age 22. She was the daughter of an Oneida chief. They had two children, Issac and Christiana. Eight years later Christine died and Brant married her sister. Within a few years she also died, leaving him no children. His third wife, a half-blood Indian, Catherine Croghan, bore him seven children and remained a faithful helpmate until his death on November 24, 1807 at Grand River. He was buried near the church he built, the first Episcopal Church in Upper Canada, located at Brantford, Ontario.

SOURCES:

Britt, Albert, *Great Indian Chiefs,* Books for Libraries Press, 1938; 67-94.

Kelsay, Isabel Thompson, *Joseph Brant, 1743-1807: Man of Two Worlds,* Syracuse University Press, 1984.

Van Every, Dale, *A Company of Heroes: The American Frontier, 1775-1783,* William Morrow and Company, 1962; 26-43, 85-104, 150-168.

Native North American Almanac, edited by Duane Champagne, Detroit, Gale Research, 1994; 107.

Dockstader, Frederick J., *Great North American Indians,* New York, Van Nostrand Reinhold, 1977; 44-45.

—Sketch by Lisa A. Wroble

Molly Brant
1736-1796
Mohawk tribal leader
Also known as Degonwadonti or Gonwatsijsiaienni

Molly Brant is considered the most influential Mohawk woman in the New World from 1759 to 1776. She and

Catherine Brant (her younger brother's wife) are the only women of the period on whose lives any extended documentation has survived. Brant was born in 1736 to "Margaret" and "Peter," Canajoharie Mohawks registered as Protestant Christians in the Anglican chapel at Fort Hunter. Some reports do not list the names of her parents, but simply say she was the daughter of a sachem (chieftain), and came from Canajoharie, a Mohawk (Iroquois) village located in New York. Molly is said to have received her surname from her stepfather, Nickus Brant, a European thought to be part Dutch. He was a close friend of William Johnson, a British official responsible for maintaining Indian relations in the colonies during the time of the American Revolution. Brant is believed to have been a strong European influence on Brant and her younger brother Joseph. Active and gregarious, she is said to have become the object of Johnson's attention when in 1753, she accepted a British officer's challenge to participate in a horse riding competition between the British and the Mohawks. She later married Johnson in a Mohawk ceremony.

Acculturation, Iroquois Women, and Cultural Difference

A time of great upheaval and cultural change took place among all the Iroquois tribes during the eighteenth century, most markedly during the later half of the century, when colonials sought independence. Perhaps the Mohawks stood out as more notable recipients of cultural change because they were known for their aggressive resistance to European occupation. With the loss of their land along the Mohawk river in eastern-central New York, there was immense pressure on the Mohawk to culturally assimilate in order to survive. European culture was most visibly different with regard to relationships between the sexes, and this succinctly cut at the basic fabric and structure of Iroquois life. For this reason, Molly Brant's life with Johnson, a powerful British official presiding over the British Indian Department's northern district, became a living illustration of acculturation. In her *Ontario History* article "Molly Brant, Catherine Brant, and Their Daughters: A Study in Colonial Acculturation," Gretchen Green terms Molly and Catherine's "individual marital conflicts" as reflections of "the larger cultural struggle, so that Molly and Catherine Brant serve as microcosms of the Mohawk people during the trying times of the late eighteenth century."

Before the advent of the Europeans, the Mohawk were a matrilineal society, deriving the identity of their kinship ties through women. Relationships between the sexes were marked by a more equal distribution of power and validation for contributions made to the needs of the community. Primarily through their agricultural achievements and role as provider, Mohawk women were able to exert a greater degree of influence upon men's decisions than their European counterparts, and thus assertion of male dominance was met with resistance by Mohawk women. By withholding food, making their opinions known at village meetings, and utilizing their appointed clan positions in choosing the village chief/sachem, women banded together to get their agendas met in a way wholly unfamiliar to women in European culture.

Because British law did not recognize the Mohawk marriage of Johnson and Brant, she is said to have been the "common-law" wife of Johnson. She is considered by some sources to have been his mistress. Having married during the Seven Years War, Green states that Johnson is thought to have married Brant out of a desire to gain stronger and more influential political connections. Their marriage took place "when Johnson was desperately seeking Iroquois support for the war effort against the French." He learned the Iraquoian dialects, adopted several Mohawk customs, but reportedly did not choose to live among Natives. Explaining his close relationship to Joseph Brant, Johnson said, according to Green, that he "expected the young Mohawk would prove useful among the Indians because of his 'connection and residence.' It seems reasonable to assume that his relationship with Joseph's sister was in part similarly motivated, for it was said of Molly that 'one word from her [was] more taken Notice of by the Five Nations than a thousand from any white man without exception.'"

Influenced the American Revolution

Brant had been well known and was politically active in her village before joining Johnson at either Fort Johnson or at Johnson Hall, his residence located near Schenectady, "on the edge of Mohawk territory." From 1754 to 1755, she is recorded as having accompanied to Philadelphia a delegate of elders to address Iroquois land conflicts. Other than these highlighted features, relatively little is known about her life in the village during her early years. Her correspondence, written in a clear and legible script, indicates that she may have attended the English school at Canajoharie as a child.

Unlike her predecessor Catherine Weissenberg who bore three children by Johnson, Brant's eight (some sources say nine) children received Johnson's surname. It is unknown whether any of the children were christened. Weissenberg, a German indentured servant, was Johnson's housekeeper at Fort Johnson. Whereas Johnson regarded Weissenberg beneath him in status, and her role in his household was kept to a minimum, it is noted that Molly Brant accepted no such strictures upon her role. She refused to do housework, leaving such chores to the servants and slaves, and in Johnson's absence, she is said to have controlled the affairs of the estate. There is some suggestion that in doing so, she also supervised the daily operations of the Indian Department, of which Johnson was superintendent.

Johnson Hall was elegant and considered plush by frontier standards. Brant was highly admired among Johnson's peers as a model hostess. She was mentioned warmly in correspondence and was as generous with her own people living in the village as she was with European guests. Using Johnson's position and line of credit with merchants, records indicate she made large purchases of blankets, clothing and alcohol, which she gave away to various Iroquois people. Traditional Iroquois custom entailed utilizing economic gain for the good of the community by distributing wealth during a ceremonial giveaway. The more one gave away, the more one rose in honor and prestige within the group. Brant participated in this practice with such purchases, in addition to distributing cash and providing meals. By so doing she gained increasing influence and thus became, in Green's words, "the most influential Mohawk woman in the valley."

After Johnson's death in 1774, Brant was turned away from his estate and she returned to Canajoharie, taking expensive clothing and luxury possessions with her. There she lived primarily on credit, engaging in commerce with the villagers. Because conflicts were rising between the Loyalists and Patriot colonials, Brant's influence among Indians was increasingly instrumental to the British. Both sides attempted to rally the support of the Six Nations, and Patriots regarded Brant as a threat to their interests. She, unlike most Mohawk, felt strongly that the interests of her people would be best served by an alliance with the Crown. Despite her tremendous popularity and respect among her people, she was unable to sway significant numbers toward action, for most preferred not to take sides in the British-American conflict.

Brant herself took an active Loyalist stance, housing Loyalist refugees, providing weapons, and infiltrating intelligence activities where possible. During 1777 she reportedly engaged in spy activities, which were instrumental in in the British gaining military ground. As a result, American colonials and Oneida Iroquois Patriots exacted revenge by driving her from her home. Angered, she fled in exile into Canada, where she fiercely resumed Loyalist activities as a liaison among the Iroquois while residing at the Niagara garrison.

She was considered controversial because she advocated for both the British as well as for the Iroquois, even when to outward appearances, the interests of these groups were in opposition. Brant spoke only her native tongue, styled her wardrobe after Mohawk tastes, and encouraged her offspring to do the same. She was an active dissident, remaining loyal to the preservation of her people, yet, she was criticized for involving them in a dispute that wrested their lands from them and left them subjugated and dispossessed. Molly Brant could not have known the outcome of the wars she attempted to influence. It may be only hindsight that her actions were considered contradictory, for she was behaving in accordance with the laws of her people, attempting to maintain progressive negotiations and an alliance with those she percieved as the greatest allies to the Iroquois.

The British supported her Loyalist endeavors, giving her provisions and doing what was necessary to foster her activism. As a political instrument among the Iroquois, she was unequaled. After the American Revolution, the British generously provided her with a pension, land in the area of her choosing, and an English home for her service to the Crown. In addition to this she received a substantial inheritance from Johnson's estate. Retiring from political affairs, Brant finally settled in Kingston, Ontario, near three of her daughters. She died in 1796 of unknown causes.

SOURCES:

Books

Native American Women, edited by Gretchen M. Bataille, New York, Garland Publishing, 1993; 36-37.
Native North American Almanac, edited by Duane Champagne, Detroit, Gale Research, 1994; 1020.
Waldman, Carl, *Who Was Who in Native American History,* New York, Facts on File, 1990; 43.

Periodicals

Green, Gretchen, "Molly Brant, Catherine Brant, and Their Daughters: A Study in Colonial Acculturation," *Ontario History,* 81, 1989; 235-250.
Gundy, H. Pearson, "Molly Brant—Loyalist," *Ontario History,* 14, 1953; 97-108.

—Sketch by Brett A. Lealand

Brave Bird, Mary
See Crow Dog, Mary

Louis R. Bruce, Jr.
1906-1989
Oglala Sioux/Mohawk government official

Louis R. Bruce, Jr., a businessman and administrator, worked for his entire life to help Indian people. He served as commissioner of Indian Affairs in 1969, and he worked to "Indianize" the Bureau of Indian Affairs (BIA). Bruce was born on December 30, 1906, on the Oglala Sioux reservation at Pine Ridge, South Dakota, to Louis Bruce, a Mohawk from St. Regis, New York, and Nellie L. Rooks, an Oglala Sioux. Bruce's grandfather, John Bruce, was a Mohawk chief and boat expert known for aiding British troops in a failed attempt to rescue General Charles Gordon in 1884 by crossing the Nile River rapids in the Sudan. Bruce's father studied dentistry at the University of Pennsylvania, where he paid his tuition by playing professional baseball (he led the Toronto International and Philadelphia American League in pitching and hitting); after working as a dentist, he followed a spiritual urge to enter the ministry and earned a place as pastor on the Onondaga Reservation and the St. Regis Reservation.

Bruce grew up on the Onondaga Reservation near Syracuse, New York. His father enrolled him in the Cazenovia Seminary at the age of 17. He was guided by his father's stern, religious convictions, advocacy of temperance, and ethics of self-achievement, but did not feel comfortable as the only Native American at the seminary. His self-consciousness was compounded because he had to work his way through high school (and later college at Syracuse University). He worked as a farmhand, construction worker, paper mill worker, clothing salesman, and waiter to his pay his tuition. To offset his discomfort with being the one Indian in a world of whites, he excelled at sports, earning a place as captain of many teams in high school and later as the star pole-vaulter at Syracuse. Still Bruce felt inferior and out of place, so he majored in psychology to better understand these feelings. He graduated from Syracuse in 1930, married former Cazenovia classmate Anna Wikoff, and took a job in a clothing store, rising quickly to department manager.

Enters Politics to Help his People

Mindful of his heritage, Bruce used his experience selling clothes to promote programs for his people. During the Great Depression, inspired by New Deal programs that put 85,000 Indians to work on reservations, Bruce conceived a program to send Indian boys to summer camps throughout New England to teach Indian lore and crafts. Bruce's plan created jobs for over 600 Indian boys and brought him to the attention of the state government. In 1935, he was appointed to a position as director for New York state of Indians for the National Youth Administration of the Works Progress Administration. Bruce was proud of running his administration with all Indian employees from supervisors to secretaries. He maintained work projects on all reservations under his jurisdiction, established committees to promote goodwill with neighboring white communities, and engineered the construction of community centers on the reservations by solely Indian labor groups. Director until 1941, Bruce attended the North American Indian Conference at the University of Toronto in 1939, and he established a section for Indian welfare in the New York State Welfare Conference.

Though he returned to politics in 1945 to represent his people at a seminar sponsored by the Carnegie Endowment for International Peace, he worked during the 1940s on two dairy farms (totalling 762 acres) that he inherited from his father-in-law. Politics found him in farming as well. He served as president of the district's chapter of the New York Youth Council program in 1943 and was active in many other local programs, mostly focusing on young people in 4-H, Boy Scouts, and his local Methodist church. He improved farm conditions as director of the Farm Bureau of Soil Conservation District, the Dairyman's League, and the Onondaga County Rural Policy Committee. And he continually found himself in charge, many times as president of an organization, such as the Six Nations Association.

Works with and for Young Indians

Bruce spent much of his life fostering a greater interest in Indian culture and traditions in young Indian people, so much so that then-Governor Dewey appointed him to the board of the Thomas Indian School. In 1949, Bruce's article "What America Means To Me" won him a Freedom Foundations Award. His interest in youth led him to create the

Louis R. Bruce, Jr.

first National American Indian Youth Conference in Washington, D.C., in 1957. He followed this by founding the National Congress of American Indians and serving as chairman of the President's Advisory Committee on American Indian Affairs. He also worked as an advertising executive, a public relations director, and as a special assistant commissioner for the Federal Housing Administration.

Serves as Commissioner of the Bureau of Indian Affairs

Capping a life of great achievements and an illustrious career of improving life for Native Americans, Bruce was appointed as commissioner of the Bureau of Indian Affairs (BIA) in 1969. Of the 33 men to hold the post before Bruce, he was the only third Indian to serve as commissioner since its inception in 1849. Despite Bruce's intentions, according to Robert C. Day in his essay "The Emergence of Indian Activism," Bruce's appointment to the post angered and drew "a vigorous, negative response" from the National Congress of American Indians [NCAI] and other groups who felt Bruce was "an Uncle Tomahawk (i.e., affluent, urbane, a New York City dweller with no recent activism record.)"

Bruce fought this characterization by the NCAI. Soon after his appointment he denigrated the termination policies of the BIA and the Department of the Interior and its "lack of consideration of Indian views during the 1950s" according to Day's essay. Bruce continually disagreed with BIA and Department of Interior policies, and he worked to turn the BIA from a management agency to a service agency. He followed the same pattern he had on the Onondaga reservation and filled as many posts as he could with Indians. Upon receiving an Indian Council Fire Achievement Award, Bruce said, "The way to Indian progress is involvement.... I want to see Indians buying cars from Indians on reservations, buying food from Indian stores, driving on Indian-planned and Indian-built roads, talking on Indian-owned telephone systems, and living in an Indian-managed economy."

The events of 1972 ended Bruce's tenure with the BIA when he and many other officials were dismissed from their posts. Struggles between the BIA and Indians had been going on ever since the BIA's beginning. In 1970, Bruce flew to Denver to quell an occupation of a BIA office there. Though he signed agreements with the protestors, after he left many were arrested and felt betrayed which led to more American Indian Movement (AIM) occupations of BIA offices across the country. In 1972, the "Trail of Broken Treaties" caravan came to Washington, D.C., and occupied the BIA national headquarters. Though the occupation lasted only six days, it deeply divided the Indian rights movement, and precipitated the firing of Bruce, John Crow, and other BIA officials. Louis R. Bruce, Jr., died in 1989. He and his wife Anna had two children Charles and Katherine.

SOURCES:

Books

Biographical Dictionary of the Indians of the Americas, second edition, Newport Beach, California, American Indian Publishers, 1991.

Handbook of the North American Indians, edited by William C. Sturtevant, Washington, D.C., Smithsonian Institute, 1983.

Indians of Today, edited by Marion Gridley, Chicago, Millar Publishing, 1947.

Insight Guides: Native America, edited by John Gattuso, Boston, Houghton Mifflin Company, 1993.

Native North American Almanac, edited by Duane Champagne, Detroit, Gale Research, 1994.

The Native Americans: An Illustrated History, edited by Betty and Ian Ballantine, Atlanta, Turner Publishing, 1993.

Native Americans Today: Sociological Perspectives, edited by Howard M. Bahr, Bruce A. Chadwick, and Robert C. Day, New York, Harper, 1972.

—Sketch by Christopher B. Tower

Joseph Bruchac III
1942-
Abenaki author, poet, and storyteller

Joseph Bruchac is an author and poet whose work emphasizes the spiritual balance and environmental concerns of

Joseph Bruchac III

his Native American heritage. His stories and poems, many of which emerge from the oral traditions passed on to him through his Abenaki elders, some of whom were relatives, have appeared in over 400 anthologies and magazines and have also been translated into several languages. Bruchac has received several awards for his writing, including a PEN Syndicated Fiction Award, a Rockefeller Foundation fellowship, and a series of National Endowment for the Arts grants that enabled him to start a publication devoted exclusively to the development of prison writers and to fund a highly acclaimed multicultural literary magazine. In addition to producing an extensive body of fictional and nonfictional work—ranging from novels and children's stories to essays on Native American culture—Bruchac has gained considerable fame as a storyteller, providing authentic interpretations of traditional Native American narratives.

The son of Joseph E. Bruchac II, a taxidermist of European descent, and Flora (Bowman) Bruchac, Joseph Bruchac III was born on October 16, 1942, in Saratoga Springs, New York. He was reared, however, by his maternal grandparents in the foothills of the Adirondack Mountains, which led him to the tribal lore and mystic songs of tribal elders who taught him to appreciate the Native American culture of the region. After completing his secondary education, Bruchac enrolled in Cornell University where he studied English, receiving his Bachelor of Arts in 1965. A year before receiving his degree, he married Carol Worthen, who shared his interest in literature and who would provide constant support to his writing and publishing efforts in the years to come. Pursuing a career as an educator, Bruchac began a program of graduate study at Syracuse University, where he was awarded his Master of Arts in 1966.

For the next three years, Bruchac taught English and literature at Keta Secondary School in Ghana, West Africa, gaining valuable experience as an educator as well as a new perspective toward the country of his birth. As he stated in the *Albany Times Union,* "I went to Africa to teach—but more than that to be taught. It showed me many things. How much we have as Americans and take for granted. How much our eyes refuse to see because they are blinded to everything in a man's face except his color. And most importantly, how human people are everywhere—which may be the one grace that can save us all." Drawing from his overseas experience, Bruchac returned to the United States to serve as an instructor in African and black literatures and creative writing at Skidmore College in Saratoga Springs. While teaching, he continued his graduate education at State University of New York at Albany before completing his Ph.D. at Union Graduate School in 1975.

Establishes Prison Creative Writing Workshops

While at Skidmore College, Bruchac also began teaching creative writing in prisons throughout the country, establishing writing workshops—often at his own expense—that provided market and manuscript information as well as artistic encouragement to numerous men and women serving time. As Nick Di Spoldo, a former prisoner who became a successful creative writer under Bruchac's tutelage, states in a contribution to *America* magazine, "[Bruchac] has given fresh motivation to countless men and women, developing and nurturing tender talents and fragile egos." For his efforts in educating prison writers, Bruchac was awarded a prestigious National Endowment for the Arts grant in 1975 that enabled him to expand his programs through the publication and distribution of *Prison Project Newsletter,* a periodical that served as a forum for thousands of aspiring prison writers and workshop instructors throughout the nation.

Founds the Greenfield Review Press

Bruchac's career as a publisher, however, has not been limited to his work with prison writing. In 1970 he founded the Greenfield Review Press, which published the critically acclaimed *Greenfield Review,* an eclectic literary magazine devoted to multicultural publishing. While providing a forum for poetry and short fiction from a variety of cultures, the magazine also featured interviews with important Native American writers such as Louise Erdrich. With his wife, Carol, serving as the managing editor, the Bruchacs were able to sustain the publication of the magazine for 17 years, through their own funds and grants from such institutions as the National Endowment for the Arts and the New York State Council on the Arts.

While Bruchac has done a great deal to encourage and develop the writing of others, he is best known for his own creative and critical publications. The author of over 20 books, including poetry anthologies, short story collections,

and novels, he has written for academics and children alike. Entering the literary world primarily as a poet, Bruchac has published numerous anthologies, including *Entering Onondaga* (1978), perhaps his most widely known collection of poetry, which deals with nature, spirit beings, and Caucasian/Native American conflicts. He has also contributed poems to over 400 periodicals, such as *New Letters, Paris Review, Hudson Review,* and *American Poetry Review,* and critical articles on various aspects of Native American culture to *National Geographic, Parabola,* and many other magazines. Bruchac has received numerous awards and grants for his poetry, including the New York State Arts and Vermont Arts Council grants in 1972 and a National Endowment for the Arts poetry fellowship in 1974.

Widely respected for his poetry, Bruchac has also received considerable acclaim for his later work in short fiction. Although long regarded for his authentic translations of Native American tales, Bruchac did not publish a collection of original stories until 1992, when *Turtle Meat and Other Stories* appeared on the young adult fiction market. The volume contains such previously awarded short stories as "Going Home," which received the 1983 PEN Syndicated Fiction Award and "Code Talkers," the winner of the 1986 Cherokee Nation Prose Award. Emerging from the Native American culture of the Adirondack wilderness, these stories present both a mythic and modern account of the Native American experience. "The Ice-Hearts," for example, recounts a battle between Native Americans and the villainous Ice-Hearts, who are later revealed to be European invaders in the guise of shiny armor. "Code Talkers," a story set in World War II, features two Native Americans from different tribes who are recruited to smuggle information past the Germans by speaking "Native American." Unable to understand each other's native tongue, the two communicate by speaking German so poorly that no one else, including the Germans, can understand them. Such a story, as Bruchac told Mary Ann Grossmann of the *St. Paul Pioneer Press,* illustrates that Native American humor is derived from knowledge, "a combination of knowing the other and knowing yourself ... it makes you laugh and think, and that's an effective way of teaching a moral lesson."

Publishes Native American Tales for Children

Bruchac's attempts to transmit the values of his Abenaki heritage have been most successful in his best-selling series of children's books, co-authored by Michael J. Caduto, an internationally known author and ecologist. Both *Keepers of the Earth* (1988) and *Keepers of the Animals* (1991) illustrate lessons of natural history and environmental science through an authentic Native American tale selected and translated by Bruchac. These books reflect the environmental concerns of Bruchac's Native American heritage, suggesting that, as he related to Grossmann, "There is a deep respect for the natural world among Native Americans, an understanding [that] we are part of creation, not above it." Popular with educators, museums, and nature centers, the *Keepers* series has over 500,000 books and tapes in print and was honored with the 1990 Art and Literary Award from the New York State Outdoor Education Association and an Association of Children's Booksellers 1992 Choice Award.

Bruchac explored similar themes from his Native American heritage in his first novel, _Dawn Land,_ published in 1993. Set 10,000 years ago in what is now New England, the novel for young adults reflects the influence of the oral traditions of the Abenaki and other Northeastern tribes, presenting the story of an ancient Native American people whose peaceful existence with each other and nature is interrupted by a mysterious dark force threatening to destroy the world. Young Hunter, Bruchac's mythic hero, is sent on a quest to save his tribe and uphold the value system of these pre-contact native people, a system built on maintaining balance and harmony with nature. Written in what Judy Sokoll has observed in the _School Library Journal_ to be a "rich, precise, gentle, yet powerful descriptive style," _Dawn Land_ enjoyed strong reviews from numerous critics.

In addition to receiving critical and popular acclaim for his various writing accomplishments, Bruchac is widely known for his skills as a professional storyteller, keeping alive the oral traditions of his Abenaki ancestors by passing on many of the tales and legends he first heard in his youth as well as stories from other cultures to thousands of people across the country. "Storytelling," as Bruchac stated in a Fulcrum Publishing press release, "is one of the most basic human activities. It keeps us humane and connects us with past generations." Not only has he passed the tradition on to his two sons, James and Jesse, but he has encouraged people of all cultures to participate in the oral traditions characteristic of his heritage.

SELECTED WRITINGS BY BRUCHAC:

Indian Mountain and Other Poems, Ithaca House, 1971.
The Buffalo in the Syracuse Zoo, Greenfield Review Press, 1972.
The Poetry of Pop, Dustbooks, 1973.
Flow, Cold Mountain Press, 1975.
The Road to Black Mountain, Thorp Springs Press, 1976.
Turkey Brother and Other Iroquois Folk Tales, Crossing Press, 1976.
The Dreams of Jesse Brown, Cold Mountain Press, 1977.
This Earth is a Drum, Cold Mountain Press, 1977.
Entering Onondaga, Cold Mountain Press, 1978.
Stone Giants and Flying Heads: More Iroquois Folk Tales, Crossing Press, 1978.
There Are No Trees inside the Prison, Blackberry Press, 1978.
Ancestry, Great Raven, 1980.
Translator's Son, Cross-Cultural Communications, 1981.
Remembering the Dawn, Blue Cloud, 1983.
Breaking Silence, Greenfield Review Press, 1984.
The Light from Another Country, Greenfield Review Press, 1984.
Iroquois Stories: Heroes and Heroines, Monsters and Magic, Crossing Press, 1985.

The Wind Eagle, Bowman Books, 1985.
Survival This Way: Interviews with American Indian Poets, University of Arizona Press, 1987.
(With Michael J. Caduto) _Keepers of the Earth,_ Fulcrum, 1988.
The Faithful Hunter, Bowman Books, 1988.
Return of the Sun, Crossing Press, 1989.
(With Michael J. Caduto) _Keepers of the Animals,_ Fulcrum, 1991.
(With Michael J. Caduto) _Native American Stories,_ Fulcrum, 1991.
Hoop Snakes, Hide-Behinds and Side-Hill Winders, Crossing Press, 1991.
With Jonathan London, _Thirteen Moons on Turtle's Backs_ (children's book), illustrated by Thomas Locker, Philomel, 1992.
Turtle Meat and Other Stories, Holy Cow! Press, 1992.
(With Michael J. Caduto) _Native American Animal Stories,_ Fulcrum, 1992.
Dawn Land, Fulcrum, 1993.
Flying with the Eagle, Racing the Great Bear, Troll Books, 1993.
(With Michael J. Caduto) _Keepers of the Night,_ Fulcrum, 1994.
Gluskabe and the Four Wishes, Cobblehill Books, 1994.
(With Michael Caduto) _Keepers of Live_ Fulcrum 1994.
The Native American Sweat Lodge, Crossing Press, 1994.

SOURCES:

Books

Contemporary Authors, New Revision Series, Volume 13, Detroit, Gale Research, 1984; 79-80.
Native North American Almanac, edited by Duane Champagne, Detroit, Gale Research, 1994; 1021-1022.

Periodicals

Albany Times Union, June 1, 1980.
Baker, Will, "Feisty Words from Native American Poets," _San Francisco Examiner and Chronicle,_ June 25, 1989.
Bodin, Madeline, "Keeping Tradition Alive," _Publishers Weekly,_ December 14, 1993; 23.
Di Spoldo, Nick, "Writers in Prison," _America,_ January 22, 1983; 50-53.
Grossmann, Mary Ann, "American Indian Author Stresses Authenticity," _St. Paul Pioneer Press-Dispatch,_ October 22, 1989.
Review of _Entering Onondaga, Choice,_ July 1979; 662.
Sokoll, Judy, review of _Dawn Land, School Library Journal,_ August 1993; 205.

Other

"Publicity Packet," compiled by Sandy Trupp, Fulcrum Publishing, 1994.

—Sketch by Jason Gallman

Diane M. Burns
1957-
Anishinabe Ojibwa/Chemehuevi poet and artist

Diane M. Burns, a contemporary Native American poet and artist of Anishinabe (Ojibwa) and Chemehuevi descent, was nominated for the William Carlos Williams Award with her first volume of poetry, *Riding the One-Eyed Ford*. Published in 1981, this collection, which Burns both wrote and illustrated, is based on the author's disparate feelings of community and individuality. In addition to her poetry, which she has been writing since early childhood, Burns is also a frequent contributor to literary journals.

Burns was born in California in 1957 to a Chemehuevi father and an Anishinabe mother. She spent the majority of her childhood both in California and in Wisconsin, where her mother's family lived. Her mother worked for the Indian boarding school system and Burns went to several boarding schools as a youth, including the Wahpeton Indian School in Wahpeton, North Dakota, and the Sherman Indian High School (then known as the Sherman Institute) in Riverside, California. She also attended an alternative high school in Scarsdale, New York, when she was 16.

After graduating from high school, Burns attended the Institute of American Indian Arts, a junior-college level program for Native Americans in Santa Fe, New Mexico. While there, she was awarded the Congressional Medal of Merit for artistic and academic excellence. In 1977, Burns moved to New York City to complete her studies at Barnard College of Columbia University, majoring in political science; she graduated in 1978.

Although Burns claims not to remember a time when she wasn't writing—and even won a poetry prize at the age of five—she began writing professionally while at Barnard, doing both newspaper articles and book reviews. Many of her reviews during this time were written for the Council on Interracial Books for Children. Shortly after her graduation in 1978 Burns gave her first poetry reading, which, as she humorously recalls in *Survival This Way: Interviews with American Indian Poets,* came about rather haphazardly: "One day somebody called up the Indian Community House in New York and said 'Do you know any Indian Writers? We need an Indian poet to read at this poetry reading.' The only writer they could think of was me, so they gave them my number. They said they were going to give me fifty bucks for this poetry reading, so I said 'Okay, I'll write some poetry.'"

Publishes First Volume of Poetry

Burns continued to write and read poetry and, in 1981, her first volume of poetry, *Riding the One-Eyed Ford*—for which she also supplied the cover illustration and additional drawings—was published by the small literary press Contact II. Nominated for the William Carlos Williams Award and cited as one of New York's St. Mark's Poetry Project's

"Ten Best of the Year," *Riding the One-Eyed Ford* was reprinted the following year.

In this slim volume, which she describes as "a true story," Burns establishes many of the themes that permeate her poetry. One of the most prominent is her interest in feeling both a part of, and separate from, society, of experiencing an ongoing sense of both community and individuality. As Burns explained to writer Joseph Bruchac in *Survival This Way:* "As American Indians, you always have the feeling of not belonging but you also have this feeling of belonging. As a woman it gets exaggerated. Living in New York it gets more exaggerated."

Burns often expresses this conflict poetically by juxtaposing images from popular culture and urban life with those from her Native American cultural heritage. As Maureen Owen has said about Burns in *Songs from This Earth on Turtle's Back,* "She crosses cultures the way most people cross a street in New York ... against the light, into full traffic with the grace that makes your eyes water." Burns' interest in both contemporary and traditional cultures is underscored by her pervasive use of all forms of music in her poetry. Musical motifs also give her poetry much of its characteristic energy and rhythmic quality.

Since publishing *Riding the One-Eyed Ford,* Burns has remained an important poetic and artistic presence. She has participated in a radio program about Native American women writers entitled *The Key is Remembering: Poetry and Interviews by Native American Women;* has contributed book reviews and poetry to the widely-circulated multi-cultural journal *Contact/II* and has published poetry in many other journals, including the *Greenfield Review, Blue Cloud Quarterly, White Pine Journal,* and *Hard Press.* She has also given poetry readings throughout the country, an activity that is of primary importance to her. As she explained in *Survival This Way,* "I would rather read poetry in front of an audience than almost anything else. I feel the most real when I am doing that because it is really expressing myself and what I am."

Consistent with Burns' love of performance is her membership in the Poet's Overland Expeditionary Troupe (POET), a travelling group that presents poetry in theatrical settings in schools and galleries. She is also a member of the Native Writer's Circle of the Americas, a project designed to enable emerging authors to be mentored by established writers; the Feminist Writers Guild; and the Third World Writers Association. Burns continues to live in New York City, where she is a full-time writer.

SELECTED WRITINGS BY BURNS:

Riding the One-Eyed Ford, New York, Contact II Publications, 1981.

SOURCES:

Books

Bruchac, Joseph, *Survival This Way: Interviews with American Indian Poets,* Tucson, Sun Tracks and the University of Arizona Press, 1987.

Native American Women, edited by Gretchen M. Bataille, New York, Garland Publishing, 1993; 48-49.

Native North American Almanac, edited by Duane Champagne, Detroit, Gale Research, 1994; 1023.

Songs from This Earth on Turtle's Back: Contemporary American Indian Poetry, edited by Joseph Bruchac, New York, Greenfield Review Press, 1983.

That's What She Said: Contemporary Poetry and Fiction by Native American Women, edited by Rayna Green, Bloomington, Indiana University Press, 1984.

Periodicals

Contact/II (special issue on women poets), 15, fall-winter 1982-1983; 102-103, 104, 108.

Greenfield Review (special issue on Native American writers), fall 1981; 167-172.

Other

The Key Is Remembering: Poetry and Interviews by Native American Women (audiotapes), produced by Helen Thorington, New York, Art, Inc., 1982.

—Sketch by Linda Cullum

Barney Furman Bush
1945-
Shawnee/Cayuga poet and teacher

Barney Bush has published four books of poetry, and made a recording of his poems. He was awarded a grant for the National Endowment for the Arts in 1981. In addition to having served as writer-in-residence at many colleges, he is known for the readings he has given across the continent accompanied by a Comanche flute player, Ed Wapp.

Importance of Family

Bush was the firstborn of many brothers and sisters. In a memoir called "The Personal Statement of Barney Bush," which was published in *I Tell You Now,* he listed as his siblings: Fred, John, Blueberry, Bobijack, Richard, David, Lance, Joe, Bernard, Johnny, Betty, Barbara, Joy, Phil, and Edsome. He claims to have so many relatives that there are kin in this extensive and farflung family he has not yet met. His family were hunters and trappers on ancestral lands near the confluence of the Ohio and Mississippi Rivers in southern Illinois. Bush was born toward the end of August when, according to legends, "snakes were regaining their eyesight after this moon of blindness." He was later told that his first cry coincided with the shriek of a hawk hovering in the fiery sky over his house. He was raised primarily in the Shawnee culture.

Studies Art

Bush spent eight years in a one-room Southern Baptist grammar school where he was harshly punished. In between the severe beatings, a female teacher taught for four grades and he learned about art experimented with colors; the male teacher who taught him for the last four years once gave him a stone axe head—"a strange act for someone who wielded the razor strap with such fury against me," Bush wrote in "The Personal Statement."

Stripminers forced the family to move from their valley. In the small Illinois town where they resettled, Bush entered a white high school. When he was 16, Bush crossed the continent by train, raft, canoe, by walking and by hitching rides when he could. He also attended pow wows and visited visiting kin. In Santa Fe, Bush studied jewelry-making at the Institute of American Indian Arts, and taught courses in folklore. He earned his bachelor's degree in 1972 from Fort Lewis College in Durango, Colorado with a major in history and art.

After some years of involvement with American Indian Movement (AIM) causes, Bush went to Haemin, Oklahoma, to help found a Cheyenne school called the Institute of the Southern Plains. Following this, he was appointed by the University of Wisconsin in Milwaukee to teach Native American studies. In 1971, he gave his first public reading at the Southwest Poetry Conference sponsored by Navajo Community College.

In 1978, Bush began work on a master's degree in fine arts and English at the University of Idaho. Bush graduated in 1980, but was summoned home by his grandparents' illness. When they died, within a year, he considered staying in the hills to hunt and fish, do crafts, and garden with his two sons, Phil Dayne and John Colin. He has taught at Milwaukee Technical College, New Mexico Highlands University, the Institute of the Southern Plains, and has served as visitng writer for the State of North Carolina. He has published four books of poetry and has recorded his poetry for a Parisian company called NATO Records. Typically written in an unpunctuated style, his poetry often reflects upon nature and family; and he keeps the past vital by comparing the stories of his grandparents with the the sights and sounds of the present. Bush is currently at work on a collection of short fiction to be called *Running the Gauntlet.*

SELECTED WRITINGS BY BUSH:

Longhouse of the Blackberry Moon, 1975.

My Horse and a Jukebox, American Indian Studies Center, University of California, Los Angeles, 1979.

Petroglyphs, Greenfield Center, New York, Greenfield Review Press, 1982.

Inherit the Blood, New York, Thunder's Mouth Press, 1985.

"The Personal Statement of Barney Bush," in *I Tell You Now: Autobiographical Essays by Native American Writers,* edited by Brian Swann and Arnold Krupat, Lincoln, University of Nebraska Press, 1987.

SOURCES:

"The Personal Statement of Barney Bush," in *I Tell You
    Now: Autobiographical Essays by Native American
    Writers,* edited by Brian Swann and Arnold Krupat,
    Lincoln, University of Nebraska Press, 1987.

—Sketch by Ruth Rosenberg

Ben Nighthorse Campbell
1933-
Northern Cheyenne legislator, jewelry designer, and athlete

Ben Nighthorse Campbell (left)

In 1994 Senator Ben Nighthorse Campbell was the only Native American serving in the United States legislature. Before entering politics he was an athlete, educator, jewelry designer, and rancher. He was born in Auburn, California, on April 13, 1933. His mother, Mary Vierra, was a Portuguese immigrant. His father, Albert Campbell, was part Apache, Pueblo, and Northern Cheyenne. Senator Campbell and his wife, the former Linda Price, have two grown children, Colin and Shanan.

Campbell dropped out of high school after his junior year. One teacher made a written observation at the time: "Born 100 yrs.' too late!" He later obtained a GED and "graduated" with the 1991 class of Placer High School in Auburn. He obtained an undergraduate degree from San Jose State in 1957. Because of his special interest in judo he also was a student at Meiji University in Tokyo in 1960. From 1951 to 1953 he served in the U.S. Air Force, including a period as a military policeman in Korea. Campbell first moved to Colorado in 1969. He served two terms in the Colorado state legislature, from 1982 to 1986, before being elected to the U.S. Congress from 1987 to 1992.

Campbell attributes much of his success outside of the political arena to the discipline acquired as a determined judo participant, at a time when it was not a standard part of American sport activity. During his association with the sport, the three-time U.S. champion earned All-American status, a gold medal at the 1963 Pan-American games, and the titles of captain of the U.S. Olympic team in Tokyo in 1964, and coach of the U.S. International Team. He is also the author of a book on the subject, *Championship Judo: Drill Training.*

Native American Identity

Biographer Herman J. Viola observes in *An American Warrior: Ben Nighthorse Campbell* that "after judo, the dominant force in Ben Campbell's life is his identity as an Indian." Since the 1960s it has been a particularly important part of his life. Before that, his search for his "roots" was obstructed by limited records and the attitude of his father, who wanted him to conceal his Indian heritage. "My father

insisted we keep our Indian background a secret," Campbell confirmed.

The scattered evidence suggests that Campbell's father's family was linked to several tribes, but at the age of ten he ran away to live with the Black Horse family on the Northern Cheyenne Reservation in Montana. The Black Horse family had been directly involved in the famous Battle at the Little Big Horn in June of 1876. Campbell's great-grandmother was one of the Indians attacked in the Sand Creek Massacre in Colorado in 1864. Campbell visited the Northern Cheyenne Reservation regularly starting in 1968 and was enrolled in 1980. He was later inducted into the Council of 44 Chiefs of the Northern Cheyenne Tribe.

Before entering politics, Campbell became prominent as a designer of jewelry. His unique all-metal patterns represented an evolution in Native American design and resulted in numerous awards, as well as an income of about $150,000 per year. Real financial independence occurred after he was featured in a 1979 issue of *Arizona Highways.* In addition to the creation of new designs, he dedicated part of his time to the training of Indian students at Folsom Penitentiary in California and Fort Lewis College in Colorado. As a member of

Congress he updated the 1936 Indian Arts and Crafts Act. Although the initial intent of the act was clear, there had never been any prosecution for the sale of fake Indian art. The new law required that the artists be able to document their background. In Campbell's words, "If an artist is proud of advertising that he is a specific kind of Indian, then he should have no problem tracing his background, even if he is not enrolled."

Entered the Political Arena

Campbell's movement into Colorado politics was quite accidental. When an airplane flight was delayed because of unfavorable weather conditions, Campbell instead decided to sit in on a local political meeting. As a result, he was drafted to be the Democratic candidate for the state legislature. At the time, he had never been to the state capitol building and his political stance was not very well defined, although he considered himself a social Democrat and a fiscal conservative. Campbell was elected by a substantial margin. Although he was not responsible for any major legislation during his first year, he worked with the Colorado Historical Society in promoting an improved marker at the 1864 Sand Creek Massacre site, where some of his Cheyenne ancestors had lost their lives. His colleagues also voted him one of the ten best legislators in the state.

Although Campbell intended to retire from politics, he was attracted by a Democratic opening for the eighth-largest congressional district in the United States. He beat the incumbent by only a four percent margin. The last Native American congressman was Ben Reifel of South Dakota, who left office in 1970. During the first term Campbell established a record that earned the praise of Colorado newspapers. He was reelected with 78 percent of the vote, and a third term followed. As a member of the House he served on the Committees on Agriculture, the Interior, and Insular Affairs.

When Campbell was elected one of Colorado's representatives to the national government, Viola noted, "As the only American Indian in Congress, he also found himself, de facto, the representative of all Indians throughout the United States." In that role he was involved in four highly symbolic events. First, along with Senator Inoye of Hawaii, he promoted the Museum of the American Indian on the Mall in Washington, D.C. Second, he was the spokesman for the 51 Native American delegates at the 1988 Democratic Convention. Third, in December 1991 he was responsible for legislation changing the name of the Custer National Battlefield Monument to the Little Bighorn National Battle Field Monument. Finally, on New Year's Day of 1992 he served as co-grand marshall of the Tournament of Roses parade with Cristobal Colon, a twentieth-generation descendant of Christopher Columbus. Campbell rode his horse Black Warbonnet in full regalia ahead of the vehicle carrying the foreign visitor.

The unexpected decision of Senator Tim Wirth not to seek reelection gave Campbell the opportunity to run for the U.S. Senate in 1992. He won by nearly a ten percent margin.

His five committee memberships include Energy and Natural Resources; Banking, Housing, and Urban Affairs; Democratic Policy; Veterans Affairs; and Indian Affairs. Upon his election, he issued a statement that included the following assurance: "I have always had a special sensitivity to Indian issues, and that will continue in the Senate." In January of 1993 Campbell, joined by other Native American riders, was a significant part of the Inaugural Parade following the election of President Clinton.

SOURCES:

Books

Viola, Herman J., *An American Warrior: Ben Nighthorse Campbell,* New York, Orion Books, 1993.

Periodicals

"Campbell Wins Senate Seat," *Medium Rare: A Publication of the Native American Journalists Association,* fall 1992; 1.

—Sketch by Keith A. Winsell

Captain Jack
1837(?)-1873
Modoc tribal leader
Also known as Kintpuash (Kientpoos or Keintpoees) ["He Has Water Brash"] and Peintpres

Kintpuash, son of a Modoc chief, was commonly known as Captain Jack because of his penchant for wearing a blue military jacket with brass buttons. Captain Jack was a major figure in the Modoc War of 1872-1873. Protesting unsuitable conditions on the Klamath Reservation, Captain Jack led a band of about 50 Modoc warriors, women and children, resisting forced removal by U.S. troops from their former ancestral lands. They secluded themselves in the Lava Beds, and held off the army for nearly a year. He was captured in June 1873 and executed by hanging on October 3, 1878 for fatally shooting General Edward Canby during negotiations. His death marked the end of a story of discrimination and infighting between Indians and whites, the Modocs and other Northern California tribes, and different factions of the Modocs themselves.

Little is known about Captain Jack's life prior to the age of 25. He was born along the lower Lost River, near the California-Oregon border, in the Wa'chamshwash Village, around 1837. The Modocs lived relatively peacefully in the territory surrounding Clear Lake, Tule Lake and the Lost River. By the 1850s, however, white pressure on the Indian lands, aggravated by the 1848 California Gold Rush, led to

Captain Jack

conflicts. In the early 1850s, a wagon train of immigrants on their way to the West Coast was attacked by Indians. Because the horses from the train ended up in the possession of the Modocs, the tribe was blamed for the raid. A reprisal party led by the miner Jim Crosby did not find the responsible parties, who were members of the Pit River tribe, and took out their frustrations on the Modocs instead. The Modocs, including Captain Jack's father, responded with violence. In 1856 the Modocs ambushed another wagon train at a place called Wagakanna, which the white survivors later labelled "Bloody Point." In response to the massacre, the well-known mountain man and Indian fighter Ben Wright organized a vigilante group specifically to stalk and kill Indians. In an attempt to preserve the peace, 45 of the Modocs leaders were invited to a conference and were ambushed by Wright and his men. Wright himself shot Captain Jack's father with a revolver.

Life at the Klamath Reservation

Captain Jack is said to have replaced his father as chief of the clan but it was actually his uncle, Old Schonchin, who compelled the Modocs to abide by the Treaty of 1864. This treaty established a reservation at Klamath Lake, across the California-Oregon boundary. All the Modocs, Klamath and Pit River Indians were to be removed to this tract of land. The reservation, however, was located on former Klamath territory and included none of the Modoc's former hunting grounds. The Klamath, feeling superior to the dispossessed Modocs, harassed and ridiculed their fellow Indians. They demanded concessions, including split wood rails, as pay-

ment for the use of Klamath territory. The Indian agents on the reservation also encouraged the Indians to establish a restructured leadership. Instead of hereditary chiefs for each tribe, the Indian men voted for a single reservation chief. The man finally selected was a Klamath native.

The treatment of the Modocs by the Klamath, together with the uncustomary rules of the reservation, caused a rift among the Modocs. Captain Jack renounced the Treaty of 1864 and left the reservation in 1865. Some of the Modoc Indians left with him, and the band returned to their hunting ground along the Lost River. Various groups of Indian agents and military officers visited Captain Jack, trying unsuccessfully to get him to return to the reservation. In December of 1869, a delegation was finally able to convince him. Alfred B. Meacham, the newly appointed Indian superintendent, organized the delegation. He took with him, in addition to soldiers, Captain O. C. Knapp and Ivan Applegate, who both served as agents for the reservation. Also included on the visit were Old Schonchin, and Frank Riddle and his Modoc wife Tobey (later known as Winema) to serve as interpreters.

The Klamath and Modoc Indians lived peacefully together on the reservation for several weeks of the new year, but conflicts soon arose again. The current agent at the reservation, Knapp, refused to become involved. The Modocs were told to work the problems out themselves. In April, 1870, Captain Jack called a meeting of all Modocs. They made plans to leave the reservation and, at the end of April, Captain Jack and 371 Modocs returned to Lost River. The rest of the tribe, led by Schonchin, remained on the reservation, although they moved away from the Klamath and settled in Yainax.

Establishment at Lost River

The Modoc presence in northern California caused unrest among the white population. Settlers in the area around the Tule Lake Basin began to demand the removal of Captain Jack and his band. In 1870, Captain Jack made a formal request for a Modoc reservation on the Lost River. The Indian agent Meacham suggested the request be granted but the settlers were enraged. In response, General Edward Canby, a distinguished Civil War veteran with experience in Indian battles, was dispatched to the area. He was placed in charge of a small troop and instructed to keep Captain Jack under control. The settlers were growing impatient with Meacham's lack of action, but neither he nor Canby would make a move until a decision was reached about a reservation site. Finally, in 1872 the Interior Department replaced Meacham as Indian superintendent with T. B. Odeneal. Keith A. Murray describes this action in *The Modocs and Their War:* "This, at this critical point in negotiations, a man who knew almost nothing of the background of the situation and had never met with Jack or the Modocs, was placed in charge of the job of getting Jack to leave Lost River. It is to be granted that Meacham was not a strong agent and that he had shamefully neglected his duty and opportunity to pacify the Modocs."

The final act of the drama began when Jack's niece fell ill. Curly Headed Doctor, the group's shaman or tribal doctor, was absent from the encampment at the time. The nearest healer was the shaman from Klamath. He was sent for, took his payment in advance, but the girl died just the same. Grieved by the unnecessary death and in accordance with tribal custom, Captain Jack killed the shaman for his inefficiency. The Klamath informed the Indian agent and a warrant was issued for Captain Jack's arrest. After a series of unsuccessful conferences, Odeneal made a recommendation to the Commissioner of Indian Affairs on June 17. His solution was to arrest Captain Jack and hold him in custody until he accepted Schonchin's leadership and returned to the reservation at Yainax. It was agreed to take action in September so additional forces could be dispatched should Captain Jack's band resist.

Captain Jack may have suspected the military's true intentions. In September, 1872, he resisted all their attempts to meet with him. The order was finally given, at the end of November, to arrest Captain Jack, Black Jim and Scarfaced Charley by the next morning, forcibly if necessary. Troops left Fort Klamath for Captain Jack's stronghold, beginning the first battle of the Modoc War. Captain Jack and 50 of his warriors fought the troops while around 175 women and children fled across the lake to the Lava Beds. The volcanic rock formations absorbed the lead as well as offered cover. Few Indians were killed or wounded, compared to casualties on the American side. The fighting Modocs held out against superior numbers, including approximately 400 reinforcements that arrived in January 1873.

At the end of January, northern California was hit by blizzard. The snow immobilized supply trains as well as the advance of additional troops. Captain Jack used the snow storm as cover in sending a messenger to the military camp. He wanted to speak with John Fairchild, a rancher who was well-liked and trusted by both settlers and Indians, about a settlement. Word was sent that Fairchild would visit when weather permitted. Captain Jack may have wanted peace but his advisors wanted land. They convinced him to continue with the war, holding out with the weather, which was working to their advantage in demoralizing the opposing troops.

Though Fairchild made several trips to and from the stronghold, no agreements were reached. Intermittent fighting continued until March when Captain Jack agreed to meet with the whites in council. By this time Lost River had officially been rejected as a reservation site. Entering the negotiations with the assumption that a compromise was sought, Captain Jack suggested two other sites as possible reservations for the Modocs. General Canby promptly refused. Albert Britt summarized the negotiation in his book, *Great Indian Chiefs*: "The only peace offered them was the peace of submission and, as each location that the Modocs would accept was rejected by Canby, it became increasingly clear that the only reservation for them would be that they would share with the unfriendly Klamath. And that had no look of peace to the Modocs."

Planning "Final" Negotiations

At this point Captain Jack called a council among his own people in the Lava Beds. Schonchin John and Black Jim, two tribesmen who were wanted by the authorities for killing soldiers, challenged Jack's leadership. They insisted he prove his commitment to the Modoc cause by killing the white representatives. Captain Jack was in a difficult position. For himself he wanted peace, an end to the fighting. As a leader of his people, however, he was obliged to meet their need for land of their own. Captain Jack spent the following two days alone in his cave, struggling with this decision. A mutual friend warned Winema (Tobey Riddle) that the negotiators would be murdered. When she, in turn, tried to warn Canby and the other representatives, they did not believe her.

The council met again on April 11, 1873. Captain Jack, Schonchin John, Boston Charley, Bogus Charley, Black Jim and Hooker Jim met with Captain Meacham, General Canby and the Reverend Mr. Thomas. Frank Riddle and his wife Winema served as interpreters. Captain Jack made a final plea for a reservation to be established for his people at Hot Creek in California. Britt describes the next events: "[A]s though the enumeration of his grievances and his thought of the home that he knew now he was not to have had broken the last thread of his resistance to violence and kindled fresh hated of the whites, he shouted in Modoc, *'Ut-wih-kutt,'* ['Let's do it,'] and fired at Canby." Captain Jack knew the fate of the Modocs was sealed. Whether judged by their fellow Indians or a jury of white men, they had committed an unforgivable act by striking down unarmed men during negotiations. Jack later stated that after killing Canby, he returned to the Lava Beds with the assumption that he would die in the fighting that followed. The Modoc representatives fled back to the Lava Beds and fighting began once more on April 14.

Capture and Trial

By May the Modoc resistance had begun to crumble. Quarrels among the Indian leaders caused the group to fragment and surrender piecemeal. Hooker Jim even offered to turn Captain Jack over to the U.S. soldiers in return for his life and liberty. Captain Jack turned in his gun in late May, accompanied by Schonchin John, Black Jim and Boston Charley. His trial began on July 5 at Fort Klamath. Steamboat Frank, Hooker Jim, and Bogus Charley—those who had convinced Captain Jack to kill the negotiators—were also present at the trial but not in custody. The four men were hung on October 3, 1873. Captain Jack was asked to name his successor, but he refused. The entire Modoc band from Lost River was forced to witness the execution. All the soldiers from Fort Klamath were also required to attend.

After the bodies were buried, Captain Jack's was exhumed and taken by freight train to Yreka. Some reports state his body was embalmed and then sent to Washington, D.C. Others suggest it was decapitated and his head then used in carnival side shows. Whatever became of his body, the Modocs gained no ground for their efforts. The cost of the Modoc War was enormous compared to its results. The tribe requested a reserve of land with a value of approximately $20,000, according to most sources. As Britt explains in *Great Indian Chiefs,* the government spent $500,000 on the war, in addition to losing "the lives of eight officers, thirty-nine privates, sixteen volunteers, two Indian scouts, and eighteen settlers—a trumpery affair, as wars go." The remaining Modocs were escorted to a reservation on Shawnee land in the Indian Territory. They arrived at their destination, Seneca Springs on the Quapaw Agency, almost one year after the war began.

Gladys Cardiff

SOURCES:

Britt, Albert, *Great Indian Chiefs,* Books for Libraries Press, 1938; 225-248.
Dockstader, Frederick J., *Great North American Indians,* New York, Van Nostrand Reinhold, 1991; 138-140.
Murray, Keith A., *The Modocs and Their War,* Norman, University of Oklahoma Press, 1959.
Native North American Almanac, edited by Duane Champagne, Detroit, Gale Research, 1994; 327, 1025-1026.

—Sketch by Lisa A. Wroble

Gladys Cardiff

1942-

Cherokee poet

Gladys Cardiff has won three prestigious awards for her poetry, which has been widely anthologized. Born in Browning, Montana, Cardiff attended school in Seattle, Washington. She graduated from the University of Washington where she studied poetry with Theodore Roethke. Other noted creative writing teachers of hers were Beth and Nelson Bentley.

Cardiff's father, a member of the Owl clan of the North Carolina Cherokee, changed his name to Harris before the family moved to Seattle, Washington, because of the racism he had experienced while working with the Indian service in the Southeast. A highly educated man, he was among the first Cherokees to leave the reservation to obtain a master's degree. In the Northwest, he became the principal of a school on the Blackfeet Reservation. Cardiff's father shared stories about his tribal heritage and researched the Cherokees throughout his life; her mother, who was Irish and Welsh, taught music and was a composer and musician.

In 1976, Cardiff published *To Frighten a Storm,* which was given the Governor's Writer's Award for a first book. In 1985 and 1986, the Seattle Arts Commission selected her work as deserving of prizes; and in 1986, she was recognized by the University of Washington for her literary endeavors when she shared the Louisa Kerns Award with another recipient. Her work has appeared in such collections as *Carriers of the Dream Wheel* and *Twentieth Century Native American Poetry, The Remembered Earth,* a collection edited by Geary Hobson for the University of New Mexico Press, Rayna Green's anthology, *That's What She Said* for Indiana University Press, and in Joseph Bruchac's *Songs from this Earth on the Turtle's Back* for Greenfield Review Press. Cardiff conceives of her poems as both celebration and affirmation of her traditions, and the names of the rivers in her homeland frequently appear in her poems: Oconoluftee, whose "ripples are Cherokee prayers," the Hiwassee which is a river that is "eating the land" with its "foam feathers." And she often uses Cherokee place names, calling them "Tsa lagi" names. Invited to read her work at the Seattle Bumbershoot Festival, Cardiff has also read at numerous public schools, universities, and libraries. She has given workshops on the writing of poetry at women's conferences at the University of Puget Sound and at the University of Washington; and she has worked as a poet-in-the-schools traveling throughout the state to teach young people to appreciate poetry by participating in the process of creating it themselves.

SOURCES:

Cardiff, Gladys, *To Frighten a Storm,* Port Townsend, Washington, Copper Canyon Press, 1976.

—Sketch by Ruth Rosenberg

Douglas Cardinal
1934-
Blackfeet architect

The firm of Douglas Cardinal, Architect, Limited of Ottawa, Ontario, Canada, has been selected to design the National Museum of the American Indian (NMAI) in Washington, D.C. It is a complex assignment because the building will house over one million objects while, at the same time, fit into the last available site on the National Mall. Douglas Cardinal became known for his innovative designs while still an undergraduate.

Cardinal was born in the village of Red Deer in the province of Alberta, Canada. His father, who served as the wildlife warden for the province, was from the Blackfeet tribe of western Canada; his mother was a nurse. Cardinal was the oldest of their eight children. In 1953, Cardinal enrolled in the School of Architecture at the University of British Columbia. Because the designs he submitted were considered too radical, he was asked, in his sophomore year, to withdraw. He continued the study of architecture in the United States, graduating from the University of Texas in 1963.

Becomes an Innovative Architect

Cardinal's first commission, upon his return to Canada was to design a private residence in sylvan Lake Alberta. The resultant round house was the Guloien House. His next design commission was St. Mary's Church in Red Deer. Again, using a circular design, he established his reputation for creative innovation and his work was acclaimed as an architectural triumph. He has achieved the reputation of one who thinks in a twenty-first century way, making powerful architectural statements and utilizing cutting-edge technology. He manages to combine ultra-modernity with ancient traditions such as circular structures commemorating the sacred hoop of creation. According to Rick West, director of the National Museum of the American Indian, "Douglas Cardinal is one of the most exciting architectural voices on the scene today." Cardinal gained fame for his daring use of state-of-the-art technology, such as computer-enhanced electronically-drawn blueprints. He designed the Canadian Museum of Civilization in Hull, Quebec; it curves gracefully along the banks of the Ottawa River across from the Parliament buildings and faces Canada's Supreme Court. West notes that the Canadian Museum "has received critical acclaim for its innovative use of fiber-optics technology to enhance its exhibitions."

Cardinal, who lives in Ottawa with his wife and six children, has extensive experience in designing Indian education centers. He recently finished the campus master plan for the Institute of American Indian Arts in Santa Fe, New Mexico. His next project is designing a new campus for the Saskatchewan Federation of Indians. His design for the National Museum of the American Indian in Washington, D.C., divides a 260,00-square-foot space into display, theater, and conference complexes. A central meeting place, "The Potomac," will provide interactive experiences such as dance, drama, music, oral history, storytelling, and Native foods.

SOURCES:

Books

Native North American Almanac, edited by Duane Champagne, Detroit, Gale Research, 1994.

Periodicals

West, Richard, Jr., "Architects Selected for NNAI," *Native Peoples,* spring 1993; 54-55.

—*Sketch by Ruth Rosenberg*

Harold Cardinal
1945-
Cree tribal leader and author

Harold Cardinal, a charismatic Cree tribal leader and author, presided over the Indian Association of Alberta, Canada, in the 1970s. His 1969 book, *The Unjust Society: The Tragedy of Canada's Indians,* powerfully motivated public opinion on the rights of indigenous people.

Early Background

Cardinal was born on January 27, 1945, one of 18 children. He grew up on the Cree reserve on Sucker Creek in Alberta, Canada. In 1965, he went east to Ontario to enroll at Saint Patrick's College, where he studied sociology for two years. In 1967, he left academia for politics, becoming associate secretary for Indian Affairs for the Canadian Union of Students. By 1968, he had been elected president of the Canadian Indian Youth Council.

Cardinal proved himself to be such a charismatic leader that by the time he was 23 he had been elected president of the Indian Association of Alberta, where he was to serve nine terms in office. He was the youngest president ever to have been elected. Under his administration, many programs to affirm Indian culture were initiated. He became, in 1968, a board member of the National Indian Brotherhood.

In 1970, he helped to draft *Citizens Plus,* which became known as "The Red Paper." It was the result of many months of consultation by him and his staff with the

42 bands of Indians in Alberta. It presented to the Canadian government the official position of these western reserves. In 1969, he published *The Unjust Society: The Tragedy of Canada's Indians* in response to a policy proposed by the Canadian government in 1966, which Cardinal characterized as "a thinly disguised program of extermination through assimilation." He opposed the claim that Indian organizations were not sufficiently developed to manage their own affairs. He mounted powerful arguments for self-determination. The Cree, for whom he spoke, are the most populous indigenous group in Canada, extending from Alberta in the West, to Quebec in the East, and having more than 60,000 registered members with countless others who have not publicly identified themselves. Divided into three major groups according to their territory they are the Plains Cree, the Woods Cree, and the Swampy Cree. They are united by their desire for self-government and economic development. These postulates were affirmed in Cardinal's *The Rebirth of Canada's Indians* in 1977.

Life in Public Service

In 1977, Cardinal left provincial Native politics to become a regional director general. He was the first Indian to receive such an appointment in Alberta. He initiated innovative reforms during his seven-month term. Then, for several years, he served as consultant to Indian bands in northern Alberta. In 1982, he was elected the chief of the Sucker Creek band; and in 1983, the Assembly of First Nations appointed him vice-chief for the prairie region.

Cardinal's activism had helped to mobilize resistance against the Canadian government's termination policies which attempted to phase out treaty obligations. Had Indians on reserves become subject to provincial laws and taxes, their depressed economic circumstances would have worsened considerably. Emboldened by new assertiveness, Canadian Indians began asking for settlement of land claims for territories which had never been formally ceded. As Alvin M. Josephy, Jr., wrote in *The Indian Heritage of America,* "In response, the government appropriated larger sums of money for the reserves and in 1973 announced a new, limited land claims policy that would seek negotiated settlements of certain 'specific' and 'comprehensive' aboriginal title claims." Cardinal's energies were instrumental in finally having given the Crees a public voice.

SELECTED WRITINGS BY CARDINAL:

The Unjust Society: The Tragedy of Canada's Indians, Edmonton, Alberta, New Press Publishers, 1969.
The Rebirth of Canada's Indians, Toronto, New Press Publishers, 1977.

SOURCES:

Getty, Ian A. L., and Donald B. Smith, *One Century Later: Western Canadian Reserve Indians Since Treaty 7,* [Vancouver], 1978.
Josephy, Alvin, Jr., *The Indian Heritage of America,* Boston, Houghton Mifflin, 1991.
Mawhiney, Anne-Marie, *Towards Aboriginal Self-Government,* New York, Garland Publishing, 1994.
Sanders, Douglas, "Government Indian Agencies in Canada" in *Handbook of North American Indians,* Volume 4, Washington, D.C., Smithsonian Institution, 1988.
Surtees, Robert J., "Canadian Indian Policies," in *Handbook of North American Indians,* Volume 4, Washington, D.C., Smithsonian Institution, 1988.
Symington, Fraser, *The Canadian Indian,* [Toronto], 1969.

—Sketch by Ruth Rosenberg

Tantoo Cardinal
1950-
Métis actress

One of North America's most widely recognized Native actresses, Tantoo Cardinal has appeared in numerous plays, television programs, and films, including the American movie *Dances with Wolves* and the Canadian picture *Black Robe.* She has received several awards for her acting achievements, as well as for her activity within the Native American community. According to Cardinal, "With acting I have found a way to do my own part to tell my people's story."

Cardinal was born in 1950 in Anzac, Alberta, a rural town 400 kilometers north of Edmonton and 40 kilometers south of Fort McMurray. She was the youngest child of a Cree woman and a white man, making Cardinal a Métis—a French term meaning one of mixed-blood. Her father abandoned the family six weeks after Tantoo was born, just before the couple's planned wedding date. When Cardinal was six months old, she and her siblings were sent to live with her maternal Cree grandmother, who had also named her; Tantoo was taken from the name of a mosquito repellent. It was her grandmother who taught Cardinal the Cree language and way of life. Regarding her upbringing, Cardinal explained, "I am an Indian woman and I was raised by my Cree grandmother; and then I'm a half breed woman, as I was also influenced in the early years by my English grandfather. So I come from two worlds in a sense. But I feel a responsibility to the Indian world."

In 1966 Cardinal attended high school in Edmonton, Alberta, and boarded with a Mennonite couple and their son, Fred Martin, who was then a university student and a Native American rights activist. Shortly after her high school graduation in 1968, Cardinal and Martin were married. While still in high school, she had joined United Native Youth and in

1971, became president of the group. That same year, without any formal theatrical education or training, she began her professional acting career with a small role in a CBC dramatized documentary entitled *Father Lacombe,* a film about a nineteenth-century Alberta priest. Recalling the incident, Cardinal asserted that "Right away I knew this is the way to get ideas into people's hearts and minds." In 1973 she and Martin had a son, Cheyenne. They were divorced in 1976.

Cardinal became progressively more active in theater; in 1979 she secured a starring role in her first feature film, *Marie-Anne.* This led to her 1982 title role in the Saskatoon production of the play *Jessica,* a psychological drama about a Canadian woman of mixed-blood, written by actress-playwright Linda Griffith. In 1986 Cardinal again played the role of Jessica in a Toronto production of the play, which won the city's best new play award and was selected by the Quebec International Theater Festival as the top play of the season. Reviewers lauded Cardinal's performance, admiring her natural instinct and realism. Griffith told *Maclean's* magazine, "There's a relentless vigilance to her. And she has this incredible sense of grounding."

In the critically acclaimed 1986 CBC movie *Loyalties,* directed and co-produced by Edmonton's Anne Wheeler, Cardinal played the role of Roseanne, a single woman whose daughter is raped by a doctor. For her stirring performance, Cardinal was nominated for the prestigious Canadian film award, the Genie, and won the American Indian Film Festival's Best Actress Award. During that time, Cardinal met actor Beaver Richards, an American Indian from South Dakota who also had a role in the film. In 1985 the couple had a son, Clifford. Only two weeks after the birth of Clifford, Cardinal had the leading role in *The Young Poundmaker,* a play written by Native Indian Ernie Carefoot and performed in Saskatoon.

In 1988 Cardinal married American actor John Lawlor and moved to Los Angeles with their new-born daughter Riel, named after Louis Riel, the famous nineteenth-century Métis leader. Two years later, Cardinal had her first supporting role in a major U.S. film. She played the role of Black Shawl, the headstrong wife of Kicking Bird (the Lakota medicine man played by Graham Greene), in the Academy Award-winning movie, *Dances with Wolves,* directed by Kevin Costner. Later that year, Cardinal won a Sterling Award for her portrayal of Kookom in the theater production *All My Relations.*

In 1991 Cardinal hosted *As Long as the Rivers Flow,* a public television series of five one-hour programs centering on the Canadian First People's movement for self-government. Also in 1991, she played the supporting role of an Algonquian woman in the award-winning Canadian film *Black Robe.* Directed by Bruce Beresford, *Black Robe* details the story of a French missionary's quest to convert Native people to Christianity.

In addition to her film work, Cardinal has made guest appearances in numerous television shows; she played the role of a Native band chief in the 1992 CBC television series *Street Legal,* and also appeared in *Gunsmoke, The Lighten-*

ing Incident, The Campbells, and *Wonderworks.* Moreover, in 1993 she won a First Americans in the Arts Totem Award for her portrayal of the character Katerina in Widows. Cardinal worked with Lou Diamond Phillips in the movie *Sioux City,* and played the title role in director Sam Shepperd's *Silent Tongue,* along with River Phoenix, Allen Bates, and Richard Harris. Cardinal received the San Francisco American Indian Film Festival's Best Actress Award in 1993 for her performance as Bangor in *Where the Rivers Flow North.* In addition, Cardinal had a leading role in the 1993 film *Legends of the Fall,* also starring Anthony Hopkins, Brad Pitt, and Aidan Quinn.

Cardinal is very particular about the types of roles she plays. She is especially concerned with realism and has convinced several directors to change the content of their projects due to inaccuracies regarding Native Americans. For her contributions to the Native American artistic community, Cardinal was awarded the Eagle Spirit Award in 1990.

SOURCES:

Books

Native North American Almanac, edited by Duane Champagne, Detroit, Gale Research, 1994; 1127.

Periodicals

Dwyer, V., "An Art with its Roots in Loyalty," *Maclean's,* December 30, 1991; 42.

Johnson, Brian D., "Masks of a Métis Star," *Maclean's,* October 20, 1986; 63-64.

Willer, Brian, "Tantoo Cardinal," *Maclean's,* December 30, 1991; 42.

Other

"Biography of Tantoo Cardinal," Toronto, Ontario, The Talent Group, 1994.

—*Sketch by tpkunesh*

Edward Castillo
1947-
Cahuilla-Luiseño educator, consultant, and activist

Edward Daniel Castillo is an educator, educational consultant, and activist. He is well aware of the need for quality education for the Native people. He was born in California on August 25, 1947, into the Cahuilla-Luiseño tribes. At that time, the Indian Reorganization Act (IRA) and the Bureau of Indian Affairs (BIA) were dividing Native tribes

Edward Castillo

and families across the United States—a political activity that was particularly damaging to the Natives of California. Because the BIA issued programs and money for food, health services, housing, and education to some Natives while ignorning others, Castillo received nothing.

Education

After receiving a B.A. in history from the University of California at Riverside, Castillo went on to the University of California at Berkeley to earn a M.A. in anthropology in 1976 and to pursue doctoral studies in anthropology. He completed the secondary education credential program at California State College in San Bernardino in 1983. He has been a lecturer on Native American subjects at numerous colleges and universities, including the University of California at Los Angeles and at Berkeley, and is a former director of the Native American studies program at the University of California at Santa Cruz. He is presently director of the Native American studies program at Sonoma State University. Castillo has worked with the California State Department of Education as a curriculum specialist. He has worked with organizations and associations across America as an ethnographer. He has also served as a consultant to several educational institutions and projects, including the Smithsonian's Museum of the American Indian in Washington, D.C., as well as the California Indian Education Association, to which he belongs. And from 1977 to 1982, Castillo belonged to the California State Native American Heritage Commission, the single organization throughout the state that takes charge of burial sites and repatriation.

Castillo has published numerous professional papers on a variety of Native topics dealing with resistance to the military invasion into California, and the armed clash with the mission system. He is widely published and has served as advisor to several artistic endeavors, including *Lost River: The Modoc Indian War of 1872-1873* for the National Endowment for the Humanities, and the *California Indians,* a documentary by Ahmium Education, both in 1990, and to the San Francisco history project, developed by public television's KQED in 1993. He has one son and one daughter, and lives in Rohnert Park, California.

SELECTED WRITINGS BY CASTILLO:

(Co-author) *A Bibliography of California Indian History,* edited by Robert Heizer, Romona, California, Ballena Press, 1978.

(Co-author) *The Missions of California,* San Francisco, American Indian Historical Society Press, 1987.

Native American Perspectives on the Hispanic Colonization of Alta, California, New York, Garland Publications, 1992.

Living Traditions: A Museum Guide for Indian People of California, Volume 5: *Southern and Coastal California,* State of California, Native American Heritage Commission, 1993.

Shared Experiences/Personal Interpretations: Seven Native American Artists, University Art Gallery Publications, Sonoma State University, 1993.

"The Ethnology and History of the California Indians," in *Native North American Almanac,* edited by Duane Champage, Detroit, Gale Research, 1994.

The Indians of Southern California, Santa Barbara, California, Bellerophon Press, 1994.

(With Robert Jackson) *Indians, Franciscans and Spanish Colonization: The Impact of Franciscan Missionaries on the Indians of California,* University of New Mexico Press, forthcoming.

SOURCES:

Castillo, Edward, untranscribed telephone interviews with Darryl Wilson, 1994.

—Sketch by Darryl Wilson

Duane Champagne
1951-
Turtle Mountain Chippewa sociologist and professor

Duane Willard Champagne is a sociologist and university professor. He is known for his writings about issues related to societal and cultural change in American Indian communities.

Champagne began life as one of seven sons in the rural setting of Belcourt, North Dakota on the Turtle Mountain Reservation on May 18, 1951. Both of his parents were enrolled members of the Chippewa tribe. He attended school on the reservation from third grade through secondary school, and in 1969 graduated from Turtle Mountain Community High School. He stayed close to home during his undergraduate study, attending North Dakota State University in Fargo directly after high school. He received his bachelor of arts degree in mathematics and sociology in summer 1973.

Champagne did not take the traditional route from undergraduate work to graduate school. He opted instead for a tour of public service via Volunteer in Service to America (VISTA), the domestic counterpart of the peace corps. During his service, Champagne collected and analyzed data for the United Tribes Technical Training Center (now United Tribes Technical College) in Bismarck, North Dakota. Since the program required him to enroll in a graduate program, he began a master's program in sociology with a minor in mathematics at North Dakota State University in Fargo, receiving his degree in 1975. Though he was accepted to a number of schools for doctoral study, Champagne chose the sociology department at Harvard University. He arrived at the school in 1975, and received his Ph.D. in sociology in 1982. A fellowship from the Rockefeller Foundation allowed Champagne to conduct post-doctoral studies with the Tlingit in southeast Alaska, and with the Northern Cheyenne in Montana in 1982. He then accepted a year-long teaching position with the sociology department at the University of Wisconsin in Milwaukee in 1983.

In 1984, he relocated to the University of California-Los Angeles, where he began work as an associate professor of sociology. Champagne became involved with the university's *American Indian and Culture Research Journal,* which had begun publication in the 1970s. Champagne became the journal's main editor in 1986. Under his direction, the journal has grown in length and scope, and has attracted more diversified writers.

After heading the journal for three years, Champagne was named associate director of the UCLA American Indian Studies Center in 1990, and in 1991, he became director of the center. As director, his main responsibility has been to oversee the daily machinery of what he termed in an interview with Jennifer Gray Reddish as "organized research." Champagne explains, "We carry on various activities [at the American Indian Studies Center]. We have a library and a publications department, where we publish the *American Indian and Culture Research Journal,* and we publish books." The center caters to a "reservation audience," and many of the books address issues of culture preservation, economic development and academia. Other publications include research aid manuals and books concerning the Child Welfare Act. Though UCLA does not have a formal undergraduate American Indian studies major, the center is closely involved with a master's program in that area. Champagne is quick to point out that the American Indian Studies Center, though primarily a research institution, also supports Native UCLA students by creating "a less threatening environment to help them adjust." The center offers counseling services, meeting rooms and computer resources in order to offset the strain some American Indian students encounter while in a dominant society environment. In addition, the center encourages students to organize a powwow each year at the university, fostering fellowship and activity among American Indian students.

Outside of his work as the director of the center, Champagne is an author in his own right. Over 30 of his articles have appeared in scholarly journals and as chapters in books. He has published two books: *American Indian Societies: Some Strategies and Conditions of Political and Cultural Survival* and *Social Order and Political Change: Constitution Governments Among the Cherokee, the Choctaw, the Chickasaw, and the Creek.* He has also written chapters for various published books. He was the main editor of the *Native North American Almanac,* published in 1994, featuring biographies of noted Indian persons throughout the United States and Canada during various time periods in history.

Despite leading an active professional career, Champagne does take time out of his work schedule for his family and recreation. He and his wife Liana have lived in Los Angeles, California, with their three children: the oldest a daughter named Talya, followed by a son Gabriel and their youngest, a daughter, Demelza. Champagne's wide-range of hobbies include playing basketball and chess. Having concentrated on his chess game, he earned a master's title in both over-the-board and correspondence chess at the national level. Champagne is actively involved with the Los Angeles American Indian community having served as a member and past chair of the Los Angeles City/County American Indian Commission, trustee for the Southwest Museum, and other community committees and boards.

SELECTED WRITINGS BY CHAMPAGNE:

Strategies and Conditions of Political and Cultural Survival in American Indian Societies, Peterborough, New Hampshire, Transcript Printing Company, December 1985.

Social Order and Political Change: Constitution Governments Among the Cherokee, the Choctaw, the Chickasaw, and the Creek, Stanford, California, Stanford University Press, 1992.

Editor and contributor, *Native North American Almanac: A Reference Work on Native North Americans in the United States and Canada,* Detroit, Gale Research, 1994.

Editor, *Chronology of Native North American History,* Detroit, Gale Research, 1994.

Native America: Portrait of the Peoples, Detroit, U•X•L, 1994.

SOURCES:

Books

Native North American Almanac, edited by Duane Champagne, Detroit, Gale Research, 1994.

Other

Champagne, Duane, interview with Jennifer Gray Reddish conducted July 6, 1994.

—*Sketch by Jennifer Gray Reddish*

Alfred Chato
1860(?)-1934
Chiracahua Apache subchief and U.S. Army scout
Also known as Chatto ["The Flat Nose"]

Alfred Chato

Of all the Apache warriors and chiefs, the United States military regarded Alfred Chato, known simply as Chato for most of his life, to be the most fearsome and daring. He was a Chiracahua Apache subchief, served as a U.S. Army scout, and was in part responsible for the Apaches' return to the Southwest during the early part of the twentieth century. Although little is known about Chato's early life, including his parents, historians estimate Chato was born about 1860. It is believed he grew up in the camp of the famous Chiracahua Apache Chief Cochise and was a close friend of Cochise's son Naiche. However, John G. Bourke in *On the Border with Crook,* speculated that Chato was actually a White Mountain Apache who married a Chiricahua woman.

The earliest activity of Chato to be discussed by historians occurred in the early 1880s. For years, the Apaches had been forced onto reservations by whites, and breakouts and subsequent raids by Apache warriors on the reservations had taken place. One such incident happened in August 1881, when Fort Apache Commander Eugene Carr attempted to arrest the prophet Nakaidoklini. Nakaidoklini had told the Apaches that their dead ancestors would soon return to destroy the white invaders of their land. During the attempted arrest, Nakaidoklini's followers objected, and fighting broke out. Nakaidoklini was killed, and a company of White Mountain scouts revolted and attacked Fort Apache along with Nakaidoklini's followers. As happened frequently during that period in the Southwest, newspapers were filled with rumors of a massacre at the fort, even though the Indians were repelled. The rumors resulted in an increase in military movements throughout the area. Feeling threatened by the activity, Chato, Naiche, Juh, Geronimo, and 74 Apache war-riors broke out of the San Carlos Reservation and headed into the mountains (Sierra Madre) in Mexico.

Determined to set the rest of the Apaches on Arizona reservations free, Chato, Naiche, Geronimo, and Chihuahua, along with a war party of about 60 men, returned to San Carlos in April 1882, cutting telegraph wires on the way. They killed the police chief and one of the Apache scouts and forced Loco, head of the Warm Springs Apaches, and his people to leave with them. After a long trek through the desert and mountains heading toward their Sierre Madre stronghold, the Apaches ran into Mexican soldiers, who killed many of the women and children. The Apaches, including Chato and Naiche, who were on horses escaped. (Later, some of those who survived the attack labeled Chato a coward and blamed those who escaped for the disaster.) Once the survivors had regrouped and rested a few days, they made a trip to Casas Grandes to trade captured goods. Mexican troops again attacked and took some 20 to 35 Apaches captive. Among the captives were Chato's wife and two children.

Leads Brilliant 1883 Raid

In March 1883, Geronimo took a raiding party south into the Sonoran Desert in search of livestock. A second group of about 25 Apaches led by Chato and Benito crossed the border into Arizona and began a daring and electrifying raid through Arizona and New Mexico. On March 21, Chato and his party crossed the border in search of ammunition. They first hit a charcoal camp near Tombstone and killed three men. On the second day, they killed three more men at a mining camp. Two of the warriors in the party, Tsoe and Beneactiney, attempted to approach a tent where a fourth man was hiding. Beneactiney, who was a close friend of Tsoe, was killed.

During the remainder of the week, many more whites were killed in raids on other mining camps and ranches. The telegraph wires were filled with rumors of the bloody scourge sweeping the territory, and the army along with citizen volunteers were out in force to try to capture the renegades. On March 28, Chato and his group crossed the path of federal judge McComas and his family near Lordsburg, New Mexico. The Apaches killed McComas and his wife and took their six-year-old son captive. The raid lasted six days, covered 400 miles, and left some 26 people dead, only one of whom was an Apache. Throughout it all, the only people who saw the raiders were their victims. According to Angie Debo in *Geronimo: The Man, His Time, His Place,* "Members of the band later told Davis that Chato slept only on horseback, standing vigilantly on guard while the others snatched brief pauses for rest." Although the raid terrified whites in the Southwest, other Apaches were less excited because Chato failed to find any ammunition. Following the McComas killing, General George Crook was ordered to find and kill the Apache warriors.

Tsoe, whom the Army would call "Peaches," had difficulty dealing with the death of his friend, so he asked Chato to let him leave. Chato allowed him to go, a move later criticized by some Apaches. Instead of heading back to the Sierre Madre, however, Tsoe went to see Crook and eventually led the army to Chato's hideout. On May 15, Crook's army caught up with Chato and Geronimo at their mountain rancheria ["camp"]. After weeks of negotiating, the parties agreed that the Apaches would come back to the San Carlos Reservation. Chato reportedly pledged to Crook that he would remain forever at peace with the United States. The Apache leaders also agreed to make their own way back to the reservation because Crook's supplies were low and would not feed the entire band of several hundred Apaches plus the soldiers. Some of the Apaches arrived in December, but Chato and 19 others did not arrive at San Carlos until February 7, 1884. Geronimo was the last to arrive, in late February.

Rift with Geronimo

During the next two years on the reservation, a rift developed between Chato and Geronimo. While things went well for Chato—Lieutenant Britton Davis made him a sergeant in the Army scouts, he learned to farm, and he was frequently consulted by Davis about the needs of the camp—Geronimo grew increasingly unhappy. He clashed with Crook about the treatment of Apache women and about the use of tizwin, an alcoholic beverage made by the Indians that Crook had forbidden. Geronimo also suspected that Chato had become one of Davis' "secret scouts," who reported everything Geronimo did to Davis.

Geronimo's discontent boiled over on May 14, 1885, when he spent the night drinking tizwin. In the morning, he asked Chato to break out of San Carlos with him. Chato refused and the two argued. In an effort to get more Apaches to leave the reservation, Geronimo told some of them that Chato was dead. He even sent two Apaches to kill Chato, but they did not carry out the plot. In the end, Geronimo was only able to sway about one-fourth of the Apaches to leave with him on the morning of May 15.

It took the Army, with Chato leading a contingent of 200 scouts that rode with the Army, two years to capture Geronimo. While Crook haggled with his Washington commanders over the terms of the surrender—a clash that led Crook to resign—Geronimo escaped again. General Nelson Miles took over the chase. Preferring to work without the help of the Apache scouts, he sent them back to San Carlos.

Chato Receives a Medal, Then Is Jailed

In June 1886, Miles decided it was time to move the Apaches from San Carlos and sent an Apache delegation led by Chato to Washington to negotiate the matter. Chato was asked to help convince the Chiricahua to move to Florida, but he refused, stating that his people should be returned to their ancestral home. While in Washington, Chato received a medal and certificate from the War Department for his service to the U.S. Army.

On September 3 or 4, 1886, Geronimo finally surrendered to Miles, who then shipped the Apaches, both from Geronimo's band and the San Carlos reservation, to Fort Marion, Florida. On Chato's return trip from Washington, he too was arrested and sent to Florida. Apparently, Miles and other U.S. government officials decided that all Apaches at San Carlos, even those who had worked as scouts for the Army, would be sent to Florida.

General Crook was livid when he found out what had happened to Chato, and he spent the next several years attempting to free his friend. The conditions at Fort Marion were bad, and the Indian Rights Association along with General Crook fought long and hard to get the Apaches at least moved to a less crowded area. In April 1887, Chato and the other Apaches were moved from Fort Marion to the Mount Vernon Barracks in Alabama, where doctors discovered that many of the Apaches were suffering from starvation. The Apaches fared better in Alabama, but Crook continued his efforts to have them moved back to the Southwest. Finally, in 1894, they were allowed to transfer to the reservation at Fort Sill, Oklahoma, which was at least closer to their ancestral home in Arizona and New Mexico.

After his arrival at Fort Sill, Chato was appointed a headman of a small village a half mile west of the Four Mile Crossing on the reservation. He also was assigned a small plot of land for farming. At some point during his stay at Fort Sill, he converted to Christianity and adopted the name Alfred Chato. Later, he was reinstated as an Army scout.

In 1913, Chato received permission to again travel to Washington to ask that the Apaches be allowed to return to their homeland. Since it had been 40 years since Chato had been home, President William H. Taft suggested that Chato survey the Arizona and New Mexico area to determine if there would be enough water, timber, and grazing land. After a trip west, Chato suggested the Apaches be resettled on the Mescalero reservation in the mountains of New Mexico. Congress had to approve the move, however. New Mexico's Congressmen relayed the fears of their voters that the Apaches might again return to raiding and effectively blocked the move for a short time. It took the intervention of two missionaries, L. L. Legters and Walter C. Roe, to convince the public and Congress that the Apaches would not resume their raids. There were 187 Apaches at Fort Sill who chose to return to the mountains in New Mexico along with Chato; 84 chose to stay at Fort Sill.

Chato was respected by both the Indians and the white community in New Mexico, where he lived the remainder of his life. He died in an automobile accident in March 1934.

SOURCES:

Books

Adams, Alexander B., *Geronimo: A Biography,* New York, G.P. Putnam's Sons, 1971; 242-241.

Baldwin, Gordon C., *The Warrior Apaches,* Tucson, Arizona, Dale Stuart King, 1965; 38-39, 42-47, 50-51.

Betzinez, Jason, and Wilbur Sturtevant Nye, *I Fought with Geronimo,* Harrisburg, Pennsylvania, Stackpole, 1960.

Biographical Dictionary of Indians of the Americas, Newport Beach, California, American Indian Publishers, 1991; 120.

Bourke, John Gregory, *On the Border with Crook,* Chicago, Rio Grande Press, 1962; 452-485.

Brown, Dee, *Bury My Heart at Wounded Knee,* New York, Bantam Books, 1970; 376-387.

Capps, Benjamin, *The Great Chiefs,* Alexandria, Virginia, Time-Life Books, 1975; 80.

Cole, D. C., *The Chiricahua Apache, 1846-1876: From War to Reservation,* Albuquerque, University of New Mexico Press, 1936.

Crook, George, *General George Crook: His Autobiography,* edited by Martin F. Schmitt, Norman, University of Oklahoma Press, 1946; 245-266, 289-301.

Debo, Angie, *Geronimo: The Man, His Time, His Place,* Norman, University of Oklahoma Press, 1976.

Geronimo, *Geronimo: His Own Story,* edited by Frederick W. Turner III, New York, Dutton, 1970; 41, 88-89.

Handbook of American Indians North of Mexico, Part 1, edited by Frederick Webb Hodge, Totowa, New Jersey, Rowman and Littlefield, 1975; 63-67, 282-285.

Lockwood, Frank C., *The Apache Indian,* New York, MacMillan, 1938; 246-247, 262-275, 310-317, 324-327.

Opler, Morris E., "Chiricahua Apache," in *Southwest,* Volume 10, edited by Alfonso Ortiz, in *Handbook of North American Indians,* edited by William C. Sturtevant,

Washington, D.C., Smithsonian Institution, 1983; 401-410.

Thrapp, Dan L., *The Conquest of Apacheria,* Norman, University of Oklahoma Press, 1967; 234-237, 262-263, 272-273, 303-309, 332-335, 363.

Utley, Robert M., *Frontier Regulars: The United States Army and the Indian,* 1866-1891, New York, MacMillan, 1973; 369, 378-383.

Utley, Robert M., and Wilcomb E. Washburn, *History of the Indian Wars,* New York, American Heritage Publishing, 1977; 311-313, 324-327.

Waldman, Carl, *Atlas of the North American Indian,* New York, Facts on File, 1985; 139-143.

Waldman, Carl, *Who Was Who in Native American History,* New York, Facts on File, 1990; 64-65, 131-133.

Washburn, Wilcomb E., *The American Indian and the United States: A Documentary History,* Volume 1, New York, Random House, 1973; 303-307.

Periodicals

Hafford, William, "Chato the Betrayed," *Arizona Highways,* 69:2, February 1993; 14-17.

—Sketch by Catherine A. Clay

Dean Chavers
1941-
Lumbee educator and fund raiser

Dean Chavers has done much to improve education for his Lumbee people and all Native Americans. He has raised large sums of money to aid students in attending college and has provided technical assistance to Indian tribes, contract schools, and health clinics.

Chavers was born on February 4, 1941, in Pembroke, North Carolina, and grew up in that region. In 1959, he was Virginia State Spelling champion among high school students. The next year, he attended college at the University of Richmond, Virginia, from 1960 to 1962.

Serves in Vietnam

The conflict in Vietnam interrupted Chavers' education, and he entered the United States Air Force. As a navigator, he flew 138 missions and won the Distinguished Flying Cross, the Air Medal, and seven other decorations. He left the service as a captain.

Instead of returning to the East, he resumed his education in the West at the University of California at Berkeley. He received a bachelor's degree in journalism in 1970. He furthered his education at Stanford University receiving master's degrees in communications in 1973 and anthropology in 1975. In 1976, he completed his doctorate from Stanford in communications with a dissertation entitled "Social Structure and the Diffusion of Innovations: A Study of Teachers at Four Indian Boarding High Schools and the Effects of their Interpersonal Communication Behavior on Their Adoption of New Ideas in Education."

While working on his degrees, he served as the managing editor of *Indian Voice* magazine in 1972. And from 1972 to 1974, he taught Native American studies as an assistant professor at Hayward State University and served as chair of the Higher Education Committee of the California Indian Education Association. This work led to membership on the board of the national Indian Education Association from 1983 to 1986 and again from 1987 to 1990. In 1972, he joined the National Congress of American Indians (NCAI) and has retained a continuous membership since then.

Raises Money for Indian Education

Between 1970 and 1978, Chavers served as president of the Native American Scholarship Fund of northern California. As part of this organization, he helped raise more than $300,000 for Indian college students. He continued his work in education as president of Bacone College in Muskogee, Oklahoma, from 1978 to 1981. He left academic administration to found his own company, Chavers and Associates, which he maintained until 1988. Chavers and Associates did fund raising work and communications consulting. He provided technical assistance in fund raising, financial management, computer software development, and training for Indian tribes, contract schools, and Indian health clinics.

With interests in Indian education and Indian economic development, Chavers has published five books and over 30 articles on these subjects. He lives and works in Albuquerque, New Mexico.

SELECTED WRITINGS BY CHAVERS:

The Feasibility of an Indian University, Muskogee, Oklahoma, Bacone College, 1979.
Funding Guide for Native Americans, DCA Publications, 1983.
How to Write Winning Proposals, DCA Publications, 1983.
Grants to Indians, DCA Publications, 1984.
The Status of Indian Education, Journal of Thought, 1984.
Tribal Economic Development Directory, DCA Publications, 1985.
The Indian Dropout, Coalition for Indian Education, 1991.

SOURCES:

Native North American Almanac, edited by Duane Champagne, Detroit, Gale Research, 1994.
Reference Encyclopedia of the American Indian, edited by Barry Klein, West Nyack, New York, Todd Publications, 1993.

—Sketch by Christopher B. Tower

Maria Chona
1858(?)-1936
Papago oral historian, medicine woman and basket maker
Also known as Cha-veela

Maria Chona is best remembered outside the Native American community for her oral autobiography *Papago Woman,* recorded by Ruth Underhill, a first-hand account of Native American life in the Southwest. Today, *Papago Woman* is used by beginning and intermediate students of social studies and anthropology. Chona is remembered by the Papago people as a medicine woman, basket maker and good homemaker. Chona was born about 1858 in the village of Mesquite Root at the base of Quijotoa Mountain on the Papago Reservation west of Tucson, Arizona. Underhill believed Chona was about 90 years old when she first spoke to the native women in 1931 and estimated that Chona was born in the mid-1840s. Based on Chona's account of her marriages and the births of her children, however, she was more likely born in the late 1850s.

Chona remembered her father, José Maríe, was the chief of the Tautaukwañi Papago, also known as the Desert People or Bean People. He was named a chief by the conquering Americans sometime after 1853 when the Gadsden Purchase brought the Papago lands under the control of the United States. Chona called her father "Con Quien" ["The Gambler"], a name that came from his love of gambling. He was the principal war chief of the Papago and often led attacks on Apache camps to the east, most often in retaliation for Apache raids on the Papago. He received the title of "Enemy Slayer" as a result of his bravery in battle. Consequently, Chona recalled, her father and his family had to undergo a purification ceremony following the battle to prevent the enemy's spirit from doing them harm.

The reason underlying this purification ceremony makes clear why we have so few details about some important facts of Chona's life. The names of Chona's mother, two brothers and her sister, for example, are not known because of the tribal taboo against speaking the name of a deceased person. The Papago believed that if an individual said a dead person's name out loud, that person's spirit might hear the individual calling and come take that individual away so the spirit would no longer be lonely.

Growing Up Papago

Chona was an active and important member of the Papago tribe from an early age. The Papago believed that children learned by example and did not scold them when they behaved inappropriately. Instead, parents instructed their children in Papago history, mythology, and community. Chona's father, José Maríe, often told her that she must work hard, be industrious, not gossip, and keep a good house if she wanted to marry a good man. But he also talked to her about tribal affairs. For instance, as chief, he often found himself having to resolve marital disputes. According to Chona's autobiography, the most frequent solution involved the beating of one of the spouses with a lash. But he did not like to beat people, so he had another tribal member, known as the Chief's Leg, carry out the punishment. The Chief's Leg also danced with young maidens during their puberty ceremony.

Much of Chona's early life was spent learning how to keep a proper Papago house. Before she was ten, she helped her mother grind seeds and corn for gruel and helped dig roots and pick yucca or cholla cactus or find other food. At ten, she was making the gruel and cooking for her entire family. During the summers ["the time of no rain"], the family packed up and moved south to Mexico where they sold pottery, or north to the River People's territory, where they worked for the Pima Indians. It was on one of the trips to Mexico that Chona was baptized and received her Christian name.

Chona spoke at great length in her autobiography about her first menstrual period, as well as the ceremonies tied to this important coming-of-age event. Before a Papago female child began menstruating, she was permitted to speak to young male relatives. Afterwards, however, she was not allowed to speak to any men until after she as married. During her monthly bleeding, she was not permitted to stay in the same house with a man because the Papago believed a woman's power during that time might harm the men. After Chona's first period, she underwent a purification ceremony and was given a new name, Cha-veela, but she was not told what the name meant. At the same time, her hair was cut short. After the purification and hair cutting, Chief's Leg led her in a dance, which was repeated every night for four nights in a row, to celebrate. Following the ceremony, Chona was allowed to paint her upper body with red dots and splashes. She also travelled with the other women to get water for the family each day and she helped to catch and saddle her brothers' horses. She thought of herself during this time as "excitable" and said she liked to run races with other women and gamble.

A few months after her coming-of-age ceremony, her father told Chona that he had decided upon a husband for her. The prospective groom was 17 and the son of a medicine man who lived at Where the Water Whirls Around. When the boy's father consented to the marriage, he sent his son to Chona's house where they stayed for four nights. After that, the newlyweds moved into his parents' home, where Chona was expected to take over her mother-in-law's cooking and cleaning duties. She did not speak to her husband until about five days after the marriage, when she found a rattlesnake in their bedding. Chona reports that "he said 'Get up and we'll shake our bedding.' After that I felt more at home." Her husband and two of his brothers all became medicine men. A third brother was referred to as a man-woman, because he preferred to do women's work and dressed as a woman. Throughout Chona's marriage to the medicine man, his man-woman brother helped her cook, make baskets and care for her children.

By the time she had her first child, Chona considered herself a modern woman, so she had a priest, rather than the Papago medicine man, name her baby. She did not know much about pregnancy and did not know the exact time to expect the delivery. As a result, she waited until the last possible moment to go to the women's hut and ended up delivering the baby on the way. Later her sister-in-law asked Chona why she had not said something about her pain and commented that Chona had been laughing just a few minutes earlier. Chona replied, "Well, it wasn't my mouth that hurt. It was my middle." She had a total of six children with her first husband. Five of them were sons and all died while they were still nursing. Chona believed that her children died because she had them too close together and she did not have enough milk to feed two babies at the same time. When she had her sixth child, a girl she named Crescenza, she had her mother nurse the baby and the child lived.

Defies Papago Tradition, Leaves Husband

Because Chona's husband was a medicine man, people traded food and clothes in exchange for his healing services. As a result, Chona said, they were rich. When his services were not required, they travelled to Mexico where they exchanged pottery for food, harvested figs, ground wheat, carried wood and water, or performed other jobs for the Mexicans in exchange for food and clothing. Her husband also encouraged Chona to go with him to various tribal celebrations, which most wives were not allowed to do. Chona, however, was an exception—she had learned to sing from her father, and her husband was proud of her singing. When Chona's daughter was 12, her husband took a second wife, which was customary among the Papago. Chona notes that most medicine men often had four wives. But Chona was not happy with the arrangement so she left her husband and returned home.

Within a few days, Chona's male relatives suggested that she marry again, this time to the Chief's Leg, whom she known from her youth. By this time, he was an old man and his first wife had died. Chief's Leg was rich, since he raised and sold horses to both the whites and to peaceful Apaches. Chief's Leg lived at Rock Stands Up, now called Standing Rock, near Tucson. Chona agreed to the marriage, although she said she did not love Chief's Leg and was not even fond of him. On her arrival at Rock Stands Up, her new husband suggested that they go to Tucson where he bought her two shawls, calico for dresses, a canvas bag and her first pair of shoes. Since the Chief's Leg was paid in cash rather than food and clothes, Chona learned to buy and eat store bought food, although she never learned to like it. She never saw her first husband again, but learned a year later that he had died after his second wife had left him.

Chona had two sons with Chief's Leg but, unlike the children she had with her first husband, she had them three years apart. That, she stated, was the reason they lived. Her oldest son was named Vincenzo, also known as Two Bits. He was married at 17 and had many children. Her second son also married at 17 but to a woman not chosen by his parents. His wife later killed him. Chona moved to Tucson and worked for white people instead of going to Mexico each year when the water dried up. She had strange dreams while she lived there and, after what she termed "a white man's disease," she learned to cure babies of illness. When her medicine man brother became ill, she returned home to Mesquite Root to take care of him. Before he died, he taught her his cures for various illnesses and asked her to take over his practice after he died. While she did continue curing children after that, she did not practice medicine on adults.

Telling Her Story

Chona said she lived with her second husband 30 years before he died. This was seven years before she met the woman who helped her record her autobiography. Until her death, she lived primarily with her daughter or son, visited relatives, and made baskets. In 1931, she met anthropologist Ruth Underhill, who recorded Chona's memories of her life as part of the first comprehensive study of Papago culture. Underhill said in *Papago Woman,* "She [Chona] was inclined to be independent and executive.... She learned a manipulation of sick babies which was much respected ... and knew other bits of practical medicine. She had a dynamic personality, which drew patients to her." According to Gretchen Bataille and Kathleen Sands in *American Indian Women Telling Their Story,* Chona was "a paradox— a woman so deeply tied to the landscape and life of traditional Papago culture that she expresses it with lyrical skill, yet so personally independent that she shatters the most firmly entrenched stereotypes applied to Indian women."

When Underhill questioned Chona about her devotion to the traditional Papago role for women, Chona replied, "You see, we *have* power. Men have to dream to get power from the spirits and they think of everything they can—song and speeches and marching around, hoping that the spirits will notice them and give them some power. But we *have* power.... Children. Can any warrior make a child, no matter how brave and wonderful he is?... Don't you see that without us, there would be no men? Why should we envy men? We *made* the men."

SOURCES:

American Indian Women Telling Their Lives, edited by Gretchen M. Bataille and Kathleen M. Sands, University of Nebraska Press, 1984; 49-68.

Dobyns, Henry F., *The Papago People,* Indian Tribal Series, 1972; 33-56.

Native American Women, edited by Gretchen M. Bataille, New York, Garland Publishing, 1993; 55-56.

Papago Indians III Commission Findings, New York, Garland Publishing, 1974; 1-16.

Native North American Almanac, edited by Duane Champagne, Detroit, Gale Research, 1994; 753-761.

Underhill, Ruth M., *Papago Woman,* Holt, 1979.

—*Sketch by Catherine A. Clay*

C. Blue Clark
1946-
Creek historian and university administrator

A member of the Creek Nation, Carter Blue Clark is Executive Vice President of Oklahoma City University. He is also a published author whose writings reflect his interest in and concern for indigenous peoples throughout the Western Hemisphere. Clark received his bachelor's, master's, and Ph.D. degrees from the University of Oklahoma at Norman. His 1970 master's thesis deals with the history of county seats in Oklahoma. His 1976 doctoral dissertation describes the history of the presence of the Ku Klux Klan in that state.

Clark has taught history at many colleges and universities, including UCLA, San Diego State University, Morningside College, the University of Utah, and the University of Oklahoma. He was professor of ethnic studies, U.S. history, and American Indian studies at California State University, Long Beach, from 1984 to 1993. While there, he was director of the American Indian Studies Program. Clark has written and edited several books and is the author of numerous book chapters, journal articles, papers, and book reviews. Thematically, his writings often center on Native peoples of the American west and federal Indian policy and its often disastrous effects on American Indians. Clark's 1994 book *Lone Wolf v. Hitchcock: Treaty Rights and Indian Law at the End of the Nineteenth Century,* which resulted from nearly ten years of research begun while he was a 1984-1985 fellow at the McNickle Center of the Newberry Library, details the 1902 Supreme Court case. The suit was initiated by Kiowa warrior and leader Lone Wolf, who challenged the legality of a 1900 Congressional act permitting the distribution of American Indian lands to non-Indians. Lone Wolf, along with other Kiowa, Comanche, and Plains Apache Indians, and assisting attorneys, argued that the 1900 act violated terms of the 1867 Treaty of Medicine Lodge. With the help of the Indian Rights Association, the case was argued before the Supreme Court in October 1902 as *Lone Wolf v. Hitchcock.* The Supreme Court justices found the act constitutional, stating that Congress had acted "in good faith." This ruling, Clark stated in an earlier article from *Western Legal History,* "marks the weakest recognition of American Indian sovereignty in United States history." As a result of this case, 3,444 land allotments were made for the Kiowas, Comanches, and Apaches, while over 11,638 homesteads were awarded to non-Indians. In 1865, the Kiowas had claimed some 90 million acres; by 1904, only one-half million acres were left to them.

In addition to his works regarding American Indians, Clark has also written extensively on the struggles of the Sumu, Rama, and Miskito Indians in Nicaragua as well as indigenous groups in Guatemala, Peru, and Brazil. Clark observed, in a 1988 commentary in the magazine *Christian-*

ity and Crisis, that while the United States government outwardly bemoaned the injustices perpetrated against oppressed peoples around the world, those within its political borders could not obtain rights of their own. Yet, he noted, Native Americans have been able to preserve their traditions. "Americans do not have to look to South Africa or to Poland for examples of strength under oppression. Indians have carried on traditional spirituality through 500 years of occupation. Tribal languages survive and articulate the innermost meanings for Indian philosophy, interpretation of the universe, and daily adjustments to a smothering alien way of life. Indian cultural traditions endure."

SOURCES:

Books

Chiang Kai-shek and the United States, edited by Carter Blue Clark, United States, IAHE, 1986.

Clark, Blue, *Lone Wolf v. Hitchcock: Treaty Rights and Indian Law at the End of the Nineteenth Century,* Lincoln, University of Nebraska Press, 1994.

Native North American Almanac, edited by Duane Champagne, Detroit, Gale Research, 1994; 1032.

Periodicals

Clark, C. Blue, *"Lone Wolf v. Hitchcock:* Implications for Federal Indian Law at the Start of the Twentieth Century," *Western Legal History,* 5:1, winter/spring 1992; 1-12.

Clark, C. B., "This Land Was Their Land," *Christianity and Crisis,* 48, August 1, 1988; 267-270.

—Sketch by Christina E. Carter

Henry Roe Cloud

Henry Roe Cloud
1886(?)-1950
Winnebago educator and administrator
Also known as Wo-Na-Xi-Lay-Hunka (Wonah'i layhunka) ["War Chief"]

As an educator, Henry Roe Cloud instigated major reforms in Native American schools. The first Native American to graduate from Yale University, Cloud founded the Roe Indian Institute (later renamed the American Indian Institute), led the noted Haskell Institute, and served in the Office of Indian Affairs. Although he felt that Native Americans had no choice but to assimilate into white society, he fought for the preservation of Native American identity and leadership.

In a 1916 autobiographical essay, "From Wigwam to Pulpit," Cloud said he was born in the winter of 1884, but most sources indicate he was born December 28, 1886, at Winnebago in Thurston County, Nebraska. He was a member of the Bird Clan, which could prevent or instigate a war. His grandfather was called "Yellow Cloud," his father was Na-Xi-Lay-Hunk-Kay or Nah'ilayhunkay, and his mother was named "Hard-To-See." The Winnebago people spoke a Siouan dialect, which was the only language Cloud spoke for his first ten years. He later became fluent in English, Latin, and Greek.

In "From Wigwam to Pulpit," he recalled that an uncle first taught him the "art of worship." "He used to lead me to the sandy banks of the Missouri River, where he would set fire to a pile of driftwood, and then, taking me by the hand, sing sacred songs to the fire and river.... I never knew the meaning of these offerings, but I always felt that some living thing actuated both the fire and the river." Around the age of seven, Cloud went to the Genoa Indian School for two years. He remembered that during his years there he herded sheep, flew kites, and fought with another boy, among other things that had nothing to do with education. When he returned home, he could not communicate with his parents for several weeks because he could not remember his native language. He relearned the language, however, before returning to school.

The Indian police, who took him to his first school, also came to take him to the Winnebago Reservation government school a short time after his return home from Genoa. It was at the reservation school that he wrote an essay in which he said he wanted Jesus as his friend. The essay resulted in a Presbyterian minister, the Reverend William T. Findley, telling the young boy the story of Jesus. "I felt a strange constraint to accept this new spirit-friend," Cloud later recalled. Since making friends among Indians was considered a special act that required the friends to stand by and defend each other, Cloud considered his new friendship with Jesus in the same way. This friendship also required that he stop fighting with other boys, but that led others to label him a coward. His family also cautioned him about following the white man's path. "A severe soul-struggle began, but I determined to remain true to my new Spirit Friend," Cloud said in his autobiography. During this same period, he was baptized and took the name Henry Cloud.

His parents died shortly after he was baptized, and not long after that he began attending the Santee Mission School, which was about 100 miles from his home. While many of the other eight Winnebago boys who were sent to the school ran away, Cloud decided to stay. He attended that school for four years. In 1902, he decided to attend Mount Hermon, a school founded by D. L. Moody in Massachusetts. It took him five years to graduate, because he worked on a farm in New Jersey to earn the money to attend.

In 1906, he entered Yale University. While there, he met Mrs. Walter C. Roe, who spoke to an assembly about American Indians. He had not met or heard much about other Indians who had become Christians until her speech. As a result of that meeting, he spent the summer of 1907 at the Fort Sill Reservation in Oklahoma, where he met Reverend Dr. Walter C. Roe, a missionary with the Dutch Reformed Church. Dr. Roe became his friend and mentor. After a time, the Roes adopted him, and he honored them by adding the name Roe to his Christian name.

In 1910, Cloud became the first Native American to graduate from Yale University, receiving a degree in anthropology. He spent a year at Oberlin Seminary College studying sociology before moving on to Auburn Theological Seminary, where he received a Bachelor of Divinity degree in 1913. The same year, he was ordained as a Presbyterian minister. The next year, he received his master's degree in anthropology from Yale. Later in his life, he returned to school in Kansas and received a doctorate of divinity from Emporia College in 1932. Cloud came to the attention of Washington officials in 1912 and 1913 when he chaired a delegation of Winnebagos that met with President William H. Taft. In 1914, Washington called upon him to serve on the Survey Commission on Indian Education.

Walter Roe had wanted to establish an inter-denominational school to train Indians from all the various tribes to be Christian leaders. Although he died before his dream could become a reality, his adopted son acted on his dream and established the Roe Indian Institute in Wichita, Kansas, in 1915. In 1920, it was renamed the American Indian Institute. Cloud thought that Indian children needed a Christian motive in their lives, and providing this motive became a central aim both in his work with the American Indian Institute and later in his career.

On June 12, 1916, Cloud married Elizabeth Georgian Bender, who was the sister of baseball figure "Chief" Bender. She was Minnesota Ojibwa (Chippewa) and helped Cloud manage the Institute. They had four daughters: Elizabeth Marion, Anne Woesha, Lillian Alberta, and Ramona Clarke Cloud. A son named for his father died in infancy.

In 1923, Cloud was appointed to U.S. Secretary of Interior Hubert Work's Committee of 100, which investigated Native American policies and produced a report entitled "The Indian Problem." The study essentially recommended increasing budgets for Native American education and scholarships, health care, and for the courts that were adjudicating land claims. The report was supposed to address the concerns of various Indian reform groups about the issue of giving Indian lands to non-Indians, but the reformers were dissatisfied, believing that the report did not go far enough in its recommendations.

Co-Authors Influential "Meriam Report"

As a result of the reformers' discontent, in June 1926, Secretary Work asked the Institute for Government Research at the Brookings Institute to investigate the problems further. The Institute, a non-government agency that received money from John D. Rockfeller, Jr., to complete the report, used a panel of Indian experts to study Indian issues. Cloud was a member of that panel and co-authored its final report, called "The Meriam Report," published in 1928. The report outlined the poor health of Indians on reservations, deficiencies in educational programs, and living conditions at Indian schools, as well as the various problems involving land claims. It also served as the match that lit the fire of Indian reorganization during the next decade.

From 1931 to 1933, Cloud served as a special regional representative to the Office of Indian Affairs and assisted in developing the plans for the Indian Reorganization Act of 1934. The Act gave Indians the right to govern themselves in addition to dealing with health, education, and land issues. Among the many changes resulting from that report was that more Indian children were encouraged to enroll in public schools rather than being sent to boarding schools. As a reward for his efforts, Cloud was appointed superintendent of the well-known Haskell Institute in Lawrence, Kansas, in 1933. In 1935, he received the Indian Achievement medal from the Indian Council Fire. The following year, he was recruited to be the supervisor of Indian education at the Bureau of Indian Affairs, where he continued to make improvements in Indian educational programs until 1947. That year, Cloud was named superintendent of the Umatilla Indian Agency in Pendleton, Oregon. In 1948, he was appointed the regional representative for the Grande Ronde and Siletz Indian Agencies in Oregon.

Cloud died of a heart attack (coronary thrombosis) in Siletz, Oregon, on February 9, 1950. At the time of his death, he was encouraging northwestern Native Americans to develop family genealogies to provide a basis for awarding a $16 million court settlement over land disputes. During his life, he also served as a vice president of the Society of American Indians, which was an Indian activist organization later renamed the National Council of American Indians. At one time, he also served as editor of *Indian Outlook.*

SOURCES:

Biographical Dictionary of Indians of the Americas, second edition, Newport Beach, California, American Indian Publishers, 1991; 133.

Cloud, Henry Roe, "From Wigwam to Pulpit," *Southern Workman,* July 1916; 400-406.

Debo, Angie, *Geronimo: The Man, His Time, His Place,* Norman, University of Oklahoma Press, 1976; 428-432.

Dictionary of American Biography, Supplement Four: 1946-1950, edited by John A. Garraty and Edward T. James, New York, Charles Scribner's Sons, 1974; 165-166.

Dockstader, Frederick J., *Great North American Indians,* New York, Van Nostrand Reinhold, 1977; 51-52.

Handbook of American Indians North of Mexico, Part 2, edited by Frederick Webb Hodge, Totowa, New Jersey, Rowman and Littlefield, 1975; 958-961.

Indians of Today, edited by Marion E. Gridley, Chicago, Millar Publishing, 1947; 24.

Native North American Almanac, edited by Duane Champagne, Detroit, Gale Research, 1994; 52, 669-673, 1033.

Tyler, S. Lyman, *A History of Indian Policy,* Washington, D.C., Bureau of Indian Affairs, United States Department of the Interior, 1973; 112-147.

—*Sketch by Catherine A. Clay*

Cochise
1823(?)-1874
Chiracahua Apache tribal leader

A tribal leader and an excellent military tactician, Cochise was perhaps the most influential Apache in the battle to retain Native land. He is known, according to Scott C. Russell in the *American Indian Quarterly,* as a "major nemesis of both the American and Mexican governments in the areas of southern Arizona and New Mexico and in northern Mexico."

Conflicting reports exist as to the exact date Cochise was born, but most written sources believe it was either during 1812 or 1823. Similarly, the location of his birth as well as the date of his death are also unknown. Some material suggests he was born about 1810, and that the history of his native Apache tribe was influenced by more than 300 years of resisting Spain's northward expansion. Sources conclude he probably was born in what was known at the time as Ari-

zona Territory, and surmise he died on either June 7 or 8, 1874. Cochise's name means "hardwood." He was a member of the Chiracahua, one of many Apache factions contributing to the tribal and band divisions that made up the group generally recognized as the Apache. It is assumed that Cochise grew to adulthood much the same way other youths of his tribe matured, and that he was affected by the constant traditional tribal fighting between groups in his region and those in northern Mexico. If he were to be caught by traditional enemies of his tribe, there would be a bounty on his head. It was this same repeated generational fighting with Mexicans that reportedly took the life of his father.

Cochise was relatively unknown to outsiders as a tribal leader until 1861, when he was brought to the attention of U.S. military personnel. In February of that year, a report came into the Arizona garrison at Fort Buchanan from a rancher. The rancher complained of an Apache raid, and highlighted the reported incident of cattle theft by saying his son had been abducted by the group. The child became known as Mickey Free, who later joined the army and became a scout. George Bascom, a garrison lieutenant, organized a posse of 50 men in response to the complaint. Bascom then led the soldiers to Apache Pass, located along heart of Chiracahua Apache country. The Southern Overland (Butterfield) Trail brought them to their final destination, a mail station from which Bascom could send word via a scout to Cochise requesting a meeting. As the story goes, Cochise acquiesced and appeared with his family members (including his youngest son Naiche) carrying a truce flag. The lieutenant accused Cochise of the raid and placed him under arrest.

Some sources report the incident as having occurred to a squatter complaining to the garrison of an abducted adopted son by a group of Pinal Apache in October of 1880. It was in February of 1861 that Bascom and Cochise first met in Bascom's tent. Bascom, young and inexperienced (having just arrived from West Point Academy), apparently was convinced that it was Cochise who led his followers to abduct the child. In this variation of the account, Bascom and his men did not pursue and then request a meeting with Cochise; instead Cochise and five companions paid Bascom a surprise visit one evening in his quarters.

Each variation of the incidents converge on four points of agreement, the first being that in each account, Bascom is certain of Cochise's guilt in the matter. The second is that Cochise, spokesperson for his group, proclaims complete innocence, denying any involvement in or knowledge of the abduction, which is the focal point of the confrontation. Third, when Bascom either arrests or threatens Cochise with arrest if he does not immediately produce the boy, Cochise and his group are forced to flee and Cochise cuts his way out of the tent. Last, one member of Cochise's group is killed in the attempted escape, and the other four members taken prisoner, leaving Cochise wounded and the sole escapee. The Apache Wars are considered to have begun with this incident, known historically as the Bascom Affair. Upon return to his camp, Cochise garnered active support in his attempts to avenge the capture of his companions who accompanied him to his meeting with Bascom. Among those who joined him were Mimbrenos, and his father-in-law Mangas Coloradas, from whom he received early leadership training, and with whom he was very close. In addition, his followers included members of the White Mountain (Coyotero) Apache tribe.

The Civil and Apache Wars

During the same time, events in the eastern United States were leading up to the Civil War. Cochise had no way of comprehending what factors beyond his immediate existence were impacting his situation. Cochise spoke no English, and the officials he encountered most likely had even less facility of his dialect. Communication was reliant upon the skills and integrity of an interpreter. Warfare was increasingly heavy in the Southwest. Some sources testify that it was specifically Apache raids that created the destruction that reverberated through Arizona and pushed Mexicans and Anglo-Americans from the state. Apache raids were also held responsible for disruption of communications between the East and West Coasts.

A variety of conflicting agendas and influences kept the region in turmoil, but a great deal of credit for the conflict was placed on the Apaches. In his book *Cochise: Chiricahua Apache Chief,* Edwin R. Sweeney provides an in-depth overview of the kinds of problems that kept the Apache factions at war with surrounding groups of Mexicans and Americans. Roger L. Nichols points out in his review of the book for *Ethnohistory* that "Sweeney's discussion shows clearly, however, that the Apaches were no more bloodthirsty than the Mexicans or the Anglo-Americans there at the time."

In an attempt to quell the turmoil resulting from the Bascom Affair, a governmental decision was made to deploy troops in the area. However, during the early years of the American Civil War, there was a shortage of men available for military duty. Western recruits were being sent to do battle in the East. As an alternative, Colonel James H. Carleton was sent in, leading 3,000 volunteers from California. In response, Cochise and his father-in-law, a highly respected leader in his own right, devised a trap for the new soldiers. While their forces only represented 500, they were able to hold Carleton and his troops at bay with breastworks until Carleton introduced short cannons (howitzers) onto the battlefield at Apache Pass. With Mangas wounded, Cochise retreated.

Reputation of Cochise

In his *Western Historical Quarterly* review of Sweeney's book *Cochise: Chiricahua Apache Chief,* Leonard R. Bruguier describes Cochise as "a powerful warrior who led by example," adding that "he possessed a discerning intellect with respect for truth, and his generosity, wisdom, and compassion earned respect from all who came within his circle." According to Russell in the *American Indian Quarterly* review of Sweeney's book, Cochise was an "American Indian leader of mythical proportions. A rela-

tively few outsiders actually talked to Cochise and his followers during these years due to the hostile relationships. Any interaction that occurred also would have been through an intermediary, an interpreter." Nichols describes Cochise as "elusive," calling attention to the leader's quietness and pointing out that "Cochise left no impassioned speeches; he spoke little, if any, English; and his ... adversaries spoke even less Apache. Few whites interviewed the elusive leader, and those who saw him did not record enough to enable any twentieth-century scholar to depict or analyze his character, desires, or motives with much hope of accuracy."

Developing Governmental Policy on Native Americans

At around the same time of Cochise's birth in the early part of the nineteenth century, government officials were pondering two primary questions with regard to Native or indigenous peoples of North America. A question of domesticity came first. Natives were perceived as uncivilized savages, and the question was whether or not they could be made civilized. Second came the matter of whether Natives were an inferior race when compared to white Europeans. As a method of addressing these questions, the sciences of craniology (the study of skull characteristics) and phrenology (the study of brain protuberances) were developed in attempts to prove racial inferiority to white Europeans, and to explore the basis of justifying westward expansion and therefore establishing policy for the removal of Native Americans from their lands.

In 1823, Samuel G. Morton, known as the originator of physical anthropology in America, began researching the question of inferiority by dissecting Native skulls from the Midwest in Pennsylvania. Within ten years, it had become fashionable among the elite to maintain collections of Native American skulls, and people were sending Morton (at his request) different geographic tribal samples for making comparisons. Operating under the assumption that Native Americans as a race would cease to exist, zoologist Louis Agassiz (Morton's contemporary) began to collect Native American bodies in the 1850s in order to form the Museum of Comparative Zoology at Harvard University. Another contemporary, anthropologist Franz Boas, is documented as having paid grave diggers and body robbers handsomely for their acquisitions. Military collection of Native American remains was documented up until 1904.

Father-in-Law Lost in Battle

One year after Carleton descended upon Cochise and his followers with troops comprised of 3,000 volunteers, his soldiers captured and killed Mangas Coloradas. Cochise and his followers, numbering less than 200, were driven into the Dragoon Mountains. For a decade he and his warriors kept the U.S. Army at bay by vandalizing and utilizing hit-and-run tactics to raid and kill whites. In an attempt to bring an end to the Apache Wars, General George Crook was sent in during June of 1871. Experienced at locating Native renegades, Crook instituted the use of Apache warriors as scouts to find Cochise. Some sources attribute Crook with tracking him down and negotiating peace, while others report that Cochise eluded him. Sources agree that Cochise declined an offer to be relocated with his people onto a reservation located in Fort Tularosa, New Mexico.

A mail carrier by the name of Thomas J. Jeffords had lost 14 of his white employees to Cochise and his warriors. He spoke a little Apache, and decided to go see Cochise regarding the matter. Risking his life, he entered Cochise's camp alone and offered his firearms in exchange for talks. In his *American West* article "Tom Jeffords, Friend of Cochise," C. L. Sonnichsen quotes Jeffords as having said that Cochise was "so astonished and impressed by this intrepid white man that he made him welcome. 'I spent two or three days with him discussing affairs with him and sizing him up.'" The result of this meeting was that Jeffords and Cochise developed a working relationship; Jeffords' carriers then passed through Cochise's territory unharmed.

With the aid of Jeffords acting as scout, General Oliver Howard was successful in arranging a negotiation meeting with Cochise during the autumn of 1872. Howard had been sent by President Ulysses S. Grant to make another attempt at putting an end to the Apache Wars. In exchange for Howard's promise to give Cochise and his people reservation land along Apache Pass (Chiracahua Mountains), Cochise agreed to stop killing whites. Cochise's one condition to the settlement was that Jeffords be the liaison between his people and the U.S. government; Jeffords reluctantly agreed. During the ensuing four years, the agreement was kept intact, but decayed after Cochise's death in 1874. Neither the cause of his death, nor the location of Cochise's burial mound has been found.

As for the settlement agreement, some sources say that at the succession of his sons, the eldest (Taza) attempted to maintain it, while the youngest (Naiche) disregarded the pact after Taza's death. All agree that Jeffords was held responsible for the breech and was subsequently dismissed from his post. The reservation was dissolved and its members either fled or were relocated to the San Carlos Agency.

Jeffords received scarce recognition for his role in ending the Apache Wars and in subduing Cochise. He was denigrated by his contemporaries for his involvements with the leader. Sonnichsen quotes a rancher acquainted with Jeffords as having said during a 1926 interview: "[Jeffords was] a no-good filthy fellow—filthy in his way of living— lived right among those damn things ... was a blood brother or something of Cochise. He wasn't very bright." Jeffords received the remaining brunt of hostilities for the failed agreement after Cochise's death. He was labeled a murderer and publicly hailed as "an incarnate demon." Jeffords died a recluse in 1914.

For many, Cochise stands as a figure of inspiration and dignity. Published in *Prairie Schooner,* John Frederick Garmon's poem "The Silence of Cochise" illustrates the leader's wisdom and integrity among his people. In addition to a number of biographies written on Cochise and his involvement with the Apache Wars, his unprecedented relationship with Jeffords has been the subject of novels and films created during the latter half of the twentieth century. Elliott Arnold's *Blood Brother,* published in 1947, depicts them as prototypes of the Western genre, while the film *Broken Arrow,* produced in 1951 and featuring actors Jimmy Stewart and Jeff Chandler, does the same. In his article on Jeffords, Sonnichsen writes that "Arnold broke new ground in his novel when he made Jeffords a spokesman for the movement, just getting under way, that idealized Indian lifestyles and downgraded white 'civilization'—a movement that produced such partisan tracts as *Bury My Heart at Wounded Knee* and *Custer Died for Your Sins.* Jeffords would surely have been surprised to find himself expressing such views."

SOURCES:

Books

Biographical Dictionary of Indians of the Americas, Newport Beach, California, American Indian Publishers, 1983; 105-106.

La Farge, Oliver, *Cochise of Arizona: The Pipe of Peace is Broken,* New York, Aladdin Books, 1953.

Native North American Almanac, edited by Duane Champagne, Detroit, Gale Research, 1994; 1033.

Roberts, David, *Once They Moved Like the Wind: Cochise, Geronimo, and the Apache Wars,* New York, Simon & Schuster, 1993.

Sweeney, Edwin R., *Cochise: Chiricahua Apache Chief,* Norman, University of Oklahoma Press, 1991.

Waldman, Carl, *Who Was Who in Native American History,* New York, Facts on File, 1990; 72.

Wyatt, Edgar, *Cochise, Apache Warrior and Statesman,* New York, McGraw, 1953.

Periodicals

Bieder, Robert E., "Why Were Native America Remains Taken to Museums for Study and Research," *Akwesasne Notes,* 23:2, 1994; 10-11 (from "A Brief Historical Survey of the Expropriation of the American Indian Remains" [dissertation], April 1990, Bloomington, Indiana; condensed for presentation by Red Arrow, Sisseton, South Dakota).

Bruguier, Leonard R., review of *Cochise: Chiricahua Apache Chief, Western Historical Quarterly,* 23, August 1992; 379-380.

Garmon, John Frederic, "The Silence of Cochise," *Prairie Schooner,* 67, fall 1993; 134.

Nichols, Roger L., review of *Cochise: Chiricahua Apache Chief, Ethnohistory,* 39, summer 1992; 359-360.

Russell, Scott C., review of *Cochise: Chiricahua Apache Chief, American Indian Quarterly,* 17, summer 1993; 431-432.

Sonnichsen, C. L., "Tom Jeffords, Friend of Cochise," *American West,* 20, September/October 1983.

—Sketch by Brett A. Lealand

Mangas Coloradas
1790(?)-1863
Mimbreno Apache tribal leader and warrior
Also known as Mangas and Mangas Colorado
["Red Sleeves" or "Red Shirt"]

Some authorities cite Mangas Coloradas as the most significant Apache war chief of the nineteenth century, although some dispute whether he was formally recognized as their chief. Americans and Hispanics of the period described Mangas as an influential statesman, diplomat, and sage, as well as a ferocious, uncompromising, and brutal butcher who laid waste huge tracts of northern Mexico, all of Arizona, and much of New Mexico. His name was synonymous with terror. Despite his apparent penchant for violence, however, he was said to be a peace-loving man whose only interest was in preventing the Hispanics and Americans from overrunning his people's lands.

A member of the Mimbreno ["Willow"] band of the eastern Chihenne ["Red Paint People"] Apache, Mangas Coloradas was born between 1790 and 1795, probably somewhere in what is now southern New Mexico. His nomadic band inhabited the area of the Mimbres Mountains and along the Mimbres River. At that time this territory was part of the Janos district of New Spain. The early nineteenth century was characterized by a low level of hostility between the Spanish and Apache. This would change around 1831, however, and Mangas would figure prominently in the Apaches' attempts to drive the Spanish, and later the Mexicans and Americans, from ancestral Apache lands.

Physically Mangas was described as very muscular and unusually tall for an Apache: over six feet. His most prominent feature was his large head, described by John Cremony in *Life among the Apaches* as having "a broad, bold forehead, a large aquiline nose, a most capacious mouth, and a broad, heavy chin. His eyes were rather small, but exceedingly brilliant and flashing when under any excitement—although his outside demeanor was as imperturbable as brass." One legend suggested he was at least half white.

Origins Are Subject of Speculation

Mangas Coloradas' name initially appeared in historical documents in 1842. He was cited as a Mogollon leader, with the Mogollons being another of the eastern Apache bands. It has been suggested that prior to 1842 he was known by some other name. He may have received his Spanish name meaning "red sleeves" or "roan shirt" either because his shirt had sleeves of red fabric, or because it was covered with his victims' blood. The latter may be applicable given Mangas' revenge for the murder in 1837 of Juan Jose Compa, his predecessor.

Prior to this event he may have been known as Fuerte, who was the dominant Chihenne leader from 1815 through the 1830s. "Fuerte," Spanish for "strong," could well have been used to describe a man like Mangas. Mangas and Fuerte seemed to be about the same age, and both were called by the title "general." Fuerte, however, is on record of officially receiving this title, while Mangas is not. Besides a similarity in their physical features, they seemed to share the practice of distancing themselves from Mexicans, taking what the administrators could be made to give them but keeping personal contact to a minimum. Fuerte lived near the Mimbres River and Santa Rita del Cobre, where Mangas had his stronghold. He disappeared around 1840. It is also possible that up until 1840 Mangas was simply overshadowed by Fuerte, and assumed power as his position weakened. Mangas reportedly became chief of the Mimbrenos about 1837.

The Apache language was a difficult one to learn and speak. This was possibly one reason why Spanish names were often assigned to people and places. Thus virtually none of the original Apache names are known. The Spanish intended to create out of the nomadic Apache a population of self-sufficient farmers. Some of the regulations they imposed on the Apache to force them into farming were requiring passports for those who wished to travel in the territory, and forbidding traditional hunting and gathering without a permit. They rewarded loyal Apache allies with gifts of horses or in some cases the return of incarcerated relatives. When the Mexicans gained independence from Spain in 1821, the region was opened to commerce from the outside, and raiding became more profitable than farming. Many Apache left their farms and assumed very successful and lucrative roles of middlemen; raiding and trading, especially in horses, mules, and captives. One of these captives became Mangas Coloradas' principal wife.

Arranged Inter-Tribal Alliances

While on a raid in Sonora, Mangas abducted an attractive, intelligent Mexican girl. She was given the name Tues-seh and bore three exceptionally attractive daughters. When Dos-teh-seh, the eldest, came of age, Mangas presented her to Cochise, leader of the Chiricahua ["Mountain of the Wild Turkeys"] Apache, for his wife. He gave his second daughter to Katu-hala, leader of the White Mountain Apache, and the third to Cosito, chief of the Coyotero Apache. While it is well-documented that Dos-teh-seh married Cochise, the identity of the husbands of the other two daughters are disputed. Some claim Mangas gave one to the chief of the Navajo and another to the head chief of the Mescalero Apache. In any case, Mangas' intent with all the marital arrangements was to forge alliances and create stronger relationships within the tribes, including the Navajo, who were enemies of the Mexicans and the Spanish before them.

Mangas was described as a statesman, actively shaping and conducting Apache policy with respect to the whites. These marriages seemed to show that he knew the threat from the Mexicans and Americans was greater than any inter-tribal or inter-band dispute, and the only hope of overcoming that threat was to unify the bands and tribes against it. If indeed this was his strategy, he was for all practical purposes the only Indian since Tecumseh to realize the value of unification. Despite this, only his alliance with Cochise was completely successful. In addition to his daughters, Mangas Coloradas had at least three sons: Seth-mooda, Casco, and Mangas. His brothers of record were Jose Mangas, Phalis Palacio, and Chaha. He may have had additional brothers or sisters.

Attempted to Drive Whites from Apache Lands

The Spanish government and the Mexican government which succeeded it had customarily provided rations to the Apache. When the Mexican government discontinued this practice in 1831, strained relations between the Mexicans and Apaches caused the Indians to intensify their raids on towns and ranches. The state of Chihuahua declared general war on Apaches on October 16, 1831. Mangas' theater of operations in the early 1840s encompassed the Chihuahua state and the Mogollon Mountains. He expanded this to include Sonora state by the 1850s. In 1856 Mexican officials offered a bounty for Mangas Coloradas' head.

Raiding allowed the Apache to maintain some semblance of their traditional livelihood; it suited their nomadic nature. But atrocities against their victims were generally not part of their raids. In the case of Mangas, however, this changed radically as a result of two notable incidents which precipitated his hatred of all whites.

The first of these concerned John Johnson, an American who made his living hunting Apaches. He traded the scalps of his victims to the Mexican government in exchange for a bounty. In April of 1837, Johnson, after befriending the Mimbreno head chief Juan Jose Compa, ambushed and massacred Juan Jose and about 20 members of his band near Santa Rita in the Sierra de las Animas (modern Hidalgo County, New Mexico). Mangas was apparently related to Juan Jose, and he retaliated by killing a group of 22 American miners as well as whatever other Americans he could find in the area. In an interesting turnaround, when he met General Stephen Kearney in 1846, he pledged his friendship to the Americans and alliance if Kearney wanted to invade Mexico. Kearney refused.

The second incident, in April 1851, also occurred near Santa Rita. An influx of gold miners angered the Apaches because it drove off game and mocked their spiritual traditions. Mangas offered to lead the miners to an area richer in gold than the mines at Santa Rita, where they could pick large nuggets off the ground. Suspecting he was trying to lure them away individually and kill them, the miners bound him to a tree and whipped him to near unconsciousness. The beating was so humiliating, Mangas hid in the mountains for two weeks until his back healed.

As a result of these experiences, Mangas' assaults against the whites became increasingly brutal and murderous. His infamous trademark was leaving the hats on the scalped heads of his victims. Since whites wore hats and Apaches did not, Mangas ordered his men to shoot anyone wearing a hat. The hat would remain even when only bones

were left, testifying to Mangas' killing of another enemy. In yet another turnaround, Mangas and a group of chiefs signed a treaty with the U.S. government in 1852 at Acoma Pueblo, but Congress refused to ratify it. Atrocities thus continued, and Colonel E. V. Sumner's official report for 1852 strongly recommended giving New Mexico back to the Indians and Mexicans.

Tortured and Murdered at Fort McLean

Mangas Coloradas and Cochise joined forces in 1861, when several of Cochise's relatives were executed by Lieutenant George M. Bascom's Seventh Infantry. Mangas and Cochise intended to drive all Americans from their lands. In 1862 Mangas was wounded in the chest by John Teal in the battle of Apache Pass in Arizona. He was taken to Janos, Chihuahua, where his band coerced a doctor to treat him. He made a full recovery.

In January 1863, he was captured by Captain Edmond Shirland's First California Volunteer Cavalry. Lured into Shirland's camp by a flag of truce, Mangas trusted Shirland and rode in alone. He was taken to Fort McLean in Arizona, where he was killed by guards when he protested against their torturing him with hot bayonets. An inaccurate report of his capture and death stated he was killed while attempting escape. Convinced the Americans could not be trusted, the Apaches began another campaign to eliminate the whites.

Mangas' murder in itself had a profound effect on the Apache, but the mutilation of his body by the soldiers (he was scalped and buried in a ditch) further excited their rage. Captain D. B. Sturgeon, fort surgeon, exhumed the body, had the head cut off, the meat boiled from the bones, and the skull sent to a phrenologist, O. S. Fowler, who pronounced it of greater capacity than Daniel Webster's.

Despite his years of savage tactics, Mangas' principal aim seemed to be obtaining a lasting peace for his people, a goal for which he continually placed himself in harm's way. A 1970s survey of Chiricahua Apaches living in New Mexico and Oklahoma revealed that while many remembered the murder of Mangas Coloradas, comparatively few recalled Pearl Harbor—despite the fact that radical changes had taken place in Chiricahua culture in the century since Mangas' death occurred.

SOURCES:

Ball, Eve, Nora Henn, and Lynda Sanchez, *Indeh, an Apache Odyssey,* Provo, Utah, Brigham Young University Press, 1980.

Betzinez, Jason, and Wilbur Sturtevant Nye, *I Fought with Geronimo,* Harrisburg, Pennsylvania, Stackpole, 1959.

Brown, Dee, *Bury My Heart at Wounded Knee,* New York, Holt, 1970.

Clum, Woodworth, *Apache Agent,* Cambridge, Massachusetts, Riverside Press, 1936.

Cremony, John C., *Life among the Apaches,* Glorieta, New Mexico, Rio Grande Press, 1970.

Griffen, William B., *Apaches at War & Peace: The Janos Presidio, 1750-1858,* Albuquerque, University of New Mexico, 1988.

Roberts, David, *Once They Moved Like the Wind,* New York, Simon & Schuster, 1993.

Santee, Ross, *Apache Land,* Lincoln, University of Nebraska Press, 1947.

Sweeney, Edwin R., *Cochise, Chiricahua Apache Chief,* Norman, University of Oklahoma Press, 1991.

Thrapp, Dan L., *The Conquest of Apacheria,* Norman, University of Oklahoma Press, 1967.

Worcester, Donald E., *The Apaches,* Norman, University of Oklahoma Press, 1979.

—*Sketch by Claudeen E. McAuliffe*

Colorado, Mangas
See Mangas Coloradas

Elizabeth Cook-Lynn

Elizabeth Cook-Lynn
1930-
Crow Creek Sioux poet and professor

Elizabeth Cook-Lynn is a poet and a professor of American Indian studies and English. She is also managing editor of *Wicazo Sa Review: A Journal of Native American Studies,* an interdisciplinary scholarly publication since 1985.

She was born Elizabeth Bowed Head Irving on November 17, 1930, at the Indian Health Service (IHS) hospital in Fort Thompson, South Dakota, on the Crow Creek Reservation. During her childhood, she lived in a traditional extended-family atmosphere. She has one sister; her brother is deceased.

Cook-Lynn grew up in a family whose names are familiar figures in Indian history, and whose dedication to their people and their culture had a profound influence on her writing, as well as her social and political views. Her grandfather, Joseph Bowed Head Irving of the Yankton Sioux, was a skilled linguist, and was instrumental in the production of Dakotah language dictionaries. An accomplished tribal politician, Bowed Head, along with Cook-Lynn's father, Jerome Bowed Head Irving of the Sisseton Sioux, served on the Crow Creek Tribal Council. At the turn of the century, Bowed Head and other tribal leaders such as Sitting Bull, with whom he was photographed on a couple of occasions, traveled to Washington, D.C., to negotiate treaties on behalf of the Dakota/Lakota people. Eliza Renville, Cook-Lynn's grandmother and namesake, was Bowed Head's wife. She was a member of a well-known French and Indian family on the Sisseton Sioux Reservation. Her father was a brother to the Santee Chieftain, Gabriel Renville. She was respected for her ability as a bilingual writer, and her skills were employed by early Christian newspapers in the area.

Later in life, Cook-Lynn married and raised a family of her own. "Cook-Lynn" is actually a hyphenation of her former spouse's and second husband's surnames—Melvin Traversie Cook (Lakota) and Clyde Lynn (Spokane), respectively. She has four adult children: David, Mary, Lisa and Margaret, and two grandsons: Tep and Kesse. Her children and grandchildren are enrolled members of the Crow Creek, Cheyenne River, Yankton, and Rosebud Sioux tribes in South Dakota.

Pursues Education and Becomes Writer

In her autobiographical essay "You May Consider Speaking about Your Art...," which appears in the book, *I Tell You Now: Autobiographical Essays by Native American Writers,* she states: "Ever since I learned to read, I have wanted to be a writer." However, her schooling in the written word did not begin with pen and pencil, but with the oral tradition shared by her family and others on the reservation. She learned that history was the key to understanding the present, and as Cook-Lynn mastered the art of story-telling, she learned about her people. When asked in an interview where she was born, Cook-Lynn not only answered with her birthplace, but with a discussion of the historical circumstances that rendered the Great Sioux Reservation into eight different reservations. Similarly, regarding her "Indian" name, Cook-Lynn answered by placing her life in the historical context of her family and her people and related how she, like many of her generation, did not receive an Indian name in the traditional way because the United States government had outlawed Indian religion for much of the twentieth century—rendering even the basic, daily life rituals illegal, anti-Christian and, therefore, dangerous for her people.

In terms of formal education, Cook-Lynn, like many Indian children at the time, attended such schools as Iron Nation Elementary and Stephen Mission All Saint's School. After graduating from high school, she attended South Dakota State College, earning a bachelor of arts degree in journalism and English in 1952. Cook-Lynn's early career was in newspaper journalism, as a writer and editor in South Dakota. She was a secondary school teacher in Carlsbad, New Mexico, from 1958 to 1964, and later for one year at Rapid City Central in South Dakota.

In 1968, Cook-Lynn took education courses at the University of Mexico, Las Cruces. She completed her master's degree in psychology, education and counseling at the University of South Dakota in 1970. After completing her master's degree, Cook-Lynn joined the faculty of Eastern Washington State University in Cheney that same year. She was an associate professor of English and American Indian studies until 1991, when she left and was awarded professor emeritus status. During this time, she did graduate study at the University of Nebraska, Lincoln, in 1974, and studied briefly at Stanford University in California in 1976. She has been a visiting professor at the University of California, Davis, and at other various universities. Cook-Lynn lives in Rapid City and writes full-time, having completed another novel and a nonfiction manuscript.

Gains Stature as Native American Writer

Cook-Lynn's work has appeared in various literary magazines and scholarly journals throughout her writing career, including *Sun Tracks, Prairie Schooner, South Dakota Review, Great Plains Observer,* and *The Ethnic Studies Journal.* Her poems and short stories have been widely anthologized in such collections as the *Anthology of Native American Literature* in 1980, the *Short Story in Native American Literature* in 1983, and *Harper's Book of Twentieth Century Native American Poetry* in 1988. She also has presented papers at numerous seminars on writing and Native American literature.

Although she has published extensively throughout her writing career, Cook-Lynn's writing began gained a larger audience after the age of 40 with the publication of two chapbooks entitled *Then Badger Said This* and *Seek the House of Relatives* in 1984 and 1986, respectively. During this time, Cook-Lynn, along with Beatrice Medicine (Lakota), Roger Buffalohead (Ponca), and William Willard (Cherokee), became one of the founding editors of the *Wicazo Sa Review: A Journal of Native American Studies* in 1985. Shortly thereafter, she published two books—a col-

lection of short stories in 1990, *The Power of Horses,* and a novel in 1991, *From the River's Edge.*

Draws Inspiration from Many Sources

Cook-Lynn's writing is representative of most Native American literature and is part of the Native American literary renaissance that began in 1968 with the publication of *House Made of Dawn* by the Kowa writer, N. Scott Momaday. The personal "I" in her poetry, along with the events and opinions expressed in her stories, reflect her own convictions and experiences. According to Cook-Lynn, "There is a self-absorption in my work that is inherent in my survival as a person, and my identity as a Dakotah." She draws inspiration for her stories and poems not only from her familial and tribal past, but also from the landscape of the northern plains and the lyrical writing style of other Native American writers, namely Momaday. His innovative writing style, which blends Western poetry and prose styles with traditional Indian chants and tales in *The Way to Rainy Mountain,* inspired Cook-Lynn to do the same in her own work. One sees this in prose-like lines of poems such as "Grandfather at the Indian Health Clinic." In this poem Cook-Lynn describes taking her once seemingly invincible elder who "came home to drive the Greenwood Woman's / cattle to his brother's place / two hundred miles / along the timber line" but now can barely walk around the hospital in his feeble, old age. The language Cook-Lynn uses is simple, but the images are powerful. She shows the difficulties of growing old on the reservation, and communicates that white culture has even taken the dignity from an elder Indian man's death. In these lines, one also finds another dimension to Cook-Lynn's writing—her anger. She sees writing as the crux of survival for herself, and for her people, in a world that considers them *persona non grata.* She recalled a class that she had once taken in college called "The Westward Movement" which neglected to mention Indian nations. The course textbook remains in her library today as a reminder of "scholarly ineptitude and/or racism."

Cook-Lynn explains in her essay "You May Consider Speaking about Your Art..." that she writes to defy the dominant society's efforts to make the Indian population invisible. As she states, writing is "an act of defiance born of the need to survive. It is the quintessential act of optimism born of frustration. It is an act of courage, I think. And, in the end ... it is an act that defies oppression." One sees this in *From the River's Edge* when the protagonist John Tatekeya consults an Anglo lawyer after his cattle are stolen. "We don't think in terms of getting your cows back or getting paid for them, necessarily," explains the lawyer. "We think in terms of what is fair." But John answers that he believes that "fairness" and the return of his cows were identical, to which the lawyer replies, "Not necessarily." Here, Cook-Lynn points out that dominant society determines what is "fair" and "just" for the American Indian. The trial in this novel is a parody of such justice.

Though her writing is rich in the history of her people, Cook-Lynn is quick to assert that she does not see herself as an official "tribal" voice for her people. The "real" poets of the Dakotah tribe, in her opinion, are the "men and women who sit at the drum and sing the old songs and create new ones." The difference between her poetry and theirs is simple: the singers' creation is communal—she speaks for herself. Perhaps Cook-Lynn's mission as a writer is best summarized in her own words: "The final responsibility of a writer like me ... is to commit something to paper in the modern world which supports this inexhaustible legacy left by our ancestors."

SELECTED WRITINGS BY COOK-LYNN:

"You May Consider Speaking about Your Art...," in *I Tell You Now: Autobiographical Essays by Native American Writers,* edited by Brian Swann and Arnold Krupat, Lincoln, University of Nebraska Press, 1987.

The Power of Horses and Other Stories, New York, Arcade-Little, Brown, 1990.

From the River's Edge, New York, Arcade-Little, Brown, 1991.

Seek the House of Relatives, Marvin, South Dakota, Blue Cloud Quarterly, 1993.

Then Badger Said This, Fairfield, Washington, Ye Galleon Press, 1983.

"As a Dakotah Woman," in *Survival This Way: Interviews with American Indian Poets,* edited by Joseph Bruchac, Tuscon, University of Arizona Press, 1987; 57-71.

SOURCES:

Books

American Indian Women: A Guide to Research, edited by Gretchen M. Bataille and Kathleen M. Sands, Garland Publishing, 1991.

Cook-Lynn, Elizabeth, "As a Dakotah Woman," in *Survival This Way: Interviews with American Indian Poets,* edited by Joseph Bruchac, Tuscon, University of Arizona Press, 1987; 57-71.

Cook-Lynn, Elizabeth, *From the River's Edge,* New York, Arcade-Little, Brown, 1991.

Cook-Lynn, Elizabeth, "You May Consider Speaking about Your Art...," in *I Tell You Now,* edited by Brian Swann and Arnold Krupat, Lincoln, University of Nebraska Press, 1987; 5-63.

Harper's Anthology of Twentieth Century Native American Poetry, edited by Duane Niatum, San Francisco, Harper, 1988.

Native American Women, edited by Gretchen M. Bataille, New York, Garland Publishing, 1993.

Native North American Almanac, edited by Duane Champagne, Detroit, Gale Research, 1994.

Reference Encyclopedia of the American Indian, sixth edition, edited by Barry T. Klein, West Nyack, New York, Todd Publications, 1993.

Other

Cook-Lynn, Elizabeth, interview with Jennifer Gray Reddish conducted July 14, 1994.

—*Sketch by Jennifer Gray Reddish*

George Copway
1818-1869(?)
Ojibway missionary, writer, and lecturer
Also known as Kahgegwagebow (Kah-ge-ga-gah-bowh) ["He Who Stands Forever" or "Stands Fast"]

George Copway was Canada's first Native American literary celebrity to gain prominence in the United States. A Christian convert and missionary among his people, he also wrote and published four books, largely autobiographical in nature, which were widely read by non-Natives. He was a well-known lecturer and briefly edited his own newspaper in New York City. During his career as a writer and lecturer, he associated with such prominent authors as James Fenimore Cooper, Henry Wadsworth Longfellow and Washington Irving. Interestingly, it has been said that Copway was Longfellow's inspiration for writing the epic poem *The Song of Hiawatha* in 1855.

Kahgegawagebow was born in the fall of 1818 at Rice Lake near the mouth of the Trent River in Ontario. His parents were full-blood Ojibway Indians. His father, a hereditary chief, was also the tribe's medicine man. Both parents converted to Christianity when Methodist missionaries, led by Peter Jones, arrived at Rice Lake around 1828. After his conversion, George's father became known by his English name, John Copway. During this period, the missionaries built a village for the Rice Lake people and started a school. George attended the Rice Lake Mission school, greatly admiring his teacher, James Evans, who would later invent the Cree syllabics.

Missionary Work Begins

During the summer of 1830, shortly after the death of his mother, Copway converted to Christianity at a Methodist camp meeting. At the age of 16 he was selected, along with his uncle, his cousin and another man from Rice Lake, to serve as interpreters at the Lake Superior Mission of the American Methodist Church. The group departed on July 16, 1834, accompanied part of the way by Peter Jones. Within a year Copway had been promoted from interpreter and teacher to preacher. He traveled to La Pointe Mission on Madeline Island, and while there helped the Reverend Sherman Hall translate the Gospel of St. Luke and the Acts of the Apostles into Ojibway.

Copway, his cousin John and Peter Marksman, traveled west, into what is now northwestern Wisconsin, to establish a another Methodist mission in 1836. Located at Lac Court Oreille on Ottawa Lake near the Chippewa River, this mission was in the midst of the war zone between the Ojibway and the Santee Sioux (eastern Dakota). The young men persevered at this remote station, however, with the promise that they would be able to attend school after two years. Upon completing their service at Lac Court Oreille, the three men entered Ebenezer Manual Labor School located near Jacksonville, Illinois, in the fall of 1837. After his graduation in 1839, Copway returned to Rice Lake to visit his father, traveling through several important cities such as Chicago, Detroit, Buffalo, Boston, and Syracuse along the way. Ironically, Copway was traveling in the opposite direction of many of his fellow Indians, who had been ordered to move to reservations west of the Mississippi by President Andrew Jackson.

During a visit with Peter Jones at the Credit River Mission, Copway met his future wife, Elizabeth Howell. She was the daughter of Captain Henry Howell, an English gentlemen from Yorkshire. Though her family disapproved, the couple married five months later, with Peter Jones performing the ceremony. According to Donald B. Smith, writing about Copway's life in the *Journal of Canadian Studies,* "Before the marriage, Peter Jones and Eliza, his English-born wife, had counselled them on what they might encounter in racially-conscious Upper Canada. Many settlers expected educated Indians to conform to their society, but then, still regarding them as inferiors, they refused to accept them as equals."

Difficulties in Acceptance

During the following two years, Copway served in the Upper Mississippi Missions. The mission had to be moved several times before a location outside of the Sioux-Ojibway war zone could be established. Copway found this a lonely time. As an educated native missionary, he had difficulty fitting in and being fully accepted by any one group. Reportedly, he did not get along well with the American missionaries, and neither the Ojibway nor the Sioux perceived him as anything but a Frenchman because of the European style of clothing he wore. Given these difficult circumstances, it is not surprising that he and his wife gladly accepted an invitation from Peter Jones to return to Canada late in 1842.

For the next several years Copway participated in missionary fund-raising tours in eastern Canada, and he served as part of a delegation that visited the Governor-General in Montreal to request the establishment of Indian Manual Schools. In records that Jones kept of this period, his evaluations characterize the young missionary as hasty and headstrong and unwilling to seek or listen to the advice of wiser and more experienced colleagues. Copway's destructive behavior reached a critical point in 1845, when he was accused of taking council funds from the Saugeen Mission on Lake Huron without permission. His own tribe disclosed a similar event involving the mishandling of funds, and Copway was arrested and imprisoned in Toronto. He was also expelled by the Canadian Conference of the Wesleyan Methodist Church.

Rapid Success with Literary Career

Upon his release from prison in 1846, Copway began to write his life story, which was published as *The Life, History, and Travels of Kah-ge-ga-gah-bowh (George Copway)* in 1847. By the end of 1848 the enormously successful book was in its seventh printing, and Copway had become a popular lecturer. He settled with his family in New York, continued to lecture, and wrote several more books. During this time, he began to advocate his strong belief that education and Christianity were solutions to the turmoil of his people; everywhere he went on the lecture circuit, he actively promoted the creation of a self-governed Indian Territory. Furthermore, Copway wrote a proposal to the United States Congress which recommended that the territory located near the Missouri River be deeded to Native Americans and governed by educated representatives, with the hope that it would eventually become a state in the Union. While the proposal was flatly rejected, Copway published his arguments in the *Organization of a New Indian Territory, East of the Missouri River* in 1850.

Copway traveled to the World Peace Conference in Frankfurt, Germany, in August 1850. His wife, Elizabeth accompanied him for part of the trip. Upon returning to New York in 1851, he published *Running Sketches of Men and Places,* a sort of travelogue of his visit abroad. He also began publishing a weekly newspaper entitled *Copway's American Indian.* During these years of prosperity and popularity, he became acquainted with several prominent literary figures, including Washington Irving, James Fenimore Cooper, and Henry Wadsworth Longfellow. However, it was not long before Copway's novelty as the "savage turned civilized" began to wane. He struggled financially and was emotionally devastated when three of his four children died within a span of less than two years. He lived the remainder of his life in relative obscurity, struggling to support his family through speaking engagements. Though he is reputed to have died in 1863, Smith reports otherwise in his *Journal of Canadian Studies* article: "His cousin, John Johnson, believed George had died at Pontiac, Michigan about 1863, and many others have cited this as his death date ... In reality, however, George Copway remained very much alive, working with his brother David as a Union Army recruiter in 1864. He collected bounty for enlisting Canadian Indians in the Civil War."

Other sources attest that Copway traveled among several Native American tribes in the territories throughout the 1860s. Acting as a healer, he collected herbs, roots, and barks for his cures, and he eventually came to be known as "Doctor Copway." One report also indicates that Copway came into contact with a Roman Catholic missionary near Lake of Two Mountains. There he served as the priest's interpreter and guide and studied the Roman Catholic religion. He is said to have been converted on January 17, 1869, and died several days later.

SELECTED WRITINGS BY COPWAY:

The Life, History, and Travels, of Kah-ge-ga-gah-bowh (George Copway), a Young Indian Chief of the Ojebwa Nation, a Convert to the Christian Faith, and a Missionary to his People for Twelve Years, Philadelphia, J. Harmstead, 1847; revised as *Recollections of a Forest Life: or, The Life and Travels of Kah-ge-ga-gah-bowh,* or George Copway, Chief of the Ojibway Nation, London, C. Gilpin, 1850.

The Life, Letters, and Speeches of Kah-ge-ga-gah-bowh, New York, S. W. Benedict, 1850.

The Ojibway Conquest, a Tale of the Northwest, New York, G. P. Putnam, 1850.

Organization of a New Indian Territory, East of the Missouri River. Arguments and Reasons Submitted to the Honorable Members of the Senate and House of Representatives of the Thirty-first Congress of the United States, New York, S. E. Benedict, 1850.

The Traditional History and Characteristic Sketches of the Ojibway Nation, London, Charles Gilpin, 1850, facsimile edition, Toronto, Coles, 1972; revised as *Indian Life and Indian History by an Indian Author: Embracing the Traditions of the North American Indians Regarding Themselves, Particularly of that Most Important of all the Tribes, the Ojibways,* Boston, A. Colby and Co., 1858.

Running Sketches of Men and Places, in England, France, Germany, Belgium, and Scotland, New York, J. C. Riker, 1851.

SOURCES:

Books

Copway, George, *The Life, Letters, and Speeches of Kah-ge-ga-gah-bowh,* New York, S. W. Benedict, 1850.

Copway, George, *The Traditional History and Characteristic Sketches of the Ojibway Nation,* London, Charles Gilpin, 1850; facsimile edition, Toronto, Coles, 1972.

Dictionary of American Biography, Volume 4, edited by Allen Johnson and Dumas Malone, New York, Charles Scribner's Sons, 1930; 433.

Great North American Indians, edited by Frederick J. Dockstader, New York, Van Nostrand Reinhold, 1977; 59.

Native North American Almanac, edited by Duane Champagne, Detroit, Gale Research, 1994; 756-57.

Periodicals

Smith, Donald B., "The Life of George Copway or Kah-ge-ga-gah-bowh (1818-1869)—and a Review of His Writings," *Journal of Canadian Studies,* 23, fall 1988; 5-37.

—*Sketch by Lisa A. Wroble*

Helen Quintana Cordero
1915-
Cochiti Pueblo potter and figurine maker

Helen Quintana Cordero is a sculptor of Pueblo Indian pottery and clay figurines; she is also the inventor of the Storyteller Doll. From the late 1800s until the invention of the Storyteller Dolls, the art of clay figure sculpturing was almost a lost tradition. Cordero has reinvented the Singing Mother and established her Storyteller Dolls in the culture of the Pueblo Indians of the Southwest. These hand-crafted clay dolls depict the traditional female Singing Mother doll; however, Cordero has changed the doll to a male figure representing her grandfather, Santiago Quintana.

Cordero, who lives in Cochiti, New Mexico, 50 miles north of Albuquerque, has won many awards and honors for her clay dolls. In 1964, she won first, second, and third place prizes at the New Mexico State Fair. She has won awards at the Indian Market and has gained fame from the national and international exhibits where her dolls are displayed. These exhibits bring Cordero numerous requests for her Storyteller Dolls. The New Mexico's Governor Award was presented to Cordero for her outstanding contributions, and her pottery is featured in newspaper and magazine articles throughout the country. In 1986, she received the National Endowment of the Arts Heritage award. Cordero has influenced Native American clay pottery and figure making by reintroducing an almost forgotten traditional art form.

Helen Quintana Cordero is the daughter of Pablo Quintana and Caroline Trujillo Quintana. She married Fred Cordero in 1932, and they have four children: Dolly, Jimmy, George, and Tony, along with two foster children, Gabriel and Leonard Trujillo. In the middle 1950s, with her children grown, she began working with leather and beads to supplement the household income. The sale of this work barely earned enough profit to purchase new leather and beading. During the late 1950s, she began working with a relative, Juanita Arquero, in making clay pottery. The bowls and pots seldom turned out quite right—they were crooked and had flaws that would not make them saleable. Cordero received advice from one of her relatives to try clay figure making. From that point, Cordero has developed into the premier clay figure sculptor that make her Storyteller Dolls a collectable artwork.

Storyteller Doll Evolves

For thousands of years, the Southwest Indians made clay figures and effigy characters. The doll figures were used by the Indians for religious purposes, ceremonies for harvesting, and seasonal changes. In the late 1800s, the railroad carried white settlers to the Southwest and Christian influences brought about the decline in clay figure making. In the past, the clay dolls were typically of women singing to the children.

Cordero started her figure making in the late 1950s. She had displayed some of her traditional Singing Mother figures; and Alexander Girard, a folk art collector, asked Cordero to make some larger figures with more children sitting around the singing mother. This request revitalized Cordero's memories of her grandfather, Santiago Quintana. She remembered that as a young girl, all the children gathered around as he told the traditional stories of the Pueblo

Indians. Children would sit on his legs, or stand and kneel around him to hear the old stories from generations long ago. In 1964, as a result of these memories, Cordero invented the Storyteller Doll. Cordero was the first to use the male figure in developing her clay dolls, and the first to place a larger than usual number of children around the figures. The dolls range in size from approximately six to 12 inches in height; they are usually in a sitting position with the mouth of the doll open telling a story to the children sitting on and around the doll. Each Storyteller Doll has from six to 30 small children arranged in various positions upon and around the doll listening to the grandfather tell traditional Pueblo Indian stories.

Since her first showing in 1964, many requests have come to her for the Storyteller Dolls. Many Indian artists have followed her in producing similar dolls. In an interview in the autumn 1988 edition of the *Journal of the Southwest,* Barbara Babcock reported Cordero as having said, "Many imitations are female figures and not really Storytellers. They may call them Storytellers, but they don't know what it means. They don't know it's after my grandfather."

Cordero uses only the old ways of making her Storytellers. She collects the clay from the Earth near her home. Most of her supplies are from traditional sources, and the painting, drying, and oven firing are done in the old way. Babcock quotes Cordero in an interview for the *Journal of American Folklore,* "I like doing it the right way, the old way. I don't just get up in the morning and start making potteries. First I talk with Grandma Clay and she tells me what to do.... It's not me, it's the fire, he decides how they'll come out.... It's my grandfather, he's giving me these. He was a wise man with lots of stories and lots of grandchildren and we're all in there, in the clay."

SOURCES:

Books

Native American Women, edited by Gretchen M. Bataille, New York, Garland Publishing, 1993; 64-65.

Periodicals

Babcock, Barbara A., "Clay Changes: Helen Cordero and the Pueblo Storyteller," *American Indian Art,* 8:2, spring 1983; 33-39.

Babcock, Barbara A., "Taking Liberties, Writing from the Margins, and Doing It with a Difference," *Journal of American Folklore,* October/December 1987; 390-395.

Babcock, Barbara A., "At Home, No Women Are Storytellers: Potteries, Stories, and Politics in Chichiti Pueblo," *American Indian Art,* 30:3, autumn 1988; 357-383.

Cordero, Helen Quintana, interview with Barbara A. Babcock, *Journal of the Southwest,* autumn 1988.

—Sketch by Russell Hellstern

Cornplanter
1732(?)-1836
Seneca tribal leader
Also known as Gä-gae-wá-gä ["By What One Plants"] and John O'Bail

Cornplanter was born sometime between 1732 and 1746, in the village of Conewaugus on the Genesee River in New York, the son of a Seneca woman and a Dutch trader named John Abeel (O'Bail). It should be noted that Lewis Henry Morgan erroneously states that it was Cornplanter's mother who was white rather than his father. This is important in that the Seneca, like other Iroquois people, are matrilineal, reckoning membership in the tribe through their mothers. Cornplanter had two half siblings who were born to his mother and a Seneca father: a brother, Handsome Lake, the Seneca prophet; and a sister who became the mother of Governor Blacksnake, the Seneca political leader. Little is known about Cornplanter during his early years, although many scholars contend that he was a warrior during the French and Indian War at the defeat of Edward Braddock in 1755 while the Indian was in his early teens. It was also noted in a letter to the governor of Pennsylvania that Cornplanter, while playing with the other Indian boys, noticed that his skin color was lighter than that of the other boys, whereupon his mother told him of his white father who lived in Albany. As a prospective bridegroom, he visited his father who treated him kindly, but gave him nothing in the way of either material goods or expected information, particularly regarding the coming rebellion of the colonists against the British. This rebellion, however, was to play a major role in Cornplanter's life.

Political Importance during American Revolution

Cornplanter's importance in American Indian history derives from his major role in Iroquois Confederacy politics before and during the American Revolution and the subsequent political adaptation of the Seneca to the new government of the United States. Although the date of its beginnings is the subject of ongoing discussion, the Iroquois Confederacy was begun as an alliance of five northern Iroquoian-speaking tribes: the Mohawk, Onondaga, Oneida, Cayuga, and Seneca. This alliance was formed in order to harness the strength of these five groups in fighting common enemies as well as to foster economic cooperation among them. The confederacy was governed by the Grand Council of 50 Chiefs, made up of the following: eight Seneca chiefs, ten Cayuga chiefs, 14 Onondaga chiefs, eight Oneida chiefs, nine Mohawk chiefs, and the person who held the title of Tadadaho, an Onondaga chief who presided over confederacy meetings. The Tuscarora, a southern Iroquoian-speaking group in coastal North Carolina, came north after their defeat in the Tuscarora War in 1711, joined the confederacy at the invitation of the Oneida, and there-

Cornplanter

fore had no direct voice in the Grand Council, speaking only through the Oneida.

Among the Grand Council, one of the cardinal governing rules was that any decision made required a unanimous vote of the chiefs. Among the major diplomatic and political decisions made in this manner were decisions of war. While it is not known if ideal rule of unanimity was always reached in such decisions, it is well known that a major disagreement arose within the confederacy over the impending colonial rebellion against the British.

The Grand Council of the Chiefs usually met before the central fire at Onondaga due to the fact that it was the home of the Tadadaho, or head chief, of the confederacy. In the months prior to the outbreak of the revolution, both the loyalists and the rebelling colonists had been busy soliciting the partisanship of the Indian nations, including the mighty Iroquois. Discussions ranged back and forth on the issue of which side to support if any. The Mohawk were firmly on the side of the British, but the Seneca, long willing to war against the British, in this case spoke for neutrality. Among those Senecas speaking strongly for neutrality were both Cornplanter and his half brother Handsome Lake, who held one of the major chiefly Seneca titles in the confederacy. In opposing this stand, Cornplanter was reminded of his clan brotherhood with Joseph Brant, a Mohawk captain for the British. This clan relationship obliged Cornplanter to support his fellow clansman, and thus he was reminded that duty lay in fighting with the British against the colonists.

In the end, the arguments of the pro-British Seneca prevailed, and the Seneca agreed to side with the British in the conflict. While the Seneca made this decision, however, several of the other members of the confederacy were not willing to accept this decision, notably the Oneidas and Tuscarora, with the latter remaining neutral for the most part and the Oneida taking the side of the colonists. Since there was no confederacy unanimity on this question, the Grand Council agreed to "cover the fire," meaning that they agreed to disagree and each member was left to decide for himself how he would affiliate in the coming war.

Despite his original misgivings about entering the war on the side of the British, Cornplanter, with Old Smoke, served as commanders for the Seneca throughout the war. It should be noted that Old Smoke was of advanced age by this time, being in his seventies or eighties. Nevertheless, these two were the primary field commanders of the tribe.

Perhaps most indicative of Cornplanter's character is a perhaps apocryphal encounter described by Governor Blacksnake during the Battle of Canajoharie, located in the Mohawk Valley, during August of 1780. Cornplanter supposedly recognized his father, John Abeel, among the captive survivors of the attack and burning of the village. Even after the earlier disappointment he felt at not receiving a wedding gift from his father at their first meeting, Cornplanter still accorded him the respect and kindness due a kinsman by offering his apology for the burning of his house and the option of his father returning to Seneca country to be supported by his son, or being released immediately. According to Thomas S. Abler in *Chainbreaker: The Revolutionary War Memoirs of Governor Blacksnake,* Abeel chose the latter and was allowed his freedom by the council of leaders out of respect for Cornplanter.

Around this time, the American revolutionaries began to discuss ideas for removing the Indians from their land. They not only wanted to punish them for their aid to the British by destroying the political importance of the confederacy, they also looked at the monetary gain to be had by first confiscating, then selling, Indian land to help pay for the expenses of the war. When General George Washington ordered an invasion of the Iroquois homeland to punish them for their role in the revolution, Cornplanter sent an urgent message in July of 1779, saying: "Father. You have said that we are in your hand and that by closing it you could crush us to nothing. Are you determined to crush us? If you are, tell us so that those of our nation who have become your children and have determined to die so, may know what to do. But before you determine on a measure so unjust, look up to God who made us as well as you. We hope He will not permit you to destroy the whole of our nation."

While this plea was not successful, it was indicative of Cornplanter's attempts to reconcile the Seneca with the colonists. He attended the treaty council held at Fort Stanwix (1784) between the Iroquois and the newly successful republic, in which large amounts of Indian land were ceded to the new government. Because of his conciliatory stance and the great loss of land with this treaty, Cornplanter became very unpopular with his tribe and his rivals, including the influential Red Jacket, who began to work against him politically. Although he was not a signatory, Cornplanter's apparent agreement to the Fort Harmar Treaty (1789), in which another great tract of land was ceded to the United States, only worsened his position with the tribe.

Involvement in "Right of Pre-emption" Controversy

Cornplanter was involved in another major dispute over land which has implications lasting to the present day. During this period of treaty-making, arguments arose over which of the newly formed states would encompass Indian territories. Recognition was made of the Indians' first right to ownership of their land, but the question was raised concerning who would have first rights to purchase the land should the Indians decide to sell it. Robert Morris, an early colonial and American financier, purchased this right, called a "right of pre-emption" from the state of Massachusetts. He eventually decided to sell this right of pre-emption to the Holland Land Company, agreeing in the bargain to extinguish Indian claim to the land by buying the land from the Indians. Finances ultimately kept him from accomplishing this, but he still attempted to extinguish Indian claim to the land through political channels. He met with Cornplanter in Philadelphia in August of 1797 to begin preliminary discussions of this issue, which led to full-scale negotiations between Morris and the Seneca at Genesee, New York. The Seneca rejected all of Morris' offers and Red Jacket eventually proclaimed negotiations to be at an end. However, other warriors and women eventually agreed to cede the land and signed a treaty in September of 1797. Since Cornplanter was one of the signers of this treaty, it signaled a major break between him and his political opponents led by Red Jacket, and for a while Cornplanter's life was in danger.

Fortunately for him, in 1795 the Pennsylvania Commonwealth awarded him in fee simple 1,500 acres of land in western Pennsylvania. Cornplanter directed the survey of this land into three strategic and valuable tracts and a patent was issued in 1796. He eventually lost two of the tracts, those at Oil City and Richland. The third tract he kept, encompassing about 750 acres along the Allegany River including the site of the old Seneca town Jenuchshadago and two islands in the river. He was also awarded a yearly pension by the U.S. government as a result of the 1797 treaty, which he collected for some time. An additional tract of land given to Cornplanter in what is now Marietta, Ohio, continues to be claimed be the contemporary heirs of Cornplanter who feel that he was defrauded out of the ownership of this land.

Imbroglio with Handsome Lake over Religious Issues

Cornplanter retired to his land grant where he raised horses and cattle and maintained his own political community. It was not, however, the end of his political strife. According to O. Turner in *Pioneer History of the Holland Purchase of Western New York,* Cornplanter later quarreled with his messianic half brother Handsome Lake over some of the religious teachings which Handsome Lake had introduced to the Seneca.

In 1807, at the primary instigation of Handsome Lake, a woman at Allegany was executed for witchcraft. Cornplanter was not present at the time, but on his return, he expressed his regret over this action. Cornplanter eventually became a Christian, against the teachings of Handsome Lake, and allowed the invited Quakers to build a school on his land grant. It is reported, however, that he became very disillusioned with white men and the effects of their culture on the Seneca and publicly destroyed the formal regalia and various awards that he had received from the president of the United States. He died on February 18, 1836, in his village on the Cornplanter Grant at about the age of 100 years. Portraits of Cornplanter were painted by F. Bartoli in 1796 (now in the collection of the New York Historical Society).

The passage of time allowed Cornplanter to regain some of the recognition that he lost through his involvement in political and religious controversies. His efforts to bring peace between the Seneca and the U.S. government were not forgotten. His delicate and successful role as mediator between the new government and the Iroquois in creating a new political balance for his people in a drastically changed Indian world is generally recognized in the history of the Iroquois and the Seneca. A monument was erected on his grave by the grateful Commonwealth of Pennsylvania, reputedly the first monument in the United States erected in memory of an American Indian.

The majority of the Cornplanter Grant acreage was flooded during the Kinzua Dam Project which created the Allegany Reservoir, spelling the end to residence on the grant by Cornplanter's heirs. As a consequence of the construction of the Kinzua Dam in the 1960s, the remaining homes and outbuildings on the Cornplanter Grant, including the church and school, were bulldozed and burned. The trees were leveled and burned and the Spring of Handsome Lake, reputedly the source of water used to initially revive the Prophet at the end of his first vision, was destroyed in the process of construction of the dam. Today, many of the nearly 600 descendants of Chief Cornplanter still meet at an annual family picnic on the Allegany Reservation in August and formally recognize their proud ties to both Cornplanter, a major figure in Iroquois history, and to the land granted to him.

SOURCES:

Books

Abler, Thomas S., *Chainbreaker: The Revolutionary War Memoirs of Governor Blacksnake,* Lincoln, University of Nebraska Press, 1989.

Abler, Thomas S., and Elisabeth Tooker, "Seneca," in *Handbook of North American Indians,* Volume 15, edited by W. C. Sturtevant, Washington, D.C., Smithsonian Institution, 1978; 505-517.

Hodge, Frederick Webb, *Handbook of American Indians North of Mexico,* New York, Rowman & Littlefield, 1965; 349-350.

Morgan, Lewis Henry, *League of the Ho-de-no-sau-nee or Iroquois,* Rochester, New York, Sage Books, 1851;

reprinted as *League of the Iroquois,* Corinth Books, 1962.

Schaaf, Gregory, *Wampum Belts and Peace Trees: George Morgan, Native Americans, and Revolutionary Diplomacy,* Golden, Colorado, Fulcrum Publishing, 1990.

Turner, O., *Pioneer History of the Holland Purchase of Western New York,* Buffalo, New York, George H. Durby, 1850.

Wallace, Anthony F. C., "Origins of the Longhouse Religion," in *Handbook of North American Indians,* Volume 15, edited by W. C. Sturtevant, Washington, D.C., Smithsonian Institution, 1978; 442-448.

Periodicals

Abrams, George H. J., "Cornplanter Cemetery," *Pennsylvania Archaeologist,* 25:2, 1965; 59-73.

—*Sketch by Martha Symes*

Crazy Horse (top center)

Crazy Horse
1840(?)-1877
Oglala Brulé Sioux military and tribal leader
Also known as Horse Stands in Sight and Curly

Crazy Horse is significant not only for his defiant and skilled military leadership during his lifetime but also for his mystical symbolism in the twentieth century. Richmond L. Clow has noted that "because the legacy of Crazy Horse must be seen through oral tradition, sighting reports, and opinions scattered through military documents and popular reports, it is less distinct than that of most other prominent Sioux leaders of the post-Civil War times." Referring to a related 1870 letter published for the first time in *Nebraska History* in 1994, R. Eli Paul comments: "Documentary references to Crazy Horse are rare before 1876, when he burst upon the national scene and they are usually as enigmatic as the great man himself. Piecing together his early movements across the Lakota landscape has challenged historians; any new information which adds to our knowledge warrants attention."

Few details are available regarding Crazy Horse's youth. The only major biography, written with an Indian perspective by Mari Sandoz in 1942, offers an atmospheric interpretation of his life. Another biography is anticipated by Texas historian Joseph C. Porter. Crazy Horse was probably born on Rapid Creek, just east of what is now the community of Rapid City, South Dakota, at the edge of the Black Hills. According to a 1975 "preliminary genealogical study" his father was an Oglala medicine man and his mother, Rattle Blanket, a Minniconjou. He had brown eyes, light skin, and yellow-brown hair. The texture resulted in his early name,

Curly. According to the 1975 study by Richard G. Hardorff his mother committed suicide in his early years and Crazy Horse's father later married two of Spotted Tail's sisters. Most historical accounts refer to Spotted Tail as his uncle.

The historical context of the life of Crazy Horse was defined by the promises of the Treaty of Laramie (1851) and a peculiar incident that followed in the same region. A malnourished cow owned by a Mormon emigrant was killed by a young Minniconjous, Straight Foretop. The owner insisted on punishment by the military. Efforts at negotiations, in which Conquering Bear offered mules and horses as compensation, were ignored. Lieutenant J. L. Grattan was sent to arrest the youth. After a boisterous move into the center of the Oglala camp one of the soldiers shot Conquering Bear's brother and Conquering Bear himself was wounded. Grattan and his 30 men were promptly killed.

Because of the mass migration to the West, spurred in part by the Gold Rush of 1849, a period of over 30 years of conflict followed. The military assumed the task of keeping the passageways clear and safe. During the early years after the Grattan incident much of young Crazy Horse's time was consumed in the quest for food for his people and demonstrating his bravery in battle with tribal enemies—the Pawnee, Arapaho, Crow, and Shoshones. His reputation was well established long before whites had heard of him. In his teens he was known as Horse Stands in Sight. At about the age of 17 his father bestowed his own name, Crazy Horse, upon him. There are numerous versions of the actual meaning of the name.

One of the major influences on Crazy Horse was a vision quest that he underwent in 1855. The imagery governed his life until the time of his death 22 years later. The vision compelled him to shun ornamentation and to act rather than speak. He was assured of invincibility in battle and was warned that his death would come only with the restraint of one of his own people. The resulting life style caused both respect and suspicion among his contemporaries. He did not join council meetings, singing or dancing, and he wore only a single red hawk feather in battle. This aloofness and his skill in battle led whites moving into the land of the Lakota to fear his power.

Crazy Horse was not always popular with his own people for other reasons as well. He was infatuated with Black Buffalo Woman, the niece of Red Cloud. However, she was married to No Water and they had three children. Crazy Horse persuaded her to leave with him. Shortly afterwards No Water borrowed a gun and entered their lodge and shot him in the face. Crazy Horse recovered, but he lost the role of shirt wearer, or special protector of his people. Crazy Horse later married Black Shawl in 1871 and they had a female child, They Are Afraid of Her, who died at the age of two.

Crazy Horse Chooses Military Response

Crazy Horse's distrust of whites intensified during the mid-1850s. In 1855 General W. S. Harney was sent with 600 troops to eliminate the threat to westward expansion. Over 100 Indians were killed in the Battle of Blue Water in September of that year. Crazy Horse saved the life of Yellow Woman, the daughter of a Cheyenne medicine man. By 1857 Crazy Horse had seen three villages destroyed by soldiers. He did not believe the promises white people made, and he considered diplomacy to be merely a form of skilled deception.

In 1857 Crazy Horse also attended a great council near the sacred Bear Butte at the eastern edge of the Black Hills. It was an unusual gathering of all the great camps of the Teton Sioux—the Oglala, Brulé, Minniconjou, No Bows, Blackfeet, Two Kettles and Hunkpapa. Among those present were Sitting Bull, Spotted Tail, and Hump. Crazy Horse saved Hump's life only three years later. The four years after leaving the Fort Laramie area had been relatively good ones and there was little sentiment to submit to the invaders of the region.

Following the Civil War President Ulysses S. Grant attempted to establish a "peace" policy. A treaty was signed assuring safe passage through the Powder River country, and several forts were built along the Bozeman Trail. But there was strong resistance. Crazy Horse was among those who refused to grant safe passage to the military and rejected the continuing flood of emigrants. In 1865 he participated in a Sioux-Cheyenne attack on the Julesburg stockade in Colorado Territory, in retaliation for the assault on the Sand Creek encampment, led by former minister John M. Chivington.

Other fights with whites were to follow. Captain William J. Fetterman boasted that he could march through the Lakota nation with only 80 men. In December of 1866 he led that number on a mission to protect wood gatherers for Fort Kearny. Crazy Horse skillfully led a decoy force that trapped the soldiers. All of Fetterman's force were killed. Only 12 Indians lost their lives and their bodies were removed before the appearance of other white forces. Another important battle, the Wagon Box Fight, occurred near the same fort in August of 1867.

Little Big Horn and the End of Resistance

The Fort Laramie Treaty of 1868 tried to set up final dividing lines between the various Native American forces and the United States. Forts were abandoned along the Bozeman Trail. Red Cloud and Spotted Tail agreed to move to their respective areas. But Crazy Horse refused to honor the treaty and took the position of war chief of the Oglala. The discovery of gold in the Black Hills in 1874 made the treaty pointless as hordes of prospectors flooded into the region. Partly to keep these miners and settlers safe, the military attempted to place all Native Americans on reservations by January 31, 1876.

The various tribes soon realized that a unified military effort was needed to preserve their traditional freedoms. The Cheyenne and Sioux gathered in a great encampment in the Rosebud area of Montana and then moved to the Little Big Horn. The unified forces showed courage in the June 17, 1876 conflict with the troops of General George Crook, but it was the Little Big Horn battle of June 25 that was the major event of the campaign. On a ridge above the river General George Custer's isolated force of 225 men confronted a group of warriors that exceeded the total number of cavalry in the entire area. Crazy Horse led the attack across the river, remarking that it was "a good day to die." In fact, only about 20 of his followers lost their lives, while Custer and all of his troops were killed.

Although Little Big Horn remains a symbolically important event, celebrated even today in the Native American community, "ironically, this Indian victory proved to be a hollow one because increased military pressure, famine, and division in the ranks of Indian allies forced the surrender of most of the hostiles in 1877," explains Richard G. Hardorff. The "weight of historical inevitability" that Wallace Stegner noted in his 1943 review of the Sandoz biography would become obvious in the next few months. There was no possibility of coexistence outside the restrictions of the predefined reservations. Even those borders were to be changed and Native American sovereignty strictly limited.

Living conditions among the tribes were made worse because of unnatural patterns of migration, influenced by the army's presence, and the fact that trade with whites was largely restricted after 1864. They were further disheartened by a harsh winter, combined with the word that the sacred Black Hills had been sold. Crazy Horse's village was attacked by soldiers under the command of Colonel Nelson A. Miles on January 8, 1877. This was the final military upheaval. As supplies and morale diminished, Crazy Horse reluctantly led his 889 followers (only 217 of them men) to

Fort Robinson, in northern Nebraska, in early May of 1877. He had been promised an agency at one of two preferred locations in Wyoming. Their horse and weapons were taken away and they were compelled to remain within three miles of the fort. During this period Crazy Horse married a third woman, Nellie Larrabee, the 18-year-old mixed child of a local French trader.

Death of the Sioux Leader

The army did not quite know what to do about Crazy Horse and his followers, and did not understand their status in relation to the nearby camps of Red Cloud and Spotted Tail. Some suggested sending Crazy Horse to Washington, D.C., as a representative of his people. However, according to General Jesse Lee, Crazy Horse replied that he "was not hunting of any Great Father. *HIS* father was with him, and there was no Great Father between him and the Great Spirit." After only four months General Crook issued an order for the arrest of Crazy Horse. He showed reluctance to cooperate with the U.S. military by serving as a scout or combatant against the Nez Percé. A distorted interpretation of his words left the impression that he would continue to fight with the whites. There was also a rumor that he would run away to Canada and join Sitting Bull.

As a result, Crazy Horse was returned to Fort Robinson on September 5, 1877, with the expectation of meeting with the local commander. There is evidence that a special train was scheduled to send him to exile in Florida a few hours after his return to the fort. The exact events after his arrival are not clear. Several "eye witnesses" give distinct accounts. Crazy Horse apparently feared that he would be imprisoned in a guardhouse near the fort headquarters. He broke away and pulled a concealed knife. Little Big Man and Swift Bear helped restrain him. In the struggle he was stabbed, probably by a private's bayonet. He died from that wound several hours later. Touch the Clouds and Crazy Horse's father were with him at the time of his death and his body was taken to an unspecified location for burial, perhaps near Wounded Knee. Within a few weeks the remaining Sioux were sent to reservations in the area that would become South Dakota. Participants in subduing the great leader were awarded "Crazy Horse medals."

Historical and Contemporary Image

Judgements about his historical role and importance varied widely among white contemporaries. V. T. McGillicuddy, the former head of the Red Cloud agency, called him "the greatest leader of his people in modern times.... In him everything was made secondary to patriotism and love of his people. Modest, fearless, a mystic, a believer in destiny, and much of a recluse.... These qualities made him a danger to the government, and he became *persona non grata* to evolution and to the progress of the white man's civilization. Hence his early death was preordained." Only two days after his death a *New York Tribune* correspondent wrote that Crazy Horse's "morals had so stiff an edge that he never permitted himself to gain any personal

advantage from his power." General Jesse Lee, the temporary agent in the area designated for Spotted Tall and his followers, was less charitable when he wrote, "There is no Indian journalist, author or reporter to present the chief's side of the story of his tragic fate. With the lapse of time his name and fame may linger for awhile in the tradition of his tribe, and then fade away forever. History will make but little record of him."

Many people—including family members—insisted that no picture was ever taken of Crazy Horse. They state that the photograph reproduced on the back and binding of the 1992 novel, *Crazy Horse,* by Bill Dugan is of someone else. Other sources, however, refer to pictures taken of the leader on horseback and state that these rare items went to a collector in California. The denial of such an image is consistent with retaining the memory of the independent spirit and mysticism of Crazy Horse. Ironically, the huge monument now under construction in the Black Hills of South Dakota will make him nearly as well known as the four presidents featured on Mt. Rushmore only a few miles away. The monument was the result of a determined effort of the skilled artist Korczak Ziolkowski, whose work was honored at the 1939 World's Fair and who worked briefly on the Mt. Rushmore project in the 1940s.

In 1948 Ziolkowski selected the massive granite Thunderhead Mountain, located only five miles from a community named after George Custer, as the site of a monumental sculpture of Crazy Horse. The uncarved mountain is featured in one of the scenes of the 1954 "Crazy Horse" feature film, which starred Victor Mature in the title role. He sculpted a figure on horse back pointing forward, representing the spirit of the Sioux leader. With the support of numerous Native American spokesmen, Ziolkowski proceeded with his project, without state or federal assistance. He felt the project should be an independent effort. He also envisioned a nearby university, medical center, and airport. Although the 1977 completion date was abandoned, the work has continued on the project after the artist's death in 1982. Under the guidance of his widow, Ruth, the outline of the monument is becoming more apparent. By September of 1994 the features of the nine-story high face were clearly identifiable and work on the total outline proceeded. Mrs. Ziolkowski predicted "a 'sudden' visual impact (from the observation area) in the not too distant future." The final carved granite structure will be 563 feet high and 641 feet long.

After many years of skepticism the effort has now captured the popular imagination. Over 1.2 million people visited the site in 1990. The work is supported by private contributions and income generated by a gallery, museum, and gift shop at the location of the massive project. A 13-cent postage stamp honoring Crazy Horse, using an image provided by the creator of the monument, was issued in 1982.

An unusual battle is taking place in the courts over the distribution of Crazy Horse Malt Liquor. Native Americans in South Dakota, including relatives of the famous warrior, have filed actions to prohibit the distribution of the product, manufactured in New York, claiming that it exploits the leader's name and perpetuates stereotypical attitudes about Indians. The issues also relate to the Indian Arts and Crafts Act and the intellectual property rights of descendants. Lakota customary law, including special patterns of descendance, are being given recognition in courts of law. The result of the case might also affect other places of business that exploit the Crazy Horse name, such as saloons, and camp grounds, as well as products such as cosmetics, spring water, pizza, tobacco, and jewelry.

SOURCES:

Books

Andrist, Ralph K., *The Long Death: The Last Days of the Plains Indian,* New York, Macmillan, 1969; reprinted, 1993.

Brown, Vinson, *Crazy Horse, Hoka Hey (It Is a Good Time to Die!),* Happy Camp, California, Naturegraph Publishers, 1987.

Clark, Robert A., *The Killing of Chief Crazy Horse,* Lincoln, University of Nebraska Press, 1988.

Clow, Richard L., "Sioux Response to Non-Indian Intrusion: Sitting Bull, Spotted Tail, and Crazy Horse," in *South Dakota Leaders: From Pierre Chouteau, Jr., to Oscar Howe,* edited by Herbert T. Hoover and Larry J. Zimmerman, Vermillion, University of South Dakota Press, 1989; 29-44.

Dugan, Bill, *Crazy Horse,* New York, HarperCollins, 1992.

The Eleanor H. Hinman Interviews on the Life and Death of Crazy Horse, edited by John M. Carroll, Garry Owen Press, 1976.

Fielder, Mildred, "Crazy Horse, the Warrior," in *Sioux Indian Chiefs,* Seattle, Superior Publishing, 1975; 11-24.

Garst, Shannon, *Crazy Horse, Great Warrior of the Sioux,* Eau Claire, Wisconsin, E.M. Hale, 1950.

Hardorff, Richard G., *The Oglala Lakota Crazy Horse: A Preliminary Genealogical Study and an Annotated Listing of Primary Sources,* Mattituck, New York, J. M. Carroll, 1985.

Lee, Major-General Jesse M., *The Capture and Death of Chief Crazy Horse,* Los Angeles, E.A. Brininstool, [n.d.]

Sandoz, Mari, *Crazy Horse: The Strange Man of the Oglalas,* Lincoln, University of Nebraska Press, 1942; reprinted, 1992.

Sneve, Virginia Driving Hawk, "Tashunka Witco, Crazy Horse," in *They Led a Nation: The Sioux Chiefs,* Sioux Falls, South Dakota, Brevet Press, 1975; 26-27.

Periodicals

Buecker, Thomas R., "The Crazy Horse Surrender Ledger—A New Source for Red Cloud Agency History," *Nebraska History,* 27;2, summer 1994; 191-194.

Fort Robinson Illustrated (special issue of *Nebraskaland*), 64:1, January-February, 1986.

Hedren, Paul L., "The Crazy Horse Medal: An Enigma from the Great Sioux War," *Nebraska History,* 27:2, summer 1994; 195-199.

Paul, R. Eli, "An Early Reference to Crazy Horse," *Nebraska History,* 27:2, summer 1994; 189-190.

"Winter Work Keeps Crazy Horse Face Ahead of Schedule," *Crazy Horse [Monument] Progress,* 26:1, May 1994; 1.

—*Sketch by Keith A. Winsell*

Crow Dog
1834(?)-1911(?)
Brulé Lakota Sioux warrior and tribal leader
Also known as Kangi-Shunka (Kangisunka, Kangi Sunka) and Sunka Kangi

Found guilty of murdering his cousin and Brulé Lakota chief, Spotted Tail, Crow Dog became the subject of a landmark United States Supreme Court case about the federal government's jurisdiction on Native American reservations. He also was one of the leaders of the Ghost Dance revival during the Lakota breakout in 1890. According to Mary Crow Dog and Richard Erdoes in *Lakota Woman,* Crow Dog was born in 1834; however, some historians believe he was born in 1832 or in 1835. He was born at Horse Stealing Creek in the Montana Territory and was believed to be the nephew of Brave Bear, chief of the Lakota Wazhazha (Orphan Band). According to family legend, Crow Dog's name was given to him after a battle with white settlers and Crow scouts. After fighting bravely and being wounded, Crow Dog was left to die following the battle. The legend says that by way of two coyotes, the Great Spirit sent Crow Dog the medicine and food he needed to heal. On his return to the Wazhazha camp, a crow guided him. Hence, he became Crow Dog.

Although known as a great and fearless leader among his people, he was not widely known among the Euro-Americans until 1877. When his good friend Crazy Horse surrendered at Fort Robinson in September of 1877, Crow Dog accompanied him to the fort. When Crazy Horse was then murdered at the fort's jail, it was Crow Dog who calmed the angry Lakota. George E. Hyde in *Spotted Tail's Folk: A History of the Brulé Sioux,* said, "Crow Dog rode coolly up and down in front of the mass of enraged Sioux who were threatening to charge into the military stockade, pushing the butt of his gun against the ponies' breasts and ordering the warriors to move back."

Feuding Worsens with Appointment as Police Chief

As a result of the bravery shown at Fort Robinson, Rosebud Indian Agent Cicero Newell appointed Crow Dog the chief of the Rosebud Indian police, which fueled an

Crow Dog

already bitter feud between Spotted Tail and Crow Dog. Hyde reported in his biography of Spotted Tail that "Crow Dog regarded Spotted Tail as an usurper who had wrongfully taken the position as head chief, which belonged to the Brave Bear family." Paul Dyck in *Brulé: The Sioux People of the Rosebud,* said that Spotted Tail had killed Crow Dog's friend, Big Mouth, in 1869 over a dispute about allowing whiskey trading, and it resulted in a blood feud. But Mary Crow Dog believed that the dispute lay solely in the fact that although Spotted Tail was a progressive, believing in cooperation with the federal government, Crow Dog was from the conservative faction, which wanted to maintain tribal traditions.

Shortly after his appointment as police chief, Crow Dog learned that white cattlemen were grazing herds on Indian land. When he and a group of police went to collect fees for the grazing, Crow Dog was told that Spotted Tail had already been paid. On his return to the Rosebud Agency, he charged Spotted Tail with keeping the money for himself. Spotted Tail replied that as chief of the tribe he had many expenses and the grazing fees rightly belonged to him. During the winter of 1879, Agent Newell removed Crow Dog as chief of police because he had sided with his friends in arguments over land claims. However, Crow Dog believed that Spotted Tail was behind his removal.

Crow Dog continued to investigate Spotted Tail's activities because he believed the chief was stealing from the tribe. As a result of Spotted Tail's negotiations for railroad right-of-ways, Crow Dog charged that the chief had actually sold Indian land to the railway companies and kept the money. He also charged that Spotted Tail had a mansion given to him by the government in exchange for helping the whites obtain more land—Spotted Tail denied the charges. Following a disagreement between the new Indian Agent, John Cook, and Spotted Tail over who was in charge of the police, Crow Dog was reappointed as chief of police by Cook.

Historical accounts do not agree on the final events leading to the murder. Some sources indicate that Spotted Tail stole or had an affair with the wife of one of Crow Dog's friends. Another report indicated that Crow Dog threatened Spotted Tail during a July 4 celebration. One source indicated that Crow Dog believed Spotted Tail did not consider the best interests of the tribe when he signed a treaty favoring the United States government. Other accounts claim that there was a conspiracy among several Indians to remove Spotted Tail as chief. However, all the accounts agree that on August 5, 1881, Crow Dog and his wife were hauling a load of wood to the agency when Crow Dog saw his rival leaving a tribal council meeting. Crow Dog stepped down from the wagon and shot Spotted Tail. Crow Dog was arrested for the murder and, according to tribal custom, gave Spotted Tail's family a number of horses and blankets, and paid them $600 in cash. For the most part, that settled the matter as far as the Indians were concerned. Washington, however, was not satisfied. They wanted Crow Dog tried in a court of law for murder. He was sent to Fort Niobrara, Nebraska, then was moved to Deadwood, South Dakota, where an all-white jury convicted him of the murder and sentenced him to hang.

First Native Case Heard by U.S. Supreme Court

Crow Dog's case went to the U.S. Supreme Court because his lawyers claimed the white courts had no jurisdiction over Indian affairs on the reservation. In 1883, the court, in *Ex Parte Crow Dog,* overturned the conviction and sentence, agreeing that the various treaties and laws dealing with the Lakota did not give the government jurisdiction. The court ruled that since the government did not have jurisdiction, the government could not try or convict Crow Dog of a crime committed on the reservation. Crow Dog returned to the Rosebud Reservation. But, according to family accounts, his blood would be tainted by the crime and it would affect the next four generations of his family. Consequently, Crow Dog was told by his cousin, Black Crow, that he had to live separately from the tribe for the rest of his days and that the next four generations of his family also would be ostracized.

In addition to affecting Crow Dog's descendants, the impact of the Supreme Court ruling played an even more important role in federal relations with Native American tribes. Congress was angered by the court's ruling and in 1885, passed the Major Crimes Act, which gave the government legal jurisdiction on Indian reservations and abolished the right of tribes to use their own systems of justice in criminal cases. That law, among others, gave the federal government the right to pursue and prosecute Crow Dog's great grandson, Leonard Crow Dog (a fourth generation descendant of Crow Dog) and other members of the American Indian Movement, following the second incident at Wounded Knee in 1975.

The Ghost Dance and the Last Indian War

In March of 1889, Congress passed the Dawes Act, which proposed dividing up the Lakota reservation. Each family was allotted 320 acres, single people were allotted somewhat less acreage. What land was not taken, some nine million acres, was to be sold to white homesteaders with the proceeds to be used for the needs of the Indians. A new treaty was drawn up and agreed upon by the various Lakota chiefs, but the land cession required the approval of three-fourths of the adult male Lakota population. Although Crow Dog refused to sign, the treaty was eventually approved. At the same time, promised government-provided food rations were being reduced and the Lakota people were going hungry. Efforts by the long-term Indian agents failed to convince Washington bureaucrats that the effect of the smaller rations and loss of land was creating a restlessness among the tribes on the various reservations. The agent at Pine Ridge resigned over the dispute and was replaced with the inexperienced, D. F. Royer, whom the Indians gave the name Lakota Kokipa-Koshkala ["Young-Man-Afraid-of-the-Lakota"].

At about the same time, the Lakota heard about the prophet Wovoka, who had a vision that the earth would be renewed and that Native American ancestors would rise from the dead to end the misery that their living relatives were experiencing. But, Wovoka encouraged the people to live in peace with the whites, to work hard, avoid lying or stealing, and in general, to be good to each other. According to Arlene Hirschfelder and Paulette Molin in *The Encyclopedia of Native American Religions,* "He also told them to perform a dance for five days at a time in order to bring about the changes." The dance became known as the Ghost Dance, and the shirts, generally decorated with stars and crescent moons, that were worn during the dance were believed to be bullet-proof.

The Ghost Dance was first practiced on the Pine Ridge Reservation in 1889. On the Rosebud Reservation, Lakota medicine man Short Bull, Crow Dog and Two Strikes became the leaders of the Ghost Dance movement. The purpose of the dance was misinterpreted by the white Indian agents, who ordered the Lakotas to stop holding the dances. For a brief time, the Lakotas at Rosebud agreed. But the Pine Ridge Lakotas ignored their new agent's request. Fearing the loss of control, Royer requested military assistance in November of 1890 to force an end to the Ghost Dance practice. His first few requests were denied. Meanwhile, Short Bull announced that the time to make the great change was then within a month and he urged all the believers to gather in one place. James Mooney in *The Ghost-Dance Religion and the Sioux Outbreak of 1890,* said that Short Bull "told them they must dance even though troops should surround them, as the guns of the soldiers would be rendered harmless and the white race itself would soon be annihi-

lated." On November 17, 1890, General John R. Brooke was ordered to the reservations to prevent a possible outbreak. They arrived November 19.

Crow Dog, Short Bull, Kicking Bear and Two Strikes, leading several thousand Lakotas, fled Rosebud at the first sign of the troops. They went into the area known as the Badlands near the edge of the Pine Ridge reservation. As word spread, other Lakotas joined them there and the Ghost Dancing was continued. Tensions mounted, especially after the military arrested and killed Sitting Bull, an Oglala Sioux chief they believed to be the instigator of the outbreak. By late December, nearly 3,000 troops had been deployed into the area and had surrounded the Lakotas taking refuge in the Badlands. Through negotiations, General Brooke convinced Crow Dog and his followers to move closer to the Pine Ridge agency office. Short Bull and the rest followed about a week later.

However, Big Foote's Cheyenne party was still trying to get to the Badlands when they were arrested and taken to Wounded Knee. On December 29, 1890, a battle broke out between the Cheyenne and the federal troops after the Natives were asked to give up their weapons. Some 200 Cheyenne men, women and children were killed. Upon hearing of the massacre, Crow Dog and Short Bull, believing that the military meant to slaughter them, opened fire on the Pine Ridge agency buildings. To put a stop to the attack, Brooke ordered the Lakota police to stand clearly in the line of fire. Crow Dog refused to fire on his brothers and prevented the other Lakotas from doing so as well. They surrendered and returned to their own reservations. Soon after, the last Indian war in the United States was over.

Several sources reported Crow Dog died on the Pine Ridge Reservation in 1910, while at least one source showed he died in 1890. However, Mary Crow Dog stated that her husband's great grandfather died in 1911, "owning a Winchester .44 repeating rifle with not a single buffalo left to use it on. He lived long enough to ride in a car and make a telephone call."

SOURCES:

Biographical Dictionary of Indians of the Americas, Volume 1, Newport Beach, California, American Indian Publishers, 1991; 167-168.

Brown, Dee, *Bury My Heart At Wounded Knee,* New York, Bantam Books, 1970; 395.

Crow Dog, Mary, and Richard Erdoes, *Lakota Woman,* New York, Grove Weidenfeld, 1990; 148-153, 177-183, 213-214.

Dockstader, Frederick J., *Great North American Indians,* New York, Van Nostrand Reinhold, 1977; 65-66, 277.

Dyck, Paul, *Brulé: The Sioux People of the Rosebud,* Flagstaff, Arizona, Northland Press, 1971; 33-34, 44, 46, 53.

Handbook of American Indians North of Mexico, Part 1, edited by Frederick Webb Hodge, Totowa, New Jersey, Rowman and Littlefield, 1975; 367.

Hirschfelder, Arlene, and Paulette Molin, *The Encyclopedia of Native American Religions,* New York, Facts On File, 1992; 98-99.

Hyde, George E., *Spotted Tail's Folk: A History of the Brulé Sioux,* Norman, University of Oklahoma Press, 1961; 277-304.

Mooney, James, *The Ghost-Dance Religion and the Sioux Outbreak of 1890,* abridged edition, Chicago, Illinois, University of Chicago Press, 1965; vii-x, 60-115, 123-140.

Native North American Almanac, edited by Duane Champagne, Detroit, Gale Research, 1994; 488-489.

Schmitt, Martin F., *General George Crook: His Autobiography,* Norman, University of Oklahoma Press, 1960; 283-288.

Waldman, Carl, *Who Was Who in Native American History,* New York, Facts On File, 1990; 87-88, 334-336.

Washburn, Wilcomb, *The American Indian and the United States: A Documentary History,* Volume 4, New York, Random House, 1973; 2655-2666.

—*Sketch by Catherine A. Clay*

Mary Crow Dog
1953-
Lakota Sioux activist
Also known as Ohitika Win ["Brave Woman"],
Mary Brave Bird

Mary Crow Dog dictated her life story, *Lakota Woman* and *Ohitika Woman,* to Richard Erdoes, a photographer and illustrator who himself became involved in political activism through having taped and transcribed that story. In these two books, 15 years apart, she told how the American Indian Movement (AIM) gave meaning to her life. The first book portrays her life from her birth to 1977, the second covers the events up to 1992 and augments the earlier history with new details.

Ancestral Background

Mary Crow Dog's mother, Emily Brave Bird, had been raised in a tent in the village of He-Dog on the Rosebud Reservation, then taken to St. Francis Mission boarding school where she was converted to Catholicism by Father Eugene Beuchel. While she studied nursing in Pierre, South Dakota, her four children were raised by their grandparents. Robert Brave Bird trapped in the winter and farmed in the summer. He was a descendent of the legendary warrior, Pakeska Maza ["Iron Shell"], who became chief of the Wablenicha ["Orphan Band"] of the Brulé ["Burned Thigh"] or Sicanju tribe of the Lakota people.

The best-known member of her tiyospaye (clan or extended family) was Mato He Oglogeca (Chief Hollow Horn Bear), whose face was on a 14-cent stamp as well as on a $5 bill and who had attended Theodore Roosevelt's inauguration. Another famous clan member was Tatanka Witko ["Fool Bull"] who fought at Little Big Horn against General George Custer. His son, Dick Fool Bull, was the last carver of traditional courting flutes and died in 1975 at the age of 99.

Caught between Two Worlds

The Iyeska's (halfbreed's) dilemma was to fit in neither world. For three generations, the Brave Bird women had been taken from their homes at the age of five to be sent to St. Francis Mission boarding school, there to be disciplined harshly and deprived by force of their own language. This loss proved particularly disruptive when Mary Brave Bird became the stepmother of Leonard Crow Dog's children. Her parents-in-law continually reminded her that Francis, their son's first wife, had been a full-blood, fluent in Lakota. She was ill-equipped to serve a traditionalist's needs. The disparity in their ages, she was 17 and he was 31, when they married in 1973, was less of a problem than their cultural differences. He had to teach her the ceremonies, the use of healing plants, and reconcile her to the role of a medicine man's life. This involved feeding multitudes of uninvited guests for the feasts following every service, and never getting enough rest because, as tribal counselor, Leonard Crow Dog was always on call, traveling constantly, and took his family along when he was summoned. Since he did not charge for healing, and gave everything away, there was never enough money to feed the family. Mary Crow Dog raised seven children. In addition to Richard, Ina, and Bernadette from Crow Dog's first marriage, she had four more with him: Pedro, Anwah, June Bug, and Jennifer Louise.

Reclaiming Indian Values

The symbolic role that AIM played for her people was re-enacted in the contours of Mary Crow Dog's life. Without the organization, she lived in despair, poverty, alcoholism, a suicidal existence of drunken car-crashes, domestic violence, joblessness, and hopelessness. Within the movement, she felt a sense of purpose. The alliance that AIM members made with the traditionalists restored for them their own ancient ways. It reinvigorated the tribal elders and returned to them their traditional roles as transmitters of their culture. Mary Crow Dog, sober, working for the cause, was heroic. Its message that pan-tribal coalitions can fortify and infuse with spiritual power those who are treated as the dregs of society made *Lakota Woman* a national best-seller, won it a movie contract, and earned it the American Book Award for best nonfiction.

The most engrossing chapters of both of her books retell the ancient myths and explain the meanings of the ceremonies. As she said, "AIM made medicine men radical activists, and made radical activists into sundancers and vision seekers.... It restored women's voices and brought them into the tribal councils." It gave urban drifters back their proud past. Instead of confrontations, AIM has organized transcontinental runs to dramatize survival issues. Through this culturally relevant mode of protest they are exempt from the federal prosecution that crippled their initial efforts. This distinction also differentiates her two books. *Lakota Woman* is a thrilling first-hand account of AIM's early demonstrations from the perspective of a teenager who had been involved in those heady events; *Okitika Woman* contextualizes them as a mature woman of 36 recapitulates her youthful adventures, setting each in its historical background.

Cankpe Opi (Wounded Knee)

The riot that occurred in Custer, South Dakota, when the murderer of Wesley Bad Heart Bull was acquitted in February 1973, resulted in a meeting attended by all the medicine men (Frank Fools Crow, Wallace Black Elk, Henry Crow Dog, and Pete Catches) to consider how to protest this racist incident. Two elders, Gladys Bissonette and Ellen Moves Camp suggested that they take a stand at Wounded Knee; and on February 27, they did so. They dug trenches, put up cinderblock walls, and became warriors. The siege lasted 71 days. On March 12, surrounded by armored cars spewing bursts of gunfire, a declaration was drafted for the independent Oglala Nation proclaiming its sovereignty. Two Native Americans were killed: Frank Clearwater and Buddy Lamont; many were wounded. Crow Dog treated them with medicinal herbs; he led sunrise prayers at Big Foot's grave, and brought back the Ghost Dance for which his ancestors had been slaughtered in 1890. For four days, and for the first time in 80 years, on sacred ground, they circled a cedar tree, dancing in the snow.

On April 11, Mary Crow Dog's baby was born. She named him after Pedro Bissonette, who was killed by Dick Wilson's tribal police for having founded the Oglala Sioux Civil Rights Organization (OSCRO). The terrorist reprisals by Wilson's "goons" (Guardians of the Oglala Nation) resulted in the deaths of 250 people, many of them children, on the reservation. Jeannette Bissonette was shot on her way home from the funeral. The great-grandson of the prophet Black Elk, Byron De Sersa, was gunned down for having written an article critical of Wilson; and Delphine, Leonard Crow Dog's sister, was beaten to death. On September 5, 1975, 180 agents broke into Crow Dog's home with helicopters whirring overhead. They took him away in handcuffs. After three trials, he was sentenced to 23 years in prison. Mary Crow Dog addressed rallies to raise funds; and it took contributions of $200,000 from friends, Amnesty International, and the World Council of Churches to get him out of prison. Attorney William Kunstler argued on his behalf. Sandy Rosen wrote the appeals. At Lewisburg Penitentiary, his cell was so small that he could not stand upright in it. At Leavenworth, they tried to disorient him by keeping a neon light glaring 24 hours a day.

Filmmakers Mike Cuesta and David Baxter made a documentary about his imprisonment; and celebrities rallied to his support, among them: Harry Belafonte, Rip Torn, Geraldine Page, Dick Gregory, Marlon Brando, Ossie Davis, and Ruby Dee. When he returned to Rosebud, the entire tribe welcomed him with honoring songs. After many separations and reconciliations with Leonard Crow Dog, Mary Crow Dog married Rudi Olguin, a descendent of Zapotecs, Mexican Indians, on August 24, 1991, in Santa Fe, New Mexico. Together they had a daughter, Summer Rose.

SOURCES:

Crow Dog, Mary, and Richard Erdoes, *Lakota Woman,* New York, Grove Weidenfeld, 1990.
Crow Dog, Mary, and Richard Erdoes, *Ohitika Woman,* New York, Grove Press, 1993.

—*Sketch by Ruth Rosenberg*

Crowfoot
1830-1890
Blackfeet tribal leader
Also known as Isapo-muxika, Astoxkomi ["Shot Close"], and Kyiah-sta-a ["Bear Ghost"]

Crowfoot was born in 1830 at Blackfoot Crossing, near present-day Calgary, Alberta, Canada. He became famous as the Blackfoot peace chief, signing a treaty with the Canadian government in 1877 and leading his people from buffalo hunting to the early reservation period. His father Istowun-eh'pata ["Packs a Knife"] and his mother Axkyahp-say-pi ["Attacked Toward Home"] were Blood Indians, one of the three tribes that made up the Blackfeet Confederacy. The Bloods, Blackfeet, and Piegans spoke a common language, intermarried, and allied to fight common enemies, including the Crow, Cree, and Sioux. The Blackfeet were buffalo hunters and warriors, ranging over the northern plains from the Upper Missouri to the North Saskatchewan Rivers and from the Yellowstone River to the Rocky Mountains.

From Blood to Blackfoot

Crowfoot's father was killed during a horse raid against the Crow. After learning of her husband's death, Crowfoot's mother took her two young sons and returned to her father's camp. While living with her father, Scabby Bull, she met a Blackfeet warrior, Akay-nehka-simi ["Many Names"]. The couple fell in love and were married. The family, including the two young boys, were adopted into the Blackfeet nation.

A Blackfeet could have several names during his or her life. For instance, when Crowfoot was born, his parents

Crowfoot

gave him the name Asotxkomi ["Shot Close"]. Attacked Toward Home called her son Shot Close as long as she lived. For the Blackfeet, names were not simply means of identification. They were owned by families and were considered heirlooms and passed on through the family. The second name given Crowfoot was Kyiah-sta-ah ["Bear Ghost"], and it was only when he reached maturity that he became Isapo-muxika ["Crow Indian's Big Foot" or "Crowfoot"], the name of a famous Blackfeet warrior.

Although the Blackfeet had suffered from epidemics of diphtheria in 1836 and smallpox in 1837, they were still a powerful and vibrant people in the 1840s. During this time, the Blackfeet nation controlled most of southern Alberta and northern Montana. They were also almost constantly at war with the surrounding tribes. As a young man Crowfoot went on many raids, earning a reputation as a warrior and a leader. Fighting in 19 battles and being wounded six times, he suffered from his war injuries the rest of his life.

Becomes Recognized as a Chief

Crowfoot grew to become a tall and lithe young man, although thinner and never quite as healthy as his comrades. A great orator, with a reserved and quiet demeanor, he also had a quick and violent temper. He seldom joined in social activities and took no part in religious activities. Nonetheless, Crowfoot became recognized as a prominent Blackfeet chief thanks to his abilities as warrior and leader. He also gained status in the summer of 1866, when he single-handedly killed a grizzly bear with only a spear. Crowfoot was an

indifferent hunter, however, and gave up hunting entirely later in life.

Crowfoot secured his position among the Blackfeet by by taking a Blackfeet woman, Sisoyaki ["Cutting Woman"], for a wife. He eventually had as many as ten wives, although there were seldom more than three or four in his household at one time. They included Nipis-tai-aki ["Cloth Woman"], Ayis-tsi ["Packs on Her Back"], Sowki-pi-aki ["Prairie Woman"], Awatoht-sinik ["Killed the Enemy with His Own Gun"], Pi-ot-skini ["Going Out to Meet the Victors"], and Asinaki ["Paper Woman"], sister of Red Crow, head chief of the Bloods.

Although he had many wives, Crowfoot had relatively few children, and only four of these, a boy and three girls, reached maturity. Most of his other children were sickly, dying of tuberculosis while still quite young. His son Bear Ghost was blind. His daughters were Charged Ahead, Little Woman and First Beaver. Little Woman outlived all the others, dying in the early 1940s. After Crowfoot's eldest son was killed by a Cree war party on the Red Deer River, he adopted a young Cree warrior, Pito-kanow-apiwin ["Pound-maker"] giving him the Blackfeet name Makoyi-koh-kin ["Wolf Thin Legs"]. Poundmaker was much like his foster father in temperament and, like Crowfoot, he could see the time coming when the Indians would have to live peacefully with the white men.

The Blackfeet leader also won prestige through his relationship with the white Canadians. The Hudson's Bay Company traders were pleased to hear that Crowfoot had become a chief. Relations between the traders and the Blackfeet were uneasy and Crowfoot had already shown a willingness to maintain the peace. He also developed a friendship with one of the chief traders, Richard Hardisty. Wealthy in horses and a recognized leader, Crowfoot began to win supporters. Originally known as the Big Pipes, his band later were known as the Tsikin-aiee ["Moccasins"]. Crowfoot was a generous leader, sending his young men through the camps helping the poor, distributing tobacco and other presents, and providing horses for those who needed them. The Moccasin band soon were calling him Manis-tokos ["The Father of His People"].

Although Crowfoot did not fully understand the white men, he did not see them as a threat to his people. They traded guns, iron kettles, beads, and woolens for buffalo hides, horses, and dried meat. As long as the white men treated him fairly, Crowfoot did the same. He expected justice from the whites, and demanded it for them from his own people. In 1865 Crowfoot met and befriended Father Albert Lacombe, a Roman Catholic missionary from Quebec. Their friendship grew after Crowfoot saved the priest's life during a battle with the Cree. Although Crowfoot showed no more interest in Christianity than he did in the Blackfeet's Sundance, he allowed the priest to preach to his people. Lacombe also assisted Crowfoot in changing his people's economy from hunting to farming.

By the early 1870s the disastrous effects of whiskey, brought across the border by American citizens on the

Whoop-Up Trail, was weighing heavily upon the Blackfeet. Although rum was always part of the Hudson's Bay Company inventory, the British had used it sparingly in the trade. The Americans did not. Trading rotgut whiskey for the Indian's buffalo robes, horses, guns, and Indian women, the rough and ready American style of commerce abused the Blackfeet. After complaints reached Ottawa from missionaries, Hudson's Bay Company men, and government officials, the Canadian government responded. In 1873 the North West Mounted Police were organized and sent to the plains, bringing the Queen's law to the Canadian West.

Crowfoot welcomed the coming of the redcoats. They cleared his country of the American whiskey traders. But they also came to make the prairie safe for settlers. In 1877 Crowfoot, representing the Blackfeet, Bloods, North Piegans, and Sarcees, agreed to a treaty with the Canadian government. Treaty No. 7 was the last treaty signed on the Canadian plains, formalizing the government's relationship with the Blackfeet. The government wanted land for a railroad and for settlers; the Blackfoot Confederacy, led by Crowfoot, ceded 50,000 acres, including most of what is now southern Alberta. The government also wanted to prevent the Blackfeet from allying themselves with Chief Sitting Bull's Sioux, who had come to Canada after defeating George Custer at the Little Bighorn in 1876.

Shortly after signing the treaty, the Blackfeet were faced with starvation. The buffalo were no longer in Crowfoot's country, and in order to survive his people had to follow them south to Montana. For several winters, bands of Canadian Blackfeet lived in Montana, chasing remnants of the once vast buffalo herds. Upon his return to Canada, Crowfoot found his people impoverished and the hunting as poor as when he had left. The Blackfeet had no other choice but to live off government rations and try their best to farm.

Adding to their problems was the turmoil arising from the Northwest Rebellion of 1885. Louis Riel, leader of the Métis, attempted to form a provisional government in Saskatchewan and tried to convince Crowfoot to join the cause. Although Crowfoot kept the Blackfeet out of the rebellion he encouraged his people to assist any Cree or Métis rebels passing through their country. Poundmaker, Crowfoot's adopted son, led the Crees against the Canadians at the town of Battleford. When the rebellion was crushed, Crowfoot's decision proved to have been the best choice for the Blackfeet.

After the Blackfeet settled on their reserve, Crowfoot's role as chief evolved into that of a mediator and magistrate. He gave counsel, confronted government officials when they attempted to swindle his people, and succeeded in maintaining relative harmony in the camps. Although he continued to live in the Indian manner, he also traveled to Montreal on the railroad, meeting government officials and the prime minister.

Crowfoot lived to see the Blackfeet fall from their role as proud hunters of the northwestern plains to a broken and dispirited people ravaged by disease, alcoholism, and starvation. He witnessed the deaths of most of his children,

including his adoptive son Poundmaker. But Crowfoot also successfully led his people without shedding blood, taking them from a nomadic life on the prairies to their reserve. He died in his tipi on the prairie of the Bow Valley on April 25, 1890.

SOURCES:

Dempsey, Hugh A., *Crowfoot, Chief of the Blackfeet,* Norman, University of Oklahoma Press, 1989.
Native North American Almanac, edited by Duane Champagne, Detroit, Gale Research, 1994; 1038-1039.
Waldman, Carl, *Who Was Who in Native American History,* New York, Facts On File, 1990; 88.

—Sketch by Michael F. Turek

Curly
1859(?)-1935(?)
Crow scout

Curly is remembered for having brought the earliest tidings of the massacre of George Custer's troops at the Battle of Little Bighorn to General Alfred Terry, who was headquartered aboard the steamer *Far West* at the mouth of the Yellowstone River. Claiming to be the only survivor of Custer's Last Stand, this 17-year-old Crow scout provided a confused and incredible account of Custer's annihilation while pursuing hostile Sioux and Cheyenne Indians in Montana; and 60 years of retelling the story added no clarity to what role Curly really played in the battle. Visiting Curly's deathbed, his long-time interpreter Russell White Bear confessed himself to be "not clear yet on your stories—tell me for the last time if you were with Custer up to the time when the gray horse troop separated from the main command."

The first mention of Curly occurs in Sergeant James E. Wilson's report to Terry's Engineer Officer, stating that the young scout, known to have served with Custer, showed up at about noon, three days after the June 25, 1876, battle. According to Wilson, Curly indicated that there had been a battle, "but there being no interpreter on board very little reliable information was obtained. He wore an exceedingly dejected countenance, but his appetite proved to be in first class order." Later, Curly told the commander of the detail sent to bury Custer's men, "I did nothing wonderful—I was not in the fight." Further, a visit to the battlefield with Curly on the first anniversary of the massacre convinced Colonel M. V. Sheridan to report to his brother and commander, General P. H. Sheridan, that the now-famous scout "had run away before the fight really began," and "the greater portion of his tale was untrustworthy."

Curly

Based on these and later reports, it became clear that Curly had apparently fled the battlefield before the massacre took place and deduced the trend of events once he was safely away. In the months and years that followed, Curly became a skilled "raconteur" among the white men, continually adding to and embellishing his original story. So the tales proliferated: Curly hid under a Sioux blanket, changed his hairstyle, and crawled two miles to safety; Curly vainly tried to persuade the gallant Custer to escape under a blanket with him; Curly hid inside a disemboweled horse; Curly appeared on a ridge top loyally beside disillusioned old soldiers.

Gradually, Curly became a celebrity, among the most-photographed and interviewed Native Americans of his time, his cabin preserved and displayed for tourists. He mocked and challenged other Crow scouts who had fought elsewhere along the Little Bighorn on the day of Custer's defeat when they could not remember seeing Curly during any of the actual fighting. However, Curly did not contest charges leveled at him by the Sioux War Chief Gall who, at the tenth anniversary reunion of the Battle of Little Bighorn, dismissed Curly's role in the battle by saying, "You were a coward and ran away before the battle began." According to another account, the formidable Gall demanded to know where Curly's wings were because "nothing but a bird could have escaped after we surrounded the whites."

Another eyewitness account of the Battle of Little Bighorn was provided by Minnie Devereaux, the daughter of Cheyenne Chief Plenty Horses and later a silent screen actress, who recalled that as a little girl she played on the fresh killing field. She asserted that the Indians deliberately trapped Custer, whom they blamed for the Washita Massacre, in which Custer's troops overran a sleeping Cheyenne village in 1868. "The women, the children and the old men went one way," Devereaux told the *Mack Sennett Weekly* in 1917. "The young men went another, but they left no trail. It was our trail, the trail of the old men, and the women, that Custer followed, and we led him to his doom." To illustrate Indian humor Vine Deloria, Jr., a Sioux, wrote in *Custer Died for Your Sins:* "The Sioux tease other tribes a great deal for not having been at the Little Big Horn. The Crows, traditional enemies of the Sioux, explain their role as Custer's scouts as one of bringing Custer where the Sioux could get at him!"

SOURCES:

Books

Berger, Thomas, *Little Big Man,* Dial Press, 1964.

Connell, Evan S., *Son of the Morning Star: Custer and the Little Bighorn,* North Point Press, 1984.

Deloria, Vine, Jr., *Custer Died for Your Sins: An Indian Manifesto,* New York, Macmillan, 1969.

Graham, W. A., *The Custer Myth: A Source Book of Custeriana,* Stackpole Company, Bonanza Books, 1953.

Gray, John S., *Centennial Campaign: The Sioux War of 1876,* Old Army Press, 1976.

Sandoz, Mari, *The Battle of the Little Bighorn,* New York, J. B. Lippincott, 1966.

Periodicals

Devereaux, Minnie, "Indian Woman Tells History," *Mack Sennett Weekly,* February 12, 1917; reprinted as "Indian Actress Recalls Little Bighorn Battle in a 1917 Article," *Native American Smoke Signals,* April 1993; 3.

—Sketch by Steven Edwin Conliff

Charles Brent Curtis
1860-1936
Kansa/Kaw-Osage attorney, legislator, and vice president

Charles Brent Curtis was born on January 25, 1860, on Kansa/Kaw Indian allotted land which would later become part of North Topeka, Kansas. He was the eldest of two children, his sister, Elizabeth, being born in 1861. His father, Orren Armes Curtis, was a white man whose English ancestors originally arrived in America in the early 1600s. Orren Curtis was born in Eugene, Indiana, in 1829. He appears to have been married several times prior to marrying

Charles Brent Curtis

Ellen Pappan, the mixed-blood daughter of his employer, in 1859. Ellen Pappan Curtis' mother, Julie Gonville Pappan, was of Kansa/Kaw, Osage, and remote remote Potawatomi ancestry. Julie had married three times, her last husband, Louis Pappan, being of French ancestry and born in St. Louis. Mrs. Pappan's mother, Wyhesee, a full-blood Kansa/Osage Indian, was the daughter of the Kansa chief Nomparawarah ["White Plume"] and the granddaughter of the Osage chief Pawhuska. It was White Plume who had his portrait painted by Charles Bird King in the 1820s. Wyhesee married Louis Gonville who appears to have been of French Canadian and one-quarter Potawatomi ancestry.

Although Charles Curtis was later variously described as being of one-half, one-quarter, and one-eighth Indian ancestry, none of these appears to be correct. Technically, based on his somewhat confused and contradictory genealogy, Curtis was of a little over one-eighth Indian ancestry, and predominantly of English and French extraction. Whatever the case, Curtis identified himself as an American Indian, although he was not sentimental about his ancestry and was not above employing his Indianness in whatever manner was most politically useful during his career.

Raised among his numerous Kansa relatives on their Indian allotments along the north shore of the Kansas River, Curtis was also influenced by his maternal grandmother, Julie Gonville Pappan. Curtis resided with her on the Kansa reservation near Council Grove some 60 miles west of Topeka, following the death of his mother from cholera in April, 1864. However, southern Cheyenne and Arapaho

raids and conflicts with the residents of the Kansa reservation, between 1866 and 1868, resulted in Curtis being returned to the relative peace of north Topeka in 1868. On his return to Topeka, Curtis came under the dominant control and influence of his white grandmother, Permelia Curtis, who was to oversee his education and employment. She also laid the groundwork for Curtis' lifelong allegiance to the Republican party.

In 1878, Charles was briefly dropped from the Kansa annuity roll because he was not present at the time of the annuity distribution and because he did not have a primary residence on the Kansa reservation. At the time, the registry regarded him as being of one-eighth Indian ancestry. This did not affect his Kansa legal enrollment, however, since his grandmother, Julie Pappan, was recorded in the treaty of 1825.

Completing three years at Topeka High School, Curtis began the study of law in 1879 with A. H. Case, a local attorney, and was admitted to the bar in 1881, at the age of 21. Almost immediately, he involved himself with local political affairs, a field of interest that was to occupy the rest of his life. In 1885 he was elected the county attorney for Shawnee County, Kansas. Curtis was elected to the United States House of Representatives as a Republican from the Fourth District in 1892 and remained in the house until January, 1907, completing 14 years of service there.

Passage of the Curtis Act

In the late nineteenth century, Curtis became involved in legislation which resulted in the General Allotment Act. Passed in 1887, the act divided reservation lands among Native Americans and the surplus land went to U.S. settlers. On June 28, 1898, the Curtis Act was passed, extending the disastrous processes of the General Allotment Act (1887) to the Five Civilized Tribes of Oklahoma. It had generally been viewed that the application of the allotment was inevitable, and Curtis, an avowed assimilationist who was an ardent supporter of allotment, achieved a compromised bill which attempted to somewhat modify the process. Nevertheless, Curtis will be remembered as being the author of the legislation that destroyed tribal sovereignty in the Indian Territory (later Oklahoma). Curtis, who held his own 40-acre Kansa allotment jointly with his sister throughout his life, actually reduced his own status as a Native American through the passage of the General Allotment Act. He felt, however, that the acculturative progress of the American Indian was being hindered by the continuation of communal ownership of lands, herds, and other tribal resources.

In 1907 Curtis was designated by the Kansas State Legislature to fill an unexpired term in the United States Senate. In the same year he was elected to the Senate, but he lost a reelection campaign in 1912. In 1914, Curtis was reelected to the Senate, defeating Senator Joseph L. Bristow, and continued in that senatorial position until 1926, some 20 years in the Senate. During his years in the Senate, Charles Curtis' name was prominent on a number of bills; however, he was recognized moreso for his politicking on the Senate floor. He was a conservative Republican and party regular who was designated party whip in 1915. Curtis replaced Henry Cabot Lodge as majority leader in 1924. That year also marked the death of his wife.

Curtis was philosophically and politically antagonistic to some forms of traditional American Indian tribal government. In his capacity as chairperson of the Senate Indian Affairs Committee in 1921, Curtis supported the bill of Secretary of the Interior John Barton Payne to minimize the sovereignty of the Pueblo tribal governments by clarifying how federal jurisdiction was to be applied over the Pueblos. With the end of the sixty-sixth Congress, the Payne Bill was not acted upon, although the complex issues involving American Indian sovereignty and land title were to be repeatedly addressed in future congresses.

According to William E. Unrau, Charles Curtis' political philosophy can be summarized as follows: "Curtis supported the gold standard, high tariffs, prohibition, restrictive immigration, deportation of aliens, and generous veterans benefits; opposed the League of Nations; and took the view that depressions were natural occurrences that inevitably would be followed by periods of prosperity ... championed female suffrage ... government assistance to farmers" especially Kansans.

Becomes Vice President

In 1928, at the Republican national convention, Curtis initially opposed Herbert Hoover's presidential nomination as their candidate. After Curtis' objections were resolved by fellow delegates, Curtis was designated as the vice-presidential candidate. The Republican victory in the 1928 national elections was achieved after an acrimonious battle.

Curtis was inaugurated as the thirty-first vice president of the United States in March, 1929, the first American Indian to have achieved this office. During his tenure, Curtis spoke for American Indians whenever the occasion arose. He has generally been viewed by political analysts as having served a rather lackluster tenure as vice president. Some have disagreed, however, pointing out the effective role that he played in the complex negotiations of policy behind the scenes, and his major place in negotiations with American Indians although he attempted to avoid controversy where possible. Although Curtis was renominated with Hoover in 1932, they were defeated. Curtis retired from active politics and returned to the practice of law in Washington, D.C.

Curtis married Anna E. Baird of Topeka in 1884. Mrs. Curtis' parents had migrated to Topeka from Altoona, Pennsylvania, and were prominent Baptists in the community. The Curtises had one son and two daughters: Harry, who graduated from Harvard Law School and established a practice in Chicago; Permelia, who married an army officer; and Leona, who married a prominent industrialist of Providence, Rhode Island. Curtis died of a heart attack on February 8, 1936, in the Washington, D.C., home of his half-sister, Dolly Curtis Gann, who had served as his official hostess during his years as vice president. Curtis' remains were returned to Topeka, the place of his beginnings.

SOURCES:

Books

"Charles Curtis: The Politics of Allotment," in *Indian Lives: Essays on Nineteen Twentieth Century Native American Leaders,* edited by L. G. Moses and Raymond Wilson, Albuquerque, University of New Mexico Press, 1985; 113-138.

Gann, Dolly, *Dolly Gann's Book,* Garden City, New York, Doubleday, Doran, 1933.

Kelly, Lawrence C., *The Assault on Assimilation: John Collier and the Origins of Indian Policy Reform,* Albuquerque, University of New Mexico Press, 1983.

Mixed-bloods and Tribal Dissolution: Charles Curtis and the Quest for Indian Identity, Lawrence, University of Kansas Press, 1989.

Seitz, Don C., *From Kaw Teepee to Capitol: The Life Story of Charles Curtis, Indian, Who Has Risen to High Estate,* New York, Frederick A. Stokes, 1928.

Unrau, William E., "The Mixed-Blood Connection: Charles Curtis and Kaw Detribalization," in *Kansas and the West: Bicentennial Essays in Honor of Nyle H. Miller,* edited by Forrest R. Blackburn, Topeka, Kansas State Historical Society, 1976; 151-161.

Periodicals

Chapman, Berlin B., "Charles Curtis and the Kaw Reservation," *Kansas Historical Quarterly,* 14:15, January 1947; 337-351.

Ewy, Marvin, "Charles Curtis of Kansas: Vice President of the United States, 1929-1933," *Emporia State Research Studies,* 10; 1-58.

"Heap Big Chief," *American Mercury,* August 1929; 409-412.

"The Kaw Indian Who Leads the Senate," *Literary Digest,* January 3, 1925; 47.

Kiel, Eric, "Curtis' Indian Blood," *Nation,* August 1, 1928; 109-110.

"Lo, The Poor Senator," *Saturday Evening Post,* February 9, 1907; 15-17.

Ross, Charles E., "Charles Curtis of Kansas," *Outlook,* May 16, 1928; 83-86.

Villard, Oscar Garrison, "Charles Curtis," *Nation,* April 7, 1928; 400-402.

—Sketch by George H. J. Abrams

Datsolalee
1835-1925
Washo basket weaver
Also known as Dabuda ["Wide Hips"], Datsolali (Datsolai), and Louisa Keyser

One of the most famous weavers in the world, Datsolalee was a major influence on the evolution of Washo fancy basketry and is recognized as the greatest basket weaver and designer among the Washo people. Born in Nevada's Carson Valley of unknown parentage, she learned the skills of traditional Washo basketry, perfecting the intricate design that used up to 36 stitches to the inch.

Datsolalee was married twice, first to a Washo man named Assu, by whom she had two children, and second to Charley Keyser in 1888. With her marriage to Keyser, Datsolalee took the name Louisa. However, it was her friendship with and patronage from a man named Dr. S. L. Lee of Carson City in the 1860s that earned her the nickname Datsolalee—a name she was known by for the remainder of her life.

In 1851, disaster struck the Washo tribe when it was attacked by the Northern Paiute, a tribe that had come to Carson Valley when white settlers forced it from its own homeland during the California Gold Rush. In a dispute over the use of certain lands, the Paiute defeated the Washo, imposing two penalties: the Washo could own no horses, and, more importantly for Datsolalee and her tribe, they could weave no baskets. The Paiute wanted to eliminate the competition in order to sell their own basketry. This restriction was disastrous for the Washo people, who had very little to offer for trade or sale without their basketry.

Datsolalee Defies Basket Prohibition

By 1895, the Washo people were living in utter poverty and their financial condition was desperate. In a defiant move, Datsolalee took some glass bottles she had covered with weaving to a clothing store in Carson City, which eventually became the major outlet for Datsolalee's weavings and those of the Washo people. The Emporium Company was owned by Abram Cohn and his wife Amy (and later his second wife, Margaret), who regretted the loss of Washo basketry through the years of Paiute rule and were surprised to find that the Washo women had continued to weave despite the nearly half-century ban. Both recognized the high quality of Datsolalee's work and bought all of her

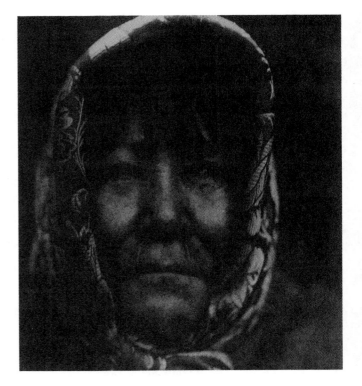

Datsolalee

baskets, requesting that she produce more and promising to purchase all of them.

After that, the Cohns handled all of Datsolalee's work, as well as baskets from other Washo weavers. Although Abram took credit for discovering Datsolalee, apparently Amy was the first to become interested in Washo basketry and in Datsolalee herself. Amy kept very detailed records of Datsolalee's work, compiling a written catalog of her basketry. Particularly with Datsolalee's major pieces, Amy's records show the dates each weaving was started and finished; Datsolalee's minor works were usually given only a finishing date or a date when she brought a group of works to the Emporium. With each sale, Amy issued certificates of authentication. In addition, she published pamphlets about Datsolalee's work and took promotional photographs, all in an effort to raise the value of her baskets.

Datsolalee's baskets combined creative and unusual design work with a rare technical skill. She wove her baskets with tiny, detailed stitches, pulled tightly into a coil. In addition, the geometrical designs in Datsolalee's baskets delineated her perception of Washo life and history. It is believed that Datsolalee interwove designs that were part of her dreams and visions. All of her baskets are distinguished by small, repetitive designs—often lines or triangles—woven with exact spacing. Her designs can be found on three major types of baskets: the singam, shaped like a truncated cone; the mokeewit, a conical burden basket; and the degikup, a spherical ceremonial basket and Datsolalee's preferred style. For tools, she used her teeth, her fingers, a piece of sharp stone or glass, and a bone or iron awl.

Most of the Washo weavers first sold their work through the Emporium, but eventually found their own patrons or sold directly to tourists at Lake Tahoe. So, too, Datsolalee found another patron for her work. Every summer, the Cohns took their inventory of baskets to their branch shop in Tahoe City, and Datsolalee attracted attention by weaving her baskets outside this store. Here Datsolalee met William F. Breitholle, who worked as a wine steward at a resort hotel at Lake Tahoe from 1907 to 1916. Because the Cohns gave her Sundays off from weaving, Datsolalee would visit the Breitholle's for breakfast and, ultimately, developed a close relationship with them. William's son, Buddy, who currently owns 17 pieces of a private collection of Datsolalee's work, has said that the baskets were given to his parents without the Cohns' knowledge and are not recorded in the Cohn ledger. Art historians have speculated that either Amy was unaware that Datsolalee was weaving on Sundays for Breitholle, or she felt she had no right to the baskets Datsolalee was making in her spare time.

The Cohn ledger lists approximately 120 of Datsolalee's pieces; however, it is estimated that she wove nearly 300 in her lifetime, including approximately 40 exceptionally large pieces. During 1904 and 1919, Datsolalee worked primarily on these large pieces, some of which took an entire year to complete. One of her most famous, called "Myriads of Stars Shine Over the Graves of Our Ancestors," contains 56,590 stitches.

Though nearly blind in the latter years of her life, Datsolalee worked until her death in Carson City at the age of 90. She experimented considerably with design, technique, and color, and, as Marvin Cohadas pointed out in "The Breitholle Collection of Washoe Basketry" in *American Indian Art* magazine was a pioneer in "introducing most of the innovations that characterize the Washo fancy or curio style, including the incurving spheroid degikup basket form, fine stitching, two-color design and expanded pattern area." Five years after her death, one of Datsolalee's baskets sold for $10,000. In the 1990s, her baskets were considered collectors' items and sold for close to $250,000.

SOURCES:

Books

Dockstader, Frederick J., *Great North American Indians,* New York, Van Nostrand Reinhold, 1977; 68-71.

Leitch, Barbara A., *A Concise Dictionary of Indian Tribes of North America,* Reference Publications, 1979; 506-508.

Terrell, John Upton, *American Indian Almanac,* New York, World Publishing, 1971; 389-392.

Waldman, Carl, *Who Was Who in Native American History,* New York, Facts on File, 1990; 93.

Periodicals

Bates, Craig, D., "Miwok-Paiute Basketry 1920-1929: Genesis of an Art Form," *American Indian Art* magazine, 4, autumn 1979; 54-59.

Cohodas, Marvin, "The Breitholle Collection of Washo Basketry," *American Indian Art* magazine, 9, autumn 1984; 38-39.

Cohodas, Marvin, "Dat So La Lee's Basketry Design," *American Indian Art* magazine, 1, autumn 1976; 22-31.

Ramo, Joshua Cooper, "A Tisket, A Tasket ... Trends: Indian Baskets Are Hot Collectibles," *Newsweek,* December 13, 1993; 79.

—*Sketch by Lori J. Sawicki*

Frank Day
1902-1976
Maidu painter and tribal historian
Also known as Lydam Lilly ["Fading Morning Star"]

Frank Day did not begin painting until late in life. He began exhibiting his work in the 1960s; within a decade, he had become California's most honored Native American artist. The spiritual energy of his pictures inspired a revitalization of the Maidu culture. A group of young Indians interested in Maidu traditions began meeting with him on weekends to hear stories of the past and to listen to his songs, which he translated so that they could interpret them. He also choreographed the traditional movements of the ancient Maidu dances, which acknowledged the animals, the birds, the earth. From this matrix, a performance group, the Maidu Dancers and Traditionalists, was formed with a repertoire of 14 ceremonials they had learned from Day.

Day's father, Twoboe, was 60 years old when his son was born in 1902 at Berry Creek, in Butte County, California. Twoboe shared the ways of the Maidu elders with his son, telling him the stories of the sacred sites and the historically significant places. Each tree, spring, boulder, canyon had its individual name which was taught to the child. Maidu children were instructed to memorize their tribal boundaries which were defined by these natural landmarks. The Maidu lived in the mountain meadows of Northwestern California about 4,000 feet above sea level surrounded by acorn-bearing oak groves, with fish and waterfowl in the sloughs and marshes. At the center of each Maidu village was a semisubterranean earth-covered dance house. Wonommi, the Creator, told the Maidu to keep the sacred dance house, the sacred rattle and the dances, and to worship at night. Boys were initiated into the Kuksu cult in order to maintain the stability and order of the world which depended upon their continuing the dances.

Ishi and Companion at Iamin Moal

One of Day's most mysterious and poignant paintings records an event 60 years after its occurrence. One day in July of 1911 when Day was nine, he had been walking with his father near the place where the forks of the Feather River join at Iamin Maol. There, he saw Ishi kneeling over a tribesman who had been shot in the stomach. Out of rock and sinew, Ishi had rigged an ingenious contrivance to extricate the bullet from his wounded companion with whom he had left his homeland in Mill Creek Canyon. Unable to resuscitate his friend, Ishi had staggered alone and disconsolate to Oroville two days later. The sheriff of Oroville had summoned Twoboe to the jail to try to communicate with Ishi who lay dazed and starving in his cell. Twoboe could not comprehend Yaki, and Ishi could not understand Maidu, but the two men recognized each other from having met on the trail. Day's picture captures the pathos of that encounter.

A 12-Year Pilgrimage

When Twoboe died in 1922, his son began an extended period of wandering. For a dozen years, he sought out other tribes, walked to faraway places, taking odd jobs to survive during his vagabond existence, which took him to places as distant as Oklahoma. According to Maidu myth, the soul of the deceased blew about like the wind, retracing each step it had taken in life before it was released to the other world; therefore, since the dead stayed with them until it was ready for departure, mourning was intense and prolonged, particularly for a father. Day depicted this in his paintings "Mourning at Mineral Springs" and "Spiritual Burial."

On his return to California in 1934, anthropologists sought him for his knowledge of the old ways. Archeologist Donald P. Jewell encouraged him to paint his recollections as well as to sing them. Herb and Peggy Puffer of Pacific Western Traders in Folsom also urged Day to paint, and then tape-recorded what he said about his pictures. Exhibits were mounted in Sacramento at American River College in 1963, in San Francisco in 1967, at California State University in 1974, at the Governor's office in Sacramento in 1975, and at the Crocker Art Museum in 1976. After his death, an important show of his works was held at the Museum of the Plains Indian at Browning, Montana in 1978; that same year, a retrospective of his work was held at Gorman on the Davis campus of the University of California. The Heard Museum in Phoenix, Arizona, paired his work with that of his fellow Maiduan, Harry Fonseca, who had begun a series of 25 drawings of the ceremonial dances of the Chico Maidu after gathering information about them from his uncle, Henry Azbill (1896-1973). The show was called "Two Views of California: Day and Fonseca."

Fulfills the Role of Tribal Historian

Because of their strong narrative content, Day's paintings, said to number about 200, have been avidly collected. Ironically, the pictures meant to serve as memorials to his own community spoke tellingly to outsiders. Intended as archives of his people's customs and legends, as historical recollections of events significant to his own tribe, they attained a universality of meaning through his innate compositional skills.

In the summer of 1992 issue of *News from Native California*, Frank La Pena, director of Native American Studies at California State University at Sacramento, recounted the founding of the Maidu Dancers and Traditionalists at the Pacific Western Traders store in Folsom. "Some young Indians who were interested in dance and tradition were only too willing to meet on weekends and learn what Frank Day wanted to teach." The dancers' families began attending the practices. The elders among them contributed what they remembered about the dance cycles, which began in the fall and continued until early May each year. These ceremonies had not been seen since 1906, when the dance leader, Holi Lafonso had died. Therefore, new materials had to be gathered: deer hides, clamshell, abalone, feathers of eagle, yellowhammer, magpie, and mallard. Pomo medicine woman Mabel McKay "doctored" these materials so that no one but the dancers might ever touch them.

Day's painting "Toto at Bloomer Hill" shows a man in an antler headdress leaping, his waist cinched with a deer-claw belt, wearing a feather necklace. The Toto was danced at the winter solstice, in buckskin skirts decorated with furs. As the participants fashioned their regalia under Day's instructions, they relearned their traditions, reclaiming their ecological bonds to their ancient environment upon which their well-being depends. They made musical instruments as Wonommi had told them to do. These included split stick rattles, deer hoof rattles, and cocoon rattles. A short stick was split halfway, and its pith removed, so that when held by the unsplit handle and shaken, it made a clacking sound. The dewclaws of deer were tied to a bone handle so that they clicked together when moved. Moth cocoons filled with seeds were tied into clusters to make a swishing sound. Whistles were made from birds' bones by plugging one end, and piercing a hole near the center. Foot drums were made from a hollowed log set over a trench that served as a resonating chamber when stamped upon by the dancers' bare feet. A photograph taken by Herb and Peggy Puffer shows these instruments in use during a rehearsal in their store is printed in the summer of 1992 issue of *News from Native California*. The Lowie Museum of Anthropology at Berkeley has some phonograph recordings of Maidu music; except for one as yet unpublished analysis by Peter Abraham, ethnomusicologists have still to study it. Had it not been for the inspiration of Day, these songs, and the rituals they accompany would have been lost. Each of the Maidu instruments was once alive and as the dancers restore motion to the seeds, branches, bird's wing bones, moth's cocoons, deer's hooves, they revivify them. All that ran, flew, rooted, sprouted are reborn. The cycle of ceremonial dances which honored each season by invoking the beings associated with it, have been restored.

SOURCES:

Books

Hill, Dorothy J., *The Indians of Chico Rancheria,* Sacramento, State of California Resources Agency, Department of Parks and Recreation, 1978.

Roberts, Helen H., *Concow-Maidu Indians of Round Valley—1926,* Chico, Association for Northern California Records and Research, 1980.

The Maidu Indian Myths and Stories of Hanc'ibyjim, edited and translated by William Shipley, Berkeley, Heyday Books, 1991.

Selected Bibliography of Maidu Ethnography and Archeology, compiled by Norman L. Wilson and Arlean Towne, Sacramento, State of California Resources Agency, Department of Parks and Recreation, 1979.

Simpson, Richard, *Ooti: A Maidu Legacy,* Millbrae, California, Celestial Arts, 1977.

Periodicals

"Chico Maidu Dancers," *News From Native California,* summer 1992; 38-41.

Dixon, Roland B., "The Northern Maidu," *Bulletin of the American Museum of Natural History,* 17:3, 1905; 119-346.

—*Sketch by Ruth Rosenberg*

Ada E. Deer

Ada E. Deer
1935-

Menominee social worker, activist, educator, and government official

Life-long advocate for social justice, Ada E. Deer was the first woman to head the U.S. Bureau of Indian Affairs (BIA). As Assistant Secretary for Indian Affairs in the Interior Department, she was "turning the BIA upside down and shaking it," as she told hundreds of Navajos in Arizona a month after taking office in late July of 1993. For Deer, an activist for the rights of American Indians, youth, and women, turning things upside down is nothing new. Her career as a social worker, leader in numerous community and political organizations, and her successful fight to restore federal recognition to the Menominee Tribe all attest to her actions on behalf of human rights and her belief in coalition building. As she told members of the Alaska Federation of Natives in August of 1993, as quoted in the Tundra Times, "I want to emphasize (that) my administration will be based on the Indian values of caring, sharing, and respect.... These values have been missing too long in the halls of government."

Deer was born in Keshena on the Menominee Indian Reservation in northeastern Wisconsin on August 7, 1935. She is the eldest of five children (her siblings are Joseph Deer, Jr., Robert Deer, Ferial Skye, and Connie Deer); four other children died in infancy. Her mother, Constance Stockton (Wood) Deer, is an Anglo-American from Philadelphia and a former BIA nurse. And her father was Joseph Deer, a nearly full-blood Menominee Indian who was a former employee of the Menominee Indian Mills; he died at the age of 85 on January 10, 1994. For the first 18 years of Deer's life, her family lived in a log cabin near the Wolf River with no running water or electricity. Deer told the Senate Committee on Indian Affairs at the hearing to confirm her as head of the BIA that "while all the statistics said we were poor, I never felt poor in spirit. My mother ... was the single greatest influence on my life. She instilled in me rich values which have shaped my lifetime commitment to service."

This service began with a solid education in Shawano and Milwaukee public schools. An outstanding student, Deer graduated in the top ten of her high school class before attending the University of Wisconsin-Madison on a tribal scholarship. She was one of two Native Americans awarded out of 19,000 applicants, and became the first Menominee to graduate from the university. She received her B.A. in social work in 1957; and in 1961, she then went on to become the first Native American to receive a M.S.W. from Columbia University.

From the time she was a graduate student and over the next ten years, Deer held several professional positions. She was employed as a social worker in New York City and in

Minneapolis Public Schools. She also worked with the Peace Corps in Puerto Rico. It was between the years of 1964 and 1967 that Deer had her first job with the BIA in Minnesota as Community Service Coordinator. From 1967 to 1968, she served as Coordinator of Indian Affairs in the University of Minnesota's Training Center for Community Programs. During the same time frame, Deer served on the Joint Commission on Mental Health of Children, Inc., and in 1969 she became a member of the national board of Girl Scouts of the U.S.A., a post she held until 1975. During the summer of 1971, Deer studied at the American Indian Law Program at the University of New Mexico and then briefly attended the University of Wisconsin-Madison Law School. She left after one semester to work on an urgent tribal matter that was to become her major focus over the next several years.

Fights to Regain Menominee Tribe Recognition

As part of the U.S. government's 1950s termination policy—an attempt to forcibly assimilate Indians—the U.S. Congress passed in 1954 the Menominee Termination Act. Fully implemented by 1961, it meant the loss of federal recognition of the Menominee Tribe and along with it, the closing of membership rolls, a loss of benefits such as health and educational services, and an imposition of state jurisdiction. The Menominees were taxed and had to sell off ancestral lands to pay the bills. As Deer testified in her confirmation hearing, the Menominees "literally went from being prosperous to being Wisconsin's newest, smallest and poorest county."

Deer left law school and returned to what was now Menominee County to help gather together tribal leaders to regain control of tribal interests from a group of Menominee elites, and to attempt to reverse termination. There, in 1970, Deer and many others created a new political organization known as Determination of Rights and Unity for Menominee Shareholders (DRUMS). With assistance from the Native American Rights Fund and local legal aid organizations, Deer and other leaders of DRUMS fought to regain federal recognition for the Menominees. Their tactics included a 220-mile "march for justice" from Menominee County to the capital in Madison. As a vital part of the restoration effort, in 1972 and 1973 Deer served as vice president and lobbyist in Washington, D.C., for the National Committee to Save the Menominee People and Forest, Inc.

Author Nicholas C. Peroff stated in Menominee Drums that Deer's positive attitude concerning restoration was evident in her comment to a Washington Post reporter in 1973: "Mainly I want to show people who say nothing can be done in this society that it just isn't so. You don't have to collapse just because there's federal law in your way. Change it!" The efforts of Deer and the members of DRUMS resulted in national publicity for the issue of termination and finally the introduction of a bill in Congress to reverse this policy for the Menominees. On December 22, 1973, President Nixon signed the Menominee Restoration Act into law.

From 1974 to 1976, Deer chaired the Menominee Tribe and headed the Menominee Restoration Committee. After its work was completed, she resigned. In 1977, she became a Senior Lecturer in the School of Social Work and in the American Indian Studies Program at the University of Wisconsin-Madison, where she taught until 1993. Deer also moved into the democratic political arena more fully at this time, serving as legislative liaison to the Native American Rights Fund from 1979 to 1981. In 1982, Deer was a candidate for Wisconsin secretary of state. And in 1984, she was delegate-at-large at the Democratic National Convention and vice-chair of the National Mondale-Ferraro Presidential Campaign. In 1992, Deer almost became the first Native American woman in Congress; after a strong showing in the Second Congressional District of Wisconsin, she lost in the general election to Republican Scot Klug. May of 1993, however, brought a nomination by President Clinton from a field of four candidates (including Navajo tribal chairman Peterson Zah) to head the BIA. Congress, with overwhelming support from its members and from tribal leaders, confirmed her nomination in July of 1993.

Turning the BIA Around

With the BIA, Deer inherited an agency that is infamous for its bureaucracy and historically poor relations with tribes. Deer has had to contend with, among many issues, budget reductions for her agency; conflicts between tribes and localities over land management, water resources, and mineral rights; tribal recognition; education; and religious freedom. Deer is a strong proponent of Indian self-determination; this coincides with the BIA's planned reorganization which will shift more power to tribes. Her approach since being in office has been to visit individual Indian tribes, bringing them together with businesses, organizations, and government entities to find ways to work cooperatively, with the ultimate goal of helping tribes gain economic self-sufficiency. Deer, in her confirmation hearing, maintained: "I want to help the BIA be a full partner in the effort to fulfill the Indian agenda developed in Indian country. The best way we can do this is for the tribes to decide what needs to be done and for the tribes to do it on their own terms, with our enthusiastic support."

Deer's motto in life is "one person can make a difference." For the difference she has made in her many spheres of activity, she has received numerous awards over her lifetime. Deer was one of the Outstanding Young Women of America in 1966. And in 1974, she received the White Buffalo Council Achievement Award, along with honorary doctorates from the University of Wisconsin-Madison and Northland College. Other honors include the Woman of the Year Award from Girl Scouts of America (1982), the Wonder Woman Award (1982), the Indian Council Fire Achievement Award (1984), and the National Distinguished Achievement Award from the American Indian Resources Institute (1991).

SOURCES:

Books

Biographical Dictionary of Indians of the Americas, Volume 1, Newport Beach, California, American Indian Publishers, 1991; 181-182.

Deer, Ada, and R. E. Simon, Jr., *Speaking Out,* Chicago, Children's Press Open Door Books, 1970.

Deer, Ada, "The Power Came from the People," in *I Am the Fire of Time: The Voices of Native American Women,* edited by Jane B. Katz, New York, Dutton, 1977.

Hardy, Gayle J., *American Women Civil Rights Activists: Biobibliographies of 68 Leaders,* 1825-1992, Jefferson, North Carolina, McFarland, 1993; 128-134.

Native American Women, edited by Gretchen M. Bataille, New York, Garland Publishing, 1993; 76-78.

Native North American Almanac, edited by Duane Champagne, Detroit, Gale Research, 1994; 1041.

Peroff, Nicholas C., *Menominee Drums: Tribal Termination and Restoration, 1954-1974,* Norman, University of Oklahoma Press, 1982.

Reference Encyclopedia of the American Indian, sixth edition, edited by Barry T. Klein, West Nyack, New York, Todd Publications, 1993; 504-505.

Periodicals

Cohen, Karen J., "Ada Deer Tries to Start Fire Under Bureaucracy," *Wisconsin State Journal,* March 20, 1994; B1.

"Female BIA Chief 'Shaking Agency Up,'" *Denver Post,* September 2, 1993; B2.

Richardson, Jeff, "Ada Deer: Native Values for BIA Management," *Tundra Times,* September 8, 1993; 1.

Worthington, Rogers, "Woman Picked to Lead Indian Bureau," *Chicago Tribune,* May 20, 1993; A1.

Other

Nomination of Ada Deer: Hearing before the Committee on Indian Affairs, United States Senate, One Hundred Third Congress, First Session, on the Nomination of Ada Deer to be Assistant Secretary for Indian Affairs, July 15, 1993, Washington, D.C., Washington, D.C., U.S. Government Printing Office, 1993.

—*Sketch by Christina E. Carter*

Deganawida
1550(?)-1600(?)
Huron prophet, leader, and statesman
Also known as Deganawidah, Dekanawidah, Dekanahwidah) ["Two Rivers Flowing Together"]

Deganawida is best known as the great leader who, with Hiawatha, founded the League of the Iroquois. Although the story of Deganawida's life is based primarily on legend, all accounts of the league's formation credit Deganawida for his efforts. In addition to his persuasive vision of unified Iroquois tribes, Deganawida was instrumental in defining and establishing the structure and code of the Iroquois league.

It is believed that Deganawida was born around the 1550s in the Kingston, Ontario, area and was one of seven brothers born to Huron parents. According to legend, Deganawida's birth was marked by a vision his mother had that her newborn son would be indirectly responsible for the destruction of the Hurons. She, along with Deganawida's grandmother, tried to protect the Hurons by attempting three times to drown him in a river. Each morning after the attempts, Deganawida was found unharmed in his mother's arms. After the third unsuccessful attempt, Deganawida's mother resigned herself to her son's existence.

Creates the League of the Iroquois

When Deganawida was grown, he journeyed south to carry out his mission of peace among the Iroquois. He met Hiawatha (not the Hiawatha of Longfellow's poem), a Mohawk, who joined him in his efforts to create an alliance of the Oneidas, Cayugas, Onondagas, Senacas, and Mohawks. Deganawida acted as the visionary and, because Deganawida had a speech impediment, Hiawatha served as his spokesman. Deganawida's message to the Iroquois was that all men are brothers; therefore, they should cease their practices of killing, scalping, and cannibalism. Together, Deganawida and Hiawatha convinced the five tribes to make peace and join together in an alliance of friendship, rather than persist with their attempts to destroy each other. The powerful Onondaga chief, Thadodaho (also known as Atotarho, Adario), who initially had been strongly opposed to the union of the five tribes, marked the beginning of the alliance when he made the decision to join. Deganawida also tried, without success, to encourage the Erie and neutral tribes to join the alliance. Their refusal resulted in their eventual dispersal by the Iroquois in the 1650s. Deganawida's effort to persuade them to join may have been prompted by their friendly disposition toward the Hurons, unlike the other Iroquois. Sometime after Deganawida's death, his mother's earlier vision was realized when the Huron nation was destroyed by the Iroquois.

The alliance of the five tribes was referred to as the League of the Iroquois (also known as The Iroquois Five Nation Confederacy; after the Tuscaroras joined in the early eighteenth century, it was known as the Six Nations). The exact date of the founding of the league is unknown. The purposes of the league were to bring peace, to build strength, and to create goodwill among the five nations in order for them to become invulnerable to attack from external enemies and to division from within. The code of the league summarized the intent of Deganawida and the confederate chiefs to establish "The Great Peace." Out of this code was created the Pine Tree Chiefs. Deganawida served as one of those chiefs, who were chosen by merit rather than by heredity.

A grand council of all the chiefs of the five tribes gathered at Onondaga, the most centrally located of the five tribes, to establish the laws and customs of the league. Each tribe had an equal voice in the council despite the fact that the number of chiefs representing each tribe varied. As the council developed over the years, it became immersed in matters of diplomacy, including war and peace, associations with other tribes, and treaties with the European settlers on their borders. Deganawida is credited with the development of the advanced political system of the league, which was primarily democratic and also allowed women a major role. Many of the principles, laws, and regulations of the league are attributed to Deganawida.

By 1677, the league had developed into the most powerful of all the North American Indian confederations and consisted of approximately 16,000 people. The successful union begun by Deganawida flourished into the nineteenth century. After its peak of influence, the league began its collapse as a result of many contributing factors, including the influence of outsiders, the supply of trade goods, the control of military posts, the old covenants with the whites, the rivalry between warriors and chiefs, and structural weaknesses. However, the league owed the several centuries of influence it enjoyed to the prominent leadership of Deganawida, as evidenced by his astuteness in negotiations and by his wisdom in framing the laws and principles that served as the basis for the entire structure of the league.

SOURCES:

Dockstader, Frederick J., *Great North American Indians,* New York, Van Nostrand Reinhold, 1977; 71-72.

Graymont, Barbara, *The Iroquois in the American Revolution,* New York, Syracuse University Press, 1972; 14, 47, 128, 296.

Handbook of American Indians, edited by Frederick Webb Hodge, New York, Rowman and Littlefield, 1971; 383-384.

Leitch, Barbara A., *Chronology of the American Indian,* St. Clair Shores, Michigan, Scholarly Press, Inc., 1975; 82.

Tooker, Elisabeth, *"The League of the Iroquois: Its History, Politics, and Rituals,"* in *Handbook of North American Indians,* edited by William C. Sturtevant, Smithsonian Institution, 1978; 422-424.

Waldman, Carl, *Who Was Who in Native American History,* New York, Facts on File, 1990; 96-97.

Wallace, Anthony F. C., *The Death and Rebirth of the Seneca,* New York, Knopf, 1969; 42, 44, 97-98.

—*Sketch by Kay A. Floyd*

Delaware Prophet
Flourished 1760s
Delaware spiritual leader
Also known as Neolin ["The Enlightened"]

The Delaware Prophet is the best known of a number of spiritual leaders of the Delaware tribe who surfaced in the Ohio Valley between 1740 and 1760. He has held a lasting place in history partly because his teachings were so clearly articulated, and partly because of his influence on his most famous convert, the Ottawa Chief Pontiac, who was to use the teachings of the prophet as the basis for the uprising he led against English forts in the Great Lakes region in 1763.

The Nativist Revival

The Delaware tribe, originally of the regions that became eastern Pennsylvania, New Jersey, and southeastern New York, were accustomed from the early seventeenth century to trading with Europeans. By these means they acquired goods such as blankets, household utensils and firearms in exchange for furs. As increased trade led to the failure of game, and as lands were ceded to white settlers, the Delaware were forced to leave their homelands and move westward toward the Ohio and Allegheny valleys. Furthermore, during the mid-eighteenth century, they became caught up in the French and Indian Wars and elected to support the French, thus earning the enmity of the British.

These events may have provided the impetus for the nativist revival which took place among the Delaware in the mid-eighteenth century. A major feature of the revival was the activity of the spiritual leaders, or prophets, who urged their people to throw off their dependence on whites and return to their traditional ways. Among those who preceded or were contemporary with the Delaware Prophet were Papounhan, who preached a pacifism which resembled Quakerism; the "Old Preast," who carried an "Indian Bible" made up of pictures which illustrated his teachings; and Wangomen, whose preaching, arose from a vision in which the Great Spirit urged reconciliation of the Indians to their god. All advocated a return to Indian traditions of earlier times, and all, with the exception of Papounhan, carried an anti-white message.

By the time the Indian revival began, white Christian missionaries had been at work for some time among the Indians. Many historians have seen a parallel between the crusading Indian prophets and the activities of the missionaries. Some have pointed to the influence of the "inner light" of Quakerism, and others to the un-Indian nature of the chart or "Bible" employed by some of the prophets. Most believe that the missionary endeavors had at least some influence on the development of Indian revivalism among the Delawares.

The Delaware Prophet

It was in this climate that Neolin, who became known as the Delaware Prophet, came to prominence. First heard of around 1762, the Delaware Prophet derived his authority from a religious experience in which he made a mystical pilgrimage to the Great Spirit, or Master of Life, who gave him instructions for the betterment of the lives of Indians and for the proper means of worship. Following a period of fasting, dreaming and incantation, Neolin undertook a journey, at the conclusion of which he was ushered into the presence of that Great Spirit. The Master of Life indicated his displeasure that the Indians allowed the white man, the English in particular, to dwell among them and that they had adopted many of his ways. He blamed the declining fortunes of the Indians on these circumstances, and he told the prophet that the way to win back his favor and once more find happiness and prosperity was to reject the ways of the whites and their trade goods, especially guns and alcohol. He instructed them to hunt with the bows and arrows and stone-pointed lances of their forefathers and to dress themselves once more in skins. He directed them to lift the hatchet against the English, who, he said, had robbed them of their hunting grounds and driven away the game.

The French were explicitly excepted from the Master of Life's condemnation of whites. He declared, "They are very dear to me, for they love the red men." The Master of Life concluded his discourse by giving the prophet some rules for a moral lifestyle, instructing the Indians to marry only one wife, to deal with one another fairly, and to avoid excessive drinking and the practice of magic.

Armed with these precepts, the prophet travelled from village to village, preaching and distributing deerskins on which were inscribed charts which illustrated the Indian's path to heaven and showed how it was obstructed by the whites. He was reportedly a powerful and emotional speaker; one observer remarked that he was constantly crying as he exhorted his listeners. His message found widespread response, and Indians of many tribes travelled long distances to hear him. His deerskin charts, which were much copied and widely distributed, did much to bring his message home to those who were unable to hear him preach.

Alliance with Pontiac

While the Delaware Prophet pursued his mission among his people, the Ottawa chief Pontiac pondered the problem of the declining fortunes of the Indians and their troubled relations with the British. Even as Pontiac formulated his plan to fashion a political and military alliance among Indians to drive the British from their fortifications along the Great Lakes, the words of the Delaware Prophet came to his ears. The prophet's message elicited a profound response from Pontiac, and the consequent alliance between the two leaders undoubtedly strengthened the authority of each. Pontiac departed from the prophet on one important point: the use of guns by the Indians. He did not believe their military aims could succeed without firearms. At the great council that Pontiac convened on the Ecorse River in April of 1763 to rally support for his planned uprising, the chief made a persuasive speech in which allusions to the teachings of the prophet figured prominently.

One outcome of the alliance of Pontiac and the prophet was the perception of the political and military mission of the nativist revival. In the months that followed the Ecorse council, Pontiac's military campaign faltered and ultimately failed, and so too did the nativist revival. The fortunes of the Delaware Prophet seem to have waned with those of Pontiac, but his career was not quenched; he continued to preach among his people during the years that followed Pontiac's

decline and death. He was described by an observer in 1765 as "an Indian of good repute among the Delawares." After 1766, he disappears from recorded history.

The best known and most complete account of the Delaware Prophet's teachings and vision has come to us through Pontiac's recorder at the Ecorse River council. The identity of the recorder of Pontiac's speech is unknown, but he is thought to have been a French priest. There has been much debate among scholars as to whether Pontiac altered the words of the prophet to suit his political ends. Pontiac's plans to drive out the British were dependent on French help, and the Master of Life's distinction between the English and the French in relation to the Indians was certainly helpful. However, the Indians had long enjoyed cordial relations with the French, while their dealings with the British had been tense. Furthermore, a number of manuscripts exist that detail the preaching of the prophet from first-hand observation, and they agree substantially with Pontiac's account.

Debate has also raged over the genuineness of Pontiac's conversion. Some writers believe that his adoption of the prophet and his teachings had a purely political motive, while others see Pontiac's vision of a united Indian effort to reclaim lost lands and traditions as the effort of a true believer. In the end, both the militaristic aspects of the revival and the prophet's injunctions against trade with the whites failed because of well-established processes. By the mid-eighteenth century, the Indians were thoroughly dependent on the goods they obtained from trade with whites, and the revival did not seriously affect the trade.

A Lasting Legacy

The Delaware nativist revival had a broader scope and more far-reaching consequences than its association with Pontiac's military campaign suggests. Arising out of conditions of economic hardship and social and spiritual chaos, it sought to point the way to a new order which would address these problems. Although the time when the Indians could have ejected the whites or ignored them economically had passed, the Indians could still turn inward to renew traditional rituals and practices and reestablish social order among themselves. The teachings of the Delaware Prophet supported such aims, addressing basic issues such as family structure, fairness, spiritual practices, rules governing alcohol use, and banning polygamy, stealing, murder, and intertribal conflict.

In the years after the Delaware Prophet's heyday, a reunification of the Delaware tribe took place. Centralized organization replaced the former loose alliance of the three major divisions of the tribe. The spiritual foundation laid down by the Delaware Prophet became the basis of a national religion, which, in its turn, served as the spiritual underpinning of a national political unit with a principal chief and a national council for centralized decision-making. What is more, the Delaware Prophet's influence went beyond his own tribe and his own time. His teachings are reflected in the careers of later spiritual leaders such as the

Shawnee Prophet Tenskwatawa and the Seneca leader Handsome Lake.

SOURCES:

Books

Parkman, Francis, *The Conspiracy of Pontiac and the Indian War after the Conquest of Canada,* two volumes, Boston, Little, Brown & Company, 1926.
Peckham, Howard H., *Pontiac and the Indian Uprising,* Cambridge, Princeton University Press, 1947.

Periodicals

Champagne, Duane, "The Delaware Revitalization Movement of the Early 1760s: A Suggested Reinterpretation," *American Indian Quarterly,* 12, 1988; 107-126.
Dowd, Gregory E., "Thinking and Believing: Nativism and Unity in the Ages of Pontiac and Tecumseh," *American Indian Quarterly,* 16, 1992; 309-335.
Hunter, Charles, "The Delaware Nativist Revival of the Mid-Eighteenth Century," *Ethnohistory,* 18, 1971; 39-49.
Wallace, Anthony F. C., "New Religions among the Delaware Indians, 1600-1900," *Southwestern Journal of Anthropology,* 12:1, 1956; 1-21.

—Sketch by Julie Henderson Jersyk

Ella Cara Deloria
1889-1971
Yankton Sioux ethnologist, linguist, and novelist

Ella Cara Deloria was a well-known linguist, ethnologist, and novelist whose work is only recently being appreciated for its depth and volume of detail, as well as for its artistry. Her contributions to the field of Native American ethnography is vast, encompassing translations of primary sources, linguistic texts on Sioux grammar, and even a Sioux-English dictionary. These accomplishments earned her the reputation as the leading authority on Sioux culture by the 1940s. She wrote a popular book on Indians in general, *Speaking of Indians,* in 1944, and an ethnographic novel about Sioux ancestral culture, *Waterlily,* which was published posthumously in 1988.

Family History and Education

Ella Cara Deloria was born into the prominent Deloria family January 31, 1889, at White Swan, South Dakota, on the Yankton Sioux Reservation. Her brother Vine Deloria,

Sr., like her own father, was a prominent minister and leader in the community. Her nephew Vine Deloria, Jr., is a well-known writer and lawyer. The Deloria family's involvement in the leadership of their community goes back a long way. In 1869, Ella's grandfather, Chief Francois Des Laurias (medicine man and leader of the White Swan band), called for the establishment of an Episcopal mission among his people. Her father, Phillip Deloria, was ordained an Episcopal priest in 1891. He was widowed by his first two wives and in 1888 married Mary Sully Bordeaux, a widow who also had children from a previous marriage. Mary, Ella's mother, was also a devout Christian, and though only one-quarter Indian, had been raised as a traditional Dakota. Thus Ella was raised in a home that valued Christian principles balanced with adherence to traditional Sioux ways; Dakota was more often than not the language spoken at home.

Deloria's first schooling took place at St. Elizabeth's school, attached to her father's church, St. Elizabeth's, on the Standing Rock Reservation. In 1902 she attended All Saints, a boarding school in Sioux Falls, South Dakota. In 1910 she matriculated at Oberlin College. She received her bachelor of science degree from New York's Columbia Teacher's College in 1915. In the same year she returned to All Saints as a teacher and stayed until 1919, when she took a job that afforded her the opportunity to travel extensively throughout the western United States. Her position as a YWCA health education secretary for Indian schools and reservations also brought her into contact with many Indian groups. In 1923 she became a physical education and dance instructor at the Haskell Institute, an Indian School in Lawrence, Kansas.

Affiliation with Franz Boas and Ethnography

Deloria is held in high esteem as an ethnologist, but in fact she never studied anthropology in an institutional setting. In a 1935 letter to anthropologist Franz Boas, published in Raymond DeMallie's afterword to *Waterlily,* she addressed the question of whether she should have gotten a degree and become an academic anthropologist: "I certainly do not consider myself as such." It was her knowledge of the Lakota language, as well as her general scholarly abilities, that attracted the attention of Boas, who taught at Columbia University from 1899 to 1942. Deloria was a student at Columbia Teachers College in 1915, when Boas hired her to work on a collection of Lakota texts which had been assembled in 1887 by George Bushotter, a Sioux, under the supervision of Smithsonian ethnologist James Owen Dorsey. She found the job of translation and linguistic analysis rewarding. Twelve years later, when Deloria was at Haskell Institute, Boas contacted her again, and work on the texts resumed. She translated some additional texts as well, and in 1929 published her first work, an article on the Sun Dance in the *Journal of American Folk-Lore.*

In 1928, Deloria moved to New York to work for Boas. It was in this year that the anthropological study of her people became her primary occupation. While in New York, she met Ruth Benedict, who encouraged her to focus on kinship, tribal structure, and the roles of women—issues that are deftly and comprehensively treated in her novel. Over the next 20 years, she worked closely with Boas and Benedict (until Boas' death in 1942 and Benedict's in 1948) and completed a body of work that added greatly to the field of Native American ethnography. She finished translation of the Bushotter collection and translated manuscripts of Oglala Sioux George Sword written around 1908, plus an 1840 text by Santee Sioux Jack Frazier. During this time, she published several books, including *Dakota Texts, Dakota Grammar,* and *Speaking of Indians,* which she wrote during the 1940s. She also assembled a Sioux-English dictionary and amassed such a wide array of Lakota and Dakota texts (conversations, autobiographies, stump speeches, jokes) that no comparable body of written work exists for any other Plains tribe. In 1943 she was awarded the Indian Achievement Medal and was esteemed the foremost authority on Sioux culture.

After Boas' death, Deloria began approaching her compiled data from an analytical standpoint. A manuscript, which she sometimes called "Camp Circle Society" and sometimes "Dakota Family Life," would later serve as the germ for her novel, Waterlily. The manuscript, which was never published, attempts to describe ancestral Sioux culture in all its aspects. In this sense it is impressionistic and idealistic, making the novel format a well-suited way to present the diverse and voluminous ethnographic material. In a 1952 letter to H. E. Beebe, she described her motivation for preparing such a work: "I feel that one of the reasons for the lagging advancement of the Dakotas has been that those who came out among them to teach and preach, went on the assumption that the Dakotas had nothing, no rules of life, no social organization, no ideals. And so they tried to pour white culture into, as it were, a vacuum. And when that did not work out, because it was not a vacuum after all, they concluded that the Indians were impossible to change and train. What they should have done first, before daring to start their program, was to study everything possible of Dakota life, to see what made it go, in the old days, and what was still so deeply rooted that it could not be rudely displaced without some hurt ... I feel that I have this work cut out for me." Deloria's sense of mission and her personal stake in the material she collected undoubtedly made it difficult for her to be the detached and objective observer that was expected of serious academic anthropology in the 1940s. She always favored a more subjective approach.

From the time when she was a student at Columbia Teacher's College onward, Deloria gave informal lectures and presentations of Sioux songs and dances at churches, schools, and civic organizations. She wished to bridge the gap of misunderstanding and ignorance between Indian and white on a directly personal level that could not be obtained through scientific monographs. In the letter quoted above, she also wrote, "This may sound a little naive, Mr. Beebe, but I actually feel that I have a mission: To make the Dakota people understandable, as human beings, to the white people who have to deal with them." Her non-technical description of American Indian culture of the past and present, *Speaking of Indians,* was assembled with this goal in mind,

and was published by one of the organizations that invited her to speak, the YMCA.

Published Novel *Waterlily*

Boas' circle of colleagues tended to search for non-technical media, perhaps even fiction, to get an anthropological point across to a wider audience. Zora Neale Hurston was a Boasian anthropologist who did just this to paint a picture of the life of African American women in the deep South. Similarly, Elsie Clews Parsons was a student and colleague of Boas who edited a book of fictional sketches of the Native Americans of the past entitled *American Indian Life* in 1922. Boas and Benedict believed that Deloria was eminently qualified for this kind of work and suggested that she write a novel about the life of a nineteenth-century traditional Sioux woman. That idea would become Deloria's best known work today, *Waterlily.*

In *Waterlily* Deloria synthesized diverse aspects of her collected data and life experience, including the texts of George Bushotter and George Sword, interviews with living elders, and the stories and values of her own family. It is in many ways a book that defies categorization. It is a work of ethnographic description, dense with cultural details; it is an historical novel firmly grounded in its geographical and chronological setting; it is a monograph on the social organization of a highly complex society; and it is a work of narrative fiction with an intricate plot and finely tuned characterizations. Like Hurston's 1937 *Their Eyes Were Watching God,* Waterlily does not focus on the tragedy of an embattled and degraded people, but chooses instead to celebrate a rich, vibrant, and healthy culture. References to the impending doom faced by *Waterlily*'s people are oblique and subtle, such as the happy chanting of the children: "While the buffalo live we shall not die!" The book did not achieve publication during the author's lifetime: Macmillan turned it down, as did the University of Oklahoma Press; both houses admired the book's depth of detail, but feared the reading public would not buy it. It was finally published by the University of Nebraska Press in 1988.

In 1955 Deloria returned to her grade school alma mater, St. Elizabeth's, to serve as director. She held that post until 1958. From 1962 to 1966 she continued her work at the University of South Dakota. She died at Vermillion in 1971. Her work remains invaluable, both to academic linguists and anthropologists for her translations and researches, and to the general reading public for her rich and polished novel, Waterlily.

SELECTED WRITINGS BY DELORIA:

Dakota Texts (first published in 1932), New York, AMS Press, 1974.
(With Franz Boas) *Dakota Grammar,* Sioux Falls, Dakota Press, 1941.
Speaking of Indians (first published in 1944), Vermillion, Dakota Press, 1979.
Waterlily, Lincoln, University of Nebraska Press, 1988.

SOURCES:

Deloria, Ella Cara, *Waterlily,* afterword by Raymond
    DeMallie, biographical sketch by Agnes Picotte, Lin-
    coln, University of Nebraska Press, 1988.
Native American Women, edited by Gretchen M. Bataille,
    New York, Garland Publishing, 1993.

—Sketch by Charles Cannon

Vine Deloria, Jr. (right)

Vine Deloria, Jr.
1933-
Yankton Sioux writer

V ine Deloria, Jr., of the Yankton Sioux, became well-
known as a political activist whose publications
explained to the American people what the Native American
rights movement was seeking. His family heritage combined
with academic training gave him credibility in his writings.
Deloria was born on March 26, 1993, in Martin, South
Dakota, the son of Vine and Barbara (Eastburn) Deloria. He
joined a distinguished family: his great-grandfather Francois Des Laurias ["Saswe"] was a medicine man and leader
of the White Swan band of the Yankton Sioux tribe; his
grandfather Philip Deloria was a missionary priest of the
Episcopal Church; his aunt Ella C. Deloria was a noted
ethnographer who published works on Indian ethnology and
linguistics; and his father, Vine Deloria, Sr., was the first
American Indian to be named to a national executive post in
the Episcopal church. Deloria's own comment about his
family gave context to his first major book. In its afterword
he wrote: "As long as any member of my family can remember, we have been involved in the affairs of the Sioux tribe.
My great grandfather was a medicine man named Saswe, of
the Yankton tribe of the Sioux Nation. My grandfather was a
Yankton chief who was converted to Christianity in the
1860s. He spent the rest of his life as an Episcopal missionary on the Standing Rock Sioux reservation in South
Dakota." From 1932 to 1982 the Indian Council Fire, an
organization in Chicago, presented 54 achievement awards
to recognize quality of Indian initiative and leadership. Of
these awards, three were to members of the Deloria family:
Vine, Sr., Ella, and Vine, Jr.

After attending grade school in Martin, South Dakota,
the younger Deloria graduated from high school at Kent
School in Kent, Connecticut. He served in the Marine Corps
from 1954 to 1956, then attended Iowa State University
where he received his B.A. degree in 1958. In his youth, he
had considered following his father in the ministry, but
exposure to his father's frustrations convinced him that
church life did not have the bearing on Indian life that he
wanted his career to have. Before he gave up the idea
entirely, however, he earned a B.D. in theology at Augus-

tana Lutheran Seminary, Rock Island, Illinois, in 1963. The
following year he was hired by the United Scholarship Service in Denver to develop a program to get scholarships for
American Indian students in eastern preparatory schools. He
successfully placed a number of Indian students in eastern
schools through the program.

He served as the executive director of the National
Congress of American Indians (NCAI) in Washington, D.C.,
from 1964 to 1967, an experience he claimed was more educational than anything he had experienced in his previous 30
years. He was expected to solve problems presented by
Indian tribes from all over the country, but found that
unscrupulous individuals made the task impossible. He was
frustrated by the feeling that the interests of tribes were
often played against one other. In addition the NCAI had
financial difficulties, and was often close to bankruptcy, so
that a majority of time had to be spent resolving funding
issues. Increased memberships and a research grant gave the
organization enough strength to successfully win a few policy changes in the Department of Interior. Although Deloria
felt the organization had been successful, especially because
of the support and hard work of organization members, he
realized that other tactics would have to be used to further
the cause for Indian rights.

Earns Law Degree

Two circumstances influenced his decision to return to
college and earn a law degree from the University of Colorado in 1970. One was learning of the success of the

National Association for the Advancement of Colored People's Legal Defense Fund which had been established to help the black community. The second was the realization that local Indian tribes were without legal counsel and had no idea what their rights were. His goal when receiving his law degree was to start a program which would assist smaller tribes and Indian communities to outline their basic rights. Throughout his career his goal in life has been twofold: to support tribes through affiliation with various advocacy organizations and to educate Native Americans on aspects of the law through teachings and writings which stress the historical and political aspects of the relationships of Indians to other people. His role as an activist in the efforts of Native Americans to achieve self-government has focused on change through education rather than through violence.

From 1970 to 1972 Deloria was a lecturer at Western Washington State College in the division of ethnic studies. While there, he worked with Northwest Coast tribes in their effort to gain improved fishing rights. From 1972 to 1974 he taught at the University of California at Los Angeles. During the same period, from 1970 to 1978, he was the chairperson of the Institute for the Development of Indian Law, headquartered in Washington, D.C. From 1978 to 1990 he was a professor of American Indian studies and political science at the University of Arizona. In 1990 he moved to the University of Colorado in Boulder to join the faculty of the Center for Studies of Ethnicity and Race in America. In addition to his teaching positions, Deloria served in leadership positions in several organizations including the Citizens Crusade against Poverty, the Council on Indian Affairs, the National Office for the Rights of the Indigent, the Institute for the Development of Indian Law, and the Indian Rights Association.

Publishes Indian Activist Views

Deloria has been an activist writer, dramatically presenting his case for Indian self-determination. *Custer Died for Your Sins: An Indian Manifesto,* written while he was attending law school, captured the attention of reviewers and critics and bolstered Native American efforts for recognition. Written at the time the American Indian Movement (AIM) was drawing public attention to Native American rights, Deloria's book was an articulation of the activist goal: to become self-ruled, culturally separate from white society and politically separate from the U.S. government. While blasting America's treatment of Indian people, Deloria explained the concepts of termination and tribalism. Although contemporaneous with the civil rights movement of other American groups, he distinguished between black nationalism and Indian nationalism, explaining that because Indian civil rights issues were based upon treaties they needed to be addressed in a different way. Deloria explained his reasons for writing the book in its afterword: "One reason I wanted to write it was to raise some issues for younger Indians which they have not been raising for themselves. Another reason was to give some idea to white people of the unspoken but often felt antagonisms I have detected in Indian people toward them, and the reasons for such antagonism."

Deloria's second book, *We Talk, You Listen: New Tribes, New Turf,* also addressed the issue of tribalism and advocated a return to tribal social organization in order to save society. His third book, *God Is Red: A Native View of Religion,* again captured a national audience. In this book Deloria offered an alternative to Christianity which he explained had failed both in its theology and its application to social issues. He proposed that religion in North America should follow along the lines of traditional Native American values and seek spiritual values in terms of "space" by feeling the richness of the land. Most critics applauded his presentation of Indian religious practice, but were offended by his attack on the Judeo-Christian tradition. His later book *The Metaphysics of Modern Existence* followed up on this theme by questioning non-Indian world views of modern life and recommending a reassessment of reality about moral and religious property.

In all of Deloria's writings, he has emphasized the failure of U.S. treaties to adequately provide for the needs of Indian people. Using his legal training, he has analyzed past relationships between the U.S. government and Native American groups and has continually pressed for renewed treaty negotiation in order to allow more Indian self-control over their culture and government. His book *Behind the Trail of Broken Treaties* provided an account of events which led to the occupation of Wounded Knee, South Dakota, by supporters of the American Indian Movement. In this work he argued for reopening the treaty-making procedure between Indian tribes and the U.S. government. As an expert in U.S. Indian treaties, Deloria was called as first witness for the defense in the trial of Wounded Knee participants Russell Means and Dennis Banks in 1974. Later, in his writing about Indian activism of the early 1970s, Deloria blamed the failure of the Indian civil rights movement on the unwillingness of the American public to forget their perception of what an Indian should be. In the second edition of *God Is Red* he stated: "When a comparison is made between events of the Civil Rights movement and the activities of the Indian movement one thing stands out in clear relief: Americans simply refuse to give up their longstanding conceptions of what an Indian is. It was this fact more than any other that inhibited any solution of the Indian problems and projected the impossibility of their solution anytime in the future. People simply could not connect what they believed Indians to be with what they were seeing on their television sets." He castigated the American public for its avoidance of the real Indian world in a series of ironic contrasts between current events of the Indian movement of the 1970s and what the American public was reading. "While Dee Brown's *Bury My Heart at Wounded Knee* was selling nearly 20,000 copies a week, the three hundred state game wardens and Tacoma city police were vandalizing the Indian fishing camp and threatening the lives of Indian women and children at Frank's Landing on the Nisqually River.... As Raymond Yellow Thunder was being beaten to death, Americans were busy ordering *Touch the Earth* from their book clubs as an indication of their sympathy for American Indians. As the grave robbers were breaking into Chief Joseph's grave, the literary public was reading his famous surrender speech in a dozen or more anthologies of Indian speeches and bemoaning the fact that oratory such as Joseph's is not used any more."

Deloria's writing style has been consistent. In his books he often attempts to peel away platitudes that his white readers have developed so that they begin to comprehend the issues and the Indian viewpoint. Not without humor, he cynically derides white culture, and then offers his replacement. He commented in an interview that Americans can be told the obvious 50 times a day and revel in hearing it, but not learn anything from it. Some critics have been disappointed that Deloria's books don't describe Indian culture. As Deloria stated in an interview in *The Progressive*, "I particularly disappoint Europeans. They come over and want me to share all the tribal secrets. Then I lecture and harangue about the white man." In the same interview he derided his own success as an Indian writer in the early 1970s. "I happened to come along when they [the media] needed an Indian. The writing is not very good at all. But Indians were new, so everybody gave *Custer* great reviews. I never fooled myself that it was a great book."

His second edition of *God Is Red,* published in 1992, built upon the arguments against Christianity he wrote in the first edition. Encouraged by trends in American society to be more concerned about religion and ecology, he raised additional issues in the revised edition. "I suggest in this revised edition that we have on this planet two kinds of people—natural peoples and the hybrid peoples. The natural peoples represent an ancient tradition that has always sought harmony with the environment." Hybrid peoples referred to the inheritors of Hebrew, Islamic, and Christian traditions who adopted a course of civilization which exploits the environment. When *The Progressive*'s interviewer asked Deloria his views on renewed interest in Native American spirituality, Deloria commented: "I think New Age shamanism is very interesting. Whites want to take our images; they want to have their Indian jewelry; at the same time, they need our valley to flood for a dam. People are desperately trying to get some relationship to Earth, but it's all in their heads.... New Age shamanism may be one of the few solutions." At the same time, he admitted his own dependence upon technology. "I wouldn't delude myself for a minute that I could go back to the reservation and live any kind of traditional life. I've been in the cities too long.... I would love to go back to the old shamanism. My great-grandfather was a very powerful man. But here I am in Tucson, Arizona, dependent upon Tucson Electric Power to stay comfortable."

Another of his major themes has been concern for the natural environment. He blames contemporary technological society for destroying the earth, and presents an apocalyptic view. He envisions the end of the earth if changes are not made soon to allow the natural environment to recover. He predicts in the Progressive interview that in 500 years "there will be fewer than 100,000 people on whatever this continent comes up as, there will probably be some Indians and all kinds of new strange animals—the Earth a completely different place, people talking about legends of the old times when iron birds flew in the air."

SELECTED WRITINGS BY DELORIA:

Custer Died for Your Sins: An Indian Manifesto, New York, Macmillan, 1969.
We Talk, You Listen: New Tribes, New Turf, New York, Macmillan, 1970.
(Compiler) *Of Utmost Good Faith,* Straight Arrow Books, 1971.
God Is Red: A Native View of Religion, New York, Grosset, 1973; second edition, North American Press, 1992.
Behind the Trail of Broken Treaties, New York, Delacorte, 1974.
The Indian Affair, Friendship, 1974.
Indians of the Pacific Northwest, New York, Doubleday, 1977.
The Metaphysics of Modern Existence, New York, Harper, 1979.
(With Clifford Lytle) *American Indians,* American Justice, Austin, University of Texas Press, 1983.
(With Clifford Lytle) *The Nations Within: The Past and Future of American Indian Sovereignty,* New York, Pantheon, 1984.
The Aggressions of Civilization: Federal Indian Policy Since the 1880s, Philadelphia, Temple University Press, 1984.
American Indian Policy in the Twentieth Century, Norman, University of Oklahoma Press, 1985.

SOURCES:

Books

Bruguier, Leonard Rufus, "A Legacy in Sioux Leadership: The Deloria Family", in *South Dakota Leaders,* edited by Herbert T. Hoover and Larry J. Zimmerman, Vermillion, University of South Dakota Press, 1989; 367-378, 471.
Contemporary Authors, New Revision Series, Volume 20, Detroit, Gale Research, 1987; 130-132.
Contemporary Literary Criticism, Volume 21, Gale Research, 1982; 108-114.
Current Biography Yearbook 1974, edited by Charles Moritz, New York, H. W. Wilson, 1974; 102-105.
Deloria, Vine, Jr., "Afterword," in *Custer Died for Your Sins: An Indian Manifesto,* New York, Avon Books, 1970; 262-272.
Deloria, Vine, Jr., "Introduction" and "The Indians of the American Imagination", in *God Is Red: A Native View of Religion,* second edition, Golden, Colorado, North American Press, 1992; 1-3, 25-45.
Indians of Today, edited by Marion E. Gridley, Chicago, ICFP, 1971; 347.
Native North American Almanac, edited by Duane Champagne, Detroit, Gale Research, 1994; 1043-1044.
Paulson, T. Emogene, and Lloyd R. Moses, *Who's Who among the Sioux,* Institute of Indian Studies, University of South Dakota, 1988; 58-59.
Reader's Encyclopedia of the American West, edited by Howard R. Lamar, New York, Thomas Y. Crowell, 1977; 295.

Something about the Author, Volume 21, Detroit, Gale
    Research, 1980; 27.

Periodicals

Warrior, Robert Allen, "Vine Deloria Jr.: 'It's About Time
    to be Interested in Indians Again,'" *Progressive,* 54:4,
    April 1990; 24-27.

—*Sketch by Karen P. Zimmerman*

Vine Deloria, Sr.
1901-1990
Standing Rock Yankton Sioux minister
Also known as Ohiya ["Champion"]

Vine Victor Deloria was born on October 6, 1901, at St.
Elizabeth's Mission, near Wakpala, South Dakota. His
grandfather, Francois Des Laurias ["Saswe"], the son of a
French fur trader and Indian mother, was a leader of the
Ihanktonwan (Yankton) Dakota half-breed band, and was valued by federal officials because of his bicultural background.
Deloria's father, Philip Joseph Deloria, was the heir apparent
to the role as leader of the half-breed band and earned a position in the warrior society. However, he joined the Episcopal
clergy in order to better serve his people in the process of
adjustment. While Vine's sister Ella C. Deloria became a
well-known scholar whose research in ethnography and linguistics brought attention to the importance of Indian studies,
Vine explored several career options before finally following
his father's path in the Episcopalian ministry.

After his mother's death in 1916, Vine Deloria
attended Kearney Military School in Nebraska, attaining the
rank of cadet colonel. From there, he moved to St. Stephens
(Bard) College in New York and received his bachelor of
arts degree. He enjoyed all sports, playing football, baseball,
and basketball and coached for a year at Fort Sill Indian
School in Oklahoma. Between school semesters he worked
in a coal mine. For a while, he considered carpentry as a
vocation.

In the late 1920s, Deloria's father took ill and
expressed the wish that Vine follow him into the priesthood.
Reluctantly, Vine completed the theological course at General Theological Seminary in New York City and was
ordained in his father's church shortly before his father's
death in 1931. Vine's first position was among his people at
the Indian Mission in Pine Ridge, South Dakota. Next, he
served on the Sisseton Reservation. The first 20 years of his
career were spent serving Indian people in South Dakota.
He made many visits to the Niobrara Deanery Convocations
and often served as the voice for Indian Episcopalians to
outsiders.

Deloria's success in the mission field led to his
appointment in 1954 to the Episcopal National Council in
New York City, where he was in charge of all Indian mission work as the Indian secretary for the Episcopal Church
of America. Frustrated by efforts to improve Indian life
through the church hierarchy, Deloria returned to local service. He spent two years in Iowa and then was appointed
archdeacon of the Niobrara Deanery. Deloria served as
archdeacon in Pierre, visiting as many as 87 churches
throughout the state of South Dakota.

In 1968, Deloria retired as archdeacon, but served as
priest at St. Paul's Episcopal mission in Vermillion for two
years. He then retired to Pierre until moving with his wife,
Barbara Sloat Eastburn, to Arizona in 1986. Deloria died on
February 26, 1990, leaving his wife, two sons, Vine Deloria,
Jr., and Sam, and one daughter, Barbara Sanchez. Vine Deloria, Jr., has carried on his father's fight for Indian rights as a
political activist and writer. Sam has contributed to the field
of Indian law.

Deloria's biographer, Leonard Bruguier, referred to
Deloria as one of the strongest personalities to emerge from
Indian society in the twentieth century. Bruguier states,
"Although Father Vine assumed an assimilationist vocation,
he maintained his Indian cultural integrity—preserving in
use both Indian language and oral tradition and, while
preaching Christian truth, teaching also the power and usefulness of traditional Indian religion." In an interview with
Bruguier in 1984, Deloria expressed disillusionment with
Christianity. He lamented that Christianity focused too
much on the spiritual Christ and too little on Jesus as a
human being, thereby losing a humanitarian approach to
people around the world.

Deloria's interest in sports was evident throughout his
life. He was proud of his own accomplishments on the football field for St. Stephens College, once completing a throw
55-yards through the air. He often used sports analogies in
his sermons to make a point.

Deloria successfully ministered through the Episcopal
Church for 37 years. He was respected by both Indians and
whites as an honest, hard-working friend. In 1986 his influence was still evident at the 114th Niobrara Episcopal Convention at the Santee Agency in Nebraska. When it was proposed that mission land be sold to raise money, people
waited expectantly for his opinion and followed his advice
to keep the land. He was considered a visionary within the
church, setting an agenda of Indian involvement at both the
national and local levels.

SOURCES:

Books

Bruguier, Leonard Rufus, "A Legacy in Sioux Leadership:
    The Deloria Family," in *South Dakota Leaders,* edited
    by Herbert T. Hoover and Larry J. Zimmerman, Ver-
    million, University of South Dakota Press, 1989; 367-
    378, 471.

Indians of Today, edited by Marion E. Gridley, Chicago, ICFP, 1971; 345-346.

Native North American Almanac, edited by Duane Champagne, Detroit, Gale Research, 1994; 1044.

Paulson, T. Emogene, and Lloyd R. Moses, *Who's Who among the Sioux,* Institute of Indian Studies, University of South Dakota, 1988; 59.

Periodicals

Kranz, David, "Missionary Deloria Dies," *Argus Leader,* Sioux Falls, South Dakota, March 6, 1990; C1.

—*Sketch by Karen P. Zimmerman*

William G. Demmert, Jr.
1934-
Tlingit/Dakota Sioux professor and administrator

While functioning as a university professor William G. Demmert, Jr. was avidly interested in the advancement of Native Americans. To accomplish his goal he served as an administrator of educational organizations on both the state and the national levels. When he served as deputy commissioner of education, then commissioner of education, and later as co-chairman of the Indian Nations at Risk Force, his recommendations helped enhance the caliber of education for Native Americans. He is also a professional writer, and one intent of his writings is to foster a better education for Native Americans.

Demmert was born on March 9, 1934, in Klawock, Alaska. He graduated from Seattle Pacific College and then went on to teach at Forks, Washington, from 1960 until 1964. In 1965 Demmert moved to Fairbanks, Alaska, where he worked until 1968 before moving back to his hometown. After returning to Klawock, he served as chief administrator of the public school system until 1970. Meanwhile, in 1969, Demmert was invited to Princeton University to attend the First Convocation of American Indian Scholars. This undertaking was organized by the American Indian Historical Society. As a result of this meeting, Demmert helped found the National Indian Educational Association. Not only was Demmert one of the founders, but he also became one of the original directors of the organization as well.

From 1970 to 1973 Demmert attended Harvard University. During these years Demmert worked for the development of the Indian Education Act of 1972 after becoming a consultant to the United States Senate to accomplish this purpose. In 1972, Demmert also became an official in the field of Indian education when he joined the United States Department of Education; he received his doctorate from Harvard the following year with a dissertation entitled "Crit-

ical Issues in Indian Education." After completing his doctorate, Demmert published many articles in the field of education; and in 1986, he co-authored the book *Characteristics of Successful Leaders.*

In addition to his many writings, Demmert has taught at several prestigious colleges and universities in the United States, including the University of Alaska at Juneau, Stanford University, the University of Washington, and Harvard University. When not in the classroom, Demmert also acted in the role of United States government official, working in the programs which helped raise the level of Indian education. From 1975 to 1976 he functioned as deputy commissioner of education at the United States Office of Education; and between the years of 1976 and 1978 Demmert served as director of Indian education for the Bureau of Indian Affairs. He also worked as commissioner of education for the state of Alaska during the 1980s.

In 1990, a series of regional mini-summits were held by the BIA Office of Indian Education Programs for the purpose of gathering information on four initiatives which had been proposed. These four encompassed community involvement, as well as parental commitment to the development of young children, raising the standards in Indian schools, and competent evaluation of the schools, students, and teachers. Another goal of the mini-summits was to formulate a definition of the more pressing concerns in Indian education which related to tribes, educators, and school board members.

Co-Chairs Indian Nations at Risk Force

The establishment of the Indian Nations at Risk Force was formed in the latter part of 1990 and 1991 in answer to a mandate from Lauro Cavazos, a former Secretary of Education. In response to this event, hearings advocated by the Department of Education were held to determine just what the condition of Native American education was. These hearings were carried on all over the country. The result was the creation of the Indian Nations at Risk Force, which was chaired by Demmert and Terrel H. Bell. The task force responsibilities were not only to deliberate the state of Indian education, but also to issue a report to recommend how the quality of Native American education could be improved. The participants hoped this would help improve the Native Americans' educational achievements as well as their economic well being.

In 1991 the task force established goals to improve federal, tribal, public, and private schools, which served not only American Indians but also Alaskan Natives. The task force expressed its conviction that these peoples should be well-educated and have their cultural and language identities renewed in order to strengthen both their self-determination and their economic success. With issues defined and specific recommendations set out, the task force under Demmert and Bell's leadership also endorsed the idea that more native teachers be trained to improve the quality of instruction. The last two strategies in the task force's strategic framework for improving schools called for holding all government officials accountable for achieving the goals, and for fostering understanding between all the levels of government and the tribes. An important need was defined, and the proposed goals solid. Time will disclose the ultimate success of the task force which Demmert co-chaired.

SOURCES:

Biographical Dictionary of Indians of the Americas, second edition, Newport Beach, California, American Indian Publishers, 1991; 188.
Native North American Almanac, edited by Duane Champagne, Detroit, Gale Research, 1994; 862-868, 1044.

—*Sketch by Wendy Pfeffer*

Lena Frank Dick
1889(?)-1965
Washoe basket weaver

Lena Frank Dick was one of the most prominent basket weavers of the Washoe "fancy basketry" period, also known as the Washoe florescence. She was an innovator in the making of fine, detailed, intricately designed baskets.

Lena Frank was born around 1889 in Coleville in the Antelope Valley of California to Charley and Lucy Frank of the Washoe (Washo) tribe. Skilled at basket making, Lucy Frank taught all three of her daughters to weave. Lena, the best known of the sisters, was described by friends as a woman of "extraordinary vitality, warmth, and generosity," according to Marvin Cohodas in *American Indian Art* magazine.

Though Lena spent most of her adult life married to Levi Dick, she was first married to and had a child with a man named George Emm. Emm deserted her and the new baby while Lena was still in her teens. Then, around 1906, she married Levi Dick. They stayed together until his death in 1963. For years, Lena Frank Dick served as a midwife to many women of the region; she also practiced Washoe traditions such as puberty ceremonies as late as the 1940s.

Major Basket Weaver of 1920s and 1930s

Dick and her sister Lillie were the two major weavers of the Antelope Valley throughout the 1920s and 1930s. Since her husband had a full-time construction job, Dick could devote her time fully to the art of basket weaving. Her early baskets were sold by the Cohn's Emporium Company of Carson City in the 1920s. In 1921, on a certificate written by Abe Cohn, he called Dick "one of the finest Washoe artists." Later, through Carson Valley rancher-turned-agent

Fred Settelmeyer, Dick and her sister Lillie were commissioned to make baskets exclusively for Roscoe A. Day, an art collector and orthodontist from San Francisco. This arrangement lasted into the early 1930s, when a heart attack caused Day to limit his collecting. Dick wove 13 baskets for Day that remain in the State of California's collection. Between the Day baskets, those sold by Cohn, and others, art historians have attributed at least 28 baskets to the artist. Dick stopped producing the fine, fancy baskets in 1935 because of failing eyesight; she spent the remainder of her life making utilitarian baskets of simpler design.

Work Mistaken for That of Another Artist

Much of Dick's artwork was mislabeled as the work of a weaver named Datsolalee. To the untrained eye, the artists' pieces bore a striking similarity to each other. Cohn had a longstanding relationship with Datsolalee and publicized her work as he sold it, but Dick only wove baskets for Cohn for a short time. Neither Settelmeyer nor Day publicized Dick's work, nor did they ever meet her. Thus, many of her baskets were mistaken for the work of Datsolalee.

Dick knew, however, which baskets were hers. She found one of her baskets in the Nevada State Museum in Carson City and showed it to her granddaughter Marjorie. The Day baskets, donated to the State of California after Roscoe Day's wife died, were all misrepresented as the work of Datsolalee. In fact, Dick did not receive full credit for her work until 1978, more than a dozen years after her death.

The most popular artistic basket form during the Washoe florescence was known as the degikup—a spherical, ceremonial basket. Unlike those of Datsolalee, Dick's degikups were small—four to seven inches high rather than 14—with tall rather than narrow coils of 25 to 33 stitches per inch.

Dick distinguished herself through her style, technique, and design from all other Washoe basket weavers of her time, even her sister. She preferred large-scale alternating designs to small repeating patterns and concentrated on shapes like serrated diamonds, V-designs, and triangles, mostly in the red and black colors of many Washoe basket makers, even after others had progressed to additional colors. Dick's later baskets show a greater uniformity and consistency than her early baskets, which were more experimental. She did not exert the same influence as other Washoe artists on her contemporaries, but her work is still very personalized and, according to some art critics, exhibits a mastery of technique and art equal to that of the famous Datsolalee.

Dick lived all her life in Coleville, California. She and her second husband joined the Native American Church there and participated in the church's peyote rituals. Once Levi Dick retired during the 1950s, the couple spent a great deal of time together taking walks, visiting relatives, and fishing. His sudden death in 1963 devastated Lena, and thereafter she refused to leave her house. She died in March of 1965.

SOURCES:

Books

The Arts of the North American Indian: Native Traditions in Evolution, edited by Edwin L. Wade, New York, Hudson Hills Press, 1986; 203-220.

Handbook of the North American Indians, edited by William C. Sturtevant, Washington, D.C., Smithsonian Institution, 1983.

Native American Women, edited by Gretchen M. Bataille, New York, Garland Publishing, New York, 1993.

Yenne, Bill, *The Encyclopedia of North American Indian Tribes,* New York, Crescent Books, 1986.

Periodicals

Cohodas, Marvin, "Lena Frank Dick: Outstanding Washoe Basket Weaver," *American Indian Art* magazine, 4, autumn 1979; 32-41, 90.

—*Sketch by Christopher B. Tower*

Olive Patricia Dickason

Olive Patricia Dickason
1920-
Métis historian, teacher and writer

Olive Patricia Dickason was one of the first scholars in Canada to write about Native American history. She has published five books and numerous articles, many of which focus on the subject of the first meeting between the native peoples of North America and the Europeans.

Dickason was born on March 6, 1920, in Winnipeg, Manitoba, to Frank Williamson and Phoebe Coté. In a rush to arrive in the world, she was born in the automobile on the way to the hospital. Dickason's father was an Englishman from northern England, employed as a banker at the time of her birth. Her mother, a grade school teacher, was of Métis heritage, a tribe of buffalo hunters in the Dakotas. Eventually, her father quit his job as a banker to open a florist business, but lost everything during the Great Depression.

When Dickason was 12 years old, Williamson decided to move his family north to mining property he owned in the bush of northern Manitoba. According to Dickason in a telephone interview with Christopher Tower: "We moved to the Ontario side of the Red Lake mining district. There were no roads, no connections to civilization. This was wild country about 34 miles from present-day Manigotogan."

Since Dickason could not continue with her education in the country, she attended a residential school run by the Oblate Order, missionaries of West Canada. Though she completed two grades by correspondence, her education stalled at the tenth grade level when she needed $60 to continue. "To ask for sixty dollars of my parents then, was like asking for six hundred or six thousand dollars now. They just didn't have the money," Dickason said.

Helped by Father Murray

At 18 years of age, Dickason left her family and life in the country and ventured south to Winnipeg. She worked at "odd jobs" as a domestic and sold magazine subscriptions door-to-door. When her sales brought her to Wilcox in southern Saskatchewan, she met Father Murray, a well-known Canadian priest who founded a college where students too poor to afford college could receive an education. "He [Father Murray] changed the course of my life," Dickason recalls. She completed her high school degree at Murray's Notre Dame of Saskatchewan, and through Notre Dame's affiliation with the University of Ottawa, Dickason received her bachelor of arts in philosophy and French in 1943.

During Dickason's college years, she met members of her mother's family and became aware of her Métis heritage. According to Dickason, she had always been remotely aware of her Indian ancestry, but it was a subject that was never discussed or even acknowledged by her parents. "Some branches of my family still deny their heritage, trying to pass as French Canadians to avoid the stigma of being Native American that still exists."

After college, Dickason married and had three daughters. Later she divorced and raised her three children as a single parent. She supported her family by working as a journalist for several daily newspapers: the *Regina Leader-Post,* the *Winnipeg Free Press,* the *Montreal Gazette,* and the *Toronto-Globe and Mail.* Once her children left home—two to become nurses and one a civil service librarian—Dickason returned to school to pursue a master's degree and a doctorate.

Recognized as a Scholar in Native American History

Having become increasingly interested in her Métis heritage, Dickason was drawn to the topic of Native American history. During this period of the 1970s professors taught Canadian history as beginning with the coming of the Europeans. Dickason was told that Indians were not a subject of history. She found that professors promoted the beliefs of historians who claimed that "before the coming of the Europeans, there was darkness, and darkness was not a subject of history." Such misconceptions set Dickason back on her heels, and she decided to pursue a dissertation topic that would reveal that such notions are myth. She refuted the idea that the first people of the Americas were "savages." "Professors of mine tried to white-wash the word 'savage.' They tried to suggest that 'savage' in French was not a pejorative word, that it meant a person who lived in the woods when definitions of the time clearly listed the word as meaning 'wild, demented, and ferocious.'"

Dickason found an ally in the history department at the University of Ottawa to mentor her on her dissertation, which went on to receive immediate respect. It was later published as a book and translated into French. Since receiving her Ph.D. in 1977, Dickason has written well over 100 articles, participated in as many conferences, and taught numerous classes at the University of Alberta, where she was made a Professor Emeritus in 1992. Also that year, she was named Métis Woman of the Year by the Women of the Métis Nation of Alberta and was awarded the Sir John A. Macdonald prize of the Canadian Historical Association for her book *Canada's First Nations,* published in 1992 by the University of Oklahoma Press.

In 1994, she was at work on new projects analyzing constitutional questions regarding the treaties which the Canadian government made with the Indian peoples after the 1871 confederation and studying the connections and similarities of the first peoples of the North American continent.

SELECTED WRITINGS BY DICKASON:

Canada's First Nations: A History of the Founding Peoples from Earliest Times, Norman, University of Oklahoma Press, 1992.
Indian Arts in Canada, Ottawa, Queen's Printer, 1972.
(With Leslie Green) *The Law of Nations and the World,* University of Alberta Press, 1989.
The Myth of the Savage and the Beginnings of French Colonialism in the Americas, University of Alberta Press, 1984.

SOURCES:

Books

Native North American Almanac, edited by Duane Champagne, Detroit, Gale Research, 1994.

Other

Dickason, Olive Patricia, interview with Christopher Tower conducted August 6, 1994.

—*Sketch by Christopher B. Tower*

Angel DeCora Dietz
1871(?)-1919
Winnebago artist, illustrator, and writer
Also known as Hinookmahiwi-Kilinaka (Henook-makhewe-Kelenaka) ["Fleecy Cloud Floating into Place"], and The Word Carrier

Angel DeCora Dietz was well known at the turn of the twentieth century as an artist and educator who championed the use of Indian design in contemporary art, lectured on Native American social and economic problems, illustrated books, and wrote in several genres. She was also an active member of the Society of American Indians. During the Allotment Period, or the early 1900s, DeCora Dietz distinguished herself as a significant influence on both Indian art and Indian affairs.

The daughter of Indian parents, DeCora was born in a wigwam, reportedly on May 3, 1871, on the Nebraska Winnebago reservation. She could trace her ancestry through her paternal lineage back to Sabvevois DesCarris, a French settler. Her father, David DeCora, also known as Hagasilikaw, was a descendant of the famous Dakaury family and was of French-Winnebago ancestry. DeCora's mother was trained in a convent, but as the artist stated in "Angel DeCora—An Autobiography," "When she married my father she gave up all her foreign training and made a good, industrious Indian wife." Angel DeCora's father died when she was still young, but he had already instilled in her the values and customs of her Native American heritage.

The first school DeCora attended was the local reservation school in Santee. She was there for only a short time when, at the age of 12, she was sent to Hampton Institute. At the time she knew very little English, but according to her autobiographical sketch, the transfer to Hampton occurred under bizarre—even sinister—circumstances. A "strange white man" is said to have made arrangements for her and five other children to attend Hampton, luring them into his care with the promise of a car ride. DeCora's family apparently knew nothing of the trip with the "stranger" until it was too late; her mother later told her that she had wept and mourned for her for months. DeCora graduated from Hampton in 1891, having studied primarily in the school's art department.

DeCora's education continued at the Burnham Classical School for Girls in Northampton, Massachusetts. Next, she enrolled in the Smith College Art Department and studied under Dwight W. Tryon. In her autobiography, she noted, "The instruction I received and the influence I gained from Mr. Tryon has left a lasting impression on me." Upon completion of a four-year course at Smith, she graduated with honors and transferred to Drexel Institute in Philadelphia. For two years she studied illustration at Drexel with Howard Pyle. Both he and Tryon were famous illustrators of the day. It was Pyle, however, who recognized DeCora's talent.

Forged New Path in Art Education

After a brief stint at the Cowles Art School, where she perfected her artistic skills under Joseph DeCamp, DeCora gained acceptance to the Boston Museum of Fine Arts School. When she completed her studies at the museum school, DeCora stayed in Boston and set up a private studio. There she did illustrations for several Boston publishing companies and lectured on Indian affairs.

DeCora later moved to New York, where she continued working for the advancement of Indian ideals. A firm believer in the importance of retaining Indian art and history in Native American curricula, DeCora strongly opposed "assimilationist" education policies that sacrificed her people's cultural traditions and forced younger generations to conform to white ways. She is credited with bringing Native American art into the mainstream by exhibiting her own original drawings, which rely heavily on American Indian symbols and images.

Around the time she moved to New York, DeCora illustrated such books as Gertrude Bonnin's *Old Indian Legends,* Elaine Goodale Eastman's *Yellow Star,* and Natalie Curtis' *Indians' Book.* While working on the illustrations for *Old Indian Legends,* she met and became friends with Bonnin, who also went by the name Zitkala-sa. This would prove to be a long-lasting friendship, marked by a dual interest in improving social, economic, and political conditions among Native Americans.

Becomes Director of Art Department at Carlisle

In 1906 DeCora was offered a position by U.S. Indian Commissioner Francis E. Leupp at the Carlisle Indian School in Pennsylvania. She enthusiastically accepted and became the first director of the school's art department. During this period at Carlisle, DeCora initiated an unprecedented educational practice—using Indian designs in art. This intensive art program encouraged Native American students to apply Indian designs to modern art media. For example, the design of one of the title pages in Natalie Curtis' *Indians' Book* showcases traditional Winnebago art; because the Winnebago people are skilled in bead and quill work, the letters are drawn in the shape of strings of Indian beads. Another piece of art shown in The *Indians' Book* symbolizes a Kiowa cradle board and consists of a necklace of beads that a Native American child might wear.

Despite opposition—mainly from white conservative elements—DeCora's ideas caught on elsewhere in Native American educational circles. By about 1910, the "San Ildefonso School" of Indian artists in the Southwest emerged. These artists were already beginning to practice DeCora's methods. This period in history is now widely viewed by art historians as a "renaissance" of Indian art.

During her nine year stay at Carlisle, DeCora met William Dietz, also known as Wicahpi Isnala or "Lone Star," a teacher and Sioux artist who illustrated the covers of the Carlisle *Red Man.* DeCora and Dietz were married in 1908, collaborated on Carlisle projects together, and were especially active in Indian activities and affairs. At the outbreak of World War I, they moved to Albany, the capital of New York State. DeCora Dietz had accepted a position at the New York State Museum there.

Ten years after their marriage, Angel DeCora Dietz and William Dietz were divorced; DeCora Dietz moved back to New York City, where she once again immersed herself in Indian politics and her art work. As a prominent lecturer and protagonist in the Indian movement, she met with President Theodore Roosevelt in an effort to enlighten him on the social and political concerns of Native Americans.

DeCora Dietz became ill during the great influenza epidemic and died in New York City on Feb 6, 1919, leaving her estate to the Society of American Indians. Her influence on Native American art and politics continues to be felt 75 years after her death. In addition to her artwork, she left behind writings, including articles on Indian art, two autobiographical sketches, and a short story titled "The Sick Child," published in *Harper's Monthly* in 1899.

SOURCES:

A Biobibliography of Native American Writers, 1772-1924: A Supplement, compiled by Daniel F. Littlefield, Metuchen, New Jersey, Scarecrow Press, 1985; 35, 199.

Biographical Dictionary of Indians of the Americas, second edition, Newport Beach, California, American Indian Publishers, 1991; 181, 189.

DeCora Dietz, Angel, "Angel DeCora—An Autobiography," in *The Red Man, by Red Men,* Carlisle, Pennsylvania, Carlisle Indian Press, 1911; 279-285.

Dockstader, Frederick, J., *Great North American Indians,* New York, Van Nostrand Reinhold, 1977; 71.

The Indians' Book, edited by Natalie Curtis, New York, Harper, 1907; reprinted, Bonanza Books, 1987; 28-29, 35-36, 219-220, 241-242.

Native American Women, edited by Gretchen M. Bataille, New York, Garland Publishing, 1993; 81-82.

—Sketch by Wendy Pfeffer

Henry Chee Dodge
1857(?)-1947
Navajo tribal leader
Also known as Hastiin Adiits'a'ii ["Man Who Interprets" or "Man Who Understands"], Ashkihih (Askihih Diitsi) ["Boy Interpreter"], Kilchii (Kilchee) ["Red Boy"], and Chee Dodge

One of the most famous of the Navajo tribal leaders, Henry Chee Dodge made significant contributions to his community throughout his long life. He is known for his service as the first official Navajo interpreter, a role he played from the 1870s through the early 1900s; his many years as a head chief; and his position as the first chairman of the Navajo Tribal Council.

There is some dispute over what year Dodge was born, as well as about his parentage. Many historians show Dodge born in 1860 and the name of his father as Juan Anea (also known as Anaya, Cocinas or Cosonisas, and Gohsinahsu). Anea was a Mexican silversmith working for Captain Henry L. Dodge, the Navajo Indian Agent at Fort Defiance. However, in an 1888 sworn affidavit, Chee Dodge stated he was the son of a white army officer and a Navaho woman, was born at Fort Defiance, and was "about" 30 years old. In 1875, Augustus C. Dodge, brother of Henry L. Dodge, wrote that he "had a nephew then 18 years old living at Fort Defiance, who was the son of a Navajo woman and of his brother," according to David M. Brugge in an essay, "Henry Chee Dodge: From the Long Walk to Self Determination." Since Henry L. Dodge was captured and killed by Apaches in late 1856, Brugge states the younger Dodge more likely was born about 1857 rather than 1860.

Dodge's mother, Bisnayanchi, was a Navajo-Jemez Pueblo woman from the Ma'iideshgizhnii [Coyote Pass] clan. She was married to Juan Anea during young Dodge's first few years of life. However, Anea died in 1862 during a Mexican raid. In 1863, Kit Carson forcibly moved the Fort Defiance Navajos to Fort Sumner at the Bosque Redondo to put an end to Navajo uprisings. During the Carson campaign, Bisnayanchi left her son in the care of a sister, then fled to Hopi territory, where she died sometime later.

Orphaned, Dodge was passed among his relatives for a time then was adopted by an eight-year-old girl and her grandfather, who found him alone and starving during the "Long Walk" to Fort Sumner. When Dodge returned to Fort Defiance with the rest of the Navajos in 1868, he lived with his mother's sister and her husband, a white man named Perry H. Williams, who taught Dodge English. He quickly learned English and Spanish, in addition to his native Navajo language. For a time, Dodge also lived with the new Indian Agent, W. F. M. Arny, who allowed Dodge to attend the Fort Defiance Indian School, where he learned to read and write.

From Interpreter to Police Chief to Head Chief

Dodge first used his language skills as a translator while working at his uncle's trading post. He earned $5 a week, most of which he saved. He also worked for a time with a freight company moving goods from Santa Fe to the fort and assisted ethnologist Washington Matthews at Fort Wingate. Dodge became so proficient at translating and interpreting, and he understood the Navajo culture so well that Agent Arny hired him in the late 1870s as the official Agency interpreter. In an effort to control crime among the reservation Indians, a police force was recruited in 1881. In 1883, Dodge was appointed chief of the Navajo patrol. He often acted as the agency interpreter during police investigations and helped to diffuse many potentially violent confrontations.

On April 19, 1884, Commissioner of Indian Affairs Dennis M. Riordan appointed Dodge to the job of head chief of the Navajos at Fort Defiance, a position held previously by the great war chief Manuelito. Later that year, Dodge and a delegation of other Navajo leaders traveled to Washington where they met with President Chester A. Arthur.

By 1890, Dodge had saved enough money from his various jobs to invest in a trading post and a sheep ranch. Near Crystal, New Mexico, he built a home at his ranch, which he called Tso Tsela ["Stars Lying Down"]. Dodge and Stephen H. Aldrich became partners in the trading post at Round Rock in the Chinle Valley. Dodge managed the post and hired Charles Hubbell as a clerk. With his business established, Dodge finally decided to marry. His first wife, Asdzaa' Tsi'naajinii, he supposedly divorced after learning she was gambling heavily. However, records at the Saint Michaels Mission indicated that his first wife was the mother of Dodge's daughter, Josephine, who was the youngest of his children.

Most historians note Dodge then married Nanabah and her younger sister, K'eehabah, an accepted practice in traditional Navajo culture. They were the daughters of the woman who, as an eight-year-old child, adopted Dodge on the trip to Fort Sumner with her grandfather. Nanabah or her sister had a daughter named Mary in 1903, according to several written accounts about Dodge. However, the Mission records indicate that during his life, Dodge had a total of eight wives and six children, named Tom, Ben, Antoinette, Annie, Veronica and Josephine. Four of his wives were sisters and a fifth was a member of the sisters' clan, the Tse' njikini clan. Another wife was a cousin of the four sisters, but belonged to the Ta'neeszahnii clan. Until the Navajos converted to Christianity, polygamy was not only accepted, but expected.

Although his business and ranch took much of his time, Dodge continued to work at the Fort Defiance Agency as an interpreter. He helped the various Indian agents resolve disputes and encouraged Navajo participation in mineral development and land rights issues and in a variety of federal programs. For example, in 1892, he helped Agent Dana L. Shipley obtain promises from a number of Navajo parents to send their children to the Fort Defiance government school. In 1907, he was a member of a committee that reviewed a request to lease land from the Shiprock Navajos. In September 1907, Dodge assisted the negotiations for surrender between federal troops and Little Singer, who had helped his wives escape jail and hid them and himself on Beautiful Mountain.

First Tribal Council Formed

The Navajos did not have a centralized form of government until 1923. Dodge, however, envisioned such a government as early as 1918 when he corresponded with Cato Sells, Commissioner of Indian Affairs. Mary Shepardson in "Development of Navajo Tribal Government," quoted Dodge as writing: "I would like to see them [all Navajos] make equal progress, but I am sure that it is only possible if we have one man at the head of the tribe, an active, strong, energetic and able man.... A uniform educational system, uniform treatment, uniform orders and regulations, and uniform progress would be the result."

In 1922, a three-man Navajo business council was formed to deal with requests for oil exploration leases in the Fort Defiance area of the reservation. Council members Dodge, Dugal Chee Bekiss, and Charley Mitchell, signed several oil leases for the jurisdiction. However, Indian Superintendent Evan Estap wanted more control over the leases and spread rumors that Standard Oil-owned companies had bribed Dodge to get leases signed. Estap, who was latter fired over the issue, appointed former New Mexico Territorial Governor Herbert J. Hagerman to sign oil leases for all six of the Navajo jurisdictions.

Under somewhat restrictive orders, the first Navajo Tribal Council was formed and met on July 7, 1923, and Dodge was elected its first chairman on July 27. The council represented all nine of the Navajo districts with 12 delegates and 12 alternate members. They approved Hagerman's position, giving him the authorization to sign all oil and mineral leases in exchange for a federal promise to obtain more land for the Navajos.

Dodge served as chairman of the Tribal Council until 1928, when he stepped down to spend more time at his sheep ranch and trading post. During his years as chairman, he often found himself at odds with Jacob C. Morgan, a council member representing the San Juan Navajo jurisdiction. Morgan believed in assimilation, which often led him into confrontations with Dodge, who wanted a unified Navajo nation. For example, in 1927, Dodge led a movement to use oil royalties to buy more land for the reservation. Morgan opposed the plan because he wanted to use the money for water development. Dodge was so upset after the council reached a compromise on the issue that he recommended the council be abolished.

While Dodge was chairman, the council steadily increased its power. It obtained the right to decide how oil lease royalties would be spent, approving a division of the royalties among the different jurisdictions, which, in turn, were allowed to determine how best to use that money within their jurisdictions. The council also opposed a federal move to use some of the funds to build a bridge off the reservation. In 1927, Dodge convinced Congress that the Navajos had a right to 100 percent of the oil royalties resulting from the oil reserves under the reservation. The Indian Oil Act of 1927, which Dodge supported, provided that states in which the oil was found would receive 37.5 percent of the royalties, but could spend those funds only on projects benefiting the Indians and only after first consulting with the Indians about those projects. Although Dodge was not a part of the Tribal Council during the next decade, he remained active in tribal politics.

The Problem with Sheep

Although the Indian Reorganization Act of 1934 provided the Navajos with more authority than in past years, it also allowed the Secretary of the Interior to limit the amount of livestock on Indian reservations. Overgrazing of reservation lands had been a problem for some years. In 1926, the Navajo Council had limited the number of horses allowed to graze on the reservation. In autumn of 1933, the Bureau of Indian Affairs (BIA) suggested that the Navajo reduce the number of sheep grazing on the reservation in an effort to reduce erosion. The government offered to buy ewes for about $1 per head, and many of the Navajo sheep ranchers agreed to cull their herds. Most of the ranchers, however, kept their most productive stock. A second stock reduction, funded by the tribe, was agreed to in the spring of 1934 but was apparently not implemented.

By 1936, stock reduction was resulting in hundreds of healthy sheep being slaughtered. In June, Dodge accused John Collier, head of the BIA, of causing hunger and sickness to spread among the Navajo as a result of the sheep reduction program. For a brief time, Morgan and Dodge formed an alliance to denounce Collier's continuing demands for more sheep reductions. During a Congressional hearing that year about expanding the boundaries of the reservation, Shepardson wrote that Dodge testified, "You take sheep away from a Navajo, that's all he knows. He isn't going to farm or anything like that; you might give a few acres to the poor ones, but stock raising is in their heart. That's their work. If you keep cutting down sheep after a while the Government will have to feed these people; give them rations; you know what that will cost." Collier later admitted that the reduction program was unfair to many Navajos.

Dodge's influence in the lives of the Navajos continued well into his 80s, when, in 1942, he was again elected as chairman of the Tribal Council. He was re-elected in 1946, but on January 7, 1947, Dodge died of pneumonia in Ganado, Arizona.

SOURCES:

Biographical Dictionary of Indians of the Americas, Volume 1, Newport Beach, California, American Indian Publishers, 1991; 123-124.

Brugge, David M., "Henry Chee Dodge: From the Long Walk to Self-Determination," in *Indian Lives: Essays on Nineteenth and Twentieth Century Native American Leaders,* edited by L. G. Moses and Raymond Wilson, Albuquerque, University of New Mexico Press, 1985; 91-112.

Dictionary of American Biography, edited by James A. Garraty and Edward T. James, Supplement 4, 1946-1950, New York, Scribner's, 1974; 237-239.

Dockstader, Frederick J., *Great North American Indians,* New York, Van Nostrand Reinhold, 1977; 75-76.

Handbook of American Indians North of Mexico, Part 2, edited by Frederick Webb Hodge, Totowa, New Jersey, Rowman and Littlefield, 1975; 41-45.

Native North American Almanac, edited by Duane Champagne, Detroit, Gale Research, 1994; 1046.

Shepardson, Mary, "Development of Navajo Tribal Government," in *Handbook of North American Indians,* edited by William C. Sturtevant, Volume 10: Southwest, edited by Alfonso Ortiz, Washington, D.C., Smithsonian Institution, 1983; 624-630.

Waldman, Carl, *Who Was Who in Native American History,* New York, Facts on File, 1990; 100-101.

—*Sketch by Catherine A. Clay*

Michael Anthony Dorris

Michael Anthony Dorris
1945-
Modoc writer, educator, and anthropologist
Also known as Milou North (joint pseudonym with Louise Erdrich)

Michael Anthony Dorris, former chair of the Native American studies department at Dartmouth College, has been a researcher on fetal alcohol syndrome, and has authored two best-selling novels. He was born January 30, 1945, in Louisville, Kentucky, to Mary Besy (Burkhardt) whose husband, Jim Dorris, was killed in World War II. Dorris was raised by a household of women—his aunts, and his grandmother, Alice Manion Burkhardt.

A prodigious reader as a child, Dorris won prizes at his local library for finishing a book a day. He also carried on a copious correspondence with foreign pen pals. Educated in Catholic schools, he applied to Georgetown University to continue his study under Jesuit teachers. In 1967, he graduated "magna cum laude" and Phi Beta Kappa. Under Woodrow Wilson and Danforth fellowships, he attended Yale University graduate school. After his first year there, he switched his major from the history of the theater to anthropology, and earned a master's degree in 1971. He did his field research in Tyonek, Alaska, a fishing village on the west coast of Cook Inlet, studying the impact of oil revenues on the local inhabitants.

Single Father Adoption

Because of the loneliness he experienced in the far north, he decided to apply to a Catholic adoption agency for a child. The three-year-old Lakota boy, whom he named Reynold Abel, had been seven weeks premature, malnourished, and diagnosed as mentally retarded, but Dorris was convinced that his problems could be solved through loving nurturance. After a year teaching anthropology at Franconia College in New Hampshire, he was invited to found a Native American studies program at Dartmouth College in Hanover, New Hampshire, in 1972. And in 1974, Dorris adopted a second son, Sava, named after his deceased Alaskan fishing partner, Sava Stephens. A daughter, Madeline Hannah, was adopted in 1976. In May of 1979, he brought all three of his children to dance at the annual Dartmouth pow wow; there he met a former student, Louise Erdrich, whom he married on October 10, 1981.

Before their wedding, however, he and the children spent seven months in New Zealand where Dorris did research on the Maori under a 1980 Woodrow Wilson faculty development grant. Dorris and Erdrich exchanged drafts, and commented extensively on each other's manuscripts. After they were married, they collaborated on short stories using the pseudonym Milou North. Many of these romantic fictions were published by a British periodical, *Woman.* With the proceeds from these jointly authored stories, they were able to pay for carpentry or plumbing repairs to the eighteenth-century farmhouse they bought in Comish, New Hampshire.

Award-Winning Achievements

In January of 1982, a short story submitted to *Chicago* magazine under Erdrich's name was judged the best of 2,000 entries. "The World's Greatest Fisherman" became the first chapter of *Love Medicine* for which Dorris served as agent, sending out chapters to magazines in advance of selling it to a publisher. He also subcontracted the movie rights to the book, which won more awards than any other first novel in publishing history. In 1983, the *Guide to Research on North American Indians* listing more than 1,000 government documents, books, and articles with evaluative annotations was selected as "Outstanding Academic Book" by *Choice* magazine. In 1985, Dorris received a Rockefeller Foundation research fellowship and became a full professor. He was given the Indian Achievement Award in Chicago, and was appointed delegate to the InterAmerican Indian Congress held in Sante Fe, New Mexico, in October. His novel, *Yellow Raft in Blue Water,* was published to good reviews in 1987. Each of its three sections deals with a different generation of the same family of courageous women. Beginning with Rayona, it moves backwards into her mother Christine's life, and concludes with the life-story of Ida, resolving the mystery of why she had insisted on being called "aunt." The book sold well and has been optioned for a movie to be directed by John Sayles.

Dorris' 1989 study of fetal alcohol syndrome, *The Broken Cord,* won the National Book Critics Circle Award for best nonfiction, as well as earning the Christopher Award and the Heartland Prize. It was chosen as a Book-of-the-Month Club selection and has been translated into eight languages. A film starring Jimmy Smits was watched by 30 million viewers and was given the Scott Newman Award, the Gabriel Award for National Entertainment program, the ARC Media Award, the Christopher Award, the Writers' Guild of America Award, and the American Psychology Association Annual Media Award. On the strength of its success, Dorris resigned from his full-time teaching to devote himself to writing. In 1991, The *Crown of Columbus* also became a great popular success. This romance between two Dartmouth faculty members, Roger Williams and Vivian Twostar, is being filmed under the direction of Michelle Pfeiffer and Kate Guinzburg.

Dorris' essays on the starvation in Zimbabwe won an Overseas Press Club citation and the Journalism Award for Excellence in 1992. They were published in book form in 1993 as *Rooms in the House of Stone.* In 1992, *Morning Girl,* Dorris' first children's book, received the Scott O'Dell Award for best historical fiction and was endorsed by *Horn Book* as one of the best books for young readers. With three daughters of his own, Persia, born in 1984, Pallas, in 1985, and Aza in 1989, Dorris plans future ventures into children's literature depicting their Indian heritage.

SELECTED WRITINGS BY DORRIS:

Books

Native Americans: Five Hundred Years After, photographs by Joseph Farber, New York, Thomas Y. Crowell, 1977.

(With Arlene Hirschfelder and Mary Lou Byler) *A Guide to Research on North American Indians,* Chicago, American Library Association, 1983.
A Yellow Raft in Blue Water, New York, Henry Holt, 1987.
The Broken Cord, New York, Harper & Row, 1989.
(With Louise Erdrich) *The Crown of Columbus,* New York, HarperCollins, 1991.
(With Louise Erdrich) *Route Two,* Northridge, California, Lord John Press, 1991.
Morning Girl, New York, Hyperion Books, 1992.
Rooms in the House of Stone, Minneapolis, Minnesota, Milkweed Editions, 1993.
Working Men (short stories), New York, Henry Holt, 1993.
Paper Trail, New York, HarperCollins, 1994.

Essays

"The Grass Still Grows, the Rivers Still Flow: Contemporary Native Americans," *Daedalus,* spring 1981; 43-70.
(With Louise Erdrich) "Sea to Sea on Route 2," *New York Times Magazine,* March 15, 1987; 530.
"The Best of Pen Pals: Corresponding with People around the World," *Seventeen,* August 1987; 128.
"Why Mister Ed Still Talks Good Horse Sense: An Anthropologist Explains How Reruns, Like Old Tribal Tales, Can Link Generations and Teach Enduring Values," *TV Guide,* May 28, 1982; 34-37.
"Rite of Passage: A Man's Journey into Fatherhood Echoes His Son's Entry into Adolescence," *Parent's Magazine,* June 1989; 246-248.
"A Desparate Crack Legacy," *Newsweek,* June 25, 1990; 8.
"What Men Are Missing," *Vogue,* September 1991; 511-513.

SOURCES:

Chavkin, Allan, and Nancy Feyl Jackson, *Conversations with Louise Erdrich and Michael Dorris,* University Press of Mississippi, 1993.
Rosenberg, Ruth, *Louise Erdrich and Michael Dorris,* New York, Twayne, 1995.

—Sketch by Ruth Rosenberg

Edward P. Dozier
1916-1971
Santa Clara Pueblo anthropologist, linguist, educator, activist, and writer
Also known as Awa Tside ["Cattail Bird"]

E dward P. Dozier was a pioneering Native American anthropologist who specialized in the study of his own people, the Pueblo Indians of the American Southwest. He also dedicated himself to improving the position of the American Indian in white society.

Dozier was born on April 23, 1916, at Santa Clara Pueblo, near Española, New Mexico, the youngest son of Thomas Sublette Dozier, a white American of French descent, and Leocadia Gutierrez Dozier, a Native American of the Santa Clara Pueblo. Dozier grew up at the pueblo, speaking both the Tewa language and Spanish and attending elementary schools sponsored by the Bureau of Indian Affairs. He learned to speak English at age 12 and later attended and graduated from St. Michael's High School in Santa Fe.

Dozier enrolled at the University of New Mexico at Albuquerque in the late 1930s. He originally planned to study medicine and become a physician like his paternal grandfather. But his interests changed following a chance meeting with anthropologist Willard Williams Hill, who asked him to become his interpreter and general assistant in his field research at the Santa Clara Pueblo. Dozier quickly became fascinated with the history and culture of his own people and excited by the prospects of a career in anthropology.

Becomes Leader in the Field of Anthropology

Dozier's undergraduate work was interrupted by over four years of military service with the U.S. Army Air Force in the Pacific during World War II. He returned to the University of New Mexico after the war and received his bachelor of arts in anthropology in 1947. Two years later, after completing a thesis on Tewa linguistics, he earned his master's degree. Dozier then transferred to the University of California and began his doctoral field research among the Hopi-Tewa of First Mesa in Arizona. He had a great advantage over most anthropologists in that he was a Native American who spoke the Tewa language and was accepted and trusted by the residents of the pueblo. He received his Ph.D. in 1952, and his dissertation was published in 1954 as *The Hopi-Tewa of Arizona.* This work solidified his reputation as a scholar of Pueblo Indian life. Around the same time, Dozier (whose first marriage had ended in divorce) married Marianne Fink, a fellow scholar. In addition to a daughter, Wanda, by his first wife, he and Fink had two children—Miguel and Anya.

Dozier was an instructor at the University of Oregon from 1951 to 1952. Following an additional year of field research as a Wenner-Gren Foundation research fellow, he joined the anthropology department of Northwestern University in 1953 and progressed through the ranks to associate professor by 1958. He published numerous papers on Pueblo Indian culture during the mid- to late-1950s, but by 1959, when he was a research fellow at the Center for Advanced Study in the Behavioral Sciences at Stanford University, he felt the need to broaden his studies. He spent the 1959-1960 academic year studying the Kalinga tribe of northern Luzon in the Philippines on a fellowship from the National Science Foundation. His research was ultimately published in 1966 under the title *Mountain Arbiters: The Changing Life of a Philippine Hill People.*

Champion of Native American Rights

Dozier became a professor of anthropology and linguistics at the University of Arizona in 1961 and remained there for a decade. Throughout the 1960s, he became increasingly concerned with the problems of Native Americans in white society, particularly with the plight of Indian students at predominantly white educational institutions. He joined the Association on American Indian Affairs, an advocacy group for Native American rights and equality, and was ultimately elected its vice president. He also began the planning of a program of studies at the University of Arizona that would specifically meet the needs of Native American students. A career retrospective published in *American Anthropologist* included a revealing quote from Dozier on his own experiences in the white world: "I've had to change so much myself over the years that I know what it's like and how hard it can be," he stated. "You have to *learn* how to change and that is hard."

By about 1970, Dozier was offered the directorship of a new program of American Indian studies at the University of Minnesota. But he was soon diagnosed as having a brain tumor and was advised to remain in Arizona following surgery. Around the same time, he published *The Pueblo Indians of North America,* a concise, fact-filled volume in which he distilled the results of his many years of study.

Dozier died of a heart attack on May 2, 1971, just after organizing a seminar on communication for a joint meeting of the American Ethnological Association and the Southwestern Anthropological Association. Alfonso Ortiz, a friend, protege, and fellow anthropologist, provided an eloquent tribute, as quoted in *American Anthropologist:* "Anthropology has lost an effective and dedicated teacher, and one of its most learned and productive scholars on native American cultures. But the loss is greatest to the Indian people, for Ed Dozier was one of a small handful of men at the very front rank of contemporary Indian leadership. He was, at the time of his passing, easily the most respected of Indian scholars. He was also the one most trusted by Indians, young and old, traditional and urban."

SELECTED WRITINGS BY DOZIER:

The Hopi-Tewa of Arizona, Berkeley, University of California Press, 1954.
Hano: A Tewa Indian Community in Arizona, New York, Holt, 1966.
Mountain Arbiters: The Changing Life of a Philippine Hill People, Tucson, University of Arizona Press, 1966.
The Kalinga of Northern Luzon, Philippines, New York, Holt, 1967.
The Pueblo Indians of North America, New York, Holt, 1970.

SOURCES:

Books

Biographical Dictionary of the Indians of the Americas, second edition, Newport Beach, California, American Indian Publishers, 1991.

Periodicals

Eggan, Fred, and Keith Basso, "Edward P. Dozier, 1916-1971," *American Anthropologist,* 74, June 1972; 740-746.

—*Sketch by John E. Little*

Frank C. Dukepoo
1943-
Hopi-Laguna geneticist
Also known as Pumatuhye ["First Crop"]

Frank C. Dukepoo was the first Hopi to earn a doctorate and among the first American Indians across the nation to earn doctorates in the sciences. He gained national recognition as a motivator of Indian students by founding and coordinating the National Native American Honor Society in 1982. In addition, Dukepoo conducted extensive research in many areas, including birth defects in Indians. The scholar is also an accomplished saxophone player and an amateur magician.

A full-blooded American Indian, Dukepoo was born on the Mohave Indian Reservation in Arizona to Anthony Dukepoo, a Hopi, and Eunice (Martin), a Laguna. His father was a laborer and house painter and his mother was a home-maker who took in laundry. Dukepoo was the fourth of 11 siblings, and he explained in an interview with Diane Andreassi that it was his older brother Freddie, who at one time worked as a lab technician, who served as his role model. Dukepoo also credited his parents with influencing him by instilling values of hard work, integrity, sharing, and caring. He went to school as a youngster in the Phoenix area, and Dukepoo recognizes a high school counselor, Abraham Lincoln Herm, as guiding him toward a path of college and success. His interest in genetics also began at an early age. "As a child, I was obsessed with birth and the miracle of life as I watched hundreds of animals reproduce," Dukepoo told Andreassi. "I even conducted a few controlled mating experiments with a myriad assortment of animals just to see what would happen."

In 1965 Dukepoo married, and he had two children, Christine and Andromeda Hope-Reminissa. In the meantime, he worked at the U.S. Department of Agriculture in Phoenix, Arizona, in 1965; at Arizona State University as a teaching assistant in 1971; for the next two years, he worked at Mesa Community College as a genetics instructor, and at Phoenix Indian School as a science and math teacher. In 1973, Dukepoo graduated from Arizona State University with a Ph.D. in zoology, or genetics. He credited one of his professors, Charles Woolf, with inspiring him to do better

with his grades. He raised his grade point average from 1.162 to nearly a 4.0. "He pulled me through," Dukepoo maintained in his interview with Andreassi.

Dukepoo's career continued to progress as he worked at the university as an assistant zoology teacher and as a laboratory instructor. San Diego State University and Palomar Junior College were his next stops, where he worked as an assistant professor staff member and instructor. Dukepoo also held administrative executive positions with the National Science Foundation from 1976 to 1979. And the next year he was assistant executive secretary for the National Cancer Institute.

Dukepoo also served as director of Indian Education at Northern Arizona University in Flagstaff, Arizona. During this time, he was director of a National Science Foundation supported program that earned a premiere rating for 100 percent retention of Indian students. Dukepoo next became a faculty member in the biology department and special assistant to the academic vice president at Northern State University, where he started working in 1980.

Founds National Native American Honor Society

A true motivator, Dukepoo founded, incorporated, and coordinated the National Native American Honor Society in 1982. According to Dukepoo, the idea for this organization was given by the Great Spirit at precisely four a.m. in Flagstaff, Arizona, on a Sunday in October of 1981. "I was in Flagstaff and I was laying in bed and I was aroused at 4 a.m. and something said to write this down: Happiness, education, achievement, Indians, success," he recalled in his Andreassi interview. "I went back to bed and four days later, it started to come together and I said: Why not? Why not an Honor Society for Indian people?" The program invites students from fourth grade up through graduation, including professional school students, who earn a 4.0 semester at any time to be members. They receive a membership certificate and an eagle pin and are required to perform some type of community service; scholarships and awards are also offered. Identifying these exceptional students, the society works to promote positive and constructive values as an example for others to follow to achieve the same personal commitments to education and high self-esteem. Dukepoo's long term goals were to establish a scholarship program, to start up an Honor Society symphonic band, and to hold the First National Conference in 1999 with 19,999 to 29,999 in attendance.

Meanwhile, Dukepoo also conducted research on the study of birth defects in Southwest Native Americans, albinism (the absence of normal pigmentation), and inbreeding among the Hopi Indians of Northern Arizona. His work was made into three films and was being considered for the basis of science instruction kits, especially in elementary schools.

The knowledge Dukepoo gained from these experiences prepared him for a position as a consultant to the Bureau of Indian Affairs, Department of Education,

National Institutes of Health, National Science Foundation, Southwest Development Laboratory, and the Far West Laboratory. He gave training to teachers, Indian tribes, and the Department of Economic Security. Dukepoo was also a member of scientific and educational societies and organizations. Commonly at the forefront of important programs and changes, Dukepoo was a founding member of the Society for the Advance of Chicanos and Native Americans in Science and the American Indian Science and Engineering Society.

Dukepoo's work has not gone unnoticed. He has earned a number of awards, including the John Hay Whitney Fellowship, Ford Foundation fellowship, Bo Jack Humanitarian Award, and Iron Eyes Cody Medal of Freedom Award. He also received the Outstanding Educator of the Year Award for the National Coalition of Indian Education and "Premier" status and "Exemplary" awards for the programs he created and directed while working with American Indian youngsters.

The scholar, however, is not always buried in books and research. Dukepoo's other interests include playing saxophone with various groups, including the Salt River Indian Band and a Latin orchestra. He is also an amateur magician who has performed "Mind, Magic and Motivation" shows around the country to audiences of youngsters and adults beginning in 1980. The shows incorporate the concepts of Eagle Force training, which is a course on communication, motivation and self-esteem that he and Lee Cannon, a communications expert and Marine veteran, developed for Indian people.

SOURCES:

Books

Biographical Dictionary of Indians of the Americas, second edition, Newport Beach, California, American Indian Publishers, 1991; 199.

Periodicals

Johnston, Scott, "'Perfect' Students Attend Conference," *Arizona Daily Sun,* April 17, 1992.
Mickela, Paul, "Banquet Celebrates Outstanding Students," *Navajo-Hopi Observer,* May 2, 1990; 9.
Reid, Betty, "College Professor Magically Inspires Students to Learn," *Independent* (Gallup, New Mexico), September 27, 1991; 9.
Ryan, Steve, "Dukepoo Organizes Native American Honor Society," *Arizona Daily Sun,* April 22, 1990.

Other

Dukepoo, Frank C., interview with Diane Andreassi conducted on July 8, 1994.

—*Sketch by Diane Andreassi*

Dull Knife
1810(?)-1883
Northern Cheyenne tribal leader
Also known as Tah-me-la-pash-me and Wo-hiev ["Morning Star"]

Best-known for leading his people in a courageous attempt to return from exile in Oklahoma to their Montana homeland in 1878, the Northern Cheyenne leader Morning Star was born in about 1810 on the Rosebud River. He was known mostly by his nickname of Dull Knife, given to him by his brother-in-law, who teased him about not having a sharp knife. A renowned Dog Soldier in his youth, Dull Knife became a member of the Council of 44 and in the 1870s was one of the four principal, or "old man," chiefs. These chiefs represented the mystical four Sacred Persons who dwelt at the cardinal points of the universe and were the guardians of creation.

Little is known of Dull Knife's early life. When he was a young man in the late 1820s, he went on a raiding party against the Pawnees. Capturing a young girl, he saved her life by asking that she replace a member of his family previously lost to the Pawnees. When he became a chief, Dull Knife made Little Woman his second wife, the union producing four daughters. Dull Knife had two other wives, Goes to Get a Drink, with whom he had two daughters, and her sister Slow Woman, by whom he had four sons and another daughter.

Dull Knife first appears in white history in 1866, when he joined Red Cloud and the Oglala Sioux in ambushing U.S. soldiers under Captain William J. Fetterman traveling along the Bozeman Trail to reach the Montana gold fields. On May 10, 1868, at the end of the Bozeman Trail War, the Northern Cheyennes signed the Fort Laramie Treaty agreeing to settle on a reservation. The U.S. government gave them the choice of joining the Crows in Montana, the Sioux in Dakota, or the Southern Cheyennes and Arapahos in Indian Territory. To force an early decision, the government withheld supplies, and the Northern Cheyennes signed an agreement on November 12, 1874, to move to Indian Territory whenever the U.S. government saw fit.

These arrangements were set aside, however, when the Black Hills Gold Rush led to war with the Sioux and their allies. The precipitating act was an ultimatum ordering the Indians to return to agencies in South Dakota by January 31, 1876. The Big Horn Expedition, intended to force the Indians back to their agencies, engaged the Sioux, Northern Cheyennes, and Northern Arapahos in several major battles, the most famous being Custer's fight on the Little Big Horn. Dull Knife was not in the Indian village that day, but his son Medicine Lodge was present and died in combat against the Seventh Cavalry.

The pivotal battle for the Northern Cheyennes occurred on the morning of November 25, 1876, when

Colonel Ranald Mackenzie's force of 600 men of the Fourth Cavalry and about 400 Indian scouts surprised Dull Knife's camp on the Red Forks of the Powder River. Reportedly killed in the fighting were one of Dull Knife's sons and a son-in-law. The dead numbered around 40, but destruction of the village and its contents sealed their fate. For all practical purposes, the campaign of 1876-77 ended the Indian wars on the Northern Plains.

Concern for their children caused Dull Knife and his people to surrender to the troops under Crook and Mackenzie in the spring of 1877. At Fort Robinson they learned that the government had decreed that all Northern Cheyennes would be sent to Indian Territory. Dull Knife and Little Wolf urged their tribesmen to abide by the wishes of the government. The Northern Cheyennes may have been led to believe that they could return to their tribal lands in a year if they did not like life in the south. The journey to Indian Territory began on May 28, 1877. In the group were 937 Northern Cheyennes. On August 5, 70 days later, they arrived at the Cheyenne and Arapaho Agency, selecting a campsite about eight miles north.

Within a year, the Northern Cheyennes were ready to return to their homeland. Starved, ravaged by disease, preyed upon by white gangs of horse thieves, unwilling to farm, critical of the civilized ways of their southern brethren, rankled by the fact that the Northern Arapahos had been allowed to remain in the north, and with 50 of their children dead, they had had enough. So at 10:10 p.m. on September 9 a party of 353 Cheyennes—92 men, 120 women, 69 boys, and 72 girls—quietly left the foreign place, leaving fires burning and lodge poles standing to fool distant military pickets. After discovery of their departure the next morning at 3 AM, the army's pursuit began, eventually involving 13,000 men in three military departments.

Following the route of the Texas Cattle Trail from Oklahoma through Kansas, Dull Knife and Little Wolf and their followers skirmished with army units on September 13 at Turkey Springs, September 14 at Red Hill, September 17 and 21-22 at Sand Creek, and September 27 at Punished Woman Creek, each time eluding the troops and continuing north. On the journey, Little Woman was killed by a horse that stampeded through the camp. When the fleeing Cheyennes reached northeast Kansas, warriors roamed the countryside, killing 40 male white settlers, some said in revenge for a mass killing of their kinsmen by whites in the area in 1875. In Nebraska, Dull Knife and Little Wolf separated, the former heading for Fort Robinson and Red Cloud Agency, the latter to the traditional Northern Cheyenne homeland in Montana.

On October 23, two companies of the Third Cavalry traveled up Chadron Creek and caught Dull Knife and his people. Taken to Fort Robinson, the Cheyennes learned on January 3 that the Washington government had decided they must be sent back to Indian Territory. When they refused, Post Commander Henry Wessells imprisoned the band in a cavalry barracks, cutting off heat, food, and water. Barricading doors and covering windows with cloth to conceal their movements, the captives tore up the floor and constructed rifle-pits to command the windows. At 10:10 PM on January 9, the Cheyennes begin firing. The men moved forward through the windows with children under their arms, while the women followed, and once again Dull Knife and his band dashed for freedom. This time they were not so fortunate. Soldiers sent volley after volley into the fleeing band. Twenty-two men, eight women, and two children died in the initial exodus, including Dull Knife's daughter, Traveling Woman, who was carrying her four-year-old sister on her back. The retreat continued for four miles in the darkness until the fugitives reached neighboring hills where pursuit was no longer possible.

Twelve days later, four companies of soldiers caught the largest number of remaining Cheyennes, pinning them down in an oblong depression about 40 miles from Fort Robinson. Twenty-three Indians were killed and nine captured, including two young girls, aged 14 and 15, discovered under the bodies of young men. The dead Indians were buried in the pit where they had hidden. In the meantime, Dull Knife, Slow Woman, and their remaining children had found a haven in the rocks, where they stayed for ten days, keeping alive by eating their moccasins. After 18 days of wandering, they reached Pine Ridge, where they were hidden by Sioux relatives in a lodge under a little bluff on Wounded Knee Creek.

After wintering in a sheltered valley near the forks of the Niobrara River, Little Wolf and his followers headed north. On March 25, they surrendered to Lieutenant W. P. Clark on the Yellowstone and were sent to Fort Keogh. In November, Indian Bureau officials permitted the Northern Cheyenne at Pine Ridge to transfer to Montana to join the rest. At the request of General Nelson A. Miles, Dull Knife was allowed to return to the valley of the Rosebud. An Executive Order of November 26, 1884, established a permanent home for the Northern Cheyenne in south central Montana east of the Crow reservation.

Dull Knife spent his remaining years, embittered and grieving, in the hills of southern Montana. Among the dead he had left behind at Fort Robinson were two daughters and a son, bringing the total of his loved ones lost in a single year to a wife, three sons, and two daughters. Dull Knife died in 1883 at his son Bull Hump's home. In 1917 Cheyenne historian George Bird Grinnell had his remains and those of Little Wolf reinterred in the cemetery at Lame Deer, where they are today.

SOURCES:

The Dull Knife Symposium, edited by John D. McDermott, Fort Phil Kearny/Bozeman Trail Association, 1989.

Grinnell, George Bird, *The Fighting Cheyennes,* second edition, University of Oklahoma Press, 1956.

Powell, Peter J., *Sweet Medicine,* two volumes, Norman, University of Oklahoma Press, 1969.

Sandoz, Mari, *Cheyenne Autumn,* Hastings House, 1953.

Stands In Timber, John, and Margot Liberty, *Cheyenne Memories,* New Haven, Yale University Press, 1967.

—Sketch by John D. McDermott

Gabriel Dumont
1837(?)-1906
Métis tribal leader

Gabriel Dumont was a Métis buffalo hunter and military leader. During the mid- to late nineteenth century the Métis, natives of mixed French and Indian descent, roamed the Canadian prairie hunting buffalo. Their culture, a combination of Indian and French-Canadian traditions, can be considered the only one truly indigenous to Canada. Dumont and the Métis played a major role in the 1885 Northwest Rebellion, led by Louis Riel. Although greatly outnumbered, Dumont led a band of no more than three hundred Métis warriors and Indian allies against the Canadian militia and the North West Mounted Police on the Saskatchewan prairie. After the Métis were defeated at Batoche in May 1885, Dumont fled to Montana, where he remained for many years before returning to Saskatchewan.

Dumont was born in 1837 or 1838 in what is now Winnipeg, Manitoba. He was the fourth of 11 children—five girls and six boys—of Isidore Dumont and Louise Laframboise. Isidore, the head of the Dumont band, had inherited the position from his father Jean Baptiste Dumont, who had come west from Québec in the 1790s and married a Sarcee Indian woman. As a Métis leader, Isidore is famous for a peace treaty he negotiated with the Sioux. As a child Dumont became proficient with bow and arrow. His uncle gave him his first gun before he was ten, and Dumont became a skilled marksman. He fired his first shot in a battle against the Sioux when he was only 12 years old.

By the time he was 25, Dumont had been elected chief of the buffalo hunt, with about 300 Métis followers. Besides being a gifted leader, Dumont was an expert horse breaker, canoeist, camp doctor, and unlike most Métis, a swimmer. He also operated a ferry on the South Saskatchewan River at the place which came to be known as Gabriel's Crossing. He ran a store, farmed a small plot of land and organized Métis labor crews, contracting for the construction of roads, trails, mail stations, and telegraph lines. Although illiterate, Dumont spoke perhaps as many as six Indian languages as well as French. His knowledge of Indian languages and cultures made him valuable as an interpreter. Dumont also had the arcane ability to "call" buffalo into a trap. As chief on the buffalo hunts he was a disciplinarian, allowing no violations of the Métis hunting code. He enjoyed horse racing, gambling, billiards, and drinking with his comrades, and he was known for a great sense of humor. Generous to a fault, he donated numerous buffalo to the poorer families in his camp. His wife Madeleine Welkey, whom he married in 1858, was the daughter of a Scottish trader and his Indian wife. Madeleine taught school at Batoche and accompanied her husband during the rebellion. She died of tuberculosis shortly after fleeing with Dumont to Montana in 1885. The couple had no children.

Métis Buffalo Hunts

The Métis reached their zenith prior to the demise of the North American buffalo. During that period, almost 3,000 Métis hunters, their families, and their Roman Catholic priests ranged over the Canadian, Montana, and Dakota prairies searching for herds of buffalo. These expeditions were complicated financial enterprises and the economic backbone of Métis society. Although the Métis did kill buffalo for their hides, it was pemmican, an essential part of the transcontinental fur trade, that drove the campaigns. Pemmican is a combination of shredded, dried buffalo meat, hot tallow or buffalo fat, marrow fat, and when available, berries. This mixture, while still hot, was poured into buffalo-hide bags capable of holding 100 pounds; the bags were then compressed as they cooled and sewn shut. Easy to transport and capable of lasting for years, pemmican could be eaten cold or heated and served as a stew. The Métis hunters transported their buffalo hides, meat, and bags of pemmican on stable, two wheeled, Red River Carts. These small, light, yet sturdy wooden carts with tall wheels, drawn by a single ox or horse, were capable of carrying loads of up to 900 pounds. With their wheels removed the carts could be turned into crude boats for crossing Saskatchewan's deep and treacherous rivers. Rolling across the prairie, accompanied by the shriek of their wooden axles, the carts could be heard for miles, announcing the coming of the Métis.

Métis buffalo hunts ware highly organized affairs, requiring firm, intelligent leadership. Governed by custom and tradition, the hunters elected officers to a general council, one of whom was in turn appointed to be chief of the hunt. It was a great tribute to Dumont's organizational and leadership skills that he was first named chief of the hunt when he was only 25. The chief commanded the officers, who maintained order and enforced the hunt's regulations. Leading expeditions of two to 300 hunters and their families was a difficult task, but Dumont excelled at it. His reputation as a chief led to his being elected leader of a local council set up by the Métis in 1873. This council petitioned the Canadian government for recognition of their territorial claims as had been awarded to the Manitoba Métis in 1870. The petition reflected the Métis' concerned reaction to an influx of white Protestant settlers encroaching on their Saskatchewan territory.

Recruits Louis Riel

By 1884 the Canadian government had still not addressed the Métis' demands to stem the tide of migration, and settlers continued flooding into Saskatchewan. That same year, Dumont and three other Métis traveled to Montana to ask Louis Riel to come to Saskatchewan and lead a rebellion. Previously, Riel had led the Manitoba Métis in a campaign which culminated in the Canadian government's recognition of the tribe in 1870, but he was a different man in 1884. After leading the fight in Manitoba, Riel suffered a mental collapse, spending time in Quebec insane asylums where he had been diagnosed as suffering from delusions of grandeur. He had also become a fanatical Roman Catholic, believing himself to be a new prophet. By the early 1880s he had moved to Montana, started a family, and was teaching school. Riel believed the arrival of four Métis horsemen at his doorstep was a sign from God that it was his destiny to lead the rebellion.

Upon arriving in Saskatchewan, Riel became the leader of a provisional government with Dumont serving as its adjutant general. Dumont's loyalty to Riel was unconditional; he rarely challenged Riel's decisions, even after Riel began interfering in military matters. After Riel's attempts to negotiate a settlement with the Canadian government failed, violence broke out in Saskatchewan. In March 1885, at the Battle of Duck Lake, Dumont led the Métis in a guerilla style confrontation with a detachment of Mounted Police and civilian volunteers, soundly defeating them. While the Métis suffered few casualties, they killed or wounded 25 percent of the Canadian force. However, one of the few Métis killed at the battle was Dumont's brother Isidore. In April the Métis and their Indian allies ware taken by surprise at the Battle of Fish Creek. Major General Frederick D. Middleton, commander of the Canadian militia, cornered Dumont and his men until 80 Métis from Batoche led by Dumont's brother Edouard arrived to fortify the beleaguered warriors. After inflicting minor casualties on the Canadians, the Métis withdrew to safety. However, the end for the Métis came one month later at their village of Batoche.

Batoche, located on the South Saskatchewan River between the present day cities of Prince Albert and Saskatoon, was the center of Métis society. The Saskatchewan River Valley, home to the buffalo and Indians for centuries, had been occupied by Métis hunters since the late 1860s. In May 1885, at the Battle of Batoche, Dumont led less than 300 Métis and other Indian allies, low on ammunition, against Middleton's 800 troops, armed with cannon and a Gatling gun. The Métis steadfastly defended Batoche from rifle pits along the edge of the bush surrounding the village, holding off the Canadians for three days. Although Dumont wanted to wage a guerilla attack on the Canadians using the hit-and-run tactics which had proved successful at Duck Lake, Riel insisted on defending Batoche by holding their present position. After running out of ammunition, having resorted to loading their rifles with nails and stones, the Métis surrendered on May 12, 1885. Both Riel and Dumont escaped.

After fleeing Batoche, Dumont searched for Riel among the scattered fugitives of the battle. He found Métis women and children everywhere, hidden in the brush and in caves carved into the coulees. In one of the caves he found Riel's wife and two children, but did not find Louis. He discovered that Riel had already surrendered to General Middleton. Refusing to surrender himself, Dumont rode 600 circuitous miles, mostly at night, hiding during the day in canyons or in Indian or Métis camps. After two weeks of successfully evading hundreds of militiamen and police, Dumont reached Montana.

While in exile in Montana, Dumont began to plot an elaborate rescue for the captured leader of the Métis rebellion. However, before he found the opportunity to implement his plan, Riel was convicted of treason and hanged in Regina, Saskatchewan, on November 16, 1885. Dumont remained in Montana for several years after Riel's execution, traveling with William "Buffalo Bill" Cody's Wild West Show. He was billed as the "Hero of the Halfbreed Rebellion," and using his rifle "Le Petit," he showcased his marksmanship to admiring audiences. Although he was no longer a young man, Dumont also gave exhibitions of his riding skills for the Wild West Show. The Canadian government granted Dumont pardon in 1886, but he continued to travel with the show for several more years before returning to Saskatchewan in 1893. Dumont's travels during this period took him from French-speaking communities in the northeastern United States, to Paris, France, where he told audiences his story of the Métis rebellion; he also dictated two memoirs of the conflict. Dumont died at Batoche in 1906 and is buried not far from Gabriel's Crossing, near the South Saskatchewan River.

SOURCES:

Dumont, Gabriel, *Gabriel Dumont Speaks,* translated by Michael Barnholden, Vancouver, Talonbooks, 1993.

Harrison, Julia D., *Métis: People between Two Worlds,* Vancouver, Douglas & McIntyre, 1985; 43-47.

Howard, Joseph Kinsey, *Strange Empire: A Narrative of the Northwest,* Westport, Connecticut, Greenwood Press, 1974.

Native North American Almanac, edited by Duane Champagne, Detroit, Gale Research, 1994; 1049-1050.

Waldman, Carl, *Who Was Who in Native American History,* New York, Facts On File, 1990; 106-107.

—Sketch by Michael F. Turek

Charles Alexander Eastman
1858-1939
Santee Sioux writer and physician

Also known as Hakadah ["The Pitiful Last"] and Ohiyesa ["The Winner"]

Born near Redwood Falls, Minnesota, of mixed Santee Sioux and white parentage, Charles Eastman was much influenced in his distinguished career as a writer, physician, and Indian spokesman by two of the last bloody Indian-white conflicts on the North American prairies and plains. He published two autobiographical accounts of his youth—*Indian Boyhood* and *From the Deep Woods to Civilization*—which were widely credited with raising white awareness of Indian issues.

His parents were Jacob Eastman ["Many Lightnings"], a Wahpeton Sioux, and Mary Nancy Eastman, a mixed-blood Sioux who died when he was a baby. His maternal grandfather was artist Seth Eastman. The youngest of five children, and given the name Hakadah ["The Pitiful Last"] because of his mother's early death, Eastman fled with his family from Minnesota to British Columbia following the Sioux Indian Uprising of 1862. Ten years later, after thorough training as a hunter and warrior, he was reclaimed by his father, who had been in prison during most of that time for his part in the uprising.

At his father's insistence, Eastman enrolled in the Flandreau Indian School and thus was abruptly introduced into an alien society that he would struggle to understand for the rest of his life. Eastman went on to study at Beloit College, Knox College, Dartmouth College (where he earned a bachelor's degree in 1887), and Boston University (where he received his doctorate in 1890). In his position as government physician at Pine Ridge Agency in South Dakota, he treated the survivors of the Wounded Knee Massacre. There he also met—and the next year married—Elaine Goodale, a poet, educator, and reformer.

A succession of positions followed with the YMCA and the Bureau of Indian Affairs (BIA), and he became much in demand in America and England throughout his life as an authority on Indian concerns. With his wife's assistance, Eastman began his career as a published author in 1893 with a series called "Recollections of the Wild Life" in *St. Nicholas* magazine. Over the next 27 years he gained increasing fame as America's distinguished Indian writer

with many more articles and ten books, one of them written jointly with his wife Elaine. In addition to collaborating as writers, the couple produced six children. In 1933, Eastman was recognized by the Indian Council Fire, a national organization, with its first award for "most distinguished achievement by an American Indian."

Throughout his life, Eastman's reputation as a writer, speaker, and advocate of Indian rights rested largely on the fact that he had made the dramatic transition from the life of a traditional Sioux Indian in the wilds of Canada to the drawing rooms and lecture halls of white America. As an articulate and accomplished physician, with a dynamic wife who spoke Lakota like a native, Eastman amazed many auditors and readers. Even some congressmen were startled, as Rob Eshman points out in the *Dartmouth Alumni* magazine. From 1897 to 1900, Eastman was a lobbyist for the Santee Sioux Tribe in Washington, D.C. Following one presentation before a Congressional committee, the only responses from the congressmen were, "Where did you go to school? Why are there not more Indians like you?"

Begins Literary Career with Autobiography

Eastman's literary career began in earnest in 1902 with the publication of *Indian Boyhood*. He had previously published a handful of short pieces, mostly in *Red Man* and *St. Nicholas* magazines, but this autobiography—dedicated to his son Ohiyesa the second—appealed to a wide non-Indian public with its depiction of "the freest life in the world," as Eastman called it. It consists of his earliest recollections from childhood; tributes to Uncheedah, his paternal grandmother who reared him, and to Mysterious Medicine, his uncle who taught him the lore of a life lived close to nature; and a moving conclusion that recounts the return of his father, just released from the federal penitentiary at Davenport, Iowa.

Of his grandmother, Eastman wrote, she "was a wonder to the young maidens of the tribe." Although she was 60 years old, she cared for Eastman as if he were her own child. "Every little attention that is due to a loved child she performed with much skill and devotion. She made all my scanty garments and my tiny moccasins with a great deal of taste. It was said by all that I could not have had more attention had my mother been living." For his uncle, his father's brother, Eastman had the greatest admiration. He characterized the warrior as "a father to me for ten years of my life," a teacher with infinite patience who knew his subject—nature—thoroughly. Said Eastman, "Nothing irritated him more than to hear some natural fact misrepresented. I have often thought that with education he might have made a Darwin or an Agassiz." But Mysterious Medicine also realized that the things he knew and taught would soon lose their value. After telling Eastman the story of one of his most exciting hunting adventures, he concluded: "But all this life is fast disappearing, and the world is becoming different."

The world became shockingly different for Eastman when his father sought him out in Canada in 1873 and returned him to the United States, to Flandreau, Dakota Territory, where a group of Santees lived as homesteaders among the whites. "Here," wrote Eastman, "my wild life came to an end, and my school days began." It was an ironic reunion and return, for Eastman had thought his father dead, had pledged himself to take revenge upon the whites for that death, and now would be living among them with his father and adopting their ways.

Eastman would go on to publish the sequel to *Indian Boyhood* in 1916, when *From the Deep Woods to Civilization* appeared. In it, as Raymond Wilson concludes in *Ohiyesa: Charles Eastman, Santee Sioux,* Eastman presents a more realistic picture of the white world, "openly attacking the evils of white society and lamenting the sorrows Indians encountered as a result of cultural contact." In particular, his versions of the controversies in which he was embroiled at Pine Ridge and later at Crow Creek are clearly presented in a one-sided way. In addition, the pervasive tone of innocence in *Indian Boyhood* is now replaced by one of frustration, expressed in its most ironic form by his comment on his years at Dartmouth College: "It was here that I had most of my savage gentleness and native refinement knocked out of me. I do not complain, for I know that I gained more than their equivalent." Above all, Eastman was profoundly depressed by the failure of Americans to practice the Christianity that they professed, so that the meek might inherit the earth and "the peacemakers receive high honor." Instead, he wrote in *From the Deep Woods to Civilization,* "When I reduce civilization to its lowest terms, it becomes a system of life based upon trade."

All told, Eastman wrote ten books, and they established him as a prominent voice for his people and a storyteller of historic significance. Other titles include *Red Hunters and the Animal People* (1904), stories and legends for youth; *Old Indian Days* (1907), divided into stories about warriors and women; *Smoky Day's Wigwam Evenings: Indian Stories Retold* (1910), written with his wife Elaine; *The Soul of the Indian* (1911), the most fully developed statement of his religious beliefs; and *The Indian Today: The Past and Future of the First American* (1915), a review of Indian history, contributions, and problems. Eastman's last book was *Indian Heroes and Great Chieftains* (1918), a collection of short biographies of Sioux leaders written for young people.

Throughout the years that Charles and Elaine Eastman lived together, she served as his editorial assistant in all of his writing. Although on occasion Eastman resented some of Elaine's rewriting, she seems to have been essential to his publishing success, for after their separation in 1921 he published nothing more. What he had done by then was to contribute substantially to a better understanding by whites of Indians in general and the Sioux in particular. For Sioux readers, Wilson explained, Eastman's books "provide a bridge to self-respect ... expressing their stories, beliefs, and customs in the language of White men." As a cultural bridge builder in the early twentieth century, Eastman was unequaled.

Serves Sioux People in Many Capacities

Throughout his career as a writer, Eastman also served his people and the larger society in a variety of roles. His training as a physician he used on the Pine Ridge Reservation (1890-1893), in private practice in St. Paul, Minnesota (1894-1897), and at Crow Creek Reservation in South Dakota (1900-1903). While in St. Paul he began to work for the YMCA, organizing chapters around the country, and from 1897 to 1900 he lobbied for the Santee Sioux. For seven years (1903-1909) Eastman was engaged, at author Hamlin Garland's urging, in a BIA project to re-name the Sioux, giving them legal names in order to protect their interests. In 1910 he began a lifelong association with the Boy Scouts of America, and from 1914 to 1925 he and Elaine operated a girls' camp near Munsonville, New Hampshire. In 1923 he entered the Indian service for the last time, working until 1925 as an Indian inspector on and off the reservations. The last years of his life, until his death in 1939, Eastman devoted principally to lecturing.

In the last analysis, Charles Eastman's most important contribution to American letters is as a writer of autobiography and as a preserver of Sioux Indian legends, myths, and history. As autobiography, his *Indian Boyhood* is without equal. As William Bloodworth concludes in *Where the West Begins,* nearly all other life stories by his contemporaries consist of "coup stories, stories that explain an individual's name, and narrative elements in oratory and prophecy." Moreover, Eastman is the most prolific teller of Sioux Indian myths and legends. In her essay for *American Indian Quarterly,* Anna Lee Stensland concludes that despite our uncertainty over which stories are tribal legends and which are Eastman's own creations, and to what degree Eastman's Christianity led him to modify incompatible Indian concepts, Eastman is still the George Bird Grinnell and Stith Thompson of his people: "In the prolific writings of Charles Eastman there is probably more Sioux legend, myth, and history than is recorded any place else."

SELECTED WRITINGS BY EASTMAN:

Indian Boyhood, New York, McClure, Phillips & Co., 1902.
Red Hunters and the Animal People, New York, Harper & Brothers, 1904.
Old Indian Days, New York, McClure Company, 1907.
Wigwam Evenings; Sioux Folk Tales Retold by Charles A. Eastman (Ohiyesa) and Elaine Goodale Eastman, Boston, Little, Brown, 1909.
With Elaine Goodale Eastman, *Smoky Day's Wigwam Evenings; Indian Stories Retold,* Boston, Little, Brown, 1910.

The Soul of the Indian; An Interpretation, Boston, Houghton Mifflin, 1911.

Indian Child Life, Boston, Little, Brown, 1913.

Indian Scout Talks; A Guide for Boy Scouts and Campfire Girls, Boston, Little, Brown, 1914.

The Indian To-day; The Past and Future of the First American, Garden City, New York, Doubleday, 1915.

From the Deep Woods to Civilization; Chapters in the Autobiography of an Indian, Boston, Little, Brown, 1916.

Indian Heroes and Great Chieftains, Boston, Little, Brown, 1918.

SOURCES:

Books

Alexander, Ruth, "Building a Cultural Bridge: Elaine and Charles Eastman," in *South Dakota Leaders,* edited by Herbert T. Hoover and Larry J. Zimmerman, Vermillion, University of South Dakota Press, 1989; 355-66.

Americanizing the American Indians: Writings by the "Friends of the Indian," 1880-1900, edited by Francis Paul Prucha, Cambridge, Harvard University Press, 1973.

Bloodworth, William, "Neihardt, Momaday, and the Art of Indian Autobiography," in *Where the West Begins,* edited by Arthur R. Huseboe and William Geyer, Sioux Falls, South Dakota, Center for Western Studies Press, 1978; 152-60.

Copeland, Marion W., *Charles Alexander Eastman,* Boise State University Western Writers Series, 1978.

Eastman, Elaine Goodale, *Pratt, The Red Man Moses,* Norman, University of Oklahoma Press, 1935.

Hassrick, Royal B., *The Sioux: Life and Customs of a Warrior Society,* Norman, University of Oklahoma Press, 1964.

Meyer, Roy W., *History of the Santee Sioux: United States Indian Policy on Trial,* Lincoln, University of Nebraska Press, 1967.

Mooney, James, *The Ghost-Dance Religion and the Sioux Outbreak of 1890,* Chicago, University of Chicago Press, 1965.

Riggs, Stephen R., *Mary and I: Forty Years with the Sioux,* Chicago, W. G. Holmes, 1880.

Sister to the Sioux: The Memoirs of Elaine Goodale Eastman, 1885-91, edited by Kay Graber, Lincoln, University of Nebraska Press, 1978.

Utley, Robert M., *The Last Days of the Sioux Nation,* New Haven, Yale University Press, 1963.

Wilson, Raymond, *Ohiyesa: Charles Eastman, Santee Sioux,* Urbana, University of Illinois Press, 1983.

Periodicals

Alexander, Ruth, "Finding Oneself through a Cause: Elaine Goodale Eastman and Indian Reform in the 1880s," *South Dakota History,* 22:1, spring 1992; 1-37.

Eastman, Charles Alexander (Ohiyesa), "A Canoe Trip among the Northern Ojibways," *The Red Man* 3, February 1911; 236-244.

Eastman, Charles, "Recollections of the Wild Life," *St. Nicholas: An Illustrated Magazine for Young Folks,* 21, December 1893-May 1894.

Eastman, Charles, "Report on Sacajawea," *Annals of Wyoming,* 13, July 1941; 187-194.

Eastman, Elaine Goodale, "All the Days of My Life," *South Dakota Historical Review,* 2, July 1937; 171-184.

Eshman, Rob, "The Ghost Dance and Wounded Knee Massacre of 1890-91," *Nebraska History* 26, January 1945; 26-42.

Eshman, Rob, "Stranger in the Land," *Dartmouth Alumni,* January/February 1981; 20-23.

Fowler, Herbert B., "Ohiyesa, The First Sioux M.D.," *Association of American Indian Physicians Newsletter,* 4, April 1976; 1, 6.

Holm, Tom, "American Indian Intellectuals and the Continuity of Tribal Ideals," *Book Forum,* 5:3, 1981; 349-356.

Johnson, Stanley Edwards, "The Indian Ohiyesa," *Dartmouth Alumni,* June 1929; 521-523.

Milroy, Thomas W., "A Physician by the Name of Ohiyesa: Charles Alexander Eastman, M.D.," *Minnesota Medicine,* 5, July 1971; 569-572.

Oandasan, William, "A Cross-Disciplinary Note on Charles Eastman (Santee Sioux)," *American Indian Culture and Research Journal,* 7:2, 1983; 75-78.

Stensland, Anna Lee, "Charles Alexander Eastman: Sioux Storyteller and Historian," *American Indian Quarterly,* 3, 1977; 199-207.

—*Sketch by Arthur R. Huseboe*

John E. Echohawk
1945-
Pawnee attorney and rights activist

John E. Echohawk was the first graduate of a special law program for Native Americans at the University of New Mexico; and he has become one of the most influential lawyers in the United States and executive director of the Native American Rights Fund (NARF). Involved in cases supporting Indian rights all over the country, Echohawk has won numerous awards for his service over the years.

Echohawk was born in Albuquerque, New Mexico, on August 11, 1945. He received his bachelor's degree in pre-law in 1967 at the University of New Mexico, and completed his law degree there in 1970. Having received the Reginald Heber Smith Community Lawyer fellowship upon graduation, he worked with the California Indian Legal Services program in Sacramento. He then joined the NARF as staff attorney. He served as deputy director from 1972 to 1973, as director from 1973 to 1975, and as vice executive

John E. Echohawk

director from 1975 to 1977, before becoming executive director of the organization in 1977.

NARF, a national non-profit organization centered in Boulder, Colorado, acts as counsel in major legal cases for Indian tribes. Since its formation in 1970, NARF has successfully represented Indian tribes and individuals in nearly every state in the nation. The hundreds of cases have spanned every area and issue in the field of Indian law. The original steering committee (later called the NARF Board of Directors) defined five priority areas for its work: the preservation of tribal existence; the protection of tribal natural resources; the promotion of human rights; the accountability of governments to Native Americans; and the development of Indian law. One of the early goals of the NARF was the development of a central clearinghouse for Indian legal materials. To accomplish this goal, NARF set up the National Indian Law Library, the only law library specializing in Indian legal materials and resources.

As a co-founder and director of NARF, Echohawk was deeply involved in those activities. Because of his efforts, he was named one of "the 100 most influential lawyers" by the *National Law Journal* in 1994. The publication described Echohawk as "a major power in the Native American rights movement."

Legal Victories

Echohawk was involved in several of NARF's legal battles. He has been a leading litigator in cases involving tribal sovereignty issues and protection of tribal natural resources. In 1989, he won a case for the Catawba tribe of South Carolina which enabled the tribe to recover 144,000 acres of land around Rock Hill. In 1993, Congress passed a Catawba tribal land claim settlement allowing restoration of the tribe and $80 million to $90 million for land acquisition, economic development, and education.

One of the significant cases Echohawk worked on in 1991 was on behalf of the Pawnee tribe of Oklahoma. He successfully blocked the Nebraska State Historical Society's attempts to avoid compliance with the state's public records law. This led to the return of burial remains and associated items to the Pawnee tribe as proscribed by the Reburial Act of 1989.

In 1992, Echohawk won a federal district court decision in North Dakota to uphold the civil jurisdiction of tribal courts on tribal lands, even in personal injury actions involving non-Native Americans. That same year, he also won recognition for the tribal status of the San Juan Southern Paiute tribe. Also in 1992, as co-counsel, he won settlement with the state of Montana recognizing rights to 90,000 acre-feet of water for the Northern Cheyenne tribe.

Outside of NARF, Echohawk has actively worked toward creating opportunities for Indian youth. He has served on the board of directors of the American Indian Resources Institute, the Association on American Indian Affairs, the National Committee for Responsive Philanthropy, the Independent Sector, the Natural Resources Defense Council, and the National Center for American Indian Enterprise Development.

In 1994, Echohawk campaigned in a legislative battle for American Indian religious freedom. As he stated in Earth Journal, "We can only regret the enormous loss of our cultural and environmental heritage as a result of government oppression of tribal religious beliefs and practices. The challenge to our generation, however, is to preserve what little is left for present and future generations."

Echohawk also served on President Bill Clinton's transition team for the Department of the Interior. He has received the President's Indian Service Award from the National Congress of American Indians and a Distinguished Service Award from the Americans for Indian Opportunity. In 1992, the NARF was co-recipient of the Carter-Menil Human Rights Foundation Prize in recognition of work on behalf of Native Americans.

SOURCES:

Books

Biographical Dictionary of Indians of the Americas, Newport Beach, California, 1983; 158.

Indians of Today, edited by Marion E. Gridley, Chicago, ICFP, 1971; 37.

Native North American Almanac, edited by Duane Champagne, Detroit, Gale Research, 1994; 1052.

Periodicals

Echohawk, John E., "Our People—Native Americans: Then and Now", *Earth Journal,* January 1994; 38-43.
NARF Legal Review, summer 1992; 1-15.
National Law Journal, April 4, 1994; C7.

—Sketch by Karen P. Zimmerman

Walter R. Echo-Hawk
1948-
Pawnee attorney

Walter R. Echo-Hawk

Walter Echo-Hawk is a prominent attorney known for his eloquent defense of Native American rights, particularly those related to burial and religious freedom. He has been on the staff of the Native American Rights Fund (NARF), the largest public interest Indian rights law firm in the country, since receiving his law degree. He has served as co-director of NARF's American Indian Religious Freedom Project and director of the Indian Corrections Project. He is a justice on the Pawnee tribe's Supreme Court. As an attorney, Echo-Hawk has appeared before the U.S. Supreme Court, the Supreme Court of Colorado, and several courts of appeals. His cases have involved religious freedom of American Indians, prisoner rights, water rights, treaty rights, and reburial rights, and he has authored numerous publications regarding those issues.

Echo-Hawk was born on the Pawnee Reservation near Pawnee, Oklahoma, on June 23, 1948. He received an undergraduate degree in political science from Oklahoma State University in 1970 and a law degree from the University of New Mexico in 1973, following the example of his cousin, John Echohawk. Echo-Hawk joined the NARF following graduation and soon became involved in protecting the rights of deceased Native Americans.

From 1989 to 1990, for example, Echo-Hawk pursued the return of Indian remains and burial offerings to native groups. He successfully negotiated agreements with archaeologists and museum directors, preferring persuasion to litigation. Pawnee burial pits in Kansas, formerly open to public viewing, were closed and covered. Furthermore, the Nebraska legislature passed a law in 1989 requiring the Nebraska State Historical Society to return Indian remains and burial offerings to the tribe of origin upon request. Also in 1989, the Smithsonian Institution eased requirements on releasing Native American remains to tribal members through provisions of the National Museum of the American Indian Act. Several other museums voluntarily agreed to return remains and artifacts. In 1990, decades of struggle culminated in passage of the Native American Graves Protection and Repatriation Act (NAGPRA), a landmark human rights law for Native people. NAGPRA provides nationwide standards for the return of Native American remains and certain protected materials from federal agencies and federally funded institutions.

Echo-Hawk has been a leading voice in all of these cases, believing strongly that the dead deserve to rest in peace. As he explained in an interview with Vicki Quade in *Human Rights,* "The issue boils down to a matter of consent." In a heated debate, Echo-Hawk argued that scientific examination of remains should not be done without consent of tribal people, and that the results of scientific examination have never been proven beneficial to tribal people. His publication with Jack F. Trope in *Arizona State Law* Journal summarizes the legislative history of the reburial and repatriation issue.

Closely related to the issue of treatment of the dead is the issue of religious freedom. Echo-Hawk has worked toward federal legislation to protect Native American religious freedom, specifically for revision of the 1978 American Indian Religious Freedom Act. Echo-Hawk argues that the Supreme Court decisions in the *Lyng* case of 1988 and the *Smith* case of 1990 have denied Native Americans the basic First Amendment right of Freedom of Religion, and that the religious freedom of all Americans has been threatened.

Echo-Hawk and his wife Pauline, a Yakima from Washington state, live near Boulder, Colorado, and have three children: Amy, Walter Jr., and Anthony. In 1991 Echo-Hawk was awarded the Civil Liberties Award from the American Civil Liberties Union of Oregon for significant contributions to the cause of individual freedom. He is also an accomplished artist: an example of his painting is used as an illustration in his book *Battlefields and Burial Grounds.*

WRITINGS BY ECHO-HAWK:

(With Dan. L. Monroe), "Deft Deliberations," *Museum News*, 70:4, 1991; 55-58.

(With Jack F. Trope), "The Native American Graves Protection and Repatriation Act: Background and Legislative History," *Arizona State Law Journal*, 24:1, spring 1992; 35-77.

(Guest editor of special edition) "Repatriation of American Indian Remains," *American Indian Culture and Research Journal*, 16:2, 1992; 1-7.

"Native American Religious Liberty: Five Hundred Years after Columbus," *American Indian Culture and Research Journal*, 17:3, 1993; 33-52.

(With Roger C. Echo-Hawk), *Battlefields and Burial Grounds: The Indian Struggle to Protect Ancestral Graves in the United States,* Minneapolis, Lerner Publications, 1994.

"Loopholes in Religious Liberty," *Cultural Survival Quarterly,* 17:4, 1994; 62-65.

SOURCES:

Books

Native North American Almanac, edited by Duane Champagne, Detroit, Gale Research, 1994; 1051-1052.

Periodicals

Brower, Montgomery, and Conan Putnam, "Walter Echo-Hawk Fights for His People's Right to Rest in Peace—Not in Museums," *People Weekly,* 32, September 4, 1989; 42-44.

NARF Legal Review, summer 1992; 15.

Quade, Vicki, "Who Owns the Past? Interview with Walter Echo-Hawk," *Human Rights,* 16:3, winter 1989-1990; 24-29, 53-55.

—Sketch by Karen P. Zimmerman

Charles Edenshaw
1839-1920
Haida artist and tribal leader
Also known as Tahayren ["Noise in the House"] and Nungkwigetklahls ["They Gave Ten Potlatches for Him"]

A member of the Eagle clan, Charles Edenshaw was a prominent Haida artist and tribal leader. His carvings, for which he is best known, were made of wood, silver, gold, copper, and argillite (a black stone indigenous to the Queen Charlotte Islands in British Columbia). Edenshaw was also a skilled illustrator and painter.

Born Tahayren ["Noise in the House"] in the village of Skidegate on Graham Island, British Columbia, he was the nephew of Eda'nsa (Albert Edward Edenshaw), the famous chief of the Sta Stas Eagle clan of Graham Island. It is likely that he learned how to carve from this uncle, as carving was passed from generation to generation within the Haida tribe, who were renowned for their expertise in woodcarvings. During his adolescence, Edenshaw became known among his people as Nungkwigetklahls ["They Gave Ten Potlaches for Him"], perhaps in recognition of his repeated participation in potlaches, a traditional Haida ceremony and feast involving the giving of food and goods.

When Edenshaw came of age, he moved to Masset, a trading community to the north and the center of Anglican activity during that time. There, Edenshaw married Si't kwuns ["Red Moon"], a member of the Raven clan who later chose Isabella as her Christian name. They had a traditional Haida wedding; but, after their conversion to Christianity sometime in the mid-1880s, they had a formal western marriage ceremony in the Anglican Church in 1885.

Becomes Tribal Leader

Upon the death of his uncle in 1894, Edenshaw was elected chief by the common assent of his tribe, partly out of respect for his lineage, but also because of his artistic talents, which were highly prized within the Haida community. Villages under Edenshaw's leadership most likely included Yatza, a village on Graham Island founded by his uncle around 1870, and Kiusta, an ancient Eagle town also on Graham Island.

Accounts of Edenshaw describe him as an individual deeply concerned for his family, his community, his homeland, and his culture. He was a consultant for government officials, scientists, and scholars throughout his life, providing significant information about the plant and animal life of the Queen Charlotte Islands as well as the Haida culture. Christianity was also important to him as was evident in his role as one of the key builders and lay ministers of the Anglican Church in Masset.

Influenced by Haida Heritage

The Haida were well-known among the Pacific coastal cultures for their woodcarvings, specifically their totem poles and canoes. It was not until the end of the nineteenth century, however, that the carving of canoes and totem poles evolved into carving for the sake of art. Many historians attribute this shift to acculturation and a population decrease in the tribe, due to a smallpox epidemic in the mid-nineteenth century. According to Florence Davidson, Edenshaw's daughter, he demonstrated artistic talent at an early age. As he matured, Edenshaw's carvings, noted for their smooth lines and fine detail, grew in popularity, and he became one of the first professional Haida carvers.

The majority of Edenshaw's carvings were made between 1870 and 1910. Their content was greatly influenced by his Haida upbringing; the mythology of the raven, eagle, beaver, grizzly, killer whale, and salmon, as well many others stories, provided inspiration for his work. Like many of his contemporaries and predecessors, Edenshaw never signed his works because he felt that the art should speak for itself. He frequently met with anthropologists and art collectors, and so provided others with insight into Haida culture and art; Edenshaw functioned as an interpreter of Haida paintings, boxes, spoons, and gambling sticks, for Franz Boas' book *Primitive Art* (1955). Many of his carvings, including model totem poles, drawings, and sketches, were collected by museums and art patrons.

SOURCES:

Books

Blackman, Margaret, *During My Time: Florence Edenshaw—A Haida Woman,* Seattle, University of Washington Press, 1982.

Boas, Franz, *Primitive Art,* New York, Dover Publications, 1955.

Drew, Leslie, *Haida: Their Art and Culture,* Surrey, British Columbia, Hancock House, 1982.

Halpin, Marjorie, *Totem Poles: An Illustrated Guide,* Vancouver, University of British Columbia Press, 1981.

Native North American Almanac, edited by Duane Champagne, Detroit, Gale Research, 1994; 1053.

Periodicals

Appleton, F. M., "Life and Art of Charlie Edenshaw," *Canadian Geographic Journal,* July 1970; 20-25.

—*Sketch by Fred White*

Edwards, Bronwen Elizabeth
See Rose, Wendy

Louise Erdrich
1954-
Chippewa novelist and poet
Also known as Milou North (joint pseudonym with Michael Anthony Dorris)

Louise Erdrich is known for her moving and often humorous portrayals of Chippewa life in North Dakota in poetry and prose. In her verse and in novels such as *Tracks, Bingo Palace,* and *The Beet Queen,* she draws on her years in North Dakota and on her German and Chippewa heritage to portray the great endurance of women and Native Americans in twentieth-century America. Erdrich's first collection of stories, published as *Love Medicine,* won a National Book Critics Circle Award in 1984.

Karen Louise Erdrich was born July 6, 1954, in Little Falls, Minnesota, and grew up in Wahpeton, North Dakota, a town on the border of Minnesota. Her father, Ralph Louis, was a teacher with the Bureau of Indian Affairs (BIA) at Wahpeton, and her mother, Rita Joanne Gourneau, was an employee of the BIA at the Wahpeton Indian school. The family lived in employee housing at the school, and Erdrich attended public schools and spent a few years at St. Johns, a Catholic school. In an interview with Jan George in the *North Dakota Quarterly,* Erdrich noted that her experience with the Catholic church affected her profoundly: "Catholicism has always been important to me even though I am not a practicing Catholic now. The ritual is full of symbols, mysteries, and the unsaid. That affects a person always, once you know it as a child."

Erdrich's German heritage comes from her father, and her three-eighths Chippewa heritage comes from her mother. She often visited her mother's people at Turtle Mountain Reservation, situated near Belcourt, North Dakota, when she was growing up. Her grandfather, Pat Gourneau, served as tribal chairman at Turtle Mountain for many years. In an interview with Joseph Bruchac in *Survival This Way,* Erdrich described her grandfather as having "a real mixture of old time and church religion.... He would do pipe ceremonies for ordinations and things like that. He just had a grasp on both realities, in both religions.... He's kind of a legend in our family. He is funny, he's charming, he's interesting. He, for many years, was a very strong figure in my life. I guess I idolized him. A very intelligent man. He was a Wobbly and worked up and down the wheat fields in North Dakota and Kansas.... He did a lot of things in his life and was always very outspoken.... I always loved him and when you love someone you try to listen to them. Their voice then comes through." Erdrich's admiration for her grandfather can be seen in several of her complex male characters.

Parents Encourage Her to Become a Writer

As a child, Erdrich's parents encouraged her to write. Her father paid her a nickel per story, and her mother made little books with construction paper covers for Erdrich's stories. Her mother found out about the Native American program at Dartmouth and helped Erdrich apply in 1972; Erdrich was in the first class of women accepted at Dartmouth, which had been previously all male. Several grants and scholarships allowed her to attend Dartmouth, and Erdrich majored in English and creative writing, winning several writing awards. While in college, she discovered that poetry came easily to her. She decided to be a writer.

After her graduation in 1976, Erdrich went back to North Dakota, telling herself, as she related to Bruchac, that she "would sacrifice all to be a writer.... I took a lot of weird jobs which were good for the writing. I worked at anything I could get and just tried to keep going until I could support myself through writing or get some kind of grant. Just live off this or that as you go along. I think I turned out to be tremendously lucky." Back in North Dakota, she worked as a publications director of a small press distributor, and as a poet for the Poets in the Schools Program sponsored by the National Endowment for the Arts. She also worked on a film depicting the culture clash between the Sioux and Europeans in the 1800s for Mid-America Television.

Returning to the East, Erdrich received an M.F.A. in 1977 from Johns Hopkins University. While at Johns Hopkins, she began writing fiction. She then served as editor of the *Circle,* the Boston Indian Council newspaper. After a poetry reading she gave in 1980, Erdrich began a relationship with Michael Dorris, who had attended the reading and been interested in her and her work. Dorris, who is three-eighths Modoc, had come to Dartmouth to found and direct the Native American Studies Program. Soon afterward, Dorris left for New Zealand on an anthropology fellowship, and their relationship was put on hold until January 1981, when both returned to Dartmouth—he to resume his position in the Native American Studies Program and she as writer-in-residence. They were married in 1981, and Erdrich subsequently adopted Dorris' three Native American children, whom he had adopted and was raising by himself. They also have three children together. They live in Cornish, New Hampshire, where both Erdrich and Dorris devote themselves full time to their writing and their family.

First Novel Wins Major Literary Award

In collaboration with Dorris, Erdrich gathered the stories she had published between 1982 and 1984 and made them into a novel called *Love Medicine* in 1984. The story is told through the voices of half-a-dozen characters, as though to someone listening to community gossip. Erdrich used this technique in several of her novels to portray the complicated relationships of the characters, many of whom appear from novel to novel and whose genealogies have become the subjects of entire scholarly essays.

Love Medicine is set in on the Turtle Mountain Reservation in North Dakota. Taking place between 1934 to 1983, the novel presents the story of Lulu Lamartine and Marie Kashpaw. Marie is married to Nector Kashpaw, but Nector desperately loves Lulu, who has had numerous husbands and romances resulting in many children. After Nector's death by some ill-fated "love medicine," Lulu and Marie unite and become tribal elders. *Love Medicine* won the National Book Critics Circle Award for the best work of fiction of 1984. The opening story, "The World's Greatest Fisherman," won the $5,000 Nelson Algren Award in 1982. Erdrich later added some other stories to *Love Medicine* and published the new and expanded version in 1993.

In *Tracks,* Erdrich's second novel, set from 1912 to 1919, the story is told through Nanapush, an elderly trickster who is the last of his family and also the last to remember when his Indian nation was free to roam and hunt before allotment, and Pauline Puyat, a mixed-breed character whose Chippewa antecedents have been forgotten. She is so desperate to fit in that she renounces her Native American heritage to become an obsessed Catholic nun. Their stories revolve around a third character, Fleur Pillager, whose spiritual powers are seen by Nanapush as necessary to save the disintegrating Chippewa nation and by Pauline as evil and destructive. Erdrich's Catholic background is perhaps most strongly reflected in *Tracks,* which portrays the interaction of Native American spirituality and the views of the church.

The Beet Queen, published in 1986, is set in Argus, a town near the reservation. It takes place from 1932 to 1972 and explores Erdrich's German roots. Abandoned by her mother, Mary Adare comes to live with her cousin, Sita Koska, whose parents own the butcher shop. Mary becomes best friends with Sita's good friend, a mixed-blood girl, Celestine James. Celestine has a child by Mary Adare's brother, Karl Adare, and the spoiled child—the Beet Queen—becomes the center of attention. Fleur Pillager makes a brief appearance as an eccentric woman who heals Karl Adare after an accident.

Bingo Palace, the story of Lipsha Morrissey (the unacknowledged son of Lulu's son Gerry Nanapush and raised by Marie), not only brings together the families from the previous books but also looks toward the future. Lipsha's great-grandmother, Fleur Pillager, appears in the novel and causes him to think about how to balance his Chippewa heritage with the business interests of his Uncle Lyman Lamartine's plan to build a bingo palace on Fleur's property.

Collaborates with Dorris

Erdrich and Dorris collaborate on nearly all of their works. Each writes his or her own drafts after they discuss various aspects of the work, such as plot and character. They then carefully review the manuscript, publishing it only after they have agreed on every word. All of Erdrich's novels have been written in this way, as well as Dorris' *A Yellow Raft in Blue Water,* in 1987, and his nonfiction piece, *The Broken Cord: A Family's Ongoing Struggle with Fetal Alcohol Syndrome.* Erdrich and Dorris co-authored the novel *The Crown of Columbus,* 1991, in which the Native-American academic, Vivian Twostar, and her Euro-American academic lover, Roger Williams, search for a fabulous relic supposedly left by Christopher Columbus on his first landing in North America.

Erdrich has also published two books of poetry, *Jacklight,* in 1984, and *Baptism of Desire,* in 1989. *Jacklight* begins the strong theme about the relationships of men and women that runs through all of Erdrich's work. In sections such as "The Butcher's Wife" and "Old Man Potchiko," the collection explores her German and Native American heritages. The first section of *Baptism of Desire* relies heavily upon Erdrich's Catholic background, but is mediated by Native American views and focused on women's religious experience. Through all her work, Erdrich continues to provide a unique and loving perspective on what it is to be a person of mixed heritage facing the problems of Native American life today.

SELECTED WRITINGS BY ERDRICH:

Love Medicine, New York, Holt, 1984; expanded version, 1993.
Jacklight: Poems, New York, Holt, 1984.
The Beet Queen, New York, Holt, 1986.
Tracks, New York, Holt, 1988.
Baptism of Desire: Poems, New York, Harper & Row, 1989.
(With Michael Dorris) *Crown of Columbus,* New York, HarperCollins, 1991.
Bingo Palace, New York, HarperCollins, 1994.

SOURCES:

Books

Bruchac, Joseph, "Whatever Is Really Yours: An Interview with Louise Erdrich," in *Survival This Way: Interviews with American Indian Poets,* Tucson, Sun Tracks and University of Arizona Press, 1987; 73-86.
Coltelli, Laura, "Louise Erdrich and Michael Dorris," in *Winged Words: American Indian Writers Speak,* Lincoln, University of Nebraska Press, 1990; 40-52.
Ruoff, A. LaVonne, *American Indian Literatures: An Introduction, Bibliographic Review and Selected Bibliography,* New York, Modern Language Association, 1990; 84-88.
Ruoff, A. LaVonne, *Literatures of the American Indian,* New York, Chelsea, 1991.

Periodicals

Bonetti, Kay, "An Interview with Louise Erdrich and Michael Dorris," *Missouri Review,* 11, spring 1988; 79-99.
George, Jan, "Interview with Louise Erdrich," *North Dakota Quarterly,* 53, 1985; 240-246.
Howard, Jane, "Louise Erdrich," *Life,* April 1985; 27-34.

—Sketch by Annette Van Dyke

Gary Dale Farmer
1953-
Cayuga actor, producer, and activist

While pursuing a career in films as both an actor and producer, Gary Dale Farmer has dedicated much of his time toward the advancement of Native American projects in the entertainment industry, including film, television, and radio. To further the advancement of the Native American and general understanding of Native American culture, Farmer has actively engaged in promoting Native American media programming, stressing the importance of literacy, advocating the protection of the environment, and emphasizing the importance of Native American participation in community affairs.

On June 12, 1953, Gary Dale Farmer was born on the Six Nations Reserve in Ohswekan, Ontario, Canada, birthplace of Jay Silverheels, who portrayed Tonto in the "Lone Ranger" television series of the 1950s. Both members of the Iroquois Confederacy, Silverheels belonged to the Mohawk nation, and Farmer was a member of the Cayuga nation.

Active in Protecting the Environment

The original frontier of the Iroquois, who refer to themselves as Haudenosaunee ("the People of the Long House"), stretched all the way from Canada to the north, Pennsylvania to the south, the Atlantic Ocean to the east, and Ohio to the west. Farmer's people of the Cayuga nation dwelled toward the east of this expanse of land in New York state and Ontario. Most of the tribe dispersed widely throughout the region. Clean rivers and lakes flourished in the land of the Cayuga people, which was once abundant with woodland and wildlife. However, with the appearance of acid rain and other forms of pollution, environmental calamities began to endanger many species of plants. Concerned with the protection of the environment, Farmer has devoted much of his energy to eradicating factors contributing to pollution and mistreatment of the environment.

Protests Neglect to Cast Native Americans

Farmer has also been active in speaking against biases towards Native Americans in media projects. For example, Farmer voiced dissent against the casting of British actor Trevor Howard as the American Indian lead in *Windwalker* in 1980. A British actor in the role of an American Indian seemed contrary to the pro-Indian movement in Hollywood filmmaking. This role casting prompted Native Americans to believe that filmmakers had little confidence in their abilities and showed little appreciation for Native Americans and their culture.

Launches a Career in Acting

Farmer received his advanced education in New York state, first at Genesee Community College and later at Syracuse University. He trained for the theater at several private studios in Toronto, Ontario, Canada and worked steadily towards developing a career in acting. A sample of his theater performances were roles in such plays as *Guys and Dolls, History of the Village of the Small Hut* (first and second), *One Flew Over the Cuckoo's Nest,* and *Of Mice and Men.*

In 1988, Farmer received the "best actor" award at the American Indian Film Festival for his role as Philbert Bono in the film *Powwow Highway;* the movie won the "best film" award. Farmer also received a nomination for best actor from the Independent Feature Project West in Los Angeles. The character Philbert Bono is a cheerful person who persuades his skeptical friend to reclaim his Indian individuality. One of the aims that this independent film accomplished, even though it was limited in its distribution, was to demonstrate how Indian spirituality and culture were essential for Indian survival.

Some of the most well-known films in which Farmer has appeared since the 1980s include *Friday the Thirteenth, The Believers, Police Academy, Renegades* (also called *Lakota*), and *Blue City Summers.* In 1992 Farmer appeared in *The Dark Wind,* a film based on Tony Hillerman's novel.

Farmer has also widely contributed his talents to television and radio programs. In the Canadian television series, "Spirit Bay," Farmer played the role of Cheemo. Some of Farmer's other television performances have been in "Miami Vice," "China Beach," and "Where the Heart Is." He has produced two series for television, one of which was "Our Native Land" for the Canadian Broadcasting Corporation and the other was "Powwow," a series of eight one-half hour programs, also hosted by Farmer, for Multilingual Television (MTV) in Canada. *Prevailing Winds,* rendered in the style of a magazine program, was a radio program produced and hosted by Farmer in 1989.

After 1989, Farmer began lecturing on Native American culture and issues on many campuses in the United States and Canada, focusing on media, environmental, social, and educational topics relevant to Native communities.

SOURCES:

Biographical Dictionary of Indians of the Americas, second
edition, Newport Beach, California, American Indian
Publishers, 1991; 217-218.
Native North American Almanac, edited by Duane Champagne, Detroit, Gale Research, 1994; 771, 1055.

—*Sketch by Wendy Pfeffer*

Donald L. Fixico

Fire, John
See Lame Deer

Donald L. Fixico
1951-
Shawnee, Sauk/Fox, Creek, Seminole professor

Donald L. Fixico is best known for his expertise in federal
Indian policy and national issues affecting Indian people. He is one of a small number of Native Americans in the
United States with a doctoral degree in history. Born January
22, 1951, in Shawnee, Oklahoma, Fixico is a full-blood
American Indian of four different tribes: Shawnee, Sauk &
Fox, Creek, and Seminole. All four tribes were eastern woodlands peoples moved to Oklahoma Territory in the 1830s as a
result of Andrew Jackson's Indian removal policy. Fixico's
parents, John and Virginia Fixico, raised him and three other
children in the typical working-class environment of the
1950s. In an interview with Catherine A. Clay, Fixico recalled
being raised in the Seminole tradition, which included annual
Green Corn ceremonies and stomp dances. Among Seminoles
and Creeks, "Fixico" is a title of war meaning "Heartless in
Battle." His Creek grandmother, Lena Fixico, continually
stressed hard work and cleanliness. His parents stressed those
values as well as the importance of individual strength, getting things done, and being pro-active.

Fixico began school near Shawnee, Oklahoma, but
moved to Oklahoma City during his fourth-grade year. The
family moved to Midwest City, where he completed junior
high school, then again moved to Muskogee, Oklahoma,
where he graduated from Muskogee Central High School.
Those years proved to be revealing ones, as Fixico learned
about racism against Indians and prejudice against minorities. He also had a curious mind and wanted to know how
things worked. While his good grades and his interest in
learning helped him to succeed, it was not an easy struggle.
"Indians, especially full-bloods, were not expected to do well
in school, and most worked as physical laborers," Fixico
explained to Clay. "It was said once to me that 'Indians work
best with their hands.' They should not aspire to do more, and

they were not expected to." Despite such prevailing attitudes,
Fixico was determined to continue his education.

Fixico began his college career at Bacone Junior College near Muskogee, Oklahoma. In 1971, he transferred to
the University of Oklahoma at Norman, where he struggled
to make good grades while majoring in chemistry. He
switched his major to history after realizing chemistry was
not the best field for him. In 1974, he received his bachelor
of arts degree in history. A class in American history taught
by the late Dr. Arrell M. Gibson led Fixico to enter graduate
school at the University of Oklahoma, where he received his
master's degree in 1976. He also was awarded a Ford Foundation Fellowship to help fund his post-graduate education.
Fixico continued his postgraduate studies and completed his
dissertation on Federal Indian Policy, receiving his doctorate degree from the University of Oklahoma in July 1980.
During his last two years in graduate school, he also taught
at Rose State College. He received an invitation to be a visiting lecturer on Indian history at the University of California at Berkeley during the spring quarter of 1980.

Teaching and Writing History

From 1980 to 1981, Fixico was a postdoctoral fellow
at the American Indian Studies Center at the University of
California, Los Angeles. During 1981, he taught as a visiting lecturer in history at UCLA. The following year he
received a postdoctoral fellowship at the D'Arcy McNickle
Center for the History of the American Indian in the Newberry Library in Chicago. He began his tenure track in 1982

as an assistant professor of history at the University of Wisconsin at Milwaukee. Four years later, he earned tenure and was promoted to associate professor. During the academic year 1984 to 1985, Fixico was a visiting professor at San Diego State University. In 1986, he published *Termination and Relocation: Federal Indian Policy, 1945-1960,* a work which received critical acclaim from other professional historians. In 1988, he edited the book *An Anthology of Western Great Lakes Indian History.* In the 1988-1989 academic year, he participated in a professor exchange program and went to the University of Nottingham in England, where he taught both American history and American Indian history. Following his year in England, he accepted the position of professor in the history department at Western Michigan University in Kalamazoo, where he is helping to build a new doctoral program and working with graduate students. He teaches both American history and American Indian history.

Fixico authored *Urban Indians* in 1991 and has contributed many articles and chapters to other books. Some of his works have been reproduced in textbooks. He has also worked as a consultant on historical documentaries. He has given numerous guest lectures and professional papers at national and international conferences. He is on the board of editors for two professional journals, the *Western History Quarterly* and the *American Indian Culture and Research Journal.* Fixico also helped to establish in 1981 the American Indian Historians Association. In the interview with Clay, Fixico said, "Because there are so few, I strive to increase the number of American Indians and the numbers of minority men and women in the history profession." He is on the Committee of Minority Historians for the American Historical Association, as well as various committees in history at the national level.

Fixico credits his success in life to his upbringing and determined attitude, forged through a personal drive of disciplined hard work to overcome obstacles of prejudice and to meet challenges. In 1990, Fixico married his long-time friend, Sharon Lynn O'Brien. She is the chairperson of the Government and International Studies Department at the University of Notre Dame in Indiana.

SOURCES:

Books

Native North American Almanac, edited by Duane Champagne, Detroit, Gale Research, 1994; 1055-1056.

Other

Fixico, Donald, interview with Catherine A. Clay conducted July 21, 1994.

—*Sketch by Catherine A. Clay*

Fixico, Fux
   See Posey, Alex

Harry Fonseca
1946-
Maidu artist

Harry Fonseca's brightly painted "Coyote" series has made him famous. From June of 1987 to March of 1989, an exhibition of his work toured the major galleries of the country, from Oakland, California, to Washington, D.C. Coyote is a tribal trickster figure known for his song, his survival strategies, and always having the last laugh. Coyotes have lived on this continent for 30,000 years, as their Nuahtl name "coyotl" testifies. The Aztecs called the god of the dance "Huehuecoyotl." Like Fonseca's traveling coyotes, Coyote is omnipresent and has outlived the extinction of other wild animals; he is an adaptable and shrewd self-transformer—he endures.

Use of the Coyote Figure

Fonseca grew up near Sacramento, California. He is of Maidu, Portugese, and Hawaiian descent. His first encounter with Coyote was when his uncle, Henry Ke'a'a'la Azbill, a Konkow Maidu elder, took him to see the Maidu dances in the Sierra foothills when he was a teenager. After the sacred dances, at about 2 a.m., came a Coyote figure who mocked the serious rituals; the Maidua Oleil was a trickster. Fonseca sketched him. He made a tape-recording of the Maidu creation story that his uncle Henry told him as he had learned it from his grandmother, Sokanneh. In 1976, Fonseca illustrated this origin myth. His 1977 painting, "Creation Story," was funded by a special projects grant from the California Arts Council. In 1980, he silkscreened "A Gift from California" in which Coyote participated in roundhouse ceremonies, spring renewal dances, and Acorn Dances. Another set, this time in ink drawings, followed in 1981: "Coyote I," and "Coyote II." And in 1982, he rendered "Coyote Flute Player" in watercolor. The pantribal aspect of Coyote was captured by Fonseca in a series of caricatures called "Snapshot or Wish You Were Here, Coyote" in 1979. He parodied tourists' consumption of "kitschy" Indian artifacts in cartoons of coyotes wearing Hawaiian shirts posing for pictures in front of adobe pueblos.

Fonseca's teacher, Frank La Pena, wrote the review for Fonseca's ten-year retrospective exhibition at the Los Angeles County Museum of Natural History. In it, La Pena said that humor is important for adaptation, because when one is laughing, it is easier to think of means for continuance—"When one is happy, it is easier to accept and learn new things." The show, "Coyote, A Myth in the Making," traveled to six major galleries after its 1987 opening.

Fonseca had studied art at Sacramento State College where he began to research Indian mythology. He paid homage to his Hawaiian background in "Coyote I," depicted in a feathered cloak. His Portugese ancestry is represented by the crossed dance-sticks that Coyote holds in his paws. The poster chosen to advertise the exhibition was "Coyote Leaves the Res, New York, New York." Fonseca said of Coyote's outfit, "The leather jacket, Levis and high-top tennis shoes are the contemporary expression of traditional trappings." His T-shirt and Converse sneakers mark him as a street-smart figure. In the 1980 "Pow Wow Club," Coyote's girlfriend Rose dances with him in high-heels and with crimson-lacquered fingernails in a dress glittering with spangled flowers. Her joy is visible in her razor-toothed grin. The couple dances in "Pas de Deux 72" in which Rose wears a tutu and ballet slippers. "Coyote, Star Dancer," "Rose and the Rez Sisters," and "Shuffle Off to Buffalo" are other dance renditions. And "Coyote's Ark" won an award at the Southwest American Indian Arts Festival in Santa Fe.

Fonseca studied at the Alvin Ailey American Dance Center in New York City for a year in order to do his ballet series, which he jokingly calls "pas de paw" art. Appropriately, these are collages in mixed media. Acrylic paint, velvet, glitter, and spray help him parody two cultures. "Albuquerque Impressions" mixes stereotypes as well. Coyote clowns as striped Hopi "koshares" are eating watermelon and wearing expensive brandname sneakers. Fonseca satirized his own duplicity in "Coyote in Front of Studio" as a warbonneted Plains figure carrying a sacred pipe bag stands in front of his office in Shingle Springs wearing a red T-shirt and a black leather jacket over jeans. He flaunts his outrageous mixture of the traditional with the modish urban fads. The same satiric irreverence appears in "Coyote and Rose Doin' It at Indian Market with a Little Help from Gail, Yazzie and Jody." Mocking tourists, the couple are in a booth, selling souvenirs of Pueblo pottery, Navajo jewelry, Hopi katsinas. Their grins deride the scavengers who collect Native American culture.

He exhibited a new series in the fall of 1991 at the gallery of the American Indian Community House in New York City. Called "Stone Poems," these are based on ancient petroglyphs that he found in California's Mojave desert. Curator, Lloyd Oxendine wrote that "in spite of 'Stone Poems' ancient sources, they look courageously modern. Their schematic simplicity recalls Egyptian hieroglyphics. Yet much remains mysterious and shrouded by secret power." Featured in this new series are animals such as buffalo, antelope, serpents. Some of the figures bear shields or carry atlatl, so they could be hunters, but rays emanate from their heads, and lightening zig-zags across their bodies, so they could also be sun gods or thunderbeings—particularly since they appear to have bird's feet. In these latest depictions, Fonseca has achieved a sense of "Indian space." There is no background. The central figures are rendered flat within a foregrounded picture plane with which they merge, showing that dieties and humans coexist within nature, of which animals are also a part. The natural and the supernatural are not set in a hierarchy distinct from one another. Instead they interact in the same environment.

SOURCES:

Books

La Pena, Frank, and Craig D. Bates, *Legends of the Yosemite Miwok,* illustrated by Harry Fonseca, Yosemite, California, Yosemite Natural History Association, 1981.

Scholder, Fritz, *Indian Kitsch: The Use and Misuse of Indian Images,* Flagstaff, Arizona, Northland Press, 1979.

Other

Archuleta, Margaret, "Coyote: A Myth in the Making: A Ten Year Retrospective of Harry Fonseca" (master's thesis in American Indian Studies), University of California, Los Angeles, 1987.

Bates, Craig D., "Interview with Harry Fonseca," November 15, 1985.

—Sketch by Ruth Rosenberg

Philip Fontaine
1944-
Sagkeeng Ojibway leader and activist

Philip Fontaine, Grand Chief of the Assembly of Manitoba Chiefs, is perhaps best known for his leading roles in the defeat of the Canadian Meech Lake Accord and in convincing the federal government to investigate child abuse at church-operated Indian schools. Born at the Fort Alexander Indian Reserve in Manitoba, Canada, on September 10, 1944, Fontaine is the son of J.B. and Agnes Fontaine. Growing up, Fontaine spoke only the Ojibway language until he began his education at the residential school on the Fort Alexander Reserve. He later attended a residential school in Winnipeg, and he graduated from Powerview High School in 1961.

Fontaine became active in Canadian and Indian politics early in his life. By 1968 he became involved with Manitoba's First Nations movement, which resulted in the establishment of the Native Indian Brotherhood. That organization, which later was renamed the Assembly of Manitoba Chiefs, provided all the Indian bands within the province a more efficient means of dealing with the provincial government and the Manitoba region's Department of Indian Affairs. At Fort Alexander, Fontaine acted as the Sagkeeng Ojibway tribal administrator for a time, and in 1972 he was elected Chief of the band. He held that position until 1976, as well as continued working in various capacities with the Manitoba Native Indian Brotherhood.

As Chief of the Fort Alexander First Nations, Fontaine established one of the first locally controlled First Nations school programs in Canada in 1973. Three years later, the first Indian Child and Family Agency with local control was also established. Neither program receives direction from the Manitoba provincial government, which is a unique situation derived under a special arrangement between the First Nations and the Canadian federal government. Fontaine also was responsible in 1976 for the development of the Sagkeeng Alcohol Treatment Centre, the first such facility in Manitoba. Fontaine also organized a boycott that forced the Department of Indian Affairs to build a much-needed new Sagkeeng Ojibway First Nations school years earlier than called for in the original plan.

From 1977 to 1981, Fontaine was the Deputy Federal Coordinator of the Native Economic Development Program and a Regional Director for the Canadian Department of Indian Affairs for the Yukon region. He also was a special advisor to the Southeast Tribal Council of Manitoba. While both holding down both a full-time job and doing volunteer work, Fontaine found the time to complete his bachelor of arts degree in political studies at the University of Manitoba in Winnipeg by 1981.

That same year, Fontaine was elected as a Vice-Chief representing Manitoba at the Assembly of First Nations, a nationwide organization that is considered a parallel form of government to the Euro-Canadian government. The national assembly takes its direction from the 600 First Nations in Canada and acts as their voice in dealing with Canada's federal government. In 1989, Fontaine returned his attention to the affairs in his home province when he was elected to the position of Grand Chief of the Assembly of Manitoba Chiefs.

First Nations and Defeat of the Meech Lake Accord

Canada's government took a paternalistic view of its aboriginal people for more than 200 years. For example, it took away large areas of Indian land through treaties and relocated the people on Reserves. Although the government viewed Indians as a distinct and separate society, it did not permit them any true form of self-government.

At the same time, Canada developed into a collection of diverse and separate cultures due to geographic, climatic, and language factors. In 1982, Canada finally approved a Constitution, similar to the U.S. Constitution, which provided a formal list of rights and freedoms already accepted as common law among the Euro-Canadians. However, the Province of Quebec demanded to be recognized as a distinct society within the framework of that Constitution, and even threatened to secede from Canada if it was not guaranteed special rights as a distinct society.

In August of 1986, the premiers of the various provinces negotiated an agreement, which became known as the Meech Lake Accord, that would allow Quebec its distinct society status. However, before the Accord could become a part of the Canadian Constitution, it had to be approved by all the other Canadian provinces. While Quebec was the only

"distinct society" mentioned in the Accord, the First Nations had been fighting for years to be allowed the right to self-government. First Nations leaders felt that the Meech Lake Accord had the potential to at least hamper, and possibly eliminate, their chances to regain that inherent right.

Fontaine, along with other leaders of the First Nations, began to mobilize support to defeat the Meech Lake Accord. Years before the final vote was cast, Fontaine was building coalitions among the Manitoba chiefs and organizing discussions, negotiations, lobbying efforts, demonstrations, and marches to insure that the aboriginals' viewpoint about the Accord would be heard by the Manitoba government. Eventually, the First Nations' argument helped convince the provincial political leaders in Manitoba and Nova Scotia to reject the Meech Lake Accord in 1990, and it was not included in the Constitution.

Since the successful defeat of the Meech Lake Accord, Fontaine has continued his consensus-building efforts. He convinced the Manitoba Constitutional Task Force to make aboriginal concerns for self-government a top priority, along with other First Nations issues, in any new Constitutional negotiations. As a result of Fontaine's efforts, the Department of Indian Affairs has agreed to dismantle their regional Indian education program as well as the medical services program. Authority to administer those two programs will be given to the First Nations. At one point, Fontaine was jailed for occupying the Indian Affairs office in Ottawa following a demonstration he organized and led to protest the department's position on post-secondary education.

A Public Stand on Child Abuse Issues

Canada did not include the schools on Indian Reserves in its regular, government-operated educational system until the 1950s and 1960s. Prior to that time, Indian schools on the Reserves were controlled by Roman Catholic or Protestant missionaries. Fontaine attended Reserve schools controlled by the Catholic Church during the two decades before the government took over control of the schools. This experience placed him in a unique position to instigate major changes in church-affiliated schools throughout Canada.

On October 30, 1990, Fontaine announced to the media that while he was in the Reserve school, at least one of the Catholic priests had sexually abused him. That announcement gave courage to hundreds of other First Nations people, who also had been abused during their years in church-operated Reserve schools. The Canadian media, as well as the media in the United States, jumped on the story. On November 5, Fontaine met with the Roman Catholic Church Bishops in Manitoba and forged an agreement with them to establish a committee to assist the abuse victims. Other Native leaders joined the cause and demanded a federal government inquiry. After more meetings and discussions, the Catholic, Anglican, United, and Presbyterian churches in Manitoba agreed on a plan to work with the Assembly of Manitoba Chiefs to ensure the public disclosure of abuse and help victims begin the healing process. In his capacity as Grand Chief, Fontaine also convinced the Canadian Human Rights Commission to join the First Nations in pushing the government for a federal inquiry into residential school abuse.

The Canadian government also has frequently allowed the adoption of Indian children into non-Indian families off the Reserves. However, this practice conflicts with the strong tradition First Nations people have of caring for their children through extended family groups. When parents died or for some other reason could not or would not care for their own children, members of the extended family usually took over so that the cultural traditions of the people could be passed on. When the children were instead adopted into non-Indian families, the traditions were often lost. Fontaine worked through the Canadian Human Rights Commission to open adoption files so that the bands could locate children who had been removed and reunite them with their extended families.

In a biographical statement, Fontaine said he hopes his work "will lead to aboriginal people assuming their own rightful place in our land." He credits a wide network of support, including his family and the Creator, for the results and success he has had in achieving his goal. When he is not travelling or working for the Assembly of Manitoba Chiefs, Fontaine enjoys playing hockey for the Sagkeeng Old Timers, listening to music, reading, and researching aboriginal history. He also jogs daily. Fontaine lives in Winnipeg and has two children, Michael and Maya.

SOURCES:

Books

Klein, Barry T., *Reference Encyclopedia of the American Indian,* sixth edition, West Nyack, New York, Todd Publications, 1993; 520.
Native North American Almanac, edited by Duane Champagne, Detroit, Gale Research, 1994; 1056.

Periodicals

Burns, John F., "Canada Abandons Accord on Quebec," *New York Times,* June 23, 1990.
Malcolm, Andrew H., "The World beyond Plain Vanilla: Immigration Has Accentuated Canada's Diversity," *New York Times,* June 8, 1990.
Mollins, Carl, "The Long Road to Unity: Exasperation Colors the Constitutional Debate," *MacLean's,* 105 (8), February 24, 1992; 16-18.
"Natives Seek Church School Probe," *Facts on File,* 50:2608, November 16, 1990; 858.
Newman, Peter C., "A New Province for First Nations?" *MacLean's,* 105:3, March 30, 1992; 36.
Newman, "Bourassa Is Just as Distinct as Mercredi," *MacLean's,* 104:36, September 9, 1991; 30.
Reuters, "Excerpts from Mulroney Address on Treaty," *New York Times,* June 24, 1990.
Stanley, Alessandra, "How Distinct Is Quebec? French, and That's That," *New York Times,* June 27, 1990.

Other

Fontaine, Philip, "Biographical Information," Scanterbury, Manitoba, Assembly of Manitoba Chiefs, 1994.

—Sketch by Catherine A. Clay

Jack D. Forbes
1934-
Renapé Powhatan/Lenapé Delaware ethnohistorian, educator, and writer

Jack Douglas Forbes chairs the Native American studies program at the University of California, Davis. He has few rivals in the scholarly field of research and writing, and he has always worked with the best interest of the Native American people as his guide. Forbes was born at Alamitos Bay, Long Beach, California, on January 7, 1934. He is of Powhatan-Renapé and Delaware-Lenapé background (Algonquian-speaking people from eastern North America), as well as being of other Native American and European heritage. Forbes is married to Carolyn L. Johnson, and has two children from a previous marriage, Nancy and Kenneth. He has a "green thumb" (acquired by planting flowers with his mother while he was a child), and enjoys nourishing plants around his Davis home, as well as planting trees and shrubs in areas of the community he discovers during his morning run that seem to be in want of additional beauty and emotional attention.

Scholarship, Research, and Writing

Forbes earned both his master's (1956) and doctoral (1959) degrees in history from the University of Southern California. He has taught at several colleges and universities in California and served as director of the Multicultural Program at the Far West Laboratory for Educational Research and Development. He also has been the recipient of a variety of fellowships, including from the John Simon Guggenheim Memorial Foundation, and is in demand to be a board member of many activities concerning the Native American people.

Forbes first served as chair of the American Indian College Committee in 1961, and he has since been on 16 other boards in various positions. In 1971, in what he considers perhaps his most important contribution to the education of Native Americans, he became a member of the D-Q University board of trustees. D-Q University is a college near Davis, California, which offers Native Americans and Mexican Americans a more culturally based education. Encouraged by his interest in and dedication to the education of the Native American people, Forbes worked with

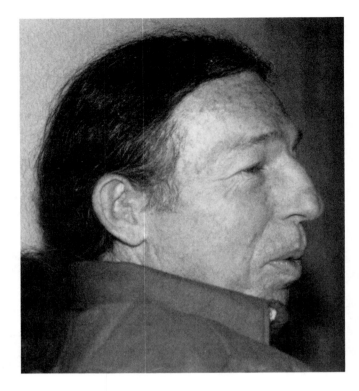

Jack D. Forbes

other educators and grassroots people to meet this need within the community.

In his research and writing, as well as his addresses to the federal government and a host of colleges and other organizations, Forbes spotlights the historical negligence of American society toward Native people. His work includes historic accounts of military conflict, the "scorched earth policy," and reservation confinement of the Native people across America. In addition, Forbes addresses the voids he perceives in the field of general and higher education that act to maintain the Native people in a posture of servility.

Forbes gained respect for his ability to approach this dilemma with openness and frankness, and as a result his credentialed opinions are weighed and in demand in many circles. For example, in his introduction to *Native Americans of California and Nevada*, Forbes states, "The author does not assign any kind of 'collective guilt' to the white population for what has happened in the past. The future, though, is a different matter; we all have a responsibility which cannot be brushed aside. The kind of society which is now being brought into existence is our collective challenge."

Fluent in His Native Language

Forbes is an eloquent speaker while defending the Native people. Since he prays in his native language, Forbes is often asked to open or close a gathering with thoughts or a prayer in his native tongue, whether the gathering takes place in a land beyond the continental limits of America or at home. The interest Forbes receives emphasizes to academics

the need for cultivation of the variety of Native American languages that are hardly being used today, in any setting.

SELECTED WRITINGS BY FORBES:

Apache, Navaho, and Spaniard, Norman, University of Oklahoma Press, 1960.
The Indian in America's Past, Englewood Cliffs, Prentice-Hall, 1964.
Warriors of the Colorado: The Quechans and Their Neighbors, Norman, University of Oklahoma Press, 1965.
Nevada Indians Speak, Reno, University of Nevada Press, 1967.
Afro-Americans in the Far West, Berkeley, Far West Laboratory, 1967.
Aztecas del Norte: The Chicanos of Aztlan, New York, Fawcett, 1973.
Tribes and Masses: Essays in Red, Black and White, Davis, D-Q University Press, 1978.
A World Ruled by Cannibals: The Wetiko Disease of Aggression, Violence and Imperialism, Davis, D-Q University Press, 1979.
Native Americans of California and Nevada, Healdsburg, Naturegraph, 1982.
Black Africans and Native Americans: Race, Caste and Color in the Evolution of Red-Black Peoples, Oxford, Blackwell, 1988; Urbana-Champaign, University of Illinois Press, 1993.

SOURCES:

Books

Forbes, Jack D., *Native Americans of California and Nevada,* Healdsburg, Naturegraph, 1982.
Voices from the Earth: An Anthology of Interviews of Native Americans from the North American Hemisphere, Austin, University of Texas Press, 1995.

Other

Forbes, Jack D., interview with Darryl Wilson conducted 1994.

—Sketch by Darryl Wilson

Billy Frank, Jr.
1931-
Nisqually activist

Billy Frank, Jr., is a Nisqually activist best known for his work in engineering a peaceful settlement to 50-year-old fishing conflicts in Washington state and throughout the

Billy Frank, Jr.

Northwest. After enduring numerous beatings and at least 40 jailings during the 1950s, 1960s, and 1970s for refusing to obey state laws restricting Native fishing rights, Frank directed his attention to reconciling the differences between the Nisqually people and state officials. From his post as chairman of the Northwest Indian Fisheries Commission, which represents 20 Washington tribes in negotiating natural resource management plans with state and federal officials, Frank was instrumental in preventing further violence and conflict in the Northwest. One of the originators of the concept of "cooperative management," a negotiating strategy that stresses common sense compromise rather than court intervention, Frank was awarded the prestigious 1992 Albert Schweitzer Award for Humanitarianism for his peacemaking efforts. Once known as "the last renegade of the Nisqually," Frank's peacemaking program has been modelled in several states, resulting in solutions to numerous natural resource conflicts throughout the United States.

The son of Willy Frank—the last full-blooded Nisqually, who died in 1983 at the age of 104—Billy Frank, Jr., was born in 1931 on a Nisqually reservation located along the banks of the Nisqually River in Washington. Instilled with a fervent pride in his Native heritage at an early age, he received his first arrest at the age of 14 while fishing with his father in a restricted area. When Frank came of age, he continued his commitment to the rights of the Nisqually tribe, leading the Native rebellion against state fishing authorities and a powerful sports fishermen's lobby during the salmon fishing wars of the 1960s and early 1970s. Frank and his followers' opponents argued that Native

Americans, like other citizens, were subject to state regulations while fishing off their reservations, thus invalidating treaties signed in the mid-1880s that guaranteed Native rights to fish at "their usual and accustomed places." After a bitter struggle in which Frank was physically attacked and arrested numerous times, the treaty fishing rights were upheld by U.S. District Judge George Boldt of Tacoma, who ruled in 1974 that Native Americans were entitled to half of the harvestable catch of salmon and steelhead in Washington. Although the state and non-Native American fishing lobbies fought the ruling, the U.S. Supreme Court refused to overturn Boldt's decision.

Promotes Negotiation Rather Than Litigation

Although Native American rights were vindicated by the high court, Frank learned from his years of fighting the state that legal solutions—even when they resulted in a victory for his people—engendered only more animosity between the opposing factions and resulted only in more problems. In an effort to effect a more lasting peace in the Northwest, Frank began bringing Native Americans and non-Native Americans together, seeking solutions at the negotiating table rather than in the courtroom. "It's a new time of cooperation, a time of healing," Frank instructed a group of state legislators and tribal leaders from Wisconsin at a 1991 seminar covered by *News from Indian Country.* Agreements negotiated by the cooperative management principle, Frank argued, provide both the state and the Native American community with an incentive to adhere to the terms of a compromise because, in the long run, neither side benefits from a court decision. "We have to work together," Frank told George Rede of the *Oregonian.* "There is no other way."

Frank's commitment to Native American causes has not been limited to the fishing rights of the Nisqually people, but rather has been demonstrated through his work on a variety of environmental issues. In 1976, for instance, he began working with the Washington state government and the timber industry for reforms in logging and spraying practices that have resulted in a dramatic increase in the bald eagle population in the Nisqually watershed. Eight years later, he helped to found the Northwest Renewable Resources Center, a nonprofit organization that mediates conflicts over natural resources in Washington and five other states.

For his humanitarian service, Frank was presented with the 1992 Albert Schweitzer Award, a $10,000 honorarium previously bestowed on such notable individuals as former President Jimmy Carter, former U.S. Surgeon General C. Everett Koop, and Marian Wright Edelman, president of the Children's Defense Fund. As Roberta Ulrich of the *Oregonian* reported, the citation honored Frank's "achievements as a mediator between opposing interest groups and as a protector of the fragile cultural and environmental heritage that all humanity share." In receiving the prestigious award, Frank characteristically directed the praise to the tribes throughout the Northwest rather than upon himself, viewing the award as a testament to the value of the Native American way of life.

SOURCES:

Books

Native North American Almanac, edited by Duane Champagne, Detroit, Gale Research, 1994; 1057-1058.

Periodicals

Craig, Carol, "Wisconsin Delegation Visits Washington to Observe Co-Management Opportunities," *News from Indian Country,* September 15, 1991; 7.

"One Rebel's Reward," *Medford Mail Tribune,* May 14, 1992.

Rede, George, "'Last Renegade of the Nisqually' Will Receive Schweitzer Award," *Oregonian,* October 13, 1992.

Ulrich, Roberta, "Indian Rights Advocate Frank Wins High Honor," *Oregonian,* October 15, 1992.

—*Sketch by Jason Gallman*

G

Gall
1840-1894

Hunkpapa Lakota Sioux warrior and tribal leader
Also known as Pizi

Gall

Gall was directly involved in more major military battles than perhaps any other warrior in the region; he acquired the title of "the fighting cock of the Sioux." Yet he spent the last 15 years of his life as an "accommodationist," recommending submission to the reality of the white man's occupation of Indian lands.

His birthplace was along the Moreau River in Dakota Territory. It would become the southern border of the Standing Rock Reservation, where he spent his final years. His father died when he was very young and he was raised by his mother. He rose from a status of obscurity to establish himself as a fearless fighter by the age of 25. Among his early associates was Sitting Bull. They were members of the Midnight Strong Heart Society.

One of the earliest reports of Gall's military prowess was in the Fetterman Massacre in 1866, a battle in which Crazy Horse had distinguished himself because of clever decoy tactics. That battle and Little Big Horn were the two clearest examples of absolute defeat of U.S. forces. In another battle that same year, while leading an assault on Fort Buford, Gall was severely wounded and left for dead; but he recovered to participate in many more violent conflicts.

Along with Red Cloud, Gall voiced his opposition to the Fort Laramie Treaty of 1868 and the sale of the Black Hills. When the treaty commission travelled to Fort Rice in North Dakota to seek support, he dramatically dropped his long skin robe to reveal wounds that had not yet healed. In a breechcloth and beaded moccasins he addressed the group: "I am not ready to take you by the hand and call you friend. The Great Father has never befriended me.... When one Indian is bad you punish all of us, even our helpless old men and women.... With your soldiers no Indians are good and no white men are bad.... Your hands are red with blood.... Not till the wounds I carry are healed and the lands that belong to us are restored will I sign a treaty with you. You ask where are my lands? I answer you—I answer you—I answer you—our lands are wherever our dead are buried." However, he later was the first to sign the document, believing, erroneously, that some significant concessions about

military withdrawal from the Missouri River area had been made.

Participant and Interpreter of Little Big Horn

According to Dee Brown, nothing occurred during the next decade to change "Gall's opinion of the white man's self-righteous arrogance, and by the summer of 1876 he was generally accepted by the Hunkpapas as Sitting Bull's lieutenant, the war chief of the tribe." Gall's role in the Battle of Rosebud on June 17, 1876, would be praised later by his opponent General George Crook. Eight days later he was one of the key figures in the Little Big Horn battle. Sergeant John Martin, a cavalry member in the misguided venture provided a summary: "The fighting strength of the Sioux that day was at least six to one; better armed, better prepared, and as well, if not better led.... Their numbers had been underestimated; their leadership and fighting capacity undervalued; their superiority in arms not even suspected. The 7th Cavalry paid the penalty for national stupidity."

Gall had the unusual role of becoming a "historian" for the event, participating in a special ceremony on the battlefield only ten years later. A Chicago newspaper reported, "Early in the day the great Sioux Chief Gall went over the entire field and described in an intelligent and straight forward manner the exact place in which Custer's command was destroyed." The forces of Major Marcus A. Reno first approached the massive combined tribal camp of up to 15,000 people. Among those killed were two of Gall's wives and three of their children. Gall reacted, this "made my heart bad. I then fought with the hatchet." A St. Paul newspaper added more detail: "Reno was whipped first and all with Custer were killed." The total Indian deaths including those who died later, according to Gall, was 43. Explaining the advantage of the victors, Gall said that "his warriors were just as many as the grass" and the Great Spirit, riding a coal black pony over the field, offered encouragement to continue.

Gall would participate in two more battles before deciding to join Sitting Bull in Canada. October negotiations with General Nelson Miles failed. During this exile, conditions continued to deteriorate for those still within the boundary of the United States. The U.S. defeat at Little Big Horn resulted in a more massive retaliation. The Black Hills treaty was signed, Crazy Horse was killed in 1877, and more formerly belligerent tribes were forced to submit to reservation life.

The Reservation Years

An argument with Sitting Bull in the fall of 1880 resulted in the movement of Gall and about 300 followers to Montana. After a brief encounter with U.S. troops, he made the decision to surrender and by June of 1881 he was on the Standing Rock Agency in North Dakota. There he supported the policies of Agent James McLaughlin who systematically sought to change the values of Native Americans.

Historian Robert M. Utley referred to Gall as "a shrewd pragmatist." He was also aided by an impressive physical appearance. McLaughlin described him as "the finest-looking Indian I had ever seen." Even Elizabeth Custer, the widow of General George Custer, expressed her admiration after seeing his photograph. In a promotional leaflet for photographer David F. Barry which displayed the chief's torso, she admitted, "Painful as it is for me to look upon a pictured face of an Indian, I never dreamed in all my life there could be so fine a specimen of a warrior in all the tribes as Chief Gall." George W. Kingsbury, author of the 1915 *History of Dakota Territory* recalled Gall's presentation at the 1886 gathering on the Little Big Horn Battlefied: "Gall is a powerful, fine looking specimen of the red race, forty six years old, and weighs over two hundred pounds."

Gall did his best to impress Agent McLaughlin. In his 1910 autobiography, *My Friend the Indian,* McLaughlin reported that Gall wished to be identified as the "best man on the reservation." McLaughlin linked his own proclaimed success to his association with John Grass and other cooperative Native Americans. "I made Gall and Crow King my friends, and they were important factors in leading the others to civilization." He also revealed, "[Gall] came to me

frankly with personal affairs that were sometimes staggering in their intimacy."

In contrast McLaughlin experienced seven years of animosity when Sitting Bull came to the reservation in 1883. Utley reviews the conflict, "Unlike other hostile leaders, notably Gall, Sitting Bull refused to be reconstructed." In the first annual report after the arrival of Sitting Bull from Canada his protagonist remarked, "Sitting Bull is an Indian of very mediocre ability, rather dull, and much the inferior of Gall and others of his lieutenants in intelligence. He is pompous, vain, and boastful, and considers himself a very important personage." McLaughlin was irritated by the constant attention paid the famous chief by visitors to the reservation. Over 25 years later, he again described this "stocky man, with an evil face and shifty eyes"—"Crafty, avaricious, mendacious, and ambitious, Sitting Bull possessed all the faults of an Indian and none of the nobler attributes which have gone far to redeem some of his people from their deeds of guilt.... I never knew him to display a single trait that might command admiration or respect."

This isolation between Gall and Sitting Bull was reflected also in the former's battlefield comments at Little Big Horn in 1886. He claimed that Sitting Bull did not even participate in the battle but chose to stay in camp. Ironically, when Kicking Bear, communicator of the Ghost Dance to Sitting Bull, did his famous pictograph of the battle, he included Sitting Bull but intentionally did not represent Gall at the scene.

Gall willingly adjusted to reservation life, doing physical labor, and being appointed as a U.S. (district) Farmer ("boss farmer") in 1885. He became an Episcopalian and made brief appearances with Wild West shows. In 1884 he was sent to represent the Sioux at the New Orleans Exposition. Duane Champagne indicates that he "adopted a way of life more European than Indian." In 1888 he was one of the envoys to Washington, D.C. That same year he expressed opposition to the sale of more reservation land but submitted to the pervasive 1889 Sioux Agreement.

Shortly before Sitting Bull's death Gall had expressed his suspicion of the Ghost Dance religion. McLaughlin claimed that Gall was fearful of Sitting Bull's supporters and requested a gun for protection. If granted, McLaughlin claimed that the December 1890 arrest, and murder, might not have been necessary. The intra-tribal conflict could have brought the same result.

Upon his return from Washington, D.C., Gall was appointed as judge of the Court of Indian Offenses. In that position he was able to have continued impact in the modification of Native American standards and behavior. He died on the reservation on December 5, 1894.

SOURCES:

Andrist, Ralph K., *The Long Death, The Last Days of the Plains Indians,* New York, Macmillan, 1964, 1993.
Brown, Dee, *Bury My Heart at Wounded Knee: An Indian History of the American West,* New York, Holt, 1970.

Champagne, Duane, "Gall (Pizi)—Hunkpapa Sioux Tribal Leader," in *Native North American Almanac,* edited by Duane Champagne, Detroit, Gale Research, 1994; 1059-1060.

Deur, Lynne, "Gall," in *Indian Chiefs,* Minneapolis, Lerner Publications, 1972; 72-75.

Fielder, Mildred, "Gall, Reno's Opponent," in *Sioux Indian Leaders,* Seattle, Superior Publishing, 1975; 57-71.

Graham, Colonel W. A., *The Custer Myth: A Source Book on Custeriana,* Lincoln, University of Nebraska Press, 1953, 1981.

Kingsbury, George W., *History of Dakota Territory,* Chicago, S. J. Clarke Publishing, 1915.

McLaughlin, James, *My Friend the Indian,* Boston, Houghton Mifflin, 1910.

Thomson, Frank, "Chief Gall's Speech," in The Thoen Stone: *A Saga of the Black Hills,* Detroit, Harlo Press, 1966; 118-120.

Utley, Robert M., *The Lance and the Shield: The Life and Times of Sitting Bull,* New York, Holt, 1993.

Utley, Robert M., *The Last Days of the Sioux Nation,* New Haven, Connecticut, Yale University Press, 1963.

—*Sketch by Keith A. Winsell*

Hanay Geiogamah

Hanay Geiogamah
1945-
Kiowa/Delaware playwright, editor, and choreographer

Hanay Geiogamah is an ambassador of Native American culture. He has used the international non-verbal language of dance to bring Native American expressiveness to the attention of the general public both at home and abroad. His plays have also toured the world showing the humor, improvisational skills, and vitality of Native American life. Through the academic journal he edited, he has won intellectual respect for Native American culture, demonstrating its importance in the university curriculum.

Creation of Native American Theatre Ensemble

When he created the Native American Theatre Ensemble (NATE) in the early 1970s, Geiogamah performed a service both to his tribal heritage and to his country. He gave tribal people a place to perform, a way of expressing their innate creativity, and recruited talented youngsters from every tribal group to be trained for performances. NATE gave America what it had lacked until then, a true national company. Appearances of the American Indian Dance Theatre are sold out months in advance. The troupe has appeared twice on national television, and videotapes of their performances have become bestsellers. The company was formed in 1987 by Hanay Geiogamah from Los Angeles, and New York producer Barbara Schwei. The repertoire of the company includes the "Eagle Dance," the "Zuni Buffalo Dance," the "Apache Crown Dance," and a "Hoop Dance" originated by Cherokee Eddie Swimmer, which interweaves 20 hoops into an earth or biosphere. New dances are learned each year by the members who have recently added Northwest coast dances using raven, whale, and cannibal masks to represent Kwakiutl potlatching. In a National Public Radio interview, Geiogamah explained that normally each of these dances takes a number of days, therefore he stages only excerpts, and severely abridges those selected episodes to heighten the dramatic interest. They constitute only the "appetizers" to the actual "feast." These can be savored through "The Great Performances" series of public television.

Geiogamah as Playwright

Geiogamah has also written a dozen plays, three of which have been published by the University of Oklahoma Press with an introduction by Jeffrey Huntsman. After receiving his bachelor's degree in drama and theater from Indiana University, Geiogamah worked for Louis Bruce at the Bureau of Indian Affairs (BIA) while writing *Body Indian*. It was composed at the typewriter, two days before the script was due in New York at Ellen Stewart's La Mama Theater, where it premiered with a cast from the American Indian Theater Ensemble in 1972. In it, he tried to convey the Kiowa sense of humor. He characterized this in an interview with Kenneth Lincoln for *MELUS* as "very, very rich, very satirical, very scatological, very screwball, loony, and yet all somehow controlled." He claims that "Kiowas are always laughing." It was the pressure of time under which he composed the play that enabled this Kiowa humor to emerge intact on the page. The anxiety he felt during rehearsals of *Body Indian* was alleviated when, during the actual performances, the audiences laughed at the tragicomic events portrayed on the stage. The Indians watching, recognized the portrayals of alcoholics taking advantage of each other. Geiogamah said that he had witnessed a great deal of such behavior at the BIA where Indians sometimes acted as their own worst enemies. The final gesture is Bobby's sardonic smile, a death grin, called "risus sardonicus" by doctors. Geiogamah meant that closure to signal that Bobby was assuming responsibility for his own suffering. It was intended as a grimace of defiance. At ground zero, cleansed, he must begin to live, to resist extermination. It is about the capacity to renew oneself.

The play *Foghorn* concerns the occupation of Alcatraz. The first version, which was later cut, projected on a screen a huge head that was gradually being lobotomized. During rehearsals, it began to seem a silly device, so it was removed. Wilfred Leach, the artistic director at La Mama, who was also a professor at Sarah Lawrence, helped Geiogamah with the play's development. He taught him about Brechtian alienation devices, gave him Martin Esslin's book, *Brecht, the Man and his Work* to read. Geiogamah, who was still in his early twenties, absorbed what he could at the time, distracted as he was by the pressures of guiding his company for their appearance in Germany in 1973. While the group was in West Berlin, the Brecht Theater invited them to come for a day's visit to the Berliner Ensemble. *Foghorn* opened in West Berlin on October 18, 1973.

Geiogamah's troupe also toured reservations. The third of his plays is called *49* after the songs sung at the conclusion of a pow wow. It is the most affirmative and celebratory of his works. His latest play is a musical comedy called *War Dancers.* His earlier plays employed energetic improvisational singing and dancing—in *Foghorn,* the Wild West Show with its singing of "Pass the Peace Pipe" had been a song-and-dance number. *49* celebrates that sense of wild, spontaneous play; and Geiogamah gives the members of his acting company the freedom to improvise their interactions.

In addition to having served as managing editor of the prestigious *American Indian Culture and Research Journal,* a scholarly quarterly for interdisciplinary contributions advancing knowledge about Native Americans published by the Regents of the University of California, he also taught at Colorado College and at the Los Angeles campus of the University of California. He also does the choreography for the Thunderbird American Indian Dancers, a troupe headquartered in New Jersey under the leadership of Louis Mofsie. The Thunderbirds meet on Tuesdays at the McBurney YMCA and hold an annual pow wow in full regalia each July at the Queens County Farm Museum, the proceeds of which are contributed to a scholarship fund for promising Indian students.

SELECTED WRITINGS BY GEIOGAMAH:

Body Indian (stage play), produced by American Indian Theater Ensemble, La Mama Theatre, New York City, 1972.
New Native American Drama: Three Plays (includes *Body Indian, Foghorn,* and *49*), edited and introduced by Jeffrey Huntsman, Norman, University of Oklahoma Press, 1980.

SOURCES:

New Native American Drama: Three Plays, edited and introduced by Jeffrey Huntsman, Norman, University of Oklahoma Press, 1980.
Lincoln, Kenneth, "Indians Playing Indians," *PLUS,* fall 1989-1990; 91-98.
Lincoln, Kenneth, "Interview with Hanay Geiogamah," *MELUS,* fall 1989-1990; 60-82.

—*Sketch by Ruth Rosenberg*

Dan George
1899-1981
Burrard Squamish actor and tribal leader

"Chief" Dan George is most widely known for his acting career, which spanned the 1960s and 1970s. He is particularly recognized for his role as the Cheyenne elder Old Lodge Skins in the 1970 film *Little Big Man,* which also starred Dustin Hoffman. Popularly known as "Chief," he came to acting late in life.

Born and raised near Vancouver, British Columbia, George worked as a logger, longshoreman, and musician before becoming, in 1951, chief of the Tell-lall-watt band of the Burrard Tribe of Coast Salish Indians outside Vancouver. He later was named honorary chief of the Squamish and Sushwap bands. Although remaining chief until 1963, he branched out into acting in 1959 when one of his sons, who happened to be playing an Indian in the Canadian Broadcast Corporation's production of the series "Caribou Country," convinced the director to give the chief a part. It was George's later role in the 1969 Walt Disney film *Smith* that brought him to the attention of the *Little Big Man* producers.

Stars in *Little Big Man*

Aside from its box office success, *Little Big Man* set the tone for a genre of films in the 1970s in which Hollywood put forth its strongest criticism ever against U.S. Indian policies. Reversing an earlier trend of the 1930s, which depicted Indians as ruthless antagonists of the white man and the cavalry, the army was now portrayed as inflicting death and destruction on innocent Native Americans.

Dan George

General attitudes surrounding the movie reflected civil rights concerns, resentment against U.S. involvement in Vietnam, and government distrust during the early 1970s. For his role in the film, George was awarded the New York Film Critics Award for best supporting actor, and was also nominated for an Academy Award.

Although George refused to endorse radical Indian political causes of the 1960s and 1970s, such as those promoted by the American Indian Movement (AIM), he eloquently spoke for Native rights and the environment throughout his career. He remained particularly interested in changing predominant images of Native Americans in the media, as well as derogatory images that many Indians had of themselves. Other movies in which he was featured include *Cold Journey, The Ecstasy of Rita Joe, Harry and Tonto,* and *The Outlaw Josey Wales.* In 1971, he received the Human Relations Award from the Canadian Council of Christians and Jews. Dan George was married and became the father of six children, Marie, Ann, Irene, Rose, Leonard and Robert. George's wife, Amy, died as he was making plans to attend the Academy Award ceremonies in Hollywood. He died in his sleep at the age of 82 on September 23, 1981, in Vancouver.

SOURCES:

Books

Biographical Dictionary of Indians of the Americas, Volume 1, Newport Beach, California, American Indian Publishers, 1991; 240.

Native North American Almanac, edited by Duane Champagne, Detroit, Gale Research, 1994; 771, 1061-1062.

Periodicals

New York Times, September 24, 1981; Section 4, 23:1.

—Sketch by William Carter

Geronimo
1827(?)-1909
Bedonkohe Chiricahua Apache warrior and tribal leader
Also known as Goyathlay ["One Who Yawns"]

The world has come to recognize Geronimo as one of history's great warriors; and his greater-than-life image is probably the result of various film portrayals. Yet, none of these accounts accurately depicts the great warrior; in addition to being a husband, father, warrior, and medicine man, Geronimo was a respected leader who preserved Apache culture and traditions, as well as the right to live on the homelands that they had occupied for generations. The story of Geronimo's life is one of the most recounted tales in Native American history. Hundreds of books have been written about his life history; however, the best storyteller is perhaps Geronimo himself. Between 1905 and 1906, Geronimo related his life story to his second cousin, Asa (Ace) Daklugie, the son of Whoa (Who, Juh) who fought in Geronimo's last campaign. Daklugie, in turn, told Geronimo's story to S. M. Barrett, a white who at the time was superintendent of education in Lawton, Oklahoma, who recorded it in 1906 as *Geronimo, His Own Story.*

Geronimo's own words best tell the trials and tribulations he endured at the hands of both the Mexican and United States governments and soldiers. The 1800s were tumultuous years for Native Americans. In 1830, one year after Geronimo's birth, President Andrew Jackson introduced the Indian Removal Act. Under the auspices of promoting progress and growth for America's expansion, Native Americans were forced to relocate to foreign and barren lands west of the Mississippi River. Due to their remote southwest geographic location, the Apaches did not experience the severe removal efforts planned by the government until later years. However, throughout the early years of attempted Spanish and Mexican control, the Apaches threatened the colonization begun by the explorers. Geronimo warded off intruders and soldiers from further land encroachment until the mid-1800s when the United States acquired southwest Apache lands from Mexico—land which Mexico claimed title to through conquest, but which rightfully was homeland occupied by Native peoples. Chastised

Geronimo

by history for their preventive measures in protecting their lands, the Apaches were described as people who raided and killed innocent and unsuspecting settlers; however, as Mexican and U.S. troops continued to invade and conquer Apache lands, the Native reaction was to retaliate and fight back.

It was Geronimo's belief that when Usen (the Apache word for God, according to historian Frederick W. Turner III, who edited and introduced the 1970 publication of *Geronimo, His Own Story)* created the Apaches, he also created their homes in the West. As more and more Apaches were removed from their homelands, Geronimo contended that the Apaches would sicken and die. As Turner explained in his introduction to *Geronimo, His Own Story,* "To the Indian mind, a man's attachment to his homeland was not a romantic nostrum but a vital necessity; a man sickened and eventually died—a whole people might die away—if cut off from the life-source of the land itself." Geronimo's strong conviction of this belief was apparent when he appealed vigorously to the Great Father, Theodore Roosevelt, to return the Apaches to their native Arizona homelands to prevent further destruction and death to the Apaches. His request was denied.

Early Years

Geronimo's story begins somewhere around the 1820s, with many historians claiming Geronimo's birth in 1827. Geronimo stated that he was born in June of 1829 in No-doyohn Canon, Arizona. According to Geronimo, his

tribe, the Bedonkohe, inhabited the region of mountainous country that lies west from the east line of Arizona, and south from the headwaters of the Gila River. To the east of his tribe lived the Chihenne (Hot Springs) Apaches whose chief was Victorio and with whom the Bedonkohe lived in relative peace. Unlike the Chihenne, the White Mountain Apaches lived to the north of Geronimo's tribe and the two tribes were not always on the best of terms. On the western border lived the Chokonen (Chiricahua) Apaches, whose chief was Cochise and later his son, Naiche. The Bedonkohe and Chokonen Apache tribes were the most friendly and often camped and trailed together. Geronimo and Naiche were to become long-time companions both as warriors and prisoners of war. To the south and west of the Bedonkohe lived the Nedni Apache whose chief was Whoa; Geronimo described the relationship between the two tribes as that of "firm friends." Fighting side by side as brothers, Geronimo explained that Whoa's enemies were his enemies and his friends were Whoa's friends.

Born the fourth member in a family of four boys and four girls, he was known as Goyathlay ["One Who Yawns"] until his late teens. Nurtured and instructed in Apache traditions and customs, Goyathlay learned about tribal legends from his mother, Juana, and the discipline of praying to Usen for strength, health, wisdom, and protection. His father, Taklishim ["The Gray One"], told Goyathlay many accounts of brave deeds by their warriors and the dangers and pleasures of warpath chases. His paternal grandfather, Maco, was a Nedni Apache chief; however, Goyathlay's father was not a chief because he joined his wife's tribe thereby losing his right to rule by heredity; consequently, Goyathlay was not entitled to become a chieftain by hereditary right due to his father's marriage outside of the tribe. Mangas Coloradas succeeded Goyathlay's grandfather and became chief of the Nedni Apaches, a position Goyathlay might have held otherwise.

At the age of 17, sometime around the year 1846, Goyathlay was invited to join the council of warriors and was then able to share in the glories of the warpath and serve his people in battle. He was also able to marry Alope, the daughter of No-po-so. As numerous movies and tales have chronicled the marriage event, Geronimo himself confirmed that Alope's father demanded many ponies in exchange for his daughter. Once the ponies were delivered, Geronimo took Alope and they went to live not far from his mother's tepee. No further ceremonies were needed to affirm the marriage, and Geronimo and Alope became the parents of three children. Throughout his life, Geronimo eventually had four full-blood Bedonkohe Apache wives and four part-blood Bedonkohe Apache and part other Apache-blood wives. Four of his children were killed by Mexicans and four were held in bondage by the U.S. government.

Mexican Raids

During the summer of 1858, Geronimo suffered a tremendous tragedy, which would affect his outlook on life and especially people of Mexican heritage. While on a peaceful trip into Old Mexico to trade, the Bedonkohe

Apache stopped at the village of Kas-ki-yeh and would travel daily into town to trade. Upon returning to the campsite, the Apache traders were met by several tribal members who informed them that they had been attacked by Mexican troops who had killed all the warrior guards, captured all the ponies, stolen their arms and supplies, and killed many of the women and children. During the aftermath, Geronimo discovered that his mother, wife and three children had all been massacred by the Mexican soldiers. Returning to Arizona quietly on the instructions of Mangas Coloradas, Geronimo vowed vengeance upon the Mexican soldiers. In the summer of 1859, Geronimo sought the assistance of the Chiricahua Apache through their chief, Cochise. Soon thereafter, he gained the additional assistance of the Nedni Apaches led by their chief Whoa; and the three tribes began their southward descent near the Mexican border. Upon arriving at Arispe, a battle broke out between the Apaches and Mexican soldiers; and while Geronimo could not bring back his loved ones, he claimed he "could rejoice in this revenge." According to Turner, the battle of Arispe is where Goyathlay acquired the name "Geronimo" from Mexican soldiers.

Geronimo sought to further punish the Mexicans. He persuaded Ah-koch-ne and Ko-deh-ne to invade Mexican country with him; both companions were killed and Geronimo returned to the Apache camp exhausted and silent. Some Apaches blamed him for the result of the expedition, but Geronimo was not discouraged. In the summer of 1860, he convinced 25 warriors to join him in another battle, during which Geronimo was struck by a Mexican trooper and was later found lying unconscious in a pool of blood. His head injuries did not heal for many months and resulted in a scar that Geronimo wore for the remainder of his life. While the Apaches appeared to have won the battle, the loss was so great that no warriors would accompany Geronimo on such warpaths for at least another year. Sometime during the summer of 1861, he once again traveled to Mexico with 12 warriors only to return without even a partial victory to his credit. The summer of 1862, however, brought several successful raids for Geronimo and for a long time the tribe had plenty of provisions, blankets and clothing. From raiding several pack mule trains, the Apache had also acquired large quantities of cheese and sugar. These successful raids continued throughout the summer of 1863 when the Apache claimed to have made their most successful raid into Mexican territory. That raid alone provided the tribe with enough food and provisions to last a year and enabled the warriors to give presents to every tribal member at the ceremonies that took place thereafter.

Geronimo's yearly raids continued throughout the fall of 1864 with 20 warriors joining him, and again in 1865 with four warriors accompanying him on foot into Mexico in pursuit of cattle. The raids continued year after year, but the number of warriors accompanying Geronimo varied greatly. Sometime around 1868, the Apaches were attacked by Mexican troops who rounded up all the tribe's horses and mules. In retaliation, the Apaches attacked, killing the cowboys who had been assigned by the Mexicans to watch over the captured livestock, and drove not only their stock but the Mexican and cowboy stock back to the Apache camp. Geronimo stated that it was a long time before they ever went back into Mexico or were disturbed by Mexicans. Another Mexican attack occurred in 1873 in the Sierra Madre Mountains; this attack lasted only a few minutes with heavy losses incurred by the Mexican troops.

In 1882, while in the Sierra Madre Mountains leading one of the bands on a raiding spree, Geronimo and his warriors were surrounded by U.S. General George H. Crook's troops and forced to surrender to government authorities. In Geronimo's description of his life, he terms this period as the break in his life from the San Carlos Reservation at a place called "Geronimo." Even though Geronimo was ordered by military authorities to remain on the San Carlos Reservation, he managed to escape in 1881. Most of his followers who accompanied him returned to the reservation in May of 1883; however, Geronimo returned with his group to San Carlos in late February or early March 1884, claiming to have returned to the reservation not on military orders, but to "get other Apaches to come with him into Mexico." In May of 1885, historical records indicate that there was tremendous disruption and fighting between the Indians and soldiers on the San Carlos Reservation. It was at this time that Geronimo steered into place his elaborate plans to break from the reservation and travel to Mexico. The battle that followed in Mexico was the last battle Geronimo ever fought with the Mexicans. During his battles with the Mexicans, Geronimo received a total of eight wounds.

Encroachment of the White Men

Around 1858, after the Massacre of Kaskiyeh, Geronimo heard about some white men coming to measure land to the south of his homelands. Accompanied by other warriors, Geronimo went to visit them. While not understanding their language and lacking an interpreter, the two groups made a treaty with one another promising to be brothers. Camping next to each other, they traded blankets, buckskins and ponies in exchange for provisions and shirts. The Apaches also brought game to trade with the white men; however, in exchange the Apaches were offered money. Unaware of its value, they kept it and later learned from their Navajo neighbors the value of this paper. After this group of surveyors left, the Apaches did not see another white man for about ten years. Trouble later developed between the two groups and Geronimo, although not wronged himself, fought with his tribe against the soldiers. Shortly after this encounter, some of the U.S. officers invited the Apache leaders to hold a conference at Apache Pass (Fort Bowie). Treachery and deceit followed on the part of the soldiers who attempted to massacre the friendly Apaches. Most of the Apaches were killed; however, Mangas Coloradas, their chief, did manage to escape. Further trouble erupted and the Indians agreed not to be friendly with the white men any longer and they never again trusted the U.S. troops. In 1872 President Ulysses S. Grant sent General O. O. Howard to Arizona to make peace with the Apaches; and Geronimo claimed to have traveled to Apache Pass to make a treaty with the general. In Geronimo's viewpoint, General Howard kept his word with the Apaches and treated them as if they were brothers; he claimed he could have lived in peace forever with him.

Although U.S. officials term Geronimo's presence as either living on or escaping from reservation lands, Geronimo did not necessarily categorize his travels as opposing any laws. For him, it was Apache land belonging to the Apaches; and as food provisions or other necessary items depleted, it was only customary that the Apache would relocate to a bountiful area to replenish their stock or to visit their homelands. This conflict in perspective continued between Geronimo and U.S. officials to the point where Geronimo, upon visiting Victorio's band in Hot Springs, was disarmed by U.S. soldiers and taken to headquarters where he was tried by court-martial. Geronimo was sentenced to the guardhouse and put in chains. When he demanded of his captors why he was treated as such, they replied that it was because he had left Apache Pass. The soldiers' actions were difficult for Geronimo to understand; as he explained, "I do not think that I ever belonged to those soldiers at Apache Pass, or that I should have asked them where I might go." He was kept a prisoner under chains for four months and then transferred to San Carlos. Upon his return to San Carlos, it appears that peace presided for a little over two years until the summer of 1883 when a rumor surfaced that officers were planning to imprison Apache leaders.

These rumors made the Apaches wary of the officers' intentions because they reminded the Apache of all the past wrongdoings by the officers. Fearing for themselves, they held a council meeting and decided that they would leave the reservation; Geronimo believed it would be better to die on the warpath than to be killed in prison. With 250 Apache followers, Geronimo and Whoa led the Apaches through Apache Pass where they encountered soldiers who battled with them for their return. Heading toward Old Mexico, they again encountered soldiers on the second day and fought well into the night. The soldiers were unaccustomed to fighting on the rough terrain, and the Apaches were well equipped with arms and supplies accumulated while living on the reservation. The remainder of the provisions was supplied by the White Mountain Apaches. After this battle, troops did not follow the Apaches and they succeeded in heading south to Casa Grande and camped in the Sierra de Sahuaripa Mountains. Geronimo claimed that the Apaches roamed the area for one year and then returned to San Carlos, taking with them their cattle and horses. Upon their return to the reservation, the officer in charge, General Crook, ignored Geronimo's pleas and confiscated all the livestock that they had obtained rightfully from the Mexicans to raise as stock on their range. Upset with the decision, Geronimo undertook plans to travel to Fort Apache. Upon instructions from General Crook, officers and soldiers were informed that they were to arrest Geronimo; if he resisted, they were to kill him. Apaches informed Geronimo of General Crook's plans and Geronimo prepared to head south to Old Mexico with about 400 Bedonkohe, Chokonen and Nedni Apaches. Camping in the mountains west of Casa Grande, the Apaches were attacked by government Indian scouts. According to Geron-

imo, one boy was killed and nearly all of the women and children were captured. Escaping to the foothills of the Sierra Madre Mountains, the Apaches were soon attacked again by a very large army of Mexican troops. Recognizing the inevitable, Geronimo claimed it was "senseless to fight when you cannot hope to win."

While holding a council of war that night, Apache scouts reported that approximately 2,000 soldiers were combing the mountains seeking the refugee Apaches. General Crook had arrived in Mexico and was camping in the Sierra de Antunez Mountains with his troops awaiting a visit from Geronimo. Upon Geronimo's arrival to Crook's camp, the general asked why Geronimo had left the reservation. Geronimo replied, "You told me that I might live in the reservation the same as white people lived. One year I raised a crop of corn, and gathered and stored it, and the next year I put in a crop of oats, and when the crop was almost ready to harvest, you told your soldiers to put me in prison, and if I resisted to kill me." According to Geronimo, General Crook denied this allegation saying he never gave any such orders and that the troops who spread these rumors at Fort Apache knew that it was untrue. Geronimo then agreed to return to San Carlos with General Crook.

Geronimo and his band of followers started to return to the United States with the general; however, fearing further treachery and deceit, he decided to remain in Mexico with about 40 of his followers. As a result of Geronimo's escape, Turner noted, General Crook resigned and was replaced by General Nelson A. Miles. Geronimo, not knowing of Crook's resignation and believing him dead, attributed Crook's death as an act of the "Almighty as punishment for the many evil deeds he committed." As General Mills' territorial powers expanded to cover more of the western frontier, U.S. troops led by Captain Lawton continually trailed the Apaches. Geronimo claimed at this point that he moved with six men and four women heading toward the mountain range near Hot Springs, New Mexico. Thinking that the troops had left Mexico, Geronimo and his followers returned to Mexico, attacking and killing every Mexican found. He believed the Mexicans had asked the U.S. troops to come down to Mexico to fight the Apaches. The Apaches discussed the situation and decided that if they returned to the reservation they would be put in prison and killed; if they stayed in Mexico, soldiers would continue to fight them. Their decision was final, "Give no quarters to anyone and ask no favors." After some time, the Apaches were reunited with their people in the Sierra de Antunez Mountains. Unbeknownst to the Apaches, the U.S. troops had not left Mexico and were soon trailing close behind the Apaches. Mexican troops near the Apaches explained that they no longer wanted to fight and would welcome the prospect of a treaty. Explaining that the U.S. troops were the real cause of these wars, the Mexican troops agreed to no longer fight the Apaches if they would return to the U.S. Agreeing to these conditions, the Apaches resumed their march northward hoping to make a similar treaty with the U.S. soldiers upon their return to Arizona. Geronimo realized there was no other course to follow.

Geronimo Becomes a Prisoner of War

On August 25, 1886, Geronimo encountered Lieutenant Charles B. Gatewood, Captain Lawton's advance scout, near Fronteras. Geronimo attempted to treat on peace terms, originally established at the famously reported conference with General Crook held at El Canon de los Embudos in March of 1886, but was refused. His final plea asked that the Apaches be immediately reunited with their families, and after serving a two year imprisonment in the East, be returned to the reservation. What happened thereafter differs according to opinion.

Knowing that General Miles was in charge of the officers, Geronimo decided to treat only with him and refused Gatewood's proposition. Turner indicated that Geronimo later changed his mind on the surrender conditions providing the Apaches would be speedily reunited with their families. This condition was apparently agreed to several days later by General Miles, however, it was never fulfilled. In a subsequent meeting with General Miles, Geronimo explained how he had been wronged and that he wanted to return to the U.S. with his people. General Miles responded by saying he was sent on behalf of the president of the United States who had agreed to treat with the Apaches if they would agree to a few words of treaty: "I will take you under Government protection ... build you a house ... fence you much land; I will give you cattle, horses, mules and farming implements.... In the fall I will send you blankets and clothing so that you will not suffer from cold in the winter time.... There is plenty of timber, water and grass in the land ... if you agree to this treaty you shall see your family within five days." Geronimo responded by exclaiming his disbelief at the general's words, but the general assured him that "this time it is the truth." Geronimo agreed to make the treaty and placed a large stone on the blanket before himself and the general. The treaty was made before the stone and was intended to "last until the stone should crumble to dust," thereby "bounding each other with an oath." Geronimo gave up his arms and stated, "I will quit the warpath and live at peace hereafter." General Miles swept a spot of ground clear with his hand and said, "Your past deeds shall be wiped out like this and you will start a new life." Geronimo did not know that the start of his new life was also the beginning of his life as a prisoner of war.

Upon his final surrender on September 4, 1886, with his companion Naiche, Geronimo and his followers were loaded onto the Southern Pacific Railroad bound for San Antonio, Texas, where he was held to be tried for crimes committed. Narrowly escaping civilian trial for murder in San Antonio, Geronimo was hurriedly swept away to Fort Pickens in Pensacola, Florida. Woodward B. Skinner noted in *The Apache Rock Crumbles* that much dissention abounded by the residents of Pensacola who demanded that "the hostiles" be sent to Fort Pickens in hopes of aiding a lucrative tourist business. There is much discussion as to the conditions of surrender for Geronimo and his followers; however, the difference of opinion appears to rest on the words of the various military officials conducting the surrender with Geronimo. Geronimo's words of surrender explained by himself and others present at the scene reflect uniform accuracy and consistency; but the discrepancy in remarks of the various military officials and agents makes it difficult to ascertain their validity. Many of the Apaches sent to Florida died in that unfamiliar climate from tuberculosis and other diseases, but all were thoroughly domesticated, according to the American mind. In 1894, after the government rejected another appeal from the Apaches to return to their homelands, their former Apache foes, the Kiowa and Comanches, offered them a home on their reservation lands near Fort Sill, Oklahoma. Geronimo spent the remainder of his life on that reservation adapting to the white man's ways and economic system. Growing watermelons and selling his signature were his methods of procuring a livelihood. Although he was still under government protection as a prisoner of war, the government allowed him to travel to numerous fairs and exhibitions at Buffalo, Omaha, and St. Louis selling his signature and photographs for 25 cents to thousands of spectators.

Attempting to understand the Christian religion, Geronimo questioned repeatedly the concept of a part of man that lived after death—the spirit—as he had never seen one. However, believing that an association with Christians would help improve his character, Geronimo joined the Dutch Reformed Church and was baptized in the summer of 1903. It was reported that he attended regularly the services at the Apache Mission, Fort Sill Military Reservation; however, he was later expelled from the church for incessant gambling. In February of 1909, Geronimo died as a result of pneumonia which he developed when he fell off his horse into a creek bed and lay exposed for several hours. He left the world as a great warrior, but he was also an individual who was dedicated to preserving his rightful place in his homeland with his family and tribal members, and to live his life in peace as his people had been doing for hundreds of years. He is most noteworthy because he had the courage to stand up and fight back for what he knew belonged to him and his people.

SOURCES:

Books

Ball, Eve, *An Apache Odyssey,* Indeh, Utah, Brigham Young University Press, 1980; reprinted, Norman, University of Oklahoma Press, 1988.

Bender, Homer, *Apache Indians V,* New York, Garland Publishing, 1974.

Betzinez, Jason, *I Fought with Geronimo,* [Harrisburg], 1960.

Bigelow, John, Jr., *On the Bloody Trail of Geronimo,* [Los Angeles], 1968.

Bourke, John G., *An Apache Campaign in the Sierra Madre,* [New York], 1958.

Brown, Dee, *Bury My Heart at Wounded Knee,* New York, Holt, 1971.

Clum, Woodworth, *Apache Agent: The Story of John P. Clum,* [Boston], 1936.

Cremony, John C., *Life Among the Apaches* (1868), New York, A. Roman, 1951.

Crook, George, *Autobiography,* edited by Martin F. Schmitt, [Norman], 1946.

Davis, Britton, *The Truth About Geronimo,* New Haven, Yale University Press, 1929.

Debo, Angie, *Geronimo: The Man, His Time, His Place,* [Norman], 1976.

Faulk, Odie, *The Geronimo Campaign,* [New York], 1969.

Forbes, Jack D., *Apache, Navajo and Spaniard,* Norman, University of Oklahoma Press, 1960.

Geronimo, *Geronimo, His Own Story,* edited by S. M. Barrett, introduction by Frederick W. Turner III, New York, Dutton, 1970.

Hayes, Jess G., *Apache Vengeance,* Albuquerque, University of New Mexico Press, 1954.

Henry, Will, I, *Tom Horn,* [Norman], 1964.

Howard, Oliver Otis, *Autobiography,* two volumes, [New York], 1907.

Miles, Nelson A., *Personal Recollections,* [New York], 1969.

Nabokov, Peter, *Native American Testimony,* New York, Penguin, 1992.

Opler, Morris E., *Apache Life-Way,* [New York], 1965.

Perry, Richard J., *Western Apache Heritage, People of the Mountain Corridor,* Austin, University of Texas Press, 1991.

Santee, Ross, *Apache Land,* [New York], 1947.

Skinner, Woodward (Woody) B., *The Apache Rock Crumbles: The Captivity of Geronimo's People,* Pensacola, Florida, Skinner Publications, 1987.

Skinner, Woodward (Woody) B., and W. George Gaines, *Adventurers in Florida History,* [Pensacola], 1974.

Sonnichsen, C. L., *Geronimo and the End of the Apache Wars* (originally published as Volume 27 of *Journal of American History,* 1986), Arizona Historical Society, 1990.

Terrell, John Upton, *The Navajoes,* [New York], 1973.

Worchenter, Donald E., *The Apaches, Eagles of the Southwest,* [Norman], 1979.

Other

History of Company I, Twelfth Infantry, 1891-1895, National Archives.

Official Records, United States Army, 1879-1914.

Senate Document No. 117, "The Surrender of Geronimo," Government Printing Office, 1887.

—Sketch by JoAnn di Filippo

Tim Giago

1934-

Oglala Sioux publisher and author

Editor and publisher of the largest independently owned American Indian weekly newspaper, Tim Giago has been known for his forthrightness in protesting trends in American society that demonstrate a lack of respect for Native culture. He has spoken out against the elevation to hero of American historical figures who took part in the injustices committed against Native Americans, and he has been active in speaking out against the use of mascots referring to Native peoples among university and professional sports teams.

Tim Giago was born on the Pine Ridge Reservation in South Dakota on July 12, 1934 in a house with no electricity or plumbing, according to a *People* magazine article. As a young boy he attended Holy Rosary Indian Mission. He later attended a Jesuit-run school. According to *People* magazine, Giago was quoted as saying, "Our teachers told us our ancestors were heathens. It was a brutal way to be raised."

Giago left the reservation after high school to join the Navy, where he served in the Korean War and was wounded in action. Afterwards, he attended San Jose Junior College. He told a *People* magazine reporter that he held several odd jobs for about 15 years, and every summer he would return home feeling that "it was the only place I ever felt comfortable." Giago continued his education at the University of Nevada at Reno and later at Harvard University on a Nieman Fellowship from 1990-1991. He was the first American Indian to be accepted into this program. Giago was also awarded an honorary doctorate degree in humanities from Nebraska Indian Community College in 1993.

His writing career started in 1979 when he became an Indian affairs columnist for the *Rapid City Journal* in Rapid City, South Dakota, earning $7.50 for each column. This opened the door to a position as a full-time reporter. In 1981, Giago founded what was to become the nation's largest American Indian newspaper, the Lakota Times, later renamed *Indian Country Today.* He launched the newspaper with $4,000 borrowed from a boyhood buddy, according to *People* magazine. The paper grew from a circulation of 3,000 free copies to a readership of 50,000 in 1991.

Giago has also written a weekly column about contemporary Indian issues, syndicated by Knight-Ridder News Service to 340 newspapers. His columns and public stands on issues have been uncompromising. During a celebration of the 215th birthday of the United States of America at Mount Rushmore, Giago adamantly expressed his resistance to the veneration of George Washington, Thomas Jefferson, Abraham Lincoln, and Theodore Roosevelt as heros and defenders of justice as displayed by the monument at Mount Rushmore. "Not only did they desecrate our sacred land," Giago was quoted as saying, "they also memorialized four presidents who committed acts of atrocity against our people."

Giago has also written articles for *USA Today, New York Newsday, New York Times, Christian Science Monitor, Newsweek, Native Peoples* magazine, and the *Atlanta Constitution* about other concerns existing among the Native population. In a *Newsweek* article about the name of the Washington Redskins, Giago wrote about the "largest protest by American Indians against a professional football team in the history of this country. Our complaint: very simply, Indians are people, not mascots." He went on to say, "I find it very hard to understand why non-Indians find it hard to understand why we consider it insulting to be treated as mascots. If white and black America is so inconsiderate of its indigenous people that it can name a football team the Redskins and see nothing wrong in this, where has our education system gone wrong?"

Giago's opinions on Indian issues have been broadcast on numerous radio talk shows, including CBS' "Nightwatch" and the "Oprah Winfrey Show." Giago did extensive work on the Indian culture in his books, *The Aboriginal Sin* and *Notes From Indian Country, Volume 1*. Giago was also editor of *The American Indian and the Media Handbook*. In the summer of 1994, he was in the process of developing a new newspaper in Scotsdale, Arizona, *Indian Country Today Southwest*.

Giago's accomplishments and activism have won him several honors. He was nominated into the South Dakota Hall of Fame to be inducted in September 1994. Three years earlier he earned a medal of honor for distinguished journalism by the University of Missouri School of Journalism. He also won the Harvard University Award for Contributions to American Journalism. In 1989, Giago was the recipient of the National Education Association's Leo Reano Memorial Award for Civil and Human Rights for providing leadership in education to resolve social problems affecting Native Americans. He received the Civil Rights and Human Rights Award given by the South Dakota Education Association in 1988. In 1985, he received the South Dakota Newspaper Association Best Column by a local writer award. Also in 1982, he won the Print Media Person of the Year award at the National Media Convention at Albuquerque in New Mexico.

SELECTED WRITINGS BY GIAGO:

The Aboriginal Sin: Reflections on the Holy Rosary Indian Mission School, San Francisco, Indian Historian Press, 1978.
Notes from Indian Country, Volume 1, Cochran Publishers, 1985.
Co-editor, *The American Indian and the Media Handbook,* National Conference C & J, 1991.
"I Hope the Redskins Lose," *Newsweek,* January 27, 1992.

SOURCES:

Books

Native North American Almanac, edited by Duane Champagne, Detroit, Gale Research, 1994.

Periodicals

Chu, Daniel, and Bill Shaw, "About Faces," *People,* July 22, 1991.
Giago, Tim, "I Hope the Redskins Lose," *Newsweek,* January 27, 1992.

Other

Giago, Tim, "Autobiographical Sketch," August 1994.

—*Sketch by Diane Andreassi*

Gist, George
See Sequoyah

James Gladstone
1887-1971
Blood Blackfeet political figure
Also known as Akay-na-muka ["Many Guns"]

James Gladstone was the first native Canadian to serve as a senator on the Canadian Parliament. During his 13-year career with the Senate, he advocated the rights of all First Nations people and fought to keep the traditions of his people alive.

James Gladstone was born May 21, 1887, to the Blood tribe of Canada. Though born at Mountain Hill in the Northwest Territory, he spent his childhood on the Blood Blackfeet Reservation in Alberta, where he was called Akay-na-muka ["Many Guns"]. Well-known for his role as politician and as a voice for all Indian peoples, he did not find his way to this career early in his life. First, he attended Calgary Industrial School, then worked briefly for the *Calgary Herald* as a typesetter. In 1911, the Royal Northwest Mounted Police asked him to be a scout and interpreter among his people. Around this time he married Janie Healy, with whom he had five children.

Gladstone was the first Indian on the Blood Reserve to have electricity or to use a tractor. He readily took advantage of modern conveniences to make his ranch of 800 acres as prosperous as possible. His excellent farming abilities won him the admiration of many, and, during World War I, he passed on his agricultural expertise, helping the other Blood farmers to properly tend their cattle and to increase the yield from their crops.

Fights for His People as Politician

Gladstone worked as many long, hard hours for his people as he did on his ranch. Like many members of Lakota and Blackfoot tribes struggling to govern themselves and keep their threatened languages alive, Gladstone fought for education and for treaty rights for his people. As a delegate to Ottawa, he repeatedly represented his people in discussions with the Canadian Federal government concerning changes to the Indian Act. In hearings held from 1946 to 1948, Gladstone led the fight against the revisions to the Indian Act because they "replaced provisions better designed for concentration camps than for reservations" according to Olive Patricia Dickason in her book *Canada's First Nations*. Still, the hearings of the Joint Senate and House of Commons Committee on the Indian Act marked the first time Canada had listened to the input of Native Americans at that level of government. The revised act was passed in 1951, and Gladstone can be credited in large part for fighting for the rights of Indians to govern themselves. Though his efforts on behalf of his people helped to make the act a reality, Gladstone would rather have abolished it altogether; he felt the act impeded the Indians' ability to govern themselves and hindered the cause of equality. Of the act, he once said: "Indians are the only ethnic group in Canada with a special act."

In addition to fighting for the rights of his people with the Canadian government, Gladstone also encouraged his people to become involved in their own administration. Gladstone, among others, founded the Indian Association of Alberta in 1939 and served as president from 1948 to 1954, again in 1956, and in 1958, he was named honorary president.

Becomes First Native Senator

In 1958, Gladstone was appointed as a senator to the Canadian Parliament; he was the first Native American to serve as senator in Canada. In a gesture that demonstrated Gladstone's commitment to preserving the traditions of his people, he delivered his first senatorial speech to the Parliament in the language of the Blackfoot nation "as a recognition of the first Canadians." In the same speech, Gladstone said, "My work will be aimed at improving the position of Canada's Indians, obtaining for them better conditions as they want them and are ready for them. I'm particularly interested in seeing more encouragement given to Indians for individual, rather than collective effort."

Gets Vote for His People

In 1959, Gladstone delivered on his promise. He was named co-chairman of a joint Senate and House of Commons committee created to study the issues involving Canada's 170,000 Native Americans. In 1960, through Gladstone's efforts, treaty Indians were given the right to vote in Canada's national elections. For this success and his other work for his people, he was named "Outstanding Indian of the Year" in 1960s All-American Indian Days. In 1969, Gladstone traveled with Canada's delegation to Japan for the Moral Rearmament Asian Assembly.

Gladstone was a long-standing member of the Crazy Dog Society. He advocated a philosophy of tradition and progress for his people, who should "hold tradition with one hand and reach forward with the other." Gladstone died September 4, 1971, in Fernie, British Columbia.

SOURCES:

Biographical Dictionary of the Indians of the Americas, second edition, Newport Beach, California, American Indian Publishers, 1991.

Dickason, Olive Patricia, *Canada's First Nations,* Norman, University of Oklahoma Press, 1992.

The Native Americans: An Illustrated History, edited by Betty and Ian Ballantine, Atlanta, Turner Publishing 1993.

Native North American Almanac, edited by Duane Champagne, Detroit, Gale Research, 1994.

Waldman, Carl, *Atlas of the North American Indian,* New York, Facts on File, 1985.

Yenne, Bill, *The Encyclopedia of North American Indian Tribes,* New York, Crescent Books, 1986.

—Sketch by Christopher B. Tower

Diane Glancy
1941-
Cherokee writer and educator

The works of Cherokee writer Diane Glancy encompass several genres, including poetry, fiction, nonfiction, autobiography, and plays, as they reveal her relationship with the land and her strong sense of tradition. Her work is well-received and has been recognized with several awards, such as the Pegasus Award in 1984 from the Oklahoma Federation of Writers for her collection of poetry *Brown Wolf Leaves the Res and Other Poems*. And in 1986 she was awarded the Lakes and Prairies Prize from the *Milkweed Chronicle* in Minneapolis for *One Age in a Dream*. Glancy has also been widely published in leading literary journals. Her other accomplishments include the distinctive honor of being laureate for the Five Civilized Tribes from 1984 to 1986.

Glancy was born in 1941 in Kansas City, Missouri, to a mother of German and English descent and a Cherokee father. The family Cherokee name in Iroquoian was Ani-yun-wiya ["Real People"]. Glancy emotionally describes the difficulties associated with her mixed-blood heritage and the frustrations of being part of two very different cultures in her autobiographical essay "Two Dresses," which was published in 1987 in *I Tell You Now: Autobiographical Essays by Native American Writers*. "Two Dresses" also reflects on Glancy's personal relationship to the land of the Plains and her sense of tradition, two elements which inspire and engulf her writing. She uses her poetry as a means to sing out against the difficulties of life, promoting stability and hope and a stay against despair.

Diane Glancy

Glancy believes in the power of education and has dedicated her life to promoting that belief in others. In 1964, she received her undergraduate degree in English from the University of Missouri. Upon her graduation, she moved to Tulsa, Oklahoma, and began working for the state art council. There Glancy traveled to high schools and spoke to Native American students about the importance of education and the need to develop personal goals. She also held the position of artist-in-residence for the Oklahoma State Art Council. In 1983, Glancy received a Master of Arts degree in creative writing from Central State University in Edmond, Oklahoma. She continued her studies at the University of Iowa where she earned a Master of Fine Arts degree in scripting in 1988.

Glancy's published credits include six volumes of poetry, two works of fiction, one nonfiction work, and seven plays. Many of her plays have received honorable awards, including *Segwohi,* which won the Oklahoma Theater Festival Award in 1987; *Weebjob,* which was awarded the Five Civilized Tribes Playwriting Prize, also in 1987; and *Stickhorse,* which won the Aspen Summer Theater Award in 1988. In addition to her poetry and plays, Glancy has also been successful in receiving awards for her fiction and nonfiction writing as well. Her collection of short stories entitled *Trigger Dance* won the Charles Nilon Minority Fiction Award in 1990. Glancy was also the recipient of a National Education Association and Minnesota State Arts Board Fellowship during that same year. In 1992, her nonfiction work *Claiming Breath* received the University of

Nebraska Press Native American Prose Award and the American Book Award from the Before Columbus Foundation.

Glancy teaches Native American literature, creative writing, scriptwriting, and college writing at Macalester College in St. Paul, Minnesota. In addition to her literary and professional accomplishments, Glancy is the mother of two children, David and Jennifer.

SELECTED WRITINGS BY GLANCY:

Traveling On (poetry), Tulsa, Myrtlewood Press, 1982.
Brown Wolf Leaves the Res and Other Poems, Marvin, South Dakota, Blue Cloud Quarterly Press, 1984.
One Age in a Dream (poetry), Minneapolis, Milkweed Editions, 1986.
"Two Dresses," in *I Tell You Now: Autobiographical Essays by Native American Writers,* edited by Brian Swann and Arnold Krupat, Lincoln, University of Nebraska Press, 1987.
Offering: Aliscolidodi (poetry), Duluth, Minnesota, Holy Cow! Press, 1988.
Iron Woman (poetry), Minneapolis, New Rivers Press, 1990.
Trigger Dance (short stories), Boulder, Fiction Collective Two, 1990.
Lone Dog's Winter Count (poetry), Albuquerque, West End Press, 1991.
"Aunt Parnetta's Electric Blisters," in *Talking Leaves,* edited by Craig Lesley, New York, Bantam Doubleday Dell Publishing Group, 1991.
Claiming Breath (essays), Lincoln, University of Nebraska Press, 1992.
Firesticks (short stories), Native American Literature/Critical Studies Series, Norman, University of Oklahoma Press, 1993.
War Cries (drama), Duluth, Minnesota, Holy Cow! Press, 1994.
Monkey Secret (short stories), Evanston, Illinois, TriQuarterly Books, Northwestern University Press, 1995.

SOURCES:

American Indian Women: A Guide to Research, edited by Kathleen M. Sands and others, New York, Garland Publishing, 1991; 314.
Native American Women, edited by Gretchen M. Bataille, New York, Garland Publishing, 1993; 93-94.
Native North American Almanac, edited by Duane Champagne, Detroit, Gale Research, 1994; 1064.
Talking Leaves, edited by Lesley Craig, New York, Bantam Doubleday Dell Publishing Group, 1991; 376-377.
Waldman, Carl, *Encyclopedia of Native American Tribes,* New York, Facts On File, 1988; 43-48.

—*Sketch by Susan Noguera*

Carl Nelson Gorman
1907-
Navajo artist and lecturer
Also known as Kin-ya-onny beyeh ["Son of the Towering House People"]

Carl Nelson Gorman is a prominent Navajo artist, who was raised in a traditional manner on the reservation, but has won acclaim as a pioneer of non-traditional Indian art forms, such as oil paintings and silk screening. His contributions to Navajo and Native American art and culture inspired the dedication of the Carl Gorman Museum at Tecumseh Center at the University of California at Davis.

Carl Nelson Gorman was born October 5, 1907 at Chinle, Arizona to Navajo parents Nelson Gorman and Alice Peshlakai. His Indian name is Kin-ya-onny beyeh, which means "Son of the Towering House People." His parents founded the Presbyterian Mission at Chinle in 1921. Through his mother's family, Gorman is a distinguished member of the Black Sheep clan. His father was a trader and cattleman, and his mother a weaver, who also translated English hymns into Navajo. Other members of his family were tribal leaders. He spent his school years at U.S. government and Indian schools—such as Rehoboth Mission—in Arizona and New Mexico; he graduated from Albuquerque Indian School in 1928. Gorman married Adella Katherine Brown in 1930, whom he later divorced in 1945. The couple had one child, Rudolph Carl Gorman, born in 1932, who followed in his father's footsteps to become an artist in his own right.

Dreaming of becoming an artist since childhood, Gorman would achieve recognition as one later in life. As a boy, he liked to draw horses even though his father discouraged him in pursuing his interest in art. Having never lost sight of his aspiration to follow his artistic ambitions, Gorman has not only been recognized as a leading Native American artist, he has also guided other Native artists into new directions in art. Known for creating non-traditional Native art, Gorman stressed in an interview with Jeanne Snodgrass in *American Indian Painters, A Biographical Dictionary*, "I believe not only in the traditional but in the adaptation of the traditional to the modern, whether in painting, silver, or music."

Immediately after graduating from high school, Gorman went to work. He first entered the trucking business in co-ownership with his brother, Wallace, until 1936. He then worked as a clerk, timekeeper, and range-rider for USDI Land Management. From 1942 to 1945, he served in the Marine Corps on the Pacific islands of Guadalcanal, Tarawa, Saipan, and Tinian during World War II as a "code talker" using coded Navajo to perplex the Japanese. Like many veterans, Gorman took advantage of the G.I. Bill after the war and attended the Otis Art Institute in Los Angeles; he graduated in 1951.

Gorman first exhibited his art in 1947, and he has continued to show his work extensively ever since, including presentations of solo exhibits throughout California, Arizona, and New Mexico. Gorman began a professional art career at Douglas Aircraft Company in Santa Monica as a technical illustrator. At the same time, he founded his own silk screen design company, Kin-ya-onny beyeh Originals. In 1963, he left Douglas and California.

When he returned to Arizona in 1964, he managed the Navajo Arts and Crafts Guild and served as the director of the Navajo Culture Center at Fort Defiance, where he demonstrated a profound concern for the Navajo people and a reverence for Navajo culture. During this time he held a variety of positions on committees for Navajo festivals and tribal affairs. He even applied his artistic talents to devise a new dance, a Navajo Gourd Rattle Dance, based on a blend of traditionally Native dance elements. In 1973, Gorman became coordinator of the Office of Native Healing Sciences at the Navajo Health Authority, representing a popular entreaty among the Navajo for improved and coordinated health care coverage. He was also active in preserving traditional ways of healing until 1976.

Ever an innovator, Gorman ventured into experimentation with a wide variety of art media which were not traditionally Native, such as oil and watercolor paintings, ceramics, mosaics, textile and industrial designs, jewelry, and silk screens. He has received numerous awards for his art, but his greatest honor came in 1973 at the dedication of the Carl Gorman Museum at Tecumseh Center at the University of California-Davis following four years as a lecturer in Native American studies. Gorman retired from the University of California-Davis in 1973; and in 1976, he retired from Navajo Community College as Navajo cultural research coordinator and lecturer. He became a part-time instructor in Native American art and studio art in 1986 at the University of New Mexico in Gallup. Upon retiring in 1992, he has been lecturing on Navajo history and culture as well as Navajo code talkers.

Honored as an Arizona Indian Living Treasure in 1989, Gorman received an honorary doctorate in humane letters from the University of New Mexico on May 12, 1990. He sums up his life's work, particularly his achievements since the early 1970s, as quoted in the *Reference Encyclopedia of the American Indian*, "[I am interested in] all phases of art, subjects chiefly Navajo, horses, rock art, but including non-Indian subjects, in a variety of styles and media. [I am interested in] improving quality, expanding markets, and promoting new and adaptive Navajo arts and crafts. I adapted the Hopi version of Navajo Yei-bi-chei song of 1917. [And now I] hope to put photos, Navajo historical and cultural material I've gathered into a book."

SOURCES:

American Indian Painters: A Biographical Dictionary, compiled by Jeanne O. Snodgrass, Museum of the American Indian, Heye Foundation, 1968.

Biographical Dictionary of the Indians of the Americas, second edition, Newport Beach, California, American Indian Publishers, 1991.

Greenberg, George, and Henry Greenberg, *Carl Gorman's World* (biography), University of New Mexico Press, 1984.

Indians of Today, fourth edition, edited by Marion E. Gridley, Chicago, ICFP, 1971.

Handbook of the North American Indians, edited by William C. Sturtevant, Washington, D.C., Smithsonian Institution, 1983.

The Native Americans: An Illustrated History, edited by Betty and Ian Ballantine, Atlanta, Turner Publishing, 1993.

Native North American Almanac, edited by Duane Champagne, Detroit, Gale Research, 1994.

Reference Encyclopedia of the American Indian, edited by Barry Klein, West Nyack, New York, Todd Publications, 1993.

Wade, Edwin, L., and Rennard Stricklan, *Magic Images: Contemporary Native American Art,* Norman, University of Oklahoma Press, 1981.

Waldman, Carl, *Who Was Who in Native American History,* New York, Facts on File, 1990.

—Sketch by Christopher B. Tower

R. C. Gorman
1931-
Navajo artist

Rudolph Carl Gorman is one of the most prominent contemporary Native American artists of the twentieth century. His art combines the traditional with the non-traditional in style and form.

Rudolph Carl Gorman was born on a reservation at Chinle, Arizona, to Navajo artist Carl Nelson Gorman and wife Adelle Kathern Brown Gorman on July 26, 1931. Like his father, he had the desire to express himself through art from an early age, but unlike his father, Rudolph had an artist father to emulate. As early as three years old, he remembers making his first drawing, tracing patterns in mud with his fingers at the base of Canyon de Chelly. As a boy, he lived in the Navajo hogan, the traditional Navajo dwelling, where he herded sheep with his grandmother. He attended school at Chinle and St. Michaels and graduated from Ganado Mission High School in Arizona in 1950. He then attended Guam Territorial College, Arizona State College (now Northern Arizona University) at Flagstaff, and San Francisco State University studying both art and literature. The Navajo Tribal Council awarded Gorman a grant to study at Mexico City College (now University of the Americas), which was the first time such a grant had been awarded to study outside the United States. From 1952 until 1956, he served in the United States Navy.

Launches a Career as a Painter

Though Gorman showed talent as a writer, he pursued a career in art and painting. He said in an interview that "the reservation is my source of inspiration for what I paint; but yet I never come to realize this until I find myself in some far-flung place like the tip of Yucatan or where-have-you. Perhaps when I stay on the reservation I take too much for granted. While there, it is my inspiration, and I paint very little, and off the reservation it is my realization." Despite these sentiments about his Navajo heritage, many feel that he is not in touch with the culture and affairs of his people. From Edwin Wade in "The Ethnic Art Market" in *Magic Images* it is noted: "Artists like Oscar Howe, Dick West, Joan Hill ... R.C. Gorman ... have all encountered protests against their work because it was too different and not Indian enough."

Part of the reason that Gorman's work has been maligned by purists is that, though he often paints Native American subjects, his style is not traditionally Native. One of his most well-known and oft-reproduced works of art "Navajo Mother in Supplication" is imaged after reservation life, but is rendered in a very modern, non-Indian style. Gorman works in ink, oil, pastel, water color, and acrylic. Aside from "Navajo Mother in Supplication," which is detailed and appears realistic, Gorman's work is usually highly abstract or at least non-representational. He often applies bleeding colors, washes, and fade-outs in his paintings, and he continually searches for innovative and original directions with his art. In addition to many group showings, he has shown his work in numerous exhibitions, more than 60 national and international one-man exhibitions, and five shows with his father.

Inclusion in Metropolitan Museum of Art Show

One of Gorman's greatest achievements was realized in 1973 when two of his works were selected for the cover of the catalog and for the show of the "Masterworks of the Museum of the American Indian" exhibit held at the Metropolitan Museum of Art in New York City. He was the only living Native American artist included. In 1975, the Museum of the American Indian in New York chose Gorman as the first artist featured in its series of solo exhibitions of contemporary American Indian artists.

Gorman has enjoyed many achievements during his lifetime. Considered one of the greatest Native American artists of the latter half of the twentieth century, he has been the subject of numerous articles; and his work has appeared in many publications. In addition, Gorman has succeeded in establishing and operating the Navajo Gallery in Taos, New Mexico, upon becoming interested in Mexican art—namely lithography, cave paintings, and petroglyphs.

SOURCES:

Books

Adams, Ben Q., and Richard Newlin, *R. C. Gorman: The Complete Graphics,* Taos Editions, 1988.

American Indian Painters: A Biographical Dictionary, compiled by Jeanne O. Snodgrass, Museum of the American Indian, Heye Foundation, 1968.

Biographical Dictionary of the Indians of the Americas, second edition, Newport Beach, California, American Indian Publishers, 1991.

Dooley, Virginia, *Nudes and Foods: Gorman Goes Gourmet,* Flagstaff, Northland Press, 1981.

Gorman, R. C., *The Man Who Sent Rain Clouds,* New York, Viking, 1974.

Green, Mary Beth, *The Drawings,* Flagstaff, Northland Press, 1982.

Handbook of the North American Indians, edited by William C. Sturtevant, Washington, D.C., Smithsonian Institution, 1983.

Henningsen, Chuck, and Stephen Parks, *R. C. Gorman: A Portrait,* Boston, Little, Brown, 1983.

Hurst, Tricia, *The Posters,* Flagstaff, Northland Press, 1980.

Indians of Today, fourth edition, edited by Marion E. Gridley, Chicago, ICFP. 1971.

Monthan, Doris, *R. C. Gorman: The Lithographs,* Flagstaff, Northland Press, 1978.

The Native Americans: An Illustrated History, edited by Betty and Ian Ballantine, Atlanta, Turner Publishing, 1993.

Native North American Almanac, edited by Duane Champagne, Detroit, Gale Research, 1994.

Wade, Edwin, L., and Rennard Strickland, *Magic Images: Contemporary Native American Art,* Norman, University of Okalahoma Press, 1981.

Waldman, Carl, *Who Was Who in Native American History,* New York, Facts on File, 1990.

Other

Gorman, R. C., interview with Christopher B. Tower, August 1994.

—*Sketch by Christopher B. Tower*

Graham Greene

Graham Greene
1952-
Oneida actor

Graham Greene, one of the most visible Native American actors working on the stage and in film today, is probably best known for his roles in the popular films *Dances with Wolves* and *Thunderheart.* Greene was the second of six children born on the Six Nations reserve near Brantford, Ontario, to John, an ambulance driver and maintenance man, and Lillian Greene. At the age of 16, Greene dropped out of school and went to Rochester, New York, where he worked at a carpet warehouse. Two years later he studied welding at George Brown College in Toronto, then worked at a Hamilton factory, building railway cars. In the 1970s Greene worked as a roadie and sound man for Toronto rock bands and ran a recording studio in Ancaster, Ontario. He has also worked as a high-steelworker, landscape gardener, factory laborer, carpenter, and bartender.

Greene took his first acting role (a Native American) in 1974 as part of the now-defunct Toronto theater company, Ne'er-Do-Well Thespians. In 1980 he played a Native American alcoholic in *The Crackwalker* by Judith Thompson, and in the 1982 theater production of *Jessica,* co-authored by Linda Griffiths, he played the role of The Crow. In the 1980s Greene worked with the Theatre Passe Muraille, acting in an "irreverent set of plays, The History of the Village of the Small Huts." When not acting, he welded sets and worked lights.

The first film role Greene took came in 1982 in the movie *Running Brave;* he played a friend of Native American track star Billy Mills. Two years later, in 1984, Greene played a Huron extra in *Revolution,* a movie about the U.S. War of Independence which was shot in England and starred Al Pacino. In the meantime, Greene had a daughter by Toronto actress Carol Lazare in 1981. The death of his father in 1984, however, started what Greene described in a *Maclean's* interview with Brian D. Johnson as a "period of fast cars and guns." Moving to the country around the same time, Greene found himself out of work and selling hand-painted t-shirts in Toronto by 1988.

Events took another upward turn in 1989 when Greene played a cameo role as Jimmy, an emotionally disturbed Lakota Vietnam veteran, in *PowWow Highway.* That same year he received the Dora Mavor Moore Award of Toronto for Best Actor in his role as Pierre St. Pierre in Cree author Tomson Highway's play *Dry Lips Oughta Move to Kapuskasing.*

Lands Key Role in Dances with Wolves

Greene's largest film success came with the 1990 production of *Dances with Wolves;* the role of Kicking Bird, a Lakota holy man who befriends Kevin Costner, brought Greene an Academy Award nomination for Best Supporting Actor in 1991. And Greene's personal life moved forward at the same time. While shooting *Dances with Wolves,* he married Hilary Blackmore, a Toronto stage manager. As his film career took off, Greene continued his theater work, playing "a toothless, beer-guzzling Indian buffoon" in an all-native cast of *Dry Lips Oughta Move to Kapuskasing.* Television also came into the picture in 1990 when Greene played a Navajo lawyer in "L.A. Law," and Leonard, a Native American shaman, on the series "Northern Exposure."

Apart from his supporting role in *Dances with Wolves,* and his brief cameo appearance in *PowWow Highway,* Greene is probably most popular for his role as the mystical, murderous, Native activist Arthur in the 1991 Canadian movie *Clearcut,* based on Toronto writer M. T. Kelly's novel *A Dream Like Mine.* Two other movie roles that display Greene's acting talents were undertaken by the actor in 1992: the role of Ishi, the last Native American in California to live completely apart from U.S.-Anglo culture, in the made-for-television movie *The Last of His Tribe;* and the role of Lakota tribal policeman Walter Crow Horse in *Thunderheart,* a drama loosely based on events in Oglala, South Dakota, in which two FBI agents were shot and killed.

Also among Greene's more recent works is the 1991 adventure movie *Lost in the Barrens;* the role of a baseball catcher in the 1992 TNT movie *Cooperstown* with Alan Arkin; the role of an Anishinabe/Ojibway grandfather living on the reservation in the made-for-television children's movie *WonderWorks—Spirit Rider;* the Native mentor in *Huck and the King of Hearts*—a loose and modern adaptation of the adventures of Mark Twain's Huckleberry Finn; a local sheriff in the movie *Benefit of the Doubt* with Donald Sutherland; and a role in the film *Maverick* with Mel Gibson, Jody Foster, and James Garner.

Greene's future is also full. He appears in the movie of Thomas King's *Green Grass, Running Water,* and in the television movie *The Broken Chain* with other Native actors Wes Studi, Eric Schweig, and Floyd Red Crow Westerman. Overall, Greene has had roles in over 13 stage performances and 30 movie and television productions. He currently lives in Toronto with his wife and cat.

SOURCES:

Books

Native North American Almanac, edited by Duane Champagne, Detroit, Gale Research, 1994; 1066.

Periodicals

"A Filmmaker's Instincts: Costner's Dances with Wolves," *Commonweal,* January 11, 1991; 18-19.
Johnson, Brian D., "Dances with Oscar: Canadian Actor Graham Greene Tastes Stardom," *Maclean's,* March 25, 1991; 60-61.
Star Tribune (Minneapolis, Minnesota), 1991-1993.

Other

Greene, Graham, personal resume from Gary Goddard & Associates, Toronto, Ontario, Canada, 1994.

—Sketch by tpkunesh

Janet Campbell Hale
1946-
Coeur d'Alene novelist, poet, and educator

Janet Campbell Hale, a member of the Coeur d'Alene tribe of Northern Idaho, is a prominent writer, poet, and teacher. Her writings have appeared in numerous periodicals and anthologies, particularly those that explore Native American and other multicultural issues. Her fictional *The Jailing of Cecelia Capture* was nominated for a Pulitzer prize and other literary awards. The mother of two grown children, Aaron Nicholas and Jennifer Elizabeth, Hale lives in New York with her husband, Muhammad Ashraf.

Born on January 11, 1946, Janet Campbell Hale is the youngest child of Nicholas Patrick Campbell and Margaret Sullivan Campbell. Her father, a World War I veteran and carpenter by trade, was a full-blooded member of the Coeur d'Alene (which translates as "Heart of Steel") tribe who died in 1969 at the age of 77. He was the son of Pauline and Gideon (Peter) Campbell, the name Campbell being derived from Hale's great-grandfather's Indian name "Colemannee." This name translates into "dust," and would have been chosen to commemorate some important incident in his life. Hale speaks with pride in her American-Book-Award-winning *Bloodlines: Odyssey of a Native Daughter* about the fact that her surname is a real Indian name and not "just a name passed out by some government clerk who needed to write down a name and record an enrollment number after the treaties were signed and all the Indians had to be counted."

Hale's mother, who died in 1987, was born in Canada to an Irish father and a Kootenay mother and was a descendent of Dr. John McLoughlin, an important figure in the history of the Northwest who came to be known as the "Father of Oregon." Hale researched the life of her maternal great-great-grandfather in the summer of 1984 while on a fellowship to the D'Arcy McNickle Center for the Study of History of the American Indian at the Newberry Library in Chicago, and writes about him in a Bloodlines essay, "The Only Good Indian."

Early Life of Poverty and Abuse

Although her family lived in Oceanside, California, Hale was born in Riverside, California, when her mother was visiting Hale's eldest sister at the Sherman Indian School there. When she was six months old, the family returned to their home on the Coeur d'Alene Reservation where they lived until Hale was ten years old. After that time, the family lived primarily in Washington, both in Tacoma and on the Yakima Reservation in Wapato, although they always maintained strong ties to the Coeur d'Alene Reservation. Hale has three older sisters, two of whom returned after many years to live on the reservation, and a brother who died in infancy a year before her birth.

Hale's young life was one of poverty, abuse, and dislocation. Much of her youth was spent moving around the northwestern region of the country with her mother as she fled from Hale's alcoholic father. Hale recalls attending classes intermittently in "21 schools in 3 states" (Idaho, Washington, and Oregon) before dropping out of school after the eighth grade. In addition to continual uprooting, she also suffered considerable verbal abuse and rejection from her mother and three older sisters, the youngest of whom is ten years older than Hale.

Hale's situation did not improve as a teenager. She briefly attended the tenth grade at Wapato High School in Washington and spent a short time as a junior at the Institute of American Indian Arts (IAIA). In 1964, when she was 18, she entered into an abusive marriage and was divorced the following year. During this time, she had a son, Aaron Nicholas; and, although she was a teenage mother on welfare—without skills or support—she found the self-courage to imagine a better future for herself and her baby, as she recalls in *Bloodlines:* "For his sake, I told myself, I can imagine a future. I can be more than I was. I can be strong."

The turning point in Hale's early life came when a friend told her that the open-admissions, tuition-free City College of San Francisco accepted students over the age of 21 even if they had not finished high school. When Hale turned 21 shortly thereafter, she took the entrance examination and passed with such high scores that she was immediately placed in a university-track program. The following year, Hale transferred to the University of California at Berkeley, receiving her B.A. in 1972. She subsequently earned an M.A. in English from the University of California at Davis in 1984, and has also completed two years of work toward a law degree at Berkeley and at Gonzaga Law School in Spokane, Washington.

An Active Writer and Teacher

Hale has been an active writer for as long as she can remember. For example, she recalls filling up tablets with "writing" at the age of four, long before she could read or write, and sending off daily batches of poetry (minus a return address) to popular magazines when she was 15. Her first published work appeared in 1972 in an anthology entitled The Whispering Wind: Poetry by Young American Indians, a collection of verse written by students at the Institute of American Indian Arts. Since that time, she has written four book-length publications, including poetry, fiction, and nonfiction, and has published works in many periodicals and anthologies, including Time to Greez!: Incantations from the Third World (1975), whose Native American section she edited; Songs from This Earth on Turtle's Back: Contemporary American Indian Poetry (1983) and The Next World: Poems by 32 Third World Americans (1987), both edited by Joseph Bruchac; and Dancing on the Rim of the World: An Anthology of Contemporary Northwest Native American Writing (1990), edited by Andrea Lerner.

Hale's first novel, The Owl's Song, was published in 1974 and reprinted the following year. One of the few works of its time to address the problems of a teenage American Indian, both on the reservation and in an urban setting, it received positive praise for its potential ability to broaden young adult readers' perceptions about Native American culture. Hale followed this publication in 1978 with a chapbook of poems entitled Custer Lives in Humboldt County, which was made possible by a Small Press Grant from the National Endowment of the Arts.

National Attention with Pulitzer Prize Nomination

Hale received national attention in 1985, when her *The Jailing of Cecelia Capture* was nominated for a Pulitzer Prize. This novel, which uses its 30-year-old title character's imprisonment for drunk driving and welfare fraud as occasion for reminiscences about her life of poverty and abuse, presents a moving and complex portrait of determination in the face of many odds as well as a quest for identity that permeates all of Hale's works. In 1993, Hale published *Bloodlines,* her first work of non-fiction, in which she weaves autobiographical tales with stories about her ancestors and her heritage to present a compelling glimpse into the history and contemporary realities of Native American life.

Although Hale's writing takes many forms, her powerful style and intense, often autobiographical, portrayal of the Native American experience inform all of her works. She also is admired for her sensitive depiction of childhood; for her acute insights into the realities of financial, emotional, and cultural deprivation; and for her insistence on the importance of establishing and being true to one's own identity.

Since the early 1980s, Hale has been actively involved in teaching both at the college level and to younger children. She has been a visiting lecturer of English and creative writing at a number of post-secondary institutions, including Northwest Indian College on the Lummi Indian Reservation and Western Washington University, both of which are in Bellingham, Washington; the University of Oregon; and the University of California at Berkeley and Davis. Hale spent a year at the University of Washington in 1985 as a Distinguished Visiting Writer. In 1987, she was Richard Thompson Lecturer at Iowa State University; and in 1992, she was Visiting Distinguished Professor of Creative Writing and Literature at Eastern Washington University. In February of 1994, she was Claremont Lecturer at College of Illinois and

will return to the Institute of American Indian Culture in Santa Fe as Distinguished Visiting Writer in November of 1994. She has also traveled across the country on speaking tours both on and off the reservations. Hale lives on the Lummi Reservation in Northwest Washington.

SELECTED WRITINGS BY HALE:

The Owl's Song (fiction), New York, Doubleday, 1974; as *The Owl's Song and Other Stories,* HarperCollins, forthcoming.

Custer Lives in Humboldt County and Other Poems, Greenfield Center, New York, Greenfield Review Press, 1978.

The Jailing of Cecelia Capture (fiction), New York, Random House, 1985.

Bloodlines: Odyssey of a Native Daughter (autobiographical essays), New York, Random House, 1993.

SOURCES:

Books

American Indian Novelists: An Annotated Critical Bibliography, compiled by Tom Colonnese and Louis Owens, New York, Garland Publishing, 1985.

Contemporary Authors, Volume 49-52, Detroit, Gale Research, 1975; 236.

Contemporary Native American Literature: A Selected and Partially Annotated Bibliography, compiled by Angeline Jacobson, Metuchen, New Jersey, Scarecrow Press, 1977.

Dancing on the Rim of the World: An Anthology of Contemporary Northwest Native American Writing, edited by Andrea Lerner, Tuscon, University of Arizona Press, 1990.

Literature By and About the American Indian: An Annotated Bibliography, edited by Anna Lee Stensland, Urbana, National Council of Teachers of English, 1979.

The Native American in American Literature: A Selectively Annotated Bibliography, compiled by Roger O. Rock, Westport, Connecticut, Greenwood Press, 1985.

Native American Women, edited by Gretchen M. Bataille, New York, Garland Publishing, 1993; 101-102.

Native North American Almanac, edited by Duane Champagne, Detroit, Gale Research, 1994; 1066-1067.

The Next World: Poems by 32 Third World Americans, edited by Joseph Bruchac, Trumansburg, New York, Crossing Press, 1987.

The Remembered Earth: An Anthology of Native American Literature, edited by Geary Hobson, Albuquerque, University of New Mexico Press, 1979.

Ruoff, A. LaVonne Brown, *American Indian Literatures: An Introduction, Bibliographic Review, and Selected Bibliography,* New York, The Modern Language Association of America, 1990.

Songs from This Earth on Turtle's Back: Contemporary American Indian Poetry, edited by Joseph Bruchac, Greenfield Center, New York, Greenfield Review Press, 1983.

The Third Woman: Minority Women Writers of the United States, edited by Dexter Fisher, Boston, Houghton Mifflin, 1980.

Time to Greez!: Incantations from the Third World, San Francisco, Glide Publications/Third World Communications, 1975.

Voices from Wah'Kon-tah: Contemporary Poetry of Native Americans, edited by Robert K. Dodge and Joseph B. McCullough, New York, International Publishers, 1974.

Voices of the Rainbow: Contemporary Poetry by American Indians, edited by Kenneth Rosen, New York, Viking, 1978.

The Whispering Wind: Poetry by Young Native Americans, edited by Terry Allen, Garden City, Doubleday, 1972.

Periodicals

Cassel, Jeris, review of *Bloodlines, Library Journal,* July 1993; 81.

Cole, Diane, review of *The Jailing of Cecelia Capture, Ms.,* 13, April 1985; 14-16.

Elmer, Cathleen Burns, review of *The Owl's Song, New York Times Book Review,* August 25, 1974; 8.

Higbie, Andrea, review of *Bloodlines, New York Times Book Review,* August 22, 1993; 16.

MacRae, Cathi, review of *The Owl's Song, Wilson Library Bulletin,* 65, April 1991; 102.

Owens, Louis, review of *The Jailing of Cecelia Capture, Western American Literature,* winter 1986; 375-376.

Review of *Bloodlines, Kirkus Reviews,* April 15, 1993; 503.

Review of *Bloodlines, Publisher's Weekly,* May 3, 1993; 288.

Review of *The Owl's Song, Kirkus Reviews,* April 1, 1974; 372.

Rosen, Kenneth, "American Indian Literature: Current Condition and Suggested Research," *American Indian Culture and Research Journal,* 3, 1979; 57-66.

Schneider, M. J., review of *Bloodlines, Choice,* December 1993; 660.

Seaman, Donna, review of *Bloodlines, Booklist,* May 15, 1993; 1669-1670; 1681.

Wolitzer, Meg, review of *The Jailing of Cecelia Capture, New York Times Book Review,* April 7, 1985; 14.

—*Sketch by Linda Cullum*

Handsome Lake
1735(?)-1815
Seneca spiritual leader
Also known as Hadawa'ko ["Shaking Snow"], Skaniadariio, Ganeodiyo, Kaniatario ["Beautiful Lake"], and Sedwa'gowa'ne ["Our Great Teacher"]

Handsome Lake, a great leader and prophet, played a major role in the revival of the Senecas and other tribes of the Iroquois League. He preached a message that combined traditional Iroquois religious beliefs with specific white values. This message was eventually published as the Code of Handsome Lake.

Handsome Lake was born around 1735 in the Seneca village of Conawagas, located on the Genesee River near Avon, New York. Very little is known of his parents. He was born into the Wolf clan and was named Hadawa'ko ["Shaking Snow"], but was eventually raised by the Turtle clan people. He was a half-brother to Cornplanter and an uncle of Red Jacket. Born during a time when the Seneca nation was at its peak of prosperity, Handsome Lake witnessed the gradual deterioration of his society.

Multiple factors led to the erosion of morale and the material welfare of the Iroquois. In the period after the American Revolution, the Iroquois lost most of their land and were forced to live on reservations. The reservations provided poor living conditions, and, within a relatively short period of time, many Iroquois began to suffer alcohol abuse, fighting, and instability of the family unit, and accusations of witchcraft. This dismal situation was due, in part, to the basic incompatibility of the Iroquois social structure and reservation existence. The traditional religious rituals alone were inadequate to lessen the harshness of this situation. As a result, the Iroquois began searching for new solutions to their difficulties.

Brings a Message of Gaiwiio ("Good Word")

In 1799, after a period of illness due to many years of excessive alcoholic indulgence, Handsome Lake had the first of a series of visions. In his first vision, he was warned by three spiritual messengers about the dangers associated with alcohol; he was also told that witches were creating chaos within his tribe and that the persons guilty of witchcraft must repent and confess. Handsome Lake was directed to reveal these warnings to the people. His nephew Blacksnake and half-brother Cornplanter were with him during this time and believed in the power of his visions and their revelations. Shortly after Handsome Lake's first vision, he ceased drinking alcohol. When he regained his health, he began bringing a message of Gaiwiio (the "Good Word") to his people. He preached against drunkenness and other evil practices. His message outlined a moral code that was eventually referred to as the Code of Handsome Lake. The Code outlawed drunkenness, witchcraft, sexual promiscuity, wife beating, quarreling, and gambling. Handsome Lake presented his message along with a threat that fire would destroy the world if this Code was not obeyed.

Handsome Lake soon became obsessed with witch hunting and demanded confessions from those whom he suspected of witchcraft; some of those who refused to confess were killed. His witch hunting nearly became a catalyst for war with another tribe when he accused a prominent young man from that tribe of being a witch and demanded his punishment. Gradually, the sentiment of the people turned against Handsome Lake for what they considered an overzealous pursuit of witches. As a result of this change in attitude, he stopped his accusatory methods and briefly assumed a less prominent leadership role. Handsome Lake once again became popular during the War of 1812 and attracted many new followers.

The rise of Handsome Lake's religion was more successful than most religions during that time, apparently because his code combined traditional Iroquois religion with white Christian values. It stressed survival without the sacrifice of the Iroquois identity and recognized the realistic need to make adjustments in order to survive in their changing world. The Code of Handsome Lake, published around 1850, played a significant role in the preservation of the Iroquois cultural heritage and was popular throughout the Iroquois nations in Canada and in the United States. Handsome Lake, referred to as Sedwa'gowa'ne, "Our Great Teacher," died on August 10, 1815, at the Onondaga Reservation. His religious beliefs were carried on by Blacksnake and other disciples, and his teachings remain a compelling force among the Iroquois.

SOURCES:

Dockstader, Frederick J., *Great North American Indians,* New York, VanNostrand Reinhold Co., 1977; 102-103.

Leitch, Barbara A., *Chronology of the American Indian,* St. Clair Shores, Michigan, Scholarly Press, 1975; 138.

Waldman, Carl, *Who Was Who in Native American History,* Facts On File, Maple-Vail Book Mfg. Group, 1990; 144.

Wallace, Anthony F. C., "Origins of the Longhouse Religion," in *Handbook of North American Indians,* edited by William C. Sturtevant, Smithsonian Institution, 1978; 445-448.

—Sketch by Kay A. Floyd

Helen Hardin
1946-1984
Santa Clara Pueblo artist
Also known as Tsa-sah-wee-eh ["Little Standing Spruce"]

Helen Hardin was an artist recognized for her masterful of designs in acrylics and casein. Her mother was the famous Pueblo artist, Pablita Velarde—also known as Tse Tsan ["Golden Dawn"]—and her father, Herbert, was a policeman of mixed European heritage. Born in Albuquerque, New Mexico, in 1946, Hardin was a Santa Clara ["Ka'Po"] Pueblo, a descendent of the ancient Anasazi civilization. The language of her people was Tewa, which she spoke fluently. Hardin's parents divorced when she was 13,

and her father later remarried and moved to Washington, D. C. When Hardin graduated from high school, she rebelled against the idea of being an artist like her mother and enrolled in the University of New Mexico, where she stayed for one year.

Although she was initially reluctant to become an artist, Hardin, who demonstrated artistic talent at an early age, was a prolific painter and, at the age of 19, she held her first one-woman show at the Coronado Monument. This monument, known locally as Kuaua, was the site of an ancient Indian ruin that was renamed after the Spanish explorer Francisco Vásquez de Coronado. It is also believed to have been inhabited by the Anasazi. Hardin's mother was upset with the idea of her daughter showing her work at the sacred monument; in a rage, she locked up all of Hardin's Indian clothes, forcing her to borrow clothes from friends for the show. This episode reflects one of the many troublesome encounters that marked Hardin's turbulent and often competitive relationship with her mother, who wanted Hardin to study business rather than become an artist.

Hardin Paints in Secret

After dropping out of college, Hardin went to live with her father in Washington, D. C., only to return to Albuquerque a short time later. She attended business college and resumed dating her high school boyfriend, Pat Terrazas. Oftentimes, Hardin would paint at home but eventually quit because she felt her mother was too critical of her work. During this time, she befriended Margarete and Fred Chase, art dealers who had worked closely with Hardin's mother for many years. They encouraged Hardin to refine her artistic voice and they helped organize her first "formal" one-woman show in 1964 at Enchanted Mesa, New Mexico. When Hardin and Terrazas moved into an apartment together, he discouraged her from developing her artistic talents, so she would only paint while he was at work and hide her canvases and paints before he came home. Also without his knowledge, she would go to the Chases' for special speaking engagements and to receive commissions for her paintings. Although Terrazas often abused her both physically and mentally, Hardin remained with him and eventually became pregnant. On November 11, 1964, she gave birth to a daughter, whom she named after Margarete Chase. Finally, when her father was transferred to Colombia to set up a police training program, Hardin and her daughter paid him an extended visit to escape the cruelty of Terrazas and the control of her mother.

A major turning point for Hardin came after she appeared on the cover of the March/April 1970 issue of *New Mexico* magazine. The publicity she received from that one magazine feature was phenomenal. Admirers wanted to buy jewelry like hers and have their hair cut like hers—and they began to buy her paintings. With a newfound confidence, Hardin began to take firm control of her life and career. On July 3, 1973, Hardin married Cradoc Bagshaw, a freelance photographer. She served on the Albuquerque Arts Board and was a member of the National League of American Pen Women, the New Mexico State Fair Committee, and the New Mexico Council of American Indians. Hardin also perfected a special painting technique which consisted of layering acrylics using drafting tools to form meticulous designs. Prior to the 1960s, many Southwest Indian artists were influenced by The Studio, founded in 1932 by Dorothy Dunn. Velarde—the most famous female graduate of The Studio—was especially influenced by Dunn's painting. For her part, Hardin was inspired by one of The Studio's harshest critics, Native artist Fritz Scholder—not because of his art—but because she saw him as a revolutionary. Perhaps some of Hardin's admiration for Scholder lay in the fact that her mother was obsessed with the superstitious notion that Scholder fraternized with evil spirits.

Hardin, who often painted in series, has been described as an obsessive, compulsive, and rebellious painter. She approached her art methodically and meticulously using ancient patterns and geometric designs. She was fascinated with metallic acrylics and robes. Hardin's paintings have been characterized as anywhere from profoundly mystical and metaphysical to merely whimsical. She was especially inspired by the kachina, or deified ancestral spirits, in one series of paintings. Hardin's mother was wary of the images she portrayed in this series because their tribal elders had warned Hardin not to paint the images. Hardin's kachina painting "Winter Awakening of the O-Khoo-Wah" ["Cloud People"], won first prize at the Scottsdale National Indian Art Competition in 1972. This was one of the most prestigious awards in Southwestern art. Another sequence of paintings that Hardin created was the Mimbres series—whimsical paintings which delineate a story.

Bouts with Cancer

In 1981, Hardin was diagnosed with a malignant tumor in her breast. Although she had a mastectomy to treat the problem, Hardin's doctors later learned that the cancer had spread to her sternum and lungs. She went through several chemotherapy treatments which seemed to force the cancer into remission; however, in December of 1983, Hardin was hospitalized after a show in New York, and there doctors found that the cancer had spread to her liver. Hardin returned to Albuquerque, and on June 9, 1984, she died at home. She was cremated and half of her ashes were scattered across Puyé Cliffs, her ancestral home, and the remainder was given to her mother for a traditional burial at Santa Clara Pueblo.

SOURCES:

Scott, Jay, *Changing Woman: The Life and Art of Helen Hardin,* Flagstaff, Arizona, Northland Publishing, 1993.

—*Sketch by Phyllis "Picturestone" Noah*

Harjo, Chinnubbie
See Posey, Alex

Chitto Harjo
1846-1911
Creek warrior
Also known as Crazy Snake and Wilson Jones

The Crazy Snake Movement of 1900-1909, named after its leader Chitto Harjo (chit-to ha-cho), marked a significant transition for the Five Nations (Cherokee, Creek, Chickasaw, Choctaw, Seminole). Members of this movement, commonly referred to as Crazy Snakes, demanded that the Creek National Council and the President of the United States enforce the Treaty of 1832, which guaranteed the Five Nations a specified amount of land in Oklahoma. Although unsuccessful, the movement is symbolic of resistance to the forces of assimilation in the twentieth century. Fear of a Snake uprising in 1901 resulted in the use of federal troops to arrest and imprison Harjo. Fear of a Snake uprising in 1909 resulted in Harjo's death and the eventual decline of the movement.

Harjo was born in 1846 in Arbeka, a Creek town on the Deep Fork River in Oklahoma, the most western town in the Creek territory. Prior to the removal of the Creek from Alabama in the 1830s, Arbeka was a sacred village located on the upper Coosa River in Alabama and held legendary significance as one of the four original Creek towns. Arbeka was known as "the gate of the Muskogees." Here, Arbeka warriors guarded the Creek Confederacy against surprise attack. Runners warned people of danger by bringing the war whoop to other Creek towns. In the summer of 1900, when Chitto Harjo spoke against allotment at Creek stomp dances, he fulfilled his traditional role of carrying the war whoop to his people.

Harjo is a common second name among Creeks. It means "recklessly brave, one who is brave beyond discretion." It is usually translated as mad or crazy. *Chitto* is a derivation of the Creek word *catto,* which means snake. Harjo's name communicated distinction based on daring and courage, with a tinge of imprudence, to Creeks. He was known more intimately to family and friends as Bill Jones, Bill Snake, and Bill Harjo.

Formation of the Four Mothers Nation

The Creeks eluded the Dawes Act (1887), which divided tribal lands, for 11 years, but the passage of the Curtis Act (1898), which eliminated tribal governments, blocked further tribal efforts to avoid the Dawes Act and escape allotment. In 1899, the majority of Creek people acquiesced to the inevitable by selecting and registering their allotments and Pleasant Porter was elected Principal Chief on a platform of cooperation with the Dawes Commission.

Dissident Creeks opposed allotment because it violated previous treaties, especially the Treaty of 1832. They initially called themselves the "adherents of the Opothle Yahola Treaty." Chitto Harjo always referred to them as "Loyal Creeks." Local newspapers often referred to them as conservative fullbloods. Creek leaders called them the "ignorant class" of Creek people. Eventually, the dissenters were called "Crazy Snakes" after their leader, Chitto Harjo.

Creek protestors of allotment formed the nucleus of the Crazy Snake movement. The majority of Snakes arrested by U.S. Marshals in 1901 were Creek. However, opposition to allotment was not uniquely Creek. Cherokees, Choctaws, Chickasaws, and Seminoles, who also opposed allotment, joined forces with Harjo. Tribal representatives attended Snake meetings and organized snake factions among their people. After Harjo's arrest in 1901, the Crazy Snakes rapidly grew into an intertribal movement against allotment. In 1908, the Snake movement culminated in the formation of the Four Mothers Nation, an Indian organization for collective political action in the state of Oklahoma.

Organization of the Crazy Snake Movement

Hickory Ground was the center of Snake activity. Located 30 miles southwest of Checotah, Hickory Ground ranked eighth in size among 48 Creek towns with a population of 343. Residents of Hickory Ground had many pre-removal attitudes, including a strong anti-American sentiment and distrust of kinsmen who cooperated with whites. Therefore, the tribal conflict over allotment was rooted in centuries of factional enmity between Hickory Ground residents and pro-American Creeks.

The nature and history of the Creeks made factional discord over allotment inevitable. Political differences between Creek factions saturate Creek history. Harjo learned about the trauma of removal from his parents. He intimately experienced the differences that led Creeks to fight against each other during the Civil War, Reconstruction, and the Green Peach War. Factions evolved around local leaders whenever there was major discord, particularly in Creek relations with Anglo-Americans. Therefore, Creeks who opposed allotment resorted to the traditional Creek method of dissension.

Chitto Harjo was not the initial leader of the opposition movement. In 1900 Lahtah Micco was the *micco* (head chief) of Hickory Ground. Harjo was his *heneha,* the eloquent orator who made announcements and speeches for Lahtah Micco. Lahtah Micco wielded the power at Hickory Ground, but Harjo's speeches attracted the most attention, establishing him foremost among the dissenters to his white neighbors.

Harjo was elected *micco* of Hickory Ground in the spring of 1900 after illness had stranded Lahtah Micco in Washington for more than six months. Lahtah Micco had led a delegation to Washington to persuade the President of the United States to enforce the Treaty of 1832. All the delegation, except Harjo, contracted small pox. Harjo left the delegation quarantined in Washington and returned to Hickory Ground to organize Creek resistance to allotment. As the movement grew in size, white neighbors and government agents called its members "Snakes" after their charismatic orator.

The Snakes sought control of Creek affairs. They elected Chitto Harjo as their Principal Chief and adopted a code of laws for Creeks living in the Hickory Ground vicinity. They also erected a new tribal emblem in the Hickory Ground square. Harjo appointed a Light-Horse unit (police force); and, in a bold move, the Snakes claimed jurisdiction over Okmulgee, the site of the Creek Council House, where the National Council met in session.

Harjo Imprisoned for Snake Activity

Harjo and the Snakes were regarded lightly until Snake Light-Horse started enforcing Snake laws. Public whippings and ear croppings generated fear among non-Creeks. After Snake leaders threatened to kill Principal Chief Porter, National Council members and Dawes Commissioners requested federal help to end Snake resistance. Troop A of the Eighth United States Cavalry from Fort Reno and a dozen deputy United States marshals set up camp near Henryetta. A bloody confrontation was expected, but the arrest of Harjo and other Snake leaders was quick and bloodless. Ninety-six Snakes, from age 14 years to 88 years, were arrested.

The Snakes appeared in the U.S. District Court of Judge John R. Thomas, where they pleaded guilty to four charges. Judge Thomas sentenced them to two years at Leavenworth, then immediately suspended the sentences upon their pledge to live in peace. He promised future imprisonment at Leavenworth if they continued their resistance. The threat of jail did not stop Harjo from further organizing Snake opposition to allotment. He eluded arrest for ten months, but deputy marshals captured him in the spring of 1902. He and nine others were imprisoned at the Leavenworth federal penitentiary in March 1902, where they served the remainder of their two-year sentence.

Harjo Appeals to the United States Senate

Harjo took his opposition directly to the U.S. Senate in the summer of 1906. A select Senate Committee came to Indian Territory to investigate matters related to the termination of the Five Nations. On November 23, 1906, Harjo attended the public hearing in Tulsa, Oklahoma. When Harjo addressed the Senators, the clash of cultures was painfully evident. Harjo's style was difficult for the Senators to understand. In traditional, eloquent Creek oratory, Harjo petitioned the committee to restore the Treaty of 1832. He did not sway action by the Senators, but he embarrassed them by challenging the ambiguous legal status of Indians.

In 1909, after years of enmity between the Snakes and their neighbors, a shootout between Checotah police officers and Chitto Harjo resulted in Harjo's death. Even though Snake activity had subsided after their Leavenworth imprisonment, white fears of an uprising never disappeared. A large gathering of Snakes at the Hickory Ground Green Corn ceremony in the summer of 1908 scared citizens of Checotah and Henryetta. In addition, much to the displeasure of Henryetta citizens, Hickory Ground had allowed many displaced Black families from Henryetta to set up a tent camp near the town. Unemployed and landless, the families resorted to theft to feed themselves.

A posse from Henryetta rode to the tent camp and a shootout ensued as they tried to arrest suspected thieves. The posse opened fire and killed several Black men. Harjo and other Snake leaders were not at the camp. Harjo was at home, located 20 miles from Hickory Ground. McIntosh County Sheriff William L. Odom blamed Harjo for the incident. He sent four deputies to arrest Harjo. At sundown, March 27, 1909, as the officers approached Harjo's cabin, one of Harjo's friends shot and killed two officers. A bullet from the officers found its way through the cabin and struck Harjo in the leg above the knee. This wound eventually proved fatal.

The death of the two officers created a furor in Checotah and Henryetta. A larger posse returned to Harjo's home to find him gone. They shot at the women in the cabin, forcing them to flee, and burned Harjo's property to the ground. Consumed with revenge, vigilante groups roamed the vicinity pillaging Snake farms in search of Harjo. An alarmed Governor Haskell called out the state militia. The First Regiment of the Oklahoma National Guard occupied Hickory Ground with 200 guardsmen. They quickly restored order, but they did not capture Chitto Harjo. His disappearance resulted in many legends about his death. He most likely died on April 11, 1911, at the home of his Choctaw friend, Daniel Bob, from the gunshot wound in his hip. Snakes continued their efforts to block assimilation through World War I.

Views about Harjo were mixed at the time of statehood. Creek leaders and mixed-bloods viewed Harjo as ignorant, backwards, and an embarrassment to the tribe. Non-Indians labeled him the most dangerous Indian in Oklahoma because they believed he intended to kill every white person in the region. Other tribes viewed him as smart and eloquent, but many refused to follow him in the later years of the movement because they feared imprisonment at Leavenworth. Today, the Creek Nation views Harjo as a sincere, honest warrior-statesman, a shrewd and charismatic leader.

Chitto Harjo did not halt the encroachment of white culture upon the Creeks. However, the significance of his efforts transcends his failure to enforce the Treaty of 1832. Harjo's inclusive oratory disseminated seeds of intertribal cooperation that blossomed into an official political organization called the Four Mothers Nation. Moreover, he built a foundation on which intertribal political activism has flourished throughout the twentieth century and forged a coalition designed to influence the United States within acceptable forms of the dominant culture.

—Sketch by Kenneth W. McIntosh

Joy Harjo
1951-
Muscogee Creek writer, educator, musician, and artist

Joy Harjo is in the forefront of a group of Native American writers and artists who have emerged into national and international prominence over the past two decades. She is a screenwriter, a teacher, and a musician, but her reputation rests largely on her widely admired poetry. Beginning with her first published collection in 1975, her poetry has evolved into a solid and influential body of work that has earned her numerous prestigious awards as well as frequent comparisons with some of the major poetic voices of our century. Having established her reputation as a writer, Harjo has increasingly turned to music: she plays alto and soprano saxophone with a group appropriately named "Poetic Justice," and she makes recordings and personal appearances with that group. Harjo's different activities as an artist do not lend themselves to strict classifications; her early work as a painter, her later work as a poet, and her more recent interest in music performance, are all parts of an ongoing, integrated whole. For example, it is noteworthy that for her 1985 Watershed recording entitled *Furious Light,* Harjo reads her own poetry to musical accompaniment and created the artwork on the front cover of the tape cassette. Harjo is a writer who has acknowledged her debt to the technique of painting even as she works with words; she is a poet who freely admits to starting with a musical sound as her inspiration for a poem; and she is a musician who calls upon more than one medium to give full expression to her artistic impulses. Harjo is also an artist who is very aware of her political and societal position and is sensitive to how others view that position in terms of her work. "I am seen as a feminist poet," she told a *Poets & Writers* interviewer in 1993. "The way I interpret feminism in my own work is the power of a woman to be a warrior—to recognize the warrior characteristics within herself, which include self-love, vulnerability, honesty, integrity, a sense of morals, and so on."

Childhood and Education

Joy Harjo was born on May 9, 1951, in Tulsa, Oklahoma, toAllen W. and Wynema (Baker) Foster. She is the oldest of four children; her parents divorced when she was eight years old. As a young child, she became involved in a local church where her own passionate sermonizing made a deep impression on the children of her neighborhood. It was also at this time that Harjo's perennial urge to travel found expression in a desire to become a missionary. All thoughts of formal religion and missionary work ended when Harjo saw the local minister embarrass two Mexican girls who were noisy in church and were told to leave. Harjo left too— and for good.

Joy Harjo

One of the most important moments in Harjo's life occurred when, at the age of 16, she went to boarding school at the Institute of American Indian Arts in Santa Fe (she would return to the same school in 1978 as an instructor). For the first time in her life Harjo found her talents appreciated and encouraged in a school situation. In the words of Susan Lepselter, writing in the *Tucson Weekly,* the fact that she was now learning alongside other Native Americans "set her artistic self in motion." That artistic self was further stimulated when Harjo studied at the University of New Mexico, where she earned her B.A. in 1976. It was at Albuquerque that she continued the painting she had begun in Santa Fe. In her early twenties, Harjo sought out another painter in the family, her Great Aunt Lois Harjo Ball, and ask for guidance; she received the direction she needed, and as the poet told Susan Lepselter in 1989, her great aunt "was very connected to what I call the dream world." It was also at the Indian school that Harjo met and heard such Native American writers as Leslie Marmon Silko and Simon Ortiz give readings of their work. These readings led to another turning point for Harjo: she decided to give up painting and devote her energies to poetry. In 1993, Harjo told *Poets & Writers* magazine that a reading by Galway Kinnell had been especially influential on her, as had the work of a Ugandan poet, Okot p'Bitek, in addition to such writers as Audre Lorde, Gwendolyn Brooks, and N. Scott Momaday.

While she was still living in Santa Fe, Harjo became pregnant with her son, Phil; before the birth of that first child in 1968 (her second child, a daughter named Rainy Dawn, was born in 1973), she moved back to Oklahoma where she held various jobs, including that of a nurse's assistant in a local hospital. Her genuine feeling for the work led to an assignment in the maternity area where she was fascinated by being so close to the elemental events of life and death. More than an echo of Harjo's experiences in the world of medical care may be found in her 1991 *Ms.* article, "Three Generations of Native American Women's Birth Experience."

Two years after completing her B.A., Harjo earned an M.F.A. from the University of Iowa. She also studied filmmaking in 1992 at the Anthropology Film Center. By 1985 she was teaching at the University of Colorado, and from 1988 to 1990 she was with the University of Arizona. In 1991 she became a full professor at the University of New Mexico.

Early Published Poetry

Harjo's first collection of poetry was a 1975 chapbook entitled *The Last Song,* and many of the poems in that anthology come out of her early life and adolescence in the Southwest. Titles such as "Isleta Woman Singing," "Too Far Into Arizona," and "for a hopi silversmith," offer important insights into some of the wellsprings of Harjo's creative imagination. All of the material in The Last Song reappears, along with 48 new poems, in Harjo's second collection, *What Moon Drove Me to This?,* published in 1980. The poet's dissatisfaction with her early work is evident in a comment she made during her 1993 interview for Poets & Writers magazine. Speaking of the poems contained in *What Moon Drove Me to This?* Harjo concluded: "It was a very young book. There are probably only two good poems in it—poems that showed promise. It was a painful book, written during a difficult period in my life. You could see the beginnings of something, but it wasn't quite cooked."

Throughout this period, Harjo was also a writer-in-residence at Navajo Community College (1978), the New Mexico Poetry in the Schools Program (1974-1976, 1980), and the State Arts Council of Oklahoma (1980-1981). The same year *What Moon Drove Me to This?* was published, she had also begun to serve on such boards and panels as the Native American Public Broadcasting Consortium, and the National Endowment for the Arts. In 1983, Harjo published one of her best known works, *She Had Some Horses,* a volume that made the poet's work more widely known than any of her previous publications; more than a decade after its publication, the book was still in print and widely used in college literature courses. The long title poem of the book is perhaps Harjo's single most famous poetic expression—and the one she does not wish to discuss. In the poet's treatment of the horse, the animal is presented in terms of what has been called "psychic dualism," a vision that permits us to see our human nature as a part of, and at the same time apart from, the world of nature.

Additional Poetry and Screenwriting

The world of nature, more specifically the Southwest of her childhood and youth, became the subject of Harjo's next effort, her 1989 *Secrets from the Center of the World,* a book of prose poems and accompanying photographs by Stephen Storm. The combination of meditative texts by Harjo and surreal images by Storm results in a book that not only evokes a special mood but also leads to insights about relationships among people, landscape, and history.

Secrets from the Center of the World, with its usage of imagery to illumine words, was not unique in Harjo's output during the 1980s; throughout that decade she had been working steadily on screen projects for various broadcasting outlets. From 1979 to 1984, the poet was co-writer on *The Gaan Story* for Silvercloud Video Productions; and from 1983 to 1984, she was assistant screenwriter on *The Beginning* for the Native American Public Broadcasting Consortium. In 1984 she also produced a series of eight 20-minute scripts for Nebraska Educational Television under the title *We Are One, Umonho;* and in the following year she wrote a one-hour dramatic screenplay entitled *Maiden of Deception Pass,* for the Native American Public Broadcasting Consortium. In 1986, her screenplay work included *The Runaway* for Nebraska Educational Television, and *I Am Different from My Brother,* a rewrite of six half-hour scripts for the Native American Public Broadcasting Consortium. That same year, Harjo wrote poetry for a PBS film, *American Indian Artist Series II,* and worked as a production assistant on the project. Perhaps the most noteworthy moment on screen for Harjo herself came in 1989, when she appeared on the Bill Moyers PBS series "The Power of the Word;" the poet was interviewed by Moyers and read selections from her own poetry, notably a lengthy section from *She Had Some Horses.*

In 1990 Harjo published her most critically acclaimed poetry collection to date, *In Mad Love and War.* While the book contains recognizable variations on the poet's continuing concerns, it represents a new and very different direction for Harjo's poetic voice. The themes she deals with in this collection range from the strictly autobiographical ("Rainy Dawn" and "Autobiography") to music in the United States ("We Encounter Nat King Cole as We Invent the Future" and "Bird") to the personal, social, and political implications of the power of love ("The Real Revolution is Love" and "City of Fire"). The reception for the book was immediate and positive; less than a year after its publication, it earned the writer both the William Carlos Williams and the Delmore Schwartz awards for poetry. Harjo also received important recognition for her work during the earlier part of her career, including a first place award from the Academy of American Poetry in 1976 and a first place prize in poetry from the Writers Forum at the University of Colorado the following year. She received another first place award in poetry at the Santa Fe Festival in 1980, and a Pushcart Prize in 1988.

Harjo's most significant publication after *In Mad Love and War* has been her 1994 volume of poems entitled *The Woman Who Fell From the Sky.* The contents of this book return to some of the poet's earlier concerns, among them music, storytelling, the land and the human spirit, and female individuality. Speaking of the book and its contents, Harjo is quoted in the fall 1994 Norton catalogue as saying

that "the word poet is synonymous with the word truth teller. So this collection tells a bit of the truth of what I have seen since my coming of age in the late sixties." It is noteworthy too that the book is accompanied by an audiocassette of Harjo performing her own work to music.

In addition to the publication of her own poetry, Harjo has been actively involved in the placement of the work of other writers. She has served as poetry editor for the *High Plains Literary Review* and as contributing editor for *Tyuonyi* and *Contact II.* She has also been on the steering committee for the En'owkin Centre International School of Writing, and has been a member of the National Third World Writers Association.

Harjo is a mystical writer but with a sense of our modern world that firmly roots her in the here and now; she is a university teacher whose greatest influence on students often takes place outside the confines of the classroom; she is a reader of poetry in the oral tradition but one who will use every part of the media to spread that ancient tradition; and she is a visionary who not only takes us toward the future but also reminds us of our common and immeasurably distant past. Dan Bellm in the *Village Voice* has commented on Harjo's position as an individualist and as an inheritor of a great tradition: "Harjo's work draws from the river of Native tradition, but it also swims freely in the currents of Anglo-American verse—feminist poetry of personal/political resistance, deep-image poetry of the unconscious, 'new-narrative' explorations of story and rhythm in prose-poem form." Just as an artist may leave a native country but still work in the tradition of that country, Harjo moves in more than one world while constantly calling upon the symbols and traditions of her Native American experience.

SELECTED WRITINGS BY HARJO:

Books

The Last Song (chapbook), Las Cruces, Puerto del Sol Press, 1975.

What Moon Drove Me to This? New York, I. Reed Books, 1980.

She Had Some Horses, New York, Thunders Mouth Press, 1983.

Secrets from the Center of the World (with photographs by Stephen Storm), Volume 17 in Sun Tracks, an American Indian Literary Series, Tucson, Sun Tracks and the University of Arizona Press, 1989.

In Mad Love and War, Middletown, Wesleyan University Press, 1990.

Fishing (chapbook; originally published in New York Times, June 21, 1991), Minnesota, Ox Head Press, 1991.

The Woman Who Fell from the Sky, New York, Norton, 1994.

Screenplays

With Henry Greenberg, *The Gaan Story,* 1979-84.

With Henry Greenberg, *The Beginning,* 1983-84.
We Are One, Umonho, 1984.
Maiden of Deception Pass, 1984-85.
Origin of Apache Crown Dance, 1985.
I Am Different from My Brother, 1986.
The Runaway, 1986.
Indians and AIDS, 1988.
When We Used to Be Humans, 1990.

Recordings

Furious Light, 1985.
Lamman Foundation (video), 1989.
Power of the Word (video), PBS, 1989.
A Moveable Feast, 1991.
New Letters on the Air, 1991.

Other

"Three Generations of Native American Women's Birth Experience," *Ms.,* July-August 1991.
"Family Album," *The Progressive,* March 1992.
"The Place of Origins," in *Partial Recall: Photographs of Native North Americans,* by Lucy R. Lippard, 1992.

SOURCES:

Books

Bruchac, Joseph, "An Interview with Joy Harjo," in *Survival This Way: Interviews with American Indian Poets,* Tucson, Sun Tracks and University of Arizona Press, 1987.

Periodicals

Bellm, Dan, "Ode to Joy," *Village Voice Literary Supplement,* April 2, 1991.
Hamburger, Susan, "A Circle of Nations: Voices and Visions of American Indians," *Library Journal,* February 1, 1994; 128.
Lepselter, Susan, "Spinning Dreams Into Words" (interview with Joy Harjo), *Tucson Weekly,* December 27, 1989.
Nizalowski, John, "Joy Harjo: A Mystical Sense of Beauty," *Pasatiempo,* August 26, 1989.
Ruppert, Jim, "Paula Gunn Allen and Joy Harjo: Closing the Distance between Personal and Mythic Space," *American Indian Quarterly,* 7:1, 1983.
Scarry, John, "Representing Real Worlds: The Evolving Poetry of Joy Harjo," *World Literature Today,* spring 1992.
Smith, Stephanie Izarek, "Joy Harjo" (interview), *Poets & Writers,* July-August 1993; 23-27.
"The Spectrum of Other Languages: An Interview with Joy Harjo," *Tamaqua,* spring 1992.

Other

"Joy Harjo," in *This Is About Vision: Interviews with Southwestern Writers,* 1990.

—Sketch by John Scarry

Suzan Shown Harjo
1945-
Cheyenne administrator

As president and director of the Morning Star Institute in Washington, D.C., the oldest and the largest Indian advocacy group in the country, Suzan Shown Harjo reminds the federal government of the treaty rights promised in return for land cessions. She tries, in the face of constant budget cuts, to get the administration to honor the education, housing, and health benefits promised to Indians.

Harjo lived on a farm in Oklahoma for her first 11 years. Then, from the age of 12 until the age of 16, she lived in Naples, Italy, where her father had been stationed with the U.S. Army. She found a familiar tribal feeling in the Italian neighborhoods where people had known one another for generations, as they had on her Oklahoma reservation. Her early years on Indian territory were spent without running water, without indoor plumbing, without electricity. At that time, her notion of wealth was the ice put into drinks in the drugstore in town. Now, she deals with a budget of nearly $1 million, and drinks iced tea.

Artistic Interests

Harjo sings, plays the guitar, composes poetry, and acts. She was one of the founders of the Spiderwoman Theatre Company, an improvisational group in New York City. She played Hamlet's mother in a repertory company production, and sang in Gilbert and Sullivan performances. With her husband, Frank Ray Harjo, she co-produced a program twice a week on WBAI-FM radio called *Seeing Red.* She also served as drama and literature director at the station. She relaxes late at night by playing tribal music on her 12-string Martin guitar. In 1974, she moved to Washington, D.C. Her daughter, Adriane, studied art in California; her son, Duke, went to preparatory school in Massachusetts in 1989.

Career

In Washington, Harjo served as legislative liaison for an international law firm. Then, under the administration of Jimmy Carter, she became congressional liaison for Indian Affairs. Although she has never attended law school, she obtained a bachelor's degree, and she plans and drafts legislation. As executive director of the National Congress of American Indians (NCAI), she plans their annual conventions, does fundraising, delivers speeches, writes articles, publishes newsletters, and lobbies on behalf of the nation's one and a half million Native Americans.

During the 1980s, Harjo fought the Reagan-era budget cuts, which sought to eliminate one-third of NCAI's funds. She is especially concerned with the decline in health clinics because of the high mortality rates among Native Ameri-

Suzan Shown Harjo (left)

Harjo, Suzan Shown, "Guest Essay," *Native Peoples,* winter 1994; 5.

Howard, Jane, "An American Crusader: Suzan Shown Harjo of Washington, D.C.," *Lear's,* July/August 1989; 135-136.

—*Sketch by Ruth Rosenberg*

cans. She points out in a New York Times article that "the highest reported incidence of diabetes in the world exists on the Gila River Reservation in Arizona ... and an epidemic of hepatitis B in Alaska." Moreover, cancer, suicide, and alcoholism rates among Native Americans have reached alarming proportions.

The organization that Harjo heads so capably was founded on November 16, 1944, in the Cosmopolitan Hotel in Chicago, Illinois, under the sponsorship of D'Arcy McNickle to provide a political voice for Indian interests affected by legislation. Harjo's family helped to establish that collective with Ben Dwight (Choctaw), Archie Phinney (Nez Percé), Charlie Heacock (Rosebud Sioux) and three Cherokee leaders: Lois Harlan, Erma Hicks, and Ruth Muskrat Bronson. One of the earliest victories of NCAI was the eight-week protest mounted by representatives of 80 tribes against Termination, which was repudiated in 1960. The repatriation of sacred objects from museums is a more recent success. As she wrote in *Native Peoples:* "We are today celebrating the recovery of much of our history. We are greeting sacred, living beings who have been 'museum pieces' during all our lifetimes, honored in our memories and customs, but never seen in their context by anyone living."

SOURCES:

Gamarekian, Barbara, "Working Profiles: Suzan Harjo, Lobbying for a Native Cause," *New York Times,* April 2, 1986.

Elijah Harper
1949-
Cree provincial legislator

Manitoba provincial legislator Elijah Harper prevented the passage of the Meech Lake Accord. The accord was a 1990 federal proposal to amend the Canadian Constitution in response to the province of Quebec's demands for home rule. Harper objected to the accord because of the document's dismissal of Native concerns. Backed by the Assembly of Manitoba Chiefs, Harper blocked the accord's passage in the Manitoba legislature on June 22, 1990. By preventing the passage of the Meech Lake Accord, Harper, the sole aboriginal member of the Manitoba legislature and former chief of the Red Sucker Lake Indian Band, put aboriginal issues at the top of Canada's constitutional agenda. In 1990 Harper was awarded the Canadian Press Newsmakers of the Year Award and, in 1991, the Stanley Knowles Humanitarian Award.

Harper, who was born in northern Manitoba on his parents' trapline near the community of Red Sucker Lake, left home at the age of eight for residential school. After completing high school, he attended the University of Manitoba in Winnipeg from 1970 to 1972. Along with studies in anthropology, Harper helped establish the university's Native students' association, organizing the association with two other future Native political leaders, Ovide Mercredi and Phil Fontaine. In 1973, Harper married Elizabeth Ann Ross; the couple have four children.

Political Career Begins as Band Chief

After returning to Red Sucker Lake and working on several community development projects, Harper began his political career in 1977. In that year he was elected chief of the Red Sucker Lake Band, serving as band chief from 1977 until 1981. In 1980 and 1981 Harper travelled to London where he participated in Native efforts to stop Prime Minister Pierre Trudeau from patriating the constitution. Upset because aboriginal people had not been recognized in the Canadian constitution, Harper refused an invitation to attend the Queen's signing of the constitution in 1982.

In 1981, Harper was elected to the Manitoba legislature, winning re-elections in 1986, 1988, and 1990. While serving in the Manitoba legislature, Harper was legislative assistant to the minister of Northern Affairs, and also served as co-chairman of the provincial cabinet's Native affairs committee. He was appointed minister responsible for Native affairs in 1986 and a year later became minister of Northern affairs. In 1990 Harper attained national recognition for his rejection of the Meech Lake Accord.

Stops Meech Lake Accord

Canada's constitutional crisis came to a head in June of 1990. With all of the other provinces agreeing to support the Meech Lake Accord, Prime Minister Brian Mulroney feared that Manitoba would not. Attempting to pacify Manitoba's Native leadership, the prime minister offered a royal commission to investigate Native affairs and several other incentives. But Harper, with the support of Manitoba's Native leaders, prevented the legislature from ratifying the accord before the June 23 deadline. Commenting on his position in the *Globe and Mail, A Constitutional Primer,* Harper said: "It was not easy for me to make this decision.... But who's going to speak for us? We've been shoved aside." Harper added that his actions were meant "to symbolize that aboriginal people are not being recognized as the first people of this country and not being recognized as founders of this country."

Harper's vote, in addition to ending hopes for the Meech Lake Accord and a new constitution for Canada in 1990, also contributed to the acquisition of political power for Canadian Natives. Harper's stand against the accord captured the public's attention and the Native legislator from Manitoba became a Canadian folk hero. The failure of the accord also convinced Canadian political leaders that Native concerns had to be addressed. By August of 1990, both British Columbia and Saskatchewan were reevaluating their Native policies. And as the 1990s progressed, other provinces followed. The constitutional crisis, amplified by the failure of the Meech Lake Accord, gave Canada's aboriginal people political power they had not had in centuries. Harper's stand and the public's reaction to it brought Native groups all across Canada together in a triumphant display of pride and determination. Not since the late 1960s had Canada's First Nations been so united. Harper, standing in the Manitoba legislature, holding an eagle feather in one hand while quietly saying "No," to the prime minister, became a symbol of Native pride and determination.

SOURCES:

Books

Miller, J. R., *Skyscrapers Hide the Heavens: A History of Indian-White Relations in Canada,* revised edition, Toronto, University of Toronto Press, 1991; 291-307.

Native North American Almanac, edited by Duane Champagne, Detroit, Gale Research, 1994; 1069.

Sweet Promises: A Reader on Indian-White Relations in Canada, edited by J. R. Miller, Toronto, University of Toronto Press, 1991; 461-468.

Periodicals

Platiel, Rudy, "Canada Reconsidered: Aboriginal Rights," *Globe and Mail, A Constitutional Primer,* January 11, 1992; 7.

—Sketch by Michael F. Turek

LaDonna Harris
1931-
Comanche political activist and economic developer

LaDonna Harris is one of the most widely involved activists in the arena of Native American economic development and human rights. An outspoken feminist and advocate for the rights of children and the mentally ill, she has been recognized both nationally and globally for her humanitarian efforts on behalf of oppressed and poverty-stricken peoples throughout the last three decades.

Harris learned about the effects of racism against Native Americans early in her life. Her Comanche mother and Irish-American father separated soon after her birth on February 15, 1931. According to the family, the discrimination her parents faced as a racially mixed couple was more than her father could endure. He moved to California, where he kept up a correspondence with his daughter, but he never returned to see her. The responsibility of raising young LaDonna fell to her full-blooded Comanche grandparents in Cotton County, Oklahoma, near her birthplace of Temple. Her grandfather, a former Indian scout at Fort Sill, was a cultural traditionalist and an Eagle Medicine Man. Harris' grandmother was a Christian, but her grandparents' loving marriage was based upon their mutual respect for each other's beliefs. Raised largely in the Comanche tradition, Harris spoke only her tribal tongue until she went to public school at the age of six. It was there that she first experienced the full enormity of the discrimination that existed against Native Americans in Oklahoma, even though the state had the largest and most tribally diverse Indian population in the country.

The Senator's Wife

In high school, Harris met her future husband, Fred, who had specific ambitions to go to law school and run for elected office. While she harbored her own aspiration to work for the equality of native peoples, Harris nevertheless put her goals on hold in order to help put Fred through college and later law school. The couple had three children, Kathryn, Byron, and Laura. In the years to come, Fred in turn supported Harris' ambition to help her fellow Native Americans. He had been a sharecropper's son and grew up in dire poverty, so, although not a Native American, he

LaDonna Harris (left)

understood some of the difficulties that many indigenous people faced; he did not turn his back on them when he was elected to office. Serving first as a state senator, and then moving on to the United States Senate, he worked on human rights issues and helped Harris gain experience and make political connections that would aid her activist efforts in the future.

In 1965, while the Old South was embroiled in the struggle for African American civil rights, Harris, too, was working against the segregation of the Southern Plains Indians in Lawton, Oklahoma. Her efforts included assembling representatives from nearly all of Oklahoma's tribes, and from one of these conferences emerged Oklahomans for Indian Opportunity. This organization, which was the state's first association to draw members from all 60 Native American tribes, identified the achievement of equality and the breaking down of racism with economic stability, which had been sorely lacking in most Oklahoma tribes since the days of the Trail of Tears. Her work on this project earned Harris the title of "Outstanding Indian of the Year" in 1965.

National Prominence

Suddenly, Harris was a national figure, much sought after for service on public issues task forces, steering committees, and pilot projects. She became involved in policy issues related to children's rights and mental health, drawing upon the skills and acumen she had developed in her work on behalf of Native Americans. The late 1960s, with its turbulent social and political milieu, saw her working with such

groups as the National Rural Housing Conference, the National Association of Mental Health, the National Committee Against Discrimination in Housing, and chairing the Health Task Force of the National Steering Committee of the Urban Coalition.

In 1967, President Lyndon Baines Johnson recognized Harris' work by appointing her to chair the National Women's Advisory Council of the War on Poverty. Johnson's administration had been the impetus for the "Great Society," a group of programs aimed at actuating the promise of equal rights for all Americans through fairness in housing, employment, health care, and education. Again, Harris approached the task with unbridled energy and a positive outlook, so impressing Johnson that he named her to the newly created National Council on Indian Opportunity, a branch of the Office of Economic Opportunity.

With the escalating war in Vietnam and increasing civil unrest at home, Johnson decided not to seek re-election. He was succeeded by Richard M. Nixon, who ushered in an era of "mixed signals" for Native Americans. His administration would ultimately prove sympathetic to religious and land rights for native people, but reforms identified as "civil rights" were sometimes slow in coming. Harris' appointment to the National Council on Indian Opportunity in 1968 had proved to be a dormant one. She had resigned as founding director of Oklahomans for Indian Opportunity to work with the national organization, but its first meeting was not held until January 26, 1970. The Council was the responsibility of Vice President Spiro Agnew, but it was only at Harris' frustrated urging that the group was called together at all. After much of the same ambivalent attitude ensued, Harris left the position and began refocusing on grassroots Native American movements and on women's issues. She became a founding member of the National Women's Political Caucus and, in 1970, founded Americans for Indian Opportunity.

Global Advocate

During these years, Harris, still the caring mother and involved senator's wife, reached out to indigenous people the world over. She became interested in the peace corps and how its projects could foster local development for aboriginal groups. Traveling to such far-flung countries as Mali, Senegal, the former Soviet Union, and numerous nations in Central and South America, she served as a representative of the Inter-American Indigenous Institute, a group formed by the Organization of American States.

Harris, a well-known activist, an insider on Capitol Hill, and a frequent official visitor to the White House, divided her time between national and international work, always keeping Americans for Indian Opportunity at the center of her plans. Already well-connected on matters of rights for Native Americans, children, and the mentally ill, she was emerging as a national figure in feminism. To applaud her efforts, President Gerald Ford named her to the U.S. Commission on the Observance of International Women's Year. She also received human rights awards from the National Association for Education and Delta Sigma Theta Sorority. Even though she had not gone to college, she received three honorary degrees, including a Doctor of Laws from Dartmouth College. Dartmouth had been founded for the purpose of providing higher education for Native Americans, so this honor was a very special one in Harris' mind.

Although proud of her recognition by the Ford administration, she once again tired of the political bureaucracy in Washington, which often caused long delays in carrying out national initiatives. Furthermore, Harris' husband, Fred, was finishing his senatorial term, and wanted to return to the Southwest. The Harris family chose to settle in New Mexico, and Americans for Indian Opportunity relocated with them in 1975. Although directing most of her efforts towards AIO, Harris nonetheless has remained active in international affairs. Secretary of State Cyrus Vance offered her a position on the Board of Directors of UNESCO, and she accepted, dovetailing her global work with her responsibilities in tribal development projects.

At the behest of President Jimmy Carter, Harris served as a special advisor to Sargent Shriver, director of the Office for Economic Opportunity. Through this venture, she was able to realize a long-held dream, that of creating an Indian version of the peace corps. Called the "Peace Pipe Project," this program trained Native North Americans to serve as local organizers and developers, assigning them to indigenous communities elsewhere in the hemisphere. The host communities felt more at ease working with other Indians, and the Peace Pipe workers learned skills which they could apply when they returned home to tribal or urban Indian communities. Although limited in actual application, this project would become the basis for another of Harris' initiatives, the sometimes controversial Council for Energy Resources Tribes. This Council's mission was to establish the fair development (or nondevelopment) of natural resources on Native American land, with an eye towards employment and an equitable market price for coal, oil, natural gas, and uranium, among others.

Carrying on Comanche Tradition

In correspondence between Harris and Cynthia Kasee (July 29, 1987), Harris indicated that she sees her many roles as extensions of the traditional roles of Comanche women. They all translate into methods for retention of Comanche values, while still equipping the next generation to survive in a changing world. Certainly her teaching post at the Washington School of the Institute for Policy Studies shows this, as does her service as a U.S. delegate to Women for a Meaningful Summit's International Assembly in Greece. She keeps quite busy at her continuing post as Executive Director of Americans for Indian Opportunity, and board memberships with the National Organization of Women, Save the Children, Common Cause, and the National Urban League, to name just a few. She is justly proud of her children: Kathryn Harris Tijerina, president of the Institute of American Indian Arts, Byron Harris, a filmmaker, and Laura Harris Goodhope, a senate staffer. Husband Fred actively supports Harris' work and has himself

served on the President's Commission on Civil Rights, chaired the Democratic National Committee, and made two election bids for the presidency.

With all her accomplishments, it is easy to see why *Ladies Home Journal* named Harris one of their "Women of the Year and of the Decade" in 1979. Her tireless work on behalf of native peoples continues today.

SOURCES:

Books

Biographical Dictionary of Indians of the Americas, Newport Beach, California, American Indian Publishing, 1983.
Contemporary American Indian Leaders, edited by Marion Gridley, New York, Dodd Mead Publishing, 1972.
Native American Women, edited by Gretchen Bataille, New York, Garland Publishing, 1993.
Native North American Almanac, edited by Duane Champagne, Detroit, Gale Research, 1994.
Vogel, Virgil, *This Land Was Ours,* New York, Harper, 1972.

Other

Harris, LaDonna, personal correspondence with Cynthia R. Kasee, dated July 8 and 29, 1987.

—Sketch by Cynthia R. Kasee

Ned Hatathli
1923-1972
Navajo educator

Ned Hatathli was an influential leader in the Navajo community; he served on the Tribal Council and had a profound effect on the educational life of the Navajo. Among the first Navajos to earn a Ph.D., Hatathli improved the Navajo Arts and Crafts Guild and became the first president of the Navajo Community College—the first college to be operated by the Navajo people.

The first of ten children, Hatathli was born October 11, 1923, in a hogan on the reservation at Coalmine Mesa, Arizona. As a very small boy, he cared for the family's sheep and horses. At that time, the federal government built boarding schools for Native Americans; therefore, to receive an education, Hatathli would have to leave his home. His uncle, an Indian policeman, convinced his parents to send him away to school. He was raised in the traditional Navajo ways until he went to school. On a field trip to the deep South, he saw a world that he had never seen before: cities, industry, people of many colors, and an ocean that fascinated him. This strange new world impressed upon him the need for an education.

When he was a teenager, Hatathli became ill and had to return to the reservation for a time. While he was home, he learned more about his Navajo heritage, beliefs, and customs. Hatathli excelled in high school and graduated as valedictorian of his high school class at Tuba City (Arizona) High School. He then attended Haskell Institute in Lawrence, Kansas, a government school for Indians. World War II began only six months after he enrolled at Haskell.

Hatathli left school to join the U.S. Navy and served on a tanker as a radio operator. The ocean had a particular fascination for him, and the Navy gave him an opportunity to see the vastness of the sea. He was stationed in the South Pacific and traveled to ports as far as Australia. After he was discharged from service, Hatathli returned to Haskell and then moved back to the reservation. He worked as a property clerk for the Bureau of Indian Affairs (BIA) and married a Navajo girl, Florence Smiley, with whom he had four children. After their first child was born, Hatathli decided to work his way through college at Northern Arizona University in Flagstaff. Hatathli made moccasins and sold paintings for his income. He excelled in college and graduated (cum laude) with a B.S. degree. Later, Hatathli went to the University of Colorado in Boulder and became one of the first Navajos to receive an honorary doctorate.

Hatathli returned to the reservation and became the firstmanager of the newly formed Navajo Arts and Crafts Guild. He greatly improved the quality of the community's arts and crafts, updating the silver work and restoring the traditional weaving styles. Hatathli's influence in the community strengthened as he worked to increase employment and develop the use of natural resources on the reservation. He served on the Tribal Council and became the first director of tribal resources. Hatathli began building and utilizing the natural resources on the reservation—gas, oil, uranium, coal, and timber. In 1967, he worked with the Navajo Indian Irrigation Project as an education specialist. In addition, he purchased ranches and made profitable land deals for the Navajo. The Navajo people flourished and Hatathli was credited with the progress and growth on the reservation.

Opens First Native American College in Country

In 1969 Hatathli helped found the Navajo Community College at Many Farms, Arizona, the first college in the United States founded by and for Native Americans. As the first president of the college, Hatathli believed that his people could learn from the "white man." For many people, the college was a "dream-come-true." Some had never seen the written Navajo language and many had never written their names before. Traditional arts and crafts were taught at the school as well as business, agriculture, English, math, history, literature, law, and government.

Hatathli received many awards for his contributions to Native American society, including the Distinguished Citi-zen Award from Northern Arizona University, an honorary doctor of laws degree from Eastern Michigan University, and the Silver Beaver Award by the Boy Scouts of America. Hatathli's contributions to his community were cut short, however, when he died on October 16, 1972, at Many Farms, Arizona. One report states that he was acidentally shot but other sources indicate that it may have been suicide since he was despondent over facing 60 days in jail for driving under the influence of alcohol.

SOURCES:

Books

Biographical Dictionary of Indians of the Americas, Volume 1, Newport Beach, California, American Indian Publishers, 1991; 270.
Contemporary American Indian Leaders, edited by Marion Gridley, New York, Dodd, Mead, 1972; 92-99.
Native North American Almanac, edited by Duane Champagne, Detroit, Gale Research, 1994; 1070.

Other

Allen, Perry, interview with Phyllis Noah conducted August 17, 1994.

—Sketch by Phyllis "Picturestone" Noah

Ira Hamilton Hayes
1923-1955
Pima military hero

Ira Hamilton Hayes is best remembered as one of the Marines who helped raise the U.S. flag on Mount Suribachi during the battle of Iwo Jima in World War II. This brave action was captured in one of the most famous photographs to come out of the war, making Hayes and the other surviving members of the group instant national heroes. They received a hero's welcome from President Franklin Delano Roosevelt at the White House, were immortalized in a larger-than-life bronze statue in Washington, D.C., and were honored with a commemorative postage stamp.

Hayes was born to Joe E. and Nancy W. Hayes on the rural Pima Reservation in Sacaton, Arizona, on January 12, 1923. Little is known about his early life before joining the Marines to fight in World War II. Hayes served his tour of duty without attracting recognition until he participated in an Allied invasion of a small Japanese-held Pacific island named Iwo Jima. On February 23, 1945, Allied troops engaged the occupying Japanese forces in a fierce battle for control of the island. Having fought foot-by-foot to establish

Ira Hamilton Hayes

a secure beachhead for the rest of the Allied troops to land, the Marines symbolically declared victory over the Japanese by planting the American flag on Mt. Suribachi, a small rise on the island. This effort cost the lives of three of the six Marines who planted the banner. Photographer Joe Rosenthal was present to capture the heroic moment on film, although it has since been alleged that Rosenthal actually restaged the event for the camera several hours later. In any case, the now-legendary photograph caused a sensation in the United States, and Hayes and the other surviving Marines became national heroes.

A Hero's Welcome

Hayes and the other two survivors of the flag raising were immediately recalled back to the states, where they were received by President Roosevelt and reassigned to participate in the campaign to sell war bonds, investment certificates which helped finance America's involvement in World War II. This non-combat assignment, the constant public attention, and the lack of commemoration of the three Marines who died at his side while raising the flag, greatly disturbed Hayes. Because he felt that he had done no more for his country than any other soldier who had died or who was still fighting in the war, he considered himself undeserving of the conspicuous adulation that he received throughout the United States. Everywhere the war heroes traveled, they were hosted to receptions, honored at parades, and enjoyed the goodwill of countless grateful civilians who wanted to buy them a drink.

While the war bond drive continued, the image of the flag raising was becoming a national symbol. The government issued a postage stamp commemorating the event and commissioned an enormous bronze statue which reenacted the flag raising, to be placed on display in Washington, D.C. Becoming increasingly dissatisfied with his stateside duties, Hayes asked permission to return to active combat; however, by this time, the war was nearly over. Eventually, Hayes completed his tour of duty and left the Marines, hoping to settle down to a peaceful life on the Pima Reservation.

A Troubled Life after the War

Returning to the reservation proved much more difficult than Hayes had imagined it would be. By now, he had become used to receiving public notice, although he still maintained a humble posture towards his celebrity status. Life in the rural Sacaton community seemed very quiet and isolated, and Hayes began to feel that he did not belong there. Hayes had never married, and with other relatives to look after his aging parents, he did not feel that he had to remain on the reservation. He began drifting around the country, trading on his name to get odd jobs, a place to sleep, and free drinks. During this period, Hayes became an alcoholic and started getting into trouble with the law.

Over the span of 13 years, Hayes was arrested more than 50 times, and most of these incidents were alcohol-related offenses. Hayes' inability to translate his fame into a stable place in life caused him to feel even more alienated from society. He moved from city to city, periodically returning to the Pima Reservation with the desire to improve his life only to move on when the rural life bored him. Never able to regain control of his life, Hayes died of exposure in the Arizona desert on January 24, 1955, the apparent result of one last drinking binge. He was buried alongside many of his fallen comrades in Arlington National Cemetery, not far from the bronze statue which captured the most noteworthy moment in the life of this reluctant hero.

In 1961, an idealized version of Hayes' life was portrayed in the film The Outsider, in which Hayes was played by actor Tony Curtis. In 1965, singer-songwriter Bob Dylan wrote a far more realistic account of the alienated hero in his song "The Ballad of Ira Hayes." For a generation of young Native Americans who came of age during the rise of Indian activism and the Vietnam War in the late 1960s and early 1970s, Ira Hayes gained a new prominence. He was held up as the ultimate symbol of the wronged Indian warrior, one who fought for the United States and gained celebrity, but who died in near-forgotten obscurity.

SOURCES:

Dockstader, Frederick J., *Great North American Indians,* New York, Van Nostrand Reinhold, 1977.
Vogel, Virgil, *This Land Was Ours,* New York, Harper and Row, 1972.

—Sketch by Cynthia R. Kasee

William L. Hensley
1941-
Inuit leader
Also known as Iggiagruk ["Big Hill" or "Little Mountain"]

W illiam L. Hensley has been a leader in the Alaskan community since he graduated from college in 1966. He was a co-founder of the Alaska Federation of Natives, which successfully lobbied the federal government for the settlement of land claims, and also served in the Alaska State Senate. Hensley was born to John ["Aqpayuk"] and Priscilla ["Naungiagak"] Hensley on June 17, 1941, in Kotzebue, Alaska. His family were hunters and fishermen. The Native language of the Inuit is Inupiaq. After attending elementary school in Northwest Alaska, Hensley, like most Native children, had to go away to receive further education. He attended a boarding school in Knoxville, Tennessee, where he graduated from high school. Hensley attended several colleges before receiving his bachelor's degree in political science and economics at George Washington University in Washington, D.C., in 1966. In 1974, Hensley married Abbe Ryan (Irish descent) and they had four children, Priscilla, Molly, James, and Elizabeth.

William L. Hensley

Begins a Life of Public Service

While attending college in Washington, D.C., Hensley wondered why his people did not have much representation in Congress. Living conditions were very poor for his people. There were few jobs and most of the villages had no electricity. "It was a very tough life hunting and fishing," Hensley told Phyllis Noah in an interview. "I just had to do something." When he returned to Alaska after earning his degree, Hensley took a constitutional law class at the University of Alaska in Fairbanks. This class proved to be a major turning point in his life. He wrote a paper, "What Rights to Land Have the Alaskan Native?," that presented a detailed account of the historical and moral obligation of the U.S. government to resolve the Alaskan land claim issue.

In 1966, Hensley was one of the founders of the Alaska Federation of Natives (AFN), representing 200 villages, 12 regional corporations, and 12 regional non-profit social service organizations. The AFN lobbied in Washington for Eskimo land claims, and as a result of their efforts, the Alaska Native Claims Settlement Act of 1971 was passed in Congress, granting nearly $1 billion and 44 million acres of land to 80,000 Alaskan Natives. Hensley served as executive director, president, and co-chairman of AFN, and was instrumental in the passage of the land claims act.

Hensley was appointed by President Lyndon B. Johnson in 1968 to the National Council on Indian Opportunity, and he was invited to an international meeting in Paris to speak on the future of the Eskimo tribes. Hensley also received the John F. Kennedy Memorial Award and was awarded a scholarship to study living conditions in Poland and the Soviet Union. He had been studying the Russian language at that time and was interested in seeing how the Russian people lived. He served in the Alaska House of Representatives for two terms (1966-1970) before being elected an Alaska State Senator in 1970. Hensley served one four-year term, then was appointed to the position again in 1986 and served two more years when the senator at that time became ill. Hensley has received several awards for his role in public service, including the National Public Service Award from the Rockefeller Foundation in 1980 and the Governor's Award for Alaskan of the Year in 1981. Also in 1981, Hensley received an Honorary Doctorate of Laws from the University of Alaska in Anchorage.

Hensley has remained active in public service. He has worked to increase public awareness of many issues, including problems in Alaskan schools, suicide prevention, and alcohol abuse. He has served as chairman of numerous committees, including the Senate Special Committee on School Performance and the Senate Special Committee on Suicide Prevention from 1986 to 1988. He has also been involved with fish and game management and the rights of Natives to hunt and fish.

Active in Alaska Native Issues

Hensley has played an active role in Alaska Native issues since the late 1960s. Besides his activity with AFN, Hensley was involved with the Alaska State Rural Affairs Commission and directed the Land Claims Task Force. While senator, his district covered over 150,000 square miles and a population of almost 20,000 people, with the majority being Eskimos. Hensley was founding president for the Alaska Village Electric Cooperative in 1967, which was a joint effort between the Rural Electric Company and the Office of Economic Opportunity. Through these efforts, 50 villages received electricity for the first time. Hensley also served as chairman of the Federal Subsistence Board, which establishes hunting and fishing regulations for over 200 million acres of land. He was vice-chairman of Charter College and a member of the Pacific Region Council of the American Red Cross. He has served as chairman of the Democratic Party in Alaska, as a National Committeeman, and as a member of the Clinton Transition Staff in Little Rock, Arkansas, after President Clinton's election in 1992.

Hensley founded the Northwest Alaska Native Association (NANA) Regional Corporation in Anchorage, and he has served as executive director, chairman, and senior vice president. The corporation is Inupiat Eskimo-owned and employs 1,000 people. It is a diversified company with interests in natural resource development, tourism, food and janitorial contracting, electric power production, and security services. In 1989, Hensley was instrumental in developing the Red Dog Lead-Zinc Mine in Northwest Alaska, working on local, state, and federal levels. This zinc mine is the second-largest in the world with 85 million tons of reserve.

Charlotte Heth

SOURCES:

Books

Biographical Dictionary of Indians of the Americas, Newport Beach, California, American Indian Publishers, 1991; 271-272.
Native North American Almanac, edited by Duane Champagne, Detroit, Gale Research, 1994; 1071-1072.

Other

Hensley, William L., "Biography and Resume," 1993.
Hensley, William L., interview with Phyllis Noah conducted on July 29, 1994.

—Sketch by Phyllis "Picturestone" Noah

Charlotte Heth
1937-
Cherokee ethnomusicologist and administrator

Charlotte Anne Wilson Heth has made a lifelong study of American Indian music. Her interests have led her to collect and publish materials from ancient ceremonies, social dances, and native hymns, to a variety of other musical expressions. As Heth explained in *Selected Reports in Ethnomusicology:* "Categories of Indian music would include music for public ceremonies and social occasions as well as for private and semi-public activities such as curing, prayer, initiation, hunting, influencing nature, putting children to sleep, storytelling, performing magic, playing games, and courting."

Heth was born October 29, 1937. She completed her public school education in Tulsa, Oklahoma, and obtained her Bachelor of Arts and Master of Music degrees at the University of Tulsa. She took a doctorate in ethnomusicology at the University of California, Los Angeles (UCLA) in 1975. Thereafter she took a faculty position at UCLA in ethnomusicology. She also served as the director of the American Indian Studies Center on campus. In 1988, Heth served as visiting professor of American Indian Studies at Cornell University for two years. She then returned to UCLA as a part of the ethnomusicology faculty, serving as head of the department, then as associate dean of the School of the Arts. In 1994, she became the assistant director for public programming of the National Museum of the American Indian in Washington, D.C.

As a member of the Cherokee Nation, Heth began her primary research in Oklahoma Cherokee music and the music of surrounding tribal groups, particularly those tribes who were removed from the southeastern region of what is now the United States. She has continued researching, doing applied work in, and publishing on American Indian music, ethnomusicology, dance, education, and other Native American studies. By 1994, she completed extensive research for an important monograph entitled "Songs of Medicine Spring," which includes Cherokee/Natchez tribal town history, ceremonial practice, music, and dance. Published work from her Medicine Spring research includes: "The Mosquito Dance," *Chronicles of Oklahoma* (1976-1977); *Songs and Dances of the Eastern Indians from Medicine Spring and Allegheny* (New World Records, 1991-1993); and *Music of the Sacred Fire: The Stomp Dance of the Oklahoma Cherokee,* with Willie Jumper and Archie Sam (UCLA, 1978).

Heth has also served as general editor for several publications, including: *Selected Reports in Ethnomusicology* (UCLA, 1980); *Issues for the Future of American Indian Studies* (UCLA, 1985); and *Native American Dance: Ceremonies and Social Traditions* (1992). *Native American Dance* is the first publication of the National Museum of the American Indian, a major installation in Washington, D. C., which is a collective part of the Smithsonian Institution. Heth described the importance of her work in the introduction to the book: "The value of this music and dance to the peoples who created them and still use them cannot be overestimated. Indian music and dance pervade all aspects of life, from creation stories to death and remembrance of death. The importance of American Indian dance is found not only in its impact on modern society, but also in the traditions and values it expresses to and for the Indian peoples. This oral tradition has survived solely because the music and dance were too important to be allowed to die. Native peoples' relationships to their creators, their fellow humans, and to nature is what American Indian dance really celebrates."

Heth has received many honors, including being named president of the Society for Ethnomusicology and being selected as keynote speaker at prestigious conferences and universities. She is fluent in French, German, Spanish, and Cherokee. In curriculum development, she has served as a member of the curriculum committee of the American Indian Studies Center at UCLA. In this capacity, she wrote and edited the curriculum for the interdisciplinary Masters of Arts degree in American Indian Studies that was initiated in 1982. She also served as organizer and team teacher of the interdisciplinary course "Racial Minorities in the United States," and as co-facilitator for the "Ford Ethnic Women's Project" for curriculum transformation at UCLA in 1989 and 1990. Heth's work to make music and song intelligible to peoples of all cultures serves the processes of mutual tolerance and understanding.

SOURCES:

Books

Issues for the Future of American Indian Studies: A Needs Assessment and Program Guide, edited by Charlotte Heth and Susan Guyette, Los Angeles, UCLA American Indian Studies Center, 1985.
Native American Dance: Ceremonies and Social Traditions, edited by Charlotte Heth, Washington, D.C., National Museum of the American Indian, Smithsonian Institution, 1992.

Native North American Almanac, edited by Duane Champagne, Detroit, Gale Research, 1994.
Selected Reports in Ethnomusicology, edited by Charlotte Heth, Los Angeles, UCLA American Indian Studies Center, 1980.

Other

Treasures (compact disc), Washington, D.C., National Museum of the American Indian, Smithsonian Institution, 1994.

—*Sketch by Howard Meredith*

J. N. B. Hewitt
1859-1937
Tuscarora ethnologist

John Napoleon Brinton Hewitt, the twentieth century's foremost authority on the Iroquois (and arguably other Woodlands Indians), was probably the most important scholar of the American Indian who was himself Indian. He shaped modern appreciation of the Iroquois (Hodenosaunee) League as having inspired the United States Constitution, with its democratic-republican impulse and institutionalized women's rights. Hewitt powerfully personified Indians' ability to compete with whites as intellectual equals and ultimately to handle their own affairs. Yet his career remained dependent on white financing, he failed to play a unifying role in the Iroquoian political crisis of his time (the Iroquois Land Claim cases of the 1920s), and as an anthropologist, he contributed to the objectifying and stereotyping of Indian cultures decried by later activists like Vine Deloria, Jr.

Born near Lewiston in Niagara County, New York, of a Tuscarora mother and a Scottish physician father, Hewitt was hired before his twenty-first birthday by Erminnie A. Smith to help her collect Iroquois myths. Smith died in 1886, and, to continue her work, the Smithsonian Bureau of American Ethnology hired Hewitt. In the bureaucratic wars between the archaeologists, who wanted to learn about Indians by digging up and analyzing their graves, and the ethnographers, who placed a higher value on linguistics and oral histories, Hewitt was a powerful voice on the side of listening.

Hewitt was a painstaking researcher. He published a tiny portion of his work, and that only in academic and government journals. In addition to various *American Anthropologist* articles on the founding of the Iroquois League, Hewitt published articles in other journals on Iroquois religion and politics, including his masterwork, "A Constitutional League of Peace in the Stone Age of America: The League of the Iroquois and its Constitution." He contributed freely to the works of others, particularly to F. W. Hodge's two-volume *Handbook of American Indians North of Mexico,* in which Hewitt made 18 contributions. Hewitt played an important role in two Iroquois studies completed after his death by William N. Fenton, among them 1944's seminal study of grieving ceremonies, "The Requickening Address of the Iroquois Condolence Council." Hewitt's manuscripts in the Smithsonian archives include important research on Wyandot and Munsee vocabularies and Tuscarora customs and beliefs.

Hewitt's manuscripts and notes at the Smithsonian Institution continued to provide a treasury of insights into Iroquois, Creek, and Algonquian history, mythology, and customs long after his death in 1937. Scholars have drawn from his research throughout the twentieth century. For example, Hewitt's Creek notes were incorporated by W. C. Sturtevant in his 1987 *A Creek Source Book.* Gill and Sullivan's *Dictionary of Native American Mythology* cites Hewitt for no less than 23 complex Indian legends, among them stories of Bean Woman's mating with Corn, Cannibal Woman, Chipmunk's Stripes, and the Midwinter Feast of Dreams. On little-documented matters of prehistory, John Upton Terrell's *American Indian Almanac* cites Hewitt as his authority on Delaware wampum-making, Susquehanna and Erie fighting qualities, Huron funeral practices, Iroquois affection for kinfolk, and Sauk clan structure.

Early in the twentieth century, Hewitt began a professional association with the flamboyant Oneida activist Minnie Cornelius Kellogg. Hewitt's New York Tuscaroras and Kellogg's Wisconsin Oneidas, descendants of Indians who fought on the American side in the Revolutionary War, were guaranteed their homelands by the 1784 Fort Stanwix Treaty. Although Hewitt was satisfied to prove on paper that the ancient Iroquois League had inspired the Founding Fathers, Kellogg wanted to resurrect the League itself. Hewitt believed that her scheme was impractical but aided her in exchange for her help in gathering information on the reservations and contacting Iroquois informants. However, Hewitt distanced himself from Kellogg in a 1932 correspondence in which he accused her of misinterpreting several fairly esoteric points of Iroquois lore. Soon thereafter, a pyramid scheme of Kellogg's collapsed and further aggravated Iroquois factionalism.

Hewitt died justified, Kellogg in disgrace. Fifty years later, Anglo academics have continued to bicker over whether Hewitt adequately proved his theories about Iroquois democracy and feminism. Although twentieth century scholars of the Iroquois have relied heavily on Hewitt's authoritative manuscripts and notes, Hewitt, the most important Iroquoian scholar, never had his work published as a book.

SOURCES:

Beyond the Covenant Chain: The Iroquois and Their Neighbors in Indian North America, 1600-1800, edited by Daniel K. Richter and James H. Merrell, Syracuse University Press, 1987.

Collier, John, *Indians of the Americas: The Long Hope* (abridged edition), New York, New American Library, 1947.

Deloria, Vine, Jr., *Custer Died for Your Sins: An Indian Manifesto,* New York, Macmillan Company, 1969.

Dictionary of Indians of North America, Scholarly Press, 1978.

Gill, Sam D., and Irene F. Sullivan, *Dictionary of Native American Mythology,* Oxford University Press, 1992.

Handbook of American Indians North of Mexico, two volumes, edited by Frederick Webb Hodge, New York, Greenwood Press, 1907, 1910, 1969.

Handbook of North American Indians, Volume 15: Northeast, edited by Bruce G. Trigger, Washington, D.C., Smithsonian Institution, 1978.

Indian Lives: Essays on Nineteenth- and Twentieth-Century Native American Leaders, edited by L. G. Moses and Raymond Moses, University of New Mexico Press, 1985.

Johansen, Bruce E., *Forgotten Founders: Benjamin Franklin, the Iroquois, and the Rationale for the American Revolution,* Gambit Publishers, 1982.

Native North American Spirituality of the Eastern Woodlands: Sacred Myths, Dreams, Visions, Speeches, Healing Formulas, Rituals and Ceremonials, edited by Elisabeth Tooker, Paulist Press, 1979.

Terrell, John Upton, *American Indian Almanac,* New York, Barnes and Noble, 1971, 1994.

—Sketch by Steven Edwin Conliff

Hiawatha
Fourished fourteenth century
Mohawk or Onondaga tribal leader

Hiawatha is the cultural hero from Iroquois mythology who is credited with the founding of the Iroquois Confederacy. He is generally thought to have been Mohawk, but other versions of the legend have described him as an Onondaga. Due to the various theories of his tribal origin, it is probable that Hiawatha was not a single person; instead, he was probably an amalgamation of two or more figures from the northern Iroquoian tribes who worked to form the confederacy, and he probably combines the best qualities of each. The time period most often ascribed to Hiawatha's actions is the mid- to late-1400s, although the exact beginnings of the confederacy have long been the subject of discussion and scholarly debate.

Confusion by Longfellow

Perhaps of most importance before beginning the actual story of Hiawatha and the founding of the Iroquois

Hiawatha

Confederacy is an explanation of the misuse of Hiawatha's name by Henry Wadsworth Longfellow. Longfellow's poem, *The Song of Hiawatha* (1855) actually tells the tale of an Algonquian mythic hero named Nanabozho. Longfellow's use of the name Hiawatha for this character seems to be the result of a rather strange series of misidentifications starting with Joshua V. H. Clark, who first confused Hiawatha and his deeds with an Onondaga culture hero named Tharaonhiawagon in his *Onondaga: Or, Reminiscences of Earlier and Later Times* (1849). According to Horatio E. Hale in his *Iroquois Book of Rites* (1883), this confusion may have arisen from the fact that Clark was collecting the story of the founding of the confederacy from two Onondaga chiefs and the Onondaga names for the two individuals sound very similar. Henry Rowe Schoolcraft published this same version of the story in his *Notes on the Iroquois; Or Contributions to the Statistics, Aboriginal History, Antiquities and General Ethnology of Western New York* (1847), although he fails to identify Clark as the source for his legend, probably because his work was published before that of Clark. Thus, when Longfellow encountered these stories while researching for his epic poem, he noted their similarities with those of the Algonquian cultural hero Nanabozho, and eventually decided to use the name Hiawatha, possibly because Hiawatha would be more pleasing to the Western ear than Nanabozho. The success of this poem led Schoolcraft to republish many of the legends, including that of "Hiawatha; or, Nanabozho," thus forever confusing the two heros and their deeds. Hale commented that "If a Chinese traveler, during the middle ages, inquiring

into the history and religion of the western nations, had confounded King Alfred with King Arthur, and both with Odin, he would not have a more preposterous confusion of names and characters."

The Legend of Hiawatha

This relating of the legend of Hiawatha and the founding of the Iroquois Confederacy is primarily drawn from Arthur C. Parker's version of the story in *Seneca Myths and Folk Tales* (1923). According to legend, the Mohawk of a certain village at the conjunction of the Mohawk River and the Hudson were particularly warlike. They continually sent out war parties to raid neighboring villages in an effort to weaken and ultimately to defeat the surrounding tribes. Among the Mohawk chiefs was one named Dekanawida, who despaired at his tribe's incessant fighting. During the council gatherings, he often spoke out against intervillage and intertribal warfare and warned his Mohawk brothers that they might all die in such pursuits. Nevertheless, the aggressive young warriors rejected Dekanawida's advice. One day, he finally grew tired of cautioning the Mohawk about their actions and moved west to avoid the conflict. During his journey, Dekanawida came to the shore of a lake where he lay down to rest. As he lay meditating, he heard the sound of a paddle in the water of the lake and looked out to see a man leaning over the edge of his canoe dipping a basket into the shallow water. When he raised the basket, Dekanawida saw that it was full of periwinkle shells. The man then paddled his canoe to shore where he lit a fire and sat stringing the shells into wampum belts. As he finished each string, he would touch the shells and talk. Dekanawida watched as he finished many strings in this fashion and then rose to his feet to make his presence known.

After the man from the canoe had introduced himself as Hiawatha, Dekanawida inquired of him the meaning of the strings of shells that he had made. Hiawatha replied that they were the rules of life and good government, asserting that the string of all white shells was the sign of truth, peace, and good will, while the string of all black shells represented hatred, war, and a bad heart. Further, the string which alternated black and white signified that peace should exist between nations, while the string with white on either end and black in the middle signified that wars must end and peace be declared. Dekanawida saw the wisdom of Hiawatha's words and realized that the warring Mohawk could benefit from such advice. Further, Dekanawida recognized that all those who spoke one tongue should stop fighting and instead join forces to strengthen their position against other tribes. Hiawatha said that he had attempted to express such ideas to Tadadaho of the mighty Onondaga nation, but the uncooperative chief had driven him away, so he had journeyed to this far lake where he could make laws that should govern all men. The strings of shells which he used to represent these laws would remind men for all time of the law and its meaning.

Dekanawida invited Hiawatha to return with him to his Mohawk village where he called a council of all the chiefs, warriors, and women so that Hiawatha could explain his laws. The people were much impressed with the laws that Hiawatha set forth and everyone agreed to live by them. Dekanawida and Hiawatha also journeyed to the Oneida and the Cayuga nations so that they might tell them, too, of the laws, and both tribes agreed to abide by them. Now Dekanawida and Hiawatha turned to the Onondaga and the mighty Tadadaho. When Tadadaho learned that three of the Iroquois nations had united and that the two emissaries wanted the Onondaga to join as well, he ran from the village into the woods. The evil spirits which inhabited him became serpents and sprouted from his head in a weaving mass, transforming Tadadaho into a Medusa-like creature. Despite Tadadaho's malevolent transformation, Dekanawida refused to fear him, and he once more asked the Onondaga chief to join the confederacy of peace and friendship. Tadadaho continued to rage until Hiawatha approached him and combed the serpents from his head; he also told Tadadaho that he would be named the head chief of the confederacy as long as he promised to govern it according to the established laws. Upon hearing this condition, Tadadaho agreed to join the union, but asked why the mighty Seneca, who numbered more than any of the other tribes, had not been visited and asked to join the confederacy. Taking Tadadaho's concern seriously, the delegates visited the Seneca as well as other tribes to the west, but only the Seneca agreed to embrace the peace and goodness of Hiawatha's laws.

Many elements of this legend correspond to what is known today about the founding of the Iroquois Confederacy. Prior to the union, there had been a great deal of warfare among all of the tribes. Around the mid- to late-1400s, there is evidence that the five northern Iroquoian speaking tribes of the Mohawk, Oneida, Cayuga, Onondaga, and Seneca came together to form an alliance based on their mutual needs for defense and economic stability. With the arrival of French traders in the St. Lawrence Valley around this time, the Indians may have seen the wisdom of facing these potential trading partners or enemies with a united Iroquois front. Moreover, the Iroquois nations probably recognized the advantages of defending themselves against their common enemies such as the neighboring Algonquians, as well as providing a strong economic compact which would assist any one of the member tribes in the event of a bad harvest or some other disaster. What is more, the Iroquois may have concluded that such a comprehensive alliance would give the five member tribes a decisive edge over other groups—both Indian and European—in the economic and political issues that affected the region.

There also appears to be some historical evidence to corroborate with Tadadaho's selection as the Chief of the Chiefs of the Iroquois Confederacy in the Hiawatha legend. While the story explains the way in which he obtained this position, it does not account for why an initially evil chief was bestowed with such an honorable title. Witchcraft was widely practiced at this time, and Tadadaho was considered to be one of the most formidable witches among the Iroquois. Because of his power as a witch, he was both feared and respected not only be his followers, but by the other

tribes as well. Therefore, in order for the Iroquois Confederacy to become a reality, this powerful and influential figure had to be appeased. It is said that Hiawatha attempted to address the Onondaga council three times with his ideas, only to be defeated by the obstinate Tadadaho on each occasion. Hiawatha then left the Onondaga village and took his plans to the Mohawk, who saw the wisdom and potential benefits of such an alliance. The Mohawk realized that they alone could not stand up to Tadadaho, however, so they enlisted the support of the Oneida and Cayuga in order to strengthen their position in persuading the Onondaga to join the confederacy. In the face of such united support and with the appeasement of Tadadaho, the Onondagas ultimately agreed to the union of tribes. Interestingly, it is possible that Tadadaho's recommendation to include the Seneca in the confederacy was an attempt to sabotage Hiawatha's plan because the Onondaga chief did not believe that the Seneca could actually be persuaded to join the membership. Nevertheless, Hiawatha's choice of Tadadaho as the head chief was a master stroke of diplomacy in that Tadadaho was now forced to support the confederacy publicly rather than to work against it.

Of collateral interest in the Hiawatha legend is the story of the Seneca woman Ja gon sah sa. This tale appears to have less historical depth than the rest of the legend, but it is significant in that it recounts how a woman played an important role in the origin of the confederacy. Ja gon sah sa was believed to have been a rather wanton woman who met and came under the influence of Dekanawida and Hiawatha when they visited the Seneca on their mission to assemble a confederacy. According to the legend, Ja gon sah sa was instrumental in convincing the Seneca to join the alliance, a role which was ultimately pivotal to the success of the whole undertaking. As a result of her contribution to the project, she was given the name of Ja gon sah sa, which means Lynx, to remind the member tribes of her importance. She is said to be buried at the present site of Ganondagan State Park near Rochester, New York.

The symbol that the five member tribes adopted for the Iroquois Confederacy is the Great Tree of Peace, which was said to be planted at the inception of the new alliance with its roots pointing in the four cardinal directions. The idea was that other nations, when they saw the roots, were to follow them to their source at the Great Tree where they would discover Hiawatha's Great Law. The eagle surmounting the Great Tree represents an ever vigilant symbol watching for any approaching threat to the confederacy. Thus, the five tribes sought to extend their ideas to surrounding groups and eventually to bring peace and prosperity to much of the area.

Political Structure of the Confederacy

The symbolic political structure of the confederacy was laid out in the form of the longhouse, the traditional form of dwelling of the Iroquois people. A longhouse is, as its name implies, a long narrow dwelling in which an extended family would live. Longhouses could be ten to 15 feet wide and up to 250 feet in length. There was a door on either end of the dwelling, and two or more shelves ran down either side from one end to the other. Clan-affiliated nuclear families lived in segmented units in the longhouse, each two families having their own fire in the center aisle and using the side shelves as sleeping and storage areas. In setting up the confederacy, the founders saw the political system as a large longhouse encompassing the territory of the five tribes. The Mohawk, being the eastern most people, were seen as keepers of the eastern door of the longhouse. The Seneca, being the western most group, were seen as keepers of the western door. The Onondaga, centrally located, were seen as keepers of the central fire of the longhouse, and their territory was where all formal confederacy meetings were to be conducted. These three nations were considered the elder brothers of the confederacy. As keepers of the doors at either end of the longhouse, the Seneca and Mohawk were expected to be the guardians of the confederacy; they officially greeted any visitors approaching the confederacy from their direction, and they warned the member tribes of any danger which might be approaching from their borders.

The governmental structure of the Iroquois Confederacy was made up of the Grand Council of Chiefs, which included 49 chiefs from the member tribes, plus the Chief of the Chiefs: the council was comprised of nine chiefs from the Mohawk, eight from the Oneida, 14 from the Onondaga, ten from Cayuga, and eight from the Seneca. When the Tuscarora nation joined the confederacy at the invitation of the Oneida sometime after 1717, they were afforded no chiefs, but the Oneida represented them in council. Thereafter, the formerly Five Nations of the Iroquois Confederacy became known as the Six Nations. All decisions of the confederacy were to be made by a unanimous vote of the chiefs. If no unanimity could be reached, provision was made to "cover the fire," meaning that the nations agreed to disagree on that subject and the individual nations were free to act on their own.

In order to assure peace and an end to the warring and blood feuding which had caused so much strife among the five nations, the Great Law established rules and regulations for settling these blood disputes. For example, an arbitrary price of ten strings of wampum each at least a cubit in length was determined as the value of a human life. In the case of a murder, the bereaved family was to be offered not only the price for their own lost member, but also the price for the murderer, who under the law must forfeit his or her life to that family. As a result of these rules, the sometimes generations-old cycle of feuding between Iroquois families and tribes was gradually resolved.

It should be noted that wampum, although given as a value for human life, was not considered a form of currency as such by the Iroquois. Wampum was made from the shell of the quahog, or round clam, and shaped into a bead about one quarter or an inch long. The beads, which generally vary between white and purple in color, were strung on elm bast (the soft inner lining of the bark), sinew, or slender thongs, and arranged in various patterns. The strings of shells referred to in the Hiawatha legend are, in fact, seen as the origin of wampum as an important mode of communication. Just as the patterns mentioned in the legend are to remind men for all time of the Great Law, other patterns of wampum

beads stand for other significant ideas and events. Some belts were made especially to commemorate events such as treaties, while others represented prominent individuals. The wampum belt which represents Hiawatha, for instance, was returned several years ago to the Onondaga by the New York State Museum in Albany. Another use for wampum belts was devised when a tribal council wished to invoke a provision under discussion at the Grand Council of Chiefs; once the issue was decided upon, a messenger would travel to the various villages in the confederacy to display the wampum belt which carried the inscribed law enacted at the grand council. Wampum belts can and do change meaning over time. If the event which a belt represented lost its importance to the confederacy, that belt would be assigned a new meaning. In the same manner, some personal wampum belts also changed significance from time to time, but those such as the Hiawatha belt, given their importance to the confederacy, have never lost their meaning.

Hiawatha held a position of great importance and authority after the Iroquois Confederacy had been founded. As one of the founding chiefs, he was given the prominent office of Keeper of the Wampum, in which he was responsible not only for the wampum which represented the Great Law and the confederacy itself, but also for all of the wampum belts which were later endowed with meaning by the Grand Council of Chiefs. In addition, the names of Hiawatha and Tadadaho have held an esteemed place in the long tradition of the Iroquois Confederacy. To the present day, when a new leader is selected to be the Chief of the Chiefs of the grand council, he assumes the name of Tadadaho; likewise, a chief who is chosen to be Keeper of the Wampum takes the name of Hiawatha. These are titles of respect which serve to remind each member of the Iroquois Confederacy of the origins of its alliance and of its founding fathers.

SOURCES:

Books

Bradley, James W., *Evolution of the Onondaga Iroquois: Accommodating Change, 1500-1655,* Syracuse, Syracuse University Press, 1987.

Clark, J. V., *Onondaga: Reminiscences of Earlier and Later Times,* two volumes, Syracuse, Stoddard and Babcock, 1849.

Hale, Horatio E., *The Iroquois Book of Rites,* Philadelphia, D. G. Brinton, 1883; reprinted, Toronto, University of Toronto Press, 1965.

Hodge, Frederick Webb, *Handbook of North American Indians North of Mexico,* New York, Rowman and Littlefield, 1965.

Longfellow, Henry Wadsworth, *The Song of Hiawatha,* Boston, Tickner and Fields, 1855.

Parker, Arthur C., *Seneca Myths and Folk Tales,* Volume 27, Buffalo Historical Society, 1923.

Schoolcraft, Henry R., *Algic Researches, Comprising Inquiries Respecting the Mental Characteristics of the*

North American Indians, two volumes, New York,
    Harper, 1839.
Schoolcraft, Henry R., *Notes on the Iroquois: Contributions
    to the Statistics, Aboriginal History, Antiquities and
    General Ethnology of Western New York,* Albany, Eras-
    tus H. Pease, 1847.
Tooker, Elisabeth, "The League of the Iroquois: Its History,
    Politics, and Ritual," *Handbook of North American
    Indians,* Volume 15, edited by W. C. Sturtevant, Wash-
    ington, D. C., Smithsonian Institution, 1978; 418-41.
Wallace, Anthony F. C., *The Death and Rebirth of the
    Seneca,* New York, Knopf, 1970.
Washburn, Wilcomb E., "History of Indian-White Rela-
    tions," in *Handbook of North American Indians,* Vol-
    ume 4, edited by W. C. Sturtevant, Washington, D. C.,
    Smithsonian Institution, 1988.

Periodicals

Gibson, John Arthur, "Concerning the League: The Iroquois
    League Tradition as Dictated in Onondaga," *Algonquin
    and Iroquoian Linguistics* (Memoir 9), edited by John
    D. Nichols, Winnipeg, 1992.

—*Sketch by Martha I. Symes*

Rosella Hightower (left) with Rudolph Nureyev

Rosella Hightower
1920-
Choctaw ballerina, dance teacher, and director

Rosella Hightower is an internationally famous ballerina,
dance teacher, and director. Among her many achievements, she was the first American prima ballerina, danced
with the Original Ballet Russe, directed the Paris Opera Ballet, and opened her own school of dance in Cannes, France.

Hightower was born in 1920 in Ardmore, in present-
day Oklahoma, to Choctaw parents. The family moved to
Kansas City, Missouri, when Hightower was still an infant.
She studied ballet at an early age in Kansas City with
Dorothy Perkins and later with private teachers, such as
Mikhail Fokine. The famous ballet master Leonide Massine
asked her to join the Ballet Russe de Monte Carlo in southern France after an audition. She danced under Massine for
two years, until 1941. Throughout her career, Hightower
danced all the major classic roles and many more, including
modern roles and roles featuring her own choreography.

In 1942, Hightower returned to the United States and
joined the Ballet Theatre (later renamed the American Ballet
Theatre) as a soloist and worked under Lucia Chase. She
danced all the classical ballets at the Ballet Theatre, after
which she joined the Original Ballet Russe and toured North
and South America until 1947. After her tour, she returned to

the Grand Ballet de Monte Carlo, later called the Grand Ballet du Marquis de Cuevas, and became prima ballerina. She
won international acclaim for her virtuoso dancing with this
company. In 1952 she married Jean Robier, with whom she
had one child, Dominique, in 1955. Hightower continued to
dance with the Grand Ballet until its demise in 1962, dancing
with Rudolf Nureyev and performing on television and in
movies. She enjoyed a successful run of performances at the
Theatre of the Champs Elysees in Paris in 1965.

Founded School of Dance

When the Grand Ballet du Marquis de Cuevas closed
in 1962, Hightower opened her own dance school, the Center
for Classical Dance, or "Le Centre de danse," in Cannes in
southern France. Hightower wished to challenge Paris' place
as the center of French dance by establishing her school and
two dance companies—Le Nouveau Ballet at the Opera de
Marseille and Le Ballet de Nancy—in the provinces. By
exposing both dancers and patrons to a variety of dance
styles, she hoped to raise the quality of dance audience and
performance, not just in France but everywhere. The school
offers students classes in all aspects of dance as well as
scholastic studies. It provides a haven for students, from neo-
phytes to experienced company dancers, to engage in year-
round training that acknowledges dance as a profession of
intellectual, artistic, cultural, and technical demands.

Hightower returned to the United States in 1967 to
appear with three other acclaimed Native American ballerinas from Oklahoma in the world premier of *The Four

Moons in Tulsa—a performance dedicated to Oklahoma's celebration of its sixtieth year of statehood. *Newsweek* afforded the show great praise: "four such illustrious moon maidens were more than enough to transform the vision of ancient tribal glory into graceful, dramatic movements."

Directed Paris Opera Ballet

Hightower danced until 1977, at which point she devoted herself full-time to teaching and directing. From 1981 to 1983, Hightower directed at the Paris Opera Ballet. She was the first American—let alone the first Native American—to direct at the opera, and she intentionally shook things up. *Hommage au ballet,* which she directed in her first year, featured a rare on-stage appearance by the entire opera company. This performance fostered the notion of one unified company, although at the same time Hightower created three distinct companies: one to perform at the opera house, one to go on tour, and one to perform modern works. Hightower suggested many changes that were considered controversial, but her work at the opera won her a prominent place in the French and the world's dance scene. The French government recognized her contributions to dance with the "Chevalier de la Legion d'Honneur" in 1975, the "Officier de la Legion d'Honneur" in 1988, and the "Grand Prix national de danse" in 1990.

SOURCES:

Books

Biographical Dictionary of the Indians of the Americas, second edition, Newport Beach, California, American Indian Publishers, 1991.
Indians of Today, fourth edition, edited by Marion Gridley, Chicago, ICFP, 1971.
International Dictionary of Ballet, edited by Martha Bremser, Detroit, St. James Press, 1993.
Waldman, Carl, *Atlas of the North American Indian,* New York, Facts on File, 1985.

Periodicals

"Moon Maidens: Five-Part Indian Ballerinas," *Newsweek,* November 6, 1967; 101-102.

—*Sketch by Christopher B. Tower*

Thomson Highway
1951-
Cree playwright and artistic director

Thomson Highway has won numerous Canadian awards for his plays, several of which have been performed in New York City. As artistic director of Native Earth Performing Arts, the only professional Native American theater company in Toronto, he has served as producer, actor, stage manager, and playwright. His Native Earth Performing Arts company is one of the few places in North America dedicated to the development of Native dramatic art. It has won major awards for its productions and has provided a training ground for talented indigenous people of Canada. An annual festival of new Native playwrights is staged at the Native Canadian Centre of Toronto during the summer season. Highway's work has been recognized by the Dora Mavor Moore Award during the 1988-1989 season, and the prestigious Wang Festival Award in 1989.

Born in 1951 to a family of Cree trappers and fishermen on the Brochet Reserve in Manitoba, Highway was the eleventh of 12 children. He studied music and literature at the University of Western Ontario, later continuing his academic work in England.

When Thomas King published an excerpt from Highway's 1986 play *The Rez Sisters* in his anthology of contemporary Canadian Native fiction, he stated that it celebrated the value of community, defining community as "the intricate webs of kinship that radiate from a Native sense of family." The characters in Highway's plays have inhabited the same place for many generations, have become intimately familiar with the local plants and animals, have been imbued by the weathers, the winds, the waters with a shared sensibility, and know each other so well that they can communicate in a kind of private code like members of a family. Highway's characters, wrote King, in his introduction, "are related to one another through blood, marriage, adoption, or acceptance." This sense of a continuous communal identity constitutes the major defining trait of Native literature, since non-Native writers "prefer to imagine their Indians as solitary figures poised on the brink of extinction." Therefore, the presentation of such inter-related survivors of all the genocidal assaults that have been endured is the most important theme, and the raucous good humor with which they celebrate their endurance is the significant tone of this drama.

The Rez Sisters takes place on Manitoulin Island in Lake Huron. Seven women fantasize about winning the million-dollar jackpot in a bingo game, feverishly imagining how it will change their lives. The dramatist set his play in a Manitoulin reservation that he called the Wasayshigan Hill Indian Reserve. Involved in the excursion are Marie-Adele Starblanket, mother of 14; Emily Dictionary, whose lover has just been killed in a motorcycle accident; Veronique St. Pierre, who has adopted a mentally-impaired daughter; Annie Cook who aspires to be a country-rock singer; Philomena Moosetail who hopes to purchase a real toilet with her winnings; Pelagia Rosella Patchnose who is trying to reshingle her little welfare house and dreams of sailing away somewhere; and Zhaboonigan Peterson. Their farcical dialogue compensates for their bleak existence, which has forced their men off-shore to attempt to make a living in far-flung places. Fragments of their traditional culture surface in references to "the old stories, the old language. Almost all gone." There are references to the mythical cannibal giant,

Windigo, to the tribal trickster, Nanabush, and off-handed uses of Anishinabe phrases such as "Aw-ni-ginaw-ee-dick" ["Oh, go on"]. *The Rez Sisters* was given a two-week run at the New York Theatre Workshop in December of 1993. It was presented in collaboration with the American Indian Community House where it previewed beginning on December 3, 1993.

The Red Brothers, which Highway later changed to *Dry Lips Oughta Move to Kapuskasing,* won the Dora Mavor Moore Award for best new play and received its Canadian staging at the Theatre Passe Muraille in Toronto from April 25 to May 21, 1989. Earlier that same year, another play of Thomson's, *The Sage, the Dancer, and the Fool,* was performed at the Native Canadian Centre of Toronto. Reviewers were struck by the gusto and courage of Highway's people. The *New York Times* singled out his "colorful creation of community" among those who "are proud of their Indian heritage but also caught by the promises of an alien culture." The spare sets and sparse stagings—a circle of birch trees and some wooden chairs—serve as metaphors for the magic of the oral tradition. An entire world is recreated in this meager setting simply by means of talk.

SOURCES:

Books

All My Relations: An Anthology of Contemporary Canadian Native Fiction, edited by Thomas King, Norman, University of Oklahoma Press, 1992.

Native Literature in Canada: From the Oral Tradition to the Present, edited by Penny Petrone, Toronto, Oxford University Press, 1991.

Periodicals

Richards, David, "Bingo as the Way of Escape, at Dismal Odds," *New York Times,* January 9, 1994; 5, 28.

—Sketch by Ruth Rosenberg

Norbert S. Hill, Jr.

Norbert S. Hill, Jr.
1946-
Oneida educator

Also known as Onan-quat-go ["Big Medicine"]

A member of the Oneida tribe, Norbert S. Hill, Jr. has achieved prominence in the field of education in a variety of roles, all of which reflect his dedication to a better quality of life for the Native American community.

Hill was born in Warren, Michigan, a suburb of Detroit, on November 26, 1946, the son of Norbert Hill, Sr. (Oneida/Mohawk) and Eileen Johnson Hill (Canadian Cree). Growing up in Warren, Hill was exposed to the activism modeled by his father who started the first Indian urban organization in the United States: the North American Indian Club. The club provided a support network for Indian people. According to Hill, role models in his family were very powerful. His father's philosophy was "speak softly, walk humbly, and act compassionately." In addition to his father's achievement, in 1899 his grandmother, Rosa Hill, was the first Native American in the United States to acquire the degree of Doctor of Medicine.

In 1962 Hill and his family moved to the Oneida Reservation, near the city of Green Bay, Wisconsin. In Warren he had learned about the white world and what he needed to survive in it. At Oneida he experienced life in the Indian community, but did not realize how much an Indian he was until he moved off the reservation. Hill told Claudeen E. McAuliffe in an interview, "I play in the white playground, but I don't have keys to the gate. White guys don't play on our [Indians'] playground."

Dedicated to Community Service

Immediately after high school, Hill enrolled at the University of Wisconsin-Oshkosh where, in 1969, he earned a bachelor's degree in sociology and anthropology as well as being presented with an Alumni Award. He pursued postgraduate work at the same institution, receiving a master's degree in guidance and counseling. After receiving his master's degree, Hill took a job as a guidance counselor at Port

Washington (Wisconsin) High School. Hill told McAuliffe, "My counseling in high school was so bad that I thought no matter what I did I could do better." At that point he accepted a position at the University of Wisconsin-Green Bay as a counselor to American Indians, eventually becoming the assistant to the dean of students, a post which he held for five years. Desiring to pursue a doctoral degree, Hill moved to Boulder, Colorado, in 1977 and was offered a job at the University of Colorado. He became director of the American Indian Education Opportunity Program there and began working toward his degree.

According to Hill, the overriding theme in his life and family has been a dedication to community service. He described this dedication as "the dominant factor; the fabric of our family." Hill's family role models were educated, articulate, and displayed leadership in a number of different areas. This provided him a foundation upon which he could securely base his own community service and educational activities. He has emphasized the importance of grass roots activities like powwows.

From 1970 to 1974 Hill chaired the Oneida tribal education committee, one of the most important career events in his life, helping him to focus his future on service and education. Adopting his grandmother's philosophy, he wanted to do something that would make life easier for Indian people, rebuilding the community in the larger context of building people, thus helping the community to help itself. In this endeavor, he has maintained that education is the common denominator for the survival of Indian people.

Hill's awards and honors include the Reginald H. Jones Distinguished Service Award which he received in 1980 from the National Action Council for Minorities in Engineering; an educational policy fellowship from the Institute of Educational Leadership in 1981; the Chancellor's award at the University of Wisconsin-Oshkosh in 1988; and a Rockefeller fellowship in 1994. Cumberland College in Kentucky conferred upon him an honorary Doctor of Laws degree in 1994. He recently published *Words of Power,* a compilation of historical and contemporary Indian quotes, and continues to publish the award-winning magazine *Winds of Change,* which he started in 1986 to help fill a void in publications designed specifically for an American Indian audience. He is chairman of the board for the Smithsonian's National Museum of the American Indian, and has held the executive directorship of the American Indian Science and Engineering Society (AISES) in Boulder, Colorado, since 1983.

Hill's avocational interests include gourmet cooking and hiking. He and his wife Mary Anne have three children: Melissa, Megan, and Norbert III. His brother Richard is the chairman of the National Indian Gaming Commission and former chairman of the Oneida tribe. Another brother, Charlie Hill, is a popular comedian. His sister Rosa is the first Indian to hold a seat on the school board of West DePere (Wisconsin) High School. His first cousin Roberta Hill is a noted American Indian poet. Additional family members include a brother, James, and a stepsister, Barbara.

SOURCES:

Books

Native North American Almanac, edited by Duane Champagne, Detroit, Gale Research, 1994.

Other

Hill, Norbert S., Jr., interview with Claudeen McAuliffe conducted August 1, 1994.

—*Sketch by Claudeen E. McAuliffe*

Geary Hobson
1941-
Cherokee, Quapaw, and Chickasaw writer and educator

During his career as an educator and author, Geary Hobson has served as a staunch advocate of Native American writing. He and his wife, Barbara Torralba Hobson, were instrumental in the coordination of Returning the Gift, An International Native Writers Festival, which spawned the Native Writers' Circle of the Americas, a national organization designed to support native authors and artists. Geary Hobson serves as associate professor of English, specializing in American Indian literature, and as historian of the International Native Writers Festival at the University of Oklahoma in Norman. Previously, he served as coordinator and instructor in the Native American Studies Program at the University of New Mexico in Albuquerque.

A Native American of mixed Cherokee, Quapaw, and Chickasaw tribal descent, Hobson was born in Chicot County, Arkansas, on June 12, 1941, to Gerald and Edythe (Simpson) Hobson, a surveyor and bookkeeper respectively. After graduating from Desha Central High School in Rohwer, Arkansas, in 1959, he joined the United States Marine Corps. Hobson served in the military until 1965, reaching the rank of sergeant. While still in the military service, he began his education at Phoenix College, where he received an A.A. degree in Liberal Arts in 1964. He enrolled at Arizona State University where he completed his B.A. in English in 1968, and his M.A. in English in 1969. After teaching Spanish and English one year at Dumas High School in Arkansas, he went to the University of New Mexico to work on his Ph.D. in American Studies, which he completed in 1986. In the interim he taught in the Native American Studies program at the University of New Mexico and English at both the University of Arkansas at Little Rock and Central Arkansas University at Conway. Hobson was married briefly in the late 1960s to Denise Reed, with whom he had a daughter, Rachel.

Hobson served as a Tribal Council Member of the Arkansas Band of Quapaw Indians. He speaks a number of languages, including Cherokee, Spanish, and French. Hobson is the author of *Deer Hunting and Other Poems* (1990) and the compiler and editor of *The Remembered Earth: An Anthology of Contemporary Native American Literature* (1979). Since 1985 he has been working on a critical and literary history of American Indian and Native Canadian writing and publishing for the period from 1968 through 1990.

Other published works include essays, literary criticism, poems, and fiction. Among the essays and literary criticism Hobson has written are "Native American Writing: A Renaissance," printed in Four Directions, 1974; "A Statement about Poems and Sissies," published in *Southwest Women's Poetry Exchange* in 1977; the foreword to the 1984 work *Rattlesnake Band and Other Poems* by Robert Conley; and "The Literature of Indian Oklahoma—A Brief History," printed in *World Literature Today* in 1990. Among his published poems are pieces including "Meeting Andrew Jackson in an Albuquerque Bar," printed in *The Beloit Poetry Journal,* 1979-1980; "Tiger People," published in the anthology *Songs from this Earth on Turtle's Back: Contemporary American Indian Poetry,* released in 1983; "The Road Where the People Cried," printed in the 1983 work *Clouds Threw This Light: Contemporary Native American Poetry;* and "Going to Water," published in *OYO: An Ohio River Anthology* in 1990. His poems have been translated into Serbo-Croatian in Sovremenost, published in 1982 and into Dutch in De Aarde is Ons Vlees, published in 1990. Hobson's fiction pieces include: "The C.O.," published in the 1976 volume *A Journal of Contemporary Literature;* "An Attitude of Dignity," printed in *New America: A Review* in 1976; and "The Talking That Trees Does," printed in the *Greenfield Review* in 1983.

On November 25, 1977, Hobson married Barbara Torralba, with whom he had a daughter, Amanda Chekoba. Hobson and his wife served as principal coordinators for the Returning the Gift, An International Native Writers Festival. This brought together several hundred published writers, poets, and storytellers of Native American heritage for several days of presentations, workshops, and panel discussions at the University of Oklahoma from July 7 through July 11, 1992. This was the first such conference which involved such numbers and which brought Native writers and students from across the United States, Canada, Mexico, Guatemala, Panama, Cuba, and Peru. The Native Writers' Circle of the Americas emerged as a continuing organization from the Returning the Gift festival. Hobson has served on the Board of Directors from its initiation. The organization has produced newsletters for native writers, has maintained a directory of Native writers, and has developed regional and international Native writers' conferences. The organization includes not only literary artists, but also storytellers, film makers, performing artists, native historians, and keepers of oral traditions.

SELECTED WRITINGS BY HOBSON:

(Editor) *The Remembered Earth: An Anthology of Contemporary Native American Literature,* Albuquerque, University of New Mexico Press, 1988.

Deer Hunting and Other Poems, Norman, Oklahoma, Strawberry Press, 1990.

SOURCES:

Contemporary Authors, Volume 122, Detroit, Gale Research, 1988.

—*Sketch by Howard Meredith*

Linda Hogan
1947-
Chickasaw poet, novelist, and essayist

Linda Hogan has received many honors for her work, including an American Book Award in 1986 for *Seeing through the Sun* and a Pulitzer Prize nomination and a Lannan Foundation award in 1991 for *Mean Spirit.* Hogan was born in Denver, Colorado, in 1947. Her father, Charles Henderson, a Chickasaw from Oklahoma, was a sergeant in the U.S. Army. Her mother, Cleo Bower Henderson, was of German descent. The family moved frequently. Her uncle, Wesley Henderson, was involved in the White Buffalo Council, and his activities in Indian tradition inspired her as a child.

"The main thing that inspired me was my family in Oklahoma," Hogan told Phyllis Noah in an interview. "My father's family were gifted storytellers and that was really important to me." Hogan, who feared that Indians were a vanishing society when she was young. When she was older, she felt that she had to write down the stories she had heard or they would be lost forever. "It was a total misconception on my part from going to public schools," she said. "The Native population has increased. There is a great movement now going back to traditional culture." In 1979, Hogan worked at the Indian Center in Denver, Colorado, with the urban Indian community, and continues to work in Native communities.

Hogan received her master's degree in creative writing and English in 1978 from the University of Colorado in Boulder, where she became a professor of English and creative writing. Hogan married in 1972 and had two daughters, Sandra and Tanya. She divorced in 1982. She lives in a Morrison, Colorado, canyon. For relaxation, she enjoys gardening and Yoga. "When I am quiet and still my body enters a place where there is no time, when I enter into an understanding that I am part of everything else is my most creative time," Hogan told Noah. Her work reflects the history, culture, and spirituality of Native Americans.

Works with Wildlife Rehabilitation

In 1984 Hogan moved to Minnesota and worked in non-raptor wildlife rehabilitation, helping deer, beaver, and other non-predatory animals and birds back to the wilds. After two years, she moved back to Colorado. She then went

Linda Hogan

to work at a birds-of-prey rehabilitation facility. Hogan claimed in the interview with Noah that working at the raptor facility was one of the most rewarding experiences of her life, even more than writing. "Releasing a bird back into the wild and the mate was waiting for it—you can see the results right away," she said. "With writing, it takes time." As her writing became more prevalent, Hogan gave up her volunteer work with animals, but she has never lost her love of wildlife. For example, she is organizing a conference scheduled for 1994 to bring traditional people together to talk about endangered species.

Recipient of Many Awards

Initially a poet, Hogan first published *Calling Myself Home* in 1979. Her second book of poetry, *Eclipse,* was published by the American Indian Studies Center Press at UCLA in 1983. Since then, Hogan has received many awards for her work. Her book of poems *Seeing through the Sun* received an American Book Award from the Before Columbus Foundation in 1986. Her historical novel *Mean Spirit* won the Oklahoma Book Award and the Mountains and Plains Booksellers Award in 1990. It was also one of three finalists for a Pulitzer Prize in 1991. The story is set in the early 1920s during the Oklahoma oil boom, and tells how it affected the Native American community. Although the characters are fictionalized, the narrative is detailed and revealing of Native American culture. Some of the events were so realistic to those who lived through the oil boom that Hogan received calls from readers correcting her on certain dates in the book.

Hogan's *The Book of Medicines* received the Colorado Book Award in 1993 and was a finalist for the National Book Critics Award in 1994. Hogan was the recipient of a Guggenheim fellowship in 1990, a National Endowment for the Arts grant in 1986, and a Lannan Foundation award in 1994. She also received a Minnesota Arts Board grant, a Colorado Writer's fellowship, and a Five Civilized Tribes Museum playwriting award. More recently, Hogan has completed a novel, *Solar Storms,* to be published in 1995 by Scribner's Publishing, and a book of essays, Dwellings, to be published by Norton Publishing.

SELECTED WRITINGS BY HOGAN:

Eclipse, Los Angeles, UCLA American Indian Studies Center, 1983.
Seeing through the Sun, Amherst, University of Massachusetts Press, 1985.
That Horse, Pueblo of Acoma Press, 1985.
Savings, Minneapolis, Coffee House Press, 1988.
Mean Spirit, New York, Atheneum, 1990.
Red Clay: Poems and Stories, Greenfield Center, New York, Greenfield Review Press, 1991.
The Book of Medicines, Minneapolis, Coffee House Press, 1993.

SOURCES:

Books

Native American Women, edited by Gretchen M. Bataille, New York, Garland Publishing, 1993; 113-114.

Periodicals

Nathan, Paul, "Rights," *Publishers Weekly,* May 17, 1991; 25.

Other

Hogan, Linda, interview with Phyllis Noah conducted July 23, 1994.

—Sketch by Phyllis "Picturestone" Noah

George Horse Capture, Sr.
1936-
Gros Ventre museum curator, writer, consultant, and cultural conservator

During his career as a museum director, consultant, writer, and public speaker, George Horse Capture, Sr., has been responsible for preserving Native American culture and educating individuals seeking insight into the lives

George Horse Capture, Sr.

of Native people, especially those of the Gros Ventre tribe. Horse Capture was born on October 20, 1936, on the Fort Belknap Reservation in Montana, home of the Gros Ventre people. He was raised in an environment where traditional culture became the center of his worldview. While growing up, Horse Capture saw formal education as a tool for keeping precious traditions alive. He received a B.A. in anthropology from the University of California at Berkeley in 1974 and an M.A. in history from Montana State University at Bozeman in 1979.

Working as an assistant professor of Native American studies at Montana State University while completing his graduate program, Horse Capture had already set his sights on museology as a career. From 1980 to 1990, he served as curator of the Plains Indian Museum of the Buffalo Bill Historical Center in Cody, Wyoming. In this capacity, he oversaw numerous exhibits focusing on Plains Indian history, art, and contemporary culture. Among these were exhibitions on cradleboards (baby carriers), powwowing, and Wounded Knee (site of the 1890 massacre of Minneconjou Sioux by the Seventh Cavalry).

While his curatorship kept him busy in Wyoming, he also maintained a full schedule of public lectures throughout the country as well as a research agenda that took him all over the world. He wrote many articles, including one on the collection of painted robes in the Musee de l'Homme in Paris (gathered by Jesuit missionary Jacques Marquette in his travels in the "New World" in the seventeenth century).

He was also featured in several interviews in Wyoming (and other western states) magazines.

Powwowing is both a personal and a professional interest of Horse Capture. His 1983 documentary film, *I'd Rather Be Powwowing,* won him the William E. Cody Motion Picture Award. His editing of the 1980 volume *The Seven Visions of Bull Lodge* won critical favor and contributed to his winning of the American Association of State and Local History Award of Merit in 1990. Never straying far from his personal commitment to preserve Gros Ventre tradition, he has continued to serve on several tribal committees and has begun plans for a Fort Belknap museum focusing on the history and cultures of the Gros Ventre and Assiniboine Sioux.

Having lectured at such prestigious institutions of higher education as Harvard and Yale universities and having served in professional capacities with the Smithsonian Institution, Horse Capture left Cody in 1990 to work as a private consultant for museums, with Fort Belknap as his home base of operations. When he was brought in as a consultant for the launching of the Smithsonian Institute-Heye Foundation's National Museum of the American Indian, the hectic pace forced him to put the Fort Belknap museum project on temporary "hold." As the project escalated, Horse Capture moved to New York City to serve as site director for the Bronx Annex Research Center and Deputy Assistant Director of Cultural Resources.

In keeping with traditional Gros Ventre values, Horse Capture is most proud of his accomplishments in cultural preservation and of his family's accomplishments in various fields. His wife, Kay-Karol Horse Capture, works with him as a private consultant, having been trained as a museum conservator. Their four children are following in their parents' footsteps of maintaining Native American culture. In an interview, Horse Capture told Cynthia Kasee that his son George, Jr., is the family's Sacred Pipe Keeper; son Joseph is a Presidential Scholar at Montana State University, studying history; daughter Daylight, former high school valedictorian, has attended the University of Montana; and son Peter has planned to enter the armed services after graduation. George Horse Capture, Jr. and Sr., have been profiled in an episode of a television series on Native Americans entitled "The Plains Indians."

SOURCES:

Books

Native North American Almanac, edited by Duane Champagne, Detroit, Gale Research, 1994.

Other

Horse Capture, George, Sr., interview with Cynthia R. Kasee, conducted July 1, 1994.

—Sketch by Cynthia R. Kasee

Allan Houser
1914-1994
Fort Sill Chiricahua Apache artist, and art instructor

Allan Houser was a master in all sculpture media, including stone, marble, alabaster, fabricated steel, clay, and bronze. He worked equally well in tempera, charcoal, pastel, and oil. His works are displayed in prominent museums and public places throughout the world, and have received numerous awards. According to the *New York Times,* his work, which reflects many different styles, exhibits the recurring themes of "mother and child, warriors on horseback, [and] Apache fire dancers."

Houser was born June 30, 1914, to Sam and Blossom Haozous on their allotment of land in the Kiowa, Comanche, and Apache reserve near Apache, Oklahoma. His father was the grandson of Mangas Coloradas, the famous Apache chief. It was from his parents and the Apache community that he received his education in Chiricahua and Warm Springs Apache tradition. Houser received mandatory English-based education in the public school at Boone and at Bureau of Indian Affairs (BIA) boarding schools until he left these to work on the family trust lands. He continued his formal education with Dorothy Dunn at the painting studio of the Santa Fe Indian School from 1934 to 1938. During that time his paintings were exhibited in Santa Fe and San Francisco. In 1939 he worked with others painting murals in the Department of the Interior Building in Washington, D.C., and exhibited his work at the World's Fair in New York, the National Gallery of Art in Washington, D.C., and the Art Institute of Chicago. In 1939, Houser married Anna Maria Gallegos.

In 1940 Houser returned to Washington, D.C., to paint additional murals in the Department of the Interior Building. he then took time to study with the Norwegian muralist Olle Nordmark in a special program at the Fort Sill Indian School, near his family home. He painted additional murals at the Indian School in Dulce, New Mexico, on the Jicarilla Apache Reservation, and at the Riverside Indian School near Anadarko, Oklahoma, on the Wichita, Caddo, and Delaware reserve.

During World War II, Houser moved his family to Los Angeles, where he worked as a pipe fitter in construction. During the wartime period, he continued to paint and sculpt at night. In 1948 Houser was commissioned to create a sculpture, "Comrade in Mourning," honoring Native Americans who died fighting for the United States in World War II. This sculpture was dedicated in 1949. That same year, one of his works on paper won the Grand Award at the Philbrook Art Center's Third Annual Indian Art Competition in Tulsa, Oklahoma. That year was also a turning point in that he received a Guggenheim fellowship in painting and sculpture. Houser used the financial support to work on his

projects at a studio established on the family trust land. In 1950, before he left Oklahoma, he received a commission to paint four dioramas within the Southern Plains Museum in Anadarko.

Becomes Notable Art Educator

Houser then began a long, productive career as an art teacher. First he taught at the Inter-Mountain School at Brigham City, Utah, from 1951 through 1961. During 1954, he received the French Government's Palmes d'Academigue for his outstanding work as a teacher and artist. From 1962 through 1975, Houser was a teacher and later head of the sculpture department at the Institute of American Indian Arts at the Santa Fe Indian School. It was in 1968 that he cast his first bronze work at Nambe in Pojoaque, New Mexico.

During the early 1970s, Houser exhibited his stone, bronze, and welded steel sculptures at such arts places as the Heard Museum in Phoenix, Arizona, and the Philbrook Art Center in Tulsa, Oklahoma. In 1977 he was commissioned to do the memorial bronze "Coming of Age" for the Denver Art Museum. In 1979, he served as artist in residence at Dartmouth College and had a one-man exhibition at Hopkins Center in Hanover, New Hampshire. He continued to create and show his work throughout the 1980s, with exhibits at the Grande Palais in Paris, the Amerika Haus in Berlin, and the Kunstlerhaus in Vienna. In 1983 he dedicated a life-size bronze—"Chiricahua Apache Family"—at the Fort Sill Apache Tribal Center near Apache, Oklahoma. In 1985 he dedicated the monumental bronze "Offering of the Sacred Pipe" at the United States Mission to the United Nations in New York City. In 1986 he created a bronze bust of Geronimo to commemorate the one hundredth anniversary of the surrender of the Chiricahua Apaches to the U.S. Army. The bust was presented to the Fort Sill Apache Tribal Center near Apache. In 1989, Houser dedicated a 15-foot bronze of an Apache woman, entitled "As Long as the Water Flows," on the grounds south of the Oklahoma State Capital Building.

In 1992 Houser became the first American Indian to receive the National Medal of Arts, presented by President George Bush. The medal is the nation's highest art achievement award. He also received the Honored One recognition as the finest Native American artist at the Red Earth Festival in Oklahoma City, as well as the Ellis Island National Medal of Freedom. During a special ceremony in Washington, D.C., at the historic 1994 meeting of 200 Native American tribal leaders and President Bill Clinton, Houser dedicated his sculpture "May We Have Peace" to the people of the United States. He died of cancer in Santa Fe, New Mexico, on August 22, 1994.

SOURCES:

Books

Allan Houser: A Life in Art, Santa Fe, Museum of Fine Arts and Museum of Indian Arts and Culture, 1991.

Native North American Almanac, edited by Duane Champagne, Detroit, Gale Research, 1994; 1076.

Perlman, Barbara, *Allan Houser,* Santa Fe, Glenn Green Galleries, 1987.

Reference Encyclopedia of the American Indian, edited by Barry Klein, West Nyack, New York, Todd Publications, 1990; 880-881.

Periodicals

New York Times, August 25, 1994; D19.

Washington Post, August 25, 1994; D6.

—*Sketch by Howard Meredith*

Oscar Howe
1915-1983
Yankton Sioux artist and professor
Also known as Mazuha Hokshina ["Trader Boy"]

One of the most influential Native American artists of the twentieth century, Oscar Howe was among the first Indian artists to combine traditional and modern forms in his paintings, and is therefore credited with pioneering a new phase of artistic expression in American Indian art.

Howe was born Mazuha Hokshina ["Trader Boy"] on May 13, 1915 at Joe Creek on the Crow Creek Reservation in South Dakota to George Tikute Howe and Ella Fearless Bear, both of the Yankton Dakota Sioux tribe. As a young boy, he was avoided by other children due to a severe skin disorder from which he suffered. Keeping to himself, Howe focused on his love for drawing, a pursuit discouraged by his parents and others in the tribe. Howe continued to draw despite these obstacles. After being sent to the Indian School in Pierre, South Dakota, Howe tried to run away many times and even contemplated suicide. Eventually, due to health problems, authorities returned Howe to the reservation.

At the age of 19, Howe entered the Santa Fe Indian School where he took several art classes under the instruction of Native artist Dorothy Dunn, who trained many of the great American Indian artists that emerged in the 1930s and 1940s. From Dunn, Howe learned the basics of art as well as the prejudices Native artists often faced when trying to win acceptance in a predominantly white art world. Like other Indian artists of the time, Howe painted in a traditional style, depicting aspects of Indian life, culture, and belief through art. "Of the Sioux artists, Oscar Howe was the outstanding painter," wrote Dunn. "He had the quiet, persevering studiousness which combined with high technical aptitude to make for intellectual achievement in art."

Developed Modern Style

Eventually, Howe began to develop a characteristically individual style which departed from traditional American Indian art. His childhood profoundly influenced this new artistic direction; Howe's paintings are firmly grounded in the stories and customs told to him by the elders of his tribe. He was further influenced by the Dakota concept of straight lines symbolizing truth and curved lines representing unity, movement, and the open sky. To these ideas, he added his interpretation of *tahokmu* ("spider web"), a design combining line, circle, and triangle. Howe continued to push the limits of the traditional styles of Dakota Indian art, expanding his palette and rethinking his aesthetics for more active, vital work, and gradually added more abstraction to his paintings.

After leaving the Santa Fe school in 1938, Howe taught art at Pierre Indian School—the same school he had tried to escape from years before. He accepted several commissions during this time, many of which were for murals. In 1940 he painted the interior dome of the Carnegie Library in Mitchell, South Dakota. Shortly thereafter, Howe was commissioned to paint ten murals in an auditorium in Mobridge, South Dakota. To prepare for this project, he studied with leading muralist Olaf Nordmark in 1941. Unfortunately, his mural work and studies with Nordmark were interrupted by the second World War. Howe was drafted by the U.S. Army in 1942 and served for three and a half years. Though he did not paint during this period, he did meet his future bride Heidi Hampel, whom he married in 1947.

Upon his release from the armed services, Howe returned to his art work. He won the Grand Purchase Prize in the 1947 Indian Art Annual sponsored by the Philbrook Art Center in Tulsa, Oklahoma for his painting *Dakota Duck Hunt.* With the notoriety the show brought him, Howe joined Dakota Wesleyan University in 1948 as an artist-in-residence. He earned a bachelor's degree from the university in 1952 and served as acting Chairman of the Department of Art. Howe earned a master's degree in fine arts from the University of Oklahoma in 1954. Though he had another short stint as an instructor in Pierre, he accepted a position at the University of South Dakota at Vermillon in 1957, where he remained until his retirement in 1980.

Challenged the Philbrook Committee

It was during Howe's tenure at USD that he fully developed the style for which he is known today, a contemporary mixture of abstraction, cubism, and true *tahokmu.* In 1958 he challenged the art world's deeply ingrained perceptions regarding Indian art when his painting *Umine Wacipi* was rejected by the Philbrook's Indian Art Annual committee for not looking like an Indian work. Howe was enraged. Like many other Native American artists of the time, he was frustrated by critics, curators, and art dealers who were only willing to accept Native work that "looked" Indian, meaning art that contained recognizable Native subjects and avoided the use of shading, foreground and background, and proper perspective. In an American Indian Art letter to Jeanne O. Snodgrass, curator of American Indian art at the Philbrook, he retaliated the committee's decision, asserting: "Who ever said that my paintings are not in the traditional Indian style has poor knowledge of Indian art indeed. There is much more to Indian Art than pretty, stylized pictures.... Are we to be held back forever with one phase of Indian painting, with no right for individualism, dictated to as the Indian always has been, put on reservations and treated like a child, and only the white man knows what is best for him? Now, even in Art, 'You little child do what *we think* is best for you, nothing different.'" Well, I am not going to stand for it. Indian Art can compete with any Art in the world but not as a *suppressed Art* ... I only hope the Art World will not be one more contributor to holding us in chains." Howe's letter was so persuasive that the rules for inclusion in the art show were immediately amended.

The time was ripe for change. Many critics and curators had already begun to question the criteria for evaluating art by Native Americans. After Howe's letter, American Indian art was evaluated by the same aesthetic standards as other art. He thus pioneered the way for many Indian painters who followed him, enabling them to find their own means of individual expression, whether traditional or avant-garde. As for Howe, his paintings became increasingly more abstract, a style that later came to be known as Indian Cubism, though Howe denied any prior knowledge of European Cubists. According to the artist, his cubism was influenced by the isolation of the South Dakota reservation and by his idea of *tahokmu,* derived from Indian ideas of abstraction.

Howe painted and taught art for many years though plagued with health problems. The recipient of numerous awards, Howe was named South Dakota's Artist Laureate in 1960. In his later years, he contracted Parkinson's Disease, from which he died in his sleep on October 7, 1983.

SOURCES:

Books

The Arts of the North American Indian: Native Traditions in Evolution, edited by Edwin L. Wade, New York, Hudson Hills Press, 1986.

Dunn, Dorothy, *American Indian Painting of the Southwest and Plains Areas,* Albuquerque, University of New Mexico Press, 1968.

Encyclopedia of the Indians of the Americas, Volume 6, edited by Keith Irvine, St. Clair Shores, Michigan, Scholarly Press, 1974.

Native America in the Twentieth Century, edited by Mary B. Davis, New York, Garland Publishing, 1994.

Native North American Almanac, edited by Duane Champagne, Detroit, Gale Research, 1994.

Reference Encyclopedia of the American Indian, fourth edition, edited by Barry Klein, West Nyack, New York, Todd Publications, 1986.

Periodicals

Dockstader, Frederick, "The Revolt of Trader Boy: Oscar Howe and Indian Art," *American Indian Art,* 4, summer 1983; 42-51.

Howe, Oscar, *American Indian Art,* April 18, 1958.

—Sketch by Christopher B. Tower

Hump
1848-1908
Minniconjou Sioux tribal leader
Also known as Etokeah

Hump, a Minniconjou Sioux, was born in 1848 near Bear Butte in western South Dakota. He served with Red Cloud during the wars of 1866-1868, when the Sioux fought to protect land rights along the Bozeman Trail. At the age of 18, he was made chief of the Minniconjou contingent, and was a leader in the ambush of Lieutenant Colonel William Fetterman's troops at Fort Phil Kearny in Wyoming in December, 1866. Along with Red Cloud, Sitting Bull, and Crazy Horse, Hump was known as a nontreaty chief for his refusal to sign the Treaty of Fort Laramie in 1866.

Also active in the Sioux War for the Black Hills in 1876-1877, Hump was among the warriors present at the Battle of the Little Bighorn where General George Custer was defeated. In May of 1877 Hump and 300 others surrendered to General Nelson A. Miles at his camp on the Yellowstone River. As a negotiator, Hump accompanied Miles in pursuit of the remaining Minniconjou militants. He hoped to negotiate a peaceful settlement, but a fight broke out, and the Minniconjou leader Lame Deer was killed. In 1877, Hump served Miles again as a scout in the Nez Percé war.

As a reward for his work as scout, Hump was appointed to the Cheyenne River Agency's Indian police force. As agents on the various reservations tried to break up traditional power structures among the Sioux bands, they created police groups to work for them. It was somewhat ironic that Hump was appointed to the police. At Cheyenne River, Hump and Big Foot were actually the most influential anti-white spokesmen on the reservation.

During the negotiations of the Crook Commission to acquire signatures on the Sioux Act of 1888, Hump arranged disturbances which disrupted the process. This act required the signatures of three-fourths of all adult males on each reservation and resulted in more loss of land to white settlers through the allotment process. Hump refused to sign originally, but under threat of military pressure, he finally signed the treaty.

When messages of a new Messiah sent to save the Indian people reached Cheyenne River in 1890, Hump exchanged his police uniform for a Ghost Dance shirt and presided over a succession of dances that attracted about 400 Minniconjous. The Paiute prophet Wovoka preached that the Ghost Dance religion would assure the Indian people of eternal peace. This brought hope to a despondent group of people who had suffered from the loss of their land, economy, religion, and traditional ways of life.

Worried that the Ghost Dance movement might turn into stronger rebellion, federal agents tried to diffuse danc-

Hump

next day events at Red Cloud's Pine Ridge Reservation reached a boiling point during a confrontation between dancers and police. Troops were requested at Pine Ridge. At Cheyenne River, an infantry company from Fort Sully was moved to Fort Bennett, the reservation's military post.

As the Ghost Dancers set up a retreat called the Stronghold, Cheyenne River dancers turned to Hump and Big Foot for leadership. General Miles sent Captain Ezra P. Ewers to convince Hump to give up the Ghost Dance. Ewers had been in charge of Hump as a scout, and there was a bond of friendship and trust between the two men. Ewers successfully convinced Hump to return to the Cheyenne River Agency, where he again wore the police uniform and worked to stop the Ghost Dance, even against Big Foot. When he was informed of Sitting Bull's death, Hump refused to join Big Foot's group, and was therefore not present at the battle at Wounded Knee. An agile negotiator, Hump was among the delegation sent to Washington, D.C., to plead for fair treatment on Sioux reservations. Thereafter, he served as a member of the police force at Cheyenne River Reservation. Hump died in 1908 and was buried in the Episcopal cemetery at Cherry Creek. Hump Creek in Haakan County, South Dakota, is named for him.

ing. At Cheyenne River, agent Perain P. Palmer sent a new captain of his police force to stop the dancing at the camps of Hump and Big Foot. Armed with Winchester rifles, the dancers easily overpowered the police. By November 10, Palmer decided to use greater strength to remove the perceived threat of the Ghost Dance from Cheyenne River. The

SOURCES:

Dockstader, Frederick J., *Great North American Indians,* New York, Van Nostrand Reinhold, 1977; 116-117.

Paulson, T. Emogene, and Lloyd R. Moses, Who's Who *Among the Sioux,* Vermillion, Institute of Indian Studies, University of South Dakota, 1988; 96.

Utley, Robert M., *The Last Days of the Sioux Nation,* New Haven, Yale University Press, 1963.

—Sketch by Karen P. Zimmerman

Ishi
1862(?)-1916
Yahi (Southern Yana) survivor and research informant

O ften identified as "the last wild Indian" in North America, Ishi was the last known survivor of the Yahi tribe of Northern California. His ancestors were the victims of 25 years of extermination following the California Gold Rush. The Native American population of the state was reduced from about 100,000 in 1848 to only 20,000 in 1910. In 1911 Ishi emerged alone from the forest and spent the remainder of his life in the urban world of San Francisco, protected by a group of academics who respected his heritage and benefited from his friendship.

Yana History and Culture

In 1961 Theodora Kroeber compiled a composite picture of Yana life and history from traditional sources and the words of Ishi himself. She believed a full understanding of the group would come only with a grasp of "the land and people of Indian California." It is concluded that the Yana population never exceeded two or three thousand people and that they existed in Northern California for a period of between three and four thousand years. The range of activity of the Yana was probably confined to an area stretching 40 by 60 miles. There were four subgroups, each with a distinct dialect. The Yahi was the most southernmost of the groups. Generally the groups remained apart, living in small settlements, searching for food, and gathering only in the autumn in large encampments. (The massacres in the 1860s occurred because of these annual meetings.) In the winter they reviewed the meaning of the yearly reunions, transmitted tribal legends and history, studied the pattern of the skies, and found meaning in personal dreams. The Yana had generally been unaffected by the Spanish and Mexican regimes in California (1769-1848). Sonoma, the mission farthest north was still out of range of these native peoples. But the Mexican land grants of 1844 and the gold rush at the end of the same decade resulted in a nearly complete destruction of the Yana by 1872.

Policy of Extermination

Violent racism, combined with occasional murders of whites by Yana—perhaps a total of 20 such acts—promoted

Ishi

a policy of extermination. Thousands of native Californians were subjected to servitude and prostitution. Streams were polluted by the mining process and natural survival became more difficult. Theodora Kroeber attempted to analyze the mental condition of the whites who arrived in California after a perilous journey from the East. She believed they often arrived in a "dehumanized" state and added, "Gold seems to work on the human psyche to its undoing." Although there are "inconsistencies and gaps in the record" it is clear that a pattern of total suppression of the Yana started by 1850. Part of the story is found in Thomas Talbot Waterman's 1918 study, *The Yana Indians*. The elusiveness and sporadic acts of revenge by the group seemed to promote anguish and violence among the whites. A military "removal" and "reservation" plan at Nome Lackee failed from 1859 to 1861.

Ishi was probably born in 1862, at the beginning of the most intense extermination period. Not only were random Indians who remained in the wild killed but even indentured men, women, and children were put to death by angry settlers. The evasive irritants had gained the name of "the Mill Creeks," which perhaps explains the intense attack on a group of Yahi on Mill Creek where Ishi's father was probably killed. Ishi and his mother were among the few survivors. Another group of Yahi were massacred in a cave by a group headed by a man named Kingsley.

A People in Hiding

Ishi apparently went into to hiding at about the age of ten. The years of 1872 to 1884 were those of almost total concealment. An earlier symbolic effort by the Yahi at a peace settlement was ignored by the settlers. Alfred L. Kroeber characterized the tiny remaining band as "the smallest free nation in the world." It was to be a virtually noiseless world, where no foot prints could be left to reveal their existence. But Ishi and his family and associates were thus able to keep both their identity and their culture. The desperate conditions, however, resulted in the renewal of raids for food a decade later in 1884. Ishi and three others were actually caught in the act as they exited a cabin window. Because they had only taken clothing in this case, a surprisingly tolerant owner let them go free. The grateful escapees later returned to the cabin and left a gift of two baskets.

The most permanent of the hiding places was a concealed area called the Grizzly Bear's Hiding Place. It was occupied by Ishi, his mother, a sister, and two men. Their solitude ended in November of 1908 when two engineers, scouting the area to build a dam for electrical power, happened upon Ishi while he was fishing with a harpoon. According to their report, he fiercely scared them away. Shortly thereafter, a party of surveyors located the abandoned Grizzly Bear site. Ishi's sick mother was still there, wrapped in a blanket. All useful items, including food and implements, were taken by the white men. The dying woman was left behind. Ishi was to return to move his mother, but she died a few days later. The others in the small group had disappeared. Ishi was totally alone for a period of nearly three years.

"The Ordeal of Civilization"

Theodora Kroeber states dramatically, "The ordeal of civilization began for Ishi at the door of the Oroville jail." Under the circumstances, both his survival and the fortunate events that followed left a generally positive result. If he had emerged from the wilderness at a different location in the summer of 1911 he might have been killed. Instead, the sheriff put him temporarily in the local jail cell for the insane. Newspapers quickly labeled him the "Wild Man of Oroville." Within a few days Thomas Talbot Waterman travelled the 50 miles from San Francisco to bring him to a new location. He soon gained Ishi's confidence by demonstrating his awareness of the Yana language. Soon "the Stone Age Man" encountered modern transportation—a train, a ferry boat, and a San Francisco trolley car. He was fascinated by the experience. His new home was the museum of the anthropology department of the University of California. It was located in Parnassus Heights, near Golden Gate Park in San Francisco. The department, which had been established in 1901, and the museum, scheduled to open to the public

only two months after Ishi's arrival, were made possible by the support of Phoebe Apperson Hearst, mother of William Randolph Hearst, who needed a home for her personal anthropological collection.

At first Ishi was quite timid and was easily startled by loud and unfamiliar noises. He shared the museum with two caretakers. Alfred Kroeber became his second significant friend. Because of public pressure, Kroeber gave him a name: "Ishi"—the Yahi name for "man." He never revealed his real name, or repeated the one that was bestowed upon him.

Because Ishi's state of mind is perhaps the most intriguing part of this unusual chapter in American social history, the revelations of Kroeber's wife about Ishi are important: He was shy and blushed frequently. He kept his dignity. "He was no king's jester: no one ever laughed at him." He was amiable and had great curiosity. "To be sure, he would sit, unbored, dreamy, and withdrawn into his own mystic center, but only if there was nothing to do, no one to talk to or to word with.... He was interested, concerned, amused, or delighted, as the case might be, with everything and everyone he knew and understood."

Naturally there were those who wished to exploit him. Among those who showed interest were promoters of vaudeville circuits, exhibitors for carnivals, and commercial phonograph producers. But Alfred Kroeber never allowed these intrusions. Kroeber promoted a pattern of life in which Ishi could be independent. He was made a junior janitor at the museum with a $25-per-month salary. His formal public appearances in the museum were limited to two and one half hours on Sunday afternoons. Ishi showed great interest in learning people's names and was able to make distinctions between ethnic groups and distinct classes in San Francisco society.

Ishi was most overwhelmed by the *number* of people he encountered in his new environment. Before his appearance near Oroville he had probably never seen more than 40 or 50 people at one time. When he attended a vaudeville show he was much more impressed by the audience than the performance. At the same time he felt uncomfortable in large groups of people. He compared the odor of sweating crowds to that of old deer hides. When he was delivered to the beach for the first time to see the Pacific Ocean his first impression was not of the water but the masses of people on the beach: "Hansi saltu, hansi saltu!" ["Many white people, many white people!"] Before long he became increasingly independent. He did his own shopping and prepared food in the museum kitchen. He considered matches more interesting than gas or electricity. He walked to Golden Gate Park where he first saw a buffalo and travelled alone to the University of California campus in Berkeley. New items, such as ice cream, became part of his diet. On a daily basis he found new things that intrigued him—glue, roller shades on windows, kaleidoscopes, etc.

In part because of his close friendship with Dr. Saxton Pope, Ishi spent much of his time at the hospital, located next to the museum. He visited and showed great concern for patients; he detected that there were more male than female patients and concluded that this was because the men spent too much time indoors. He even watched actual operations, was distressed by anaesthesia (believing that artificially induced sleep resulted in the removal of the soul from the body), and concluded that tonsillectomies were unnecessary—having his own special cure.

Return to the Wilderness

As many as 1,000 visitors would gather on Sunday afternoons to observe Ishi's unique skills as a craftsman. Supplies of special woods, obsidian, flint, and other items were delivered to him. He prepared hunting implements and shaped nearly perfect arrowheads. In May of 1914 Ishi had the unanticipated, and unwanted, opportunity to use his survival skills in his former environment. Kroeber, Waterman, and Pope pushed Ishi into joining them on a month-long camping expedition in the region where Ishi had lived his solitary existence only three years before. Waterman demonstrated his own enthusiasm to Kroeber in a memo, "I think the three of us, working in cordial cooperation for a summer could do the ethnography, ethnobotany, ethnogeography and ethno-everything else of the Southern Yana (Yahi) up brown." The troop, which also included Pope's 11-year-old son, took a Pullman sleeping car to Oroville. Ishi casually tipped the porter upon their departure from the train. Soon he was riding a horse for the first time and upon reaching his wilderness home, he abandoned his formal attire for a breechcloth. Once in his former setting he accepted the mission of this grand ethnological venture and became a perfect host for his amateur "primitives." Theodora Kroeber claims he also had "a sudden comprehension of a sense of history." Much of the summer activity was recorded in photographs. A return visit to the region in the autumn was cancelled because of the beginning of World War I.

Ishi's Journey Ends

The Bureau of Indian Affairs (BIA) showed a brief interest in Ishi and offered him the option of going to a reservation. His reply to the California Special Agent was: "I will live like the white man for the remainder of my days. I wish to stay here where I am now. I will grow old in this house, and it is here I will die." A formal reply from the BIA accepted his decision and concluded, "Owing to his previous manner of life, his mental development as far as understanding of our manner of life was concerned, was not beyond that of a six year old child." Kroeber, perhaps wishing not to provoke a change in Ishi's status, replied with civility: "Ishi has taken readily to civilization ... his mental development was by no means stunted or sub-normal." Kroeber told his wife, "He [Ishi] was the most patient man I ever knew." She added comments about his orderliness and observed, "The impulse of any sort of exhibitionism was totally foreign to him.... Affectionate and uncorrupt, he was denied the fulfillment of wife and children, or of any sex life whatever." However, Ishi was to fall victim to another element of civilization—tuberculosis. He developed a severe

cough in December of 1914 and soon required medical care. After some time in the nearby hospital, and as a guest in Waterman's home, a major exhibit was removed to give him a special room in the museum. It was there that he died on March 25, 1916.

Because of a European sabbatical, Kroeber was not with him in his final months, but he communicated by mail two or three times a week. The day before his death Kroeber sent an urgent message not to violate his body in any way. An autopsy would be a sacrilegious ending for the Yahi. "If there is any talk about the interests of science, say for me that science can go to hell." But the message was not received in time and Ishi's brain was removed. Consistent with Yana custom, his body was cremated. The ashes, and some of his artifacts, were buried in the Mt. Olivet Cemetery in the small town of Colma, near San Francisco. He left an estate of $523 in cash.

Waterman blamed himself for pushing Ishi too hard during the summer of 1915. During that period, he worked daily with the great language specialist Edward Sapir. Although 1,500 feet of valuable documentary film of Ishi was lost because of improper preservation, fortunately, about 400 wax-cylinder sound recordings survived and were relocated again in 1957. Waterman wrote to Kroeber, "He was the best friend I had in the world." Pope added his own epitaph: "And so, stoic and unafraid, departed the last wild Indian of America. He closes a chapter of history. He looked upon us as sophisticated children—smart, but not wise.... His soul was that of a child, his mind that of a philosopher."

The Image Remains

Kroeber was so disillusioned that he abandoned his profession for a time and studied psychoanalysis. He choose not to write the story of his friend. It would have been lost had not his wife decided to write a biography nearly a half century later. Theodora Kroeber's 1961 biography, published by the University of California Press, created a general public awareness of the life of Ishi again. In a beautifully illustrated 1976 edition of the biography, she reveals the remarkable reaction to the book 15 years before: "I could not know that ahead of me lay the real experience of Ishi: the greatest human experience of my life.... All sorts of people came, wanting sometimes to question, more often to talk, to express complex reactions, to philosophize, to wonder, even to cry—shamelessly, men and women—to put into words their feeling for Ishi's humanity." Three years later she issued a fictionalized account of his life. Nearly 30 years after the initial publication, during a wave of interest in Native American life, her novel was transformed into a film with Graham Greene in the title role. A documentary film about his life, in "The American Experience" series, was also completed.

In 1966 a monument was dedicated near Oroville by the white man who first saw Ishi in 1911. Conservationists have also been active in preserving an Ishi Wilderness in the region of his original home.

SOURCES:

The Indians of California: A Critical Bibliography, compiled by Robert F. Heizer, Bloomington, Indiana University Press, 1976.

Ishi: The Last Yahi; A Documentary History, edited by Robert F. Heizer and Theordora Kroeber, Berkeley, University of California Press, 1979.

Karttunen, Frances, "Two Survivalists: Dersu Uzala and Ishi," in *Between Worlds: Interpreters, Guides, and Survivors,* New Brunswick, New Jersey, Rutgers University Press, 1994.

Kroeber, Theodora, *Ishi in Two Worlds: A Biography of the Last Wild Indian in North America,* Berkeley, University of California Press, 1961.

Kroeber, Theodora, *Ishi: Last of His Tribe,* Berkeley, Parnassus Press, 1964.

Meyer, Kathleen Allan, *Ishi: The Story of an American Indian,* Minneapolis, Dillon Press, 1980.

Waterman, Thomas Talbot, *The Yana Indians,* 1918.

—Sketch by Keith A. Winsell

Alice Mae Jemison (right) with Joseph Bruner

Alice Mae Jemison
1901-1964
Seneca-Cherokee activist and politician

Alice Mae Lee Jemison was born October 9, 1901, on the Cattaraugus Reservation of the Seneca Nation of Indians (SNI) in New York. She was the eldest of three children born to Daniel A. Lee and Elnora E. Seneca. Her mother was a Seneca from a prominent political family in the SNI; her father was a Cherokee cabinetmaker. Both of Alice Mae Lee's parents were graduates of Hampton Institute in Virginia, where they met as students. Given the matrilineal descent rule of the Seneca and the prominence of the family in Seneca politics, the Lee family resided on the Cattaraugus Reservation. Alice Mae Lee graduated from Silver Creek High School (a public school just off the reservation in the town of Silver Creek, New York) in 1919, having worked both as an usher and beautician in the evenings in order to help the family financially. She married LeVerne Leonard Jemison, a Seneca steelworker from the Cattaraugus Reservation, on December 6, 1919, separating from him in December, 1928. During their marriage, the couple had two children, LeVerne "Jimmy" Lee, born in 1920, and Jeanne Marie, born in 1923.

Political Beginnings

Jemison held a number of different jobs during this period, but perhaps most crucial was her position as secretary to her cousin, SNI President Ray Jimerson in 1929.

Always interested in the living conditions of her people, Jemison was, in this position, provided entree into the inner circle of Seneca politics which made her privy to political workings both within the SNI and in the world outside the Nation. She demonstrated her political skills the following year, in 1930, when she, along with other Iroquois leaders, came to the aid of the defense in a celebrated murder case which involved two Seneca women from the Cattaraugus Reservation accused of killing the wife of an artist in Buffalo, New York. Since the crime reputedly involved witchcraft, the case was quite sensational. Following this involvement, Jemison stayed involved with Indian affairs by writing columns for the North American Indian Newspaper Alliance, and working as a lobbyist in Washington, D.C., for the SNI.

Opposes Indian Reorganization Act

Jemison held two strong political beliefs which were to color all her later activities. She was a firm believer in the sovereignty of Indian treaty rights, and she strongly believed that the Bureau of Indian Affairs should be abolished. During the presidency of Franklin D. Roosevelt, Jemison opposed the New Deal, particularly as it pertained to Indians. In the interest of fighting for her beliefs, Jemison joined the American Indian Federation, an activist organization. The federation was formed in 1934 under the leadership of Joseph Bruner, a full-blood Creek from Oklahoma, who believed that Indians should fully accept both American citizenship and culture.

In 1934, Commissioner of Indian Affairs John Collier proposed the Indian Reorganization Act, which presented as its goal the opportunity to provide Native Americans with the chance to reaffirm the sovereignty of tribal governments and adopt tribal constitutions. Bruner, however, felt that the act was an attempt to impose communism on Indians as a way of establishing communism in the United States. The vice president of the American Indian Federation, Jacob Morgan, a Navajo tribal councilor and missionary of the Christian Reformed Church, joined Bruner in his beliefs. Bruner also contended that the Indian Reorganization Act—rather than empowering tribal governments—would cause a "divide and conquer" situation among Indian tribes within the United States. In 1935, Jemison became district president of the federation, editor of the federation's newspaper, The First American, and spokesperson for Bruner, spurred on by her belief that the Indian Reorganization Act should be repealed.

Jemison also personally opposed the act—which included provisions for providing Native American groups with the opportunity to borrow money from a revolving fund—on the basis that it was impossible for any single act or program to satisfy the economic, political, and cultural needs of all American Indian groups throughout the country. During hearings of the House Indian Affairs Committee, Jemison argued for the abolition of the Bureau of Indian Affairs as well as the repeal of the Indian Reorganization Act, feeling that Indians would do better if freed from federal control. She further questioned Collier's qualification to head the Bureau of Indian Affairs based on his membership in the American Civil Liberties Union, which she and her colleagues thought to be communistic, as well as on the basis of administrative incompetence and fiscal irresponsibility.

Based on her belief that SNI sovereignty extended to the right to declare war independent of the United States, Jemison also opposed Seneca participation in the Selective Service Act, which required members of the tribe to register for the military draft. This was a natural extension of Jemison's strong belief in Indian sovereignty over any outside governmental control including federal control.

Jemison's fight against the Bureau of Indian Affairs, the Indian Reorganization Act, and the Selective Service Act brought her into association with many self-styled fascists who appeared at many of the same hearings Jemison attended. In fact, the American Indian Federation sought support from Nazi organizations, such as the German-American Bund, in their attempt to discredit the Bureau of Indian Affairs, Collier, and the Indian Reorganization Act. These fascist organizations supported Indian activists based on a declaration by the German government that Indians were members of the Aryan race. Such connections caused Jemison to be branded an Indian Nazi, although she herself was neither a member of these organizations nor a supporter of their basic beliefs.

Jemison remained in the Washington, D.C., area for the rest of her life where she continued to campaign for various Indian causes. Her strong family ties and the continued political activities of her family helped her to maintain contact with the SNI and to continue her awareness of Seneca feelings on federal issues. Jemison died in March, 1964, from cancer. She is buried at the United Mission Cemetery on the Cattaraugus Reservation. Jemison lives in the memory of her people who recognize her as a powerful advocate for Indian causes who was instrumental in shaping federal Indian policies during the 1930s and continued to lobby for Indian causes until her death.

SOURCES:

Ballantine, Betty, and Ian Ballantine, *The Native Americans: An Illustrated History,* Atlanta, Turner Publishing, 1993.

Hauptman, Laurence M., "Alice Mae Lee Jemison," in *Notable American Women; The Modern Period: A Biographical Dictionary,* edited by Barbara Sicherman and Carol Hurd Green, Cambridge, Massachusetts, Belknap Press, 1980.

Philip, Kenneth R., *John Collier's Crusade for Indian Reform, 1920-1954,* Tucson, University of Arizona Press, 1977.

Watkins, Tom H., *Righteous Pilgrim: The Life and Times of Harold L. Ickes, 1874-1952,* New York, Holt, 1990.

—Sketch by Martha I. Symes

Emily Pauline Johnson
1861-1913
Mohawk author and performer
Also known as Pauline Johnson and Tekahionwake ["Double Wampum"]

Emily Pauline Johnson was the first Native Canadian (and the first author) to have her likeness and name commemorated on a postage stamp. She is remembered for her contributions to First Nations literature (as work by indigenous Canadians is called) and to the acceptance of Native women of letters. Johnson was descended from the well-known Brant and Johnson families of the Mohawk Nation. Her distant relative Joseph Brant (also known as Thayendanegea ["He Who Places Two Bets"]) was a steadfast ally of the British during the French and Indian War and the American Revolution. Joseph's sister, Molly Brant (also known as Degonwadonti) had married William Johnson, British trader and Superintendent of Indian Affairs for the Crown. She became something of a diplomat and liaison for her people and the English-Canadians.

Often called "Pauline Johnson" by Canadian writers, Emily was born March 10, 1861, in Chiefswood, Ontario, not far from Brantford and next to the Six Nations (Iroquois) Indian Reserve. Her father, Henry Martin Johnson (Onwanonsyshon) was a Mohawk chief whose full name is sometimes reported as George Martin Henry Johnson. Her mother was Emily S. Howells, an Englishwoman and an aunt of American writer William Dean Howells. Some contemporary accounts erroneously list Brant's parents as George Mansion and Lydia Bestman. This may be the result of the sheer size and prominence of the Brant and Johnson families, and their frequent use of first names such as "Emily" and "Molly."

As a youngster, Johnson loved to read. She particularly enjoyed the classics of British literature, and as was the custom for Victorian ladies of her day, she paid close attention to the Romantic writers as well as Shakespeare. She tried her hand at writing early on, but doubted her own talent. Coupled with her shyness, this lack of confidence kept her from sharing much of her early pieces. Taught at home until she was ready to enter Brantford College in her mid-teens, she also lacked an audience in front of which to gain recitation experience.

Begins Writing Career

Still in her teens and attending college, Johnson began winning accolades from teachers for her poetry. She took drama classes and branched out into theatrical performance, appearing in plays and learning to develop a charisma that held her listeners. In the mid-1870s, Johnson sent a manuscript of a single poem to the Brantford newspaper, hoping it might be published. Although she aspired to a professional writing career, she had not as yet had any of her efforts reviewed for publication. With modest dreams, Emily mailed off the poem and was delighted to receive a favorable critique from the newspaper's editor. Suggesting that she set her sights higher, even for a first effort, he advised her to send it to poetry journals or a large-scale magazine.

When magazines such as *Harper's* and the *Athenaeum* published her poems, Johnson was elated. Her confidence growing, she was determined to begin public readings in order to interpret her work in front of an audience. Her local readings led to an invitation to present her poetry at a Canadian literature forum in Toronto. The 1892 event was sponsored by the Young Liberals Club of Toronto, and the highlight of the evening was Johnson's reading of her poem entitled "A Cry from an Indian Wife." The story of the Northwest Rebellion, Johnson's tome was enhanced by the visual impact of the author dressed in traditional clothing. The coupling of Johnson's message—that Canada was still Indian land wrested unfairly from indigenous hands—with the stunning drama of her recitation literally stole the show. Soon, Johnson was a national sensation. As word spread, eager audiences queued up for her full evening performances, and she tailored several new works for dramatic reading, the most popular of which was "The Song My Paddle Sings." Her performances centered clearly on indigenous themes and Native rights, but were presented in the Romantic lilt of Victorian-style cadences. Johnson's famil-

iar form arose out of her love of British literature and the popular style of the day, making it understandable to most audiences. In 1885, however, just as her professional career blossomed, Johnson's beloved father died. To be closer to her newly famous daughter, Emily Howells Johnson moved into Brantford, and the two supported each other in their shared grief.

Songs of the Great Dominion, Johnson's first book-length collection, appeared in 1889. Soon, she was on a poetry recital tour of Canada, and word of her talent spread to the United States and England. She was invited to London in 1894, and she fulfilled a girlhood dream of being introduced to famous British authors. Wherever she went, Johnson's readings were well-attended and her public praises grew. John Lane Publishers of London contracted with Johnson to print her next poetry collection. *White Wampum* was released in 1895, again to critical success. On the strength of the new volume, she returned to Canada for a triumphal tour, including several U.S. cities.

Gains Wide Popularity with the Public

Throughout the 1890s, Emily Pauline Johnson traveled and read her poems, donning her now famous Mohawk clothing. A popular place for dramatic readings in those days in Canada was saloons, and through such venues, Johnson was able to bring her poetry to working-class Canadians and rural residents in the northern and western reaches of the country. That she did not confine her tours to large halls in major cities or to places where only cultured intellectuals would venture endeared her to the common folk of Canada. Her 1903 edition, *Canadian Born,* was a reflection of this growing interest; Johnson stressed the shared heritage of Canadians, while still keeping the integrity of Native cultures and history central to her themes. Although she still loved interacting with her audiences, Johnson tired of the continual travel, and her health began to suffer.

Johnson subsequently scaled back her touring to focus more on writing. She committed to paper the traditional stories she had collected from many First Nations in her years of travel. Settling far from her Mohawk homeland, she now made her home in Vancouver and the traditional tales of British Columbia Natives captured her heart. In 1911, she offered *Legends of Vancouver,* recounting and interpreting tribal stories she had learned from Chief Joe Capilano. Although the collection of tribal stories was already a mainstay of academically oriented writing on Native people, her innovative and articulate commentary aimed at a general reading audience. It has since become a commonly held belief that the authorship of fiction and nonfiction alike by Native women is "preservative"—that Native women writers preserve traditional stories and customs by weaving them into their narratives, creating a "printed museum."

Meanwhile, Johnson's fiction was developing new themes. She continued to write about Native characters, usually women, but now she included the experiences of white pioneer women (especially from the prairie provinces of Alberta, Saskatchewan, and Manitoba) and their commonality with Native women in their struggles to survive. She also began to focus more keenly on the difficult position of the "métis," the large mixed-blood segment of Canada's population. Métis were often interpreters for both Indian and non-Indian interests, and Johnson saw her work as an author and performer as the natural outgrowth of this role. She dramatically explored the alienation many Métis felt in trying to find their identity in Canadian society. In this, she anticipated a common genre of modern Native writing.

While 1912's *Flint and Feather* carried on the now-familiar format of collections of Johnson's Indian-themed poetry, her 1913 work, *The Moccasin Maker*, introduced her new interests in pioneer women and métis. Critically acclaimed and widely popular, the work put Johnson squarely in a ground-breaking position. Women were then generally believed to be incapable of writing long works of prose. That a Native woman could accomplish this feat was almost unthinkable. In fact, prior to Johnson's *The Moccasin Maker*, the only widely read fiction written by a Native woman had been the works of Sarah Callahan (a Creek author). Johnson's contemporary, Okanogan writer Humishuma (also known as Chrystal Quintasket), wrote a short novel, *Coqewea, the Half-Blood,* which eclipsed Johnson's in sales. However, Johnson is considered the more influential Native woman author due to her breadth of writing styles and to the success of her poetic performances.

For some time, Johnson had been suffering from cancer, a battle she lost on March 7, 1913, just three days before her fifty-third birthday. She died in her home in Vancouver and was honored by her adopted hometown when she was interred in Stanley Park. Johnson's last work, *The Shagganappi*, was published posthumously, and her work continued to sell briskly for several years after her death. *Legends of Vancouver* was reprinted in 1922, and a revised *Flint and Feather: The Complete Poems of Pauline Johnson* appeared in 1972.

Johnson has often been called the unofficial poet laureate of Canada. The country issued a commemorative five-cent postage stamp 1961, coinciding with the hundredth anniversary of her birth. Its design shows Johnson in profile in Victorian apparel in the foreground, with a traditionally-clad figure appearing in the background, arms spread skyward in a dramatic gesture reminiscent of her public performances. In 1974, she was the subject of a biographical study of her life and times, *Pauline Johnson and Her Friends,* authored by Walter McRaye and published by Toronto's Ryerson Press.

SELECTED WRITINGS BY JOHNSON:

Songs of the Great Dominion, 1889.
The White Wampum, London, John Lane Publishers, 1895.
Canadian Born, Toronto, George N. Morang, 1903.
The Legends of Vancouver, first published 1911; Toronto, McClelland and Stewart, 1922.
Flint and Feather, Toronto, Musson Book Company, 1912.
The Moccasin Maker, Toronto, William Briggs, 1913.

The Shagganappi, Toronto, William Briggs, 1913.
Flint and Feather: The Complete Poems of Pauline Johnson, Ontario, Don Mills, 1972.

SOURCES:

American Indian Women: A Research Guide, edited by Gretchen M. Bataille and Kathleen Sands, New York, Garland Publishing, 1991.
Biographical Dictionary of Indians of the Americas, Newport Beach, California, American Indian Publications, 1983.
Dockstader, Frederick, *Great North American Indians,* New York, Van Nostrand Reinhold, 1977.
Native North American Almanac, edited by Duane Champagne, Detroit, Gale Research, 1994.
That's What She Said, edited by Rayna Green, Bloomington, Indiana University Press, 1984.

—Sketch by Cynthia R. Kasee

Basil H. Johnston
1929-
Ojibway (Chippewa) author and educator

Basil H. Johnston is the author of numerous stories, articles, poems, essays, and books, including several guides for teaching and learning the Ojibway language. His writings describe the diversity of the Ojibway culture and the changes it has undergone in the past century. His essays strive to preserve aspects of his heritage, such as the native language and accomplishments, before they are lost or integrated into mainstream society. For his work on behalf of the Native community, he received the Centennial Medal in 1967. In 1976 he received the Samuel S. Fells Literary Award for his essay "Zhowmin and Mandamin," and in April of 1989 he received the Order of Ontario for his many contributions to society in Ontario and elsewhere; and on June 8, 1994, the University of Toronto awarded him an honorary doctorate.

Johnston was born on July 13, 1929, to Rufus and Mary Lafreniere Johnston on the Parry Island Indian Reserve in Ontario. There, he attended elementary school at the Cape Croker Indian Reserve school until the age of 10. By this time, his parents had separated and Johnston, his mother, and four sisters were living with his grandmother. Johnston and one sister were "selected" by an Indian agent and the local priest to attend residential school in Spanish, Ontario. He attended St. Peter Claver's Indian Residential School, commonly referred to as "Spanish" after the town where it was located. The school, run by Jesuit priests, offered discipline, education, and taught the boys trades that they could pursue once they were released at the age of 16. Subsidized by the government, the boys generally performed every task necessary to keep the institution running. Under the guidance of the Jesuits, they grew their own vegetables, helped to bake and prepare food, made their clothes and shoes, maintained the buildings and grounds, and raised and sold cattle, chickens, and hogs.

Plans for the Future

Johnston was released from St. Peter Claver's in 1944 to enter secondary school. Three months short of completing the ninth grade, he dropped out of Regiopolis College in Kingston at the end of March 1945. After spending the following months at miscellaneous jobs, including fishing, farming, and trapping, Johnston found it difficult to support himself. He describes his decision to return to school in *Indian School Days:* "Maybe it would be better to go back to school. I had heard vague rumors that Spanish was offering a high-school program. If it were true, I would return. It was my only chance to escape a life of cutting wood."

During Johnston's absence, many changes had taken place at St. Peter Claver's. The trades that the boys were being taught had become obsolete. Jobs for chicken farmers, cobblers, and tailors were scarce due to machines and equipment that had replaced human labor. The new Father Superior, R. J. Oliver, appointed in 1945, believed that the boys needed a solid secondary school program if they were to have any advantage in life. He began to institute changes to prepare for a high school curriculum and interscholastic sporting events. Johnston wrote to the Father Superior, requesting to return to the institution. He re-enrolled in what was now called the Garnier Residential School for Indian Boys in 1947.

In 1950 Johnston graduated valedictorian from Garnier and then attended Loyola College in Montreal. Again graduating with honors, he earned a B.A. from Loyola in 1954. From 1955 through 1961 he was employed by the Toronto Board of Trade. After receiving a Secondary School Teaching Certificate from the Ontario College of Education in 1962, he took a position teaching history at the Earl Haig Secondary School in North York until 1969. He then joined the Ethnology Department of the Royal Ontario Museum where he served as lecturer. He has presented academic lectures at universities and conferences across Canada and the United States.

Preserves Ojibway Heritage

Johnston's writings began appearing in print in 1970. His first essay, "Bread Before Books or Books Before Bread," which appeared in *The Only Good Indian: Essays by Canadian Indians,* recounts events contributing to the deterioration of the Native American culture. The essay concludes with a summary stressing the accomplishments of the Native people from the Incas through the North American Indians. Johnston writes, "Men like to be judged not only by the great men and great works they have fostered, but also for standards of courage, perseverance, and endurance. Indian people in addition to these attributes like to be known for magnanimity, fortitude and resourcefulness."

For the Ministry of Indian and Northern Affairs Johnston wrote the *Ojibway Language Course Outline and the Ojibway Language Lexicon* in 1978. He is often sought as a translator, perhaps because his translations display a sensitivity to both the Ojibway and English languages. A respected author, many of his books have been credited with presenting his tribal mythology in a way that both renews and reveals the Ojibway attitudes and insights toward life.

SELECTED WRITINGS BY JOHNSTON:

"Bread Before Books or Books Before Bread," in *The Only Good Indian: Essays by Canadian Indians,* edited by Waubageshig, Chicago, New Press, 1970; 126-141.

"Zhomin and Mandamin," *Toronto Native Times,* 5:11, 1974; 11-12.

Ojibway Heritage, Toronto, McClelland & Stewart, 1976; New York, Columbia University, 1976.

Moose Meat and Wild Rice, Toronto, McClelland & Stewart, 1978; as Ojibway Tales, Lincoln, University of Nebraska Press, 1993.

How the Birds Got Their Colours, Toronto, Kids Can Press, 1978.

Ojibway Language Course Outline, Ottawa, Ministry of Indian and Northern Affairs, 1978.

Ojibway Language Lexicon for Beginners, Ottawa, Ministry of Indian and Northern Affairs, 1978.

Tales the Elders Told: Ojibway Legends, Toronto, Royal Ontario Museum, 1981.

Ojibway Ceremonies, Toronto, McClelland & Stewart, 1982.

By Canoe and Moccasin: Some Native Place Names of the Great Lakes, Toronto, Royal Ontario Museum, 1986; Lakefield, Ontario, Waapoone Publishing & Promotion, 1992.

Indian School Days, Toronto, Key Porter Books, 1988; Norman, University of Oklahoma Press, 1989.

SOURCES:

Dictionary of Literary Biography, Volume 60: Canadian Writers Since 1960, Second Series, 60, Detroit, Gale Research, 1987; 146-149.

Johnston, Basil H., "Bread Before Books or Books Before Bread," in *The Only Good Indian: Essays by Canadian Indians,* edited by Waubageshig, Chicago, New Press, 1970; 126-141.

Johnston, Basil H., *Ojibway Heritage,* Toronto, McClelland & Stewart, 1976; New York, Columbia University, 1976.

Johnston, Basil H., *Indian School Days,* Toronto, Key Porter Books, 1988; Norman, University of Oklahoma Press, 1989.

Native North American Almanac, edited by Duane Champagne, Detroit, Gale Research, 1994; 1079.

Reference Encyclopedia of the American Indian, sixth edition, edited by Barry T. Klein, West Nyack, New York, Todd Publications, 1993; 553.

—Sketch by Lisa A. Wroble

Ted Jojola
1951-
Isleta Pueblo educator and administrator

Ted Jojola is a prominent Isleta Pueblo educator and administrator known for his research on various aspects of Native American culture. His numerous publications, which have appeared in a variety of scholarly journals, books, and government documents, have addressed a wide range of topics, including urban planning, preschool computer teaching, architecture, and ethnography. Jojola's research at such places as the Institute of Philippine Culture, the University of California, Los Angeles, and the University of New Mexico has earned him the recognition and financial support of several grants and honors, including a public grant from Honolulu's Atherton trust in 1976 and a fellowship from the American Indian Studies Center at UCLA in 1984.

The son of Jose Levi and Juanita Bautista, Theodore Sylvester Jojola was born on November 19, 1951, in Isleta Pueblo, New Mexico. After completing his secondary education, Jojola enrolled at the University of New Mexico, earning his Bachelor of Arts degree in archeology in 1973. After graduation, Jojola worked for one year as an internal planner with the National Capital Planning Commission in Washington, D.C., before pursuing an advanced degree in city planning at the Massachusetts Institute of Technology. He received his Master of Arts degree two years later, enabling him to accept a position as the legal and historical researcher for the Institute for the Development of Indian Law in Washington. Jojola's work at this research post led to his first major work, *Memoirs of an American Indian House: The Impact of a Cross-National Housing Program on Two Reservations,* which was published in 1976.

During the next ten years of his career, Jojola continued to build upon his already wide base of expertise through further education and research opportunities. In 1977, for instance, while working towards a Ph.D. in political science at the University of Hawaii, Manua, he obtained a two-year position as a visiting researcher at the Institute of Philippine Culture in Manila. In 1980, the same year in which he married Adelamer Novino Alcantara, he was appointed the director of Native American Studies at the University of New Mexico. Upon the 1982 completion of his doctoral dissertation, "Tribal Survival and Outside Contact: The Spanish Colonial and American Territorial Occupation of the Bontoc and Isleta Villages," he became an assistant professor at New Mexico. In 1984, Jojola's research efforts were rewarded with a post-doctoral fellowship at the American Indian Studies Center at UCLA, where he also served as a visiting professor of urban planning. Before returning to New Mexico, Jojola received a certificate in human rights law from the University of Strasbourg in France.

Ted Jojola

Research Reveals an Evolving Isleta Culture

While Jojola has engaged in a variety of research projects during his tenure at New Mexico, he has devoted the majority of his attention to studying the various ways in which Native Americans—specifically, the Isleta Pueblo—have attempted to preserve and transform their civilization in response to modernization and the influx of non-Native culture. Previous scholars have argued that, since the invasion of Europeans, the descendants of ancient cave dwellers have sought only to preserve their traditional way of life. Jojola, however, has demonstrated that this model of Pueblo history is far too simplistic. He has shown that, throughout history, Isleta culture has not remained static but, rather, has continually evolved to accommodate the various changes occurring in the outside world. As Jojola stated in "Modernization and Pueblo Lifeways: Isleta Pueblo," which appeared in the 1990 publication of *Pueblo Style and Regional Architecture,* "The processes of persistence, adaptation, and innovation have been the basic prescriptions of community settlement since Pueblo prehistory. The community settlement has not been a process of maintaining 'tradition.' What was regarded as traditional in one period would not have been considered traditional in another.... Overall, Isleta is a dynamic community. To assume that its community traditions remain static is to underestimate the abilities of its culture to survive."

Although Jojola is known primarily for his contributions to the academic world, he has been an active participant in numerous programs devoted to the interests of

Native Americans. He has served on the United States organizing committee of the Ninth International American Indian Congress, held in Santa Fe, New Mexico. He has also served as the series editor of *Public Policy Impact on American Indian Development* and the contributing editor of *Wicazo sa Review,* an Eastern Washington University journal devoted to Native American studies emphasizing contemporary issues, literature, and culture. The father of one son, Manoa Alcantara, Jojola has taken an active role in local education affairs as well, donating his talents to the Isleta Elementary School in New Mexico by serving as a director of the school board and as the chairman of the Indian Education Parent's Committee.

SELECTED WRITINGS BY JOJOLA:

Memoirs of an American Indian House: The Impact of a Cross-National Housing Program on Two Reservations, 1976.
"Modernization and Pueblo Lifeways: Isleta Pueblo," in *Pueblo Style and Regional Architecture,* New York, Van Nostrand Reinhold, 1990; 78-99.

SOURCES:

Native North American Almanac, edited by Duane Champagne, Detroit, Gale Research, 1994; 1079-1080.
Reference Encyclopedia of the American Indian, fourth edition, edited by Barry T. Klein, New York, Todd Publications, 1993; 136.

—Sketch by Jason Gallman

Peter Jones
1802-1856
Ojibwa Missisauga ruling chief, missionary, and author
Also known as Kahkewaquonaby (or Kahkewagonnaby) ["Sacred Feathers"]

Sacred Feathers, better known by his English name Peter Jones, was an Ojibwa Missisauga chief and Christian missionary. He was revered for his work in bridging the European and Indian cultures in early Upper Canada, and for his endless pursuit of equality and advancement for the Missisauga Credit Indians. He was born to a white land surveyor named Augustus Jones, and to Tuhbenahneequay, daughter of a Missisauga chief. However, since Augustus was unable to convince Tuhbenahneequay to become a Christian, and she was unable to convince him to live like the Indians, they parted. Augustus later married Sarah Tekarihogen, a Mohawk

Christian convert, although he remained in contact with Tuhbenahneequay. Tuhbenahneequay did not mind Augustus having two wives, but she insisted on keeping Sacred Feathers and his older brother Tyenteneged to raise as Indians.

Sacred Feathers spent his childhood with the Missisauga tribe on the north shore of Lake Ontario. However, when he was about ten years old the War of 1812 devastated the tribe. Pressure caused by increasing numbers of white settlers in the following years brought a rapid deterioration of Missisauga society. "Sacred Feathers knew of relatives and friends who had perished in the winter from exposure while intoxicated or in the summer from drowning," states Donald B. Smith in his biography *Sacred Feathers.* "Others had died from wounds and internal injuries received in brawls." His father, now retired, believed that the Credit River Indians were near extinction and he sought his sons' help to save them. "The native people in the years immediately after 1815," Smith explains, "needed a go-between, an individual versed in the practices of both the Indians and the Europeans, someone who could articulate their needs to the government officials." Sacred Feathers and his brother went with Augustus, choosing to live with the white settlers, and taking new names: Peter and John Jones.

Peter Jones had first learned about Christianity when he lived with the Missisaugas. Initially, he rejected the religion, but in 1820 he changed his mind and was baptized as a Christian near Brantford, Ontario. Jones became active in the Wesleyan Methodist Church and went on a missionary tour throughout Ontario in 1827. He also began his literary work, translating a book of hymns into Chippewa. His translation work later expanded to include parts of the Scripture and additional hymns, making Christian texts accessible to his native people.

Jones is Appointed Ruling Chief

Jones was ordained a deacon of the Wesleyan Methodist Conference in 1830, and consecrated as a minister in 1833. In September of that year, he also married an English woman named Eliza Field. They had seven children together, four of them sons. One of his sons, Peter E. Jones, later became editor of the *Indian,* a periodical for local Indians published in Hagersville, Ontario, during the mid-1880s.

Jones spent his life after his marriage to Eliza as a missionary among the Missisauga, Chippewa, and Iroquois, working to convert the Indians to Christianity. Jones had great influence over his people and other tribes, particularly the Chippewas. As the Christian pastor of his tribe, he was eventually appointed the ruling chief of the Missisauga Credit Indians. In his dual role of leadership, Jones traveled to many parts of the world lobbying on behalf of his people while at the same time performing his missionary work. He petitioned the government for promised pieces of land at the Credit River, worked to protect the Indian's economic interests, and tried to develop a solid financial foundation for the settlement. He met with many high officials, trying to convince them that Indians could equal white men if supplied with proper education, housing, and title to their lands.

Throughout the 1830s Jones wrote secular works as well as hymnbooks and religious tracts. *The Life and Journals of Kah-Ke-Wa-Quo-Na-By,* was published in 1860, after his death. In this journal, Jones described his travels during the years 1825 to 1855 and his missionary work with various tribes, particularly the Canadian Ojibwa (Chippewas). Also included in this journal was a short autobiography. In his second and more familiar work, *History of the Ojebway Indians: With Especial Reference to Their Conversion to Christianity,* Jones explained how white culture had impacted the Indians, and praised the role of Christianity in the life of the Chippewa.

Mixes Missionary and Ethnological Work

During the 1840s, Jones grew discouraged by a number of events, including an argument with Thomas Hurlburt, involving a five-year controversy over the quality of his Scripture translations, his half-brother's defection from the church, and the death of his brother John in London. After 1845, he abandoned his work on Ojibwa history, a project that had been of extreme importance to him. It was his wife Eliza who ultimately gathered his notes and had them published several years after his death.

Jones was diagnosed with Bright's kidney disease in 1856. Many people came to see him as his health failed, including boyhood Missisauga and Mohawk friends, white ministers, his sister Polly, and his mother Tuhbenahneequay. He died on June 29, 1856, at his home, "Echo Villa," near Brantford, in the company of Eliza and their four sons. In 1857, the Ojibway and other Indian tribes erected a monument in Jones' memory.

"Above all else," Smith declares, "Peter Jones' intercultural skills made Christianity familiar and accessible to his native audiences," showing similarities between Christianity and the traditional religious beliefs and using his translating skills to convert many Indians. In addition, Jones used his mixed racial background to communicate with both white and Indian cultures and, as Smith summarized, quoting Jones' own diary, "spend nearly half his life working for the moment when the Ojibwas could 'walk side by side with their white neighbours, and partake in all the blessings and privileges enjoyed by the white subjects of her most gracious Majesty, the Queen.'"

SELECTED WRITINGS BY JONES:

(Translator) *Ojibway Spelling Book,* 1828.
(Translator) *The New Testament* (partial), 1829.
(Translator) *The Discipline of the Wesleyan Methodist Church in Canada,* (partial), 1835.
(Translator) *The First Book of Moses,* 1835.
The Life and Journals of Kah-Ke-Wa-Quo-Na-By, Anson Green, 1860.
(Translator) *Additional Hymns,* 1861.
History of the Ojebway Indians: With Especial Reference to Their Conversion to Christianity, A. W. Bennett, 1861.

SOURCES:

American Indian and Eskimo Authors, compiled by Arlene B. Hirschfelder, Association on American Indian Affairs, 1973; 49-50.
Dockstader, Frederick J., *Great North American Indians,* New York, Van Nostrand Reinhold, 1977; 126-127.
Handbook of American Indians North of Mexico, Part I, edited by Frederick Webb Hodge, Pageant Books, 1959; 633-634.
Handbook of North American Indians, edited by William C. Sturtevant, Washington, D.C., Smithsonian Institution, 1978; 765, 771.
Smith, Donald B., *Sacred Feathers,* University of Nebraska Press, 1987.
Waldman, Carl, *Who Was Who in Native American History,* New York, Facts on File, 1990; 173.

—Sketch by Lori J. Sawicki

William Jones
1871-1909
Fox ethnologist and writer

An eloquent writer, William Jones was among the first to research and document Algonquin religious practices. A member of the Fox (Mesquakie) tribe, which belongs to the Algonquian Nation, Jones was born March 28, 1871, on the Sac and Fox Reservation in Oklahoma. His mother died shortly after he was born and Jones was raised by his grandmother, who taught him the Fox language and traditional ways of life. When he was about nine years old, his grandmother died and he went to live with his father. This relationship did not prove satisfactory and Jones was sent to boarding school. After three years, Jones returned to his father's home and worked herding cattle.

Jones longed for further education. In 1889 he was sent to Hampton Institute and later transferred to Andover for college preparatory work. Jones did well there and was admitted to Harvard College, where he had planned to study medicine. Upon his arrival, advisors encouraged him to study anthropology. When he was unable to obtain a medical scholarship, Jones eventually gave in to what he considered the inevitable. He graduated from Harvard with a Bachelor's Degree in 1900 and went on to graduate school at Columbia, where he received his Masters of Arts degree in 1901 and his Ph.D. in 1904.

Conducts Work in Algonquian Spiritual Expression

While in school, Jones had spent his summers conducting field work with the Fox, Sac, and Kickapoo tribes, among others. In time, he became engrossed in tribal spiritual expression among the various communities, specifically the Fox, within the Algonquian language speaking group. According to Henry Rideout, in his unpublished book *William Jones* (1909), "The Iowa Foxes initiated him into many ancient mysteries of their religion, which have never been disclosed to a white man. Jones committed to paper an account of these, with sketches, diagrams, and the full interpretation which probably no other man could have supplied." After conducting this research, he published a number of tracts, the most important of which is *Fox Texts* (1907). Other significant publications include: "Oskaie Legend of the Ghost Dance," *Journal of American Folk-Lore* (1899); "Some Principles of Algonquian Word-Formation," *American Anthropology* (1904); "The Algonquian Manitou," *Journal of American Folk-Lore* (1905).

Jones brought a sophistication to ethnological discourse that did not previously exist. Prior to his research, conventional scholarship regarding Algonquian religious practices referred to an unsystematic belief in a mysterious cosmic power. In his discussions of the Gitche Manitou, or Great Spirit, Jones explained that the Manitou has many manifestations and is therefore present in all things, including plants, animals, the earth, and stars. He also argued that the Manitou is derived from an individual's feelings rather than knowledge and, consequently, is awakened through emotion.

Jones wanted to go to Labrador, Canada to continue his work on Algonquian spirituality by investigating the Naskapi and their religious practices in comparison with other Algonquian tribes. Despite the fact that he was the premier scholar among the Algonquian speaking peoples, he could not obtain permanent employment to support these efforts. In 1906 the Field Museum of Chicago gave him his choice of three expeditions—to Africa, to the South Pacific, or to the Philippines. He finally consented to travel to the Philippine Islands and, in August, he left Seattle for Luzon. In the spring of 1909, shortly after completing his research, he was murdered by natives.

SELECTED WRITINGS BY JONES:

"Fox Texts," *Publications of the American Ethnological Society,* 1, 1907.
"Notes on the Fox Indians," *Journal of American Folk-Lore,* 24, 1911.
"Kickapoo Tales," translated by Truman Michelson, *Publications of the American Ethnological Society,* 9, 1915.
"Ojibwa Tales from the North Shore of Lake Superior," *Journal of American Folk-Lore,* 24, 1916.
"Ojibwa Texts," edited by Truman Michelson, *Publications of the American Ethnological Society,* two parts, 4, 1917-1919.

SOURCES:

Books

Fisher, Margaret Welpley, *William Jones' "Ethnography of the Fox Indians,"* Philadelphia, University of Pennsylvania, 1939.

Rideout, Henry, *William Jones,* 1909.

Periodicals

Jones, William, "Fox Texts," *Publications of the American Ethnological Society,* 1, 1907.
Jones, William, "Notes on the Fox Indians," *Journal of American Folk-Lore,* 24, 1911.
Jones, William, "Kickapoo Tales," translated by Truman Michelson, *Publications of the American Ethnological Society,* 9, 1915.
Jones, William, "Ojibwa Tales from the North Shore of Lake Superior," *Journal of American Folk-Lore,* 24, 1916.
Jones, William. "Ojibwa Texts," edited by Truman Michelson, *Publications of the American Ethnological Society,* two parts, 4, 1917-1919.

—Sketch by Howard Meredith

Jones, Wilson
See Harjo, Chitto

Joseph
1790(?)-1871
Nez Percé leader
Also known as Old Chief Joseph, Tuekakas, and Wellamotkin

Old Chief Joseph was the principle chief of the Wallowa Nez Percés and father of the better known Chief Joseph, Hin-mah-too-Yah-lat-kekt ["Thunder Rolling in the Mountains"], celebrated leader of the Nez Percés during the 1877 war. According to Lucullus Virgil McWhorter in *Hear Me My Chiefs! Nez Percé History and Legend,* Joseph's father was "a great Umatilla or Cayuse chief." He married Khapkhaponimi, a Nez Percé of the Grand Ronde Valley, and they had at least two other children besides Chief Joseph. Another son, Ollokot ["Frog"], was a hunter, warrior, and leader of the young men during the Nez Percé War of 1877.

Relations with Americans Began Peacefully

Joseph's relations with the United States began peacefully when he met Captain Benjamin L. E. Bonneville in 1834 and by 1836 he was showing an interest in the Christian teachings of American missionaries. He was especially fond of Henry H. Spalding, the Presbyterian missionary who baptized him, giving him the name Joseph. Joseph and Chief Timothy were the first two Nez Percés to be baptized. For many years Joseph proudly carried a copy of the New Testament he received from the missionary. He attended the governor of Washington Territory, Isaac Stevens, Walla Walla Council. He reluctantly agreed to Stevens' 1855 Nez Percé Treaty, satisfied that he had retained possession of the Wallowa Valley for his people. Although Joseph did not fight in the Yakima War which followed the Walla Walla Council, he did become disenchanted with the Americans and Chief Lawyer, leader of the Christian Nez Percés. He aligned himself more closely with Chief Looking Glass, a militant non-Christian Nez Percé. By 1856 Joseph's bitterness and frustration increased and he denounced his Christian faith, tearing up his copy of the New Testament and becoming one of principal spokesmen of the anti-treaty Nez Percés. Joseph refused to accept annuity goods or treaty payments, insisting that he had signed away nothing and therefore was owed nothing by the Americans.

After gold was discovered in Nez Percé country, the government called for another treaty council. Although Joseph was against the 1863 Nez Percé Treaty, Lawyer agreed to it, driving a wedge between the two Nez Percé factions. Joseph now tried to isolate himself and his people in Wallowa country.

Retreats to Wallowa Valley

The Joseph, or Wallowa band of Nez Percés retreated to their homeland in northeast Oregon. A mountainous country sliced by a network of deep, rugged canyons, with the Wallowa River meandering through the valley floor. With altitudes ranging from approximately 2,000 to 4,000 feet, it was of little value for agriculture. But the lush grasses in the canyons and on the plateaus made it a natural grazing country. Wild horses were plentiful and the Nez Percés' cattle herds prospered. The mountains and valleys were alive with deer, bighorn sheep, elk, and bear, and the rivers ran with salmon and trout. The Americans did not invade Joseph's country until the early 1870s when gold was discovered in the Wallowa mountains and miners and cattlemen rushed into the valley. The American onslaught resulted in conflicts with the Nez Percés, culminating in the Nez Percé War of 1877.

Joseph and his people desired to be left alone in their valley home, maintaining many of their old ways. The non-Christian Nez Percés were influenced by the teachings of the Wanapum prophet, Smohalla, who lived at Priest Rapids on the Columbia River. Smohalla's Dreamer faith corresponded to traditional Nez Percé beliefs and the prophet's teachings inspired the non-Christian Nez Percés, giving them hope for the future. But by the early 1870s the Nez Percés time in the Wallowa Valley was running out.

By 1871 Joseph was completely blind and his son, the young Chief Joseph had already assumed leadership of the Wallowa Nez Percés. Late that summer, Joseph died. According to Alvin M. Josephy, Jr., in *The Nez Percé Indians and the Opening of the Northwest,* Chief Joseph recounted his father's dying plea to an eastern writer in 1879: "My son, never forget my dying words. This country holds your father's body. Never sell the bones of your father or mother." Chief Joseph buried his father in the lower part

of the Wallowa Valley. In 1886, nine years after the Nez Percés had been removed from the Wallowa, the owners of the property on which old Joseph was buried opened the grave and removed the chief's skull. Later, it was put on display in a Baker, Oregon dentist's office. In 1926 a group of Wallowa Valley citizens removed Joseph's remains and reinterred them at the foot of Wallowa Lake. A modest granite monument was placed on Joseph's grave.

SOURCES:

Haines, Francis, *The Nez Percés: Tribesmen of the Columbia Plateau,* Norman, University of Oklahoma Press, 1978.

Josephy, Alvin M., Jr., *The Nez Percé Indians and the Opening of the Northwest,* Lincoln, University of Nebraska Press, 1979; 442.

McWhorter, L. V., *Hear Me My Chiefs! Nez Percé History and Legend,* edited by Ruth Bordin, Caldwell, Caxton Printers, 1986; 598-603.

Waldman, Carl, *Who Was Who in Native American History,* New York, Facts on File, 1990; 173-174.

—Sketch by Michael F. Turek

Joseph
1840(?)-1904
Nez Percé tribal leader
Also known as Chief Joseph, Joseph the Younger, and Hin-mah-too-Yah-lat-kekt ["Thunder Rolling in the Mountains"]

Chief Joseph, the statesman-leader of his people during the Nez Percé Indian War of 1877, was born in Wallowa Valley, Oregon, in about 1840. Known to his tribesmen as Hin-mah-too-Yah-lat-kekt ["Thunder Rolling in the Mountains"], he was the son of Old Chief Joseph of the Wallowas, a half-Cayuga and half-Nez Percé married to a Nez Percé woman. Young Joseph had two brothers, one of whom died in early maturity, and Ollokot (Frog), who became an accomplished hunter and warrior and Joseph's chief confidant. When grown to manhood, Joseph was very striking in appearance. About six feet in height, he was powerfully built, with strong features and a regal bearing. He married three times during his lifetime, fathering a set of twins.

Discovery of Gold

Joseph lived his early years in the quiet of the Wallowa and Imnaha valleys of northeastern Oregon. However, in 1860, the discovery of gold brought thousands of adventurers pouring into neighboring Idaho, and pressures by white interests resulted in a series of treaties and executive orders

Joseph the Younger

that reduced Indian holdings. A split in the tribe came in 1863 when those bands who had become Christianized signed a treaty reducing Nez Percé lands by seven million acres. Since agreement deprived the Wallowas and allied bands of their traditional homeland, they refused to sign, becoming known as the non-treaty Nez Percé. In protest, Old Chief Joseph tore his copy of the treaty to shreds, destroyed his New Testament, and continued to oppose white settlement until his death in 1871.

Although the Wallowa Valley proved barren of gold, stockmen were covetous of its grassy meadows. Finally, officials ordered the non-treaty bands to occupy unallotted lands inside the boundaries of the reservation, authorizing force if necessary. On May 14, 1877, General O. O. Howard gave the non-treaty Nez Percés 30 days to comply. Trouble began on June 13 a few miles from the reservation border when three young men decided to avenge earlier grievances with white settlers. A two-day raid followed in which 21 whites were killed, causing the non-treaty bands to flee. On June 17, Captain David Perry, two companies of the First Cavalry, and 12 civilian volunteers engaged the Nez Percés in the Battle of White Bird Canyon, suffering a resounding defeat, and losing 33 soldiers. The Nez Percés did not lose not lose a single warrior. In this battle, like all those that followed, Joseph fought like any other warrior, leaving military strategy to others.

"I will fight no more forever"

During the next four months, the Nez Percés fled more than 1,000 miles over the Bitterroot Mountains, through what would become Yellowstone National Park, and across the breadth of Montana. Of the 700 who began the journey,

only 155 were able-bodied warriors. At Clearwater, Big Hole, and Canyon Creek, they fought troops with great success, only to suffer defeat at Bear Paw Mountain, just a few miles from refuge in Canada. On October 5, after a few made good their escape, 414 Nez Percés surrendered to General Nelson A. Miles, ending what General William T. Sherman referred to as one of the most extraordinary Indian wars of record. Joseph's poignant surrender speech ended with the oft-quoted lines, "Hear me, my chiefs, I am tired; my heart is sick and sad. From where the sun now stands, I will fight no more forever."

The Nez Percé prisoners were eventually sent to Indian Territory in Oklahoma. In 1884, officials permitted Joseph and 150 of his band to live on Colville Reservation in Washington. There, the Nez Percé leader spent his remaining years, urging the young to pursue education and speaking out against gambling and alcohol abuse. The agency physician attributed his death on September 21, 1904, to a broken heart.

For many years, writers pictured Joseph as the Red Napoleon who had outwitted U.S. generals, a misconception created by General O. O. Howard, his pursuer, in several books. Only recently have historians more precisely defined Joseph's role as that of an orator, diplomat, and statesman. An inspiration to his people, he remains a symbol of the tragedy suffered by nineteenth-century Native Americans.

SOURCES:

Brown, Mark H., *The Flight of the Nez Percé,* New York, G. P. Putnam's Son's, 1967.

Josephy, Alvin, *The Nez Percé Indians and the Opening of the Northwest,* New Haven, Connecticut, Yale University Press, 1965.

McDermott, John D., *Forlorn Hope: The Battle of White Bird Canyon and the Beginning of the Nez Percé War,* Boise, Idaho State Historical Society, 1978; xii-xv, 11, 12, 83, 113, 126-27.

McWhorter, Lucullus, *Hear Me My Chiefs!: Nez Percé History and Legend,* Caldwell Printers, 1952; 598-603.

—Sketch by John D. McDermott

Betty Mae Tiger Jumper
1923-

Seminole nurse, tribal leader, journalist, and story-teller

Betty Mae Tiger Jumper is a woman of "firsts." She was the first Seminole woman to graduate from high school, the first to become a nurse, the first female elected to the

Seminole Tribal Council, and the first woman to lead it. As an administrator and storyteller, she has worked for much of her life to communicate and preserve Seminole cultural traditions.

Jumper was born in 1923 in Indiantown, a small village in the Florida Everglades. Her mother, Ada Tiger, was a full-blood Seminole woman who spoke little English and kept the "old ways"; her father was a white man. As Jumper herself related in Miami at the 1988 conference "Native American Culture: A View from Within," "half-breed" children at that time were thrown in the Everglades immediately after birth. But her grandfather, a Baptist, would not allow angry relatives to kill either Betty Mae or her younger brother Howard. The children grew up in very traditional surroundings, and their father's culture was not part of their early years.

In order to keep the effects of cultural assimilation to a minimum, the Seminoles avoided contact with mainstream white culture. When a land boom in southern Florida caused many whites to move to the area, the Seminoles (and the related Miccosukees) found it harder to remain isolated. Jumper's grandmother was opposed to the children's going to school or learning to read. But Jumper's discovery of a comic book at a church piqued her interest, and she became determined to go to school. Jumper attended a day school operated near Indiantown (on the eastern shore of Lake Okeechobee) until it closed in 1936. She then prevailed upon her family to let her and her brother, Howard, go to an Indian boarding school nearly 1,000 miles away in Cherokee, North Carolina. The youngsters found the colder, more seasonal climate of the Smoky Mountains a drastic change from that of the tropical Everglades, but their close friendship with the four other Seminoles at the school helped ease their homesickness. It was not long before the teachers at Cherokee saw how determined Jumper was to learn, and she made great strides in her years at the school. She became, with a cousin, the first Seminole to graduate from high school.

After her graduation in 1945, Jumper moved to Oklahoma to study nursing at the Kiowa Indian Hospital. She finished a year-long course in public-health nursing, and then returned to Florida and married Moses Jumper, a friend from the Cherokee school. Howard Tiger also met his future spouse—a young Cherokee woman named Winifred—at the Cherokee school; they later married and moved to Florida to live with the Tiger family.

Like the well-known Navajo public-health worker Annie Dodge Wauneka, Jumper used her nursing skills to earn the respect of her people with tireless work to eradicate disease and improve health on Indian reservations. Throughout the 1950s, she traveled between the reservations at Dania (in Hollywood, Florida), Big Cypress, and Brighton, speaking with tribal members in traditional Muskogee/Creek and Miccosukee/Hitchiti languages.

The Seminole Tribe of Florida was chartered in 1957 when the termination policy of the Bureau of Indian Affairs threatened the Seminole tribe's status as a recognized Indian nation. The Seminole charter was followed a couple of years later by the charter of the Miccosukee Tribe of Florida, Inc. In their first formal tribal election, the Seminoles chose Jumper as one of their representatives. After her term expired in 1959, Jumper became a member of the board of directors of the tribe. She remained a board member until 1963, helping direct the economic endeavors of the Seminoles.

Elected to Lead Seminole Tribal Council

Throughout the 1960s, Jumper worked in tribal administration. Between 1963 and 1967, she held the position of "secretary-treasurer and vice-chairman." She made headlines throughout the Native-American world in 1967, when she was elected "chairman" of the tribe, the first Seminole woman so designated. When Jumper took office, many issues faced her and the tribe, and over the next four years, she strove to improve social, educational, and housing conditions for the Seminoles, moving them toward economic self-sufficiency. She also worked to incorporate the Seminole people into a regional support network of tribes called the United Southeastern Tribes, now known as the United Southern and Eastern Tribes (USET), of which Jumper was a founding signatory. In 1968 the leaders of the Seminoles, Cherokees, Choctaws, and other federally recognized tribes signed the group's Declaration of Unity. For her work, Jumper was honored as one of the "Top Indian Women of 1970" and awarded an invitation to attend that year's national seminar for American Indian women. At about the same time, the Nixon administration recognized her with an appointment to the National Congress of Indian Opportunity.

Having served her people for nearly a decade in a political capacity, Jumper took another path after she left office in 1971, when she assumed the post of director of operations for Seminole Communications, publisher of the *Seminole Tribune,* a biweekly newspaper detailing local and national Indian news and the Seminole nation's official publication. Jumper's work with the organization is only one of the ways in which she has served her people using modern communication tools.

In 1980, the Seminole Print Shop published Jumper's history of Christianity among the Seminoles, *...and with the Wagon Came God's Word.* She frequently speaks at Indian church conferences, often working with a singing group that includes family members. Jumper also lectures widely on Seminole history and culture, tribal administration, Indian education, health care, and economic development. Although she is known throughout the country, Jumper focuses her efforts in Florida. A regular at the Folklore and Folklife Festival in Brooksville each summer, she also appears at cultural events at colleges across the state, sometimes with her son, Moses Jumper, Jr. (one of her three children), who is himself a poet and author. In the early 1990s, Jumper and the Seminole tribe produced a video portraying several traditional stories, with Jumper in the roll of the storyteller/title character called "The Corn Woman," for whom the video is named.

Honors bestowed on Jumper in the 1990s have included a Woman of the Year award sponsored by the Jewish War Veterans of the U.S. Ladies Auxiliary of Florida. In May, 1994, she was recognized by the Florida Department of State's Bureau of Florida Folklife Programs with the Folklife Heritage Award. The award featured an inscription that lauds, as quoted in the Seminole Tribune, Betty Mae Tiger Jumper's "outstanding contributions to the folklife of Florida, through her telling of Seminole traditional stories and her folk-cultural advocacy."

SELECTED WRITINGS BY JUMPER:

...and with the Wagon Came God's Word, Hollywood, Florida, Seminole Tribe of Florida Print Shop, 1980.

SOURCES:

Books

Biographical Dictionary of Indians of the Americas, Newport Beach, California, American Indian Publications, 1983.

Native American Women, edited by Gretchen M. Bataille, New York, Garland Publishing, 1993.
Native North American Almanac, edited by Duane Champagne, Detroit, Gale Research, 1994.

Periodicals

Wickman, P. R., "State Awards Highest Folklife Honor to Tribune Editor, Tribal Leader, Betty Mae Jumper," *Seminole Tribune,* June 10, 1994; 1.

Other

Jumper, Betty Mae, public lectures at Miami-Dade Community College's "Native American Culture: A View from Within" conference, October 1988.

—Sketch by Cynthia R. Kasee

Fred Kabotie
1900-(?)
Hopi artist and teacher

Fred Kabotie was an internationally recognized painter whose work is exhibited in the permanent collections of major museums, including the Museum of Modern Art in New York, the Corcoran Gallery in Washington, D.C., and the Peabody Museum of Harvard University. Honored by the countries of France, India, and Mexico, he created employment for Hopi veterans by founding a silverworkers guild after World War II. And in 1949, his research on Mimbres designs was published in *Designs from the Ancient Mimbrenos with a Hopi Interpretation.*

Kabotie was born in Arizona, at Shongopavi, Second Mesa on February 20, 1900. Shongopavi is one of the 13 Hopi villages in northeastern Arizona clustered around the southern rim of Black Mesa. So little rain falls there that the people practice dry farming, planting corn kernels so deep that their roots can tap underground water. Elders say that this barren sandstone village was selected because no one else would ever want to live there so they could inhabit it in peace. Shongopavi has maintained its traditional ceremonies, not permitting non-Indians to observe the katsina dances. Michael Kabotie, the artist's son and noted abstract expressionist who co-founded Artist Hopid, said that through participating in this great communal art form, it was inevitable for all Hopi to become artists. When visitors noted signs of Picasso's influence in this art, Kabotie proudly contradicted them, claiming, "No, Picasso was the one who was influenced by the Hopis."

In 1915, Kabotie was sent to the Santa Fe Indian School. His talent was recognized immediately by superintendent John De Huff who encouraged him to paint in his home after class; he also got him commissions at the Museum of New Mexico and enabled him to sell his paintings while still a student. Kabotie's teacher, Dorothy Dunn, marveled at his "masterly draftsmanship, perfect proportion, anatomical correctness, adroit perspective and foreshortening," all of which the boy achieved without formal academic instruction. He particularly excelled in his depictions of Katsinas which struck her with their supernatural power. These were not, she commented, mere impersonations: "His performers are not men dressed as gods; they are gods."

Fred Kabotie (right) with Frederick H. Harvey

Patrons of the Santa Fe Movement

A prominent artists' colony in Santa Fe used its influence to arrange exhibits of student art. Among these patrons were Mabel Dodge Luhan, the poet Mary Austin, Olive Rush, and John Sloan who was then president of New York's Society of Independent Artists which exhibited annually at the Waldorf-Astoria Hotel in New York City. Austin arranged for an exhibit at the Museum of Natural History and shows followed at Salt Lake City, Utah. A fund was established by Rose Dougan for an annual art prize to be given by the Museum of New Mexico during fiesta week. The first award was given in September of 1922 to Fred Kabotie. An exhibit at the Riverside Museum (then called the Corona Mundi International Art Center) featured Kabotie's work in 1927 to excellent reviews. By 1928, John D. Rockefeller, Jr., had granted $200,000 for a new building on a 50-acre site donated by Senator Bronson M. Cutting. In 1930, Kabotie's early paintings were permanently hung in the Museum of New Mexico, thus establishing him on a par with the modern artists displayed in the other galleries. Kabotie's paintings traveled for two years across this continent visiting all the major galleries as part of the Exposition of Indian Tribal Arts. Also shown at the Venice Biennial, the show of indigenous American art was the most popular of all the displays.

Kabotie's Important Commissions

In 1932, Kabotie was hired by the architect Mary Colter to paint frescos based on kiva murals in the Watchtower, which is a reconstruction of an Anasazi tower at the eastern entrance of the Grand Canyon. There he painted the Snake legend on the walls. Later in the thirties, he reproduced the Amatovie prehistoric murals for Harvard University's Peabody Museum. He was asked by the Museum of the American Indian to record daily Hopi life for the Heyes Collection and was invited to New Delhi to lecture and demonstrate Hopi crafts.

In 1963, under the auspices of the United States Information Agency's cultural exchanges, his work toured from Athens to southern Asia. Commercial establishments such as the Painted Desert Inn near Holbrook, Arizona, called on his talents; in 1947, he painted murals in oil colors on three of its walls. He was also empaneled to jury art shows such as the 1961 American Indian Artists' Exhibition in Philbrook Art Center where he had been the very first grand prize winner decades earlier. Honored with a Guggenheim Foundation fellowship in 1945, the French government elected him to its national Academy of Arts in 1954. In 1958, he was awarded the Certificate of Merit from the United States Indian Arts and Crafts Board. Nearly every major museum in the country has bought Kabotie's paintings, including the Museum of Modern Art in New York, the University of Oklahoma, Gilcrease Museum and Philbrook Art Center, the Corcoran Gallery in Washington, D. C., the Cincinnati Art Museum and Columbus Gallery of Fine Arts in Ohio, Dartmouth College in New Hampshire, the Heard Museum and the Amerind Foundation in Arizona, the Museum of Northern Arizona, the McNay Art Institute in Texas, and the Taylor Museum in Colorado.

Becomes a Teacher

From 1937 to 1959, Kabotie taught art in Oraibi, Arizona. A number of his disciples have gone on to achieve fame, particularly his son, Michael, who paints the sacred clowns, the striped koshares and the mudheads, who perform on the plaza. In the Hopi tradition of always giving something back to the people, Kabotie ameliorated the joblessness of World War II veterans by employing them as silversmiths. He created the Hopi overlay style of silverwork with Paul Saufkie and taught this new craft to returned servicemen. One of the most gifted of his proteges was Charles Loloma. The Hopi Silvercraft Cooperative Guild, which Kabotie founded in 1941, produced outstanding craftsmanship using traditional motifs.

SOURCES:

Dunn, Dorothy, *American Indian Painting of the Southwest and Plains Areas,* Albuquerque, University of New Mexico Press, 1968.

Grattan, Virginia, *Mary Colter: Builder Upon the Red Earth,* Northland Press, 1980.

Kabotie, Fred, *Designs from the Ancient Mimbrenos with a Hopi Interpretation,* San Francisco, Grabhorn Press, 1949.

Trimble, Stephen, *The People: Indians of the American Southwest,* Santa Fe, School of American Research Press, 1993.

—Sketch by Ruth Rosenberg

William Wayne Keeler
1908-1987
Cherokee tribal leader and businessman

A controversial figure during a controversial period in Cherokee history, William Wayne Keeler served as chief of the Cherokee Nation of Oklahoma while simultaneously serving in the highest ranks of Phillips Petroleum Company, one of the largest and most powerful of the oil companies in Oklahoma. Keeler was also active in the federal government, serving with the Department of the Interior. He is perhaps best remembered for accusations of misuse levelled against him of tribal and company funds in the late 1960s and early 1970s, but he also helped put the Cherokee tribe on a solid financial footing, won national attention for Native American issues, and promoted nonviolent activism to win Cherokee goals.

After the Civil War, in which the Cherokees had been allied with the Confederacy, the tribe was stripped of much land and rights by the federal government. Later, the tribal government was abolished by the U.S. Congress, primarily through the Dawes Act of 1898. The Cherokee lands and the rest of Indian Territory, along with the Oklahoma Territory, was officially proclaimed the state of Oklahoma by President Theodore Roosevelt on November 16, 1907. From that time on, the chieftanship of the tribe was given or withheld by the President of the United States. The President appointed a "chief for a day" when official signatures were needed on certain documents. Later, though, the U.S. Congress passed the Oklahoma Indian Welfare Act, which specifically allowed Oklahoma tribes to reorganize their tribal governments. A Cherokee government, called the United Keetoowah Band of Cherokee Indians and composed mainly of full-blood Cherokees, was organized under this act.

Keeler Appointed Principal Chief of the Series

William Wayne Keeler was appointed principal chief of the Cherokee Nation of Oklahoma by President Harry Truman on December 1, 1949, thus creating two separate and competing Cherokee governments. On July 21, 1954, Keeler was appointed chief "indefinitely," and kept this position through succeeding presidents. Finally, in 1970

William Wayne Keeler

Congress passed a law which allowed the Five Civilized Tribes to hold elections. Keeler was elected chief in 1971 with about 75 percent of the votes. Keeler, who was only one-sixteenth Cherokee, did not speak or understand the Cherokee language and did not mingle socially with the traditional full-blood Cherokees. He was descended from two of the wealthiest and most well-known families in the Bartlesville, Oklahoma area and enjoyed an upper-class lifestyle far removed from that of the Cherokees whom he was appointed to represent. Both of his grandfathers were white men who had emigrated to Indian Territy, and both married women who were one-eighth Cherokee.

Keeler's maternal grandfather, Nelson Carr, settled in Indian Territory in the 1860s and opened the area's first trading post. Although he and his wife had been married in 1867, he re-married her once more according to the laws of the Cherokee Nation in order to be adopted into the tribe and obtain land as a tribal member. He then began buying all the Indian land he could, owning around 5000 acres, and became a gentleman farmer. However, once oil was discovered, he began leasing his land to drillers. At one time, 100 producing wells were located on Carr's land.

George Keeler, Keeler's paternal grandfather, was in the vanguard of the oil boom, and used his Cherokee Nation connections to his advantage. With the discovery of oil in the area, he leased over 200,000 acres from the Cherokee Nation, and then persuaded the U.S. Secretary of the Interior to approve his plans for drilling for oil on the land. He then made an agreement with Michael Cudahy, the millionaire meat-packer, for Cudahy to provide the financing. In 1897 they made the first big strike in the area.

Keeler was born April 5, 1908 in Dalhart, Texas. He and his parents moved to Bartlesville while he was a small child. He attended elementary school in Bartlesville, and graduated in 1926 as valedictorian of his Bartlesville High School class. In 1924, while still in high school, Keeler began working for Phillips during his summer vacations as a part-time employee in the engineering department. He entered the University of Kansas in 1926 and earned a degree in chemical engineering. In 1928, he joined Phillips full time at the company refinery in Kansas, advancing to chemist, engineer and supervisor. On September 15, 1933, he married Ruby L. Hamilton, and the couple had three sons; William, Bradford, and Richard. Except for a few years when Phillips stationed Keeler at different parts of the country, he and his wife made their home in Bartlesville, and also owned a working ranch just outside the city.

Keeler continued to rise in the executive ranks of Phillips, and was made manager of the company's refining department in 1945, and vice president for refining in 1947. He became vice president of the executive department in 1951, and was appointed to the board of directors that same year. He then became a member of the executive committee in 1954, executive vice president in 1956, and chairman of the executive committee in 1962. Keeler was named chief executive officer and chairman of the board of Phillips Petroleum Company in 1967, and served in those positions until he retired in 1973.

Keeler began his long relationship with the federal government during World War II, when he served on various refining technical committees of the Petroleum Administration for War, including chairman of the Military Petroleum Advisory Board. In 1952 Keeler served as deputy administrator of petroleum for defense in the Interior Department under Secretary Oscar Chapman, and in 1960 he was the head of the first U.S. Petroleum Industry Exchange Delegation to tour Russia's oil industry. He also served on numerous federal economic development committees such as President Lyndon Johnson's National Advisory Committee on the War on Poverty Program. Keeler was also active with Oklahoma state government and was on the Oklahoma Governor's Committee for Eastern Oklahoma Economic Development. He was appointed by Governor Henry Bellmon as a member of the Board of Directors of The Oklahoma Academy for State Goals. In 1966, Oklahoma elected him to its Hall of Fame.

As chief of the Cherokee Nation, Keeler was interested in economic development and hired persons with the expertise to establish Cherokee Industries, a tribally operated electronics assembly business. At the tribal office complex near the old Cherokee capital of Tahlequah, Keeler's business people established an arts and crafts center selling Cherokee handcrafts and a motel with a restaurant. The tribe also operated a Phillips 66 gas station. In 1957 Keeler received the All-American Indian Award, and was named the outstanding American Indian of the Year in 1961 at the American Indian Exposition in Anadarko, Oklahoma.

Also in 1961, Keeler was named by the Secretary of the Interior to head the Special Task Force on the American Indian to develop plans for reorganizing the Bureau of Indian

Affairs in the U.S. Department of the Interior. In 1962, Keeler was appointed by Secretary of the Interior Morris Udall as chairman of a three-man task force to study operations of the Bureau of Indian Affairs in Alaska, and to meet with Alaskan native groups on such things as native land and fishing rights. He also chaired the group that represented the Inter-American Indian Conference in Ecuador in 1964.

Questionable Dealings

From the very start many traditional Cherokees had questioned why a man who was to all intents and purposes a white man should be considered chief of the Cherokee. They also questioned the political implications of how Keeler's position as chief could be used to benefit Phillips Petroleum. The U.S. Department of the Interior, with which Keeler was associated, has authority over both Indian affairs, through the Bureau of Indian Affairs, and oil drilling and production on national lands, through its Bureau of Land Management. Keeler was convicted in federal court on December 4, 1973, of making an illegal contribution of $100,000 to Richard Nixon's 1972 presidential campaign.

The money he used came from a slush fund he and his company established. In March 1975, he and other former executives of Phillips Petroleum were charged by the Securities Exchange Commission in U.S. District Court with keeping false corporate records and shifting over $2.8 million in Phillips corporate funds to two Swiss corporations. Over $1.3 million was converted into cash and returned to the United States, of which approximately $600,000 was used for mostly illegal political contributions. Keeler and the company later pleaded guilty to concealing the $2.8 million of corporate funds from the U.S. Internal Revenue Service.

Keeler's tribal dealings also came under harsh criticism, and in 1968 the first public picket line by Cherokees was held against him and his policies. Keeler had used funds from a land judgement the Cherokee Nation won in 1961 from the federal government to establish what was called a Cherokee traditional ancient village, and a play on Cherokee history. Tradition-minded Cherokees protested Keeler's hiring of a white man to head the project, They also protested the authenticity of both the village and the play, which was also written by a white man. Keeler, however, failed to heed the protests and proceeded with his plans.

In addition, the fullblooded Cherokees questioned Keeler's dealings with his tribal attorney Ross Swimmer, president of Tahlequah's First National Bank. Keeler and Swimmer formed a trust company called Jelanuno Cultural and Economic Development Authority. They also made Cherokee County, the location of the Cherokee capital of Tahlequah, the beneficiary of the trust, rather than the Cherokee Nation. In 1972, for only $1, the Jelanuno company became the trustor for all property and proceeds of the Cherokee Nation Historical Society. In 1973, for $10, the company secured a deed for the Cherokee Nation land where the Cherokee Nation's restaurant, craft shops, and motel were located. Keeler signed the deed in his position as chief. The next day, he signed another document in which

the Cherokee Nation agreed to pay Jelanuno over $11,000 per month to lease the land. Keeler's elected term ended in 1975. He decided to retire as chief and campaigned heavily for Swimmer, who was elected as chief with only 23 percent of the vote. No provisions had been made for a run-off. Although there were many protests of election fraud, the Bureau of Indian Affairs declared the election valid.

Between the time Keeler left office in 1975 and his death in 1987, feelings about him within the Cherokee community gradually cooled. In the spring of 1987 a new group of buildings, named the W. W. Keeler Complex, opened at the Cherokee Nation headquarters near Tahlequah. Swimmer, Cherokee principal chief Wilma Mankiller, and others honored Keeler for his contributions to the Nation, including putting the Cherokee on a solid financial footing and bringing Indian issues to national attention. Keeler himself, who had been in ill health for four years, died in Bartlesville at the age of 79 on August 24 of that same year.

SOURCES:

"Cherokees Mourn Former Chief W. W. Keeler," *Cherokee Advocate,* 11:9, September 1987; 2.

"First Cherokee Picket Line Surprises Village Guests," *Indian Voices,* winter 1968; 13-15.

"Former Cherokee Chief Dies," *Muskogee Phoenix,* August 25, 1987.

"Former Phillips, Cherokee Leader Dies," *Tulsa World,* August 25, 1987.

Gourd, Charles Allen, "No Contest: Dependent Sovereignty from Tribe to Nation," (doctoral thesis), Department of Anthropology, University of Kansas, 1984; 109, 111.

"Keeler Exhibit Showing at Heritage Center," *Green Country Neighbor,* December 16, 1990; 6.

"Keetoowah Band of Cherokee Indians," *Cherokee One Feather,* 23:1, January 4, 1989; 2.

"Shadow of W. W. Keeler—'A Cherokee Watergate,'" *Akwesasne Notes,* autumn 1975; 20.

"Tribal Complex Named for W. W. Keeler," *Cherokee Advocate,* 11:4, April 1987; Section A, 1.

"W. W. Keeler, Cherokees' Ex-chief, Dies," *Tulsa Tribune,* August 24, 1987.

—Sketch by Sandra Sac Parker

Kenojuak
1927-
Inuit artist

Kenojuak is generally regarded as Canada's foremost Inuit artist. Since her first print appeared in the 1959 Cape Dorset collection, she has established an international reputation for her talents, with her work appearing in exhibitions throughout Canada, the United States, and Europe. Although most widely renowned for her prints, two of which have appeared on Canadian postage stamps, Kenojuak has worked in a variety of two- and three-dimensional media, developing a vast corpus that also includes sewing, sculptures, copperplate engravings, paintings, and drawings. In recognition of her artistic achievements, she was among the first group of Canadians to receive the prestigious Order of Canada Medal of Service—an award honoring achievement in all fields of Canadian life—from Governor General Roland Michener in 1967. Elected into the Royal Canadian Academy in 1974, Kenojuak has also been awarded numerous commissions, including the mural for Osaka '70, the Sunday Mass Book, and the Waddington portfolios.

On October 3, 1927, in south Baffin Island, Northwest Territory, Ushuakjuk, an Inuit hunter and fur trader, and his wife Seelaki named their newborn daughter Kenojuak, after the infant's deceased maternal grandfather. By participating in this Inuit naming tradition, the parents believed that all of the love and respect that had been given to the deceased during his lifetime would now be bestowed upon their daughter.

Although remembered by Kenojuak to be a kind and benevolent man, her father caused conflict within the Ikerrasak camp and was murdered by other members of the camp in 1933. After his death, Kenojuak went to live with her grandmother, Koweesa, who taught her the sewing skills that would resurface in her first works of art years later. While learning to repair sealskins being readied for trade at the Hudson's Bay Company, Kenojuak also devoted many of her childhood hours to chasing small birds, which would later serve as the subjects for many of her prints.

When Kenojuak was 19, her mother and stepfather, Takpaugni, arranged for her to marry Johnniebo, a local Inuit hunter. A spirited young woman, Kenojuak initially resisted the marriage, throwing rocks at her new husband whenever he approached her. In time, however, she came to regard him as a kind, gentle man, whom she loved a great deal. Years later, he developed his own artistic talents and sometimes collaborated with his wife on large projects. During the first few years of her marriage, Kenojuak gave birth to three children: two daughters, Jamasie and Mary, who died in childhood of food poisoning, and a son, Qiqituk, whom another family adopted at birth—a common Inuit custom.

In 1950, the first nurse arrived in the North, providing the Inuit people with their first access to modern medical care. After testing positive for tuberculosis, Kenojuak was sent to the Parc Savard Hospital in Quebec City, where she stayed from early 1952 to the summer of 1955, narrowly escaping death several times. While convalescing, she learned to make dolls and beadwork in the hospital crafts program and received the notice of James Houston, an early promoter of Eskimo art.

Launches Career as an Artist

Upon her return to her family in the North, Kenojuak officially launched her career as an artist, selling her seal-

skin and beaded crafts through a program started by Houston's wife, Alma. She also began carving, selling her work primarily through the Hudson's Bay Company. At the encouragement of Houston, who provided her with supplies, she tried her hand at drawing. After destroying her first effort, she gained enough confidence in her abilities to show her drawings to Houston, who praised her work and urged her to continue. In 1958, her first print, *Rabbit Eating Seaweed,* was produced from a design on one of her sealskin bags at a Cape Dorset printshop. Shortly thereafter, several of her original drawings were reproduced as prints, making her work accessible to a wider audience.

Encouraged by the income their art work might generate, Kenojuak and several other Inuit of Cape Dorset, under Houston's guidance, formed the West Baffin Eskimo Cooperative in 1959. The organization, in which the Inuit could purchase shares, served as a *senlavik*—"a place where one works"—for aspiring Inuit artists. Several of the early drawings, including a stencil by Kenojuak, were collected that same year and displayed in an exhibit in Stratford, Ontario. Viewing the Eskimo art for the first time, the southern audience responded favorably, providing the artists of West Baffin with the encouragement they needed to continue their work.

Fame Spreads Following Documentary

By 1962, Kenojuak's art had garnered enough recognition to be featured in a National Film Board production, *Eskimo Artist—Kenojuak,* which showed the artist at work and provided a detailed account of the stone printing process. The documentary, which took three months to film, also attempted to show Kenojuak and her family participating in the traditional ways of Eskimo life. While the filmmaking process was tiresome and artificial, the money she earned from it enabled Johnniebo to purchase his own canoe and achieve his independence as a hunter. This was an added benefit to the family, which by this time had added a daughter, Aggeo, and an adopted son, Ashevak. Kenojuak's financial success, however, was not always well received within her own community. The fact that she was a woman in her early thirties earning significantly more money than anyone in the camp angered many of the men, but it did not prevent her from continuing her work.

As more of her prints were released to the public in subsequent Cape Dorset print collections, Kenojuak's fame spread throughout Canada. In 1967 she was honored with the Order of Canada Medal of Service from the Governor General and had her work featured in the National Gallery of Canada. Three years later, her famous work *The Enchanted Owl* was commemorated by an appearance on a six-cent Canadian postage stamp. Full-size printed versions of the work would sell for as much as $14,500 several years later, further demonstrating the strength of her reputation. By 1972, two years after the death of Johnniebo, she had been selected for membership in the Royal Canadian Academy and her work had been exhibited in several European countries, as well as throughout Canada and the United States.

Experiments Go Beyond Traditional Art

Despite her considerable fame, Kenojuak has never thought of herself exclusively as an artist, but rather has considered her artistic career to be only one facet of her life. "I don't put any aspects of my experience first as the main thing," she stated in Jean Blodgett's *Kenojuak,* a book-length study of her work. Kenojuak's unwillingness to view herself primarily as an artist is consistent with the traditional Inuit culture, in which living conditions demanded that men and women develop competence in a wide range of skills in order to survive. What is conventionally considered to be a work of art is valued by the Eskimo people primarily for its utility—as a ritual item, as a piece of clothing, or as a source of income. As Kenojuak told Blodgett, "The main reason why I create things is because of my children, my family."

While Kenojuak has placed her work within the Inuit tradition of functional art to some degree, she has also expressed the desire to simply create something beautiful. "And rather what I do is I try to make things which satisfy my eye, which satisfy my sense of form and color," she told Blodgett. Consequently, the subject matter of Kenojuak's work seldom reflects any mythological meaning or portrays scenes from Inuit life. She chooses her subjects instead for their inherent beauty and their adaptability to the print medium. As Charlotte Townsend Gault concluded in *Maclean's,* "She is voicing the Inuit tradition in which making and decorating things is simply a part of daily life, and at the same time putting herself in the Western tradition of 'art for art's sake.'"

With these two contrasting threads of artistic philosophy intertwined in her work, Kenojuak has created an original style that many have sought to duplicate. What has continued to set her work apart from her imitators, however, is her continual experimentation with form and color. While working within the familiar Inuit patterns of birds and animals, Kenojuak has developed unique systems of color by adding, superimposing, altering, and embellishing shapes and motifs. As Blodgett argued, "What makes her work stand out in the context of contemporary Inuit art is the degree of formal experimentation she has pursued."

Although Kenojuak has achieved unprecedented financial success for an Inuit artist, earning over $30,000 a year during the 1980s, she has remained firmly within the culture of the Inuit people. While she has replaced her traditional igloo with a modern frame house, she has not given up her love for the outdoors and still travels with her third husband, Joanassie Igiu, and six children to some of her old campsite areas to hunt and fish during the summer, living off the land as she did as a child. While family obligations have limited the amount of time she devotes to her work, she has not given up drawing and carving. "I continue to do so primarily for the future these works of art will guarantee for my children," she stated in *Kenojuak.* "When I am dead, I am sure there will still be people discussing my art."

SOURCES:

Books

Blodgett, Jean, *Kenojuak,* Toronto, Firefly Books, 1985.

Katz, Jane B., *This Song Remembers: Self-Portraits of Native Americans in the Arts,* Boston, Houghton Mifflin, 1980; 21.

Native North American Almanac, edited by Duane Champagne, Detroit, Gale Research, 1994; 1083.

Periodicals

Gault, Charlotte Townsend, "Master of Decoration and Delight: Inuit Artist Kenojuak's One-Woman Show Has Been 20 Years Coming," *Maclean's,* April 20, 1981; 62.

—Sketch by Jason Gallman

Keokuk
1780(?)-1848
Sauk and Fox tribal leader
Also known as He Who Has Been Everywhere and Kiyo'kaga ["One Who Moves Warily" or "Watchful Fox"]

Keokuk and his great rival Black Hawk were the two principal tribal leaders of the Sauk and Fox Indian confederacy from about 1813 until their deaths in the mid-1800s. The guiding theme of Keokuk's life seems to have been his contest with Black Hawk. Black Hawk was a militant warrior and war leader who strongly resisted the loss of the tribe's ancestral lands to white Americans. Keokuk, though nominally a war leader, was primarily a politician and compromiser who believed that his people had little choice but to surrender their ancient lands to the whites in return for whatever concessions they could get. He presided over the disposal of the Sauk and Fox tribal lands first in Illinois and then in Iowa.

Keokuk was born in the principal Sauk Indian town of Saukenuk, also the birthplace of Black Hawk, located at the junction of the Rock and Mississippi Rivers near what is now Rock Island, Illinois. He is believed to have been born in 1780, though some historians place his year of birth at 1783, 1788, or 1790. Keokuk probably had some French blood in him, but it is uncertain whether this came from his father or his mother. Like Black Hawk, Keokuk was technically not entitled to become a tribal civil leader because he was not descended from one of the hereditary ruling clans. Instead, he rose to power because of his prowess as a warrior and his skills as a politician and orator. Nothing is known of his early life.

Black Hawk, in his well-known dictated autobiography *Life of Black Hawk,* related the story of Keokuk's ascent to power over the Sauk and Fox peoples. Around 1813,

Keokuk

Black Hawk, an ally of the British, returned to Saukenuk from fighting against U.S. forces during the War of 1812. He was shocked to find that during his year-long absence, Keokuk had become a war chief. Black Hawk then asked about the circumstances leading up to this appointment. Other warriors informed him that Keokuk had been standing outside the council lodge while the civil leaders of the tribe discussed the possibility of abandoning the town because of a report that an American army was approaching. Having overheard the discussion, Keokuk asked permission to address the council. As Black Hawk related in his memoir, Keokuk stated: "I have heard with sorrow, that you have determined to leave our village, and cross the Mississippi, merely because you have been told that the Americans were seen coming in this direction! Would you leave our village, desert our homes, and fly, before an enemy approaches? Would you leave all—even the graves of our fathers, to the mercy of an enemy, without trying to defend them? Give me charge of your warriors; I'll defend the village, and you may sleep in safety."

The leaders thereupon appointed Keokuk war chief, and he sent out scouting parties who found no Americans in the area. (This seems to have been the only occasion on which Keokuk seriously proposed to fight white Americans.) Thus began Black Hawk's great rivalry with Keokuk.

Dissenting Opinions

After the War of 1812, Black Hawk strongly resisted the attempts of the U.S. government to remove the Sauk-Fox

confederacy westward by negotiation or by force; Keokuk, however, made every possible effort to meet the demands of the Americans in order to avoid what he regarded as an unwinnable conflict that would destroy his people.

Federal officials soon realized the value of cultivating Keokuk's friendship and appealed to his vanity and avarice with frequent presents. A prime example of the influence Keokuk had obtained in Sauk and Fox affairs was his selection by the tribal leaders in 1824 as one of ten chiefs to travel to Washington, D.C., to confer with Secretary of War John C. Calhoun about tribal land claims east and west of the Mississippi River. The result of the meetings was a treaty signed on August 4, 1824, by which the tribe surrendered all claim to the disputed territory in return for cash and other considerations.

U.S. officials then took the Indian leaders on an East Coast tour, including stops in Washington, D.C., Baltimore, Philadelphia, and New York. In a significant move, Black Hawk boycotted this trip to Washington and the other cities. But Keokuk maintained his close relationship with the federal government. In 1825 he was a prominent participant in the peace conference held in Prairie du Chien, which included representatives of the U.S. government and of the Sioux, Chippewa, Winnebago, Ottawa, Menominee, Potawatomi, Iowa, and Sauk and Fox nations.

Claims to the Land

From about 1827 on, the rivalry between Keokuk and Black Hawk centered on the pressing question of whether or not the Sauk-Fox tribe should abandon the town of Saukenuk and their other territory east of the Mississippi and take up residence on lands reserved by the government in the present state of Iowa. Officials of the United States insisted that the tribe had already ceded the eastern territory in exchange for the western lands in several treaties dating as far back as 1804. Keokuk basically supported this contention; Black Hawk vehemently denied that the tribe had ever made any valid cession of these lands east of the Mississippi. He later claimed in his autobiography that the chiefs who had signed the Treaty of 1804 actually had no right to do so and, furthermore, had agreed to the terms while intoxicated by the white man's whiskey. The land claim question grew more acute as white settlers came increasingly close to Saukenuk.

In May of 1828, the U.S. Indian agent assigned to the Sauk-Fox tribe informed its leaders that they must leave the territory east of the Mississippi within a year. Black Hawk and his followers refused to do so. When members of the tribe left Saukenuk late in the summer of 1828 to go on their annual buffalo hunt, white squatters moved in. An outraged Black Hawk and his band returned in the spring of 1829 and remained through the summer, thus creating a potentially explosive confrontation with the white settlers.

Despite unpleasant incidents, a violent conflict was avoided. But the same cycle was repeated in 1829, 1830, and 1831. U.S. Army General Edmund P. Gaines then called all of the leaders of the Sauk-Fox tribe to a conference and warned that the Indians would be expelled by force if they did not vacate the land. Black Hawk once again refused to leave.

Keokuk, however, worked hard to persuade his fellow tribesmen to comply with the general's demand. In his autobiography, Black Hawk later contrasted his attitude with that of Keokuk: "We were a divided people, forming two parties. Ke-o-kuck being at the head of one, willing to barter our rights merely for the good opinion of the whites; and cowardly enough to desert our village to them. I was at the head of the other party, and was determined to hold on to my village.... Ke-o-kuck, who has a smooth tongue, and is a great speaker, was busy in persuading my band that I was wrong—and thereby making many of them dissatisfied with me."

On June 26, 1831, General Gaines and his army, supported by Illinois militia, bombarded Saukenuk and then marched in, only to find that Black Hawk and his followers had fled across the Mississippi River the previous night. The militiamen then burned the town. Gaines demanded that Black Hawk return for a conference, and on June 30 he did so. The Indian chief was then forced to sign an agreement stating that he and his followers would never return to the site of Saukenuk—and that they would submit to the authority of Keokuk.

As time passed, Black Hawk's boldness and resentment against the white settlers resurfaced, and he decided to return to Saukenuk in the spring of 1832. Keokuk argued fiercely against Black Hawk's plan, and when he was unable to prevent the march, he warned the American government of Black Hawk's intentions. An army of regulars and volunteers was hastily assembled to pursue Black Hawk and his band. From April through August of 1832, the resistant Indians retreated, first eastward across northern Illinois, then westward through the southern part of the present state of Wisconsin, experiencing a major defeat on the Wisconsin River on July 21 and suffering near annihilation while trying to cross the Mississippi on August 3. Black Hawk survived but was turned over to U.S. authorities by Winnebago Indians.

Keokuk Recognized as Civil Chief by U.S. Government

General Winfield Scott and Governor John Reynolds of Illinois were chosen by the U.S. government to negotiate a treaty of peace with the Sauk-Fox tribe in September of 1832. They took it upon themselves to proclaim Keokuk civil chief of the united tribe, and Keokuk accepted the title. He was the first tribesman to sign the treaty of September 21, 1832, by which the Indian nation not only made peace with the American government but also ceded some 6 million acres adjacent to the west bank of the Mississippi in the present state of Iowa in return for a small reservation of 400 square miles along the Iowa River. Shortly thereafter, in March of 1833, Keokuk interceded with the American government for the release of Black Hawk; by August, the old warrior was released to the custody of his hated rival, who assumed responsibility for his good behavior.

Keokuk seemed to be the unchallenged leader of the Sauk-Fox faction, but his influence waned in the remaining years of his life. Although he had secured from the American government the control of annuity funds provided to the tribe by the United States, his use of the money and goods was frequently contested by other tribal leaders. In 1836 Keokuk and other tribal leaders sold most of the 400-square-mile reserve in Iowa country to the U.S. government, and the next year they sold another 1.25 million acres. By the early 1840s, American government negotiators had persuaded Keokuk and his tribe to sell the remaining land in Iowa. They were allowed to occupy part of the area until 1845, when they were finally relocated to a reservation in Kansas. Meanwhile, Keokuk's health—and his prestige within the tribe—had been declining. He died in April of 1848 after having lost his position of authority. His son, Moses Keokuk, succeeded him as chief.

SOURCES:

Books

Black Hawk, *Life of Black Hawk,* edited by Milo Milton Quaife, Chicago, R. R. Donnelley & Sons, 1916.

Dockstader, Frederick J., *Great North American Indians,* New York, Van Nostrand Reinhold, 1977; 134-36.

Fixico, Don, "The Black Hawk-Keokuk Controversy," in *Indian Leaders: Oklahoma's First Statesmen,* edited by H. Glenn Jordan and Thomas M. Holm, Oklahoma City, Oklahoma Historical Society, 1979; 64-78.

Hagan, William T., *The Sac and Fox Indians,* Norman, University of Oklahoma Press, 1958; 194-233.

Josephy, Alvin M., Jr., *The Patriot Chiefs: A Chronicle of American Indian Leadership,* New York, Viking Press, 1961; 226-53.

Periodicals

Metcalf, P. Richard, "Who Should Rule at Home? Native American Politics and Indian-White Relations," *Journal of American History,* 61, December 1974; 651-665.

—Sketch by John E. Little

Keyser, Louisa
See Datsolalee

Khanshandel, Chiron
See Rose, Wendy

Kicking Bird
1835(?)-1875
Kiowa tribal leader
Also known as Tené-angop'té (Tay-nay-angopte) and Watohkonk ["Black Eagle"]

Kicking Bird was a Kiowa tribal leader who believed that peace and accommodation with white America was necessary to the survival of the Indians. His opinions and actions caused considerable dissent among his people. When he actively worked for friendly relations with the whites, he was frequently denounced by more militant Native American leaders who demanded war to the death against white civilization. As a result of such criticism, he seemed obliged to engage in aggressive actions that made him appear hostile to the whites. His conflicting motives pursued him to his final days—and may have even cost him his life.

Kicking Bird was born about 1835, probably in what is now southwestern Oklahoma, where his Great Plains tribe had migrated from the north in the early nineteenth century. His paternal grandfather was a member of the Crow tribe who had been adopted by the Kiowas. His father, Tsain-hayte ["Big Horse"] was a Kiowa chief.

Not much is known of Kicking Bird's early life. He first appeared as a Kiowa leader of some importance on October 18, 1865, when he was one of the signers of the Treaty of the Little Arkansas River. According to this agreement, the Kiowa and Comanche tribes accepted a reservation in what is now the Oklahoma panhandle and adjacent areas of Texas; the treaty was later nullified by the government of Texas.

In August of 1866, some members of the Kiowa tribe conducted a raid into Montague County, Texas, where they killed a white settler named James Box, and abducted his wife and daughters. Major General Winfield S. Hancock reported later that Kicking Bird had been a member of the raiding party and was involved in the crime. However, General William Tecumseh Sherman, the Civil War hero turned commander of the U.S. Army's Division of the Mississippi, knew Kicking Bird well and trusted that he was not responsible for the murder.

Believed His People Could Not Triumph Over Whites

In late April of 1867, General Hancock had a conference with Kicking Bird and urged the Kiowas and associated tribes not to ally themselves with the Sioux and Cheyennes on the warpath against the white settlers. Kicking Bird responded that he had always advised his tribesmen to maintain peace and friendship with the whites, and he professed agreement with Hancock's assertion that the white man would ultimately win in any prolonged conflict with the Indians.

Kicking Bird attended the important peace conference between representatives of the U.S. government and those of the Cheyenne, Arapaho, Kiowa, Comanche, and Kiowa Apache nations held in October of 1867 at Medicine Lodge, Kansas. He signed two of the treaties agreed upon at the conference, providing, among other things, for a new but smaller reservation for the Kiowas and Comanches and for the establishment of individual Indian families on 160-acre plots, which they would own and farm.

The steady westward advance of white settlers and their ever-increasing encroachments on the Native Americans and their reservations largely undermined the agreements reached at Medicine Lodge. The U.S. Army found it necessary to fight repeated battles to put down Indian revolts in the region, culminating on November 27, 1868, in a battle at the Washita River in the western part of what is now the state of Oklahoma. During the conflict, a major Cheyenne village was destroyed and Cheyenne Chief Black Kettle was killed. This battle seems to have motivated Kicking Bird to become a fairly consistent advocate of peace and accommodation between Indians and whites.

Torn between Revenge and Accommodation

Kicking Bird's new peace policy led many of the younger, more militant members of the Kiowa tribe to regard him as a coward. In an effort to regain his lost prestige and influence, he organized and led a raiding party of 100 warriors across the Red River into Texas. Deliberately provoking the U.S. Army unit stationed near Fort Richardson, they seized a mail stagecoach. A force of 53 soldiers pursued Kicking Bird's band and caught up with them on July 12, 1870, near the present town of Seymour, Texas. Kicking Bird led an assault against the army troops, impaling one soldier on his lance. The army unit spent the rest of the day in retreat, with 12 wounded and three killed by the end of the incident. Some historical observers view the Texas assault as a necessary evil that functioned to confirm Kicking Bird's bravery and, thereafter, allowed him to influence his tribe in the direction of peace. The U.S. military authorities ignored Kicking Bird's transgression, apparently in the belief that he remained the best hope for Indian-white peace.

In May of 1871, several of the more aggressive Kiowa chiefs, including Satanta and Satank, led another raiding party into Texas and attacked a wagon train, killing seven teamsters. General Sherman was at that time visiting Fort Sill, in the present state of Oklahoma, and he decided that the principal leaders of the conflict must be captured, sent to Texas, and tried for murder. When a number of the Kiowa chiefs, including Satanta, Satank, Big Tree, and Kicking Bird went to the Indian agency at Fort Sill to receive rations, Sherman asked who had been responsible for the wagon train raid. Satanta defiantly said that he had been the leader.

Sherman then announced that Satanta, Satank, and Big Tree were to be arrested and transported to Texas for trial. Records indicate that at that instant, white soldiers—armed with carbines and ready to shoot—appeared on the scene. A melee ensued, during which Kicking Bird vehemently objected to Sherman's actions. Soon thereafter, Lone Wolf, another militant Kiowa chief, rode up and somehow was able to supply several of the Indians with guns. One of them attempted to shoot Sherman but was wrestled to the ground by an army officer.

In all the confusion, Lone Wolf and several others escaped, but Satanta, Satank, and Big Tree remained in custody. Satank was later killed in a scuffle while being transported to Texas, but the others were tried and sentenced to death. (Their death sentences were later commuted to life imprisonment.) Kicking Bird devoted much of his time during the remainder of his life to bargaining with the white leaders for the release of the two chiefs, apparently in the hope that this would promote peace.

Expressed True Feelings in Schoolmaster's Book

On several occasions in 1873 and 1874, Kicking Bird was able to keep most of the Kiowa tribe off the warpath, a considerable achievement in light of the fact that their close allies, the Comanches, did make extensive attacks on the whites. However, he was under constant harassment from the more militant members of his own tribe who favored a policy of war. It was at this time that he became friendly with a Quaker schoolmaster named Thomas C. Battey, who had come to the Kiowa Indian agency in 1873 to teach at the Indian school there. Battey later published a book, *The Life and Adventures of a Quaker among the Indians,* in which he included transcripts of several conversations with Kicking Bird. These notes highlight the tenuous relationship between the Indians and the whites and suggest the reasons for Kicking Bird's often conflicting actions. Battey quoted Kicking Bird as saying: "I long ago took the white man by the hand; I have never let it go; I have held it with a firm and strong grasp. I have worked hard to bring my people on to the white man's road. Sometimes I have been compelled to work with my back towards the white people, so that they have not seen my face, and may have thought I was working against them; but I have worked with one heart and one object. I have looked ahead to the future, and have worked for the children of my people, to bring them into a position, that, when they become men and women, they will take up with the white road."

By 1874 Kicking Bird was regarded—at least by the army leaders and other whites in and around Fort Sill—as the principal chief of the Kiowa tribe. The militant factions of the Kiowa and other tribes who had insisted on making war against the whites were decisively defeated in a battle at Palo Duro Canyon on September 27, 1874. However, many of the Indian leaders escaped capture, and in early 1875 Kicking Bird was heavily involved in the negotiations leading to the surrender of most of the militants at Fort Sill. The army officers at the fort asked Kicking Bird to identify the tribal leaders who acted as ringleaders in the revolt so that they might be sent to St. Augustine, Florida, for imprisonment. The persons chosen by Kicking Bird included Lone Wolf, his former occasional ally but a strong militant, and Maman-ti, a Kiowa medicine man commonly considered the leader of the faction warring against the whites. The prisoners departed for Florida on April 28, 1875.

In a dramatic encounter on that same day, Maman-ti denounced Kicking Bird for his support of the whites and declared that he would bring about his death. On May 4,

1875, after drinking a cup of coffee, Kicking Bird became very ill and died within hours. Shortly before his death, according to Battey, he said once again that he had "taken the white man's road [and] was not sorry for it," and that he "was dying holding fast [to] the white man's hand." An army physician in attendance suggested in his report that Kicking Bird had died of strychnine poisoning. Most Kiowas believed that his death was caused by the magic or "medicine" of Maman-ti. Thus, even in death, Kicking Bird was caught in an ambiguous position between the white world and that of his Native American people. He was buried at Fort Sill.

SOURCES:

Books

Battey, Thomas C., *The Life and Adventures of a Quaker among the Indians,* Norman, University of Oklahoma Press, 1968.

Dockstader, Frederick J., *Great North American Indians,* New York, Van Nostrand Reinhold, 1977.

Indian Affairs: Laws and Treaties, compiled and edited by Charles J. Kappler, Volume 2, Washington, D.C., U.S. Government Printing Office, 1904; 892-895, 977-984.

Jones, Douglas C., *The Treaty of Medicine Lodge,* Norman, University of Oklahoma Press, 1966.

Leckie, William H., *The Military Conquest of the Southern Plains,* Norman, University of Oklahoma Press, 1963.

Mayhall, Mildred P., *The Kiowas,* second edition, Norman, University of Oklahoma Press, 1971.

Nye, Wilbur Sturtevant, *Carbine & Lance: The Story of Old Fort Sill,* centennial edition, Norman, University of Oklahoma Press, 1969.

Tatum, Lawrie, *Our Red Brothers and the Peace Policy of President Ulysses S. Grant,* Lincoln, University of Nebraska Press, 1970.

Periodicals

Taylor, Morris F., "Kicking Bird: A Chief of the Kiowas," *Kansas Historical Quarterly,* 38, autumn 1972; 295-319.

—Sketch by John E. Little

Kirke Kickingbird
1944-
Kiowa attorney and educator

A prominent lawyer and defender of Indian legal rights, Kirke Kickingbird has served as director of the Native American Legal Resource Center at Oklahoma City Univer-

Kirke Kickingbird (center)

sity School of Law since 1988. Kickingbird has taught American Indian law, conducted seminars and special projects for the tribal courts and governments, and served as vice-chairman of the board of commissioners for the Oklahoma Indian Affairs Commission. He also co-founded and serves as executive director of the Institute for the Development of Indian Law in Washington, D.C.

Kickingbird was born in Wichita, Kansas, to Carl and Sue Kickingbird. He is the great-great-grandson of Chief Kicking Bird, a leading Kiowa peacemaker who played a key role in the Little Arkansas and Medicine Lodge treaties and who was named to the Hall of Fame for Famous American Indians in 1994.

Kickingbird began practicing Indian law after earning a law degree from the University of Oklahoma in 1969. From 1969 to 1971, he worked in the office of congressional relations for the Bureau of Indian Affairs. In 1971, Kickingbird co-founded the Washington, D.C.-based Institute for the Development of Indian Law, with which he is still affiliated. As executive director of the Institute from 1971 to 1975 and again from 1978 to the present, Kickingbird has been responsible for ultimate policy and decision making and has served as chief administrator for project financing and execution. He has also conducted fund raising, litigation, research, writing, editing, and public relations efforts. In addition, he served as editor-in-chief of the Institute's *American Indian Journal,* from 1975 to 1981.

Kickingbird has also held positions with the American Indian Policy Review Commission of the U.S. Congress, a two-year joint commission that studied U.S. Indian policy and developed legislative recommendations for change, and the Legal Services Corporation. In 1988, he was named director of the Native American Legal Resource Center and assistant professor of law at the Oklahoma City University School of Law. The Center was designed as a focal point for research, writing, teaching, and publication in federal Indian law.

Consulting and Writing Activities

In addition to the above activities, he also founded Kickingbird Associates, a consulting firm that specializes in Indian affairs and Indian economic development. He has provided training and technical assistance to more than 150 tribal governments in the United States, Australia, New Zealand, Japan, Namibia, and Russia on matters of indigenous peoples' rights. In addition, he has represented the U.S. government in conventions dealing with the treatment of indigenous peoples. In 1993, he was co-curator of "Moving the Fire: The Removal of the Indian Nations to Oklahoma," an exhibit for the International Monetary Fund Visitor's Center that coincided with the United Nation's declaration of 1993 as the International Year of the World's Indigenous Peoples.

Kickingbird has also written extensively about Indian law. He has contributed to or written numerous books, including *Behind the Trail of Broken Treaties, 100 Million Acres,* and *Indians and the U.S. Constitution: A Forgotten Legacy.* The latter book, published in 1987 and written with his wife, Lynn, won an award from the U.S. Commission on the Bicentennial of the Constitution. Kickingbird has also contributed to several periodicals, including *American Indian Journal* and *American Criminal Law Review.*

His numerous memberships include the Oklahoma and District of Columbia bars, the Oklahoma Indian Bar Association, and the Native American Bar Association. His work has earned him proclamations and letters of appreciation from the State of Oklahoma, the City of Oklahoma City, and the Office of International Visitors of the United States Information Agency. March 3, 1994, was designated Kirke Kickingbird Day by the governor of the state of Oklahoma and the mayor of the City of Oklahoma in recognition of his outstanding achievements. He and his wife have two children.

SELECTED WRITINGS BY KICKINGBIRD:

(With Karen Ducheneaux) *100 Million Acres,* New York, Macmillan, 1973.

(Contributor) Deloria, Vine, Jr., *Behind the Trail of Broken Treaties,* New York, Delacorte, 1974.

Economic Perspectives of American Indian History, Washington, D.C., Institute for the Development of Indian Law, 1979.

(With Lynn S. Kickingbird) *Indians and the U.S. Constitution: A Forgotten Legacy,* Washington, D.C., Institute for the Development of Indian Law, 1987.

SOURCES:

Books

Native North American Almanac, edited by Duane Champagne, Detroit, Gale Research, 1994; 1084-1085.

Periodicals

Daily Oklahoman/Oklahoma City Times, June 20, 1994; 6.

—*Sketch by Diane Andreassi*

Clara Sue Kidwell

Clara Sue Kidwell
1941-
Choctaw/Chippewa author, educator, and historian

Clara Sue Kidwell's research and writings concern the historical interactions between Native Americans and Europeans, as well as contemporary Native American women's issues. She has taught history at several colleges and universities and acted as assistant director for cultural resources at the Museum of the American Indian in Washington, D.C. Kidwell was born July 8, 1941, in Tahlequah, Oklahoma, to Hardin Milton Kidwell, Choctaw, and Martha Evelyn St. Clair, Chippewa. She grew up in Muskogee, Oklahoma. Her Choctaw grandmother raised her while her mother and father worked. Her father worked in civil service at the Bureau of Indian Affairs, then later at the Veterans Administration Hospital. After attending a Catholic elementary school, Kidwell graduated from Muskogee Central High School in 1959. She then went on to earn her bachelor's degree from the University of Oklahoma in Norman. She received two pieces of advice growing up—one from her grandmother and one from her mother. Her grandmother always said, "If you want something done right, do it yourself." And her mother, who worked in personnel at the Bureau of Indian Affairs, told her, "Always make a carbon copy of everything."

Kidwell read every copy of her grandmother's treasured *Reader's Digest* when she was young. Little did she know at the time that the trivia and information she garnered from the magazine would be instrumental in her later decision to pursue graduate school studies in History of Science. Kidwell had an opportunity to go on the College Bowl team, where she impressed two professors in History of Science—Tom Smith and Duane Roller. "They thought I was a whiz kid," Kidwell told Phyllis Noah in an interview. She attributes her success on the College Bowl team to her grandmother's *Reader's Digest*. Kidwell later received both her M.A. and Ph.D. degrees in History of Science.

Begins Teaching Career

Both of Kidwell's parents graduated from Haskell Institute in Lawrence, Kansas. When Haskell became a junior college in 1970, Kidwell had just received her Ph.D. Her mother found out there were job openings at the college for a Ph.D. and told her daughter to "hurry and call." Kidwell ended up teaching American history at Haskell for two years. She taught history at several other colleges and universities, and also worked as coordinator of publications at the Experimental Education Unit at the University of Washington in Seattle. Since 1974, she has been an associate professor of Native American studies at the University of California, Berkeley.

Kidwell's interests are focused on the Native American culture and Native American women's issues. She has written books and essays on Native American women in education, civil rights, ecology, and medicine, the Choctaw tribe, and various studies of the historical interaction between Native Americans and Europeans. Kidwell has been the recipient of many fellowships during her career from such organizations as the Rockefeller Foundation, the Newberry Library, and the Smithsonian Institution. Kidwell's work has been published in numerous journals and magazines and several books, including *The Choctaws: A Critical Bibliography*. She has lectured in colleges and universities throughout the United States.

Accepts Post at National Museum

In June 1993, Kidwell left Berkeley and moved to Washington, D.C., to become assistant director for cultural resources at the Smithsonian Institution's National Museum of the American Indian. She is responsible for collections and a staff of over 50 people. She often travelled to New York to prepare for opening a new Indian museum, George Gustav Heye Center, in 1994. A new museum is also planned to open on the Mall next to the U.S. Capitol in early 2000.

Cooking is one of her hobbies, especially baking bread. "It's wonderful smelling a fresh loaf of bread in the house," she told Noah. When Kidwell moved from Berkeley to Washington, D.C., she claimed that there were three essentials needed to establish a new house—"my cat, Betsy, my asparagus fern, and my sourdough starter."

SOURCES:

Books

Kidwell, Clara Sue, and Charles Roberts, *The Choctaws: A Critical Bibliography,* Bloomington, University of Indiana Press, 1980.
Native American Women, edited by Gretchen M. Bataille, New York, Garland Publishing, 1993; 139.
Native North American Almanac, edited by Duane Champagne, Detroit, Gale Research, 1994; 1085-1086.

Other

Kidwell, Clara Sue, interview with Phyllis "Picturestone" Noah conducted July 28, 1994.

—Sketch by Phyllis "Picturestone" Noah

Thomas King
1943-
Cherokee writer and educator

Thomas King is a Cherokee writer best known for his two novels, *Medicine River* and *Green Grass, Running Water,* which depict the complexities of Native American life in the late twentieth century. Noted for his adept handling of dialogue and his wit, King has continually challenged the prevailing stereotypes of Native America through various types of writing, running the gamut of fiction and non-fiction. A well-respected academic, he chairs the Native American Studies department at the University of Minnesota and has written and edited a number of academic publications dealing with various aspects of Native American identity and culture. King has received several awards and fellowships for his writing, including the 1990 PEN Oakland/Josephine Miles Award for Excellence in Literature and runner-up for the 1990 Commonwealth Writer's Prize.

The son of a Cherokee from Oklahoma, King was born in 1943 in Roseland, California, a small town located in the central part of the state. When he was around five years of age, his father deserted the family and was never heard from again, leaving King and his younger brother to be reared by their mother. Although the family occasionally travelled to Oklahoma when the boys were small to see Cherokee relatives, they grew up for the most part outside of the Cherokee culture. Careful to include his Greek and German heritage as part of his ethnicity, King resists stereotypical categorization. As he told Jace Weaver in a *Publisher's Weekly* interview, "I don't want people to get the mistaken idea that I am an 'authentic Indian,' or that they're getting the kind of Indian that they'd like to have ... some 19th-century Native on a pinto pony in a teepee." In fact, it was not until after he went to college that he remembers knowing another Native American.

After graduating from Chico State University in California, King pursued his lifelong interest in photography, working as a photo-journalist in a number of places, including Utah, Canada, New Zealand, and Australia. While overseas, he made his first attempts at fiction, writing short stories that he described to Weaver as "blithering messes, romantic slop." He also tried his hand at a few novels, which he recalls with equally disparaging remarks as "penny-dreadful things about American astronauts hidden away on college campuses pursued by Russian agents—real pukey stuff." The itinerant phase of King's career, however, provided him with material for his more mature fiction—for instance, the narrator of his first novel, *Medicine River,* is a photographer. It also enabled him to see that there were other aboriginal peoples in the world that were subject to the same forms of colonial abuse faced by Natives in the United States and Canada.

King's travels eventually circled back to the United States, where he began working towards his doctorate in Native American Studies. In 1980, while completing his dissertation on "Inventing the Indian," he accepted a position teaching Native American Studies at the University of Lethbridge in Alberta. This move marked the turning point of both his personal and professional life. Divorced and living alone with his first son, King entered into a spousal relationship with Helen Hoy, a fellow academic who later accompanied him to the University of Minnesota in St. Paul, where they live with their three children. He also started writing again, this time with a focus on the Native American experience. During his ten-year stint in Canada, King worked with Blackfeet and Cree people, providing him with the basis for much of his writing. In his free time, the six-foot, six-inch professor played basketball on an all-Native team, an experience that furnished him with additional material for the short fiction he was producing at the time, which later served as the foundation for *Medicine River.*

Completes Highly Regarded First Novel

King did not have the opportunity to complete the novel until nine years later, when he received a one-month writer's residency at the Ucross Foundation in Wyoming.

Shortly after King completed the program, Denise Bukowski signed on as his agent and within a month sold the rights of his first novel to Viking Penguin, who published the book in both Canada and New York in 1990. *Medicine River* follows the life of its half-Native narrator, Will, who has left Toronto for the Native community of Medicine River, Alberta. Through his eyes the reader is introduced to various members of the town—the players on the Medicine River Friendship Centre Warriors basketball team, a marriage doctor, a battered wife, and a Native activist—who collectively provide a complex view of Native life and its relationship to Western culture. "King does not use the novel as a platform from which he can lecture non-natives about native Canadians; he chooses the harder, and more effective, route of drawing the reader into the daily lives of [its characters]," concluded M.A. Gillies in *Canadian Literature.* "He succeeds where polemics would surely fail.... By weaving together past and present, native and non-native, humorous and insightful accounts, King creates a subtle and rich novel."

Despite the novel's strong critical reception—it won the PEN/Josephine Miles Award and was runner-up for the Commonwealth Writer's Prize—it was poorly promoted by Viking in New York and did not sell especially well in the United States. *Medicine River,* however, did receive enough attention to be converted into a screenplay, which King wrote for a television movie that was filmed in Canada and starred Native actor Graham Greene. King also had a small acting part in the movie, taking advantage of his height to play an over-the-hill basketball player.

Second Novel Receives Acclaim

Green Grass, Running Water, King's second novel, is also a product of his work at the Ucross Foundation, where he completed a 300-page draft during his 30-day residency. Like his first novel, this work addresses questions surrounding contemporary Native life. More heavily publicized than his first novel, *Green Grass, Running Water* has received a host of rave reviews. Publisher's Weekly, for instance, has given the novel its highest rating, labelling King as "a sort of Native American Kurt Vonnegut, addressing contemporary Native American life with a wild and comic imagination." Louis Owens, author of *Other Destinies: Understanding the American Indian Novel,* has described the novel as "a brilliant addition to Native American writing and to all of American literature," concluding that "Never have the real people and the real issues of Indian America been presented more movingly or more persuasively."

King's critique of America's treatment of Native peoples is cogently summarized through the novel's title, which is borrowed from the language of treaties that Native Americans were coerced to sign with the United States government—treaties which guaranteed Native claims to land "as long as the grass is green and the water runs." The irony, of course, cuts in more than one direction. It is not only a stark reminder of the government's failure to uphold their end of the bargain; it also serves as a warning to those who abuse the environment. "If we don't straighten up the world," King stated in a *Philadelphia Inquirer* interview, "we will wake up one morning to find that the grass is no longer green and the water has vanished."

King's "tour de force," a label commonly affixed to *Green Grass, Running Water,* is set in the fictional town of Blossom and its nearby reservation. It tells the story of five Blackfeet Indians whose lives represent various constructions of Native identity. A university professor, lawyer, and salesman among them, these characters all hold jobs that are affirmed by the dominant white culture. Intertwined with the conflicts surrounding these characters are the intermittent appearances of four mysterious aged Natives—amusingly named Hawkeye, Ishmael, Robinson Crusoe, and the Lone Ranger—who have fled from a mental institution in an attempt to prevent an environmental disaster about to occur in Canada. Their actions and the stories they tell elicit various responses from the modern Natives, who both help and hinder the escapees' efforts to restore nature's harmony.

The interactions between these two groups affords King the opportunity to reevaluate ethnic stereotypes, uncovering the truth and fabrication in the various stories—both Native and Western—that are a part of the cultural identity of contemporary Natives. King attempts to present contemporary characters that are more challenging and complex. "I like to demonstrate a viable present and, more important, promise a future," he stated in the *Philadelphia Inquirer.* "Someplace in [Native culture], there's a strength. And someplace in there, people are managing, not just surviving, but actually prospering. And I want to see these people in my fiction."

Demonstrates Wide Range of Writing Talents

Although King is most widely known for his two novels, he has also performed well in other genres of writing. A full-fledged academic chairing the Department of Native American Studies at the University of Minnesota, King has had a hand in a number of academic publications, editing *The Native in Literature: Canadian and Comparative Perspectives,* a collection of essays dealing with ethnicity and Native culture, and *All My Relations,* an anthology of short fiction by Canadian Native writers. Demonstrating the wide scope of his writing talents, he has also published *A Coyote Columbus Story,* a children's book that puts a humorous Native spin on Columbus' arrival in America. According to Sarah Ellis of *Horn Book,* the story captures "a bold, outrageous iconoclastic energy that incorporates warmth and inclusiveness."

In addition to maintaining his academic duties at the University of Minnesota and writing screen adaptations for his short stories, King has started work on a third novel. He promises to address similar themes of Native American cultural identity, but this time from a more pan-Native perspective and in a manner less dependent upon comedy. Although King's literary reputation most certainly is on the rise, he remains largely indifferent to the reactions of his non-Native audience. However, as Weaver predicted, "With *Green Grass,* Thomas King is likely to attract them regardless, and in the process, to interest and educate an impressive number of readers."

SELECTED WRITINGS BY KING:

Medicine River, New York, Viking Penguin, 1990.
All My Relations: An Anthology of Contemporary Canadian Native Fiction, Norman, University of Oklahoma Press, 1992.
A Coyote Columbus Story, Groundwood, 1992.
Green Grass, Running Water, Boston, Houghton Mifflin, 1993.

SOURCES:

Butler, Jack, "Dad Was with the Rodeo," *New York Times Book Review,* September 23, 1990; 29.

Carlin, Margaret, "Challenging the Myth of the Stone-faced Indian," *Rocky Mountain News,* April 18, 1993.
Ellis, Sarah, "News from the North," *Horn Book,* September 1993; 637-639.
Gillies, M.A., "Temporal Interplay," *Canadian Literature,* winter 1991; 212.
Howells, Coral Ann, "Imagining Native," *Canadian Literature,* spring 1990; 307.
"Thomas King: Native Intelligence," *Pennsylvania Inquirer,* May 9, 1993.
Weaver, Jace, "Thomas King," *Publishers Weekly,* March 8, 1993; 56-57.

—*Sketch by Jason Gallman*

Francis La Flesche
1857(?)-1932
Omaha ethnologist
Also known as Zhogaxe ["Woodworker"]

Francis La Flesche was one of the first Native Americans to have a noteworthy career as a research scholar and writer of scholarly books. This achievement was all the more remarkable in view of the fact that he had only a few years of primary and secondary education at an Indian mission school, followed many years later by academic training in law while working as a clerk for the federal government in Washington, D.C. With the aid of his extraordinary family and a devoted friend, he remade himself into a widely respected ethnologist.

He was born on the Omaha Indian Reservation, some 70 miles north of the present city of Omaha, Nebraska, the son of Joseph La Flesche (Estamahza or "Iron Eye") and Elizabeth Esau (Ta-in-ne). La Flesche's obituary notice in the *American Anthropologist* gives his exact date of birth as December 25, 1857, but it is not absolutely certain that even the year is correct because of the absence of official records for that period. His father, of half Omaha and half French blood, was the principal chief of the Omaha tribe, and his mother, a full-blooded Omaha, was the second of at least three wives of Joseph. La Flesche was the half-brother of Indian rights activist Susette La Flesche Tibbles and physician and missionary Susan La Flesche Picotte. He shared in many of the traditional tribal activities and rituals as a child and adolescent, such as participation in several of the last great buffalo hunts before the near extinction of the animals was caused by white hunters. However, his father was determined that all of his children should learn to live in the white man's world. La Flesche attended the Presbyterian mission school on the reservation where he began the study of English, a language of which he was in time to have an impressive command.

La Flesche got his first major exposure to white civilization in 1879, when he and his half-sister Susette served as interpreters for the Ponca Chief Standing Bear on his famous lecture tour to Chicago, Boston, New York, Washington, and other cities. It was at this time that La Flesche first met Alice Cunningham Fletcher, the pioneering ethnologist and crusader for Indian rights, with whom he was to have a close relationship until her death in 1923. He also came to the attention of Samuel Jordan Kirkwood, a United States Senator from Iowa who, when he became Secretary of the Interior in 1881, appointed La Flesche as a clerk in the Office of Indian Affairs. For the rest of his life, Washington, D.C., was his place of residence, though he often spent time working on various Indian reservations and always returned to the Omaha reservation for vacations.

Began Collaboration with Fletcher

La Flesche was twice married but soon separated from each of his wives. The closest personal, as well as professional, relationship of his life was with Alice Fletcher, a woman some 20 years his senior. She became crippled with rheumatism in the early 1880s and La Flesche became her close associate and interpreter, providing not only physical assistance in her frequent travels to Indian reservations but also assistance in her efforts to improve the condition of the Indians and in her later studies of the life of the Plains Indians. He did much of the research over a period of some 20 years that ultimately resulted in the monumental study *The Omaha Tribe,* published in 1911 with himself and Fletcher as coauthors. He was particularly skilled at persuading elderly tribal leaders of the Omaha to reveal the words and ceremonies of the ancient tribal rituals, which were rapidly dying out. Alice Fletcher ultimately proposed to legally adopt La Flesche as her son, a plan which fell through only because he did not want to change his surname, as the law required. From 1891 onward, they lived together with another female companion in a house in Washington. La Flesche also studied at the law school of the National University in Washington and was granted a bachelor's degree in law in 1892 and a master's degree in 1893.

In 1900 La Flesche published his first book as sole author: *The Middle Five,* a charming autobiographical sketch of his school days at the Omaha Indian mission school. It did not sell well at the time but was reprinted in 1963. Following the publication of *The Omaha Tribe* in 1911, he turned his scholarly research to the Osage tribe, a group closely related to the Omahas. In 1910 he transferred from the Office of Indian Affairs to the Bureau of American Ethnology in the Smithsonian Institution. There he could devote his full time to exhaustive research on the Osage tribe, the first results of which appeared in 1921 in *The Osage Tribe: Rite of the Chiefs; Sayings of the Ancient Men.* Later products of his studies included a monumental *Dictionary of the Osage Language,* published in 1932, and *War Ceremony and Peace Ceremony of the Osage Indians,* published posthumously in 1939.

La Flesche's friend and mentor Alice Fletcher died in 1923. Thus she did not live to see the numerous honors which came to him for his work on the Osages, including membership in the Washington Academy of Sciences and an honorary Doctor of Letters degree from the University of Nebraska in 1926. His own health began to fail in 1927 and he ultimately suffered several paralytic strokes. He died at his younger brother's home on the Omaha Indian Reservation near Macy, Nebraska, on September 5, 1932. He was buried on the reservation.

SELECTED WRITINGS BY LA FLESCH:

With Alice Cunningham Fletcher, *The Omaha Tribe,* Washington, D.C., Government Printing Office, 1911.

The Osage Tribe: Rite of the Chiefs; Sayings of the Ancient Men, Washington, D.C., Government Printing Office, 1921.

A Dictionary of the Osage Language, Washington, D.C., Government Printing Office, 1932.

War Ceremony and Peace Ceremony of the Osage Indians, Washington, D.C., Government Printing Office, 1939.

The Middle Five: Indian Schoolboys of the Omaha Tribe, Madison, University of Wisconsin Press, 1963.

SOURCES:

Books

Dockstader, Frederick J., *Great North American Indians,* New York, Van Nostrand Reinhold, 1977; 144-145.

Green, Norma Kidd, *Iron Eye's Family: The Children of Joseph La Flesche,* Lincoln, Nebraska, Johnsen Publishing Company, 1969.

Notable American Women, 1607-1950: A Biographical Dictionary, edited by Edward T. James and Janet Wilson James, Cambridge, Massachusetts, Harvard University Press, 1971; 630-633.

Periodicals

Alexander, Hartley B., "Francis La Flesche," *American Anthropologist,* 35, April-June 1933; 328-331.

—*Sketch by John E. Little*

Susan La Flesche Picotte
1865-1915
Omaha physician and community leader

Susan La Flesche Picotte was the first Native American woman to become a physician. She served her community tirelessly in this capacity, and in others as well—as a missionary, as a representative of her people in the East and in the nation's capital, and as a politically active temperance advocate. La Flesche Picotte was born June 17, 1865. She was the daughter of Joseph La Flesche (Insta Maza, or "Iron Eye"), who was half Omaha and half white and had become a chief of the Omahas in 1853. Her mother was Mary Gale (Hinnungsnun, or "One Woman"). Her half-brother, Francis La Flesche, was a noted ethnologist and interpreter.

Both her parents worked closely with Presbyterian missionaries in the region. The Omaha tribe was considered by missionaries to be exemplary of what other tribes could become. The federal government had already begun individual allotment of Omaha tribal lands by the 1870s, a process which did not get started among many tribes until the next century. La Flesche Picotte grew up in a frame house on a plot of land in her father's name. Her family was Christian, influential, and respected, and emphasized the importance of education. La Flesche Picotte attended Protestant missionary schools until she was 13, at which time she followed in the footsteps of her sister Susette La Flesche Tibbles and went off to the Elizabeth Institute, a finishing school for young ladies in New Jersey. In 1882 she returned to teach at a mission school on the reservation.

Education and the Connecticut Indian Association

In 1884 La Flesche Picotte enrolled at Hampton Normal and Agricultural Institute. Hampton had been founded with the goal of educating black freedmen, but was experimenting at the time with Indian education as well. During her tenure at Hampton, La Flesche Picotte came into contact with the Connecticut Indian Association, which had been founded in Hartford in 1881 and was a branch of the nationwide Women's National Indian Association (founded in Philadelphia in 1879). This group was one of many Protestant women's organizations of the late nineteenth century dedicated to improving the welfare and morality of Native Americans according to the standards and values of middle-class Protestants.

La Flesche Picotte's Presbyterian background provided her with the qualities that would make her an ideal symbol of a "progressive" Indian—an Indian eager to embrace change for her people along Euro-American lines. In 1886 she graduated from Hampton and gave a speech, reprinted in *Relations of Rescue,* which demonstrates the nature of her sense of mission: "From the outset the work of an Indian girl is plain before her.... We who are educated have to be pioneers of Indian civilization. We have to prepare our people to live in the white man's way, to use the white man's books, and to use his laws if you will only give them to us." She went on to underscore her religious beliefs, saying, "the shores of success can only be reached by crossing the bridge of faith."

The Connecticut Indian Association was interested in training "native missionaries" who would foster the development of Christian lifestyles among their own people. La Flesche Picotte seemed a perfect candidate, so they agreed to fund her medical training at the Woman's Medical College at Philadelphia. She began study there in October 1886, a few months after finishing at Hampton. Throughout medical school she corresponded with her friend Sara Kinney, the president of the Connecticut Indian Association, assuring her that her professional goals were linked to her desire to return to Nebraska and help her people. When not busy studying, she exhibited her community-oriented nature by speaking to church groups and visiting the Lincoln School for Indian children near Philadelphia. Yet despite her time-consuming extracurricular activities, she graduated at the top of her class in 1889.

Soon after graduation La Flesche Picotte departed on a speaking tour to association branches in Connecticut, which added greatly to the group's membership rolls. Then she returned to Nebraska, as promised, and won a government appointment as physician for the Omaha Agency. Since she was the first Native American woman to become a physician, this was the first such post to be occupied by a Native American woman, and among the first to be filled by any Native American. In 1893 she resigned in order to care for her ailing mother.

Marriage and Temperance

La Flesche Picotte herself was suffering from ill health at this time, too. The break from medical practice afforded her the time not only to convalesce and to care for her mother, but also to get married. She had promised her sponsors at the Connecticut Indian Association, who took an active interest in her personal life, that she would delay getting married until after she had practiced medicine for a few years. This promise she had kept and was married in 1894 to a Yankton Sioux who had gained popularity among the Omaha as a good storyteller. Henry Picotte also had a reputation as a heavy drinker, which may be why her family opposed the marriage. The La Flesche family already had ties with the Picottes, because Henry's brother Charles had married Susan's sister Marguerite six years earlier. The couple settled at Bancroft, Nebraska, and had two sons, Caryl and Pierre. La Flesche Picotte also found time for active involvement in the Presbyterian church at Bancroft.

Despite her marriage to a man who was fond of drinking, La Flesche Picotte herself was a teetotaler and was developing a strong dedication to temperance. This probably caused some tension in her marriage, and it certainly created rifts between her and her tribe. Members of the Omaha tribe had been granted citizenship a great deal earlier than other Indians (citizenship for all Indians did not come until 1924), but citizenship carried with it the right to buy alcohol—a right that previously had been closely curtailed.

After citizenship, there was no more government supervision of the sale of alcohol on the reservation and there was no longer enforcement of the prohibitive laws by the tribal police. La Flesche Picotte viewed the increase in drinking on the reservation with trepidation. According to *Relations of Rescue,* in 1914 she looked back on this time and wrote, "Intemperance increased ... men, women, and children drank; men and women died from alcoholism, and little children were seen reeling on the streets of the town;

drunken brawls in which men were killed occurred, and no person's life was considered safe." The drinking affected her in direct personal ways as well. She worried not only about her husband's drinking, but about her brother's, too. She took a direct involvement in the lives of women who faced abuse from drunken husbands.

La Flesche Picotte's vocal and active opposition to the sale and drinking of alcohol on the reservation caused controversy and was resented by other progressive, white-educated Indians, who found her views condescending. They failed to understand why Indians were less capable than whites when it came to exercising their right to use alcohol. La Flesche Picotte felt that such legalistic arguments were out of place in the midst of what she considered a dire social crisis. She exacerbated the division between herself and members of her community by supporting white politicians who, for reasons different from her own, supported prohibition of the sale of liquor to Indians. She boasted of her influence in banning alcohol sales in the newest reservation town of Walthill, Nebraska, by the Bureau of Indian Affairs, a federal office which was of course not universally admired by Indians. While many Omaha leaders were enraged by the brutal treatment of Indians arrested for drunkenness by white officials, she defended the arrests. This kind of controversy was not new to her, though, as her father had also long been an advocate of temperance. In *Relations of Rescue,* she excused the resentment held for her by many of her tribespeople with statements like: "I know that I shall be unpopular for a while with my people, because they will misconstrue my efforts, but this is nothing, just so I can help them for their own good."

Final Years and New Directions

After her husband died in 1905 of an illness that may well have been related to alcoholism, La Flesche Picotte was appointed by the Presbyterian Board of Home Missions as missionary to the Omaha. In the years following, animosities toward her by some members of her tribe would be eclipsed by her positive work on their behalf. One of her activities was to improve public health by pressing for modern hygienic and preventative standards among the Omaha. In 1913 she realized a lifelong goal and saw the opening of a hospital for the Omaha at her new home in Walthill, Nebraska. But she served her tribespeople in other ways as well. In 1910 she headed a tribal delegation to Washington, D.C., to discuss issues of citizenship and competency—a fuzzy and often abused legal prerequisite for Indian citizenship—with the Secretary of the Interior.

In the years after her husband's death she began to distrust the role of the government in supervising tribal life, a role which she had heretofore always encouraged. Part of her change in attitude resulted from the difficulty she had in assuming control of the inheritance left by her husband for their two sons. Government officials insisted that care of the inheritance should be given to a hard-drinking distant relative of Henry's who had only visited the children once and lived in another state. Only after submitting references from white friends was she granted the right to supervise the monies. This encounter with government bureaucracy angered her and fueled a major turnaround in the way she viewed the relationship between Indians and the Bureau of Indian Affairs. She had once likened her tribe to "little children, without father or mother." Now she said, as quoted in *Relations of Rescue*, "this condition of being treated as children we want to have nothing to do with ... the majority of the Omahas are as competent as the same number of white people."

Shortly before her death in 1915, La Flesche Picotte demonstrated her newfound distance from former white mentors (women like Sara Kinney and anthropologist Alice Cunningham Fletcher) by expressing her support for a new Native American religious movement that worried Protestant missionaries: the Peyote Religion, a pro-temperance Christian denomination that later became known as the American Indian or Native American Church.

Susan La Flesche Picotte became a great deal more than the first Native American woman physician. She was a symbol for many marginalized groups who sought empowerment in the nineteenth century. She was a shining light not only for the Indian rights movement, but for the women's movement as well. She was ahead of her time as a Native American activist because she was among the earliest Indian leaders to look beyond the interests of her own tribe and address the broad issues facing Native Americans in general. She never failed to speak her mind in the face of castigation either from fellow tribespeople or from white supporters. Her courage, in concert with a rare physician's compassion, made her a unique and effective leader for her people.

SOURCES:

Native American Women, edited by Gretchen M. Bataille, Garland Publishing, 1993.
Pascoe, Peggy, *Relations of Rescue: The Search for Female Moral Authority in the American West,* 1874-1939, Oxford, Oxford University Press, 1990.

—*Sketch by Charles Cannon*

Susette La Flesche Tibbles
1854-1903
Omaha advocate of Indian rights
Also known as Inshtatheamba ["Bright Eyes"]

Susette La Flesche Tibbles became a well-known Native American advocate of Indian rights partly by design and partly by chance. The design grew out of her father's and her own passionate desire for an education that would enable her to make her way in white America. This led her to seek and obtain an excellent primary and secondary education in white schools, which gave her a strong command of both spoken and written English as well as an enduring devotion to much of white culture. She became a speaker and writer on Indian rights in her mid-twenties, when she became involved in a great national controversy over the treatment of the Ponca Indians. An extended tour of the eastern United States in 1879 made her something of a celebrity under her Indian name, Bright Eyes.

La Flesche Tibbles was born in 1854 (the month and day are unknown) in a village of the Omaha Indian tribe located near the present town of Bellevue, Nebraska, the second child and eldest daughter of Joseph La Flesche (Estamahza, or "Iron Eye") and Mary Gale La Flesche. Her father, of half Omaha and half French blood, was the last principal chief of the Omaha tribe. Her mother was of half white American and half mixed Indian blood. Joseph La Flesche had several wives in the traditional Omaha culture and had eight children who lived to maturity. Two of La Flesche Tibbles' siblings became well-known: her sister Susan La Flesche Picotte, who became probably the first Native American woman physician, and her half-brother Francis La Flesche, who became a widely respected ethnologist. Joseph La Flesche was a remarkable and far-seeing leader who realized that both his children and his tribe would have to adapt to and make their way in white America. He did all in his power to influence his often reluctant tribesmen to move in that direction, and he inspired his children to seek education in the English language and in American life and culture.

La Flesche Tibbles grew up on the Omaha Indian reservation on the Missouri River some 70 miles north of the city of Omaha, to which the tribe moved in 1854 after giving up their former hunting lands to the United States government. She received her early education at the Presbyterian mission school on the reservation. In about 1872, she went to Elizabeth, New Jersey, to attend the Elizabeth Institute for Young Ladies, her way being paid by various white philanthropic groups. There she received an excellent secondary education and acquired a thorough command of the English language and a lifelong enthusiasm for English literature and for much, if not all, of American culture. She graduated in 1875 and returned to the Omaha reservation with the intention of becoming a schoolteacher. At first she was unable to obtain a teaching position at the Indian Agency elementary school. Ultimately, she discovered that Bureau of Indian Affairs (BIA) policy required that Indians be given preference for positions in the Indian service, including teaching. She wrote to the Commissioner of Indian Affairs in Washington demanding her right, and in 1877 she finally obtained a job as teacher in the Omaha Agency school.

Joined in Defense of Ponca Land Rights

La Flesche Tibbles' life was transformed in 1879 when she became involved in the famous affair of the Ponca Indians and their chief Standing Bear. The Ponca, a small tribe of about eight or nine hundred people, closely related to the Omahas, had been guaranteed a small reservation near the mouth of the Niobrara River in what is now northeastern Nebraska in a treaty which they had signed with the United States in 1858. In 1868 their reservation had been included, apparently by mistake, in a much larger grant to the Sioux Indians. In 1877 the United States Bureau of Indian Affairs attempted to resolve this problem by forcibly transporting the Ponca tribe to the Indian Territory in what is now the state of Oklahoma. A sizable portion of the tribe sickened and died in the hot, humid southern climate. In 1879 Standing Bear, then chief of the tribe, led a band of about 30 Poncas back to Nebraska. The Omaha tribe offered to allow them to settle on their reservation, but the U.S. Army soon arrested Standing Bear and his followers under orders from the Secretary of the Interior to transport them back to the Indian Territory.

At this point, Thomas Henry Tibbles, then a newspaperman in the city of Omaha, took up the cause of Standing Bear and the Poncas. Tibbles, a former follower of the abolitionist John Brown, an army scout in the Civil War, and a one-time itinerant preacher, was a large, flamboyant man who was a born crusader for good causes and underdogs. He first secured the support of many leading citizens in Omaha, and then arranged to file a writ of habeas corpus on Standing Bear's behalf in the federal district court in Omaha against the army general who had ordered the arrest of the runaway band of Poncas. In a famous trial held in April and May 1879, the judge ruled that an Indian was a person within the meaning of the law and thus entitled to a writ of habeas corpus, that the government had no right to remove the tribe to Indian Territory by force, and that the Indians had the right to expatriate themselves to whatever location they wished. He ordered the release of the Poncas.

Tibbles wished to carry the case to the U.S. Supreme Court in order to secure a definitive statement on Indian citizenship and rights and also to regain the reservation of the Poncas in Nebraska. La Flesche Tibbles and her father became involved in the case when Tibbles sent them, together with a white lawyer involved in the case, to Indian Territory to gather evidence as to how the Poncas who had remained there were faring. They found them living in very poor conditions and reported this finding to Tibbles and other white advocates of the Poncas in Omaha. Soon after this, La Flesche Tibbles, though very nervous, made her debut as a public speaker at a meeting of supporters of the Ponca cause in Omaha.

Carrying the Ponca case to the Supreme Court and securing their rights to their land in Nebraska required the raising of considerable money. Following a fundraising trip to the East Coast by himself in the summer of 1879, Thomas Tibbles conceived the idea of a much more extensive speaking and money-raising tour. He decided to take Standing Bear along to speak for the Poncas. Since the old chief spoke no English and the Ponca language was very similar to that of the Omahas, Tibbles proposed to take La Flesche Tibbles along to interpret. After much discussion, her father allowed the young woman to go, provided that her half-brother Francis La Flesche went along as a chaperon and second interpreter.

Toured the East Coast with Standing Bear

The tour began in October 1879 in Chicago and was well-publicized in the press from the beginning. The coming of Standing Bear and Bright Eyes (as everyone insisted on calling La Flesche Tibbles) was keenly anticipated on the East Coast. The party spent over a month in Boston, where Standing Bear and Bright Eyes created a sensation among the cultural and philanthropic elite. Many Boston reform leaders, such as the old abolitionist Wendell Phillips, became active in the cause of Indian rights. La Flesche Tibbles soon became a most effective advocate and symbol of the Indian cause in her own right. In a famous encounter at a dinner party given by the publisher Henry O. Houghton, the poet Henry Wadsworth Longfellow declared of La Flesche Tibbles, "*This* is Minnehaha," referring to the heroine of his epic poem about Indians, *The Song of Hiawatha* (1855). At this time, La Flesche Tibbles also met and befriended Helen Hunt Jackson, who was inspired by the Ponca cause to become a famous writer on Indian rights. La Flesche Tibbles was to make important contributions to Jackson's *Century of Dishonor: A Sketch of the United States Government's Dealings with Some of the Indian Tribes* (1881).

The tour continued with lengthy stays in New York City, Philadelphia, and Baltimore. Standing Bear and La Flesche Tibbles also testified on several occasions before committees of Congress. The party finally returned to Nebraska in April 1880. La Flesche Tibbles, or Bright Eyes, had by now become a well-known public figure who would find a ready audience for both her speeches and writings for the rest of her life. As it turned out, the Ponca case never did go to the Supreme Court, but Congress in March 1881 did pass legislation which compensated the tribe for its forced removal to Indian Territory and declared that the tribesmen could live wherever they chose.

Married Journalist/Activist Thomas Tibbles

Susette La Flesche and Thomas Tibbles made another lecture tour to the East in the autumn of 1880. Thomas, whose first wife had died in 1879, and Susette were married on July 23, 1881. The couple had no children of their own but raised Tibbles' two daughters by his first marriage. Their marriage seems to have been a happy one, though the overbearing and mercurial Tibbles was often in conflict with his wife's family. The Tibbles made frequent lecture trips together during their married life, most frequently in the eastern United States. In the late 1880s, they also made a successful lecture tour of England. La Flesche Tibbles confined her public speaking almost exclusively to the subject of Indian rights.

La Flesche Tibbles, writing under the name Bright Eyes, became a frequent contributor of semi-fictional stories of Indian life to children's magazines, such as *St. Nicholas*. She also wrote stories and political editorials for adults which appeared in many newspapers and magazines. She was also an artist of some talent who provided the illustrations for at least one book. In the late 1880s and the 1890s, Thomas and Susette alternated living on a small farm which had been allotted to Susette on the Omaha Indian reservation, and in Lincoln, Nebraska, where Tibbles once again took up newspaper work. In the 1890s, Tibbles joined the Populist political party and became the editor of a Populist weekly newspaper in Lincoln, *The Independent*. La Flesche Tibbles frequently wrote for the paper. La Flesche Tibbles' health grew poor in 1902, and she died at her home on the Omaha reservation on May 26, 1903. Tibbles made an unsuccessful run for Vice President of the United States on the Populist party ticket in 1904. He lived until 1928.

SOURCES:

Being and Becoming Indian: Biographical Studies of North American Frontiers, edited by James A. Clifton, Chicago, Dorsey Press, 1989; 137-159.

Green, Norma Kidd, *Iron Eye's Family: The Children of Joseph La Flesche,* Lincoln, Nebraska, Johnsen Publishing Company, 1969.

Notable American Women, 1607-1950: A Biographical Dictionary, edited by Edward T. James and Janet Wilson James, Cambridge, Massachusetts, Harvard University Press, 1971; 461-462.

Tibbles, Thomas Henry, *Buckskin and Blanket Days: Memoirs of a Friend of the Indians,* Garden City, New York, Doubleday, 1957.

Wilson, Dorothy Clarke, *Bright Eyes: The Story of Susette La Flesche, an Omaha Indian,* New York, McGraw-Hill, 1974.

—*Sketch by John E. Little*

Lame Deer
1903-1976
Minniconjou herbal healer, tribal leader, and activist

Also known as Tacha Ushte and John Fire

Lame Deer was born in South Dakota between the Pine Ridge and Rosebud reservations, and spent the last decades of his life in the small town of Winner in a dilapidated shack without electricity or plumbing. But his engaging humor made him a welcome guest on radio talk shows, television interviews, and intertribal ceremonies. The book, which he persuaded artist/photographer Richard Erdoes to write with him, has been translated into several languages and is required reading in many Indian studies and anthropology classes.

Lame Deer's Distinguished Ancestry

Lame Deer's great-grandfather, Tacha Ushte, as chief of the Minniconjou had won renown as a warrior. As a youth, he had fought against 50 Crow. He also led his people in the battle at the Little Bighorn in June of 1876 in southeastern Montana against Lieutenant Colonel George Armstrong Custer's forces. The first of his three wives had three sons: Did Not Butcher, Flying By, and Cante Witko ["Crazy Heart"], who was Lame Deer's grandfather.

Cante Witko escaped from the troops of General Nelson Miles on May 7, 1877, when surrender negotiations between him and Tacha Ushte turned into a slaughter. Tacha Ushte had signed the Treaty of Fort Laramie of 1868 with his mark and his thumbprint. His son, Cante Witko, was a "wicasa Yatapka" (shirt-wearer). His blue and yellow shirt, fringed with hair, was a sign of the honor by which he was regarded among his people.

Lame Deer's father was noted for his generosity, which was considered the highest of the four Lakota virtues. He sponsored many give-away ceremonies and feasts. His name Wawi-YohiYa meant "Let Them Have Enough." He came from Standing Rock Reservation, a prosperous man who owned more than 200 horses. A patient, taciturn, kind man who taught his son the arts of horsemanship without talking, he gave away all his horses and cattle and returned to Standing Rock when the communally held land was fenced off into 180 plots in 1920.

Maternal Ancestors

Lame Deer's mother, Sally Red Blanket, was renowned for her fine beadwork. She had 12 children, most of whom died young of such diseases as measles and influenza. Only Lame Deer and one sister survived. His mother died of tuberculosis in 1920 and he was raised by his maternal grandparents, Good Fox and Pte-Sa-Ota-Win ["Plenty White Buffalo"]. Good Fox had fought in the Custer battle, and was a survivor of the Wounded Knee Massacre of December 29, 1890. Respected by all for his wisdom, he served as sun dance intercessor who was given the honor of smoothing the ground which served as the altar, the "owanka osnato."

Education

Forced to attend Bureau of Indian Affairs schools for eight years, Lame Deer learned neither to read nor write since all instruction was in English in a punitive, military environment. He spent eight years in the third grade. From 1926 to 1939, he learned about the white world on a "find-out." During his "roaming" he was a rodeo rider and clown, a powwow dancer, a shepherd, a potato picker, a farmer, a bootlegger, a tribal policeman, an army recruit until he settled down "to my only full-time job—being an Indian." In his book, he recounts his activism on behalf of his people whose suffering from racism, inadequate education, poverty, and exploitation he had shared. Without having experienced these depths, he felt he would not have been able to heal.

The spiritual disciplines he explains in detail are their means of endurance. His mission was to preserve "our old Sioux ways—singing the ancient songs correctly, conducting a sweat lodge ceremony as it should be, making out old beliefs as pure, as clear and true as I possibly can, making them stay alive, saving them from extinction."

SOURCES:

Books

Crow Dog, Mary, and Richard Erdoes, *Lakota Woman,* New York, HarperCollins, 1991.

Lame Deer, Archie Fire, *Gift of Power: The Life and Teachings of a Lakota Medicine Man,* Santa Fe, New Mexico, Bear & Company, 1992.

Lame Deer, John Fire, and Richard Erdoes, *Lame Deer Seeker of Visions;* New York, Washington Square Press, 1972.

Lincoln, Kenneth, "Historical Slippage," in *Indi'n Humor: Bicultural Play in Native America,* New York, Oxford University Press, 1993; 58-88.

Matthiessen, Peter, *Indian Country,* New York, Penguin, 1992.

Periodicals

Sanborn, Geoff, "Unfencing the Range: History, Identity, Property, and Apocalypse in *Lame Deer Seeker of Visions,*" *American Indian Culture and Research Journal,* 14:4, 1990; 39-57.

—*Sketch by Ruth Rosenberg*

Arlinda Faye Locklear
1951-
Lumbee attorney

Locklear was the first Native American woman to argue a case before the United States Supreme Court. A published writer on Native issues, she has lectured on Native American and women's legal rights throughout the United States and has served on the boards of the National Indian Policy Center of George Washington University, the Institute for the Development of Indian Law, and the *Encyclopedia of Native Americans in the Twentieth Century.* Locklear is a member of the North Carolina, District of Columbia, Maryland, and the U.S. Supreme Court bars.

Born in 1951, Locklear is a member of the Lumbee Tribe of North Carolina, a tribe living primarily in North and South Carolina. She graduated with high honors from the College of Charleston in Charleston, South Carolina, in

1973 with a B.A. in political science, and in 1976 received her J.D. from the School of Law at Duke University in Durham, North Carolina. Locklear was the winner of the 1975-1976 Moot Court Competition, sponsored by the New York City Bar Association. Based upon an actual case, this competition attracts law students from across the country. The most outstanding among them eventually reach the national competition and confront real judges.

Locklear began her legal career as a staff attorney with the Native American Rights Fund (NARF) in Boulder, Colorado in 1976, where she was responsible for all major litigation involving tribes from Arizona, Florida, Nebraska, New York, South Dakota, Wisconsin, and Virginia. In April 1977 she moved to the Washington, D.C., office where, in August 1982, she became directing attorney of NARF's Washington staff. Locklear held that position through October 1987. She then left NARF, took the position of Lumbee tribal attorney, and established her private practice in Jefferson, Maryland. Locklear specializes in U.S. federal Indian law, including tribal land claims, jurisdictional issues, federal recognition of tribes, taxation, and water rights.

Appeared before the United States Supreme Court

In 1983 Locklear became the first Native woman to argue before the U.S. Supreme Court. In the case of *Solem v. Bartlett,* she challenged the jurisdiction of the State of South Dakota to prosecute a member of the Cheyenne River Sioux Tribe for on-reservation conduct. She won the case unanimously. Locklear further established herself as a leading authority on tribal issues, particularly tribal land claims, in 1985 when she argued and won her second case before the U.S. Supreme Court. In the *Oneida Indian Nation v. County of Oneida* case the Oneida of New York sought to reclaim control of lands from the local county government. She argued that federal common law enables tribes to claim homelands taken without the consent of the federal government.

Testified before Congress

Locklear first testified before Congress in 1982 while representing the Oneida Indian Nation of Wisconsin and the Oneida of the Thames Band, along with Eastern tribal chiefs and other tribal attorneys, who were opposed to the Ancient Indian Land Claims Settlement Act of 1982, which retroactively approved and validated pre-1912 transfers of Native lands and resources to non-Native peoples in New York State and South Carolina. In 1983 she gave extensive testimony before Congress in favor of federal Bureau of Indian Affairs (BIA) recognition of Native tribes not officially recognized by the United States, including the Tulalip, Samish, Snohomish, Snoqualmie (Washington State), and Lumbee tribes. Locklear's last testimony as a NARF attorney was delivered before Congress in December 1987. Here, she argued for federal recognition of the contributions made by the Iroquois Confederacy of Nations to the United States Constitution, particularly in Articles I and II.

After leaving NARF, Locklear represented her own tribe in 1988 when she testified before Congress in favor of improved procedures for federal recognition of Native tribes, including those of Washington State, in order to secure recognition of the Lumbee Tribe. In 1989 she again testified before Congress, voicing her approval of the Indian Federal Acknowledgment Administrative Procedures Act of 1989, and arguing for federal recognition of various tribal groups within the United States.

Among Locklear's many notable awards and honors is the 1984 American Heroine Award from *Ladies Home Journal,* the Young 1985 Woman of Promise Award from *Good Housekeeping* magazine, and the 1987 Outstanding Woman of Color Award from the National Institute for Women of Color. In 1990 she received an honorary doctorate from the State University of New York.

SOURCES:

Indices & Abstracts to Congressional Publications and Public Laws, Congressional Information Service, Washington, D.C., 1983, 1984, 1988, 1989.

Native North American Almanac, edited by Duane Champagne, Detroit, Gale Research, 1994.

—Sketch by tpkunesh

Charles Loloma
1921-1991
Hopi jewelry designer, potter, and educator

Although Charles Loloma was praised for his work as a potter, painter, and illustrator of children's books, he was best known as one of the world's great jewelers. His innovative jewelry designs, which combined traditional Hopi motifs with nontraditional materials and techniques, earned him worldwide recognition. Not only did his designs inspire other Native American artists, but he contributed much of his time to instructing others in his craft. Later in life, he was also leader of the Badger Clan at the Hopi village where he was born.

Loloma was born January 7, 1921, to Rex and Rachael Loloma in Hotevilla, Arizona, at the Third Mesa Hopi village. He attended Hopi High School in Oraibi, Arizona, a student of Fred Kobotie, and later went to Phoenix Indian High School, where he studied under Lloyd Kiva New. New, who became president emeritus of the Institute of American Indian Arts and was a consultant to the Smithsonian Institution's National Museum of the American Indian, became a lifelong friend of Loloma.

At the age of 18, Loloma was commissioned to paint murals at the Golden Gate International Exposition for the Federal Building on Treasure Island in the San Francisco Bay. Then in 1940, he and Fred Kobotie painted murals at the Haskell Institute in Lawrence, Kansas, which were moved one year later to New York as part of an exhibit at the Museum of Modern Art, "Indian Art of the United States." Around this time, Loloma illustrated several books, including *Hopihoya* (1940) and *Little Hopi* (1948) by Edward Kennard. During World War II, Loloma joined the U.S. Army and spent three years in the Aleutians.

When he returned from the army, Loloma used his G.I. Bill to attend the School for American Craftsmen at Alfred University, New York. In an unconventional step, Loloma studied ceramics there, a craft traditionally reserved for women among the Hopi. In 1947, he married Ottelie Pasivaya, who was from Shipaulovi, Second Mesa, Arizona. The same year, Loloma received his journeyman's certificate in ceramics; then, two years later, he was awarded the John Hay Whitney Opportunity Fellowship to study Hope clays and glaze materials. In 1954 he and his wife opened a ceramic shop in Kiva Craft Center in Scottsdale, Arizona. They had moved off the reservation because Loloma found it too conservative.

Begins Making Jewelry

During this time, Loloma became interested in jewelry making and, without any formal training, he began casting silver in handcarved sandstone molds. He began by using this traditional Navajo technique to form Hopi motifs, but later he experimented with other techniques, including the lost wax method and soldering. Loloma also began using natural materials in his designs, such as ivory, bones, shells, and pebbles. Although most Native American jewelers used silver, Loloma combined these natural materials with gold. Loloma would arrange the stones and shells into a sculptured setting and into mosaic arrangements with the finest quality semiprecious stones, such as turquoise, coral, and lapis lazuli. In another departure from traditional Hopi design, he incorporated diamonds, emeralds, and pearls into some of his jewelry. Loloma's friend and former teacher, Lloyd Kiva New, said of his jewelry designs in *American Craft,* "His design genius is characterized by an unusual treatment of sculptural form and a talent for balancing color and texture.... [He] combined the oldest of Hopi design forms with a seemingly limitless vision."

Loloma's career as an artist was paralleled by his work as an instructor. Loloma began teaching pottery and jewelry making at Arizona State College in Tempe and Sedona, and for three summers he was an instructor with the Southwest Indian Art Project, sponsored by the Rockefeller Foundation at the University of Arizona in Tucson. According to New in American Craft, As he became more recognized for his jewelry, Loloma traveled extensively, giving workshops in such places as Japan, Korea, and the Philippines. From 1962 to 1965 Loloma was an instructor and the chairman of the Plastic Arts and Sales Departments of the Institute of American Indian Arts (IAIA) in Santa Fe. In 1965, he divorced his wife, Ottelie, after 18 years of marriage and moved to Hotevilla, Arizona. In 1972 he was appointed to a three-year term on the Arizona Commission on the Arts and Humanities.

Loloma's steadily increasing prestige as an artist led to numerous exhibits of his work throughout the 1960s and 1970s. In 1963, he had a private showing in Paris, France, which brought him international attention. From 1965 to 1975 Loloma was an exhibitor at the Scottsdale National Indian Arts Exhibition and won first award for seven years in a row. The Heard Museum featured a one-man show of his work in 1971, and, the same year, he again exhibited his work in Paris. He was sought after for numerous one-man shows throughout the world, and in 1978 he was artist-in-residence in Manila, Philippines, in the Pacific Program for the National Endowment for the Arts and the Department of Defense.

Loloma was at the pinnacle of his career when, in 1986, he was in an automobile accident that severely injured him. In 1990 Loloma received the Arizona Governor's Award for his contributions to the arts in the state. The next year, on June 9, Loloma died at the age of 70.

SOURCES:

Books

Native North American Almanac, edited by Duane Champagne, Detroit, Gale Research, 1994; 1094-1095.
Younger, Erin, *Loloma: A Retrospective View,* Santa Fe, Heard Museum, 1978.

Periodicals

New, Lloyd Kiva, "Remembering Charles Loloma," *American Craft,* 51, October/November 1991, 18-19.

—*Sketch by Phyllis "Picturestone" Noah*

Otellie Loloma

clay pieces. "She was always artistically inclined," her sister Jewel "Kay" Wauneka told Phyllis Noah in an interview, but working in clay was not encouraged at Second Mesa. In the Hopi tradition, Second Mesa women made woven plaques and coiled woven baskets; First Mesa women worked with clay and were known as the potters. The traditional pottery was polychrome and black-on-yellow. On the Third Mesa Hopi women made baskets with wicker and dyed with native plants. The men on the Mesas were known as the weavers and made blankets with ceremonial clothing.

Receives Scholarship to College

In 1945, Loloma received a three-year scholarship to the School of the American Craftsmen at Alfred University in New York. At the time she was a substitute teacher at Indian Day Schools in Shungopovi, Keams Canyon, Polacca, and Oraibi. She almost turned down the opportunity to stay at Second Mesa but decided to go away to school. Loloma began working in clay only after she left Second Mesa. She and her future husband Charles Loloma, the world-famous Hopi jewelry designer from Third Mesa, Hotevilla, decided to go to Alfred to study ceramics. He attended school on the G.I. Bill after being discharged from the U.S. Army in 1945 as a noncombat camouflage expert in the Aleutian Islands. Loloma broke tradition by studying ceramics instead of making coiled baskets and he broke tradition by studying ceramics instead of weaving.

They married in 1947 in Winslow, Arizona. Loloma was at a farm near Winslow when they decided to get mar-

Otellie Loloma
1922-1992
Hopi artist
Also known as Sequafnema ["The Place in the Valley Where the Squash Blossoms Bloom"]

Otellie "Okie" Loloma received world acclaim for her ceramic art and was known as the "single most influential Indian woman creator in clay." She was born in Second Mesa, Arizona, at Shipaulovi. Her father was El Capitan Pasivaya, a trader, and her mother was Susan Masabenka, a midwife at Second Mesa. Loloma was from the Sun Clan. She attended the Bureau of Indian Affairs (BIA) school. When Loloma was a little girl, she would go into the apple and peach orchards with her grandmother and make small

ried; the way in which she was married still brings a chuckle to her sister. "We didn't know about it," said Wauneka. "She didn't have any wedding clothes. Charles, Okie, and a friend just got on horses and rode into Winslow and went to a Justice of the Peace. She was a natural-born horsewoman."

After returning from New York, Loloma taught children to work in clay at the Shungopovi Day School. Later, she attended the College of Santa Fe and Northern Arizona University. The Lolomas moved to Scottsdale, Arizona, and until their divorce in 1965, they worked together on numerous projects. She set up a studio in her home; and from 1954 to 1962, they opened a studio-shop at the Kiva Craft Center in Scottsdale, Arizona. The Lolomas made "Lolomaware" at the center, which contained several small studio-shops for artists to work and sell their art to the public. Lloyd Kiva New, Cherokee textile designer and art teacher, founded the center and sold his textiles and leather goods at the center. Paolo Soleri, architect, made bells at one of the studios and he became famous for his work.

When Charles Loloma received a Whitney Foundation grant to research and develop clay resources, they moved to the Shungopovi Village. Loloma assisted her husband in his research and incorporated her knowledge of wheel-throwing techniques with the traditional hand-made techniques to develop her original style of pottery. Loloma began teaching at Arizona State University during the summers and from 1960 to 1962 she became an instructor for the Southwest Indian Art Project, funded by the Rockefeller Foundation at the University of Arizona in Tucson. The project was an innovative move to return artists to their individual styles using their tribal background for expressing their work. In the early 1930s, Dorothy Dunn promoted a "studio style" of painting at the Santa Fe Indian School—a style of realism in Indian art. At the time, Native Americans were discouraged from creating any art depicting Indian culture and Dunn was considered a revolutionary. But by the 1960s, "individualism" and a return to tribal heritages in Indian art were encouraged. Loloma and her husband were recognized as two of the first successful Native American artists and business owners.

Devoted to Students and Children

Although Loloma did not have any children, she would keep children who needed a home. "There were many children she helped along the way," said Wauneka. When the Institute of American Indian Arts (IAIA) opened in 1962, Loloma worked on the faculty as an instructor. Until her retirement in 1988, Loloma devoted herself to her students and the children who needed her help. She did not concentrate on her own work during this time. Some of her students became well known artists: Pete Jones, Onondaga; Jacquie Stevens, Winnebago; Robert Tenoria, Manuelita Lovata, Santo Domingo; Luke Simon, Micmac; and Erika Eckerstrand, Swedish. "She was more like a nurturer," long-time friend, Linda Lomahaftewa, told Noah in an interview. "I looked on her as an aunt because she was Sun Clan as was my father." At IAIA, Loloma taught painting, ceramic sculp-

ture, basic design, and traditional Hopi dance. Loloma performed traditional dance with the students at various functions including the 1968 Mexican Olympics and a special program at the White House.

Loloma became highly recognized for her work and won numerous awards. She credited her ideas from the Hopi life and legends but used different nontraditional methods to manipulate the clay. She would construct sculptures with textured surfaces and use leather and turquoise to dress the sculpture. Some of her sculptures were maiden figures using the traditional Hopi hairstyle of butterfly buns behind the ears. Loloma accredited her ideas to Hopi stories and memories from her childhood. "She loved texture," Craig Locklear told Noah in an interview. "Even her paintings were textured using collage and experimentation with various textures." Locklear met Loloma when he was a printmaking instructor at IAIA. "She treated me like a son and was very fostering," said Locklear. "She always took time to tell me stories. She was full of love and had a wonderful sense of humor." Loloma loved to cook and bake traditional breads, pikami and piki.

Her work as been in exhibitions throughout the United States, Europe and Latin America and is in numerous public and private collections. Although Loloma worked on canvas and in bronze, her ceramics brought her the most acclaim. She won many awards including the Arizona State Fair, the Scottsdale National Indian Arts Exhibition, and the Philbrook Art Center in Tulsa, Oklahoma. Her work is at the Museum of the American Indian, Heye Foundation, New York; the Heard Museum; the Philbrook Indian Art Center; Blair House, Washington, D.C., the Wheelwright Museum, and at the IAIA Museum.

One of the last awards she received was in February of 1991 at the twelfth annual National Women's Caucus for Art conference in Washington, D.C. She was one of five women to receive the Outstanding Achievement in the Visual Arts award. The prestigious Women's Caucus for Art was founded in 1972 and began bestowing awards in 1979; the first award ceremony was held in the Oval Office of the White House with President Jimmy Carter presenting. The WCA Honor Awards program book states: "Otellie Loloma, we honor you for your dedication to what is creative, beautiful and eternal in your Hopi Indian culture. You are honored for your ancient tradition of working in clay and teaching what is important of Hopi values and your continuing tradition of creating new forms of art from the traditions of your Hopi People. You have made your Hopi traditions visible for all of us to share through your art."

Throughout her life, Loloma continued to return to Second Mesa for traditional ceremonies. The last ceremony she attended was in 1992. On the way home, she developed the hiccups; unable to stop, she went to the emergency room at St. Vincent's hospital in Santa Fe. Loloma remained in the hospital on a ventilator. At first, the doctors thought she had suffered a stroke, then they thought it was cancer, but they never could determine the cause of her illness. Her sister Kay sat by her side every day. Sometimes it was difficult for her to talk, so she would write notes. Then after almost six months in the hospital, Loloma appeared to be getting better and the doctors were going to take her off the ventilator when she had a relapse and died.

SOURCES:

Books

Biographical Dictionary of Indians of the Americas, Volume 1, Newport Beach, California, American Indian Publishers, 1991; 368.

Cirillo, Dexter, *Southwestern Indian Jewelry,* New York, Abbeville Press, 1992; 143-147.

Euler, Robert C., and Henry F. Dobyns, *The Hopi People,* Phoenix, Indian Tribal Series, 1971; 70-74.

McGrath, James, "Otellie Loloma," in *WCA Honor Awards,* edited by Charleen Touchette, Washington, D.C., 1991; 5-6.

Native American Women, edited by Gretchen M. Bataille, New York, Garland Publishing, 1993; 156-157.

Other

Feil, Jerry, interview with Phyllis Noah, September 11, 1994.

Locklear, Craig, interview with Phyllis Noah, September 11, 1994.

Lomahaftewa, Linda, interview with Phyllis Noah, September 11, 1994.

Wauneka, Jewel "Kay," interview with Phyllis Noah, September 11, 1994.

—Sketch by Phyllis "Picturestone" Noah

Linda Lomahaftewa
1947-
Hopi/Choctaw artist and educator

Linda Lomahaftewa is an accomplished Hopi/Choctaw artist and art instructor. Her work, which reflects the spirituality and storytelling traditions of her Hopi background, has garnered numerous awards and exhibitions.

Lomahaftewa was born July 3, 1947, in Phoenix, Arizona, to Clifford and Mary Lomahaftewa. The family participated in pow wows and ceremonies together and their home was filled with Native American art. Her father carved Kachina dolls and is a drummer and singer, and her mother quilts and makes intricate beadwork designs. Lomahaftewa has three brothers: Dan, who is a painter and printmaker; Newton, who is an award-winning fancy dancer; and Woody, the oldest brother, who is a Vietnam veteran and

Linda Lomahaftewa

likes living in the country. She has one sister, Gloria, who is assistant curator at the Heard Museum, a beadworker, and a pow wow dancer.

In 1962, Lomahaftewa attended the Institute of American Indian Arts in Santa Fe, New Mexico, for two years and received a high school diploma in art. She earned a B.A. in fine arts in 1970 and an M.A. in fine arts in 1971 from the San Francisco Art Institute. After college, Lomahaftewa featured her work in more than 40 exhibitions around the United States. Since then she has been involved in teaching at various colleges and universities, including California State College and the University of California at Berkeley. Since 1974 she has been a drawing and painting instructor at the Institute of American Indian Arts.

Wins Numerous Awards

Lomahaftewa's work has won many awards, including first place at the Indian Festival of Arts in LaGrande, Oregon, in 1974, the Helen Hardin Award for creative excellence in painting at the Southwestern Association of Indian Art's (SWAIA) sixty-seventh annual Indian Market in Santa Fe, New Mexico, in 1988, and first place in handpulled prints at the SWAIA seventieth annual Indian Market in 1991. Lomahaftewa's art has also appeared in numerous shows throughout the world. For example, "Shared Visions—Native American Painters and Sculptors in the Twentieth Century," a Heard Museum exhibition, went on national and international tours.

Lomahaftewa's art reflects the symbolism of the Hopi—rainbows, lightning, and clouds—with colors and designs she draws from her Hopi traditions. Some of the symbols and images that she uses in her work are parrots, petroglyphs, mountain lions, shamans, and cloud maidens. Lomahaftewa was particularly influenced by her father's philosophy. He told her, "Whatever you work on, any kind of artwork or whatever you're doing, pray for it to come out well," she recalled in publicity for her limited edition *Migration of the Parrot*. As a result, she views each painting as a prayer for all people. Lomahaftewa feels her paintings tell stories about being Hopi, and reveal her memories of the colors and shapes she has seen at ceremonies and in the landscape. There is a certain spiritual element in her work—reflecting her belief that all things are sacred.

In 1992, Lomahaftewa and her brother Dan participated in a two-person exhibit, "Looking for Beauty in the Future," at Galleria Posada in Sacramento, California. Many museums and galleries display her paintings in their permanent collections, including the Southern Plains Indian Museum in Anadarko, Oklahoma, the Millicent Rogers Museum in Taos, New Mexico, the American Indian Historical Society in San Francisco, and the Center for the Arts of Indian America in Washington, D.C.

In 1993, her art was featured in the "Bridges and Boundaries" exhibit at the Peiper-Riegraf Gallery in Frankfort, Germany. In 1994, Lomahaftewa was the featured artist in several shows, including the thirty-sixth annual Heard Museum Guild Indian Fair and Market in Phoenix, Arizona, "The Book as Art" exhibit at the Institute of American Indian Arts Museum in Santa Fe, New Mexico, and "The Spirit of Native America" exhibit's Latin American tour with American Indian Contemporary Arts of San Francisco. At the Heard Museum in 1994, her "Cloud Maiden Series, #10," an oil pastel monotype, was featured on posters and t-shirts for the event.

SOURCES:

Books

Biographical Dictionary of Indians of the Americas, Newport Beach, California, American Indian Publishers, 1991; 369.
Reference Encyclopedia of the American Indian, fifth edition, edited by Barry T. Klein, West Nyack, New York, Todd Publications, 1992; 919.

Periodicals

"Heard Uses Lomahaftewa Art," *Navajo-Hopi Observer,* March 2, 1994.

Other

"Limited Edition by Linda Lomahaftewa" (publicity), Vancouver, British Columbia, Garfinkel Publications, 1994.

—*Sketch by Phyllis "Picturestone" Noah*

K. Tsianina Lomawaima
1955-
Creek educator and anthropologist
Also known as K. Tsianina Carr

Kimberly Tsianina Lomawaima, an associate professor of anthropology, specializes in studies about the indigenous people of North America. Her name, "Tsianina," for which there is no English translation, was a family name also used by her grandmother's sister, Tsianina Redfeather Blackstone. Born March 30, 1955, in Kansas City, Kansas, Lomawaima spent much of her early life moving from one place to another with her parents. In addition to Kansas City, she lived in Denver, Colorado; Wheaton and Aurora, Illinois; and Cincinnati, Ohio. She attended both junior and senior high school in Cincinnati. Her father was Curtis Thorpe Carr, a Creek Indian who was employed as a salesman until his retirement. Her mother, F. Marilyn Voth Carr, worked as an office manager. Because her family moved often, she found herself relying more on her family for support than on outside friends. In correspondence with Catherine A. Clay, Lomawaima wrote, "My family was so close and supportive. It gave me confidence to do things, such as starting college early, at age 16."

Becomes Interested in Anthropology

Lomawaima did not know anything about anthropology when she first started college in 1972 at DePauw University in Greencastle, Indiana. After two years there, she moved to the University of Arizona in Tucson where she took her first class in anthropology as an introduction to the study of linguistics. With her interest aroused, she found the study of the history of humans and their relationships within the context of their environment a challenge. In 1976, she received her bachelor's degree from the University of Arizona. From 1978 to 1979, Lomawaima continued her studies as a Ford doctoral fellow at Stanford University in California, where she received her master's degree. While at Stanford, she met Hopi Indian Hartman H. Lomawaima, whom she married in 1980. She also worked from 1979 to 1980 as a curriculum developer at the Lame Deer Public School on the Northern Cheyenne Reservation in Lame Deer, Montana.

Lomawaima began the long trek to a doctoral degree at Stanford University in 1983 mostly because her undergraduate professors and advisors thought she would do well in postgraduate work and would like it. Once she had started the final chapter in her education, Lomawaima said stubbornness helped motivate her to finish to prove to herself she could do it. She received support in the form of a National Research fellowship from the National Institute of Mental Health, as well as grants from the L. J. and Mary C. Skaggs Foundation and the Phillips Fund. In 1984, Lomawaima also was honored with the Dorothy Danforth Compton fellowship. During her last year at Stanford, she was a lecturer in the Native American studies program at the

University of California at Berkeley. She received her doctorate degree in anthropology in 1987 from Stanford.

While it was her determination that helped her through the long hours of studying, her father's life provided the inspiration for her doctoral dissertation. "My father grew up, and was educated at Chilocco Indian Agricultural School in north-central Oklahoma," she told Clay. "He and his brother were placed there in 1927 as wards of the court (their mom was a single mother, having a very hard time raising three children). My dad was eight or nine at the time. He ran away in 1935, so his stories of childhood were mostly stories of Indian school." As a result, "They Called It Prairie Light: Oral Histories from Chilocco Indian Agricultural School, 1920-1940," became the title of her dissertation. A book she wrote later based on the same subject received the North American Indian Prose Award in 1993.

Begins Teaching and Consulting Career

In 1988, Lomawaima was appointed an assistant professor of anthropology and American Indian studies at the University of Washington in Seattle. In 1990, she received a research grant from the Institute of Ethnic Studies in the United States to examine American Indian education and early twentieth century federal policy. Working as a consultant in 1991, she assisted *Newsweek* with its special publication *1492-1992, When Worlds Collide.* In 1992, she received a grant from the Institute of Ethnic Studies for work on "Southwest Pueblos and the Atchinson Topeka and Santa Fe Railway." Also in 1992, Lomawaima began consulting on the new Hall of Native American Cultures at the Carnegie Museum of Natural History in Pittsburgh, Pennsylvania.

While research has played a large role in her career, Lomawaima also taught anthropology and American Indian studies, which resulted in a Distinguished Teaching Award in 1991. "I devote a lot of time and effort to my students to help them discover their strengths, whatever they may be," Lomawaima wrote in correspondence with Clay. She also was appointed in 1993 as an adjunct assistant professor in the Department of Women Studies at the University of Washington, in addition to her position in the American Indian studies program.

In 1994, Lomawaima was enticed back to the University of Arizona with an offer of an associate professor's post in American Indian studies. At the same time, her husband accepted the job of associate director of the Arizona State Museum, located on the University of Arizona's campus. Living in Arizona allowed the couple to continue their joint research project on the social history of Native American employees of the Atchinson Topeka and Santa Fe Railways. Lomawaima has written numerous journal articles based upon her research and is a manuscript and proposal reader for several journals.

SOURCES:

Books

Native North American Almanac, edited by Duane Champagne, Detroit, Gale Research, 1994; 1095-1096.

Reference Encyclopedia of the American Indian, sixth edition, edited by Barry T. Klein, West Nyack, New York, Todd Publications, 1993; 569.

Other

Lomawaima, K. Tsianina, correspondence with Catherine A. Clay, July 18, 1994.

—Sketch by Catherine A. Clay

Looking Glass
1823(?)-1877
Nez Percé tribal leader
Also known as Allalimya Takanin

Looking Glass was one of the principal Nez Percé leaders during the 1877 Nez Percé War. Born Allalimya Takanin in 1823, he did not become known as Looking Glass until his father's death 40 years later. He was the son of Apash Wyakaikt ["Flint Color" or "Flint Necklace"], also known as Looking Glass, headman of the Asotin band and a leader of the non-treaty Nez Percés. The father had worn a small trade mirror on a thong around his neck; when he died his son inherited both the pendant and the name. He also inherited the leadership of the Asotin band. A proud and opinionated man standing almost six feet tall, Looking Glass was a warrior and a buffalo hunter who was familiar with the northern plains hunting grounds. He was a realist about the whites; he knew their numbers and strengths, refusing to go to war with them until his village was attacked in 1877. Although he was not as forceful as his father, he was appointed a Nez Percé war leader in 1848. His father, who had not supported the 1855 Nez Percé Treaty, remained at peace with the Americans until his death. Looking Glass followed his father's example of passive resistance as long as he could.

In the early 1860s, after gold was discovered in the Nez Percé country, prospectors, followed by another wave of land-hungry immigrants, invaded the reservation. The government decided that all of the Nez Percés would now have to move from Oregon onto the relatively small reservation at Lapwai, Idaho. Negotiations between the government and selected chiefs led to the 1863 Nez Percé Treaty. In spite of protests from many of the Nez Percés, including Looking Glass and Chief Joseph, the treaty was signed by Chief Lawyer and several other Christian Nez Percés. Even though the treaty did not directly impact Looking Glass and his people—they escaped removal because their lands were on a tributary of the Clearwater River, within the eastern boundary of the reservation—Looking Glass did not sign the 1863 treaty, siding instead with the non-treaty Nez Percés. Even as more Americans came into his country, Looking Glass

Looking Glass

continued to follow a peaceful policy, urging the other head-men to do the same. But by 1877 peaceful negotiations were no longer an option for the non-treaty Nez Percés.

The Nez Percé War Begins

In May 1877 General Oliver O. Howard told Chief Joseph's Wallowa Nez Percés and other chiefs who were still living off the reservation that they were to move onto the reservation voluntarily within 30 days. If the chiefs refused, Howard warned, the Army would move them forcibly. The chiefs, still desiring peace and aware of the military forces aligned against them, reluctantly consented. Their impending removal, combined with the bitterness and anger that already existed between the Nez Percés and the white settlers, increased tensions in the country and led to violence: two young Nez Percé warriors, seeking revenge for a previous incident, killed several settlers, and the Nez Percé War of 1877 began. Once violence erupted Howard decided to move the Nez Percés onto the reservation immediately. The Indians' large herds of cattle and horses, and the Nez Percé elders and children, were forced to cross rivers swollen by spring runoff. The Nez Percés wanted more time to round up their herds, collect their possessions, and allow the rivers to drop. But Howard was adamant that the Indians must move now. On June 17 he attacked Chief Joseph's village, thereby drawing the Wallowa Nez Percés into the war.

Looking Glass' Village Attacked

On July 11 a combined force of volunteer militia and regular army troops under Lieutenant Stephen C. Whipple approached Looking Glass' village. Looking Glass, still desiring peace, sent an emissary to meet Whipple. But the lieutenant, wanting to speak personally with Looking Glass, rode past the emissary and into the village with his men. With Whipple were several Idaho volunteers, undisciplined men with grudges against the Nez Percés. One of the volunteers fired at a warrior he apparently resented, and then firing broke out all around. Whipple did nothing to stop it, and the soldiers and militia attacked the village, looting, burning, and rounding up the Indians' cattle and horses. Looking Glass and most of his people escaped, joining Joseph and the other non-treaty Nez Percés on what would be an epic 1600-mile flight.

On July 15 a council of the non-treaty chiefs was held at Weippe. Looking Glass urged the people to cross the Lolo Trail and continue traveling east to the buffalo country of the Crow tribe, with whom they were friendly. He knew the country, having hunted buffalo with the Crows, and he believed they would welcome the Nez Percés. Supported by the other chiefs and warriors, Looking Glass became the leader of the Nez Percés. Believing that their fight was with the people of Idaho, not Montana, the Nez Percés set a leisurely pace while crossing the Bitteroot Mountains. Their relatively peaceful crossing into Montana reinforced their assumption that Howard was not following them. Looking Glass assured his people it was safe to rest. When two Nez Percés who had been living on the Flathead Indian Reservation came into camp and recommended a short route to Canada through the Flathead country, Looking Glass disagreed. He did not trust the Flat-heads, and if the Nez Percés must retreat to Canada he would lead them east over the mountains first. They could then join up with Sitting Bull's Sioux, who had fled to Canada after the Battle of the Little Bighorn in 1876.

Leisurely travel and Looking Glass' assurances that the army would not follow them into Montana proved disastrous for the Nez Percés. On August 7 the Nez Percés set up camp in the Big Hole Valley, believing that here they could rest, hunt, and repair their equipment. Ignoring some of the warriors' fears that the army may still be following them, Looking Glass did not post scouts. Just before daybreak on August 9, government forces attacked, killing and wounding many Indians. The Nez Percés, initially taken by surprise, rallied and drove off the soldiers and volunteers. But the Indians' losses had been high: between 60 and 90 Nez Percés had been killed, including 12 of the best warriors. Looking Glass was discredited, and Joseph took over as principal leader.

Although Lean Elk was now the war leader and Joseph had overall authority over the Nez Percé retreat, Looking Glass remained influential. His opinions and suggestions were still taken seriously in the councils, and he was included in planning an attack on Camas Meadows. When the chiefs went into council during the stops, Looking Glass continually pointed out that the Nez Percés were tired and needed rest. Once again, he was arguing that they had out-distanced the soldiers and that they could go more slowly and linger in their camps. By September, with Canada less than 100 miles away, the Nez Percés crossed a pass between the Little Rockies and the Bear Paw Mountains in north central Montana. With the weather growing colder and the people and horses nearing exhaustion, Looking Glass resumed command. In spite of some of the warriors' fears that maintaining a leisurely pace would prove fatal, the column slowed down once again. They also began making camps earlier in the day, giving the warriors a chance to hunt and the people a rest from their long march. Forty miles from Canada, near the northern flank of the Bear Paws, on a bleak and desolate plain, the Nez Percés made their last camp.

Once again, Looking Glass' underestimation of the army's persistence brought tragedy to his people. Colonel Nelson A. Miles, with fresh troops and Cheyenne scouts, attacked the Nez Percés on September 30, 1877. The Nez Percés dug in, inflicting casualties on the troops and holding off Miles for four days. But the winter weather and the Indians' fewer numbers, combined with the arrival of army reinforcements, signaled the end for the Nez Percés. Exhausted and demoralized, the Nez Percés considered surrender.

To Looking Glass, White Bird, and some of the other warriors, surrender was unthinkable, as they believed they would be hanged if taken alive. Looking Glass and White Bird decided to make a break for Canada at the first opportunity. The opportunity never came for Looking Glass. On October 5, 1877, shortly after a council ended, someone called out that a mounted Indian was approaching from the north. Thinking that it was a messenger from Sitting Bull, Looking Glass sprang up to see if it was a Sioux warrior. As he turned to call out to the rider, he was struck in the forehead with a bullet. He was the last casualty of the war.

After a few days of fighting, Chief Joseph reached an agreement with the Army whereby the Nez Percés would agree to surrender as long as they were allowed to settle on the reservation in Idaho. Although Howard and Miles agreed to these terms, General William Sherman voided the agreement and forced the Nez Percés to move first to Kansas and then to Oklahoma. Joseph struggled for years to persuade government officials to allow his people to move back to their traditional homeland. Finally, in 1885 the government allowed the tribe to move back to Idaho.

SOURCES:

Dockstader, Frederick J., *Great North American Indians,* New York, Van Nostrand Reinhold, 1977; 157-159.

Haines, Francis, *The Nez Percés: Tribesmen of the Columbia Plateau,* Norman, University of Oklahoma Press, 1978; 223, 263, 264, 274, 275, 299, 318.

Josephy, Alvin M., Jr., *The Nez Percé Indians and the Opening of the Northwest,* Lincoln, University of Nebraska Press, 1979.

McWhorter, L. V., *Hear Me My Chiefs! Nez Percé History and Legend,* edited by Ruth Bordin, Caldwell, Caxton Printers, Ltd., 1986.

Native North American Almanac, edited by Duane Champagne, Detroit, Gale Research, 1994; 1097.

Waldman, Carl, *Who Was Who in Native North American History,* New York, Facts on File, 1990; 210-211.

—Sketch by Michael F. Turek

Phil Lucas
1942-
Choctaw film producer, director, writer, and actor

Native American film producer, director, and writer Phil Lucas creates realistic images of his people in an effort to combat the stereotypical picture held by most Euro-Americans, and even some Native Americans. Lucas was born January 15, 1942, in Phoenix, Arizona, the son of Charles W. and Sally Lucas. His father was a Tennessee-born Choctaw and Crow Indian who was sent across country by the government to attend Phoenix Indian School in Phoenix, where he eventually decided to make his home and worked as the athletic equipment manager at Phoenix Community College.

Filmmaker Lucas grew up in Phoenix, attending North Phoenix High School from 1956 to 1960, and Phoenix Community College from 1960 to 1961. He spent the next seven years as an entertainer, travelling around the United States playing guitar and singing folk music. He returned to Arizona in 1966 and spent another year in school at Mesa Community College. From there he went to Bellingham, Washington, to work on a bachelor of science degree in visual communication, which he completed in 1970 at Western Washington University. While he was at the university, he taught a class on the basics of black and white photography.

Since it typically took several years to get to the account executive level at advertising agencies in the United States, Lucas decided to move to Honduras following college, where he opened an advertising agency with several other people. After several years there and a brief stint shooting stills for a couple of photography agencies in New York, he found that he disliked the advertising business and decided to return to his first love—making films. In January of 1974, he began work at the United Indians of All Tribes Foundation in Seattle, Washington, where he created a media center, trained other young Native Americans in the art of filmmaking, and began making films in earnest. One of his first films for the foundation, *An Act of Self Determination,* was funded by the Bureau of Indian Affairs (BIA) in 1974 to explain the BIA's policy on the subject.

The Shaping of American Thought

Since Europeans first came in contact with Indians, white people have recorded images of the Native people in America, first with drawings, then paintings and photographs, and finally with moving pictures, beginning in 1894 with Thomas Edison's kinetoscope pictures. In accounts ranging from silent films to made-for-television movies, Indians were portrayed as savage, ignorant, lazy, shrieking murderers who scalped their victims. Although many movies featuring Indians were filmed on location at reservations around the country to give them an aura of authenticity, white men typically wrote the scripts, directed the action, and even played the roles of the Indians. As a result, perceptions held by the writers, directors, and even actors shaded the image of what the American public saw on the screen.

The films did not show the immense diversity that existed among the hundreds of different Native American cultures. The films also did not show the moral conflict created with the invasion of the white culture, or the devastation wrought when Euro-Americans took land, split up families, and destroyed whole villages. One of the better known examples of the dominant film caricature of Indians was the 1939 Oscar-winning western *Stage Coach,* starring John Wayne. In that film, Geronimo supposedly has broken out of the reservation and is dashing across Arizona and New Mexico killing, raping, and burning anyone and anything in his path. When the stage coach on which Wayne is riding is attacked by the "savage Apaches," Wayne fends off the attack until the cavalry arrives to save the day. It was a movie designed to make viewers walk away feeling good about themselves and the world in which they live.

"I clearly remember sitting, at the age of 12, in a darkened theater on a Saturday afternoon watching the larger than life images of the movie *Stage Coach,*" Lucas wrote in an introduction to his "Images of Indians" film series. "I suddenly found myself spontaneously cheering for the cavalry along with the rest of the audience. As the realization of what I was doing hit, I was devastated." Lucas then realized that film had the power to influence and manipulate not only white people's thoughts, feelings, and opinions, but also the way Native Americans thought and felt about themselves. He claimed that on that day, his idea for "Images of Indians" was born.

In 1979, Lucas began the long process of bringing his youthful idea into reality. It resulted in a five-part, Public Broadcasting Service (PBS) series, which he wrote, co-produced, and co-directed. The film examined the distortions, misrepresentations, and stereotypes of Indians that Hollywood filmmakers perpetuated in films and on television. It also questioned the impact those images have had on the self-esteem and self-image of Native Americans. In an interview with Catherine A. Clay, Lucas explained his primary goal as a filmmaker: "The underlying issue is how to get non-Indians to look at us as human beings ... even to get Indians, who often lack self-esteem, to see themselves as human beings." The "Images of Indians" series won a special achievement award for documentary film in 1980 from the American Indian Film Institute, and in 1981 won the Prix Italia Award.

Forms Independent Film Production Company

In 1980, Lucas decided it was time to strike out on his own, and he formed the Phil Lucas Production Company, of which he is president. He not only produced many of his early films, but also wrote and directed them. Much of his work reflects his desire to bridge the gap of understanding between the white world and Native Americans, while also dispelling the myths surrounding the latter. In 1989 he

applied his multiple talents to the television program *Beyond Hunting and Fishing,* which documents the economic successes of British Columbian Indians. Also that year he produced a 15-part series, "Native Indians: Images of Reality," for the Canadian Knowledge Network. That series and another 11-part series produced the following year by the same title examine from the Indians' perspective what their lives are like. *Broken Chain,* which Lucas co-produced in 1993 for Turner Network Television, is a historical drama that looks at the Iroquois Confederacy's relationships to Americans and the British during the American Revolution. It starred Native American actors Wes Studi, Floyd Westerman, and Graham Greene, as well as English actor Pierce Brosnan. Among other things, the film emphasizes the contributions the Iroquois Confederacy made to democracy and the influence the Constitution of the Five Nations had on the American Constitution.

Although making films to help non-Indians better understand Native Americans has been part of his focus, Lucas also uses the medium to address some of the problems facing many Native Americans. For example, treatment for alcoholism, AIDS, and sexual abuse have been featured in several of his documentaries. In 1985 and 1986, he produced, directed, and wrote a two-part documentary, *The Honor of All,* about the Alkali Lake Band's successful rehabilitation from alcoholism, and how they combined modern treatment methods with traditional Native beliefs to achieve it. That film also aired on PBS and was selected in 1988 for an INPUT Award. Lucas produced and directed "Lookin' Good" for the U.S. Department of Education in 1988, which was a two-part series featuring drug and alcohol prevention for junior high school students. The series was distributed to all the major public schools in the country and to schools at U.S. military bases. His 1990 documentary *I'm Not Afraid of Me* profiled a young mother and her daughter infected with the AIDS virus. Lucas later made a music video featuring a song written by the mother. His 1992 film, *Healing the Nation,* focused on the efforts of the Nuu-Chan-Nulth Nation to end the sexual abuse cycle in families within their community.

A New Form of Storytelling

Storytelling is one of the highly honored tribal traditions among Native Americans, and film has provided a new medium to pass along the myths, legends, and traditions to young people more interested in Saturday morning cartoons than in elders reminiscing about the past. Lucas, who does not see himself as a storyteller, does put his skills to use to pass along some of the history and morality lessons that help make up the Native American culture. In 1982, he wrote, directed, and produced *Nez Percé: Portrait of a People* for the National Park Service. Two years later, he wrote, directed, and produced *The Great Wolf and Little Mouse Sister* and *Walking with Grandfather,* which were pilot programs for PBS. Those two films won the 1984 award for best animated short subject from the American Indian Film Institute. The pilot program *Walking with Grandfather,* which brought to life some of the traditional Native American children's stories, was expanded into a six-part series in 1988 and aired on PBS. Lucas also wrote, directed, and produced for television *Voyage of Rediscovery,* which tells the story of a troubled British Columbian Indian youth, Frank Brown, who is exiled from his village for eight months by a judge (with his family's consent). The boy is sent to an island, where he learns to survive in the traditional manner of his people. As a result of his experiences, the boy later helps revive the making of ocean-going canoes once used by the Native people of the West Coast.

Sometimes for fun or when in a bind, Lucas also has appeared in front of the camera. He has acted in the Columbia Broadcasting System (CBS) series "Northern Exposure" twice, first as an accountant in the segment *Soapy Sanderson* in 1990, and then as an Indian in the segment *What I Did for Love* in 1991. He also has been a technical and cultural content advisor for that acclaimed series, as well as for the series "MacGyver." In 1992, the actor scheduled to play an Iroquois Sachem ["Chief"] in Lucas' movie *Broken Chain* became ill with a kidney infection shortly before filming began and was unable to work. Since producers are responsible overall for obtaining the actors, and the director and crew thought he fit the role, Lucas filled in as the Sachem.

Producers of films also must find the money to pay the costs of making the movie or television program. That has not been an easy task for Native American producers wanting to make films from the Indians' point of view. It is an especially difficult task when the production is a documentary instead of a potential blockbuster drama or comedy.

Lucas stays busy tracking down government agencies, tribal groups, and other organizations willing to invest the capital needed for his productions. He has succeeded in finding funds for the more than 60 films and television programs he has to his credit.

SOURCES:

Books

Hirschfelder, Arlene, and Martha Kreipe de Montaño, *Native American Almanac,* New York, Prentice Hall, 1993; 177-188.

Native North American Almanac, edited by Duane Champagne, Detroit, Gale Research, 1994; 763-767, 795, 1097-1098.

Periodicals

Weatherford, Elizabeth, "Starting Fire with Gunpowder," *Film Comment,* 28:3, May-June 1992; 64-67.

Other

Lucas, Phil, "Biography and Resume," 1994.
Lucas, Phil, "Images of Indians," 1994.
Lucas, Phil, interview with Catherine A. Clay conducted July 28, 1994.

—Sketch by Catherine A. Clay

Peter MacDonald
1928-
Navajo tribal leader

Peter MacDonald served as a popular but controversial tribal chairman of the Navajo Tribal Council for almost four terms. He was born on a goatskin in a hogan on the Navajo reservation near Teec Nos Pos ["Cottonwoods in a Circle"] on December 16, 1928. His maternal grandfather Left Curley Hair, who had been the second chairman of the Navajo Tribal Council, and his maternal grandmother, Little Grandmother, were imprisoned in 1864 for four years after having walked 300 miles to Fort Sumner, New Mexico. After the Treaty of 1868, they were released and walked the 300-mile trip back to the Navajo Reservation. MacDonald's father was Daghalani Begay ["Many Whiskers' Son"] and his mother was Glahhabath ["Many Warriors Over the Hill"].

MacDonald was taught as a child to become a medicine man. When he went to school, his teacher could not pronounce his Indian name so he took the name MacDonald from the children's song, "Old MacDonald Had a Farm." MacDonald dropped out of school in the sixth grade; and when he was 15, he lied about his age and joined the U.S. Marines. During World War II, he was one of the Navajo Code-Talkers of the South Pacific who spoke their Native language to deliver secret messages over the radio. Later he finished his high school equivalency and in 1951 attended Bacone Junior College where he earned an associates degree. In 1957, MacDonald earned a degree in electrical engineering from the University of Oklahoma. After graduating from college, MacDonald was hired by Hughes Aircraft Company in El Segundo, California. Beginning as a junior engineer, within a few years he advanced to management in the Aerospace Group working on the Polaris missile guidance system.

Returns to Reservation to Lead His People

In 1963, Perry Allen, first chief prosecutor for the Navajo Nation under tribal chairman Raymond Nakai, asked MacDonald to return to the reservation to direct the newly formed Manage Methods and Procedures office. MacDonald accepted the position and took a leave of absence from Hughes. He was later appointed director of the Office of Navajo Economic Opportunity (ONEO) by Nakai. Because the Bureau of Indian Affairs (BIA) wanted to manage the

Peter MacDonald

$900,000 ONEO budget itself and MacDonald wanted to have the money sent directly to ONEO, a battle ensued and MacDonald won; he then decided to stay on the reservation. In 1970 MacDonald was elected tribal chairman and continued as chairman for three four-year terms. Before MacDonald became chairman, the BIA negotiated for the tribe and failed in their efforts to improve conditions for the Native Americans.

The unemployment rate was 40 percent and his people were spread out over 17 million acres encompassing three states—Arizona, New Mexico, and Utah. Throughout his career as tribal chairman, he was a controversial and often outspoken representative of the nearly 200,000-member tribe. In 1975, the American Indian Movement (AIM), seized Fairchild Camera and Instrument Corporation in New Mexico and MacDonald was asked to get them out. When he refused, the plant closed. Within a few years, MacDonald raised employment from 900 to over 5,000 by approaching big companies in the private sector to bring business to the reservation. But during his reign as chairman, he made enemies along the way.

Credited with bringing the Navajo people into the modern world, MacDonald promised to bring his people independence from government interference and gain control over the natural resources on the reservation. Federal regulations and bureaucracy had prevented the Navajos from developing much of the land. His first goals were to bring jobs and self-determination to the Navajo people. He referred to this as the time of "nation-building." He traveled to Washington to lobby for his people and during that time, he worked in Republican politics on the Committee to Reelect the President—then Richard M. Nixon. At that time a land dispute between the Hopi and Navajo tribes concerning 1.8 million acres became a major issue in Congress. The Democratic candidate for President, George McGovern, who was chairman of the Senate Subcommittee on Indian Affairs, supported the Navajo position on the land dispute. MacDonald, who had been scheduled to speak at the Republican Convention in Miami in 1972, announced he might back McGovern for President. This angered Barry Goldwater, Republican senator from Arizona, who later took the side of the Hopi in the land dispute. However, in 1974, the law was passed granting the Hopi control of the land; and more than 7,000 Navajos had to be relocated in one of the largest forced relocations in the United States. After MacDonald's reelection in 1976, Goldwater asked for an investigation into Navajo tribal finances, and MacDonald was indicted for filing false travel vouchers. Represented by F. Lee Bailey, MacDonald was acquitted for lack of evidence; moreover, Bailey charged Goldwater with holding a political vendetta against MacDonald.

After serving three terms as tribal chairman, MacDonald lost to Peterson Zah in 1982. MacDonald then accepted a position as a marketing director for a nuclear-power-plant-equipment manufacturer. He was very successful in this position but when the next election for tribal chairman came up in 1986, he ran again and won by a narrow margin over his opponent Zah. MacDonald's lavish lifestyle of using chartered planes, taking expensive trips, and riding in chauffeur-driven cars did not help his popularity while many Navajo people still lived without electricity. But he was still considered an asset to the Navajo people; he was an aggressive negotiator for the tribe, persuading government and business alike to build and develop on Navajo land. After his reelection in 1986 he created 2,000 construction jobs and 800 full-time jobs in many different industries.

Scandal Haunts MacDonald

MacDonald organized and held the first Navajo Economic Summit in July of 1987. Notable leaders from government and business attended the two-day meeting, including five U.S. senators, congressmen, and other government officials, executives from major businesses, as well as journalists from across the country. At the same time, it was reported that MacDonald had been involved in a land deal which had reaped a profit of $7.2 million, and that the brokers involved in the deal had been close friends of his. MacDonald had purchased the Big Boquillas Ranch for the Navajo tribe for $33.4 million immediately after the 491,000-acre ranch was purchased by Tracy Oil and Gas Company from California for $26.2 million. The president

of Tracy was also a MacDonald associate. During the investigation, a special Senate committee was formed and received permission to use surveillance and telephone taps spurred by a series of stories in the *Arizona Republic* about allegations of fraud between the BIA and energy companies. After an investigation into allegations that MacDonald had taken bribes from outside businesses, the Senate Select Committee on Indian Affairs held hearings looking into the charges. MacDonald asked the tribal council to support him with legal help and to allow him to retain his $55,000 annual salary. The council gave him his annual salary but put him on indefinite leave. Although Zah and his followers had pushed to remove MacDonald for more than a year, the tribe's constitution made it almost impossible for the 88-council members to recall the chairman. Later in 1989, the council suspended MacDonald after he was charged with corruption by the U.S. Senate Committee.

The turmoil created by the charges against MacDonald caused a rift among his people. Some of MacDonald's supporters stormed into tribal headquarters in Window Rock, Arizona, in 1989 and the ensuing battle with tribal police left two of the protesters dead and several people severely injured. At the hearings, his son Peter "Rocky" MacDonald, Jr., the broker who had sold the Big Boquillas Ranch to the tribe, and other associates claimed that MacDonald had taken bribes and kickbacks from many deals with outside "white" or "Anglo" businesses. MacDonald's nickname on the reservation was "MacDollar." Although MacDonald denied the charges, in October of 1990, he and his son were both convicted on corruption charges. MacDonald received six years in prison, an $11,000 fine and five years of community service. In 1992, he was charged with racketeering and sentenced to five years; and in 1993 he received a sentence of 14 and a half years on charges of conspiracy and burglary in a 1989 riot at Window Rock.

Receives Awards and Commendations

During his career, though, MacDonald received many awards and commendations. In 1970, he received a Presidential Commendation for exceptional services to others, and a citation as Distinguished American from the National Institute for Economic Development. In 1971 he received a citation as Distinguished Baconian from Bacone Junior College, Oklahoma, and he was chosen as Arizona Indian of the Year. His other awards and honors include the Good Citizenship Medal, National Society of Sons of the American Revolution in 1972, the Silver Beaver Award from the Kit Carson Council of the Boy Scouts of America in 1973, and a *Time* magazine citation as "One of the 200 Rising American Leaders" in 1974. He was also inducted into the Engineering Hall of Fame at the University of Oklahoma in 1975.

SOURCES:

Books

Dobyns, Henry F., and Robert C. Euler, *The Navajo People,* Indian Tribal Series, 1972.

Reference Encyclopedia of the American Indian, fifth edition, edited by Barry T. Klein, Todd Publications, 1992; 931-932.

MacDonald, Peter, and Ted Schwarz, *The Last Warrior: Peter MacDonald and the Navajo Nation,* Crown (Library of the American Indian), 1993.

Periodicals

Atchison, Sandra D., and Peter Finch, "Suddenly Peter MacDonald is Business' Best Friend," *Business Week,* August 10, 1987; 64.

Atchison, Sandra D., "Bad Day at Window Rock," *Business Week,* March 6, 1989; 32.

Baker, James N., and Michael Reese, "Casting a Long Shadow," *Newsweek,* January 2, 1989; 32.

Lamar, Jacob V., Jerome Cramer, and Nancy Harbert, "Letting Down the Tribe," *Time,* March 6, 1989; 30.

Shapiro, Joseph P., "Up by the Bootstraps is an Uphill Fight for Indians," *U.S. News & World Report,* February 22, 1988; 26-27.

Tolan, Sandy, "Showdown at Window Rock," *New York Times,* November 26, 1989; 28.

Trewhitt, Henry, "A Mighty Tribe's Dilemma," *U.S. News and World Report,* November 26, 1990; 33.

"Turmoil in the Navajo Nation," *Time,* February 27, 1989; 25.

—*Sketch by Phyllis "Picturestone" Noah*

Wilma Pearl Mankiller (right) with Phillip Martin

Mangas
See Coloradas, Mangas

Wilma Pearl Mankiller
1945-
Cherokee tribal leader

Wilma Pearl Mankiller is both the first woman Deputy Chief and first woman Principal Chief of the Cherokee Nation of Oklahoma. She overcame many personal tragedies and returned home to Mankiller Flats, Oklahoma, to establish herself as a political power working for the betterment of all people. Mankiller was born at Tahlequah, the capitol of the Cherokee Nation, in November 1945, and was raised until she was ten years old at Mankiller Flats. Her father is Charlie Mankiller, Cherokee, and her mother is Irene Mankiller, Dutch-Irish. She has four sisters and six brothers.

Trail of Tears

Mankiller's great-grandfather was one of the over 16,000 Cherokees, Choctaws, Creeks, Chickasaws, Seminoles, and African slaves who struggled along the Trail of Tears to Oklahoma during the removal period, under Andrew Jackson's presidency in the 1830s. According to Carl Waldman in *Atlas of the North American Indian,* their journey was one of much pain and death: "At least a quarter of the Indians died before even reaching the Indian Territory. And many more died afterward, as they struggled to build new lives in the rugged terrain, with meager supplies and surrounded by hostile western Indians."

The Mankillers were very poor in Oklahoma, their ancestors being deposited there in 1838 and 1839, and it was difficult for Mankiller's father to maintain his family with any semblance of dignity. Although they did not want to move to California, Charlie Mankiller thought he could make a better life for them there and accepted a government offer to relocate. However, program promises faltered, money did not arrive, and there was often no employment available, so their life did not improve after their arrival in San Francisco.

The children were homesick even before they started for California. As Mankiller recalled in her autobiography, *Mankiller: A Chief and Her People,* "I experienced my own Trail of Tears when I was a young girl. No one pointed a gun at me or at members of my family. No show of force was used. It was not necessary. Nevertheless, the United States government through the Bureau of Indian Affairs, was again trying to settle the 'Indian problem' by removal. I learned through this ordeal about the fear and anguish that occur when you give up your home, your community, and everything you have ever known to move far away to a strange place. I cried for days, not unlike the children who had stumbled down the Trail of Tears so many years before. I wept tears that came from deep within the Cherokee part of me. They were tears from my history, from my tribe's past. They were Cherokee tears."

In California, cringing at the snickering that always followed the school roll call when the teacher said "Mankiller," she finished high school and pursued higher education. In the 1960s she attended Skyline Junior College in San Bruno then San Francisco State College. At San Francisco State she met and married Hector Hugo Olaya de Bardi. In 1964 they had a daughter, Felicia, and in 1966 another, Gina. In college, Mankiller was introduced to some of the Native Americans who would soon occupy and reclaim Alcatraz Island for the Native American people.

Alcatraz Occupation Fuels Political Awakening

The "invasion" of Alcatraz by the Native Americans quickly became a focal point for many Native people, Mankiller included. Her political activist "button" flipped to "on." Because of the bold move onto Alcatraz by San Francisco State student and Mohawk Richard Oakes, along with his "All Tribes" group, Mankiller realized that her mission in life was to serve her people. She yearned for independence, something that caused a conflict with her marriage. "Once I began to become more independent, more active with school and in the community, it became increasingly difficult to keep my marriage together. Before that, Hugo had viewed me as someone he had rescued from a very bad life," she noted in her autobiography. In 1974 she was divorced and became a single head of the household. Mankiller longed to do more for her people. Soon she was volunteering to work for attorney Aubrey Grossman of San Francisco, who was defending the Pit River people against charges from Pacific Gas and Electric Company.

There were many political and social movements across America during the 1960s. To many Native people across America, however, the defiant occupation of Alcatraz in a challenge of treaty rights, which led to the arrest of many people, ushered in a new and real feeling of self-determination. "When Alcatraz occurred, I became aware of what needed to be done to let the rest of the world know that Indians had rights, too. Alcatraz articulated my own feelings about being an Indian," Mankiller stated in her autobiography. She became involved in the movement and began a commitment to serve the Native people to the best of her ability in the area of law and legal defense.

Endures Personal Tragedies and Health Problems

In 1960, Mankiller's brother Bob was badly burned in a fire. Not wanting to be an added burden to the survival of the family, he had traveled north to pick apples in Washing-

ton State. In the chill of early morning, he mistakenly started a fire with gasoline instead of kerosine, and his wooden shack exploded in flames. Bob survived for only six days. He was Mankiller's role model for a "care free" spirit.

In 1971, Mankiller's father died from a kidney disease in San Francisco, which she indicated in her autobiography, "tore through my spirit like a blade of lightning." The family took Charlie Mankiller home to Oklahoma for burial, then Mankiller returned to California. It was not long before she too had kidney problems, inherited from her father. Her early kidney problems could be treated, though later she had to have surgery and eventually, in 1990, she had to have a transplant. Her brother Donald became her "hero" by donating one of his kidneys so that she could live.

In 1976, Mankiller returned to Oklahoma for good and found time to pursue higher education. She enrolled in graduate courses at the University of Arkansas, Fayetteville, which required her to drive the distance daily. She was returning home one morning when an automobile approached her on a blind curve and, from seemingly nowhere, another automobile attempted to pass it. She swerved to miss the approaching automobile, but failed. The vehicles hurtled together, almost head on.

Mankiller was seriously injured, and many thought she would not survive. The driver of the other automobile did not. It turned out to be Sherry Morris, Mankiller's best friend. It was terribly difficult, both physically and emotionally, but Mankiller recovered. Shortly after this accident, she came down with myasthenia gravis, a muscle disease. Again her life was threatened, but her will to live and her determination to mend her body with the power of her mind prevailed.

Becomes Principal Chief of the Cherokee Nation

In 1983, Ross Swimmer, then Principal Chief of the Cherokee Nation of Oklahoma, asked Mankiller to be his Deputy Chief in the election, and she accepted. They won the election and took office on August 14, 1983. On December 5, 1985, Swimmer was nominated to head the Bureau of Indian Affairs in Washington, D.C., and Mankiller was sworn in as Principal Chief.

Mankiller overcame many tragedies to become a guiding power for the Cherokee people of Oklahoma and a symbol of achievement for women everywhere. Yet through all the trying times, she worried for all people everywhere and planned for their happiness. She herself found love and strength in Charlie Soap. She gives him much credit for her successes and her will to overcome the many obstacles that threatened her political and physical life after her return to Oklahoma.

Throughout her life, Mankiller has managed to not complain about how bad things are for herself, for her people, and for Native people in general, but instead to help make life better. Fittingly, she was entered into the Woman's Hall of Fame in New York City in 1994. She may not run for re-election as Principal Chief of the Cherokee Nation in 1995, but people everywhere have already benefitted from her display of endurance and courage.

SOURCES:

Mankiller, Wilma, and Michael Wallis, *Mankiller: A Chief and Her People,* New York, St. Martin's Press, 1993.
Waldman, Carl, *Atlas of the North American Indian,* New York, Facts on File, 1985.

—*Sketch by Darryl Wilson*

George Manuel

George Manuel
1921-1989
Shuswap tribal leader, activist, and author

George Manuel was a noted chief of the Shuswap tribe and a leader in several Native American organizations, including the National Indian Brotherhood, the Union of British Columbia Indian Chiefs, and the World Council of Indigenous Peoples. From positions of authority within these tribal alliances, Manuel fought with federal authorities for the advancement of aboriginal land claims in British Columbia. An articulate spokesman as well as a gifted writer, Manuel skillfully presented his arguments supporting the rights of Native Americans numerous times before the Canadian government and outlined the philosophical and spiritual foundations of his people in several publications. The most notable expression of Manuel's personal philosophy can be found in *The Fourth World: An Indian Reality,* which was published in 1974.

The son of Louie Manuel, a Shuswap farmer, and his wife, Maria Andrew, George Manuel was born on February 17, 1921, in the Shuswap village of Neskainlith, which is located on the South Thompson River, about 30 miles east of Kamloops, in south-central British Columbia. Manuel spent much of his childhood with his grandparents, where he was exposed to the spiritual and medical philosophy of his grandfather, an influential tribal doctor who lived to the age of 101. These teachings later formed the foundation of Manuel's own philosophy and served as a motivating force behind his activities as a tribal leader and writer. At the age of 12, while attending a Kamloops industrial school, Manuel contracted tuberculosis of the hip, or what is today known as osteomyelitis (an inflammatory bone disease), and was transported to a children's hospital in Coqualeetza, British Columbia. In the years it took to recover from the disease and rehabilitate his legs, Manuel learned to read from the compassionate nurses who brought him books and sat with him for many hours. "I honour those women who kept me alive as though they were grandmothers of our own nation," wrote Manuel in *The Fourth World.* However, the instruction that the nurses provided Manuel marked the end of his formal education.

At the age of 21, Manuel left the hospital for good, and returned home to work at a lumber mill and, later, to start farming. After several years of rigorous work at both occupations, he developed a steady income and began to take an active political role in fighting for the rights of less fortunate Native Americans. Angered by the Bureau of Indian Affairs' (BIA) decision to stop paying for medical services rendered to natives, Manuel made his first formal initiative to organize the tribes of British Columbia in opposition to the Canadian government. From his position as Shuswap chief, he began to bring the native people of the Interior Salish region together, forming, in 1958, the Aboriginal Native Rights Committee of the Interior Tribes, an organization whose composition represented an unprecedented level of direct intertribal involvement. Under Manuel's leadership, the group submitted to the Ottawa parliamentary committee a lengthy report protesting government policies on liquor prohibition, education reform, voting rights, and land claims. While the government supported the rhetoric of the proposal, their response, as Manuel writes, "came to sound as hollow as a gutted rabbit." Nevertheless, a foundation upon which future tangible reforms could build was put in place as a result of the organization's and the committee's work. During the next three decades, Manuel continued to fight for the rights of Native Americans as the leader of several intertribal groups, serving as president of the National Indian Brotherhood from 1970 to 1976, the Union of British Columbian Indian Chiefs from 1977 to 1981, and the World Council of Indigenous Peoples in 1975 and 1981. At his death in 1989, Manuel was survived by eight children, the product of two marriages which had ended in divorce.

The importance of Manuel to his people and to the world's understanding of the Native American experience, however, cannot be limited to his actions within these organizations. The impact of his life must also be measured by the force and insight of his autobiographical and philosophical writings. In his development of the concept of "the Fourth World," Manuel called for a new relationship between aboriginal and European cultures. Rather than considering indigenous people within the concept of the Third World, as inferior to the technologically advanced First and Second Worlds, Manuel argued that Western culture had much to learn from his people. He suggested, for instance, that the future of the world depended upon "the utilization of technology and its life-enhancing potential within the framework of the values of the peoples of the Aboriginal World." The clarity of this vision led Vine Deloria, Jr., to conclude in the introduction to *The Fourth World,* that "George Manuel may be Canada's greatest prophet and to refuse to consider his words of advice may be the ultimate folly of our times."

SELECTED WRITINGS BY MANUEL:

District Six, Longmans, Green, 1967.
White Man's Whitewash, National Indian Brotherhood, 1972.
With Michael Posluns, *The Fourth World: An Indian Reality,* New York, Free Press, 1974.
Indian Control of Indian Education, edited by Bruce Gealy and V. Kirkness, 1977.

SOURCES:

Contemporary Authors, Volume 107, Detroit, Gale Research, 1983; 311.
Manuel, George, and Michael Posluns, *The Fourth World: An Indian Reality,* New York, Free Press, 1974.
Native North American Almanac, edited by Duane Champagne, Detroit, Gale Research, 1994; 1099.

—*Sketch by Jason Gallman*

Manuelito
1818(?)-1894
Navajo tribal leader
Also known as Hastin Ch'ilhajinii/Childhajin ["The Man of the Black Weeds"], Hashkeh Naabah ["The Angry Warrior"], Little Manuel, and Pistol Bullet

Manuelito was a tribal leader who led his warriors in the Navajo wars of 1863-1866. He and his followers were the last to surrender after Kit Carson's scorched earth cam-

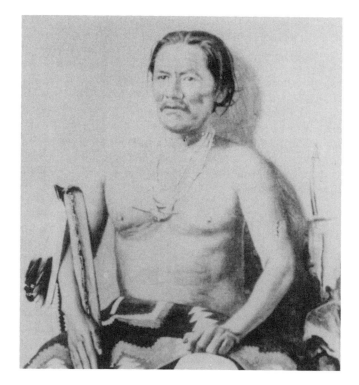

Manuelito

paign to force them to relocate to the Bosque Redondo Reservation near Fort Sumner. As their leader, Manuelito was a source of support and encouragement during their days in confinement. He pleaded with the government for the release of his people to be returned to their homeland, and lead them back from exile in 1868. There he was selected to be the head of tribal police. In his later years he advocated education for his people in the hopes that they might improve their lives.

Manuelito was born a member of the To'Tsohnii ["Big Water"] clan in 1818, in southeastern Utah, probably near Bears' Ear Peak. He was a powerful warrior who rose to prominence among his people during years of attacks and raids against Mexicans, U.S. army troops, and neighboring Indian tribes. In 1855, he became headman of his tribe, succeeding Zarcillas Largas ["Long Earrings"] who resigned because of his inability to control his warriors. Manuelito had two wives—the first was the daughter of Narbona, the great Navajo leader, and the second a Mexican woman named Juana.

The Navajo Indians then lived in the southwest, in what is now the states of Utah, Colorado, Arizona, and New Mexico. Their territory was bordered by four mountains which they considered sacred. They believed they could only be happy if they stayed within the confines of those boundaries. They called themselves Dineh or Diné, which means "the people." Navajo was a name given to them by the Spanish. They made their living by raising sheep, by hunting wild game, by growing wheat, corn, melons, and peaches, and by gathering wild pinon nuts and berries.

The Navajo's territory had been claimed by many nations, including the Spanish, the Mexicans, and the Americans, for many years. The signing of the Treaty of Guadalupe Hidalgo in 1848, marked the end of the Mexican-American War. Under this treaty Mexico ceded to the United States the present-day states of Texas, New Mexico, Arizona, Colorado, Utah, Nevada, and California. All Mexicans who were living in that region became U.S. citizens automatically, but the Indians did not. The U.S. Government considered itself responsible for the protection of its citizens in the territory from the Indians and instructed the Navajos to stop all raids against Americans and Mexicans.

The Government Moves In

In 1855, Fort Defiance was built in the heart of Navajo country in Canyon de Chelly. The same year the Navajos signed a treaty decreasing the size of their territory to 7,000 square miles, of which only 125 square miles were suitable for cultivation. The Navajo leaders found it too difficult to keep their people from raiding neighboring Indian or American settlements, and clashes between the Indians and the settlers continued.

In 1858, the pasture land around Fort Defiance became a point of contention when the new post commander, Major William T. H. Brooks decided that he wanted to use the land as grazing ground for the army's horses. Brooks ordered Manuelito to move his livestock or they would be killed. Manuelito, whose father and grandfather before him had used the land to graze their livestock, refused to give it up. Under Brooks' orders, the army shot and killed 60 of Manuelito's horses and over 100 of his sheep. The Navajos were outraged by the slaughter of their leader's livestock and retaliated by killing a negro slave who belonged to Major Brooks. Brooks ordered the killer to be found and turned in, and the army began to harass the Indians. Manuelito attempted to settle the matter, but assaults against the Navajos continued. After several weeks of fighting, the Navajo chiefs went to the fort to sign a peace treaty promising to remain on their land.

In 1860, many of the troops began to leave the fort to join the Civil War. With the strength of the army decreased, the Indians saw an opportunity to attack the fort and run the intruders out of their country. The headmen held a council to discuss their plans. Manuelito, Barboncito, and Herrero Grande were in favor of the attack. Ganado Mucho, another headman, opposed the plan. The Navajos invited other tribes of the region, including the Utes, Apaches, and Pueblos to join them in war. On April 30, 1860, between one and two thousand warriors stormed the fort. However, the army had been warned of the impending attack and was prepared with canons and guns ready when the Indians arrived. The warriors made an impressive show against the well armed troops, but were driven back. Many warriors were killed, and the rest retreated to their stronghold in the Chuska Mountain canyons. Colonel Edward R. S. Canby pursued them but the Indians eluded him in the many hiding places of Canyon de Chelly.

The government stepped up its efforts to control the hostiles. On June 23, 1863, General James H. Carleton sent a message from Fort Wingate to the Navajo headmen, demanding that they turn themselves in by July 20 or face the possibility of war if they did not. Carleton wanted to convince the Indians that they could no longer resist the power of the U.S. government. He believed that they had no choice but to give up their land and relocate to a new home beyond the Rio Grande. The deadline passed but the Navajos refused to surrender. Carleton then recruited Colonel Christopher "Kit" Carson to help him to persuade the Indians to leave their homeland. Carson began a scorched earth campaign to drive the Navajos out. He and his troops confiscated as much of the crops and livestock as they could use for their own purposes and destroyed the rest. Fields of crops were burned, hogans were destroyed, and livestock was slaughtered.

With nothing left to eat but wild berries and pinon nuts, some of the Indians moved on to join other tribes. Manuelito and his band, however, went down into the Grande Canyon. Kit Carson and his men went back to Fort Defiance to wait for the winter when the Indians would be forced by starvation to surrender. The Indians who stayed struggled to survive as best they could on whatever wild foods they could gather in the Chuska Mountains. Many died of starvation or froze to death during the winter, yet they still refused to surrender. It was not until February of 1864 that thousands of weak, sick, and hungry Indians began to turn themselves in at Fort Defiance.

The Long Walk

On March 6, 1864, the soldiers at the fort formed the 2,500 refugees into a long line and started them on a long trek past the borders of their homeland to the reservation of Bosque Redondo near Fort Sumner. This was "the Long Walk", a part of Navajo history still remembered with great sorrow and bitterness. Many people died or were killed on that journey. The army had not supplied enough food, but the Indians were forced to continue marching onward in spite of hunger and cold. Those who were too sick, weak, or old to keep up were killed or left behind.

By the time the group reached the Rio Grande the spring melt had flooded the river, making it very treacherous to cross. The Indians tried to get across any way they could but many were swept away and drowned. At the end of their ordeal they arrived at the wasteland that was to be their new home, the Bosque Redondo reservation. This place that Carleton had promised would be a "garden of Eden" was nothing but a desolate, barren flatland with no means of support for the Indians. Carleton had not provided enough food or supplies for the large number of new inhabitants to the remote reservation, nor had he realized how difficult it would be for the Indians to become self-supporting as farmers on such a worthless piece of land.

Delgadito, Herrero Grande, Armijo, and Barboncito had all surrendered with their bands by September of 1864.

However, Manuelito and his followers held out longer than any of the others. Carleton sent Herrero Grande and five other Navajo headmen to find Manuelito and give him a message. He was advised to turn himself in peaceably or be hunted down and killed. Dee Brown records Manuelito's response in his book, *Bury My Heart at Wounded Knee.* According to Brown, Manuelito replied to his fellow tribesmen, "My God and my mother live in the West, and I will not leave them. It is a tradition of my people that we must never cross the three rivers—the Grande, the San Juan, the Colorado. Nor could I leave the Chuska Mountains. I was born there. I shall remain. I have nothing to lose but my life, and that they can come and take whenever they please, but I will not move. I have never done any wrong to the Americans or the Mexicans. I have never robbed. If I am killed, innocent blood will be shed." Herrero Grande went back to Carleton alone.

In September of 1866, however, Manuelito and 23 of his still surviving people were forced by hunger to surrender at Fort Wingate. He then joined the others at Bosque Redondo. The conditions at the reservation continued to worsen as each year the crops failed. About 2000 Navajos died at Bosque Redondo of disease or starvation. The horrific conditions that the Indians were forced to live under, as well as their continued longing to return home, increased anger and unrest among them.

In the late 1860s Manuelito traveled to Washington, D.C., to petition on behalf of his people for their return to their homeland. On May 28, 1868, General William T. Sherman and General Samuel F. Tappen called a council with the Navajo headmen Manuelito, Barboncito, Delgadito, Herrero Grande, Armijo, Largo, and Torivo. Manuelito pleaded for his people to be allowed to return to the Chuska mountains. General Sherman offered them land in Indian territory in Oklahoma instead. After much debate it was finally decided that the Navajos would be allowed to return home. They were happy to agree to any terms just to be in their beloved lands again.

The new treaty was signed June 1, 1868, at Fort Sumner. The Navajos promised never to fight again and to remain on the 5,500 square mile reservation in their former homeland that the treaty provided for them. The U.S. government promised to provide sheep, goats, farm tools and a yearly clothing allowance, as well as schools for their children.

Home from Exile

In the early morning hours on June 18, 1868, more than 7,000 Navajo people began their six week journey home from exile. Manuelito was one of two men in charge of leading the people safely home. Once they were back in their familiar environment the Navajos began to rebuild their lives. The area of land that was allotted to them was much less than what they had been accustomed to before their forced evacuation. They were no longer free to roam between the four sacred mountains that had previously been their boundaries. The U.S. government was slow to follow through with their promises and the Indians had many setbacks with their crops.

To try to maintain some sense of order the people were divided into groups with appointed leaders. Barboncito was appointed head chief; Manuelito and Ganado Mucho served as subchiefs. All three of them urged their people to live peacefully on the reservation and work hard to rebuild their herds and fields. Slowly the Navajo people began to recover and prosper. In 1870, Barboncito died and Ganado Mucho became head chief, while Manuelito became second in command. A Navajo police force, led by Manuelito, was established in 1872 to guard the reservation. He lived in an area the people called the "place dark with plants," which is now called Manuelito Springs. He was a popular leader, and his hogan was always full of his followers.

Even though Manuelito still commanded the respect of his people, the pressures of reservation made living difficult. After traders brought whiskey to the reservation, Manuelito began to drink. His last years were spent in and out of prison for drinking. Even so he continued to represent his people. In 1875, he traveled again to Washington, D.C., to meet with President Ulysses S. Grant to discuss his concerns about the construction of the railroad through Navajo grazing lands. Before his death in the winter of 1893, he traveled to the World's Fair in Chicago, where he was once again impressed by the white man's accomplishments. His counsel to his people is recorded by Marie Mitchell in her book, *The Navajo Peace Treaty,* 1868. On his return home he advised his people for the last time, "The white men have many things we Navajo need but we cannot get them unless we change our ways. My children, education is the ladder to all our needs. Tell our people to take it."

SOURCES:

Brown, Dee, *Bury My Heart at Wounded Knee,* New York, Holt, 1970; 11-33.

Dockstader, Frederick J., *Great North American Indians,* Van Nostrand Reinhold, 1977; 164-165.

Loh, Jules, *Lords of the Earth: A History of the Navajo Indians,* New York, Crowell-Collier Press, 1971; 9, 19, 23, 49, 87, 92, 104.

Mitchell, Marie, *The Navajo Peace Treaty,* 1868, Mason & Lipscomb, 1973; 46, 73, 105, 122.

Native North American Almanac, edited by Duane Champagne, Detroit, Gale Research, 1994; 1100.

Navajo Stories of the Long Walk Period, Navajo Community College Press, 1973.

Underhill, Ruth M., *The Navajos,* Norman, University of Oklahoma Press, 1956; 119, 134, 142, 152, 206.

Waldman, Carl, *Who Was Who in Native American History,* New York, Facts On File, 1990; 219.

Wood, Leigh Hope, *The Navajo Indians,* Chelsea House, 1991; 30.

—Sketch by Denise Marecki-Arriola

Mungo Martin
1879(?)-1962
Kwakiutl tribal leader and artist
Also known as Naqapenkim

Mungo Martin (right) with Dave Martin

Mungo Martin was the third highest chief of the Kwakiutl—or Kwagiulth/Kwak woka'wakw as they are often known—and an internationally known artist and craftsman highly regarded for his original carvings and restorations of totem poles. At a time when the Canadian government attempted to legislate the extinction of Native American art and language, Martin was instrumental in the survival of tribal traditions. By 1952, the political climate for Native Americans had changed and he was commissioned by the Provincial Government of British Columbia to display his work at Thunderbird Park, Victoria, enabling him to preserve numerous Native poles. Among his most famous original creations are a 127-foot pole—the tallest in the world—located in Victoria's Beacon Hill Park and a 100-foot totem commissioned by Queen Elizabeth to stand in Windsor Great Park as a celebration of the British Columbian provincial centennial in 1958. For his many contributions to Canada's artistic, cultural, and intellectual life, Martin was posthumously awarded a Canada Council medal in 1962, becoming the first Native American to receive the prestigious honor.

Martin, who was born in Fort Ruport, British Columbia, was the son of Yanukwalas ["No one leaves the house without a gift"], a leading Kwakiutl man, and Sarah Finlay, the daughter of a Hudson's Bay company man and a Kwakiutl girl. Martin estimated his date of birth—sometime in the spring of 1879—from the great Seattle fire of 1889, which he remembered witnessing as a boy of nine or ten during a trip south to pick hops with his family. As a baby, he was symbolically endowed with artistic gifts through a ritual in which four of his eyebrows were plucked to form a paintbrush. He was then placed in a wooden box drum, which was beaten to give him musical gifts. While still a young child, Martin's father died, and his mother married Charlie James, a noted carver who instructed Martin in the art forms of the Kwakiutl.

Defies Laws to Preserve Culture

Despite the proscriptions on Native American cultural expression enacted by the Canadian government in the earlier years of this century, Martin continued carving pieces in the tradition of his ancestors, openly defying the laws of the state while many others abandoned their art. In addition to painting and carving, Martin sought to preserve the language and folklore of the Kwakiutl, tape recording numerous traditional songs and stories. These cultural artifacts have made their way into such museums as Alert Bay, British Columbia's U'mista Cultural Centre, which stated in the *Seattle Times* that "Without Mungo Martin, many artistic features of the Kwakwaka'wakw, and much cultural knowledge, would have been lost forever." Or as *Seattle Times* art critic Deloris Ament concluded, Martin "represents the slender thread that carried tribal traditions from the past into the present."

Martin's artistic talents were presented in a 1991 U'mista Cultural Center display, the first international traveling museum exhibit of this breadth ever arranged by a Canadian native cultural center or museum. The exhibit, entitled "Mungo Martin: A Slender Thread," provided a younger audience with an opportunity to view more than 40 of Martin's productions, including masts, rattles, model totem poles, and other carvings, as well as 30 more carvings by Native artists who worked under his tutelage. One of the most stunning achievements in the collection, according to Ament, was a Chief Shakes Killer Whale hat, the "royal crown" of the Nanyaayi clan of the Stikene Tlingit, an elaborate crest carving made with alder, human hair, and abalone shell.

In addition to leaving an artistic legacy of his own, Martin went to great lengths to pass his skills on to future generations and preserve the fragile culture of his tribe. During the last ten years of his life, a period in which he was no longer encumbered by laws against native art, Martin restored many of the old poles that stood in the park of the Royal British Columbia Museum in Victoria and, while there, instructed novice artists in the traditional Kwakiutl carving style. One of his best students was his son-in-law, Henry Hunt, who became a famous carver himself, carrying on the restoration work of his stepfather at the museum and passing his skills on to two of his own sons, Tony and

Richard Hunt, and a cousin, Calvin Hunt, all of whom are recognized as notable artists in their own right.

Mungo Martin drowned on August 16, 1962, at the age of 83 while on a fishing trip off the Victorian coast. The events of his funeral served as testimony to the strength of his art and tribal leadership. After a day-long Kwakiutl mourning service authenticated by Martin's ritual art and his own tape-recordings of tribal songs, he was buried at sea by the Canadian Navy with every flag in port dropped to half mast, an honor unprecedented for a Native American. As Frederica De Laguna of *American Anthropologist* magazine concluded after attending the day's events, "Perhaps no Canadian Indian did more than Chief Martin to secure recognition and honor for the culture of his people."

SOURCES:

Books

Dockstader, Frederick J., *Great North American Indians,* New York, Von Nostrand Reinhold, 1977; 167-168.

Periodicals

Ament, Deloris Tarzan, "Burke Show Displays Tribal Art," *Seattle Times,* December 15, 1991.
De Laguna, Frederica, "Mungo Martin, 1879-1962," *American Anthropologist,* 65, August 1963; 894-896.
New York Times, obituary, August 18, 1962; 19.

—*Sketch by Jason Gallman*

Maria Montoya Martinez (left)

Maria Montoya Martinez
1887(?)-1980
Tewa San Ildefonso Pueblo potter
Also know as Poveka ["Pond Lily"]

Maria Montoya Martinez has been described by Richard L. Spivey, author of the biography *Maria,* as the most famous Indian artist of all time. Together with her husband, Julian Martinez, she brought about a revival of indigenous pottery-making techniques and led to innovations that transformed their craft into high art.

Martinez was the second daughter born to Tomas and Reyecita Peña Montoya in the San Ildefonso Pueblo of the Tewa linguistic family, about 20 miles northwest of Santa Fe, New Mexico. Guided by her aunt, Nicolasa Peña Montoya, a respected potter, Martinez made her first pottery as a child of seven or eight. She attended the government school in her pueblo and then was selected by the council to attend St. Catherine's Indian School in Santa Fe. She considered

becoming a school teacher, but her marriage to Julian Martinez directed her interests toward family life and pottery making. The couple shared artistic talents and sensitivities, as well as an openness to innovation, which shaped their successful pottery-making career for over 40 years. Martinez produced, shaped and polished vessels. Julian decorated and helped fire them. Martinez continued her work for more than 30 years after her husband died in 1943. Biographer Alice Marriot, in the foreword of her book *Maria: The Potter of San Ildefonso,* referred to Martinez as "a woman who has become in her own lifetime a legend."

Beginnings

Martinez and her husband Julian spent their honeymoon at the St. Louis World's Fair in 1904, demonstrating Pueblo pottery-making techniques and Pueblo dancing. By then pottery making in the Pueblo had been almost entirely replaced by inexpensive manufactured wares. In 1907 Julian began working at the Pajarito Plateau excavations of prehistoric Pueblo sites. Edgar Hewett, director of the project, asked him to copy pottery and wall designs. Hewett asked Martinez to try to duplicate a potsherd found at the site. Persistent experimentation with a variety of clays, polishings, and firings, led Martinez and her husband to recreate the ancient pottery which was thinner, harder, and more highly polished than pottery made in their Pueblo.

In 1911 the Museum of New Mexico in Santa Fe allowed Martinez and her husband, who worked there as a janitor from 1909 to 1912, to demonstrate their craft on site and to sell directly to the public. By 1915 Martinez had learned to create large pottery and was acknowledged as the master potter of San Ildefonso. Her classical shapes were perfectly rendered, her new shapes elegantly proportioned. Julian's decorative designs worked in harmony with the shapes and surfaces. He kept a notebook of designs and rarely repeated decorative drawings except for his famous avanyu, a mythical water serpent, and his feathers, adapted from the prehistoric Mimbres feather designs. By 1919 the couple had developed a black-on-black vessel.

Encouraged by the Museum of New Mexico, and Kenneth M. Chapman, who purchased the best examples of their black pottery, the couple witnessed continued increase in the worth of their work. Demand from the public led them to create prodigious amounts of dinnerware and housewares. Their black-on-black pottery gained distinction throughout the United States and in many museums worldwide. A critic of their work at the Museum of New Mexico in 1920, according to Spivey, compared it to "the best of the Orient or the Occident, ancient or modern." In 1923, in response to the demand from collectors, Martinez began to sign her pottery on a regular basis. As her fame and success grew, other Pueblo natives wanted to learn her craft. Eager to help others, Martinez held pottery classes at San Ildefonso and at the Indian School in Santa Fe.

Martinez and Julian had four children, Adam, Juan, Tony, and Philip. A daughter died in infancy. After Julian's death in 1943, Martinez collaborated with her daughter-in-law, Santana Martinez, Adam's wife. In 1956 her son Tony Martinez, who took his Indian name Popovi Da, became her partner. Many experts felt that this collaboration enabled Martinez to express the highest level of her creativity. After her death, the family tradition of pottery making was carried on by Maria's grandchildren, great-grandchildren, and great-great-grandchildren. Her grandson Tony Da and great-granddaughter, Barbara Gonzales are the most famous crafters. The younger potters, like Martinez, extended the boundaries of their craft, creating new styles while maintaining the family tradition of excellence.

Achieves National and International Acclaim

Throughout her lifetime Martinez received hundreds of awards and commendations, both national and international. Her first award came at the Santa Fe Indian Market in 1922 for pottery she created with other family members. In 1934, Martinez was awarded a bronze medal for Indian Achievement by the Indian Fire Council—the first Native American woman to receive the nation's most prestigious emblem of recognition for Native Americans. In 1954 the presented her with the Craftsmanship Medal, the nation's highest honor for craftsmanship. Martinez received several honorary degrees, and four invitations to the White House. Many of her awards recognized not only her superior craftsmanship, but her leadership in reviving a nearly extinct ancient craft and in developing and preserving it for her people.

Martinez's efforts transformed San Ildefonso from an economically poor farming community into one of the Pueblo Indian arts and crafts centers in the Southwest. A

gifted, generous woman of great humility, she told Spivey, "I just thank God because it's not only for me; it's for all the people. I said to my god, the Great Spirit, my Mother Earth gave me this luck. So I'm not going to keep it. I take care of our people." Her legacy lives on in the generations of potters she inspired and in the timeless art she created.

SOURCES:

Dittert, Alfred E., Jr., and Fred Plog, *Generations in Clay: Pueblo Pottery of the American Southwest,* Flagstaff, Northland Publishing, 1980.

Marriott, Alice, *Maria, the Potter of San Ildefonso,* Norman, University of Oklahoma Press, 1945.

Native American Women, edited by Gretchen M. Bataille, New York, Garland Publishing, 1993; 165-166.

Native North American Almanac, edited by Duane Champagne, Detroit, Gale Research, 1994; 84, 699, 718-719, 728.

Peterson, Susan, *Maria Martinez: Five Generations of Potters,* Washington, D.C., Smithsonian Institution Press, 1978.

Spivey, Richard L., *Maria,* Flagstaff, Northland Press, 1979.

—Sketch by Roberta Kaplan Gelatt

Massasoit
1600(?)-1661
Wampanoag tribal leader
Also known as Great Chief, Massassoit, Ousamequin, Woosamequin, and Yellow Feather

In concluding his article on Massasoit for the *Dictionary of American Biography,* James Truslow Adams sums up the standard view of this influential New England chief: "Always inclined to peace, even among his own race, Massassoit remained a faithful friend to the English throughout his entire life." Though there is a large measure of truth to this opinion, along with generations of schoolbooks presenting a eupeptic and rather bland portrait of Massasoit, it also misses many of the likely conflicts both within this powerful Indian leader and swirling about him.

Massasoit and the Pilgrims

As to the bare facts of the matter, from his home village in Pokanoket, near present-day Bristol, Rhode Island, Massasoit held sway over a number of related tribes in southeastern New England. Some months after the Pilgrims arrived in Plymouth in 1620, the Indian leader appeared in the new colony and offered friendship. After some negotiations, the chief signed a peace treaty with the English, one

Massasoit

vowing nonaggression and mutual defense in case either were attacked. It was a treaty and a friendship that Massasoit would keep for the next 40 years of his life.

Over the decades, the two groups exchanged amiable visits. When Massasoit took ill, Plymouth sent emissaries on the two-day trek through the forest to Pokanoket to help cure their ally. On several occasions, Massasoit or his fellow Wampanoags probably saved the colonists from slaughter by warning them of mischief brewing in warring tribes. When Roger Williams, a renegade religious thinker forced out of the rigid theocracy of the English towns, appeared cold and starving at Massasoit's door, the chief took the desperate man in and made him feel welcomed.

Little is known personally of Massasoit except that he was physically vigorous and when treating with the whites was "grave of countenance and spare of speech." Still, as might be expected, when in March of 1621 the great chief first appeared at the head of 60 warriors, face painted red and wearing a thick necklace of white beads, the sign of his authority, on a hill overlooking the hovels of tiny Plymouth, striking fear into the little band of Europeans huddled below, much more was going on than the beginning of friendship between a good-souled Wampanoag holding out the olive branch and the English settlers eager to return the gesture to their new Indian brothers.

For his part, despite his authority, Massasoit was in a threatened state. Disease had recently swept through the tribe, ravaging his people, and he had enemies eager to take advantage of the sharp reduction in the number of his warriors. To the west, across Rhode Island's Narragansett Bay

roved the powerful Narragansett tribe, eager to slaughter both Massasoit and the Wampanoags. To the east, the English, whatever their troubles, were rumored to have valuable trade goods and strange, new, fire-breathing weapons. Caught in the middle, then, between his traditional enemies to the west and the English on the coast to the east, Massasoit may well have thought he had little choice than to throw in his lot with the potentially helpful newcomers.

As to the situation of the English, when the Mayflower sailed back to England in the winter of 1620, it left behind a group of men, women, and children almost totally unprepared to deal with the realities of their new situation in a wild land. Around them as they shivered in their brush huts against the New England cold was the "howling wilderness," an endless, impenetrable forest full of, so they had heard, bloodthirsty savages, wolves, and, some thought, devils. The new settlers knew neither how to hunt, fish, plant, or build adequate shelters. They had few supplies to carry them through to spring. In their grinding circumstances, staying alive itself became the foremost issue. One by one they started dying of malnutrition, disease, and gnawing hunger. Only half of them survived that first winter, and those who remained, weakened, confused, had little hope for the future. It seemed they would soon all be gone, dying thousands of miles from home on this wild, foreign shore, their bones dragged into the forest by the fierce beasts who would consume their dead flesh.

Thus, when Massasoit and his 60 warriors stepped out of the wilderness and stood on the hilltop fearsomely looking down on Plymouth, and the few able-bodied colonists left scrambled for their guns, the settlers slowly realized they were confronting not enemies capable of killing off the remainder of the weakened settlers but friendly human beings who would give them food in exchange for baubles and, on top of that, help protect them against marauding tribes, Massasoit seemed a godsend, a blessing sent by Providence.

Massasoit and Squanto

What we have, then, in this meeting is not so much two human groups coming together in mutual benignity but in pledged cooperation, each for its own, self-serving advantages. Actually, the situation was far more convoluted than the immediate interactions of these two, small groups, and to catch the complexities requires some comment on the historical background behind the meeting of Massasoit and the colonists. Insights into this can be seen in the related story of Squanto, famous to schoolchildren for helping the Plymouth settlers even before the friendship with Massasoit began.

Years before, in 1614, an English sea captain had kidnapped a number of Indians in the area where the Plymouth colonists would later land and sold them as slaves in Spain. Through a fantastic turn of events, monks ransomed Squanto, who made his way to England and from there gained passage to his homeland. To his dismay, however, upon his arrival Squanto found his home village abandoned, ravaged by disease. Tribeless, he became a subject of Massasoit. When a year later the Pilgrims arrived, Squanto stepped out of the forest to greet them in English, and through his woodcraft he helped them survive their harsh conditions. Squanto's earlier friendship, then, helped ease the way for the friendship of the far more powerful Massasoit. Whatever the twists and turns of Squanto's story, it illustrates a larger set of negative circumstances. European contact with the Indians in the New England area had gone on for decades before the colonists set foot on Plymouth Rock, and it often was not kindly. Not only kidnappings and other violence took place between the sea captains and fishermen touching the New England shore and the Indians they met, but the Europeans unwittingly introduced diseases, among them smallpox, typhus, and measles. Lacking immunity to the new maladies, whole Indian villages fell before wave on wave of virulent epidemics sweeping up and down the coast. Understandably, most of the Indians, even those who had not yet seen white men, considered the newcomers to be both ruthless deprecators and bearers of deadly illnesses. In short, Indian societies already were in an unfriendly turmoil upon the colonist's arrival, and in light of this Massasoit's friendship was the decided exception.

Given the problems, despite some earnest efforts at good will, such as Massasoit's, the situation almost inevitably became worse. New colonists starting other settlements cared nothing about an old, carefully nurtured friendship. Land-poor in Europe, they had not pulled up stakes and risked the dangerous, months-long voyage across the stormy Atlantic Ocean to be restrained upon their arrival. What they wanted was land of their own, land that seemed theirs for the taking, except for the obstacles the native peoples, waxing ever fiercer in their resistance as the pressures of the invasion increased, represented. Further complicating the situation was the diversity of the settlers and the consequent rivalry among them. Originally conceived as a religious community with central and, hence, consistent, authority, Plymouth soon found itself assailed by Englishmen with a variety of often conflicting sacred and secular notions. In light of the turmoil within the white community itself, it was impossible to carry out a humane and consistent policy toward the Indians. Massive, bloody conflict was all but inevitable.

In the face of these building pressures and loss of land to the new colonists, Massasoit kept mending his good relations with the whites. In hindsight, depending on the perspective one wishes to take, the chief of the Wampanoags might be seen as exchanging his people's birthright for the trade goods, renown, and personal power he gained against the enemy Narragansetts through his associations with the whites. Whatever one's view, however, in Massasoit's friendship lies one of the grand ironies of New England history. Massasoit had taken a minority position by casting his fortunes with the English. As pressures against the Indians mounted, many of them resolved to unite and either drive out the invaders or die in the attempt. In this the peacemaker Massasoit became an unwilling instrument. Fourteen years after his death, his son Philip angrily burst into patriotic fervor and flew to the opposite extreme of his father by becoming the leader of what is known as King Philip's War, the bloodiest Indian-white conflict to rake New England.

SOURCES:

Adams, James Truslow, "Massasoit," in *Dictionary of American Biography,* Volume 6, Part 2, New York, Scribner's, 1933; 380-381

Biographical Dictionary of Indians of the Americas, Volume 1, Newport Beach, American Indian Publishers, 1991; 400-401.

Peirce, Ebenezer W., *Indian History, Biography, and Genealogy: Pertaining to the Good Sachem Massasoit,* North Abington, Zerviah Gould Mitchell, 1878.

Weeks, Alvin Gardner, *Massasoit of the Wampanoags,* Fall River, privately printed, 1919.

Wood, Norman B., *Lives of Famous Indian Chiefs,* Aurora, American Indian Historical Publishing Company, 1906; 65-84.

—Sketch by Peter Wild

John Joseph Mathews
1894-1979
Osage tribal leader and writer

John Joseph Mathews was a highly regarded writer who produced five significant books, two of which are important scholarly studies of his own Osage tribe. In addition, he was a widely respected leader of his tribe, serving on the Osage Tribal Council for eight years.

Mathews was born in Pawhuska, Oklahoma, the capital of the Osage Indian Reservation, on November 16, 1894. He was the eldest child of William Shirley Mathews, who ran an Indian trading post in Pawhuska and later founded the Citizen's National Bank of Pawhuska, and Eugenia Girardeau Mathews. Mathews was one-eighth Osage Indian by blood on his father's side of the family and therefore, possessed the minimum amount of Osage blood to be on the official tribal role. This was to bring great monetary benefits from 1917 onwards, when the Osage reservation became the site of an oil drilling bonanza, providing Mathews with financial independence for the remainder of his life.

Mathews played football and basketball at the Pawhuska high school and went on to study and play football at the University of Oklahoma, which he entered in 1914. His college career was interrupted by almost three years of service in the United States Army during World War I, first in the cavalry and later in the aviation section of the Signal Corps in France. Mathews then returned to the University of Oklahoma where he graduated a member of Phi Beta Kappa in 1920, majoring in geology. He was offered a Rhodes Scholarship to study at Oxford University but turned it down, choosing instead to attend Merton College at Oxford. Mathews received his Oxford B.A. in natural science in 1923.

Feeling no financial pressure to work right away, Mathews next studied at the School of International Relations at the University of Geneva. He then traveled extensively throughout Europe and North Africa. Following his return to the United States in the late 192Os, Mathews spent several years in the real estate business in Los Angeles. He was also briefly married during this period. Mathews returned to Pawhuska in 1929. It was at this time that he began writing magazine articles about his frequent hunting trips and the Osage tribe, which appeared in the University of Oklahoma's alumni magazine.

Launched Writing Career

In 1931 Mathews was bequeathed the diaries and notes of Laban J. Miles, who had been the federal agent assigned to the Osage tribe from 1878 to 1884 and again from 1889 to 1892. A friend of Mathews, Joseph Brandt, the founder and director of the University of Oklahoma Press, urged him to write a book about the Osages, based upon Miles' papers. Mathews did so in about five months during the summer and fall of 1932. The work was published under the title *Wah'Kon-Tah: The Osage and the White Man's Road* and became a surprising commercial success when it was recommended by the Book-of-the-Month Club in November 1932. Critics hailed the book as a lyrical evocation of the often difficult accommodation of the Osages to the white man's world. Writing the volume inspired Mathews to a lifetime of study of his tribe.

Mathews' next large literary project was a semi-autobiographical novel entitled *Sundown,* published in 1934. Probably because of the Great Depression, this book was not financially successful. However, it later attracted considerable attention as one of the earliest novels written about American Indians by an author of Indian blood.

Elected Tribal Leader

In 1934, Mathews was elected by popular vote to the Osage Tribal Council, despite the fact that he was only partially Osage. He was re-elected in 1938 and served until 1942. He was thus active in all tribal political affairs through the difficult years of the Depression and often served on delegations sent to Washington to seek federal assistance. One of the enduring results of Mathews' period on the council was the establishment of the Osage Tribal Museum in 1938. Under Mathews' leadership, the Museum became a showcase for tribal artifacts and a depository for tribal papers, as well as a meeting place and center of tribal life. In the 193Os, he built a stone house on tribal lands where he lived for the remainder of his life. Mathews wrote about his time there in *Talking to the Moon,* published in 1945. At this time, he also married Elizabeth Palmour, who thereafter assisted him in his scholarly research and typed his manuscripts.

Mathews' next book was *Life and Death of an Oilman: The Career of E. W. Marland,* published in 1951. Here Mathews drew on his training as a geologist, as well as his own political experiences, to paint a vivid portrait of his lifelong friend, Ernest Whitworth Marland, the oil tycoon and

Governor of Oklahoma from 1935 to 1939. His final and perhaps his most impressive work, *The Osages: Children of the Middle Waters* (1961), is a massive history of the Osage Indian Tribe, amounting to over 800 pages. Basing this piece upon exhaustive archival research, Mathews made judicious use of oral interviews of old persons within the tribe that were gathered over many years. The result was a nearly definitive history of the Osages.

Mathews lived happily on his small ranch for 18 years after the publication of *The Osages.* Though he wrote a long autobiography, it was never published. He died on June 11, 1979, leaving behind his wife Elizabeth; a daughter, Virginia Mathews; a stepson, John Hunt; and a stepdaughter, Ann Hunt Brown.

SELECTED WRITINGS BY MATHEWS:

Wah'Kon-Tah: The Osage and the White Man's Road, Norman, University of Oklahoma Press, 1932.
Sundown, London, Longmans, Green, 1934.
Talking to the Moon, Chicago, University of Chicago Press, 1945.
Life and Death of an Oilman: The Career of E. W. Marland, Norman, University of Oklahoma Press, 1951.
The Osages: Children of the Middle Waters, Norman, University of Oklahoma Press, 1961.

SOURCES:

Lottinville, Savoie, "In Memoriam: John Joseph Mathews, 1895-1979," *American Oxonian,* 67, fall 1980; 237-241.
Wilson, Terry P., "Osage Oxonian: The Heritage of John Joseph Mathews," *Chronicles of Oklahoma,* 59, fall 1981; 264-293.

—Sketch by John E. Little

McGinness, Duane
See Niatum, Duane

D'Arcy McNickle
1904-1977
Flathead writer, historian, and activist

As a writer, historian, activist, government project manager, community organizer, and university professor, McNickle's career was as diverse as his accomplishments. His voice was heard in the halls of Congress and the halls of universities, in homes on the reservation and homes in urban America. He was an advocate for Native rights both when Indian causes were championed and when Indian rights were being eliminated. Not only was he able to speak to non-Natives about the Native world, but he talked to the Natives about the changes coming from the non-Native world. Throughout it all, he was a cultural mediator, thoroughly at home in both worlds.

He was born William D'Arcy McNickle on January 18, 1904, in St. Ignatius, Montana. His mother, Philomena Parenteau married Irish rancher William McNickle and lived with him on the Flathead reservation. The Parenteaus, of Cree descent, had fled to Montana after the failure of the Métis uprising in 1885 and were formally adopted into the Flathead tribe.

In his early years, McNickle attended school on the reservation. Then over his own and mother's objections, he was sent to the Bureau of Indian Affairs boarding school at Chemawa for three years. He was shocked by the harsh, culturally insensitive attitude that permeated the school, preferring the schooling in Washington State and Montana. When he entered the University of Montana at the age of 17, he was drawn to the world of literature and the study of languages, including Greek and Latin. He was encouraged by one of his professors to attend Oxford. In 1925, he sold his tribal allotment and traveled to England. Difficulty with the transferability of his college credits kept him from matriculating, and, with money running out, he moved to Paris with uncertain thoughts of being a writer or a musician.

Returning to New York, McNickle took a series of jobs, including positions as editor for the Encyclopaedia Britannica and the National Cyclopaedia of American Biography. In November 1926 he married Joran Birkeland and they had a daughter, Antoinette. During his years in New York, he periodically attended courses at the New School for Social Research and at Columbia. However, he was continually working on his writing. He finished a number of short stories and revised his novel, which was published in 1936 as *The Surrounded*. During this period he changed his name from Dahlberg back to McNickle. When his mother had remarried, he had taken his step-father's last name to please them. After he and Joran divorced in 1938, he married Roma Kauffman and had a daughter, Kathleen.

Joins Collier Administration

When the Collier administration took over the Bureau of Indian Affairs (BIA), McNickle joined the staff as an administrative assistant. During his 16 years with the BIA, he held a number of positions, including field representative and director of tribal relations. He was a tireless advocate of Indian rights, believing in change, but change with respect and Native initiative. By 1944 he was aware of the necessity of unified political action on the part of tribal groups. He cofounded the National Congress of American Indians to create an effective Indian political voice.

In 1949 he published *They Came Here First: The Epic of the American Indian,* which drew on anthropological sources to chronicle Indian history and the interaction of Indians and settlers. This work initiated a series of publications that included his juvenile novel, *Runner in the Sun: A Story of Indian Maize* (1954), *Indians and Other Americans: Two Ways of Life Meet* (1959) with Harold Fey, and *Indian Tribes of North America* (1962). These last two books reviewed Federal Indian policy and the history of white/Indian interaction so as to explain the clash of values and cultural misunderstanding that have resulted in so much tragedy.

In the early 1950s the federal government increasingly strove for the termination of tribal groups and their relocation to urban centers. McNickle did not agree with the federal goals and resigned from BIA to pursue community development work with the American Indian Development Corporation. He worked extensively in Crownpoint, New Mexico, for a number of years before he moved on to other work with students and Indian communities. He sat on the United States Civil Rights Commission and worked on leadership workshops for Native students.

In 1966 he was awarded an honorary doctorate from the University of Colorado. Moving from community work to academia, McNickle accepted a professorship at the new Regina campus of the University of Saskatchewan. He was given the position of chairman and asked to set up a small anthropology department. In 1969, he married Viola Pfrommer.

In 1971, he published a biography of Oliver La Farge, *Indian Man: A Life of Oliver La Farge,* which was nominated for a National Book Award, and retired to Albuquerque to work on his writing. He remained on the editorial board of the Smithsonian Institution's revision of the *Handbook of North American Indians*. He also agreed to serve as founding director of the Newberry Library's Center for the History of the American Indian. During his retirement, he revised two of his books and wrote numerous book reviews and entries, but most importantly he worked on his novel, *Wind from an Enemy Sky*. In October of 1977, he died in Albuquerque of a massive heart attack.

SELECTED WRITINGS BY McNICKLE:

The Surrounded, New York, Dodd-Mead, 1936; reprinted, Albuquerque, University of New Mexico Press, 1978.

They Came Here First: The Epic of the American Indian, New York, Lippincott, 1949; reprinted, New York, Octagon, 1975.

Runner in the Sun: The Story of Indian Maize, New York, Winston 1954; reprinted, Albuquerque, University of New Mexico Press, 1987.

With Harold Fey, *Indians and Other Americans: A Study of Indian Affairs,* 1959; reprinted, New York, Harper, 1970.

The Indian Tribes of the United States: Ethnic and Cultural Survival, 1962; reprinted as *Native American Tribalism: Indian Renewals and Survivals,* New York, Oxford University Press, 1973.

Indian Man: A Life of Oliver La Farge, Bloomington, Indiana University Press, 1971.

The Hawk Is Hungry and Other Stories, edited by Birgit Hans, Tucson, University of Arizona Press, 1992.

SOURCES:

Owens, Louis, *Other Destinies: Understanding the American Indian Novel,* Norman, University of Oklahoma Press, 1992.

Parker, Dorothy, *Singing an Indian Song: A Biography of D'Arcy McNickle,* Lincoln, University of Nebraska Press, 1992.

Purdy, John Lloyd, *WordWays: The Novels of D'Arcy McNickle,* Tucson, University of Arizona Press, 1990.

Ruppert, James, *D'Arcy McNickle,* Boise, Boise State University, 1988.

—Sketch by James Ruppert

Russell C. Means

Russell C. Means
1939-
Lakota Sioux activist

Russell C. Means has been an outspoken Indian rights activist for more than two decades. The organizer of numerous protests against the U.S. government's treatment of Native Americans and a major figure in the American Indian Movement (AIM), Means is perhaps best known for leading a 71-day siege at Wounded Knee, South Dakota, which drew national attention to Indian-rights issues in the early 1970s. The head of the American Indian Anti-Defamation League since 1988, Means continues to fight for the unique identity and independence of Native Americans.

Russell Charles Means, who prefers the traditional term "Lakota" rather than the term "Sioux", which he views as a derogatory white word, was born November 10, 1939, on the Pine Ridge Reservation in South Dakota, the oldest son of Harold ("Hank") Means, a mixed-blood Oglala Sioux and Theodora (Feather) Means, a full-blood Yankton Sioux. He attended the Bureau of Indian Affairs (BIA) school on the reservation and later public schools in Vallejo, California. During his high school years, he transferred from the racially mixed Vallejo school to the almost all-white San Leandro High School where he experienced daily ethnic taunting. Not knowing how else to respond, Means at first fought back and then retreated into drugs and delinquency. After barely graduating from high school, he worked through various jobs and attended five colleges without graduating. He spent much of the 1960s drifting throughout the West, working as a cowboy, day laborer, and at an advertising firm. In 1969 he moved from a position on the Rosebud Sioux tribal council on the Rosebud Reservation in South Dakota to the directorship of the government-funded American Indian Center in Cleveland, Ohio.

In Cleveland, Means met Dennis Banks, one of the cofounders of the newly organized American Indian Movement, a militant Indian civil rights group. Inspired by Banks and his movement, he set up AIM's second chapter in Cleveland. Means became a national media figure representing dissident Indians on Thanksgiving Day in 1970 when he and a small group of other Indians confronted costumed "Pilgrims" on the Mayflower II in Plymouth, Massachusetts. Dressed in combination western and Indian style, he became an effective symbol for AIM. Eloquent and charismatic, he inspired support from local Indian people while his inflammatory statements riled non-Indians.

That same year, Means participated in a prayer vigil on Mount Rushmore, a symbolic demonstration of Lakota claims to Black Hills land. His next protest was to file a $9 million lawsuit against the Cleveland Indians baseball club for use of Chief Wahoo as a mascot, asserting in the suit that the symbol demeaned Native Americans. This latter action provoked Cleveland ball club fans, and led to Means' decision to resign his position at the Cleveland Center in 1972. He returned to South Dakota and participated in further activities intended to bring attention to Indian rights.

In February, 1972, Means led 1,300 angry Indians into the small town of Gordon, Nebraska, to protest the suspicious death of Raymond Yellow Thunder. The demonstration convinced town authorities to conduct a second autopsy, which eventually led to the indictment of two white townsmen for manslaughter. The Indian protest gained further success when the city council suspended a police officer accused of molesting jailed Indian women and then organized a multiracial human rights council. Violence against Indians increased all over the country that summer, leading to further defensiveness among local Indian people who felt they needed to arm themselves if they were to be the targets of murderous attacks.

At the annual Rosebud Sun Dance celebration, Means helped plan a mass demonstration to occur in Washington, D.C., during election week of 1972. He urged a march to demand a federal law that would make it a crime to kill an Indian, even if it had to be added as an amendment to the Endangered Species Act. A series of cross-country caravans called "The Trail of Broken Treaties" arrived in Washington on November 2 only to find that the adequate housing promised by the Department of the Interior was in fact crowded and rodent-infested. Feeling that the government officials sent out to investigate were officious and patronizing, Means then led the group to the Bureau of Indian Affairs where they successfully seized the offices and renamed the building the Native American Embassy. On November 6 a U.S. District Court Judge ordered the group's forcible eviction. Angry and frustrated, the Indians destroyed furniture and equipment and removed files they felt exploited Indian people. The next day the group agreed to leave the building peaceably after government officials promised to investigate federal programs affecting Indians and to consider the issue of Indian self-government. The government also offered $66,000 to cover travel expenses.

Occupies Town of Historic Massacre

When Means returned to South Dakota, he learned that the president of the Oglala Tribal Council, Dick Wilson, had obtained a court order prohibiting members of AIM from attending public meetings on the reservation. Wilson, a conservative opposed to the extreme activities of AIM, received government support to increase his police force, and had Means arrested twice for challenging the court order. When a white man was charged for second degree manslaughter instead of murder for the stabbing death of an Indian man, Means was among the leaders of a protest through the town of Custer where court was held. He and nearly 80 others were arrested for rioting and arson. The internal tribal governance conflict escalated as traditional leaders requested AIM's help in getting rid of council president Wilson, whom some viewed as representative of Washington bureaucracy. On February 27, 1973, Means and a group of nearly 200 armed supporters occupied the community of Wounded Knee, the site of the 1890 massacre of some 350 Sioux men, women, and children by the U.S. military. Tensions mounted as heavily armed FBI agents and federal marshals surrounded the area. More than a month later, Means agreed to fly to Washington to negotiate an agreement to end the siege, but the government refused to negotiate until all arms were laid down. Means refused the unconditional surrender and left the meeting. He was arrested and detained for the remainder of the siege when he announced his intention to return to Wounded Knee. On May 8, 1973, the remaining Indians surrendered when the government agreed to meet with tribal elders to begin an investigation into tribal government, which had been accused, under Wilson, of ignoring the tribal con-

stitution, among other things. Highly publicized in the national media, the ten-week siege became known as "Wounded Knee II" and garnered the support of many white Americans, including several Hollywood personalities.

Means ran against Wilson in the 1974 election of tribal council president while under federal indictment for actions during the Wounded Knee occupation. He lost the election, receiving 1530 votes to Wilson's 1709, but claimed that his election results indicated strong support for AIM causes on the reservation. His trial opened on February 12, 1974, and continued until September 16, when U.S. District Court Judge Fred Nichol dismissed the charges against Means and Banks and denounced the prosecution's handling of the case, which had included the use of information obtained from a member of Means' defense team by a paid FBI informant. When asked years later about the beneficial results of the Wounded Knee occupation, Means related a story of watching three little Indian boys playing, one pretending to be Banks, one pretending to be Means, and the third refusing to be Wilson. Means felt that the protests influenced the development of a different sense of Indian identity: that "government" Indians were considered traitors.

During the Wounded Knee occupation, Means was shot by a BIA officer. In the following six years, he survived four other shootings and was stabbed while serving a term in South Dakota's prison. These attempts on his life sent a message to other Indian people that they were not safe from violent attacks. In 1975 Means was indicted for a murder in a barroom brawl, but his attorney, William Kunstler, who had been one of the defense attorneys during the Wounded Knee trial, argued that the government had created such a climate of fear that Indians were armed in self-defense. The jury acquitted Means of the murder charge on August 6, 1976. He was convicted of riot charges relating to the 1973 Custer demonstration and served one month in jail. In November 1977, he served a term for rioting in a South Dakota state penitentiary.

Reclaims Indian Land at Yellow Thunder Camp

Russell Means was also among the group who occupied federal land at Yellow Thunder Camp. In April 1981, a group of Dakota AIM and traditional Lakota people established a camp on federal land in Victoria Creek Canyon, about 12 miles southwest of Rapid City, South Dakota. Named in honor of Raymond Yellow Thunder, the man murdered in Gordon, Nebraska, in 1972, the camp was established as the first step in reclaiming the Black Hills land for Lakota use. When the U.S. Forest Service denied a use permit for the camp, Means acted as a lay attorney in the complaint against the Forest Service for violating the American Indian Freedom of Religion Act of 1978. In 1985, Judge Donald O'Brien ruled in favor of the Indian camp, but a higher court overturned the decision.

After the Yellow Thunder trial, Means became involved in native rights issues in other countries, including supporting the cause of the Miskito Indians of Nicaragua. He has been associated politically with the Libertarian Party. In 1992, he turned actor, playing the role of Chingachgook in the movie *The Last of the Mohicans.* While on the set, Means served as liaison between Indian extras and the movie producers during a labor dispute. He claimed that he had not abandoned his role as activist. In an article in *Entertainment Weekly,* Means commented, "I have been asked whether my decision to act in *The Last of the Mohicans* means that I've abandoned my role as an activist. On the contrary, I see film as an extension of the path I've been on for the past 25 years—another avenue to eliminating racism."

In the spring of 1994, AIM cofounder Clyde Belle-court accused Means of selling out the AIM cause by accepting a $35,000 settlement from the 1972 suit against the Cleveland Indians baseball organization. Means, who left the American Indian Movement in 1988, responded that his current organization, the American Indian Anti-Defamation League, would be filing another lawsuit against the ball club since he never received any of the money.

Although Means generally detests writing as a European concept, he agreed to have his words published as a chapter in *Marxism and Native Americans* in order to communicate with a wider audience. He urged each American Indian to avoid becoming Europeanized, using traditional values to resist. He criticized the European intellectual traditions, including Christianity and capitalism, and accused the Europeans of despiritualizing the universe. He also warned that Marxism, as a European tradition, is also no solution for American Indians' problems. He concluded:"I am not a 'leader.' I am an Oglala Lakota patriot. That's all I want or need to be. And I am very comfortable with who I am."

SOURCES:

Books

Current Biography Yearbook 1978, New York, H. W. Wilson, 1978; 294-297.

Deloria, Vine, Jr., *God Is Red: A Native View of Religion,* second edition, Goldon, Colorado, North American Press, 1992; 18-24.

Matthiessen, Peter, *In the Spirit of Crazy Horse,* New York, Penguin Books, 1991.

Means, Russell, "The Same Old Song," in *Marxism and Native Americans,* edited by Ward Churchill, Boston, South End Press, 1983; 19-33.

Native North American Almanac, edited by Duane Champagne, Detroit, Gale Research, 1994; 1106.

Paulson, T. Emogene, and Lloyd R. Moses, *Who's Who Among the Sioux,* Vermillion, Institute of Indian Studies, University of South Dakota, 1988; 150.

Political Profiles: The Nixon/Ford Years, edited by Eleanora W. Schoenebaum, New York, Facts On File, 1979; 431-432.

Periodicals

Little Eagle, Avis, "Means Accused of Selling Out for $35,000," *Indian Country Today,* 13:45, May 4, 1994; A1-2.

Means, Russell, "Acting Against Racism," *Entertainment Weekly,* October 23, 1992; 34-37.

—*Sketch by Karen P. Zimmerman*

Beatrice A. Medicine
1924-
Lakota Sioux anthropologist

One of a few Native American women to earn advanced degrees in anthropology, Beatrice Medicine was born August 1, 1924, on the Standing Rock Reservation in Wakpala, South Dakota. Throughout her childhood, her family maintained her interest in their Lakota Sihasapa tribal traditions. She carried this interest into her college studies and later professional life. She received a B.S. from South Dakota State University, and after earning her M.A. from Michigan State University, and Ph.D. from the University of Wisconsin, Madison. Medicine taught anthropology at several universities and directed one Native American studies program. Among them were the University of Washington, the University of British Columbia, the University of Calgary, Alberta, Michigan State University, the University of South Dakota, Dartmouth and Stanford. At the time of her retirement, she was associate professor of anthropology at California State at Northridge. She currently serves as a research coordinator for Women's Perspectives for Canada's Royal Commission on Aboriginal Peoples.

She has contributed articles to more than 60 journals and chapters to several books. Her published work reflects her interest in the changing American Indian cultures and in Native American women's roles. She has also participated in research with aboriginal people in Canada, Australia, and New Zealand. Outside of academic life, she has helped to develop leadership among Indian people and has worked in establishing urban Indian centers.

Medicine has received numerous honors in academic life and in the Lakota traditional setting. In 1977 she was chosen Sacred Pipe Woman in a revival of the Lakota Sun Dance. She has been a member of several U.S. and Canadian organizations, and has been active in political affairs as well. Her strong traditional ties influenced her decision to return to South Dakota upon her retirement. After her marriage and divorce, she raised her son, Ted Garner, in the traditional Lakota culture.

SELECTED WRITINGS BY MEDICINE:

Native American Women: A Perspective, Austin, Texas, National Educational Laboratory, 1978.

(Editor, with Patricia Albers) *The Hidden Half: Studies of Plains Indian Women,* Washington, D.C., University Press of America, 1983.

"Indian Woman: Tribal Identity as Status Quo," in *Woman's Nature: Rationalizations of Inequality,* edited by Marion Lowe and Ruth Hubbard, New York, Pergamon, 1983; 63-73.

"'The Hidden Half' Lives," in *Cante Ohitika Win (Brave-Hearted Women): Images of Lakota Women from the Pine Ridge Reservation, South Dakota* by Carolyn Reyer, Vermillion, University of South Dakota Press, 1991; vii-viii.

SOURCES:

American Indian Women: A Guide to Research, edited by Gretchen M. Bataille and Kathleen M. Sands, New York, Garland Publishing, 1991; 74-75, 159-160, 334.

Indians of Today, fourth edition, edited by Marion Gridley, Chicago, ICFP, 1971; 187-188.

Native American Women, edited by Gretchen M. Bataille, New York, Garland Publishing, 1993; 170-171.

Native North American Almanac, edited by Duane Champagne, Detroit, Gale Research, 1994; 1106-1107.

Paulson, T. Emogene, and Lloyd R. Moses, *Who's Who Among the Sioux,* Vermillion, Institute of Indian Studies, University of South Dakota, 1988.

—Sketch by Karen P. Zimmerman

Billy Mills

Billy Mills
1938-
Oglala Sioux athlete

Billy Mills was the first American to win a gold medal in a distance race in the Olympics. Against tremendous odds he set a world record during the 1964 Olympic games in Tokyo, Japan, becoming a celebrated athlete in the United States. William M. Mills was born in on the Pine Ridge Reservation in South Dakota, in 1938. His mother died when he was seven and his father died six years later, leaving eight orphaned children. His father had boxed for a living but after his death there was no one to support the family. As was often the custom, Billy was sent away to a Bureau of Indian Affairs boarding school.

He entered Haskell Indian School in Lawrence, Kansas. Taking after his father, he tried out for the boxing team. Although he was of relatively small stature, only 5-foot-2-inches tall and 104 pounds, he joined the football team. He was attracted to the vigorous discipline of football and felt, at that time, that track was a "sissy" sport. But when he eventually turned to track, he discovered that it was extremely demanding, and he began to develop physical stamina through the robust training. The physical and mental training along with his inherent natural abilities helped him develop into a successful competitive runner. He won the Kansas State two-mile cross country championship three years in a row as well as the state mile championship as a junior and senior. When he graduated from high school, the University of Kansas awarded him a full athletic scholarship.

In college, Mills often felt lonely and isolated. He had little contact with his scattered brothers and sisters, and no one person really took an interest in him or his running. Despite the lack of attention that he received individually, Mills set a conference record of 31 minutes in his first 10,000-meter race and became the Big Eight cross country champion during that time. His team won the National Track Championships two years in a row while he was a junior and senior. Still, he did not gain prominence or recognition as a runner.

After trying and failing to qualify for the Olympic team, he became discouraged, finishing poorly in races and occasionally dropping out of events. In an interview for *Contemporary American Indian Leaders,* he reminisced about his period in his life. "I didn't realize then, but it was because of my attitude. I just didn't want to make the effort. I wasn't interested and because I wasn't, it was impossible for me to win. I blocked myself off from winning." Just before graduation, Billy married his college sweetheart and, during the same period, accepted an officer commission from the U.S. Marine Corps.

Some of his fellow marines were aware of his extraordinary running ability, and one of them encouraged him to begin running again. He began training and won the inter-service 10,000 meter race, with a time of 30:08, in Germany. Also, concentrating on the one-mile race, he got his time down to 4:06 minutes.

The 1964 Olympic Games—Astonishing Victory

The marines sent Mills to Tokyo, Japan, to compete in the Olympic games in 1964. This was an opportunity and a privilege for the young Sioux athlete. He entered the games as a complete unknown, a dark horse with odds of 1000-to-1 against him—no American had ever won a distance race in the Olympics. Just minutes before the race, the American coach was calculating the possibilities of any of his athletes placing in the race. Billy Mills' name was not even mentioned. He began the race with silent determination. By the last 300 yards he was actually leading the other 36 world class track stars. Suddenly he was pushed by another runner and he stumbled, dropping 20 yards behind. In the next few seconds he charged ahead, capturing one of the biggest upsets in Olympic history. He won the race in 28:24.4, establishing a new Olympic record and winning the gold medal."My Indianness kept me striving to take first and not settle for less in the last yards of the Olympic race," he said in his interview. "I thought of how our great chiefs kept on fighting when all of the odds were against them as they were against me. I couldn't let my people down."

The world was astonished at Mills' run and he became an instant international hero. Yet he remained modest and dignified. The president of the International Olympic Committee commended Mills for his ability to respond to pressure, saying never in 50 years had he seen a better reaction to such circumstances.

The honor of successfully representing the United States meant a lot to Mills, but his most cherished tributes came from his own Lakota people in the form of traditional gifts. He became a role model to generations of young people growing up in Pine Ridge. He traveled all over the world speaking in over 51 countries. Be always emphasized his tremendous desire to win as well as his Indianness. "I wanted to make a total effort, physically, mentally, and spiritually," he stated in his interview. "Even if I lost, with this effort I believed that I would hold the greatest key to success."

His story was respected around the world, and a movie—*Running Brave*—was filmed about his early life of hardship, his determination, and his Olympic victory. An honored spokesperson for Indian athletes, Mills stated in his interview: "[Other Indians] have ability far greater than mine, and if they are given the opportunity to explore and develop their talents, they can achieve any personal and educational goal they choose, especially if they make this total physical, mental and spiritual effort."

After the Olympics, Further Discouragement

After the Olympics, Billy Mills continued to train and to run, setting another record in the six-mile race. At the same time he was living in California with his family and working as an insurance salesperson. He tried out for the 1968 Olympic games but due to a technicality regarding his application form, he was denied a place on the team. He ran in the qualifying 5000-mile trial, even though he was not a contestant for the team, finishing 13 seconds ahead of the fastest runner who qualified for the games in Mexico City.

For a time he felt bitter and discouraged. It seemed that politics had kept him out of the 1968 Olympic games. Then, as he had done so often, he put the bitterness behind him and went on with his life. "A man can change things," he explained in his interview. "A man has a lot to do with deciding his own destiny. I can do one of two things—go through life bickering and complaining about the raw deal I got, or go back into competition to see what I can do." His positive attitude has made him a role model for all young people. He has devoted a great deal of his time to being a spokesperson for Indian causes, speaking out about the benefits of physical discipline and self esteem. In 1977 he was named one of ten outstanding young men of the U.S. by the U.S. Junior Chamber of Commerce. In 1994 he published a book, *Wokini: A Lakota Journey to Happiness and Self-Understanding.*

SOURCES:

Books

Contemporary American Indian Leaders, edited by Marion E. Gridley, New York, Dodd, Mead & Company, 1972.
Mills, Billy, *Wokini: A Lakota Journey to Happiness and Self Understanding,* New York, Crown, 1994.
Native North American Almanac, edited by Duane Champagne, Detroit, Gale Research, 1994.

Periodicals

Link, Martin, review of Wokini: *A Lakota Journey to Happiness and Self-Understanding, Indian Trader,* June 1994.

—*Sketch by Nancy Maryboy and David Begay*

N. Scott Momaday
1934-
Kiowa writer, poet, and educator
Also known as Tsoai-talee ["Rock Tree Boy"]

One of the most distinguished Native American authors writing today, Navarre Scott Momaday is chiefly known for novels and poetry collections that communicate the fabulous oral legends of his Kiowa heritage. In 1969 he became the first American Indian to win the Pulitzer Prize in fiction for his novel *House Made of Dawn,* which had a

N. Scott Momaday

tremendous impact on the development of Native-American literature in the United States. Published during a time of heightened cultural awareness in the late 1960s and early 1970s, *House Made of Dawn* not only influenced but also brought attention to other gifted Indian writers, including Vine Deloria, Jr., Leslie Marmon Silko, and James Welch.

Born in a Kiowa Indian hospital in Lawton, Oklahoma, on February 27, 1934, Momaday was the only child of Kiowa artist Alfred Morris Momaday and teacher Mayme Natachee Scott Momaday. A descendant of early American pioneers, Momaday's mother derived her middle name from a Cherokee great-grandmother, Natachee. His father inherited the Kiowa family name "Mammedaty" from Momaday's grandfather. "At that time," Momaday explains in an essay appearing in *Something about the Author*, "People had but one name. That was the name that was given to him as a child, and that was the only name he had. But during his lifetime the missionaries came in, and the Indians adopted the Christian tradition of the surname and the Christian name. And so my grandfather was given the name John, and he became known as John Mammedaty, and Mammedaty simply became the surname of his family. It was passed down. Some of my relatives in Oklahoma still use that spelling, but my father abbreviated it to Momaday."

Growing up on Indian reservations in the American Southwest, Momaday attributes many of his childhood and lifetime memories to his parents. "Some of my mother's memories have become my own. This is the real burden of the blood; this is immortality," he relates in *The Names: A*

Memoir. Born of mixed blood, Natachee began to identify with her Indian heritage around the age of 16. A beautiful girl, she called herself "Little Moon" while her cousins referred to her as "Queen of Sheba"—both of which pleased her mightily. To pursue a degree and to learn more about her Indian heritage, Natachee attended the Haskell Institute, the Indian school at Lawrence, Kansas, in 1929. Her intense love of books and English literature was a great pleasure that she passed on to her son. Through their shared experiences, Momaday learned to develop a mental repository for his vast collection of memories. As Momaday recalls, "Memories ... qualify the imagination, to give it another formation, one that is peculiar to the self. I remember isolated, yet fragmented and confused, images—and images, shifting, enlarging, is the word, rather than moments or events—which are mine alone and which are especially vivid to me."

Cultivates Vivid Early Memories

Momaday remembers that the first notable event in his life occurred when he was just six months old and he accompanied his parents on a journey to the Black Hills in Wyoming to see Devil's Tower. Referred to in Kiowa as Tsoai ["Rock Tree"], Devil's Tower became the source of Momaday's Kiowa name, Tsoai-talee, given to him by Pohd-lohk ["Old Wolf"], a Kiowa elder. Pohd-lohk had in his possession a ledger that he had secured from the supply office at Fort Sill and which depicted the calendar history of the Kiowa people from 1833. Momaday would later derive much of his knowledge about the origin of his people from that book.

Being an only child, Momaday learned at an early age to give free reign to his imagination, or as he states, "to create my society in my mind. And for a child this kind of creation is accomplished easily enough." Momaday's mother encouraged him to learn English as his native language, and this circumstance sometimes led the boy to experience brief periods of cultural dislocation. In describing these strange incidents, Momaday relates that he was able to see "Grendel's shadow on the walls of Canyon de Chelly, and once, having led the sun around Hoskinini Mesa, saw Copperfield at Oljeto Trading Post." When he was 12, his family moved to the Pueblo village of Jemez. Momaday remembers "not being able to imagine a more beautiful or exotic place," and Jemez offered the boy a child's natural delight full of canyons and mountains. In Momaday's interpretive mind, Jemez became a landscape full of mystery and life, and many of his descriptive details of those childhood days can be found in his later writings. Once referring to Jemez as having "horses in the plain and angles of geese in the sky," Momaday later reflected on this image when writing *Angle of Geese and Other Poems* (1974).

Embarks on a Writing Career

Uncertain about his future after graduating from high school, Momaday contemplated attending West Point before deciding to enroll in the University of New Mexico in 1952. He earned a bachelor's degree in Political Science in 1958, while distinguishing himself as a public speaker and creative writer. Taking a one year break from his studies, Momaday taught school on the Jicarilla Apache reservation before pursuing a graduate studies program in literature. By this time, he had received his first academic recognition as a talented writer when he was awarded the John Hay Whitney fellowship in creative poetry writing and the Stanford Wilson dissertation fellowship at Stanford University. While at Stanford, Momaday met Yvor Winters, who later became a close friend and advisor. Momaday obtained his master's degree in 1960 and his Ph.D. three years later. In 1965 he published his first book, *The Complete Poems of Frederick Goddard Tuckerman,* which was based on his doctoral dissertation. Momaday credits Winters for his decision to analyze the writings of Tuckerman, a reclusive New England naturalist. According to the 1971 edition of the *Penguin Companion to World Literature,* Momaday's thesis led to an increased awareness of Tuckerman's poems on the part of poets and critics alike.

Following his graduate studies, Momaday joined the faculty of the University of California at Santa Barbara in 1963 as assistant professor of English. Further literary research led him to pursue a Guggenheim fellowship at Harvard University during the 1966-1967 academic year, after which he returned to Santa Barbara to resume teaching. Two years later, he was named professor of English at the University of California, Berkeley, where he taught creative writing and introduced a new curriculum centered around American Indian literature and mythology. Also during this period, Momaday published his influential novel *House Made of Dawn* (1968). The story follows the adventures of Abel, a disenchanted Native-American World War II veteran who attempts to balance his identity between culturally disparate native and non-native worlds. Unable to exist peacefully in either world, Abel gradually reaches the conclusion that he is lost, and he returns to the reservation heal his shattered psyche. In an analysis of *House Made of Dawn* in the *New York Times Book Review,* Marshall Sprague observes that "while mysteries of culture different from our own cannot be explained in a short novel," Momaday's book is "as subtly wrought as a piece of Navajo silverware." Momaday was accorded one of literature's highest honors when he was awarded the Pulitzer Prize for fiction for *House Made of Dawn.*

In his next novel, *The Way to Rainy Mountain* (1969), Momaday incorporated several Kiowa myths and legends into a quasi-fictional account of the 300-year-old migration of the Kiowa tribe from their place of origin in the Yellowstone region to the plains, where they learned to domesticate horses and developed into a sophisticated society. Relating the legend of how the Kiowas came into the world through a hollow log, Momaday explains that the Kiowas are a small tribe because when they entered the log "there was a woman whose body was swollen up with child, and she got stuck in the log. After that, no one could get through, and that is why the Kiowas are a small tribe in numbers." *The Way to Rainy Mountain* features illustrations by Momaday's father, Alfred, and it has been characterized by a reviewer for *Choice* (September 1969) as "a beautiful book—honest, unique, dignified, and told with a simplicity that approaches the purest poetry.... It is a book for all seasons, for all readers."

In subsequent years, Momaday's reputation has ascended to the international level. In 1979 he was awarded Italy's highest literary award, the Premio Letterario Internationale "Mondello." Moreover, in 1990 Momaday was selected to be a keynote speaker in Moscow before the Conference on Environment and Human Survival, the Global Forum, and the Supreme Soviet. That same year, he was asked to be a member of the Pulitzer Prize jury in fiction. The father of four daughters, Momaday continues to write and teaches classes on oral tradition at the University of Arizona.

SELECTED WRITINGS BY MOMADAY:

The Complete Poems of Frederick Goddard Tuckerman, New York, Oxford University Press, 1965.
House Made of Dawn, New York, Harper & Row, 1968.
The Way to Rainy Mountain, Albuquerque, University of New Mexico Press, 1969.
Colorado: Summer, Fall, Winter, Spring, Chicago, Rand McNally, 1973.
Angle of Geese and Other Poems, Boston, David R. Godine, 1974.
The Gourd Dancer, New York, Harper & Row, 1976.
The Names: A Memoir, New York, Harper & Row, 1976.
The Ancient Child, New York, Doubleday, 1989.
In the Presence of the Sun: A Gathering of Shields, St. Martin's Press, 1992.

SOURCES:

Books

Current Biography 1975, New York, H. W. Wilson Company, 1975; 281-283.
Shubnell, Matthias, *N. Scott Momaday: The Cultural and Literary Background,* Norman, University of Oklahoma Press, 1985.
Something about the Author, Volume 48, Detroit, Gale Research, 1987; 158-162.
Twentieth Century Western Writers, second edition, edited by Geoff Sadler, Chicago, St. James Press, 1991; 470-471.
Woodward, Charles, *Ancestral Voice: Conversations with N. Scott Momaday,* Lincoln, University of Nebraska Press, 1989.

Periodicals

Review of *The Way to Rainy Mountain, Choice,* September 1969.
Sprague, Marshall, review of *House Made of Dawn, New York Times Book Review,* June 9, 1968.

—Sketch by JoAnn di Filippo

Carlos Montezuma
1867(?)-1923
Yavapai physician and activist
Also known as Wassaja (Wasagah) ["Signaling" or "Reckoning"]

Carlos Montezuma, a renowned physician and surgeon, was also a strong and vocal proponent for Native American independence from reservations and assimilation into the mainstream culture. Born about 1867 in Arizona, he was the son of Cocuyevah, a Yavapai man, and an unidentified mother, perhaps an Apache. Called "Wassaja" as a youth, he was captured by Pima Indians during a raid on his village when he was only five years old. They sold him to a traveling photographer named Carlos (Charles) Gentile for $30. Wassaja's mother found out that the Pima had taken him alive and asked for permission to leave her reservation to find him. When the Indian agent refused, she tried to go after him anyway. She was shot and killed as she fled.

After traveling to Santa Fe, New Mexico, and Pueblo, Colorado, Gentile and Wassaja moved east, finally arriving in the Chicago area. There, Wassaja was baptized as a Christian and renamed. He took "Carlos" after his "benefactor," and Gentile provided "Montezuma," after the ancient ruins of the same name in Wassaja's homeland. Although Gentile and the newly named Carlos sometimes lived as far east as Brooklyn, New York, most of their time was spent in Illinois.

Montezuma was apparently a talented student, as records indicate that he graduated with a B.S. degree from the University of Illinois in 1884 at the age of 17. Gentile had committed suicide during Montezuma's early teen years, so he worked his way through the school. At this time, he began to speak about his determination to force a change in the way in which Indians were being assimilated into the dominant culture. He believed that the maintenance of traditions would "hold back" Natives and that they should be acculturated as soon as possible.

By 1888, Montezuma had earned his M.D. from the Chicago Medical College of Northwestern University. His first professional post was with the Indian School at Fort Stevenson, North Dakota. Subsequent jobs on the Western Shoshone reservation in Nevada and the Colville reservation in Washington proved to Montezuma that he did not belong on a reservation. He thought that the "isolation" of Indians on reservations set Natives up for failure. In this period of his life, he started calling for citizenship for indigenous people and was reportedly distraught that citizenship had been granted to African Americans in 1888, but not to those Indians who were not already made citizens by Acts of Congress.

Montezuma started his private practice in Chicago in 1896. He specialized in gastroenterology and was often linked professionally with Fenton Turck, a nationally recognized expert in stomach disorders. Montezuma also taught in the College of Physicians and Surgeons in the Postgraduate Division of Rush Medical School.

Political Activist

The call for the abolition of the Bureau of Indian Affairs (BIA) was being heard from many quarters at the beginning of the twentieth century. Perhaps its most articulate spokesperson was Montezuma. To counteract his protests, President Theodore Roosevelt offered him the position of BIA director in 1906. Montezuma refused, as he would later attempts to place him at the helm of "the Indian Department." That same year, he published *The Indians of Today and Tomorrow*, a book detailing a more accurate history of Natives than was then commonly accepted. The book was not primarily a history though; its message was that Indians must be allowed into the American Dream, and that this could best be accomplished by doing away with cultural traditions and providing public, nonreservation education to young Indians.

The first two decades of this century saw increased activism on the part of Native Americans who had been educated formally. Montezuma was one of the most vocal of these "Educated Indians," as they were then commonly called. In April of 1911 he was invited to join a conference in Columbus, Ohio, to discuss the formation of an organization of these activists. Out of their efforts was born the Society of American Indians (SAI), a group whose influence would be felt keenly in the policy-making centers of Washington, D.C.

Montezuma, although part of the first conference, opposed SAI. In particular, he opposed their support of the continuance of "wardship" status for Indians and the creation of an annual American Indian Day. To offset the power of the SAI, Montezuma wrote his 1914 book, *Let My People Go*, which continued his arguments for the dissolution of the BIA and for mainstream public education for Indians. An equally strident but opposing voice belonged to Seneca activist Arthur Parker, who worked with SAI. When Parker was elected president of the SAI in 1916, Montezuma urged him to bring the group into line with the ideas expressed in *Let My People Go*. Parker refused.

"Wassaja" Is Born

Because the SAI's publications would not give space to Montezuma's work, he launched a monthly journal in 1916 bearing his childhood name, "Wassaja." The motto of the journal was "Let My People Go," Montezuma's continuing allusion to Indian wardship. In its pages, he decried the efforts of so-called "Friends of the Indians" groups, including SAI. The journal was published until 1922.

With World War I looming, the federal government announced its intention to draft Native men into the armed services. In 1917, Montezuma publicly protested the move and was jailed. Garnering even more publicity for his stand against the policy, Montezuma was now being listened to by a much larger audience. He was released from jail through the intervention of President Woodrow Wilson, who again offered to appoint him head of the BIA, an offer Montezuma again declined.

Although his public career as an activist was overshadowing his personal and professional life, Montezuma still attempted to maintain his thriving private practice. He worked long hours, taught, lectured on Indian policy, and generally taxed his health. Little is printed on his first wife, other than that she was Romanian by birth and that they divorced. Not long after, Montezuma married his second wife, Marie Keller. In addition to all his other commitments, Montezuma was also quite active in a local Masonic chapter, becoming a Master Mason.

For some time, Montezuma had suffered from diabetes. As he aged, the condition worsened and other health complications arose. Overall, his constitution declined as he worked, to near exhaustion, both for his patients and for Indian rights as he saw them. By 1922, Montezuma had apparently contracted tuberculosis and was no longer able to work. Montezuma and Marie relocated to the Fort McDowell reservation in Arizona, living not far from where Montezuma was born.

On January 31, 1923, Carlos "Wassaja" Montezuma died. He was buried in the Indian Cemetery at Fort McDowell and a Masonic monument was set on his resting place. Although controversial, his legacy remains with Native people today, and none doubt the sincerity of his efforts. In honor of his unswerving convictions, a contemporary Indian topics journal was started in California in 1972. Called *Wassaja: The Indian Historian,* it sought to illustrate the links between Native history and current topics.

SOURCES:

Biographical Dictionary of Indians of the Americas, Newport Beach, California, American Indian Publications, 1983.

Contemporary American Indian Leaders, edited by Marion Gridley, New York, Dodd, Mead and Co., 1972.

Dockstader, Frederick, *Great North American Indians,* New York, Van Nostrand Reinhold, 1977.

Native Americans in the Twentieth Century, edited by James Olson and Raymond Wilson, Urbana, University of Illinois, 1984.

Native North American Almanac, edited by Duane Champagne, Detroit, Gale Research, 1994.

Vogel, Virgil, *This Country Was Ours,* New York, Harper and Row, 1972.

—Sketch by Cynthia R. Kasee

Norval Morrisseau
1932-
Ojibwa artist
Also known as Copper Thunderbird

Norval Morrisseau is considered the father of Canadian woodland Indian art and a major influence on the younger Cree and Ojibwa artists of today. Morrisseau was the first native artist to break into the world of mainstream Canadian art with his pioneering pictographic style. His acrylic paintings, silkscreen works, and pen-and-ink drawings have been exhibited in galleries in North America and Europe. His work has been influenced both by the rock paintings found along the northern shores of Lake Superior and by the birch bark scrolls of the Midewiwin or Grand Medicine Society, a native religious group. Awarded the prestigious Order of Canada in 1978, Morrisseau describes himself as a shaman-artist. In *The Art of Norval Morrisseau,* he wrote, "My paintings are also icons; that is to say, they are images which help focus on spiritual powers, generated by traditional belief and wisdom."

Norval Morrisseau was born on Sand Point Reserve, near Beardmore, Ontario, on March 14, 1932. The eldest of seven boys, Morrisseau, following the native custom, was raised by his maternal grandparents, Moses (Potan) Nanakonagas, a shaman, and his wife Vernique, on the shores of Lake Nipigon. The native legends and spiritual teachings related by Nanakonagas form the basis of Morrisseau's art. When the artist published *Legends of My People: The Great Ojibway* in 1965, he dedicated the book to his grandfather.

Contracting Tuberculosis Changes Life

As a child, Morrisseau earned only a fourth-grade education at an Indian residential school in Fort William (now Thunder Bay) before returning home to the reserve. Here, he struggled against poverty and isolation for many years. At age 19, the malnourished Morrisseau developed tuberculosis and was sent to a Fort William sanatorium. One of the doctors there encouraged the young native to paint. The same year, Morrisseau began having visions that showed that his role in life was to be a shaman-artist. It was also at the hospital that Morrisseau met his wife, Harriet Kakegamic, a Cree Indian. The couple had six children before the marriage dissolved. The artist traditionally signs his work with his native name, Copper Thunderbird, written in the Cree syllabics his wife taught him.

In 1962, Jack Pollock, a Toronto artist and gallery owner, met Morrisseau when Pollock was teaching painting on a summer project in northern Ontario. So impressed was Pollock with the vibrant imagery of Morrisseau's paintings, that he organized a one-man show for the artist at the Pollock Gallery. Morrisseau's work sold out on the first day of the show. Although the artist's work was immediately popular with critics and collectors, some of his fellow Ojibwa felt the artist should not reveal the tribe's legends and beliefs to outsiders. Morrisseau defended his actions, stating his desire to restore the pride of the once-great Ojibway people through the images in his art.

Survived Alcoholism and Health Problems

Morrisseau has struggled to reconcile his native religious beliefs with his Christian faith, both in his paintings and his life. The artist has always been a wanderer and a loner, moving restlessly across Canada, often living on the streets. In 1976, he adopted the Eckankar religion, with its strong belief in soul travel, which comes closer to native religious teachings. Writer Lister Sinclair in *The Art of Norval Morrisseau* observed, "Morrisseau is a romantic artist in the tradition of Baudelaire and Rimbaud, pushing his body, his consciousness, his experiences to the further limits of possibility, and then one inch more. He returns shaken from these interior voyages, some of which are perilous indeed, not only to the integrity of the emotions and the spirit, but also to the actual life of the body."

Morrisseau's first brush with death occurred in 1972, when the artist suffered second-degree burns to more than one-third of his body in a Vancouver, British Columbia hotel fire. Three years later, staying at a Catholic detoxification center, he painted "Lily of the Mohawk" and other paintings filled with Catholic imagery. Morrisseau has continued to be plagued by health and alcohol-related problems. Each tragic experience in his life, however, has seemed to bring fresh ideas, which he translates into his art. The artist, now living on the coast of British Columbia and again exhibiting his work, remains one of Canada's most celebrated Native artists.

SOURCES:

Books

McLuhan, Elizabeth, and Tom Hill, *Norval Morrisseau and the Emergence of the Image Makers,* Toronto, Art Gallery of Ontario, 1984.

Morrisseau, Norval, *Legends of My People: The Great Ojibway,* edited by Selwyn Dewdney, Toronto, Ryerson Press, 1965.

Schwarz, Herbert T., *Windigo and Other Tales of the Ojibways,* illustrated by Norval Morrisseau, Toronto, McClelland and Stewart, 1969.

Sinclair, Lister, and Jack Pollock, *The Art of Norval Morrisseau,* foreword by Norval Morrisseau, Toronto, Methuen, 1979.

Southcott, Beth, *The Sound of the Drum: The Sacred Art of the Anishnabec,* Erin, Ontario, Boston Mills Press, 1984.

The Canadian Encyclopedia, second edition, Edmonton, Hurtig Publishers, 1985.

Other

Colours of Pride (film), National Film Board of Canada, 1974.

The Paradox of Norval Morrisseau (film), National Film Board of Canada, 1974.

Spirits Speaking Through: Canadian Woodland Artists (film), CBC Spectrum Series, 1982.

—*Sketch by Alice Gibb*

Mountain Wolf Woman
1884-1960
Winnebago writer
Also known as Haksigaxunuminka ["Little Fifth Daughter"] and Kéhachiwinga (Xehaciwinga) ["Wolf's Mountain Home Maker"]

Mountain Wolf Woman is best known for her autobiography, *Mountain Wolf Woman, Sister of Crashing Thunder,* which provided a document of one Native American woman's adaptation to the twentieth century. Set down by her adopted niece, Nancy Oestreich Lurie, and published in 1958, this account was hailed both in academic circles and among critics as a contribution to the literature of cultural crisis and change.

Mountain Wolf Woman was the daughter of Charles Blowsnake and Lucy Goodvillage, both of whom were pure Winnebago (a Siouan-speaking tribe that lived in the Green Bay area of Wisconsin). Mountain Wolf Woman's father belonged to the Thunder Clan. The baby of the family, Mountain Wolf Woman had four sisters and three brothers: Hinuga ["White Thunder"] was the eldest child and daughter. Hinuga was followed by eldest son, Kunuga ["Crashing Thunder"]; second daughter, Wihanga ["Bald Eagle"]; second son, Henaga ["Strikes Standing"]; third son, Hagaga ["Big Winnebago"]; third daughter, Haksigaga, who died when she was small; fourth daughter, Hinakega ["Distant Flashes"]; and finally Mountain Wolf Woman, who was born in April of 1884 at East Fork River, Wisconsin. She was given her name after a woman named Wolf Woman, who cured her of a life-threatening illness when she was a child.

The family moved within the state to Black River Falls, and, at age nine, Mountain Wolf Woman began attending school in Tomah. She studied there for two years until her family took her out to travel with them. She liked school, but because the family followed the hunting and harvesting seasons, she had to journey with them. As a teenager she attended school again for a short time at the Lutheran Mission School in Wittenberg. There she met an Oneida woman, Nancy Smith, who was the girls' matron. They became friendly and attended tribal dances and other events together. Her family then took her out of school for the last time, as she was to be married. Mountain Wolf Woman noted, "Alas, I was enjoying school so much, and they made me stop."

Marriages and Motherhood

One of her older brothers had arranged for her to marry in order to relieve himself of a debt of gratitude. After her mother explained to the unhappy Mountain Wolf Woman that she had to cooperate with her brother since marriage was an economic arrangement among the Winnebago, she did so. The union was very unhappy; she never referred to her first husband by anything other than "that man." She spent several unpleasant years with him, leaving him after she gave birth to their second child. Subsequently, with the intervention of her brother Crashing Thunder, she made a happy marriage with Bad Soldier, a member of the Bear Clan; this clan acted as a police force in Black River Falls. They remained together until his death in 1936. In this way, Mountain Wolf Woman accommodated the traditional rules about arranged marriages but eventually managed to marry a man of her choosing.

After her second marriage, Mountain Wolf Woman moved several times in search of better employment or housing situations. She had 11 children, three of whom died, at least 38 grandchildren, and at least nine great-grandchildren. (Lurie notes that Mountain Wolf Woman was not absolutely sure about the numbers, and that these figures represent the minimum number of her descendants.) Mountain Wolf Woman was unafraid of the many changes that occurred during her lifetime. As Lurie wrote, "Mountain Wolf Woman has lived far longer than I have and has seen the transition from horse to airplane without feeling a sense of threat to her individuality." She was one of the first Winnebago women to own a car and once took a train to visit her daughter in Oregon. She made her first airplane journey at 74, when she flew to Ann Arbor, Michigan, to collaborate with Lurie.

Mountain Wolf Woman's upbringing included participation in the Scalp Dance and the Medicine Dance. From her grandfather Náqisaneinghinigra or Náqiwankwax-opiniga ["Spirit Man"], Mountain Wolf Woman learned to practice tribal medicine. She was also a practicing Christian. But Mountain Wolf Woman deemed her conversion to the Native American Church and consequent participation in peyote meetings as her most important life experience. Church members gathered weekly to eat peyote "buttons" (from the cactus plant *Lophophora williamsii*) that would bring on intense religious and mystical experiences. Mountain Wolf Woman spoke of having seen Jesus during one of these occasions. Wherever Mountain Wolf Woman, her husband, and their family traveled, they lived among other peyote eaters because, as she explains in her narrative, "The others hated us."

Throughout her autobiographical narrative, Mountain Wolf Woman stressed the differences between the society in which she grew up and the present day. Although she was flexible and showed no bitterness about the changes to her way of life; she was in her seventies at the time her history was recorded. As an older woman, she recalled the respect with which the elderly tribe members were treated when she was young and remarked that "we respected the old people, but today they do not respect old people." She also remembers a time when "the Indians were real Indians!"

Family relations were of paramount importance to Mountain Wolf Woman, though her conception of relation lay beyond the more immediate, nuclear sense. For example, her autobiography came about because her niece Nancy Lurie asked her to tape record her life story. Mountain Wolf Woman could not but comply, even though Lurie was not a blood relative. The women were linked through Mountain Wolf Woman's cousin Mitchell Redcloud, Sr. According to Winnebago tradition, Mountain Wolf Woman and Redcloud are classified as brother and sister because their fathers were brothers. Lurie met Redcloud when she was doing field work in 1944. He was ill, and she visited him often to learn about the Winnebago. Fearful that he would not survive an upcoming operation, Redcloud offered to adopt Lurie. She was given a Winnebago name, a clan affiliation, and many relatives on whom she could call in order to pursue her work. He wrote to Mountain Wolf Woman of his decision, and she welcomed Lurie as her niece.

Collaborates on Her Autobiography

Lurie sensed that Mountain Wolf Woman's autobiography would be interesting both from a literary and an ethnographic standpoint. She was also aware that the first full-length autobiography of a Native American, edited by anthropologist Paul Radin, had been of Crashing Thunder, Mountain Wolf Woman's brother. Although quite a few other autobiographies of Native Americans were collected after Radin's work, very few had been taken from women. Most accounts of Native Americans were written by outsiders to whom the women's culture was foreign or who had very little idea of women's roles within the culture.

In making her autobiography, Mountain Wolf Woman narrated her life in Winnebago and translated it into English, and then Lurie crafted it into a written narrative. Lurie also included detailed appendices and notes as well as an earlier version of Mountain Wolf Woman's life that was far shorter. In the preface, Lurie noted that her subject made the transition from traditional tribal life to life in the twentieth century with relative effortlessness, particularly in comparison with her brother Crashing Thunder.

The autobiography was very well received, and Mountain Wolf Woman achieved a certain level of fame during the last two years of her life. She died of pneumonia at the age of 76 on November 9, 1960, in Black River Falls, Wisconsin. Eve Merriam chose to include excerpts from Mountain Wolf Woman's autobiography as an example of Native American writing in her collection titled *Growing Up Female in America, Ten Lives*. Later, a videotape was also produced in which Mountain Wolf Woman's granddaughter narrated her grandmother's life with the use of still photographs. In her 1983 book *Native American Women: A Contextual Bibliography*, Rayna Green described *Mountain Wolf Woman, Sister of Crashing Thunder* as "the classic and still fine autobiography" of a Native American woman.

SOURCES:

Books

American Indian Women: A Guide to Research, edited by Gretchen M. Bataille, New York City, Garland Publishing, 1991.

Brumble, H. David, III, *An Annotated Bibliography of American Indian and Eskimo Autobiographies,* Lincoln, University of Nebraska Press, 1981.

Dockstader, Frederick J., *Great North American Indians,* New York City, Van Nostrand Reinhold Company, 1977.

Green, Rayna, *Native American Women: A Contextual Bibliography,* Bloomington, Indiana University Press, 1983.

Josephy, Alvin, Jr., *The Indian Heritage of America,* Boston, Houghton Mifflin, 1991.

Mountain Wolf Woman, Sister of Crashing Thunder, edited by Nancy Oestreich Lurie, foreword by Ruth Underhill, Ann Arbor, University of Michigan Press, 1961.

Native American Women, edited by Gretchen M. Bataille, New York, Garland Publishing, 1993.

Wong, Hertha Dawn, *Sending My Heart Across the Years: Tradition and Innovation in Native American Autobiography,* New York City, Oxford University Press, 1992.

Other

Riley, Jocelyn, *Mountain Wolf Woman, 1884-1960,* Women Writers Series, Her Own Words Productions, Madison, Wisconsin, 1990.

—*Sketch by Megan Ratner*

Mourning Dove
1885(?)-1936
Colville Salishan writer and activist
Also known as Christine Quintasket, Humishuma ["Mourning Dove"]

Mourning Dove is the pen name of Christine Quintasket. She is considered the first Native American female novelist. According to her writings, she was born in a canoe crossing the Kootenai River near Bonner's Ferry, Idaho. Although the exact year of her birth is uncertain, most sources indicate that she was born in April of 1888. Her parents were Joseph Quintasket, an Okanogan from British Columbia, Canada, and her mother was Lucy Stukin, a Colville (Salishan) from north central Washington State. Her grandfather, Seewhelhken, was head chief of the Colville tribe for many years. His nephew, Kinkannawh, also known by the white people as Pierre Jerome, was chief around 1872. Mourning Dove was married twice. In 1909, she married Hector McLeod, a Flathead; in 1919, she married Fred Galler, a Wenatchee. Her mother died in 1902; and although Quintasket had no children of her own, she was responsible for rearing her younger brother and two younger sisters—Julia born in 1891, Mary Margaret in 1892, and Louis in

1896. Two other younger siblings, John and Marie, both died before age five.

Mourning Dove's Childhood

There are several accounts reflecting different ages for Quintasket. In June of 1891, her name appears on a tribal census as an eight year old. Some of her classmates were interviewed in later years, and because she was bigger than the other children, it is likely she was older than she reported. In 1895, Quintasket entered the Sacred Heart School at the Goodwin Mission in Ward, Washington. She could only speak Salishan and the nuns were hard on her for not speaking English. After several months, she became ill from the constant punishment and was sent home. In 1896, she returned to school and remained there until 1899. At that time, the U.S. government funding for Indian schools was cut, and all the Indian students were sent to school at Fort Spokane.

In 1902, when Quintasket's mother died, she returned home to care for her brother and sisters. When her father remarried in 1904, Quintasket was then able to return to school. She enrolled at Fort Shaw Indian School at Great Falls, Montana. While at school, she saw the last roundup of a wild buffalo herd in 1908. This roundup made a strong impression on Quintasket, and she used this event as a base for her first novel, a love story, *Cogewea, the Half Blood: A Depiction of the Great Montana Cattle Range.* Quintasket also met her first husband, Hector McLeod, a Flathead Indian, while she was at Fort Shaw Indian School. They married in 1909 and divorced several years later. His abusive nature lead to his shooting death while playing cards in April of 1937.

Quintasket worked as a housekeeper to support herself. She was able to purchase a typewriter with money she had saved. In 1912, Quintasket was living in Portland, Oregon where she began writing her first novel. When she began to write, she used the pen name Morning Dove, but changed it to Mourning Dove when she saw the name on a bird exhibit at a museum in Spokane, Washington. The Okanogan tribal name for this bird is Humishuma. In 1913, she entered Calgary Business School and stayed until 1915. There she developed a greater understanding of writing styles and typing skills.

First Novel

Around 1915, she went to the Walla Walla Frontier Days Celebration. There she met Lucullus Virgil McWhorter. He was a local businessman and took a serious interest in the Yakima tribe from the central Washington state area. He was an advocate for their rights and was responsible for the Yakima's receiving compensation on past due government promises. The Yakima tribe held him in high regard and gave him the Indian name of Hemene Kawan ["Old Wolf"]. Because of his size, he was also called Big Foot, which is the name Quintasket used most often when corresponding with L. V. McWhorter. He befriended Quintasket and helped her with her writing, using his influence to get her first book published in 1927. Fifteen years had passed since she first began writing the Cogewea novel.

The delay was due to the endless editing and rewriting, but also to World War I. Criticism by some influential local people also played a part in the delay. They said that McWhorter wrote the book and Quintasket just put her name on it. During these collaborations, McWhorter insisted that Quintasket interview her elder tribal members to record the traditional stories. He thought these old stories would soon be lost in the process of assimilation into the white culture. This was the basis for Quintasket's second book, *Coyote Stories.*

Second Novel

In 1919, Mourning Dove married Fred Galler. He was a Wenatchi Indian from the Colville Indian Reservation in north central Washington state. This marriage also had difficulties, but they stayed together. They lived on the Colville Reservation. During her adult life, she was recognized by her various names. Through her writing, she was known as Mourning Dove, people on the reservation knew her as Christine Quintasket, and when she and her husband worked in the orchards and fields she was called Mrs. Fred Galler. Quintasket and her husband earned a living by picking fruit and vegetables. As migrant workers, they found themselves moving around, living in a tent, or finding meager housing on the labor farms. It was during this time that Quintasket began to use McWhorter's advice and collected the stories from the elders on the reservation. McWhorter again helped her edit and rewrite the legends. He called upon his friend, Heister Dean Guie, who worked as the editor at the newspaper in the town of Yakima. Letters from Quintasket and Guie passed through McWhorter. He would make his comments and would try to pacify the detail-minded Guie. Quintasket did not have a full command of the English language because of her limited education; therefore, some interpretation was usually needed from McWhorter. In the evenings, Quintasket found the energy to type her novels and correspond with McWhorter. She was constantly overworked and found herself with periods of illness and fatigue. She suffered from pneumonia, rheumatism, and general poor health throughout her entire life.

L. V. McWhorter knew that Quintasket could go to the elders on the reservation and hear the traditional stories and legends told for centuries. He urged her constantly to collect the stories for her book about the tribal heritage. *Coyote Stories* is a collection of legends and traditional stories told to Quintasket by her elders on the Colville Indian Reservation. Quintasket went to the elders and found that each family group usually had slightly different versions of the same story. She heard some of the most influential stories by attending Colville funerals which would last throughout the night. To help relieve the grief and to help keep everyone awake during the funerals, the older Indian women would tell the most colorful and humorous of the coyote stories. The coyote is an important central animal figure in the Colville culture. He is a hero and a villain; a prankster and practical joker. The coyote can transform himself into any shape and animal he chooses. He can even take on a human form to deceive or play jokes. According to these legends, the coyote made the world and everything in it the way it is today.

Mourning Dove, the Activist

When Quintasket's book, *Cogewea,* was finally published in 1927, she became a well-known personality in the Washington state area and especially on the Colville Indian Reservation. Quintasket and her husband settled down, and she became active in local Indian politics. She joined with other Indian women and started social organizations and clubs for their handicrafts. She began to speak at gatherings locally and several times went east to speak. She found these long trips tiring and expensive since she paid for most of the travel expenses herself.

From the late 1920s until her death in 1936, she was an activist for Indian rights. In 1930, she and others organized the Colville Indian Association. Through their efforts, unresolved land claims, past due payments for lands purchased, and money owed to the tribe on leases for land, timber, and water rights, were secured for the tribe. She was the first woman elected to the Colville Tribal Council.

Quintasket continued with her activism and writing. She worked on her autobiography throughout the late 1920s and early 1930s. These combined efforts of writing, activism, and family were a strain on her fragile health, and she became more despondent. At times she became disoriented; and on July 30, 1936, she was taken to the state hospital at Medical Lake for treatment. Mourning Dove died on August 8, 1936; exhaustion from manic depressive psychosis was listed on her death certificate. Her grave marker plainly says, "Mrs. Fred Galler." In the introduction to the book, *Mourning Dove: A Salishan Autobiography,* editor Jay Miller writes, "Mourning Dove had bought a plot in a local white cemetery. After a life devoted to providing a bridge between Indian and white, she decided to leave the reservation."

The Autobiography

Heister Dean Guie collaborated with Mourning Dove and L. V. McWhorter for many years. The year before *Coyote Stories* was published, Quintasket had stayed with the Guies. Quintasket wanted Guie to review and edit her autobiography. The manuscript was stored away and several years later Quintasket died. Guie's widow found manuscript pages stored away in a trunk in the home attic in 1981. She turned them over to a scholar friend who was unable to put the manuscript into any order. The papers were then sent to the University of Washington Press where the editor, Jay Miller, put the autobiography together. Quintasket's autobiography was published in 1990, 54 years after she died.

SELECTED WRITINGS BY MOURNING DOVE:

Co-Ge-We-A, the Half-Blood: A Depiction of the Great Montana Cattle Range, Boston, Four Seas Company Publishers, 1927.
Coyote Stories, Caldwell, Idaho, Caxton Printers, 1933.
Mourning Dove: A Salishan Autobiography, edited by Jay Miller, Lincoln and London, University of Nebraska Press, 1990.

SOURCES:

Books

Mourning Dove, *Cogewea, the Half-Blood: A Depiction of the Great Montana Cattle Range,* edited by Dexter Fisher, Lincoln and London, University of Nebraska Press, 1981.

Mourning Dove, *Coyote Stories,* edited by Jay Miller, Lincoln and London, University of Nebraska Press, 1990.

Native American Women, edited by Gretchen M. Bataille, New York, Garland Publishing, 1993; 178-179.

Periodicals

Brown, Alanna Kathleen, "Mourning Dove's Canadian Recovery Years, 1917-1919," *Canadian Literature* (Vancouver, University of British Columbia), 124-125, spring-summer 1990: 113-121.

—Sketch by Russell Hellstern

Raymond Nakai
1918-
Navajo tribal leader

Raymond Nakai is credited with helping to modernize the largest Native American nation in the United States—the Navajo nation. Nakai was born on the reservation in Lukachukai, Arizona. He attended Indian schools in Fort Wingate and Shiprock then joined the U.S. Navy, serving during World War II in the South Pacific. After returning to the reservation, he became well known to the Navajo people when he worked in radio as a disc jockey and announcer in Flagstaff, Arizona. He married Ella Crawford, a women of mixed Ute and Navajo heritage, and together they had five children, one of whom, R. Carlos Nakai, became a prominent composer and musician.

Nakai, Peter MacDonald, and Perry Allen, all of whom share professional ties, played crucial roles in the development of enterprise for the Navajo nation. Allen, first chief prosecutor for the tribe, served as Nakai's public relations director and administrative assistant during Nakai's bid for the chair of the Navajo Council in the 1960s. Nakai ultimately served as chair of the council from 1963 to 1971. In addition to assisting with Nakai's campaign, Allen was the creator of the Manage Methods and Procedures Office. At Allen's request, Peter MacDonald—then an employee of Hughes Aircraft in California—was called upon to serve as director of the office. MacDonald was later appointed director of the Office of Navajo Economic Opportunity (ONEO), which Nakai set up with funds from Washington. MacDonald ultimately succeeded Nakai as chair of the Navajo Council in the 1970s.

Nakai, early in his administration as Navajo Council chair, was flying with Allen to California on business. On the ground below, they saw a canal and large aqueduct through which water was begin transported from Navajo land in Arizona for use by Californians. "He was always concerned about that," Allen told Phyllis Noah in an interview. "He wondered how the Arizona government could sell water from Navajo land to California."

Expands Industry, Tourism, and Agriculture

Nakai was instrumental in industrializing the Navajo community. He was the first chair of the Navajo Council to implement the use of a computer for the council budget.

Raymond Nakai

Nakai also emphasized the production of the reservation's natural resources—uranium, coal, gas, oil, and timber. But when factories were built on the land, environmental problems—such as pollution and land erosion—and labor problems haunted him. Throughout his tenure, Nakai worked on correcting such problems and improving the quality of life for his people in many areas. He promoted agriculture and built a huge irrigation system for farmers, built roads, and created the first legal service for the Navajo people. Nakai also saw the advantage of tourism and promoted luxury motels and tribal parks—all owned and operated by the Navajo people.

Nakai and President John F. Kennedy were close personal friends. Kennedy once said that he had never heard a politician who spoke as well as Nakai. Influenced by Nakai, the Kennedy administration granted funds to the Navajo nation to set up ONEO. During his time in office Kennedy also signed a bill to guarantee loans for Indian people to build homes. Others associated with the Kennedy administration, such as Hubert Humphrey and the president's brother, Robert F. Kennedy, paid visits to the Navajo during the 1960s. Nakai also met with Kennedy himself on many occasions and he was highly respected by the Kennedy administration.

Nakai built the first reservation post office and instituted the first Social Security program on the reservation, which successfully distributed governmental monies to elderly Navajos. Nakai also helped his people obtain loans for buildings in their community which they then leased to the government. Nakai did this so that the money would go back to his people. Nakai developed the Navajo housing authority under the Housing and Urban Development (HUD) program and built thousands of homes on the reservation. He also fought for farmers' rights to raise sheep, cattle, and horses that previously had been limited by the Bureau of Indian Affairs (BIA) and the federal government.

Develops the First Bill of Rights for Navajo Nation

Nakai was the first chair to creating shopping centers, a housing authority, a school board, and banks for the Navajos. In 1968, Nakai developed the Navajo Bill of Rights and he tried to draw up a constitution for the Navajo people. At the time, however, many council members from the previous administration, the "Old Guard", rejected the idea of a constitution. He became frustrated when the Old Guard made stalled the progress and development of the Navajo nation. They called Nakai "Little Caesar" and "Dictator" opposing him just for the sake of opposing him. After the first term, many of the "Old Guard" were replaced by new people. This second group's opposition to his constitution was the biggest frustration of Nakai's administration.

In 1969, Nakai signed an agreement to build a $309 million electric generating plant. The plant was built in Page, Arizona. A coal mine on Navajo mountain shipped coal to the plant. The Hopis were part owners of coal mine and complained that ground water was being taken by the mine. But the mine brought in over $1.8 million annually for the Hopis and the Navajos. General Dynamics built a factory on the reservation at Fort Defiance, and Nakai signed an agreement with the unions to come into the reservation so that Navajos would have preference for jobs. Fairchild Semi-Conductor opened an electronic assembly plant in Shiprock at the Shiprock Community Center which was leased from the Navajos. Later they built a permanent facility there.

Brings Schools to the Reservation

Nakai emphasized education for the Navajo and created cultural programs and public schools on the reservation which did away with government boarding schools. He was founder of the Navajo Community College at Many Farms, Arizona, in 1969 and created the Navajo Library in Window Rock, Arizona, in 1970. Ned Hatathli, one of the first Navajos to earn a Ph.D., was appointed the first president of the college. This was the first Indian college in the country.

Before Nakai became tribal leader, thousands of Navajo children did not go to school unless they left home and attended government boarding schools. He encouraged the return to traditional practices of weaving and silversmithing with the formation of the Navajo Arts and Crafts Guild. Hatathli was the first manager of the guild and after his appointment as president of the college, Carl Gorman was asked to manage the Arts and Crafts Guild.

Although lacking formal education, Nakai was successful in his years as chair of the Navajo nation and was admired by his people. One of Nakai's biggest supporters was the Native American Church. Previously, the church was prohibited from practicing their religion on the reservation; Nakai was instrumental in developing the church and legalizing peyote to be used in ceremonies. The Bill of Rights gave the church the right to practice their religion.

Nakai wanted the Navajo nation to have their own flag and he asked Perry Allen to have a flag designed. The first Navajo flag was created, featuring tribal border lines (white with brown) on the perimeter and the four sacred mountains in the center in white, yellow, blue and black. Cattle, sheep, horses, and corn are included in the design and the sun shines down on the land from above the mountains. The four sacred mountains are called Blanco Peak, Mount Taylor, San Francisco Peak, and the LaPlata Mountains.

Nakai had a problem with his eyes and had two pairs of glasses—one dark and one light. He had a habit of wearing dark glasses even inside because of the reflection from light. Nakai was an avid reader of Greek philosophy and great books of the West. He incorporated philosophy and his Navajo beliefs into his methods of leadership. His hobbies were photography and hunting turkey and deer. "On his days off, which were very seldom," Allen said, "he would walk over the mountains and into the canyons and take hundreds of pictures." Nakai currently lives in Lukachukai, Arizona.

SOURCES:

Books

The American Indian, 1492-1976, second edition, compiled and edited by Henry C. Dennis, Dobbs Ferry, New York, Oceana Publications; 76-77.

Biographical Dictionary of Indians of the Americas, Volume 2, Newport Beach, California, American Indian Publishers, 1991; 459-460.

Native North American Almanac, edited by Duane Champagne, Detroit, Gale Research, 1994; 1112-1113.

Young, Robert W., *A Political History of the Navajo Tribe,* Tsaile, Navajo Nation, Arizona, 1978; 162-164.

Other

Allen, Perry, interview with Phyllis Noah conducted August 17, 1994.

—Sketch by Phyllis "Picturestone" Noah

Nampeyo
1860(?)-1942
Hano potter

Also known as Num-pa-yu (Nampeya, Nampayu, Nampeyjo) ["Snake That Does Not Bite"] and Tcu mana ["Snake Girl"]

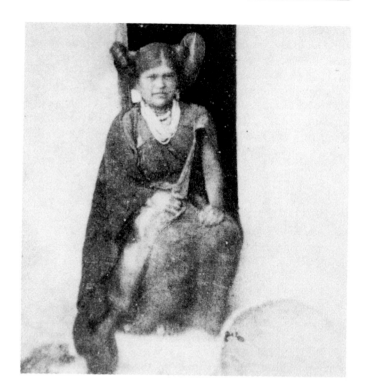

Nampeyo

When Nampeyo was featured at the United States Land and Irrigation Exposition in Chicago in 1910, the *Chicago Tribune* proclaimed her to be "Nampeyo, squaw, regarded as the greatest maker of Indian pottery alive." Reintroducing ancient styles and designs to Hopi pottery, Nampeyo led the Sityatki Revival Movement that changed the nature of Hopi pottery, helped the economy of the Hopi-Tewas, and began a family tradition extending through many generations.

Born about 1860 at Hano on First Mesa in Northern Arizona, Nampeyo was the daughter of Qotsvema, a Hopi from Walpi and member of the Snake Clan, and Qotcakao, a Tewa woman of Hano and member of the Tobacco Clan. According to Hopi tradition, they lived with the wife's family at Hano, sometimes called Hopi-Tewa village. As a young girl, Nampeyo often visited her grandmother, her father's mother, at Walpi. From that grandmother she began learning the skills of pottery making.

At first, Nampeyo probably made the usual, useful pots and utensils: cook pots, water carriers, and stew bowls. At that time, pottery was made chiefly for those purposes, with little attention given to style and decoration. At Walpi, pots were sometimes decorated with designs borrowed from the Zuni. The pots were painted with a slip or thin clay mixture that, when fired, produced a crazed or crackle-glazed surface. In the late nineteenth century, however, handmade clay pots were beginning to be replaced by metal cook pots and china dishes available through traders. Fascinated by the pottery-making process, Nampeyo began experimenting with different styles and designs. Perhaps she walked to the site of Sityatki, an ancient ruin three miles from Hano and found potsherds, fragments of pottery, marked with bright designs, made by potters who had lived there three or four hundred years before.

Becomes a Leader in the Sityatki Revival Movement

After a brief marriage to a man named Kwivioya, Nampeyo married Lesou, a native of Walpi, in 1881, and they lived at Hano. When Walter Fewkes came in 1895, to excavate Sityatki, Lesou worked for him. Nampeyo visited the dig often, borrowing pencils to sketch designs and symbols for her pots. Discovering sources of the kinds of clays used in the early pots, she began shaping her pots like the ancient ones. She used a white slip that turned yellow during the firing, and she matched the pigments used to paint the designs.

Soon her work was noticed by the tourists and traders who visited the pueblo. Her pottery became much in demand, and she was recognized as an artist. Fewkes wor-ried that her pots might be sold by unscrupulous traders as genuine Sityatki pots. However, Nampeyo's were not replicas or exact copies of the ancient pots. Instead, she captured the spirit of those long-dead potters, using the symbols and designs to create original works of art that evoked the past and began the Sityatki Revival, a movement that spread through her village and family.

William Henry Jackson had photographed Nampeyo when she was about 15, still wearing the butterfly whorls or squash blossom hairdo signifying eligibility for marriage. When he published the photo later, he noted that she had become a famous potter. She was renowned most for her oversized pieces—low, wide-shouldered, graceful pots—in shades ranging from cream to bright yellow, the designs painted in red and black. She also made many small pieces to sell through railroad hotels and tourist shops and to tourists and traders who visited the reservation. Other Hopi potters began copying her styles and designs, making pots that brought better prices than the crackle-glazed ware.

Nampeyo left the reservation at least three times: in 1905 and 1907, to spend time at Fred Harvey's Hopi House in the Grand Canyon where she manufactured and displayed her pottery, and in 1910, to demonstrate her pottery making at the Chicago Land Show. As her grandmother had taught her, Nampeyo taught the art of pottery making to her daughters and granddaughters. Almost blind, in the last years of her life, she still shaped the pots, but her daughters painted the designs.

Nampeyo died on July 20, 1942, leaving a tradition of beautiful Hopi pottery, based on ancient materials, methods, and designs. She also left many descendants to continue the work. One daughter, Fannie Nampeyo, was among four potters called by S. Peterson "Matriarchs of Pueblo Pottery." In 1983 an exhibit in Albuquerque, New Mexico, featured the creative work of Nampeyo and five generations of her descendants. An exhibition of Hopi Crafts in New York in 1991 included the works of ten of those descendants. Daisy Hooee Nampeyo, a granddaughter and Dextra Quotskuyva Nampeyo, a great granddaughter, are among at least 73 family members who have continued to make Sityatki-style pots, gaining fame for themselves and keeping the spirit of Nampeyo alive.

SOURCES:

Books

Bartlett, Katherine, "A History of Hopi Pottery," in *Hopi and Hopi-Tewa Pottery,* Flagstaff, Arizona, Museum of Northern Arizona, 1977.

Collins, John, *Nampeyo, Hopi Potter: Her Artistry and Her Legacy,* Fullerton, California, Muckenthaler Cultural Center, 1974.

Lisa, Laurie, "Nampeyo," in *Native American Women,* edited by Gretchen M. Bataille, New York, Garland Press, 1993; 183-184.

McCoy, Ronald, "Nampeyo: Giving the Indian Artist a Name," in *Indian Lives: Essays on Nineteenth- and Twentieth-Century Leaders,* edited by L. G. Moses and Raymond Wilson, Albuquerque, University of New Mexico Press, 1985; 43-57.

Nampeyo of Hano and Five Generations of her Descendants, Albuquerque, New Mexico, Adobe Gallery, 1983.

Seven Families in Pueblo Pottery, Maxwell Museum of Anthropology, Albuquerque, University of New Mexico Press, 1974.

Periodicals

Ashton, Robert Jr., "Nampeyo and Lesou," *American Indian Art,* 1, summer 1976; 24-33.

Colton, Mary Russell F., and Harold S. Colton, "An Appreciation of the Art of Nampeyo and Her Influence on Hopi Pottery," *Plateau,* 15, January 1943; 43-45.

Freudenheim, Betty, "Crafts: 'Ancient Ones' Inspire Hopis," *New York Times,* April 21, 1991; Section 12NJ, 11.

Hough, Walter, "A Revival of the Ancient Hopi Pottery Art," *American Anthropologist,* 19, April-June 1917; 332.

Kramer, Barbara, "Nampeyo, Hopi House and the Chicago Land Show," *American Indian Art,* 14 winter 1988; 46-53.

Monthan, Guy, and Doris Monthan, "Dextra Quotskuyva Nampeyo," *American Indian Art,* 2, autumn 1977; 58-63.

"Nampeyo," *Arizona Highways,* 50, May 1974; 16-21.

Nequatewa, Edmund, "Nampeyo, Famous Hopi Potter," *Plateau,* 15, January 1943; 40-42.

Peterson, S., "Matriarchs of Pueblo Pottery," Portfolio— *The Magazine of the Fine Arts,* 2:5, 1980.

—*Sketch by Blanche Cox Clegg*

Nora Naranjo-Morse
1953-
Tewa Pueblo poet and potter

Nora Naranjo-Morse, an artist who works in clay, metal and words, struggles, as she stays, "in two worlds, between Pueblo tradition and modern values." Her work, described as modern and unique, is, nevertheless, deeply rooted in Pueblo culture and traditions. Through her work found in exhibitions, audiovisuals, and a book combining poetry with pictures of her clay figures, Naranjo-Morse tries to make sense of those two worlds.

Ninth of ten children of Mitchell and Rose Naranjo of Santa Clara pueblo, Naranjo-Morse was born into a family known for pottery-making; her mother and sisters are all potters. Converted by Baptist missionaries, her father became a minister, setting the family apart from the Pueblo community, causing them to be viewed as different. He served first in Santa Clara and then at Taos, New Mexico, but eventually left the ministry. The family returned to Santa Clara, but still felt alienated by the Pueblo, leading Naranjo-Morse and other members of her family to pursue their own dreams in their own ways.

After graduating from Taos High School in 1971, Naranjo-Morse left New Mexico and went on to travel a great deal. She sorted mail in Washington, D.C., and sold firecrackers in South Dakota. This period was also one of rebellion against the church. She finally returned to Santa Clara reuniting with her family. In her poem, "Two Worlds," she asks, "Had I forgotten who I was, where I'd come from?" At the Pueblo she married Greg Morse from Connecticut and became the mother of twins, Eliza and Zachary. In 1976, she began seriously working with clay, and soon, in addition to making bowls, she began sculpting clay figures of animals and people, blending Pueblo traditions with her own images of the outside world.

In 1980, she graduated from College of Santa Fe with a degree in social welfare, but as a recognized potter she continued with her art career. Combining micaceous clay with Santa Clara clay she made figures, often humorous and inspired by her personal experiences and observations and her culture. The figures have immense appeal because, as Linda Eaton points out in *A Separate Vision: Case Studies of Four Contemporary Indian Artists,* "Her people are made not of earth, but of us.... Inspired by our most human attributes, [she] celebrates and consoles them in the clay."

Sometimes Naranjo-Morse's figures achieve an identity continuing through a series of sculptures. One such figure was Pearlene, wearing tight, short skirts and purple "tennies." Pearlene, Naranjo-Morse explains in *Mud Woman,* "fluctuates between confusion and clarity, reverence and mischief, while searching for her niche in life." Craig Womack remarks in *American Indian Quarterly,* "Pearlene is the one brave enough to actually do the things the rest of us only fantasize about ... Pearlene's life demonstrates both the problems and potential of merging past and present." When someone offered to mass-produce Pearlene, Naranjo-Morse, struck with the horror of a multitude of identical, plastic Pearlenes, made one final Pearlene and went on to other things.

Participates in "A Separate Vision"

Besides displaying her work in galleries and Indian markets, Naranjo-Morse was part of a two-year project beginning in 1987 at the Museum of Northern Arizona, Flagstaff. Called "A Separate Vision," it sought to foster support and understanding for the efforts of Native American artists to, as Eaton writes, "move away from expected forms and techniques and find creative artistic synthesis out of their own late twentieth century experiences ... both reservation and non-reservation life." As one of four artists in the project, Naranjo-Morse spent a month in residence at the museum gallery, displaying and practicing her art. She participated in the making of a videotape called "Separate Visions" and in an educational program for children and adults.

In 1989, she was one of seven poets in the annual Taos Poetry Circus, sponsored by Society of the Muse of the Southwest (SOMOS). Her book, *Mud Woman: Poems from the Clay,* juxtaposes poems and pictures of her clay sculptures. In the preface she says, "This collection of poems and clay forms documents a fifteen-year milestone of creating." Janice Gould, a well-known Native American poet, calls the book "gentle, thoughtful, expressive of the rituals of daily life." Joy Harjo, another famous Native American poet, asserts, "Nora Naranjo-Morse reminds us that the Sky and the Earth are relatives of the artist and are part of each conception, as is the human family—most importantly the unforgettable character Pearlene, the wild thing in all of us."

Speaking of her vision and her creative processes, Naranjo-Morse mentions *Gia* "mother" and *Nan chu Kweejo* "Clay Mother" as most responsible for her approach to art. From *Gia* she learned respect for the clay and the steps in making pottery, from the gathering, sieving, soaking, and draining of the clay through pillowcases hung from trees to the shaping and firing of the clay. A prayer of thanks is offered to *Nan chu Kweejo* at the site of the clay gathering, a disordered area covered with branches and earth. As her mother taught her, Naranjo-Morse has taught her children of pottery-making, and she had encouraged them to help with the adobe house she and husband Greg built. Other art projects include creating a series of masks and working with bronze. She wants to be remembered, Eaton mentions, "as an artist who listened to the clay, who followed her art where it led, and had faith that it would take care of her."

SELECTED WRITINGS BY NARANJO-MORSE:

Mud Woman: Poems from the Clay, Tucson, University of Arizona Press, 1992.
A First Clay Gathering, Cleveland, Modern Curriculum Press, 1994.

SOURCES:

Books

Babcock, Barbara A. "Naranjo-Morse, Nora," *Native American Women,* edited by Gretchen M. Bataille, New York, Garland Publishing, 1993.
Eaton, Linda B., *A Separate Vision: Case Studies of Four Contemporary Indian Artists,* Flagstaff, Arizona, Museum of Northern Arizona Press, 1990.

Periodicals

Gould, Janice, "Gentle and Imaginative Text: Mud Woman: Poems from the Clay by Nora Naranjo-Morse," *American Book Review,* April 1993; 5-6.
Lichtenstein, Grace, "The Evolution of a Craft Tradition: Three Generations of Naranjo Women," *Ms.,* April 1983; 59-60, 92.
Naranjo-Morse, Nora, "The Heart of the Vein," *Studio Potter,* December 1991; 54.
Trimble, Stephen, "Brown Earth and Laughter: The Clay People of Nora Naranjo-Morse," *American Indian Art,* autumn 1987; 58-65.
Womack, Craig, "Nora Naranjo-Morse, Mud Woman: Poems from the Clay," *American Indian Quarterly,* winter 1993; 102.

—Sketch by Blanche Cox Clegg

Lloyd Kiva New
1916-
Cherokee artist, fabric designer, artisan, administrator, and arts educator

Artist and craftsperson Lloyd Kiva New, a half-Cherokee, is best known for his work in textile or fabric design. Throughout his career he has also worked as an administrator and arts educator and has done much research into the history of Indian art, crafts, and performing arts. Throughout his career he has worked with various government and private organizations for the support of Indian art.

He was born Lloyd H. New on February 18, 1916, in Fairland, a small community in the northeastern corner of Oklahoma, and attended several universities, including Oklahoma State University and the Art Institute of Chicago, before receiving his bachelor of arts in education from the University of Chicago in 1938. While in Chicago, he also studied textile printing and dyeing with D. D. and Leslie Tillett.

One of his first positions after receiving his degree was as an instructor in arts and crafts at the U.S. Indian School in Phoenix, Arizona, where he worked until 1941. While at the school, he also became director of the Indian Exhibit at the Arizona State Fair, a position which he held from 1939 to 1950.

In the mid-1940s, New began what ultimately became the internationally known Lloyd Kiva Studio in Scottsdale, Arizona. There, he and other Indian artists and artisans worked in leathers, hand-woven tweeds, and hand-dyed fabrics. New, discussing the establishment of the studio in the 1993 *Reference Encyclopedia of the American Indian,* noted that "during this period [I] was devoted to the problem: Can Indian craftsmen produce contemporary craft items for general use, enabling the craftsmen to earn a living, pursuing their crafts in a general society? This implies some understanding of design inspiration from Indian tradition, careful craftsmanship, fashion, and marketing."

In 1959, New became co-director of the Southwest Indian Arts Project at the University of Arizona, which was sponsored by the Rockefeller Foundation. Later, in 1962, he moved to Santa Fe, New Mexico, where he became arts director of the new Institute of American Indian Arts. He became president of the institute in 1967 and remained in that position until 1978. New served a number of years as a commissioner and later was appointed a chair of the Indian Arts and Crafts Board of the U.S. Department of the Interior by the Secretary of the Interior. During his time on the board he was a main player in chartering the National Foundation for American Indian Art, which promotes traditional contemporary Indian arts, regardless of media.

New was a charter-member trustee and member of the national advisory board of the Heard Museum of Anthropology and Primitive Art in Phoenix, Arizona, and also has served or currently serves on the boards of other historical art museums. Some of these positions are senior advisor of the National Museum of the American Indian of the Smithsonian Institution in Washington, D.C.; member of the advisory council of the Museum of the American Indian, Heye Foundation, New York; and member of the national advisory board of the Plains Indian Museum and Buffalo Bill Historical Society in Cody, Wyoming.

New has been featured at such major exhibitions as the Textile Exhibit at the Museum of Modern Art in New York, the World Crafts Country Exhibit in Peru, and the International Touring Exhibit sponsored by the U.S. Department of the Interior. New has held an honorary membership in the American Institute of Interior Design and is an honorary fellow in the American Crafts Council. He also belongs to the World Crafts Council and has been the chair of the Intercultural Committee of the American Council of Arts Education.

In 1994, he was selected by Red Earth, a major Native American art and cultural exhibit held annually in Oklahoma City, to receive its Honored One Award. The award, the highest given by Red Earth, is presented to a Native American who has a distinguished record of service on behalf of promoting and contributing to Native American art.

SOURCES:

Books

Havlice, Patricia Pate, *Index to Artistic Biography,* first supplement, Metuchen, New Jersey, Scarecrow Press, 1981; 619.
Reference Encyclopedia of the American Indian, sixth edition, edited by Barry T. Klein, West Nyack, New York, Todd Publications, 1993; 594.

Periodicals

"New 'Honored One' at Red Earth," *Cherokee Observer,* 2:8, August 1994; 20.

—*Sketch by Sandra Sac Parker*

Duane Niatum
1938-
Klallam poet, short story writer, essayist, and editor
Also known as Crow's Son, Little Crow, and Duane McGinness

Duane Niatum has achieved international recognition as editor of the two most widely read and best-known anthologies of Native American poetry, and as author of several volumes of his own award-winning poetry. He has also published essays and short stories that have been translated into more than 12 languages, and was invited in June of 1983 to address an international conference on world literature in Rotterdam.

Born in Seattle, Washington, as Duane McGinness, Niatum spent most of his life there. Raised by his maternal grandfather, he changed his name to Niatum, which was his maternal great-grandfather's Indian name. His grandfather's name was Francis Patsy ("Old Patsy"). In a poem to him ("Old Tillicum") Niatum imagines his grandfather thinking: "Pitch-dry with age I am here / to see that my daughter's son starts / the long journey back to the clearing of Old Patsy." That grandson was given the guardian spirit of a crow, and so, was called "Little Crow."

The Klallam are a Salishan tribe of salmon fishermen whose name means "strong people." In the turmoil of Niatum's early childhood, he found the strength that restored him to psychic stability when he internalized his grandfather's values. From the age of four he learned the Klallum traditions, "Fishing, hunting, which gave me a strong sense of my relationship to the sea, to the land, to the animals, which I retain," he told Joseph Bruchac. From the time that his father left, and his parents divorced, until he joined the

Duane Niatum

Navy at 17, Niatum learned from Old Patsy. His first book, called *After the Death of an Elder Klallam,* constituted an elegy. In it, he acknowledged all the survival strategies he had been taught—the use of every element of his environment, including every plant, tree, bird, fish, animal. He had learned how to recognize each in every season. He knew how to identify clams by the shape and the level of their holes, and to differentiate those that were edible from those that were not. A poet could not have any better training than such habits of minute observation of particular details of the natural world.

The poem "Street Kid," in his book *Digging Out the Roots,* tells about his surviving three incarcerations by looking out toward the natural world in which he had been free. He spent two months in a reform school in Martinez, California, and was held twice in the Youth Service Center in Seattle, Washington. His youthful rebellions have matured into adult protests against social injustice expressed in demonstrations, marches, and letters.

From 1955 until 1959 he was in the United States Navy stationed for two years of his service in Japan. There he found many parallels with his own Native American traditions. He learned restraint and understatement from Japanese art. At 21, after his service in the Navy, he enrolled at the University of Washington. Teachers who influenced him were Theodore Roethke, Nelson Bentley, Elizabeth Bishop, and Leonie Adams. Later, he studied with Susan Sontag who encouraged him to discover European culture. He paid tribute to Roethke's reverence for old forms by composing a Shakespearian sonnet sequence in his honor.

Uses Puget Sound Images

The sacred tree of the Northwest Coast was the cedar. It was made into everything used in daily life: spoons, forks, bowls, canoes, houses, totems were carved from it, and clothing was made of its bark. The references to Ceder Man combine associations with his grandfather and with the tree upon which the Salish depended for survival. He called his second collection *Ascending Red Cedar Moon.* His powerful short story, "Crow's Sun" ends with a young sailor's being locked up in the brig, as Niatum himself had been by brutal, racist officers for 30 days. But the protagonist has summoned his spiritual guardian, the crow, to sustain him; and as he is dragged off, "a crow rises from a red cedar branch, upward to the mountain peaks." As it ascends to the clouds, the protagonist thanks his grandfather, his people, and the sunrise glinting from the black feathers.

Cultural Mediations

From 1973 to 1974 he served as editor of the Native American Author Series at Harper and Row in New York City. He sought out young writers' work from small periodicals and gave it permanence between the covers of a 1975 anthology called *Carriers of the Dream Wheel.* This collection and the 1986 *Harper's Book of Twentieth-Century Native American Poetry* became the best-known volumes of contemporary Indian work. The dream wheel alludes to the Sacred Hoop, which is not only the tribal circle of inter-related kin, but also the great cycles of the seasons, the stellar circles, the earth's rotation, the circling of danced prayers in the Sun Dance around the sacred tree in the center, and the need for pan-Indian coalitions to join in affirmations of the circle without end. Niatum believes that only an art grounded in Nature has wholeness of vision.

Niatum has sustained himself on part-time jobs. From 1970 to 1972 he was an instructor at Johns Hopkins; he taught at Immaculate High School in Seattle from 1974 to 1975; from 1977 to 1978, he taught the elderly for the Seattle Arts Commission; and he worked for three years as an assistant librarian. He was a visiting instructor at the University of Washington, Evergreen State College, Eastern Washington University, and Seattle Central Community College. He has been invited to read at 40 colleges, and in 1976, at the Library of Congress. He also worked as a poet-in-the-schools in Arizona, New Mexico, and Oregon.

Wins Many Honors

He has won first prize in poetry twice (1966 and 1970) at the Pacific Northwest Writers' Conference. The Seattle Music and Art Foundation gave him its Literature Award in 1968; and he received the Washington Governor's Award in 1971. He has won grants from Carnegie in 1975, and from PEN in 1976. And in 1977, he was invited to the Yaddo Artist's Colony in Saratoga Springs, New York. His book, *Songs for the Harvester of Dreams* was honored by the American Book Award in 1982 by the Before Columbus Foundation.

In addition to having composed an experimental verse drama, *Breathless,* which was performed in 1968 at the University of Washington, he has contributed over 100 reviews, essays, short stories, and poems to a variety of newspapers and periodicals; and he has published a number of chapbooks. His work, which has been translated into Frisian, Icelandic, Macedonian, Danish, Spanish, German, Polish, French, Dutch, and Italian, attests to its worldwide appeal.

SELECTED WRITINGS BY NIATUM:

Ascending Red Cedar Moon, New York, Harper, 1969.
After the Death of an Elder Klallam, Santa Fe, Baleen, 1970.
Taos Pueblo: Poems, Greenfield Center, Greenfield Review, 1973.
A Cycle for the Woman in the Field (chapbook), Laughing Man Press, 1973.
Editor, *Carriers of the Dream Wheel,* New York, Harper, 1975.
Digging Out the Roots, New York. Harper, 1977.
Turning to the Rhythms of Her Song (chapbook), Jawbone Press, 1977.

To Bridge the Dream (chapbook), A Press, 1978.
Songs for the Harvester of Dreams, Seattle, University of Washington Press, 1981.
Pieces (chapbook), Strawberry Press, 1981.
Raven and the Fear of Growing White (chapbook), Bridge Press, 1983.
"On Stereotypes," in *Recovering the Word: Essays on Native American Literature,* edited by Brian Swann and Arnold Krupat, Berkeley, University of California Press, 1987.
Editor, *Harper's Anthology of Twentieth Century Native American Poetry,* New York, Harper, 1988.
Drawings of the Song Animals: New and Selected Poems, Duluth, Holy Cow Press, 1990.
"Crow's Bun," in *Talking Leaves: Contemporary Native American Short Stories,* edited by Craig Lesley, New York, Dell, 1991.

SOURCES:

Bruchac, Joseph, *Survival This Way: Interviews with American Indian Poets,* University of Arizona Press, 1987.

—Sketch by Ruth Rosenberg

O

Richard Oakes
1942-1972
Mohawk political activist

In the mold of the Iroquois warriors of long ago, Richard Oakes stood up for the rights of his people and of all indigenous Americans, playing an important role both in the activist organization Indians of All Tribes (IAT) and in the Pit River Indians' efforts to regain tribal land. His work for Native Americans ended abruptly, however, when he was cut down in the prime of life. Whether he was a victim of institutionalized racism or a personal conflict remains a question to this day.

Many Mohawk people live on the St. Regis Reservation in upstate New York. The reservation straddles the U.S.-Canadian border, but the Native Americans do not formally recognize the boundary. Into this community, Richard Oakes was born in 1942. Little is recorded of his early years, except that he left school in his junior year, disillusioned, certain that his future would not require "the white man's schools."

Oakes drifted into construction work, a viable option for many Mohawk men, who are famous for their high-steel crews. This work took him throughout New England, where he was exposed to many Native groups striving for recognition and rights. He softened to the idea of formal education, attending both Adirondack Community College and Syracuse University. His trade took him to California, and as he traveled to the West Coast, he visited several reservations. Settling in San Francisco, Oakes set to work, both as an iron-worker and as a college student at San Francisco State College. It was the winter of 1969. The 29-year-old man met a Pomo woman, Annie Marufo, from the Kashia people. She was already the single mother of five, and when they married, Richard took on the role of father with earnest sincerity.

The Alcatraz Occupation

By this time, the rising tide of Red Power/Indian Pride had swept Oakes up. He and the whole family had become involved with Bay Area Indian groups. Members of the organization Indians of All Tribes (IAT), the Oakes' were part of the defining event of that Indian rights movement. On November 21, 1969, a small party of IAT members landed on Alcatraz Island, site of the infamous federal prison of the same name. It was actually the group's second take-over of Alcatraz, but the first occupation five years earlier

Richard Oakes (left) with Earl Livermore

had gained little media attention. Oakes actually swam ashore from the tiny landing vessel and found the island uninhabited and the massive prison in terrible disrepair.

IAT intended to use the landing to get media attention for Indian issues, with the call for an Indian center to be built on the island. They were using a provision of the Fort Laramie Treaty of 1868, a treaty with the Sioux/Lakota that ended Red Cloud's War. This provision noted that unused federal land or structures could be claimed by Indians for their own use. The spirit of the law would probably indicate the clause meant Sioux people claiming unused federal land or structures in the vicinity of South Dakota at the time of the treaty signing; nevertheless, the seizure was legal.

In the early days of the occupation, Oakes was the acknowledged leader of IAT. His compatriot, Santee Sioux John Trudell, would become the official spokesperson for the media, and so, Oakes would remain a shadowy figure to many reporters. Several days after the occupation began, Oakes met with government officials. He told the group of IAT's demands, including their plans to seize property in Northern California and Fort Lawton in Seattle. Among the things Oakes addressed were the poor economic, educational, and social conditions in most Indian communities. He spoke of the restriction of tribal religions, the intransigence of many tribal leaders, and the failure of the Bureau of Indian Affairs (BIA) to support Indians on "Relocation" programs in urban centers. Oakes came away from the meeting not having created a confrontation with government officials, but with the promise that they would do what they could to bring public attention and policy analysis to bear on the issues.

Government pressure was not the only issue for IAT. The Oakes family would suffer a devastating loss when their 12-year-old daughter, Yvonne, fell from a well-constructed, safety-railed walkway. Speculation still exists about the suspicious nature of the accident; because intergroup fighting had by then emerged, pro-Oakes factions feared that the anti-Oakes faction might have caused the fall. In any case, the Coast Guard removed Yvonne to San Francisco General Hospital, where she died a few days later from massive head injuries. The bickering that had simmered just below the surface now broke into full-fledged fighting. The anti-Oakes faction was led by Gary Leech and Stella Leech. While Oakes and his family were on the mainland, at Yvonne's bedside and, later, attending her funeral, Oakes was voted out as council head and replaced with Gary Leech. Richard Oakes and his family did not return to Alcatraz, but continued their Indian political activism.

Attacked for His Activism

The next front on which Oakes fought was the Northern California Pit River Indians' attempts to retrieve tribal land. Oakes again made headlines on June 12, 1970, when he made a citizen's arrest of the president of Pacific Gas and Electric, one of the companies operating on land claimed by the Pit River people. Returning to San Francisco several hours after the incident, Oakes was attacked and beaten by three assailants, requiring his hospitalization.

For the next two years, Richard Oakes continued his efforts on behalf of Native people, particularly those of California, primarily small tribes with little political power or no federal recognition of their Indian status. He also believed in personal responsibility in the Indian movement; his family took in a young Native boy. In the fall of 1972, the teenager got into an argument with a young white man over the issues of Indian fishing rights. Oakes stopped the fight, but the white man's companion, 34-year-old Michael Morgan, shot over Oakes' head. Morgan worked at the Santa Clara YWCA camp in Sonoma County where the Indian teenager was visiting.

Oakes had been threatened before, even assaulted and hospitalized. Described as powerfully built but extremely gentle, Oakes rarely engaged in physical fights. In the late afternoon of September 20, 1972, Oakes was walking along a rural road leading to the YWCA camp, on his way to retrieve the Indian teenager. He encountered Morgan, who would later say that Oakes "jumped" him, although the activist was unarmed. Pulling a .9mm pistol, Morgan fired,

killing Oakes. He was charged with manslaughter, but was acquitted on the grounds of self-defense.

The murder of Richard Oakes, combined with the equally pointless killing of Lakota Sioux Raymond Yellow Thunder around that same time, galvanized the Indian movement. In particular, the leaders of the American Indian Movement (AIM) were outraged over the incidents. In large part as a tribute to the fallen warrior, the 1972 Trail of Broken Treaties caravan to Washington, D.C., carried on the spirit of Richard Oakes' battles. Richard Oakes is considered by Native Americans to be a martyr in the cause of Indian rights. His legacy evokes a much older tradition of those Iroquois warriors who fought for their people, whether on the battlefield, in the Council House, or in parlay with Europeans.

SOURCES:

Kickingbird, Kirke, and Karen Ducheneaux, *One Hundred Million Acres,* New York, Macmillan, 1973.

Matthiessen, Peter, *In the Spirit of Crazy Horse,* New York, Viking, 1983.

Matthiessen, Peter, *Indian Country,* New York, Penguin, 1984.

Native American Testimony, edited by Peter Nabokov, New York, Viking, 1991.

Native North American Almanac, edited by Duane Champagne, Detroit, Gale Research, 1994.

Shorris, Earl, *The Death of the Great Spirit,* New York, New American Library, 1971.

Steiner, Stan, *The New Indians,* New York, Harper, 1968.

Viola, Herman J., *After Columbus: The Smithsonian Chronicle of the American Indians,* Washington, D.C., Smithsonian Books, 1990.

Vogel, Virgil, *This Country Was Ours,* New York, Harper, 1972.

Weyler, Rex, *The Blood of the Land: The Government and Corporate War Against the American Indian Movement,* New York, Everest House, 1982.

—Sketch by Cynthia R. Kasee

Alanis Obomsawin
1932-
Abenaki filmmaker and singer

In addition to being an accomplished producer, director, and singer, Alanis Obomsawin is one of Canada's foremost documentary filmmakers on Native life, culture, and the arts. Born in Lebanon, New Hampshire, in 1932, she grew up on the Odonak Reservation located in Quebec. In 1967, she began working with the National Film Board of

Canada in conjunction with her first film. Completed in 1971, *Christmas at Moose Factory* delves into Cree life as it is perceived through the artwork of Native children.

Her early films reflect the richness of Native American culture and the diversity of Native peoples. Traditionally, many Native cultures are matrilineal if not matrilocal, placing emphasis upon women's activities and their direct influence upon culture. Produced in 1977, *Mother of Many Children* is a celebration of Native oral tradition, focusing on traditional women's use of language and storytelling in transmitting culture. Also produced in 1977, *Amisk* highlights Native artistic expression in the forms of dance and music.

In the years following her singing debut at New York City's Town Hall in 1960, Obomsawin traveled extensively through Canada, the United States, and Europe, performing at schools, universities, museums, prisons, and art centers for a variety of age groups and audiences. Her performances also include folk festivals and various fundraising functions. Like her film work, her singing has focused on and been inspired by Native themes. In 1988 she released her first solo album, *Bush Lady,* which is a compilation of her own compositions in her Native tongue (Abenaki), as well as in French and English.

Using Documentary to Further Humanitarian Causes

Obomsawin's affinity for humanitarian causes is especially reflected in her later films, which are dedicated to bringing to light to the systematic and often severely punitive oppression of Native Americans. One such example is *Incident at Restigouche,* a 1984 documentary portraying the brutal raid of Quebec Provincial police on the Restigouche Reserve concerning Native fishing activities. Her focus on such inequities sometimes has positive repercussions. As a result of bringing such governmental cruelty to the attention of the public, some Native American groups have, despite extensive commercialization of fishing, secured subsistence (survival) fishing rights. Such is the case with Natives of Kodiak and the Aleutian islands of Alaska.

Obomsawin created seven more films from 1986 to 1992 which all serve to illustrate governmental injustices toward Indians. Produced in 1986, *Richard Cardinal: Cry from a Diary of a Métis Child* tells the true story of a Cree boy whose abuse and neglect by the Child Welfare system culminate in his suicide during adolescence. *Poundmaker's Lodge: A Healing Place,* produced in 1987, focuses on the treatment provided by a drug and alcohol center geared towards the rebuilding of Natives' lives devastated by the abuse of these substances. Homelessness, another dilemma faced by many Indians and often an economic plight of disenfranchised groups, is the topic of her 1988 film *No Address.*

In 1983, the Canadian government awarded Obomsawin its highest honor, the prestigious Order of Canada, for her continual commitment to indigenous peoples. In addition to her 16 films and documentaries, she has directed and produced a number of different filmstrips, two vignettes,

and two multimedia packages, entitled *Manowan* and *L'ilawat.* Amidst these many and varied activities, she has continued to pursue her career as a singer. Obomsawin resides in Montreal, Canada, where she is an active board member of the Native Women's Shelter and Canada Council's Native Advisory Committee. She is dedicated to the preservation of Native culture and continues her interest in singing while working with the National Film Board.

SOURCES:

Canadian Who's Who, edited by Kieren Simpson, Toronto, University of Toronto Press, 1993; 839.
Native North American Almanac, edited by Duane Champagne, Detroit, Gale Research, 1994; 1117.

—*Sketch by Brett A. Lealand*

Samson Occom
1723-1792
Mohegan preacher, diarist, epistolarist, and hymn lyricist

Samson Occom, a Mohegan Indian who became a preacher, holds the significance of being the first Native American to write and publish a text, in 1772, in the English language. Its full title, of customary length for the eighteenth century, was *A Sermon, Preached at the Execution of Moses Paul, an Indian; Who Was Executed at New Haven, on the Second of September, 1772; For the Murder of Mr. Moses Cook, Late of Waterbury, on the 7th of December, 1771. Preached at the Desire of Said Paul. By Samson Occom, Minister of the Gospel, and Missionary to the Indians.* Over the next decade ten editions of this *Sermon* were printed. Simplistically written, it possesses a narrative focus and an organizational structure that, along with Occom's diaries and letters, reveal an unusual life for a Native American of his time.

Occom figures in the religious life of eighteenth-century North America, a man of prudence, selfless devotion to his calling, and an Indian whose solemnity proved to be an asset as he defended the autonomy and pride of his people. His writings offer little in terms of literary style; terse and lackluster best describe his diary entries. The book of hymns he published in 1774 probably interested him more than any notions about taking himself seriously as a writer. As a preacher, he sponsored solicitations for Reverend Eleazer Wheelock's school for Indians, some moneys which he obtained in England, led indirectly to the establishment of Dartmouth College as the first institution of higher learning intended for Native Americans. Occom had detractors who used race to justify criticizing him for alleged excesses.

Despite such confrontations upon his character and the impoverished circumstances of his family, Occom maintained an inner strength and disciplined will while preaching tirelessly to Indian communities in Connecticut, Long Island, and in New York's Mohawk Valley.

In one brief account of his early years, written in Boston on November 28, 1765, Occom felt compelled to defend the integrity of his early life and education: "I was Born a Heathen in Mmoyouheeunnuck alias Mohegan in N[ew]. London—North America. my [sic] Parents were altogether Heathens, and I was Educated by them in their Heathenish Notions.... [They] in particular Were very Strong in the Customs of their fore Fathers." When he reached age 16, he says "there was a great Stir of Religion in these parts of the World both amongst the Indians as Well as the English, and about this Time I began to think about the Christian Religion, and was under great trouble of Mind for Some Time."

Occom reported being born in a wigwam in 1723 to Sarah, a descendant of the legendary Mohegan leader Uncas, and Joshua, "a great Hunter" and one of three sons of Tomockham, also called Ashneon. His sister Lucy died in 1830 and his brother Jonathan served in the French and Indian and the Revolutionary wars. By "great Stir of Religion" Occom meant the Great Awakening and its widespread impact on evangelical communities throughout the colonies. Sarah, a Christian convert, found attractive the principles of "cleanliness, frugality, and industry," according to Occom biographer Harold Blodgett. She dissuaded her son from remaining with sachem Ben Uncas as one of his 12 councillors, and she implored the widely known Reverend Eleazer Wheelock of Lebanon, Connecticut, to accept her son in 1743 as a pupil. Occom would respond valorously to a life of Christian sacrifice that demanded of him frequent preaching tours despite his health being constantly fragile and his being susceptible to eyestrain. He underwent conversion and commenced religious study with Wheelock, driven by the desire to learn how to read so that he could study the Bible. Because he enjoyed the tutelage of the famous Wheelock, what he believed would be a short stay extended into the late 1740s; and although he had not completed his studies by that time, he was sent by Wheelock to teach the Gospel to the Montauk Indians on the eastern tip of Long Island. Their minister had left them in a state of spiritual uncertainty when he decided to preach to the westerly Shinnecock Indians.

Marriage and Financial Struggles

The Montauks encouraged Occom to extend his assignment to them. In 1751, against the objections of Wheelock, Occom married one of his students, Mary Fowler. The marriage lasted until his death, but despite his being a domestically responsible man and a loving husband and father, the marriage was never financially secure. The Occoms had ten children. When her husband was away preaching, Mary Occom often had to humble herself to beg for money from Wheelock and others in order to buy food and menial necessities.

The annual remuneration Occom received from the Boston Commissioners who oversaw religious affairs was a pittance of £15. Blodgett indicates Occom received none of the assistance given generally to clergy and teachers, and as a result he soon owed New York £50. He had to purchase his own wood and raise his own corn, and he was allowed to keep no sheep. This kind of short-shrifting of his income and the poverty it placed him in plagued Occom all his life. He felt himself exploited because of his race, particularly after 1759, the year of his ordination when he learned how a certain young minister was granted £180 annually, a sizable portion being his stipend. Financial solvency also eluded him that year when he was considered for a ministry among the Cherokees in the South, only for the venture to be prohibitive when the Cherokees engaged in a series of battles against settlers illegally invading their territory. Occom's physical labors, meanwhile, further affected his health and during this time he suffered from bleeding ulcers of the thigh. Yet, he continued visiting the Montauks and other tribes, preaching as opportunities arose. He ventured into New York City and Yonkers, describing them collectively as comparable to the biblical Sodom. After preaching to the Oneidas in the summer of 1761, he was given a wampum belt signifying a bond of friendship between this member of the Six Nations of the Iroquois and himself. He would return to them at their occasional requests over the next three decades.

Wheelock's Indian Charity School

Indian students from New England and New Jersey joined Occom when Reverend Wheelock established his Indian Charity School in 1754. Relations with the famous religious figure always fluctuated, but for many years Occom was an effective fundraiser for the school, despite his own scant livelihood and the reputation as a spendthrift that various Wheelock associates claimed him to be. Wheelock's mission was to prepare young Indians for a life of Calvinism's "light in pure truth." By 1764 some Iroquois and white charity students enlarged the student body. Then Wheelock conceived the idea of sending Occom and the Reverend Daniel Whitaker to England and Scotland on a fundraising campaign. The circumstances of this 1765-1767 journey and Wheelock's intentions about the future of the school eroded Occom's faith in his old teacher. Occom and Whitaker's relationship was tenuous and uneasy; Blodgett describes Occom as a plodder and his partner as "too preoccupied with grandiose schemes." The Indian minister never forgot his Indian identity, and while his hosts showered him with adulation, Whitaker reported by letter to Wheelock accusing Occom of extravagant spending and deportment unbefitting a Christian minister.

The Wheelock-Occom relationship deteriorated further when, upon Occom's return from abroad, his lingering sense deepened that Wheelock wished to change the Charity School from its Indian educational and missionary goals to a college. He objected strenuously to Dartmouth College as a "fraudulent diversion of the endowment from the Indians to the whites," and to Wheelock's relocating it to New Hampshire. In addition to this, Occom came to realize that his teacher had been patronizing him as a successful "creature" rather than a devoted Christian human being.

Occom's Active Life and his *Sermon*

For several years Samson Occom had withstood Wheelock's paternalism, conflicts with adversarial ministers, and his virtual powerlessness to receive the kind of income for his duties that would keep his growing family out of poverty. Most of all, he disliked being dependent upon Wheelock, who sent him on preaching assignments at his own discretion. While he tried to remain politically independent in affairs affecting his people, he would be drawn into situations where taking a position was unavoidable. One of these was the Mohegan Land Case or Mason Controversy. This far-reaching case, stemming from an "ambiguous agreement" in 1640 involving the Mohegans, the Colony of Connecticut, and Major John Mason, signifies the conflicting tone and conditions of land sales and land usage in trust as Indians and whites interpreted them. The Mohegans trusted Mason and his heirs and for over a century accused the Colony of fraud. Litigation was complex and continual, and by the time Occom returned from the Montauks in 1764 it had factionalized his people. He sympathized with the larger pro-Mason group; but the case fell victim to the preoccupations of the Revolutionary War and with the defeat of the British the Mohegans lost this substantial portion of their land.

Occom's role in the Mason Controversy infuriated the Reverend David Jewett, whose jurisdiction included Mohegan lands. Jewett issued charges of misconduct, public clamor, and heresy against Occom before Connecticut's Board of Correspondence. At its hearing on March 12, 1765, the Board exonerated Occom except for his actual participation in the Mason issue; and Occom, under the heavy influence of Wheelock, submitted a humble apology for trying to protect his tribe's land claim. English cunning against Indians distressed Occom, adding to his personal difficulties of the late 1760s and precipitating occasional though temporary bouts with alcohol by 1770.

Sermon for the Execution of Fellow Indian Moses Paul

Occom kept an extensive diary, but his entries are bland and hardly effusive, reading like a listing of tasks performed and things to do and offering no reflection of the inner personality. His sermons too are straightforward, following a simple format, and they are imbued with Calvinist exhortations about sin, death, and eternity. They avoid theological subtleties and are elementary as persuasive discourse. However, his most famous sermon, for the execution of fellow Indian Moses Paul, assumes social and political levels of interest as well as being the product, in light of the fame it brought him, of an ironical situation.

One December night in Waterbury, Connecticut, in 1771, Moses Paul, "a vagabond Indian" ejected from a tavern, enacted revenge on the first patron to emerge. Sentenced to be hanged, this former soldier and sailor gained a three-month reprieve and asked, possibly by his own writing, Occom to preach his execution sermon. Numerous Indians were among the clergymen, lawyers, and judges attending the sermon on a stormy September 2, 1772. All came to witness the execution—the first in New Haven since 1759—and hear the Indian preacher. Occom found himself in a dubious position as an Indian preacher having to preach a sermon for a condemned Indian on the topic of sobriety to whites and Indians that, from a rhetorical standpoint, demanded formidable skills of balance in referring to the effects of alcohol; he realized how the English used strong drink to weaken the spirit of his people.

For all its absence of stylistic flourish, *A Sermon* is a minor masterpiece of American "gallows literature." Conventional quotes from Scripture and the stern admonition that man's plight is rooted in sin characterize it; Occom goes on to address the sentenced Paul, then whites, before proceeding to remind Indians of the sin of drunkenness in his lengthy conclusion. The printing history of *A Sermon* is phenomenal. The New Haven press of Thomas and Samuel Green issued the first edition on October 31, 1772; the second was issued from New London two weeks later; the tenth appeared in 1780; and there were several more. Blodgett reports that some later editions contain an introduction with a contrived dialogue between preacher and condemned on the eve of the execution.

Writes Hymns

Occom began enjoying hymns while studying with Wheelock; and in England he met several hymn writers with whom he would later correspond. The number of hymns he actually composed which are included in his *Collection of Hymns and Spiritual Songs* of 1774 is unknown, but most possess his naivete and fundamental quality. One hymn widely agreed to be his is "Awaked by Sinai's Awful Sound," published posthumously.

Toward the end of his life Samson Occom and his wife settled in the New York community of the Stockbridge Oneidas—Stockbridge Indians are those tribes from the Hudson valley and westward who became Christian converts and were referred to as "praying Indians." In yet further ironical circumstances, Occom found himself defending these Oneidas from traditional Oneidas in land disputes. On July 14, 1792, he completed writing an article, collapsed while walking back to his house, and was found dead by his wife. Occom had been experiencing pains in his "vitals." He was 69. Over 300 Indians attended his funeral.

Occom preached the stern admonitions derived from the Great Awakening. He lived a prudent and joyless but busy life and he did not challenge his teachings. Blodgett describes him as affectionate and "intensely domestic.... He did not have an unusual intellect, but he possessed a solidity, an integrity of character, which preserved his independence in an alien culture.... He never 'sold out.'"

SOURCES:

Books

Blodgett, Harold, *Samson Occom,* Hanover, Dartmouth College Publications, 1935.

Love, W. Deloss, *Samson Occom and the Christian Indians of New England,* Boston, Pilgrim Press, 1899.

Murray, David, *Forked Tongues: Speech, Writing and Representation in North American Indian Texts,* Bloomington, Indiana University Press, 1991.

Richardson, Leon Burr, *An Indian Preacher in England, Being Letters and Diaries Relating to the Mission of the Reverend Samson Occom and the Reverent Nathaniel Whitaker,* Dartmouth College Manuscript, Series 2, Hanover, Dartmouth College Publications, 1933.

Ruoff, A. LaVonne Brown, *American Indian Literatures: An Introduction, Bibliographic Review, and Selected Bibliography,* New York, Modern Language Association, 1990.

Periodicals

Occom, Samson, "A Sermon Preached by Samson Occom ... at the Execution of Moses Paul," tenth edition (1780), *Studies in American Indian Literatures,* 4:2 and 3, summer/fall 1992; 82-105.

Ruoff, A. LaVonne, Brown, "Introduction: Samson Occom's *Sermon Preached by Samson Occom ... at the Execution of Moses Paul, An Indian,"* *Studies in American Indian Literatures,* 4:2 and 3, summer/fall 1992; 75-81.

—*Sketch by Ron Welburn*

Barney Old Coyote

Barney Old Coyote
1923-
Crow educator and administrator

Barney Old Coyote is a Crow educator and administrator who has served the interests of Native Americans in a variety of capacities. In addition to holding several different positions during his 21 years with the Bureau of Indian Affairs (BIA), he served as the first president of the American Indian National Bank (AINB), becoming the nation's first Native American bank president. Since his retirement from federal service in 1970, Old Coyote has been a professor and the director of the American Indian studies program at Montana State University. For his promotion of Native American affairs in both the public and private sector, Old Coyote has received an honorary Doctor of Humane Letters from Montana State University and a Distinguished Service Award from the U.S. Department of the Interior.

A descendant of several generations of Crow warriors, Old Coyote was born April 10, 1923, on a reservation in St. Xavier, Montana, where he attended Big Horn County Schools. At the age of 17, on the day Pearl Harbor was attacked, he enlisted in the Air Force where he was trained as a pilot. Carrying on a family tradition of bravery in battle that dates back to Mountain Sheep, a renowned Crow chief, and Big Forehead, a hero in the Battle of Rainy Butte, Old Coyote, along with his older brother, completed over 50 missions during World War II, despite the setback of a crash landing in Puerto Rico. After receiving several decorations during his five-year stint in the Air Force, including the Air Medal and the 14 Oak Clusters award, he was honorably discharged from military service. Upon his return to the United States, Old Coyote was honored by the Crow people with the official war ceremonies of the tribe, in which he proudly took full participation, carrying the pipe traditionally given to leaders of Crow war parties. Upon returning to civilian life, he quickly finished his secondary education and entered Haskell Institute in Kansas before transferring to Morningside College in Sioux City, Iowa, where he earned his Bachelor of Science degree. He also married Clara Teboe, who would give birth to seven children: Kenneth, Patricia, Gary, Bernard, Rachel, Jacqueline, and Edwina.

Promotes Native American Interests through BIA

After finishing college, Old Coyote began a distinguished career in government service. Affiliated primarily with the BIA, he was employed as an agricultural engineer, realty officer, and superintendent. During his long career in public affairs, Old Coyote also served as special assistant to the secretary of the U.S. Department of the Interior from

1964 to 1969, working with young men and women as the coordinator of a job corps training program. In 1968, he received a Distinguished Service Award from the Department of the Interior for his efforts. In 1970, he concluded his career in federal service, retiring from his position as assistant area director of the BIA office in Sacramento, California, where he helped to promote the interests of the California tribes.

Old Coyote learned through his experiences with the BIA that gaining access to the financial segment of the economy would enable Native Americans to expand their opportunities in a capitalist society. Armed with this knowledge, he became involved in a federal project that gave birth to the American Indian National Bank. He received the charter for the Federal Deposit Insurance Corporation (FDIC) supported bank in 1973 and served as its first president. With its 100,000 shares of stock under the sole ownership of Native Americans, the bank was able to fill the capital needs of Native American individuals and tribes that could not be met by other financial institutions. The Oklahoma Creek Nation, for instance, received a $375,000 loan—the first made to a tribe—that enabled them to build a commercial office building and a complex of tribal offices on Creek land. As Old Coyote told *Banker's* magazine, the AINB was "the first real opportunity for Indians to put their money to work for themselves and for others in the Indian community."

Bringing with him a wealth of wide-ranging practical experience, if not a great deal of formal education, Old Coyote channelled his respect for his Native American heritage to the university setting, serving as professor and director of American Indian studies at Montana State University in Bozeman since 1970. From his position as an academic, he has contributed a variety of publications on Native American culture, addressing Native American education and general involvement in U.S. society. Having demonstrated earlier in his life the ability to skillfully serve his country and his people through governmental channels, Old Coyote's role as an educator has enabled him to pass on the cultural values of the Native American tradition to students of all races.

SOURCES:

Books

Indians of Today, fourth edition, edited by Marion E. Gridley, ICFP, 1971; 227-229.

Native North American Almanac, edited by Duane Champagne, Detroit, Gale Research, 1994; 1120.

Periodicals

"Barney Old Coyote and the American Indian National Bank," *Banker's,* 157, autumn 1974; 17-18.

—Sketch by Jason Gallman

Earl Old Person
1929-
Blackfeet tribal leader

Earl Old Person is the Blackfeet tribal chairman and a Native American political leader. At the age of 25, he became the youngest member of the Blackfeet Tribal Business Council, the governing body of the tribe. Ten years later, in 1964, he was elected tribal council chairman, a position he maintained with distinction for multiple terms. In July of 1978 he was awarded an honorary lifetime appointment as chief of the Blackfeet Nation.

Old Person was born on April 13, 1929, in Browning, Montana, to Juniper and Molly (Bear Medicine) Old Person. His parents were from respected Blackfeet families and were leaders in their community. Raised on northern Montana's Blackfeet Indian Reservation, Old Person attended grade school in the community of Starr School and graduated from Browning (Montana) High School. Old Person and his wife, Doris (Bullshoe) Old Person, have six children: Erlina Old Person, Glenda Eaglefeathers, Rose Eaglefeathers, Marty Eaglefeathers, Alfred Eaglefeathers, and Earl Old Person, Jr.

Old Person began his career as a representative of the Blackfeet in 1936 at the age of seven. As a child he was taught many of the cultural traditions of his people and performed the songs and dances of the Blackfeet for audiences across Montana. Old Person often performed for tourists at the lodge in East Glacier, Montana. The lodge at East Glacier is within Glacier National Park on the western boundary of the reservation. When Old Person was a child, tribal members camped on the expansive lawn of the beautiful old hotel during the summer tourist season. The eastern half of the park remained part of the reservation until 1895 when the Blackfeet sold it to the government. The Blackfeet consider the park part of their homeland. Tribal members can still be found camping, horseback riding, working, and performing there. Old Person has officiated at numerous ceremonies in the park. One area he has been particularly involved in is the naming of traditional Blackfeet sites within Glacier National Park.

The Blackfeet have lived on Montana's northern plains for several hundred years. Sometime during the early part of the twentieth century, the Indians on the Montana reservation began referring to themselves as the Blackfeet, in order to differentiate themselves from the Blackfoot tribe in Alberta, Canada. The Blackfeet Indian Tribe is now the official name of the tribe. The Montana reservation also includes many people who trace their ancestry to the Piegans (pronounced "Pay-gans") and the Bloods. Montana's Blackfeet were once part of the larger Blackfoot confederacy, which originally consisted of three tribes: the Pikuni (or Piegan), the Kainah ["Blood"], and the Siksika ["Blackfoot"]. Each tribe spoke the same language, shared many customs, intermarried, and fought common enemies.

Earl Old Person

Today's Blackfeet Indian Reservation in northern Montana, consisting of more than 1.5 million acres, is but a remnant of the vast territory the Blackfeet once controlled. Primarily buffalo hunters until the late nineteenth century when the northern herd was wiped out, the tribe currently bases its economy on timber, oil and gas, and agriculture. The reservation is home to about 7,000 tribal members with total tribal enrollment reaching 13,000. Under Old Person's leadership, the Blackfeet have constructed a community college, an industrial park, housing developments, tourist facilities, and a community center. The Museum of the Plains Indian in Browning, and a tribal buffalo herd have also received his enthusiastic support.

Develops Education and Business Opportunities

Old Person has actively pursued educational and business opportunities for the Blackfeet. In recent years, the reservation's manufacturing plants have produced pencils, pens, gloves, coats, and hats. From the Headstart program to the Blackfeet Community College, educational programs have also grown under Old Person's leadership.

Old Person was president of the National Congress of the American Indians (NCAI) from 1969 to 1971 and was elected vice president in 1990. The NCAI, one of the oldest national Indian organizations, was established in 1944 by representatives of Indian tribes with the goal of representing tribal interests. The NCAI works to preserve Indian cultural values and monitors federal Indian policy, lobbying on behalf of U.S. tribes. The Blackfeet tribe was also one of the first tribes to join the Council of Energy Resources Tribes

(CERT), headquartered in Denver, Colorado. Old Person was one of the 25 tribal leaders who organized CERT in 1975.

Old Person has been a leader in efforts to promote a better understanding between Native Americans and the larger society. A highly esteemed and honored Indian leader, Old Person has always been willing to listen to the concerns of tribal members. He has met with several United States presidents, England's royal family, Canada's prime minister, as well as numerous congressmen, governors, and movie celebrities. He is as comfortable in the company of dignitaries and celebrities as he is with tribal members.

SOURCES:

Books

Native North American Almanac, edited by Duane Champagne, Detroit, Gale Research, 1994; 1121-1122.

Other

Old Person, Earl, interview with Michael F. Turek conducted July 11, 1994.

—*Sketch by Michael F. Turek*

Opechancanough
1556(?)-1646
Powhatan-Renapé leader
Also known as Opechankino, Apechancanough, Appochankeno, and Apitchan-kihneu ["Sharp Opposition"]

Opechancanough was a leading Native American figure of the seventeenth century. He befriended Captain John Smith and the English settlers in Virginia, but later grew disillusioned with the land-greed the settlers displayed and led two rebellions against the settlers in 1622 and 1644. He was described in later years as "a man of large stature, noble presence, and extraordinary parts." His birthplace is unknown but, like his elder brother Powhatan ("Wahunsonacock"), he may have been born at Powhatan Village (present-day Richmond). If he was 90 when he died in 1646, his birth occurred around 1556, which would make him about eight years younger than Wahunsonacock.

Contemporary rumor suggested that Opechancanough was not a full-blooded Renapé. He was supposed to be from a Spanish-controlled area, perhaps Mexico, although he probably shared the same mother with Wahunsonacock. She

Opechancanough

but Opechancanough and his tribe were probably more familiar with the English, who were colonizing and slave-raiding from what is now North Carolina to Newfoundland. The English were adventurers sent out by a private company, the London Company, to find ways to exploit the resources of the new colony. Their major center in Virginia Colony was at Jamestown, located on a marshy area of the coast. Late in 1607 Opechancanough discovered John Smith, one of the adventurers, making an unauthorized ascent of the upper reaches of the Chickahominy River near the treasury houses of Orapacks.

Smith was arrested and could have been easily killed but the Renapé spared his life. He was taken to the nearby hunting camp of Rasawrack and there he observed Opechancanough "well guarded with 20 bowmen, 5 flanck and rear, and each flanck before him a sword and a peece [gun], and after him the like, then a bowman, then one on each hand a bowman, the rest in file in the reare ... each his bowe and a handful of arrowes, a quiver at his back grimly painted: on each flanck a sargeant, the one running alwaies towards the front, the other towards the reare, each a truepace and in exceeding good order." Opechancanough took Smith northward to the Mattapanlent River and then on to Toppahannock, where he was examined to see if he had been the captain of the ship which had enslaved Native Americans from the Rappahannock River a year or two before. Fortunately for Smith the ship captain had been a much taller man then he.

Smith records that he made friends with Opechancanough and the Renapé. In 1608 he reported that "Opechan-kanough his wife, Weomen, and children came to meete me: with a naturall kind affection hee seemed to rejoyce to see me." One of these children might have been Wecuttanow, a young man whom Smith later accused of attempting to poison him. When the English first met him, Opechancanough was staying in a house five miles north of Apamatuk belonging to the *Werowans* of Winau (Weanoc). Smith describes the meeting in great detail, stressing the riches of the native people: "This Wyroans Panaunche I holde to inhabite a Rychland of Copper and pearle. His country lyes into the land to another [Pamunkey] Ryver.... The Copper he had, as also many of his people, was very flexible,.... They weare it in their eares, about their neckes in long lynckes, and in broade plates on their heades.... The Kyng had a 'Chaine of pearle about his neck thrice Double, the third part of them as bygg as pease." Smith added that Opechancanough's territory was "full of Deare" and that he had "many rich furres." One hundred acres were planted with beans, corn, peas, tobacco, gourds, pumpkins, and other crops.

Near to Opechancanough's village of Menapacunt was the sacred center of Uttamussak, located on "top of certaine red sandy hils." In the woods there were "three great houses filled with images of their kings, and Devils, and Tombes of their Predecessors. Those houses are neare sixtie foot in length built arbour-wise, after their building [style]. This place they count so holy as that but the Priests and Kings dare come into them." People going up the adjacent Pamunkey

was presumably the sister of a Powhatan-Renapé leader, since inheritance among the Renapé ran first to brothers and then to sisters and their children. Opechancanough would have been about 14 in 1570 when the Spaniards attempted to establish Jesuit missions in Virginia. His father (if a Mexican) would have been a survivor of the large numbers of Native Americans brought north with the De Soto expedition in the early 1540s. The Native American opposition to the Jesuits in Axacan (the Hispano-Mexican name for Virginia) might have been partly due to the experiences of Opechancanough's father. Opechancanough had two brothers, Opitchapam and Katataugh, who lived at Cinquoateck, a major village located at the eastern tip of Pamunkey Neck. Captain John Smith refers to Opitchapam and Katataugh as the "two kings of Pamaunke."

Some time before 1607, Opechancanough became *Werownsi* or *Werowance* ["Good Person"] of Pamunkey. His "kingship" was centered on the neck of land lying between the Mattaponi (Mattapanlent) River and Pamunkey River. Most likely it was consisted of several villages located along the Pamunkey side of the neck. Opechancanough's major village seems to have been at Menapacuts (Menapacunt), somewhat farther up the Pamunkey River and near the sacred center of Uttamussak.

English Settlers Disrupt Renapé Life

The Renapé knew about the European presence in the New World in the late sixteenth century. Spanish and French activity was centered in the Florida-South Carolina region,

River "solemly cast some piece of copper, white beads, or Pocones [red paint powder] into the river" to honor *Oke*, or *Okee* (probably *Auki*) ["Earth-Spirit"]. Opechancanough had similar places in the territory of his brothers. Smith noted that near Katataugh's house, "the great King hath foure or five houses, each containing fourscore or an hundred foote in length, pleasantly seated upon an high sandy hill, from whence you may see westerly a goodly low Country, the river before the which his crooked course causeth many great Marshes of exceeding good ground. An hundred houses, and many large plaines are here togither inhabited."

Opechancanough played a major role in negotiations between the English settlers and other tribes from 1607 to 1618. He took the settlers' side in a significant attempt to conquer the Chickahominy Indians in 1616. For many years the English had been forcing the Chickahominy to give them corn and other food. In 1616, the Chickahominy refused to pay. However, according to English sources, Opechancanough also took advantage of this situation to try to impose his own dominance in the area. In 1618 Opechancanough allegedly granted a Chickahominy town to the English as punishment for the killing of five Englishmen. In the same year Wahunsonacock died, and Opitchapam and Opechancanough confirmed their league of friendship with the English.

Old Allies become Enemies

The league did not last. On March 22, 1622, the Renapé people turned against the settlers, probably led by Opechancanough. Some 350 English were killed on the first day, but the Renapé failed to seize the major fortified positions. Fighting continued for almost ten years, with losses on both sides. Negotiations finally brought a truce to central Virginia, from 1632 through 1644. Opechancanough and his people had been greatly weakened, and English immigrants continued to stream into the country, paying little attention to Native American property rights. The Cheskoyack retreated to later Gloucester County, while other groups, including the Paspahegh, Kecoughtan, Arrohateck, and Weanoc, moved south of the Powhatan River or disappeared. For its part, the English government recalled the London Company's charter, bringing the settlers in the Virginia colony under the control of the English crown.

By the early 1640s, it must have been clear to Opechancanough and his "cawcawassoughs," or councilors, that the settlers were indeed insatiable. They were beginning to occupy land in Maryland and the Rappahannock River region, including territory belonging to Native American villages. An earlier English writer expressed a common attitude among the settlers when he stated that in Virginia "there are an immense quantity of Indian fields cleared already to our hand by the Natives, which till we grow over populous may every way be abundantly sufficient." In 1612, William Strachey had argued that the Native Americans ought to lose their national territories and only "hold their landes as free burgers and cittizens with the English and Subjects to King James." They should to pay a tribute in corn to provide for the 8necessary English garrisons, which would make them

"clense double as much ground as they doe." The Native Americans were also expected to provide a great deal of cheap labor and domestic service.

In 1644 Opechancanough led another widespread rebellion against the invaders. He was said to command with his wife 32 "kingdomes," the same number as his brother Wahunsonacock. Many settlers were killed but, as in 1622, the major fortified positions were not taken. In 1646 Opechancanough was captured and murdered while a prisoner. Necotowance ("He who is first") succeeded Opechancanough. A treaty was signed with the English which required that all groups living between the Pamunkey (York) and Powhatan (James) Rivers remove their homes and fields to either southside Virginia or Pamunkey Neck. The area north of the Pamunkey River and south of the Rappahannock was "forever" reserved to the Native Americans.

Forever, in this case, lasted for three years. In 1649, the Virginia Assembly ordered that Native American town boundaries should be clearly marked and defined. This served to open up the lands in-between for white settlers. During the 1650s English planters rushed into areas previously held by native tribes. The Treaty of 1646 was violated in the same way as future treaties with Native Americans.

SOURCES:

Books

Beverly, Robert, *The History and Present State of Virginia* (1705), University of North Carolina Press, 1947.

Potter, Stephen R., "Early English Effects on Virginia Algonquian Exchange and Tribute in the Tidewater Potomac," in *Powhatan's Mantle: Indians in the Colonial Southeast* by Peter H. Wood, Gregory A. Waselkov, and M. Thomas, University of Nebraska Press, 1989; 151-172.

Powhatan Foreign Relations 1500-1722, edited by Helen C. Rountree, University Press of Virginia, 1993.

Purchas, Samuel, *Hakluytus Posthumus or Purchas His Pilgrimes,* Volume 19, MacLehose, 1906.

Rountree, Helen C. Pocahontas' People: *The Powhatan Indians of Virginia through Four Centuries,* University of Oklahoma Press, 1990.

Rountree, Helen C., *The Powhatan Indians of Virginia: Their Traditional Culture,* University of Oklahoma Press, 1989.

Smith, John, *The Generall Historie of Virginia New England and the Summer* (1624), Volume 1, MacLehose, 1907.

Strachey, William, *The Historie of Travell into Virginia Britania* (1612), edited by Louis B. Wright and Virginia Freund, Hakluyt Society, 1953.

Travels and Works of Captain John Smith, Volume 1, edited by Edward Arber, Grant, 1910.

Periodicals

Bushnell, David I., Jr., "Virginia—From Early Records," *American Anthropologist*, 9, 1907; 31-44.

Forbes, Jack D., "Anglo-Powhatan Relations to 1676," The *Masterkey,* November-December 1956; 179-183; January-February, 1957; 4-8.

—*Sketch by Jack D. Forbes*

Alfonso Ortiz
1939-
San Juan Tewa educator, author, and anthropologist

Alfonso Ortiz

A noted educator and author, Alfonso Ortiz has lectured widely on the cultures of the various Pueblos, and is a respected authority on indigenous knowledge and its applications for contemporary problems. Ortiz was born on April 30, 1939, in San Juan Pueblo, New Mexico to Sam and Lupe (Naranjo) Ortiz. The stories and traditions of his Tewa people influenced him in later years, both as a central philosophy and as a wellspring of information he interprets for students and the public alike. While studying anthropology at the University of New Mexico in Albuquerque, he worked as a teaching assistant, going on to earn his B.A. in 1961. On July 26 of that year, he married Margaret Davisson. Seeking a career in university teaching, he moved on to the University of Chicago, where he received his M.A. in anthropology in 1963, earning the Roy D. Albert Prize for Outstanding Thesis in 1964.

From his teaching post at Claremont, California's Pitzer College, Ortiz completed his dissertation, and he received a Ph.D. in anthropology from the University of Chicago in 1967. Ortiz then spent seven years teaching at Princeton University, where he earned tenure while also pursuing private consultancy contracts with such entities as the Xerox Corporation. It was during this period that he was awarded a Ford Foundation Fellowship, a highly respected honor for academics.

Although his academic reputation grew, Ortiz never forgot his roots. Founder of the San Juan Indian Youth Association, he was elected to the board of directors of the Association on American Indian Affairs, in part in recognition of this work with young Tewa people. He would also hold the positions of vice president, and later, president of the AAIA.

Ortiz's first book, *The Tewa World: Space, Time, Being and Becoming in a Pueblo Society,* was published in 1969 by the University of Chicago Press. A formal version of his dissertation research, it also provides a conceptual framework for much of his ongoing work. Professional accolades for the book and Ortiz's growing reputation as an articulate public speaker were contributing factors in the National Indian Education Conference's invitation to Ortiz to deliver the keynote address at their second annual meeting in 1970. That same year, he chaired the first Convocation of American Indian Scholars.

After teaching stints at Rutgers University, Colorado College, and the University of California, Los Angeles, among other institutions, Ortiz returned to the University of New Mexico in 1974 as a full professor, following the institution's 1972 publication of his book, *New Perspectives on the Pueblos.* He edited two volumes of the Smithsonian Institution's *Handbook of North American Indians* and then received postdoctoral fellowships from the John Simon Guggenheim Memorial Foundation and the Center for Advanced Study in the Behavioral Sciences at Stanford University. Ortiz's 1984 book entitled *American Indian Myths and Legends,* a collaboration with Richard Erdoes, is considered a classic in contemporary anthropology, and is widely used in courses ranging from cultural studies to Native American history to literature.

In addition to his academic work, Ortiz is also well known as an activist. During his presidency at the AAIA, the organization was integral in the return of the sacred Blue Lake to the Taos Pueblo people, the assessment of the Alaska Native Claims Settlement Act, and the passage of the Indian Child Welfare Act. While politically active as an advisory board member of the Native American Rights Fund, which provides legal expertise to Native communities, Ortiz was also a fellow of both the American Anthropological Association and the Royal Anthropology Institute.

Ortiz is the father of three children, Juliana, Elena, and Antonico. He is fluent in Tewa and also speaks some Maricopa and Pima. While Ortiz is the only son of his parents to venture away from the family tradition of religious service, his brothers and ancestors are leaders of the Winter People "moiety" at San Juan Pueblo (the Tewa divide the population into "Winter" and "Summer" groups). Ortiz told contributor Cynthia R. Kasee that the achievements of which he is most proud are his work with the Association on American Indian Affairs, his chairing of the advisory board of the D'Arcy McNickle Center for the Study of the History of the American Indian at the Newberry Library in Chicago, and the fiftieth anniversary Indian Achievement Award (1982) from the Indian Council Fire of Chicago, for his contributions to the field of Native studies.

The author of more than 60 articles and essays, Ortiz values the help he received as a "junior scholar" and sees a part of his professional mission as identifying and connecting young Native academics in a supportive network, so they can go on to make significant contributions.

SELECTED WRITINGS BY ORTIZ:

The Tewa World: Space, Time, Being and Becoming in a Pueblo Society, Chicago, University of Chicago Press, 1969.
Indian Voices: Proceedings of the 1st Convocation of American Indian Scholars, 1970.
New Perspectives on the Pueblos, Albuquerque, University of New Mexico Press, 1972.
(Editor), *Handbook of American Indians,* Washington, D.C., Smithsonian Institution, Volume 9, 1979, Volume 10, 1983.
(With Richard Erdoes) *American Indian Myths and Legends,* New York, Pantheon, 1984.
The Pueblo, New York, Chelsea, 1994.

SOURCES:

Books

Biographical Dictionary of Indians of the Americas, Newport Beach, California, American Indian Publications, 1983.
Contemporary Authors, Volumes 29-32, Detroit, Gale Research, 1972.
Native North American Almanac, edited by Duane Champagne, Detroit, Gale Research, 1994.
Reference Encyclopedia of American Indians, second edition, Volume 2, West Nyack, New York, Todd Publications, 1974.
Steiner, Stan, *The Vanishing White Man,* New York, Harper, 1976.
Vogel, Virgil, *This Country Was Ours,* New York, Harper, 1972.

Other

Ortiz, Alfonso, interview with Cynthia R. Kasee conducted July 2, 1994.

—Sketch by Cynthia R. Kasee

Simon J. Ortiz
1941-
Acoma Pueblo poet, writer

"When I see Native people, it assures my existence," expressed Simon J. Ortiz in a recent interview. A noted poet and writer with an international following, Ortiz acknowledges his origins from the Acoma Pueblo, or "Aacqu" as it is called in his language. Born on May 27, 1941, he is a member of the Eagle or Dyaamih Clan, his mother's clan. As there are no words in his native tongue for "cousin," "aunt," or "uncle," each member is thought of as a "brother," "sister," "mother," or "father." When Ortiz speaks about his family, one senses the deep cultural ties that bind not only the family together, but the people to the land. His father, an elder in the clan, was charged with keeping the religious knowledge and customs of the Acoma Pueblo people. Ortiz is the father of three children: a son, Raho Nez, an attorney for the Tohono O'odham Nation in Sells, Arizona, and two daughters, Rainy Dawn and Sara Marie, both students.

A Young Boy in His Community

Ortiz spent his early childhood years in the village of McCartys, or "Deetzeyaamah" in his language, attending McCartys Day School through the sixth grade. It was more or less required at that time for Indian children to leave home and attend boarding schools, and Ortiz was no exception; soon after, he went to St. Catherine's Indian School in Santa Fe, but his attendance was curtailed as he became homesick. Ortiz kept a diary in which he expressed his teenage thoughts. Reading whatever was available became a passion for Ortiz—especially dictionaries, which would allow his mind to travel to a "state of wonder." St. Catherine's, while attempting to provide Indian children with an education, also encouraged the Indian children to abandon their cultural ways and adopt a more "American" lifestyle. "The fear of God was instilled in each child ... penance and physical duty were the day's rigor," Ortiz stated. "I spoke and had known only the Acoma world." Disillusioned with St. Catherine's, Ortiz heard that Albuquerque Indian School taught trade classes such as plumbing and mechanics, and decided that they would be good classes to take in order to be considered employable. Ortiz' father, a railroad worker in addition to his community activities, was opposed to his sons learning a trade and encouraged his children to get an education and training in a field other than hard, manual labor. Although Ortiz attended sheet metal and woodworking classes, his interest did not remain in those areas. He liked to read and study, to learn about the world. In retrospect, he claimed that it was "an escape from a hard life. Study, dream and read ... escape to fantasy. It became the food for my imagination." Ortiz did not consider becoming a writer—writing was not something Indian people practiced. When asked why, he replied that "it is a profession

Simon J. Ortiz

only whites did." His thoughts would later change—if whites could do it, so could he.

In the 1950s, public schools were beginning to receive funding from Johnson-O'Malley legislation, which provided opportunities for greater numbers of Indian students to attend school. Ortiz enrolled in one such school, Grants High School in Grants, New Mexico—the largest non-Indian town near Acoma. Education had always been a significant priority with the people of Acoma Pueblo. It was the means by which they could better their own lives and their community. Ortiz believed this approach stemmed from the "indoctrination" of the Bureau of Indian Affairs (BIA) which tried to make Indians "good American citizens." Yet, in those days Indian children received no further encouragement to pursue an education beyond high school. While attending high school, his leadership skills began to emerge. Although he often refers to himself as a "not too social kid," he became a school leader by "default." He did not agree with the manner and treatment accorded Indian students, as if they were of lesser status or inferior people, and advocated to Indian students that they did not have to accept a subordinate position.

A Search for Meaning in Education

The day after Ortiz graduated from high school, he began work in the uranium industry at Kerr-McGee as a laborer. Wanting to be a chemist, Ortiz applied for a technical position at Kerr-McGee but was employed instead as a clerk typist because he was "good at typing." He was ulti-

mately promoted "down to the pit" as a crusher, and later a semi-skilled operator. His work experience as a laborer would later provide the material resource for his writings in *Fight Back: For the Sake of the People, For the Sake of the Land.* Using his savings and funds from a BIA education grant, Ortiz left the mining industry to pursue a university education. In 1962, he attended Fort Lewis College majoring in chemistry. While his interest in science prevailed, his grades did not. He was more interested in learning about life and being a part of it. The study of chemistry did not encompass elements about understanding or respecting life. Barely passing his biology and organic chemistry classes, he decided to try English because he had been "remotely" contemplating becoming a teacher. "It was *remotely* because what I really wanted to do was read, think and write," he explained. The prescribed university curriculum did not favor Ortiz's search for knowledge, and he "felt an intuitive resistance to the knowledge being learned." University structure was attempting to change who he was as a natural person. Drama interested him and he played a part in the university play, *Death of a Salesman.* Through drama, he was able to express his thoughts visually, and he temporarily found a new form of artistic freedom.

As a leader of the Indian student organization, Ortiz found himself confronting many different issues. No matter where he turned, he was surrounded with the inferior treatment of Native peoples. Ortiz began seeking something different, something to answer the questions and reasons of life. He found it in alcohol, which provided a false sense of relief. Security soon faded and bouts with alcohol abuse would haunt Ortiz for many years to come.

Ortiz enlisted in the United States Armed Forces in 1963 because he wanted something different to experience. His commander later assigned him to the battalion newspaper editor; however, the army discontinued the publication shortly after. Ortiz was sent to Texas for training and was assigned to a Hawk missile battalion as a missile defense specialist. While still in the army, he thought about attending the University of New Mexico to study English literature and creative writing because, by this time, he considered himself a "writer."

At the University of New Mexico, Ortiz found himself once more confined by the structured curriculum, and he soon discovered that virtually no ethnic writers had entered the closed domain of American literature. He became aware that a new age of Native American writers was beginning to emerge because of the current political activism. Ortiz credits the political climate and activities of the day as one of the fundamental reasons for altering his writing style. Writing previously from absolute self-expression, he now focused on the unheard Native American voice. The duration of university life lasted two more years until 1968 when he received a fellowship for writing at the University of Iowa in the International Writers Program. "I don't have any college degrees," explains Ortiz in his autobiographical statement. "I've worked at various jobs ... and had a varied career, including ups and too many downs." Ortiz served as public relations director at Rough Rock Demonstration

School from 1969 to 1970. He taught at San Diego State University and at the Institute of American Arts in Santa Fe, New Mexico, in 1974, and at summer sessions at Navajo Community College from 1974 to 1977. He also taught at the College of Marin in Kentfield, California, from 1976 to 1979, and the University of New Mexico from 1979 to 1981. Beginning in 1982, he served as consulting editor for the Pueblo of Acoma Press.

Returns to Acoma Pueblo Origins

In 1988 Ortiz was appointed as tribal interpreter, and in 1989 he became First Lieutenant Governor for Acoma Pueblo in New Mexico. Being connected to his Aacqu community has been of major importance in his life. "Helping others in the community are the very reasons for purpose and meaning in life," according to Ortiz's interpretation of traditional Aacqumeh way. "To help or to be helpful ... is a quality associated with the responsibility each individual has to the community," not only in traditional Acoma ways, but with Native Americans in general, observes Ortiz in his autobiographical statement, adding that "leadership is a way of showing that each person is meant for some larger or extended purpose, for the true meaning of his existence is to be helpful to his community. Leadership is not a personal choice, you are appointed to serve the people as completely as possible, and you offer to help achieve happiness and wholeness for all the people." For Ortiz, there is a certain valuable element in being with elders to hear their stories and wisdom. It is under the guidance and direction of their leaders, Ortiz explained, that the "coming together of community members is a responsibility we all have to carry out in order to assure the continuance of our community."

In 1988 Ortiz was appointed to be the Acoma Tribal Interpreter, but he was not sure what responsibilities this task entailed. He learned through family and community members that he was "working for the people and for the land." These leadership roles in the community afforded him the path in which to connect himself spiritually, in wholeness, with the continuance of his culture. In his "What We See: A Perspective on Chaco Canyon and Pueblo Ancestry," Ortiz refers to a thought from Vincent Scully: "All human construction involves a relationship between the natural and the man-made. That relationship physically shapes the human cultural environment. In historical terms, the character of that relationship is a major indication of the character of a culture as a whole. It tells us how the human beings who made it thought of themselves in relation to the rest of creation."

Writing with a Native Voice

The writings of Ortiz are emotionally charged and complex. His expressions of anger, passion, love, fear, and threats to our existence make the reader question the backdrop of the society in which he or she exists. Essayists have compared his writing to other present day poets and authors, but Ortiz stands on his own. Pertinent to both Native and non-Native readers, Ortiz' subjects are those that affect daily life. In his *Simon Ortiz,* Andrew Wiget notes that Ortiz has "committed himself to articulating what he saw as a distinctly Native American perspective on fundamental human experiences ... a consciously assumed purpose which came from a clear sense of the power and function of language derived from Ortiz's immersion in the oral tradition."

With his first collection of poems, *Going for the Rain,* Ortiz's editors found themselves in an unusual position. They favorably accepted the collection, but could not understand how a person of Indian culture could write with such a style of verse. Ortiz himself found it interesting that he could write in such a manner using the English language, a language that had usually only served to oppose Indian favor. His writings serve to confirm, verify, and affirm the essence of the land and people together, and their existence based on the concept of "wholeness."

In his collections and stories, Ortiz not only attempts to "assure ourselves of our willingness to be recipients, but also the other concept of willingness to give back. There must exist a reciprocal relationship for humanity to take care of itself as well as for the environment." His storytelling relates traditions of his culture, and evokes visions familiar and foreign to the reader. His second collection of poems, *A Good Journey,* includes the remarkable Ortiz trait of awakening the reader's senses while leaving a message for his children to always be aware of their Indian traditions and the beauty of nature and the environment.

Ortiz blends experience and oral tradition. In his *Stories* selections, he illustrates a deep, personal experience about his not speaking until he was almost four years old. He then takes the realistic experience and combines it with an oral tradition story involving his grandfather. Having taken a key from his pocket, the grandfather spoke of speech and its importance to knowing the world; he then "turned the key, unlocking language." Later, Ortiz speaks. Ortiz emphasizes that language provides for the "discovery of one's capabilities and creative thought." Language has many uses, and one of those uses implemented by Ortiz is to convey a message with political overtones. In *A Good Journey,* Ortiz describes his camping trip in which he encounters the National Park Service. Collecting firewood for his camp, he is told that he must first buy a permit. He considers this a ridiculous concept since his grandfathers "ran this place," and ignores the permit request. He then cuts his firewood, mumbling along the way, "Sue me."

In considering material for his works, Ortiz relies on the stories that he "likes and believes the most; it's as simple as that." These stories are the ones that let him know where he has been, or locate for him a place that is distinct, special, and true because everything about it is familiar. Questioned about his subject matter, Ortiz confided, "The best stories told are those that provide for me, the listener-reader, a sense of grounding even when I've never been in the locale or setting where the storyteller or writer sets his story." Ortiz often refers to his mother's ability to lead him as a child into envisioning the words of the stories as she told him about days past of gathering and roasting pinion cones. As a child, his father told him stories about the desperation and cold the community had to endure; he knew the essence of those words because "it was the experience of his people and he is part of them." Ortiz further explained that these stories are believable "when we are intimately involved or linked to them because they are who we are, or when we become intimately and deeply involved and linked with them." As a poet, fiction and nonfiction writer, Ortiz captures life on paper. It is not a fancy, superficial life, but one in which words come alive in the heart and mind; they are words that tell the story of Ortiz himself and the world he knows most and loves. Ortiz is a writer of accomplishment who combines the often hurtful knowledge of reality with mythic wholeness.

In each of his travels, Ortiz incorporates his journey into his writings. In 1970 he went in search of "Indians." He concluded that Indians were not a part of America's history, other than the bare mention of the Indian wars and savagery. He then asked himself if the Indian were a myth. Were there no more Indians? Had the movie industry absorbed Indians into savage portrayals? He soon understood that the vanished "Red Man" was vanished only from the public mind; it was intentional, for if Indians existed, then there would be claims to the land, water, and all things residing in western civilization. Ortiz traveled to the South where he found 45,000 Lumbee Indians living in the North Carolina region. His writings have dealt with the debunking of the vanished-Indian myth and the fact that Indians do exist—everywhere. Wiget's tribute summarizing Ortiz's work is that "it is not about a race that is vanishing, a way of life that is passing, or a language that is dying, but about a nation of those who have preserved their humor, their love for the land that is their mother, and their sense of themselves as a distinctive people. It is about journeying, about survival, about the many significances of being a veteran."

Ortiz continues to write for both book and television production. In reading and listening to his work, one is left with the indelible printed image in Chaco Canyon and Pueblo ancestry that "from the moment in creation, life moved outward, and from that moment, human consciousness began to be aware of itself. And the *hanoh*, the people, began to know and use the oral tradition that would depict the story of their journey on the hiyaanih, the road, of life. The oral tradition of Acoma Pueblo, and of all the other pueblos, is central to the consciousness of who they are, and it is basic to their culture. It is through oral tradition that the journey is told ... in order that the people may be secure and fully aware within their cultural environment." The works of Simon Ortiz ensure that for generations to come there will be the opportunity to see "life, as always life will be."

SELECTED WRITINGS BY ORTIZ:

Naked in the Wind (chapbook), Pembroke, North Carolina, Quetzal-Vihio Press, 1971.

"The San Francisco Indians" and "The Killing of a State Cop," in *The Man to Send Rain Clouds*, edited by Kenneth Rosen, New York, Viking Press, 1974.

Going for the Rain (verse), New York, Harper, 1976.

A Good Journey (verse), Berkeley, Turtle Island, 1977; reprinted, Tucson, University of Arizona Press, 1985.

Song, Poetry and Language (essays), Tsaile, Arizona, Navajo Community College, 1977.

Howbah Indians (fiction), Tucson, Blue Moon, 1978.

The People Shall Continue, San Francisco, Children's Book Press, 1978.

With Roxanne Dunbar Ortiz, *Traditional and Hard-to-Find Information Required by Members of American Indian Communities: What to Collect, How to Collect It, and Appropriate Format and Use,* Washington, D.C., Office of Library and Information Services, 1978.

Fight Back: For the Sake of the People, For the Sake of the Land (prose and poetry), Albuquerque, INAD-University of New Mexico, 1980.

From Sand Creek (verse), New York, Thunder's Mouth, 1981.

A Poem Is a Journey (verse), Bourbonais, Illinois, Pteranadon, 1981.

Editor (with Rudolfo A. Anaya), *A Ceremony of Brotherhood 1680-1980,* Albuquerque, Academia, 1981.

"Towards a National Indian Literature: Cultural Authenticity in Nationalism," *MELUS,* 8:2, 1981; 7-12.

Blue and Red, Acoma, New Mexico, Acoma Partners in Basics, 1982.

The Importance of Childhood, Acoma, New Mexico, Acoma Partners in Basics, 1982.

Fightin': New and Selected Stories, New York, Thunder's Mouth Press, 1983.

Editor, *Earth Power Coming,* Tsiale, Arizona, Navajo Community College Press, 1983.

"Always the Stories: A Brief History and Thoughts on my Writing," in *Coyote Was Here: Essays on Contemporary Native American Literary and Political Mobilization,* edited by Bo Scholer, Aarhus, Denmark, English Department of University of Aarhus, 1984; 57-69.

Editor, *These Heats, These Poems,* Acoma, New Mexico, Pueblo of Acoma Press, 1984.

"The Creative Process ['That's the Place Indians Talk About']," *Wicazo Sa,* 1:1, 1985; 45-49.

Woven Stone, Tucson, University of Arizona Press, 1992.

After and Before the Lightening, Tucson, University of Arizona Press, 1994.

"What We See: A Perspective on Chaco Canyon and Pueblo Ancestry," in *Chaco Canyon: A Center and Its World,* Museum of New Mexico Press, 1994.

SOURCES:

Books

Ortiz, Simon J., "What We See: A Perspective on Chaco Canyon and Pueblo Ancestry," in *Chaco Canyon: A Center and Its World,* Museum of New Mexico Press, 1994.

Twentieth Century Writers, second edition, edited by Geoff Sadler, St. James Press, 1991.

Wiget, Andrew, *Simon Ortiz,* Boise, Idaho, Boise State University Printing and Graphic Services, 1986.

Other

Ortiz, Simon J., biographical statement, March 27, 1993.
Ortiz, Simon J., interviews with JoAnn di Filippo during May, June, and September, 1994.

—*Sketch by JoAnn di Filippo*

Osceola

Osceola
1804-1838
Seminole tribal leader
Also known as Asi-Yaholo (Assiola) ["Black Drink Singer"] and Billy Powell

Osceola rose to prominence during the Second Seminole War, where his brilliant guerrilla tactics in the Florida swamps earned him the admiration and respect of the many United States Army officers who tried to capture him. He remained unconquered in war. Originally an Upper Creek Red Stick born in Alabama, accounts vary on Osceola's lineage because of his early name of Billy Powell and his later denial of any white ancestry. According to William and Ellen Hartley in *Osceola: The Unconquered Indian,* some historians decided that white trader William Powell was Osceola's stepfather and that Billy Powell was a nickname for the young Indian who was really fathered by a Creek warrior. However, because Creek and Seminole inheritance was matrilineal, Osceola was correct in his later insistence that, "No foreign blood runs in my veins; I am a pure-blood Muskogee [Creek]." Osceola's mother was Polly Copinger, a Creek woman. Whether his stepfather or not, for at least a time William Powell lived with the family as Osceola's father, but Powell was frequently gone and later left permanently.

The Creek War of 1813-1814 was a civil war between the White Sticks and the Red Sticks, but the United States became involved and fought the Upper Creek Red Sticks, who were against U.S. encroachment on Creek lands and culture. Young Osceola and his mother went into hiding when the fighting came close to their village. In March of 1814 General Andrew Jackson ended the Creek War by killing close to 1,000 Indians. Osceola and his mother were part of the migration of Red Sticks who fled to Florida, where Spain claimed the land and the swamps that would prove so useful to the survival of the Seminoles. The migration was led by Osceola's great uncle Peter McQueen, a Creek tribal leader. The Creeks joined the Seminoles, which were made up of Creeks from earlier migrations as well as other tribes, their black slaves, and maroons, who were fugitive black slaves harbored by the Seminoles. Although his heritage would always be Upper Creek Red Stick, Osceola would eventually consider himself Seminole.

Billy Powell Receives His Indian Name

After Osceola's first few years in his new home, the First Seminole War broke out in 1819 as a result of white and Indian aggressions along the Georgia-Florida border. The Seminole chief, Neamathla, was angry with continued white intrusions and declared the intention to defend Seminole lands. The U.S. Army became involved, attacking and burning Neamathla's village. Seminole retaliation on a party of soldiers and their wives and children as they traveled to Fort Scott began the war. Osceola was growing up, and, although not a warrior at 14, the war affected him by making him a fugitive and contributing to his developing hatred for the Creeks his people had fought and his distrust of the whites. After the war ended Osceola and his mother rejoined Peter McQueen at Tampa Bay. Osceola spent the next few years developing his athletic, hunting, and warrior skills. He served as a medicine man's helper during the annual Green Corn Dance when adult names were given and the bitter black drink was used to purge and purify the body. It was at one of these ceremonies when he was about 18 that Osceola, who up until now had been called Billy Powell, was named Asi-Yaholo ["Black Drink Singer"], for as he served the black drink he sang out the long, ritual cry. His duties during these ceremonies established him as a future leader.

Spain had sold Florida to the United States in 1819, and the U.S. government wanted to concentrate the scattered bands of Seminoles in one place. However, the government could not decide whether to send them west to a reservation or have them remain somewhere in Florida. The Seminoles disliked the unsettled situation and asked that a decision be made. Times were hard for many of them because they had not planted crops, believing that the tribe would be removed before harvest time. Finally, in 1823, the Treaty of Moultrie Creek, which was to last for 20 years, directed the Seminoles to cede their present lands and move south. However, their reservation was poor for grazing their cattle or raising crops, it cut them off from fishing in the Atlantic Ocean or the Gulf of Mexico, and it stopped their trade with Cuba. However, this treaty also forbade white intrusion. At the age of 19, Osceola was still not a leader and therefore had no voice in the proceedings, but he probably attended the treaty as most young warriors did. During the early to mid-1820s Osceola served as a guide and worked with surveyors to mark the boundaries of the reservation. He was recognized by whites and Seminoles alike as a fine hunter and athlete, and, as he explored the reservation and lands beyond, he met other Seminole bands and became known and admired by many.

Becomes War Chief

The poor reservation lands and inadequate government rations to the Seminoles found many of them in dire circumstances by 1825. They knew Big Swamp was fertile land and had asked to have it granted to them. Osceola moved to Big Swamp around 1826 and had a growing band of followers. Also in 1826 he married his first wife, Che-cho-ter ["Morning Dew"], who was said to be quite beautiful. As was customary for Seminole men, Osceola took two wives, marrying the second in 1834, but very little is known about her. By 1832 Osceola had become a Tustenuggee ["War Chief"]. Osceola did not inherit leadership; however, a Seminole warrior could become a leader if other men and young braves chose to follow him out of admiration for certain qualities, such as his warrior or hunting skills.

In 1832 the Treaty of Payne's Landing was negotiated, calling for the removal of the Seminoles to a reservation in Arkansas, where they would be reunited with the Creeks. This infuriated the Seminoles, including Osceola. The Creeks who had migrated to Florida and become Seminoles had no intention of giving up their new identity as Seminoles, nor would they unite with the Creeks they had fought during the Creek War. In addition, the treaty called for all blacks to be turned over to white authorities upon removal. Slaves had been an integral part of the tribe for many years and had even intermarried. Osceola, even though he personally owned no slaves, was bitterly against the treaty. In 1833 the Treaty of Fort Gibson was drawn up, enforcing the Treaty of Payne's Landing. General Wiley Thompson was determined to enforce these treaties, even though the terms of the Moultrie treaty had not expired and many chiefs claimed they had not signed the new ones.

A Formidable Opponent

In 1834 the Seminoles decided that they would fight to stay on their lands. Osceola was made the head war chief and was instrumental in organizing stores of ammunition and making plans for warfare. He was also given prominence in the tribe and sat beside head chief Micanopy at many councils, and, even though a subchief, he gave many speeches. Osceola also performed a powerful action that would be repeatedly recounted in the history books: As the chiefs met with Wiley Thompson and other officers to sign treaty papers, Osceola drew his hunting knife, pierced the document, and walked away.

Sometime later, when Osceola and Wiley Thompson argued, possibly over Thompson's halt of gun powder to the Indians, Thompson had him arrested. To be imprisoned was a great humiliation for a warrior, and Osceola was wild with rage. Eventually he calmed down and planned for his release. The next day he apologetically told Thompson that he would sign the treaty papers and convince others to move to the reservation as well. Thompson released him, little knowing that he would pay for his action. Although Osceola signed the document, his only thoughts were revenge for his imprisonment and the fight to retain Seminole lands. The Seminole leaders decided not only would they kill white settlers and soldiers if they had to, they would also kill any of their own people who would honor the treaty by agreeing to relocate to Arkansas. Shortly after this decision was made, Osceola killed Charlie Emathla, a Seminole chief who insisted on moving to the reservation.

The Second Seminole War broke out in 1835. Osceola had been preparing the tribe for war, instilling discipline in his warriors, for he knew it was the only way their smaller numbers could succeed against the might of the U.S. Army. The hostilities began with raids on white settlements, but the first battle of the war came at Black Point with the ambush of a government supply train and the killing of militia. Osceola made good his vow for revenge on Wiley Thompson by killing him in December 1835. Osceola hid members of the tribe, their cattle, and food stores in the swamps to avoid retaliation on his people for his actions. Before long, the army leaders realized that the only way to stop the Seminoles was to stop Osceola, but as the war raged on he proved to be a formidable opponent and avoided capture by the many officers and troops who tried.

Betrayal

The war lasted for seven years, but Osceola was to see the action for only three of those years. He had sickened with malaria in 1836 and continued to suffer bouts of the fever and weakness. By 1837 Osceola, weary of fighting, was ready to talk peace. Unfortunately, his reign ended with the deceit of General Thomas Jesup. When Osceola came to a meeting under a flag of truce with several other chiefs, General Jesup betrayed him, as he had earlier done to the Seminole leader Coacoochee ["Wildcat"]. Osceola and the chiefs were imprisoned with Coacoochee at Fort Marion in St. Augustine. The fever and weakness, which continued to plague Osceola, was in part responsible for his refusal to join Coacoochee in his successful escape from the prison. Osceola had sent for his wives and children to be sure they would safely join him.

After Coacoochee's escape, Jesup ordered Osceola and the other chiefs moved to Fort Moultrie, South Carolina. The fort was on an island in the harbor of Charleston, and the chance of possible rescue by the Seminoles was deemed nonexistent. Osceola and his companions were well treated and given freedom to move about. It was here that Osceola's portraits were made by George Catlin and Robert John Curtis. After three months of imprisonment, Osceola had weakened and was dying. It has been suggested that heartbreak and disillusionment with white treatment contributed to Osceola's death. Whether it was heartbreak or malaria, neither the post doctor or a Seminole medicine man were able to save him, and Osceola died on January 30, 1838, surrounded by his wives, Seminole chiefs, and the fort's officers. In a military funeral, he was buried at Fort Moultrie, headless because the post doctor had cut Osceola's head from the body and taken it home with him. Later, it ended up in a museum in New York, but was lost when the museum burned in 1866.

The Second Seminole War continued with Coacoochee assuming Osceola's leadership, but by 1843 over 3,800 Seminoles and related blacks had been captured and sent to Arkansas. Approximately 300 Seminoles remained in the Florida Everglades swamps. Osceola had fought courageously to retain Seminole lands, and American Army officers would always remember him as the noble, brilliant opponent they both feared and admired. To the Seminole people his name would be a reminder of their proud heritage.

Oshkosh

SOURCES:

Alderman, Clifford Lindsey, *Osceola and the Seminole Wars,* New York, Julian Messner, 1973.

American Heritage Book of Indians, edited by Alvin M. Josephy, Jr., American Heritage Publishing, 1961; 228, 233.

Dockstader, Frederick J., *Great North American Indians,* New York, Van Nostrand Reinhold, 1977; 199-200.

Famous Indians: A Collection of Short Biographies, United States Department of the Interior, Bureau of Indian Affairs; 22-23.

Hartley, William, and Ellen Hartley, *Osceola: The Unconquered Indian,* New York, Hawthorn Books, 1973.

—Sketch by Sandy J. Stiefer

Oshkosh
1795-1858

Menominee tribal leader

Also known as ["Claw"], Oskas ["His Claw"], Os'koss (Uskasha, Oshkushi) ["Hoof" or "Nail"]

Oshkosh was a leader known for his tribal dedication and desire for peaceful co-existence with white settlers. During his time of leadership, he coped with the influx of settlers into the Menominee domain of Wisconsin and was determined that his people and lands would not be lost or destroyed. Despite the pressures placed upon him as his homelands were swallowed up, he did not believe in resorting to violence upon white settlers as other tribal leaders did.

The son of Akwinem'i ["The Feathered One"], Oshkosh was born near Green Bay, Wisconsin, a member of the Owasse, or bear clan. Oshkosh was named for his grandfather, TsheKatch'ake'mau ["Chief of the Bear Clan" or "Head Chief of All"], who was later known as the old king. Oshkosh was called Little Bear as a child, and although he was small in size he later earned the name Oshkosh the Brave. Oshkosh received much of his schooling from his grandfather and from his mentor, Chief Tomah. Their teachings served Oshkosh well as he became highly respected among his people. During the War of 1812 Chief Tomah supported the British, and 17-year-old Oshkosh accompanied him and his warriors in the capture of Fort Mackinaw from the Americans. Oshkosh proved to be a skilled warrior in subsequent battles during the war.

Becomes Head Chief

Chief Tomah died in 1818, and when TsheKatch'ake'mau, the old king, died in 1821 the Menominees were left without a head chief. The 1827 Treaty of Butte des Morts was the occasion for Oshkosh's appointment as head chief by General Lewis Cass, commissioner of Indian Affairs.

Cass announced that he would choose their chief after three day's study of the tribal members. His choice of 32-year-old Oshkosh was consented to by the Menominees. Oshkosh's leadership carried the burden of trying to hold on to ancestral lands while preserving the unity of his tribe. A million acres of Menominee lands were sold by 1831 despite Oshkosh's desire to retain it for his people. Although he was a proven warrior and was unhappy with the land transfers, he would not resort to warfare against the settlers. In fact, he supported the Americans in the Black Hawk War of 1832.

A City Named for Oshkosh

By 1836 Wisconsin had become a territory, and with the Treaty of the Cedars it gained for white settlement and the lumber trade almost 190,000 acres from the Menominees. This cession included the Fox River valley, home of Oshkosh and his clan. According to the treaty they had to move west of the Wolf River, and Oshkosh chose to settle at Lake Poygan. In 1840 the nearby community of Athens was renamed Oshkosh for the Menominee chief.

Although historians state that Oshkosh succumbed to alcohol in his latter years, according to the anonymously written *A Merry Briton in Pioneer Wisconsin,* he spoke strongly against it, saying at a treaty payment meeting, "I am resolved to preserve order in the camp, and I set my face against the whiskey."

By 1848 government policy called for the removal of all Indians to west of the Mississippi River. The Menominee lands at Lake Poygan were wanted for settlement, and the Indians were pressured to give up this area as well. When Oshkosh refused to go, federal agents convinced him to visit the Crow Wing country in Minnesota where they wanted the Menominee tribe to move. Oshkosh went to examine the area, only to announce, "The Crow Wing country is not suitable to the needs of my people." Troubled by the pressure to leave his homeland, Oshkosh went to Washington to speak to the "Great White Father," President Millard Fillmore. Oshkosh was a skilled orator, and according to Phoebe Jewell Nichols in *Oshkosh The Brave,* his convincing words to the president ended with, "My tribe is small and we want to live in peace for the little time remaining to us." Fillmore responded by drafting of a document that would allow the Menominees to stay in Wisconsin.

When Oshkosh returned to his home the agents were still determined to remove the Menominees from their Lake Poygan lands. However, this time the agents ordered the Menominees to move to the upper Wolf River, which was part of their original domain. Oshkosh had succeeded in keeping his people in Wisconsin, although this reservation of approximately 400 square miles was but a small portion of their once vast homeland. The Menominees moved to the reservation in 1852. Oshkosh the Brave died at Keshena, Wisconsin, on August 20, 1858. His son Akhwinem'i Oshkosh became chief, holding that position until 1871 when Oshkosh's second son, Neopit, replaced him.

SOURCES:

Academic American Encyclopedia, Volume 14, Danbury, Connecticut, Grolier, 1994.

Dockstader, Frederick J., *Great North American Indians,* New York, Van Nostrand Reinhold, 1977.

Handbook of North American Indians, edited by William C. Sturtevant and Bruce G. Trigger, Washington, Smithsonian Institution, 1978.

Nichols, Phebe Jewell, *Oshkosh the Brave,* Menominee Indian Reservation, 1954.

—Sketch by Sandy J. Stiefer

Ouray
1833(?)-1880
Uncompahgre Ute tribal leader
Also known as "The Arrow," Oo-ay ["Yes"], Ulay (Yulay), Yuray (U-ray or U-re), and Willie Ouray

Ouray was an Uncompahgre Ute tribal leader best known for his treaty negotiating skills and his efforts to maintain the peace between his people and the Euro-Americans moving west into Colorado Territory. He was born during the year of the "Shooting Stars" in Taos, New Mexico, probably in 1833, although some sources indicate he was born in 1820. Most historians agree that his father was Guerra Murah, an Uncompahgre Ute warrior, who was captured by Jicarillo Apaches, and later adopted by them. However, Marshall Sprague reported in *Massacre: The Tragedy at White River* that Ouray's father was a Ute warrior named Salvador. There is agreement that his mother was a Jicarillo Apache woman, who may have been the sister of the Jicarillo Apache chief Wherro-Moondo. Sometime before 1845, his parents returned to the Uncompahgre tribe at the request of Ute Chief Nevava. After their arrival there, they had a daughter named Shoseen ["Shining River"], who was later named Susan. But, Ouray and his older brother, Quenche, were left in Taos with a Spanish couple. The boys tended sheep, hauled pinon wood, learned to speak Spanish and were "taken to a Catholic mass regularly," according to author Val J. McClellan in *This Is Our Land.* Later in his life, he would practice the Methodist religion.

On February 4, 1847, Ouray witnessed the Pueblo Indian attack at Taos, in which New Mexico's first governor, Charles Bent, was killed. Bent was described by McClellan as Ouray's friend, and the governor's death apparently left a strong impression on the teenager. It also was during this time that Ouray met his life-long friend, Christopher "Kit" Carson. In 1848 or 1849, Ouray and his brother followed their parents to the Uncompahgre territory in southwestern Colorado, where he learned to be a Ute war-

Ouray

rior. His youthful Ute companions often mocked his "half-breed" status, and throughout his life, he was frequently referred to as "half-Ute" or even "Apache," particularly by his enemies. At the age of 18, Ouray was adopted by the Uncompahgre and acquired a reputation as a courageous and skilled warrior. In 1852, he married a woman named Black Mare following the annual Ute Bear Dance. In 1858, she gave birth to Ouray's only son, named Cotoan, but more often called Queashegut ["Little Left Hand"]. Black Mare died shortly thereafter and in 1859, Ouray married Chipeta, a 16-year-old Ute maiden. Chipeta adopted Cotoan, but she and Ouray never had children of their own.

Learned to Negotiate Treaties Early in Life

In 1855, Muache Ute Chief Kaneache asked Ouray to join him in a raid on a white settlement. Ouray refused and instead alerted the settlement and, with other Uncompahgre warriors, attacked Kaneache's war party. Ouray wounded Kaneache, then took him prisoner until his wounds healed. Although Ouray later released Kaneache to his people, Kaneache "would never forgive Ouray for his deeds," according to McClellan.

In 1854, Kit Carson was named the Indian Agent for the Taos Muache Utes and sometime later established a sub-agency at Conejos for the Uncompahgre Utes. It was Carson's belief that the Utes would be wise to seek a separate treaty with Washington to confirm their right to their land. As Ouray watched more and more Euro-Americans enter the Colorado territory in search of gold, he frequently discussed

the problem with Carson. Finally in 1860, Ouray tried to convince Chief Nevava that the Utes needed a treaty with Washington to ensure that the tribe kept its land. Nevava believed the Utes had enough weapons to keep the miners and settlers from encroaching into Ute territory and refused to consider such a treaty. Finally, Ouray decided to present the issue to Nevava's council and received their permission, over Nevava's objections, to pursue talks. Although the council left Nevava as chief, their actions stripped him of most of his power and, in effect, gave Ouray control of Uncompahgre affairs. Carson, who was impressed with Ouray's accomplishment, then began to teach Ouray the fine art of negotiating treaties. Meanwhile, Nevava became another of Ouray's enemies, and moved north to join the Yampa and White River Ute bands.

With the new Conejos Indian Agent, Lafayette Head, Ouray went to Denver in 1862 to discuss the treaty with Colorado Territorial Governor John Evans. Dee Brown said in *Bury My Heart at Wounded Knee,* "A treaty was signed there, giving the white men all the Colorado land east of the mountaintops (the Continental Divide), leaving the Utes all the land west of the divide. In exchange for $10,000 in goods and $10,000 in provisions to be distributed annually for ten years, the Utes agreed to relinquish mineral rights to all parts of their territory, and they promised not to molest any citizen of the United States who might come into their mountains to dig." Agent Head then selected 13 Utes, including Ouray, to travel to Washington for the formal signing of the treaty in 1863. While other Native American tribes were losing vast amounts of land, the Utes were able to retain much more than their brothers as a result of the 1863 agreement. The treaty applied to all Utes. However, only Uncompahgre chiefs and a few of the subchiefs from White River actually signed the final document. It was also at this meeting that Ouray was introduced as "Chief of the Utes" to President Abraham Lincoln, which at the time was not true. McClellan said, "Ouray did not like to be introduced as a chieftain when he was but a mere warrior, but, perhaps due to courtesy, he did not embarrass Head before the president by stating otherwise."

For the next several years, Ouray worked hard to get the other Ute bands to go along with the treaty he had signed for all of them. In hopes of mending the rift between himself and Nevava, Ouray encouraged his 16-year-old sister, Susan, to marry a Yampa Ute medicine man by the name of Canalla (also known as Johnson). However, Nevava continued to oppose all Ouray's efforts and even worked to turn the rest of the Yampa and White River Utes against him. Kaneache also was one of the Ute chiefs who refused to sign the 1863 treaty. He and Colorow, another White River subchief, claimed Ouray had "overstepped his authority by signing, and that by so doing had usurped the authority of the rightful leaders," according to McClellan. During the next several years, these Utes, believing they were not bound by the treaty, continued to harass miners, steal livestock and frighten Colorado's newest residents.

By 1868, the Euro-Americans who had settled in Colorado decided the tribe had been allowed to retain too much land, and were tired of the harassment from the renegade

Utes. Again, Ouray travelled to Washington with several other Ute leaders for treaty negotiations. The delegation was wined and dined, and generally treated like royalty (his wife Chipeta was called "Queen of the Utes"). In the end, though, the new treaty reduced somewhat the area reserved for the Utes and established two more government agencies to oversee the activities of the tribe. But, most historians agree the pact represented Ouray's excellent negotiating skills and protected his people better than other treaties of that time. As noted by both McClellan and Brown, however, Ouray told a group of newspaper reporters after the talks, "The agreement an Indian makes to a United States treaty, is like the agreement a buffalo makes with his hunters when pierced with arrows. All he can do is lie down and give in."

Many Utes Believed Ouray Betrayed Them

In 1864, Ouray, his son Cotoan, and about 30 braves went hunting along the South Platte River. They were attacked by several hundred Arapaho Indians, who managed to abduct Cotoan. The six-year-old was kept and raised by the Arapahos. Ouray was devastated by his loss and he spent many years attempting to find his son.

By 1872, silver was discovered in the San Juan Mountains, which increased pressure on the Utes to give up more land. In an effort to entice Ouray into another round of negotiations, Indian Agent Felix Brunot told Ouray that he would find and return Cotoan to him. In October of 1873, another Ute delegation travelled to Washington to revisit the Treaty of 1868. Ouray was told that he "had to assist the government in getting the San Juans," according to McClellan, in exchange for finding Cotoan. Ouray refused the offer because he was aware that his now-grown son had been raised by and adopted the ways of the Arapahos. Brown also records that Ouray did not give into the bribe readily. McClellan reported that "he was willing to sell the mountains, but not all the fine hunting land around them. [Ouray said,] 'The whites can go and take the gold and come out again. We do not want them to build houses there.'" Ouray did see his son briefly during the seven days of negotiations, but his son spurned him, as any Arapaho brave might have done upon seeing a Ute warrior.

Eventually, the Ute delegation agreed to the government's terms of $25,000 in exchange for the four million acres of San Juan mountains. In addition, Ouray was given a salary of $1,000 a year for the remainder of his life. After the treaty was signed, the government also appointed Ouray "Chief of the Utes." In nearly all the reports about this particular treaty, writers emphasized that Ouray's main goal was to maintain the peace between the Utes and the Euro-Americans. However, many Utes believed that he had betrayed his people by giving so much away. During the next several years, a number of unsuccessful attempts were made by Utes to kill Ouray as a result that belief.

Massacre at White River

In the spring of 1878, Nathan C. Meeker arrived at the White River Ute Agency to take over as Indian Agent.

Meeker, who, according to Brown, "was a former poet, novelist, newspaper correspondent, and organizer of cooperative agrarian colonies," fervently attempted to transform the Utes from a hunting society into a farming community. When Meeker ordered land reserved by the Utes for grazing horses to be plowed, several armed Ute warriors confronted the plowman and told him he could not plow the land. When Meeker ordered the plowman to get back to the field and finish the job, the Natives fired warning shots at him. Canalla, who owned the horses, then argued with Meeker about the plowing. Angry about the confrontation, Meeker wrote to Colorado's governor to request troops for protection. On September 15, 1879, Meeker was informed that Major Thomas T. Thornburgh and 175 soldiers were on the way. About 300 warriors attempted to stop Thornburgh's troops before they reached the White River Agency, and on September 28, the first shots were fired near the Milk River. When Utes at the Agency heard about the fight, they killed Nathan Meeker and abducted three women. The fight at Milk River continued for a week leaving 12 soldiers, including Thornburgh, and 37 Utes dead. Another 43 soldiers were wounded. When Ouray heard about the confrontation, he sent a messenger with orders to cease the hostilities. The messenger arrived at the same time the cavalry's reinforcements arrived. On October 21, Ouray negotiated the release of the women captives.

In early 1880, Ouray again travelled to Washington to negotiate a new peace agreement. As a result of that treaty, the White River and Uncompahgre Utes were relocated to reservations in Utah. Shortly after the treaty was signed, Ouray travelled to the Southern Ute Agency in Ignacio. He died there August 27, 1880, from a kidney disease, known as Bright's Disease. His wife, Chipeta, died in 1924. In 1882, the Uncompahgre Ute Reservation in Utah was named, Ouray.

Ouray believed in peace and wanted to avoid violence between the Euro-Americans and the people he loved, the Utes of Colorado. He was wise, dignified, gentle and nearly always diplomatic in his dealings with the Euro-Americans. As a result, whites viewed Ouray as a friend, who truly wanted to protect both their interests as well as those of his fellow Utes. Throughout his life, Ouray lived the traditions of his Ute culture, which taught that fights that shed blood unnecessarily were foolish and should be avoided at all costs.

SOURCES:

Biographical Dictionary of Indians of the Americas, New Port Beach, California, American Indian Publishers, 1991; 504-505.

Brown, Dee, *Bury My Heart at Wounded Knee,* New York, Bantam Books, 1970; 349-367.

Dockstader, Frederick J., *Great North American Indians,* New York, Van Nostrand Reinhold Company, 1977; 202-203.

Handbook of American Indians North of Mexico, Part 2, edited by Frederick Webb Hodge, Totowa, New Jersey, Rowman and Littlefield, 1975; 175, 875-876.

Handbook of North American Indians, edited by William C. Sturtevant, Volume 11: *Great Basin,* edited by Warren L. D'Azevedo, Washington, D.C., Smithsonian Institution, 1986; 339, 354-356, 532.

McClellan, Val J., *This Is Our Land,* Volume 1, New York, Vantage Press, 1977.

North American Indians in Historical Perspective, edited by Eleanor Burke Leacock and Nancy Oestreich Lurie, New York, Random House, 1971; 271-275.

Sprague, Marshall, *Massacre: The Tragedy at White River,* Lincoln, University of Nebraska Press, 1957; 75-99.

Utley, Robert M., *Frontier Regulars: The United States Army and the Indian,* New York, Macmillan, 1973; 337-339.

Utley, Robert M., and Wilcomb E. Washburn, *History of the Indian Wars,* edited by Anne Moffat and Richard F. Snow, New York, American Heritage Publishing, 1977; 306-310.

Waldman, Carl, *Who Was Who in Native American History,* New York, Facts On File, 1990; 260-262.

Washburn, Wilcomb E., *The American Indian and the United States: A Documentary History,* Volume 1, New York, Random House, 1973; 246-301.

—Sketch by Catherine A. Clay

Elizabeth Anne Parent
1941-
Athabascan and Yupik educator

Elizabeth Anne Parent, a well-known Native American educator, lives by the words her aunt instilled in her at an early age, "Never give up." Also, her desire to follow the motto, "If you can run ... keep moving," has prompted her to pursue higher education as well as dedicated service to Native American peoples.

Parent was born in 1941 in the small Alaskan village of Bethel. Describing her homeland as being "mostly Indian in the middle of Alaskan country," she remembers Bethel as at one time having the highest infant mortality rate in the United States. Her ability to survive and flourish in a harsh environment was one of the first challenges she faced in life. During the early years of her life, Parent lived in her father's village of Crooked Creek, Alaska, until ten years of age. With the loss of her parents, she was sent to live with her aunt in western Massachusetts, where she attended junior high school; the following year she was sent to Park City, Montana, to begin high school. Due to her aunt's efforts to provide a fundamental education for her, Parent was sent to the Holy Name boarding school in Seattle, Washington, where she completed her high school studies. Education was beginning to become an important element in her life. In June 1964, she returned to Alaska, where she achieved the beginning of her many educational goals, receiving a bachelor of arts degree in anthropology with secondary studies in political science and English.

The Road to Higher Education

Education had always been an important goal in Parent's life, and she succeeded in securing the best possible education for herself. As a land grant institution originating from the incorporation of the Indian College from the Society for the Propagating of the Gospel Among the Heathen in 1650, Harvard University had an agreement in place to offer education to 25 American Indian students per year. Parent was one of those selected, and she went on to earn a master's degree in education (1973) and a C.A.S. in education (1974). While at Harvard, she was appointed editor of the Harvard Educational Review (1973-1974), focusing on the rights of children; she subsequently became a book review editor for the Harvard Educational Review (1974).

Elizabeth Anne Parent

While pursuing her academic studies, Parent expressed an interest in the study of Native cultures and societies. Her ability to "keep moving" soon found her relocating to the San Francisco Bay area in 1976 in acceptance of a teaching assistantship at the University of California-Berkeley in the Native American Studies Program. Initially afraid of teaching, her fears subsided, and she soon developed one of the most comprehensive and innovative curriculums dealing with Native American issues, which was a breakthrough in curriculum offerings at the time. Her courses contained a curriculum which enabled students to study the history of the Alaskan Native experience, American Indian psychology, and indigenous women's and children's issues; courses of these type were not offered and rarely considered by universities previously. Parent's academic travels during the next ten years led her to pursue additional studies at Stanford University, where she received a master's degree in anthropology (1978) and a Ph.D. in education (1984). Throughout her academic career, she has received many prestigious awards, including a Danforth fellowship (1975-1979) and an honorary Ford Foundation fellowship (1975-1978).

In recognition of her dedication in creating an outstanding American Indian studies curriculum, she was offered a lecturer position in 1979 at San Francisco State University. It was apparent that her professional leadership skills and extensive Native American educational background were qualities the university was seeking to help expand its Ethnic Studies Department. Throughout the next 14 years, she continued to advance her academic career as a faculty member of the American Indian Studies Program at San Francisco State University, later becoming department chair.

Beyond the Window of Education

Encouraging people to grow and achieve their goals has been one of the highlights of Parent's career. As a single mother raising her children, she recognized that the road is not always paved with "ease" for individuals attempting to reach their goals. Her numerous community service activities have enabled her to extend assistance to others in need. A staunch supporter of women's rights, she has contributed to the establishment of an American Indian Women's Support Group in conjunction with Stanford University and has labored extensively promoting children's rights while working at the Urban Indian Child Resource Center in Oakland, California.

Sensitive to the impending health needs and high infant mortality rates of American Indian communities, Parent was determined to offer assistance and knowledge to those health care workers serving native communities. In 1982, she developed and implemented a series of cultural sensitivity workshops for Indian and non-Indian personnel in health care delivery programs to American Indian populations.

Fostering social awareness of the needs and histories of Native communities is one way that she has attempted to break the cultural barrier between Western societies and native communities. In her article, "An Equal Chance for American Indians in the Home of the Brave and the Land of the Free," she stressed that "the presence of the Indian student will continue to be minimal until institutions of higher education do some fundamental rethinking of their services to the populations from whom they got the land." She stressed, "television is an important vehicle which can be utilized to teach others about native peoples. Through mass media outreach one can learn about their history, cultures and traditions."

Parent's appearance as a Native elder in Steven Seagal's film, *On Deadly Ground,* affirmed her conviction in utilizing film and television to educate the masses. She has maintained that through the media the public can have opportunity to learn not only about Native American communities, but all indigenous peoples. In an interview with JoAnn di Filippo, when asked of her plans for the future, she responded, "I love my career, teaching and educating people. It is my desire to pursue a television career, educating people about the history of the United States, and more importantly, teaching the truth of history and its native peoples—not some fictionalized account created by western civilization." Since 1993, she has been involved in the production of "Reality, Mind, and Language," a television series.

Parent has served on various committees and organizations dealing with Native American issues. In 1994, she was appointed to the tribally controlled committee of the Hewlett-Packard Foundation, as well as to the Hiring Committee for Director of Residential Education for California State University at Seaside, California. A true example and living legend of what she pronounces, she offered the following advice to everyone, "Don't take your eye off the prize ... go for it!"

SOURCES:

Periodicals

Parent, Elizabeth Ann, "An Equal Chance for American Indians in the Home of the Brave and the Land of the Free," in *Minorities in Graduate Education: Pipeline, Policy, and Practice,* Princeton, Educational Testing Service, 1992.

Other

Parent, Elizabeth Anne, telephone interviews with JoAnn di Filippo conducted May, June, and July, 1994.

—*Sketch by JoAnn di Filippo*

Arthur C. Parker
1881-1955
Seneca anthropologist and activist
Also known as Gawasowanah ["Big Snowsnake"]

One of the most prominent Native American intellectuals of the early to mid-twentieth century, Arthur C. Parker made significant contributions to the fields of anthropology, social activism, and museology. Through his various endeavors, Parker advocated an awareness of the changing culture of the American Indian in modern society, and the need to adapt to a culture in flux.

Arthur Caswell Parker was born on Cattaraugus Indian Reservation in New York in 1881, the son of Frederick Ely Parker, a half-blood Seneca, and Geneva H. Griswold, a white teacher who had worked on both the Cattaraugus and the Allegany Reservations. Frederick Parker was the son of Nicholson Henry Parker (1824-1892), brother of General Ely S. Parker, and Martha Hoyt, a niece of Mrs. Laura Sheldon Wright. Mrs. Wright, and her husband the Reverend

Asher Wright, were long time missionaries to the Seneca Indians. Considered among the "progressves," the Parker family was one of the most prominent on the reservation. In addition to General Parker, many notabe Senecas were represented in Parker's family, including the prophet Handsome Lake, Red Jacket, Governor Blacksnake, Cornplanter, and Disappearing Smoke, all individuals who had become Seneca and Iroquois culture heroes in the fight for Indian rights and causes in their day. Frederick Parker, a graduate of Fredonia State Normal School (located near his home on the Cattaraugus Reservation), was employed by the New York Central Railroad. Arthur's grandfather Nicholson had attended the State Normal School in Albany and was a prosperous farmer. He also had held the office of chief clerk of the Seneca Nation of Indians for many years. This greatly respected grandfather was a role model for Arthur during his formative years; Nicholson Parker read the classics to his grandson and passed on the story of the Seneca Indians' long and turbulent history.

Because of the matrilineal rule for legally determining tribal and clan affiliation among the New York Iroquois, neither Arthur Parker nor his father were legally recognized as Seneca, although both were adopted into a clan. In his early twenties, Parker was adopted into the Seneca Bear Clan and given the adult name Gawasowanah ["Big Snowsnake"] at the Newton Longhouse on the Cattaraugus Reservation. In addition, he was also inducted into the Little Water Society, one of the so-called secret medicine societies of the Iroquois; Parker's acceptance into this group was a particular honor, for many of the members practiced native religions while Parker himself was a recognized Christian. As a result of these traditional rites, Parker considered himself to be a Seneca by birth, culture, and affiliation.

The majority of Parker's childhood was spent on the reservation; however, in 1892 Arthur's father was transferred to White Plains, New York. Despite having to relocate to White Plains, the family continued to make frequent visits to the Cattaraugus Reservation, presumably assisted by his father's affiliation with the New York Central Railroad. Arthur and his sister attended public schools, and he graduated from high school in White Plains in 1897. For a brief period in 1899, Parker was a student at Centenary Collegiate Institute in Hackettstown, New Jersey, but apparently left after a school fire in October. Later in the fall of 1899, he went on to study for the ministry at Williamsport Dickinson Seminary in Pennsylvania. He left Dickinson in 1903, not having graduated.

Embarks on a Career in Anthropology

During this time, Parker worked as a newspaper reporter, developing the facility to write well, an ability which later became evident in his scientific writing. He also attended informal classes at the American Museum of Natural History in New York City, conducted by the early anthropologist Frederick Ward Putnam. There, Parker met anthropologists Frank G. Speck and Alanson Skinner, among others, and he accepted a brief appointment as an archaeological assistant at the museum in 1900. While in

New York, Parker also became a frequent visitor at the salon of Harriet Maxwell Converse, an amateur Iroquoianist scholar who had also been adopted by the Seneca. It was at "Aunt Hattie's" salon that Parker made the acquaintance of a number of intellectuals, both Indian and white, who became important figures in his life.

Parker also became acquainted with Franz Boas at Columbia College, but he ultimately rejected Boas' urging to pursue a degree in anthropology under his tutelage. This was a professional decision which Parker later regretted, but his reluctance may have been due, at least in part, to Boas' vehement rejection of Lewis Henry Morgan's evolutionary theories. Parker felt that he owed a particular debt to Morgan, who was an important part of Parker's link to his Indian background and who had achieved an established place in the anthropological study of the Iroquois. At this time, Parker became a field archaeologist with Mark R. Harrington, under the direction of Putnam and the Peabody Museum at Harvard, and he conducted his first formal archaeological excavation on the Cattaraugus Reservation. Harrington later became an in-law of Parker's, and he also initiated Parker into the archaeology of the Oyster Bay shell mounds on Long Island. While engaged in the archaeology in the Cattaraugus Reservation area, Parker systematically began to collect the folklore and oral history of the Seneca. In 1904, he received an offer of a temporary job from the New York State Library and Museum to collect ethnographic materials and art. Also that year, Parker married his first wife, Beatrice Tahamont, an Abenaki Indian.

The next year, Parker successfully completed the Civil Service examination for the position of archaeologist with the State Museum. Thus began his important and prolific anthropological career, in which he published extensively on the subjects of archaeology, ethnology, folklore, race relations, and museology. After nine years, Parker left the State Museum to become the director of the Rochester Museum (now the Rochester Museum and Science Center). His leadership of the museum helped to elevate that institution to a professional and highly regarded presence in the field. Parker continued his professional affiliation with the Rochester Museum until his death in 1955.

Becomes an Advocate of Pan-Indianism

Parker is considered to have been one of the major intellectual personalities in the Pan-Indian movement prior to World War I. On October 12, 1911, his commitment to progressive reform of Indian policy in the United States brought him into affiliation with the Society of American Indians (SAI) at its founding on Columbus Day, in Columbus, Ohio. This organization, the leading Pan-Indian advocacy group of its day, was comprised of the foremost educated Indian activists of the early twentieth century. Through his involvement with the SAI, Parker became the founder and editor of the *Quarterly Journal*, the official publication of the organization. He eventually became secretary-treasurer and later president of the Society as well.

Parker's leadership in the early efforts of Pan-Indian reform has directly influenced subsequent movements up to the present day. According to Hazel W. Hertzberg in *The Search for an American Indian Identity: Modern Pan-Indian Movements,* two major themes dominated Parker's professional life: his work in anthropology, and the integration of the American Indians into the fabric of the larger American national identity. In the former, Parker was able to make concrete contributions to the scientific field in a generally non-threatening and academically recognized manner. In the latter case, however, he was faced with attempting to reconcile major questions which continue to remain unsettled to this day. Chief among those critical issues were the effect of acculturation processes on the traditional cultures of Indian tribes and the problem of defining Indian identity. Parker and his associates in the SAI were philosophically committed to the concept that the American Indian was not vanishing through culture change, and that Indians could and would adapt to contemporary American culture without losing their identity as Indians. Ultimately, Parker embraced the melting-pot theory regarding the future of the American Indian, both as individuals and as a race. By 1920, he had become President of the New York Welfare Society, and he resigned from the SAI because he did not have the time to devote to the organization.

Remains Politically Active

In May 1923, Parker was elected to chair the first meeting of the Committee of One Hundred, the National Advisory Committee of the newly appointed Secretary of the Interior, Dr. Hubert Work. The committee had been created as a consequence of the uproar among dispossessed Pueblo Indians over the proposed Lenroot Bill, which legitimated the past confiscation of Indian Land while claiming to settle the issue of continuing disputed land titles. The Commissioner of Indian Affairs, John Collier, had drafted an alternative plan, the so-called "Indian Bill," which was introduced to Congress by Senator Charles Curtis of Kansas on January 16, 1923. Curtis, himself of Indian ancestry, was later to become Vice President of the United States. In the end, the reformers in the Committee of One Hundred failed to control the agenda, little positive assistance to the Pueblos resulted, and Collier's attempt to make the Committee a permanent advisory body failed. Eventually, a compromise was agreed upon which gave great concessions to the Pueblos. This bill, the Pueblo Lands Act, was signed into law by President Calvin Coolidge on June 3, 1924, one day after legislation was signed granting citizenship to all American Indians.

Beginning during the Great Depression and continuing up to the start of World War II, Parker obtained federal money for the Rochester Museum to fund an Iroquois arts and crafts program which greatly assisted the revitalization of Seneca material culture. By paying wages to Iroquois craftsmen and artists to produce the multitude of traditional items, Parker stimulated the continuation of the Seneca arts and crafts tradition. This program was instrumental in providing the material that is the basis of the magnificent Iroquois collection at the Rochester Museum. In later years, Parker continued to maintain both his anthropological interests and his role as an activist. He founded the Philosophical Society of Albany and

the New York State Archaeological Association; and, in 1944 he attended the inaugural meeting of the National Congress of American Indians (NCAI) in Denver, Colorado. The NCAI continues the Pan-Indian effort that Parker and his associates attempted at the turn of the century.

Although he never received an earned Ph.D., in recognition of his great contribution to the field of anthropology and museology, Parker was awarded an honorary M.S. from the University of Rochester in 1922, an honorary doctorate in science from Union College in 1940, and an honorary doctorate of Humane Laws from Keuka College in 1945. His bibliography consists of over 360 entries, the content of which includes perhaps his greatest contribution to his people. The breadth of his interests ranged from archaeology, ethnobotany, social and political organization, history, museum studies, biography, contemporary art, and current social activism, among others. Indeed, Parker made a lasting contribution to both the Iroquois tradition and the scientific field of anthropology. Parker died suddenly of a heart attack on New Year's Day, 1955. He was survived by his second wife, two daughters, and a son. His eldest daughter, the late Bertha, or "Birdie," was the wife of the show business personality, Cooper "Iron Eyes" Cody.

SOURCES:

Books

"Arthur C. Parker—Seneca, 1881-1955," *American Indian Intellectuals, 1976 Proceedings of the American Ethnological Society,* edited by Margot Liberty, St. Paul, West Publishing Company, 1978; 128-138.

Hertzberg, Hazel W., *The Search for an American Indian Identity: Modern Pan-Indian Movements,* Syracuse, Syracuse University Press, 1971.

Kelly, Lawrence C., *The Assault on Assimilation: John Collier and the Origins of Indian Policy Reform,* Albuquerque: University of New Mexico Press, 1983.

Parker, Arthur C., *Seneca Myths and Folk Tales,* Buffalo Historical Society, 1923; reprinted, University of Nebraska Press, 1989.

Parker on the Iroquois: Iroquois Uses of Maize and Other Plant Foods; The Code of Handsome Lake, the Seneca Prophet; The Constitution of the Five Nations, edited by William Fenton, Syracuse, University of Syracuse Press, 1968.

Periodicals

Hauptman, Lawrence, "The Iroquois School of Art: Arthur C. Parker and the Seneca Arts Project, 1935-1941," *New York History,* 60, July 1979; 283-312.

"Nationality, Anthropology, and Pan-Indianism in the Life of Arthur C. Parker (Seneca)," *Proceedings of the American Philosophical Society,* 123, 1979; 47-72.

Parker, Arthur C., "The Iroquois Uses of Maize and Other Food Plants," *New York State Museum Bulletin,* 144, 1910; 5-113.

Parker, Arthur C., "The Code of Handsome Lake, the Seneca Prophet," *New York State Museum Bulletin*, 163, 1913.

Parker, Arthur C., "The Constitution of the Five Nations," *New York State Museum Bulletin*, 184, 1916; 7-158.

Parker, Arthur C., "The Life of General Ely S. Parker, Last Grand Sachem of the Iroquois and General Grant's Military Secretary," *Publications of the Buffalo Historical Society*, 23, 1919.

Parker, Arthur C., "The Archaeological History of New York," *New York State Museum Bulletin*, 1922; 235-238.

Ritchie, William A., "Arthur Caswell Parker 1881-1955," *American Antiquity*, 21, 1956; 293-295.

Thomas, W. Stephen, "Arthur Caswell Parker: 1881-1955, Anthropologist, Historian and Museum Pioneer," *Rochester History*, 27, July 1955.

Thomas, W. Stephen, "Arthur Caswell Parker, Leader and Prophet of the Museum World," *Museum Service Bulletin*, 27; 18-25.

—*Sketch by George H. J. Abrams*

Ely Samuel Parker

Ely Samuel Parker
1828-1895

Seneca tribal leader, military leader, government official, and engineer

Also known as Ha-sa-no-an-da

Ely Samuel Parker (Ha-sa-no-an-da) was born in 1828 at Indian Falls on the Tonawanda Indian Reservation, near Akron, New York, the second of six children of a distinguished Seneca family. His mother was Elizabeth Johnson (Ga-ont-gwut-ywus), a Seneca Indian and member of the wolf clan who was born about 1786 and died in 1862. It has been speculated that Elizabeth may have desended from a white Quaker captive, Frances Slocum, although this has not been definitively sustantiated. His maternal grandfather, Jimmy Johnson (So-So-Ha'-Wa), was a grandson of the Seneca prophet Handsome Lake, the founder of the Iroquois religion, Gai-wiio. Ely Parker's father was the Seneca Chief William Parker (Jo-no-es-do-wa), who was born about 1793 and died in 1864; he was a veteran of the War of 1812 and a grandson of Disappearing Smoke (also known as Old King) a prominent figure in the early history of the Seneca.

Parker was also a collateral relative of many major figures in the history of the Iroquois, including the tribal leader Cornplanter, Governor Blacksnake, and the great orator Red Jacket. This familial background was a factor which influenced his later role in service to his people. Chief William Parker owned a large farm on the reservation and became a converted member of the newly formed missionary Baptist church. Ely reputedly received his first name from Ely Stone, one of the local founders of the mission. Supposedly, the Parker surname is derived from a Congregational missionary friend of Chief William Parker, Reverend Samuel Parker (1779-1866), the son of a Revolutionary War veteran who briefly served in western New York until 1812 when he become prominent in missionary activities in the West. According to Arthur C. Parker's biography, William Parker, his two brothers, and Elizabeth Johnson, Ely's mother, had migrated to Tonawanda from the Allegany Reservation at the same time that Handsome Lake was driven from Allegany to Tonawanda.

Ely Parker received his preliminary formal education at the Baptist boarding school associated with the mission church on the Tonawanda Reservation. Leaving the mission school at ten years of age, Parker had only a rudimentary knowledge of English, being able to understand but not speak the language. He was taken to Canada for several years where he was taught to hunt and fish, but returned to the Tonawanda Reservation at the age of 12, resolved to learn English and to further his formal education. He eventually was assigned the job of interpreter for the school and the church.

Becomes Intermediary with Government Delegations

Recognizing Parker's abilities in his early teens, the Seneca chiefs designated him to assist in numerous Seneca tribal delegations to Albany and Washington, D.C. He served as a translator and intermediary, accompanying his father and other Seneca chiefs on official trips. It was during one of these trips to Washington that Ely attended a dinner in the White House at the invitation of President James K. Polk. The experience of direct involvement in Seneca and Iroquois political and diplomatic affairs provided Parker with a valuable and practical educational foundation that served him later in life.

He attended Yates Academy from 1843 to 1845 and Cayuga Academy from the fall of 1845 to 1846, where he received the typical classical education of the time, leaving school at the age of 18. Lewis Henry Morgan (1818-1881), who had previously attended Cayuga Academy in Aurora, New York, assisted Parker in being admitted to the institution. Parker ultimately left Cayuga Academy to, once again, accompany a Seneca delegation to Washington. Parker's early role during this period was critical in the fight of the Tonawanda Seneca to regain the title to their reservation taken from them by the Buffalo Creek Treaty of 1832. The Tonawanda Reservation was not restored to the Seneca in the so-called "Compromise" Treaty of Buffalo Creek of 1842 and occupied the diplomatic and legal attention of the Tonawanda Seneca for many years. A portion of their former reservation was finally purchased in 1857, following a treaty of that year.

Parker met Morgan during one of his visits to Albany in 1844, in the company of his maternal grandfather Sachem Jimmy Johnson and Chief John Blacksmith. This meeting with the Seneca delegation provided the initial opportunity for Morgan to begin the collection of data on the Seneca, with Parker serving as interpreter. Their friendship was to last for the rest of their lives. Parker became the major informant for the continuing anthropological data that provided the ethnographic basis of Morgan's famous *League of the Ho-de-no-sau-nee, or Iroquois* (1851), considered to be the first and one of the finest ethnographies of an American Indian group. Morgan acknowledged his great debt to Parker and his collaboration by dedicating this major scientific publication to him when Parker was still a teenager.

Parker's value to the Seneca was formally recognized by his tribespeople and further enhanced in 1852 when he was designated to fill the vacant Seneca chief's wolf clan title of Do-ne-ho-ga-wa (Keeper of the Western Door), one of the major titles in the Iroquois Confederacy. This title had previously been held by the venerable Chief John Blacksmith who had died in 1851. At that time, Parker received the Red Jacket medal that had been given to Red Jacket by President George Washington in 1792 and inherited by Jimmy Johnson, Parker's grandfather. Parker retained his title and the medal for the remainder of his life.

Becomes Engineer

Beginning in 1847, Ely Parker aspired to become a lawyer and studied law in the offices of Angel & Rice in Ellicottville, New York, north of the Allegany Reservation. This firm had represented the Seneca Indians in several cases, and Parker had been previously acquainted with W. P.

Angel when he served as sub-agent from 1846 to 1848 for the New York Indian Agency. Parker, however, was denied admittance to the bar in the State of New York on the basis of his race. Indians were not recognized as citizens of the United States until 1924.

Parker turned his attention to the field of civil engineering and attended Rensselaer Polytechnic Institute. In this field he quickly became a recognized success, obtaining a number of important positions, beginning with work on the Genesee Valley Canal in 1849, and later on the Erie Canal. After a political difference of opinion, Parker left the Canal Office in Rochester in June, 1855. He moved on to engineering positions in Norfolk, Detroit, and finally, in 1857, he accepted the position of superintendent of construction for a number of government projects in Galena, Illinois, where he resided for a number of years. It was here that Parker initially became acquainted with a store clerk and army veteran, Ulysses S. Grant. They established a life-long friendship.

Begins Military Career during Civil War

With the outbreak of the Civil War, Parker tried to obtain a release from his engineering responsibilities at Galena but did not receive one. The decision resulted in his resignation in 1862. Parker then returned to the Tonawanda Reservation to request and gain his father's approval to go to war. Once again, his race proved to be an obstacle to obtaining and he was unable to obtain an army commission from either the governor of New York or the Secretary of War. In fact, Secretary William H. Seward informed Parker that the rebellion would be suppressed by the whites, without the aid of Indians. Eventually, Parker was commissioned in the early summer of 1863 as a captain of engineers and was briefly assigned to General J. E. Smith as division engineer of the Seventh Division, Twenty-seventh Corps. Later that year, on September 18, Parker became Grant's staff officer at Vicksburg. A year later, on August 30, 1864, Parker was advanced to lieutenant-colonel and became Grant's military secretary. It was Parker who made draft corrections in the terms of surrender at Appomattox Court House on April 9, 1865, and penned the final official copies that ended the Civil War. Parker later reported that General Robert E. Lee was momentarily taken aback on seeing Parker in such a prominent position at the surrender. Apparently, Lee shook hands with Parker and said, "I am glad to see one real American here." Parker replied, "We are all Americans."

At the conclusion of the Civil War, Parker continued as Grant's military secretary. He was also commissioned a brigadier-general of volunteers at the date of surrender at Appomattox. In addition, two years later, on March 2, 1867, Parker's gallant and meritorious service was recognized through his appointment to first and second lieutenant in the cavalry of the Regular Army, and brevet appointments as captain, major, lieutenant-colonel, colonel, and brigadier-general, also in the Regular Army.

On Christmas Day, 1867, with Ulysses S. Grant as best man, Parker married Miss Minnie Orton Sackett (1850-

1932) of Washington, D.C., the stepdaughter of a soldier who had died in the war. In 1878, Ely and Minnie had a daughter, Maud Theresa Parker (d. 1956), from whom Ely Parker's descendants are derived.

Enters into Troubled Political Career

Following the election to the presidency, Grant appointed Parker as Commissioner of Indian Affairs on April 13, 1869; he was the first American Indian to hold the office. Parker resigned from the army on April 26. Although a strong advocate for the assimilation of the American Indian and a supporter of Grant's Peace Policy, directed to the improvement of the American Indian, Parker also sought major reform and restructuring of the Bureau of Indian Affairs, an unpopular policy in some political quarters. In addition, his humanitarian and just treatment of western Indians created many influential political enemies in Washington. Especially troublesome was the relationship with the Sioux and the implementation of the provisions of the Fort Laramie Treaty, which had been signed in 1868, ending Red Cloud's War of 1866-1868.

Finally, accused of defrauding the government, a committee of the House of Representatives tried Parker in February, 1871. The charges against Parker involved the assignment of contracts at the Spotted Tail Agency (formerly the Whetstone Agency) on the White River. He was completely exonerated of any misconduct, but nevertheless resigned from government service in July, feeling that the office of commissioner had been greatly reduced in authority and effectiveness.

Parker entered the stock market on Wall Street and made a fortune which he eventually lost in settling a defaulted bond of his business partner. Other attempts at business opportunities also proved unsuccessful. Later, Parker served with the New York City Police Department. Ely Samuel Parker died on August 31, 1895, at his home in Fairfield, Connecticut, where he was initially buried. In 1897, his remains were reinterred with those of Red Jacket and his ancestors in Forest Lawn Cemetery, Buffalo, New York.

SOURCES:

Armstrong, William H., *Warrior in Two Camps: Ely S. Parker, Union General and Seneca Chief,* Syracuse, NY, Syracuse University Press, 1978.

Morgan, Lewis Henry, *League of the Ho-de-no-sau-nee, or Iroquois,* Rochester, New York, Sage, 1851; reprinted, Corinth Books, 1962, 1990.

Olson, James C., *Red Cloud and the Sioux Problem,* Lincoln, University of Nebraska Press, 1965.

Parker, Arthur C., *The Life of General Ely S. Parker: Last Grand Sachem of the Iroquois and General Grant's Military Secretary,* 23, Buffalo, New York, Buffalo Historical Society Publication, 1919.

Tooker, Elisabeth, "Ely S. Parker, Seneca, ca. 1828-1895," in *American Indian Intellectuals: 1976 Proceedings of the American Ethnological Society,* West Publishing, 1978; 14-29.

Waltmann, Henry G., "Ely Samuel Parker, 1869-71," in *The Commissioners of Indian Affairs: 1824-1977,* edited by Robert M. Kvasnicka and Herman J. Viola, Lincoln, University of Nebraska Press, 1979; 123-131.

Yeuell, Donovan, "Ely Samuel Parker," *Dictionary of American Biography,* Volume 7, edited by Dumas Malone, New York, Charles Scribner's Sons, 1934; 219-220.

—Sketch by George H. J. Abrams

Quanah Parker
1852(?)-1911
Comanche tribal leader and businessman

Quanah Parker was a leader of the Comanche people during the difficult transition period from free-ranging life on the southern plains to the settled ways of reservation life. He became an influential negotiator with government agents, a prosperous cattle-rancher, a vocal advocate of formal education for Native children, and a devout member of the Peyote Cult.

Quanah ["Fragrant"] was perhaps specially able to help his people bridge the two worlds because of his own mixed ancestry. He was born to Peta Nocona, a Quahadi (Kwahado, Quahada) Comanche war leader, and Cynthia Ann Parker, a white woman who had been captured by the Comanche and raised as an Indian. Cynthia's family, the Parkers, were influential people in prestatehood Texas, so the raid on Fort Parker on May 19, 1836, is considered a major event in Texas history. Several family members died in the raid, but nine-year-old Cynthia was one of those taken alive. She and her brother were adopted by the Natives, but her brother apparently died soon after. Cynthia was renamed Preloch and was brought up in a traditional Quahadi village.

In her middle teens, Cynthia married Peta Nocona. About 1852 (some sources say as early as 1845), Quanah was born to them as their band camped at Cedar Lake, Texas. Approximately three years later, Quanah's sister Topsannah ["Prairie Flower"] was born. Their childhood coincided with major changes in Comanche life, as American settlement increased and free range for Indians and buffalo decreased. Cynthia's family kept up the search for her throughout the years. Finally, in 1861, Texas Rangers recaptured Cynthia and brought her and Topsannah back to her relatives. Although she knew about her early years, Cynthia had become completely Comanche, and she mourned for her Indian family and friends. It is believed that Prairie Flower died in the mid-1860s, and Cynthia followed her to the grave in 1870.

Quanah Parker

Back amid the Quahadi, Quanah was trying to adjust to the loss of his beloved mother and sister. The death of Peta Nocona in 1866 or 1867 was a further blow to the young man. For all intents and purposes now an orphan, Quanah found himself at the mercy of the charity of other relatives, while becoming the object of taunts from other Quahadi for his mixed ancestry. He must have been a striking figure among his people, taller and thinner than other Comanches, with a lighter complexion and grey eyes. Still, he felt himself to be unquestioningly Comanche in his beliefs and way of life.

The Move to Indian Territory

In 1867, the Treaty of Medicine Lodge was signed, which called for the settlement of the Comanche, Cheyenne, Riowa, Kiowa-Apache, and Arapaho onto reservations in Indian Territory (later the state of Oklahoma). Most of the Comanche bands accepted the treaty, but the Quahadi would resist settlement the longest, refusing to recognize the document. Seven years of periodic raiding and open hostility towards white settlers and frontier towns ensued, with retaliation against the Comanche for these incidents. The final insult in the minds of the Quahadi was the increasing presence of buffalo hunters, professionals hired to hunt the huge animals for the eastern market and to undercut the basis of Plains Indian life, forcing them onto reservations to avoid starvation. In June of 1875, a group of 700 allied tribes' warriors attacked a group of buffalo hunters at a fortification called Adobe Walls, in the Texas Panhandle. Three days of bitter fighting led to an eventual turning back of the Indian

raiding force, and the beginning of two years of relentless pursuit of the Quahadi by General Ranald Mackenzie. Until recently, published accounts of Quanah Parker's life reported that he led the Indians against Adobe Walls, became the war chief of the Quahadi during Mackenzie's pursuit, and reluctantly surrendered to reservation life as the last fierce war leader of the free Comanche. Recent works show that Quanah was too young to have been a war chief, but report that he did fight at Adobe Walls.

The Quahadi surrendered to reservation settlement in 1875. The person who was most likely their leader at that time was Eschiti ["Coyote Droppings"], who had been the leader who incited the raid on Adobe Walls. A medicine man as well as a civil leader, Eschiti would see his influence decrease as Quanah Parker's increased with the favor of the Indian Agent. Early on, the agent had courted Parker's good graces, believing that, as a mixed-blood, Parker could be more easily converted to white ways and could then influence his people to change also. However, the agent had not taken into account that Parker's mixed ancestry was the reason many staunchly traditional Comanche refused to accept his leadership. That he was being "created" as an Indian leader by white officials caused further conflict.

A Chief Emerges

These first years of settled life took quite a toll on the Quahadi: Not only was their old way of life dying, many Indian people sickened and died as well. Perhaps this alarmingly high death rate also accounted for a lack of rivals to contest Quanah Parker's rising power. In fact, his most potent competitor, Mowaway, who had been a war chief, chose to rescind his position in 1878, virtually clearing the way for Quanah to become the "principal chief" of the Comanche around Fort Sill.

Quanah Parker then moved quickly from the status of a "ration chief" (one who is recognized as the leader of a small band of reservation-dwellers who count collectively as one unit for the purpose of handing out rations) to a member of the Comanche Council. Throughout the late 1870s, the council functioned mainly to agree to whatever the Indian Agent decided. The single major disagreement between the agency and the council in this period arose over the Indian Department's decision to consolidate the Wichita, Kiowa, Kiowa-Apache, and Comanche agencies and to move the headquarters from Fort Sill to the Washita River. This change would place the source of rations some 60 miles distant from the Comanche settlements. With rations being handed out three times per week, most Comanche would be constantly in transit to or from the headquarters. Parker joined in with other, more traditional leaders in opposing this move. The growing anti-Quanah faction regarded this as one of his last "loyal" acts. Already, Parker's accommodation of whites was earning him enemies.

Heading into the 1880s, Texas cattlemen were regularly driving cattle across Comanche lands on the way to railheads at Dodge City and Abilene, Kansas. The sparingly grazed grasslands were lush and provided a last chance for cattle barons to fatten their stock before sale. At first, the Comanche ignored this trespassing, as the cattlemen also ignored the occasional poaching of a cow by the Indians. Eventually though, the ranchers in the areas adjoining Comanche land intentionally ranged their herds on Comanche grasslands. In 1881, the Comanche Council formally protested the actions. Sensing that Quanah Parker was a man who could see both sides of the issue, the cattlemen agreed to put him (and Eschiti) on their payroll to ride with white "cattle police" keeping an eye on property lines. Later, Permansu (also known as "Comanche Jack") would join them.

Being on the cattlemen's payroll provided Quanah Parker with money, "surplus" cattle, and influence among the cattle barons. He started his own herd with gift cattle and a blooded bull, courtesy of the king of the cattle barons, Charlie Goodnight. Parker started his own ranch, where he would eventually build his famous residence, the Star House. More a mansion than a house, it was two-storied with a double porch, its metal roof was decorated with prominent white stars, and the interior was richly appointed in the manner of wealthy non-Indians of the day. Some of Quanah's detractors said he had built the Star House to lord over the more traditional leaders of the Comanche; others said he needed the room for his seven wives and seven children.

The Indian Agency was appalled that Quanah, a strong believer in formal education for his people and their participation in the developing money economy of Indian Territory, was an equally strong believer in polygamy and the Peyote Cult. It is not certain when Quanah was introduced to the peyote rite (originally a religion of the native peoples of northern Mexican deserts), but he was well respected in the Comanche branch of the faith, becoming a "road man" (a ritual leader). When the Ghost Dance swept the Plains tribes, and people from the Lakota to the Paiute were dancing themselves into trances, trying to make the buffalo return, Parker rejected the movement. He remained true to his peyotism, but would accept the inclusion of elements of Christianity, some said in honor of his mother.

"Progressive" in Two Worlds

In 1884, Quanah Parker made his first of 20 trips to Washington, D.C. This one dealt with changes in the lease arrangements the Comanche had been able to work out with the cattle ranchers. The Comanche were profitably leasing grasslands they were not using themselves, and they resented the property changes that would come with allotment in severalty, the process of dividing tribally held land into individually owned plots. Despite several trips, Quanah was unable to stave off the allotment under the terms of the Jerome Commission, but he did improve the deal for his people.

The ever-present anti-Quanah Parker faction on the reservation criticized Quanah for trying to arrange a larger allotment for himself and a higher price per acre payment for the sale of surplus land. However, he was still a very influential leader. In the 1890s, the Indian Agent was issuing official "chief certificates," a sort of identification, and Quanah was able to convince the agency that he should be issued the cer-

tificate for the principal chieftainship. This done, Eschiti was finally completely deposed, and Parker went so far as to have letterhead printed with his name and the emblazoned title of principal chief. The action further impressed white men, but further embittered the more traditional Comanche.

Starting in 1886, Quanah Parker had been a judge of the Court of Indian Affairs, but lost his position as the tribe made the final move towards allotment near the end of the century. The breakup of communally held lands and the resulting breakdown of age-old tribal traditions greatly angered many Comanche and they saw Quanah as the source of their problems. They saw that Quanah courted a public image as a "progressive" Indian in the eyes of white America, becoming something of a national celebrity. Visitors to the Star House would include Theodore Roosevelt and British Ambassador Lord Bryce. In fact, Quanah would be one of the four Indian chiefs to ride in President Theodore Roosevelt's inaugural parade.

The Circle Is Completed

In the first decade of the twentieth century, Quanah Parker's influence began to wane. On a personal level, two of his wives left him, angered over what they saw as a self-important pursuit of plural wives. Tonarcy was considered his principal wife, but among his others were Topay, Chony, Mahcheettowooky, and Aerwuthtakum. Since most of his wives were widows when he married them, Parker saw this arrangement as a way to take care of women who would otherwise have had to rely on relatives for their survival, due to their young ages. In the sphere of tribal politics, Quanah was also losing ground. Allotment had reduced his land base and therefore his personal fortune, and he would eventually resort to taking a paid position with the Indian Service as an "assistant farmer."

By the beginning of 1911, Quanah Parker was in obvious poor health. He had rheumatism and his heart was weakening. In February, after a long and tiring train ride, he took to his bed, suffering from heart trouble. On February 25, 1911, Quanah Parker died at the Star House, Tonarcy at his side. Despite criticism during his life from traditional Comanche, Quanah Parker was so revered that the procession to his resting place was said to be over a mile long. After a Christian service in a local church, Quanah was buried next to his mother's and sister's reinterred remains in Cache County, Oklahoma. Four years later, graverobbers broke into his grave, taking the jewelry with which he had been buried. The Parkers ritually cleaned and then reburied him. Quanah Parker, Cynthia Ann, and Topsannah were all moved to Fort Sill Military Cemetery in 1957. The life of Quanah Parker is today seen as the extraordinary story of a person successfully living in two worlds, two minds, two eras.

SOURCES:

Andrews, Ralph W., *Indian Leaders Who Helped Shape America, 1600-1900,* Seattle, Superior Publishers, 1971.

Dockstader, Frederick J., *Great North American Indians,* New York, Van Nostrand Reinhold, 1977.

Edmunds, R. David, *American Indian Leaders: Studies in Diversity,* Lincoln, University of Nebraska, 1980.

Hagan, William T., *Quanah Parker, Comanche Chief,* Norman, University of Oklahoma, 1993.

—Sketch by Cynthia R. Kasee

Jeanine Pease-Windy Boy
1949-

Crow educator, administrator, and college president

Many contemporary Native leaders believe that education is the path for Native self-sufficiency, cultural preservation, and economic security; Jeanine Pease-Windy Boy not only espouses this belief but she has devoted her life to making it a viable option for Crow people. A life in education seemed almost predestined for Jeanine Pease-Windy Boy. The daughter of two teachers (her father, a Crow Indian and her mother, of English and German ancestry), she was born in 1949 in Nespelem, Washington, on the Colville Reservation, where her parents were then assigned. She was one of four children, all of whom have established professional careers, and all of whom credit their parents' emphasis on education as the root of their success.

Although well versed in the expectations of the "outside world," Pease-Windy Boy was also brought up with her Crow culture, an ever-present source of security. Jeanine was given a Crow name by an elder clan member. The name, which, according to Crow tradition reflects the attributes of the name giver, translates as "One Who Likes to Pray." During many summers, she lived with relatives on the Crow reservation in southeastern Montana. As a young adult, Pease-Windy Boy attended Central Washington University, from which she graduated in 1970 with a bachelor's degrees in sociology and anthropology. She counseled Indian students at Navajo Community College (Arizona) and directed Big Bend Community College's Upward Bound Program (Washington). She married in 1975, started a family, and went to work for the Crow Tribe of Indians. While serving as the tribe's director of the Adult and Continuing Education Commission, she was raising a daughter, Roses, and a son, Vernon, with her husband.

But a split from her husband in 1979 left Pease-Windy Boy in precarious financial straits. The couple had decided that she would take two years off from her career to spend with the children, the family supported wholly by Windy Boy. Soon, he lost his job and Pease-Windy Boy had to accept public assistance in order to provide for Roses and Vernon. Unwilling to let the situation stand as it was, Pease-Windy Boy began job-hunting. By 1981, she had secured a position with Eastern Montana College, helping Native students enter college and find jobs after graduation. Inspired by the success of some of her clients, she decided to direct her efforts toward making higher education more available to Crow people.

In 1982, Pease-Windy Boy was appointed President of the Little Big Horn College. Pease-Windy Boy directed the college as its chief operating officer, taught several subjects, worked as a part-time janitor, occasionally brought students to school when Montana winters make driving difficult, and even donated a portion of her modest salary back to the school. Since that time, Little Big Horn College has experienced continual growth, now enrolling more than 280 students in two-year degree programs that prepare them for jobs or for continued education at four-year colleges and universities.

Pease-Windy Boy has not ignored her own education. She finished her Master of Education program at Montana State University in 1987. In an interview with contributor Cynthia Kasee, Pease-Windy Boy indicated that she received her Ed.D. from MSU in 1994. She was the National Indian Education Association's "Educator of the Year" for 1990. She has received several honorary doctorates from universities and a human-rights award from the Torah Academy of Suffolk County (New York) for her public stand against anti-Semitism. She was lead plaintiff in *Windy Boy v. Bighorn County,* a landmark voting rights case.

The U.S. Federal District Court found intentional discrimination in county voter registration procedures. The court ordered zoning that provided a means for the election of Indian county commissioners and school board trustees.

Pease-Windy Boy remains an active lobbyist for more funds for the more than 20 tribally controlled colleges in the United States, never turning her back on her concern for preservation of tribal cultures. In recognition of these joint efforts, she has been appointed as a trustee of the National Museum of the American Indian and received a Clinton appointment to NACIE.. She is frequently called upon to deliver commencement speeches and is a much sought-after speaker at education conferences, particularly those that focus on Native issues.

SOURCES:

Books

Native American Women, edited by Gretchen Bataille, New York, Garland Publishing, 1993.

Native North American Almanac, edited by Duane Champagne, Detroit, Gale Research, 1994.

Periodicals

"Crow College," *Life,* August, 1988.

Mooney, Carolyn J., "Head of Blossoming Tribal College: A Product of My Community," *Chronicle of Higher Education,* November 29, 1989; A3.

Other

Pease-Windy Boy, Jeanine, interview with Cynthia Kasee conducted May 16, 1994.

—Sketch by Cynthia R. Kasee

Leonard Peltier

1944-

Ojibwa-Lakota activist and political prisoner
Also known as Gwarth-ee-lass ["He-Leads-the-People"]

Leonard Peltier

A leader in the American Indian Movement (AIM) in the early 1970s, Leonard Peltier is serving two consecutive life sentences at Leavenworth Prison in Kansas, after being convicted of killing two Federal Bureau of Investigation (FBI) agents in 1975 at the Pine Ridge Reservation in South Dakota. Peltier continues to assert his innocence in the deaths of these agents. He is considered by many to be a political prisoner. With the support of hundreds of tribes, lawmakers in the United States and Canada, Amnesty International, religious leaders such as Archbishop Desmond Tutu and the Archbishop of Canterbury, Nobel Peace Prize winner Rigoberta Menchu, the Princess of Belgium, a U.S. Court of Appeals judge, and support groups throughout the world, he works for his release from prison and for justice and betterment for all Native Americans.

Peltier was born on September 12, 1944, in Grand Forks, North Dakota. At that time, Peltier's large family worked in the potato fields, migrating from Turtle Mountain to the Red River Valley. Peltier's maternal grandmother was a full-blood Lakota Sioux. His father Leo (who died in 1989) was three-quarters Ojibwa, one-quarter French. Peltier's father and mother (Alvina Showers) separated when he was four, and Peltier and his younger sister Betty Ann then went to live with his paternal grandparents, Alex and Mary Peltier. Peltier moved with his grandparents to Montana to look for work in the logging camps and copper mines. After Peltier experienced a racist incident in Butte, his grandparents returned with him and his sister to the reservation in North Dakota. After spending some time in Wahpeton Indian School, Peltier returned to the Turtle Mountain Reservation to live with his father. There, he became interested in traditional medicine and ceremonies. In 1958, Peltier participated in his first sun dance on Turtle Mountain, but because such activity was illegal at that time, he and other participants were placed in jail.

During the 1950s termination era, Peltier witnessed poor conditions among the Ojibwa that had a profound effect on him. He recounted to Bud Schultz and Ruth Schultz in *It Did Happen Here:* "When I was a teenager, I heard an old Ojibwa woman, a relative of mine, get up and speak at an Indian meeting. She was pleading for food for her children. 'Are there no more warriors among our men,' she asked, 'who will stand up and fight for their starving children?' That day, I vowed I would help my people the rest of my life."

Becomes Active in the American Indian Movement

In 1959, Peltier's mother moved to the West Coast as part of the government's relocation program and Peltier soon followed. In Oakland, Peltier and his cousins Bob and Steve Robideau learned carpentry and machine work from Bob's father. Peltier and Steve Robideau then worked as welders in shipyards in Portland. By the age of 20, Peltier was part-owner of an auto body shop in Seattle. At this time, he became more active in Native American issues, participating in the local fishing rights fight. His first "AIM-style" confrontation was as a participant in the takeover of surplus Indian land at Fort Lawton outside of Seattle in 1970.

After the Fort Lawton episode, Peltier began traveling the country with leaders such as Dennis Banks and Vernon Bellecourt of the relatively new American Indian Movement. In November of 1972, Peltier went to Washington, D.C., with other AIM members as part of the Trail of Broken Treaties march. AIM leaders had alerted Washington officials that they would be in town to discuss treaty matters, yet they ended up barricading themselves in Bureau of Indian Affairs (BIA) offices for a week when they were asked to leave. AIM leaders had drafted a list of "20 points" which focused on validation of Indian treaties, including the Fort Laramie Treaty of 1868. This treaty recognized Indian sovereignty and Indian lands, including that of Peltier's people, the Sioux. Violations of this treaty left the Oglala Sioux with only a fraction of their original homeland. The government's promise to consider the 20-point proposal was never carried out. Rather, after the incident at the BIA building, AIM was classified by the FBI as an "extremist organization" and its leaders—including Peltier—were added to the Bureau's list of "key extremists."

Events quickly escalated against Peltier and other AIM members. In late November 1972, Peltier was beaten by two off-duty policemen in Milwaukee. When they found a gun (which did not work) in Peltier's possession they charged him with attempted murder. After he spent five months in jail, AIM raised bail for his release and he went underground. Instead of appearing at a pre-trial hearing in July 1973, Peltier headed for the Dakotas.

Meanwhile, members of the Pine Ridge Reservation in South Dakota had begun experiencing a "reign of terror" under the tribal chairmanship of Richard "Dick" Wilson, the BIA police, and the reservation police known as the "GOON squad" ("Guardians of the Oglala Nation"). There were many incidents of harassment and abuse of tribal members. When Wilson and the FBI did not respond to efforts to resolve the murder of an Oglala Indian named Raymond Yellow Thunder, Pine Ridge traditional elders appealed to AIM for help. Violent incidents and unrest continued, and in February 1973, 300 traditionals and AIM members, including Peltier, occupied the village of Wounded Knee to protest the abuses of Wilson and the GOON squad. A 71-day siege by the FBI, U.S. Marshals, and BIA Police ended when U.S. government representatives agreed to investigate conditions on the Pine Ridge Reservation and Fort Laramie Treaty violations; the investigations never took place. An estimated 300 largely unexplained murders or "accidents" occurred during this period. At the request of Oglala Sioux chiefs, including Francis He Crow who stated that "there is no law on the reservation," Peltier and six other AIM members returned in March 1975 to establish a spiritual camp near Oglala to protect the Pine Ridge people.

Convicted of Deaths of FBI Agents

In the late morning of June 26, 1975, FBI agents Ronald Williams and Jack Coler entered the Jumping Bull property near Oglala, ostensibly to serve a warrant for robbery on a young Oglala Indian named Jimmy Eagle. A firefight ensued in which the two agents and a young Coeur d'Alene Indian named Joe (Killsright) Stuntz were killed. FBI agents, BIA police, and other law enforcement agencies moved in and the standoff continued for the remainder of that day. While police searched for someone to charge with the murder of the FBI agents (no one has yet been charged with the death of Joe Stuntz), the U.S. Civil Rights Commis-

sion was called in to investigate tactics that the FBI was using in their search; no investigation was ever conducted by the Justice Department of civil rights violations.

In November 1975, Peltier, Jimmy Eagle, Bob Robideau, and Darrelle Dean ("Dino") Butler were indicted for the deaths of agents Williams and Coler. Peltier had fled to Canada because, as he related in *It Did Happen Here*, "I realized the possibility of getting a fair trial was very slim." Peltier asked for asylum in Canada, but on February 6, 1976, he was arrested in Alberta, Canada. On February 18, extradition hearings began in Vancouver in which, under duress from the FBI, a Lakota woman named Myrtle Poor Bear alleged that she saw Peltier commit the murders. She later recanted, saying that she had been threatened by an FBI agent with a similar fate to that of AIM member Anna Mae Aquash, who had been found shot in the head on February 24, 1976, on the Pine Ridge Reservation. Aquash had earlier told the FBI she knew nothing about the murders of the agents and said she would not cooperate with them. In the summer of 1976, Dino Butler and Bob Robideau were acquitted of the murders of the FBI agents on the grounds of self-defense; in September, charges were dropped against Jimmy Eagle for lack of evidence. That left Peltier; and on December 18, based on Myrtle Poor Bear's faulty affidavits, he was extradited to the United States.

Peltier's murder trial began in Fargo, North Dakota, on March 4, 1977. The prosecution alleged that Peltier and others "ambushed" the FBI agents. The largely circumstantial evidence centered around a single shell casing from a .223 caliber AR-15 rifle that was linked to Peltier. The other piece of evidence connected to him was a red and white van in which Peltier was allegedly seen entering and leaving the Jumping Bull property. No one testified in court that they had seen Peltier commit the murders. Even the prosecution claimed as "unbelievable" an FBI Special Agent's statement that he saw Peltier at the scene through his seven-power rifle telescope from one-half mile away. The evidence of violence on the Pine Ridge Reservation, the persecution of AIM by the FBI, as well as FBI tampering were kept from the jury. On April 18, 1977, the all-white jury convicted Peltier of both murders. On June 1, Judge Paul Benson sentenced Peltier to two consecutive life terms; he was eventually sent to Marion Federal Penitentiary in Illinois.

Appeals for New Trial Denied

Peltier's lawyers appealed his conviction before the U.S. Court of Appeals for the Eighth Circuit in December 1977. The appeal was denied, based on the supposed evidence of the murder weapon. A petition was also filed with the U.S. Supreme Court, but in March 1979, the Court refused to review Peltier's case. In April 1979, Peltier was transferred to Lompoc Prison in California. There, upon learning of an assassination attempt against his life, he and three other inmates escaped from Lompoc. Peltier was recaptured in late July 1979. He was tried, convicted, and given seven additional years in prison for the escape but the conviction was reversed by the Ninth Circuit Court of Appeals. A second appeal was filed a few years later, when it was revealed in FBI documents released through a Freedom of Information suit that the critical shell casing could not be linked to the rifle allegedly used by Peltier. Prosecutor Lynn Crooks testified that they "do not know who killed those agents." But again, in December 1982, Peltier was denied a new trial. Another hearing in 1984 on ballistics evidence failed to overturn Peltier's conviction, and in October 1987, the U.S. Supreme Court again refused to hear his case.

Peltier's third and final appeal to the Eighth Circuit Court was denied on July 7, 1993. This time, the Court upheld his conviction on the "alternative theories" ruling, stating that he would either be guilty of the murders or of "aiding and abetting" them. In December 1993, the U.S. Parole Commission denied Peltier parole; he was told to reapply in 15 years.

Public Interest in and Support for Peltier Grows

Over 20 million people worldwide have signed petitions and written letters of support for Peltier. There are some 150 support groups around the country, and support organizations also exist in Canada, Europe, Australia, and Japan. After Peltier's final, unsuccessful appeal, his lead attorney Ramsey Clark submitted a formal application for executive clemency on November 22, 1993. Petitions for clemency with more than 500,000 signatures were submitted to President Bill Clinton in December 1993. Also, in the spring of 1994, the Justice Minister of Canada authorized a review of Peltier's extradition from Canada.

In the epilogue of the 1991 edition of *In the Spirit of Crazy Horse,* the most well-known account of the events on the Pine Ridge Reservation, Peter Matthiessen described meeting the individual—"X"—who maintains that he is the one who actually shot the FBI agents. This individual told Matthiessen that he wished others to know of Peltier's innocence but did not intend to reveal his own identity to authorities.

In 1986 Peltier received Spain's Human Rights Award for "defending the historical and cultural rights of his people against the genocide of his race." In 1993, he was nominated for the Nobel Peace Prize. From Leavenworth Prison, Peltier directs the efforts of the Leonard Peltier Defense Committee (LPDC), established in 1985 to lobby support for his release. He is involved in social and charitable causes and the Native American rights movement. He also paints. Yet, as Peltier has written in the LPDC's newsletter, *Spirit of Crazy Horse,* "I have had to stare at photographs of my children to see them grow up. I have had to rely on restricted telephone calls to be linked to my mother and grandchildren. I miss having dinner with friends. I miss taking walks in the woods. I miss gardening. I miss babies. I miss my freedom." And of his ordeal in the summer of 1975, Leonard Peltier has said, "In honesty, I wish I hadn't been at that camp, but I do not regret that I was one of those who stood up and helped to protect my people."

SOURCES:

Books

Biographical Dictionary of Indians of the Americas, second edition, Volume 2, Newport Beach, California, American Indian Publishers, 1991; 524-525.

Churchill, Ward, and Jim Vander Wall, *Agents of Repression: The FBI's Secret Wars Against the Black Panther Party and the American Indian Movement,* Boston, South End Press, 1990.

Deloria, Vine, Jr., *Behind the Trail of Broken Treaties,* New York, Delacorte, 1974.

Matthiessen, Peter, *In the Spirit of Crazy Horse,* New York, Viking, 1991.

Messerschmidt, Jim, *The Trial of Leonard Peltier,* Boston, South End Press, 1983.

The Native North American Almanac, edited by Duane Champagne, Detroit, Gale Research, 1994; 1130.

Stern, Kenneth S., *Loud Hawk: The United States Versus the American Indian Movement,* Norman, University of Oklahoma Press, 1994.

"War Against the American Nation: Leonard Peltier," in *It Did Happen Here: Recollections of Political Repression in America,* compiled by Bud Schultz and Ruth Schultz, Berkeley, University of California Press, 1989; 213-229.

Weyler, Rex, *Blood of the Land: The Government and Corporate War Against First Nations,* Philadelphia, New Society Publishers, 1992.

Periodicals

Knickerbocker, Brad, "U.S. Is Under Pressure to Ask if Justice Was Done in Case Against Native American," *Christian Science Monitor,* February 3, 1994; 1,4.

Matthiessen, Peter, "Who Really Killed the FBI Men," *Nation,* 252, May 13, 1991; 613-16.

Payne, Diane, "A Brief History of Leonard Peltier v. U.S.: Is There Recourse for Justice?", *American Indian Journal,* 5, March 1979; 2-6.

Peltier, Leonard, "Peltier Pleads: Please Don't Forget Me," *News from Indian Country,* 7, September 30, 1993; 25.

Peltier, Leonard, "Statement of Leonard Peltier," *Spirit of Crazy Horse,* September-October 1993.

Rydell-Janson, Elisabet, "*Notes* Interviews Leonard Peltier," *Akwesasne Notes* 21, fall 1989; 7-11.

Specktor, Mordecai, "U.S. Court of Appeals Rejects Peltier's Plea for New Trial," *Circle,* 15, January 1994; 14.

Other

Akwesasne Notes, 1968-82.

Incident at Oglala (documentary), Miramax, 1992.

Spirit of Crazy Horse (a bimonthly newsletter published by the Leonard Peltier Defense Committee, National Office, P.O. Box 583, Lawrence, Kansas, 66044).

Warrior: The Life of Leonard Peltier (documentary), Westport, Connecticut, Cinnamon Productions, 1991.

—*Sketch by Christina E. Carter*

Petalésharo
1797(?)-1832(?)
Pawnee tribal leader

**Also known as Pitalesharu (Patalacharo, Pitale-
sharo, Petalésharoo, and Pitaresharu) ["Man
Chief" or "Chief of Men"]**

The son of chief Lachelesharo ["Knife Chief"] of the
Skidi Pawnee tribe, Petalésharo is primarily recognized
for his brave and determined opposition to the Morning Star
Ceremony. Though he is sometimes hailed for having put an
end to this ritual of human sacrifice, he did not succeed in
fully abolishing it. He did, however, wield a great deal of
influence among the Skidi and is credited with raising the
collective consciousness of the Pawnee people.

Petalésharo's life is shrouded by legend. He was born
in a village on the Loup ["Wolf"] River, probably near the
present site of Fullerton, Nebraska, around 1797. More than
a century earlier, French traders began referring to the Skidi
band of Indians as "Loups," and the Loup River was so
called after the French custom of naming rivers for the tribes
that lived on them. The Pawnees' relatively isolated plains
location in the center of U.S. territory prevented much contact with whites before 1800, and there are few detailed written records of this tribe prior to 1833, a year or so after
Petalésharo's death. By the time he died, however, a once-
prosperous population of 15,000 had been reduced to only
1,300 people. They were nearly wiped out by the combined
effects of smallpox epidemics, encroachment from surrounding tribes disenfranchised by whites, and a lack of
close friends or allies with whom they could seek protection. A few Pawnee Indians survive today in Oklahoma, but
hardly any can claim full blood.

Challenged an Enemy Chief

The Skidi were one of four Native American peoples
(Skidi, Chaui, Kitkehahki, Pitahauerats), collectively known
as the Pawnee. Unlike the other three bands, the Skidi did
not appear cannibalistic; however, they did practice human
sacrifice. Once a separate tribe, the Skidi had arrived in
Nebraska territory some time prior to the other Pawnee
bands and were subsequently conquered by them, possibly
around the mid-1700s. But the Skidi managed to maintain a
high degree of independence, camping and hunting apart
from the others. They held their conquerors in some con-
tempt, calling them "Big Shields": timid ones who resorted
to hiding behind unusually large shields.

The Chaui were the nominal leaders of the confederation. Around 1809, head chief Long Hair of the Chaui joined
forces with another Great Plains tribe, the Ponca, to attack

Petalésharo

the Skidi. Petalésharo's first appearance in history is this
confrontation with Long Hair. When Petalésharo realized
the odds were hopelessly against him and his band of warriors, he challenged Long Hair to single combat. Long Hair
refused to fight him, and Chief Lachelesharo was then able
to negotiate an amicable agreement that actually resulted in
Long Hair joining the Skidi.

Pawnee tribes followed a matrilineal system of succession, and the role of chief was usually inherited by a deceased
ruler's younger brother or nephew. Occasionally, however,
sons did succeed their fathers, and this seems to have been
the case with Petalésharo. In all cases, the man ultimately
selected as chief was the one who had displayed most
strongly the traits of a leader. Petalésharo's confrontation of
Long Hair made him a prime candidate for the position.

Despite the strength and courage of the Skidi chiefs,
historians have noted that the tribal leaders often found
themselves in a power struggle with Skidi priests. This was
especially true in the case of human sacrifice, which was
vital to the Morning Star Ceremony. While the priests
upheld this ritual, by the early nineteenth century the chiefs
wanted to abolish it.

Defied Priests and Rescued Sacrificial Victim

The Pawnee had astronomer priests who were said to
be empowered directly by the stars, and it was from the stars
that the Skidi band received much of their ritual and life
direction. The Skidi organized their 18 villages according to
stellar patterns, carefully observing celestial events. Each

village had a connection to a different star. Possibly because of the human sacrifice ritual, some observers suggest that the Skidi Morning Star Ceremony had a tie to the Aztec religion; however, the Aztec were sun rather than star worshippers. In fact, the Skidi Pawnee were unique among North American tribes because of their stellar rather than solar orientation.

The Morning Star rite was not necessarily an annual event. Its frequency was based on whether or not a warrior had a vision or dream of Morning Star and whether tribal conditions warranted the ceremony. During periods of prosperity, the priests might see no need to placate Morning Star, since he was already providing well for the tribe.

In 1816 or 1817, when Petalésharo intervened in a Morning Star ritual, the Skidi priests had a firmer grip over the people than the chiefs. The tribe believed that abandoning the ancient sacrificial rite would cause every conceivable misfortune to fall upon the tribe, including crop failure and the disappearance of the buffalo. But the chiefs knew how much the white Americans hated the ritual, and because they wanted to stay on good terms with the white settlers, they tried their best to discourage it. Outraged over the violent, murderous aspect of the ritual, many whites failed to see its spiritual significance. But Morning Star was viewed as the source of the Skidi lifeways. Through his ritual, which served as an expression of the essence of Skidi existence, the people reenacted their creation myth.

According to George E. Hyde's dramatic account of the 1816-1817 Morning Star Ceremony in *The Pawnee Indians,* the Skidi had kidnapped a young Ietan (Comanche) girl and planned to sacrifice her at planting time. Knife Chief, seeking to keep peace with the Anglo-Americans, tried to persuade the Skidi to release the girl. The people, however, believed that if they didn't appease Morning Star with this sacrifice, their crops would fail, hunting would be poor, and they would be overcome by their enemies. Accounts of the incident indicate that the Ietan girl had been tied to a scaffold—with priests poised and ready to shoot an arrow into her heart—when Petalésharo came before the crowd. He reminded them of his father's feelings about the ritual and vowed he would either rescue the girl or die trying. With Petalésharo's reputation for courage, no one tried to stop him as he cut the girl free, placed her on a horse, and escorted her some distance from the camp.

The Skidi priests maintained a strong hold over the people, however, and the next year, a Skidi party traveling through Oklahoma captured a young Spanish boy from a group of New Mexican hunters and immediately dedicated him to Morning Star. When the party arrived at the Skidi village, Knife Chief and Petalésharo unsuccessfully attempted to negotiate a release. Knife Chief then called a council of the other Skidi chiefs and the French trader Pappan, where he asked the participants to give him items that he might use to buy the boy from the warrior who had captured him. According to Hyde, "Contributions were generous but the warrior refused, which caused Knife Chief in a fury to spring at him with a war club.... [But] by a great effort of

will [he] withheld the blow." After Knife Chief added selected items of his personal property to the ransom, the warrior finally agreed to release the boy. The June 19, 1818 edition of the *Missouri Gazette* erroneously attributed the boy's rescue to a Missouri River trading post operator. Three years later, Knife Chief and Petalésharo were finally given credit for their heroic feat. However, the Morning Star Ceremony did not end with the release of the Spanish boy. Much controversy exists over when the last ritual occurred, but records indicate that an Oglala girl was secretly sacrificed in 1838.

Joined Delegation to Washington

In October of 1821, Major Benjamin O'Fallon, an Indian agent, persuaded a delegation of chiefs, including Petalésharo, to accompany him on a visit to several eastern cities, hoping to impress the Pawnee with the power of the whites. The delegation drew throngs of people, since Petalésharo's rescue of the Ietan girl was, by then, well known in the East. Upon reaching Washington, D.C., he was presented with a commemorative silver medal by the students of an all girls' school, and he had his portrait painted by Charles Bird King.

At the time his portrait was painted, Petalésharo had become the Skidi war chief, having distinguished himself through many acts of bravery. But despite his reputation as a warrior, he was, by all accounts, a peace-loving man. In the fall of 1825, Petalésharo and his father made what many historians feel was their final appearance in history, co-signing a treaty at Fort Atkinson on the Missouri River, a few miles north of present-day Omaha. By agreeing to the terms of this treaty, the Skidi pledged they would not attack Anglo-Americans traveling to and from Santa Fe. In return, as documented by Hyde in *The Pawnee Indians,* the United States agreed to give the Pawnee "from time to time such benefits and acts of kindness as may be convenient or seem just and proper to the President."

The Skidi band of Pawnees declined rapidly after 1832; they were preyed upon by the Comanche and continually at odds with the whites. But smallpox was probably their worst enemy. Affecting all four of the Pawnee tribes, it reportedly killed nearly everyone over 30 years of age—an estimated 3,000 persons—within a few days. Knife Chief and Petalésharo were probably among the victims. Records exist of later treaties that were signed by Pawnee chiefs in Nebraska with names similar to Petalésharo, but most scholars agree that these leaders were not the same Petalésharo who fought for the abolition of the Morning Star Ceremony.

SOURCES:

American Indian Ethnohistory: Plains Indians, edited by David Agee Horr, New York, Garland Publishing, 1974.

Champe, John L., Franklin Fenenga, Thomas M. Griffiths, and Waldo R. Wedel, *Pawnee and Kansa (Kaw) Indians,* New York, Garland Publishing, 1974.

Dockstader, Frederick J., *Great North American Indians,* New York, Van Nostrand Reinhold, 1977.

Hyde, George E., *The Pawnee Indians,* second edition, Norman, University of Oklahoma Press, 1974.

The Indians' Book, edited by Natalie Curtis, New York, Bonanza Books, 1987.

Tyson, Carl N., *The Pawnee People,* Phoenix, Indian Tribal Series, 1976.

Waldman, Carl, *Who Was Who in Native American History,* New York, Facts On File, 1990.

Williamson, Ray A., *Living the Sky: The Cosmos of the American Indian,* Norman, University of Oklahoma Press, 1984.

—*Sketch by Claudeen E. McAuliffe*

Helen White Peterson
1915-
Oglala Sioux government advisor

Initially intending to become a teacher, Helen White Peterson has centered her career around creating improved race relations and working to resolve minority issues. A supporter of retaining tribal identity and culture, she became a lecturer and negotiator in Indian and minority affairs. She has also been active in Hispanic issues and is well known as a writer and editor of American Indian and Hispanic publications.

Born on the Pine Ridge Reservation in South Dakota on August 3, 1915, Peterson is Cheyenne in heritage, but enrolled in the Oglala Sioux Tribe. As the first grandchild, she received special direction and training in her tribal culture from her grandmother. Peterson left the reservation to pursue studies at Chadron State Teachers College in Nebraska, Colorado State College, the University of Colorado, and the University of Denver Law School. She was married to Richard F. Peterson and has son, Robert.

A Career in Race Relations

Peterson's professional ambitions have been related to improving Native and minority living conditions and status. Her first position was as secretary in the Education Department at Colorado State College. She later became director of the Rocky Mountain Council of Inter-American Affairs at the University of Denver Social Science Foundation while serving in Nelson Rockefeller's National Office of Inter-American Affairs. She founded the Colorado Field Service Program, which was incorporated into the extension division of the University of Colorado, and consisted of American community service clubs, including the Latin American Education Foundation in Colorado. The program strived to promote education and improved human relations through administering civic projects and educational scholarships. While in Denver, in 1948, Peterson created and directed the Mayor's Committee on Human Relations for the city of Denver, which was later renamed the Denver Commission on Community Relations.

Peterson's career evolved into that of acting as negotiator and consultant in Native affairs. In 1949, she attended the second Inter-American Indian Conference in Cuzco, Peru, where as advisor to the U.S. delegation she wrote and presented a resolution on Indian education, which was ratified by conference delegates. From 1953 to 1961 Peterson served as executive director of the National Congress of American Indians. As director, she was heavily involved with the 1961 Chicago Conference of Indians, which created a significant document compiling current Native issues with various congressional positions. According to Peterson, the conference was an exciting event, because it raised public awareness of Native issues and brought together many Native writers and activists. Freed from the normal drudgery of working on carefully documented tribe-by-tribe statements, they created a more comprehensive document outlining Indian concerns.

Peterson returned to Colorado in 1962 to her earlier position as the director of the Denver Commission on Community Relations and was appointed executive director of American Indian Development in 1968. As the first female assistant to the Commissioner of Indian Affairs (1970), Peterson established the first Bureau of Indian Affairs (BIA) intergovernmental relations office in Denver in 1972 and also functioned as tribal government services officer in the Portland Area Office. She retired from the BIA in 1985.

One of her most significant contributions to Native education was her involvement with leadership training summer workshops from 1956 to 1970, where Native American students from all over the country could earn college credit. Many of these students have succeeded as business professionals, artists, and tribal leaders.

Peterson has lectured nationally and has served as a consultant to communities in race relations. She has also been involved in many organizations addressing Native concerns in education, health, and human relations, including NAIRO, Commission on Religion and Race, the National Council of Churches, Opportunities Industrialization Center, Denver West Side Health Board, Intercultural School of the Rockies, Intercultural Advisory Committee to the Colorado State Department of Education, White Buffalo Council of American Indians, and Delta Kappa Gamma.

Awards and Honors

Peterson has received numerous awards and recognitions. In 1968, she was recognized as "Outstanding American Indian Citizen" at the American Indian Exposition in Anadarko, Oklahoma. She was also named "Outstanding Woman of Color" and received the Distinguished Service Award from Columbia University. Other lifetime honors include recognition for "Outstanding Contribution in

Human Relations," the "Dolls for Democracy Award" from the Anti-Defamation League, a citation as "Woman of the Year" by the Business and Professional Club, a nomination for the first annual Eleanor Roosevelt Award, and the Friendship Award by the White Buffalo Council of American Indians. In 1994, Peterson was named Elder of the Year by the Northwest Indians Veterans Association and received an award from the non-denominational Four Winds Worshiping Community. Also in 1994, she received an honorary Ph.D. from her alma mater, Chadron State College.

Peterson's work in 1994 involved establishing an endowment at Chadron State College in Nebraska, endeavoring to promote and continue amiable human relations with Oglala Lakota College on Pine Ridge Reservation in South Dakota, fostering a bond between tribal and border towns, an undertaking much aligned with Peterson's active career as peacemaker.

SOURCES:

Books

Biographical Dictionary of Indians of the Americas, Newport Beach, California, 1983; 370.
Indians of Today, edited by Marion Gridley, Chicago, ICFP, 1971; 299-300.
Native American Women, edited by Gretchen M. Bataille, New York, Garland Publishing, 1993; 203-204.
Native North American Almanac, edited by Duane Champagne, Detroit, Gale Research, 1994; 1131.
Paulson, T. Emogene, and Lloyd R. Moses, Who's Who Among the Sioux, Vermillion, Institute of Indian Studies, University of South Dakota, 1988; 168.
Reader's Encyclopedia of the American West, edited by Howard R. Lamar, New York, Crowell, 1977; 907.

Other

Peterson, Helen White, interview with Karen P. Zimmerman conducted July 13, 1994.

—Sketch by Karen P. Zimmerman

Archie Phinney
1903-1949
Nez Percé anthropologist and activist

Archie Phinney was a Nez Percé anthropologist and ethnographer credited with preserving a great deal of the language and folklore of traditional Nez Percé culture through his seminal work as a scholar. During the course of an academic career cut short by his untimely death at the age of 46, he authored two anthropology books as well as several journal articles. The recipient of an honorary degree from the Academy of Science in Leningrad, a prestigious academic award from the former Soviet Union, Phinney was internationally recognized for his study of various aspects of Native American culture. Also a noted activist, he held positions of leadership with the Bureau of Indian Affairs and the National Congress of American Indians. For his efforts as both a scholar and community leader, he was awarded the prestigious Indian Council Fire Award in 1946.

Archie Phinney was born in Idaho on a Nez Percé reservation in 1903. He was reared in a traditional Nez Percé home, where he learned to appreciate the cultural heritage of his people, often listening to the stories and legends of his people from his mother, Wayi'latpu, who was noted for her great ability as a narrator. In addition to learning the nuances of his own native language, Phinney quickly demonstrated his mastery of English, winning the Idaho State Spelling Tournament at the age of 14. Noted for his outstanding ability as a high school student, he enrolled at the University of Kansas, where he received his bachelor of arts degree in 1926, becoming the first Native American to graduate from the university. He then moved on to graduate work in anthropology at George Washington University and New York University before finishing his program of study at Columbia University, where he specialized in the study of Native American reservation life.

Phinney's training as an anthropologist and his appreciation of his own cultural heritage led him back to the reservation of his childhood. Having discovered that the Nez Percé stories and legends his mother had first told to him years ago were quickly disappearing from the cultural fabric of the reservation, he took it upon himself, as a respected academic, to preserve this rich segment of his people's heritage. In 1934, with the help of his then 60-year-old mother, Wayi'latpu, he published Nez Percé Texts, a collection of authentic translations of traditional Nez Percé stories. In the introduction to the volume, he maintained that the "penetration of floating myth elements, the permeation of new ideas and interpretations, the growing use of the English language on the reservation, and the changing forms of native speech, all within historical times have caused a superficial knowledge of tales." Phinney's unique position as both a scholar, who was able to trace such influences, and a native Nez Percé, who thoroughly knew the native language, enabled him to present a deeper understanding of the mythology of his people.

In publishing Nez Percé Texts with the prestigious Columbia University Press, Phinney not only presented an accurate recording of the ancient tales for an academic audience, but he attempted to show that folklore was a legitimate field of Native American study. Whereas other expressions of native culture—such as dances, potlatches, and spirit ceremonies—sometimes survived because of their ritual value, folklore had "disintegrated under a morbid reservation consciousness," according to Phinney. Because the tales often contained what was considered ribald material, sometimes dealing with sexuality and bodily functions, they were generally labeled "vulgar" or "puerile" and were not taken seriously. By placing the tales within their proper cultural context—one in which such activities were viewed as an integral part of human existence and were not meant to be simply humorous—Phinney was able to portray the complexity and genius of Nez Percé mythology.

Phinney's contributions to preserving the ways of his people were not limited to the academic world. Within the umbrella of the Bureau of Indian Affairs, he served as superintendent of the Northern Idaho Agency. This high administrative position enabled him to tend to the affairs of a local reservation community. On the national level, Phinney was a central figure in the National Congress of American Indians, an intertribal organization created in the 1940s. Through this association, Phinney helped to lobby Congress for legislation protecting the rights of Native Americans, addressing such issues as education and land claims. In recognition of his accomplishments as an activist and as an academic, he received the Indian Council Fire Award in 1946. When Phinney died three years later, in his prime at the age of 46, he left behind a rich legacy of scholarship and service that enabled the world to better understand the complex culture of the Nez Percé.

SOURCES:

Native North American Almanac, edited by Duane Champagne, Detroit, Gale Research, 1994; 1131-1132.
Phinney, Archie, *Nez Percé Texts,* New York, Columbia University Press, 1934.

—*Sketch by Jason Gallman*

Peter Pitseolak
1902-1973
Inuk photographer

Peter Pitseolak was an Inuk photographer responsible for recording the cultural transformation of his people from the late 1930s to the early 1970s through his pictures and autobiographical writings. His legacy of over 2,000 photographs and negatives captured the last days of Eskimo camp life and the changes engendered by southern and European influences. Also an accomplished artist and a noted leader within his community, Pitseolak himself played a significant role in the history that he attempted to preserve through his camera. Without his efforts, many of the visual details of traditional Eskimo culture would have been lost. Equally important, however, is the personal narrative that he left to accompany his pictorial account, thus providing historians with an authentic native perspective on the changes in Eskimo life during the twentieth century.

Peter Pitseolak, in his autobiography *People from Our Side,* which he wrote in Inuit syllabics, estimated that he was born in 1902, one year after the "first religious time," the period in which Christianity made its first inroads into Cape Dorset, Baffin Island. The son of Inukjuarjuk, a hunter, and his third wife, Kooyoo, Pitseolak claimed to have actually remembered in detail the circumstances of his birth. Recalling a dreamlike process of travelling through a narrow channel, like a "crevice in the ice," and then opening his eyes to find the "two little cliffs" of his mother's thighs, Pitseolak stated that he was born with a smile and did not cry, recollections that were supported by family members. Reported to have been a precocious youngster, Pitseolak learned both the Eskimo and English alphabet before he was able to talk from the first Christian minister to come to the North, Okhamuk, who taught the Eskimos through song. As Pitseolak matured into adulthood, he was known for his great intelligence and wisdom and was placed in positions of leadership with fur trading companies such as Hudson's Bay and the Baffin Trading Company.

While hunting one day in the 1930s, Pitseolak was asked by a white man wary of approaching a polar bear to take a picture for him. Though a bit apprehensive himself, Pitseolak took the photograph, his first, and began a lifelong career in the art. In the early 1940s, while working for Baffin, he obtained his first camera, which he described as a box that "was simple to use; you didn't have to set it." A few years later, he received a more advanced model—a large 122 with focus settings—from a Catholic missionary, enabling him to improve the quality of his pictures. Pitseolak gained proficiency in various film developing techniques as well. Having first learned the process by watching a white man, he soon grew dissatisfied with his efforts and began to try his own methods. By washing the film longer and with a lower temperature of water, for instance, Pitseolak was able to produce higher quality pictures and was often solicited for his expertise by white men, including the Catholic missionary who gave him his camera.

Pitseolak's photographs capture various aspects of Eskimo life and usually feature family members, such as his wife Aggeok and their five children, and friends in representations of everyday activities. Although the best of Pitseolak's pictures showcase his photographing abilities, his work is generally valued more for the perspective it provides on an Eskimo culture in transition. As Dorothy Harley Eber, who compiled and edited *People from Our Side,* concluded, "Peter Pitseolak photographed the people around him and their everyday life. In doing so he photographed an era—a period when people still got their food from the land, but when camp bosses sometimes put up small wooden houses in their camps, when planes made mercy flights, and when, eventually, a plastic igloo went up in Cape Dorset." Aware that he was documenting a vanishing culture, Pitseolak dedicated his work to his 35 grandchildren, setting up many of his pictures so that the camera might "show how for the future."

In addition to leaving behind a vast corpus of photographs to various museums in Canada, Pitseolak preserved in his autobiographical writings his own feelings toward the changes he witnessed in his lifetime. Taking care to note both the advantages and disadvantages of southern and European influence, Pitseolak provided commentary on topics ranging from Christianity to igloo construction. Rather than simply mourning the loss of the past ways or completely embracing the ways of the "kadluka"—the Eskimo word for white man—he emphasized the importance of adapting to the changes in his environment while preserving his heritage. For instance, he spoke of his acceptance of the "kadluka's" religion, but condemned the hypocrisy of the materialism that often accompanied it. He found praise for the new methods of igloo construction while taking pride in the "taoteeghroot," a type of violin invented "way before the white men came," an instrument that was "true Eskimo." When Pitseolak died in 1973, he left behind a personal account that captured in pictures and in words the final moments of Eskimo camp life and the feelings of ambivalence that accompanied the entrance of a new era.

SELECTED WRITINGS BY PITSEOLAK:

Pictures Out of My Life, Seattle, University of Washington Press, 1972.
People from Our Side, compiled and edited by Dorothy H. Eber, Bloomington, Indiana University Press, 1975.
Peter Pitseolak's Escape from Death, 1977.

SOURCES:

Native North American Almanac, edited by Duane Champagne, Detroit, Gale Research, 1994; 1133.
Pitseolak, Peter, *People from Our Side,* compiled and edited by Dorthy H. Eber, Bloomington, Indiana University Press, 1977.

—*Sketch by Jason Gallman*

Plenty Coups
1848(?)-1932
Crow chief and tribal leader
Also known as Alaxchíiaahush ["Bull That Goes Against the Wind"] and Plenty Coos

Plenty Coups was the last of the traditional Crow chiefs and led the tribe in its transition from the "buffalo days" to reservation life. He served with the U.S. Army at the Battle of the Rosebud in 1876. However, Plenty Coups is best remembered for his leadership of the tribe after reservation settlement. He was among the first of the Crows to settle down, begin farming, open a store and build a two story log home. He often negotiated for his people with U.S. repre-

Plenty Coups

sentatives, both in Washington and on the reservation, in the many attempts to reduce or open Crow lands to further white settlement between 1880 to 1920. After 1904, he was effectively recognized as the single most important Native American tribal leader both by the federal government and his own people. He represented all American Indians at the burial of the Unknown Soldier in Washington in 1921. He died in 1932, still fighting for the rights of his people at the end of his life.

The last of the traditional Crow chiefs was born not far from present day Billings, Montana around 1848. His name was given to him by his grandfather, from a dream that the boy would count many coups (a war deed), live to an old age, and become a chief. At some point in his life, he was also given the name Bull That Goes Into (or Against) the Wind. He was a member of the Sore Lips clan of the Mountain Crow, one of the three divisions of the tribe. His father Medicine Bird died when Plenty Coups was young. His mother was named Otter Woman and he had a sister named Goes Well. Plenty Coups was first married at the age of 24 to Knows Her Mother. His last two wives were Kills Together and Strikes the Iron. Though he married about 12 different times, he had only two children, both of whom died young. Plenty Coups adopted and raised some poor children, but he told Frank Bird Linderman in his biography *American* that he considered all the Crows as his children.

The Crow were often at odds with their neighbors the Lakota Sioux, and Plenty Coups was no exception. At the age of nine, he lost a brother who was killed by the Lakota. Grant Bulltail, whose grandfather was raised by Plenty

Coups, explained that in all two brothers and the parents of Plenty Coups were killed by the Lakota. According to Linderman. after his brother was killed Plenty Coups went on a fast, as he did on several occasions throughout his life, in hopes of receiving a vision which would give him power and direction. In his greatest vision, he saw the buffalo disappear and spotted buffalo, or cattle, appear in their place. A forest was destroyed by a storm, except for a single tree. This tree held the lodge of the Chickadee, who survived the storm because he was a sharp listener who learned from others and knew where to pitch his lodge.

The dream was interpreted to mean that the cattle which replaced the buffalo represented the whites taking over Crow country. The tree which survived was the Crows, who would survive the coming of the white man because, like the Chickadee, they listened and learned from the experiences of other tribes and placed themselves (pitched their lodges) in the right place. This powerful vision guided Plenty Coups throughout his life. It told him to adapt to and cooperate with the whites so the Crows would survive and prosper. It guided him as leader of the tribe through the difficult times ahead.

War Deeds and Chieftainship

With the aid of his powerful visions and medicines (objects with spiritual power), Plenty Coups became a feared warrior. He joined the Fox warrior society early in his career. Tribal historian Joseph Medicine Crow explained that Plenty Coups was particularly noted for horse capturing, one of the four war deeds required to become a Crow chief. The four deeds were: the capturing of a horse picketed in front of an enemy lodge (tipi), the leadership of a successful war party, capturing a weapon from an enemy in combat, and striking the first coup (hitting an enemy with the hand or an object) in a battle. Plenty Coups was able to achieve each of these deeds many times over. He became a chief by the age of 25 or 26, and, by the age of 30, had completed each of the deeds four times. In 1876, he fought alongside General George Crook and Chief Washakie of the Shoshones against the Lakota and Cheyenne in the Battle of the Rosebud. Eight days later, other Crows served as scouts for George Armstrong Custer at the Battle of the Little Big Horn.

Reservation Life and Rise to Tribal Leadership

Though Plenty Coups earned a strong reputation as a war chief, he did not become a peacetime leader of his people until he became a reservation chief. He began to rise in importance in the mid to late 1870s or early 1880s. As noted by Frederick Krieg in "Chief Plenty Coups: The Final Dignity," the government recognized him as head chief by 1890. However, it may not have been until after the death of Chief Pretty Eagle in 1904 that his people gave him the same honor. Plenty Coups demonstrated his power in 1908, when the tribe abandoned an internal factional struggle and united behind him to fight the first of the bills which proposed to open the reservation to white settlement. From that time on,

he played the leading role in the political struggles over this issue, which eventually resulted in the Crow Act of 1920.

Plenty Coups' strong dedication to his people was evident. He advocated a policy of cooperation with and adaptation to the whites. However, he also expressed resentment toward the white man. He told Frank Linderman in *Plenty Coups* that "[w]e made up our minds to be friendly ... but we found this difficult, because the white men too often promised to do one thing and then, when they acted at all, did another. They spoke very loudly when they said their laws were made for everybody; but we soon learned that although they expected us to keep them, they thought nothing of breaking them themselves ... we know that with all his wonderful powers, the white man ... is smart, but not wise, and fools only himself." In 1914, artist Joe Scheurle accompanied Plenty Coups on a tour of a Chicago zoo. As quoted in C. Adrian Heidenreich's article "The Crow Indian Delegation to Washington, D.C., in 1880," Scheurle wrote that "the superintendent of the zoo brought out a trained chimpanzee which immediately began searching Plenty Coups' pockets. When asked how he liked the animal, Plenty Coups replied, 'No! No like him, much like white people.'" Toward the end of his life, having witnessed about 50 years of the new reservation life with its changes, Plenty Coups told Glendolin Wagner in the book *Blankets and Moccasins* that "nothing the white man has given can make up for the happy life when vast plains were unfenced."

Plenty Coups preferred the old lifestyle of the "buffalo days" to the new ways. Even in his adaptation to the new lifestyle forced on the Crows, he tried to retain many of the tribal traditions. Plenty Coups became a Catholic in 1917, when he was baptized at St. Xavier, Montana, yet he also continued to practice traditional Crow religion. On one occasion, as Norman Wiltsey noted in his article "Plenty Coups: Statesman Chief of the Crows," Plenty Coups once scolded his men by telling them to work in the new way, but also to continue to fast and sweat in the traditional way. He said, "I am ashamed of you, self-pity has stolen your courage, robbed you of your spirit and self-respect; stop mourning the old days—they are gone with the buffalo. Go to your sweat lodges and cleanse your bodies so you may be fit to pray to Ab-badt-dabt-deah ["Akbaatatdía", God] for forgiveness. Then clean out your dirty lodges and go to work!"

Although Plenty Coups supported many of the tribe's traditional ways, he also fought to preserve his people's control over Crow land, resources, and lives. In these battles, Plenty Coups proved himself a strong leader. Krieg describes an 1890 meeting in which Plenty Coups stated, "I would like to see all of [the Crows] supplied with wagons, plows, mowing machines, and such farming implements as they may need.... I want the men who have cattle here on the Crow lands ... to make them work and teach them the white man's ways so that they may learn.... we want to cut our own hay; we want the white man to buy hay from us; we don't want to beg and buy our hay from them. This is our land and not white men's ... if they won't employ Crows to work, put them off entirely." In 1893, while negotiating with the

Chicago, Burlington, and Quincy Railroad over the construction of a railroad in the Little Big Horn valley, Plenty Coups demanded that Indians be hired by the railroad company. On another occasion, he asked that the tribal herd be distributed among the Crows and that the Crows be consulted in management of tribal affairs.

Plenty Coups also realized early that good education was necessary for the tribe to prosper. As cited in Norman Wiltsey's book *Brave Warriors,* he told the Crows that "education is your most powerful weapon. With education you are the white man's equal; without education you are his victim." Yet, he did not see education as a way for the Crows to blend into white society while forgetting their own people. As he told Glendolin Wagner for *Blankets and Moccasins,* he wished them "to go to school and become well educated ... then ... to come back home on the reservation and work their land." Even even with a partial adoption of white ways, Plenty Coups encouraged a strong loyalty to the tribe and tribal self sufficiency.

It is easy to say that Plenty Coups was an assimilationist, eager to cooperate with the whites at the expense of his own people. However, the circumstances and historical context suggest that the Crows were threatened with not just cultural, but actual physical, extinction. In addition, though Plenty Coups was friendly to whites, it was not any great love for whites or admiration of their ways that guided his actions, but what was best for the Crows. Just as the military alliance with the United States in the 1860s and 1870s was the best policy at that time for the tribe—to preserve Crow lands and lives—so too did the adoption of the new ways enable the people to survive a new threat—starvation and the taking of the remainder of Crow lands by the government and white farmers and cattlemen.

Plenty Coups demonstrated his leadership during the difficult period of adjustment to reservation life in three ways: in his advice to the people, in his own life, and in his political leadership and statesmanship. He urged the people to get a good education and to farm their land, as well as to continue to practice their traditional Crow religion. Plenty Coups put his beliefs into practice in his own life. He was one of the earliest and most successful farmers on the reservation. He had established a garden by 1882. After he settled in what is now Pryor, Montana in the mid 1880s, he often exhibited at agricultural fairs the largest potatoes in Yellowstone County. Eventually, he developed a farm where he also raised apples, grain, wheat, hay, and oats. Plenty Coups also lived in a log house, eventually building the only two story log house among the Crows. This building and his barn can still be seen today in Pryor.

Plenty Coups in Politics

Few other old Crow chiefs had accomplished more war deeds than Plenty Coups, but none could match him as a political leader and statesman around and after the turn of the century. An impressive, dignified speaker, he showed his negotiating skill in dealing with ranchers, railroad companies, and often with the U.S. government. He met with

Indian agents, tribal attorneys, and congressmen over such issues as irrigation projects, grazing leases, and land cessions. At times, he requested that the government provide farm equipment and training, improved schooling, and that it lease out tribal lands for oil and gas mining with the revenues going to tribal members. He often called meetings with tribal members over these same issues. Officials of railroad companies also found that he was a tough bargainer, yet fair.

While Plenty Coups may have been cooperative with the whites regarding such issues as farming and education, land was quite a different matter. Between 1880 and 1921, he traveled to Washington, D.C., at least ten times to fight proposed land concessions by the Crows. The heaviest period of travel took place in the ten years between 1908 and 1918. During this time, the Montana congressional delegation made its strongest effort to open the reservation to general homesteading. The Crows recognized these proposals as threats to the wellbeing of the tribe, and the people ended their factionalism and united behind Plenty Coups to defeat the measures. Although other leaders played roles in uniting the Crows, it was Plenty Coups who was the guiding figure, especially in the Congressional hearings in Washington D.C.

Still, Plenty Coups and the other older chiefs were aided in their victory by young Crows and mixed bloods, the first generation to be educated in the white man's schools. Young men such as Robert Yellowtail were especially valuable as interpreters, and their schooling also served as their training ground for future tribal leadership. The victory over the general opening of the reservation served as the ultimate proof of the wisdom of Plenty Coups' vision. The chief's advice that education is "your most powerful weapon" with which "you are the white man's equal" was correct. Yet, true to the spirit of the old ways of the warrior, after Senator Thomas J. Walsh withdrew his bill at a Senate hearing in 1917, Plenty Coups approached the senator and reached out toward him with his cane, symbolically striking a coup.

Plenty Coups in Retirement

The defeat of the general opening of the reservation ended Plenty Coups' heavy involvement in tribal affairs. Although he no longer wielded political power, he still occupied the role of an elder statesman for Native Americans. In 1921, the War Department chose him to represent all Indian tribes at the Burial of the Unknown Soldier of World War I in Arlington National Cemetery near Washington, D.C. On November 11, 1921, in the presence of the President and high ranking men from the victorious Allied nations, Plenty Coups placed a wreath of flowers, his war bonnet, and his coup stick at the tomb. The war bonnet can still be seen today at the cemetery. Though informed that only the President was to speak, Plenty Coups did make a speech which was actually a prayer. It was the last speech made before the coffin was lowered.

On March 4, 1928, Plenty Coups executed a deed of trust that set apart 40 acres of his land in Pryor to be used as a park and recreation ground for both Crows and whites.

Plenty Coups had been inspired by a visit to Mt. Vernon with the 1880 delegation and wished to create a similar memorial. The deed also arranged for a museum to be set up in one room of his two story house. According to Wiltsey's article, Plenty Coups stated that the park was to be a memorial not to him, but to the Crow nation, and that it should be "a reminder to Indians and white people alike that the two races should live and work together harmoniously." Since 1962, the house and grounds have been administered as a state park. The museum was transferred from a room in the old house to a new museum building in 1973.

In the last years of his life, Plenty Coups took on the role of the official greeter of important visitors to Crow country. In addition to General James Harbord, who had ceremoniously accepted the 40 acres on the part of the government, and World War I supreme Allied commander Marshall Ferdinand Foch of France, Vice President Charles Curtis, who was part Kansa Indian, visited in 1928. Even in his last months of life, Plenty Coups was thinking of the good and future of his people. On November 7, 1931, the old chief made one of his last official statements. He wanted the Pryor and Big Horn Mountains on the reservation reserved from allotment, the trust period for allotments extended for 26 years, and the money from the Crow Land Claim given to the children of the tribe. He passed away a few months later on March 4, 1932.

SOURCES:

Books

Curtis, Edward S., *The North American Indian,* Volume 4: *The Apsaroke, or Crows*; *The Hidatsa,* Johnson Reprint Corporation, 1980.

Hoxie, Frederick E., "Building A Future On the Past: Crow Indian Leadership in an Era of Division and Reunion," in *Indian Leadership,* edited by Walter Williams, Sunflower University Press, 1984.

Hoxie, Frederick E., *Parading through History: The Making of the Crow Nation, 1805-1935,* Oxford University Press, 1995.

Linderman, Frank Bird, *American: The Life Story of a Great Indian, Plenty-coups, Chief of the Crows,* John Day, 1930; published as *Plenty-Coups, Chief of the Crows,* University of Nebraska Press, 1962.

Medicine Crow, Joseph, *From the Heart of the Crow Country: The Crow Indians' Own Stories,* Orion Books, 1992.

Wagner, Glendolin Damon, and William A. Allen, *Blankets and Moccasins: Plenty Coups and His People, the Crows,* Caxton Printers, 1933; reprinted, University of Nebraska Press, 1987.

Wiltsey, Norman B., *Brave Warriors,* Caxton Printers, 1964.

Yellowtail, Robert Summers, *Robert Summers Yellowtail, Sr., at Crow Fair,* 1972, Wowapi, 1973.

Periodicals

Ewers, John C., "A Crow Chief's Tribute to the Unknown Soldier," *American West,* 8:6, November 1971; 30-35.

Heidenreich, C. Adrian, "The Crow Indian Delegation to Washington, D.C., in 1880," *Montana, the Magazine of Western History,* 31:2, spring 1981; 54-67.

Krieg, Frederick C., "Chief Plenty Coups, the Final Dignity," *Montana, the Magazine of Western History,* 16:4, October 1966; 28-39.

Wiltsey, Norman B., "Plenty Coups: Statesman Chief of the Crows," *Montana, the Magazine of Western History,* 13:4, September 1963; 28-39.

Other

Bradley, Charles Crane, "After the Buffalo Days: Documents on the Crow Indians from the 1880s to the 1920s" (master's thesis), Montana State University, 1970.

Bulltail, Grant, interview with Timothy Bernardis conducted March 15, 1985.

Lowie, Robert H., "Notes on Crow Chiefs," in Robert Harry Lowie Papers, Bancroft Library, University of California, Berkeley.

Medicine Crow, Joseph, personal communication to Timothy Bernardis, May 15, 1985.

Plenty Coups Papers, held at Plenty Coups Museum, Pryor, Montana.

Wildschut, William, unpublished manuscript on the life of Plenty Coups based on interviews conducted with Plenty Coups, held in the Archives of the National Museum of the American Indian, Heye Foundation, New York, New York.

Yellowtail, Robert Summers, class lecture for "Crow History—Post-Settlement" (tape-recording), May 15, 1984, held at Little Big Horn College Archives, Crow Agency, Montana.

Yellowtail, Robert Summers, "Notes on Crow Chiefs," held in Little Big Horn College Archives, Crow Agency, Montana.

—Sketch by Timothy Bernardis

Pocahontas
1595(?)-1617
Powhatan-Renapé diplomat
Also known as Matoaka ["She Is Playful"],
Rebecca Rolfe

The story of the Powhatan-Renapé princess Pocahontas is one of the earliest and most deeply rooted legends of the American past. "Americans who know nothing else about early American history," wrote history professor Martin Fishwick in *American Heritage,* "can recount the dramatic tale of [John] Smith's rescue ... by the beautiful Indian

Pocahontas

princess." If the story is true, Pocahontas may have decisively influenced the course of English settlement in the New World. Her relationship with Smith and the English settlers helped preserve the colony through the long winters when the colonists were threatened with starvation. With the benefit of hindsight, many Native Americans have vilified her for preventing her father from killing off the colonists. Had she not done so, the English might never have colonized North America and many Native cultures might have been preserved from extinction. On the other hand, Pocahontas has been regarded by white Americans as a savior of their race and a foremother of the United States. The truth probably lies somewhere in-between.

Much of what we know about Pocahontas' early life comes through the writings of Captain John Smith. Smith was an adventurer with the Virginia Company, the corporation licensed by King James I to explore the coast of North America and exploit its resources. The company established the settlement of Jamestown, named after the English king, in May, 1607, on the shores of the James River in Virginia, near Chesapeake Bay. The settlement was plagued in its early years by jealousy and disagreement among its leaders. Smith himself was imprisoned for some time for insubordination. In December of 1607, Smith was on an expedition up the Chickahominy River, exploring the region for new tribes to trade with, places to prospect for gold, and possible access to the Pacific Ocean. He apparently got too near a treasure house of the local overking, a man named Powhatan after the primary tribe he ruled. Powhatan's agents caught him there and brought him before the king.

What happened after that is confusing. Smith claimed that he wrote a letter to Queen Anne, wife of James I, in 1616, stating that "at the minute of my execution," he declared, Pocahontas "...hazarded the beating out of her own braines to save mine." Writing about himself in the third person, Smith told a fuller account in his *Generall Historie of Virginia,* published in 1624. He says that Powhatan fed him well, but then "two great stones were brought before Powhatan: then as many [of the Indians] as could layd hands on him, dragged him to them, and thereon laid his head, and being ready with their clubs, to beate out his braines, Pocahontas the Kings dearest daughter, when no intreaty could prevaile, got his head in her armes, and laid her owne vpon his to saue him from death."

Some modern historians have questioned Smith's version of the events that took place in Powhatan's camp. They believe that Smith, a self-promoter, created the story of Pocahontas to enhance his own prestige. In fact, in Smith's earliest version of his meeting with Powhatan, there is no mention of Pocahontas at all, and no threat of an execution. According to an account Smith wrote only a year after the incident, he was brought before Powhatan and was questioned about the presence of the English in the territory. After Smith answered Powhatan's questions, the king sent him back to Jamestown. On the other hand, there is nothing in Smith's story of Pocahontas that can be disproved. When young Indian men were initiated into full tribal membership, they often went through an initiation ceremony that involved a mock execution like the one Smith describes. At some point during the execution a sponsor had to speak up for the young man. If this was Smith's initiation ceremony, then Pocahontas served as Smith's sponsor in the tribe. This interpretation makes her behavior toward the English colonists more understandable.

The Willful One

Pocahontas seems to have well deserved her name, which means something like "the willful one." Smith believed that her father indulged her and could refuse her nothing. William Strachey, a Jamestown resident and official secretary and historian for the colony, called her "a well featured but wanton young girle," adding that she, "sometymes resorting to our Fort, of the age then of 11. or 12. yeares, [would] gett the boyes [to go] forth with her into the markett place and make them wheele, falling on their hands turning their heeles upwardes, whome she would follow, and wheele so her self naked as she was all the fort over." The picture of a teenaged princess turning handsprings in public, exposing herself as she did so, was not one that fit with English ideas of proper behavior.

If Pocahontas did regard the English colonists as her responsibility, then she took her duties toward them seriously. During the hungry early months of 1608, she supplied the colonists with food after their own stores and homes burned down. "Now ever once in foure or fivedayes," Smith recalled, "Pocahontas with her attendants brought him [Smith] so much provision, that saved many of their lives, that els for all this had starved." "James towne with her wild traine she as freely frequented, as her father's habitation," Smith continued, "and during the time of two or three yeeres, she next under God, was still the instrument to preserve this Colonie from death, famine and utter confusion; which if in those times, [it] had once been dissolved, Virginia might have [lain] ... as it was at our first arrivall to this day."

Pocahontas also served as a go-between for further negotiations between her father and the English settlers. In April of 1608, one of Smith's fellow captains of the Virginia Company had made the mistake of exchanging English steel swords for turkeys. When Smith refused to barter any more of his limited supply of weapons, the natives began to ambush settlers for their swords, guns, axes, spades and shovels. Smith led a punitive expedition, taking seven Native hostages, who confessed that they were acting under their king's orders. In mid May of 1608 Powhatan sent Pocahontas to Smith as a negotiator, and it was to her that Smith released his captives.

Despite Pocahontas' efforts, relations between her father and the colonists deteriorated. The overking was alarmed by the arrival of more colonists and believed that the English intended to take his land away from him. An attempted coronation of Powhatan according to English rituals (the plan of some Virginia Company officials in London) did nothing to ease his suspicions. In the autumn of 1608, Powhatan forbade all trade with the English. Faced with another hard winter on inadequate rations, Smith decided to confront Powhatan at his capitol, Werowocomoco, and force him to trade under threat of war. In January of 1609, Smith and Powhatan met on the banks of the Pamunkey River. According to Smith, Powhatan's major concern was when the English would be leaving: "Some doubt I have," Smith quotes him as saying, "of your comming hither, that makes me not so kindly seeke to relieve you as I would: for many doe informe, your comming hither is not for trade, but to invade my people, and possesse my Country."

This was the major break between the English and the Powhatan Indians. Recognizing that Smith did not intend to leave without the grain he wanted, Powhatan decided to remove himself and his family—including Pocahontas—to the town of Orapaks, about 50 miles from Jamestown. Smith and his men were stranded at Werowocomoco because the barge they had brought to transport the grain had been grounded by low tide. They were forced to spend the night in the partly deserted town. Powhatan had laid plans to beseige and destroy the English party, but Smith and his men were saved once again by the princess. "For Pocahontas [Powhatan's] dearest jewell and daughter, in that darke night came through the irksome woods, and told our Captaine [Smith] ... if we would live, shee wished us presently to be gone," he explains in his *Generall Historie.*

So Pocahontas took upon herself the role of betrayer assigned to her by some modern Native American commentators. She was at most 14 or 15 years old, yet she came alone, at night, in winter weather, in defiance of her father's wishes. Whether this was because of her feelings of responsibility toward the English she had sponsored or for some personal love she had for Smith, we do not know. The Eng-

lish captain was insensitive enough to offer her trinkets for her news: "Such things as shee delighted in, he would have given her: but with the teares running downe her cheekes, shee said shee durst not be seene to have any: for if Powhatan should know it, she were but dead, and so she ranne away by her selfe as she came." It was the last Smith would see of her for about eight years.

Travels to England

At this point Pocahontas largely drops out of the history of the Jamestown colony. There is some evidence suggesting that she helped hide occasional fugitives who fell into Powhatan's hands, sending them back to the settlement. Smith himself suffered a serious wound—some gunpowder he had in a pouch at his side exploded, stripping the flesh off one leg—and he returned to England in early September, 1609. He returned under a cloud of suspicion as well; the men he had removed from power to preserve the Jamestown settlement had returned, and they levied charges in turn against Smith, which he would have to answer for in London. Reports that reached the Indians were confused. Frances Mossiker, in her biography *Pocahontas: The Life and the Legend,* declares, "Pocahontas, believing Smith to be dead, and being under injunction of her father to sever relations with the English colony, would never again—of her own free will and accord—set foot in Jamestown."

There is very little in the English records about Pocahontas for the next four years. About 1610, according to Strachey, Pocahontas married one of her father's supporters, a man named Kocoum. He may have been a member of another tribe, possibly the Patawamakes, who lived further north on the shores of the Potomac River. Whether for this or some other reason, by 1613 Pocahontas had left her father's territory and was living with friends among the Patawamakes. It was there that the English came into her life once again.

After John Smith's departure, his function in the Jamestown colony was largely taken over by a sea captain named Samuel Argall. The Jamestown colonists were still suffering from the trading sanctions imposed by Powhatan. In late December, 1612, while looking for new trading partners, Argall made contact with the chief of the Patawamakes, a man named Iapazaws. According to Ralph Hamor, the new historian of the colony, "Captaine Argall, having entred into a great acquaintance with Iapazaws ... heard by him there was Pocahontas, whom Captaine Smiths Relations intituleth the Numparell of Virginia, and though she had beene many times a preserver of him and the whole Colonie, yet till this accident shee was never seene at James towne since his departure." Argall realized that Powhatan, who had been waging a sort of guerilla war against the English for years, might be brought to negotiate if he knew his daughter was in the hands of his enemies. He coaxed Pocahontas on board his ship and sailed off with her to Jamestown.

Despite Pocahontas' presence in their midst, negotiations with the Powhatan tribes did not go as smoothly as the English wished. Powhatan was willing to release the Eng-

ovi Da
1971

efonso Pueblo artist

Da, whose name means "Red Fox," is considered
uential and innovative pottery artist whose work
m wide renown. He was born April 10, 1923, as
artínez, the first son of Julián and María Montoya
t the San Ildefonso Pueblo. Known for their
, Da's parents are credited with reviving the
Pueblo pottery. His father was hired to work as
an archaeological site at Pajarito Plateau, an
lo ruin, directed by Edgar L. Hewett, who
Maria to reproduce the ancient pottery shards
rs uncovered. Maria, whose Indian name was
ond Lily"], had been making pottery for such
ing and collecting rain water, but she did not
an art form until this time. Eventually, Maria
ized as one of the great ceramic artists of the
family became a major influence in the
n art world. Julian assited his wife by paint-
on the pottery and firing them for Maria.
er died in 1943 his sister-in-law, Santana,
painter. Later, Santana became well known
gns.

studying art at the Santa Fe Indian School,
aduated in 1939. He married a high school
Cata Montoya, from Santa Clara Pueblo,
tion. They had two daughters, Janice and
ns, Bernard and Tony. Like his father and
ny Da has also been recognized as a fine
ars after he graduated from high school,
ded the Canyon Art School in Santa Fe,
how pottery was made by non-Indians and
rawing and painting. During World War II
nto the U.S. Army and stationed at Oak
, and Los Alamos, New Mexico—without
h basic training. After two and a half years
cial engineering detachment, he left the
ained his job. He worked there for three
ving back to San Ildefonso. Da became
mily's pottery business, and in 1949—with
,000—he and his wife opened an arts and
he named Popovi Da ["Red Fox"], which
ne. He borrowed $3,000 and traveled to dif-
ern tribes to purchase a variety of the best
n arts and crafts he could find. He also
his name to Popovi Da (his family called

th Innovative Techniques

s brother, Adam, dug clay for their mother

and collected dung that was used as fuel in the firing
process. Around 1950 Da began working with Maria and
Santana on the pieces. Da also encouraged other Pueblo
artists and was instrumental in getting them accepted into
arts and crafts shows that were usually for non-Indians.
Experimenting with different techniques, Da designed an
unusual matte ware that was black and sienna, and he re-
introduced Polychrome ware—the art of combining different colors on a piece of pottery. He won "Best of Show"
with his Polychrome ware at the Gallup Ceremonial in 1957.
Since the mid-1920s, black-on-black ware had been the
standard in Pueblo pottery. He described his technique in
creating Polychrome as a "two-firing" process but never
revealed how he did it. He also developed Gunmetal ware,
which has an unusual shiny gunmetal finish, and—with the
help of his son Tony—he added turquoise pieces to his pottery, a practice that had never been done before.

By the 1960s, Popovi Da became a recognized artist,
sought after for art conferences throughout the world as a
lecturer and master Pueblo craftsman of Southwestern art.
Da was best known for the pieces he created with his
mother, which carried the double signature of "Maria/
Popovi." In fact, it was not until 1965 that he introduced his
first solo piece. The pottery that Da created alone remains
rare and valuable.

Proud of his Pueblo Indian heritage, Popovi Da
became a spiritual and ceremonial leader of his people. In
1952 he was elected to the post of governor of San Ildefonso
Pueblo, in which capacity he served three terms. He also
served as chairman of the All-Indian Pueblo Council for two
years. On October 17, 1971, Popovi Da died in Santa Fe,
New Mexico. After his death the prices on the pottery that
he and his mother designed skyrocketed. This shift in market value had a remarkable impact on other Native-American pottery as well, raising prices on the creations of less
well-known potters. Da was an eloquent speaker, and at one
of his many public speeches, he said: "Our culture and our
creative arts are interwoven and inseparable. Everything in
our lives is all-inclusive. We must preserve what has been
created and what can be created.... Out of the silences of
meditation come purity and power which eventually become
apparent in our art." The pottery of Maria and Popovi Da is
now displayed permanently in several museums, including
the Heard Museum in Phoenix, Arizona; the South Plains
Museum in Anadarko, Oklahoma; and the Philbrook Art
Museum in Tulsa, Oklahoma.

SOURCES:

Sando, Joe S., *Pueblo Nations: Eight Centuries of Pueblo
Indian History,* Santa Fe, New Mexico, Clear Light
Publishers, 1992.

Spivey, Richard L., *Maria,* third edition, Flagstaff, Arizona,
Northland Publishing Company, 1994.

—Sketch by Phyllis "Picturestone" Noah

Alexander Lawrence Posey
1873-1908
Creek poet, journalist, and humorist
Also known as Chinnubbie Harjo and Fus Fixico

Before his death on May 27, 1908, at the age of 34, Creek Indian Alexander Lawrence Posey (who preferred to be called Alex Posey) had established himself as a wise and distinguished voice on Native American issues. He is best remembered as a poet, journalist, and humorist, but he also dabbled in politics and business, serving at various times as a school administrator, a newspaper editor and publisher, a real estate speculator, and a member of the Creek House of Warriors. Although poetry was his first love—his work made him the first Native American lyric poet to gain national notice—Posey's lasting literary contributions come from his newspaper writings, which also earned him the respect of his contemporaries. He had a distinct and original journalistic voice that caught people's attention and made them laugh, most notably in the series of humorous editorials known as the *Fus Fixico Letters*. These made him the most widely appreciated Native American humorist before Will Rogers.

Alex Posey was born into the Creek nation near Eufaula (what is today McIntosh County, Oklahoma), on August 3, 1873. His father, Lewis Henderson Posey, was of Scottish-Irish descent and claimed to be one-sixteenth Creek Indian. The elder Posey's Creek lineage has been disputed, but it has been verified that he was born in the Creek section of Indian Territory, around 1841, and was raised by a Creek woman after the death of his own parents, who had probably come from Texas. It is also known that he spoke fluent Creek.

In October of 1872, after his first wife died, Lewis Posey married a 15-year-old full-blooded Creek girl whose English name was Nancy Phillips; she would eventually bear him 13 children. Nancy was the daughter of Pahosa Harjo, a member of one of the oldest and most prominent Creek families. From her mother (Thlee-sa-ho-he, also called "Eliza"), Nancy and her children inherited membership in the Upper Creek town of Tuskegee, a "peace" town whose change-oriented political and social attitudes would have an impact on the development of the young Alex's thinking. Alex's mother also belonged to the Wind Clan, the most elite and powerful of the Creek clans. Although she did not speak English, she was a devout Christian and a member of the Baptist Church, which was the fastest growing denomination among the Creeks at that time.

In a memoir included in *The Poems of Alexander Lawrence Posey,* William Elsey Connelley quoted Posey's comments on his childhood: "It is enough to say, concerning my youth, that I was raised on a farm and accounted a pretty weedy crop. The cockle-burrs and crab-grass grew all the more prolifically after I had been given a good thrashing.... I

often look back to [these] 'days of lost sunshine.'" By his own account, Posey's childhood was idyllic—aside from the occasional "thrashings" he received in response to his penchant for pranks. Until he was about 12 years old, he spoke almost no English. His father found tutors for him, though, and Posey soon grasped the new language.

Begins Writing for School Newsletter

At the age of 17, Posey was sent to Bacone Indian University (BIU), a Baptist school named after its president, A. C. Bacone. There he began to discover the voice and motivation that would lead him on his writing career. He set type for the school's monthly newsletter, the *BIU Instructor;* this paper was the first public forum for his writing, which at that time was mostly poetry. Before his graduation in 1895, Posey published a number of poems in the *Instructor,* including one that attracted national attention, "Death of a Window Plant." By this time he was a minor celebrity among the so-called "Five Civilized Tribes" (Creek, Choctaw, Chickasaw, Cherokee, and Seminole) populating the area that is today Oklahoma.

Ventures into Politics

After his graduation from BIU, Posey retreated from public view briefly, then reappeared as a candidate for the seat in the House of Warriors (the lower house of the Creek legislature) that had earlier been held by his maternal grandfather, Pahosa Harjo. Posey was elected to this post on September 3, 1895. The Creek nation, like the other tribes of the Indian Territory, faced dire questions at this time. Back in 1887, U.S. Congress had passed the Dawes Act, which authorized the formation of a commission to negotiate the nullification of treaties that existed between the federal government and various Native American peoples, including the Creeks. On March 3, 1893, the Dawes Commission was established for this purpose. Massachusetts senator Henry Dawes was convinced that the treaties had outlived their usefulness. He envisioned a plan that would diminish Indian sovereignty and force Native Americans into the broader national political culture by enhancing their stake as private, individual U.S. citizens. Under the plan, tribal titles would be invalidated, tribal assets would be liquidated, and tribal land allotted in severalty (meaning pieces of land would be individually owned as a sole and exclusive possession—a concept contrary to the ancient Native American way of thinking about land).

Supporters of allotment believed that such a plan would diminish intratribal corruption and economic disparity. Every Creek would be given title to his or her own tract of land and become a propertied citizen with ownership rights. This, some believed, would lead to greater political participation and civic responsibility and decrease the potential for abuse of tribal holdings by tribal elites. Opponents of allotment, among them members of the Creek National Council, feared that the practice would lead to wholesale loss of land by those Native Americans who were not well versed in the jargon and complexities of the law. Congress, however, made it clear that the tribes had no real choice: as in the period leading up to the Indian Removal Act (1830), which relocated tribes of the southeastern United States to Oklahoma, the Creeks could either concede to the federal government's wishes or face implementation of the law by force.

Alex Posey had an astute political mind and strong feelings about the issues facing his people. His political thinking gave rise to a new writer's voice that eventually surpassed his poetry in originality of style. While still at BIU, he had conceived a persona called Chinnubbie Harjo, whose character is summed up by the title of the first tale in which he appeared: "Chinnubbie Harjo, the Evil Genius of the Creeks." This first story has been lost, but it was followed by several "tall tales" in which the hero accomplishes strange but dubious feats. Posey became so found of his character that he adopted the name as a pseudonym.

In February of 1894, as he watched the airing of the Dawes Commission's arguments before a specially convened intertribal council, Posey voiced his political thoughts on allotment through the character of Chinnubbie, who came to represent the entire Creek nation as it mused on the permanence of the choices it faced. To a certain extent, Posey supported the Dawes Commission's recommendations; he hoped for the formation of a separate Indian state.

Posey was surrounded by Creek leaders who bitterly opposed allotment and was happy to distance himself from the combative atmosphere by accepting a post as superintendent of the Creek Orphan Asylum at Okmulgee. The Creek National Council later established its own commission to negotiate with the Dawes Commission.

From Administrator to Newspaper Publisher

It was at the Creek Orphan Asylum that Posey fell in love with his future wife, Minnie Harris (whom he affectionately called "Lowena") of Fayetteville, Arkansas. She had been employed by Posey as matron of the home. They were married on May 9, 1896, and had two sons, Yohola and Pachina, but the latter child survived only one year. Posey resigned as superintendent of the orphanage in October of 1897 and served a brief stint as head of public instruction of the Muskogee (Creek) nation.

The following year he returned to farm life and poetry writing, but his administrative abilities were in demand and he consented in 1899 to supervise the National High School at Eufaula. The *Indian Journal* was published there, and its editorial staff often invited Posey to submit work—both poetry and prose. It was his first regular affiliation with a newspaper since he was involved with the school paper at BIU, and he found that he liked it. In 1902, after one more short-lived educational administration post—this time at the Wetumpka National School—he bought the *Indian Journal* and took over as editor.

Fus Fixico Letters Read Nationwide

Over the next couple of years, Posey perfected a journalistic style that brought him contemporary recognition as well as lasting praise. The commitment he demonstrated to newspaper work did not entail a retreat from the political arena, just a new approach to it. His literary style was not only unique and well-suited to him, it was seen as a fresh way to write political commentary. He found that the best way to discuss towering issues like the disintegration of the Creek nation was in the form of witty conversations as reported by his fictional persona, *Fus Fixico,* in the English dialect of a full-blooded Creek. Biting potshots were launched against many of the players who were instrumental in bringing about the end of the traditional way of life for members of the Creek tribe. The *Fus Fixico Letters* were an immediate hit in the Indian Territory and were soon widely read throughout the United States. Posey wrote 72 letters between 1902 and his death six years later; they stand today as one of the quintessential expressions of American political humor.

In 1904 Posey returned to public service in the form of an enrollment officer for the Dawes Commission. A prelude to allotment of Indian lands in severalty was the enrollment of all the members of the tribe, many in remote regions who harbored neither the desire to put their names down on paper for the federal government nor an understanding of the purpose of such an action. Posey spent three years performing this tedious task, during which time he came into contact with many highly conservative Creeks, who he felt would be unable to engage in the kind of self-government that would be expected of them after statehood.

Still, Posey managed to hold on to the dream of a separate Indian state. After the Civil War, Oklahoma Territory had been carved out of Indian Territory as punishment for Native American support of the Confederacy. Now that statehood was imminent, many Native Americans in the territories hoped for two separate states. Posey acted as secretary to the convention convened at Muskogee in the summer of 1905 to discuss the formation of a constitution that would settle the matter.

Posey continued with his Dawes Commission fieldwork, began to have a go at the real estate business, and had resumed editing the *Indian Journal* when he accidentally drowned in 1908. He had become the symbol of the progressive Native American, facing challenges to his traditions and culture with wisdom, humor, and optimism. Many critics credit him with producing a body of work in a distinctly American voice that rests among the most original, most sincere, and funniest expressions of American maverick journalism. Having lived through a tumultuous time in his people's history, Posey looked forward to the emergence of a new and enduring Creek people—challenged, but stronger than before.

SELECTED WRITINGS BY POSEY:

The Poems of Alexander Lawrence Posey, collected and arranged by Minnie H. Posey, Topeka, Crane, 1910.
Fus Fixico Letters, edited by Daniel F. Littlefield, Jr., Lincoln, University of Nebraska Press, 1993.

SOURCES:

Connelley, William Elsey, "Memoir of Alexander Lawrence Posey," in *The Poems of Alexander Lawrence Posey*, Topeka, Crane, 1910.

Littlefield, Daniel F., Jr., *Alex Posey: Creek Poet, Journalist, and Humorist,* Lincoln, University of Nebraska Press, 1992.

—*Sketch by Charles Cannon*

Poundmaker

1842(?)-1886

Cree tribal leader

Also known as Pitikwahanapiwiyin, Pito-kanow-apiwin, Opeteca Hanawaywin, Makoyi-koh-kin ["Wolf Thin Legs"]

Poundmaker was one of the most capable chiefs of the Cree Confederacy in Canada. He is perhaps best remembered for his role in the Riel Rebellion of 1885. Born about 1842 in west central Saskatchewan, Canada, Poundmaker was raised in the House band of the Paskwawininiwug ["people of the plains"]. His mother was a métis [part French-Canadian and part Indian] and his father was a Stony Cree Indian called Sikakwayan ["Skunk Skin"]. Poundmaker spent his early years in Cree camps, although his parents apparently died when he was a young man. His name came from his proficiency at attracting buffalo and other animals into corrals known as pounds.

In 1873, the Cree and the Blackfeet, traditionally enemies, signed a temporary peace treaty. During this short peace the young Poundmaker met the famous Blackfoot chief, Crowfoot ["Isapo-Muxika"]. Poundmaker reminded Crowfoot of his recently deceased son, and the Blackfoot warrior invited the Cree youth to his camp at Blackfoot Crossing. Shortly after that, Crowfoot adopted Poundmaker and gave him the Blackfoot name of Makoyi-koh-kin. The two were alike in many ways: Poundmaker was as inclined toward peace as was Crowfoot, and both men foresaw a time when they would have to live in peace with the white man. During his time with Crowfoot, Poundmaker also learned to speak the Blackfoot language fluently.

When Poundmaker returned to his people, he brought with him many horses given to him by Crowfoot. They made him wealthy and gave him a high status among his own people. He married a Cree woman on his return and had at least one son, who later attend the Big Lake Indian School at Saint Albert. Poundmaker was named a sub-chief under Pihew-kamihkosit ["Red Pheasant"] of the Sipiwininiwug ["River People"], one of the subdivisions of the Paskwaw-ininiwug. Becau... ...telligence, Poundmaker became a councillor to t... ...y Cree chief and helped to secure a lasting peace b... ...is people and the Blackfoot.

Poundma... ...ects to Treaty

D... ...1860s and 1870s, the United States government... ...onstant costly battles with the Indians over land... ...alone, the Indian conflicts cost the government some... ...illion. Canada's entire federal budget during the same ye... was less than that amount, and an Indian war like the ones in the United States would have destroyed the Canadian economy. The Canadians recognized the potential problem as early as 1867, when the Dominion of Canada was first formed. They included in their constitution a recognition of responsibility for Native Americans, and set aside lands for them. Beginning in 1868, legislation was passed based on the principal that Indians should be free and active citizens of Canada. However, the Canadian government did not believe the western Indian nations were civilized enough to exercise their citizenship properly. Also, the government wanted to insure peace with the Native Americans before too many settlers moved into the territory. As a result, the government began to make treaties with the various Native American nations to cede much of their land to the government for later settlement, and to establish reserves for the Indians.

In August, 1876, at Fort Carlton, the Canadian government began negotiations for Treaty Number 6 with the Cree nation. Poundmaker was one of the spokesmen for the Cree. Alexander Morris, the lieutenant governor of the Manitoba province and governor of the Northwest Territories, outlined the terms of the treaty, which provided each family with one square mile of land. Poundmaker was not impressed. Hugh Dempsey in *Big Bear* reports that Poundmaker said, "This is our land! It isn't a piece of pemmican to be cut off and given in little pieces back to us." Later in the negotiations, he insisted that the government provide the Indians with training in how to farm, and other assistance once the buffalo were gone, in exchange for land. Morris hesitated to make such a commitment. According to John Maclean in *Native Tribes of Canada,* Poundmaker said, "I heard what you said yesterday, and I thought that when the law was established in the country it would be for our good. From what I can hear and see now, I cannot understand that I shall be able to clothe my children and feed them as long as the sun shines and water runs.... I do not know how to build a house for myself ... I do not know how to cultivate the ground for myself." Despite his concerns, Poundmaker signed the treaty on August 23, 1876. When his chief, Pihew-kamihkosit, finally agreed to settle on a reserve in 1878, Poundmaker formed his own band and continued to hunt the ever-smaller number of buffalo.

By 1879, however, the buffalo were gone, and Poundmaker finally agreed to settle on his own reserve just west of Battleford near the point where the Battle River and Cut Knife River joined. The government's promised assistance was not what Poundmaker had hoped. The farm instructors knew little about farming practices, especially in the Northwest Territory, and there were not enough oxen, seed and other materials to make the farms productive. The government's failure to follow through on the treaty laid the groundwork for future discontent among the Cree nation.

"The Whites Will Dictate to Us"

In 1881 the Marquis of Lorne, who was Governor-General of Canada and the son-in-law of Queen Victoria, toured the country, and Poundmaker was chosen to accompany him on the trip from Battleford to Crowfoot's Blackfoot Reserve. During the discussions with Crowfoot, where Poundmaker interpreted for the Blackfoot chief, Lorne advised that the old days were gone and the Indians would have to turn to agriculture to survive. At a New Year's festival following his return, Maclean reported, Poundmaker told the Cree, "We can do a good deal of work with the help we get now from the Government, ... but let us not forget it is the last year to receive rations. The Governor-General told me so, and it will be so. Next summer, or, at the latest, next fall, the railway will be close to us, the whites will fill the country, and they will dictate to us as they please. It is useless to dream that we can frighten them, that time has passed. Our only resource is our work, our industry, our farms." He was concerned that the Cree would fight among themselves and encouraged them to love one another. He also encouraged them to send their children to mission schools.

By 1883, federal funds were low and Indian rations were the first to be cut along with the services of many Indian Agency employees. Delays in the delivery of supplies further inflamed the situation and, by the winter of 1883, many Indians were starving. It was difficult for Poundmaker to maintain the peace among his warriors. In June, 1884, some 1,000 Cree Indians came to the Poundmaker Reserve to discuss the need for more food and supplies as well as to celebrate the annual Thirst Dance, at which the natives reaffirmed their beliefs in the sun spirit. During the dance, Lucky Man's two sons were accused of assaulting John Craig, a farm instructors. Expecting violence, the Northwest Mounted Police sent 90 men to arrest the two brothers. They forced their way into the Medicine Lodge in the midst of the sacred ceremony. Because they could not recognize the brother, the police left with the promise that the culprits would be brought to them at the end of the ceremony. On June 20, all the Indians started toward the ration house where the police waited. Then an argument started among the Cree about turning over the accused men. Finally, Dempsey reports, Poundmaker said, "As you will not give up this man, I will go down and surrender myself sooner than blood be shed." After the police arrested the two brothers, they handed out bacon and flour to all the natives that promised not to cause more trouble.

Lack of Food Leads to Rebelliom

After the Hudson Bay Company sold its land to the government of Canada, the federal bureaucrats assumed that any land not specifically granted by them to individuals belonged to the Crown. The métis, who had been farming this land for several generations, were now required to register their holdings as if they were new settlers. But the government was slow in surveying those holdings and when they did, the surveyors demanded that the lots be square rather than oblong, the way the métis had laid out their tracts. The result was that many of the new survey lines were drawn through houses, or cut off the houses from the fields. The métis appealed the results of the survey, but they were ignored. They turned to Louis Riel, who had led a land rebellion in Manitoba 15 years earlier. In March 1885, Riel and his followers took over the métis village Batoche, set up their own government, ransacked federally owned stores and took hostages. Another of Riel's followers, Gabriel Dumont, took over the trading post at Duck Lake. Northwest Mounted Police Superintendent Leif Crozier moved swiftly against Riel. Leaving Fort Carlton on March 26, Crozier and 55 Mounted Police headed toward Duck Lake. After brief negotiations, Crozier fired on the rebels, but found himself outnumbered and outgunned, so he retreated.

After Duck Lake, Riel met with various tribal chiefs in the area to encourage them to join his rebellion. About the same time Riel started his rebellion, Poundmaker decided it was time to ask the government for the delayed supplies, since food still was in short supply on the Reserves. Leading 200 warriors, Poundmaker headed for Battleford to request the overdue rations. Upon hearing about the events at Duck Lake and that Poundmaker was moving toward them, the

500 residents panicked and took refuge at the Mounted Police garrison just outside the village. The Indian agent refused to leave the protection of the garrison to talk with Poundmaker, but sent a telegraph message to his superiors requesting authority to issue the rations.

Poundmaker, however, was not able to control his warriors. The warriors, angry and impatient, decided to ransack the abandoned town. Farmhouses were burned and a white settler, caught outside the fort, was killed. The raiding continued for three weeks, but the warriors finally decided to return to the Reserve without attacking the garrison. Meanwhile, Stony Cree Chief Big Bear and some 400 warriors ransacked stores at Frog Lake and took over the Catholic mission there. That raid ended with nine whites dead.

Immediately after Riel defeated the Mounted Police at Duck Lake, the Canadian government mobilized 8,000 soldiers and began moving them to the troubled area. By mid-April, the military was ready to launch an offensive against the rebels and Indians. While the main force moved toward Batoche where Riel was headquartered, a second group of 325 soldiers under Colonel William Otter headed to Battleford to relieve the barricaded settlers and Mounted Police. Meanwhile, many of the Stony Crees involved in the confrontation at Frog Lake also moved onto Poundmaker's Reserve. When Otter discovered the Indians had left Battleford, he proceeded to the Reserve intent on punishing the Indians. On May 2, 1885, the Stony Cree Indians heard about the advancing column and set a trap. After seven hours of fighting, Otter retreated.

Some sources indicate Poundmaker did not participate in the fight. However, Hugh A. Dempsey in *Crowfoot* said the Blackfoot chief was proud of his adopted son, who "had turned the tide of the battle. Armed only with a whip, he had been an inspiration to all those around him and had forced the white attackers to withdraw. Then, showing results of Crowfoot's teachings, he had refused to let the young warriors pursue and destroy the retreating soldiers." After the attack, the métis persuaded the warriors at Poundmaker's Reserve to move to Batoche. Poundmaker did not want to go and instead tried to reach Devil's Lake, but the Stony warriors under Big Bear prevented him from going. Attacks on forts and settlers continued. Still, when the métis captured a wagon train a few days later, Poundmaker was able to protect the prisoners.

Tried for Treason

Riel surrendered on May 15, 1885. Upon hearing of his surrender, Poundmaker attempted to negotiate a peace treaty with Major-General Frederick Dobson Middleton, who had led the main Canadian forces against Riel. Middleton, however, demanded an unconditional surrender. Finally, on May 26, Poundmaker and his followers travelled to Fort Battleford to surrender. Big Bear did not surrender until July 2. Poundmaker was tried for treason in July, 1885 and was sentenced to three years in prison. Both Maclean and Dempsey reported that Poundmaker told the court, "I am not guilty. A lot has been said against me that is untrue.... When

my people and the whites met in battle, I saved the Queen's men.... Everything I could do was done to stop bloodshed. Had I wanted war, I would not be here now but on the prairie. You did not catch me. I gave myself up. You have got me because I wanted peace." During his first year at the Stony Mountain Penitentiary, Poundmaker was baptized and admitted to the Catholic church by Archbishop Tache. Unfortunately, his health deteriorated as well. As a result, and at the urging of Crowfoot and various government officials, Poundmaker was released on March 4, 1886, after serving about seven months of his sentence.

Five weeks after his release from prison, Poundmaker went to visit his adopted father, Crowfoot at the Blackfoot Reserve. His health improved during his stay there and he began to make plans to return to his own people. During the annual Sun Dance, however, some food caught in Poundmaker's throat and he started coughing violently, breaking a blood vessel in his lung. He died on July 4, 1886.

SOURCES:

Biographical Dictionary of Indians of the Americas, second edition, Newport Beach, California, American Indian Publishers, 1991; 565.

Dempsey, Hugh A., *Big Bear,* Lincoln, University of Nebraska Press, 1984; 69, 95, 123-132, 135-138, 194-195.

Dempsey, Hugh A., *Crowfoot,* Norman, University of Oklahoma Press, 1972; 70-73, 136-138, 189-191, 194-200.

Dempsey, Hugh A., "Pitikwahanapiwiyin," in *Dictionary of Canadian Biography,* Volume 11, University of Toronto Press, 1982; 695-697.

Dockstader, Frederick J., *Great North American Indians,* New York, Van Nostrand Reinhold, 1977; 223.

Doenecke, Justus D., "Louis Riel," in *Historic World Leaders,* Volume 5, Detroit, Gale Research, 1994; 706-711.

Handbook of American Indians North of Mexico, Part 1, edited by Frederick Webb Hodge, Pageant Books, 1960; 359-361.

"History of Indian-White Relations," edited by Wilcomb E. Washburn, in *Handbook of North American Indians,* Volume 4, edited by William Sturtevant, Washington, D.C., Smithsonian Institution, 1988; 89-92.

The Illustrated History of Canada, edited by Craig Brown, Lester & Orpen Dennys, 1987; 328-357.

Maclean, John, *Native Tribes of Canada,* Toronto, William Briggs, 1896; reprinted, Coles Publishing, 1980; 371-390.

Native North American Almanac, edited by Duane Champagne, Detroit, Gale Research, 1994; 1136-1137.

Samek, Hana, *The Blackfoot Confederacy 1880-1920,* Albuquerque, University of New Mexico Press, 1987; 14-15, 40-51.

Tanner, Ogden, *The Canadians,* New York, Time-Life Books, 1977; 185-221.

Waldman, Carl, *Who Was Who in Native American History,* New York, Facts On File, 1990; 283-284.

—Sketch by Catherine A. Clay

Powell, Billy
See Osceola

Powhatan
1548(?)-1618
Powhatan-Renapé leader
Also known as Wahunsonacock (Wahunsenacawh,
Wahunsenacawk) ["He Makes an Offering by
Crushing with a Falling Weight" or "He Knows
How to Crush Them"], Ottaniack ["Possessor"],
Mamanatowick ["He Who Exceeds" or "He Who
Is Very Superior"], Priest, and "I Dream"

Powhatan was a major indigenous leader of the Renapé speaking people of what is now Virginia. He formed a confederacy of more than 30 tribes and was the major political force in the area at the time the English were trying to establish their first permanent settlement. Powhatan was born between 1532 and 1548, at a place called variously Poetan, Pawatah, Powahtan, Powetan, and Pawetan (present-day Richmond), from which he acquired his best-known name. The name Powhatan first appears in the *Walam Olum,* the epic history of the Lenapé, as *powatanep* and *powatapi.* It has been translated as "priest" or "religious leader." The name also refers to dreaming and divination and is related to the modern word "pow-wow," but in the sense of spiritual or sacred dreams directed toward hearing something. Wahunsonacock may perhaps have earned the name Powhatan from his visions or dreaming as well as from being born at the place known by that name. The term Powhatan was not only used for a specific place but also for the river flowing through it, known today as the James River. A local group of Renapé people continued to be known as the "Powhite" tribe long after the English settlement, and the name also seems to have been used (at least by the English) to include all of Powhatan's confederated "kingdoms" or "tribes."

Captain John Smith described Powhatan around 1608 as "a tall well-proportioned man ... his head somewhat gray.... His age is near 60; of a very able and hardy body to endure any labour." William Strachey wrote that "he is a goodly old man, not yet shrincking [in 1612], though well beaten with many many ... wynters.... Of a tall stature, and cleane lymbes, of a sad aspect, round fat visag'd with gray haires.... He hath bene a strong and able Salvadge [sic], synowie, active and of a daring spiritt, vigilant, ambitious."

Powhatan also had a large family. In 1612, his family reportedly numbered 20 sons and ten daughters, along with a young child by Winganuske ["Pretty or Handsome Woman"]. Strachey gives the names of 12 of his wives, including Oweroughwough (Werowo, probably "Good Woman"). Another daughter was Pocahunta (Pocahontas) who was around 1612 (at 14 or so) married to Kocoum but later married John Rolfe. Powhatan's sons included Naukaquawis and Parahunt, the leading man at the village of Powhatan.

Powhatan probably inherited his rank from the sister of the previous leader. In an often-quoted speech, Powhatan stated that "my bretheren, namely Opichapam, Opechankanough, and Kekataugh, my two sisters, and their two daughters, are distinctly each others successors" to his position as leader of the Powhatan confederacy. Opichapam ["The Opposer"] and Kekataugh ["The Speaker"] lived together in Pamunkey Neck at Cinquoteck (West Point). Smith also wrote: "His kingdome descendeth not to his sonnes nor children but first to his brethren, whereof he hath 3 ... and after their decease to his sisters ... but never to the heires of the males." Opichapam was Powhatan's immediate successor, followed by Opechankanough.

Powhatan and his society were greatly influenced by the Spanish attempts to establish a mission in the area in 1570, and the English efforts to colonize the Roanoke region in the 1580s. The Europeans may have introduced new diseases, including venereal disease, which could have reduced the population of the region. In the early 1600s, English ship captains also began to raid for slaves along the American coast. In 1605 or 1606 a ship raided the Powhatan and Rappahannock river areas, killing the chief person of Toppahannock and carrying off others as slaves. Because of this, Powhatan was extremely suspicious of the English colonists who arrived in 1607. The independent Chesapeake people at the mouth of the bay attacked the settlers when they came ashore, probably for the same reason. Smith's writings and the works of other colonial figures reveal that the English were capable of continuous duplicity in their greed to exploit the wealth of Virginia and to control the Renapé people. Powhatan responded in kind, at first indulging the strangers and, finally, trying to expel them.

In the early 1600s Powhatan usually resided at Werawocomoco ["Good House"], located on the north side of the lower Pamunkey (York) River. There English visitors found him "proudly lying upon a Bedstead a foote high, upon tenne or twelve mattes, richly hung with mannie Chaynes of great Pearles about his necke, and covered with a great Covering of Rahaughcums [Raccoon furs]. At [his] heade sat a woman, at his feete another; on each side sitting upon a Matte upon the ground, were raunged his chiefe men on each side the fire, tenne in a ranke, and behind them as many young women, each a great Chaine of white Beades over their shoulders, their heade painted in redde: and [he] with such a grave and Majesticall countenance." In front of his house "stood fortie or fiftie great Platters of fine bread" for his guests.

Reportedly, Powhatan had a large house in the territory of each of the "kingdoms" which he had inherited. These were located roughly from the area of present-day Petersburg north to the Mattaponi River. Powhatan also maintained a treasure house on the upper Chickahominy called Orapacks. A mile from there "in a thicket of wood, hee hath a house, in which he keepeth his kind of Treasure, as skinnes, copper, pearle, and beades; which he storeth up against the time of his death and buriall. Here also is his store of red paint for ointment, and bowes and arrowes. This house is 50 or 60 yards in length, frequented only by Priestes. At the 4 corners of this house stand 4 Images as Sentinels; one of a Dragon, another of a Beare, the [third] like a Leopard [puma], and the fourth like a giantlike man." Smith was made prisoner in late 1607 or early 1608 for coming too close to Orapacks. He was threatened with execution but, according to his own story, he was rescued by the intervention of Pocahontas, who later persuaded her father to send food to the starving colonists.

English writers tend to assign great power to Powhatan as the head *werowans* of the tribal confederacy. As befitted an honored leader, Powhatan kept "about his person ... a guard of 40 or 50 of the tallest men his Country doth afford. Every night upon the 4 quarters of his house are 4 Sentinels, each standing from [the] other a flight [arrow] shoot: and at every halfe houre, one from the Corps du guard doth hallowe; unto whom Sentinall doth answer round from his stand." Certainly Powhatan received tribute from many republics but many others were only weakly attached to his confederacy. Several tribes on the north side of the Powhatan River had at least some degree of autonomy. Further north, Powhatan's power seems to have ended at the Mattaponi River. The English may have overrepresented Powhatan's power, calling him an "emperor," for their own purposes. They wished to make him a subject of the King of England and to seize overlordship over all of the region. The more territory and power Powhatan controlled, the more land and authority the English could grab through a single act of obedience.

Powhatan proved to be a very capable adversary of the English, thwarting their schemes while gathering arms and intelligence for a war to expell the invaders. His strategy included sending several of his counselors to England, to discover the English strength and intentions. Uttamatamakin (Tomocomo), sent with Pocahontas in 1616, was one such observer. He was a vigorous defender of Renapé religion and values in arguments with the English elite of the court of James I. In 1617, Pocahontas died suddenly as she was returning to Virginia, and in the following year her father died also. It remained for Powhatan's brother Opechankanough to start the planned war of liberation.

SOURCES:

Books

Potter, Stephen R., "Early English Effects on Virginia Algonquian Exchange and Tribute in the Tidewater Potomac," in *Powhatan's Mantle: Indians in the Colonial Southeast* by Peter H. Wood, Gregory A. Waselkov and M. Thomas Hartley, Lincoln, University of Nebraska Press, 1989; 151-172.

Powhatan Foreign Relations 1500-1722, edited by Helen C. Rountree, University Press of Virginia, 1993.

Purchas, Samuel, *Hakluytus Posthumus or Purchas His Pilgrimes,* Volume 19, MacLehose, 1906.

Rountree, Helen C., *Pocahontas' People: The Powhatan Indians of Virginia through Four Centuries,* Norman, University of Oklahoma Press, 1990.

Rountree, Helen C., *The Powhatan Indians of Virginia: Their Traditional Culture,* Norman, University of Oklahoma Press, 1989.

Smith, John, *The Generall Historie of Virginia. New England and the Summer Isles (1624),* Volume 1, MacLehose, 1907.

Strachey, William, *The Historie of Travell into Virginia Britania (1612),* edited by Louis B. Wright and Virginia Freund, Hakluyt Society, 1953.

Tracts and Other Papers, edited by Peter Force, New York, Smith, 1947.

Travels and Works of Captain John Smith, Volume 1, edited by Edward Arber, Edinburgh, Grant, 1910.

Periodicals

Bushnell, David I., Jr., "Virginia—From Early Records," *American Anthropoligist,* 1907; 31-44.

Forbes, Jack D., "Anglo-Powhatan Relations to 1676," *Masterkey,* November-December 1956; 179-183, and January-February 1957; 4-8.

"Newport's Virginia Discovery, 1607," *Virginia Magazine of History and Biography,* 1907; 373-378.

—Sketch by Jack D. Forbes

Pushmataha
1764(?)-1824
Choctaw tribal leader

Also known as Apushmataha ["The Scalp Is Ready to Take" or "He Has Won All the Honors of His Race"], Apushim-altitaha ["The Sapling Is Ready to Bend"], A push matahaubi ["One Whose Tomahawk Is Fatal in War or Hunting"]

Pushmataha was a simple man who distinguished himself as a warrior and statesman. It was said that on all occasions and under all circumstances he was the white man's friend, because he often managed to balance his intense loyalty to the Choctaw Nation with his desire to maintain peaceful relations with the U.S. government. He became principal chief of the Choctaw Nation in 1805, distinguished himself in battle during the Creek War of 1813, and was a leading negotiator in several important treaties. Andrew

Pushmataha

Jackson frequently expressed the opinion that Pushmataha was the greatest and bravest Indian he had ever known.

Pushmataha was born in June 1764 on the east bank of Noxuba Creek (in present-day Noxubee County, Mississippi) in one of the villages of the Six Towns people, a division of the Choctaw Nation. He belonged to the Iksa or Kinsah-a-hi clan ["Potato-Eating People"]. The names of his parents are unknown because Choctaw tradition was never to speak of the dead; however, Pushmataha, who was a great orator and storyteller, liked to say of himself, "I had no father. I had no mother. The lightning rent the living oak, and Pushmataha sprang forth." He also said he "was raised in blood," a reference to the belief that the Creeks killed his parents in a massacre.

At five feet ten inches tall, Pushmataha had a full chest, square, broad shoulders, a fine forehead, a large mouth with rather thick lips, and keen eyes with a look of kindness and understanding. His fine forehead was probably the result of head deformation. The Choctaws used a hinged piece of wood to apply pressure over a period of time to the foreheads of male infants. They believed head-flattening made men more handsome. Pushmataha grew stouter with age.

He was not always called Pushmataha, since in accordance with Choctaw tradition, he had to do something worthy to get a name. During his teens he was called Hochifoiksho ["I Have No Name"], often shortened to Hoh, until one night he told a good story at a hunting camp and became Ishtilawata ["The Bragger"]. He was more than a good talker, though. He killed more game and preserved a greater number of skins than any other hunter in the camp, giving his excess to those less successful.

Pushmataha led many raids on enemy Osage and Caddo villages across the Mississippi River. On one expedition he was captured. When he escaped he lived among the Spanish, an experience which gave him the firsthand knowledge of the territory he later used during treating. An another occasion he singlehandedly killed five men. The incident earned him the name "Eagle" and probably led to his having the name Pushmataha bestowed on him, which is derived from a combination of words meaning "The Scalp Is Ready to Take." Some historians believe his name originally was A push matahaubi, meaning a messenger of death, or more literally "One Whose Tomahawk Is Fatal in War or Hunting." Still others think the name derives from Apushim-altitaha ["The Sapling Is Ready to Bend"] and refers to the oak tree, as Pushmataha claimed. Yet another definition, given by an early historian of Alabama, was "He Has Won All the Honors of His Race."

Contributions as a Soldier and Statesman

Pushmataha was one of the few prominent Indian leaders who, though intensely loyal to his people and race, acknowledged the growing power of the United States. He advocated a policy of conciliation with the United States, yet warned his people not to let anyone with a drop of white blood participate in the Choctaw Nation, since whites did not love the land. Nevertheless, he felt honored to represent the United States as an army officer and believed the Choctaws need not lose independence or racial identity if they cooperated. The Choctaws believed Americans would protect them and give in return the same honor and loyalty. However, this reciprocity never proved to be the case.

In 1804 Pushmataha was part of a delegation that went to Washington, D.C., to meet with President Thomas Jefferson. The delegation signed a treaty ceding a large tribal area in Alabama and Mississippi in exchange for the forgiveness of debts individual Choctaws had with the Spanish trading posts, as well as cash and annuities for the signers. Pushmataha made a speech in Washington and impressed the audience with his earnestness. Later, his oratory abilities would become a hallmark. When the delegation returned to Mississippi, he helped present the proposed treaty to the whole Choctaw Nation.

In 1805 Pushmataha was selected principal chief of the Choctaw Nation after Tuscana Hopaia died. Although he only had authority over his own Six Towns district, he held the highest position of honor and good opinion of all Choctaws and used his influence to promote friendly relations with whites. He never surrendered or disguised his convictions, and he was always proud of his race, stating often, "Chaeta sia hoke" ["I am a Choctaw"].

The Shawnee chief Tecumseh visited the Choctaws in 1811 to propose they join an all-Indian Confederacy to oppose the Americans. The alliance would have extended the length of the frontier from Canada to Florida. Push-

349

mataha went to many of the meetings Tecumseh held and, though he agreed with some of the things Tecumseh said, he spoke out against his methods. Pushmataha persuaded his people not to join the Indian Confederacy and prevented an all-out Indian war against the United States as well as a civil war within the Choctaw Nation. When the Creeks decided to join the Indian Confederacy, Pushmataha offered Choctaw assistance to the Americans.

Pushmataha, who served under General Andrew Jackson in the War of 1812, served under the general again during the Creek War of 1813-1814. Pushmataha's rigid discipline succeeded in converting his warriors into efficient soldiers and earned him the name "The Indian General." During the Creek War, Pushmataha led about 500 of his warriors to defeat the Creeks in the Battle of Holy Ground. He received full military honors for his participation, including the rank of brigadier general and a resplendent $300 uniform with regimentals, gold epaulets, sword, silver spurs, and hat with ostrich feathers. He never put his uniform on again after the Creek War, because he wanted his people to remember him as the chief of the Choctaws, not as a former general in the U.S. Army.

Role as Treaty Negotiator

On November 16, 1816, Pushmataha, Moshulatubbee, and Puckshenubbee signed the Mount Dexter Treaty. Recognizing the importance of education to succeeding in the white man's world (and to bargaining treaties), Pushmataha used portions of the $1,000 annuity he received for his work on the treaty to support a school and a blacksmith shop. He developed a Choctaw educational system based on white methods.

By 1819, the lands ceded in the 1816 treaty were not enough for the white settlers—Mississippi wanted all of the Choctaw territory east of the Mississippi River. But when General Jackson, whom Pushmataha considered a friend of the Choctaws, failed to show up to negotiate for the United States, Pushmataha came out against the proposal and it failed. The following year Jackson came to discussions with the Choctaws and used trades in bargaining the Treaty of Doak's Stand. Nonetheless, the Americans still relied on "diplomatic tricks"—economic pressure, the prospect of war, and blackmail—to win acceptance. Jackson chose Pushmataha to make the opening speech at the treaty council because he held the most important position among the Choctaw chiefs. What Jackson did not realize was that Pushmataha was familiar with the lands west of the Mississippi being traded and would effectively parley with Jackson. Each time Jackson acknowledged Pushmataha's position, Pushmataha would say "Sia Hoka" ["very well" or "that is all right with me"]. He said it so frequently, both while serving in the U.S. Army and while treating, that Jackson began to use the expression "O.K.," mimicking the accent the Choctaws placed on "Hoka."

Pushmataha and other principals signed the Treaty of Doak's Stand on October 18, 1820. Congress appropriated funds the same year to put the treaty into effect. However, homesteaders in Arkansas, whom U.S. troops had attempted to drive out in 1819, objected to giving up their homes to resettling Choctaws. In 1823 Congress decided to divert the appropriation to revise instead of implement the treaty. But the chiefs who had signed in good faith the "perpetual" Treaty of Doak's Stand refused to call another general council to consider its revision. Instead Pushmataha and the other chiefs decided to go to Washington and talk only with the president. The delegation was lodged in a Washington hotel and provided with food, drink, and entertainment, but was largely ignored by government officials and refused access to the president. Officials reasoned that if they kept the chiefs waiting, their opposition to new proposals would break down.

On December 23, 1824, Pushmataha was stricken by a throat infection while taking a walk and died at midnight of croup. General Jackson showed his respect for Pushmataha by visiting his deathbed and attending his funeral. Pushmataha received full military honors, with a procession of 2,000 military and civilian persons, several military companies, two bands, and marines from the naval yard. He was buried on Christmas Day at the Old Congressional Cemetery. Per his deathbed request to General Jackson, three volleys were fired over his grave, an honor of war corresponding to rank of major general. His request, "When I am gone, let the big guns be fired over me," also appears on his cemetery monument. In the Choctaw Nation, Pushmataha's family and friends set up poles ornamented with white and red streamers at his old home and held a "great cry." He left one son, Johnson Pushmataha, known as Mingo. Following Pushmataha's death, the dispirited chiefs, without a strong leader, finally signed a revised treaty on January 14, 1825, giving up all land in Arkansas.

SOURCES:

Dockstader, Fredrick J., *Great North American Indians: Profiles in Life and Leadership,* New York, Van Nostrand Reinhold, 1977; 226.

Lewis, Anna, *Chief Pushmataha, American Patriot: The Story of the Choctaws' Struggle for Survival,* New York, Exposition Press, 1959.

Waldman, Carl, *Who Was Who in Native American History,* New York, Facts On File, 1990; 287-88.

—*Sketch by Doris Morris Maxfield*

Quintasket, Christine
See Mourning Dove

Rain-in-the-Face
1835(?)-1905
Hunkpapa Sioux tribal leader and warrior
Also known as Iromagaja (Iromagaju), and Ama-
razhu

Rain-in-the-Face

Rain-in-the-Face was a Sioux leader in several battles with the U.S. military in the 1860s and 1870s, including the Battle of the Little Bighorn in June, 1876, in which George Armstrong Custer was killed. He is perhaps best known for a story about revenge he allegedly took against George Custer's brother Tom following the Little Bighorn battle. The legend asserts that Rain-in-the-Face, after murdering Tom Custer, cut out his heart and ate it. It was also believed for a time that the Indian warrior personally killed George Custer, but this has never been proven true.

Rain-in the Face was born at the forks of the Cheyenne River in present-day North Dakota about 1835. According to James McLaughlin, an Indian Agent at Standing Rock Reservation, there were five other sons in the family: Bear's Face, Red Thunder, Iron Horn, Little Bear, and Shave Head. McLaughlin related in *My Friend the Indian* that Rain-in-the-Face received his name as an infant when raindrops fell on his face as he was hanging from a tree branch in a cradle board. However, according to Charles Eastman who interviewed Rain-in-the Face shortly before his death and related in *Indian Heroes and Great Chieftains,* the name came from two other incidents in his life. One was when he was in a fight with a Cheyenne youth and blood washed his face paint away. The second incident occurred when he was a young man fighting the Gros Ventre. Eastman related the tale as he said Rain-in-the-Face told him: "I had wished my face to represent the sun when half covered with darkness, so I painted it half black, the other half red. We fought all day in the rain, and my face was partly washed and streaked with red and black: so again I was christened Rain-in-the-Face. We considered it an honorable name."

Begins Fighting against Whites Early in His Life

Rain-in-the-Face became a warrior at a very young age. His first important battle as a warrior was in December, 1866 in the fight against Captain William Fetterman's troops at Fort Phil Kearny, Wyoming. This battle was one of the Sioux victories in Red Cloud's War to gain back control of the land along the Bozeman Trail in Wyoming and Montana.

Two years later, Rain-in-the-Face was injured in a raid on Fort Totten in North Dakota. He also joined several war parties against the Crow, Mandan, Gros Ventre, and Pawnee, trying to gain respect as a warrior. One chance he had to gain distinction was to join in the raids on expeditions passing through Sioux country to the gold mines in South Dakota's Black Hills. His words, as reported by Eastman, were: "It was when the white men found the yellow metal in our country, and came in great numbers, driving away our game, that we took up arms against them for the last time.... We young warriors began to watch the trails of the white men into the Black Hills, and when we saw a wagon coming we would hide at the crossing and kill them all without much trouble. We did this to discourage the whites from coming into our country without our permission. It was the duty of our Great Father at Washington, by the agreement of 1868, to keep his white children away." This referred to the Treaty of Fort Laramie which did in fact recognize the Sioux claim to the Black Hills.

In 1873 Rain-in-the-Face was involved in a skirmish that led to a great controversy. That summer General George Armstrong Custer led troops from his Seventh cavalry to the

Yellowstone River area to serve as military escort for surveyors of the Northern Pacific railroad. A band of Indians attacked them at the mouth of the Tongue river. The same band of Indians attacked them again near the mouth of the Big Horn. During this second skirmish four men were killed. During the first skirmish one soldier was wounded, but two civilians lagging behind the soldiers were killed. These two were a sutler named Balliran and a veterinary surgeon named Honsinger.

A year later a scout took word to Custer at Fort Abraham Lincoln, near Bismarck, North Dakota, that Rain-in-the-Face was boasting that he had killed the two men. Custer sent out his brother, Captain Tom Custer, and Captain Yates to the Standing Rock Agency to arrest Rain-in-the-Face. Accompanied by 100 men, Captain Custer arrested Rain-in-the-Face and returned him to Fort Abraham Lincoln, where Rain-in-the-Face confessed to the murders. He was then imprisoned until a sympathetic guard allowed his escape. Several years later Rain-in-the-Face was arraigned in a federal court and charged with the murder of Balliran and Honsinger. The defense attorney successfully argued that the men had been killed as an act of battle, and that it was therefore not murder. The judge agreed and the case was dismissed.

Thomas Marquis wrote concerning this case that Rain-in-the-Face later indicated that he presumed he was in jail beause of killing a lone soldier. Eastman reported that Rain-in-the-Face said, "I had not yet become noted for any great deed. Finally, Wapaypay and I waylaid and killed a white soldier on his way from the fort to his home in the East.... I was seized and taken to the fort near Bismarck, North Dakota." Marquis surmised that Rain-in-the-Face was most likely "bewildered by the whole proceedings in his case, and that he never did learn precisely what was the charge against him when he was arraigned in court."

Story of Revenge against Tom Custer Arises

It was said by some that Rain-in-the-Face threatened to kill Tom Custer and tear out his heart in revenge. In 1876, Rain-in-the-Face was a leading warrior in the defeat of Custer at the Battle of the Little Bighorn in southern Montana. Publicity immediately following the battle accused Rain-in-the-Face of having completed his revenge by taking Tom Custer's heart. Reports of the condition of Tom Custer's body were consistent. Although mutilated, the chest cavity was not opened. Some supporters who did not believe Rain-in-the-Face was guilty of such a mutilation even denied that he had been a part of the battle. As one writer would relate of Rain-in-the-Face's confession in an interview, another would write that he denied it. Henry Wadsworth Longfellow immortalized the controversy about the warrior in his poem "The Revenge of Rain-in-the-Face."

Each of the early writers wrote about Indian events with a particular political agenda in mind. As well-known Indian photographer D. F. Barry wrote in a 1921 letter, "Men have written articles about him [Rain-in-the-Face] claiming to be an interview with him at Standing Rock. Major James McLaughlin says the partys [sic] never saw Rain-in-the-Face and were never at the agency." Even Charles Eastman's interviews are considered suspect, although Eastman himself was a fullblood Sioux. According to George Hyde, "It [the interview] presents a spectacle of poor and distorted memory that is appalling, as nearly every date and statement of fact is incorrect.... Wherever we can check them from reliable sources they turn out to be apocryphal." Eastman's interview with Rain-in-the-Face in fact has the dates reversed on the attack at Fort Totten and the Fetterman fight. On the other hand, it was often to the advantage of an Indian being interviewed to tell the story they knew was expected. The historical record seems to indicate that Rain-in-the-Face was involved in the Custer battle, but that there is no evidence supporting the accusations that he removed Tom Custer's heart.

Sources also disagree about how Rain-in-the-Face received the leg injury which left him crippled. An account in Cyrus Townsend Brady's history *The Sioux Indian Wars from the Powder River to the Little Big Horn* states that Rain-in-the-Face was wounded in the Custer battle, and that he had to conduct his own surgery using a razor retrieved from a fallen soldier. Judson Elliott Walker's account, *Campaigns of General Custer in the North-West, and the Final Surrender of Sitting Bull*, states that Rain-in-the-Face's leg was injured in 1880 during a buffalo hunt. Furthermore, Walker gives the accidental injury as the reason Rain-in-the-Face was willing to surrender in 1880-1881. Rain-in-the-Face was among the warriors who accompanied Sitting Bull to Canada. In the winter of 1880-1881 he surrendered with others at Fort Keogh, Montana and lived the remainder of his life on the Standing Rock Reservation in North Dakota. He died there on September 14, 1905, and was buried near Aberdeen, South Dakota.

According to Eastman, Rain-in-the-Face stated shortly before his death: "I have lived peaceably ever since we came upon the reservation. No one can say that Rain-in-the-Face has broken the rules of the Great Father. I fought for my people and my country. When we were conquered I remained silent, as a warrior should. Rain-in-the-Face was killed when he put down his weapons before the Great Father. His spirit was gone then; only this poor body lived on, but now it is almost ready to lie down for the last time. *Ho, hechetu!* [It is well.]" Whether or not Rain-in-the-Face actually spoke those words, they eloquently serve to summarize his later years.

SOURCES:

Books

Biographical Dictionary of Indians of the Americas, Newport Beach, California, 1983; 396-397.

Brady, Cyrus Townsend, *The Sioux Indian Wars from the Powder River to the Little Big Horn* (originally published under the title Indian Fights and Fighters), New York, Indian Head Books, 1992; 209-215; 279-292.

Dockstader, Frederick J., *Great North American Indians,* New York, Van Nostrand Reinhold, 1977; 229-230.

Opposes Christianity and Cultural Assimilation

Despite the attacks of Handsome Lake and his followers, Red Jacket was probably at the height of his influence with his tribe at the time of the War of 1812. Though he was now strongly opposed to the introduction of American ways among the Indians, he consistently followed a policy of friendship toward the United States government. He opposed the efforts of the Shawnee tribal leader Tecumseh to create a new Indian confederation to halt the westward expansion of the United States. When war broke out between Great Britain and the United States in 1812, he urged the Seneca and the other tribes of the Iroquois confederacy to remain neutral. Later the Seneca Indians did go to war on the side of the United States. Red Jacket, though now approaching 60 years of age, fought bravely in several battles during this conflict.

By the 1820s, Christianity was gaining many adherents among the Seneca tribesmen, including many of its political leaders. Red Jacket's strong opposition to Christianity, as well as his increasing tendency to alcoholic excess, led the so-called "Christian party" to initiate a council in September of 1827 to remove his chieftainship. Twenty-five chiefs set their marks to the document that deposed him. Red Jacket then went to Washington, where he told his story to the Secretary of War and the head of the Indian Bureau. They advised him to return home and show a more conciliatory attitude toward the Christian party. He did so and a second meeting of the tribal council restored him to his leadership post.

Red Jacket's final years were not happy. His second wife and her children had become Christians. This so distressed Red Jacket that he left her for a time, though they were ultimately reconciled. He was once again commonly believed to be drinking heavily. He died on January 20, 1830, at his tribal village near Buffalo. His wife had him buried in a Christian cemetery following a Christian religious service, neither of which he would have approved. In 1884, his remains, along with those of other Seneca tribal leaders, were reinterred in Forest Lawn Cemetery in Buffalo, where a memorial now stands.

SOURCES:

Dockstader, Frederick J., *Great North American Indians: Profiles in Life and Leadership,* New York, Van Nostrand Reinhold, 1977; 234-235.

Handbook of American Indians, two volumes, edited by Frederick Webb Hodge, Washington, D.C., U.S. Government Printing Office, 1907-1910; Volume 2, 360-363.

Parker, Arthur C., *Red Jacket: Last of the Seneca,* New York, McGraw-Hill, 1952.

Stone, William L., *Life and Times of Red-Jacket, or Sa-go-ye-wat-ha,* New York, Putnam, 1841.

Wallace, Anthony F. C., *The Death and Rebirth of the Seneca,* New York, Knopf, 1969.

—Sketch by John E. Little

Ben Reifel
1906-1990
Brulé Sioux political figure
Also known as Wiyaka Wanjila ["Lone Feather"]

Ben Reifel spent a lifetime working to bridge both white and American Indian cultures, a task in which he reaped large success. As the first member of the Sioux Nation to serve in the United States Congress, he campaigned for improved education on reservations, recommending consolidation of reservation and county schools, which enabled integration among Indian and non-Indian school children.

Reifel was born near Parmalee on the Rosebud Reservation in South Dakota on September 19, 1906. His mother, Lucy Burning Breast, was a full blood Brulé ("Burnt Thigh") Sioux, descendant of tribesmen Yellow Hair and Burning Breast. His father, William M. ("Shorty") Reifel, was a German-American farmer. Reifel married a college classmate, Alice Johnson, in 1933, and had one daughter, Loyce Reifel Anderson. After Alice died in 1972, Reifel married lifelong friend, Frances Ryland Colby.

Although Reifel's mother knew little English, she raised her son in a bilingual environment and encouraged him to become educated. In spite of his father's efforts to keep him on the farm, Ben attended South Dakota State University in Brookings, majoring in chemistry and dairy science. He later earned a master's degree and Ph.D. in public administration at Harvard University.

Reifel's first employment after graduating from college in 1932 was a year as Boys' Advisor at the Episcopal Hare School in Mission, South Dakota. In 1933, he was given the position of U.S. Farm Extension Agent at Pine Ridge Indian Reservation, where he had opportunity to utilize his experience and education in farm science. In 1935, he was transferred to Pierre, South Dakota, where he was Organizational Field Agent for North Dakota, South Dakota, Nebraska, Montana, and Kansas under the Indian Reorganization Act. Reifel's role was to help tribes develop organizational skills in order to improve tribal business management.

His work was interrupted by World War II when he went on active military duty as a second lieutenant in the U.S. Army. Throughout most of the war, he served in the states with the Military Police. After V-E Day, he was among those sent to Europe to retrain combat troops for service as military police. By the time he left the service in 1946, he had achieved the rank of Major.

In July 1946, Reifel went back to work for the newly reorgan.0ized Bureau of Indian Affairs (BIA) as the first District Tribal Relations Officer for the Northern Great Plains states. Almost immediately, he was promoted to the office of Superintendent on the Fort Berthold Reservation in North Dakota, home of the Three Affiliated Tribes (Arikara, Mandan, and Hidatsa). During his term there, the U.S. Con-

Ben Reifel

gress mandated the construction of Garrison Dam and Reservoir on mainly Indian land, resulting in a feeling that the government had unfairly forced the contract on the tribes.

Upon gaining access to graduate studies at Harvard through a scholarship, Reifel used his experience working at Fort Berthold on which to base his dissertation topic, namely to explain differences between Native and non-Native cultures and how to best alleviate conflict. In later interviews, Reifel offered advice to both cultures, admonishing Native people for clinging to the past and failing to adjust to new economic realities and recommending to non-Natives patience, tolerance, and understanding in relation to Native issues and concerns. He believed that it was possible to be both an American Indian and an active member of American society.

After receiving his degree at Harvard in 1952, Reifel returned to Fort Berthold during the controversy about government policies of relocation and termination. In 1954, he was transferred to Pine Ridge Reservation, where he became the first Indian to serve as Superintendent. The following year he became Area Director for the Aberdeen Area Office of the BIA. Until his election to Congress in 1961, Reifel successfully applied modern management practices and public relations skills as an administrator. As a congressman, he demonstrated his commitment to personal integrity and public responsibility.

After fulfilling four terms in Congress from 1961 to 1971, Reifel was credited for several political contributions

to his home state of South Dakota. He aided in the efforts to keep Ellsworth Air Force Base open, secure the presence of the Earth Resources Observation System Data Center (EROS) in the state, and upgrade the veteran's hospital in Sioux Falls, South Dakota. He also assisted in establishing the National Endowment for the Humanities. Reifel retired from Congress in 1971, but returned briefly to public service as the last Commissioner of Indian Affairs in 1976. His own dual heritage provided his success throughout his career as he continuously promoted intercultural understanding. After a lifetime of public service, Reifel died on January 2, 1990, in Sioux Falls.

SOURCES:

Books

Biographical Dictionary of Indians of the Americas, Newport Beach, California, American Indian Publishers, 1983; 403-406.
Biographical Directory of the United States Congress 1774-1989, Washington D.C., U.S. Government Printing Office, 1989; 1705.
Fielder, Mildred, *Sioux Indian Leaders,* Seattle, Superior Publishing, 1975; 127-148, 155.
Indians of Today, edited by Marion Gridley, Chicago, ICFP, 1971; 2-4.
Native North American Almanac, edited by Duane Champagne, Detroit, Gale Research, 1994; 1142-1143.
Painter, John S., "Transitional Sioux Leader: Benjamin Reifel", in *South Dakota Leaders,* edited by Herbert T. Hoover and Larry J. Zimmerman, Vermillion, University of South Dakota Press, 1989; 331-354.
Paulson, T. Emogene, *Sioux Collections,* Vermillion, University of South Dakota, 1982; 131-132.
Paulson, T. Emogene, and Lloyd R. Moses, *Who's Who Among the Sioux,* Vermillion, Institute of Indian Studies, University of South Dakota, 1988; 196-197.
Reader's Encyclopedia of the American West, edited by Howard R. Lamar, New York, Crowell, 1977; 1008.

Periodicals

Giago, Doris, "U.S.'s First Indian Congressman Dies," *Argus Leader* (Sioux Falls, South Dakota), January 3, 1990; A1-2.
Hunhoff, Bernie, "Ben Reifel on Bridging the Culture Gap," *South Dakota,* 4:5, 1989; 11-14.
"Straight Shooter Reifel's Mark in History Will Grow," *Argus Leader* (Sioux Falls, South Dakota), January 6, 1990; 8A.
Trahant, Mark, "Reifel Proved Indian, White Cultures Can Come Together, Find Harmony," *Argus Leader* (Sioux Falls, South Dakota), January 28, 1990; C3.
Young, Steve, "'Hero' Reifel Buried," *Argus Leader* (Sioux Falls, South Dakota), January 7, 1990; C1.

—Sketch by Karen P. Zimmerman

Carter Revard

1931-

Osage poet and professor
Also known as Nompehwahthe

Carter Revard, an inheritor of Osage traditions, is a recognized authority on the literature of the Middle Ages; he is also a poet who combines aspects of all the traditions he has mastered. Revard grew up in Pawhuska, Oklahoma. His great grandmother spoke only Osage and could remember when the tribe had come from Kansas into Oklahoma in the 1870s. His grandmother, who still cooked the traditional foods, had been put into a convent school at the age of ten and learned a little English while she was there. Revard has recordings of his grandmother's Osage-accented speech and when he writes about Native American subjects, he listens to the pitch and cadence of her talk to find his rhythms.

Early Years

Revard attended a one-room school at Buck Creek under a single teacher, who soon discovered his writing talents. Still proud of having won the school spelling contest when he was only in the third grade, Revard reminisces about the country school he and his twin sister attended daily, and from which they graduated as valedictorian and salutatorian at the age of 13. They earned $9 a month during these Depression years by serving as janitors. After eight grades together in a single room, the shock of attending high school in Bartlesville with more than 3,000 students was considerable. In the afternoons, Revard cleaned dog kennels, and groomed and fed the greyhounds. He also had to rise at 4:30 every morning to run the dogs three to five miles before school. On weekends, he took them to the races.

Revard entered college with the idea of pursuing a career in engineering. He got into the University of Tulsa through a radio show called *Going to College,* and won a Rhodes scholarship to Oxford University where he studied English literature. Before he left for England, a naming ceremony was held in September of 1952 in the Pawhuska Legion Hall, followed by feasting, dancing, and a hand game. He was given John Joseph Mathews' *Talking to the Moon,* signed by all the guests. Mathews had attended Merton College (as did Revard) in Oxford before returning to the family mansion beside the Osage Agency to write his books. Revard took his Ph.D. at Yale, after which he taught in Amherst until 1961, when he moved to St. Louis. He lived in the top half of the house once owned by Mabel Loomis Todd where Emily Dickinson's poems had lain in a camphor chest. It was at this time that he began to suffer from otosclerosis which, eventually required him to wear hearing aids.

One night, during a thunderstorm, he recalled how at the age of 14 he had hidden in a coyote cave from another storm. Thinking of how much more acute coyotes' ears were than human ones, and how well they sing, led him to compose a sonnet, which became the opening poem in *Ponca War Dancers.* Once he had used coyote's voice he was able to write about the Osage and felt, finally, that he had recovered the sound of Oklahoma. The line, "The storm made music when it changed my world" is especially meaningful to him because he was initiated into the Thunder clan, and thunder is considered one of the forces of transformation. That sonnet liberated him from the strict forms in which he had been trained at Oxford and Yale, and enabled him to sound less literary.

Family and Traditions Figure in His Work

Revard's poems are distinguished by their narrative line and their mythic resonances, and they are often inspired by Osage traditions. "Dancing with Dinosaurs," written for the naming ceremony of a young girl in 1979, exemplifies both his sense of story and his sense of ceremonial cycles. The girl's grandparents had taught him the gourd dances so that he could join the St. Louis Gourd Dancers. According to the Osage creation myth, people came from the stars and made their bodies from birds. In commemoration of these origins, they donned feathers and danced the seasons into being, just as birds migrate, fleeing winter, seeking spring. To Revard, the survival of Native Americans is as miraculous as the transformation of dinosaurs into winged beings; therefore, the poem celebrates the ability of a species to rescue itself from extinction.

Revard has a large extended family from which he gleaned a world of stories; and his family often figures in his work. The poem, "Ponca War Dancers," tells the story of his uncle Gus McDonald, the athlete with a warrior's presence who introduced fancy wardancing to the powwow circuit. He had been trained to become a traditional leader, having fasted and sought a vision. His sister, Aunt Jewel, makes her presence felt in his 1993 book, *An Eagle Nation,* and is one of the characters in his short story, "Never Quite a Hollywood Star." The poem, "How the Songs Came Down" is about the Ponca song she sang them to sleep with when they were children. It was a strongheart song to drive out fear and encourage warriors. In the title poem of this collection, Aunt Jewel says "Kahgay" [brother] to a caged eagle who makes a shrill response to her. Revard's many cousins also figure in his work. He and his twin sister stayed with them on the Ponca reservation for some time, just as those cousins spent months with them on the Osage reservation. And to each of his uncles, he has fashioned a "giveaway talk," which is the speech at the end of a dance when gifts are distributed during which the good feelings for that person are articulated to the assembled crowd, affirming the bonds of kinship. Revard considers his poems, which honor a relative or esteemed elder, to be such public affirmations.

Inspired by the birds that nested and sang around his boyhood home, Revard fills his work with references to birds. In the memoir, "Walking Among the Stars," he lists them: "If there are so many birds in the poems that come to me ... [it is because] our trees were where the orchard orioles, robins, turtledoves, scissortails, bluebirds, kingbirds, dickcissels came to perch." He pities urban children who have only television for diversion, instead of mockingbirds, shrikes, indigo bunting, flickers, and sapsuckers to entertain them. Therefore, he has made his muses from these "Okie" singers that trilled in the Osage Hills. He has mythicized his meadowlarks.

Revard has been a professor of medieval literature since 1961 at Washington University in St. Louis. The campus is situated on the grounds of the great St. Louis Exposition where Geronimo had been exhibited in chains for tourists. In March of 1973, Revard went to Wounded Knee in support of his cousin, Carter Augustus Camp, one of the national leaders of the American Indian Movement (AIM), who had become a spokesman of the occupation. Through his cousin, he learned much during the protests of the 1970s; and with his cousin, he is collaborating on a history of AIM.

SELECTED WRITINGS BY REVARD:

My Right Hand Don't Leave Me No More, Eedin Press, 1970.
Ponca War Dancers, Norman, Oklahoma, Point Riders Press, 1980.
"Walking Among the Stars," in *I Tell You Now: Autobiographical Essays by Native American Writers,* edited by Brian Swann and Arnold Krupat, Lincoln, University of Nebraska Press, 1987.
Cowboys and Indians, Christmas Shopping, Norman, Oklahoma, Point Riders Press, 1992.
An Eagle Nation, Tucson, University of Arizona Press, 1993.

SOURCES:

Revard, Carter, "Something That Stays Alive," in *Survival This Way: Interviews with American Indian Poets,* edited by Joseph Bruchac, Tucson, University of Arizona Press, 1987.
Revard, Carter, "Walking Among the Stars," in *I Tell You Now: Autobiographical Essays by Native American Writers,* edited by Brian Swann and Arnold Krupat, Lincoln, University of Nebraska Press, 1987.

—Sketch by Ruth Rosenberg

Everett Ronald Rhoades

Everett Ronald Rhoades
1931-
Kiowa physician, administrator, and educator
Also known as Dau-ahlm-gya-toyah ["One Who Makes a Quest for Healing Power"]

Everett Ronald Rhoades was the first person from the Kiowa Tribe of Oklahoma to receive a medical doctorate degree. He worked to improve Native American health care as director of the Indian Health Service, and received many honors for his distinguished service. Rhoades was born in Lawton, Oklahoma, to Lee J. Rhoades (of European descent) and Dorothy Rowell Rhoades (Kiowa). After graduating from Elgin High School in Oklahoma, he attended Lafayette College in Easton, Pennsylvania, under the Zeta Psi Indian Scholarship. Rhoades also received the John Hay Whitney Opportunity Fellowship, and he entered the School of Medicine at the University of Oklahoma in 1952 and graduated with his M.D. degree (Phi Beta Kappa, Alpha Omega Alpha, and Sigma Xi) in 1956. Rhoades specialized in internal medicine during residency training and then specialized in health administration and infectious disease. He is considered an authority in his field. He married Bernadine H. Toyebo (Kiowa) in 1953 and they have five children.

Rhoades joined the U.S. Air Force in 1957 and worked at the University of Oklahoma Medical Center through the Air Force Institute of Technology until 1961. He was then promoted and served as chief of the infectious disease section at Wilford Hall USAF Hospital at Lackland Air Force Base through 1966. He was promoted to major in 1964. Rhoades worked as area consultant in infectious disease and internal medicine to the USAF Surgeon General from 1965 until his discharge in 1966.

After leaving the Air Force, Rhoades returned to the University of Oklahoma as associate professor of medicine and assistant professor of microbiology, and later became professor of medicine and adjunct professor of microbiology and chief of infectious disease. He was also chief of infectious disease at the Veterans Administration Medical Center in Oklahoma City until 1982.

Becomes Director of Indian Health Service

Rhoades was commissioned rear admiral for the U.S. Public Health Service (USPHS) in 1982 and became the director of Indian Health Service (IHS) and assistant surgeon general until he retired in 1993. As director of Indian Health Service, Rhoades oversaw the health care for nearly 1.5 million Native Americans and Alaska Natives in 50 hospitals and several hundred clinics throughout the United States. He worked with a budget of up to $1.85 billion and employed almost 14,000 people around the country. Ten hospitals and 12 ambulatory centers were built during his directorship. Under his direction, the IHS established many programs to improve health care, including preventative disease programs, cancer prevention and detection, and a chronic diseases center. During Rhoades' tenure, the IHS also established a national adolescent alcohol and substance abuse prevention and treatment program, mandated a smoke-free environment in all clinical and administrative areas, established the first clinical fellowship in community injury control, created a national child protection team, and initiated the country's leading fetal alcohol syndrome program.

Rhoades then became associate dean of community affairs and adjunct professor of medicine at the University of Oklahoma School of Medicine, as well as adjunct professor of international health and director of education initiatives at the Center for American Indian and Alaska Native Health at Johns Hopkins University. He has written prolifically throughout the years and has been published in numerous medical journals and books in his field of medicine and on Native American life. Rhoades has received many honors, including the Public Health Service Distinguished Service Medal in 1991, the Surgeon General's Medallion and the President's Council on Physical Fitness Recognition Award in 1992, and the Indian Health Service first St. Martin-Beaumont Award in 1993.

Since 1967, Rhoades had been involved in the Kiowa community as a member of the Kiowa Tribal Council, the Kiowa Tribal Business Committee, and the Kiowa Tribal Land Management Committee. He is also a member of the Kiowa Gourd Clan and the Kiowa Blacklegging Society, and he dances at powwows. He was the founder and donor of the Dorothy Rowell Rhoades award to an outstanding graduating Indian student of Elgin High School, established in 1968. In the early 1970s, he was the primary force in the establishment of the Association of American Indian Physicians, and the United Tribes of Western Oklahoma and Kansas, and was a founding member of the Oklahoma City Urban Indian Health Program. Rhoades has been a speaker on a local and national level for hundreds of presentations to civic, academic, scientific, and government organizations on various topics, including infectious disease, history, public health, Indian health, and the delivery of health care.

SOURCES:

Books

Biographical Dictionary of Indians of the Americas, Newport Beach, California, American Indian Publishers, 1991; 609.

Native North American Almanac, edited by Duane Champagne, Detroit, Gale Research, 1994; 1043.

Reference Encyclopedia of the American Indian, fifth edition, edited by Barry T. Klein, West Nyack, New York, Todd Publications, 1992; 988-989.

—*Sketch by Phyllis "Picturestone" Noah*

John Rollin Ridge
1827-1867
Cherokee poet, editor, journalist, and author
Also known as Chees-quat-a-law-ny ["Yellow Bird"]

As noted Oklahoma historian Edward Everett Dale said in *Chronicles of Oklahoma,* "There is no more picturesque and romantic figure in all the annals of the Cherokee people than that of John Rollin Ridge, poet, scholar, adventurer, argonaut, journalist and man of letters." After he witnessed the assassination of his father when he was 12, Ridge fled to Arkansas with his family, was educated in the East, and made his name in California as an author and editor. He never returned to the Cherokee Nation. Shortly before Ridge's death at age 39, his uncle Stand Watie named him a delegate from the Southern Cherokees to treaty negotiations in Washington, D.C. He took part in the talks and then returned to California, where he died of "brain fever" in October 1867.

Ridge, either three-eighths or one-half Cherokee (accounts vary), was born in the Cherokee Nation East on March 19, 1827. This area, soon to be part of Georgia (near the city of Rome), was home to many of the Ridges and their relatives. His father, John Ridge, and grandfather, Major Ridge, were outstanding and prosperous Cherokee citizens and tribal leaders of the time. Ridge's mother was Sarah Bird Northrup of Connecticut. She had married John Ridge when he attended the Cornwall Indian School in Connecticut. His parents' marriage "was opposed by both families and so scandalized the Yankee 'do-gooders' that they soon closed their Indian school," Ridge wrote in an essay published in *A Trumpet of Our Own.*

Both Ridge's father and grandfather were active in Cherokee politics and in the acculturation of the tribe with white society. They were key members of the "Treaty Party," which believed that the Cherokee land in Georgia

John Rollin Ridge

should be sold to the U.S. government and that the Cherokees should be voluntarily, peacefully relocated to new lands west of the Mississippi. They believed that resistance to leaving Georgia would prove devastating to the Cherokees, both individually and collectively as a nation. The "Ross Party," led by Cherokee principal chief John Ross, on the other hand, believed that negotiation with the federal government and use of the U.S. court system would allow the Cherokees to stay in what was left of their ancestral lands. In accordance with this majority position, Major Ridge was the author of legislation providing that any Cherokee who sold or bargained away tribal land would be guilty of a capital offense against the tribe. Notwithstanding this, Major Ridge and John Ridge, along with their relatives Elias Boudinot and Stand Watie, signed the Treaty of New Echota in 1835. The treaty led to the death of many Cherokees during relocation along the Trail of Tears, and most of its signers were assassinated in the Cherokee Nation West on June 22, 1839. The murders, never solved, were attributed to followers of John Ross.

Ridge witnessed his father's murder when he was 12. The scene and its story haunted him for the rest of his life and he told it whenever possible. His father was dragged from the house and stabbed to death by armed men. His mother took the children and fled to Fayetteville, Arkansas, some 50 miles away, but out of the Cherokee Nation. In 1841 Ridge was sent east to Great Barrington School in Massachusetts. This was not successful, however, and he returned to Arkansas, where he worked with the missionary Cephas Washburn. Ridge flourished under this tutelage and enjoyed studying the classics.

In 1847, before Ridge was 23, he married Elizabeth Wilson and they had one daughter, Alice Bird Ridge (Beatty). Ridge always had a quick temper and a strong desire for revenge against the Ross faction. Ridge claimed to be actively involved in the guerilla warfare between the Ross and the Ridge factions in the late 1840s. When he shot and killed David Kell, a Ross follower and local judge, in May 1849, he fled to Missouri (leaving his wife and daughter in Arkansas) rather than risk a trial in the Ross-controlled Cherokee Nation—even though it was widely thought that the dead man had been assigned to kill Ridge and the intended victim had merely gotten the advantage over him. Ridge's thirst for revenge is revealed in his correspondence of the time. For example, in a letter to his uncle, Stand Watie, he says "The feeling here is that of indignation against the Ross party. They would be glad to have every one of them massacred."

Sought His Fortune in California

Ridge had seen the estates and fortunes of his father and grandfather depleted, and he himself was never prosperous financially. He decided to go to California in an effort to seek his fortune. This move was probably endorsed (and possibly financed) by his mother and grandmother, who did not want him to return to the Cherokee Nation because he would have faced trial for the Kell murder. Gold had been discovered in California, and Ridge knew he could earn a living with his pen or his hands, or both. He set out with his brother Aeneas and their black slave Wacooli on the "Northern route" to California. Their trip was full of hardships, but they arrived in California in August 1950. Ridge went to Yuba City, where he tried trapping, trading, and mining. Lacking much success in these, he became deputy clerk, auditor, and recorder for the county. He moved to Shasta City in late 1851, and his wife and daughter joined him in 1852, the year he wrote his famous poem "Mount Shasta." Critics in California considered it one of his best.

Ridge spent his time in California in various pursuits before he turned to editing and part ownership of a newspaper. During his residence in California he made his home at Marysville, Weaverville, Red Bluff, Sacramento, San Francisco, and Grass Valley. In 1854, he published his one book-length work, *The Life and Adventures of Joaquin Murietta.* Ridge apparently realized no financial gain from the book, telling people that the publishing house failed. He continued to write poetry and articles for whichever newspaper he worked for or owned at the time. He was the first editor of the *Sacramento Bee,* which was started in February 1857 and was still published in 1994. In 1857 he edited the *California Express,* and in August of 1858 he left the *Express* for part ownership and editorship of the *Daily National Democrat.* In the period preceding the Civil War, he was outspoken against secession. In 1861, Ridge became the political editor of the *San Francisco Herald,* where he supported Douglas against Lincoln in the presidential race. In 1863, he founded the *Trinity National,* after moving to Weaverville in Trinity County. His last move was to Grass Valley, where in June 1864 he bought a quarter interest in the *Grass Valley National.*

Represented Cherokee Interests in Washington, D.C.

Following the American Civil War, delegations from the Five Civilized Tribes went to Washington, D.C., to negotiate new treaties. The Cherokees had split during the war, with John Ross heading the group supporting the Union and Stand Watie heading the group supporting the Confederacy. Watie had been, according to most accounts, the last Confederate general to surrender. The Confederate Cherokees were not optimistic about the coming negotiations and, to make matters worse, the Cherokees sent two delegations to Washington. Ridge was asked by his uncle to be a part of the Southern group. Their aim was to divide Cherokee country into two nations, so that Confederate sympathizers would have their own territory and government. The delegation was composed of Ridge's cousin Elias Cornelius Boudinot, Stand Watie and his son Saladin Watie, William Penn Adair, Richard Fields, Joseph Absolom Scales, and Ridge. During the negotiations, Ridge quarreled bitterly with Boudinot, the Cherokees' former representative to the Confederate Congress at Richmond, and this family feud was in part responsible for the failure of their mission. The U.S. government at last recognized the Northern delegation as the one to represent the Cherokee Nation, which remained undivided. This was the only Cherokee work Ridge ever undertook after leaving the nation as a young adult. He stated many times that he longed to return to his own people, even at the risk of facing trial on the earlier murder charge, but it was not to be.

Ridge returned to California and died within a year, on October 5, 1867. He is buried in California, next to his wife and daughter, in Green Wood Cemetery near Grass Valley. Ridge combined the heart and soul of a poet and writer with the brooding dream of killing John Ross—the overriding thought of revenge which rendered his mind "darkened with a perpetual shadow." Although Ridge stated several times that he wanted to use his pen on behalf of his people, his only real efforts in that direction came in 1862, when he produced a three-part series on the American Indian for the *Hesperian,* a southern California women's periodical.

SOURCES:

Books

Biographical Dictionary of Indians of the Americas, second edition, Newport Beach, California, American Indian Publishers, 1991.
Cherokee Cavaliers: Forty Years of Cherokee History as Told in the Correspondence of the Ridge-Watie-Boudinot Family, edited by Edward Everett Dale and Gaston Litton, Norman, University of Oklahoma Press, 1939.
Dictionary of American Biography, edited by John A. Garraty, New York, Charles Scribner's Sons, 1951.
Dockstader, Frederick J., *Great North American Indians,* New York, Van Nostrand Reinhold, 1977.
Native North American Almanac, edited by Duane Champagne, Detroit, Gale Research, 1994.
Parins, James, *John Rollin Ridge: His Life and Works,* Lincoln, University of Nebraska Press, 1991; 3, 32, 105.

Reference Encyclopedia of the American Indian, fifth edition, edited by Barry T. Klein, West Nyack, New York, Todd Publications, 1990.
Starr, Emmet, *Old Cherokee Families: "Old Families and Their Genealogy,"* Norman, University of Oklahoma Foundation, 1972; 381, 473.
A Trumpet of Our Own: Yellow Bird's Essays on the North American Indian, Selections from the Writings of the Noted Cherokee Author John Rollin Ridge, edited by David Farmer and Rennard Strickland, San Francisco, Book Club of California, 1981; 15f.
Waldman, Carl, *Who Was Who in Native American History,* New York, Facts on File, 1990.
Wardell, Morris L., *A Political History of the Cherokee Nation, 1838-1907,* Norman, University of Oklahoma Press, 1977.
Wilkins, Thurmond, *Cherokee Tragedy: The Story of the Ridge Family and of the Decimation of a People,* New York, Macmillan, 1970.
Woodward, Grace Steele, *The Cherokees,* Norman, University of Oklahoma Press, 1963.

Periodicals

Dale, Edward Everett, "John Rollin Ridge," *Chronicles of Oklahoma,* 4:4, December 1926; 314.
Debo, Angie, "John Rollin Ridge," *Southwest Review,* 17:1, October 1931; 59-71.
Ellis, Clyde, "'Our Ill Fated Relative': John Rollin Ridge and the Cherokee People," *Chronicles of Oklahoma,* 67:4, winter 1990-1991; 376-395.
Foreman, Carolyn Thomas, "Edward W. Bushyhead and John Rollin Ridge, Cherokee Editors in California," *Chronicles of Oklahoma,* 14:3, September 1936; 299-311.
Ranck, M. A., "John Rollin Ridge in California," *Chronicles of Oklahoma,* 10:4, December 1932; 560-569.

—*Sketch by Philip H. Viles, Jr.*

Louis Riel
1844-1885
Métis resistance leader

Louis David Riel, Jr., was the leader of Métis resistance to the encroachment of English-speaking white settlers in Manitoba in the mid-1800s. Following the First Riel Rebellion, he drafted the Métis List of Rights and acted as president of the newly created nation Assiniboia. When white settlers and the Canadian government still refused to recognize Métis land rights, he led the unsuccessful Second Riel Rebellion. He was executed for high treason in 1885.

Riel was born in the Red River colony, in what is today part of metropolitan Winnipeg, Manitoba, the eldest of 11 chil-

Louis Riel

dren. Baptized "Louis Riel," he later added the name David. His father, Louis Riel Sr., was a Métis gristmill operator. His mother, the former Julie Lagimodiere, was a deeply religious Frenchwoman who had grown up in the West. Her early influence, and his Catholic education which began at age seven, formed the basis for Riel's deep religious convictions.

With a solid Catholic upbringing and education, Riel entered the seminary of the Gentlemen of St. Sulpice at Montreal College at the age of 14. There he excelled in English, French, Latin, Greek, and philosophy, as well as math and science. His father's death in 1864 caused Riel to become moody and withdrawn. He finally left the college in March 1865 without receiving a degree. Riel abandoned his dream of becoming a priest. He obtained a clerical position in a Montreal law firm and worked there for a year, intending to pursue a career in law.

Riel intended to marry a young Montreal woman with whom he had fallen in love, but her parents forbade the union. It is unclear if they objected on the grounds of his Métis heritage or his poverty—arguably it was both. In any event, he decided to abandon law and return to Red River, leaving Montreal in June of 1866. From 1866 to 1868, Riel worked a variety of odd jobs in Chicago and St. Paul, finally coming home to Red River in July 1868. Within a year he led the First Métis Rebellion, also called the First Riel Rebellion or the Red River Rebellion.

To understand the rebellions, it is important to first understand some background about the Métis. Métis is French for "mixed blood." When used with a capital letter it refers to a particular group of people who possess a distinc-

tive cultural heritage and ethnic self-identification. Their history dates back to the early seventeenth century when French fur traders came to the Canadian wilderness. Through casual relations with, and often marriage to Native American women, these traders cemented relations with the Native Americans and succeeded in the fur trade. The children of these unions were the Métis. The majority of these early Métis were French-Cree, but some were Scots-Cree. Many were also French-Ojibway, as in the case of the Riels. Caught between two very disparate worlds, the Métis often formed their own communities. These communities had roots in both the Native American and the French-Catholic traditions. By the nineteenth century the Métis of Manitoba had became a marked socio-political entity.

The First Rebellion and Exile

The First Riel Rebellion primarily involved land rights. In 1867, the Canadian colonies united and formed the newly independent Dominion of Canada. Two years later the Hudson's Bay Company sold its land holdings—known as Rupert's Land—to the new government. The government feared the intrusion of American Civil War veterans and so encouraged quick settlement.

In response to available new land and the government's call, people began streaming into the Red River area. Being Protestant Englishmen, prejudiced against French, Catholics, and Indians, they did not recognize Métis land rights. Prime Minister John MacDonald sent in surveyors to divide the land into 800 acre-square townships. This would destroy Métis property lines, traditionally laid out in strips that extended from the river, through woods, and then to fields. In October 1869, Riel and 16 others chased off the surveyors.

Meanwhile, William McDougall was on his way to Red River to assume the territorial governorship. He brought 300 rifles to form and arm a militia. Louis Riel organized the Comité National des Métis, an independent Métis government, and sent men to barricade the border. His army of 400 caught up with McDougall at Fort Garry near Winnipeg. After a bloodless takeover, Riel used the fort to establish his base. He then sent a List of Rights to the Prime Minister in Ottawa. Métis demands included land rights, freedom of language and religion, representation in the Canadian government, and prior consultation for any decisions pertaining to Red River country.

The central government initiated negotiations with the Métis. In the meantime, McDougall, acting on his own, recruited and armed a militia of Canada Firsters—annexationist members of the Canada Party. Discovering this, Riel's men forced the militia to surrender. By December, McDougall had returned to Ottawa. Riel declared the Comité a provisional government and named the Red River area Assiniboia.

Riel was elected to the presidency of Assiniboia, although he was only 25 years old. He declared a state of amnesty and released all prisoners. One of the released, Thomas Scott, a Canada Firster, plotted an attack on Fort Garry. The Métis army captured him and brought him back to Fort Garry. In a subsequent trial, a jury of seven Métis sentenced Scott to death for attempted murder. Scott's execution turned eastern public sentiment, with the exception of Québec, against Riel.

By terms of the Manitoba Act of 1870, Assiniboia entered the Canadian confederacy as part of Manitoba. The central government guaranteed most of the Métis List of Rights, but did not offer amnesty for Scott's execution or other actions during the rebellion. Riel, however, continued to oppose the settlement. When troops were dispatched to control the inflammatory situation, he fled. Riel went from one Métis settlement to another, in Canada and the United States, during this period. In that time, the Métis twice elected him as their representative to Parliament. However, he never assumed the office.

In 1875 the Prime Minister pardoned Riel for his part in the rebellion. However, the conditions of the pardon stipulated that he remain in the United States for five more years. He returned to Canada from 1876 to 1878, spending most of this time under an assumed name in two mental institutions in Québec. Upon his release, Riel returned to the United States and became a citizen. He eventually found his way to Montana where he married a Métis woman, Marguerite Bellehumeur, and settled down to teach Native American children at a Jesuit mission.

The Second Rebellion, Trial, and Death

While Riel forged a new life for himself in the United States, white Protestants continued to violate the Manitoba Act and settle Métis lands. Having lost much of what they fought for, many Métis moved west to the Saskatchewan River. The railroad was not far behind. By the 1880s white settlers were moving into the Saskatchewan River area and once again ignoring Métis rights. Once again the Métis sought Riel's help.

It was in Montana that famed horseman and hunter Gabriel Dumont found Riel in June 1884 and asked him to once again come to defend the rights of the Métis. Riel agreed on the condition that the rebellion not be a violent one. On his return to Canada, Riel formed the Provisional Government of Saskatchewan, drafted a bill of rights, and organized the Métis into a cavalry force of 300. When the government ignored their appeals, Riel approved a campaign of sabotage. The Métis occupied government lands, cut telegraph wires, and took hostages. They also demanded the surrender of Fort Carlton.

Against Riel's wishes, the situation escalated and became violent. On March 26, 1885, at Duck Lake, Dumont's men defeated a band of Royal Canadian Mounties. Sympathetic Crees, sensing a possible Métis success, joined in the fight. On March 28 Poundmaker's band attacked Battleford, and on April 2 Big Bear raided Frog Lake. The Canadian government responded by sending 8,000 troops to the region.

On April 24, Dumont's men routed General Frederick Middleton's column at Fish Creek. That same day, Colonel William Otter's forces retook Battleford, then turned their attentions to the Cree camp on Cut Knife Creek. The tide began to turn for the Métis. On May 9 government troops routed the Métis at Batoche. After four days the Métis surrendered, having suffered 16 dead and 30 wounded.

Riel surrendered after the disaster at Batoche, knowing he faced prosecution for treason and for Thomas Scott's murder 15 years prior. He hoped his trial would become such a public spectacle that it would embarrass the Canadian government and they would set him free. Unfortunately, Riel was wrong. While his lawyers tried to plead insanity, even bringing in doctors to testify to that effect, Riel refused as a matter of pride. The six-man jury found him guilty of high treason and the judge sentenced him to death. He repeatedly appealed his sentence, but in vain. He was hanged on November 16, 1885, at Regina, Northwest Territories, the site of his trial. To this day, Riel remains a hero to the Métis and his fate a divisive issue between French and English-speaking Canada.

SOURCES:

Davidson, William McCartney, *Louis Riel,* 1844-1885; a Biography, Calgary, Alberta, Albertan Publishing Company, 1955.

The Diaries of Louis Riel, edited by Thomas Flanagan, Edmonton, Alberta, Hurtig Publishers, 1976.

Flanagan, Thomas, *Louis "David" Riel: "Prophet of the New World,"* Toronto, University of Toronto Press, 1979.

Giraud, Marcel, *The Métis in the Canadian West,* translated by George Woodcock, Lincoln, University of Nebraska Press, 1986.

Images of Louis Riel in Canadian Culture, edited by Ramon Hathorn and Patrick Holland, Lewiston, New York, Edwin Mellon Press, 1992.

MacEwan, Grant, *Métis Makers of History,* Saskatoon, Saskatchewan, Western Producer Prairie Books, 1981.

Native People, Native Lands: Canadian Indians, Inuit and Métis, edited by Bruce Alden Cox, Ottawa, Carleton University Press, 1987.

Sprague, D. N., *Canada and the Métis,* 1869-1885, Waterloo, Ontario, Wilfrid Laurier University Press, 1988.

—Sketch by Tina Weil

David Risling
1921-
Hoopa, Yurok, and Karok educator

David Risling, a Native American of Hoopa, Karok, and Yurok heritage, and a former director and professor of Native American studies at the University of California-Davis, has been generally regarded as one of the nation's most influential and effective leaders in the field of Native American education, legal rights, and economic advancement. In addition to championing Native American causes through his pioneering work in the field of Native American Studies at U-C Davis, Risling helped to create and manage numerous state and national organizations dedicated to promoting and protecting Native American legal, economic, and social interests. In 1992, he was awarded the U-C Davis Distinguished Public Service Award for his tireless commitment to various Native American educational and social programs both on the U-C Davis campus and throughout the nation.

Risling was born on April 10, 1921 in Weitchpec, California, where he grew up on the Hoopa Indian Reservation in Humboldt County. After completing his secondary education, Risling entered California State Polytechnic University. His progress towards a degree, however, was slowed by a period of military service during World War II. After serving as a lieutenant commander in the Naval Reserves from 1943 to 1946, he returned to the university, where he received his bachelor of science degree the following year. Risling is believed to have been the first American Indian from California to have graduated from a university. In preparation for a career in academia, he continued his studies at California State, earning a master of arts degree in 1953.

In 1970, Risling officially entered the field of higher education as a lecturer and director of a Native American studies program at U-C Davis, with the goal of preserving the heritage and culture of Native peoples and preparing Native American students for life in American society. As the leader of one of the pioneering programs in Native American studies, Risling published the influential *Handbook of Native American Studies*, which provided a model for other universities and colleges to follow in establishing Native American studies programs. Risling also helped to found D-Q University, a junior college located in Davis, California, in dedication to the progress of Native American and Chicano people. As the chairman of the board of directors at D-Q, a position he held during the formative years of the college in the 1970s, he published *The Establishment of D-Q University*, a book recording the events of the college's founding and early development.

While Risling's career as an educator was primarily defined by his 20 years at U-C Davis, he has exercised his influence in various types of community service efforts, working as a consultant on programs involving vocational and Native American education, as well as community development and management. In 1968, for instance, he joined the California Indian Association, serving as its president for his first two years of membership. From 1970 until 1977, Risling was elected to the board of the National Indian Education Association. Other national Native American run organizations in which he has taken a leadership role include the Association on American Indian Affairs and the Native American Rights Fund. Throughout his career, Risling is credited with helping to form more than seven state and national associations, all of which are managed by Native Americans.

Throughout Risling's career as an educator and administrator, he has attempted to assist Native Americans by encouraging them to cultivate skills and develop solutions to problems that have not been remedied by the government. According to a *Native Nevadan* profile, "An underlying principle of Risling's efforts has been to guide Native Americans toward self-determination, autonomy and mutual assistance in these areas by encouraging them to chart their own course, independent of the actions, or inactions, of mainstream political institutions." Risling's practical philosophy of self-reliance has provided encouragement for those wishing to jettison the often unsuccessful bureaucratic solutions to Native legal and economic problems.

A year after retiring from his position at U-C Davis in 1991, Risling was honored with the U-C Davis Distinguished Public Service Award. Established in 1990 by university administrators as a means for recognizing substantial contributions to the community, state, nation, and world, the award—which included a $1000 honorarium—served as a tribute to Risling's dedication to Native American education in both the public and private sectors. Although no longer affiliated with the university, Risling continues to travel throughout the Americas visiting Native peoples of many different tribes in an effort to expand his own knowledge of Native heritage and culture while fostering the preservation of these traditions for future generations.

SELECTED WRITINGS BY RISLING:

Handbook of Native American Studies, University of California-Davis, 1970.

The Establishment of D-Q University, Davis, California, D-Q University, 1972.

Parliamentary Procedure, Hints for Successful Meetings, University of California-Davis, 1974.

SOURCES:

Books

Reference Encyclopedia of the American Indian, edited by Barry Klein, New York, Todd Publications, 1978.

Periodicals

"Risling Wins Distinguished Service Award," *Native Nevadan,* May 31, 1992; 13.

—Sketch by Jason Gallman

Will Rogers
1879-1935
Cherokee entertainer and humorist

Will Rogers was America's preeminent humorist during the first three decades of the twentieth century. He

Will Rogers

began his entertainment career as a Wild West show trick rider and roper but easily and successfully made the transition into other venues, including the stage, silent and sound films, the after-dinner speaking and lecturing circuit, nonfiction writing, and radio broadcasts. His down-home style and wit appealed to audiences of all types. Rogers' trademarks were his ever-present mouthful of gum, his unmistakable drawl, and his easygoing demeanor.

Born on November 4, 1879, on the family ranch near Oolagah, Indian Territory (now Oklahoma), Rogers was the last of eight children of Clement Vann Rogers, a former Confederate army officer, rancher, banker, and leader in Cherokee affairs, and his wife, Mary America Schrimsher. His parents named him William Penn Adair Rogers after his father's Civil War comrade in arms and friend. Rogers proudly proclaimed throughout his life that he was an Oklahoma cowboy and one-quarter Cherokee Indian. "My ancestors didn't come on the Mayflower but they met the boat," he was quoted as saying in *Will Rogers: His Life and Times.*

Rogers attended the local one-room Drumgoole School for a while, but was such a restless student that his parents enrolled him in Harrell International Institute in Muskogee, Oklahoma. Harrell was a girls' boarding school that his sister Mary attended. Until the school's president suggested he be removed, Will went to class with the president's son. He then spent four years at Willie Halsell College, a private boarding academy in Vinita, Oklahoma. Next he attended Scarritt Collegiate Institute in Neasho, Missouri, but his passion for roping led to his expulsion.

At yet another school, Kemper Military Academy in Booneville, Missouri (where his father hoped he would finally settle down), he earned 150 demerits. After a two-year stay at Kemper, the 18-year-old Rogers quit school for good to travel and work. Though he never graduated, he had roughly the equivalent of a high school education.

Rogers always liked doing riding and roping tricks more than anything else. He went on his first roundup when he was just a toddler and learned to throw a rope from Uncle Dan Walker, a black cowboy, before he was five. Rogers won his first prize in a roping contest on July 4, 1899, in Claremore, Oklahoma, the place he always called "home." He entered roping contests whenever he could, picking up tricks from his competitors, and he continued to practice his repertoire of fantastic rope stunts throughout his life.

Launched Career as Actor and Entertainer

After leaving school, Rogers worked on cattle drives and managed his father's ranch until he decided to make his way to Argentina. In 1901 he sold his father the herd he had been given and set off. This trip was his first one around the world and marked the beginning of his entertainment career. His travels eventually landed him in South Africa, where he tended cattle for a couple of months before joining Texas Jack's Wild West Show in 1902. Rogers started as a trick rider in the show, but soon his rope act earned him the billing "The Cherokee Kid—The Man Who Can Lasso the Tail Off a Blowfly." Texas Jack reportedly gave him some advice that he followed throughout his professional life: get off the stage before the audience has had enough. For eight months in 1903, Rogers, billed as "The Mexican Rope Artist," toured with a circus in New Zealand and Australia before returning home, having traveled 50,000 miles in two years.

Rogers was home only a few weeks before performing in St. Louis in Colonel Zach Mulhall's Wild West Show at a fair and a burlesque house. In 1905 he made his New York debut in Madison Square Garden and even garnered newspaper coverage when he roped a wild steer that went up to the balcony. He broke into vaudeville the same year at Hammerstein's Roof Garden in New York City. His act consisted of riding his pony, Teddy (clad in felt-bottom boots buckled like galoshes), onto the stage and doing a variety of rope tricks to soft orchestra music.

Between 1905 and 1916, Rogers worked regularly without becoming a headliner. During the same period, he also married his longtime, long-distance sweetheart, Betty Blake, and they had three of their four children. Rogers' career began to develop when he started talking while doing tricks, more because of his delivery and superb timing than any particular jokes; he would concentrate on his lassoing, then make an impromptu remark half to himself. He was on the verge of being fired from a vaudeville show that was a property of Florenz Ziegfeld, Jr., when he followed his wife's suggestion and started using newspaper stories as a source for his humorous topical comments. His voracious newspaper reading made it possible for him to produce enough new material for three daily performances, which he prefaced with: "Well, all I know is what I read in the papers." (He later used the same phrase in his newspaper column.) Known as "the columnist of the theatre," Rogers found over the years that the more serious the situation, the more the audiences laughed at his parody. In 1916 he joined the Ziegfeld Follies and appeared in several editions of the show until 1924.

Rogers' entertainment career extended beyond the vaudeville stage. He opened in his first Broadway musical, *The Wall Street Girl,* in 1912. He went on to perform in many legitimate stage successes in the United States and England. Rogers maintained a strong sense of public decency in his acting career, later giving up his role in a California production of Eugene O'Neill's *Ah, Wilderness!* (1932) when a Pasadena clergyman wrote him that he had been embarrassed when he took his 14-year-old daughter to a performance.

In 1918 Rogers appeared in his first motion picture, a silent film titled *Laughing Bill Hyde.* After signing a two-year contract with Sam Goldfish (later known as Samuel Goldwyn), he moved his family from New York to California. During the same period, he made weekly shorts for Pathé, a film distributor, that were a takeoff on "The Literary Digest Topics of the Day." Called "The Illiterate Digest," the clips consisted of Rogers' comments on the daily headlines, flashed on the screen along with his picture.

By 1929 Rogers had made the transition to talkies, starring in his first sound movie, *They Had to See Paris.* Rogers was one actor who benefited from the advent of talking movies; they allowed him to showcase his on-stage persona and play himself. In all, he appeared in 17 motion pictures, including *A Connecticut Yankee* (1931), *David Harum* (1934), and *Steamboat 'Round the Bend* (1935). He was probably the highest paid actor of his time, and he was definitely one of the best loved. His name showed up on several "most popular actor" lists, and he headed the *Motion Picture Herald's* Top Ten box office stars list in 1934.

In 1921 Rogers formed a company to write, produce, direct, and star in his own films. Pathé distributed the company's three films, none of which was a financial success. (One was called *The Ropin' Fool,* in which he performed 53 rope tricks, ranging from simple to nearly impossible.) On the brink of bankruptcy, Rogers returned to the New York stage. Soon he added public speaking to his entertainment repertoire, sometimes speaking at as many as four luncheon and dinner meetings a week. Rogers usually began his speeches by startling or insulting his audience. His manager billed him as "America's Greatest Humorist."

Rogers made his first radio broadcast in 1926. Beginning in 1930, he gave a series of popular weekly broadcasts. At first he had trouble fitting his comments to the radio program's time requirements: he was used to timing his act to the response he was receiving from his audience (and following Texas Jack's advice to get off while they wanted more). His solution was an alarm clock; when it rang, he stopped talking.

Became a Columnist and Commentator

Rogers' stage, film, broadcasting, writing, and commentating careers overlapped considerably. In 1920, then widely known as a theatrical performer and movie actor, he wrote a series of articles for the *Los Angeles Record* about the Republican and Democratic conventions. Although asked to run for legitimate public office, he never did. *Life* magazine persuaded him to accept the Anti-Bunk Party's presidential nomination in 1924. He ran his campaign through columns and articles in the magazine. The party's platform was "Whatever the other fellow don't do, we will." When "candidate" Rogers was in a rollover plane accident in Kansas City, he quipped he was "the first candidate to land on his head, and being a candidate, it didn't hurt the head." By 1928 he was a recognized commentator on political conventions.

Earlier, in 1922, Rogers started writing a weekly humorous newspaper column for the *New York Times.* Syndicated by the McNaught Newspaper Syndicate, the column appeared in America's Sunday papers until his death more than a dozen years later. Through the years, the column evolved from staccato to longer anecdotes and fewer punchy gags, but it always conveyed his tone of voice and personality. Without the help of gag writers or researchers, Rogers wrote more than 2 million words over his career. He is said to have been the most widely read—with an estimated 20 million readers—and frequently quoted newspaper columnist of his time.

After two years, Rogers collected his favorite newspaper columns for publication in *The Illiterate Digest* (1924)—the same title he had used for his weekly film shorts several years earlier. The well-received book prompted reviewers to recognize him as "The Cowboy Philosopher," an "everyman" who skillfully articulated the feelings of the average American. The targets of his nonpartisan epigrams included the U.S. government, American business, and world disarmament.

The *Saturday Evening Post* sent Rogers to Europe in 1926 to cover a conference. The resulting series of articles was later published in book form as *Letters of a Self-Made Diplomat to His President.* (After his trip he actually visited and "reported to" President Calvin Coolidge.) In addition, Rogers sent a daily telegram to the *New York Times* while he was in Europe. The telegrams became a syndicated daily wire, "Will Rogers Says." An excursion to Russia during the same trip provided material for the book *There's Not a Bathing Suit in Russia* (1927). He later drew on his 1929 gallstone operation for the witty collection *Ether and Me.* Although he was quite ill for a few months, he only missed writing one daily telegram message.

Will Rogers, the Humanitarian

From early in his entertainment career, Rogers expressed concern for victims of misfortune, donating both his earnings and talents to charitable causes. He pledged ten percent of his 1918 salary to the American Red Cross and gave the organization $100 per week for the duration of World War I. As his popularity increased rapidly in the late 1920s, the press gave generous coverage to his continued humanitarian activities. In 1927 he toured the then-devastated Mississippi flood areas, gave benefit performances for the victims, and testified in favor of flood relief before Congress. During the 1930s Rogers toured areas ravaged by a Central American earthquake and gave benefits for the homeless.

Aside from donating his own funds to the needy during the Great Depression, Rogers appeared at many benefit performances for relief and charitable organizations, raising money for (and the hopes of) thousands of heartsick Americans. He also was an advocate of relief for farmers and the unemployed. In 1933 he donated his earnings from a series of radio broadcasts to the American Red Cross and Salvation Army for unemployment relief.

Death of An Aviation Booster

Rogers was an early booster of air travel and safety and often flew around the country to his engagements. (He visited every state of the Union and traveled around the world three times.) Rogers flew with most of the outstanding aviators of the time. When he could not take a commercial flight, he would catch a ride on an airplane carrying the U.S. mail, weighing himself outfitted in flight gear and paying the equivalent sum as if he were a package. Rogers was in several plane crashes during his career. The third crash, which occurred in Chicago in 1929, left all of his ribs fractured.

In 1935 Rogers and his fellow Oklahoman Wiley Post set off for what Rogers called "a vacation." It probably would have been a flight to the former Soviet Union via Alaska if fate had not intervened. A world aviation record holder, Post had given his historic airplane to the Smithsonian Institution. For the Arctic trip, which Rogers was financing, Post piloted a craft assembled from parts of more than one airplane model. Though certified as airworthy, the plane was hard to control in some situations because of heaviness in the nose and the wrong-sized pontoons. On August 15, Post and Rogers stopped on Walakpa lagoon near Point Barrow, Alaska, to ask some Eskimos fishing there for directions to that outpost. Shortly after they took off for their destination, their airplane lost power and nosedived into the water, splitting apart and killing them both instantly. The last word Rogers typed on his typewriter was "death." Betty Rogers is said to have learned of her husband's death in Connecticut where their daughter, Mary, was starring in the play *Ceiling Zero*, about a young woman whose father dies in an airplane accident.

Rogers died at the pinnacle of his career, having joined the ranks of such contemporary American heroes as aviator Charles Lindbergh and baseball great Babe Ruth. Paradoxically, his death fulfilled something he once wrote: "This thing of being a hero, about the main thing to it is to know when to die. Prolonged life has ruined more men than it ever made." He died at the age of 55.

Never before had the nation and the world mourned the passing of a mass-media personality as they did when Rogers died. The *New York Times* dedicated four full pages to him; general newspaper and radio coverage lasted for a week. In his memory, the nation's movie theaters were darkened; CBS and NBC television stations observed a half-hour of silence; and in New York, a squadron of planes, each towing a long black streamer, flew over the city in final tribute to the hero and friend of aviation.

Originally buried in California, Will Rogers' body was moved in 1944 to a gravesite beside that of his wife and their fourth child, Fred, who had died of diphtheria as an infant. The tomb sits in the garden of the Will Rogers Memorial at Claremore, Oklahoma. His chosen epitaph was one of his favorite sayings, "I never met a man I didn't like." In the 1990s Rogers' legend lives on in the Tony award-winning musical *Will Rogers Follies* and in various advertising mentions. Much of his wisdom remains pertinent because it addressed the fundamental human condition in a timeless, simple way.

SELECTED WRITINGS BY ROGERS:

Rogers-isms: The Cowboy Philosopher on the Peace Conference, New York, Harper, 1919.
Rogers-isms: The Cowboy Philosopher on Prohibition, New York, Harper, 1919.
The Illiterate Digest, New York, A & C Boni, 1924.
Letters of a Self-Made Diplomat to His President, New York, A & C Boni, 1926.
There's Not a Bathing Suit in Russia, New York, A & C Boni, 1927.
Ether and Me, New York, Putnam, 1929.
Twelve Radio Talks Delivered by Will Rogers during the Spring of 1930, New York, E. R. Squibb & Sons, 1930.
The Autobiography of Will Rogers, edited by Donald Day, Rogers Company, 1949.
Sanity Is Where You Find It, edited by Donald Day, Boston, Houghton Mifflin, 1955.

SOURCES:

Alworth, Paul E., *Will Rogers,* New York, Twayne, 1974.
Dictionary of Literary Biography, Volume 11: American Humorists, 1800-1950, Detroit, Gale Research, 1982; 404-09.
Dockstader, Fredrick J., *Great North American Indians,* New York, Van Nostrand Reinhold Company, 1977; 243-45.
Ketchum, Richard M., *Will Rogers: His Life and Times,* New York, American Heritage Publishing, 1973.
Rogers, Will, *The Autobiography of Will Rogers,* edited by Donald Day, Rogers Company, 1949.
Sterling, Bryan B., and Frances N. Sterling, *Will Rogers' World: America's Foremost Political Humorist Comments on the Twenties and Thirties—and Eighties and Nineties,* New York, M. Evans, 1989.

The Will Rogers Scrapbook, edited by Bryan B. Sterling, New York, Grosset & Dunlap, 1976.

Yagoda, Ben, *Will Rogers: A Biography,* New York, Knopf, 1993.

—*Sketch by Doris Morris Maxfield*

Roman Nose (right)

Roman Nose
1830(?)-1868
Cheyenne tribal leader
Also known as Bat, Woquini, and Wo o hki nih'

Roman Nose was a prominent southern Cheyenne warrior best remembered for his key role in the ongoing battle against white advancement in the West throughout the 1860s. During this time, white railroad builders, gold seekers, buffalo hunters, and politicians invaded the Kansas-Nebraska-Colorado frontier, which was homeland to the southern Cheyenne and Arapaho peoples. Roman Nose's bold tactics and seemingly impenetrable demeanor made him something of a legend in the Native American conflicts with white settlers; he became a virtual epic hero, riding on horseback, his flowing feathered medicine hat topped by a lone buffalo horn, which in battle resembled an eagle's beak. Some observers equate his death at Beecher's Island on September 17, 1868, to the final conquest of the Old West.

Not much information is available on Roman Nose's early life, but scholars generally agree that he was born around 1830 in the Great Plains region of the United States. After more than 200 years of fighting, the white invasion and destruction of Native American territories had reached its final phase. Scandals like the notorious Sand Creek Massacre—the 1864 annihilation of southern Cheyenne villagers, including women and children, by U.S. troops—marred President Abraham Lincoln's attempts to quell hostilities and brought cross-cultural tensions to a boiling point. By that time, Roman Nose was the most renowned warrior of the Crooked Lances, one of several American Indian war societies composed of embittered Indians who raided the settlements of their white enemies in the nation's heartland.

The Magic of the War Bonnet

In battle Roman Nose would always strike first and draw enemy fire. He had an unflinching faith in the protective power of the war bonnet given to him by an old medicine man named White Bull. Roman Nose believed that as long as he wore the bonnet and adhered to a strict set of rules of conduct, he would possess a hypnotic power over his enemies and be immune to bullets. The strong belief in the supernatural among Native Americans stems from a cultural worldview—one that centers on balance and justice, the conservation of energy, and the notions of reciprocity and retribution.

On July 24, 1865, at Platte Bridge, Nebraska, Roman Nose led a huge Cheyenne-Sioux expedition that annihilated an entire U.S. cavalry column. However, his inability to draw troops out of a nearby stockade disappointed him. Another noted warrior, High Backed Wolf, died in this fight; according to legend, he forgot White Bull's warning to touch no metal to his lips and, while reloading his six-gun, held a bullet in his mouth. Roman Nose's brother Left Hand also died in the same battle.

A Slim Chance for Peace

In Roman Nose's famous fight on Powder River in September of 1865, the protective magic of his war bonnet held. His pony was shot from under him, yet he survived unscathed. To draw fire from U.S. soldiers, Roman Nose is said to have galloped repeatedly up and down their line while his warriors encircled them. With few firearms, the Indians could neither break the line nor lure them out. Nonetheless, the army withdrew for a full year while Roman Nose raged against the westward expansion of railroads and stagelines: "We will not have the wagons which make a noise in the hunting grounds of the buffalo," the warrior is said to have declared, according to T. C. McLuhan's *Touch the Earth: A Self-Portrait of Indian Existence.* "If the pale-faces come farther into our land, there will be scalps of your brethren in the wigwams of the Cheyennes."

In late 1866 in Dakota Territory, a Native American attack destroyed an entire army command, with only nine U.S. veterans offering serious resistance. Roman Nose fought in this fray where Sioux and Cheyenne warriors acquired blue greatcoats and modern guns from among the 81 dead soldiers. Variously reported as displaying a Spencer repeating rifle and a huge Henry buffalo gun, which he waved over his head like a lance, he was rarely seen to fire his rifle because he usually lacked ammunition.

In the spring of 1867, Roman Nose met with General Winfield Scott Hancock, a pompous Gettysburg hero who arrived at Fort Larned, Kansas, with 1,400 men, including George A. Custer's new Seventh Cavalry. As indicated in Thomas B. Marquis' *Keep the Last Bullet for Yourself,* the Seventh Cavalry was specifically charged with "clearing the central and southern parts of the western Plains of those Indians who had been harassing white settlers."

The Cheyenne nation had become increasingly combative toward federal government troops. The whites had invaded their land, killed their people through war and disease, and virtually destroyed their culture. Killing Hancock would have made Roman Nose the biggest man on the Plains; sparing him transformed Roman Nose from a warlord to a distinguished leader of his people. But subsequent acts of violence by Hancock and other U.S. military leaders against the Native American people shattered any hope of a lasting peace.

Roman Nose later played a major role in the devastating attack on Captain G. A. Armes' Tenth Cavalry. In October of 1867, after an uneasy peace was declared, Roman Nose was among the few prominent Cheyenne who refused to sign the Medicine Lodge Treaty. Journalist Henry Stanley called it a "mock treaty" and "a burning brand—a signal for war," never even read or explained to the Indians. Even as the chiefs were cajoled to sign it, they vowed not to give up their country "as long as the buffalo and elk are roaming."

The Cheyenne seethed at the government's reluctance to supply arms promised by the treaty for hunting. Disgruntled young warriors ravaged white settlements on the Saline and Solomon Rivers. The U.S. Army reported 99 civilians killed in 26 separate clashes over six weeks before the cavalry closed in. To draw out the Cheyenne fighters, a 50-man command of scouts was sent into action under Major George Alexander Forsythe at Beecher's Island, Colorado. Roman Nose was among those who died in the battle.

Death at Beecher's Island

According to eyewitness accounts included by George Bird Grinnell in his book *The Fighting Cheyennes,* Roman Nose arrived at the battleground late on the first day of the conflict with a troublesome dilemma: "At the Sioux camp the other day something was done that I was told must not be done. The bread I ate was taken out of the frying pan with [a fork]. I have been told not to eat anything so treated. This is what keeps me from making a charge. If I go into this fight, I shall certainly be killed." In *The Cheyennes: Indians of the Great Plains,* E. Adamson Hoebel explained that one taboo associated with Roman Nose's magical war bonnet was that he could not eat food served with a pointed iron untensil. "The psychological association is clear. As the pointed implement pierces the food, so will a pointed metal bullet pierce the flesh."

Pressured by other Indians to lead his men into battle, Roman Nose was unable to complete a long purification rite to counteract the damage done by eating the pierced bread. He reportedly donned his warpaint and the war bonnet he no longer trusted to protect him, mounted his horse, and galloped toward the shooting. Many Indians followed. Before they could charge, two scouts hidden in the tall grass fired from such close range that Roman Nose's horse nearly trampled them. Roman Nose died of the wounds he sustained in that first day of battle at Beecher's Island.

SOURCES:

Brady, Cyrus T., *Indian Fights and Fighters,* originally published in 1904, Lincoln, University of Nebraska Press, 1971.

Brandon, William, *American Heritage Book of Indians,* Bonanza Books, 1982.

Brown, Dee, *Bury My Heart at Wounded Knee,* New York, Holt, Rinehart and Winston, 1970.

Grinnell, George Bird, *The Fighting Cheyennes,* New York, Charles Scribner's Sons, 1915.

Hoebel, E. Adamson, *The Cheyennes: Indians of the Great Plains,* New York, Holt, Rinehart and Winston, 1970.

Hoig, Stan, *The Battle of the Washita: The Sheridan-Custer Indian Campaign of 1867-69,* New York, University of Nebraska Press, 1976.

Llewellyn, Karl N., and E. Adamson Hoebel, *The Cheyenne Way: Conflict and Case Law in Primitive Jurisprudence,* Norman, University of Oklahoma Press, 1941.

Marquis, Thomas B., *Keep the Last Bullet for Yourself: The True Story of Custer's Last Stand,* Algonac, Michigan, Reference Publications, 1976.

Mooney, James, *The Ghost-Dance Religion and Wounded Knee,* Washington, D.C., U.S. Government Printing Office, 1896.

The Reader's Encyclopedia of the American West, edited by Howard R. Lamar, New York, Harper & Row, 1977.

Touch the Earth: A Self-Portrait of Indian Existence, edited by T. C. McLuhan, New York, Promontory Press, 1971.

Waldman, Carl, *Atlas of the North American Indian,* New York, Facts on File, 1985.

—Sketch by Steven Edwin Conliff

Wendy Rose
1948-
Hopi/Miwok poet, artist, and educator
Also known as Bronwen Elizabeth Edwards and Chiron Khanshandel

Wendy Rose is a major contributor to American poetry. She has published ten collections of poems, and her

Wendy Rose

poetry, essays, reviews, and autobiographical writings have appeared in many periodicals and anthologies. Rose is also a visual artist whose watercolors and pen-and-ink drawings illustrate her own and other authors' books. Rose's academic and teaching work has focused on social sciences; since 1984 she has been coordinator of the American Indian studies program at Fresno City College.

Rose was born Bronwen Elizabeth Edwards in Oakland, California. She grew up in the San Francisco Bay area with her mother, her older brother, and her mother's husband. Her childhood during the 1950s and 1960s was tumultuous; she dropped out of high school, and as a teenager on her own became connected with some of the bohemian artistic circles in San Francisco. Her earliest poems date to this period.

Early Publications and Academic Study

From 1966 through 1980 Rose was enrolled at various times in Cabrillo and Contra Costa Junior Colleges and the University of California at Berkeley. In 1978 she received a Master of Arts degree in cultural anthropology and went on to complete coursework for a Ph.D. in anthropology. During this period she published five volumes of poetry, including her first major collection, *Lost Copper*. The 1960s and 1970s also saw major rights movements among Native Americans. One of the most visible actions was the protracted occupation of Alcatraz Island by Indians from many tribes seeking to create a new community and awaken the consciousness of fellow citizens. Rose's first collection, *Hopi Roadrunner Dancing*, contains several poems alluding to this event. "Oh My People

I Remember," for instance, describes the gathering of people as the fulfillment of a sacred dream vision. Other poems in this volume reflect Rose's ongoing search for personal, cultural, and ethnic identity. "Oh Father" is dedicated to her father and ends with the question, "oh father, who am I?" Another poem, "Newborn Woman, May 7, 1948," refers to the poet's birthdate and recreates the birth experience of a strong, vocal girl child into an "already alien world."

Many of the poems in Rose's early collections are concerned with the perceptions of anthropologists (and other scientists) versus the perceptions of the people whom the anthropologists are trying to study. The title of her third book, *Academic Squaw: Reports to the World from the Ivory Tower,* announces this as a major theme, which is then expanded in *Long Division: A Tribal History.* One of the poems frequently reprinted from Academic Squaw is untitled and begins "I expected my skin and my blood to ripen." A brief epigraph opens the poem; the note is taken from a publication called *Plains Indian Art Auction Catalog* and gives the prices of items stolen from the bodies of Lakota men, women, and children massacred in 1890 at Wounded Knee, South Dakota. The poem text that follows is spoken in the voice of one of the murdered women. The speaker recalls with chilling understatement what it was like to have her infant taken away and bayoneted and then to be killed, stripped, and dismembered. This poem introduces a characteristic structure in Rose's poems. She frequently opens a poem with an explanatory note or fragment of text from a journalistic or scholarly source. The body of the poem that follows then functions as a second voice, creating a dialogue between the persona speaking in the poem and the voice of the opening text. Poems like "I expected ..." and "Three Thousand Dollar Death Song" from *Long Division* make use of this method to create an intensely ironic, deeply felt sense of sorrow and outrage.

In *Lost Copper,* Rose's first retrospective collection, it is possible to identify important themes that pervade all of her work. One of these major themes is identification with the earth. The "Frontispoem" to *Lost Copper* strongly evokes this identification. The persona speaking in the poem tells of tending fields with a bone-handled spade and remarks how the dust remains on her hands. Eventually the persona describes rolling like a horse on the earth, seeking to "grow from the ground that bears me." Almost every poem in the collection contains some expression of oneness, identity, and love of the earth.

Builder Kachina, a 12-page chapbook containing four poems, is included in *Lost Copper.* This short series of poems explores another pervasive theme in Rose's poetry: her search for ancestry, roots, and family connection. The title page carries the explanatory note: "Journey from the land of my mother in California to the land of my father in Arizona, August, 1977," and each poem is identified with a point on the itinerary from the San Joaquin Valley in California to the Hopi village of Hotevilla, Arizona. While publishing her poems and illustrating her own books and those of others, Rose was also completing academic coursework and research. One project was a monograph, *Aboriginal Tat-*

tooing in California, which was published at the University of California at Berkeley.

Marriage, Teaching, Further Publications

In 1976, after having been married briefly some years earlier, Rose married magician and judo instructor Arthur Murata. They lived in the Bay Area while Rose attended the University of California at Berkeley, later teaching there and at Contra Costa College in San Pablo. In 1983 Rose took a permanent position with the Native American studies program at Fresno State University in Fresno, California, and, in 1984, at Fresno City College. Rose and Murata live in the foothills of the Sierra Nevada mountains, near Yosemite National Park. One of Rose's abiding interests is her plant and reptile collections; as early as her first publication she described herself as an "amateur herpetologist." A garage converted into a greenhouse contains her extensive collection of euphorbias, cactuses, and other tropical plants, as well as several rare lizards.

Before moving to Fresno, Rose published *What Happened When the Hopi Hit New York.* The vision of different landscapes is a strong theme throughout *What Happened.* Several poems describe landscapes as seen from airplanes or on brief stopovers, such as Alaska, Denver, Iowa City, and New Orleans. Another series in the collection centers on the urban scene of Brooklyn. "Subway Graffiti, An Anthropologist's Impressions" incorporates the cryptic messages scrawled on subway surfaces and offers a personal view of the speaker's responses to and speculations about the origins of the anonymous messages.

Two subsequent books, *The Halfbreed Chronicles & Other Poems* and *Going To War with All My Relations,* contain some of Rose's strongest poems. The "Halfbreed Chronicles" poems frequently make use of the dialogue form of note-plus-poem as seen earlier. They reach out to embrace individuals from many places, historical eras, and backgrounds who have suffered injustice and misunderstanding, including: Truganinny, a Tasmanian woman whose body was displayed in museums; Julia Pastrana, a woman exhibited in a freak show; and an anonymous Salvadoran mother describing a massacre. A more overtly political statement emerges in *Going To War with All My Relations.* Rose notes in the preface to this collection that the poems are "a memoir of sorts" documenting "thirty years of observation and activity within the Fourth World (Indigenous Peoples) Movement." Some of these poems spring from observations of academic activities: excavation of a mission church where human bones were discovered embedded in the walls; conferences of scholars reporting on research among so-called primitive peoples; the insensitivity of educational bureaucracies. Other poems reflect isolated moments of personal insight, like "men talking in the donut shop," which relates the conversation of several workmen describing a husband shooting his wife. Rose has indicated that this book is one of her favorites among her work, expressing directly some of her most deeply held convictions.

Bone Dance: New and Selected Poems, 1965-1993 is Rose's second major retrospective collection. It contains poems from all her previous books as well as new poems, including some written early in Rose's poetic career but not previously published. Many of these poems explore perceptions of feminism and identity as woman. "Is It Crazy to Want to Unravel," for instance, expresses the sensations and feelings of a woman who feels her identity and sense of selfhood dissolving into nothing. Other poems derive from fantasy and science fiction, a longtime interest of Rose's that is also expressed in her color-pen drawings. The section of *Bone Dance* called "What the Mohawk Made the Hopi Say" continues a longstanding literary dialogue with Mohawk poet Maurice Kenny. The title poem alludes to Rose's acknowledgment that the New England and New York landscape does include mountains, although they are not as imposing as the Sierra and Rockies of the West.

In addition to writing, drawing and painting, teaching, research, and caring for her plants and animals, Rose has been consultant, editor, panelist, and advisor for many community and academic projects. She has given dozens of poetry readings, exhibited her art in the western states and on the East Coast, and has granted numerous interviews. Her prose publications include essays, reviews, and "Neon Scars," an autobiographical narrative. An important indication of her distinguished reputation is the number of anthologies of American and contemporary literature that include her work.

SELECTED WRITINGS BY ROSE:

Hopi Roadrunner Dancing, Greenfield Center, New York, Greenfield Review Press, 1973.
Long Division: A Tribal History, New York, Strawberry Press, 1976; expanded edition, 1981.
Academic Squaw: Reports to the World from the Ivory Tower, Marvin, South Dakota, Blue Cloud Press, 1977.
Builder Kachina: A Home-going Cycle, Marvin, South Dakota, Blue Cloud Press, 1979.
Aboriginal Tattooing in California, Berkeley, Archaeological Research Facility, University of California, 1979.
Lost Copper, Banning, California, Malki Museum Press, Morongo Indian Reservation, 1980.
What Happened When the Hopi Hit New York, New York, Contact II Publications, 1982.
The Halfbreed Chronicles & Other Poems, Los Angeles, West End Press, 1985.
"Neon Scars," in *I Tell You Now,* edited by Brian Swann and Arnold Krupat, Lincoln, University of Nebraska Press, 1987.
Going To War with All My Relations, Flagstaff, Arizona, Northland Publishers, 1993.
Bone Dance: New and Selected Poems, 1965-1992, Tucson, University of Arizona Press, 1994.

SOURCES:

Rose, Wendy, interview with Helen Jaskoski conducted April 30, 1994.

—Sketch by Helen Jaskoski

Sacagawea
1784(?)-1812(?)
Lehmi-Shoshone interpreter and guide
Also known as Boinaiv ["Grass Maiden"], Saca-
jawea ["Boat Launcher"], and Tsakakawia ["Bird
Woman"]

Sacagawea

Sacagawea was an interpreter and guide for and the only woman member of the Lewis and Clark Expedition of 1804-1806. She was born somewhere between 1784 and 1788 into the Lehmi band of the Shoshone Indians who lived in the eastern part of the Salmon River area of present-day central Idaho. Her father was chief of her village. Sacagawea's Shoshone name was Boinaiv, which means "Grass Maiden." The primary documentation of Sacagawea's life is contained in the journals of Meriwether Lewis and William Clark, a lawyer and a clerk of a fur trading company who led an expedition authorized by President Thomas Jefferson in 1803 to explore the recently purchased Louisiana Territory. In addition, the Shoshone Indians have many stories in their oral tradition about Sacagawea, and many living Shoshone trace their ancestry to her. Nevertheless, there is much controversy surrounding the life of this intrepid woman.

Captured by Hidatsa War Party

In 1800, when the Shoshone girl Boinaiv was about 12 years old, her band was camped at the Three Forks of the Missouri River in Montana, when they encountered some Hidatsa warriors. The warriors killed four men, four women and a number of boys. Several girls and boys, including Boinaiv, were captured and taken back to the Hidatsa village. At the Hidatsa camp, Boinaiv was given the name Sacagawea by her captors, which means "Bird Woman." There is more than a little argument over the derivation and spelling of her name. The *Original Journals of Lewis and Clark* support a Hidatsa origin. On May 20, 1805, Lewis wrote of "Sah-ca-ger-we-ah or Bird Woman's River" as a name for what is now Crooked Creek in north-central Montana. Another spelling of her name is often given as Saca-jawea, a name meaning "Boat Launcher" in Shoshone. Sometime between 1800 and 1804, Sacagawea and another girl were sold to (or won in a gambling match by) trader Toussaint Charbonneau, a French-Canadian who was residing among the Hidatsa. He eventually married both girls.

Joins the "Corps of Discovery"

In 1803, Jefferson and the U.S. Congress authorized a "Voyage of Discovery" by which a group of men would explore the territory between the Mississippi and Columbia Rivers and attempt to find a water route to the Pacific Ocean. Jefferson's secretary and confidante, Lewis, and Lewis' friend Clark were assigned to lead the corps of explorers. The expedition of some 45 men left St. Louis, Missouri, on May 14, 1804. They arrived at the Mandan and Hidatsa villages near the mouth of the Knife River in North Dakota on October 26, 1804. There, they built cabins in a clearing below the villages and settled in for the winter.

On November 4, 1804, Clark wrote in his journal: "A Mr. Chaubonie [Charbonneau] interpreter from the Gross Ventre nation came to see us ... this man wished to hire as an interpreter." Clark's field notes for the same day state that both Charbonneau and Sacagawea were hired: "a french man by name Chabonah who speaks the Big Belley language visited us, he wished to hire and informed us his 2 Squaws were Snake [Shoshone] Indians, we engaged him to go on with us and take one of his wives to interpret the Snake language." Lewis and Clark realized that they would need someone to help interpret and help secure supplies from the Shoshone when they passed through their territory. As it later turned out, the process of interpretation was a cumbersome matter. Sacagawea conversed with her husband in Gros Ventre. Charbonneau then passed on Sacagawea's words in French to another individual in the party who spoke French and English; that individual then relayed the information along to Lewis and Clark in English. Sacagawea also made extensive use of sign language, which many in the party could interpret.

At the time the party had come to the Mandan villages, Sacagawea was pregnant. Lewis duly noted in his journal the birth on February 11, 1805, of a "fine boy," although Sacagawea's "labor was tedious and the pain violent." The boy was named Jean Baptiste Charbonneau. Even with an infant, Sacagawea and her husband were hired as interpreters. On April 7, 1805, Sacagawea—carrying her infant in a cradleboard—accompanied the expedition out of the Mandan villages for the trek west. Clark listed among the 32 members of the party "my servant, York; George Drewyer, who acts as hunter and interpreter; Sharbonah and his Indian squaw to act as Interpreter & interpretess for the Snake Indians ... and Shabonah's infant."

Sacagawea quickly demonstrated her knowledge of edible plants along the course. Lewis wrote on April 9 that when the expedition stopped for dinner Sacagawea "busied herself in search for the wild artichokes.... This operation she performed by penetrating the earth with a sharp stick about some collection of driftwood. Her labors soon proved successful and she procured a good quantity of these roots." At many other points in the trip, Sacagawea gathered, stored, and prepared wild edibles for the party, especially a plentiful root called *Year-pah* by the Shoshones.

On May 14, the party encountered heavy winds near the Yellowstone River. Charbonneau was at the helm of the pirogue, or canoe, which held some supplies and valuables gathered during the expedition. Lewis noted that "it happened unfortunately for us this evening that Charbono was at the helm of this perogue...; Charbono cannot swim and is perhaps the most timid waterman in the world." Both Lewis and Clark were on shore and could only watch in horror at what occurred next. Clark wrote: "We proceeded on very well until about 6 o'clock. A squall of wind struck our sail broadside and turned the perogue nearly over, and in this situation the perogue remained until the sail was cut down in which time she nearly filled with water. The articles which floated out were nearly all caught by the squaw who was in the rear. This accident had like to have cost us dearly; for in this perogue were embarked our papers, instruments, books, medicine, a great proportion of our merchandise." Lewis noted in his journal: "The Indian woman, to whom I ascribe equal fortitude and resolution with any person on board at the time of the accident, caught and preserved most of the light articles which were washed overboard." About a week later, Lewis recorded that a recently discovered river was named in Sacagawea's honor, no doubt in recognition of her important service to the party. According to Lewis: "About five miles above the mouth of Shell river, a handsome river

of about fifty yards in width discharged itself into the Shell river on the starboard or upper side. This stream we called Sah-ca-ger-we-ah or 'Bird Woman's river,' after our interpreter, the Snake woman."

On June 10, Sacagawea became ill and remained so for the next several days. This event is discussed at length in the journals of both Lewis and Clark, who were extremely concerned for her welfare. Both took turns tending to her. On June 16, Clark wrote that Sacagawea was "very bad and will take no medicine whatever until her husband, finding her out of her senses, easily prevailed upon her to take medicine. If she dies it will be the fault of her husband." Lewis wrote that Sacagawea's illness "gave me some concern as well for the poor object herself, then with a young child in her arms, as from the consideration of her being our only dependence for a friendly negotiation with the Snake [Shoshone] Indians on whom we depend for horses to assist us in our portage from the Missouri to the Columbia River." Sacagawea recovered from this illness, but a few days later, on June 29, she, her infant son, Charbonneau, and the servant York nearly drowned in a flash flood. Fortunately, Clark hurried the group to safer ground and all were spared.

Reunion with the Shoshones

On July 30, 1805, the party passed the spot on the Three Forks of the Missouri where Sacagawea was taken from her people some five years previously. A little over one week later, at Beaverhead Rock, Sacagawea recognized her homeland and notified the expedition that the Shoshones had to be near. On August 13, Lewis took an advance party on ahead to find and meet the Shoshones while Clark remained behind with Sacagawea and the rest of the group. The next day, Charbonneau was observed by Clark on two occasions to strike his wife, for which Clark severely reprimanded him.

On August 17, Clark, Sacagawea, and the rest of the party came upon Lewis who had met the Lehmi-Shoshone chief Cameahwait. Clark described what happened: "I saw at a distance several Indians on horseback coming towards me. The interpreter and squaw, who were before me at some distance, danced for the joyful sight, and she made signs to me that they were her nation." The Biddle edition of the journals of Lewis and Clark notes that Sacagawea was sent for to interpret between Lewis and Clark and Cameahwait: "She came into the tent, sat down, and was beginning to interpret, when in the person of Cameahwait she recognized her brother; she instantly jumped up and ran and embraced him, throwing over him her blanket and weeping profusely...; after some conversation between them she resumed her seat, and attempted to interpret for us, but her new situation seemed to overpower her, and she was frequently interrupted by tears." Sacagawea learned that her only surviving family were two brothers and a son of her eldest sister, whom she immediately adopted. She also met the Shoshone man to whom she had been promised as a child; however, he was no longer interested in her because she had borne a child with another man. While among her people, Sacagawea helped to secure horses, supplies, and Shoshone guides to assist in the expedition's trip across the Rocky Mountains.

Leaving her adopted son in the care of her brother Cameahwait, Sacagawea and the rest of the party traveled on, eventually following the Snake River to its junction with the Columbia, and on toward the Pacific Ocean. On October 13, 1805, Clark again commented on the value of having Sacagawea as a member of the expedition: "The wife of Shabono our interpreter we find reconciles all the Indians as to our friendly intentions a woman with a party of men is a token of peace." In November 1805, a lead party from the expedition reached the ocean. Having heard that this group had discovered a beached whale, Sacagawea insisted that Lewis and Clark take her to see the ocean. Lewis wrote on January 6, 1805: "The Indian woman was very importunate to be permitted to go, and was therefore indulged; she observed that she had traveled a long way with us to see the great waters, and that now that monstrous fish was also to be seen, she thought it very bad she could not be permitted to see either."

When the party separated on the return trip in order to explore various routes, Sacagawea joined Clark, directing him through the territory of her people, pointing out edible berries and roots, and suggesting that Clark take the Bozeman Pass to rejoin the other members at the junction of the Yellowstone and Missouri rivers. Clark noted on July 13, 1806, that "The Indian woman, who has been of great service to me as a pilot through this country, recommends a gap in the mountains more south which I shall cross."

Two days after the parties were rejoined, on August 14, 1806, the expedition arrived back at the Mandan villages. Here Charbonneau and Sacagawea decided to remain. Clark offered to adopt their son Jean Baptiste, whom he had affectionately called "Pomp" on the trip. They accepted Clark's offer for a later time after the infant was weaned. On the return trip to St. Louis, Clark wrote a letter to Charbonneau, inviting him to come live and work in St. Louis and commenting: "your woman, who accompanied you that long dangerous and fatiguing route to the Pacific Ocean and back, deserved a greater reward for her attention and services on that route than we had in our power to give her at the Mandans." While Charbonneau was paid for his services, Sacagawea, as his wife, received no financial remuneration separate from her husband.

Controversy Remains Over Sacagawea's Later Years

There is strong evidence to indicate that Sacagawea lived for only a few short years after parting ways with the Lewis and Clark expedition. It may be that Charbonneau accepted Clark's invitation to come to Missouri and farm land. On April 2, 1811, a lawyer and traveler named Henry Brackenridge was on a boat from St. Louis to the Mandan, Arikara, and Hidatsa villages of North and South Dakota. He noted in his journal for that day (cited in Ella E. Clark's and Margot Edmonds' *Sacagawea of the Lewis and Clark Expedition*): "We have on board a Frenchman named Charbonet, with his wife, an Indian woman of the Snake nation, both of whom had accompanied Lewis and Clark to the Pacific, and were of great service. The woman, a good creature, of a mild and gentle disposition, was greatly attached to the whites, whose manners and dress she tried to imitate; but she had become sickly, and longed to revisit her native country; her husband, also, who had spent many years amongst the Indians, was become weary of a civilized life."

It is believed by many scholars that Charbonneau and Sacagawea, having left their son Jean Baptiste with Clark to raise in St. Louis (Jean Baptiste later became a respected interpreter and mountain man) took their infant daughter named Lizette, and traveled to the Missouri Fur Company of Manuel Lisa in South Dakota. An employee of the fur company, John C. Luttig, recorded in his journal on December 20, 1812: "this Evening the Wife of Charbonneau, a Snake Squaw died of a putrid fever she was a good and the best Woman in the fort aged abt 25 years she left a fine infant girl." Sacagawea was buried in the grounds of the fort. In addition, William Clark published an account book for the period of 1825-1828, in which he listed the members of the expedition and whether they were then either living or dead. He recorded Sacagawea as deceased.

Another theory of Sacagawea's life, supported among others by an early biographer, Dr. Grace Hebard of the University of Wyoming, relates that Sacagawea actually left her husband, took her son Jean Baptiste and adopted son—named Bazil—and went to live with the Comanches. There she married a man named Jerk Meat and bore five more children. Later, Sacagawea returned to her homeland to live with her Shoshone people at what was now the Wind River Agency. She was called Porivo ("Chief") at Wind River and became an active tribal leader. She was reported by some Shoshones, Indian agents, and missionaries to have died at the age of about 100 in 1884 and to have been buried at Fort Washakie. Opponents of this theory argue that the woman who called herself Sacajawea was actually another Shoshone woman.

The Shoshones of Fort Washakie have started a project to document the descendants of Sacagawea. As of mid-1993, more than 400 Shoshones who can trace their ancestry to Sacagawea have been counted. Many among them believe that she indeed lived a long and full life.

From the time of her marriage, Sacagawea's life became inextricably bound to a group of Anglo explorers and their quest for westward expansion. In spite of separation from her people, illness, physical abuse from her spouse, and an infant to care for, Sacagawea made key contributions to the success of the Lewis and Clark Expedition. Her skills as an interpreter and as liaison between the Shoshone and the expedition, her knowledge of the flora and fauna and of the terrain along much of the route, and her common sense and good humor were key elements that contributed to the successful resolution of the journey.

Sacagawea has become one of the most memorialized women in American history. A bronze statue of her was exhibited during the centennial observance of the Lewis and Clark Expedition in St. Louis in 1904. Another statue was commissioned by a women's suffrage group in Oregon, with the unveiling set to coincide with the Lewis and Clark Centennial Exposition in Portland in 1905. Statues also reside in Idaho, Montana, North Dakota, Oklahoma, and Virginia. In addition to the river in Montana named for Sacagawea by Lewis and Clark, other memorials include three mountains, two lakes, and numerous markers, paintings, musical compositions, schools, and a museum.

SOURCES:

Books

Biographical Dictionary of Indians of the Americas, Volume 2, Newport Beach, California, American Indian Publishers, 1991; 642-647.

Clark, Ella E., and Margot Edmonds, *Sacagawea of the Lewis and Clark Expedition,* Berkeley, University of California Press, 1979.

Dictionary of American Biography, Volume 16, edited by Dumas Malone, New York, Scribner's, 1935; 278.

Dockstader, Frederick J., *Great North American Indians,* New York, Van Nostrand Reinhold, 1977; 248-249.

Dye, Eva Emery, *The Conquest: The True Story of Lewis and Clark,* Chicago, A. C. McClurg, 1902.

Hebard, Grace Raymond, Sacajawea: *A Guide and Interpreter of the Lewis and Clark Expedition, with an Account of the Travels of Toussaint Charbonneau, and of Jean Baptiste, the Expedition Papoose,* Glendale, California, Arthur H. Clark Company, 1933.

Howard, Harold P., *Sacajawea,* Norman, University of Oklahoma Press, 1971.

Letters of the Lewis and Clark Expedition, with Related Documents, 1783-1854, edited by Donald Jackson, Urbana, University of Illinois Press, 1962.

Lewis, Meriwether, and William Clark, *Original Journals of the Lewis and Clark Expedition, 1804-1806,* eight volumes, edited by Reuben Gold Thwaites, New York, Dodd, Mead, 1904-1905.

Lewis, Meriwether, William Clark, and Nicholas Biddle, *History of the Expedition Under the Command of Captains Lewis and Clark, to the Sources of the Missouri, Thence Across the Rocky Mountains and Down the River Columbia to the Pacific Ocean, Performed During the Years 1804-5-6, by Order of the Government of the United States,* three volumes, New York, A. S. Barnes, 1904.

Liberty's Women, edited by Robert McHenry, Springfield, Massachusetts, Merriam, 1980; 362-363.

Native American Women, edited by Gretchen M. Bataille, New York, Garland Publishing, 1993; 219-222.

Native North American Almanac, edited by Duane Champagne, Detroit, Gale Research, 1994; 1151.

Notable American Women, 1607-1950: A Biographical Dictionary, Volume 3, edited by Edward T. James, Cambridge, Harvard University Press, 1971; 218-219.

Reader's Encyclopedia of the American West, edited by Howard R. Lamar, New York, Crowell, 1977; 1055.

Reid, Russell, *Sakakawea: The Bird Woman,* Bismark, State Historical Society of North Dakota, 1986.

Remley, David, "Sacajawea of Myth and History," in *Women and Western American Literature,* edited by Helen Winter Stauffer and Susan J. Rosowski, Troy, New York, 1982; 70-89.

Ronda, James P., *Lewis and Clark among the Indians,* Lincoln, University of Nebraska Press, 1984.

Waldman, Carl, *Who Was Who in Native American History,* New York, Facts on File, 1990; 309-310.

Weatherford, Doris, *American Women's History,* New York, Prentice Hall, 1994; 303-304.

Periodicals

Anderson, Irving, "Probing the Riddle of the Bird Woman," *Montana, the Magazine of Western History,* 23, October 1973; 2-17.

Chuinard, E. G., "The Bird Woman: Purposeful Member of the Corps or Casual 'Tag-Along'?," *Montana, the Magazine of Western History,* 26, July 1976; 18-29.

Dawson, Jan C. *"Sacagawea: Pilot or Pioneer Mother?,"* *Pacific Northwest Quarterly,* 83, January 1992; 22-28.

Morrison, Joan, "Sacajawea's Legacy Traced," *Wind River News* 16, June 22, 1993; 4.

Schroer, Blanche, "Boat-Pusher or Bird Woman? Sacagawea or Sacajawea?," *Annals of Wyoming* 52, Spring 1980; 46-54.

—Sketch by Christina E. Carter

Buffy Sainte-Marie
1942(?)-
Cree singer, composer, actress, and activist

It is likely that the first awareness many contemporary non-Indian Americans had of Indian rights came to them through the lyrics of a Buffy Sainte-Marie song. A unique and versatile performer with an eye toward informing her audiences about the wrongs done to Native Americans, she is a highly respected spokesperson for indigenous people.

Early Life

Buffy Sainte-Marie, a full-blooded Cree, was born on February 20 in either 1941 or 1942 on the Piapot Reserve in Craven, Saskatchewan, Canada. She was orphaned in the first months of her life and adopted by Albert C. Sainte-Marie and Winifred Kendrick Sainte-Marie, a part-Micmac couple in Massachusetts, who had lost an infant daughter about her age. Beverly was nicknamed Buffy as a child. She learned Micmac stories from her mother and taught herself to play an old piano at the age of four. Later, she composed poems and set them to her own tunes and taught herself to play the guitar. Sainte-Marie credits the gift of her own gui-

Buffy Sainte-Marie

tar at 16 or 17 as a pivotal event in her life. She quickly mastered the instrument and more than 30 tunings, developing a distinctive style for her haunting songs about Native history and modern social concerns. While enrolled at the University of Massachusetts, she played at local coffee houses and clubs and drew large audiences, combining original compositions with folk and jazz favorites. She earned a B.A. in philosophy (with an emphasis on Oriental traditions) in 1963, and was named one of the top ten graduating seniors at the university that year.

A Folk Artist and Activist

Soon after graduation, Sainte-Marie moved to New York City's Greenwich Village which, as the center of the burgeoning folk culture in the 1960s, supported a creative explosion of music and poetry. Enthusiastically embraced by the movement, Sainte-Marie regularly appeared at such clubs as the Gaslight Cafe, the Bitter End and Gerde's Folk City. She signed with Vanguard Records, which released her first long-playing album, *It's My Way,* in 1964; and in 1965, she played Carnegie Hall. She possesses a unique singing style that includes traditional Native "vocables" (characteristic syllables without meaning that are repeated again and again) and the use of the Creek mouthbow. Praising Sainte-Marie's power to communicate, Irving Kolodin noted in a *Saturday Review* piece, "She can sing on, off, or around the pitch, as she chooses; her sense of phrasing is superb." With her riveting songs about Indian oppression, Sainte-Marie soon became an activist, using her music to relate the tragedies and triumphs of aboriginal North Americans. Her song "Now

That the Buffalo's Gone" is frequently cited as the first Indian protest song. Other Sainte-Marie compositions have met with both critical and popular acclaim; among the better known of these songs are "Until It's Time for You to Go" and "Up Where We Belong" (the Oscar-winning theme song, which she co-wrote with Jack Nitzche, for the film *An Officer and a Gentleman*). In the early 1970s, she wrote a song that is sometimes referred to as the theme song of the American Indian Movement (AIM), "Starwalker."

Although Sainte-Marie's early career focused on music, she was soon offered acting roles. She appeared on several television programs in the 1960s, including an important episode of "The Virginian" in which she insisted that all Indian roles be played by Indians. This episode, which also benefited from Sainte-Marie's assistance with the script, was highly praised for its authenticity. She narrated portions of the Oscar-award winning documentary *Broken Rainbow* about the Hopi-Navajo land dispute, and appeared as the Iroquois Clan mother/matriarch in Turner Entertainment's made-for-television movie, *The Broken Chain*. A frequent guest on the children's television series "Sesame Street," she has written for children (including the 1986 book, *Nokomis and the Magic Hat*), and for periodicals such as *Akwesasne Notes*. Never one to take herself too seriously, she has also done commercials for Ben and Jerry's ice cream.

Although performers are public people professionally, some are able to maintain relative privacy in their personal lives. Little is reliably known about Sainte-Marie's life offstage; however, in 1967, she married Dewain Kamaikalani Bugbee, a person of Hawaiian-American Indian-white ancestry; and it is believed that she has an adult son, Cody Starblanket. Her name has also been linked with composer-musician Jack Nitzche and actor Sheldon Peters Wolfchild. Sainte-Marie is best known, though, in her public persona.

Buffy Sainte-Marie continues to be an active voice in Indian affairs. She performs frequently to large audiences and has played at concerts in support of Leonard Peltier, the AIM activist and political prisoner who is currently serving two life sentences at Leavenworth Prison. She founded the Native North American Women's Association, which sponsors art and education projects, and instituted a scholarship fund, Nihewan Foundation, for Native Americans who wish to attend law school. Although her recording schedule has slowed, she remains a unique singer-songwriter with an international following.

SOURCES:

Books

Biographical Dictionary of Indians of the Americas, Newport Beach, California, American Indian Publications, 1983.
Biography Almanac, Detroit, Gale Research, 1981.
Native American Women, edited by Gretchen M. Bataille, New York, Garland Publishing, 1993.
Native North American Almanac, edited by Duane Champagne, Detroit, Gale Research, 1994.

Contemporary American Indian Leaders, edited by Marion Gridley, New York, Dodd, Mead, 1972.
Current Biography, New York, H. W. Wilson, 1969.
Vogel, Virgil, *This Country Was Ours,* New York, Harper and Row, 1972.

Periodicals

Kolodin, Irving, *Saturday Review,* November 11, 1968.

—*Sketch by Cynthia R. Kasee*

Ramona Sakiestewa
1949-
Hopi weaver

Ramona Sakiestewa is a contemporary fiber artist of the Southwest who dreams in color and pattern. Those dreams, translated into blankets, rugs, and tapestries, have brought her awards, important commissions, and a business of her own. Incorporating elements of ancient design and processes into modern weaving methods and techniques, she is creating new directions and new traditions in Native American arts.

Born at the former Albuquerque Indian Hospital and raised by her German/Irish mother in the city, Sakiestewa still felt a closeness to the heritage of her Hopi father. She always loved fabric, and even sewed doll clothes at age four. Her mother and stepfather were avid collectors of Native American art, and she worked with Indian art at an Albuquerque trading post. Especially interested in weaving, she studied books by two anthropologists, Ruth Underhill's *Pueblo Craft* and Kate Peck Kent's *Weaving of Cotton in the Prehistoric Southwestern United States.* Later in her life, she was able to work directly with Kent, and they became close friends. While still in high school, she taught herself to weave on the vertical loom.

In the late 1960s, Sakiestewa spent time in New York studying color and design at the School of Visual Arts. She became skilled at using the treadle loom and took a variety of short-term classes in Santa Fe. At first, weaving was just a hobby; she worked in arts administration and planned training programs for the Museum of New Mexico. She also helped establish ATLATL, a national Native American arts and cultural service organization. She married Arthur Sze, a poet, and had a son, Micah.

Combines the Contemporary with the Traditional

In 1975, Sakiestewa received her first commission from the Park Service at Bandelier National Monument in Los Alamos, New Mexico, to replicate an Anasazi turkey feather blanket like those found at archaeological sites there. Through study and research, she learned the process of fab-ricating yarn from plant fibers. She made one-of-a-kind rugs, using wool in its natural colors or hand-dyeing it with natural vegetable dyes. Becoming expert on the horizontal loom greatly increased her production, but her techniques remained linked to tradition. "My weaving comes out of Pueblo weaving," Sakiestewa told Betty Freudenheim in *American Craft.* "Unlike Renaissance and modern tapestries, mine are completely finished on both sides."

Patricia Harris enumerates the sources of Sakiestewa's designs in *Fiberarts* magazine: "architecture, natural landscape formations, the colors of the land and vegetation ... traditional Navajo and Pueblo tribal designs, patterns from tapestry, pottery and basketry, ceremonial dance movements." Often, the patterns and designs come to Sakiestewa in dreams. She told Freudenheim that she has extraordinary dreams, in "full color, like a Cecil B. DeMille movie." She began using fine wool yarn in 260 colors, imported from Sweden, and likes to see colors from different cultures, different eras. Always she uses intense colors and tries to get to the essence of particular color combinations.

She founded Sakiestewa Ltd., her own company, in 1982, a year after she began weaving full time. At first her products were strictly functional: floor rugs, upholstery fabrics, and pillows. Then she began producing one-of-a-kind rugs, with designs from historic textiles. By 1992 she had four looms, and with two part-time assistants working in a studio cottage next to her home, she was producing up to 30 tapestries a year. She sold her work at the annual Santa Fe Indian Market, at the Native American Arts show at the Heard Museum in Phoenix, and through Indian-oriented art galleries.

Receives Wright Commission

In 1989 Sakiestewa received a commission for a series of 13 tapestries from the Taliesen Foundation, to be based on the drawings of Frank Lloyd Wright. Their purpose was to support the Taliesen West traveling museum project. Many of her works are done in series; she often works on several series simultaneously. Each series develops from her experience, her observations, her heritage, or her multicultural studies. For example, the "Basket Dance" series emerges from early Southwestern basketry and textiles; the "Eastern Horizon" series uses astronomical configurations from Anasazi ruins; and the "Katsina" series is drawn from the many figures in the Hopi ceremonial calendar. From her experience in South America, she derived the "Kutij" series; her trip to Japan led to the "Tenryuji" series. In collaboration with Pendleton Woolen Mills of Oregon, she undertook the "Southwest Trails" blanket series to commemorate the historic trails of the Southwest.

An exhibit titled "Ramona Sakiestewa: Patterned Dreams" was held at the Wheelwright Museum of the American Indian in Santa Fe in 1989. Her tapestry was also included in a touring show, "Women of Sweetgrass, Cedar, and Sage," an exhibition of contemporary Native American women artists, sponsored by ATLATL. In 1991, 12 of her Wright tapestries were united in an exhibit in New Jersey. The thirteenth was touring with the "Wright Automatic House" traveling museum. "An appreciation of Sakiestewa's work,"

Suzanne Baizerman concluded in *Ramona Sakiestewa: Patterned Dreams,* "is linked to an understanding of the cultural and historical context of Southwest fiber arts." Her tapestries, rooted in her culture, filled with history, yet boldly contemporary, chart new directions in Native American art.

SOURCES:

Books

Baizerman, Suzanne, *Ramona Sakiestewa: Patterned Dreams: Textiles of the Southwest,* Santa Fe, Wheelwright Museum of Indian Art, 1989.
Native American Women, edited by Gretchen M. Bataille, New York, Garland Publishing, 1993; 225-226.

Periodicals

Colton, Mary R., "Ramona Sakiestewa: The Wright Commissions," *Shuttle, Spindle and Dyepot,* spring 1989; 17-19.
Freudenheim, Betty, "The Newark Museum, New Jersey Exhibit," *American Craft,* August/September 1991; 64-65.
Freudenheim, Betty, "A Dozen Tapestries Right from Wright," *New York Times,* April 11, 1991; C5.
Freudenheim, Betty, "Crafts: 'Ancient Ones' Inspire Hopis," *New York Times,* April 21, 1991; 11.
Harris, Patricia, and David Lyon, "The Tapestries of Ramona Sakiestewa: Patterned Dreams," *Fiberarts,* November/December 1990; 31-34.
Lindenfeld, Lore, "The Frank Lloyd Wright Tapestries: Themes and Variations," *Fiberarts,* September/October 1991; 61.
Miller, Bobbi, "Ramona Sakiestewa," *Shuttle, Spindle and Dyepot,* spring 1992; 34-37.
Pontellon, Jacqueline, "Modern Classic," *Southwest Art,* October 1991; 37.
Ruch, Teresa, "The Southwest Trail Blanket Project and Pendleton Woolen Mills," *Shuttle, Spindle and Dyepot,* spring 1992; 37.
Zimmer, William, "Art: Seeing through to the Past," *New York Times,* September 15, 1991; 12.

—Sketch by Blanche Cox Clegg

Samoset
1590(?)-1653(?)
Abenaki tribal leader
Also known as Captain John Somerset

The friendly Native American who welcomed the English to Massachusetts in March of 1621 was Samoset, a chief of the Abenaki (also spelled "Abnaki" or "Wabanaki,"

Samoset

meaning "People of the Eastern Dawn") at Pemaquid in southern Maine. Historical memory favors more turbulent characters than this gentleman leader, who, in the words of nineteenth-century Pequot minister William Apess, "was so good to the Pilgrims." The most-traveled diplomat of his generation, Samoset recognized that possibilities for mutual benefit lay in alliance with the Anglo-Americans. For more than 30 years he acted on his vision with shrewdness and courage. Samoset was the first chief to negotiate the treaties and land sales that enabled his nation to survive an era of plague, warfare, and slavery. New England's half-century of multiracial prosperity, finally broken by King Philip's War in 1675, has been held up by generations of patriotic writers to exemplify America's truest egalitarian spirit, epitomized by the legendary first Thanksgiving at Plymouth.

Samoset's home lay on the southeastern coastline of Maine, opposite Monhegan Island, where John Smith and other English sea captains had begun competing with the French for fish and furs. In the early 1600s, warfare and disease had reduced the landscape of the Northeast Coastal Indians' world to a patchwork of confederacies held together by dynamic dynasties like that of Massasoit Ousamequin ["Big Chief Yellow Feather"] of the Wampanoag and Nahanada (Dohoday), a Pemaquid chief who is said to have lived for many years in England. At Monhegan, fishermen and traders long had trucked with Indians from modern-day Maine and Nova Scotia, while marooned or mutinous sailors unfailingly made their way to this busy rendezvous.

But when the Micmac Grand Sagamore (or chief) Membertou converted to Catholicism in 1610 and allowed French

Jesuits to open a mission, Micmac raiders armed with steel tips for their arrows terrorized the countryside. Monhegan had become dangerous ground. Desperate not to fall too far behind the French in their imperial competition, English explorers kidnapped dozens of Native Americans, mainly to guide future commercial expeditions. One Indian named Squanto from Patuxet—the ghost town which the Pilgrim Separatists renamed Plymouth—had been taken off to Europe so many times that he spoke English better than Samoset, who had picked up bits of the language from white settlers.

Pemaquid's Seafaring Sagamore

Around 1615 Captain Thomas Hunt escalated the abductions to a wholesale level, luring 27 Indians on board his ship to trade, then delivering them into slavery in Malaga, Spain, for 20 pounds each. Native Americans launched retaliatory attacks on the English traders, fatally wounding one of Samoset's friends, Captain Thomas Dermer. Meanwhile, in raids of unprecedented brutality, Micmac warriors ravaged the vast coastal farmlands, while other northeastern tribes like the Wampanoag and neighboring Narragansetts turned against each other.

But commercial competition, feuds, and warfare over the fur trade were far less devastating to the Plymouth settlers—and the Native American population—than the illnesses that swept the area during this time. Diseases introduced by European traders spread, aggravated by a growing reliance on alcohol and contact with corpses too numerous to bury—some of them *Mayflower* passengers who died during the colonists' first three months ashore in 1620. The Plymouth settlement's seven able-bodied men had failed in three tries to organize a militia when suddenly Samoset strode into their town and astounded them with his English salutation.

Traveling five days' journey from home by land but only a day's sail with a strong wind, Samoset had arrived in the Patuxet region eight months earlier. William Bradford and the mysterious G. Mourt (likeliest Edward Winslow) both wrote of the encounter, Mourt at length in his promotional journal published a year later. Both called Samoset's English "broken" but quickly understood the value of his information. The Sagamore asked for beer; they gave him liquor and food. Naked except for a leather breechclout, Samoset carried a bow and two arrows, only one of them tipped, apparently to show his willingness for war or peace. He walked boldly and confidently, stood tall and straight, and wore his black hair long in back but short in front. "He was a man free in speech, so far as he could express his mind, and of a seemly carriage," according to *Mourt's Relation*. "We questioned him of many things; he was the first savage we could meet.... He discoursed of the whole country, and of every province, and of their sagamores, and their number of men, and strength."

Samoset told them about the slave traders and wars, the plague (which the Pilgrims saw as divine preparation for their colonization), and the powerful Massasoit, nearby with 60 Wampanoag warriors. The next day, Samoset departed, saying he would return with furs to trade and emissaries from Massasoit. Later the next week, he returned with Squanto—more articulate by virtue of his various imprisonments—and a meeting was arranged with Massasoit. From this emerged the remarkable mutual defense pact which for the next 55 years allied the English, with their terrible guns and hunger for furs, and the Wampanoag, no longer vulnerable to attack.

Diplomacy Stabilized New England

Samoset reemerges in history in 1624, back home in Maine, where he greeted English trader Christopher Levett as "cousin." "Somerset," as Levett called him, swore his "cousin" should have all the tribe's fur trade. This monopoly so angered rival traders that one company actually assaulted Samoset. By the 1630s sporadic retaliation for traders' beatings and cheatings had resumed among the Northeast Coastal Indians. These ultimately culminated in the full-scale wars of the late seventeenth century.

Samoset, however, continued to live in peace with the English. On July 15, 1625, Samoset, alternately known as Captain John Somerset by Monhegan seafarers, deeded land near his village. This was the first land sale transaction between eastern Indians and English colonists; as such, it legally established the Indians—not the Crown—as the land's owners. Samoset sold another piece of land in 1653 and is believed to have died soon after. His grave is in present-day Bristol, Maine.

Remembered dimly as half-naked, pidgin-speaking, noble (but gullible and brutal) savages, instead of the sophisticated statesmen, peacemakers, and cultural mediators they really were, Samoset and other coastal chiefs are often criticized for beginning the erosion of the Native American land and cultural base. Some historians, however, feel these tribal leaders deserve some credit for how much they were able to save. Samoset and Massasoit, they argue, were not motivated to befriend English colonial enterprise or preserve Native American solidarity, but to do the best job possible to help their dependents and descendants endure life in a tumultuous and deadly new world.

SOURCES:

Apess, William, *On Our Own Ground,* originally published in 1836; reprinted, Amherst, University of Massachusetts Press, 1992.

Bakeless, John, *America As Seen by Its First Explorers: The Eyes of Discovery,* New York, Dover, 1950.

Bonfanti, Leo, *Biographies and Legends of the New England Indians,* Wakefield, Massachusetts, Pride Publications, 1968.

Bourne, Russell, *The Red King's Rebellion: Racial Politics in New England,* 1675-1678, New York, Oxford University Press, 1990.

Dawnland Encounters: Indians and Europeans in Northern New England, compiled and edited by Colin G. Calloway, Hanover, New Hampshire, University Press of New England, 1991.

Handbook of North American Indians, Volume 15: The Northeast, edited by Bruce G. Trigger, Washington, D.C., Smithsonian Institution, 1978.

Mourt's Relation: A Journal of the Pilgrims at Plymouth, edited by Dwight B. Heath (from the original 1622 text), Boston, Applewood Books, 1986.

Parker, Arlita Dodge, *History of Pemaquid with Sketches of Monhegan, Popham and Castine,* Boston, MacDonald & Evans, 1925.

Russell, Howard S., *Indian New England before the Mayflower,* Hanover, New Hampshire, University Press of New England, 1980.

Utley, R. M., and Wilcombe E. Washburn, *American Heritage History of the Indian Wars,* Bonanza, 1977.

Weeks, Alvin G., *Massasoit of the Wampanoags,* privately printed, 1920.

Whitehead, Ruth Holmes, *The Old Man Told Us: Excerpts from Micmac History, 1500-1950,* Nimbus Publishing, 1991.

Willison, George F., *Saints and Strangers,* New York, Time-Life Books, 1945.

—*Sketch by Steven Edwin Conliff*

Will Sampson, Jr.

Will Sampson, Jr.
1934-1987
Creek actor and artist

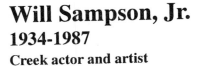ith his acting debut as Chief Bromden in the hit movie *One Flew Over the Cuckoo's Nest,* Will Sampson, Jr., became one of the most widely recognized Native American actors in recent memory. Sampson was born and raised on the Creek Nation Reservation in Okmulgee, Oklahoma. After a brief stint in the U.S. Navy, he pursued a variety of jobs as a construction worker, oil field worker, forest ranger, lumberjack, rodeo cowboy, and professional artist.

Begins Acting Career

Sampson was 40 years old when he began his acting career in 1974. While directing an art exhibition in Yakima, Washington, an old rodeo friend informed him that producer Michael Douglas was looking for a "big Indian" to play in his latest movie. An imposing six feet, seven inches tall, Sampson was easily "discovered." After meeting with Douglas and actor Jack Nicholson, Sampson read the Ken Kesey book on which the film was based before signing on for the part in *One Flew Over the Cuckoo's Nest.* Sampson portrayed the mysterious, alienated Indian who pretends to be mute to protect himself against the hostile, inhumane treatment by doctors, nurses, and orderlies in a mental hospital, which serves as a microcosm of society. The patients, including Bromden, find strength and sanity in the Nichol-son character, Randall McMurphy, a rebel whose heroic demise at the end of the story serves as inspiration for the Indian to once again pursue his own path of freedom and self-respect. For his role in the movie, Sampson was nominated for an Academy Award as best supporting actor, and his acting career looked very promising.

Sampson took advantage of a variety of opportunities in the entertainment industry. His movies included *Buffalo Bill and the Indians, The Outlaw Josie Wales, The White Buffalo, Orca, Fighting Back, Alcatraz: The Whole Shocking Story, Poltergeist II: The Other Side,* and the lead role in *Old Fish Hawk.* In 1982, Sampson was awarded best narration honors by the Alberta film commission for his work on *Spirit of the Hunt,* a major Canadian film. He also worked in television and on stage. Television work included regular appearances in the series "Vegas," "Born to the Wind," and "The Yellow Rose." He also narrated the PBS documentary "Images of Indians," which recounted a history of the dominant perceptions that Europeans and Americans have had of Indians.

Continues Work as Artist

While his acting career grew, Sampson's foremost passion remained painting. His work was exhibited in the Smithsonian Institution and the Library of Congress, as well as galleries and other notable contexts. Sampson once said that he prepared for his paintings of cowboys, Indians, and western landscapes in the same manner he studied for his acting roles: "I research thoroughly."

With success and fame, Sampson contributed his influence, knowledge, and money to Native American causes. He frequently educated students on the topics of Western art and Indian traditions. He also contributed to the fight against alcoholism.

He had suffered from scleroderma, a chronic degenerative disease, for years. However, after complications associated with a heart-lung transplant, Sampson died from kidney failure in Houston, Texas, on June 2, 1987. He was 53 years old and married to his fourth wife.

SOURCES:

Books

Biographical Dictionary of Indians of the Americas, Volume 2, Newport Beach, American Indian Publishers, 1991; 652-53.
Native North American Almanac, edited by Duane Champagne, Detroit, Gale Research, 1994; 771, 1153.

Periodicals

New York Times, June 4, 1987; Section 4, 26.

—*Sketch by William Carter*

Sanapia
1895-1984
Comanche medicine woman

Also known as Mary Poafpybitty, Memory Woman, and Sticky Mother

Sanapia, the last known Comanche eagle doctor, was one of the most powerful Native American women on the Great Plains. She was a member of one of the northern bands of the Comanche community, the Yapai ["Root Eaters"], also known as Yamparika ["Yap Eaters"]. In the spring of 1895, a group of Yapai Comanches traveled from Medicine Park, Oklahoma, to Fort Sill to obtain government rations. It was there that Sanapia was born—the sixth of 11 children—to a Comanche father who had converted to Christianity, and a traditional Comanche-Arapaho mother.

Sanapia's ties to her tribe were strong: her paternal grandfather was a revered Yapai leader, and one of her mother's brothers was an Arapaho chief. According to custom, she was raised mainly by her maternal grandmother, who repeatedly stressed to her the value of the Comanche life and oral tradition. The elder woman directed young Sanapia to follow in the footsteps of her mother and another maternal uncle, both of whom were eagle doctors.

Sanapia's Comanche ancestors shared cultural and historical roots with the Shoshone people of the Great Basin, speaking the same language and beginning a southward migration sometime in the 1700s. Sanapia's people, the Yapai, were members of the northernmost of the Comanche bands and were probably the last to split from the Shoshone. They were also the most traditional and conservative. The Yapai Comanche today live south of the Washita River near Anadarko, Oklahoma, north of Fort Sill.

Having acquired horses from the Spanish in the late 1600s, Comanches became quite mobile and skilled at hunting buffalo. Theirs was a male-dominated society; women were normally of low status in this culture, while shamans and medicine men wielded the most influence. The tribe's religion acknowledged a "Great Spirit" as the source of all power: humans could gain access to this power through dreams of spirits and other beings, or it could be passed from one person to another through appropriate rituals. Sanapia's guardian spirit and bestower of supernatural power was the eagle—hence her designation as an eagle doctor.

As the buffalo population decreased in the nineteenth century, the Comanche people began raiding their neighbors as well as trading with them, and prior to the reservation years (1870-1901), their trade enterprises formed an important part of the economy in Texas, Old Mexico, and New Mexico. Subsequent contact with Anglo-Americans moving westward eventually put an end to the Comanche's nomadic life: first they were confined to reservations, then to allotments on which they were expected to pursue an agricultural existence. Their final transition, assimilation into white society, eroded their traditional culture. Inability to cope with the stresses of assimilation was said to cause "ghost-sickness" among many Comanches, for which the eagle doctor had specific spiritual, herbal, and psychological remedies.

Becomes an Eagle Doctor

When she was seven, Sanapia started her formal education at Cache Creek Mission School, where she studied for seven years. At the age of 13, she reluctantly agreed to allow her mother to begin training her in the ways of the eagle doctor. Sanapia understood well the taboos, obligations, and responsibilities associated with the eagle doctor profession and was not sure she wanted that kind of life for herself. But she had little choice. Earlier, her uncle had given her his blessing while treating her for a childhood bout with influenza—and made her recovery conditional on her consent to devote her life to healing. He named her "Memory Woman," so that she might never forget her promise.

Following a prescribed ritual, Sanapia first learned to identify, gather, and process native plants used in medicines; then she spent the following four years practicing healing skills and acquiring the eagle power, working under the tutelage of her mother, grandmother, grandfather, and uncle. They insured that she developed the proper attitude toward her profession, as well as the needed skills and knowledge.

In early twentieth-century Comanche society, such training elevated her status to that of a man.

The supernatural power that Sanapia received in the last stage of her training was considered potentially dangerous. There was always a chance that new doctors could use their power for evil, so family approval was required before Sanapia's mother could pass the eagle power on to her. The final days of training—when the transfer of power occurred—were a period of solitude, reflection, and fasting for Sanapia; her worthiness and courage were tested by supernatural beings during this time. Once she completed her training, though, Sanapia could not begin to practice as an eagle doctor until many years later. Strict taboos prevented premenopausal women from exercising the powers of a medicine women.

Guided toward Healing through Personal Tragedy

Three separate religious concepts influenced Sanapia's life. Her mother represented the traditional Plains Indian spiritualism, which was in direct conflict with her father's Christianity. Her uncle and paternal grandfather were Peyotists, practitioners of a religion that combined aspects of Christianity with Native American beliefs and relied heavily on sacramental ritual. Never an advocate of organized religion—and true to the individualistic Comanche nature—she combined elements of all three concepts into a unified philosophy that she felt was consistent with her future role of medicine woman.

All of the varying influences on her beliefs converged in her adult life. Sanapia married three times. Her first marriage, at the age of 17, produced a son. She left her husband shortly after and remarried within a year. She had two more children, a son and a daughter, from this second marriage. The death of Sanapia's second husband in the 1930s was emotionally devastating to her, and she dealt with her grief by engaging in excessive drinking, gambling, and reckless sexual behavior. It was during this time of instability that Sanapia was asked by her sister to cure a sick child. Sanapia's cure was successful, and this led her to follow the path for which her mother had trained her many years earlier. She married her third husband some years later and at that time committed herself to the role of medicine woman.

An Uncertain Future

Cultural norms dictate that one's medicine power should be transferred to a younger person who is worthy and willing to accept the position's responsibilities. Sanapia was concerned that she would not live long enough to pass on her power to another generation, so she allowed anthropologist David E. Jones to write a detailed account of her life and medicine ways, hoping the book would serve as a training manual. She predicted, however, that changing times would eventually bring about the end of the medicine way in the Comanche community. Sanapia died in Oklahoma in 1984. It remains unclear whether she passed her power to a successor.

SOURCES:

Foster, Morris W., *Being Comanche,* Tucson, University of Arizona Press, 1991.

Hagan, William T., *United States-Comanche Relations: The Reservation Years,* New Haven, Yale University Press, 1976.

Johnson, Michael G., *The Native Tribes of North America,* London, Windrow & Greene, 1993; 85-86.

Jones, David E., *Sanapia: Comanche Medicine Woman,* New York, Holt, Rinehart and Winston, 1972.

Native American Women, edited by Gretchen M. Bataille, New York, Garland Publishing, 1993; 227-228.

—*Sketch by Claudeen E. McAuliffe*

Joe Sando
1923-
Jemez Pueblo author, historian, and educator
Also known as Paa Peh

As a scholar, Joe Simon Sando has worked hard to improve life for the Jemez Pueblo people, primarily in the areas of education, the law, and housing. He has written three books that chronicle the lives, culture, and history of the Pueblo Indians.

Sando was born on August 1, 1923, in Jemez Pueblo, New Mexico, and named Paa Peh in the language of the Pueblo Indians. He attended Santa Fe Indian School like many Pueblos of that time. He married and had three children with Louisa Parker, who worked as a realty specialist with the Bureau of Indian Affairs (BIA). Later, their son Parker Sando helped revise the Pueblo Land Status reports for the BIA.

During his younger years at Santa Fe, Sando struggled due to his low proficiency in English. He found, however, that his knowledge of the Pueblo Indian language would be one of his assets later in life. In addition to language barriers, his smallness in stature was initially an obstacle to him playing football, one of his greatest desires as a young person. However, he finally made the team in his senior year.

Upon completion of his secondary studies in 1941, Sando entered Eastern New Mexico University (ENMU), financing his education by working in a cabinet shop repairing furniture. During his first college year in 1943, he decided to postpone college to enlist in the U.S. Navy. Later, in the preface to *Nee Hemish: The History of the Jemez Pueblo,* Sando wrote: "I am fortunate that I survived World War II to take advantage of the G.I. Bill, which opened up a new world for me." Sando participated in the U.S. invasion of the Gilbert

Joe Sando

and Marianas islands in the Pacific. Having earned a Pacific Campaign Ribbon with four stars, Sando ended his naval career after serving as a petty officer second class.

Sando returned to ENMU and completed his bachelor of arts in 1949. Still harboring a dream to play football, he made second-string varsity quarterback. He pursued further studies at the University of New Mexico in 1950 to 1951 (and again in 1973). Later, he went on to receive a master of science from Vanderbilt University in audiology and speech pathology in 1960. During the time between undergraduate and graduate school, he worked as a counselor in government schools for eight years. After receiving his master's, he worked as an audiologist in Albuquerque, New Mexico, testing astronauts and pilots among others.

Active in serving the Jemez Pueblo community, Sando has held chairmanships on three committees: the New Mexico Judicial Council, the All Indian Pueblo Housing Authority, and the Educational Committee of the All Indian Pueblo Council. His work for the Housing Authority included a $2 million project for the construction of new homes for Pueblo Indians. He also worked to improve the legal system in New Mexico while working for the Judicial Council. As a member of the Educational Committee, he worked to send Pueblo Indians to college. In addition, he created the All-Indian Track Meet at Jemez Pueblo, resulting in the awarding of scholarships to students in the community. He has also served on the boards of Americans for

Indian Opportunity and the Northern New Mexico Economic Development District.

Sando has also functioned as a visiting scholar. He taught ethnohistory at the Institute of American Indian Arts in Santa Fe, specializing in Pueblo Indian history. He traveled to New Zealand to study the Maori tribe and its similarities to Native American tribes. In addition, he also toured as a lecturer throughout the United States, Switzerland, and Germany.

Since the late 1970s and 1980s, he has written four books on Pueblo history and culture: *The Pueblo Indians, Pueblo Indian Biographies, Nee Hemish: The History of the Jemez Pueblo,* and *Pueblo Nations: Eight Centuries of Pueblo Indian History.* On the purpose and significance of his historical writings, Sando writes the following in the preface to *Nee Hemish:* "It became apparent to me early in my career as an educator that there was no history of American Indians written by a member of that American subculture. Through the years Indian students have asked me where relevant history such as they had heard from their parents and grandparents might be found. Fellow tribal members of mine from Jemez, in quest of information for school term papers, and out of their own curiosity, have called me, asking about their history." Sando, thus, felt compelled to research and write about the history of his people, the Jemez Pueblo. From his work, he experienced both joy and sadness. Referring to his writings as "a dream come true" but also as "heartbreaking" as he has seen the mournful faces of older Pueblo as he explained the events surrounding the loss of tribal lands.

SELECTED WRITINGS BY SANDO:

The Pueblo Indians, Indian Historian Press, 1976, 1982.

Pueblo Indian Biographies, Albuquerque, SIPI Press, 1976.

Nee Hemish: The History of the Jemez Pueblo, University of New Mexico Press, 1982.

"Pope," in *World Book Encyclopedia,* 1970.

SOURCES:

Biographical Dictionary of the Indians of the Americas, second edition, American Indian Publishers, 1991.

Handbook of the North American Indians, edited by William C. Sturtevant, Washington, D.C., Smithsonian Institution, 1983.

Native North American Almanac, edited by Duane Champagne, Detroit, Gale Research, 1994.

Reference Encyclopedia of the American Indian, edited by Barry Klein, West Nyack, New York, Todd Publications, 1993.

Sando, Joe, *Nee Hemish: The History of the Jemez Pueblo,* Albuquerque, University of New Mexico Press, 1982.

—Sketch by Christopher B. Tower

Satanta
1820-1878
Kiowa war chief

Also known as Set-tainte ["White Bear"] and "The Orator of the Plains"

Satanta

Satanta was a celebrated Kiowa warrior and the tribe's principal war chief, known for his flamboyant style, his great speaking ability, and his determined resistance to the white man's invasion of his territory. He was born in 1820, the son of Do-guadal-kap-tah ["Old Man Red Tipi"], who was a Kiowa priest and keeper of the medicine bundles, or Tai-me. The Kiowas, along with their allies the Comanches and the Kiowa-Apaches, inhabited the southern plains in an area that is now western Oklahoma, part of New Mexico, and the panhandle of Texas. These tribes lived a nomadic lifestyle, relying on horse breeding and buffalo hunting as the mainstay of their culture.

Satanta was a colorful and clever warrior. During battles, he wore a red and yellow buckskin war shirt and decorated his face with red war paint. He carried a medicine lance with red ribbons and a buffalo hide shield that had been given to him by Black Horse, another great warrior. He also carried a brass bugle that he had won during a raid on a military camp when he was 25 years old. During battles, he used the bugle to confuse enemy troops, and, at more peaceful times, he used it to call his people together for dinner or ceremonial dances. Satanta lived in a flaming red tipi with red streamers flying from the lodge poles, just as his father had done before him.

In 1866, when he was 46 years old, Satanta was appointed second chief of his band. He rose to leadership during a time of war on the southern plains. An increasing number of white immigrants were severely and adversely affecting the Indian way of life, as they settled ranches and farms in the heart of the Kiowas' territory. The traffic of wagons and cattle along the Santa Fe Trail was destroying the buffalo grazing land so crucial to the existence of the Kiowas and their allies. Frustrated and angry, the Indians in that region began striking out against the travelers. Before long the Santa Fe Trail was known to be an extremely hazardous route—in fact, it was considered nearly impassable.

In April of 1867, the government called the Kiowa chiefs to a council at Fort Dodge, Kansas, to discuss peace. General Winfield S. Hancock represented the U.S. government. Chiefs Kicking Bird and Stumbling Bear spoke for the peaceful faction of the Kiowa tribe, while chiefs Satanta, Lone Wolf, and Satank represented the militant war faction. Satanta did not trust the whites, but was present at the peace council and made an impressive speech. Afterwards, General Hancock presented Satanta with a full dress uniform of a U.S. army major-general. A few weeks later Satanta returned to Fort Dodge, in his new uniform, leading a raid and stealing horses from the cavalry. As he rode off, pursued by soldiers, he saluted them with a tip of his new plumed hat.

"The Orator of the Plains"

In October of 1867, a great peace council took place at Medicine Creek Lodge in southern Kansas. The government peace commission planned to negotiate a treaty with the 5,000 Kiowas, Comanches, and Arapahos who were assembled. At this council, Satanta demonstrated his usual style. He shook hands with each commissioner present before delivering the prophetic and moving speech that earned him the title of "the orator of the plains." Speaking of his frustrations, Satanta said, "I love the land and the buffalo and will not part with it.... I have heard that you intend to settle us on a reservation near the mountains.... I love to roam over the prairies. There I feel free and happy, but when we settle down, we grow pale and die. A long time ago this land belonged to our fathers, but when I go up the river, I see camps of soldiers on its banks. These soldiers cut down my timber; they kill my buffalo; and when I see that, my heart feels like bursting; I feel sorry."

General William Tecumseh Sherman spoke for the commissioners. He reminded the chiefs of the power of the U.S. government and told them that they could not stop the wave of progress from sweeping through their territory. He said that they would have to give up their old ways and learn to live like the white settlers by farming and ranching. After several more days of negotiating, Satanta and most of the other Kiowa chiefs present signed the Medicine Lodge Treaty. Under the terms of the treaty, the government promised payments of food, clothing, tools, and other supplies in exchange for much of the Indians' territory. The Comanches and Kiowas were to settle on a reservation in Oklahoma, but would still be allowed the right to hunt on their former lands.

Peace did not last long. The treaty-signing Kiowas and Comanches had settled on the reservation, but had never intended to live as farmers. The warriors continued to hunt and raid in the Texas panhandle; however, they found the buffalo all but gone. White hunters were slaughtering entire herds, taking the hides and leaving the meat to rot. In the face of such atrocities, the Indians grew increasingly restless, frustrated, and dissatisfied with reservation life. They did not adjust well to the rations of the government or to a sedentary lifestyle. Many of the warriors left the reservation to join the non-treaty bands still living and hunting in their old territory on the plains.

In the spring of 1871, Satanta organized a war party of over 100 Kiowa and Comanche warriors, including Satank, Big Tree, and Maman-te, who accompanied him on a raid into Jack County, Texas. Attacking some supply wagons on their way to Fort Richardson, Texas, they killed seven teamsters, looted and burned the wagons, and stole 41 mules. Satanta lost three warriors during the fighting.

Several days later, the chiefs were called to council with Lawrie Tatum, the agent in charge at Fort Sill. When Tatum asked the chiefs about the raid, Satanta confessed, implicating Satank and Big Tree as well. The next day General Sherman arrested the three chiefs and took them to Jacksboro, Texas, to be tried for murder. Satank made an attempt to escape and was killed. Satanta and Big Tree were convicted of murder and sentenced to hang. Their sentences were reduced to life imprisonment after humanitarian groups protested that the death penalty was too harsh a punishment. Subsequently, the two men were sent to the Texas State Prison at Huntsville.

In 1873, after serving two years of their sentences, Satanta and Big Tree were granted parole by President Ulysses S. Grant, with the condition that they must remain on the reservation. Upon his release from prison, Satanta stated that he no longer wanted to be a warrior or a chief. He gave his medicine lance to his friend, Ato-t-ain ["White Cowbird"], and his buffalo hide shield, which he had carried in over 100 battles, to his son.

Raids by the Kiowa and Comanche continued in Texas. General Sherman ordered all of the Indians to report weekly to their reservation agency for a roll-call. Many of the chiefs, including Kicking Bird, reported regularly to the agencies with their bands. Others, including Lone Wolf, continued to live and hunt on the plains according to their old ways.

Satanta and Big Tree were off the reservation hunting when, in 1874, fighting broke out at the Wichita Agency Uprising. They were afraid to return to the reservation, for fear of being accused of involvement in the hostilities. Finally, they turned themselves in, proclaiming that they had not taken part in the fighting. Because they had broken the terms of their parole by being off the reservation, they were arrested. Big Tree was held for several months at Fort Sill and then released. Satanta was sent back to prison in Huntsville to serve the remainder of his life sentence.

After four more years in prison, Satanta began to grow weak and ill, just as he had predicted seven years earlier in his much noted speech at Medicine Lodge. The commissioner of Indian affairs, Edward Smith, as well as the superintendent of the prison, Enoch Hoag, argued for the release of the chief; but General Sherman continued to oppose it. Satanta was told by a prison official that he would never be released. Discouraged and disheartened, he sent word to his people that he could no longer live confined behind bars. On September 11, 1878, he sang his death chant and jumped from the balcony of his second story hospital room. He died several hours later at the age of 58, and was buried at Huntsville prison cemetery. Satanta's relatives made repeated requests to the Texas State Legislature to be allowed to move his remains back to his former homeland. His grandson, James Auchiah, finally received permission to do so in 1963, and Satanta's remains were reinterred at the cemetery in Fort Sill, Oklahoma, in the heart of his old hunting grounds, with full Kiowa and military honors.

SOURCES:

The American Heritage Book of Indians, edited by Alvin M. Josephy, Jr., American Heritage Publishing, 1961; 381.

Boyd, Maurice, *Kiowa Voices: Myths, Legends, and Folktales,* Volume 2, Fort Worth, Texas Christian University Press, 1983; 173, 226-232.

Dockstader, Frederick J., *Great North American Indians,* New York, Van Nostrand Reinhold, 1977; 252-253.

Freeman, Russell, *Indian Chiefs,* New York, Holiday House, 1987; 29-51.

Mayhall, Mildred P., *The Kiowas,* University of Oklahoma Press, 1962; 227, 275, 300.

Native North American Almanac, edited by Duane Champagne, Detroit, Gale Research, 1994; 1155.

Saul, Terry C., *Biographical Dictionary of Indians of the Americas,* Newport Beach, California, American Indian Publishers, 1983; 434-435.

Waldman, Carl, *Who Was Who in Native American History,* New York, Facts On File, 1990; 312-313.

—Sketch by Denise Marecki-Arriola

Katherine Siva Saubel
1920-
Cahuilla educator and tribal leader

Katherine Siva Saubel is an internationally known Cahuilla scholar whose work on the history, literature, and culture of her people has appeared in numerous publications. In addition to making significant contributions in such varied fields as ethnobotany and linguistics, she helped to found the Malki Museum, the first non-profit tribal museum on a Native American reservation in California. While teaching at various universities in California, she has exhibited her expertise on Native American culture and history before the California legislature and the United States Congress. For her work as a historian responsible for protecting numerous sacred sites and remains, she was named Riverside County Historian of the Year in 1986, and the following year recognized as the Elder of the Year by the California State Indian Museum.

Saubel was born on a Los Coyotes Reservation in 1920. She was reared by her father, Juan C. Siva, and her mother, Melan Seivatily, in Palm Springs, California. As a child, she was taught by her parents to value the rich traditions of her people, learning both the folklore and language of the Cahuilla. Her long-held love for Native culture was fostered by her marriage to Mariano Saubel, a fellow historian. Together they began compiling various cultural artifacts relating to Native Californians. With the aid of other Natives and the University of Riverside, they founded the Malki Museum on the Morongo Indian Reservation in Banning, thereby establishing one of the first on-site reservation museums in California. Especially noted for its Cahuilla display, the museum boasts an impressive collection of a variety of artifacts from prehistoric and historical periods, including basketry, pottery, ceremonial equipage, and hunting materials. The museum has also served as a forum for publishing numerous scholarly works on Native Californians, including several by Saubel herself.

Preserves Cahuilla Language and Culture

One of Saubel's greatest achievements as both a scholar and tribal leader can be seen in her efforts to preserve the language of the Cahuilla people. As early as 1960, she began working closely with linguistics professor Hansjakob Seiler on the arduous process of writing down and providing an authentic translation of the Cahuilla language, which had previously existed only in spoken form. Their collaborative effort resulted in the publication of both a Cahuilla grammar book and dictionary in the late 1970s. As Saubel joyously wrote in a tribute to Professor Seiler in 1978, "Now we know our language, and it's been written. That way, we have seen that in the future anyone who wants to know how we speak will see this and know it." A noted linguist on her own terms, Saubel has published her own dictionary, *I'sniyatam Designs, a Cahuilla Word Book.* Her work also includes several authentic transcriptions and English translations of Cahuilla folklore, including a native version of the famous European tale of "The Three Pigs," which appeared in *Wege zur Universailien Forschung,* a 1980 German linguistic study.

The depth of Saubel's expertise in Cahuilla culture can be demonstrated in the second major focus of her scholarship: Native ethnobotany, the study of the plant lore of a specific ethnic group. Considered a leading authority on the unique Cahuilla uses of such plants as mesquite, screwbean, and oak, she has written several works in collaboration with anthropology professor John Lowell Bean. *Temalpakh: Cahuilla Indian Knowledge and Uses of Plants,* a wide-ranging study in Cahuilla ethnobotany published in 1972, is perhaps the best known of these works. Her research as an individual scholar has also appeared in a variety of government, academic, and museum publications. While conducting her research, Saubel has taught on various aspects of Cahuilla history, literature, and culture at such institutions as the University of California, Riverside and Los Angeles; California State University, Hayward; and the University of Cologne.

In addition to her work within the academic community, Saubel has taken an active role in government service, working to preserve the remnants of Cahuilla culture in California. Having witnessed her exemplary performance at the Malki Museum and with the Riverside County Historical Commission, California Governor George Deukmejian in 1986 appointed her to the state Native American Heritage Commission, where she has successfully led the fight to preserve sacred locations throughout the state. Also a member of numerous commissions and agencies, Saubel has been asked to demonstrate her knowledge of Cahuilla ethnobotany and tribal affairs before state and federal legislative bodies. For her efforts as a museum historian, author, teacher, and activist, Saubel is generally acknowledged to be one of California's most respected Native American leaders.

SELECTED WRITINGS BY SAUBEL:

With John Lowell Bean, *Cahuilla Ethnobotanical Notes: The Aboriginal Uses of Oak,* Archaeology Survey Annual Report, Los Angeles, UCLA Press, 1961.

With John Lowell Bean, *Cahuilla Ethnobotanical Notes: Aboriginal Uses of Mesquite and Screwbean,* Archaeology Survey Annual Report, Los Angeles, UCLA Press, 1963.

With John Lowell Bean, *Temalpakh: Cahuilla Indian Knowledge,* Banning, California, Malki Museum Press, 1972.

I'sniyatam Designs, a Cahuilla Word Book, Banning, California, Malki Museum Press, 1977.

SOURCES:

Bean, John Lowell, and Sylvia Brakke Vane, *California Indians: Primary Resources,* Ramona, California, Ballena Press, 1977.

Native American Women, edited by Gretchen M. Bataille, New York, Garland Publishing, 1993; 229-230.

Saubel, Katherine Siva, "Professor Seiler and the Cahuilla Language," *Wege zur Universalien Forschung,* edited by Gunter Brettschneider and Christian Lehmann, Tubingen, Narr, 1980; 479-481.

Saubel, Katherine Siva, "The Three Pigs: A Modern Cahuilla Text," *Wege zur Universalien Forschung,* edited by Gunter Brettschneider and Christian Lehmann, Tubingen, Narr, 1980; 482-493.

—*Sketch by Jason Gallman*

Fritz Scholder
1937-
Luiseño artist

Fritz Scholder is a leading American artist credited with revolutionizing the style and content of Native American art. His paintings and lithographs focus on a broad range of subjects and are characterized by dynamic brush strokes and luminous colors. Scholder is the recipient of numerous awards, including New Mexico's Governor's Award in Visual Arts (1983) and the Golden Plate Award (1985).

Scholder was born on October 6, 1937, in Breckenridge, Minnesota. While his grandmother was a member of the Luiseño tribe, Scholder is also part German, English, and French. He began drawing and painting as a child. "For me," Scholder commented, "there was never any question about what I would do and that I would be successful." His father was employed with the Bureau of Indian Affairs (BIA) and, as a result, Scholder moved frequently throughout his childhood. In South Dakota he met Oscar Howe, an esteemed Sioux cubist painter. Regarding the experience, Scholder remarked, "It was interesting for me to see somebody who was serious about being an artist." He attended Wisconsin State University before graduating from Sacramento City College in 1960. Also that year, Scholder won first prize in the Tenth Southwestern Painter's Festival. In 1964 he received his Masters of Fine Arts degree from the University of Arizona. Upon graduation, he found employment as a professor at the Institute of American Indian Arts in Santa Fe, where he remained until 1969.

Scholder began his "New Mexico" series in 1965. This was followed by an examination of butterflies, and finally an "Indian" series, for which he is perhaps best known. "I vowed that I would not paint the Indian," Scholder once stated. "Non-Indian artists had painted the subject as a noble savage and the Indian painter had been caught in a tourist-pleasing cliché. I retracted my vow of 1964 for several reasons, one of these being a teacher's frustration upon seeing students with a good idea fall short of the solution. One winter evening early in 1967 I decided to paint an Indian. It soon became evident that it was time for a new idiom in Indian painting." In these somewhat controversial works, which combine surrealist pop imagery and American Indian mysticism, he addressed such issues as alcoholism, assimilation into mainstream American society, and the degradation of Native American culture. While some critics felt that he reduced the vital issues of his people to popularized art with little aesthetic value, others praised Scholder for depicting American Indians as individuals rather than stereotypes.

In 1972 Scholder began traveling in Europe and Africa. His travels in Rumania led to his "Vampire" series. He also did numerous paintings influenced by Egyptian figures. In 1980, Scholder began "The American Portraits" and followed it with his "Dream" series in which androgynous lovers embrace. He then returned to painting the American Indian in a "Shaman" series. More recently, he has created sculpture and designed jewelry. Scholder, who has fought to maintain his artistic freedom throughout his career, has claimed, "I have never lived my life in an orthodox way. Most artists realize that there are so many possibilities and the need for introspection."

In 1992 Scholder created the lithograph *Indian Contemplating Columbus.* Regarding the 40-by-60-inch work, Scholder stated, "I'm very divided about Columbus because I grew up thinking of him as a hero. When I was a boy, I didn't think about my being part Indian.... But now, I can understand the other side, and now, after much more reading as an adult, I realize that Columbus' trip was the beginning of the end for many cultures." The lithograph portrays a silhouetted figure sitting in a chair, facing the corner. A brightly colored moccasin on his foot is the only clue that the figure is Native American. Concerning the celebration of the 1992 Columbus Quincentenary, Scholder felt that all viewpoints had a right to be heard: "If someone puts up a statue to Columbus, they have that right, and people should be dignified about it and not protest. But the American Indian should also make his stand clear."

SOURCES:

Adams, Clinton, *Fritz Scholder: Lithographs,* Boston, New York Graphic Society, 1975.

Highwater, Jamake, *Anpao: An American Indian Odyssey,* Philadelphia, Lippincott, 1977.

Native North American Almanac, edited by Duane Champagne, Detroit, Gale Research, 1994; 1156.

Scholder, Fritz, *Fritz Scholder,* New York, Rizzoli, 1982.

Scholder, Fritz, *Fritz Scholder, Paintings and Monotypes,* Altadena, California, Twin Palms, 1988.

World Artists: 1980-1990, edited by Claude Marks, New York, H. W. Wilson Company, 1991; 342-346.

—*Sketch by Brett A. Lealand*

Seattle
1788(?)-1866
Suquamish-Duwamish tribal chief
Also known as Seathl (Seatlh, Sealth), See-yat, and "Noah"

Generally regarded as the last great leader of the native bands that lived in the Pacific Northwest, Seattle was responsible for continued good relations between Native Americans and the new white settlers. He was born around 1788 to Schweabe, his Suquamish father, and Scholitza, his Duwamish mother, in the area of central Puget Sound, Oregon Region (now Washington State). As a member of a patrilineal society, Seattle learned and spoke the Suquamish dialect of his father.

When Seattle was four years old, whites arrived at in the Puget Sound area, and the process of cultural assimilation began. By the 1830s, when he was in his mid-forties, Seattle had converted to the Catholicism of the French missionaries and was baptized as "Noah." With his new-found faith, he instituted morning and evening church services among Native Americans that were continued even after his death.

The City

The California Gold Rush of 1849 deluged the Pacific Northwest with white settlers intent on exploring the natural wealth of the area. Seattle, then principal chief of the united Suquamish and Duwamish nations—both Coast Salishan bands—counseled friendship, open trade, and accommodation of whites settlers.

In respect for their friend and ally, the whites at Puget Sound took Seattle's name for their own settlement in 1852. Among the Salishan Indians of the Pacific Northwest, however, it was believed that the frequent mention of a dead person's name would disturb that person's eternal rest. In order to use his name—Seattle—as the name of their city, white settlers agreed to prepay the chief for the trouble that his spirit would later experience when his name was mentioned; Seattle was compensated with moneys from a small tax imposed on the settlers prior to his death.

The Land

As white settlers continued to pour into the area, the U.S. Government pressed the issue of land purchase from the Indians. In December of 1854, Seattle met with Washington territorial governor Isaac Stevens to discuss the sale of native lands in exchange for smaller reservations and government annuities. His speech at this meeting was translated into English and transcribed by Henry A. Smith, a poet. Seattle agreed to accommodate the whites and the U.S. Government by moving the Puget Sound bands to a reservation.

Seattle

In 1855, at the age of 67, Seattle became the first signer of the Port Elliott Treaty between the Puget Sound Indians and the United States. But soon after the treaty was made, the terms were broken by whites, leading to a series of Native American uprisings from 1855 to 1858, including the Yakima War of 1855-1856 east of the Cascade Mountains, and the unsuccessful 1856 attack on Seattle's village by Nisqually warriors from west of the Cascade Mountains.

In accordance with the treaty stipulations, Seattle and his people moved to the Port Madison reservation, located west-northwest across the Puget Sound from the current city of Seattle, on the east shore of Bainbridge Island. There he lived in the Old Man House—a large community building.

The Speech

Seattle's 1854 address to the Washington territorial governor regarding the status of his people and their future was said to be eloquent and moving, but today there are at least four variations of the text, which raises the question of cultural authenticity. Seattle spoke in either Suquamish or Duwamish, which was then translated immediately into Chinook, and then into English for the U.S. Government representatives. The only surviving transcript of Seattle's oration was derived from the notes in English that were purportedly taken by Dr. Smith as Seattle spoke. On October 29, 1887, the *Seattle Sunday Star* published what Dr. Smith claimed was a representative transcription of Chief Seattle's spoken words, although he noted his text "contained none of the grace and elegance of the original." The text begins: "Yonder sky that has wept tears of compassion upon my people for centuries untold, and which to us appears changeless and eternal, may change. Today it is fair. Tomorrow it may be overcast with clouds. My words are like the stars that never set. Whatever Seattle says, the great chief at Washington can rely upon with as much certainty as he can upon the return of the sun or the seasons."

Two years later, in 1889, Washington became a state. A year after that, the city of Seattle erected a monument to its ancestral namesake, chief of the Suquamish and Duwamish peoples. Both of these Native American tribal bands are now extinct, but Seattle's speech has continued to fascinate scholars throughout the twentieth century. In the 1960s poet William Arrowsmith revised the speech into modern-day English. Arrowsmith's version begins: "Brothers: That sky above us has pitied our fathers for many hundreds of years. To us it looks unchanging, but it may change. Today it is fair. Tomorrow it may be covered with clouds." Perry's letter, featured in an ecology movie titled *Home,* is based loosely on Dr. Smith's transcription of Seattle's 1854 oration: "The Great Chief in Washington sends word that [he] wishes to buy our land. The Great Chief also sends us words of friendship and goodwill. This is kind of him, since we know he has little need of our friendship in return. But we will consider your offer. For we know that if we do not sell, the white man may come with guns and take our land. How can you buy or sell the sky, the warmth of the land? The idea is strange to us."

Seattle was married twice and had six children, four of whom died in childhood. He passed away on June 7, 1866, at the age of 78, on a Washington reservation. His famous speech and its current interpretations and use continue to challenge academics, but according to Native American history expert Herman Viola, as quoted in *Newsweek,* Seattle's discourse—whether accurate or embellished—undoubtedly "conveys the feeling a lot of Indians had."

SOURCES:

Books

Kaiser, Rudolf, "Chief Seattle's Speech(es): American Origins and European Reception," in *Recovering the Word: Essays on Native American Literature,* University of California Press, 1987.

Leitch, Barbara A., *A Concise Dictionary of Indian Tribes of North America,* Algonac, Michigan, Reference Publications, 1979.

Native North American Almanac, edited by Duane Champagne, Detroit, Gale Research, 1994; 1157.

Waldman, Carl, *Who Was Who in Native American History,* New York, Facts On File, 1990; 318.

Watt, Roberta Frye, *Four Wagons West,* Portland, Binsford & Mort, 1934.

Periodicals

Buerge, David, "Seattle's King Arthur: How Chief Seattle Continues to Inspire His Many Admirers to Put Words in His Mouth," *Seattle Weekly,* July 17, 1991.

"Chief Seattle's Treaty Oration—1854," *Seattle Sunday Star,* October 29, 1887.

Jones, Malcolm, Jr., and Ray Sawhill, "Just Too Good to Be True: Another Reason to Beware of False Eco-prophets," *Newsweek,* May 4, 1992; 68.

Other

Information from Nancy Zussy, State Librarian, Washington State Library, Olympia, Washington.

—Sketch by tpkunesh

Sequoyah
1770(?)-1843
Cherokee linguist

Also known as Sequoya (Sikwaji, Sikwayi), Sogwali (Sogwili), George Guess, George Gist, and George Guest

Generations of American schoolchildren have known Sequoyah from his famous nineteenth-century portrait hanging in the Library of Congress. Head wrapped in a traditional turban, smoking a long pipe, Sequoyah points to a tablet of 86 strange letters. The painting captures both Sequoyah's main accomplishment and the public's heroic conception of him. He was the untutored genius who single-handedly invented a written language for the Cherokees and thus led his people from illiteracy onto the path of progress and civilization. It was an astounding accomplishment. Up until then, so it was believed, no American Indian tribe had an alphabet. That a lone, uneducated person developed one full-blown in a relatively brief time was a stroke of extraordinary inventiveness. It marked a first in world history.

Outline of Sequoyah's Life

Standard reference books expand on this view of the Cherokee linguist. Because few solid facts are known about Sequoyah, such details as the year of his birth sometimes differ; nonetheless, most modern accounts generally agree on the following outline of Sequoyah's life.

He was born in an Indian village in Tennessee, the son of Nathaniel Gist, a white trader, and a part-Cherokee mother. The father abandoned the pregnant woman, and Sequoyah grew up uneducated and speaking no English. A hunter, trader, and accomplished silversmith, Sequoyah served in the U.S. Army in the war against the Creek Indians of 1813-1814. Sometime in this adult period, Sequoyah adopted George Guess as his English name, the "Guess" a misspelling of his father's last name. Crippled, some sources say by a war wound, others by a hunting accident, Sequoyah

Sequoyah

was thereafter forced into a less active life. In this more contemplative state, he became fascinated by the "talking leaves" of nearby whites, the books and letters allowing them to communicate over long distances. Determined to equip his people with a similar advantage, about 1809 he set his mind to the task, and after years of trial and error completed a Cherokee alphabet.

At first, the Cherokees held his discovery suspect. They thought Sequoyah was practicing witchcraft. In 1821, however, boldly appearing before the Cherokee council, he explained the invention of his writing and demonstrated its practical values to the tribe. The system was easy to learn, and the Cherokees rapidly took to it. Sequoyah began traveling, a teacher to his far-flung people; and within a few years thousands of Cherokees could read and write. Soon, books and newspapers began tumbling from the Indian's own presses, and the Cherokee people, blessed with the new literacy as was no other Indian tribe, quickly adopted the technological advantages of the white civilization overwhelming them.

Not stopping at that, Sequoyah served the Cherokees as a representative to the whites, trying to ameliorate a difficult time for his people when thousands of Cherokees were forcibly removed from their homelands in the Southeast to new lands in Oklahoma. Always curious, late in life Sequoyah set off on a long search to make contact with a Cherokee band rumored to have migrated to Mexico many years earlier. In this last effort he failed, dying in the Mexican state of Tamaulipas. Among the many honors accorded

to Sequoyah, subsequent generations named a genus of giant redwood and a national park in California after him.

Despite this widely accepted rendition of Sequoyah, heroes rarely are as simple as their pictures indicate, and cracks quickly appear in Sequoyah's bright image when one looks beyond the surface of its popular appeal. There are three basic approaches to this famous Native American, all variations of the above outline and all lacking solid supporting evidence. If each comes with its rather large set of factual problems, each nonetheless shows how different groups readily spin versions of historical figures to serve their own particular ends.

A Nineteenth-Century Romance

Weaving its subject in a gauzy web of the nineteenth century's preference for melodrama, George E. Foster's *Se-Quo-Yah: The American Cadmus and Modern Moses* reads more like a romantic novel than an historical work. It is a biography peopled with heroes and villains whose exaggerated vices and virtues, though soaring far beyond the human norm, agreeably excited white readers of the day. The impulse rings strong in the book's very subtitle, associating Sequoyah with two larger-than-life figures of divine favor. The reference to Cadmus links the Indian to the famed slayer of a sacred dragon and subsequent founder of Thebes. The Moses reference compares the Cherokee to the Biblical figure who led the ancient Jews from slavery to the Promised Land. Foster's shameless abandon to wanton comparison was effective for its day, cloaking the Indian in the mantle of the two main strains of Western civilization, Greek myth and the Judeo-Christian tradition, and thereby giving Sequoyah immediate cultural entrée.

Though laughable in terms of today's tastes, the book's wayward progress is worth following for more than its entertainment value. Immediately dubbed "noble" and hailed for his "high place among the great benefactors of mankind", Sequoyah is turned into a cultural contortionist by a Foster who at once touts the superiority of Indian culture and the superiority of his own. Before the coming of the white man, Cherokee life was so "charming and bright," so ideal that the Indians knew not the least discomforts, not even the minor maladies of stomachaches. Sequoyah's father, however, in Foster's account a lazy German trader representing the invasion of the evil white men, is a scofflaw so shiftless and disreputable that he's off philandering at the moment of the hero's birth. Yet it is a birth accompanied by near divine attention, by a "sighing of the forest" and a "musical rustle of leaves" that initiate the babe into his later genius. Be that as it may, Foster forces a valiant Sequoyah to overcome a series of difficulties that burnish his soul before he achieves fame. Sequoyah thus fulfills the earnest Horatio Alger model popular in the day's white culture.

Foster continues spinning his enthusiastic balderdash. In the process he displays a heady ignorance, one substituting wishful imagination both for his subject and for knowledge of the Cherokee way. Nineteenth-century prejudices are blithely imposed upon a far-off racial group. For instance, Foster instructs his readers, the Cherokee religion is "crude and undeveloped," lacking a moral code; yet how could such an unlettered person saddled with primitive concepts of the universe score the remarkable achievement of inventing an entire language? Foster has a ready answer. Though Sequoyah's father was a scalawag, he nonetheless passed on good genes. From the wayward German trader Sequoyah inherited "German transcendentalism" and the best of European "instinct and thought." These were so powerful that they lifted the Indian, allowing him intellectual flights far beyond his static Indian heritage. This, then, accounts, Foster tells us, not only for Sequoyah's linguistic genius but for the self-mending of his ways so that he falls in line with the white preachments of the day, to the extent of signing the temperance pledge. Sequoyah, therefore, is a "good Indian" to the measure that he fits European habits and ideals, a sentiment applying to Indians generally throughout the book's pages.

Yet it should be kept in mind that Sequoyah is not only a "good" Indian, he is an extraordinary Indian, in fact, a figure shining throughout history. His is no mere case of good genes and a talented person pulling himself up by his own bootstraps. Here, Foster brings into play his earlier comparison with Moses. For with Sequoyah we have yet another case of divine intervention, of God singling out Sequoyah for a purpose. And that purpose is nothing less than leading the Cherokee people to God, that is, to the Christian God.

Still, to Europeanize Sequoyah completely would lose him a great deal of his audience appeal. Whatever his accomplishments and conversion to white behavior, the mystery and exotic Indian romance clinging to him keeps awed readers turning Foster's pages. Foster has his hero meeting his end not in Mexico but in a pass in the shining Rocky Mountains. There, somewhat in the mode of Cooper's earlier Natty Bumppo, the aging Indian has a vision of the future, one of near Wagnerian proportions, before he expires—a vision, of course, of his people completely happy and prospering because they now follow white ways.

From visionary euphoria, the writer slides into sentimental speculation. No one knows the place where Sequoyah's bones lie high in the Rocky Mountains. Still, "It is not impossible, that in some future day, some traveler, student or explorer, in searching in some of the rocky caverns along the Colorado, for traces of silver or gold, shall find there a heap of human bones, the skull of which will indicate, that he who died there, was a man of more than common intellect. Should the finder be a phrenologist, he might stoop to study the skull and to wonder at the revealed capacities, and then, perhaps, as he holds his lamp nearer to this funeral pile, he may see something like a silver coin just where there was once a human heart—and it may prove to be the silver medal given to Se-quo-yah by his race." So Foster concludes his rhapsodic version of Sequoyah's life. However, in a long sermon Foster extolls the virtues of the Cherokee people, condemns the depredations of the whites, and curries favor for the missionary work bringing Christian blessings to the Cherokees. One notes further that *Se-Quo-*

Yah was published by the Indian Rights Association. In such circumstances, then, lies a clue to the outlandish biographical distortions visited upon Sequoyah. Most causes, whether for good or ill, benefit from erecting simple icons stirring widespread support. In creating an inaccurate but heroic image of Sequoyah, groups sympathetic to Indians rallied public excitement and thereby promoted their agendas.

An Accepted Modern View

At least one modern reference guide cites Grant Foreman's *Sequoyah* as the "standard biography," that is, the one we can now trust. Foreman's account has little of the bombast of its nineteenth-century predecessor. In fact, it makes bold to disagree on certain details, arguing, for instance, that Nathaniel Gist was not German but American, and it offers a plausible account of Sequoyah's demise in Mexico. All in all, the book follows the widely accepted outline of Sequoyah's life as initially presented above. However, Foreman passes on, without question, pictures of Sequoyah that ring with romanticized and overdramatized constructs. Thus, one traveler who claims to have visited Sequoyah reports that the Indian linguist reminded him of "an old Greek philosopher" whose eyes flash wildly before his face subsides into "a gentle & most benignant smile". Sounding suspiciously like the stereotype of what the nineteenth century thought Sequoyah *should* be, this and other passages undermine the sense of an encounter with a flesh-and-blood individual.

Moreover, nowhere does Foreman deal with a central conundrum: the unlikelihood of an uneducated person, whatever his exceptional abilities, inventing an entire alphabet out of whole cloth. Lastly, any study purporting to set the record straight on such a significant figure should as a matter of course offer copious documentation; one fears that the book largely repeats the romanticized version of Sequoyah, though this time made more palatable by stripping the earlier account of its most egregious hoopla.

A Recent Revisionist Theory

Traveller Bird's *Tell Them They Lie* does deal with the question of the origins of the Cherokee alphabet, along with many other doubts surrounding Sequoyah, but his answers are so bizarre as to call the whole fabric of his Sequoyah story into question. This Sequoyah descendant claims that the Cherokees had an alphabet for many years before Sequoyah's time. In the dim past, a "lost tribe" wandered out of the west and presented the Cherokees with a language written on "thin gold plates." Traveller Bird's approach turns the Sequoyah story inside out, claiming that the standard version is a white conspiracy. Here, Sequoyah becomes a hero of a different sort and to a different end. Now a full-blooded Cherokee, instead of helping the whites, he's a fierce warrior resisting their advances. As with the nineteenth-century account, Sequoyah has visions, but this time they spur Sequoyah to reclaim his birthright. Instead of dying in Mexico, he was killed by soldiers in Texas.

The story certainly has its appeal, if for no other reason than for its novelty. However, it smacks of an absolutist diatribe, the nineteenth-century version reversed, painting whites as "evil and foul-talking" and reviving the "Devil theory" of history. Even at that, this version could have some truth to it. Yet the book, supposedly based on original writings by Sequoyah and other Indians and found in caves, as with other accounts fails to produce the documentation. Very little for certain is known, then, of the historical Sequoyah and his contributions. Lacking sufficient verifiable information, perhaps the best that can be said is that the appealing stories surrounding this major figure have been spun to serve the wishes of their tellers.

SOURCES:

Biographical Dictionary of Indians of the Americas, Volume 2, Newport Beach, California, American Indian Publishers, 1991; 672-674.

Bird, Traveller, *Tell Them They Lie: The Sequoyah Myth,* Los Angeles, Westernlore Publishers, 1971.

Dockstander, Frederick J., *Great North American Indians,* New York, Van Nostrand Reinhold, 1977; 259-261.

Faulk, Odie B., "Sequoyah," in *McGraw-Hill Encyclopedia of World Biography,* Volume 9, New York, McGraw-Hill, 1973; 516-517.

Foreman, Grant, *Sequoyah,* Norman, University of Oklahoma Press, 1938.

Foster, George E., *Se-Quo-Yah: The American Cadmus and Modern Moses,* Philadelphia, Office of the Indian Rights Association, 1885.

"Sequoya," in *Handbook of American Indians North of Mexico,* Volume 2, Washington, D.C., Smithsonian Institution, 1912; 510-511.

Kilpatrick, Jack Frederick, *Sequoyah of Earth And Intellect,* Austin, Encino Press, 1965.

Woodward, Grace Steele, *The Cherokees,* Norman, University of Oklahoma Press, 1963.

—Sketch by Peter Wild

Kathryn W. Shanley
1947-

Assiniboine (Nakota) scholar
Also known as Kathryn Shanley Vangen

Active in the scholarship and teaching of Native American, American, and Third World literature, as well as feminist theory and criticism, Kathryn Winona Shanley is a member of the English faculty of Cornell University. She currently serves as co-chair of the university's American Indian Program Steering Committee and has served on important national boards and commissions, including the Committee on Languages and Literatures of the Americas

Kathryn W. Shanley

and the American Indian Literature Discussion Group of the Modern Language Association.

Born on December 1, 1947, in Wolf Point, Montana, Shanley is of the Assiniboine (Nakota) tribe of the Fort Peck Reservation. Her father, Ervin James Shanley, was a jazz musician and surveyor, and her mother, Winona Kathryn Simons Shanley Peabody, worked as a nurse's aide. According to Shanley, her parents divorced when she was quite young, and her mother held a position as a clerk for the Bureau of Indian Affairs (BIA) before becoming a nurse's aide. Shanley was married to James H. Vangen from 1968 to 1973, and during that time the couple had a son, Jay Marcus Vangen. In 1990, Shanley married David L. Moore, who is also involved in American Indian education.

In 1973, Shanley began a career in the field of medicine upon completing an associate degree in nursing at Metropolitan State University in Minneapolis. She worked as a nurse from 1973 to 1980. Shanley left a career in nursing to pursue scholarship in the field of literature. In 1980, she completed a bachelor of arts in English, graduating with highest honors from Moorhead State University in Moorhead, Minnesota. During her second year as a graduate student at the University of Michigan, she obtained a research assistantship in the university's Center for Afro-American and African Studies and English with Lemuel Johnson. She completed her Ph.D. in 1987, after two years as an acting assistant professor at the University of Washington.

Since her student days, Shanley's research and writing projects have been recognized by many prestigious awards and citations. Her essay titled "The Devil's Domain: Leslie Silko's 'Storyteller'" received second prize in the Dorothy Gies McGuigan essay competition at the University of Michigan in 1985; this essay examines Silko's short story as an example of post-colonial literature and appeared in *Coyote Was Here: Essays on Contemporary Native American Literary and Political Mobilization,* edited by Bo Scholer and published in Aarhus, Denmark. Shanley's other scholarly achievements include an A. D. White Society for the Humanities Fellowship in the fall of 1994, a Ford Foundation post-doctoral fellowship for the academic year 1988 to 1989, the Alison Tennant Myers scholarship from the alumni association of the University of Michigan in 1986, a Wellesley Women's fellowship for the year 1985 to 1986, and a Mellon Foundation fellowship during 1980 to 1984.

The writings of fellow Montana author James Welch have been one of the main subjects of Shanley's criticism and scholarship. Welch's poetry and fiction centers on historical and modern Blackfeet and Gros Ventre community life. Shanley has contributed articles on Welch's writings to scholarly books and journals published in the United States, Denmark, Canada and France, primarily focusing on comedy in Welch's fiction, his use of cinematic technique, and political overtones in his poetry and prose. Several of Shanley's articles and papers on Welch have been devoted to analyzing his historical novel, *Fools Crow.*

Shanley's writings and achievements reveal a sense of social obligation to communicate multicultural issues, and her commitment to community service is evident in her teaching and consulting activities. At scholarly conferences she has addressed topics such as "Mixed Bloods, Postcolonial Discourse, One World," "American Literary Pluralism: Rhetoric and Reality," "Ethnicity, Popular Culture, and the Law," and "A Sisters' Quarrel?: American Indian Women and Feminism." She taught a course in American Indian autobiography at Fort Peck Community College in Poplar, Montana, in 1994, and continues her commitment to bring her subjects to tribal colleges and historically black colleges and universities. She also participated as a faculty member in a program at the University of Washington Northwest Center for Research on Women titled "Different Voices: Integrating the Experience and Expression of American Ethnic Minority Women into Undergraduate American History and Literature Courses." Shanley has maintained a deep commitment to increasing academic opportunities for people of color, out of which evolved her participation on committees on racism and cultural diversity, recruitment and retention of minority faculty, and minority mentorship at the University of Washington. She is a founding member of Open Mind, The Association for the Achievement of Cultural Diversity in Higher Education.

SOURCES:

Shanley, Kathryn Winona, interview with Helen Jaskoski conducted July 1994.

—Sketch by Helen Jaskoski

Leslie Marmon Silko
1948-
Laguna Pueblo novelist and poet

Leslie Marmon Silko is best known for her 1977 novel *Ceremony,* in which she took the stories she had learned as a child and retold them in a contemporary setting. She illustrates her belief in the power of stories by using the novel form to create a powerful and moving experience for her readers in the Native American tradition of storytelling as healing, unifying, and contributing to continuance. In 1981, Silko was given a five-year grant by the MacArthur Foundation, which searches annually for men and women of genius and high potential.

Silko was born in Albuquerque on March 5, 1948, and raised in Old Laguna on the Pueblo Reservation in New Mexico. Her father, Lee Marmon, and her mother, a Native American of mixed Plains ancestry born in Montana, created a home that reflected Silko's background of Euro-American, Laguna and Mexican lineage. She was kept for her first year on a cradleboard by her mother, and her father treated her and her two younger sisters in ways that were not restrictive because they were girls. He took them hunting, and at age eight, Silko owned a horse. Later, she helped round up and drive the family's cattle. In the Laguna tradition, the people who came to repair the plaster were women. Silko's paternal grandmother, Lillie Marmon (born Francesca Stagner) was a Model A mechanic. An influential role model for Silko, she continued to use her mechanical skills to fix the machines in her son's coin-operated laundry even as an elderly woman. Lillie had been educated at Carlisle Indian School and Dickinson College in Carlisle before her marriage to Hank Marmon. Her mother, Helen, was from an old Spanish family in the area, and Silko's Mexican ancestry can be traced to them.

Hank (Henry) Marmon, Silko's grandfather, had attended Sherman Institute, an Indian School, in Riverside, California. He wanted to be an automobile designer, an occupation closed to Indians at the time, so he returned home to clerk in a store. He maintained an interest in automobiles all his life.

The culture in which Silko grew up was female-centered. The Lagunas are matrilineal, and women own the houses and the fields; the deities are female, the most prominent being Thought Woman, sometimes referred to as Spider Woman. Because of the importance of the female in Laguna culture and Silko's strong female and male role models, it is not surprising that she incorporates male and female characters into her novel with equal ease and feels herself to have grown up without restrictions. Because her mother was away at work, Silko was raised primarily by her great-grandmother, Marie Anaya Marmon, who was a full-blood from Paguate village north of Old Laguna. Marie or "A'mooh" as she was called had attended the Indian School

Leslie Marmon Silko

at Carlisle, Pennsylvania, and had married Robert G. Marmon, becoming a strong Presbyterian. She also saw much of her grandmother Lillie and her great-aunt Susie, wife of Walter K. Marmon, Hank's brother. Lillie, "Aunt" Susie and her great-grandmother were primarily the persons who told Silko the old stories.

In an interview with Kim Barnes, Silko discussed the representation of men and women in her work. Remarking that people have asked her why her male characters are vulnerable and complex and the women are less so, she said, "I grew up with women who were really strong, women with a great deal of power ... within the family.... If someone was going to thwart you or frighten you, it would tend to be a woman; you see it coming from your mother, or sent by your mother." The women are the authority figures, and "your dad is the one who's the soft touch, and it's the mother's brother who reprimands you."

The Marmons, the Euro-American men who figure so prominently in Silko's background, had come to New Mexico after the Civil War with other men including John Gunn (Paula Gunn Allen's great-grandfather) to work as surveyors. They married Laguna women and stayed in the area. The Marmon brothers, Walter G. and Robert G. (for Gunn), became traders, and both were Presbyterian. Robert Marmon, Silko's great-grandfather, was elected as Laguna governor for a year about the time that traditionalists reacting to the prohibition placed on their religious activities left Laguna. The Marmons were influential at Laguna, but also controversial and when the ceremonies were revived, they maintained somewhat of an outsider status. Silko grew up in the Marmon home in which her father was born, which was located outside the village proper. She helped with the revived ceremonies, but did not herself dance in them.

Education and Storytelling

Silko attended Catholic school in Albuquerque, which seemed to her always a bit foreign, but she was secure enough in herself and her culture not to feel that the strangeness was in herself. Silko attended the University of New Mexico at Albuquerque, marrying and then bearing her first son, Robert, in 1966 when she was just 18 and a first-semester sophomore. In 1969 she graduated from the University of New Mexico *Summa cum laude* in English honors and *Magna cum laude* in general honors. She attended law school at the University of New Mexico in a program intended to produce Native American lawyers until 1971 when she received her first National Endowment for the Arts (NEA) discovery grant for short fiction. This discovery grant was awarded for her story, "The Man to Send Rain Clouds," about an incident she read in the paper. In 1967, she had written the story for a creative writing assignment and discovered that writing came easily to her. The story was subsequently published in the *New Mexico Quarterly* and was the beginning of her writing career.

Silko believes that storytelling is a birthright of the Lagunas. Children hear stories from the time they are very small, and storytelling is a way of life. She feels fortunate to come from such a culture and believes that her skill is not just an accident. As a child, she loved to read stories from different places, which adds to her range. When she was in high school, she was interested in American authors such as William Faulkner, John Steinbeck, Flannery O'Connor, and Edgar Allan Poe. She particularly admired O'Connor's ability to take the same landscape and make new wonderful stories, and many of Silko's stories are set in and around Laguna.

Silko is never sure how much of her stories come from her imagination and how much she has heard and does not remember hearing. A case in point is "Tony's Story," which appeared in the 1974 collection, *The Man to Send the Rainclouds: Contemporary Stories by American Indians,* and was written while she was in college. The story is about the killing of a state policeman when Silko would have been only about four years old; it is from the perspective of a Native American man who had killed the policeman because he thought the policeman was a witch, a perspective that Silko thought she had invented. Later when the trial records were investigated, she found that what she thought she had imagined was fact. Her only conclusion was that she must have heard about the case as a small child and forgotten it.

Writing Career Accelerates

The early 1970s were very busy for Silko both in her personal life and in her writing career. In 1972, Silko gave birth to her second son, Cazimir. In 1973, she was awarded an NEA writers fellowship and a *Chicago Review* poetry prize, and her poetry chapbook, *Laguna Woman,* was published.

Silko's poetry demonstrates a finely tuned sense of place, and she often recreates old Laguna stories in her poetry, sometimes giving them a modern twist. In the foreword to *Laguna Woman,* she says: "I suppose at the core of my writing is the attempt to identify what it is to be a halfbreed or mixed blooded person; what it is to grow up neither white nor fully traditional Indian." Silko's double vision is evident in all her work, and allows her to write from the inside as well as the outside.

Silko taught two years at Navajo Community College at Tsaile and learned about Navajo witchcraft beliefs, which figure in some of her works. She then moved with her husband, John Silko, to Ketchikan, Alaska, where he took a position as the supervising attorney for Alaska Legal Services. During the next two years, while Silko was writing her novel, *Ceremony,* she was having migraines and was chronically ill. Her illness paralleled that of her main character, Tayo, a mixed-breed Laguna man back from World War II, and she said in an interview with Dexter Fisher that "as Tayo got better, I felt better." Silko named the novel, *Ceremony,* because "writing the novel was a ceremony for me to stay sane."

Ceremony was received with wide acclaim, the first Native American novel to be so noticed since N. Scott Momaday's 1968 novel, *House Made of Dawn.* Like Momaday's novel, *Ceremony* explores the plight of World War II Pueblo veterans; but unlike Momaday's novel, which has a rather ambiguous, depressing ending, *Ceremony* speaks to the continuance of the Pueblo people. Silko weaves the old stories into the text, paralleling the modern story of her veterans, culminating in a magnificent healing story inspired by and dedicated to Thought Woman. Set mostly on the Laguna Reservation, a prominent part of the story has to do with the uranium mining which has been carried on there since the 1940s and first atomic blast which was set off only 150 miles away. The deepest uranium mine shaft was sunk into Mount Taylor, a mountain sacred to the Pueblos and the Navajo and featured in the novel.

Shortly before the publication of *Ceremony,* Silko's short story, "Yellow Woman" had been included in Martha Foley's *Two Hundred Years of Great American Short Stories,* put out in time for the Bicentennial. Yellow Woman is a retelling of an old tale with a contemporary view. Yellow Woman is a kind of Pueblo everywoman who is taken away by a supernatural being, a Ka't'sina, sometimes returning home with twins. In the modern story, the woman goes off with a man who tries to convince her he is a Ka't'sina and she is Yellow Woman, but the reader sees her ambivalence and her passionate interest in him. Silko combines perfectly the old and the new in this gem of a story.

Personal Difficulties

Silko returned to New Mexico and taught at the University of New Mexico, finding it increasingly difficult to teach and find time to write. She moved to Tucson and

taught at the University of Arizona. She had met poet James Wright at a writer's conference in 1975, and after the publication of *Ceremony,* he wrote to tell her how much he liked the novel, thus beginning their correspondence which ended at his death from cancer in 1980. In her letters of 1978 which were collected by Wright's wife, Anne, and published in 1986 as *The Delicacy and Strength of Lace,* Silko admits she is having a very hard time; she is going through a second divorce, a custody battle, and money is tight. Wright's supportive letters were important to her. In the Spring semester of 1979, Silko was on leave from the University of Arizona and taught writing at the University of Washington in Seattle and did a three-week writing workshop at Vassar. The campus newspaper made much of her absence from the University of Washington, even though the English department had approved it, and Silko was upset. Money and time continued to be a pressing problem.

Situation Improves

Upon returning to Arizona, Silko continued to teach, and worked on four videotapes on Laguna stories funded by the National Endowment for the Humanities (NEH). Things began to improve; in 1980 Silko won a Pushcart IV prize. Silko had also written a short story, "Storyteller," while she was in Alaska, which demonstrated the process of storytelling and of being a Native American storyteller. This became the title story for her collection of photographs, short stories and poetry, entitled *Storyteller* and published in 1981. Most of her previously published short stories and poetry appear in this volume.

Also in 1981, Silko won the prestigious John and Catherine MacArthur Prize fellowship for work in fiction, poetry and film—$159,000 tax-free over five years. She used this money to free herself from her teaching responsibilities so that she could work full-time on her filmmaking and writing. After the publication of letters between her and James Wright, the *Boston Globe* awarded the book their prize for nonfiction. In 1988, Silko won the New Mexico Endowment for the Humanities, "Living Cultural Treasure" award. In 1989, she was given the University of New Mexico's Distinguished Alumnus award. 1991 saw the awarding of the Lilla Wallace-Reader's Digest Fund Writers award and the publication of Silko's 763 page opus, *Almanac of the Dead,* her most controversial work to date.

Silko sees *Almanac* as a sort of trial by novel. Her father in his capacity as tribal treasurer used stories to testify for the Laguna land boundaries, and Silko is collecting stories in the form of a novel to document 500 years of European abuse and oppression of Native Americans and the land, and is hoping to foretell a bit of the future. A vast tale of drug dealers, military tyrants, self-serving land developers, and even corrupt Native Americans, *Almanac* is a graphic and disturbing novel. In an appearance at Ohio University's Spring Literary Festival in Athens, Ohio, in 1992, when questioned about the depressing nature of the novel, Silko said that maybe it wasn't supposed to be read. Nevertheless, Silko's complex and passionate work is a testimony in her belief in the power of words to preserve and sustain a culture and will not soon be forgotten.

SELECTED WRITINGS BY SILKO:

Laguna Woman: Poems, Greenfield Center, New York, Greenfield Press, 1974.
Ceremony (novel), New York, Viking Press, 1977.
Storyteller, New York, Seaver Books, 1981.
With James Wright, *The Delicacy and Strength of Lace: Letters Between Leslie Marmon Silko & James Wright,* edited by Anne Wright, Saint Paul, Greywolf Press, 1986.
Almanac of the Dead (novel), New York, Simon & Schuster, 1991.

SOURCES:

Books

Allen, Paula Gunn, "The Feminine Landscape of Leslie Marmon Silko's Ceremony," in her *The Sacred Hoop: Recovering the Feminine in American Indian Traditions,* Boston, Beacon, 1986; 118-126.
The Man to Send Rain Clouds: Contemporary Stories by American Indians, edited by Kenneth Rosen, New York, Viking, 1974.
Ruoff, A. LaVonne, *American Indian Literatures: An Introduction, Bibliographic Review, and Selected Bibliography,* New York, Modern Language Association, 1990; 78-80.
Ruoff, A. LaVonne, *Literatures of the American Indian,* New York, Chelsea, 1991; 89-90.
Seyersted, Per, *Leslie Marmon Silko,* Boise, Boise State University Western Writers Series, Number 45, 1980.
"Stories and Their Tellers—A Conversation with Leslie Marmon Silko" in *The Third Woman: Minority Women Writers of the United States,* edited by Dexter Fisher, Boston, Houghton Mifflin, 1980; 18-23.
Van Dyke, Annette, "Curing Ceremonies: The Novels of Leslie Marmon Silko and Paula Gunn Allen" in her *The Search for a Woman-Centered Spirituality,* New York, New York University Press, 1992.

Periodicals

Barnes, Kim, "A Leslie Marmon Silko Interview," *Journal of Ethnic Studies,* 13:4, winter 1986; 83-105.
Evers, Lawrence, and Dennis Carr, "A Conversation with Leslie Silko," *Sun Tracks,* 3, fall 1976; 28-33.
"Indian Storyteller Wins Pot of Gold," *Greenfield Review: American Indian Writings,* 9:3/4, 1981; 103-105.
Seyersted, Per, "Two Interviews with Leslie Marmon Silko," *American Studies in Scandinavia,* 13, 1981; 17-33.
Work, James C., and Pattie Cowell, "Teller of Stories: An Interview with Leslie Marmon Silko," *Colorado State Review,* 8:2, spring-summer 1981; 68-79.

—Sketch by Annette Van Dyke

Jay Silverheels
1918(?)-1980
Mohawk actor
Also known as Harold J. Smith

A popular Native American actor, Jay Silverheels is perhaps best remembered as Tonto, the loyal Indian sidekick to the Lone Ranger in the notable television series, which ran from 1949 to 1957. He also performed in a number of films throughout the 1950s, the 1960s, and the 1970s. The first American Indian to be given a star on Hollywood's Walk of Fame, he has been credited with contributing to the development of favorable Hollywood portrayals of Native Americans in both television and film.

Silverheels, a full-blooded Mohawk Indian, was born Harold J. Smith on Six Nations Indian Reservation in Ontario, Canada. The Mohawks are a powerful tribe of the Iroquois Confederacy who still occupy a large reservation in New York State and Ontario. The son of Captain A.G.E. Smith, a decorated Canadian soldier of World War I, Silverheels was a strong athlete who achieved early fame in Canada as a champion lacrosse player. He was also skilled in hockey, football, and track, and had won several awards in boxing and wrestling.

Launched Acting Career

Silverheels first traveled to the United States in 1938 while playing on Canada's national lacrosse team. Shortly thereafter, he met Joe E. Brown, who launched his acting career. For nine years Silverheels had only minor roles in western films, in which American Indians were generally portrayed as villains. He had his first important role in 1947 when he played an Aztec warrior in *The Captain from Castile.* Despite being cast opposite the then famous actor Tyrone Power, Silverheels performed exceptionally well in several scenes, drawing the attention of numerous directors and producers. In 1949 Silverheels was cast as Tonto in "The Lone Ranger" television series, an offshoot from the popular radio program created by Fran Striker in 1933. The part of Tonto was originally played on the screen by veteran actor Chief Thunder Cloud, a Cherokee Indian. Silverheels adapted the role to his own personal style and became immensely popular in the process. As Tonto, Silverheels, along with Clayton Moore as the masked ranger, fought for law and order in the old American West. Overall, Silverheels appeared in 221 television installments of "The Lone Ranger" before the series was cancelled in 1957. Reruns of the program were shown through 1961; afterwards, the program was widely syndicated.

Prospered in Film

Silverheels' performance as Tonto, as well as his notable appearance in *The Captain from Castile,* greatly contributed to his later success in film. A tall and handsome

Jay Silverheels

man, Silverheels was well-liked by American audiences. He was therefore most often cast as a "good Indian," providing for a sharp contrast to the villainous roles usually given to Native Americans in early American film. Consequently, Silverheels has been credited, in part, with changing public opinion regarding American Indians through film.

While Silverheels appeared in many western pictures, a few performances were particularly important to his career. Among these was his 1950 portrayal of the Apache Indian chief, Geronimo, in the movie *Broken Arrow,* a picture often hailed as the first film to depict American Indians in a sympathetic light. In 1964 Silverheels starred in *Indian Paint,* which is a rite of passage movie about an Indian boy and his love for his horse, and in 1973 he co-starred in *Santee,* a film centering on the relationship between a bounty hunter and the son of a man he killed. Silverheels also co-starred in three "Lone Ranger" films during this period: *Lone Ranger* (1956), *Lone Ranger and the Lost City of Gold* (1958), and *Justice of the West* (1961). Throughout his career, Silverheels purposely selected non-violent projects in which American Indians and white people were able to co-exist peacefully. Also characteristic of his work is a thematic emphasis on good prevailing over evil. According to Silverheels, "children had better examples in those days."

Contributions to the Native American Community

In the 1960s, Silverheels founded and directed the Indian Actors Workshop in Hollywood. Through this workshop, he helped further the acting careers of several Native Americans during a time when roles for American Indians

were scarce and often limited. Silverheels was also active in numerous public service projects focusing on substance abuse and the elderly. On July 21, 1979, he became the first American Indian actor to have a star placed in Hollywood's Walk of Fame along Hollywood Boulevard.

On March 5, 1980, Silverheels died of complications from pneumonia at the Motion Picture and Television Country House in Woodland Hills, California. At the time of his death, he was survived by his wife, Mary, and four children, Marilyn, Pamela, Karen, and Jay Anthony. Since then, a sports recreation center has been built in his honor on his home reservation in Ontario.

SOURCES:

Books

Biographical Dictionary of Indians of the Americas, second edition, Newport Beach, California, American Indian Publishers, 1991; 687.
Corneau, Ernest N., *The Hall of Fame of Western Film Stars,* North Quincy, Massachusetts, Christopher Publishing House, 1969; 253-254.
Halliwell, Leslie, *Halliwell's Filmgoer's Companion,* ninth edition, New York, Harper; 1008.
Indians of Today, fourth edition, edited by Marion Gridley, ICFP, 1971; 126.
Native North American Almanac, edited by Duane Champagne, Detroit, Gale Research, 1994; 770, 1160.

Periodicals

New York Times, March 5, 1980.
Time, March 17, 1980; 65.

—Sketch by Wendy Pfeffer

Sinte Gleska
See Spotted Tail

Sitting Bull
1831(?)-1890
Hunkpapa Sioux tribal leader and warrior
Also known as Tatanka Iyotake

Sitting Bull is arguably the best-known Indian in American history. He was respected as a great warrior, chief, and holy man in the Sioux Nation. His reputation among his

Sitting Bull

own people gave him the unprecedented rank of primary chief of several Sioux bands. Also a singer and songwriter, Sitting Bull left a legacy of songs, many composed for special spiritual occasions and others of more secular content. He also left an autobiographical record of pictographic images of many of his exploits. Sitting Bull fought during the conflicts of the late nineteenth century, when the Sioux persistently resisted the white man's occupation of their land, destruction of their lifestyle, and desecration of their sacred places in the Black Hills of South Dakota. He is perhaps most remembered for his leadership during the Battle of the Little Big Horn, which occurred when General George Custer unsuccessfully attacked a massive group of Indians gathered to resist white domination. Known to the public through his appearances in Buffalo Bill Cody's Wild West Show and for his lifelong refusal to accommodate treaties and compromises that were detrimental to his people, Sitting Bull was killed during his arrest by government officials for supporting the ill-fated Ghost Dance movement. The movement, in turn, led to the massacre of several hundred Indians at Wounded Knee, South Dakota, in 1890.

Although Sitting Bull's year of birth has been reported to be various dates from 1831 to 1837, the most recent consensus is that Sitting Bull was born near the Grand River during the Winter-when-Yellow-Eyes-Played-in-the-Snow, interpreted as 1831. Until he first distinguished himself as a warrior at the age of 14, his name was Jumping Badger, but he was nicknamed "Slow." After "Slow" displayed courage in battle with the Crows, his father gave him the name of Sitting Bull and took for himself the name Jumping Bull.

By 1856, Sitting Bull was one of the two honored sash wearers of the Hunkpapa's Strong Heart warrior society. After receiving a bullet wound in the foot, which left him with a permanent limp, he was named leader of the Strong Hearts, and he was a cofounder of the elite Midnight Strong Hearts. As a leader, he successfully fulfilled his role as tribal hunter and kept the tribal hunting grounds cleared of competition from other tribes.

Sitting Bull's first wife died in childbirth in 1853, and his four-year old son died in 1857. That same year he adopted his sister's four-year old son, One Bull. In a raid on the Assiniboin that year, Sitting Bull adopted a young captive as his brother. This eventually led to a temporary truce between the Hunkpapa and Assiniboin. One Bull and his brother White Bull later in life provided firsthand information about Sitting Bull for researchers.

In 1862, the eastern Sioux in Minnesota rebelled against pressure of white settlement. Several of the Dakota Sioux fled west and found refuge with the western Sioux, bringing white troops behind them. For the next few years, Sitting Bull's Hunkpapas participated with several other bands of Sioux in fighting the troops of Generals Henry H. Sibley and Alfred Sully. Sully's victory at the battle at Killdeer Mountain in 1864 caused factionalism to develop among the Sioux leaders. Some were ready to surrender after seeing the firepower of the white army. Others, like Sitting Bull, became more aggressive. The first official mention of Sitting Bull in white documents was in Sully's report on the raid at Fort Rice in 1865.

Fights against Indian Relocation to Reservations

Although Sitting Bull was instrumental in the rout of Cole and Walker's Powder River march on September 8, 1865, generally he was located to the north of Red Cloud's War around Fort Laramie. While Red Cloud's Oglalas fought against development of the Bozeman Trail, Sitting Bull mounted a campaign against the forts on the Upper Missouri River. In 1867 he was inaugurated chief of several Sioux bands, with the Oglala Crazy Horse as second in command. This was a very untraditional political organization for the Lakota, but indicates the respect and trust that many of the Sioux had in Sitting Bull as a leader.

As part of the government's peace policy, the Jesuit missionary Father Pierre-Jean De Smet met with Sitting Bull to try to persuade him to give up the fight against the white plan to settle the Sioux on reservation lands. Sitting Bull's speech summarized his terms for peace: he did not propose to sell any part of his country; the whites must quit cutting timber along the Missouri River; and the forts of the white soldiers must be abandoned. Although Sitting Bull refused to sign the 1868 Treaty, government officials believed that signatures by Gall and Bull Owl represented Sitting Bull's Hunkpapas. In reality, Gall and Bull Owl probably did not even understand what they were signing, and they in no way represented the sentiments of Sitting Bull who was adamantly opposed to white settlement. Later government accusations that Sitting Bull did not live up to the treaty consequently held no meaning for him.

Sometime between 1867 and 1870, Sitting Bull adopted a rescued mail carrier. This man, Frank Grouard, provided information and advice about dealing with the white world. Sitting Bull's last offensive attack was the war expedition against Fort Buford in 1870. In 1871, again willing to negotiate for peace, Sitting Bull settled near Fort Peck. The difficult winter of 1872 caused a number of Sioux to go into the Milk River Agency for rations and clothing. This "temporizing" policy of the government led to further factionalism within Sioux bands, but was not strong enough to sway most bands permanently into the white system.

Throughout these years, Sitting Bull's bands also maintained their traditional warfare with the Crows and the Flatheads. Internal tribal society continued to change. Sitting Bull became a powerful leader in a newly formed secret society called the Silent Eaters. In 1875 or 1876, he also formed a visible group called the White Horse Riders, a kind of *akicita,* or police guard. In 1872, Sitting Bull acquired two new wives, replacing two earlier wives, one whom he had thrown out and the other who had died. These two new wives, daughters of Gray Eagle, stayed with him until his death.

On August 14, 1872, Sitting Bull led warriors out to warn off Stanley's soldiers protecting the surveyors of the Northern Pacific Railroad line in the Yellowstone valley. To convince his warriors to quit the battle once it became obvious they had lost, Sitting Bull, sat down in the midst of the fight to smoke. Several others joined him, and all were unharmed. This display of his bravery and power encouraged all but Crazy Horse and White Bull who made one last run at the soldiers. Crazy Horse's horse was shot from under him, and he had to return to camp riding with another warrior.

Sees Vision and Unites Tribes with "Sun Dance"

After George Custer's discovery of gold in Black Hills 1874, white miners and settlers increased pressure on the government in Washington to clear the land of Indians. In 1875 the government ordered all Sioux to come to agencies on the White River. Busy negotiating a truce with the Assiniboin and fighting the Canadian mixed bloods, Sitting Bull ignored the demand. In 1876 the government launched a military campaign to capture the rebel bands of plains Indians. In March 1876, General George Crook, led by Sitting Bull's former friend and now army scout Frank Grouard, attacked a Northern Cheyenne village on the Powder River. The victims from the village joined Crazy Horse and retreated to Sitting Bull's village between the Powder and Little Missouri rivers. Sitting Bull and Crazy Horse began planning strategies for the combined bands gathered at the village. Of the Lakota people, there were gathered more than 10,000 Hunkpapa, Oglala, Sans Arc, Minniconjou, Blackfeet, and Brulé Indians. Other bands included Cheyenne and the remaining Dakota refugees from the 1862 Minnesota conflict, along with some Yanktonais. The groups moved gradually toward the Rosebud and Little Big Horn rivers.

Sitting Bull experienced a series of visions which were interpreted as signs of a great Indian victory. At a sun dance, known as "Sitting Bull's Sun Dance," Sitting Bull gave 100

pieces of skin from his arms as sacrifice and had another vision of hundreds of soldiers coming toward an Indian village, and all the soldiers were upside down. Again interpreted as a victory image, the vision gave new force to the feelings of outrage and invincibility in the camps.

Helps Lead Battle of the Little Big Horn

On June 17, 1876, Crazy Horse and Sitting Bull led warriors against the soldiers at the Battle of the Rosebud. Still recovering from his sun dance sacrifice, Sitting Bull dropped out of the battle. Sensing victory, the village relocated in the valley of the Greasy Grass (the Little Big Horn) river and celebrated for six days. Although it was a great victory, it did not fulfill the sun dance vision of white soldiers falling upside down into their camp. On June 25, the prophecy was fulfilled when Custer and Reno engaged them in the famous Battle of the Little Bighorn, a massive and historic defeat for U.S. troops in which Custer and his troops were killed.

Sitting Bull went back to his camping area on the Grand River near Twin Buttes. On September 9, 1876, word came to the camp of an attack on the camp near Slim Buttes. Sitting Bull led his warriors to help in defense, but Crook's troops were too strong. The white retaliation for Custer's loss pressured many of Sitting Bull's allies to abandon him and surrender with American Horse and his combined Oglala and Minniconjou bands. October 1876 Sitting Bull and General Nelson A. Miles attempted to negotiate, but misunderstanding and lack of patience caused another battle to break out. Throughout the winter, continual military pressure forced the surrender of Dull Knife's Northern Cheyenne, Lame Deer's Minniconjou and finally Crazy Horse's Oglalas.

Escapes to Wander in Canada

In early May 1877, Sitting Bull crossed the international boundary into Queen Victoria's Canada, the land of the "Great Mother." After Crazy Horse was stabbed to death while resisting incarceration at Camp Robinson in September, several of his followers escaped to join Sitting Bull. Delegations met with Sitting Bull to convince him to return to the United States, but he refused. In 1879, he followed the buffalo south of the border to obtain food and supplies for his people, but General Miles drove him back into Canada. Canadian officials gradually eroded the support of several of Sitting Bull's followers. Some of them, including Rain-in-the-Face, left in 1880, surrendering at Fort Keogh. Finally in July, 1881, because of scarce food and lack of support from the Canadian government, Sitting Bull allowed the trader Jean Louis Legare to escort him to Fort Buford. Again mistrusted, he was confined at Fort Randall for the next two years while his followers were placed at the Standing Rock reservation. Once at the Standing Rock reservation, Sitting Bull was embroiled in a constant feud with agent James McLaughlin, who almost immediately enrolled Sitting Bull in exhibition tours. For almost two years, Sitting Bull was a feature attraction in Buffalo Bill's Wild West show.

Throughout the 1880s, the government policy became one of "civilization." The tribal economy vanished. Vanishing buffalo herds also meant vanishing social structure and material culture. Red Cloud, Spotted Tail, and Sitting Bull hung tenaciously to the institutions of chief and tribal council. Agents were encouraged to strip "nonprogressive" chiefs of their power and to break up tribal relationships. At the same time, they rewarded "progressive" chiefs with nice houses and more power than they would have had traditionally. Indian police forces, supported by agents, replaced the traditional *akicita* societies. Christianity was to replace traditional religion, and children were sent to day schools and off-reservation boarding schools to become educated in the white traditions. By the end of the decade, the Sioux were full of bitterness, helplessness, and futility.

To exacerbate the Indians' loss further, the government took away more land in the Sioux Act of 1889. This act, left only three sections of land from the original Great Sioux Reservation. It was then divided into six reservations. The size of each was to contain only enough land to allow for individual allotments, the remainder to be sold off to white settlers as part of Henry L. Dawes' General Allotment Act of 1887. Sitting Bull was part of a group of leaders taken to Washington, D.C., in October of 1888 to negotiate a compromise. Although Sitting Bull held fast, General George Crook exploited Sioux factionalism to get the necessary signatures of three-fourths of the adult males, in spite of overwhelming opposition to the agreement. After the harsh winter of 1889-90 spawned starvation and epidemics, the Sioux had lost hope. When word spread of a new Messiah, their hope was revived. A Paiute prophet called Wovoka declared that by embracing his new religion and dancing the Ghost Dance, Indians would find eternal peace.

Tribes Attempt to Unite through "Ghost Dance" Ritual

First at Pine Ridge, then at Rosebud and Cheyenne River reservations, ghost dancers gathered. Sitting Bull invited Kicking Bear, a witness of the dance's power, to bring the message to Standing Rock. Kicking Bear arrived October 9 and began teaching the Ghost Dance. By the time McLaughlin had Kicking Bear escorted off the reservation, Sitting Bull was already a supporter of the new religion. Whether he actually believed the Messiah's message or whether he saw the religion as a new weapon in his ongoing war with agent McLaughlin, Sitting Bull did act the part of apostle of the Ghost Dance at Standing Rock. Fearing an uprising from the Messiah influence, McLaughlin urged Sitting Bull's removal from Standing Rock reservation.

General Miles, who sent troops to Pine Ridge and Rosebud, also believed that Sitting Bull should be removed. A battled ensued between the military and Indian affairs bureaucracies as to how best to arrest Sitting Bull. Miles hired his old friend Buffalo Bill Cody to arrest Sitting Bull, but McLaughlin had his translator, Louis Primeau intercept Cody on his way to Sitting Bull's camp and convince him that Sitting Bull had already returned to the agency. McLaughlin's plan was to use agency police to arrest Sitting Bull during the harsh winter, and to withhold rations from those participating in the Ghost Dance. In order to prevent Miles from bringing troops to arrest Sitting Bull, he devised a plan whereby he would have agency police arrest him on ration day. The plan was to be implemented December 20. However, worried that Sitting Bull would leave the reservation to go to Pine Ridge to learn more of the Ghost Dance, McLaughlin decided he could wait no longer. With mixed feelings, the Hunkpapa police force entered Sitting Bull's cabin at daybreak December 15. Sitting Bull submitted without a fight until his followers gathered around his cabin and encouraged him not to surrender. Sitting Bull was killed in the ensuing fight, along with his son, Crow Foot, and several other supporters and policemen. Two weeks later, as the Seventh Cavalry attempted to disarm Big Foot, a Minniconjou who had fought with Sitting Bull at Spotted Elk, the massacre at Wounded Knee unfolded, ending the Ghost Dance, and further poisoning Sioux-white relations for generations to come.

Sitting Bull was originally buried without ceremony in the post cemetery at Fort Yates, but Hunkpapas requested his removal to the Grand River. In 1953, to keep the burial site from being flooded by the construction of dams on the Missouri River, Sitting Bull's nephew Clarence Gray Eagle may have taken the warrior's bones from Fort Yates to a site on the Grand River, where a memorial sculpted by Korczak Ziolkowski was constructed. Because the Fort Yates burial site was not flooded by the dams, a marker remains there which states only: "He was buried here but his grave has been vandalized many times." No one can say for sure where Sitting Bull's remains are. In 1892, Sitting Bull's cabin was moved to Chicago to become part of North Dakota's exhibit at the World's Columbian Exhibition, and his gray circus horse was purchased by Buffalo Bill and used to lead his grand procession at the fair.

By his two wives of 1872, Sitting Bull was known to have twin sons born just before the Battle at the Little Bighorn in 1876, a daughter born in 1878, twin boys (including Crow Foot) born in Canada 1880, a son in 1887, and a daughter in 1888. Sitting Bull's memory has been an inspiration to generations of Sioux, and while sometimes he has been overglorified, there is no question that he was in fact a great Hunkpapa patriot, true to the values and institutions of his culture, and one who remained adamantly opposed to white influence.

SOURCES:

Biographical Dictionary of Indians of the Americas, Newport Beach, California, 1983; 460-462.

Dockstader, Frederick J., *Great North American Indians,* New York, Van Nostrand Reinhold, 1977; 266-269.

Native North American Almanac, edited by Duane Champagne, Detroit, Gale Research, 1994; 1161-1162.

Paulson, T. Emogene, and Lloyd R. Moses, *Who's Who Among the Sioux,* Vermillion, Institute of Indian Studies, University of South Dakota, 1988; 220.

Utley, Robert M., *The Lance and the Shield: The Life and Times of Sitting Bull,* New York, Henry Holt, 1993.

Utley, Robert M., *The Last Days of the Sioux Nation,* New Haven, Yale University Press, 1963.

Vestal, Stanley, *Sitting Bull, Champion of the Sioux; a Biography,* Norman, University of Oklahoma Press, 1957.

—Sketch by Karen P. Zimmerman

Smith, Harold J.
See Silverheels, Jay

Juane Quick-to-See Smith
1940-
Salish/Cree/Shoshone artist

Juane Quick-to-See Smith's art work is contemporary as well as traditional. Shown nationally in prestigious art galleries, her art is described as expressing the traditionally abstract art enjoyed by the Native American, showing the merging of the animate with the landscape, and revealing Smith's appreciatiation for modern art. As an ardent supporter of Native American scholarship and education, Smith has donated her time and talent by offering professional and educational oppportunity to aspiring artists, and the experience of the beauty of her world to the general public.

Smith was born in 1940 on the Flathead Indian Reservation in St. Ignatius, Montana. Her lineage is of Salish, French-Cree/Shoshone descent. Her father, a horse trader, was a significant influence in her decision to pursue a career as an artist. As an amateur artist and a collector of Charles Russell prints, he put value in art and passed on his appreciation for art and beauty to his daughter. Smith owned a horse, "Cheyenne," of which she placed an image in every art work. In 1976, Smith earned a bachelor of arts in art education from Farmingham State College, and in 1980, a master of fine arts in Painting from the University of Mexico. She has since made her home in New Mexico.

Artistic Influences

Appying knowledge gained through her Native heritage and through university studies, Smith has created paintings that are both traditional and contemporary, revealing her Native influence and also an appreciation for the work of artists like Kooning, Klee, Miro, and Picasso. The strength of her work is in the traditional images of animals and landscape, rock art, and cave paintings. She is quoted in *Native American Women* as saying that she "makes parallels from the old world to contemporary art ... like being able to speak two languages and find a word that is common to both." She has consistently included in her work a circle of flame-like tufts representing the sites where tepees were once located but are now overgrown with grasses, and much of her work has been done in earth colors.

Honors and Achievements

Smith has merged the two generes of traditional or Native abstract and contemporary successfuly in her paintings. An excellent artist in both Native American and contemporary art circles, Smith's paintings have been included in permanent collections in both the United States and Europe, including the Heard Museum in Phoenix, the Museum of Modern Art in San Francisco, and the Corcoran Art Gallery in Washington, D.C. Her work has been shown in over 25 solo exhibits and more than 50 group exhibits. Some of her honors include the Purchase Award of Arts and Letters in 1987 and fellowship award from the Western States Art Foundation in 1988. In 1989, she was named honorary professor and Beaumont Chair at Washington University in St. Louis.

Smith has contributed to the field of art as a founder and administrator of art programs and as a contributor to and judge and curator of various art exhibits. As a patron of art and education for the Flathead Reservation, she has assisted in granting scholarships for the Salish-Kootenai College on the reservation. She established both the Coup Marks artists' cooperation on Flathead Reservation, as well as the Grey Canyon artists' cooperation in Albuquerque, which evolved into a nationwide program. Smith has also served on the panels of arts commissions in Washington and Idaho and on the board for ATATL, a Native American organization for the arts. In New York she was one of the curators for the Indian Women's Exhibit for AIR Gallery and for "Sweetgrass, Cedar, and Sage" at the Gallery of the American Indian Community House.

A major achievement in her career as an artist has been the opening of her first solo show in New York, where her work exhibited a bold blend of Native-American art and modernism in her landscape series entitled "Kalispell" and "Porcupine Ridge." In each painting, the Native American influence is manifest in the portrayal of the land and its relationship to the people and animals that dwell there. The colors and images she chooses represent events, such as hunting, which are common on the prairie. Figures are represented abstractly, the horses as outlined tubular bodies and the people as stick figures, borrowed from presentations found on painted skins. She also taps from abstract designs found on Indian blankets, which are displayed in primary colors and simple geometric shapes.

SOURCES:

Books

Native American Women, edited by Gretchen Bataille, New York, Garland Publishing, 1993; 239-240.

Periodicals

Bass, Ruth, "Juane Quick-to-See Smith," *Art News,* March 1984; 224.

Cohen, Ronny, "Juane Quick-to-See Smith at Kornblee," *Art in America,* 68, March 1980; 116-117.

—*Sketch by Wendy Pfeffer*

Smohalla

1815(?)-1895

Wanapam spiritual leader

Also known as Yuyunipitqana ["The Shouting Mountain" or "Big Talk on Four Mountains"]

Smohalla was the Wanapam dreamer-prophet and spiritual leader responsible for revitalizing the traditional Washani religion of the Pacific Northwest. He lived along the Columbia River in present-day Washington state during the mid- to late-nineteenth century and advocated a return to the Wanapams' ancient ways and values. Smohalla's teachings combined traditional native beliefs with elements of Christianity. He also taught that the coming of the white man had put the world on a course of self-destruction and the only way to avert the end of the world was for the Indians to restore the balance of nature by returning to traditional ways. He opposed the government's attempts at putting Indians on reservations and was against farming and ranching, advocating peaceful resistance to the U.S. government and missionaries. With his followers he remained on ancestral lands along the Columbia River, continuing to live a traditional life based on fishing, hunting, and gathering. A variant of Smohalla's teachings, the Washat, or Seven Drums religion, is still being practiced by Indians along the river and on the Yakima, Nez Percé, and Warm Springs reservations.

Smohalla was born sometime between 1815 and 1820 on the Columbia River in what is today Wallula, Washington. Wallula ["many streams"], was a mecca for the Columbia Plateau's tribes and bands coming to fish, trade, and socialize on the Columbia River. Like most Native Americans, Smohalla possessed several names; he did not receive the name Smohalla until he was an adult and recognized as a spiritual leader. The name Smohalla, from the Shahaptian language, has been translated as "dreamer," although some sources claim it meant "preacher." At birth he was named Wak-wei, or Kuk-kia ["Arising from the Dust of the Earth Mother"]; he was later named Yuyunipitqana ["The Shouting Mountain"], because of a revelation that came to him during a dream. This vision of a mountain speaking inside his soul was rendered into English as "Big Talk on Four Mountains." Another of his names was Waipshwa ["Rock Carrier"].

Becomes a Spiritual Leader

The Wanapams were peaceful people with a tradition of spiritual leaders, prophets, and shamans. Prior to Smohalla's ascendancy another dreamer-prophet, Shuwapsa, had predicted the coming of the white man, warning his people that the newcomers would destroy the Indians. Smohalla, who came from a long line of shamans and prophets began his spiritual training with the traditional vision quest. Eventually he became what his people called a yantcha, a leader with strong spiritual qualifications. Smohalla's rise to leadership was precipitated by the arrival of white missionaries, soldiers, settlers, and the diseases they brought with them. Traditional shamans appeared powerless against the threats posed by whites, the old ways were especially ineffective against the white man's diseases. The Indians of the Columbia Plateau needed special leaders who could offer them hope and a revitalized spiritual power. These spiritual leaders had to give their people a vision of a future in which the Indians not only survived but flourished. Smohalla was such a spiritual leader.

Smohalla was a small man with a hunched back and an inordinately large head. Neither a great warrior nor a hunter, Smohalla's power was based solely on charisma and his spiritual teachings. He had perhaps as many as ten wives and numerous children, and all of his children and grandchildren, except for his son Yo-Yonan, died prior to his own death. Smohalla's failure to save a beloved adolescent daughter's life, combined with the deaths of other Indian children, contributed to his development as a dreamer-prophet.

Contacts with fur traders, Christian Indians, and missionaries exposed Smohalla to Christian ideas. The Christian doctrine of resurrection was one of the ideas that influenced Smohalla's teachings, and resurrection became one of the tenets of the Dreamer religion. Both Smohalla and his followers claimed that he had died twice, each time returning to life. By going into a trance, or dying and returning to life, the dreamer-prophet received revelations from the Great Spirit. Smohalla said that he received the Great Spirit's revelations from a small bird, gaining as many as 120 power songs and numerous rituals while in trances. The idea that wisdom came to one in dreams was an ancient Wanapam belief and a fundamental teaching of the dreamer-prophets. Smohalla's creed included two other essential teachings: all Indians were to return to their traditional rituals and religious practices, abandoning all aspects of "civilization," and a supernatural intervention was going to destroy the whites. On this "Millennial Day" all of the dead Indians would return to life to carry on the old ways with their living relatives.

Opposes Farming and Ranching

Smohalla was adamant in his opposition to farming and ranching, stressing the importance of the Indians' traditional ways. He preached that hunting, fishing, gathering berries, digging roots, and maintaining "first foods" and other traditional ceremonies was the path to salvation. Smohalla's well-known and eloquent statement concerning his disdain for farming is quoted in Robert H. Ruby and John A. Brown's, *Dreamer-Prophets of the Columbia Plateau: Smohalla and Skolaskin:* "You ask me to plough the ground! Shall I take a knife and tear my mother's bosom?... You ask me to dig for stone! Shall I dig under her skin for bones?... You ask me to cut grass and make hay and sell it, and be rich like white men, but how dare I cut off my mother's hair?"

Smohalla's teachings not only led to conflicts with whites, he also alienated other Indian leaders. Chief Moses of the Columbia Sinkiuses offered the greatest challenge to Smohalla. According to one story, Moses nearly killed Smohalla in a fight. Smohalla then fled the country, returning after wandering as far south as Mexico. Whether or not the story is true, a rivalry certainly existed between these two influential leaders. Another conflict existed between Smohalla and the Wallawalla chief Homily, who tended to be more open to white ideas. Smohalla's rise to leadership also challenged another powerful Wallawalla chief, Peopeomoxmox. Desiring to be free of whites and Indian leaders who opposed him, Smohalla left Wallula, moving north with his followers to P'na Village on the Priest Rapids of the Columbia River. The Wanapams, who never signed a treaty, had been lumped in with the Yakima Nation during treaty negotiations in 1855. When the Yakima War broke out shortly after the treaty was signed, Smohalla and his Wanapams refused to take up arms against the whites, alienating the Yakima war chiefs.

The Washat dance or Pom Pom ["drums beating like hearts"], was the primary religious ceremony performed by the dreamer-prophet's followers. Other dreamer-prophets besides Smohalla also conducted Washat dances, aiding in the revival of the Washani amongst the Indians of the Northwest. Followers of the dreamer-prophets existed amongst the Columbia Plateau's Umatillas, Yakimas, Wascos, Nez Percé, and the Modocs of southern Oregon and northern California. Although Smohalla's teachings emphasized nonviolence, most whites failed to understand that. Rumors of war dances at Priest Rapids and of an Indian uprising led by Smohalla were common in the Northwest's white communities. Smohalla's notoriety and his refusal to move onto a reservation led the whites to label him a renegade and troublemaker. Government officials and most other whites could not comprehend the Dreamers' beliefs; to them the Dreamer religion was nothing more than superstition and its followers "fanatics."

One exception to the Northwest's anti-Smohalla rhetoric was an article appearing in the July 1886 issue of a local publication, the *North Yakima Farmer.* A writer recommended that the name Smohalla be adopted for the proposed state of Washington. In 1886 the suggestion found no support. A century later, in 1989 during Washington State's centennial celebrations, Smohalla was selected for the state's Hall of Honor as one of the 100 persons whose contributions were influential to both the state and the nation.

By 1890 the government's efforts to round up Indians living off the Northwest's reservations increased. With access to their root grounds and fishing sites becoming more

difficult, and constant pressure from authorities to give up their traditional beliefs and practices, the Indians had few options besides moving to the reservations. Although some stayed on lands along the Columbia River, most moved to reservations. By 1895, at the time of his death, even Smohalla had left Priest Rapids for the Yakima Indian Reservation. Although he left his village on the Columbia River, Smohalla continued to believe in his religion, passing on the leadership to his son Yo-Yonan. After his son's death during a hunting expedition in the winter of 1917, Smohala's nephew Puck Hyah Toot ["Birds Feeding in a Flock"], took over as the leading Priest Rapids prophet. He conducted Washat ceremonies in the Priest Rapids longhouse until his death in 1956. Another Wanapam, Rex Buck took over after Puck Hyah Toot's death. Buck's son Rex Jr., succeeded him in 1975.

Smohalla's impact on the Indians of the Columbia Plateau was significant: it gave them hope for the future and pride in their traditions. One hundred years after Smohalla's death, Indians in the Northwest continue to practice a variant of his teachings. The Pom Pom, Seven Drums, or Longhouse Religion and its ceremonies, such as the first-foods feasts, are still being held on reservations and in Indian communities in the Northwest.

SOURCES:

Mooney, James, *The Ghost-Dance Religion and the Sioux Outbreak of 1890,* edited and abridged by Anthony F. C. Wallace, Chicago, The University of Chicago Press, 1965; 49.

Native North American Almanac, edited by Duane Champagne, Detroit, Gale Research, 1994; 1164.

Relander, Click, *Drummers and Dreamers,* Seattle, Pacific Northwest National Parks and Forests Association, and Caxton Printers, Ltd., 1986.

Ruby, Robert H., and John A. Brown, *Dreamer-Prophets of the Columbia Plateau: Smohalla and Skolaskin,* Norman, University of Oklahoma Press, 1989.

—Sketch by Michael F. Turek

Reuben Snake, Jr.
1937-1993
Winnebago tribal and religious leader

Former Winnebago tribal chairman Reuben Snake, Jr., was a prominent voice in the struggle for Native American rights. Members of the Winnebago tribe lived for years in the state of Wisconsin but were forcibly "removed" from their homeland and resettled in the Nebraska region of the

Great Plains as whites moved westward. As a political, spiritual, and educational leader, Snake typified the strength, dignity, and resilience of the Winnebago people.

Reuben Snake, Jr., was born in 1937 in Winnebago, Nebraska. Snake grew to manhood on a settlement adjoining the reservation of the Omaha tribe. The Nebraska Winnebagos had long been actively involved in the Native American Church, a religious movement that combines Native American philosophy and beliefs with certain aspects of Christianity. (Church ritual centers on the use of mescaline, a hallucinogenic drug from the button of the peyote cactus, as a sacrament.) With the strong identity of the Winnebago people, the positive values fostered by the Native American Church, and the friendship of the neighboring Omaha around him, Snake learned a deep, abiding pride in his Indian heritage from an early age. He went on to become a respected church leader.

Although he did not earn a college degree, Snake attended the University of Nebraska in Lincoln from 1964 to 1965 and Peru State College from 1968 to 1969. He was a staunch advocate of education for Indian people and eventually became a teacher in adult education.

Draws National Attention as Activist

Snake's position as a road man and prayer chief in the Native American Church brought him to national prominence in 1972. American Indians from all corners of the United States—urban and reservation dwellers, teenagers and elders, political activists and traditional religious leaders—traveled in caravans across the country in what was called the Trail of Broken Treaties, a mass movement intended to focus national attention on the abuses of Native American rights by federal, state, local, and tribal governments. The caravans eventually converged on the Bureau of Indian Affairs (BIA) in Washington, D.C., and Snake emerged as a leader in the chorus of dignified protest. Though known for his fairness, tact, and diplomacy, he is remembered as an uncompromising fighter for Native rights.

Snake was elected national chairman of the American Indian Movement (AIM) in 1972. His election was an indicator of AIM's overall commitment to the integration of traditional religions into the organization. Snake was an effective leader and his wisdom was especially appreciated by AIM's urban Indian membership. These urban people—often one or more generations removed from their reservations, religions, customs, and languages—seemed to be drawn to the traditional style of leadership that Snake exemplified with great distinction.

Becomes Winnebago Leader and Spokesperson

After his service as AIM chairman, Snake ran for tribal office, becoming chairman of the Winnebago tribe in 1975. He was such a competent and respected leader that he held this position for more than a dozen years. During this time, he also kept up his duties with the Native American Church and spoke widely on subjects ranging from Indian education to Native American religious rights. In addition, he worked as a conflict resolution manager and, later, as a teacher at Winnebago Community College and the Institute of American Indian Arts in Santa Fe, New Mexico.

Snake's efforts on behalf of Indian peoples earned him considerable recognition, including the Nebraska Indian Commission Citizenship Award, the Distinguished Nebraskan Award, and the U.S. Secretary of the Interior's Certificate of Recognition. Other honors came in the form of positions with national Indian organizations. He headed the National Congress of American Indians (NCAI; the oldest still-functional intertribal organization in the United States) from 1985 to 1987—a difficult time for Indian leaders. The U.S. federal government, under a Republican administration sometimes seen as "unfriendly" to Native concerns, dealt cutback after cutback to programs serving Natives Americans. As national president of NCAI, the most visible lobbying group for upholding Indian rights, Snake was especially outspoken about the sanctity of treaty obligations.

Snake also served as a consultant to prominent Comanche activist LaDonna Harris' organization, Americans for Indian Opportunity. The group was designed to encourage appropriate economic development on reservations and in other Indian communities, and Snake's expertise as the chairman of a tribe that was succeeding in the dominant economic system made for a perfect match. In addition, Snake's integrity as a traditional religious leader and cultural preservationist helped him to guide the organization in the observance and conservation of Native American values.

Reuben Snake, Jr.'s last professional posting was as an instructor and cultural resource person with the Institute of American Indian Arts in Santa Fe. While there, his health began to fail, and he returned to his beloved Winnebago people in the northeastern Nebraska grasslands. Snake died there a few months later in 1993. Friends recall how he had always signed his personal correspondence "Your Faithful Serpent," a phrase reported to be the working title of the autobiography he was composing at the time of his death. He is fondly remembered and greatly respected by Native American people throughout the United States but will remain a special "favorite son" of the Winnebago.

SOURCES:

Books

Crow Dog, Mary, and Richard Erdoes, *Lakota Woman,* New York, Grove, 1990.
Native North American Almanac, edited by Duane Champagne, Detroit, Gale Research, 1994.

Other

Blackhawk, John, interview with Cynthia R. Kasee conducted July 3, 1994.

Ortiz, Alfonso, interview with Cynthia R. Kasee conducted July 3, 1994.

—Sketch by Cynthia R. Kasee

David Sohappy, Sr.

David Sohappy, Sr.
1925-1991
Yakima fisherman and activist

David Sohappy, Sr., was a leading figure in the battle for Northwest Coast Indian fishing rights. He staunchly defended the historic and religious traditions that allowed the region's Native Americans to live and fish freely in the waters of the Columbia River. Sohappy followed the Waashat or Seven Drums religion, also known as the Dreamer religion, which is practiced by members of the Yakima, Nez Percé, and Warm Springs reservations in the Northwest coastal region of the United States. Dreamers believe in the sacredness of traditional values and in the need for the Indian people to return to their ancient ways. A steadfast disciple of his great-granduncle Smohalla, the Wanapam prophet who revived the Dreamer religion in the 1800s, Sohappy was arrested and harassed for more than 25 years for his convictions. His continued resistance brought the issue of Indian fishing rights to the forefront of a budding cross-cultural debate in the late 1960s, when his pioneering case, *Sohappy vs. Washington State,* led to the Boldt Decision. His beliefs in his right to live and fish along the Columbia River were repeatedly tested until his death in 1991.

Sohappy was born on April 25, 1925, on the Yakima Indian reservation, near Harrah, Washington. It was there that he met his wife, Myra, when they were just children. They were both raised in strict, traditional families. Sohappy only attended school through the fourth grade: His family believed that the only things worth learning in the white man's schools were reading and writing. Beyond that, they felt that the white influence might be detrimental to a young Indian child's culture and beliefs. Sohappy and Myra eventually married and had nine children: Steve, David, Jr., Andy, Sam, Aleta, Barbara, Donna, Dean, and Alfred.

After serving in the U.S. Army during World War II, Sohappy lived and worked with his family on the reservation for many years. He was employed in a sawmill until the early 1960s, when he became a victim of a layoff. The Sohappys then moved to Cook's Landing, Washington, on the north bank of the Columbia River, in order to live and fish as their ancestors had done for thousands of years before them. Cook's Landing was a temporary fishing camp allotted to the Yakima, Nez Percé, and Warm Springs Indians after the flooding of the Indian village of Celilo and the destruction of the Celilo Falls fishing site, one of the nation's last remaining traditional Indian fishing spots. The flood, which occurred on March 9, 1957, was caused by the construction of a government-sponsored dam in the area. The village of Celilo had been part of the land accorded to the Indians in the Yakima Nation's Treaty of 1855, which granted them the right to fish in their "usual and accustomed times and places."

Challenged Treaty Rights in Court

In 1968 Sohappy was arrested for fishing out of season on the Columbia River. He held an uncompromising belief that he was protected by the Treaty of 1855 and was anxious to test Native American treaty and religious rights in U.S. courts. His landmark case against Washington State brought about a federal court ruling that the state could regulate Indian fishing only when necessary for conservation purposes. Judge Robert C. Belloni, who presided over the case, also ruled that the region's Native American fisherman were entitled to a "fair and equitable" share of the fish caught in Washington waters. Later rulings further defined the meaning of "fair and equitable": the Boldt Decision of 1970 established that the treaties gave the Columbia River Indians the right to 50 percent of the harvestable salmon from the river. The ruling, handed down by U.S. District Court Judge George Boldt, met with controversy from non-Indian commercial and sports fishermen.

Over the course of two and a half decades, the Sohappy family lived and fished along the banks of the Columbia River and encountered mounting opposition from federal and state officials. During that time, Washington State officials confiscated approximately 230 fishing nets from Sohappy. The family also had to fight a federal move to evict them from their home. Nonetheless, Sohappy was persistent in his convictions and continued to live and fish as his forebears and his religion dictated. In an interview with Michal Conford and Michele Zaccheo for the documentary *River People—Behind the Case of David Sohappy,* Myra Sohappy declared: "The white man says I'm breaking his laws. But what about my laws? The laws we got, unwritten laws—our laws come from the Creator. That's the way you gotta live. Is it a crime to try to survive and eat in this country?"

Imprisonment Captured National Attention

In 1983, as a result of "Salmonscam," an undercover operation by the federal government, Sohappy and his son, David, Jr., were arrested and convicted of selling more than 300 fish out of season. They were sent to Geiger Federal Prison in Spokane, Washington, to serve a five-year sentence. The Yakima Tribal Council, Democratic senators Brock Adams of Washington and Daniel Inouye of Hawaii, and Sohappy's lawyer, Thomas Keefe, Jr., protested that the sentence was ridiculously severe. This chorus of voices, combined with the news that Sohappy's health was failing, led to his release on May 17, 1988, after serving about 20 months of the sentence. Sohappy then returned to Cook's Landing to live with his wife and family. During his incarceration, he had suffered a series of strokes and endured transfers to prisons in three other states.

Sohappy fished only occasionally after his release from prison but continued to fight for his right to remain on the land. During the late 1980s and early 1990s, the Columbia River became known as some of the best waters for windsurfing in the United States, second only to Hawaii. Land prices increased—and so did the government's attempts to evict Sohappy. In August of 1990, the eviction case against the Sohappys was thrown out by the Ninth Circuit Court of Appeals. In a statement made for the River People video, Sohappy offered his thoughts on the continued efforts by the U.S. government to remove the family from their home: "They says, David, you can only stay here temporary. I says, I'm only here temporary to begin with. I'm not here forever. Nothing is." David Sohappy, Sr., died in a nursing home in Hood River, Washington, on May 7, 1991, at the age of 66.

SOURCES:

Books

Native North American Almanac, edited by Duane Champagne, Detroit, Gale Research, 1994; 322, 679, 1164, 1165.
Schuster, Helen H., *The Yakima,* New York, Chelsea House Publishers, 1990; 91, 93.

Periodicals

Geranios, Nicholas K., "Sohappy Battles On for Indian Fishing Rights," *Oregonian,* November 12, 1990.

Senior, Jeanie, "Indian Activist Sohappy Dies," *Oregonian,* May 9, 1991.

Other

Conford, Michal, and Zaccheo, Michele, *River People—Behind the Case of David Sohappy* (documentary film), New York, Filmmakers Library, 1990.

—Sketch by Denise Marecki-Arriola

Spokane Garry
1811(?)-1892
Spokane tribal leader, scholar, and Christian convert
Also known as Spokan Garry and Chief Garry

Spokane Garry was one of the first Native Americans of the northwestern United States to be schooled and baptized by Protestant missionaries. Garry's ability to speak English earned him the respect of his tribesmen and that of the neighboring Indian peoples. His education and conversion to Christianity is thought to have indirectly affected United States history, leading an influx of missionaries—and the homesteaders that followed them—to the Oregon territory.

Garry was born around 1811 in the territory along the Spokane River, in what is now the state of Washington, to Chief Illim Spokanee ["Child of the Sun and the Moon"]. The Spokane people are one of many Plateau Indian groups, so named because they occupy the plateau area between the Rocky Mountains and the Cascade Range. Garry belonged to a band of Middle Spokane Indians known as "Sin-ho-man-naish," or "salmon-trout people," hunters and fishers whose domain was the area around Spokane Falls, where the Spokane and Little Spokane Rivers meet. The first white settlers to visit the area named the tribe, the rivers, and the Indians' territory after Garry's father.

Becomes a Scholar and Christian Convert

In the spring of 1825, Garry was one of two boys chosen to be sent to the Red River Settlement School, an Episcopal institution in what is now Winnipeg, Canada. (The Anglican church in the United States is known as the Episcopal church.) Both children were the sons of chiefs from two different tribes—the Spokanes and the Kootenais. Their benefactor was Sir George Simpson of the Hudson's Bay Company. Simpson sought to educate some of the Indian youths in Anglo-American ways in the hopes that they would, in turn, pass their newfound knowledge on to other members of the Native American population. Combining their tribal names with those of two of his company's directors, he renamed the youths Spokane Garry and Kootenai Pelly.

At the Episcopal school, Garry and Pelly were educated in the ways, language, and religion of the white settlers. They were baptized as Christians on June 27, 1829, becoming the first Indians west of the Rockies to be become Protestants. In the fall of that same year, they returned to their homeland with enthusiastic reports of all that they had learned while they were away.

Shared Religion and Education

Garry was eager to share his new religion and education. Armed with his Bible and a burgeoning religious zeal, he began to do missionary work among his people, as well as among the neighboring Flathead, Coeur d'Alene, and Nez Percé peoples. Garry's words spread wherever Indians gathered—in villages, hunting and fishing grounds, and trading posts. In 1830 he and Pelly returned to the Red River Settlement, bringing with them a few other young Indians who were later converted and baptized as Christians. Garry's friend Kootenai Pelly died at Red River in 1831, and Garry returned to Spokane Falls the following autumn to continue his preaching alone.

Upon the death of his father, Garry became the principal chief of the Spokanes, in part because of his ability to speak English and French. He directed his people to build a 20 by 50 foot lodge to use as a schoolhouse and church. He then called his people to gather and worship there both morning and evening. Garry read to the tribe from the Bible and attempted to teach them to read and write English. He also taught them how to cultivate wheat fields and grow vegetable gardens. But among his own people, his attempts at teaching were misunderstood and unappreciated. Eventually, this caused him to abandon his missionary endeavors, though he continued to be interested in the Anglo-Christian religion and culture throughout his life.

Garry's teachings did, however, play a key role in the growing interest in Christianity among neighboring Plateau Indians. The Northwest came to be perceived as fertile ground in which to sow the seeds of Christian ideals. The Protestants responded to the need before the Catholics did, and so began the trek of many Protestant missionaries to the area. Among them were the Reverends Jason W. Lee, H. H. Spalding, Elkanah Walker, and Dr. Marcus Whitman, followed by more American settlers. The census of U.S. citizens in the Oregon territory was thereby substantially increased.

Spokane Garry was anti-Catholic, perhaps because of his allegiance to the Anglican Missionary School were he was educated. Clifford Drury made reference to Garry's relations with the Catholic missionaries, as well as to the competition between the Protestants and Catholics, in his book *Nine Years with the Spokane Indians: The Diary, 1838-1848, of Elkanah Walker.* Walker wrote in a letter to the Reverend William Cochran: "The priests have told the Indians, all over whom they had any influence, not to hear us or come near us as we were unfit to teach.... Spokane Garry,

although a profligate wretch, has ever opposed the priests and they tried hard to bring him under their influence without success."

Garry's allegiance to the Protestants, along with the early response of the Protestant missionaries to the Indians' needs, made it difficult for Catholic missionaries to gain a foothold in the Oregon territory. Many of the Catholics were French-Canadian, and their failure to become established in the region had a profound effect on the course of U.S. history: The Pacific Northwest had been sought after by both Canada and the United States for years, and if the Catholic missionaries had succeeded in populating the area, it might well have been annexed to Canada. Instead, the Oregon territory became part of the United States in 1846.

After Garry abandoned his educational efforts among his own people, he was reluctant to help the other missionaries in the area. Their ongoing attempts to recruit him to teach the Indians were met with disappointment. He did continue to visit the missionaries from time to time, trading goods and services with them and acting as a letter courier and translator. He visited Tshimakain, Elkanah Walker's mission village, for the first time on January 5, 1841. During his subsequent stops there, he would at times assist Walker with translating portions of the Bible into the Salish language, but he is said to have refused to read to the Indians himself. Walker is credited with writing and printing the first book in the Salish language, and Garry may have been of some help to him in the translations.

Garry was regarded with favor by U.S. government officials. He met with Governor Isaac I. Stevens of the Washington territory in October of 1853. Stevens called Garry a man "of education, of strict probity, and great influence over his tribe," according to Robert H. Ruby and John A. Brown in *Indians of the Pacific Northwest.* In *A Tepee in His Front Yard,* Clifford M. Drury recorded General O. O. Howard's description of Garry as "short in stature, dressed in citizen's clothing, [with] his hair cut very short for an Indian. He was ... wiry and tough, and still able to endure great fatigue, though he must have been at least seventy years of age." Of his speaking ability, Howard remarked that "Garry could make the longest speech of any Indian I ever listened to, and he knew how to filibuster like a congressman when he had a point to gain by continuous talking."

Garry was present at many important councils with the U.S. government, including the council at Walla Walla on April 1, 1855, out of which came the establishment of three major reservations: one for the Yakimas; one for the Nez Percés; and one for the Cayuses, Umatillas, and Walla Wallas. Many of the Indians of the Columbia River basin were dissatisfied with the terms of the treaty, which deprived them of their lands and restricted them to the reservations.

In the summer of 1855, war broke out between the whites and the Oregon Indian tribes, including the Yakimas, Cayuses, Walla Wallas, Palouses, and Umatillas. Garry was opposed to the fighting and attempted to use his influence among his people to restrain them from joining the hostilities. Many young Spokanes were against him and did eventually fight. Garry lost several brothers and other family members in the battle, and although he sympathized with their cause, he continued to rally for peace with the whites.

Removed from His Land

Garry hoped for a treaty between the government and the Spokane people. He was opposed to the filing of land claims by Indians because he feared that the claims would prevent the establishment of a reservation. Although he made repeated requests to the government to preserve some parts of their homelands as a reservation—and commissioners promised many times to hold council to discuss the issue—no action was ever taken. Instead, U.S. government officials continued to insist that the Spokanes move to one of the already established reservations. Finally, in 1887, the Spokanes signed a treaty ceding their land to the government. Under the terms of the treaty, Garry and some of the other chiefs were to receive payments of $100 per year as part of the payment for their lands.

During the 1870s, increasing numbers of immigrants began settling in the village then called Spokane Falls, which in 1881 became incorporated and known as Spokane. Eventually, the growing tide of settlers drove Spokane Garry from his home. While Garry and his family were away at their fishing camp, white farmers took possession of the farm that Garry had cultivated for years. Homeless, he moved to Indian Canyon, outside of Spokane, where he set up a tent camp with his family. He never received any of the payments promised in the 1887 treaty, and so he lived his last years still waiting for the whites he had befriended throughout his life to compensate him. He died of pneumonia on January 12 (some sources say 14), 1892, and was buried at Greenwood Cemetery, outside of Spokane.

SOURCES:

The American Heritage Book of Indians, edited by Alvin M. Josephy, Jr., American Heritage Publishing, 1961; 308.

Dockstader, Frederick J., *Great North American Indians,* New York, Van Nostrand Reinhold, 1977; 91-92.

Drury, Clifford M., *A Tepee in His Front Yard,* Portland, Oregon, Binfords & Mort, 1949; 102, 103, 105, 154, 165.

Drury, Clifford M., *Nine Years with the Spokane Indians: The Diary, 1838-1848, of Elkanah Walker,* Glendale, California, Arthur H. Clark Company, 1976; 70, 71, 129, 174, 181, 183, 202, 244, 500.

Lewis, William S., *The Case of Spokane Garry,* Fairfield, Washington, Ye Galleon Press, 1987.

Ruby, Robert H., and John A. Brown, *Indians of the Pacific Northwest: A History,* Norman, University of Oklahoma Press, 1981; 68, 70,78,79.

Waldman, Carl, *Who Was Who in Native American History,* New York, Facts On File, 1990; 334.

—Sketch by Denise Marecki-Arriola

Spotted Tail
1823(?)-1881
Brulé Sioux warrior, civil leader, and negotiator
Also known as Sinte Gleska

Spotted Tail, whose name resulted from a raccoon tail gift from a fur trader, established himself as a warrior as a young man. During the last 25 years of his life, he was the leading Sioux proponent of a nonviolent resolution with the dominant white population, while insisting on the retention of traditional culture.

Spotted Tail's birth in the winter of 1823 or 1824 occurred at the end of over 40 years of relative prosperity and freedom for the nomadic Sioux. His parents were affiliates of the Sicangu Nation (Burnt Thigh). His father, Tangle Hair, was a Saone of the Blackfeet-Sioux and his mother, Walks with a Pipe Woman, was a Brulé.

The signs of change started with the first migration of whites along the Platte River in 1834. But Spotted Tall's early obsession had been with the hated Pawnees with whom the Sioux were in constant struggle over hunting areas. By the time he was about 30, Spotted Tail had been chosen as an Ogle Tanka Un ["Shirt Wearer"] or war leader. According to Victor Douville, chair of the Lakota studies program at the university that bears Spotted Tail's Lakota name, "His shirt was said to have been adorned with over 100 locks of hair, each representing coups, scalps taken, and horses captured."

The most detailed account of the warrior's life was written by self-trained historian George E. Hyde in 1961. Hyde noted that little is recorded about Spotted Tail's life from 1841 to 1854. During these years, Crazy Horse's father apparently married two of Spotted Tail's sisters, after the death of the other famous warrior's mother. But the paths of Spotted Tail and Crazy Horse were to become quite distinct during the final years of their lives.

Both men were directly affected by an incident near Fort Laramie in 1854. A Mormon emigrant had insisted on military intervention after the disappearance of one of his cattle. The animal had been killed by a young Minniconjou. Attempts at negotiation were ignored and Lieutenant J. L. Grattan and his troops marched into a Brulé village and initiated a conflict. Spotted Tail led the forces that immediately retaliated, killing all of the cavalry men. But the event led to inevitable retaliation by the U.S. forces. General William S. Harney, with 600 men under his command, was sent to oust the Sioux. He encountered Spotted Tail at the Bluewater Battle in 1855. There were 86 Brulés killed at Ash Hollow and 70 taken prisoner, including Spotted Tail's wife and baby daughter. Spotted Tail escaped but suffered two bullet and two saber wounds. The first printed references to Spotted Tail are found in regional newspaper accounts of the battle.

Spotted Tail

Imprisonment at Fort Leavenworth

After Harney moved on to Fort Laramie to meet with friendly tribes the word was sent that key figures would have to surrender or further slaughter would result. On October 18, 1855, Spotted Tail and four others came to Fort Laramie, anticipating execution. The group was actually brought to Fort Leavenworth in Kansas, later moved to Fort Kearney, and released about a year later. The episode was a great turning point in the life of the Brulé leader. Hyde described the transformation: "This journey into Kansas was an education to Spotted Tail.... The number and power of the whites was frightening." During the balance of his years his approach was generally one of diplomacy, recognizing that military victory was highly improbable. The long-term interests of his people were substituted for the glory of warfare. It was not always an easy choice and there would be powerful criticism. But the immediate impact of his submission to military authority is summarized by Victor Douville: "Sinte Gleska's surrender and ordeal of imprisonment led the people to view this as an unselfish sacrifice for the good of the tribe and they continued to follow him as a war leader. Furthermore, 11 years after his release from confinement at Fort Leavenworth, the Southern Sicangu remembered and elevated Sinte Gleska, now an experienced leader, to Wicasa Itancan (civil leader), the highest leadership ranking found among Siangu."

But upon his return from the federal prison he joined the camp of Little Thunder. Again, Hyde suggests a relative lack of historical documentation regarding the life of Spot-

ted Tail from 1856 to 1863. He probably did not participate in the great council near Bear Butte in 1857. Although not a "chief," Spotted Tail retained the status of Shirt Wearer and head soldier of the camp. The struggle with the Pawnees continued. Spotted Tail's goals of reconciliation and the government's effort to seek resolution are disrupted by the Minnesota uprising of 1862. The random attacks on settlers in the area put all Sioux under suspicion and resulted in a period of repression.

Spotted Tail was annoyed by the efforts to restrict the movement of the Sioux along the Platte River and was affected by the Chivington Massacre at Sand Creek in 1864. He was pulled into an intertribal alliance in late 1864 and early the next year led assaults on the community of Julesburg, Colorado. He later brought his band to Fort Laramie to seek peace with the whites. During the 1866-1868 war for the Bozeman Trail he advised accommodation and met with a commission to discuss the subject. A treaty signed in June of 1866 indicated Spotted Tail's status as head of the Brulés. The Indian Peace Policy put a temporary restraint on U.S. military violence. But the ultimate goal was to assure railroad development and the white settlement of Kansas and Nebraska. Restricting Native Americans to reservations was the only guarantee for these ventures.

Although the Treaty of Laramie of 1868 offered great promise and established a Great Sioux Reservation many of the participants did not realize they had also lost their hunting rights and would have to move to a new reservation in Dakota Territory. Particularly affected were the Loafers who had been virtual wards at Fort Laramie for 25 years. Many of that weakened and bewildered group lost their lives to a smallpox epidemic on the way to the new agency. Among the survivors was Big Mouth, who disputed Spotted Tail's leadership and in October of 1869, after a drunken harangue, attempted to shoot the Brulé leader. Spotted Tail then killed his opponent with a pistol.

Uncertainty of Agency Life

Spotted Tail would not live at the agency near the Missouri but selected a camping spot about 40 miles distant. Several other agency locations would be tested before the location was finally chosen on Rosebud Creek. One sign of the instability was the fact that there were ten different agents and acting agents on Spotted Tail agencies from 1868 to 1880. Part of the reason was Spotted Tail's reaction to the unrealistic attempt to convert the Brulés into farmers—in areas where farming was nearly impossible. At Whetstone Creek in the late summer of 1868 they were greeted with heavy agricultural equipment—"Proof," in Hyde's judgement, "that the officials in Washington knew nothing whatever about the Sioux.... These Indians had been hunters and warriors since the beginning of time."

But since 1855 Spotted Tail had learned a great deal about white men and their motives. Mildred Fielder noted that as early as 1868, "he was beginning his own brand of battle with the whites through negotiation." His personality made him effective. He was sociable and genial, demonstrating good humor with his directness. William Seagle described him as having "a melancholy dignity which impressed all beholders." Upon confronting the Secretary of the Interior during his first visit to Washington, D.C., in 1870, he immediately scolded him for government violation of the 1868 treaty. When the Secretary lectured him on how he "must expect some trouble in his life and should face it in a manly way, not complaining," Spotted Tail laughed and told the translator: "Tell him, that if he had had as much trouble in his life as I have had in mine, he would have cut his throat long ago."

A review of his activities and comments shows patience as well as firm resolve. He knew when to make demands and when to submit. The contrasts between his methods and those of Crazy Horse and Sitting Bull are quite clear. In Richmond L. Clow's comparative study he evaluates the utility of the two approaches: "From 1868 to 1877 Sitting Bull and Spotted Tail endured crucial years that required the most consummate leadership. Both wanted to preserve Sioux culture and protect tribal members. Each refined a separate strategy to accomplish these goals. In the role of a leader, Spotted Tail had the advantage over Sitting Bull. The Hunkpapa's unwavering commitment to resistance with arms left no room for compromise. The Brulé pressed for a non-military solution with concessions. Spotted Tail's flexibility created options. Sitting Bull's rigidity forced confrontation."

Spotted Tail had good reason to be annoyed in the months between the Laramie Treaty and his first visit to the national capital. "Already in 1869," Hyde observed, "the officials were meddling in every phase of Sioux life and attempting to twist the Indians into new and officially approved shapes." The Poncas, traditional Brulé enemies, were sent from Nebraska to be part of the agency. The government had also initiated a policy of trying to acknowledge heads of families but not chiefs chosen by the people. The tribes were even expected to wear "white" clothing. Among the items received were discarded military coats, with the army brass buttons still on them.

Spotted Tail's approach to trying to establish a definable future for his people attracted individuals from bands with less certain destinies. The Brulé population increased to 300 lodges between 1872 and 1875. A 1876 census showed the Red Cloud agency (later Pine Ridge) and the Spotted Tail agency (later Rosebud) had nearly the same populations: 4,760 and 4,715. Spotted Tail's last battle with the Pawnees occurred in July of 1873.

Invasion of the Black Hills

The events of 1874 through 1876 made a position of neutrality difficult. General George Custer, in violation of the 1868 treaty, marched to the Black Hills with 1,200 troops. Surveys were conducted and the discovery of gold confirmed. Spotted Tail recognized the potential value of the findings and did his own inspection of the region in 1875. So, when the U.S. government offered either a $400,000 annual lease arrangement or an outright purchase of the small volcanic mountain range (about 150 miles by 50 miles), which was also the location of many sacred Lakota sites, the tribal leaders were ready to respond. Spotted Tail demonstrated his understanding of the white man's money market when he told a federal commission, "As long as we live on this earth we will expect pay.... I want to live on the interest of my money. The amount must be so large that the interest will support us.... We want some good cattle every year. Every year we want some guns.... Until the land falls to pieces we want these things.... There is no use for the troops here now, and we want them removed." The ultimate demand was for $60 million, a figure that was rejected by the government representatives.

President Ulysses S. Grant took a rigid position on December 3, 1875, when he ordered that all Indians be placed on agencies by January 31, 1876. Not only was the order not widely known, but it was an impossible request in the middle of winter. This was followed by the climactic events in the Rosebud and Little Big Horn region of Montana in the summer of 1876. But military glory did not translate into improved conditions for the victors. In early 1877 Spotted Tail, at the height of his personal prestige, completed a 55-day journey seeking the submission of those who remained hostile. Sitting Bull had taken his band to Canada. Crazy Horse avoided a personal meeting with Spotted Tail, but was to acknowledge the futility of further resistance and led his followers to Fort Robinson in May of 1877.

Spotted Tail was able to continue to manipulate the agency representatives of the U.S. government. For example, he temporarily blocked the denial of tribal authority with the government creation of an agency police force. He limited their authority over full-bloods by selecting only "squaw men" and half-breeds to be a part of the force. Farming activity was again delayed by a massive Sun Dance sanctioned by a naive new agent. Carl Schurz, the Secretary of the Interior, was so annoyed by the activity that he made a personal visit to the agency to try to establish order.

Another significant episode was the decision of Spotted Tail to send four of his sons, two grandchildren, and 34 other students from Rosebud to the new Carlisle Indian School in Pennsylvania. His motive was to allow them to learn English in order to help his people. Within a few months he found that the group had been baptized as Episcopalians, given Christian names, dressed like soldiers, and were doing farm and industrial work. He was outraged and personally removed the members of his family in 1880. Hyde explained the impact of this decision: "Spotted Tail, who had started East as the darling of the church people, educators, and idealists, because he had given his children to Captain [Richard Henry] Pratt to experiment with, was now a pariah." Victor Douville, Lakota scholar, adds this perspective: "Although this was a major setback for Sinte Gleska (Spotted Tail) he, nevertheless, raised one of the first and significant issues of bilingual and bicultural education. It was this concern that set the stage for the founding of Sinte Gleska College 100 years later."

The Carlisle incident provided a context for opponents of Spotted Tail's leadership to express their views openly. A 1880 petition signed by chief of police Crow Dog and others insisted that Spotted Tail should follow the orders of the new agent, John Cook. It was ignored by Spotted Tail. Crow Dog lost his position but was later reinstated. An effort was made to establish Yellow Hair as the head chief. But the tribal council supported the long-time leader. Crow Dog wrote another letter to the Secretary of Interior making additional charges against his adversary.

The two men had an encounter in a space between buildings at the agency on July 4, 1881. Crow Dog drew a gun and threatened to shoot Spotted Tail. The latter challenged him to do so in the presence of a large crowd and Crow Dog withdrew. But on August 5, as Spotted Tail was returning from a council meeting Crow Dog saw him approaching, knelt down, and killed him with a rifle shot. Victor Douville argues that "the motives behind the assassination and death of Sinte Gleska are complex, controversial, and so sensitive that, for the time being, no complete picture of what occurred can be drawn." The detailed study of the subsequent legal proceedings by attorney William Seagle reveals little more about the motives, but the pattern of leadership conflict is clear from the events of the two previous years.

Ex Parte Crow Dog

The local punishment of Crow Dog and his descendants would be generations of ostracism in the Lakota community, as well as the traditional compensation under Indian civil law. However, to outsiders, it appeared that the punishment for the killing of Spotted Tail would be limited to the transfer of eight horses, a blanket, and $50 in cash. But, because of press coverage and Spotted Tail's image as a negotiator for peace, his death, in Seagle's words, "became an event of national importance." By the end of August, Crow Dog was arrested and brought to Deadwood and tried in the District Court of the First Judicial District of the Territory of Dakota. After a lengthy trial a murder verdict was given on March 24, 1882. But there was a question about proper jurisdiction in the case, and Crow Dog was actually allowed to spend about a month on the Pine Ridge agency during the appeal process.

The case went to the Supreme Court of the United States. In addition to legal issues, such as the extradition of an individual who had committed an offense against a member of his own tribe, there was the political fear that the killing of another Sioux leader at this time would hamper future negotiations about land concessions with the tribe. On November 26, 1883 the Supreme Court reversed the conviction, Justice Stanley Matthews arguing, in part: "It tries them [Native Americans], not by their peers, not by the customs of their people, nor the law of their land, but by superiors of a different race, according to the law of a social state of which they have an imperfect conception, and which is opposed to the traditions of their history, to the habits of their lives, to the strongest prejudices of their savage nature;

one which measures the red man's revenge by the maxims of the white man's morality."

But there was an angry congressional response, perhaps again reflecting positive attitudes about Spotted Tail, but also the implication that a serious crime like murder, under some unusual circumstances, might go unpunished. As a result, a few months later the Major Crimes Act gave Federal courts jurisdiction over major offenses on Indian reservations, even when the acts were committed by Indians upon other Indian victims. As Seagle concludes, "The white man's laws were now applicable not only to the Sioux but to the whole Indian race."

The Legacy of Spotted Tail

Donald E. Worcester offers this tribute to Spotted Tail: "Even after his death his program continued, and the Brulés remained in spirit much as they were in 1881, still restless and mobile, but not quite ready to take up farming seriously. For enabling them to escape an abrupt and thorough change in their way of life, they can thank Sinte Gleska, the warrior-diplomat of the Sioux." Only a small monument, not the bronze statue predicted by Captain John B. Bourke in 1876, is found at the gravesite near the Rosebud agency. But a more significant memorial was created in the form of a tribal college, now Sinte Gleska University, on the Rosebud Sioux Reservation in South Dakota. The institution was chartered in 1971, based on the concept of retaining the elements of Lakota culture while utilizing the survival tools of the white world. The school has had a great impact on the local population and has gained national recognition. A *New York Times* writer referred to it in July of 1994 as "the jewel of the reservation."

SOURCES:

Books

Andrist, Richard K., *The Long Death: The Last Days of the Plains Indian,* New York, Macmillan, 1964; reprinted, 1993.

Clow, Richmond Lee, "Sioux Response to Non-Indian Intrusion: Sitting Bull, Spotted Tail, and Crazy Horse," in *South Dakota Leaders: From Pierre Chouteau, Jr., to Oscar Howe,* edited by Herbert T. Hoover and Larry J. Zimmerman, Vermillion, University of South Dakota Press, 1989; 29-44.

Fielder, Mildred, "Spotted Tail the Strategist," in *Sioux Indian Leaders,* Seattle, Superior Publishing Company, 1975; 25-39.

Hyde, George E., *The Sioux' Chronicle,* Norman, University of Oklahoma Press, 1956.

Hyde, George E., *Spotted Tail's Folk: A History of the Brulé Sioux,* Norman, University of Oklahoma Press, 1961; reprinted, 1974.

I Have Spoken: American History through the Voices of Indians, compiled by Virginia Irving Armstrong, Athens, Ohio University Press, 1971.

One Feather, Vivian, *Makoce* (Curriculum Materials Resource Unit), Spearfish, South Dakota, Black Hills State University, 1974.

Poole, Captain DeWitt Clinton, *Among the Sioux of Dakota: Eighteen Months Experience as an Indian Agent,* New York, Van Nostrand, 1881; reprinted, St. Paul, Minnesota Historical Society, 1988.

Utley, Robert M., *The Last Days of the Sioux Nation,* New Haven, Yale University Press, 1963.

Periodicals

Clow, Richmond Lee, "The Whetstone Indian Agency, 1868-1872," *South Dakota History,* 7:3, 1977; 291-308.

Johnson, Dirk, "In Bleak Area In South Dakota, Indians Put Hopes in Classroom," *New York Times,* July 3, 1994.

Seagle, William, "The Murder of Spotted Tail," *Indian Historian,* 3:4, fall 1970; 10-22.

Worcester, Donald E., "Spotted Tail: Warrior, Diplomat," *American West,* 1:4, 1964; 38-46, 87.

Other

Douville, Victor, "History of Sinte Gleska (Spotted Tail)," *Sinte Gleska University Catalog,* 1990-1993; 2-3.

—*Sketch by Keith A. Winsell*

Squanto

Squanto
1600(?)-1623
Wampanoag translator and guide
Also known as Tasquantum (Tisquantum)

Squanto is remembered as the interpreter, guide, and agricultural advisor who shepherded the Pilgrim settlers of Plymouth Colony through their precarious early existence in the New World and did more than anyone else to secure the survival of the settlement.

Squanto was a member of the Patuxet band of the Wampanoag tribe, which dominated the area in which the colonists eventually settled. He first enters written history in 1614, as one of 20 Patuxet Indians kidnapped by English explorer Thomas Hunt. Hunt carried his captives to Spain, where he sold them into slavery. Squanto, however, was one of a number who were rescued by Spanish friars, and he eventually made his way to England, where he next surfaced in the employ of John Slaney, whose interests extended to exploration in the New World. He sent Squanto along on an expedition to Newfoundland in 1617; there the Indian met explorer Thomas Dermer, with whom he returned to England the following year. Squanto's relation to Slaney and Dermer may have been in the nature of indentured servant;

he may have hoped to earn his passage home. In any event, he traveled once again to the New World with Dermer in 1619, coming to rest in the Patuxet region of his birth.

In 1617, during Squanto's absence, a great epidemic—perhaps the plague—swept the Indian populations in the Massachusetts Bay region, and the Patuxet band was particularly hard hit. Indeed, they were virtually wiped out. Squanto returned to find the village of his youth abandoned. He left Captain Dermer to go in search of survivors, but returned to his aid when Dermer ran afoul of hostile Indians. Squanto remained with Dermer until Dermer was mortally wounded in a skirmish with the Pokanoket Wampanoag. Squanto was then taken prisoner.

Some historians have theorized that when Squanto was dispatched in 1621 as emissary to the English settlers, he may have still been living with the Wampanoag as a captive. This would explain the later reports of antagonism between him and Massasoit, who had become Sagamore, or civil chief, of the Wampanoag confederation in the wake of the epidemic. It was Massasoit who sent Squanto to the English at Plymouth, Massachusetts, where they had settled on the former lands of the Patuxet in November of 1620.

The English—weakened from their journey, hungry, and ill—kept their distance from the Indians during the first winter of their residence; half of the Pilgrims died before spring. The Wampanoag, who had had mixed experiences with Europeans, watched the newcomers with a wary eye. In March, Massasoit felt the time was right to approach the English and sent Squanto and a companion to reassure them of the friendly intentions of the Indians. The two arranged for a conference between the English leaders and Massasoit. That meeting resulted in the historic treaty in which the Wampanoag and the English pledged mutual peace and friendship.

"Sent of God"

Squanto was sent to live with the English settlers. His guidance proved so indispensable to them that Plymouth Governor William Bradford was moved to declare him a "spetiall instrument sent of God for [their] good."

Squanto's role in introducing the English to neighboring tribes was particularly crucial. His extensive travels had provided him with unique qualifications as intermediary between the cultures. Thus it was possible for the colonists to establish vital trade relationships, thereby enabling them to secure seeds and other supplies necessary to life in New England, as well as animal pelts which they sent to England to repay investments and secure English goods.

Tradition has it that Squanto taught the English, most of whom had not been farmers in their native country, to plant Indian corn and other local vegetables, and to insure the success of the crop by the use of fish fertilizer. The English believed the practice of fertilizing with fish to be traditional among the Indians. In recent years, however, this has come into question among historians, some believing that Squanto learned the practice in Europe or in Newfoundland.

Steeped in Conflict

Squanto's career was not without controversy. There are reports that he sought to increase his status among the Indians by exaggerating his influence with the English and alarming neighboring Native American groups with reports that colonists kept a plague (he may have meant gunpowder) buried underground that could be released at any time. There is also evidence that he tried to undermine Massasoit's relationship with the English. A crisis developed in 1622 when Squanto perpetrated an elaborate ruse to try to convince the English that Massasoit was plotting with the hostile Narragansett tribe to destroy the Plymouth Colony and that an attack was imminent. The deception was quickly discovered; however, Massasoit was sufficiently incensed to demand Squanto's life. The Plymouth settlers were very angry with Squanto in the wake of the fiasco, even to the extent that Governor Bradford admitted to Massasoit that Squanto deserved death for his act of betrayal. It was a measure of the colonists' dependence on him that they nevertheless protected him from Massasoit's vengeance.

In November of 1623, with the arrival of additional English settlers who came ill-prepared for the approaching New England winter, Squanto guided an expedition from Plymouth to trade with Cape Cod Indians for corn. He fell ill with what William Bradford, who led the foray, described as an "Indian fever" and died within a few days. According to Bradford, as quoted by John H. Humins in *New England Quarterly,* the dying Squanto expressed his wish to "go to the Eng-

lishmen's God in Heaven" and "bequeathed his little property to his English friends, as remembrances of his love." Some observers, including Humins, contend that Squanto's legendary role as the Pilgrims' savior has been largely exaggerated. "His struggle for power with Massasoit ... has not been adequately noted in histories about the period," noted Humins, "[and] in fact jeopardized the plantation's relationship with the Indians." However, Squanto remains a key figure in American folklore—and the classic symbol of Thanksgiving.

SOURCES:

Books

Salisbury, Neal, *Manitou and Providence: Indians, Europeans, and the Making of New England, 1500-1643,* New York, Oxford University Press, 1982.

Thacher, James, *History of the Town of Plymouth from its First Settlement in 1620, to the Present Time,* third edition, Yarmouthport, Massachusetts, Parnassus Imprints, 1972.

Vaughan, Alden T., *New England Frontier: Puritans and Indians, 1620-1675,* Boston, Little, Brown, 1965.

Periodicals

Ceci, Lynn, "Squanto and the Pilgrims," *Society,* 27, May/June 1990; 40-44.

Humins, John H., "Squanto and Massasoit: A Struggle for Power," *New England Quarterly,* 60, March 1987; 54-70.

—Sketch by Julie Henderson Jersyk

Standing Bear
1829(?)-1908
Ponca tribal leader
Also known as Ma-chu-nah-zhay (Mochunozhin)

Standing Bear was a respected leader of the small Ponca Indian tribe that resided for years in northern Nebraska. In the late 1870s, at a crucial point in the tribe's existence, he took heroic action to reverse the wrongs inflicted upon his people at the hands of the U.S. government and its Indian agents. He remains a heroic and symbolic figure in the long struggle for Native American rights.

Nothing is known of Standing Bear's early life, although he is generally assumed to have been born around 1829. He was a member and a chief of the Ponca Indians, a small tribe—apparently never more than 800 or 900 persons

Standing Bear

strong in the nineteenth century—closely related to the much larger Omaha tribe. Since at least the mid-seventeenth century, the tribe had lived near the region where the Niobrara River enters the Missouri River in what is now northeastern Nebraska.

The Loss of Ponca Land

In a treaty between the U.S. government and the Ponca Indians signed on March 12, 1858, the tribe ceded to the United States all the land they held except for an extensive tract near the mouth of the Niobrara River, which was reserved for the Poncas as their permanent home. In a second treaty, signed on March 10, 1865, the Poncas ceded another 30,000 acres to the federal government, retaining a total of 96,000 acres as their permanent reservation. However, in a separate treaty negotiated with the Sioux Indian tribes three years later, U.S. government negotiators inadvertently included the Poncas' 96,000 acres as part of a much larger reservation granted to the Sioux nation. Since the Poncas had not been consulted in the matter, they continued to occupy the tract. However, the much larger and more warlike Sioux tribes carried out repeated attacks on the Poncas during the next few years, seeking to drive them off land that they regarded as part of Sioux territory. The Indian Bureau in the U.S. Department of the Interior decided in 1876 that the only solution to the problem was to relocate the Ponca tribe to a new reservation in the Indian Territory, located in the present state of Oklahoma.

Early in 1877, a delegation of ten Ponca chiefs, Standing Bear among them, was escorted by agents of the Indian

Bureau to the Indian Territory to survey the land and choose a location for their reservation there. Standing Bear and seven of the other leaders found all the suggested sites unsatisfactory and decided to return to their home in Nebraska; the agents refused to assist them in their return, so the eight chiefs walked the 500 miles from Oklahoma back to Nebraska in 40 days in the late winter of 1877. When they arrived home, they found that their Ponca tribe was already being moved to the Indian Territory under military escort.

About 170 Ponca members had begun the long trek in late April of 1877. Standing Bear and his brother, Big Snake, were briefly imprisoned when they urged that the remainder of the Poncas resist the removal. By May, the remaining 600 or so Poncas—including Standing Bear and his brother—were forced to join in the march, leaving behind their homes, farms, and many of their possessions. Nine persons died in the course of the journey, including a daughter of Standing Bear.

The nine deaths turned out to be a grim prelude to much further hardship and death for the Poncas in their new locale. They suffered from diseases, such as malaria, which afflicted a large number of Indians transported from northern climates to the humid Indian Territory. Estimates of the number of deaths vary greatly, but even Indian Bureau reports indicate that a sizeable portion of the tribe perished in the course of the first year. Standing Bear and several other leaders went to Washington, D.C., in the autumn of 1877, seeking President Rutherford B. Hayes' approval of their request to return to Nebraska. Hayes reportedly vetoed the request, but allowed the Ponca leaders to select a more desirable location for their reservation within the Indian Territory. Although the Poncas eventually settled on a more favorable site 150 miles away, the ravages of disease and poverty continued. Standing Bear's last living son was among those who had died by 1878.

Standing Bear's Trial

Despair over the situation of the Poncas in Indian Territory, together with the more personal desire to bury his son in the tribe's Nebraska homeland, led Standing Bear to make the move that made him famous—though it cost him the leadership of his tribe. In early January of 1879, he led a small band of Poncas on a return march to Nebraska, determined to resettle on the old land or die in the attempt. Most of the roughly 600 members of the tribe chose to remain in the Indian Territory, but Standing Bear and several dozen followers arrived at the Omaha Indian agency at Decatur, Nebraska, on March 4, 1879. The Omahas welcomed their kinsmen and invited them to settle there; temporarily at least, they did so.

The Indian Bureau had been informed of Standing Bear's flight from the Indian Territory soon after his departure. Secretary of the Interior Carl Schurz ordered General George Crook, commander of the U.S. Army Department of the Platte, at Omaha, to arrest the chief and his followers and return them to the territory in Oklahoma. Schurz and his advisers feared that if Standing Bear and his band were allowed to remain in Nebraska, it would set a precedent for all Native Americans in the Indian Territory to demand a return to their respective homelands.

Although General Crook obeyed the order and arrested Standing Bear and his followers, he is said to have personally sympathized with the Poncas and believed that they had been repeatedly wronged by the government. Crook convinced Thomas Henry Tibbles, an Omaha newspaperman, to undertake a publicity campaign and institute a case in the federal district court to have Standing Bear and his group released.

Tibbles saw to it that the plight of Standing Bear and his followers was well publicized not only in his own Omaha newspaper but in papers nationwide. He also persuaded two young Omaha lawyers to file a writ of *habeas corpus* (a claim of unjust detention) in the federal district court at Omaha for the release of Standing Bear and his group. The trial of *Standing Bear vs. Crook* was held from April 30 to May 2, 1879. The case was of great significance not only as a means of righting the wrongs inflicted on the Ponca tribe, but also because it raised the larger question of Native American citizenship and the rights of Indians to appear in and to sue in the courts of the nation.

The federal district attorney argued that Standing Bear was not entitled to the protection of a writ of *habeas corpus* because he was not a citizen or even a "person" under American law. Standing Bear spoke briefly but eloquently on his own behalf. Judge Elmer S. Dundy, in the decision he handed down several weeks later, held that an Indian was, indeed, a person within the meaning of the laws of the United States, though he avoided the larger question of what rights of citizenship an Indian might have. He also ruled that the federal government had no rightful authority to remove the Poncas to the Indian Territory by force; Native Americans, he stated, possessed an inherent right of expatriation— that is, a right to move from one area to another as they wished. Dundy therefore ordered the release of Standing Bear and his followers from custody.

Became a Symbol of Human Rights Struggle

Thomas Tibbles and other leaders of the movement for Indian rights hoped to carry the case of Standing Bear to the U.S. Supreme Court in order to secure a more definitive statement on Indian citizenship and rights. Tibbles himself made a tour to Chicago, New York, and Boston in the summer of 1879 to publicize the case and to raise money for the Supreme Court appeal. By October of that year, he had arranged for Standing Bear to lecture in key cities in the eastern United States. As interpreters for the chief, who spoke no English, Tibbles included in the party two Omaha Indians: Susette La Flesche (better known by her Indian name, "Bright Eyes") and her brother, Francis La Flesche, both of whom had been educated in English-speaking schools.

The tour generated great enthusiasm in urban social and literary circles, especially in Boston. Standing Bear, an impressive figure in his full Indian regalia, including feather headdress, related his story and that of his people in simple but emotional terms, while Bright Eyes, also in Indian dress,

translated it into poignant English. A good deal of money was raised for the court appeal and for relief of the Poncas, and reform leaders were moved to become active in the cause of Indian rights. Standing Bear and Bright Eyes also testified before committees of Congress in Washington. The tour finally ended in April of 1880.

As it turned out, Secretary of the Interior Schurz was able to quash the proposed appeal of the Ponca case to the Supreme Court. However, the agitation over the affair did lead to both congressional and presidential investigations. On February 1, 1881, President Hayes recommended to Congress that the Poncas be allowed to live where they chose and that they be compensated for lands relinquished and losses sustained during the forced removal to the Indian Territory in Oklahoma. Congress voted the necessary legislation and funds on March 3, 1881.

The majority of the Ponca tribe did in fact remain in the Indian Territory, but Standing Bear and his group lived quietly on the old Nebraska reservation near the mouth of the Niobrara River. Standing Bear died in September of 1908.

SOURCES:

Books

Biographical Dictionary of Indians of the Americas, second edition, Newport Beach, California, American Indian Publishers, 1991; 711-713.

Dockstader, Frederick J., *Great North American Indians,* New York, Van Nostrand Reinhold, 1977; 279-281.

Green, Norma Kidd, *Iron Eye's Family: The Children of Joseph La Flesche,* Lincoln, Nebraska, Johnson Publishing, 1969.

Mardock, Robert Winston, *The Reformers and the American Indian,* Columbia, University of Missouri Press, 1971; 168-191.

Mardock, Robert Winston, "Standing Bear and the Reformers," in *Indian Leaders: Oklahoma's First Statesmen,* edited by H. Glenn Jordan and Thomas M. Holm, Oklahoma City, Oklahoma Historical Society, 1979; 101-113.

Tibbles, Thomas Henry, *Buckskin and Blanket Days: Memoirs of a Friend of the Indians,* Garden City, New York, Doubleday, 1957.

Tibbles, Thomas Henry, *The Ponca Chiefs: An Account of the Trial of Standing Bear,* Lincoln, University of Nebraska Press, 1972.

Periodicals

Clark, Stanley, "Ponca Publicity," *Mississippi Valley Historical Review,* 1, March 1943; 495-516.

Hayter, Earl W., "The Ponca Removal," *North Dakota Historical Quarterly,* July 6, 1932; 262-273.

King, James T., "'A Better Way': General George Crook and the Ponca Indians," *Nebraska History,* 50, fall 1969; 239-256.

—Sketch by John E. Little

Ross Swimmer
1943-
Cherokee tribal leader, government official, attorney, and businessman

Ross Owen Swimmer is currently the president of Cherokee Nation Industries, Inc., in Stilwell, Oklahoma, an electronics subcontractor wholly owned by the Cherokee Nation of Oklahoma. One-quarter Cherokee, he served as Principal Chief of his tribe from 1975 until he was appointed to head the Bureau of Indian Affairs (BIA) in late 1985. He served in that post until resigning in 1989 to practice law in Tulsa with Hall, Estill, Hardwick, Gable, Golden, and Nelson. He was named to his current position at Cherokee Nation Industries in February 1992. Swimmer's commanding presence, ambition, and numerous achievements have combined to make him one of the foremost representatives of not only his Nation, but of all Indian peoples.

Swimmer was born in Oklahoma City, Oklahoma, on October 26, 1943, to Robert O. Swimmer and Virginia (Pounder) Swimmer. His father practiced law and was elected as a member of the 15-person Cherokee Council during his son's first term as chief. The elder Swimmer, one-half Cherokee, was re-elected to the Council in 1979 and died in the summer of 1982. Virginia, Ross' mother, obtained her law degree, attending Oklahoma City University part-time, while working for the Federal Aviation Agency. She continued to work there until retirement.

Swimmer attended public schools in Yukon and Oklahoma City before entering the University of Oklahoma in 1961. He was awarded a bachelor's degree in political science four years later. This was the formal training in politics that was to stand him in good stead in later life. Swimmer then attended the University of Oklahoma School of Law, where he developed strong negotiating skills and a persuasive public speaking technique, talents which made him a good campaigner and effective spokesman in the years to come.

His first position after passing the bar examination was with Hansen, Peterson, and Thompkins in Oklahoma City. He became a partner in that firm in 1970, but resigned two years later to accept the post of general counsel for the Cherokee Nation in Tahlequah, Oklahoma, offered to him by Chief W. W. Keeler. At that time, the Cherokee Nation had approximately 8,500 enrolled members, and Tahlequah had been its capital since 1839. Swimmer was destined to spend only a brief time as counsel, however, as the tribe's top job became open in 1975.

Runs Three Successful Campaigns for Chief

The Cherokees had had their chief appointed by the U.S. President since Oklahoma had become a state in 1907. A Cherokee election was held for the first time in 1971, and

Ross Swimmer

Keeler, who had been chief since the death of Chief J. Bartley Milam in 1949, won that campaign. However, toward the end of this term the chief announced that he would not be a candidate in the 1975 election. After Keeler's announcement, Swimmer declared his candidacy for chief, secured the endorsement of Keeler, and won the election. In the 1979 election, Swimmer received nearly 67 percent of the vote in a field of five candidates, although the election was the subject of two protests which were heard and resolved by tribal officials. During these four years, the old Cherokee Capitol Building in the town square of Tahlequah was returned to the Nation. The building had become the Cherokee County Courthouse at Oklahoma statehood and was returned to the tribe under a complex arrangement involving federal, state, county and tribal officials. Named for W. W. Keeler, the tribe's new headquarters building opened on September 30, 1979.

Swimmer won a bitter election contest in 1983 with 50.4 percent of the vote. His running mate was Wilma Mankiller, who served as Deputy Principal Chief for two years and succeeded Swimmer as Principal Chief in December of 1985 when he went to Washington and the U.S. Department of Interior. Swimmer's health had been made an issue in the campaign because he was diagnosed with non-Hodgkins lymphoma, a skin cancer, in 1981. Having received treatment in Oklahoma and at M. D. Anderson cancer center in Houston, Texas, he was pronounced fit to run for re-election, but his opponents questioned the reports. Swimmer's main opponent was Perry Wheeler, who had served as Deputy Principal Chief from 1979 to 1983. Even after a recount, the election results were not finally put to rest until 1985 when a federal judge in Tulsa dismissed a $33 million lawsuit alleging that Swimmer and 27 others conspired in fraudulent election practices.

Accomplishments During Tribal Service

In the ten years he was chief, Swimmer saw the tribal budget grow from $5 million to $20 million annually. Tribal assets increased by $23 million during that 1975 to 1985 period, and in his last year in Tahlequah, the tribal payroll stood at $9 million. Also during Swimmer's tenure, the percent of funding from federal and state grants dropped from 90% of the annual budget to 58%, as he developed the self-determination programs and asset utilization programs that he would champion for all tribes as head of the BIA. He was instrumental in obtaining funding for the $18 million W. W. Hastings Hospital in Tahlequah (part of the Indian Health Service), and he lobbied Congress to pass legislation allowing the Cherokees to sue for the value of minerals taken from the bed of the Arkansas River. The Cherokees obtained their Oklahoma land in fee simple title from the federal government. Notwithstanding this agreement, sand and gravel operators have taken leases on the Arkansas River from the state government and have extracted these commodities for years from Cherokee land. The value of the land, the removed minerals, and the trespass is still being negotiated.

A report in the October 1985 issue of *Cherokee Advocate* listed Swimmer's principal achievements as the funding of the W. W. Hastings Hospital in Tahlequah; congressional maneuverability and lobbying skills; business development; the revision of the Constitution of the Cherokee Nation of Oklahoma; his emphasis on self-determination; and administration. With regard to the Cherokee constitution, the tribe was ostensibly operating under the original 1839 document when Swimmer took office in 1975. This constitution was obviously outmoded in many respects and, with the suspension of tribal government earlier in the century, it had not been used in almost 70 years. One of Swimmer's first acts as chief was to name a committee to draft and push for adoption of an updated constitution, a draft of which had first been prepared in 1973. The document was officially ratified by a 6,028-785 vote of the Cherokee people in June 1976. During his period of residence in Tahlequah, Swimmer served as chairman of the city's planning and zoning commission, as an active in the chamber of commerce, as a Cub Scouts volunteer, and as a member of the vestry of St. Basil's Episcopal Church.

Named Assistant Secretary of the Interior

Swimmer was appointed as one of six Assistant Secretaries of the Interior by President Ronald Reagan on September 26, 1985. The White House announcement ended months of speculation that Swimmer would be selected. His assignment was the head of the Bureau of Indian Affairs, the highest Indian post in the federal government. His nomination required Senate approval, which came in December

1985. Swimmer resigned as Cherokee Chief at the same time and Wilma Mankiller was sworn in to take his place, first on December 6 (Swimmer's Senate confirmation) and again in a public ceremony during a Cherokee Council meeting on December 14. Both of Oklahoma's senators (one from each party) had enthusiastically recommended Swimmer to the Senate Select Committee on Indian Affairs. The full committee approved him on a voice vote without debate. Testifying on Swimmer's behalf were LaDonna Harris, native Oklahoman and founder of Americans for Indian Opportunity, Chief Robert S. Youngdeer of the Eastern Band of Cherokees, and Richard LaFromboise, president of the National Tribal Chairman's Association. Senator Mark Andrews, committee chairman, commented on "the totally bipartisan support" for Swimmer.

Reagan had already shown his confidence in the Cherokee chief by naming him to co-chair the President's Commission on Indian Reservation Economies in 1983. This group was a panel of tribal leaders who focused on improving economic conditions as a means of helping their people. During his period of government service, Swimmer was particularly interested in tribal self-governance and self-sufficiency, goals upheld by the Reagan administration as well. At that time, Donald Hodel was Reagan's Interior Secretary, and he had actively recruited Swimmer to become head of the BIA. Upon Swimmer's nomination, Hodel said, "We are extremely fortunate that Ross Swimmer is willing to be considered for this position. He has the extraordinary qualities of leadership and business experience that are vital to the success of U.S. Indian programs. He is dedicated to helping tribes achieve economic success in a competitive society, while preserving the rich Indian heritage."

A Balance Between Family, Civic Duty, and the Job

Swimmer married Margaret McConnell in 1966. They have two sons: Joseph, who entered Stanford Law School in 1994, and Michael, who is a student at the University of Tulsa. Margaret is a 1982 graduate of the University of Tulsa Law School and is a practicing attorney in Tulsa. She was a partner in the Hall, Estill, Hardwick, Gable, Golden & Nelson firm when Ross joined them in 1989, and she remains in that capacity. The couple have resided in Tulsa since 1984, where Ross serves on the boards of the University of Tulsa, Holland Hall School, and Gilcrease Museum. He remains active in banking as an owner and director. His hobbies include landscaping and woodworking. He enjoys hunting and fishing when his busy schedule permits.

Swimmer's business ability had been honed by serving as executive vice president of the First National Bank in Tahlequah for a year before being elected president of that bank in 1975. He held the bank presidency the entire time he was tribal chief. Swimmer also served as President of The Cherokee National Historical Society during the time he was chief, resigning upon his federal appointment in 1985. When he returned to Oklahoma, he rejoined the board, and in late 1993, he was named to the same Society post, then called Chairman of the Board of Trustees.

As President of Cherokee Nation Industries, Swimmer oversees a work force of 350 employees, many of whom are Cherokees. The firm provides much-needed employment to residents of Adair County, Oklahoma—a county with one of the highest unemployment rates in the state. During the 1980s, CNI was heavily involved in defense sub-contracting work, and one of Swimmer's challenges has been to find other markets for the firm's products after the downsizing of the military, which began in the early 1990s. Recruited to the job by Chief Wilma Mankiller, Swimmer enjoys her confidence and is using his skills and experience to manage one of the tribe's most valuable and productive assets.

SOURCES:

Books

Native North American Almanac, edited by Duane Champagne, Detroit, Gale Research, 1994.

Reference Encyclopedia of the American Indian, fifth edition, edited by Barry T. Klein, West Nyack, New York, Todd Publications, 1990.

Periodicals

Cherokee Advocate, June 1979, 1, 6, 19; October 1979, 1; August 1982.
Cherokee Voices, June/July 1976, 1; November 1976, 8-9.

Other

Chief's "State of the Nation" Report; September 1984, 1; October 1985, 1, 10-12, 17; November 1985, 1, 12; December 1985, 1; January 1986, 1B, 3B; January 1993, 3; January 1994, 5.
Swimmer, Ross, interview with Philip H. Viles, Jr., conducted on July 1, 1994.

—Sketch by Philip H. Viles, Jr.

Maria Tallchief
1925-
Osage ballerina

Raised in a wealthy family, Maria Tallchief is an internationally renowned ballerina. The resources and prestige belonging to her family came as a result of her grandfather's aide in negotiating the Osage treaty, an agreement that led to the establishment of the Osage Reservation in Oklahoma. Later the reservation was found to contain large quantities of oil, which yielded great amounts of revenue for some Indians. Tallchief's family was one of the few who gained financially through alliances with the federal government and the discovery of oil on reservation land. Tallchief began studying ballet and taking music lessons at age four. By the age of eight, she had gone beyond the level of training offered in her native state of Oklahoma, and her family relocated to Beverly Hills, California. She was trained by noted ballet specialists Bronislava Nijinska, David Lichine (student of Maria Pavlova), and George Balanchine.

When Tallchief was 15, she performed her first solo at the Hollywood Bowl in a piece choreographed by her instructor Madame Nijinska. In lieu of college, she began her formal career as a member of the highly acclaimed Ballet Russe. As a dancer with the prestigious Russian troupe, she met with prejudice and disbelief in her talents. Yet, when Balanchine took over as head of the troupe, he had no difficulty recognizing her worth and appointed her as understudy for *The Song of Norway*. Creator of such works as *Orpheus, Swan Lake, The Four Temperaments,* and a contemporary of Stravinsky, Balanchine himself was an unrecognized talent at the time. As Balanchine's technique developed, he helped shape Tallchief's abilities and her reputation as a ballerina grew rapidly.

Achieved Several Ballet "Firsts"

She married Balanchine in 1942, and they moved to France. Although meeting with some resistance in Paris as a Native American, she won audiences over with her gifted performances, after making her debut as the first American ballerina to perform with the Paris Opera Ballet. After returning to the United States, she became the ranking soloist—and the first American prima ballerina—in the Balanchine Ballet Society (later known as the New York City Ballet). In 1949 Tallchief danced the leading role in *Firebird,* a role Balanchine choreographed specifically for her

Maria Tallchief

and one which showcased her accomplishments. The performance, as well as her portrayal of the leading role, is heralded as one of her finest. A decade later she retired from performance and began directing her own ballet troupe. In later years she revisited the leading role she created for *Firebird* as she painstakingly taught it to others.

Tallchief's dream of creating a Chicago-based resident ballet company first began to take form in 1974, when she was asked to develop a small troupe that would meet the needs of the Chicago Lyric Opera. In addition, she was invited to direct the Opera Ballet School. During her tenure there from 1974 to 1979, she established the same high standards for her students that she received in her own training. An organizational split took place in January of 1980. The Chicago City Ballet was formed when the Lyric Opera Ballet separated from the Lyric Opera.

During an interview with John Gruen in *Dance* magazine, Tallchief recounted her early years with Balanchine, and her exposure to his masterful teaching. "He was forging a whole new technique—a whole new system of dancing," she said of the choreographer, whom she divorced in 1952.

"He literally created a new style of classical dancing—and that's what we mustn't lose. It's what I'm promulgating at the Chicago City Ballet because I know it's right." Tallchief and dancer/choreographer Paul Mejia seek to carry on Balanchine's style and artistic vision at the Chicago City Ballet. Both proteges of Balanchine, each feels a strong depth of commitment to continuing the late choreographer's creative ideals.

Although Tallchief officially retired from dancing in 1966, she is remembered as a ballerina with verve and a "charismatic presence" that is virtually "undimmed." During her interview with Gruen, Tallchief reflected her excitement and enthusiasm when she articulated her sentiments about working with her troupe: "What's important is that I'm working with very talented young people. Yes, we're in the process of growth, but I feel that if you have a choreographer like Paul Mejia and a syllabus based on Balanchine, you really can't go wrong. What I do for the company is teach, and what I teach is what Balanchine taught me." According to Gruen, "she retains the dynamics that made her America's prima ballerina for over two decades—a figure still capable of making temperatures rise."

SOURCES:

Books

Bird of Fire, the Story of Maria Tallchief, New York, Dodd, Mead, 1961.
Native North American Almanac, edited by Duane Champagne, Detroit, Gale Research, 1994; 1172-1173.

Periodicals

Gruen, John, "Tallchief and the Chicago City Ballet," *Dance,* 58, December 1984; HC25-27.

—*Sketch by Brett A. Lealand*

Mary TallMountain

Mary TallMountain
1918-
Koyukon Athabaskan poet and fiction writer

Mary TallMountain is the best-known poet and fiction writer of the Athabaskan people of interior Alaska. Winner of a Pushcart Prize in 1982, she is the author of seven books of poetry and fiction, and a frequent contributor to magazines and anthologies. Her work is characterized by its focus on women's perceptions, on the feminine role in culture, and on the interplay of the spiritual and the physical.

Mary TallMountain was born Mary Demoski in 1918 in the small Koyukon Athabaskan village of Nulato, Alaska, located 100 miles south of the Arctic Circle and 120 miles west of Fairbanks. Her Athabaskan-Russian mother, Mary Joe, was a member of this small village on the banks of the Yukon river. Her Scots/Irish father, Clem Stroupe, was a soldier stationed nearby. They lived together for ten years and also had a son, Billy. During Mary's early childhood, tuberculosis was rampant in the Arctic. Mary Joe developed the disease and appeared to be dying. The attending Doctor Randle and his wife Agnes expressed a desire to adopt the children and move to Oregon, but the village council was not in favor of the children's being taken from the village. However, the council compromised with the Randles and allowed them to take Mary, but returned Billy to his mother. Both Mary Joe and Billy died of tuberculosis.

At the age of six, Mary moved with the Randles to Oregon, where she felt alienated because of her heritage. The poem "Indian Blood" describes one of the many difficulties Mary experienced at this time, relating an incident of being teased by other children. The doctor later moved the family to Unalaska on the Aleutian chain, and Mary felt more at home. She was instructed in literature by her adopted mother and spent much time writing. Her first story was published by *Child Life* when she was ten.

When Mary was 14, the family moved to central California. After graduation from high school, she married Dal Roberts. She divorced and remarried. In 1945, she moved to Las Vegas and began a career as a legal secretary. Later she moved to San Francisco, and living alone, continued to work in law offices. During this period she continued to write. One weekend, she and four girlfriends went camping in the mountains, hoping to write and discuss each other's work. On this trip, TallMountain created her pen name, after a mountain near the Yukon river that she remembered from her childhood.

TallMountain sees her life as one of continual struggle. The pain of her early separation from her family was eased only by the letters her mother and brother wrote until they died. The deaths of her adoptive parents, the failure of two marriages, a bout with alcoholism, and battles against cancer built resentment and anger, but throughout adversity, she has relied on her strong spiritual orientation for direction. Her native spirituality has been colored by her explorations of the Catholic mystical tradition. Paula Gunn Allen, writing in *The Sacred Hoop,* described this mixture as the essential crux of TallMountain's perception. "The work of Mary TallMountain reveals a deeply spiritualized sensibility. Her tribal consciousness is tempered with a mystical Roman Catholic perspective, and this makes for a difficult and uneasy alliance between pagan awareness that characterizes tribal thought and the less earthy, more judgmental view of medieval Christianity."

In the mid-1960s, the Friars Press began to publish TallMountain's poems and stories. For many years, starting in 1969, her thoughts appeared regularly in a column called "Meditations for Wayfarers" in *Way* magazine, a Franciscan publication. In 1970 her poem "Ashes Unto Eden" won a second place award from the Catholic Press Association. TallMountain's career continued to move ahead after she met writer/teacher Paula Gunn Allen at San Francisco State University in the mid-1970s. Allen began to work closely with TallMountain on her writing, and TallMountain threw herself into intense creative labor. TallMountain credits Allen with molding her unshaped talent. Allen also shared and appreciated TallMountain's profound spirituality. The two continue to be close friends and colleagues.

Returns to Alaska after 50 Years

In 1976, TallMountain returned to Nulato. After reveling in her return to the Alaskan landscape and the Athabaskan people, she came to sense a great distance between herself and the villagers. But although she could no longer feel the rhythm of the people, and her relatives seemed cold and remote, the experience was an important one for TallMountain's sense of identity and for her writing. She came to terms with her marginality, realizing that she had come to possess the strengths of her people while overcoming their weaknesses. In her autobiographical essay for *I Tell You Now,* she wrote, "My roots are here, I feel them deep in my memories, in the hidden spaces of my blood. It doesn't matter where I live; I will see the rounded cabins set together. I will see the hill where my mother lies clean and shining under the roots of this ground." TallMountain sees herself as essentially linked to Nulato through memory, experience, imagination, and spirit. In an autobiographical statement in the TallMountain collection, she declared, "I write from the Indian viewpoint about the country and the people where I was born."

Later in 1976, TallMountain found her father after attempting to locate him for many years. She lived with him for two years until his death in 1978. He helped her understand a great deal about her mother, her relatives, and the mood of the village in those years of disease and death. Much of TallMountain's lingering bitterness was dispelled as they talked about Alaska and her early life. Her father was able to deliver a message from her dying mother, who wanted Mary to know that she loved her and that she allowed the adoption because she was afraid her daughter would die if not taken from Nulato. She knew Mary would be all right. In the foreword to *The Light on the Tent Wall,* Allen describes the experience of reading TallMountain's writing, which has been deeply influenced by the hardships of her life. "The works in this volume are to be contemplated more than read. They can be savored by those who have themselves seen the precipice and taken the fall. By those who have seen their own flesh and bones scattered about the floor of the plain, and who have wit and strength to reconstitute themselves and keep on keeping on."

Spirituality Central to Her Writing

While the Friars Press had published a small chapbook of her poems in 1977, it was not until the early 1980s that TallMountain began to receive national attention. Blue Cloud Quarterly Press published a collection of poetry entitled *There Is No Word for Goodbye;* the title poem won a Pushcart Prize in 1982. She soon received wide notice and her work was subsequently included in many anthologies, such as *The Harper's Anthology of Twentieth-Century Native American Literature, That's What She Said, The Remembered Earth, Earth Power Coming,* and *A Gathering of Spirit.* Over the years, she has been working on many pieces of short fiction as well as continuing to write poetry. She has also been working for a number of years on an autobiographical novel tentatively titled *Doyon.*

TallMountain is keenly aware of the marginalized position of contemporary Native-American writers, many of whom are of mixed ancestry and cultural orientation. In an autobiographical statement from the TallMountain Archives, she explained: "The works of Native American writers in this time form a bridge between this vastly ancient culture and that of the new arrivals. We stand between the two, bicultural. Our work tries to express this; but first of all it wants to express the connection of Earth with the spirit of a people."

For TallMountain this spirit is nothing abstract. She views her writing as forging a channel of communication between her and her departed female relatives. In a televised interview with Bill Moyers, TallMountain spoke of the importance of spiritual communication with her mother and grandmother. In a poem for her grandmother entitled "Matmiya," she wrote, "Your spirit remains / Nourished / Nourishing me." This personal, family connection forms the basis of her connection with the spirit of her people. In addition, TallMountain sees women as the creators of culture and the protectors of spirit; as such they are central to tribal experience. For her, women epitomize the earth, establishing physical and spiritual connections. In an interview published in *Studies in American Indian Literature,* she told Joseph Bruchac, "I think they operate everything and the men are really the figureheads."

TallMountain's strength of spirit has seen her through loss, despair, anger, and death. Only later in life has she found a comfortable role. In *Continuum,* she concluded, "When the time came, I slipped as comfortably into my niche as a hand into a silk glove, realizing it as my vocation, my obligation, to observe and to write of any alienated people I encountered, chiefly of the Alaskan Native." Her works, papers, and journals have been collected at Rasmuson Library Archives of the University of Alaska-Fairbanks.

SELECTED WRITINGS BY TALLMOUNTAIN:

Nine Poems, San Francisco, Friars Press, 1977.
There Is No Word for Goodbye, Marvin, South Dakota, Blue Cloud Quarterly Press, 1981.
Green March Moons, Berkeley, New Seed Press, 1987.
Continuum, Marvin, South Dakota, Blue Cloud Quarterly Press, 1988.
The Light on the Tent Wall: A Bridging, Los Angeles, University of California at Los Angeles, American Indian Studies Center, 1990.
Matrilineal Cycle, Oakland, California, Red Star Black Rose Printing, 1990.
A Quick Brush of Wings, San Francisco, Freedom Voices Publications, 1991.

SOURCES:

Books

Allen, Paula Gunn, *The Sacred Hoop: Recovering the Feminine in American Indian Traditions,* Boston, Beacon Press, 1986.
Lincoln, Kenneth, "Mary TallMountain," in *Native American Women,* edited by Gretchen M. Bataille, New York, Garland Publishing, 1993.
TallMountain, Mary, "You Can Go Home Again: A Sequence," in *I Tell You Now: Autobiographical Essays by Native American Writers,* edited by Brian Swann and Arnold Krupat, Lincoln, University of Nebraska Press, 1987.

Periodicals

Bruchac, Joseph, "We Are the Inbetweens: An Interview with Mary TallMountain," *Studies in American Indian Literature* 1, summer 1989; 13-21.

Other

Moyers, Bill, *Ancestral Voices,* "The Power of the Word" Series, PBS, 1989.
TallMountain Collection, University of Alaska-Fairbanks archives.

—*Sketch by James Ruppert*

Luci Tapahonso
1953-
Navajo poet

Luci Tapahonso is one of a group of Native American women poets who speak for their people. Encouraged and applauded by her peers, Tapahonso is a poet of the Navajo, of Native Americans, of the minority, and of women. She incorporates into her poetry the landscape of the Southwest and the stories and experiences of those she knows both on and off the reservation. Her use of language and the interweaving of Navajo expressions and American speech make her poetry accessible far beyond the boundaries of her homelands. Her voice is one of hope and of acceptance of change without losing what is important from the past. Besides publishing several books, she has taught at two universities and has given readings and lectures in many different places.

Born in 1953 at Shiprock, New Mexico, the sixth of 11 children of a farming family, Tapahonso grew up on a Navajo reservation and attended school at the Navajo Methodist Mission in Farmington, 30 miles from Shiprock. In 1971, she graduated from Shiprock High School. At the University of New Mexico, encouraged by Leslie Marmon Silko, she changed her major from journalism to English, and received her B.A. in 1981 and an M.A. in creative writing in 1983. She had already published two books of poetry by that time: *One More Shiprock Night* and *Seasonal Woman.* Her masters thesis, *A Sense of Myself,* included, besides poetry, a short Navajo play, written with bilingual dialogue in Navajo and English. Funded by the New Mexico Arts Council, this play was performed and taped for television, produced by Geraldine Keams, and directed by Deborah Blanche.

"My sense of language, my awareness of words," said Tapahonso in the introduction of her thesis, "becomes entangled with songs, memories, history and the land." She spoke Navajo mostly while she was growing up and seems to have no difficulty putting her thoughts into English, mingling new and old. Even so, she does not hesitate to use Navajo words and phrases, especially for dialogue, usually adding a translation in parentheses. She uses both Navajo and English in her poems and readings. "As I write in English," Tapahonso explained in her thesis, "I am aware of how this particular line or feeling would be in Navajo first—so that I am translating roughly into English ... whatever I happen to be writing about."

In a 1984 interview with Joseph Bruchac in *MELUS,* Tapahonso spoke about her use of language. Asked about a poem called "Hills Brothers Coffee," she said, "It's a translation, a direct translation from Navajo ... a lot of the words are probably different than if I had written in English." She added that she was writing a lot of poetry in Navajo then because sometimes she could find no real translation into

Luci Tapahonso

song—in the sense that it stirs one's mind or that it creates a dance within a person's imagination." Her third book of poetry, *A Breeze Swept Through,* was published in 1987. That same year she was appointed assistant professor of English, women's studies, and American studies at the University of New Mexico.

In a 1988 interview with John Crawford and Annie O. Eysturoy in *This Is about Vision,* Tapahonso spoke again of her fascination with the English language and of how it is connected to the written word, and to the world outside. For the writer, Navajo was mostly spoken, not written; it represented home, family, tradition, and emotion. "It's just the writing that is English, and otherwise it's still on the periphery," she said. Tapahonso told the interviewers that her writing is all in English because she has difficulty in reading or writing well in Navajo. She can say poems in Navajo; the trouble comes in writing them down because she cannot hear all the sounds, or separate the sounds. Still, that language connects her to home and family, to food, to sounds, and to conversation and storytelling; her reactions to surprises are in Navajo first. Putting those things into English is a slow, careful process for her. "It's still a matter of finding the exact way to say it that's as close to Navajo as it can be," Tapahonso said, "but it will never be like Navajo, and that's the real challenge." It is this ability to put her thoughts and experiences into English that lends power to her poetry, enabling it to reach far beyond the borders of the Navajo community. Sometimes, in giving readings to mixed audiences of Navajos and others, she will read in Navajo without translating. It works, she says, and people respond because "poetry is much more than just words."

Importance of the Landscape in Her Writings

In the preface, "The Kaw River Rushes Eastward," to her fourth book, *Saanii Dahataal,* Tapahonso says, "The place of my birth is the source of the writing presented here." It is the place and circumstance of her birth that give her identity. Navajo people identify themselves by their clan, which is the clan of the mother. Tapahonso's mother's clan is *Todikozhi,* which means salt water. Her father's clan is *Todich'iin'ii,* which means "Salt Water." Her last name, Tapahonso, means "edge of the big water." Though she grew up on the reservation, she has lived much of her adult life in the city—in Albuquerque, and Lawrence, Kansas. This is a choice she had to make in order to write and to teach. Tapahonso cannot abandon the land. She plans to go back, to build a house where she can live full-time, she told Crawford, as soon as is possible. Her characters, too, are connected to the land. Even those who live in the city bring with them ritual and traditions from the land. Tapahonso's singular voice has been described as having come from the Navajo landscape, creating a multiplicity of voices connected to the lands and to the stories of the people. The writing is first person narrative, with the "I" of each poem belonging to a character with her or his own voice.

Tapahonso's fourth book, *Saanii Dahataal, The Women Are Singing: Poems and Stories,* was published in 1993. Writing about that book in the *New York Times,* David

English. When Bruchac asked her if she saw the Navajo language as a sort of force for herself and her poetry, she said, "That's true, I think ... if you lose, if we lose the language, then we're really not anything anymore."

Tapahonso married artist Earl Ortiz, who illustrated her first book, *One More Shiprock Night.* She has two daughters, Lori Tazbah and Misty Dawn, who appear first in the poem, "A Breeze Swept Through," which is dedicated to them. This poem became the title poem of Tapahonso's third book of poetry. The daughters also appear in other poems. "Feel good about yourselves," she tells them in "A Spring Poem." Family members—aunts, uncles, brothers, and her grandfather and their conversations, memories, and songs—fill her poems.

Through her writing, Tapahonso tells the history of her people, meshing it with the present. In her story, "The Snake Man," the oral literature of the Native American past is interwoven with events at a Christian boarding school on a Navajo reservation. Tapahonso tells of some homesick little girls at the boarding school. "The tale is at once a piece of psychological and sociological realism," wrote Patricia Clark Smith in *Earthly Relations, Carnal Knowledge.* "Though set in modern times, it is an old story, or part of one."

Publishes Her Third Book of Poetry

Song, prayer, and ritual are all important and interwoven into Tapahonso's writing. "In Navajo ... there's a song for everything," Tapahonso told Bruchac. "Poetry, too, is a

Biespiel noted, "At her best when describing the human voice, revealing an intimacy with the sound of speech.... Ms. Tapahonso speaks the observed and spiritual world into existence." In a review of the book for *Parabola,* Linda Hogan wrote, "Luci Tapahonso writes the world into balance and harmony."

Tapahonso lives in Lawrence, Kansas, where she is associate professor of English at the University of Kansas. In September of 1992, she was one of five Native American poets to participate in the Geraldine R. Dodge Poetry Festival in New Jersey, the largest poetry festival in North America. In April of 1994, she was a featured speaker at the Associated Writing Programs annual conference held in Phoenix, Arizona. Her poems, stories and essays have been published in many journals and anthologies, including *A Circle of Nations: Voices and Visions of American Indians, Sign Language: Contemporary Southwest Native America, Earth Power Coming, and Frontiers: A Journal of Women's Studies.*

SELECTED WRITINGS BY TAPAHONSO:

One More Shiprock Night: Poems, San Antonio, Tejas Art Press, 1981.
Seasonal Woman, Santa Fe, Tooth of Time Press, 1982.
"A Sense of Myself" (thesis), University of New Mexico, 1983.
A Breeze Swept Through, Los Angeles, West End Press, 1987.
Saanii Dahataal, The Women Are Singing:Poems and Stories, Tucson, University of Arizona Press, 1993.

SOURCES:

Books

Bruchac, Joseph, *Survival This Way: Interviews with American Indian Poets,* Tucson, University of Arizona Press, 1987; 271-285.
Crawford, John, and Annie O. Eysturoy, "Luci Tapahonso," in *This Is About Vision: Interviews with Southwestern Writers,* edited by William Balassi, John F. Crawford, and Annie O. Eysturoy, Albuquerque, University of New Mexico Press, 1990; 195-202.
Earth Power Coming: Short Fiction in Native American Literature, edited by Simon J. Ortiz, Tsaile, Arizona, Navajo Community College Press, 1983; 288.
Native American Women, edited by Gretchen M. Bataille, New York, Garland Publishing, 1993; 253-255.
Smith, Patricia Clark, and Paula Gunn Allen, "Earthy Relations, Carnal Knowledge: Southwestern American Indian Women Writers and Landscape," in *The Desert Is No Lady: Southwestern Landscapes in Women's Writing and Art,* edited by Vera Norwood and Janice Monk, New Haven, Yale University Press, 1987; 174-188.
Tapahonso, Luci, "The Kaw River Rushes Westward," in *A Circle of Nations: Voices and Visions of American Indians,* edited by John Gattuso, Hillsboro, Oregon, Beyond Words Publishing; 106-110, 120.

Tapahonso, Luci, "The Way It Is," in *Sign Language: Contemporary Southwest Native America,* New York, Aperture, 1989.

Periodicals

Biespiel, David, *"Saanii Dahataal, The Women Are Singing: Poems and Stories,* By Luci Tapahonso," New York Times, October 31, 1993; Section 7, 40.
Bruchac, Joseph, "A MELUS Interview: Luci Tapahonso," *MELUS,* 11, winter 1984; 85-91.
Hogan, Linda, *"Saanii Dahataal, The Women Are Singing: Poems and Stories,* by Luci Tapahonso," *Parabola,* winter 1993; 96-97.
Moulin, Sylvie, "Nobody Is an Orphan: Interview with Luci Tapahonso," *Studies in American Indian Literatures: The Journal of the Association for the Study of American Indian Literatures,* fall 1993; 14-18.

—Sketch by Blanche Cox Clegg

Tecumseh
1768-1813
Shawnee warrior and tribal leader
Also known as "The Panther Passing Across," "Moves From One Place to Another," and "Shooting Star"

Tecumseh was a Shawnee war chief and one of the most influential Indian leaders of his time. He envisioned an Indian confederacy which would transcend tribalism and enable his people to stand united against the tide of white settlement which threatened their way of life. He spent much of his career campaigning among the tribes of the Old Northwest and, despite obstacles, won many recruits for his cause. In the end, however, the superior numbers and technology of the whites, combined with differences of opinion among the Indians themselves, put an end to Tecumseh's great plan.

Tecumseh has become equally famous for his strong moral character. Although little is known for certain about his personal life, he married at least twice, according to R. David Edmunds, in *Tecumseh and the Quest for Indian Leadership,* and others. The name of his first wife is unknown; they apparently separated after a disagreement. His second wife, Mamate, died young, leaving him with a young son Pachetha, who was raised by Tecumseh's sister, Tecumpease. There may have been another son and perhaps a daughter with a Cherokee woman. Contemporary accounts also indicate that Tecumseh stood out because of his special concern for others, freely sharing game and other provisions with the less fortunate.

Tecumseh

Early Life

Tecumseh (probably originally pronounced "Tekamtha") was born at Old Piqua, a Shawnee village on the Mad River in what is now western Ohio. Tradition has it that a large meteor or comet passed through the sky at the moment of his birth, suggesting his name (which can also be translated as "Moves From One Place to Another," or "Shooting Star.") His father was Puckeshinwa, a respected Shawnee war chief, and his mother, was Methoataske, of Creek or possibly Cherokee origin. The number of children in the family is not known for certain, but they certainly included Chicksika, the eldest, who served in the role of father to Tecumseh following the early death of Puckeshinwa; Tecumpease, an older sister to whom Tecumseh was devoted all his life; another brother, Sauwauseekau; and a younger brother, Lalawethika, who seems to have been one of a set of triplets.

Tecumseh's childhood was passed during a time of crisis for the Shawnee people. From prehistoric times they had inhabited the Ohio valley, living in villages along the river, the women farming and the men hunting, fishing and, from time to time, warring with neighboring tribes. They had long been accustomed to contact with the Long Knives, as they called the white frontiersmen, trading with them and generally maintaining good relations. But throughout the 1760s and 1770s, whites arrived in ever increasing numbers. Preceded by their surveyors, they established permanent settlements, clearing and fencing the land, and driving away the game on which the Indians depended. The Indians objected

to the intrusion, and by 1774, there was war between the Shawnee and the Long Knives. Tecumseh's father, Puckeshinwa, was a casualty of this war, and Chicksika reportedly promised his dying father that he would never make peace with the Long Knives.

After the death of Puckeshinwa, it fell to Chicksika to teach his younger brother the skills of the hunter and warrior which were so necessary for success in the tribe. Chicksika, an able hunter and warrior himself, was an excellent teacher, and there was a close bond between the two. Tecumseh learned quickly. Contemporary accounts indicate that he displayed at an early age the leadership qualities which would mark his later career, organizing and leading hunting parties of youngsters and always bringing home more game than anyone else.

When the colonies went to war with Great Britain in 1776, the Shawnee remained neutral. When their principal chief, Cornstalk (Hokolesqua), was seized and murdered by white settlers while on a peace mission to Fort Randolph in 1777, however, the Shawnee retaliated with a vengeance, attacking white settlements and killing many settlers. In 1779, the Long Knives responded in kind with an attack on Chillicothe, principal village of the Shawnee and residence of Tecumseh's family. The Shawnee repulsed the attack easily; nevertheless, this incident, which brought war to hearth and home, disturbed them deeply. There was disagreement among them as to how to respond to white aggression, and before the year was out, the tribe had split. Nearly 1,000 Shawnee, including Tecumseh's mother Methoataske, migrated to southeastern Missouri. Tecumseh was eleven years old when his mother left the village, commending her younger sons to the care of Chicksika and the recently married Tecumpease, who had elected to stay and resist the Long Knives.

Young Warrior

Tecumseh's first brush with battle seems to have been in 1782, when at age 14 he accompanied Chicksika, now a war chief in his own right, in an attack against a party of invading Kentuckians. Chicksika was slightly wounded in the engagement and Tecumseh, momentarily unnerved, fled into the forest. He soon returned, however, and was forgiven this brief lapse, which was never repeated. Subsequently, Tecumseh routinely accompanied Chicksika's war parties. He made a name for himself not only as a brave and skillful fighter, but also, in an age when hostilities between whites and Indians were often marked by extreme cruelty on both sides, as a compassionate one. He is said to have objected strongly to the burning of a prisoner following a raid on a river party, speaking so persuasively that his fellow warriors promised to abandon such practices in the future. Throughout his life, Tecumseh remained steadfast in his insistence on the humane treatment of prisoners.

During the years that followed the American Revolution, the new government set about acquiring more Indian land to satisfy settlers and recoup financial losses from the war. "Government chiefs," as the Indians referred those among them who had dealings with the Americans, sold off huge tracts of land that they did not own. Tecumseh's people remained aloof from these proceedings and never recognized their validity. It may well have been during these years that Tecumseh formulated his lifelong philosophy that the land belonged to all the Indians in common and therefore no one tribe or group had the right to sell it.

Tensions between the Shawnee and the Long Knives continued to build, and the years 1787 to 1788 found Chicksika's war party, including Tecumseh, roaming the south, raiding white settlements. In the summer of 1788, Chicksika was killed in an abortive attack on Buchanan's Station in Tennessee. Most of the party returned home following the loss of their leader. Tecumseh, however, remained in the south for another two years, hunting and raiding white settlements with a small party. He did not return home until 1790.

While Tecumseh was away, the U.S. government had created the Northwest Territory from his homeland, federalizing many of the disputed Indian lands. They opened the lands to white settlement by confronting Indian resistance with military action. Forays led by General Josiah Harmar in 1790 and by Arthur St. Clair, governor of the territory, in 1791, were decisively routed by the Indians. Tecumseh was home in time to play an important role in the action against St. Clair, leading the scouting party which kept the Indians informed of St. Clair's advance.

Following these defeats, the Americans took stronger measures. Major General Anthony Wayne, who became military commander of the west in 1792, mounted a carefully planned, well supplied expedition which clashed with the Indians in August of 1794 at a place called Fallen Timbers. The Indians, badly outnumbered, suffered a crushing defeat, made worse by the failure of promised aid from the British. Tecumseh was in the forefront of the fighting at Fallen Timbers, and his brother, Sauwauseekau, was among those killed.

Tecumseh took no part in the negotiations which followed in the wake of the Battle of Fallen Timbers. These proceedings resulted in the Treaty of Greenville, by means of which the Indians relinquished their claims to lands in southern, central and eastern Ohio. Grieved by his brother's death and disappointed at the failure of British support, he withdrew to northern Ohio, where he spent the winter hunting with a small party of family and friends. Edmunds assesses Tecumseh's position at this point, noting that by 1795, he had become "an influential young war chief with a growing following among many of the younger, more anti-American warriors."

Influential Among the Long Knives

The years following Fallen Timbers were relatively peaceful for Tecumseh. He lived with his followers for a time at Deer Creek in western Ohio, and then moved west to Indiana, where he remained for several years. Interludes between hostile encounters with the Long Knives were marked by attempts at friendship, and the force of Tecum-

seh's personality brought him to the forefront of many of these efforts. Government officials often asked him to negotiate for them and he often responded. On one such occasion, following a panic by white settlers who had abandoned their farms in the wake of Indian attacks, he spoke calmly and eloquently to assembled whites, assuring them that the Indians intended to abide by the Treaty of Greenville and wished to live in peace. The settlers were reassured and returned to their homes. Whites who heard Tecumseh speak commented on the force and eloquence of his oratory, in spite of the fact that he always spoke in the Shawnee language and had his words translated by an interpreter.

The Indian Movement

In 1805 Tecumseh's younger brother, Lalawethika, initiated a religious revival which became known as the Indian Movement. He attracted large numbers of followers from many tribes to a community he established at Greenville, Ohio, where his preaching advocated a return to traditional Indian values and a general rejection of the ways of the white man. Perhaps most importantly, he emphasized that the whites had no right to the lands they had taken from the Indians. In honor of his new-found status, Lalawethika changed his name to Tenskwatawa, the Open Door. He was also known as the Shawnee Prophet.

Tecumseh joined his brother at Greenville where, under his influence, the thrust of the movement shifted from religious to political. According to Edmunds, Tecumseh had two major goals: the common ownership of all remaining Indian lands by the tribes, and a political and military confederacy to unite the tribes under his own leadership. Soon government officials became alarmed at the growing number of warriors arriving at Greenville. From his headquarters at Vincennes, William Henry Harrison, governor of the Indiana Territory, watched the Greenville community closely, often sending messages to the Indians, asking them what they meant to do. Tecumseh and Tenskwatawa responded with reassurances of their peaceful intentions.

Tippecanoe

By 1808, the game and other resources at Greenville were depleted, and the community was hard pressed to support its growing population. The brothers moved their supporters to a location on the Tippecanoe River where it meets the Wabash. There, game and fish were more plentiful, and they would be further away from the Long Knives. The establishment of this new village, called Tippecanoe or Prophetstown, with its ever increasing number of warriors, caused further alarm among the white settlers, and Governor Harrison kept a wary eye on the settlement.

Meanwhile, Tecumseh looked for more support for his confederacy. In the fall of 1808, he made a trip to Canada and established political links with the British. During the next three years, he traveled widely among the tribes of the northwest and the south in search of recruits. He met with mixed success. Older leaders, particularly the "government chiefs," felt threatened by Tecumseh's leadership and warned their followers against him. Furthermore, it was often difficult for some of the more traditionally-minded to picture themselves as part of a confederacy that united them, in some cases, with ancient enemies.

However, Tecumseh's following increased in the next year with the unwitting help of Governor Harrison. In September of 1809 Harrison entered into new land negotiations with government chiefs. The result was the Treaty of Fort Wayne, which netted for the government about two and a half million acres of Indian lands. As word of this loss spread among the northwestern tribes a flood of warriors, disgusted with the leaders who had thus betrayed them, joined Tecumseh's cause.

In 1810 Governor Harrison, convinced of the Tippecanoe community's hostility, made a final effort to subdue the Indians without warfare. He suggested that Tenskwatawa, Tecumseh's younger brother, visit Washington to meet the president—a familiar ploy by means of which officials sought to overawe Indians with the power of the federal government. Tecumseh himself travelled to meet Harrison at Vincennes in July to deliver a reply to this invitation. He was accompanied by several hundred warriors. The progress of the party was recorded by the commander of Fort Knox, who halted the Indians' canoes briefly. The commander wrote home, as quoted in Benjamin Drake's *Life of Tecumseh:* "They were all painted in the most terrific manner.... They were headed by the brother of the Prophet (Tecumseh) who, perhaps, is one of the finest looking men I ever saw—about six feet high, straight, with large, fine features, and altogether a daring, bold looking fellow."

At Vincennes, Tecumseh and Harrison met for the first time. A council was held at which Tecumseh spoke at length, reciting the long list of injustices that had been committed against the Indians, emphasizing his opposition to the Treaty of Fort Wayne, and admitting that he headed a confederacy dedicated to preventing further invasion of Indian lands. He concluded by saying that he was not at that time able to accept the invitation to Washington. Harrison came away from the meeting convinced that it was Tecumseh, not his brother, who was the real power at the Tippecanoe community.

By 1811 Harrison had become openly hostile toward the community at Tippecanoe. Tecumseh was absent from the village that autumn, recruiting among the tribes of the south, and Harrison took advantage of the opportunity. On September 26, he marched his army out of Vincennes and proceeded toward Tippecanoe. Tenskwatawa, monitoring Harrison's progress, also prepared for war but took no action until Harrison's forces crossed the river and camped within a mile of the village on November 6. During the night, the Indians surrounded Harrison's camp and attacked before dawn. The Battle of Tippecanoe lasted just over two hours. At that time the Indians began to disengage, even though they had inflicted heavy losses on Harrison's troops. They abandoned their village and scattered. Harrison's troops burned Tippecanoe. Although the Battle of Tippecanoe was not the glorious victory for the Long Knives that Harrison later claimed, the defeat was a severe blow to the absent Tecumseh, and also to Tenskwatawa, who had taken no active role in the fighting. It ended his career as a prophet.

To the Thames

Following the Battle of Tippecanoe, Tecumseh established a temporary village on nearby Wildcat Creek and set about rebuilding his confederacy. His plan included appeasing the Americans. He assured Harrison that he would give careful consideration to a renewed invitation to visit Washington. As war between the British and Americans approached, both sides courted the support of the Indians of the northwest.

For Tecumseh, the choice was not difficult. In June 1812, he headed for Canada, where he offered his support to the British. As American troops under General Hull advanced toward Detroit to protect American interests, Tecumseh campaigned among the Indians of the region, seeking support for the British cause. Many of the tribes in the region made no distinction between the British and the Americans, but Tecumseh, by the force of his personality, won many converts. He participated in a number of engagements in Canada and the Detroit area during the summer, as the tide of events ran in favor of the British. At the Battle of Brownstown, he turned back an army of over 150 American troops with only 24 warriors. Shortly afterward, he was slightly wounded at the Battle of Monguagon, which the Americans claimed as a victory.

Tecumseh was pleased when General Isaac Brock took command of the British base of operations at Fort Malden in August. Brock's forceful manner won his immediate approval, and the general had similar confidence in Tecumseh. He informed the Shawnee leader of his plans to march on Detroit and placed him in command of all the Indian forces. Tecumseh played a pivotal role in the British conquest of Detroit on August 15. Soon, however, reverses set in. Brock was killed in October and was succeeded by Colonel Henry Procter. Although he had less confidence in Colonel Procter's abilities, Tecumseh remained with and supported the combined forces. When Procter announced his intention to abandon Fort Malden after the British naval defeat at the Battle of Lake Erie, Tecumseh made such an inspiring speech before the assembled British and Indian troops that Procter reconsidered his position. Instead, he agreed that, after a strategic withdrawal to Chatham, he would make a stand against the approaching American forces led by William Henry Harrison.

In fact, Proctor retreated to Moraviantown as Tecumseh's forces guarded the rear. The colonel finally made a stand at the Thames River. However, the British positions quickly collapsed under pressure from the Americans, allowing American troops to flank the Indian positions. Tecumseh and his warriors fought until they were overwhelmed by superior numbers. Tecumseh himself was fatally wounded by a bullet in the chest. The Indians gradually withdrew, and the Battle of the Thames ended in an American victory. With the death of Tecumseh, the Indian movement ended.

Tecumseh is still one of history's more elusive figures. The extent of the impression he made on William Henry Harrison is illustrated in a letter Harrison wrote to the secretary of war, in which he described the war chief as "one of those uncommon geniuses, which spring up occasionally to produce revolutions and overturn the established order of things." If Harrison's words marked the distance between the Long Knives and the Shawnee, they are still those of one who knew Tecumseh personally. No words of Tecumseh himself survive. There is no known transcript of any of his speeches, nor do we have accounts from any of the Indians who followed him and believed in his cause. His story is told through the eyes of his opponents, who both fought and respected him.

SOURCES:

Books

Drake, Benjamin, *Life of Tecumseh,* Anderson, Gates & Wright, 1858; reprinted, Ayer Company Publishers, 1988.

Eckert, Allan W., *A Sorrow in Our Heart,* New York, Bantam, 1992.

Edmunds, R. David, *Tecumseh and the Quest for Indian Leadership,* Boston, Little, Brown, 1984.

Gilbert, Bill, *God Gave Us This Country : Tekamthi and the First American Civil War,* New York, Anchor/Doubleday, 1989.

Sugden, John, *Tecumseh's Last Stand,* Norman, University of Oklahoma Press, 1985.

Periodicals

Dowd, Gregory E., "Thinking and Believing: Nativism and Unity in the Ages of Pontiac and Tecumseh," *American Indian Quarterly,* Volume 16, 1992; 309-335.

Sugden, John, "Early Pan-Indianism: Tecumseh's Tour of the Indian Country, 1811-1812," *American Indian Quarterly,* Volume 10, 1986; 273-304.

—*Sketch by Julie Henderson Jersyk*

Kateri Tekakwitha
1656-1680
Mohawk Catholic nun and candidate for sainthood
Also known as Catherine Tekakwitha, (Tegaskouita, Tegakwitha, or Tagaskouita), "Lily of the Mohawks" and La Sainte Sauvagesse

Kateri Tekakwitha is the first Native American convert to Roman Catholic Christianity to be venerated by the

Kateri Tekakwitha

church. She was born in 1656 in Ossernenon (Auriesville), New York, to a Mohawk father and a Christianized Algonquin mother captured by Mohawks around 1653. This capture took place amidst a great deal of fighting among Native factions and Europeans attempting to penetrate the New World. Tribal warfare, as well as cultural and religious battles with Europeans, set the climate and stage for Kateri's life to unfold.

Although the French Jesuits were making some headway in their attempts to Christianize and colonize New France, native hostilities remained. The 16-year interval between 1632 and 1648 was reportedly the "most difficult and least productive period" for the Jesuit Mission. In *The Impact of Katherine Tekakwitha on American Spiritual Life,* Justin C. Steurer highlights the conflict of this period with the death of eight Jesuits who were "tortured and martyred between 1642 and 1649, three being slain by the Mohawks of Tekakwitha's village, Ossernenon." After the slayings a constant state of war presided over the region until finally, in 1667, the French government sent an expedition to avenge the killings. As a result of extensive destruction, the Mohawks (known among the Five Nations of the Iroquois particularly for their violence) were forced into requesting missionaries from the French.

Eleven years prior to the capture of Kateri's mother, a Jesuit missionary by the name of Isaac Jogues had been captured by a band of warriors in 1642 and brought to Ossernenon. He, like other missionaries, received a good deal of pressure from French officials to convert the natives, bringing them under French rule. Jogues encouraged the tribe to believe that his Catholic mass kit and attendant altar were powerful tools of sorcery and magic. David Blanchard states in *Anthropologica* that "on one occasion Jogues threatened to use these tools to bring death and disease to the Mohawk if they did not accept his religious teachings." Some years after his capture, Jogues left for France, and upon his return found that a wave of smallpox had swept the village during his absence. He was killed by a war ax when he reappeared in the village after the fulfillment of his prophesy. This smallpox epidemic took the lives of Kateri's mother, father, and younger brother. At the age of four, she was orphaned and left facially disfigured as well as visually impaired by a bout with the disease. Kateri's uncle, who was a village chief of some repute and the husband of her mother's sister, took her in.

The Virginity of Kateri Tekakwitha

Kateri's uncle was violently opposed to Christianity. However, he was obliged to host the three missionaries sent to Ossernenon after their defeat. In 1667, when she was eleven, Kateri was appointed the task of looking after them during their short stay. The young girl was reportedly taken with the docile, courteous behavior of the Jesuits. Later, two of the three missionaries returned to the area to settle and continue their work. During these years, Kateri reached puberty and, according to missionary reports, refused all overtures made toward her as well as every attempt to marry her off. Her family responded to her resistance with violence and extreme deprivation. Meals were withheld from her and her life was threatened. It is suspected that some of the Christian Algonquins and Hurons, who now made up about two-thirds of the village population, approached Kateri with stories of the unwed Ursuline nuns of Quebec, influencing her decision.

The Mohawks were not traditionally opposed to the idea of perpetual virginity and chastity. In Anthropologica, Blanchard reveals that "traditionally the Iroquois believed that virginity created great power in an individual and communities maintained special residences for women who chose to remain virgins." Members of these enclaves in the community held to specific codes of behavior expected of those of their stature. However, some evidence suggests that the Indians had been greatly shamed in the past when the virgins broke their vows. In *Customs of the American Indians Compared with the Customs of Primitive Times,* Joseph Lafitau reports this custom was being practiced up until "the arrival of Europeans who made foolish virgins of them by giving them brandy" and intoxicating them. The women then embarrassed themselves and their village by acting outside the expected behavioral code. The elders confessed shame and dishonor, thereby disbanding the enclave. This incident undoubtedly had an effect upon surrounding villages, including Ossernenon.

Conversion and Subsequent Personal Trials

In his writings, Lamberville reports finding a teenage Kateri in her dwelling, unable to work because of a foot injury. By all accounts, she was regularly a very industrious, generous worker. Lamberville states: "I conversed with her about Christianity and I found her so docile that I exhorted her to be instructed and to frequent the chapel, which she did.... I noted that she had none of the vices of the girls of her age, that encouraged me to teach her henceforth." Kateri thereafter attended his catechism through the summer and winter. Lamberville was so impressed with her learning that he baptized her the following Easter, in 1676, earlier than usual for new converts. She then received the name Kateri. For six months she remained in her village, a focus of ridicule and scorn for her open practice of Christianity. She was accused of sorcery, repeatedly accosted on her trips to and from the village chapel, and food was withheld from her on Sundays and Christian holidays when she chose not to work. Her life was once threatened on her way to chapel by a Mohawk warrior who held a war ax above her head, and she was accused by her maternal aunt of enticing her uncle to engage in sex.

Lamberville dismissed the charges and counseled her to leave the village to join the Jesuit mission of Saint Francis Xavier, at Kanawake, Quebec, at the straits of Sault Saint Louis. Kanawake was a village well known for the discipline of its inhabitants. It was formed in 1667 as a response to the bad effects of alcohol on the Iroquois. When three Native convert members of the mission came recruiting to Ossernenon, Kateri left with them. One of them was the husband of her half-sister, her uncle's adopted daughter, who resided at the mission. Her uncle was gone from the village during her departure, but upon learning of her absence, he vowed to have her and the three others killed. He pursued them, but they eluded him.

Upon her arrival at the mission, Kateri was given into the spiritual care of Anastasie Tegonhatsiongo, a former friend of her mother. She received intensive Christian training and was viewed as a gifted student of the subject. She was allowed to receive Communion within months of her arrival. Anastasie, like many other inhabitants of the mission, was opposed to Katari's desire to remain a virgin. She and others attempted to dissuade Katari from this and pressured her to marry, reminding her that to do so would secure her a life free from poverty. But Kateri had formed close friendships with two other women at the mission. After having visited the nuns of Hotel-Dieu hospital in Ville-Marie (Montreal), and learning of their lives and ascetic practices, the three women wished to form their own cloister. As a final resort, Anastasie entreated one of the three head priests, Father Cholenic, to mediate the situation. While he and the Catholic authorities felt it premature for the forming of a Native American cloister, Kateri was allowed to take a vow of chastity on the Feast of Annunciation in 1679. According to K. I. Koppedrayer in *Ethnohistory,* it was on this day that Kateri Tekakwitha became "the 'first Iroquois virgin.'"

Kateri's life at the mission was not without difficulties. Her half-sister later charged her with having sexual relations with her husband during an annual winter hunting expedition. After the incident, Kateri no longer participated in the hunt. Instead, she is said to have remained at the nearly deserted mission, where she increased her religious activities.

Iroquois Spiritual Beliefs and Catholicism

Observers at the mission recorded that one of the most noticeable features of Kateri's Catholicism was her strict observance of frequent, regimented penances. She consumed very little. What she did eat was often mixed with ashes. Kateri was known to stand barefoot for hours in the snow at the foot of a cross, saying the rosary. She once spent three continuous nights on a bed of thorns, secured an agreement to have a companion regularly flagellate her, and spent many hours upon her bare knees in an unheated chapel during severe winter weather. Onlookers were amazed at the severity of her practices, and mission priests attributed such extreme behavior to virtue, Godly reverence, and holy dedication.

However, Kateri's dedication also had significant roots in Iroquois spirituality, which placed great value on dreams and dreaming. Dreams were considered by the Iroquois to be the language of the soul. Dreaming was extremely important to insure a healthy, functioning society. Dreams were ritualized, interpreted, and fulfilled by all members of the community. It was believed that to deprive the soul of dreaming would result in sickness. If people did not or could not dream, Iroquois culture provided ritual means for encouraging a trance state. Taking a sweat-bath, fasting, singing, chanting, performing self mutilations, and various types of sensory deprivation were all employed to bring the individual back in touch with the soul. Food was sometimes mixed with ashes. After the introduction of alcohol by the Europeans, it was sometimes used as well.

Kateri's devotion to these practices probably cut her life short. At age 24, in frail health, she died during Holy Week. The Last Sacraments were administered to her at her bedside, rather than in the chapel. Kateri is said to have promised intercession to those present at her death. It is also said that shortly after her death, her badly scarred face became radiant with beauty and all scarring completely disappeared. In *The Impact of Katherine Tekakwitha on American Spiritual Life,* Steurer reports that the priests believed the timing of her death on Wednesday of Holy Week to be fitting, "for they all recalled that Katherine had particular devotion to Christ in the Eucharist and on the Cross." Since her death, there have been miraculous cures attributed to her. As a result of these, as well as the view of her life as being one of extreme devotion and piety, the Jesuits submitted a petition in 1884 for her canonization. In 1932 her name was formally presented to the Vatican, and in 1943 she was venerated. In 1980, Kateri was beatified (declared blessed).

Fifty biographies have been written about Kateri Tekakwitha, as well as numerous pamphlets and tracts. More than 100 articles have been dedicated to her life and influences. Kateri's life stories mostly draw on the accounts of two of the priests at Kanawake: Fathers Cholenec and Chauchetiere. Only one year after her death, Chauchetiere drew a portrait of her inspired by a visitation he received and compiled a short biography at that time. Cholenec drew

upon this material as a resource from 1696 (16 years after her death) to 1717, when he produced several biographies addressing her life and devoted followers. Chauchetiere also later wrote a longer biography.

At least one modern scholar has cast doubts on Kateri's actual existence. In his *Ethnohistory* article review of the literature and biographical materials dedicated to Kateri, Koppedrayer points out that upon close examination, "this point becomes obvious: the Jesuits created Kateri Tekakwitha. It was they who wrote and rewrote her biographies; they are the ones who compiled her life story, modelling it on the well-known hagiography collection, *Lives of the Saints.* Take away this creation and there is no independent oral tradition on Kateri; it is all response and comment." Koppedrayer contends that the Jesuits not only created Kateri Tekakwitha, but also fashioned her to be an instrument of Christian mission.

Many other people accept her existence and her holiness on faith. Two American quarterly magazines are devoted to Kateri, keeping a record of the favors granted via her intercession. One of these, *Kateri,* is published by the Kateri Tekakwitha Guild, and the other, *The Lily of the Mohawks,* is published by the Tekakwitha League. More than 10,000 Americans are associated with these organizations to foster support for her canonization. Radio broadcasts and television and film dramatizations, two operas, and several plays draw on her story. In addition, more than 84 organizations, including camps, clubs, and missions, have been named after her, dedicated to her, or named in her honor. An international Kateri Tekakwitha Movement is dedicated to constructing a unique form of Native American Catholicism built on her influences.

SOURCES:

Books

Biographical Dictionary of Indians of the Americas, second edition, Newport Beach, California, American Indian Publishers, 1991; 256-257.

Native North American Almanac, edited by Duane Champagne, Detroit, Gale Research, 1994; 353.

Peterson, Jacqueline and Mary Druke, "American Indian Women and Religion," in *Women and Religion in America,* San Franciso, Harper & Row, 1981; 1-11.

Periodicals

"American Indian Group Finds New Catholic Path," *New York Times,* August 9, 1992; 18.

Blanchard, David, "... To the Other Side of the Sky: Catholicism at Kahnawake, 1667-1700," *Anthropologica,* Volume 24, 1982; 77-102.

Koppedrayer, K. I., "The Making of the First Iroquois Virgin: Early Jesuit Biographies of the Blessed Kateri Tekakwitha," *Ethnohistory,* 40, spring 1993; 277-306.

Mathes, Valerie Sherer, "American Indian Women and the Catholic Church," *North Dakota History,* Volume 47, 1980; 20-25.

Other

Steurer, Justin C., "The Impact of Katherine Tekakwitha on American Spiritual Life" (dissertation), Catholic University of America Press, 1957.

—Sketch by Brett A. Lealand

Grace F. Thorpe

Grace F. Thorpe
1921-
Sauk and Fox activist and craftsperson

Grace F. Thorpe is an important figure in Indian activism. A former lobbyist for the National Congress of American Indians (NCAI), she is also the daughter of the Sauk and Fox Olympic athlete, Jim Thorpe, and has devoted much time and effort to the reinstatement of her famous father's Olympic medals and to the establishment of a museum in his honor.

After World War II, Thorpe learned that there were other battles to be fought. When the American Indian Movement (AIM) occupied Alcatraz Island in November of 1969, she was there. During the occupation, she arranged visits by such celebrities as Jane Fonda and Candice Bergen. Famous people were necessary to bring attention to the plight of Indian people, but Thorpe knew that wars were not fought in the headlines. She attended to practical matters as well, like getting an emergency generator delivered to the island. After the occupation, she headed to Washington to lobby for the National Congress of American Indians. Along the way, she earned a paralegal degree and studied urban issues as a fellow at the Massachusetts Institute of Technology.

A Tireless Worker

Thorpe retired to Yale, Oklahoma, and enjoys painting wildflowers, making pottery, and visiting family and friends. Part of her time has been spent working for the reinstatement of her father's decathlon and pentathlon medals. With the help of her sister, she has been working to establish the Jim Thorpe Museum in Yale. She serves as a part-time Sauk and Fox tribal court judge and is a member of the tribal health council.

Thorpe's retirement ended in January of 1992 when she read about her tribe applying for a nuclear waste Monitored Retrievable Storage (MRS) grant from the Office of the Nuclear Waste Negotiator. Director David Leroy had sent out two-pound packages of information to all 50 states and American Indian tribes offering a $100,000 grant to any entity willing to look into the possibility of temporarily storing spent nuclear rods. The money was supposedly offered with no strings attached but Thorpe was aware of the inherent fallacy in that. Armed with only the meager resources from her social security check, Thorpe went to war again—this time against her own tribal government. Initially, she knew little about radioactivity, but after researching it at the library, she knew that it was considered the most lethal poison in man's history and that her tribe should not be associated with it. After researching the health hazards of nuclear waste, she talked with tribal members at the Black Hawk health clinic, at meetings of elders, at the senior citizens' center, and at the bingo hall. This resulted in a tribal membership meeting to vote on the issue; and, of the 75 members present, 70 voted to return the MRS grant—the five who voted in favor of the grant were tribal council members, who were voted out of office.

Her former employer, the National Congress of American Indians, has also felt the strength of Thorpe's will. NCAI has accepted nearly $350,000 from the Department of Energy (DOE) to hold nuclear energy forums to push nuclear waste storage among Indian tribes. Thorpe believes that the Department of Energy has completely seduced national Indian organizations with money and with assurances of safety. Partly because of her tireless efforts, the MRS program has fallen out of favor in Congress and funding has stopped to push nuclear waste in Indian country. However, the war is not over. Now the Mescalero Apache has a joint agreement with private energy companies to store their spent nuclear fuel rods on Apache land. As long as Indian people are in danger from the nuclear industry, Thorpe will continue to spread the word of the hazards of nuclear waste.

SOURCES:

Thorpe, Grace F., "The Jim Thorpe Family," *Chronicles of Oklahoma,* 59:2, summer 1981; 91, 179.

—*Sketch by Scott Morrison*

Jim Thorpe
1887-1953
Sauk and Fox athlete and Olympic champion
Also known as Wa-tho-huck ["Bright Path"]

James Francis Thorpe was already famous as a three-time all-American football player when he went to the Summer Olympics in Stockholm in 1912. There, he won both the pentathlon and the decathlon and achieved international fame. Six months after his return to the United States, however, officials learned that he had played semi-professional baseball in 1909 and 1910. Since the Olympics then allowed only amateur athletes to participate, he was stripped of his medals and his name and performances were removed from the record books. He then played professional baseball in the minor and major leagues, as well as professional football, where he was a player and a player/coach until 1930. He held a series of jobs (none long-term or certain) until his death in 1953. Thorpe was adept in every sport he attempted: swimming, boxing, wrestling, lacrosse, golf, tennis, and others. Even in 1912, with 17 years left in his professional career, he was recognized as "the world's greatest all-around athlete," according to the New York Times. An Associated Press poll in 1950, more than 20 years after he had quit professional sports, selected him as the greatest male athlete of the first half of the twentieth century, as well as the greatest American football player for the same period. In 1982, the International Olympic Committee restored Thorpe's amateur status, his medals, and his place in Olympic history.

Thorpe was born near Prague, Oklahoma, on May 22, 1887, the son of Hiram Thorpe, a farmer, and Charlotte Vieux, a Potawatomi Indian fluent in Potawatomi, French, and English. Thorpe's mother was Catholic and brought her children up to be Catholics. Thorpe was a twin, but his twin brother, Charlie, died at age nine. There had been one child born in the family before the twins, and three more siblings were born afterward. The Thorpe children had the typical upbringing of the time: a smattering of school and much time spent out of doors, hunting, fishing, and playing. Thorpe attended the Sauk and Fox Mission School at age 6, and then went to Haskell Institute at Lawrence, Kansas, for three years, ending his term there in the summer of 1901.

Thorpe's mother was a descendant of the last great Sauk and Fox chief, Black Hawk, renowned not only as a

Jim Thorpe

warrior but as an outstanding athlete as well, strong and fast afoot. In *Jim Thorpe and the Oorang Indians,* Robert L. Whitman states: "Many believe that much of Thorpe's athletic prowess traces back to Black Hawk, particularly his mother who was convinced that in Thorpe was the living reincarnation of the great chief." Thorpe was very proud of his Sauk and Fox heritage and, in later life, always had a likeness of Black Hawk in his home. Thorpe also had Potawatomi, Kickapoo, and perhaps Menominee blood, although it was as a Sauk and Fox that his parents registered him and that he participated in the land allotment of 1891.

Begins Football Career at Carlisle

Beginning in 1904, Thorpe attended Carlisle Industrial Indian School in Pennsylvania, the first off-reservation school for American Indians to be established in the United States. The school provided practical training in more than 20 trades, in addition to farming and horticulture. Emphasis was placed on practical experience and pupils were urged to take an "outing," a period of time spent working on nearby farms, or in homes or industries. By 1912, Thorpe's last full year at Carlisle, the students represented 87 different tribes, speaking 75 different languages. This diversity was not appreciated, however, since uniforms were required to be worn, and it was prohibited to speak one's native language.

Thorpe played football and began to run track at Carlisle. He was selected as a third-team All-American in 1908, and first team in 1911 and 1912, as a halfback. (He was on leave from Carlisle during the school years of 1909 and 1910.) His coach at Carlisle was the legendary Glenn S. "Pop" Warner, whose teams, according to the *Dictionary of American Biography,* "regularly began to defeat the eastern powers of the day—Harvard, Dartmouth, and the University of Pennsylvania—and in 1907 overcame Amos Alonzo Stagg's mighty University of Chicago eleven." The Carlisle Indians played almost all their games away from home, lacking a stadium of their own.

It was generally acknowledged that the team would have been severely limited without Thorpe. Highlights of his 1911 season included the Harvard game, when he scored all of Carlisle's 18 points (including field goals of 23, 43, 37, and 43 yards) to defeat the home team by three points. He also scored 17 points in 17 minutes against Dickinson and punted better than 70 yards against Lafayette. In 1912, he scored 22 of Carlisle's 27 points against Army, including returning two Army kickoffs for touchdowns on consecutive plays, the first having been called back due to a Carlisle penalty. One of the hapless Army defenders was a cadet named Dwight D. Eisenhower. The same superlatives applied to the Pittsburgh game; he scored 28 of 34 points and again punted more than 70 yards. At the end of the season, he had scored a record 198 points.

Dominates 1912 Stockholm Olympics

Thorpe was 24 at the time he sailed with the American Olympic team aboard the *S.S. Finland* from New York on June 14, 1912, headed for Stockholm with a two-day stop in Antwerp, Belgium. This Olympic team had been groomed to represent the best of American athletics. Starting in 1906, with the encouragement of President Theodore Roosevelt, the American Olympic Committee had solicited private funds for the training and development of a world-class Olympic team. The 1912 team was the finest to date and would be for many years to come. Tryouts were truly national, having been conducted at Stanford University (Palo Alto, California), at Chicago's Marshall Field, and at Harvard University in Cambridge, Massachusetts.

Thorpe trained aboard ship and was ready to compete when the group reached Sweden. Twenty-eight nations had sent teams. Thorpe's events were the pentathlon and the decathlon. The pentathlon, held on July 7, consisted of five track and field events. Thorpe won the long jump with a distance of 23 feet, 2.7 inches; as well as the discus throw with 116 feet, 8.4 inches; and placed third in the javelin throw at 153 feet, 2.95 inches. He also won the 200-meter dash with a time of 22.9 seconds, as well as the 1,500-meter race in 4 minutes, 44.8 seconds.

Five days later, on July 13, the decathlon, consisting of ten track and field events, was held. Thorpe won the shot put with a distance of 42 feet, 5.45 inches; the high jump with a height of 6 feet, 1.6 inches; the 110-meter hurdles with a time of 15.6 seconds; and the 1,500-meter run with a time of 4 minutes, 40.1 seconds. He placed second in the running broad jump with 22 feet, 2.3 inches; and in the discus throw with 21 feet, 3.9 inches. He placed third in the 100-meter dash in a time of 11.2 seconds; in the pole vault

with 10 feet, 7.95 inches; and in the javelin throw with 149 feet, 11.2 inches. His worst finish was fourth place in the 400-meter run, with a time of 47.6 seconds. His total for the decathlon was 8,412 points out of a possible 10,000—almost 700 points ahead of the Swedish second-place finisher. Thorpe's performance in the decathlon was not eclipsed for 36 years, and his truly amazing records in both the pentathlon and decathlon may never be repeated; the classic pentathlon was discontinued after the 1924 Paris Olympics.

To a thunderous ovation, King Gustav V presented Thorpe with the medal for winning the pentathlon and, later in the same ceremony, presented him with the prize for the decathlon. As Bob Berontas recalled in *Jim Thorpe, Sac and Fox Athlete:* "Before Thorpe could walk away, the king grabbed his hand and uttered the sentence that was to follow Thorpe for the rest of his life. 'Sir,' he declared, 'you are the greatest athlete in the world.' Thorpe, never a man to stand on ceremony, answered simply and honestly, 'Thanks, King.'"

Unfortunately, Thorpe's glory lasted only about six months, enough time to tour parts of the United States as a national hero. In late November 1912, he told the New York Times that he wanted to leave Carlisle after the Brown game on Thanksgiving Day, citing an "absolute dislike of notoriety and utter abhorrence of the public gaze, which his athletic prowess has brought him." Soon, however, the public gaze was to become intense. On January 22, 1913, a reporter for the *Worcester (Massachusetts) Telegram* interviewed Thorpe's former baseball coach, Charles Clancey, and broke the story that Thorpe had played minor league baseball for money in the summers of 1909 and 1910, between his years at Carlisle. The first summer, he played 44 games with the Rocky Mount, North Carolina, team in the Class D Carolina Association. He batted .253 and went 9-10 as a pitcher, playing for "meal money" of $15 a week. The next year he split his time between Rocky Mount and Fayetteville, also in North Carolina.

Thorpe acknowledged the two semi-professional seasons in a letter to James E. Sullivan of the Amateur Athletic Union, published in the *New York Times,* but he stated that he did not play for the money, but rather "because I liked to play ball. I was not very wise in the ways of the world." Later in the letter he said, "I hope I will be partly excused by the fact that I was simply an Indian schoolboy and did not know all about such things." Despite the fact that Thorpe was unaware that this baseball experience might compromise his amateur status in track and field, the International Olympic Committee stripped Thorpe of his medals and removed his name from the record books—thus tarnishing his image as a national hero.

Makes Impact in Professional Sports

Soon thereafter, Thorpe left Carlisle and signed up to play baseball with the New York Giants, his choice among the six teams courting him. With his limited playing experience, he spent much time under option to Milwaukee in the minor leagues. Thorpe played outfield with the Giants for the next three seasons, 1913 through 1915. His batting averages were low, as were the numbers of games in which he appeared each season. He did not play in the majors in 1916, but rather was sent again to Milwaukee, with predictions that he would never again play in the majors. However, he proved these predictions wrong when he opened the 1917 season on loan to the Cincinnati Reds, playing 77 games before returning to the Giants for 26 games. This combined total of 103 games was the peak season for Thorpe in terms of both games played and attainment, since his team reached the 1917 World Series and he played in one game, though the Giants lost the series to Chicago, four games to two.

Thorpe stayed with the Giants through the 1918 season and two games of the 1919 season, and then went to the Boston Braves to complete his final and best year in major league baseball, posting a .327 batting average. He was used at both first base and in the outfield while in Boston. It was said that his weakness was, "He couldn't hit the curve ball." However, there is evidence that his easygoing demeanor did not sit well with his fiery Giants manager, John J. McGraw. Thorpe last played professional baseball in 1928 for Akron in the minor leagues; he was 40 years old.

During his major league baseball years, Thorpe was also playing professional football. From 1915 to 1920, he was with the Canton (Ohio) Bulldogs, and in 1921, he played with the Cleveland Indians pro football team. The next two years he organized, coached, and played with the Oorang Indians, a promotional vehicle of Walter Lingo, owner of the Oorang Airedale kennels. This pro football team was composed entirely of American Indians. They played their two 1922 home games in Marion, Ohio, at Lincoln Park. From 1924 through 1929, Thorpe played with six different teams, including a return to the Canton Bulldogs. He finished his pro football career with the Chicago Cardinals in 1929. In 1919, Thorpe was instrumental in forming the American Professional Football Association, and he served as its first president. That group later became the National Football League. Besides being an outstanding halfback, Thorpe was a leader off the field and helped to increase football's popularity.

Retires from Professional Sports

After Thorpe's retirement from football, a series of jobs and situations came his way. He travelled to California in 1930 to be master of ceremonies for the cross-country marathon staged by C. C. Pyle, known as "the bunion derby". (The event was won by the Cherokee Andy Payne.) He settled in the California town of Hawthorne and worked as an extra in motion pictures, but was never very successful. He served as superintendent of recreation in the Chicago Park System and, in the late 1930s, lived in Oklahoma and became active in Indian affairs. This led to a national tour as a popular lecturer in the early 1940s on the subjects of sports and Indian affairs. In November 1951, he had an operation for lip cancer. He returned to the public eye as various groups throughout the United States, realizing that Thorpe was impoverished and remembering his Olympic perfor-

mance, raised funds for his medical care and welfare. At the time, he was leading an all-Indian song and dance troupe, "The Jim Thorpe Show."

In 1945, at age 58, Thorpe joined the Merchant Marine, since he was past the age where the other services would accept him. His ship, the *U.S.S. Southwest Victory,* sailed to India loaded with ammunition for the American and British war effort. When his identity became known, he made a series of personal appearances and hospital visits to bolster troop morale. In 1949, his life story was made into the film *Jim Thorpe—All American,* with Burt Lancaster in the title role. Thorpe served as an adviser on the film, having sold his rights to the story some years earlier.

In 1950, two unprecedented honors came Thorpe's way. First, the Associated Press asked sportswriters and broadcasters to review the athletes of the first half of the twentieth century in a variety of categories. In late January, Thorpe was named "the greatest American football player" and the "greatest overall male athlete" in the first half of the century. Interestingly enough, Jesse Owens, the hero of the 1936 Berlin Olympics, was named first among track athletes with 201 votes to Thorpe's 74.

Jim Thorpe died in his trailer home in Lomita, California, a suburb of Los Angeles, on March 28, 1953, at age 64. He was stricken with a heart attack (his third) while eating dinner with his wife. Initial efforts to revive him were successful, but after a short period of consciousness, he died. His death was front page news in the *New York Times,* which stated that he "was a magnificent performer. He had all the strength, speed and coordination of the finest players, plus an incredible stamina. The tragedy of the loss of his Stockholm medals because of thoughtless and unimportant professionalism darkened much of his career and should have been rectified long ago. His memory should be kept for what it deserves—that of the greatest all-round athlete of our time."

The call to restore his Olympic medals was first sounded in 1943, when the Oklahoma Legislature adopted a resolution that the Amateur Athletic Union be petitioned to reinstate the records, but no action was taken. In 1952, a group in Congress made another unsuccessful attempt to have the medals restored. It was not until 1973 that the AAU restored his amateur status, and it was nine years later (1982) by the time the International Olympic Committee followed suit. The IOC not only restored his amateur status but, more importantly to his family, put the name of Jim Thorpe back in the 1912 records.

Thorpe had married three times and had eight children. In 1913, he married Iva Miller. Their first son, James Jr., died at age three from an influenza epidemic during World War I, but their three daughters, Gail, Charlotte, and Grace, lived into the 1990s. In 1926, he married Freeda Kirkpatrick, and they had four sons, Carl Phillip (deceased), William, Richard, and John (Jack). Jack Thorpe, the youngest, became principal chief of the Sauk and Fox in the 1980s. At the time of his death, Thorpe had been married to Patricia Askew for almost eight years.

Thorpe's body lay in state in Los Angeles wearing a beaded, buckskin jacket and moccasins—garments he wore in lecture appearances in his last years. Both Oklahoma and Pennsylvania asked for the right to bury Thorpe. The family held a Roman Catholic funeral service in Shawnee, Oklahoma, as well as secret rites with Thorpe's Thunderbird clan at the farm of Mrs. Ed Mack, the last descendant of Chief Black Hawk. After the funding for several memorial proposals fell through, Thorpe was buried in February 1954 in Mauch Chunk, Pennsylvania. The townspeople voted to change the town's name to "Jim Thorpe, Pennsylvania" and erect a suitable monument to him in exchange for Thorpe's burial there.

After Thorpe's death in 1953, the National Football League renamed its "Most Valuable Player" award the "Jim Thorpe Trophy." In 1961, Thorpe was named to the Pennsylvania Hall of Fame, reflecting his many successes at Carlisle. In 1963, he was placed in the Professional Football Hall of Fame and in 1975 in the National Track and Field Hall of Fame. (He had joined the National College Football Hall of Fame in 1951.) In 1977, Sport magazine conducted a national poll and announced Jim Thorpe as the "Greatest American Football Player in History."

In 1973, the Yale, Oklahoma, house in which Thorpe's family lived from 1917 to 1923 was opened as an historic site by the Oklahoma Historical Society. In addition, a portrait of Jim Thorpe (by noted Oklahoma artist Charles Banks Wilson) was unveiled in the Oklahoma State Capitol in 1966. It hangs alongside three other noted Oklahomans: U.S. Senator Robert S. Kerr, and the Cherokees Sequoyah and Will Rogers. In December 1975, the portion of Oklahoma Highway 51 running from State Highway 18 east of Yale to Tulsa was renamed "The Jim Thorpe Memorial Highway." Finally, in May 1984, a postage stamp bearing the likeness of Thorpe was issued by the U.S. government.

SOURCES:

Books

The Baseball Encyclopedia, seventh edition, edited by Joseph L. Reichler, New York, Macmillan 1988.

Berontas, Bob, *Jim Thorpe: Sac and Fox Athlete,* New York, Chelsea House Publishers, 1992.

Biographical Dictionary of Indians of the Americas, second edition, Newport Beach, California, American Indian Publishers, 1991.

Dictionary of American Biography, edited by John A. Garraty, New York, Charles Scribner's Sons, 1990.

Dockstader, Frederick J., *Great North American Indians,* New York, Van Nostrand Reinhold, 1977.

Encyclopedia of American Biography, edited by John A. Garraty, New York, Harper & Row, 1974.

Newcombe, Jack, *The Best of the Athletic Boys; The White Man's Impact on Jim Thorpe,* Garden City, New York, Doubleday, 1975.

Strickland, Rennard, *The Indians in Oklahoma,* Norman, University of Oklahoma Press, 1981.

Wheeler, Robert W., *Pathway to Glory,* New York, Carlton Press, 1975.

Whitman, Robert L., *Jim Thorpe and the Oorang Indians: The NFL's Most Colorful Franchise,* Defiance, Ohio, Hubbard, 1984.

Wright, Muriel H., *A Guide to the Indian Tribes of Oklahoma,* Norman, University of Oklahoma Press, 1951.

Periodicals

American Way, January, 1, 1992; 50.

"Athlete Thorpe to Quit Indian School: World's Champion Does Not Like to Remain in Spotlight of Fame," *New York Times,* November 26, 1912; 13.

"Jim Thorpe: An Athlete's Legacy," *Stillwater NewsPress,* May 3, 1989; special section.

"Jim Thorpe Is Dead on West Coast at 64," *New York Times,* March 29, 1953; 1.

"Jim Thorpe Named Greatest In Sport: Indian of Many Talents Voted Best Male Athlete of Past Fifty Years—Ruth Is Next," *New York Times,* February 12, 1950; 6.

"Johnson Broke Thorpe Story," *Stillwater NewsPress,* February 21, 1989; 3C.

"The Passing of Jim Thorpe," *New York Times,* March 30, 1953; 2.

"Thorpe Admits Playing Professional Ball," *New York Times,* January 27, 1913.

Thorpe, Grace F., "The Jim Thorpe Family," *Chronicles of Oklahoma,* 59:2, summer 1981; 91, 179.

"Thorpe Hailed as Greatest Player on Gridiron in Past Fifty Years," *New York Times,* January 25, 1950; 31.

Other

"The Carlisle Indian School Athletic Association" (program), Carlisle, Pennsylvania, 1912.

Prough, Meredith (director of the Jim Thorpe Home), interview with Philip H. Viles, Jr., conducted April 23, 1994.

—Sketch by Philip H. Viles, Jr.

Clifford Earl Trafzer
1949-
Wyandot historian, educator, and author

Clifford E. Trafzer is a high-profile educator, author, scholar, editor, publisher, and historian. He also encourages new writers in the publishing arena and has worked extensively with a variety of genres of the multi-faceted Native history and experience. His works emerge vividly in Native American history, an area in which he has enormous interest.

Clifford Earl Trafzer

Early Years and Education

Trafzer was born March 1, 1949, in Mansfield, Ohio. His Wyandot grandfather was Earl Henry, and his German grandfather was Clifford Nelson Trafzer. When Trafzer was ten years old, his grandfather drove him to the campus of the University of Arizona, stopping in front of Old Main (one of the oldest buildings on campus). After a brief silence, his Wyandot grandfather told him that he wanted him to attend college and become a lawyer. The following year his grandfather died; and although Trafzer did not attend the University of Arizona Law School, he remembers being determined to get a college education. He eventually attended Northern Arizona University, earning a B.A. in 1970 and a M.A. in 1971, both in history. Two years later in 1973, he earned a Ph.D. in history from Oklahoma State University.

In 1981, Trafzer married Lee Ann Smith and they have three daughters, Tess Nashone, Hayley Kachine, and Tara Tsaile. Trafzer's writings are laced with thoughts concerning his daughters and he often speaks of his manner in guiding them through life along a path that will lead to success and happiness. In an interview collected in *Voices from the Earth*, Trafzer said, "I recall one night when I was frightened by the darkness. My mother sat me down and we talked about the beauty of the night, the beauty of the sounds we were hearing from the crickets. I remember seeing the lightning bugs down in the field below us. She told me that the earth is not really dark during the night—that we have the stars up above us and it ... is a time when we can reach out beyond earth." And in Wyandot tradition, he passes this expression on to his daughters. "I take the girls out in the night and tell them that they were once stars and that the stars are so beautiful that I wanted particular stars to come down and live with me. Those stars became my children. So they believe they are star people and I certainly believe they are star people."

Much of Trafzer's expression has its origin in a dream, a narrative, or a legend that has come to him in a quiet moment. And it is through the influence of his mother, Mary Lou Henry Trafzer, more than his father Donald, that Trafzer realized the importance of history—a history tying the Native spirit to the earth and to the universe. Trafzer indicates that as a young boy, his mother "instilled in me a sense of history, a sense of being—being part Wyandot and part of the earth. The way to transfer this is to give it to our children at a very young level." He does this by spending time with them, telling them stories and reading to them.

Trafzer is currently professor and chair of ethnic studies and history as well as director of Native American studies at the University of California, Riverside. He has also taught at San Diego State University, Washington State University, and Navajo Community College. During the middle 1970s, he served as museum curator for the Arizona Historical Society. Trafzer's award-winning work has achieved wide recognition. He has collected original narratives of the Palouse people, has studied religion, prophecies and prophets, has written about the military campaigns against the original Native people of the northern hemisphere, and constantly encourages his students to become writers.

SELECTED WRITINGS BY TRAFZER:

Yuma: Frontier Crossing of the Far Southwest, Wichita, Western Heritage Press, 1980.

The Kit Carson Campaign: The Last Navajo War, Norman, University of Oklahoma Press, 1982.

Editor, *American Indian Identity: Today's Changing Perspectives,* San Diego State University Press, Publications in American Indian Studies, 1985; reprinted, Sacramento, Sierro Oaks Publishing, 1989.

Editor, *American Indian Prophets: Religious Leaders and Revitalization Movements,* Sacramento, Sierra Oaks Publishing, 1986.

Editor, Indians, *Superintendents and Councils: Northwestern Indian Policy, 1850-1855,* Lanham, Maryland, University Press of America, 1986.

Editor, *Northwestern Tribes in Exile: Modoc, Nez Percé, and Palouse Removal to the Indian Territory,* Sacramento, Sierra Oaks Publishing, 1986.

With Richard D. Scheuerman, *The Renegade Tribe: The Palouse Indians and the Invasion of the Inland Pacific Northwest,* Pullman, Washington State University Press, 1986.

Grandmother's Christmas Story: A True Quechan Story (for children), Sacramento, Sierra Oaks Publishing, 1987.

Grandfather's Origin Story: The Navajo Beginning (for children), Sacramento, Sierra Oaks Publishing, 1988.

A Trip to a Pow Wow (for children), Sacramento, Sierra Oaks Publishing, 1988.

A, B, C's the American Indian Way (for children), Sacramento, Sierra Oaks Publishing, 1988.

Grandfather's Story of Navajo Monsters (for children), Sacramento, Sierra Oaks Publishing, 1988.

Creation of a California Tribe (for children), Sacramento, Sierra Oaks Publishing, 1988.

California's Indians and the Gold Rush (for children), Sacramento, Sierra Oaks Publishing, 1989.

The Chinook, New York, Chelsea House, 1990.

Editor, *Looking Glass,* San Diego, Publications in American Indian Studies, San Diego State University Press, 1991.

Editor, with Richard D. Scheuerman, *Mourning Dove's Stories,* San Diego, Publications in American Indian Studies, San Diego State University Press, 1991.

American Indians as Cowboys (for children), Sacramento, Sierra Oaks Publishing, 1992.

The Nez Percé, New York, Chelsea House, 1992.

Yakima, Palouse, Cayuse, Umatilla, Walla Walla, and Wanapum Indians: An Historical Bibliography, Metuchen, New Jersey, Scarecrow Press, 1992.

With Richard D. Scheuerman, *Chief Joseph's Allies,* Newcastle, California, Sierra Oaks Publishers, 1992.

Editor, *Earth Song, Sky Spirit: Short Stories of the Contemporary Native American Experience,* New York, Doubleday/Anchor, 1993.

SOURCES:

Books

Native North American Almanac, edited by Duane Champagne, Detroit, Gale Research, 1994.

Voices from the Earth (anthology of Native American interviews), Austin, University Press of Texas, forthcoming.

Other

Untranscribed interviews between Darryl Wilson and Clifford E. Trafzer and family members, 1994.

—*Sketch by Darryl Wilson*

John Trudell
1947-
Santee Sioux activist, actor, and musician

The name of John Trudell is often thought of as synonymous with Indian rights and activism, whether through his work with the American Indian Movement (AIM), his acting roles, or his music. An early organizer of political action, he has worked both in the forefront and behind the

John Trudell

scenes in trying to secure a guarantee of basic freedoms for indigenous Americans.

The son of Thurman Clifford Trudell, a Dakota (Santee) Sioux, and an unidentified mother, Trudell is a native of Niobrara, Nebraska. Little is known of his early years until he began actively organizing Natives for political action in California in the 1960s. A resident of Los Angeles in 1969, he and first wife, Lou, along with their children, Maurie and Tara, went to the San Francisco Bay area to join the group occupying Alcatraz Prison. They landed on the island on November 30, just over a week after the organization, Indians of All Tribes, Inc. (IAT) had "seized" it in accord with the Fort Laramie Treaty of 1868. That treaty included the provision that unused federal land could be taken by Native people; IAT took the island in order to set up an educational facility.

Wovoka Trudell, Lou and John's son was born on Alcatraz, as was John's future as a spokesperson. He hosted a daily radio program called *Radio Free Alcatraz,* in which he called for the founding of the Native Studies center, archives and a religious retreat, and interviewed some notable Natives, including activist Grace Thorpe (daughter of athlete Jim Thorpe). The Trudells stayed on Alcatraz until the end of the occupation in June of 1971.

By the time they returned to the mainland, Trudell was a member of the American Indian Movement, and went on to become its national spokesperson. He took part in the 1972 Trail of Broken Treaties, a mass movement of Natives across the country, which converged on the Bureau of Indian

Affairs (BIA) headquarters in Washington, D.C. The event was intended to focus public awareness on Native rights and abuses of them, but the eventual occupation of the BIA and subsequent property damage cast a negative light on their effort in the eyes of the general public.

Trudell's effectiveness as a speaker throughout the turbulent event gained him the scrutiny of the FBI. When he was elected co-chair of AIM the next year, that scrutiny intensified. When AIM and their supporters took over the small settlement of Wounded Knee, South Dakota on the Pine Ridge Reservation in 1973, John Trudell was there. When two FBI agents and one Indian were killed in a shoot-out at the Jumping Bull Compound at Pine Ridge in 1975, catapulting AIM members "Dino" Butler, Rob Robideaux, and Leonard Peltier into national headlines, Trudell parried with the press about the possible illegalities involved in the government's presence on the reservation.

An articulate master of irony, Trudell continued to make enemies with his public statements concerning Peltier, AIM, Native rights, and federal policy. A 1975 incident in Owhyee, Nevada, in which Trudell fired a pistol into the ceiling of a trading post to protest alleged overpricing of goods by the non-Indian owner, did not discredit him as many of those enemies had hoped; however, Trudell ultimately served short sentences on several occasions. In one facility, he reports that he was told by another inmate that unless he stopped his activist efforts, his family might be harmed. At the time, such threat seemed to be part of political organizing and Trudell let the matter drop.

Years of absences from home for various causes contributed to the incompatibility that brought the marriage of Lou and John Trudell to a "friendly" end. John remarried, this time to a Duck Valley Shoshone-Paiute activist, Tina Manning. They lived on her people's Nevada reservation, working for AIM and other Indian rights groups. They had three children, Ricarda Star, Sunshine Karma, and Eli Changing Sun. On February 11, 1979, Trudell was away from home speaking in Washington, D.C., on abuse of Native rights by the federal government. To bring more attention to the Peltier case, Trudell burned an upside-down American flag and was arrested. Within twelve hours, the Manning-Trudell house on the Duck Valley Reservation was set afire. Burned to death were Leah Manning, Tina's mother, Ricarda, Sunshine, Eli, and a pregnant Tina Manning-Trudell. Later investigation proved the cause was arson; John Trudell has repeatedly asserted that he suspects government complicity in the fire and the consequent arson-murders.

In the 1980s, Trudell began to shift his focus from AIM. He continued to speak on Indian rights, lobby for Leonard Peltier, and recount his personal loss as an object lesson. He was also testing the waters to branch out into other fields. He played a cameo role in Hand-Made Film's production of Powwow Highway. In 1992, he appeared in the film Thunderheart, playing a character based on Peltier. That same year, he released his first album, AKA Graffiti Man on Rykodisc, an independent label. Johnny Damas and Me, his second effort, was released in 1994, and he has played numerous concerts on behalf of Native rights groups.

SOURCES:

Books

Crow Dog, Mary, and Richard Erdoes, *Lakota Woman,* New York, Grove Weidenfeld, 1990.

Mankiller, Wilma, and Michael Wallis, Mankiller: *A Chief and Her People,* New York, St. Martin's Press, 1993.

Matthiessen, Peter, *In the Spirit of Crazy Horse,* New York, Viking, 1983.

Native Americans in the Twentieth Century, edited by James Olson and Raymond Wilson, Urbana, University of Illinois Press, 1984.

Native North American Almanac, edited by Duane Champagne, Detroit, Gale Research, 1994.

Weyler, Rex, *Blood of the Land: The Government and Corporate War Against the American Indian Movement,* New York, Everest House, 1982.

—Sketch by Cynthia R. Kasee

Pablita Velarde

1918-

Santa Clara Pueblo artist

Also known as Tse Tsan ["Golden Dawn"]

Pablita Velarde has won a place as one of the greatest Native American artists of the century by chronicling the lives of her Pueblo people and reviving traditional forms of making art. She has won many awards and has shown her work in major exhibitions and solo shows.

Velarde was born September 19, 1918, as the third daughter of a Tewa family Herman and Marianita Velarde of Santa Clara, New Mexico. Her mother died three years later of tuberculosis. Her Pueblo name Tse Tsan means "Golden Dawn." An eye disease caused Velarde blindness as a child. Once healed and her sight returned, Velarde became voracious for visual experience, and as she told one biographer "I wanted to see everything." Once she regained her sight, the smallest details became as important as large vistas, and noticing and studying these details fueled her desire to become an artist.

Starting in 1924, Velarde and her two older sisters attended St. Catherine's Indian School in Santa Fe. But she did not forget or forsake her people. In the summers, back in Santa Clara, she stayed with her grandmother, Qualupita, a medicine woman. Velarde learned a great deal from her grandmother including the traditional customs and arts of her Pueblo people. Her father—a respected storyteller—taught her the traditional myths and legends of her people. All these influences gelled later in her art. In 1942, Velarde married Herbert Hardin, a non-Indian, white man. Though their marriage did not survive the conflicts of their divergent ethnic origins and careers, they had two children: Helen Hardin, who later became an artist herself, and Herby. In 1959, Velarde and Hardin divorced.

Studies at Studio School Influence Life's Work

In 1932, at 14 years old, Pablita Velarde began her studies at the Santa Fe Indian School run by the Bureau of Indian Affairs (BIA). Velarde became a student at the Studio, the first school of art for Native Americans, which was a part of the Santa Fe Indian School. The art program was founded, despite the "prevailing educational philosophy ... that Indians were best suited for manual labor jobs," according to Sally Hyer in *One House, One Voice, One Heart:*

Native American Education at the Santa Fe School. Despite these attitudes, the art school gained international recognition and produced many Indian artists who became quite well-known, among them Pablita Velarde. In 1933, at 15 years old, Velarde was selected to work on murals for the Chicago "Century of Progress" World's Fair with artist Olive Rush. In 1934, after the fair, she continued to work with Rush on WPA art projects.

At the Studio, Velarde studied with Dorothy Dunn, who had a profound influence on Velarde and her art. Dunn encouraged Velarde and many other art students under her tutelage to draw upon their roots and their tribal culture, for their art. The Puye Ruins is where Velarde studied the designs of her ancestors in the petroglyphs found there.

According to Christian Feest in *Native Arts of North America,* "Dunn is generally credited with influencing her students to adopt a flat, two-dimensional 'Indian' style and to use pastel colors." For the rest of her life, Velarde would create images of the experiences of Pueblos and of all Native Americans. But despite Dunn's influence, Velarde's art, like many others at the Studio, began to shine with individuality all her own. Throughout her career, she has continued the traditional art of her people. Although she has experimented, she has painted in this style, consistently improving it throughout her career.

Completes Bandelier Murals

Velarde graduated from the Indian School in 1936 and began teaching art at Santa Clara Day School. In 1938, she traveled through the United States with the Setons and then returned to Santa Clara and built a studio. She worked with Olive Rush again in 1938 on a mural in Albuquerque; and in 1939, the Park Service of New Mexico commissioned her for murals in the Bandelier National Monument Visitors' Center which depict the life of her ancestral Pueblos in Frijoles Canyon. The murals portray the daily lives of the Pueblos of the Rio Grande, including seasonal and religious ceremonies, political structures, craftmaking, and other facets of their lives. Native lore and attention to details—such as costumes and personal appearance—are so authentic in the paintings that the murals serve as secondary, ethnographic and archeological sources. Velarde left nothing out of the murals in terms of depicting Pueblo life. The murals show all varieties of basket making, drillwork, beadwork, dyework on buckskin, drum making, sex division of labor, tanning, smithing, uses of indigenous plants, and even a scene of a Kiva ceremony.

Velarde's primary medium was casein and tempera though she worked in oil at times. Her later work uses "earth colors," paints she makes herself from found rocks that she grinds and mixes to create the colors she desires. Critics like Edwin Wade, in his book *Magic Images: Contemporary Native American Art* echo the charge by many that Velarde, like other Indian artists, "became producers for white tastes" with paintings that often display a "bankruptcy of the conflict over traditionalism versus modernism." Nevertheless, Velarde continued to paint in the traditional styles of her Pueblo people, continually improving them. She abandoned two-dimensionality for three-dimensions with shading and perspective in paintings like "Her First Dance." Her abstract paintings blended lush colors, especially in earth paints, with symbolic design and unique compositions. For this work, she has won awards. In 1948, she won top prize at the Philbrook Art Center's Annual Indian Art Show, and in 1954, the French government awarded her the Palmes Academiques.

With the possible exception of the Bandelier murals, the work for which she was most well-known was the book of her father's stories that she illustrated, *Old Father, the Storyteller.* Those who write about and study art, like Clara Tanner, consider these illustrations among Velarde's finest work, especially the title illustration "Old Father, the Storyteller." Velarde's work is on display in many museums across the country. Her work has been featured in many exhibitions and one-woman shows. She has won the Walter Bimson Grand Award, the New Mexico governor's award, the awards at Gallup's Inter-Tribal Indian Ceremonial, the Scottsdale Grand Award, and an Honor Award from the National Women's Caucus for Art.

Velarde's importance was best phrased by Clara Tanner in her book *Southwest Indian Painting: A Changing Art:* "Pablita Velarde has long and rightfully been the leading Indian woman painter of the Southwest. Her place will be strong in the history of art in this area. Posterity's debt to her will be great, for she has sensitively communicated through her painting a wealth of Pueblo lore, from everyday living, through ritual life, into the significant fields of myth and legend."

SOURCES:

Biographical Dictionary of the Indians of the Americas, second edition, Newport Beach, California, American Indian Publishers, 1991.

Feest, Christian F., *Native Arts of North America,* New York, Thames and Hudson, 1992.

Handbook of the North American Indians, edited by William C. Sturtevant, Washington, D.C., Smithsonian Institution, 1983.

Hyer, Sally, *One House, One Voice, One Heart: Native American Education at the Santa Fe School,* Santa Fe, Museum of New Mexico Press, 1990.

Native American Women, edited by Gretchen M. Bataille, New York, Garland Publishing, 1993.

The Native Americans: An Illustrated History, edited by Betty and Ian Ballantine, Atlanta, Turner Publishing, 1993.

Native North American Almanac, edited by Duane Champagne, Detroit, Gale Research, 1994.

Tanner, Clara Lee, *Southwest Indian Painting: A Changing Art,* second edition, Tucson, University of Arizona Press, 1973.

Velarde, Pablita, and Herman Velarde, *Old Father, the Storyteller,* Arizona, Globe Publications, 1960.

Wade, Edwin, L., and Rennard Strickland, Magic Images: *Contemporary Native American Art,* Norman, University of Oklahoma Press, Norman, 1981.

—Sketch by Christopher B. Tower

Victorio
1820(?)-1880
Mimbreno Apache tribal leader
Also known as Victoria, Vitoria, Vittorio, Beduiat, Bidu-ya, Lucero ["Light"], and Laceres

The Mimbreno Apache guerilla leader Victorio is relatively unknown, perhaps because many of his fiercest fights were against Afro-American and Mexican troops. In 1879, however, he demonstrated his military ability by leading small bands of warriors—sometimes not more than 35 to 50—in successful resistance to U.S. and Mexican troops. For 15 months from 1879 to 1880 he and his tiny band held off the forces of two countries. He was finally caught by Mexican soldiers at Tres Castillos in the state of Chihuahua in October of 1880, and killed himself rather than be taken alive by his enemies.

Unlike his contemporary and fellow resistance leader Geronimo, Victorio did not befriend any future authors, and he let few white soldiers or bureaucrats get near him. An exception was one small detachment of Texas Rangers and the famed Civil War raider Benjamin Grierson with his son and a tiny cavalry guard. Victorio's only known photograph was taken after such a struggle. Two men not shown pin his arms, and he stares at the photographer with a wild look in his eyes and disheveled hair—in contrast to Geronimo, who once had his picture taken while sitting serenely in an automobile.

Certainly Victorio was respected by his fellow Apaches. His followers so loved him, legend holds, that they once threatened to kill and eat him so soldiers could never boast they captured him. In Geronimo: His Own Story, Victorio's noted neighbor declared, "No one ever treated our [Chiricahua] tribe more kindly than Victoria and his [Ojo Caliente] band. We are still proud to say that he and his people were our friends." In the opinion of Jason Betzinez, an Ojo Caliente youth who lived to be an old man and wrote a memoir called *I Fought with Geronimo,* Victorio "stood

Victorio

Gila River in southwestern New Mexico in 1837 by Mangas Coloradas. Victorio served under him in the successful war to expel the Santa Rita del Cobre copper miners.

By 1853 Victorio was himself a chief. In that year "Vitoria" (one of the many variant spellings of his name) signed a supplemental treaty between the Apaches and the United States. He does not appear in U.S. records again until after the end of the Civil War (which in Apache history coincided with the first half of the Cochise Wars). Described at that time as a well-known and powerful war chief, he told the Americans: "I and my people want peace. We are tired of war. We have little for ourselves and our families to eat or wear. We want to make a peace, a lasting peace, one that will keep.... I have washed my hands and mouth with cold fresh water, and what I said is true."

Camps of Apache Concentration

Victorio did not, however, interpret his desire for peace with the Pinda Lick-o-yi ["White Eyes"] as affecting the longstanding Apache tradition of raiding. At Warm Springs, Pionsenay and other renegades from Old Mexico attracted reservation youth to a raider's lifestyle. In July, 1873, the uneasy truce between the Apaches and the black garrison troopers and white settlers in New Mexico Territory broke for the first time. Some cattle rustlers from Warm Springs clashed with a ten-man detachment of the Eighth Cavalry. Three Indians were wounded, including Victorio's nephew. Victorio refused to surrender the rustlers to white justice and threatened to fight. In 1877 Victorio led over 300 of his people away from their Warm Springs Reservation, which he had allowed Geronimo and other raiders to use as a base for operations into Old Mexico. After losing about 56 of his people, he negotiated a peaceful return. Finally land speculators, railroad entrepreneurs, newspaper editors and corrupt government contractors pushed through the Apache Concentration policy, intended to stop the raiding by confining the nomadic, faction-ridden Apaches onto Arizona's barren San Carlos Reservation.

In the autumn of 1879, the Indian Bureau ordered the Ojo Caliente Apaches removed from their farms, orchards and homes, to be crowded onto San Carlos among their traditional enemies. When Captain B. F. Bennett told him Warm Springs would be taken and thrown open to white settlement, Victorio answered, "No! This country belongs to my people as it did to my forefathers. A few years ago the Government set aside for us the Warm Springs Reservation. Now the white people want it. If you force me and my people to leave it, there will be trouble. Leave us alone, so that we may remain at peace." He pleaded: "This is our home, our country. We were born here and we love it." Bennett cited orders he must obey. Victorio replied that if the Army wished to take the women and children away in its wagons "I cannot stop you. But I will not go. My men will not go." An indictment for murder and horse-stealing was returned against Victorio. Fearing he would be slapped in irons, as Geronimo had been, or murdered in custody like Mangas Coloradas, Victorio jumped the reservation, never to return.

head and shoulders above the several war chiefs such as Mangas, Cochise, and Geronimo who have bigger names with the white people. At the time of this [1879] outbreak both Victorio and Nanay were well along in years, Nanay being quite an old man. But together they caused more fear among the settlers and killed more people in a shorter time than any other Apaches."

Although not as well known as some of his associates, Victorio's life is fairly well documented. He stood about 5' 9 1/2", slightly taller than the average Apache male. Perhaps because of this, some Mexican authorities suggest that Victorio was half-Mexican. There is nothing necessarily impossible about such a union—Apaches often adopted war orphans and captives to replace family members enslaved in Mexico, and mixed blood disqualified no one from high status or position. In addition, descent was reckoned on the female side. Apache sources, however, declare that Victorio was a full-blooded Apache. Betzinez believed Mexicans corrupted the Apache name "Beduiat" to Victorio. He had just one wife, even though polygamy was a status symbol among powerful chiefs, and he fathered five children. Three of his sons died in battle before he himself fell.

Victorio was the last hereditary chief whose D'ne band roved freely in their ancestral homelands of present-day southwest Texas, New Mexico and southern Arizona and the northern Mexican states of Sonora and Chihuahua. This rugged region of mountain and desert favored small, mobile, self-contained bands of hardy and inventive raiders. Victorio's band, the Ojo Caliente (or Warm Springs) Eastern (also Mimbreno or Mimbres) Apaches, were first united on the

He visited his friend Dr. J. H. Blazer to shake hands good-bye, saying, "From now on it will be war. War to the death. There is no other way."

In the past, Victorio had been able to operate as an independent warlord, negotiating private treaties with ranchers and mayors on both sides of the border, extracting protection money in return for peaceful behavior—a policy which arms dealers and crooked contractors charged extended into the Army and Indian Bureau. When he left the San Carlos reservation, he had a force of about 40 warriors. Still, he conducted offensive operations over a wider area, involving more actual conflicts with troops, than any of his peers. As many as 500 Americans and Mexicans may have died during Victorio's War.

"War to the Death!"

Victorio spent the winter of 1879-80 ambushing and exhausting various detachments of the Buffalo Soldiers in the mountains and resupplying himself at their expense. A thousand U.S. troops pursued from two directions. In the diabolically brilliant "double massacre" of January 1880 he ambushed and wiped out 52 Mexican scalp-hunters at Carrizal, then killed 32 and wounded 18 more who came looking for survivors. The frustrated White Eyes retaliated as best they could. General Edward Hatch suspected the Mescalero Apaches at Sierra Blanca Reservation of helping Victorio and disarmed them. Some were massacred; grim survivors joined the warrior's band. On New Mexico's Polomas River, a picked command of Indian scouts under Captain H. K. Parker managed to pin Victorio, kill 30 of his people and wound the chief in the leg. But they were forced to disengage when their ammunition ran out, while Hatch ignored their calls for assistance. A few days later, in a fight at Cook's Canyon, Victorio lost ten more warriors, including his son Washington.

In the next month, May of 1880, Victorio launched a series of reprisal. He and his warriors killed 78 persons and ran troops from two U.S. military departments ragged. In July he invaded Texas, where the Black Ninth and Tenth Cavalry hunted him relentlessly. But it was Mexican forces under two cousins, Governor Luis Terrazas and Colonel Joaquin Terrazas, who finally trapped Victorio at Tres Castillos (Three Peaks), 50 miles south of the Texas border. Gringo soldiers and Texas Rangers who rushed to the scene were ordered by Mexican authorities to leave the country.

On October 15, 1880, Tarahumara Indian scouts, known both for running great distances and for their inveterate hatred of the Apaches, closed in. The four-year-old survivor Kawaykla recalled that the Tarahumari went from pocket to pocket among Victorio's rock fortresses, blasting the Apache out one by one with dynamite. In all some 61 warriors and 18 women and children were killed. Sixty other women and children, including two of Victorio's sons, were captured and taken into slavery. Victorio's body was found with his own knife in its breast. The Mexican government later honored a Tarahumara sharpshooter, Mauricio Corredor, as Victorio's killer, giving him a beautiful, silver-inlaid rifle.

Victorio was lacking part of his force at Tres Castillos. He and Nanay had quarrelled and separated. The Apaches say Victorio's wife, small son Istee and married daughter with her family hid out in the mountains among Nanay's survivors. The ancient warrior helplessly watched the massacre. Then, leading no more than 20 warriors, and so arthritic he had to be lifted into the saddle, Nanay launched a reprisal: history's greatest series of Apache raids. One six-week escapade covered 1000 miles, killed or wounded 150 whites, and stole 200 horses. To retaliate for Victorio's death, old Nanay killed 400 Mexicans and Americans. But even though Apache raids sparked private wars by Mexican ranchers as late as 1929, the D'ne Nation could never control Arizona after Victorio's death.

SOURCES:

Betzinez, Jason, and Wilbur Sturtevant Nye, *I Fought with Geronimo,* Lincoln, University of Nebraska Press, 1959.

Brandon, William, *American Heritage Book of Indians,* Bonanza Books, 1961.

Chronological List of Actions, Adjutant General's Office, Old Army Press, 1891.

Debo, Angie, *Geronimo: The Man, His Time, His Place,* Norman, University of Oklahoma Press, 1976.

Geronimo: His Own Story, edited by S. M. Barrett, New York, Dutton, 1906.

Stout, Joseph A., Jr., *Apache Lightning: The Last Great Battles of the Ojo Calientes,* New York, Oxford University Press, 1964.

Terrell, John Upton, *Apache Chronicle: The Story of the People,* World Publishing, 1972.

Thrapp, Dan L., *Victorio and the Mimbres Apaches,* Norman, University of Oklahoma Press, 1974.

Wellman, Paul I., *The Indian Wars of the West, Volume 2: Death in the Desert,* Garden City, New York, Doubleday, 1935.

—*Sketch by Steven Edwin Conliff*

Gerald Vizenor
1934-
Ojibwa/Chippewa author and teacher

A multifaceted writer, Gerald Robert Vizenor is an acclaimed novelist, poet, and teacher. The themes and content of his works have arisen not only from his personal and cultural experiences, but also from the strong oral traditions of his American Indian ancestors. Born on October 22, 1934, in Minneapolis, Minnesota, Vizenor is of mixed-blood descent. His father, Clement William, was an Ojibwa Indian, originally from the White Earth Reservation in Minnesota, and his mother, LaVerne Peterson, lived in the city of Minneapolis. The two met when Vizenor's father first came to the city.

In 1950 Vizenor joined the Minnesota National Guard and from 1952 to 1955, he served with the U.S. Army in Japan. Vizenor attended New York University from 1955 to 1956 and acquired his bachelor of arts degree from the University of Minnesota in 1960. He also did some graduate study there from 1962 through 1965 and later studied at Harvard University. Since then, he has been a social worker, a civil rights activist, a journalist, and a community advocate for Native people living in urban centers. Vizenor organized the Indian Studies program at the Bemidji State University and has taught literature and tribal history at Lake Forest College, the University of Minnesota, the University of California at Berkeley, and Macalester College.

Early Poetic Influences

While serving in Japan, Vizenor became familiar with haiku, a Japanese style of poetry characterized by simple verse and poignant imagery. "The Japanese and their literature were my liberation," he later wrote in the *Chicago Review*. "That presence of haiku, more than other literature, touched my imagination and brought me closer to a sense of tribal consciousness.... I would have to leave the nation of my birth to understand the wisdom and survivance of tribal literature." During the following decade, he produced several volumes of haiku, including *Raising the Moon Vines* and *Seventeen Chirps,* both published in 1964, and *Empty Swings,* published in 1967.

In the years following, Vizenor explored many different genres. In 1973 he published his first novel, *Darkness in Saint Louis Bearheart,* in which he explores his own Native American experience, particularly the impoverished circumstances of his youth. He has also published several translations of collected Ojibwa songs and prose and in 1978, Vizenor published *Wordarrows: Indians and Whites in the New Fur Trade,* his first of many short story collections. In 1984 Vizenor wrote a historical account of his tribe, The People Named Chippewa: Narrative Histories.

In the 1980s Vizenor forewent a tenured position at the University of Minnesota to explore a teaching opportunity in China. Originally planning on writing situational essays during his stay, Vizenor's poetic outlook underwent a radical transformation after attending a theatrical production which included scenes from the Monkey King opera. The Monkey King is a mischievous figure from Chinese myth similar to a character found in Native American legend. In an interview with Larry McCaffery and Tom Marshall for Chicago Review, Vizenor confided this to be a significant if not pivotal experience that altered his perspective and "changed everything" for him. Seeing a dynamic Chinese audience "so completely engaged in the production," led Vizenor to rethink his original, graduate school reading of the Monkey King. The text literally came alive. Experiencing the performance transformed the material from mere cultural documentation to a work beyond socio-political ramifications, encompassing the consciousness of the Chinese people as folk literature. Sensing he had a "powerful theme" for a book born of this experience, Vizenor then developed Griever, a trickster main character, for his award-winning novel Griever, an American Monkey King in China, published in 1987. This piece was not his first (nor his last) work to embody the theme of the trickster character. The Trickster of Liberty: Tribal heirs to a Wild Baronage, published in 1988, also boldly elicits the trickster theme and imagery.

In 1990 Vizenor published an autobiographical piece, Interior Landscapes: Autobiographical Myths and Metaphors. He has also written several Native American novels and a number of works concerning the economic, social, and political plight of American Indians, specifically his own Ojibwa tribe.

SELECTED WRITINGS BY VIZENOR:

Born in the Wind, privately printed, 1960.
The Old Park Sleepers, Obercraft, 1961.
Two Wings the Butterfly, privately printed, 1962.
South of the Painted Stone, Obercraft, 1963.
Raising the Moon Vines, Callimachus, 1964.
Seventeen Chirps, Nodin, 1964.
Empty Swings, Nodin, 1967.
Thomas James White Hawk, Four Winds, 1968.
The Everlasting Sky, Crowell, 1972.
Darkness in Saint Louis Bearheart, Truck Press, 1973.
Anishinabe Adisokan: Stories of the Ojibwa, Nodin, 1974.
Anishinabe Nagomon: Songs of the Ojibwa, Nodin, 1974.
Wordarrows: Indians and Whites in the New Fur Trade, University of Minnesota Press, 1978.
Earthdivers: Tribal Narratives on Mixed Descent, Minneapolis, University of Minnesota Press, 1981.
Summer in the Spring: Ojibwa Songs and Stories, Nodin, 1981.
Matsushima: Pine Islands, Nodin, 1984.
The People Named the Chippewa: Narrative Histories, Minneapolis, University of Minnesota Press, 1984.
Griever: An American Monkey King in China, Fiction Collective, 1987.
Touchwood: A Collection of Ojibway Prose, St. Paul, Minnesota, New Rivers Press, 1987.
The Trickster of Liberty: Tribal Heirs to a Wild Baronage, Minneapolis, University of Minnesota Press, 1988.
Narrative Chance: Postmodern Discourse on Native American Indian Literatures, Albuquerque, University of New Mexico, 1989.
Bearheart: The Heirship Chronicles, Minneapolis, University of Minnesota Press, 1990.
Crossbloods: Bone Courts, Bingo, and Other Reports, Minneapolis, University of Minnesota Press, 1990.
Distant Voices: Thunder Words, Lincoln, Nebraska, NETCHE, 1990.
Interior Landscapes: Autobiographical Myths and Metaphors, Minneapolis, University of Minnesota Press, 1990.

The Heirs of Columbus, Hanover, New Hampshire, University Press of New England, 1991.

Landfill Meditation: Crossblood Stories, Hanover, New Hampshire, Wesleyan University Press, 1991.

Dead Voices: Natural Agonies in the New World, Norman, University of Oklahoma Press, 1992.

Summer in the Spring: Anishinaabe Lyric Poems and Stories, Norman, University of Oklahoma Press, 1993.

From Different Shores: Perspectives on Race and Ethnicity in America, New York, Oxford University Press, 1994.

Manifest Manners: Postindian Warriors of Survivance, Hanover, New Hampshire, University Press of New England, 1994.

SOURCES:

Books

Native North American Almanac, edited by Duane Champagne, Detroit, Gale Research, 1994; 1182.

Periodicals

McCaffery, Larry and Marshall, Tom, "Head Water: An Interview with Gerald Vizenor," *Chicago Review,* 39, 1993; 50-54.

Vizenor, Gerald Robert, "The Envoy to Haiku," *Chicago Review,* 39, 1993; 55-62.

—*Sketch by Brett A. Lealand*

Nancy Ward
1738(?)-1824
Cherokee warrior and tribal leader
Also known as Nan'yehi ["One Who Goes About"],
Tsistunagiska ["Wild Rose"], and Ghigau
["Beloved Woman"]

The role of Beloved Woman (sometimes translated as "War Woman" or "Pretty Woman") among the Cherokee was an influential role indeed. The most noted of the Cherokee Beloved Women was Nancy Ward, who served her people during the difficult times of cultural transition at the end of the eighteenth century. She wisely counseled against land cession, but did not live to see her warnings proven true as the Cherokee were dispossessed of their eastern lands.

Earns Title Beloved Woman

Born about 1738 at Chota, a "Peace Town" or "Mother Town" in the Overhill region of the Cherokee Nation, Nan'yehi came into the world at the beginning of a crucial era in Cherokee history. Raised by her mother, Tame Deer, and her father, Fivekiller (who was also part Delaware or Lenni Lenapé), Nan'yehi learned at a young age that her people were in cultural turmoil. Missionaries, Moravians in particular, were trying to gain access to the Cherokee people in order to convert them. At that time still very conservative in their retention of custom and religion, the Cherokees had a mixed reaction to the missionaries; many regarded them as a threat, others saw them as a blessing. One of those who straddled the fence in his opinion was Nan'yehi's very influential maternal uncle, Attakullakulla ["Little Carpenter"]. He eventually struck a deal which allowed Moravians into Cherokee territory, but only if they would build schools that would instruct Cherokee youth in English and the ways of the white man. Later critics would see this as evidence of Attakullakulla's desire to acculturate the Cherokee to white ways; others say he saw what could be an advantage in dealing with whites, a sort of "know your enemy" tactic.

Nantyehi too would try to find the middle ground between tradition and innovation. She married a Cherokee man named Kingfisher while in her early teens. Kingfisher was a great warrior, and Nan'yehi was at his side in battle, helping prepare his firearms and rallying Cherokee warriors when their spirits flagged. In 1755, the Cherokees fought the Creeks at the Battle of Taliwa. During the fighting, Kingfisher was killed. A distraught Nan'yehi, about 18 years old at this time, took up his gun and, singing to the Cherokees a war song, she lead them in a rout of the enemy. Out of her loss was born a decisive victory for her people and a title of honor for her: "Beloved Woman."

The role of Ghigau (or Agigau) was the highest one to which a Cherokee woman could aspire. It was unusual for one as young as Nan'yehi to be so named, but since the name also translates as "War Woman," and was usually awarded to women warriors (or warrior's mothers or widows), Nan'yehi had duly earned it. Much responsibility went with the many privileges of the rank, and although young, Nan'yehi showed herself capable. Among the privileges accorded Nan'yehi as a Beloved Woman were voice and vote in General Council, leadership of the Women's Council, the honor of preparing the Black Drink (a ritually-purifying tea) and administering it to warriors before battle, and the right to save a prisoner already condemned to execution. Nan'yehi would exercise all these rights, as well as serving as her people's sage and guide.

Another of the Beloved Woman's duties was as "ambassadress," or peace negotiator. It is through this role that Nan'yehi became a figure in non-Cherokee history. Having been "apprenticed" as a diplomat at her uncle's side, Nan'yehi was a shrewd negotiator who tempered her dealings with a realistic view of how to help the Cherokee people survive. Continued white settlement on Cherokee lands (in violation of the Royal Proclamation Line of 1763) brought constant tension into Indian-white relations.

When militant Cherokees prepared to attack illegal white communities on the Watauga River, Nan'yehi disapproved of the intentional taking of civilian lives. She was able to warn several of the Watauga settlements in time for them to defend themselves or flee. One of the settlers unfortunate enough to be taken alive by the Cherokee warriors was a Mrs. Bean. The woman was sentenced to execution and was actually being tied to a stake when Nan'yehi exercised her right to spare condemned captives. Taking the injured Mrs. Bean into her own home to nurse her back to health, Nan'yehi learned two skills from her which would have far-reaching consequences for her people.

A Time of Change

Mrs. Bean, as did most "settler women" wove her own

cloth. At this time, the Cherokee were wearing a combination of traditional hide clothing and loomed cloth purchased from traders. Cherokee people had rough-woven hemp clothing, but it was not as comfortable as clothing made from linen, cotton, or wool. Mrs. Bean taught Nan'yehi how to set up a loom, spin thread or yarn, and weave cloth. While this would make the Cherokee people less dependent upon traders, the association of women with weaving and house chores would undermine their power, as men became farmers and women became "housewives."

Another aspect of Cherokee life that changed when Nan'yehi spared Mrs. Bean was that of animal husbandry. The white woman owned dairy cattle, which she brought to Nan'yehi's house. Nan'yehi learned the skill of dairying, which provided some reliable foodstuffs even when hunting was bad. However, because of Nan'yehi's introduction of cattle-keeping to the Cherokee, they would begin to amass large herds and farms, which required even more manual labor. This would soon lead the Cherokee into the practice of slaveholding. In fact, Nan'yehi herself had been "awarded" the Black slave of a felled Creek warrior after her victory at the Battle of Taliwa.

From these many accommodations to the "Americans," one might get the idea that Nan'yehi was selling out the Cherokee people. However, her political efforts proved to the contrary. She did not seek war, but neither did she counsel peace when she felt compromise would hurt her tribe. In her peace parlay with John Sevier at the Little Pigeon River (Tennessee) in 1781, she had called for peace, but warned Sevier to take the treaty back to "his women" for them to ratify. It did not occur to the Cherokee that women did not decide matters of war and peace in the white man's world, as was the case in many southeastern tribes. Nan'yehi was also a negotiator for the Cherokee at the 1785 signing of the Treaty of Hopewell, the first treaty the Cherokee made with the "new" United States.

By the turn of the nineteenth century, it was already becoming apparent to the Cherokee that the Americans intended to get as much Cherokee land as possible and that the day might come when the Natives would be forced off their homeground. Nan'yehi, by now being called "Nancy" by the many whites she had befriended, feared that each voluntary land cession whetted the white man's appetite and that someday, his hunger would overcome her people. In 1808, the Women's Council, with Nancy at its head, issued a statement to the Cherokee people, imploring them to sell no more land. Again, in 1817, Nancy took her seat in Council, but her desperation was ill-concealed. She told the younger people to refuse any more requests for land or to take up arms against the "Americans" if necessary.

The Road Back to Chota

Too aged to make the effort to attend further General Council meetings, Nancy sent her walking-stick in her place thereafter. Some contemporary sources say she "resigned"

her position as Beloved Woman with this action, but the mere absence from Council did not indicate the end of a woman's tenure as Beloved Woman. Nancy was well aware that Cherokee "removal" west of the Mississippi River was almost a foregone conclusion. Rather than face the sorrow of leaving her homeland, she decided to find a way to blend in to the white world. Nan'yehi had become Nancy Ward when she married Irish (or Scots-Irish) trader Bryant Ward. By now, her three children were grown, so she was accorded the indulgence of "modern conveniences" due to her advanced age and the great integrity with which she had long discharged her duty to her people. Therefore, when she and Ward took to the innkeeping trade, there was no disrespect voiced toward the Beloved Woman. Their inn was situated near the Mother Town of Chota, on Womankiller Ford of the Ocowee River, in eastern Tennessee.

Ward returned to Chota, her birthplace, in 1824. She was cared for by her son, Fivekiller, who reported seeing a white light leave her body as she died. The light was said to have entered the most sacred mound in the Mother Town. Ward was spared the sight of her people's exile to Indian Territory in 1838, but with her spirit's presence at Chota, they knew she would forever connect them to their eastern home. The last woman to be given the title of Beloved Woman until the late 1980s, Ward remains a powerful symbol for Cherokee women. She is often referred to by feminist scholars as an inspiration, and is as revered a figure by the Cherokee people of Oklahoma as by the Eastern Band Cherokees of North Carolina.

SOURCES:

Allen, Paula Gunn, *The Sacred Hoop,* Boston, Beacon Press, 1992.

American Indian Women: A Research Guide, edited by Gretchen Bataille and Kathleen Sands, New York, Garland Publishing, 1991.

Biographical Dictionary of Indians of the Americas, Newport Beach, California, American Indian Publications, 1983.

Concise Dictionary of American Biography, fourth edition, edited by Frederick I. Burkhardt and others, New York, Scribner's, 1990.

Gender, Race and Identity, edited by Craig Barrow, and others, Chattanooga, Tennessee, Southern Humanities Press, 1993.

Green, Rayna, *Women in American Indian Society,* New York, Chelsea House, 1992.

Mankiller, Wilma, and Michael Wallis, *Mankiller: A Chief and Her People,* New York, St. Martin's Press, 1993.

Native American Women, edited by Gretchen M. Bataille, New York, Garland Publishing, 1993.

Native North American Almanac, edited by Duane Champagne, Detroit, Gale Research, 1994.

—Sketch by Cynthia R. Kasee

Washakie
1804(?)-1900
Shoshoni tribal leader

Also known as Pinquana (Pina Quanah) ["Sweet Smelling" or "Smell of Sugar"], "Shoots Straight," "Sure Shot," "Scar Face," and "Two Scar Chief"

Washakie

An ally of the white fur trappers, traders, immigrants, and the U.S. government, Chief Washakie (whose name translates as "Gourd Rattle," "Rawhide Rattle," or "Gambler's Gourd") and the Eastern Shoshonis were instrumental in assisting the Anglo-Americans in settling the western United States. His father, Paseego, was an Umatilla or Flathead Indian; his mother was a Shoshoni, possibly of the Wind River or Lemhi band.

Shortly after his birth in Montana's Bitterroot Mountains, he was named Pinquana ["Sweet Smelling"]. Later in life, he took the name Washakie—derived from Shoshonean Wus'sik-he, variously interpreted as "Gourd Rattle," "Rawhide Rattle," or "Gambler's Gourd." Washakie did not acquire this name until he had killed his first buffalo: after skinning the buffalo and curing the hide, he made a stone-filled rattle out of a dried, pouch-like piece of the animal's skin. During battle, Washakie would ride toward his enemies and shake his rattle to frighten their horses. Early on, he earned a reputation as a fierce warrior against the Sioux, Blackfeet, and Crow Indian nations. He also gained several other names from his fighting exploits: "Scar Face" or "Two Scar Chief" because of the deep scars on his left cheek, which had been pierced by a Blackfoot arrow, as well as "Shoots Straight" and "Sure Shot," for his keen eye and steady hand.

Becomes the Eastern Shoshonis' Leader

The Shoshonis were known as the Snake Indians, among not only whites but also the Great Plains tribes, apparently because they painted snakes on sticks to frighten their enemies. The origin of the word "Shoshoni" is unknown, but the name is believed to have been given them by whites. Bands of Shoshoni Indians—Southern, Western, Eastern, and Northern—occupied vast portions of the Rocky Mountain and plains areas of the American West. Washakie's Eastern or Wind River Shoshonis roamed over most of Wyoming and a small part of southeastern Idaho.

When Washakie was a small child, his father was killed during a Blackfoot raid on their village. His mother escaped with her five young children and returned to her people, who lived along the Rocky Mountains in Wyoming. Washakie stayed with them until he was a young man, then is believed to have lived for about five years with the Bannocks.

As chief of the Eastern Shoshonis during the second half of the nineteenth century, Washakie became the most powerful leader of the migratory horse-owning tribe. He was chief at a time when his people's way of life was being threatened by the westward expansion of white American society. Washakie exerted great influence over the Northern Shoshonis and was temporarily allied with other Shoshoni and Bannock chiefs. Chief Pocatello, for whom a city in Idaho was named, had an alliance with Washakie. The Bannock chief Taghee of the Northern Paiutes, also offered Washakie his allegiance for a time.

Forbids His People from Fighting the Whites

During the 1820s through the 1830s, Washakie and the Shoshonis were on good terms with Anglo frontiersmen, trappers, and traders. They attended the fur trappers' Rocky Mountain rendezvous, establishing an alliance with their brigades and joining them in battles against the Sioux, Blackfeet, and Crows—all traditional enemies of the Shoshonis. By the mid-1840s, Washakie was principal chief of the Eastern Shoshoni band and waves of settlers were crossing his country on their way west along the Oregon Trail.

Washakie continued to maintain cordial relations with this new group of immigrants, assisting them in many ways. The Shoshonis helped the settlers recover lost stock and cross the region's swift rivers. Washakie also provided regular patrols of Shoshoni warriors to protect the immigrants from Sioux, Cheyenne, and Arapaho raiding parties. Perhaps even more important was his refusal to allow Shoshoni reprisals against settlers who were wiping out game and whose stock was destroying valuable Indian root grounds. According to Russell Freedman's *Indian Chiefs*, Washakie told his people: "You must not fight the whites. I not only advise against it, I forbid it!" The settlers were so appreciative of Washakie's assistance that 9,000 of them signed a document commending the Shoshonis and their chief. He was even on friendly terms with the Mormon leader "Big-Um" or Brigham Young.

Between the fall of 1858 and the spring of 1859, Washakie fought at the Battle of Crowheart Butte, the climax of the intertribal warfare between the Shoshonis and the Crows. He also met and became friends with famous mountain man Jim Bridger and Missouri hunter, trapper, and guide Christopher "Kit" Carson. In 1863 Washakie led his people to the safety of Fort Bridger, keeping them out of the Americans' Bear River Campaign against Bear Hunter's band of Northwestern Shoshonis.

In exchange for a 20-year-long payment agreement, Washakie signed the 1863 Treaty of Fort Bridger, guaranteeing U.S. travelers safe passage through his band's territory. His good relations with the U.S. government made it possible for him to secure the Wind River reservation, in present-day Wyoming, for the Eastern Shoshonis. In 1868 Washakie signed a second treaty establishing the 3-million-acre reservation; his people had given up their claims to other lands in Wyoming and Utah for the reservation, a remnant of their traditional territory. He also agreed to a clear path through the Green River Valley for the Union Pacific Railroad Company.

Even after the Shoshoni treaties were signed, the Sioux continued to hunt and raid the Eastern Shoshoni reservation. Washakie complained to the U.S. Army, but they did little to stop the Sioux, adding to the animosity the chief already felt towards his traditional enemies. Washakie had old scores to settle with the Sioux: they had raided his people's villages many times and killed and scalped his oldest son. Later, when the army requested assistance in their war against the Sioux, Washakie jumped at the proposition.

The Eastern Shoshonis served as scouts and warriors for the U.S. Army against the Arapahos, Cheyennes, Sioux, andUtes. In 1876 Washakie and 200 warriors rode to the aid of General George Crook. Arriving too late to help Crook fight the Sioux at the Battle of the Rosebud in southern Montana, he joined forces with the general's troops and together they followed Crazy Horse's warriors all the way to the Powder River in eastern Montana.

A big and imposing man, Washakie took great pride in his appearance. He is said to have enjoyed looking at a framed photograph of himself hanging on the wall of a reservation store. Washakie was also proud of his possessions. With the help of his son Charlie, he painted pictures of his war exploits and then decorated his cabin with them. He was especially fond of a handsome saddle, decorated in silver, given to him by President Ulysses S. Grant. And he proudly posed for photographs wearing a silver peace medal sent to him by President Andrew Johnson. Always popular with politicians, Washakie was visited by President Chester A. Arthur in 1883.

But the United States did not always satisfy Washakie. In 1878 the government decided to put Chief Black Coal's Northern Arapahos on the Wind River reservation. The Arapahos were traditional enemies of the Shoshonis, but since they were destitute and starving Washakie agreed to let them stay on his reservation for a limited time. In spite of

Washakie's protests, the Arapahos' temporary stay turned into a permanent one. Washakie had other complaints against the government; he objected to white hunters killing off large numbers of deer and antelope on the reservation. He also protested against trespassing gold miners and cowboys who were rustling the Shoshonis' cattle. Washakie reminded officials that the government had promised to keep both whites and other Indian tribes off Shoshoni land, but his arguments seemed to fall on deaf ears.

Washakie's Importance in Native American History

Washakie's peaceful relations with Anglo-Americans kept the Eastern Shoshoni from experiencing the devastating effects of removal to the Indian Territory, located in what is today the state of Oklahoma. Their alliance with the Americans also kept the Native American band from suffering casualties at the hands of the U.S. Army. Washakie's cooperation with the Americans benefited his people more than a war with the white settlers could have.

In 1897 Washakie was baptized an Episcopalian. He died three years later at Flathead Village in Montana's Bitterroot Valley and was buried with full military honors at Fort Washakie, Wyoming. In a life that spanned nearly an entire century, he had married twice and fathered at least 12 children, including a son, Cocoosh (Dick Washakie), who succeeded him as chief of the Eastern Shoshonis.

SOURCES:

Dockstader, Frederick J., *Great North American Indians,* New York, Van Nostrand Reinhold, 1977; 323-325.

Freedman, Russell, *Indian Chiefs,* New York, Holiday House, 1987; 73-89.

Native North American Almanac, edited by Duane Champagne, Detroit, Gale Research, 1994; 1184.

Trenholm, Virginia Cole, and Maurine Carley, *The Shoshonis: Sentinels of the Rockies,* Norman, University of Oklahoma Press, 1964; 97-99.

Waldman, Carl, *Who Was Who in Native American History,* New York, Facts On File, 1990; 372.

—Sketch by Michael F. Turek

Stand Watie
1806-1871
Cherokee political leader and Confederate general
Also known as Degataga and Takertawker
["Standing Together" or "Stand Firm"]

S tand Watie was born in the old Cherokee Nation (now Georgia) and became politically active as a young man, serving as clerk of the National Supreme Court in 1829. As a relative of Major Ridge and Elias Boudinot, he became a prime mover in the "Treaty Party," which favored relocation of the Cherokee people to the West under a treaty with the U.S. government. In contrast, the elected Cherokee government, headed by John Ross, held out hope that they could retain their ancestral lands. Although they had no authority to do so, Watie and others signed the Treaty of New Echota in 1835, which ceded tribal lands to the U.S. government and resulted in the tragic deaths of thousands of Cherokees during relocation along the Trail of Tears. Once the relocation was completed in 1839, the Treaty Party leaders were assassinated in a single day, with the sole exception of Stand Watie, who was forewarned. He remained politically active and became a superb commander of Indian forces during the American Civil War. Often called "the last Confederate general to surrender," Watie later led a delegation of Southern Cherokees who attempted to have the U.S. government split the Cherokee Nation in two in an effort to solve the Cherokees' internal political battles. This effort failed, and Watie lived only a few years more.

Watie was born on December 12, 1906, near present-day Rome, Georgia, in the old Cherokee Nation. His father was David Oowatie, the younger brother of Major Ridge, a noted Cherokee leader. His mother was a half-Cherokee, half-Scot woman of the Deer Clan named Susannah Catherine Reese. Watie attended the Moravian Mission schools at either Spring Place or Brainerd or both. At school, he learned to speak English and took the English equivalent of his name, "Standing Together," and shortened the last name of Oowatie, so that he was thereafter known as "Stand Watie." Watie's brother Elias Boudinot and his cousin John Ridge had been sent to a related school in Cornwall, Connecticut, but Watie was educated only in the Cherokee Nation.

Signs Treaty of New Echota

Watie was a planter, and he also helped his brother publish the bilingual newspaper *Cherokee Phoenix* while Boudinot was away. Watie, Boudinot, and their Ridge relatives came to be the leaders of the "Treaty Party," which felt that the answer to white encroachment on what was left of their ancestral lands lay in a treaty with the U.S. government, ceding land in exchange for new land in the West. The "Treaty Party" members negotiated unofficially on behalf of the Cherokees in Washington, D.C., in 1835, and they signed the Treaty of New Echota on December 29. Since this document called for surrender of Cherokee lands and removal of the people to Indian Territory (now Oklahoma), the lawful government of the Cherokee Nation was outraged and sent petitions with signatures of more than 90 percent of the tribal members to the Senate, pleading against ratification. Nonetheless, the treaty passed on May 23, 1836, by one vote.

Watie and his family travelled to the West in 1837, before the infamous Trail of Tears. Their journey was reasonably comfortable and they settled near Tahlequah. Watie farmed and was a slave holder, having brought his black slaves west with him, as did many well-to-do Cherokees. The Old Settlers who had moved west voluntarily were at odds with the remainder of the Cherokees, who were marched over the Trail of Tears, about the form a new government should take. This dissension turned violent as Major Ridge, John Ridge, and Elias Boudinot were all murdered on June 22, 1839. Stand Watie was able to avoid his ambush by being warned just in time. The murders were never solved—in part because it was a capital offense to cede any tribal land and many Cherokees felt that justice had been done. The heartache of the Trail of Tears, during which many Cherokees died en route to Indian Territory, spurred action against the most visible treaty signers.

Watie had relished his home life before this tragic turn of events. He had married Sarah Caroline "Betsy" Bell in September, 1842. They were blessed with three sons, Saladin, Solon Watica, and Cumiskey, and two daughters, Ninnie Josephine and Charlotte Jacqueline. He now became the leader of the Treaty Party and was on his guard thereafter. The Treaty of 1846 settled the internal difficulties of the Cherokees and there was a brief period of peace and prosperity. Watie served as speaker of the Cherokee National Council from 1857 to 1859 and, in all, was a member of the council from 1846 to 1861.

Becomes Celebrated Confederate General

At the outbreak of the American Civil War, Watie had organized a troop of both Cherokees and whites for the purpose of protecting Indian Territory from federal forces stationed at Humboldt, Kansas. Captain Watie also guarded the Cherokee Nation from the Osages, nearly all Unionists, and ancient enemies of the Cherokees as well. Watie became a colonel in May 1861, when he came under the command of General McCulloch of Texas, who commanded the military district of the Indian Territory. Watie's two regiments were called "The Cherokee Mounted Rifles."

In 1862, John Ross, the principal chief of the Cherokees, rethought the Treaty of Alliance he had signed with the Confederacy. He went to Washington and stayed there until the end of the war. A national convention of the Cherokees was held and Stand Watie, in Ross' absence, was elected chief. There was a dispute about a quorum among the Federal and Southern members of the council; the outcome was that there were two tribal governments from that convention through 1866, when the U.S. government recognized Ross and his group at Watie's expense.

Though small in stature, Watie had great physical strength and endurance, and while not a great orator, he was a good writer. His men, particularly the full-bloods, were convinced that he could not be killed and willingly followed this "man of great personal magnetism." Watie served as a raider and cavalry leader. His troops fought both in Indian Territory and along its border, including the battles of Wilson's Creek (near Springfield, Missouri) in August 1861, Chustenahlah in December 1861, and Pea Ridge (Arkansas). In this last battle, fought in March 1862, Watie captured enemy artillery positions and covered the retreat of his own forces. The Union, although victorious, suffered great losses. In the Second Battle of Cabin Creek, Watie's men captured a wagon train carrying $1 million of supplies bound for Fort Gibson. His victory at Pleasant Bluff prevented the local Confederates from becoming completely demoralized.

On June 15, 1864, Watie led his troops in the taking of the steam ferryboat *J. R. Williams* on the Arkansas River. The ship had a load of supplies bound for Fort Gibson. In September of that same year, he captured a Union supply column of 300 wagons journeying from Fort Scott, Kansas, to Fort Gibson. He was generous with his wartime booty and showed a special interest in those refugees displaced by the war, especially women and children. He never ordered a charge that he did not lead, yet he never received a wound in battle.

On May 10, 1864, Jefferson Davis, President of the Confederacy, appointed Watie as Brigadier General in the Confederate Army. He was the only Indian of this rank on either side in the Civil War and apparently only the second in U.S. history. With his promotion, "General Watie's Indian Brigade" included all Confederate Cherokees, as well as members of the other Five Civilized Tribes, at the end of the war. Watie continued the fight until June 23, 1865, when he surrendered at Doaksville, in the Choctaw Nation, two and one-half months after Lee's surrender. Watie had been able to exact partial revenge for the 1839 assassinations of his relatives by burning John Ross' splendid house, Rose Cottage, at Park Hill in November 1863.

Watie's property suffered greatly during the war, as did that of many others in Indian Territory. He served as head of a delegation to Washington, D.C., composed of his nephew Elias Cornelius Boudinot, his son Saladin Watie, his cousin John Rollin Ridge, and three others. During the negotiations, Ridge quarreled bitterly with Boudinot, the Cherokees' former representative to the Confederate Congress at Richmond, and their feud was partly responsible for the failure of their mission. The U.S. government at last recognized the Northern delegation as the one to represent the Cherokee Nation, which remained one political unit.

After his return from Washington, Watie entered the mercantile business in Webbers Falls and the tobacco manufacturing business with his nephew Boudinot. In 1870, this enterprise and its taxation gave rise to the "Cherokee Tobacco Case" in the U.S. Supreme Court. Watie had moved to a farm at Grand River near Bernice, where he lived the rest of his life. Part of that time he spent providing Cherokee ethnological information for Henry Rowe Schoolcraft's *Information Respecting the History, Condition, and Prospects of the Indian Tribes of the United States.*

Watie died on September 9, 1871, and was buried in the Ridge Cemetery, also known as Polson Cemetery (now in Delaware County, Oklahoma), near his home on Honey Creek.

SOURCES:

Books

Biographical Dictionary of Indians of the Americas, second edition, Newport Beach, California, American Indian Publishers, 1991.

Cherokee Cavaliers: Forty Years of Cherokee History as Told in the Correspondence of the Ridge-Watie-Boudinot Family, edited by Edward Everett Dale and Gaston Litton, Norman, University of Oklahoma Press, 1939; 144f.

Cunningham, Frank, *General Stand Watie's Confederate Indians,* San Antonio, Naylor, 1959; 13.

Dictionary of American Biography, edited by John A. Garraty, New York, Charles Scribner's Sons, 1951.

Dockstader, Frederick J., *Great North American Indians,* New York, Van Nostrand Reinhold, 1977.

Gabriel, Ralph Henry, *Elias Boudinot, Cherokee & His America,* Norman, University of Oklahoma Press, 1941; 132.

Native North American Almanac, edited by Duane Champagne, Detroit, Gale Research, 1994.

Parins, James, *John Rollin Ridge: His Life and Works,* Lincoln, University of Nebraska Press, 1991; 214.

Schwarze, Edmund, *History of the Moravian Missions among the Southern Indian Tribes,* Bethlehem, Pennsylvania, 1923.

Starr, Emmet, *Old Cherokee Families: "Old Families and Their Genealogy,"* Norman, University of Oklahoma Foundation, 1972; 381, 473.

Waldman, Carl, *Who Was Who in Native American History,* New York, Facts on File, 1990.

Wardell, Morris L., *A Political History of the Cherokee Nation, 1838-1907,* Norman, University of Oklahoma Press, 1977.

Wilkins, Thurmond, *Cherokee Tragedy: The Story of the Ridge Family and of the Decimation of a People,* New York, Macmillan, 1970.

Woodward, Grace Steele, *The Cherokees,* Norman, University of Oklahoma Press, 1963.

Periodicals

Anderson, Mabel Washbourne, "General Stand Watie," *Chronicles of Oklahoma,* 10:4, December 1932.

Franzmann, Tom, "The Final Campaign," *Chronicles of Oklahoma,* 43:3, fall 1985.

Hancock, Marvin J., "The Second Battle of Cabin Creek," *Chronicles of Oklahoma,* 39:4, winter 1961-1962; 420-423.

Hood, Fred, "Twilight of the Confederacy in the Indian Territory," *Chronicles of Oklahoma,* 41:4, winter 1963-1964; 429-437.

Kremm, Thomas W., and Diane Neal, "Civil War Controversy," *Chronicles of Oklahoma,* 70:1, spring 1992; 37.

Lewis, Kenneth E., "Archaeology at Fort Towson," *Chronicles of Oklahoma,* 50:3, autumn 1972.

Rampp, L. C., "Civil War Battle of Barren Creek," *Chronicles of Oklahoma,* 43:1, spring 1970.

Shadburn, Don L., "Cherokee Statesmen: The John Rogers Family," *Chronicles of Oklahoma,* 50:1, spring 1972.

Warde, Mary Jane, "Civilian Civil War," *Chronicles of Oklahoma,* 71:1, spring 1993; 80, 82.

Warren, Hanna R., "Reconstruction in the Cherokee Nation," *Chronicles of Oklahoma,* 45:2, summer 1967.

"Webbers Falls Noted Historic Site in Muskogee County," *Chronicles of Oklahoma,* 51:1, spring 1973.

Wright, Muriel H., "Notes on Colonel Elias Cornelius Boudinot," *Chronicles of Oklahoma*, 41:4, winter 1963-1964; 384.

Wright, Muriel H., and LeRoy H. Fischer, "Oklahoma Civil War Sites," *Chronicles of Oklahoma*, 44:2, summer 1966.

—Sketch by Philip H. Viles, Jr.

Annie Dodge Wauneka
1910-
Navajo health educator, and tribal leader

Annie Dodge Wauneka

Annie Dodge Wauneka is one of the best-known Native American leaders in America. A public-health educator responsible for largely eliminating tuberculosis among the Navajo Indians, Wauneka was the first woman elected to the Navajo Tribal Council and the first Native American to receive the Presidential Medal of Freedom.

Between Two Worlds

The daughter of Henry Chee Dodge (Kiil'chii; also known as Adits'aii ["Interpreter] or Ashkihih Diitsi ["Boy Who Hears and Understands"]), successful Navajo rancher and politician, and K'eehabah, Annie Dodge Wauneka was born April 10, 1910 in a hogan near Sawmill, Arizona. During her first years on the Navajo reservation Annie was exposed both to Navajo tradition and to the innovations of a changing world. In fact, although Henry Chee Dodge was able to navigate in the "white world" very well, Annie's birth to K'eehabah was indicative of just how many of the "old ways" surrounded her. K'eehabah was Dodge's "temporary wife," and Henry Chee Dodge was married to two of K'eehabah's relatives. As was the Navajo custom in polygamous marriages, a man's wives were usually relatives. Since children's identity derived from their mother's family, all children born to related wives would be considered full siblings. Annie was eventually taken from K'eehabah and raised by Dodge and his wives (a very untraditional practice). Although she should have been considered a full sister to their other children, Annie would speak in later years of growing up with a distinct sense that she was not seen as a full sibling.

Also very untraditional in Annie's early life was Dodge's wealth. His ranch was large and had all the modern features then available. However, in order to keep his children from feeling superior to other Navajos, he made sure they did customary chores, such as herding sheep. Annie would sometimes rise before dawn to check on her flock, then sit down to a breakfast prepared by paid servants.

Finds Calling in Nursing

At the age of eight, Annie left home to attend boarding school at the government-run facility at Fort Defiance, Arizona. From there, she moved on to the Albuquerque, New Mexico, Indian School. She eventually left after her junior year of high school. It was at the Indian School that she met George Wauneka, whom she would marry. Also at the Albuquerque Indian School she saw many students die from influenza. During the outbreak, she assisted nurses and found her calling in life.

While she was away at school, Henry Chee Dodge was appointed as the first Chairman of the Navajo Tribal Council, a formal body set up to govern the tribe as a corporation under the Indian Reorganization Act (1934). Upon Annie and George's return, Henry Chee Dodge began to introduce his daughter to the duties of a modern Navajo leader. It is not known whether George Wauneka (after their 1929 marriage) approved of the influence Dodge exerted on Annie, or of his very innovative attitude towards women in politics, but the lifelong endurance of the marriage indicates that George Wauneka accommodated his decidedly "modern" wife's career.

Between 1931 and 1950, the Waunekas had six children. Born at Klagetoh near Window Rock, Arizona, Georgia Anne, Henry, Irma, Franklin, Lorencita, and Sallie grew up in an unconventional family, where their father stayed home and tended their property and herds, while their mother traveled the reservation as her father's aide. Irma and

Franklin died while still young, losses that deeply affected the Waunekas.

Becomes a Public-Health Crusader

In her work with her father, Wauneka saw the devastation that disease, particularly tuberculosis, had brought to her people. Remembering her experiences with the nurses in Albuquerque, she knew that "white man's medicine" might be the answer to the problem. She made efforts to explain to traditional families in the Navajo language ways to improve their health by simple changes in sanitation and food preparation. Soon she determined that a concerted effort at improving Navajo health could only be coordinated through the tribal government. With that in mind, she ran for a seat on the Tribal Council in 1951, winning the position, and with it, the designation of the first Navajo woman elected to office.

During her three terms in office, Wauneka spearheaded the tuberculosis eradication project. An essential tool in this effort was the dictionary she wrote, in which she translated English words for modern medical techniques into Navajo words. She took concepts such as inoculation and vaccination, which were seen by Navajos as "shooting corpse poison" or witchcraft, and explained them as healing techniques, just like those used by Navajo "singers" (medicine men/women). Wauneka also made use of the growing communication network that radio afforded the widespread Navajo communities. She hosted a program in the Navajo language, in which she further explained how modern medicine could be seen as an extension of Navajo medicine. With the radio show reaching Navajo families, and the dictionary aiding government doctors in talking with their patients, tuberculosis was greatly reduced among the Navajos.

While tuberculosis was a major problem, it was not the only threat to Navajo health. Wauneka also campaigned for better pre- and postnatal care, and for regular eye and ear exams (eye and ear infections such as trachoma and otitis media were often rampant on reservations). She was a vocal opponent of alcohol abuse. She addressed everything she saw as a problem for Navajo survival. In fact, when her own husband ran against her in 1953 for a Tribal Council seat, she won handily. She loved him, but believed she could do more to help their people than he could.

In the mid-1950s, Wauneka decided to gain the educational expertise to back up her practical knowledge. She earned a bachelor's degree in public health from the University of Arizona. Her commitment to education was not just a personal one; she saw it as a way for the Navajo not only to survive in the contemporary world, but also to maintain their traditions, and to be more self-sufficient. Her efforts were recognized with Arizona State Public Health Association's Outstanding Worker in Public Health Award in 1959.

Beginning in the early 1960s, Wauneka's focus turned outward. Although Navajo health and well-being remained her first concern, she widened her circle of resources and reached out to help others with her own hard-won knowledge. She received the Josephine Hughes Award and the Arizona Press Women's Association Woman of Achievement Award. She served on New Mexico's Committee on Aging and the advisory boards of both the U.S. Surgeon General and the U.S. Public Health Service. Perhaps her most prestigious honor was the 1963 Presidential Medal of Freedom; she was the first Native American to receive it.

In 1976, Wauneka received an honorary doctor of public health degree from the University of Arizona. A highly respected member of the Navajo Nation, a forward-thinking yet traditional-minded person, she remained involved with Navajo health issues even as she aged. Wauneka, at the age of 84, still advises the Navajo Tribal Council, and she is an inspiration for Native people of all tribes.

SOURCES:

American Indian Women: A Research Guide, edited by Gretchen Bataille and Kathleen Sands, New York, Garland Publishing, 1991.

Biographical Dictionary of Indians of the Americas, Newport Beach, California, American Indian Publications, 1983.

Contemporary American Indian Leaders, edited by Marion Gridley, New York, Dodd, Mead and Company, 1972.

Native American Women, edited by Gretchen M. Bataille, New York, Garland Publishing, 1993.

Native North American Almanac, edited by Duane Champagne, Detroit, Gale Research, 1994.

Vogel, Virgil, *This Country Was Ours,* New York, Harper and Row, 1972.

Washburn, Wilcomb, *Red Man's Land, White Man's Law,* New York, Charles Scribner's Sons, 1971.

—Sketch by Cynthia R. Kasee

James Welch
1940-
Blackfeet/Gros Ventre novelist

James Welch has been hailed as one of the foremost Native American writers of his time, although his career as a novelist was not his first choice. A contemporary of authors N. Scott Momaday, Leslie Marmon Silko, and Gerald Vizenor, Welch had a variety of different jobs before settling into writing. He has worked for the forest service, been a laborer and a firefighter, and at one point was a counselor for Upward Bound. He is highly visible as a Native American writer because his themes revolve around the controversial issue of Indian acculturation. There has been a significant amount of critical interest in the origins of Welch's images, and in his opinions about how Indians should deal with assimilation in light of the U.S. government's historical attempts to exterminate indigenous peoples. Welch was born in 1940 on the Blackfeet Indian Reservation in Browning, Montana—a reservation belonging to the southern branch of the Blackfeet band. Another name for this group is Piegan or Pikuni. Welch's heritage can also be traced to Gros Ventres tribal members from the Fort Belknap Indian Reservation. He draws upon the histories of both branches of his ancestry in developing his literary themes.

Welch occasionally teaches a contemporary American Indian literature course at Cornell University in New York. During a 1990 *Publishers Weekly* interview, Welch told Will Nixon that he had problems gathering materials for the course: "it's just a pain to get enough good novels by Indians to make the course as rich and varied as I want it to be.... I think Indians tend toward poetry instead. A lot of people have said that poetry more approximates the rhythms of their own traditions, such as songs. And Indians prefer to write poetry because they have something to say about their culture and society and it's harder to be political or polemical in fiction."

Welch began his own writing career as a poet. His first published collection was *Riding the Earthboy 40,* a volume which heavily foreshadowed in concept his later works. After 11 or 12 years of writing poetry, he began to branch out, producing his first novel in 1975. *Winter in the Blood,* he told Nixon, is a short piece made up of "scenes that are like prose poems, little chapters that are almost self-contained." It represented his first step from poetry toward epic writing, garnering him the attention of critics.

Groundwork of Welch's Writing

In a *MELUS* analysis of Welch's use of language, Charles G. Ballard points out that he employs "two surrealistic tendencies: the cryptic,... and the effort to somehow dredge up peculiar images from the unconscious." Ballard traces the influences upon Welch's writing, giving particular emphasis to the vision quest common to Native American culture and spirituality. Parallels of similar imagery dealing with characters, symbolic color, terrain, and the four directions are drawn between Welch's poem "Magic Fox," published in *Riding the Earthboy 40,* and the dream imagery found in a scene from *Winter in the Blood.*

In 1977, Peter G. Biedler organized a seminar on *Winter in the Blood* for the Modern Language Association's annual convention. Biedler has categorized critical interest in three major areas of the novel. First is Welch's use of imagery and the forms thereof in distance, motion, animals, and fish. The second critical interest is concerned with the untouched, unassimilated Native qualities of the work—how myth, ownership/property concepts, tribal tradition, heritage, history, and ancestry play a role. Third, Biedler contends there is critical interest in the novel as it represents human opportunity for identity development, spiritual growth, and the role of spiritual helpers/guides in these endeavors. In other words, critics are questioning whether there is something to be learned about the human experience from Native American culture and storytelling.

Others have gone on to explore some of Biedler's categorizations further, as with the subject of motion in John Purdy's article for the *American Indian Quarterly.* Purdy explains that it is the tendency of Native authors to "employ, in various ways and to varying degrees, ancient verbal literary traditions that reflect long-standing associations with specific landscapes." Purdy concludes that it is the "preponderance of minute, detailed descriptions of motion in relation to setting" that sets Indian writing apart.

Dimensional Aspects of Welch's Writing

Welch's historical novel, *Fools Crow,* published in 1986, tells the story of a small group of Blackfeet Indians who escape from the Marias River massacre of 1870. He was inspired to write the novel by his great-grandmother, who was wounded at the massacre. Purdy focuses on Fools Crow as a "book of movement" in two ways: first, as an instrument for exploring the dynamic link between individual relational movements, as well as movements within a community; and second, as it illustrates and "explains the relationship between actions and movements, between the mundane performance of the 'everyday occurrences, the prosaic and undramatic elements of small things' and the epic, such as journey or vision quest." Exploration defines appropriateness of behavior vis-a-vis acting within the balance between self and others. When Purdy defines the novel as a "book of movement," he is not only addressing the particulars along with the individual, he is drawing attention to the whole, the community, that is mysteriously enlivened as an entity greater than the sum of its parts. When the whole is greater than the sum of its parts, it encompasses dimensions beyond time and space. Welch has tapped into this in his layering of narrative voice.

Summing up Welch's influence, Ballard writes: "The reputation of this Native American writer continues to grow and his work continues to challenge the reader, not only because it functions well in the western humanistic tradition but because it also offers specific details and insights into Indian life and thought." It is primarily the author's Gros Ventre and Blackfeet traditions which fuel the literary images Welch uses to breathe life into his stories. While *Winter in the Blood* utilizes the dream and vision quest imagery Welch is becoming known for, it, like its successors, also weaves an epic tale rooted in the mythology and folklore of Indian culture heroes and animal allies and guides. Welch addresses the plight of the modern Indian in light of personal and historical tragedy, moving progressively from an assimilated, European perspective into a more Indian point of view as the tales of his novels progress.

According to Robert F. Gish in the *American Indian Quarterly,* both *Winter in the Blood* and Welch's second novel, *The Death of Jim Loney,* represent examples of Welch's striving "to work backward into history, into the times and tellings of older generations, older ways of knowing and perceiving. He does this ... by juxtaposing stories of the present with stories of the past, the stories, histories, biographies, myths and dreams, of an individual—a central protagonist and center of consciousness—with the larger stories and histories of that protagonist's friends, family, and culture, all augmented and given texture by glimpses of the life stories of non-Native Americans who pass through the lives of Welch's protagonists as acquaintances."

Welch weaves layer upon layer, as do his critical readers in their myriad of interpretations, when he designs a three-dimensional written tapestry. Although critics have varying interpretations of Welch's work, there are those who appear to feel, as Gish does, that Welch has achieved a visual-aural synthesis of sorts; a literary transcendence by re-cultivating oral tradition in the novel genre. Gish calls Welch's third highly praised novel, *Fools Crow,* "a masterwork of linguistic and narrative transporting, an affirmation of the power of the word—the word as medicine ... and the absolute necessity for an individual, a family, and a culture not only to rely on but to identify itself, know its very dreaming, becoming, and ending in and through storytelling and myth."

Most critics agree that Welch's novels are successively maturing along lines of the protagonist's personal growth and dealings with (modern) communal re-integration. *The Indian Lawyer,* his fourth novel, was inspired by a ten-year board membership with the local parole commission. The protagonist, struggling (as all Welch's protagonists have) with his Indian identity, finds his cultural self in his relationship to the land. Far from being the despairing loner Welch's protagonists have been, the Saab-driving main character of this book is as assimilated and "successful" as the American dream could possibly envision him. There is one problem, his Indian consciousness can not be completely erased—it refuses to forget or to become extinct. From there Welch unravels the story. Reviewer Gary Davenport of the *Sewanee Review* found the plot for Welch's fourth novel "neatly tailored to his thematic concerns."

The Indian Lawyer, like its predecessors, is a quest for the self and for community. It is an odyssey, fashioned by everyday encounters, formed by everyday dramas made all the more dimensional by the warp and weave of ancestral ties—ties which Welch's work has a knack for presenting simultaneously in the past, present, and future. These are the qualities which have brought him to the forefront of cultural and political arenas of dialogue, and have put his writing at the forefront of Indian authorship.

SELECTED WRITINGS BY WELCH:

Riding the Earthboy 40: Poems, New York, Harper & Row, 1971.
Winter in the Blood, New York, Harper & Row, 1975.
The Death of Jim Loney, New York, Harper & Row, 1979.
Fools Crow, New York, Penguin Books, 1987.
The Indian Lawyer, New York, Norton, 1990.

SOURCES:

Books

Native North American Almanac, edited by Duane Champagne, Detroit, Gale Research, 1994; 1186-1187.

Velie, Alan R., *Four American Indian Literary Masters: N. Scott Momaday, James Welch, Leslie Marmon Silko, and Gerald Vizenor,* Norman, University of Oklahoma Press, 1982.

Periodicals

Ballard, Charles G., "The Theme of the Helping Hand in *Winter in the Blood,*" *MELUS,* 17, spring 1991-1992; 63-74.
Barry, Nora, "'A Myth to Be Alive': James Welch's *Fools Crow,*" *MELUS,* 17, spring 1991-1992; 3-20.
Davenport, Gary, review of *The Indian Lawyer, Sewanee Review,* 100, spring 1992; 323-330.
Franks, Kenny A., *review of Four American Indian Literary Masters: N. Scott Momaday, James Welch, Leslie Marmon Silko, and Gerald Vizenor, Western Historical Quarterly,* 15, January 1984; 86-87.
Gish, Robert F., review of *The Indian Lawyer, American Indian Quarterly,* 15, summer 1991; 369-374.
Gish, "Word Medicine: Storytelling and Magic Realism in James Welch's *Fools Crow,*" *American Indian Quarterly,* 14, fall 1990; 349-350.
McFarland, Ron, "'The End' in James Welch's Novels," *American Indian Quarterly,* 17, summer 1993; 319-327.
Nixon, Will, *Publishers Weekly,* 237, October 5, 1990; 81-82.
Purdy, John, "'He Was Going Along': Motion in the Novels of James Welch," *American Indian Quarterly,* 14, spring 1990; 133-145.
Thackeray, William W., "Animal Allies and Transformers of *Winter in the Blood,*" *MELUS,* 12, spring 1985; 37-64.
Warrior, Robert Allen, review of *The Indian Lawyer, Christianity and Crisis,* 51, March 18, 1991; 94-96.
Wydeven, Joseph J., review of *Four American Indian Literary Masters: N. Scott Momaday, James Welch, Leslie Marmon Silko, and Gerald Vizenor, Modern Fiction Studies,* 29, summer 1983; 322-323.

—Sketch by Brett A. Lealand

Floyd Westerman
1936-
Sisseton-Wahpeton Dakota Sioux songwriter and performer

Floyd Red Crow Westerman was born on the Sisseton-Wahpeton Reservation in northeast South Dakota. After several years at an Indian boarding school, he began supporting himself by entertaining others. He was originally labeled as a country folksinger, but has become most well-

Floyd Westerman

known for his role as Ten Bears in the film *Dances with Wolves.* Through his songs and acting roles, he translates traditional values for modern life.

His first album, *Custer Died for Your Sins,* was released shortly after publication of the book of the same title by Vine Deloria, Jr. The lyrics reflect the mood of contemporary Indian pride and some of the bitterness toward "experts" who try to explain Indian affairs. Among the song titles on this album are "Red, White and Black," "Here Come the Anthros," "B.I.A.," "Missionaries," and "They Didn't Listen." As Vine Deloria, Jr., stated on the album cover, "Floyd was born to sing these songs and they were written in search of a singer like Floyd. Like the *eyapaha,* the cryer of old who summoned the camp to action, Floyd will provide the spark, the badly needed war songs that thousands have waited to hear."

Westerman's second album, *The Land is Your Mother,* continued the lament. Titles include "How Long Have You Been Blind," "B.I.A. Blues," "Quiet Desperation," and "Wounded Knee." As bitter and full of feeling as the songs may be, however, Westerman always performs with a sense of good humor and wit, softening the blow of the lyrics. In a performance at the University of South Dakota, Westerman called out good naturedly to an anthropology professor in the audience that "this song is dedicated to you" when he sang a revised version of "Here Come the Anthros" updated to include the reburial issue.

Westerman has performed at concerts throughout North, South and Central America and Europe, often in support of human rights benefits. His appearances have included singing and songwriting collaborations with Jackson Brown, Willie Nelson, Joni Mitchell and Kris Kristofferson. One of his recent worldwide tours was in concert with Sting and the Chief of the Kayapo Indian Nation from the Zingu River in the Amazon. This tour was for the benefit of the Rain Forest Foundation Project. He has had audiences with Pope John Paul II, Prince Charles and France's President Mitterand. He is strongly committed to preservation of the rain forests and has also been involved in the recognition of treaty rights, land issues and religious freedom of Indians in the United States.

Westerman has made over 55 trips to Europe. In 1994 he was invited to Germany to participate in a health symposium where experts were combining their knowledge of stress, society and spirituality to discuss whole body health treatment. Because of his role in *Dances with Wolves,* Westerman was also invited to appear on several television shows and to perform his music.

Becomes an Actor

In recent years Westerman has had several acting roles, playing a character with his own name of Red Crow in the 1989 film *Renegade,* a Chippewa elder in Clearcut, and as Walker's uncle in the television series *Walker, Texas Ranger.* He played the role of Jim Morrison's spirit guide in the movie The Doors, and he has guest-starred on several television series, including "MacGyver," "Hardball," and the ABC movie *Son of the Morning Star.* He acted in two of Ted Turner's ten-part television series, "Broken Chain" and *Lakota Woman.* In 1994 he had a role in the film *Siringo.* He also has narrated video productions, among them *The Dakota Conflict* and *Legends of the West.*

Westerman's most visible acting role, that of Ten Bears in *Dances with Wolves,* earned him an interview in the German periodical *W & M (Weiterbildung und Medien),* in which he stated that the movie helped to change Indian stereotyping by showing that Indian actors can act and that it is not necessary to use non-Indian actors to portray Indian characters. He felt it was unfortunate that Hollywood generally has a tendency to portray Indians as savages. Westerman accused Americans of not being as interested in learning about Indians as Europeans are. He praised the media for trying to publicize the Indian point of view on the interpretation of Columbus Day and on the issue of Indian mascots for sports teams. "I think a lot because *Dances with Wolves* has made the media pay more attention to Indians— to the Indian point of view. They're listening to what the Indians say now. They'll put it out like that in front of the American people.... One by one the issues come to the surface."

When asked about independence for Indian nations, Westerman commented that Indian people are beginning to think about sovereignty. "I'm one of those who feel very strongly about sovereignty, and I think there's a tendency in the world for world leaders to see the possibility that people can govern themselves better without big central government." He stressed that sovereignty is dependent on two things: language and spirituality. Indian nations who understand that will succeed.

In an interview with Karen Zimmerman, Westerman spoke further on the image of Indians in present films and television series. He stated that finding good movies like *Dances with Wolves* is difficult. He criticized the film *Geronimo* for not giving the character of Geronimo a chance to explain the Indian point of view. "When Geronimo accuses the General of killing women and children, the General said 'You killed them, too.' Wes Studi should have been able to say 'We were defending our land; we are freedom fighters.'" Westerman also explained that although many of the films present a historical viewpoint, the view is from the official state or national viewpoint, not necessarily from the Indian viewpoint.

Westerman said that he enjoys acting, and is impressed by the treatment he is given as an actor. However, he said that Indians actors have a responsibility to the roles that they play. "They need to make a more sensitive and accurate portrayal of true stories. Every Indian actor is involved in that responsibility." The next step for Hollywood, in Westerman's view, is to have Indian producers and directors for feature films. He would like to direct a film about the last days of Sitting Bull, showing the historic leader as a Holy Man, rather than as the "redskin savage" of newspaper headlines. As he told Zimmerman, "I would like to emphasize the last year of Sitting Bull's life, the personal and intimate thoughts that he had. It would be like the Ten Bears role; he had personal thoughts about the white man coming."

SOURCES:

Books

Biographical Dictionary of Indians of the Americas, second edition, Newport Beach, California, American Indian Publishers, 1991.

Paulson, T. Emogene, and Lloyd R. Moses, *Who's Who Among the Sioux,* Vermillion, Institute of Indian Studies, University of South Dakota, 1988; 262.

Periodicals

"Americans Don't Know Anything About Indians: Interview with the Indian Actor Floyd Red Crow Westerman" (reprinted from *W & M* [*Weiterbildung und Medien*]), Adult Education and Development, 38, 1992; 119-127.

"Movie Features Dakotans," *South Dakota,* 6:6, 1991; 11.

Other

Westerman, Floyd, interview with Karen Zimmerman conducted July 25, 1994.

—*Sketch by Karen P. Zimmerman*

Roberta Hill Whiteman
1947-
Oneida poet and educator

Roberta Hill Whiteman, an Oneida of Wisconsin, is an accomplished contemporary Native American poet, best known for her book *Star Quilt,* published in 1984. She was born February 17, 1947, in Baraboo, Wisconsin, to Eleanor Smith and Charles Allen Hill.

Early Years and Education

Whiteman's mother died when she was very young. As she grew up, her family moved back and forth between two Wisconsin cities, Oneida and Green Bay. Whiteman characterized her childhood as pretty tough. "I was happy part of the time and I was really sad part of the time," she told Joseph Bruchac in *Survival This Way: Interviews with Native American Poets.* Several early experiences guided her toward her future as a poet. Her grandmother often recited poetry, told stories, and read out loud to her. After her grandmother died, Whiteman liked to sit underneath the dining-room table reading her grandmother's huge leather-bound books of poetry—Wordsworth and Shakespeare. Whiteman's father, a musician and teacher, insisted that music be part of her life and she grew to love it along with dance. Nurtured by these influences, her passion for language, pattern and rhythm blossomed.

Though Whiteman kept journals and wrote poems as a child, she pursued a pre-medical degree at the University of Wisconsin because her father expected her to become a doctor like her grandmother. About 1970, when her father died, she realized that she did not have the mathematical ability needed to pass college chemistry and majored instead in creative writing and psychology. She received her B.A. at the University of Wisconsin and when she could not find a job, she went to Montana for her M.F.A., which she received in 1973. There she studied under Richard Hugo, a former student of Theodore Roethke, who helped her recognize her love for writing as a legitimate basis for her life's work.

Becomes a Poet

To develop as a poet, Whiteman read continuously and talked with scores of poets. "Other Indian writers really helped, to sit and just be able to *talk* with them, see what they're doing and see insights into things," she told Bruchac, mentioning Lance Henson, Leslie Silko and fellow student James Welch as some of the many Native American poets she met. Richard Hugo, influenced her poetic method, Kenneth Lincoln pointed out in *Native American Women,* "by tutoring the patterned natural rhythms of the blank verse line, the essentially iambic foot of Euro-American traditional verse." Hugo also helped her, Ken McCullough stated in *North Dakota Quarterly,* "to discover the magic syllables

Roberta Hill Whiteman

tration by her artist husband which captures the fluidity of Whiteman's images and the link between a season and a direction (i.e., autumn for west, winter for north).

Her poems speak to her Oneida roots. In "In the Longhouse: Oneida Museum," she delineates her Oneida heritage—its history, traditions, and dispossession. The Oneida people, once concentrated on land which became New York, scattered to four states and two Canadian provinces. Whiteman felt this dispossession personally as a child, but could not put it into words. Other poems such as "For Heather, Entering Kindergarten" and "Love, the Final Healer," written for her son Jacob, address her life as a woman and mother.

Throughout her poetry, Whiteman's eloquence with detail stands out as one of her signatures. "She discovers the emotional force within the exquisite detail," fellow student Welch said of her work in the cover copy of *Star Quilt.* In Whiteman's poem "Currents," a poem dedicated to her mother-in-law, Eva Whiteman, Ken McCullough noted that her handling of domestic detail "renders them exquisite ... through her eyes, her vision." Discussing her poem "Star Quilt" with Bruchac, Whiteman alluded to her visual acumen, "I do, though feel this intense love for looking at things, earth and sky and people and I think it does come through."

Another of her signatures, according to McCullough, is "a kind of ethereal sweetness. Words can be and sometimes must be swords, but the words of this poet serve, instead, to bind open wounds which have been left untended for many years." Likewise Carolyn Forché stated in the foreword to *Star Quilt,* "There is spiritual guidance here uncommon in contemporary letters." Whiteman observed in an interview with Bruchac, that her writing has been "in some way to just look at life, to appreciate life, its mystery." It is, perhaps, her ability to appreciate even jarring realities with serenity that infuses her writing with grace.

in the English (American) language, and how to sing them." In the *Third Woman: Minority Woman Writers of the United States,* Whiteman said of her writings, "I work as hard (consciously, unconsciously) as I can to hear the music of the voice that speaks through me. Perhaps it is my thoughts, perhaps it is the music of what I can perceive around me. I sense that I am trying to regain an image of wholeness."

Her poems appeared first in literary magazines and then from the middle 1970s, in anthologies of prominent Native American poets. After leaving Montana, Whiteman worked as poet-in-residence in St. Paul, Minnesota, for the Poets-in-the-Schools Program and taught in Rosebud, South Dakota, atSinte Gleska College. In 1976, she returned to the Oneida of her childhood to teach. She also traveled to Arizona, Wyoming, South Dakota, Oklahoma, Montana, and Wisconsin to participate in Poets-in-the-Schools programs, finally settling in Eau Claire, Wisconsin, to teach American literature at the University of Wisconsin. In 1980 she married Arapaho artist Ernest Whiteman. Together they have three children, Jacob, Heather, and Melissa. In 1993 Whiteman took a leave from her position in Eau Claire to work on a doctorate in American Studies at the University of Minnesota.

The writing for Whiteman's book of poetry, Star Quilt, was supported, in part, by a National Endowment Fellowship grant; the plan for the book germinated for many years. "The collection itself is arranged in west, north, east, south, seasonal kinds of images," she told Bruchac, "not as categories, but where images kind of flow back and forth into each other." Each section of her book begins with an illus-

SELECTED WRITINGS BY WHITEMAN:

Star Quilt, Minneapolis, Holy Cow Press, 1984.

SOURCES:

Books

Bruchac, Joseph, "Massaging the Earth: An Interview with Roberta Hill Whiteman," in his *Survival This Way: Interviews with Native American Poets,* Tucson, Sun Tracks/University of Arizona Press, 1987; 323-335.
Carriers of the Dream Wheel: Contemporary Native American Poetry, edited by Duane Niatum, New York, Harper, 1975; 68.
Harper's Anthology of Twentieth Century Native American Poetry, edited by Duane Niatum, New York, Harper, 1988; 377.
Native American Women, edited by Gretchen M. Bataille, New York, Garland Publishing, 1993; 278-280.

That's What She Said: Contemporary Poetry and Fiction by Native American Women, edited by Rayna Green, Bloomington, Indiana University Press, 1984; 326.

The Third Woman: Minority Women Writers of the United States, edited by Dexter Fisher, Boston, Houghton Mifflin, 1980; 122.

Voices of the Rainbow: Contemporary Poetry by American Indians, edited by Kenneth Rosen, New York, Viking, 1975; 228.

Periodicals

McCullough, Ken, "Star Quilt as Mandala: An Assessment of the Poetry of Roberta Hill Whiteman," *North Dakota Quarterly,* 53, spring 1985; 194-203.

—*Sketch by Roberta Kaplan Gelatt*

Wilson, Jack
See Wovoka

Sarah Winnemucca

Sarah Winnemucca
1844(?)-1891
Northern Paiute interpreter, lecturer and diplomat
Also known as Thocmetony ["Shell Flower"]

Sarah Winnemucca was a skilled interpreter, an Army scout, a well-known lecturer, a teacher, and the first Indian woman to publish a book. She was born near Humboldt Lake about 1844 in the part of Utah Territory that later became Nevada, the fourth child of her father, Chief Winnemucca, called Old Winnemucca and mother, Tuboitonie. They named her Thocmetony, meaning Shell Flower. Later she took the name Sarah, a name she kept the rest of her life. The homelands of the Northern Paiutes extended over parts of present day Idaho, Nevada and Oregon. Over those lands, the Paiutes hunted, gathered seeds (especially pine nuts), and fished in the rivers and lakes. During Sarah's lifetime, however, they were crowded onto reservations and deprived of much of their land. Sarah became nationally known for her fight for her people's rights and for her struggle to keep the peace between her people and the white newcomers.

Sarah's own friendship may have been influenced by her maternal grandfather, the leader of the tribe. He was known as Truckee, from a Paiute word meaning "good" or "all right." The name was given to him by Captain Fremont when they met soon after Sarah was born. Truckee and 11 Paiutes went with Fremont to California to help fight Mexican influence there. They returned full of stories of the ways of white people. Truckee, impressed by Fremont and the culture he had been exposed to in California, told his people to welcome the "white brothers."

As more emigrants moved west, however, the Paiutes heard horror stories about the killing of Indians. They apparently also heard a garbled account of the Donner Party, who survived a winter trapped in the Sierra Nevadas by eating their dead. These stories terrified Sarah. Her fears were intensified by an experience she described in her book *Life Among the Piutes.* Truckee was in California, and Old Winnemucca had become chief. One morning, hearing that white men were coming, the entire tribe fled in terror. Tuboitonie, who was carrying a baby on her back and pulling Sarah by the hand, found that she couldn't keep up. She and another mother decided to hide their older children by partially burying them in the ground and arranging branches to shade their faces. "Oh, can any one imagine my feelings," Sarah says, "*buried alive,* thinking every minute that I was to be unburied and eaten up by the people that my grandfather loved so much?"

At nightfall, the mothers returned and dug up the girls. It was an experience Sarah never forgot. It was long before she would look at white people or forgive her grandfather for his love of them. Finding that the white men had set fire to the tribe's stores of food and that all their winter supply was gone, Chief Winnemucca could no longer agree with his father-in-law that the white men were his "brothers."

Sarah's distrust of white folk lasted for some time. In the spring of 1850, Truckee traveled again to California, taking 50 people, including Tuboitonie and her children. Carrying a letter of commendation given him by Fremont, Truckee was able to get friendly receptions and occasional gifts of food or clothing from the settlers they met. Sarah herself hid from the strangers, refusing to speak or to look at them. Her attitude changed, however, after she fell sick with poison oak and was nursed back to health by a white woman. Although she never came to believe as strongly as her grandfather in the goodness of the "white brothers," she did try to understand them and to learn about their customs, without losing touch with her own traditions.

Serves as Interpreter and Scout as the Wars Begin

Sarah showed an early facility for languages, learning English, Spanish, and several Indian languages during the time she spent in California. She also came in close contact with white people when she, her mother and her sisters started to work in the houses of white families. When Sarah was 13, she lived with her younger sister Elma in the home of Major William M. Ormsby, a trader. Ormsby's wife, Margaret, and their daughter taught the girls to sew and cook. They learned and became quite proficient at English, even began to learn to read and write.

As contacts between the whites and Indians increased, Sarah often served as interpreter for her father when he met with Indian agents, army officers and in inter-tribal councils. In 1875, she was hired as interpreter for the Indian agent S. B. (Sam) Parrish at Malheur Reservation, which had been established three years earlier. In 1868 Sarah served as interpreter at Camp McDermit, while her father and almost 500 of his followers lived at the camp, under the protection of Captain Jerome and the U.S. Army. Parrish and Jerome were two men that Sarah trusted, men she believed treated her people fairly.

Sarah served as scout, along with her brother, Natchez, while she was at Camp McDermit, but it was during the Bannock War in 1878 that she met her greatest challenge. On her way to Washington, D.C., where she hoped to get help for her people, she learned that the Bannock tribe was warring with the whites and that some Paiutes, her father among them, were being held by the Bannocks. On the morning of June 13, she left the Camp McDermit for the Bannock camp with two Paiutes, arriving at nightfall of the second day. Wrapped in a blanket, her hair unbraided so she wouldn't be recognized, she crept into the camp. There she found her father, her brother, Lee, and his wife, Mattie, among those held captive. They escaped during the night, but were soon pursued by the Bannocks. Sarah and her sister-in-law raced their horses to get help, arriving back at Sheep Ranch at 5:30 on June 15. She had ridden a distance of 223 miles. "It was," Sarah said, "the hardest work I ever did for the army."

Sarah was poorly rewarded for her hard work for the U.S. Army. Both she and Mattie served as scouts during the Bannock War. After the war, the Paiutes were to be returned to Malheur Reservation, but to Sarah's distress, they were ordered to be taken to Yakima Reservation on the other side of the Columbia River, a distance of about 350 miles. It was winter, and the Paiutes did not have adequate clothing. Many people died during the terrible trip, and others, including Mattie, died soon after.

Writes and Speaks Out for Her People

Over the years the situation worsened. Sarah sent messages, complaints and entreaties to anyone she thought might help. She traveled to San Francisco and spoke in great halls, telling of the mistreatment of her people by the Indian agents and by the government. She was labelled "The Princess Sarah" in the *San Francisco Chronicle* and her lecture was described as "unlike anything ever before heard in the civilized world—eloquent, pathetic, tragical at times; at others her quaint anecdotes, sarcasms and wonderful mimicry surprised the audience again and again into bursts of laughter and rounds of applause." News of her lectures reached Washington, and in 1880 she was invited to meet with the President. Together with Chief Winnemucca, and her brother Natchez, she met with Secretary of the Interior Carl Schurz and, very briefly, with President Rutherford B. Hayes. However, Sarah was not allowed to lecture or talk to reporters in Washington, and the small group were given promises that were not kept.

Elizabeth Palmer Peabody and her sister, Mary Peabody Mann, the widow of Horace Mann, helped arrange speaking engagements for Sarah in Boston and many other cities in the East. They encouraged her to write, as well as speak. She wrote many letters, at least one magazine article and a book. Her friends also encouraged Sarah in her dream to start an all-Indian school. Sarah had been an assistant teacher on the Malheur Reservation, even though her formal education was limited to three weeks at a Californian Catholic school. In 1884, she founded the Peabody School for Indian children near Lovelock, Nevada, on land that had been given to Natchez. It was to be a model school where Indian children would be taught their own language and culture as well as learning English. Unable to get government funding or approval, however, she had to close the school after four years.

Sarah's own life was cut short a few years later by disease. After brief marriages to First Lieutenant Edward Bartlett and to Joseph Satwaller, she married Lewis H. Hopkins in 1881. He traveled east with her when she went to lecture there. Hopkins died at their ranch at Lovelock on October 18, 1887 of tuberculosis. On October 16, 1891, Sarah died at the home of her sister Elma at Henry's Lake, Idaho, probably of tuberculosis as well. In his book *Famous Indian Chiefs I Have Known,* General Oliver Otis Howard said of Sarah's Army career, "She did our government great service, and if I could tell you but a tenth part of all she willingly did to help the white settlers and her own people to live peaceably together, I am sure you would think, as I do, that the name of Thocmetony should have a place beside the name of Pocahontas in the history of our country."

Although Sarah ended her life believing that she had failed to make the changes she worked for, she has not been forgotten. Her name is in most reference books about North American Indians. Many books have been written about her life and accomplishments, several especially for young people. The book she wrote in 1883, with the encouragement and editorial assistance of Mary Peabody Mann, *Life Among the Piutes: Their Wrongs and Claims,* was republished in 1969 and remains an important source book on the history and culture of the Paiutes. In Nevada, on the McDermit Indian Reservation, there is a historical marker, erected in 1971, honoring Sarah Winnemucca with the words "she was a believer in the brotherhood of mankind." The name of Sarah Winnemucca, as General Howard hoped, stands high among those Native Americans who have fought for the rights of their people.

SELECTED WRITINGS BY WINNEMUCCA:

Life Among the Piutes: Their Wrongs and Claims, edited by Mrs. Horace Mann, privately printed, 1883; reprinted, Chalfant Press, 1969.

"The Pah-Utes," *California: A Western Monthly Magazine,* September 1882; 252-256.

"The Way Agents Get Rich," in *Native American Testimony: A Chronicle of Indian-White Relations from Prophecy to the Present, 1492-1992,* edited by Peter Nabokov, with a foreword by Vine Deloria, Jr., Penguin Books, 1992.

SOURCES:

Books

American Indian Intellectuals, edited by Margot Liberty, West Publishing, 1976.

American Indian Women: A Guide to Research, edited by Gretchen M. Bataille and Kathleen M. Sands, New York, Garland Publishing, 1991.

Brumble, H. David, III, *American Indian Biography,* University of California Press, 1988.

Canfield, Gae Whitney, *Sarah Winnemucca of the Northern Paiutes,* University of Oklahoma Press, 1983.

Egan, Ferol, *Sand in a Whirlwind: The Paiute Indian War of 1860,* University of Nevada Press, 1985.

Gehm, Katherine, *Sarah Winnemucca: Most Extraordinary Woman of the Paiute Nation,* O'Sullivan Woodside & Co., 1975.

Gridley, Marion E., *American Indian Women,* Hawthorn, 1974.

Handbook of American Indians North of Mexico, edited by Frederick Webb Hodge, Pageant Books, 1959.

Heizer, Robert F., "Ethnographic Notes on the Northern Paiute of the Humboldt Sink, West Central Nevada, in *Languages and Cultures of Western North America,* edited by Earl H. Swanson, Jr., Idaho State University Press, 1970.

Hirschfelder, Arlene B., Mary Gloyne Byler, and Michael A. Dorris, *Guide to Research on North American Indians,* American Library Association, 1983.

Howard, O. O., *Famous Indian Chiefs I Have Known,* Century Co., 1908.

Kloss, Doris, *Sarah Winnemucca,* [Minneapolis], 1981.

Luchetti, Cathy, and Carol Olwell, *Women of the West,* Antelope Island Press, 1982.

Miluck, Nancy Christian, *Nevada, This is Our Land: A Survey from Prehistory to Present,* Dragon Enterprises, 1978.

Morrow, Mary Frances, *Sarah Winnemucca,* Steck-Vaughn, 1992.

Notable American Women 1607-1950: A Biographical Dictionary, edited by Edward T. James, Janet Wilson James, and Paul S. Boyer, Belknap Press/Harvard University Press, 1974.

Peabody, Elizabeth P., *The Piutes: Second Report of the Model School of Sarah Winnemucca,* John Wilcox & Son, 1887.

Peabody, Elizabeth P., *Sarah Winnemucca's Practical Solution of the Indian Problem,* John Wilcox & Son, 1886.

Scordato, Ellen, *Sarah Winnemucca: Northern Paiute Writer and Diplomat,* Chelsea House, 1992.

Waltrip, Lela, and Rufus Waltrip, *Indian Women,* David McKay, 1964.

Periodicals

Brimlow, George F., "The Life of Sarah Winnemucca: The Formative Years," *Oregon Historical Quarterly,* June 1952; 103-134.

Egan, Ferol, "Here in Nevada a Terrible Crime," *American Heritage,* June 1970; 93-100.

Egan, Ferol, "Victims of Justice: Tragedy at Carson City," *American West,* September 1972; 42-47, 60-61.

Stewart, Patricia, "Sarah Winnemucca," *Nevada Historical Society Quarterly,* winter 1971; 23-28.

—Sketch by Blanche Cox Clegg

Elizabeth Woody
1959-
Wasco/Navajo poet, writer, artist, and photographer

Elizabeth Woody was born in Ganado, Arizona, in 1959. As a child, she lived in Madras, Oregon, 14 miles from the Warm Springs Reservation, about 160 miles from the Columbia River. Her maternal grandparents had been born on that reservation, the first of several generations of the family to live there, far from the river and the salmon pathways that had been so important to the Plateau people for centuries.

Though the adults spoke Native dialects, the children were encouraged to learn English; and Woody worked for true expression through that language. She studied creative writing at the Institute of American Indian Arts at Santa Fe, where she was encouraged and guided by Joy Harjo and Phil Foss. She also studied at Portland State University and graduated from Evergreen State College in Washington. She won a northwest poetry contest in 1985 and was juried into the Literary Readings of the National Women's Studies Conference at the University of Washington.

Receives Award for First Book

In 1988, Woody published her first book of poetry, *Hand into Stone,* illustrated by Jaune Quick-to-See Smith. Changes to the Columbia River and the loss of fishing rights of the Plateau people were central themes in the book. She also wrote of the dangers posed by nuclear energy, voiced her concern for the environment, and cried out against the oppression of Native peoples. *Hand into Stone* won the American Book Award from the Before Columbus Foundation, bringing Woody national recognition. In September of 1992, Woody was one of five Native American poets participating in the Geraldine R. Dodge Poetry Festival in New Jersey, said to be the largest poetry festival in North America.

From her grandfather, Lewis Pitt, Sr., who spoke several Sahaptin and Chinookan dialects, Woody came to have great respect for language, to see more closely the connections between culture and language, and to better understand the difficulty of expressing the passions of her people through a different language, through English. "Eradication of the native languages through colonization," says Woody, "has impacted massive stores of knowledge. Losing the indigenous language meant that I had to become proficient in a language entirely different from that of my Sahaptin-Wasco Dine ancestors."

This growing concern for the languages and culture of her people has begun to permeate her work. In "Translation of Blood Quantum," a poem published in *Chicago Review* in 1993, Woody speaks for the rights of the Confederated Tribes at Oregon, under the "Declaration of Sovereignty" of 1992, "to conduct our business in respect of our ancient law and languages."

From her grandmother, Elizabeth Thompson Pitt, Woody has begun to seek the skills and knowledge that will bring her nearer to the culture of her people. She has learned to weave root bags and to bead, taking in, through the movements of her fingers, strength, a greater sense of belonging, a return to tradition. And always there are the stories that fill Woody's imagination and fire her poetry. "We listen, absorbed in the story by blood, by association," Woody says, "and the memory in its own language tells the story well." In a short story called "HomeCooking," Woody talks about the magic of the stories of old times. "The magic is this soft rumble of blood-life, laughter, our great heart under the land." She also speaks of home, of grandparents, of the wonderful everyday quality of life.

Woody's poems, short stories, and essays have appeared in many anthologies and journals, including *Talking Leaves, A Circle of Nations, Reinventing the Enemy's Language, Dancing on the Rim of the World, Songs from This Earth on Turtle's Back, Returning the Gift, Greenfield Review, Tyuonyi, The Native American Today, Chicago Review, Ploughshares,* and *Image,* a Seattle Arts Commission project. Also a visual artist and photographer, Woody's art has been featured in exhibits, and she has worked closely with well-known Northwest artist, Lillian Pitt. Her second book, *Luminaries of the Humble,* was published in 1994.

Co-founder of the Northwest Native American Writers Association, Woody lives in Portland, Oregon, where she continues to write and speak out for Native peoples. She also speaks of a hope for the future, for unity. "To thrive," she says, "is to learn how to respect others and how to act with courage, humility, generosity and compassion." Simon Ortiz says of her, "There is no greater vision than the poetic insight that Woody articulates with amazing lucidity and the gently skilled, yet sturdy, language of her poems. This gift of language, honed with compassion, wisdom, and love, offers the wonderfully affirming mythic power of her Native heritage."

SELECTED WRITINGS BY WOODY:

Hand Into Stone, illustrations by Jaune Quick-to-See Smith, New York, Contact II Publications, 1988.
Luminaries of the Humble, Tucson, University of Arizona Press, 1994.

SOURCES:

Books

Lerner, Andrea, "Woody, Elizabeth," in *Native American Women,* edited by Gretchen M. Bataille, New York, Garland Publishing, 1993; 285-286.
We the Human Beings: 27 Contemporary Native American Artists; An Exhibition, Wooster, Ohio, The Museum, 1992.
Woody, Elizabeth, "By Our Hand, Through the Memory, The House is More than Home," in *A Circle of Nations: Voices and Visions of American Indians,* Hillsboro, Oregon, Beyond Words Publishing, 1993.
Woody, Elizabeth, "HomeCooking," in *Talking Leaves: Contemporary Native American Short Stories,* edited by Craig Lesley and Katheryn Stavrakis, New York, Dell, 1991; 365-371, 384-385.

Periodicals

Emblem, Mary L., "New Jersey Guide," *New York Times,* September 13, 1992; Section 13NJ, 7.
Woody, Elizabeth, "Translation of Blood Quantum," *Chicago Review,* 39:3/4, 1993; 89-90, 312.

—*Sketch by Blanche Cox Clegg*

Rosita Worl
Contemporary
Tlingit tribal leader, anthropologist, activist, and educator

Also known as Yeidiklatsokw

Rosita Worl is a research anthropologist in her own firm and with the Smithsonian Institution's National Museum of Natural History. Her scientific work has emphasized Alaska Native subsistence activities and the impacts of industrial development on Native communities. Her research and writing on subsistence economies has contributed to the public awareness of Tlingit and other Alaska Native cultures. She also helped to develop the first Native Policy adopted by the State of Alaska. With her three children she founded the *Alaska Native News* and was publisher and editor from 1982 to 1987. She was awarded the Gloria Steinem Award for Empowerment in 1989.

Mother and Extended Family Important in Her Life

Worl's Tlingit name is Yeidiklatsokw. She is an Eagle and a member of the Chilkat Thunderbird clan from Klukwan and the Thunderbird House and House Lowered from the Sun. She is a child of the Sockeye clan from Chilkoot. Worl was born in Petersburg, Alaska and raised in Haines, Juneau, and Petersburg. Her traditional home village of Klukwan is located in southeast Alaska, on the Chilkat River. Brought up in a large, traditional family, she credits much of her early education to her grandparents, her mother, and other Tlingit elders. When Worl was very young she was taken by social services to the mission school in Haines, Alaska, staying at the boarding school for three years. After returning home Worl attended public school and learned Tlingit traditions from her mother and grandparents. Her mother, Helen Marks Lanott, a union organizer in southeast Alaska's salmon canneries, was a major influence on Worl's life. Through her example of devoting herself to improving the working conditions of southeast Alaska Natives, Worl's mother instilled a commitment to social justice in her young daughter. As a young woman Worl worked with her mother in the canneries, learning the intricacies of union organizing. She also worked as a commercial fisherman during this period. Another of Worl's Tlingit mentors was the lawyer and Alaska legislator, William Paul, the first Alaska Native lawyer and one of the people responsible for the remarkable stability of the Alaska Native Brotherhood. Paul is also considered the founder of the land claims effort in Alaska. Worl's grandfather, Austin Hammond has also been one of her mentors.

Worl graduated from Juneau High School and attended Alaska Methodist University, becoming interested in anthropology and graduating magna cum laude in 1972. She went to Harvard University, earned a master of science degree in social anthropology in 1975 and was awarded a fellowship from the Ford Foundation, pursuing postgraduate work from 1972 to 1977. Worl's professional experience has included service as research anthropologist and co-curator for the National Museum of Natural History's exhibition "Tlingit Clans and Corporations." From 1987 until 1989, she served as special staff assistant for Native affairs to Steve Cowper, governor of Alaska. She was also the Alaska Native specialist advisor to the Honorable Thomas Berger and the Alaska Native Review Commission. The commission investigated the impact of the Alaska Native Claims Settlement Act (ANCSA) on Alaska Natives. She was intimately involved in writing the commission's report which was published as Thomas R. Berger's *Village Journey,* in 1985.

Field Work Takes Her North

Worl's field work on Alaska's North Slope, the Beaufort Sea, the Clyde River in Canada's Northwest Territories, and in the Arctic villages of Barrow, Wainwright, and Kaktovik has required many hours under extremely difficult conditions—in small boats, on snow machines, and on foot. While conducting postgraduate work on Alaska's North Slope, Worl began her research on the impacts of oil development on Alaska Native cultures. During this period Worl also began working with the Innuit, northern Alaskan Eskimos. Her work with Innuit whalers included assisting them in their efforts to preserve their right to hunt whales, a traditional food source. Working with the Innuit led to an appointment on the Scientific Committee of the International Whaling Commission (IWC). Worl was also a delegate to the 1979 International Whaling Conference. While working with the Innuit and the IWC, she visited every whaling village in Alaska. The project also required spending two whaling seasons on St. Lawrence Island in the Bering Sea. Worl's work has brought her into contact with many fascinating and unique people in harsh environments. While working on Norton Sound's Golovin Bay, Worl met an Apache Indian who was herding reindeer on a shaggy little Icelandic pony.

After working and living in the far north, Worl moved to Anchorage, Alaska, where she worked as an assistant professor of anthropology at the University of Alaska. She has also been a lecturer in anthropology at Anchorage Community College. While living in Anchorage, Worl also worked for the Chilkat Institute, a corporation specializing in applied social science.

Worl was also involved in developing a statewide higher education program for Alaska, and served as chairperson of the Alaska Native Education Association. She served as the chairperson of the first Alaska Native Women's Statewide Caucus in 1977. That same year Worl was the Alaska state delegate to the International Women's Year Houston Conference. Worl belongs to the Alaska Native Brotherhood, founded in 1912 by 12 men and one woman, all of whom, except one Tsimshian, were Tlingits. She also belongs to the Alaska Native Sisterhood, established in 1923. These two organizations promote the social and civil welfare of southeast Alaska Natives and are two of the oldest and most stable Native organizations in the United States.

Worl has been one of the people responsible for the Tlingit's cultural renaissance. Personally involved in Tlingit culture, she actively participates in community organizations that promote cultural awareness of the Tlingit. A people of the northwest coast, the Tlingit retain strong clan identifications and continue the potlatch, their central ceremony of mutual exchange of property between clans. Worl was instrumental in developing the Marks Trail Tlingit Dancers, Tlingit youths who perform throughout Alaska. She has also served on the boards of the Klukwan Heritage Foundation, the Alaska State Arts Council, Traditional Native Arts Panel, and the Folk Arts Panel of the National Endowment for the Arts.

Worl's research and writing include projects on Tlingit subsistence practices and traditional property law, an area she began working in under the guidance of William Paul. She has also been studying the Russian colonial period in southeast Alaska and the Tlingit War of 1804, a subject she finds fascinating. She won the Alaska Press Club Award of Excellence for Return of Native Artifacts, 1987-1988. And she is an active member of the Keepers of the Treasures, Cultural Council of American Indians, Alaska Natives and Native Hawaiians. Worl has also served as vice chair of the Board of Trustees of the Sealaska Heritage Foundation, dedicated to preserving Tlingit culture and traditions.

After running as an independent, Worl was elected to the board of the Sealaska Corporation, the major Native economic institution in southeast Alaska. Since she has been on Sealaska's board, Worl has stressed the importance of including cultural values in the board's decision-making process. Her advocacy on behalf of Tlingit cultural traditions, combined with her membership on the Board of Directors of Sealaska Timber Corporation, has changed how the corporation does business. She has also worked with the Sealaska board in acquiring and/or retaining land for five Native villages, effecting at least 3,000 people. She has also been instrumental in developing Sealaska's environmental policy and is on the board of Northwest Environmental Watch. She has also served as the Juneau and Anchorage representative to the Central Council of the Tlingit and Haida Indian Tribes of Alaska, the governing body of the Tlingit and Haida Indians in southeast Alaska. She is presently serving as the Tlingit and Haida Central Council Business and Economic Development Council chairperson. Worl's many board memberships and her community activism reflect her concerns for Alaska Native cultures, Alaska's rural economies, and the Alaskan environment. She continues her lifelong work while serving on the boards of the Alaska Federation of Natives, and the State of Alaska Raven Commission. In the past she has also been a board member of the Prince William Sound Science Center, the National Science Foundation Polar Programs Committee, and the National Quality Review Board of the Exxon Oil Spill Scientific Committee.

Worl has published and presented numerous papers, book reviews, and articles. One example of her work, "History of Southeastern Alaska Since 1867" is included in the *Handbook of North American Indians, Volume 7, Northwest Coast,* published by the Smithsonian Institution Press. Worl's work as a research anthropologist, writer, and social activist reflects years of personal experience and academic knowledge of Alaska Native cultures and the Great Land, Alaska.

Besides her exhausting professional schedule, community development work, and participation in Tlingit cultural activities, Worl enjoys travel and horseback riding. When contributor Michael F. Turek asked Worl where she finds time for her many interests, she replied, "I require very little sleep."

SOURCES:

Books

Berger, Thomas R., *Village Journey: The Report of the Alaska Native Review Commission,* New York, Hill and Wang, 1985.
Native North American Almanac, edited by Duane Champagne, Detroit, Gale Research, 1994; 1192.
Worl, Rosita, "History of Southeastern Alaska Since 1867," in *Handbook of North American Indians,* edited by Wayne Suttles, Smithsonian Institution, 1990; 149-159.

Other

Worl, Rosita, interview with Michael F. Turek conducted June 27, 1994.

—Sketch by Michael F. Turek

Wovoka
1856(?)-1932
Numu (Northern Paiute) spiritual leader
Also known as Jack Wilson

Based on a personal vision, Wovoka created the Ghost Dance religion of the late 1880s. A distorted interpretation of his beliefs and teachings was a contributing factor in the events leading to the Wounded Knee Massacre in late December of 1890. Wovoka's impact on the local Paiute people, and Native Americans throughout the West, continued beyond his death in 1932.

Until 1990 the documentation about Wovoka's life was scattered, and he was the subject of both speculation and misrepresentation. He was considered to have little importance after 1890. The only general account of his life was Paul Bailey's 1957 biography, which leaves the reader

Wovoka (left) with Tim McCoy

with the impression that Wovoka was a benign huckster. However, the meaning and effects of his life are much more complex. Key primary sources and a biographical summary are provided in *Wovoka and the Ghost Dance* by Michael Hittman, a Long Island University anthropologist. Hittman began studying the Yerington Paiute Tribe of Nevada in 1965, and the source book, completed 25 years later, is an extraordinary compilation (over 300 pages) of commentary and sources, including original manuscripts by personal acquaintances of Wovoka, photographs, newspaper accounts, government letters and reports, ghost dance songs, the views of other anthropologists, comments of surviving tribal members, and an extensive bibliography. Any serious study of the life of this famous prophet should start with this publication. According to Hittman, Wovoka was "a great man and a fake."

Wovoka was born about 1856 in Smith Valley or Mason Valley, Nevada, as one of four sons of Tavid, also known as Numo-tibo's, a well-known medicine man. (A link of Wovoka's father to an earlier Ghost Dance of 1870 in the region is unclear.) Both Wovoka's parents survived into the twentieth century. At about the age of 14, Wovoka was sent to live with and work for the Scotch-English family of David Wilson. During this period he acquired the names Jack Wilson and Wovoka, meaning "Wood Cutter."

The religious influences upon Wovoka were diverse. Wovoka was clearly affected by the religious values of the pious United Presbyterian family. Mr. Wilson read the Bible each day before work. He lived in a region where travelling preachers were common and Mormonism prevalent. There

is a possibility that Wovoka travelled to California and the Pacific Northwest, where he may have had contact with reservation prophets Smohalla and John Slocum.

At about the age of 20 he married Tumm, also known as Mary Wilson. They raised three daughters. At least two other children died.

The Ghost Dance Religion

Wovoka had promoted the Round Dance of the Numu people and was recognized as having some of his father's qualities as a mystic. A long-time acquaintance described the young Wovoka as "a tall, well proportioned man with piercing eyes, regular features, a deep voice and a calm and dignified mien." A local census agent referred to him as "intelligent," and a county newspaper added that he resembled "the late Henry Ward Beecher." Wovoka was known to be a temperate man during his entire life.

The turning point in Wovoka's life came in the late 1880s. In December of 1888 Wovoka may have been suffering from scarlet fever. He went into a coma for a period of two days. Observer Ed Dyer said, "His body was as stiff as a board." Because Wovoka's recovery had corresponded with the total eclipse of the sun on January 1, 1889, he was credited by the Numus for bringing back the sun, and thereby saving the universe.

After this apparent near death experience, Wovoka proclaimed that he had a spiritual vision with personal contact with God who gave him specific instructions to those still on earth. According to Wovoka, God told him of a transformation by the spring of 1891 when the deceased would again be alive, the game would again flourish, and the whites would vanish from the earth. He had also been instructed to share power with the President of the East, Benjamin Harrison. Until the time of the apocalypse, Wovoka counselled the living to work for the dominant population and attempt to live a morally pure life. The plan for the future could only be assured if believers followed the special patterns and messages of the Ghost Dance, which Wovoka taught his followers.

Local believers had already adopted a dependence on him to bring much needed rain. The national setting for Native Americans was such that the message of Wovoka would soon spread throughout the western territory of North America. Scott Peterson, author of Native American Prophesies, explains, "Wovoka's message of hope spread like wildfire among the demoralized tribes." Before long, representatives of over 30 tribes made a pilgrimage to visit Wovoka and learn the secrets of the Ghost Dance.

A Pyramid Lake agent dismissed Wovoka in November of 1890 as "a peaceable, industrious, but lunatic Pah-Ute," who "proclaimed himself an aboriginal Jesus who was to redeem the Red Man." Two weeks later, a writer for the *Walker Lake Bulletin* expressed concern about the 800 "sulky and impudent" male Indians who were participating in a dance at the Walker Lake Reservation. A day later the first known formal interview with Wovoka was conducted by United States Army Indian Scout Arthur I. Chapman. He had been sent to find the "Indian who impersonated Christ!" Chapman was not disturbed by what he found.

The most dynamic evidence of Wovoka's impact took place near the Badlands of South Dakota. Regional Sioux delegates, including Short Bull and Kicking Bear, returned with the message that wearing a Ghost Dance shirt would make warriors invulnerable to injury. Among those who accepted the assurance was the famous chief, Sitting Bull. The conditions were ideal for a message of deliverance in the Badlands: the buffalo were vanishing; the native residents were being pushed onto diminishing reservation lands as the designated area was opened to white settlement in 1989. The atmosphere is skillfully presented in a 1992 novel about the Lakota people, *Song of Wovoka,* which describes, "The end of their [Lakota] way of life seemed trivial compared to the very real possibility of extermination." The Lakota misinterpreted the teachings of Wovoka, namely of passivity and patience to wait for divine intervention, as a call to proactively rid the land of white settlers.

There emerged fear among white settlers and the military in the region. The uncertain future of the newly established states of North and South Dakota was being threatened by "the Ghost Dance craze." Memories of both the 1862 uprising in Minnesota and the debacle at Little Big Horn were still strong. Unable to enforce the ban of the Ghost Dance among the Lakota, Agent James McLaughlin of the Standing Rock Reservation in North Dakota ordered the arrest of Sitting Bull, a respected Lakota leader, intentionally disrupting a plan for Sitting Bull's arrest by old colleague Buffalo Bill Cody, who would have secured the arrest without harming Sitting Bull. As reported by Indian scout Charles A. Eastman, on December 15, 1890, a protest broke out as soldiers ceased Sitting Bull, which resulted in gunfire killing Sitting Bull, six Indian defenders, and six Indian police.

A few days later a seriously ill Big Foot and his band were marching to a place of surrender on the Pine Ridge Reservation in South Dakota. An overwhelming force of 470 soldiers confronted them at Wounded Knee. In the process of a final disarmament, gunfire broke out. Over 200 Native Americans, many of them women and children, were killed. The next day, without ceremony, frozen bodies stripped of their Ghost Dance garments were tossed into a mass grave. For many this symbolized the end of resistance.

There is certainly no evidence that Wovoka intentionally promoted the type of confrontation that occurred at Wounded Knee. He later referred to his idea of an impenetrable shirt as a "joke." His associate Ed Dyer evaluated the situation: "I was thoroughly convinced that Jack Wilson had at no time attempted deliberately to stir up trouble. He never advocated violence. Violence was contrary to his very nature. Others seized upon his prophecies and stunts, and made more of them than he intended ... in a way, once started, he was riding a tiger. It was difficult to dismount."

Within a few days of the atrocities at Wounded Knee, the local newspapers in Wovoka's region expressed concern

about the fact that there were "within the radius of 40 miles ... 1,000 able-bodied bucks, well armed." The Paiutes were getting "very saucy," claiming that "pretty soon they will own stores and ranches and houses ... that county all belonged to them once, and that pretty soon they will take the farms and horses away from the white man." Government sources also expressed concern. Acknowledging that "the Messiah Craze" was "headquartered" in Nevada, Frank Campbell wrote to the Commissioner of Indian Affairs on September 5, 1891: "The cause of its spreading so generally among Indians is the hope that these people have that some power greater than themselves may arrest and crush the oncoming flood of civilization that is destined soon to overwhelm them."

A month later, C. C. Warner, the openly antagonistic United States Indian Agent at Pyramid Lake, said he would not give Wovoka added "notoriety" by having him arrested. "I am pursuing the course with him of nonattention or silent ignoring." In December of 1892 he reported that although he found no local agitation, he "became suspicious that the 'Messiah' Jack Wilson was using an evil influence among foreign Indians which might result in a spring uprising among the Indians." His Farmer-In-Charge of the Walker River Reservation did a personal investigation. The following August, Warner announced that the Ghost Dance "fanaticism" was "a thing of the past" and that "the strongest weapon to be used against the movement is ridicule."

The Middle Years, 1890-1920

The role of Wovoka in the years after Wounded Knee has been generally overlooked. But it is clear that he did not fade into oblivion or hesitate to use his unusual fame and powers. An Indian Agent reported in June 1912 "that Jack Wilson is still held in reverence by Indians in various parts of the country, and he is still regarded by them as a great medicine man." Two years later he reinforced that statement, adding, "the influence of Jack Wilson the 'Messiah' of twenty five years ago is not dead." Indian Agent S.W. Pugh took a position quite different than that of C.C. Warner. When Jack Wilson sought an allotment on the reservation, he encouraged the Commissioner of Indian Affairs to help make it possible. "I would like to have him as he is still a power among his people and could be used to excellent advantage if here. He is a very intelligent Indian, and peaceably inclined apparently.... These people will follow him anywhere, and he has advanced ideas.

Although Wovoka had established a reputation as a strong, reliable worker as a young man, the reknown of the Ghost Dance phenomenon resulted in other uses of his time during the balance of his life. Attempts to bring him to both the World's Columbian Exposition in Chicago in 1893 and the Midwinter Fair in San Francisco in 1904 apparently failed, but he made trips to reservations in Wyoming, Montana, and Kansas, as well as the former Indian territory of Oklahoma. Some trips lasted as long as six months. He was showered with gifts and as much as $1,200 in cash on a single trip. In 1924, historian-actor Tim McCoy delivered

Wovoka by limousine to the set of a movie he was making In northern California. There he was treated with absolute reverence by Arapahos who had been hired for the film.

While at home Wovoka practiced another brisk form of enterprise. With the aid of his friend Ed Dyer and others he replied to numerous letters and requests for particular items, including thaumaturges and articles of clothing that he had worn. He had a fee for red paint, magpie feathers, etc. Conveniently, Dyer, his frequent secretary, was also a supplier. One of the most popular items was a hat that had been worn by "the Prophet." The usual price to a correspondent was $20. Dyer noted, "Naturally he was under the necessity of purchasing another from me at a considerable reduced figure. Although I did a steady and somewhat profitable business on hats, I envied him his mark-up which exceeded mine to a larcenous degree." Surprisingly, none of the response letters that Wovoka dictated have been found.

Despite his relative notoriety and financial security, Wovoka continued to live a simple life. As late as 1917, he was living in a two-room house built of rough boards. A visitor reported, "He lives purely Indian customs with very little household effects. They sleep on the floor and from all appearances also use the floor as their table for eating.'"

Wovoka also had an interesting peripheral role in the "political" world. As early as November 1890 an ex-Bureau of Indian Affairs employee suggested that an official invitation to Washington, D.C., for Wovoka and some of his followers "might have a tendency to quiet this craze." His early vision of course included the view that he would share national leadership with then President Benjamin Harrison. In 1916, the Mason Valley News reported that Wovoka was considering a visit to President Woodrow Wilson to help "terminate the murderous war in Europe" (Wovoka's grandson, following the prediction of his grandfather, became a pilot and died a hero in World War II.) In the 1920s, Wovoka was photographed at a Warren G. Harding rally. Perhaps the selection of Charles Curtis, a Sac-Fox from Kansas, as Vice President of the United States was a sign of the predicted millenium. Wovoka sent him a radiogram on March 3, 1929 stating, "We are glad that you are Vice President and we hope some day you will be President."

It is not possible to make an absolute judgement about the real talents of this Nevada mystic to determine which of his activities were the product of true inspiration and which were merely a display of skill. There are many accounts of his accomplishments varying from making prophesies that came true and returning people from the dead to predicting weather, making rain, surviving shots from guns, and producing ice in the middle of summer. His associate Ed Dyer reflected, it is "very human to believe what we want to believe."

Final Years

Anthropologist Michael Hittman explains most of Wovoka's shamatic practice and beliefs in the context of his native culture and concludes, "Wovoka appears to have maintained faith in his original revelation and supernatural powers to the very end." Ed Dyer commented later, "His prestige lasted to the end." His services as a medicine man were in demand until shortly before his own death on September 29, 1932, from enlarged prostate cystitis. His wife of over 50 years had died just one month before. Yerington Paiute tribal member Irene Thompson expressed a local Numu reaction, "When he died, many people thought Wovoka will come back again."

A Reno newspaper, although giving a lengthy account of his life, basically dismissed him as a fraud: "'Magic' worked with the aid of a bullet-proof vest; white men's pills and some good 'breaks' in the weather made him the most influential figure of his time among the Indians." Scott Peterson, in his 1990 study of Native American prophets, argues that if Wovoka had not "set a date for the apocalypse ... the Ghost Dance, with its vision of a brighter tomorrow, might still very well be a vital force in the world today."

In fact, elements of the Ghost Dance religion pervaded the practices of many tribes even after the tragedy of Wounded Knee. A form of the original dance is still performed by some Lakota today. Historian L. G. Moses describes Wovoka as "one of the most significant holy men ever to emerge among the Indians of North America." John Grim, in *The Encyclopedia of Religion,* gives the mystic credit for promoting "a pan-Indian identity." Hittman asserts that the key elements of "the Great Revelation" remain "honesty, the importance of hard work, the necessity of nonviolence, and the imperative of inter-racial harmony."

Wovoka's role as an "agitator" also remains significantly symbolic. In 1968, a former publisher of the *Mason Valley News* (which ignored the death of the famous resident in 1932) recalled Wovoka's stoical appearance in his elegant apparel on the streets of the small town: "Best human impression of a wooden Indian I ever seen. Oh, he was the only kind of individual that shook up the Army and Washington, D.C. Somebody today should." Five years later, after Dee Brown reminded Americans of the forgotten atrocity of American frontier history, members of the American Indian Movement occupied the original site of Wounded Knee and engaged U.S. forces in battle.

SOURCES:

Books

The American Indian Ghost Dance, 1870 and 1890, an Annotated Bibliography, compiled by Shelly Anne Osterreich, Westport, Connecticut, Greenwood Press, 1991.

Bailey, Paul, *Wovoka, The Indian Messiah,* Los Angeles, Westernlore Press, 1957.

Bailey, Paul, *Ghost Dance Messiah: The Jack Wilson Story,* Tucson, Westernnlore Press, 1970.

Brown, Dee, *Bury My Heart at Wounded Knee; An Indian History of the American West,* New York, Holt, Rinehart and Winston, 1970.

Eastman, Charles, *Indian Heroes and Great Chieftains,* Boston, Little, Brown, and Company, 1926.

Euler, Robert C., *The Paiute People,* Phoenix, Indian Tribal Series, 1972.

Forbes, Jack D., *Native Americans of California and Nevada,* Healdsburg, California, Naturegraph Publishers, 1968.

Forbes, Jack D., *Nevada Indians Speak,* Reno, University of Nevada Press, 1967.

Grim, John A., "Wovoka," in *The Encyclopedia of Religion,* New York, Macmillan, 1987; 486-487.

Hittman, Michael, *Wovoka and the Ghost Dance, a Source Book,* Carson City, Grace Dangberg Foundation, 1990.

Hultkantz, Ake, "Ghost Dance," in *Native American Religions: North America,* New York: Macmillan, 1989; 201-206.

Kehoe, Alice B., *The Ghost Dance: Ethnohistory and Revitalization,* New York, Holt, Rinehart and Winston, 1989.

Labarre, Weston, *The Ghost Dance: The Origins of Religion,* Garden City, New Jersey, 1970.

McCoy, Tim and Ronald McCoy, *Tim McCoy Remembers the West,* Lincoln, University of Nebraska Press, 1977.

Miller, David, *Ghost Dance,* New York, Duell, Sloan and Pearce, 1959.

Mooney, James, "The Ghost Dance Religion and the Sioux Outbreak of 1890," *Fourteenth Annual Report of the Bureau of Ethnology to the Smithsonian Instiution, 1892-1893,* Part 2, Washington, D.C., U.S. Government Printing Office, 1896; reprinted by University of Chicago Press, 1965.

Moses, L.G., *The Indian Man: A Biography of James Mooney,* Urbana, University of Illinois Press, 1984.

Murray, Earl, *Song of Wovoka,* New York, Tom Doherty Associates, 1992.

Peterson, Scott, *Native American Prophecies,* New York, Paragon House, 1990.

Utley, Robert M., *The Lance and the Shield, the Life and Times of Sitting Bull,* New York, Henry Holt, 1993.

Utley, Robert M., *The Last Days of the Sioux Nation,* New Haven, Yale University Press, 1963.

Periodicals

Fletcher, Alice C., "The Indian Messiah," *Journal of American Folklore,* 4, 1891; 57-60.

Hittman, Michael, "The 1870 Ghost Dance at the Walker River Reservation: A Reconstruction," *Ethnohistory* 20:3, 1973; 247-278.

Johnson, Dorothy M., "Ghost Dance: Last Hope of the Sioux," *Montana,* 6:3, July 1956; 42-50.

Logan, Brad, "The Ghost Dance among the Paiute: An Ethnohistorical View of the Documentary Evidence, 1889-1893," *Ethnohistory,* 27:3, 1980; 267-289.

Moses, L. G., "The Father Tells So! Wovoka, the Ghost Dance Prophet," *American Indian Quarterly,* 9:3, 1985; 335-357.

Moses, L. G., "Jack Wilson and the Indian Serrvice: The Response of the BIA to the Ghost Dance Prophet," *American Indian Quarterly,* 3:3, 1979; 295-316.

Overholt, Thomas W., "The Ghost Dance of 1890 and the Nature of the Prophetic Process," *Ethnohistory,* 21:1, 1974; 37-63.

Overholt, Thomas W., "Short Bull, Black Elk, Sword, and the 'Meaning' of the Ghost Dance," *Religion,* 8, 1978; 171-195.

Walker, Deward S., Jr., "New Light on the Prophet Dance Controversy," *Ethnohistory,* 16, 1969; 245-255.

—Sketch by Keith A. Winsell

Rosebud Yellow Robe
1907-1992
Dakota-Brulé/Hunkpapa Sioux author and performer

Rosebud Yellow Robe was born February 26, 1907, the oldest of three daughters born to the prominent family of Chauncey and Lily Yellow Robe. Throughout her life, she worked to introduce Native American culture and traditions to others. She was best known as a story-teller, repeating her father's stories to school children for over 20 years as the Director of the Indian Village project at Jones Beach on Long Island, New York.

Chauncey Yellow Robe was the son of the Brulé Sioux leader Tasinagi (Yellow Robe) and Tahcawin (Female Deer), who was Sitting Bull's niece. Yellow Robe's father was only six years old in 1876 when warriors returned from the Battle of the Little Big Horn, and he often told the story of watching the warriors return from battle. He was also one of the first Sioux students to attend Carlisle Indian School in Pennsylvania, and he spent his lifetime educating other Indian students. At the time of Yellow Robe's birth, her father was disciplinarian at the United States Indian School at Rapid City, South Dakota; her mother was a nurse. Yellow Robe's father instilled in his daughters a love of education, and each became successful in her own career.

Yellow Robe was educated in a one-room school house a mile from her home until she attended high school in Rapid City, South Dakota. As one of the first Indian students to attend the University of South Dakota in the late 1920s, Yellow Robe impressed the other students with her performances at Strollers, the annual student stage production. Her first national recognition came in 1927 when President Calvin Coolidge visited the Black Hills of South Dakota for the summer. On August 4, during a special ceremony, President Coolidge was named an honorary member of the Sioux tribe; Yellow Robe placed the Sioux warbonnet on Coolidge's head, and after her father's congratulatory statement, she then conducted President and Mrs. Coolidge back to their seats. Rosebud's grace and beauty were not lost on the press reporters, who commented on the "beautiful Indian maiden." One of the newspapermen covering the event, A. E. Seymour, married Rosebud within a few years, and they moved to New York.

Yellow Robe's father also received attention after the ceremony and was given a role in the film, *The Silent Enemy*. He resigned from the Indian School to research and work on the movie. As early as 1913, Yellow Robe's father had become an Indian activist. He had criticized Buffalo Bill Cody's motion picture of the Wounded Knee conflict of 1890, and had accused the early filmmakers of exploiting the event for their own glory. The producers of *The Silent Enemy* promised to be honest in their presentation of Indians. In 1929, he returned briefly to Rapid City and was convinced to pose in his film costume for photographer Della B. Vik. He returned to New York with a severe cold which turned into pneumonia, and died April 6, 1930.

Vik also photographed Rosebud on several occasions. Mildred Fielder quotes from one of Vik's letters written in 1969: "The oldest daughter, Rosebud, was married before Chauncey's death. She was exceptionally beautiful. I photographed her many times. Chauncey was always present even when I photographed her atop Hangman's Hill, and another pose of her down on her knees by Rapid Creek looking at her reflection in the water. Rosebud had all the full blood Sioux looks and in a very refined way. She was exceedingly graceful and naturally gracious." The famous movie director Cecil B. de Mille was also struck by her beauty, calling her "most beautiful."

Continues Father's Work in Education

From the 1930s through the 1950s, Yellow Robe continued her father's work in education, teaching school children about real American Indians. A newspaper article in the *Rapid City Journal* in 1975 quoted her recollections: "When I first lectured to public school classes in New York, many of the smaller children hid under their desks, for they knew from the movies what a blood-thirsty scalping Indian might do to them." In the course of her years, she met thousands of children, told them Indian stories, showed them her costumes and played games with them. Many New Yorkers got their first impression of a real Indian from her work.

In a letter written in 1975, Yellow Robe described her work. She credited her father for providing her with a background in their folklore, legends and history, which enabled her to speak to groups from the New York schools and the Long Island State Park Commission. "This in turn led to a recreation project at Jones Beach called 'The Indian Village.' There children from L.I. and N.Y. City came to take part in craft work, games, listening to stories, etc. During the winter months we worked with the teachers in the Indian studies classes, and the culmination of this activity resulted in an Annual American Indian Art Exhibit. The judges were people who were not only authorities on Art but also knew a great deal about the American Indian. The youngsters and their teachers soon found out that they did not win prizes when a picture of Plains Indian life included a totem pole standing next to a tipi. The prizes were Indian made artifacts which were to be placed in the schools' museums."

Becomes an Author

In addition to her work at Jones Beach, Yellow Robe educated Americans through radio, television and written communication. During two years in the mid-1930s, she wrote and read her own scripts on CBS radio. According to an obituary in the *New York Times,* Yellow Robe and Orson Welles worked on several dramatic shows during the 1940s and he may have been inspired to have "Rosebud" be the last word uttered by the protagonist in his classic *Citizen Kane* through his association with Yellow Robe. In the 1950s, she appeared regularly on an NBC program for children and also on "Bob Montgomery Presents" series. Her first book, *Album of the American Indian* was published in 1969. Ten years later in 1979, her second book was published. *Tonweya and the Eagles* compiled the stories she learned from her father. It was later published internationally in translation and excerpted in textbooks.

Literary editor John Milton of the University of South Dakota stated in his letter recommending her for an honorary degree: "What Rosebud Yellow Robe has done is carry the oral tradition into the more widely disseminated literary form that does justice to the orally told stories in three ways. First, from an impeccable source she has preserved the traditional stories. Second, she has written them in such a way that children can enjoy them as they listen to them being read. And third, she has managed also to make the stories meaningful and artistic on a level appreciated by adults."

In May 1989, Rosebud was granted an honorary doctorate from the University of South Dakota, paying tribute to Yellow Robe as a gifted communicator "who, though her talents and native background, promotes an authentic view of Indian life and character and who is able through her techniques of cultural exchange to pass her scholarly knowledge on to mixed audiences of young and old which numbered many thousands throughout the years."

As the oldest daughter, Yellow Robe helped take care of her two sisters after their mother died in 1922. When their father died in 1930, Evelyn Yellow Robe, the youngest daughter, moved to New York to live with Yellow Robe; and later married Dr. Hans Finkbeiner and pursued a career in laryngeal physiology, working in Europe and at Northwestern Medical School. She and her husband worked in the area of cytology, specializing in the early recognition of cancer. In 1951 Yellow Robe married Alfred A. Frantz. She had one daughter from her first marriage with Arthur Cinq-Mars, Tahcawin de Cinq-Mars Moy. Yellow Robe's other sister Chauncina White Horse was active in Indian affairs after her retirement from a career in advertising and sales. She was elected to the National Indian Council on Aging and served on the Board of Directors until her death in the early 1980s.

Rosebud wrote in a letter in 1975 that she and her sisters owed their success to their parents. She wrote: "We were very fortunate in having parents who gave us great pride in and knowledge of our family background. My father was very active in American Indian society. As in old times, he told us the folklore, legends and history of the tribe. He was anxious to keep alive the good of the old culture and combine it with the good of the new. He taught us that we could not isolate ourselves from people. He urged us to always seek knowledge from our own and from other friends we would meet."

Rosebud Yellow Robe died from cancer October 5, 1992. In 1993 the MacMillan/McGraw-Hill School Publishing Company released a textbook in her honor entitled *Write Idea.* In 1994 the National Dance Institute's event of the year, *Rosebud's Song,* was presented "in honor of and inspired by Rosebud Yellow Robe, a woman of the Lakota nation who devoted her life to teaching children through storytelling." Her collection of ethnographic materials has been donated to the W. H. Over State Museum in Vermillion, South Dakota.

SELECTED WRITINGS BY YELLOW ROBE:

Album of the American Indian, New York, F. Watts, 1969.
Tonweya and the Eagles, and Other Lakota Indian Tales, New York, Dial Press, 1979.

SOURCES:

Books

Biographical Dictionary of Indians of the Americas, Newport Beach, California, 1983; 174.
Fielder, Mildred, *Sioux Indian Leaders,* Seattle, Superior Publishing Company, 1975; 112-126, 154.
Indians of Today, edited by Marion Gridley, Chicago, ICFP, 1971; 277.
Paulson, T. Emogene, *Sioux Collections,* Vermillion, University of South Dakota, 1982; 139.
Paulson, T. Emogene, and Lloyd R. Moses, *Who's Who Among the Sioux,* Vermillion, Institute of Indian Studies, University of South Dakota, 1988; 75, 81, 265.

Periodicals

Daniels, Lee A., *New York Times* (obituary). October 7, 1992.
Moses, George, "Rosebud's Talents Remembered," *Rapid City Journal,* November 22, 1992; D11.
Moses, Lloyd, "Rosebud Yellow Robe Day," *Friends of the W. H. Over State Museum Newsletter,* 31:1, March 1989, 1-2.
"Museum Honors Yellow Robe," *Volante* (University of South Dakota student newspaper), May 3, 1989; 5.
"USD Receives Page from Famous American Bible," *Rapid City Journal,* June 14, 1975; 10.

Other

Milton, John, Letter to Committee on Honorary Degrees, October 21, 1988, in University of South Dakota Archives, Vermillion, South Dakota.

Moses, Lloyd, Letter to Committee on Honorary Degrees, October 18, 1988, in University of South Dakota Archives, Vermillion, South Dakota.

Weinberg, Marjorie, "A Biography of Rosebud Yellow Robe," in program for National Dance Institute's 1994 Event of the Year, *Rosebud's Song,* 1994; 14.

Yellow Robe, Rosebud, Letter to Webster Two Hawk, October 9, 1975, in University of South Dakota Archives, Vermillion, South Dakota.

—Sketch by Karen P. Zimmerman

Young Man Afraid of His Horses
1830-1900
Oglala Sioux tribal leader

Also known as Tasunka Kokipapi ["The Young Man of Whose Horses They Are Afraid" or "Young Men Fear His Horses"]

Young Man Afraid of His Horses

Young Man Afraid of His Horses, a chief among the Oglala Sioux of the great plains, served as President of the Pine Ridge Indian Council, negotiating with the Whites and trying to help his people make the transition from old ways to reservation life before and after the massacre at Wounded Knee. Born in 1830 as Tasunka Kokipapi, his name has often been misinterpreted. Tasunka Kokipapi translates as either "The Young Man of Whose Horses They Are Afraid" or "Young Men Fear His Horses." He was named Tasunka Kokipapi not because he was afraid of his own horses, but rather because he was such a powerful warrior that enemies even feared his horses. He was the son of "Old Man Afraid of His Horses." "Talks Asleep," Young Man Afraid of His Horses' brother, recounts the tale of how Young Man Afraid of His Horses earned and kept his name in *Tunkashila,* a book of stories compiled by Gerald Hausman.

Young Man Afraid of His Horses Earns His Name

For Native Americans, in particular the Lakota and other Sioux, horses were sacred gifts. A warrior's power was measured by his ability to ride his horse into battle as if both were one being and by the number of horses a warrior possessed. Stealing horses from an enemy's camp fueled the passions of great warriors. Riding a stolen horse away from an enemy camp was one of the greatest thrills to which a warrior could aspire. Young Man Afraid of His Horses loved horses; he had never seen anything as beautiful as a horse. He was afraid that someday horses might "pass from the land," so he kept many horses. Talks Asleep says that "they followed him about like dogs."

As Talks Asleep tells the story, Young Man Afraid of His Horses coveted the horses of other warriors. He devised a plan to trick some other warriors, known in the tale as "The Crooked Nose People," out of their horses. As the warriors watered their horses at a river, Young Man Afraid of His Horses tied a large, fake fish fin to this back and masqueraded as a giant "fish cat." As the warriors searched the water hoping to kill this enormous fish, comrades of Young Man Afraid of His Horses stole their horses. Still disguised as the fish, he lured these warriors into an ambush where his companions set upon them and "struck them down." Young Man Afraid of His Horses also became known as "Young Man Who Knows What Is His."

Defers Leadership to Chief Red Cloud

Although he was a hereditary chief with the seniority to rule, Young Man Afraid of His Horses allowed Chief Red Cloud to lead the Oglala Sioux. As white settlers moved into Sioux land, Young Man Afraid of His Horses acted as a sub-warrior chief under Red Cloud. The Whites came into Indian lands despite treaties between the United States and the plains tribes, including the Cheyennes, Arapahos, Crow, and Sioux. They came with stagecoaches, forts, the pony express, telegraph wires, and prospectors digging gold out of Indian soil. Through decade of the 1860s, Young Man Afraid of His Horses and his people struggled to hold back the tide of settlers.

An ally in this struggle was the Bent family of Fort Bent along the Arkansas River. William Bent, known to

Indians as The Little White Man, had two sons with Indian mothers—George and Charlie. George Bent joined the Cheyenne in their fight against the Whites at Sand Creek in 1864. A year later, he continued to aid the Indians when the combined tribes, including the southern Sioux, raided White camps in revenge for Sand Creek, ripping out miles of telegraph wire and raiding and plundering supplies. After the raids, the southerners fled north. Bent met Young Man Afraid of His Horses in the spring of 1865 near the Tongue River. The two became close friends, and Bent inducted Young Man Afraid of His Horses into the Crooked Lances, his Cheyenne clan.

Young Man Afraid of His Horses fought with the Oglala Sioux, the Cheyenne and the Arapaho through these years in the Red Cloud War, also called the Bozeman Trail War. This was a struggle over a route that ran between the Powder River and Big Horn River enroute to gold fields in Montana. The war parties of Red Cloud and the others raided and ambushed the Whites who tried to use the trail. In one attack, known as the Fetterman Massacre, Red Cloud and Young Man Afraid of His Horses lured 81 soldiers from their fort and killed them all.

Works for Peace with Whites

Peace was hard won. Red Cloud refused to negotiate unless the "bluecoats" abandoned their forts. Realizing they were beaten, the U.S. forces pulled out of the area. Red Cloud and his war party burned the empty forts, and then signed the Fort Laramie Treaty of 1868 agreeing to never again raise a hand in aggression against Whites. In return, the United States agreed to seek the consent of at least three-quarters of the tribe's adult males before taking any more Indian land. What Red Cloud and the other Oglala did not understand about the treaty is that it included a provision to place them on a reservation at Raw Hide Buttes. Red Cloud refused to move so far north, and he secured a closer, temporary site for the Sioux agency near Fort Laramie. This was just the beginning of a long and painful struggle between Whites and the plains Indians over both the location of the reservation and Indian control of it.

Red Cloud kept his word and never attacked the Whites again. Young Man Afraid of His Horses followed Red Cloud's example, even though other Sioux leaders, such as Sitting Bull and Crazy Horse, continued to fight. Though Red Cloud and Young Man Afraid of His Horses had moved to the new Sioux reservation established in what was then northwestern Nebraska, they soon learned of some white men, including General Custer (Long Hair) and his soldiers, travelling into the Black Hills to settle and dig for gold in Sioux land. The Black Hills were sacred lands to the Oglala Sioux, holy mountains where warriors went to speak with the Great Spirit.

Many young warriors expressed great anger at the actions of the Whites, especially Custer. Though Red Cloud did not join in their attacks, he refused to stop them. In 1874 in one near tragic incident, Young Man Afraid of His Horses protected the U.S. cavalry, led by Lieutenant Crawford,

against his fellow Oglala Sioux warriors. Young Man Afraid of His Horses and other Sioux formed a protective wall of warriors around the bluecoats and escorted them through reservation lands to Fort Robinson.

The Whites continued to fight with the Indians over the ownership of the Black Hills. In 1875, a group of senators and commissioners came west from Washington to negotiate with the Sioux for mining rights and ownership of the Black Hills. Red Cloud called for council meetings to discuss the situation. Red Cloud and Young Man Afraid of His Horses opposed giving hunting grounds to Whites but wanted to consider selling the land instead of fighting. Warriors like Crazy Horse and Sitting Bull, on the other hand, refused to relent and wanted to fight the Whites to the death. Young Man Afraid of His Horses was continuing his peacekeeping efforts when on September 23, 1875, Little Big Man—Crazy Horse's envoy—rode into the assembled council. He shouted, "I will kill the first chief who speaks for selling the Black Hills!" Young Man Afraid of His Horses and a group who supported him surrounded Little Big Man and forced him away from the council.

Thanks in part to his peacekeeping efforts, Young Man Afraid of His Horses had forged a strong bond with the Whites. As his fellow Sioux fought with Custer and the U.S. Army, Young Man Afraid of His Horses fought with Red Cloud for control of the Sioux agency, siding with the white agent Valentine T. McGillicuddy. Finally he won and was appointed as President of the Pine Ridge Indian Council, as the agency/reservation came to be known. During this time, he made many trips to Washington D.C. to find a peaceful, mutually beneficial solution to the land disputes. Ultimately, however, government officials disregarded the wishes of the Indians, paid them money, and seized the hills as U.S. property.

Even as late as 1890, Young Man Afraid of His Horses was still working for a solution to disputes over Sioux lands. He tried to convince his fellow Sioux not to follow Wovoka's message communicated through the Ghost Dance. Wovoka preached that through the Ghost Dance ceremony—in which Dancers joined hands and circled continuously until they became and dropped nearly dead from exhaustion—the dead would return, buffalo would again be plentiful, and the Whites would disappear. Though Young Man Afraid of His Horses was as starved and frustrated by the unfulfilled treaties, duplicity, and the struggle to survive that plagued all his people, he tried to convince them that the Ghost Dance led to disaster.

Young Man Afraid of His Horses did not succeed. Many of his people died as a result of Wovoka's teachings, especially at Wounded Knee where over 200 Indians were killed. After Wounded Knee, Young Man Afraid of His Horses pleaded with the few remaining "wild Indians" to surrender. Young Man Afraid of His Horses realized that their present course of opposing Whites might eventually lead to the complete destruction of all Indian people. However, Chiefs Short Bull and Kicking Bear, maddened by the slaughter at Wounded Knee, threatened to kill any Indian who left the prairies for reservation life. Eventually the hold-outs—who feared punishment more than they wanted to stay on the prairie—reported to Pine Ridge. Within two weeks time, 3500 Indians moved onto the reservation.

Dies Before His Dreams Are Realized

With the Indian people finally confined to reservations, Young Man Afraid of His Horses used his favor with the Whites to work for fairer treatment of the Sioux. At the time of his death in 1900, Young Man Afraid of His Horses knew his people did not and might never enjoy equal justice with the Whites. Some Indians viewed Young Man Afraid of His Horses as an apologist for the cruel behavior of the Whites. Others knew Young Man Afraid of His Horses as a great diplomat, a wise man who sought to protect the interests of his people through peace rather than war. Young Man Afraid of His Horses died at the Pine Ridge Reservation in South Dakota; he was 70 years old.

SOURCES:

Books

Brown, Dee, *Bury My Heart At Wounded Knee,* New York, Holt, 1970.

Dockstader, Frederick J., *Great North American Indians,* New York, Van Nostrand Reinhold, 1977.

Hausman, Gerald, *Tunkashila; From the Birth of Turtle Island to the Blood of Wounded Knee,* New York, St. Martin's Press, 1993.

Insight Guides: Native America, edited by John Gattuso, Houghton Mifflin Company, 1993.

The Native Americans, An Illustrated History, edited by Betty and Ian Ballantine, Turner Publishing, Atlanta, 1993.

—*Sketch by Christopher B. Tower*

Peterson Zah
1937-
Navajo leader

Peterson Zah has devoted his life to the service of the Navajo people. He has been active in the field of education, in legal matters, in attempts to reconcile disputes with the Hopi, and in efforts to resolve the issues of depletion of natural resources on the reservation. In 1990, he was elected as the first president of the Navajo Nation. He also received the Humanitarian Award from the City of Albuquerque and an honorary doctorate from Santa Fe College.

Peterson Zah (right)

Traditional Background

Zah was born December 2, 1937, in Low Mountain, Arizona, the disputed joint-use area. Henry and Mae (Multine) Zah raised their son to respect his heritage. Considering his mother his best teacher, Zah often quotes her sayings in his addresses. She speaks no English and is one of the 125,000 who are still fluent in the Navajo language which he, as educator, is attempting to restore on the reservation. A striking illustration of the binding force of the old language came from his assertion that his mother had always told him to use his culture "as a canoe with which to stay afloat." The metaphor, so inappropriate in a desert setting, is over six centuries old and refers to the Athapaskan ancestors who migrated from the North to New Mexico perhaps 1,000 years ago. Zah attended Phoenix Indian School until 1960, then went to Arizona State University on a basketball scholarship; he graduated with a bachelor's degree in education in 1963.

From 1963 to 1964, he worked for the Arizona Vocational Education Department in Phoenix as a journeyman carpenter instructing adults in employable skills. He then participated in the domestic peace corps known as Volunteers in Service to America (VISTA). Zah served as field coordinator of the training center at Arizona State University at Tempe from 1965 to 1967. This assignment enabled him to utilize his considerable gifts of cultural mediation, since his job was to teach cultural sensitivity to those volunteers who would work on Indian reservations. From 1967 to 1981, Zah was executive director of the people's legal services at Window Rock. This nonprofit organization, chartered by the state of Arizona, was called DNA—Dinebeuna Nahiilna Be Agaditiahe or "Lawyers Who Contribute to the Economic Revitalization of the People." During his decade directing DNA, Zah was in charge of more than 100 employees at nine reservation offices, and 33 tribal court advocates, as well as 34 attorneys. He succeeded in having several cases reach the U.S. Supreme Court, which established Indian sovereignty, and in winning some landmark cases. This grassroots legal aid system offered hope to impoverished Native Americans who would have otherwise had no recourse to the law courts.

Teaches Navajo Language and Culture

Misguided educational policies have hindered the Navajo for decades. Ever since the conquest, in 1868, reservation agents have tried to send children away to Bureau of Indian Affairs (BIA) boarding schools to speed their assimilation. Competing institutions were the mission schools run by various religious denominations, or public schools in towns neighboring the reservations. By 1946, only one in four Navajo children was enrolled in any of these schools. The Window Rock Public School District compiled the evidence that led to significant changes, more relevant curriculum and parental involvement led to increased enrollment.

Zah was elected in 1972 to the first all-Navajo school board at Window Rock, and assumed its presidency in 1973. In this capacity, he hired more Navajo teachers, installed a Navajo curriculum, developed Navajo textbooks, renewed religious ceremonies and restored knowledge of tribal history. Zah believed that to preserve the language, it must be taught in all classes, including science and math, before the introduction of English, because it conveys concepts that cannot be translated. The ecological wisdom of the elders who sought to preserve the harmony of the natural world is retained in the earth-derived vocabulary; to live as a good Navajo, for example, one must "speak the language of the earth."

Under the guidelines of Public Law 93-638, school boards made up of local community people set up contract schools; under the control of the Navajo Tribal Council, these institutions flourished. Materials were created in a Navajo spelling system devised by Oliver LaFarge and John Peabody Harrington. Medicine men were invited into classrooms to lecture. Students set up a local television station, and published a Navajo newspaper. One of the Rock Point graduates, Rex Lee Jim, went on to Princeton, and then returned to the reservation to compose a libretto for the first Navajo opera and to try to found a school for the performing arts on the reservation. By the 1990s, there were twice as many applicants for college-level professional training as could be accommodated by the tribal scholarship funds.

Zah also began fundraising in 1987 for a group soliciting scholarships for worthy Navajo students from the private sector. The Navajo Education and Scholarship Foundation enabled many impoverished young people to attend school. In 1989, Zah founded the Native American Consulting Services to obtain congressional assistance for constructing new schools on the reservation. From 1989 to 1990, he was director of the western regional office of the Save the Children Federation.

Becomes Tribal Chair

From 1983 to 1987, Zah served as chairman of the Navajo Tribal Council at Window Rock. This site was selected as a capital by John Collier who began its construction under federal work programs in the 1930s. The council meets in an eight-sided stone building modeled after a traditional hogan. There, the elected delegates govern the largest reservation in the United States—about 24,000 square miles or close to 16 million acres in Arizona, New Mexico, and southeastern Utah. These desiccated and badly-eroded lands house over 200,000 Navajo whose population is increasing at the rate of more than two percent per year. Zah invested his energies in reforming education as one way of coping with the intractable troubles of poverty.

Elected President of the Navajo Nation

From 1990 to 1994, Zah was the first elected president in the history of the Navajo Nation. His childhood friend and classmate, Ivan Sidney, became the tribal leader of the Hopi, with whom Zah tried to work out the difficulties of government-imposed relocation. A film, *Broken Rainbow,* was made about this Hopi-Navajo land dispute. Underneath this disputed land is coal; and each year, the Peabody Coal Company extracts seven million tons from this area, ruining the landscape and sullying the air. The two longtime friends worked to resolve hostilities generated by their predecessors, Peter MacDonald and Abbot Sekaquptewa, by ordering a suspension of all lawsuits over land in April of 1983, and by pledging cooperation in all areas of mutual concern including negotiations of future contracts with mining companies.

Zah's administration has been grievously tested. Just as plans had been drawn up and sites approved for the construction of six sorely needed hospital facilities, the government announced a 30 percent cut in health services. While Zah was in Washington, D.C., attempting to reverse this measure, an outbreak of hanta virus afflicted his people. Epidemiologists from the Centers for Disease Control worked frantically to find the causes of the mysterious deaths occurring on the reservation. Also, an extraordinary number of miners who had worked for Kerr-McGee extracting uranium have died of anaplastic cancer of the lungs. The Atomic Energy Commission, who bought the uranium ore, refused to clean up the radioactive tailings which are blown by the winds over the reservation, and seep into the drinking water. Drilling for petroleum and gas by Mobil, Standard Oil, and Exxon has poisoned the ground, desecrated sacred sites, and polluted the air. The stripmining of coal subjects the Navajo to a perpetual fallout of toxic fumes from the power plants. According to Stephen Trimble, Zah has tried to warn his people to think of the future when these nonrenewable energy sources have been depleted: "Someday the coal, oil, and gas are going to be gone. What's going to happen to the Navajo children then? Pete Zah won't be around then ... you have to think about the future."

Zah lives at the capital, Window Rock, with his wife, Rosalind (Begay), and his children, Elaine, Eileen, and Keeyonnie.

SOURCES:

Books

Mattheissen, Peter, "Four Corners," in *Indian Country,* New York, Penguin, 1984.

"Navajo Education," in *Handbook of North American Indians; Southwest,* Volume 10, edited by Alfonso Ortiz, Washington, D.C., Smithsonian Institution, 1983.

Tome, Marshall, "The Navajo Nation Today," in *Handbook of North American Indians, Southwest,* Volume 10, edited by Alfonso Ortiz, Washington, D.C., Smithsonian Institution, 1983.

Trimble, Stephen, "The Navajo," in *The People,* Santa Fe, New Mexico, School of American Research Press, 1993; 121-194.

Periodicals

"Proceedings of the First National Conference on Cancer in Native Americans," *American Indian Culture and Research Journal,* 16:3, 1992.

Trebay, Guy, "Bad Medicine: Illness as Metaphor in Navajoland," *Village Voice,* August 3, 1993; 39-43.

—*Sketch by Ruth Rosenberg*

Ofelia Zepeda

1954-

Tohono O'odham educator and linguist

"I am just a human being. I did try and work as hard at this as I could, but I did try ... even though I might not have accomplished everything." These words begin the story of the life of Ofelia Zepeda. In an interview with JoAnn di Filippo, she warmly described her home community as a rural center dependent upon the production of Pima cotton and other seasonal agricultural products. Yet, it was her resistance to working as a laborer in the fields which contributed to her quest for education. This combined with her respect for Native heritage led her to become a linguist with focus on Papago and Pima language and bilingual and sociolinguistic issues with respect to Native languages. The preservation of O'odham traditions and culture, including Papago and Pima, through linguistic scholarship has remained the foundation of Zepeda's professional achievements.

Acquires Appreciation for Culture and Tradition

One of seven children, Zepeda was born on March 24, 1954 in Stanfield, Arizona, a rural Indian community. The homeland of parents Alber (a farmer) and Juliana (Velasco) Zepeda was in Mexico. Zepeda fondly remembers her childhood years in Stanfield and the well-defined O'odham history which existed in the community. Although her family traveled each summer to Mexico for tribal ceremonies and visits with extended family members, the O'odham traditions and culture remained a distinct entity in Zepeda's life and the Native community of Stanfield. In describing the O'odham people of her community, she explained in an interview with JoAnn di Filippo that most community members elected to live outside the boundaries of the O'odham Reservation because, "That's not where we are from. It would be like being an intruder, living on the edges. We are traditional O'odham people who are put in a funny space in time."

As the first member of her family to graduate from high school and enter college, Zepeda vividly recalled her two reasons for seeking higher education. In the 1970s American Indian activism had reached a stage where its influence could be felt in all Native communities. While not aligning herself to any particular activist group, she felt that she should take advantage of the rights being advocated by the Indian peoples. Education was one of those rights, and Zepeda pursued the same educational track which several years earlier had discriminated against Indian peoples. "It is sort of a philosophy that we have in O'odham culture ... a lot of responsibility made sense," she related to di Filippo. "My second reason for attending college was to avoid working as a farm laborer. It was hard work, work that children were required to do. More than any of my other siblings, I was disinclined to do farm labor work."

Expands Horizons in Sociology and Literature

Her academic career began at Central Arizona State studying social sciences and literature. Later, she transferred to the University of Arizona where she pursued a career focusing on the sociological aspects of culture. A brief interruption in her studies afforded her the opportunity to work with her tribe's native O'odham language. As part of her work, Zepeda was responsible for collecting and translating traditional O'odham stories. Only one problem prevented her from completing that task; she had to learn the O'odham system of reading and writing her native language. While at the university, Zepeda began working with Kenneth Hale, a visiting MIT professor, to critically examine the O'odham language structure. With guidance and direction from Professor Hale, Zepeda changed the course of her studies from sociology to linguistics. This change ultimately altered the course of her career and led to publishing the highly regarded O'odham language dictionary, *A Papago Grammar.* Once on the university track, a reluctance to continue abandoning her studies ensued. To compensate and alleviate this resistance, she attended the university year-round and succeeded in obtaining several degrees in a very short time—a bachelor of arts (1980), a master of arts (1981), and a Ph.D. (1984) in linguistics.

A respected educator, Zepeda has been associated with the University of Arizona for over 15 years in various research and teaching positions. Her focus on the sociological impact of culture in societies has enabled her to teach a broad range of classes structured around studies in oral tradition, language and social issues, bilingual curriculum development, and Papago/Pima linguistics. In 1986, Zepeda became director of the American Indian Studies Program at the University of Arizona. Simultaneously, in 1989 she became co-director of the American Indian Language Development Institute (ALDI), an organization which emerged from a group of academic linguists and 18 American Indian parents interested in learning to read and write in their native languages. The ALDI has received overwhelming response to the program and its charter continues to promote the fact that "American Indian tribes have great knowledge of their language and culture which should be utilized and incorporated within the educational systems that their children attend.... The community should have input and control of the curriculum taught to their children." Following interdisciplinary studies is the center of Zepeda's advice to students. She revealed to di Filippo, "Some of the best experiences I have had with students is when they pursue multidisciplinary coursework, and yet feel they do not have a deficit after completing their studies ... it makes school not as intimidating."

Expanding her artistic horizons, she began to flourish and develop her own creative writings. Describing her work as originating from "personal experiences" and attempting to avoid the use of stereotypical phrasing, she imparted, "We must look at language in other ways ... it can be much more holistic. Try to get different knowledge or experiences not only by being there, but by reading. When you combine the personal experience with reading knowledge you build an overlap. It's like water ... it cannot be separated."

During the period 1984-1994, Zepeda served as a consultant to various projects and organizations in the areas of culture and linguistics, including the video production of "Code Talkers: The First 29," funded by the National Endowment for the Humanities; "Pathways," a permanent exhibit at the Arizona State Museum; and the U.S. Justice Department on the Reauthorization of the United States Voting Rights Acts.

A serene and soft-spoken woman, Zepeda views her career choice as one whose position is respected in the community. "It is a way to convey knowledge. Traditionally, a teacher was a very prestigious position to hold in a Native community. It is a position of responsibility, not power. One hundred years ago, a Native teacher might have been accorded the responsibility of a ceremonial leader. They would then have the responsibility to make things happen so the tribal community could perpetuate or continue."

Throughout her career she has been presented with numerous fellowships, recognized for her community service programs and volunteer work, and was the recipient of the Distinguished Service Award from the University of Arizona. Ofelia Zepeda has continued to write and teach, preserving the cultural and linguistic traditions of Native Americans, and has been a role model for women of all generations, Native and non-Native, in recognizing that goals can be achieved when the responsibility for those goals is accepted.

SELECTED WRITINGS BY ZEPEDA:

"O'odham Ha-cegïtodag/Papago and Pima Thoughts," *International Journal of American Linguistics,* 1980.

"Thoughts On My Mother's Grave," in *South Corner of Time,* edited by Larry Evers, University of Arizona Press, 1980; reprinted, Tlalocan-Universidad Nacional Autonoma de Mexico, 1982.

Editor and contributor, *Mat Hekid o Ju/When It Rains: Papago and Pima Poetry,* University of Arizona Press, 1982.

"Desiderative-Causative in Papago," in *Coyote Working Papers in Linguistics from A-Z,* edited by Tom Larsen, 1982.

A Papago Grammar, University of Arizona Press, 1983; reprinted, 1993.

"Desiderative-Causative in Tohono O'odham," *International Journal of American Linguistics,* 1987.

(With Jane Hill) "Situation des Langues Indigenes aux Etats-Unis," *Diogene,* 153, Patrimoine Culturel, Langues en Peril, January-March, 1991.

"People of the Desert," in *Apa Insight Guide to Native America,* Hong Kong, Apa Guides Publications, 1991.

(With Jane Hill) "Derived Words in Tohono O'odham," *International Journal of American Linguistics,* 1992.

Gawulig Ñiokï: Dialect Variation in Tohono O'odham, 1992-93.

Southwest Memory: Indigenous Arizona Tribal Histories, 1992-93.

Editor (with Larry Evers), *Home Places* (an anthology of Native American literature in celebration of 25 years of publishing by Sun Tracks), 1992-93.

(With Jane Hill) "Mrs. Patricio's Trouble: The Distribution of Responsibility in an Account of Personal Experience," in *Responsibility and Evidence in Oral Discourse,* edited by Jane Hill, Cambridge University Press, 1993.

(With Teresa McCarty) "Indigenous Memory: Indigenous Voices and Views in School Humanities," *Journal of Navajo Education,* 1993.

SOURCES:

Books

Contemporary Authors, Volume 114, Detroit, Gale Research, 1985.

Other

ALDI brochure, Department of Language, Reading and Culture, Tucson, University of Arizona, 1994.

Zepeda, Ofelia, interview with JoAnn di Filippo conducted May 16, 1994.

—*Sketch by JoAnn di Filippo*

Zitkala-Sa
See Bonnin, Gertrude Simmons

Subject Index